# Handbook of Feminist Research

# EDITORIAL ADVISORY BOARD

# Handbook of Feminist Research

## Theory and Praxis

Editor
# Sharlene Nagy Hesse-Biber
*Boston College*

**SAGE Publications**
Thousand Oaks ■ London ■ New Delhi

*For information:*

Sage Publications, Inc.
2455 Teller Road
Thousand Oaks, California 91320
E-mail: order@sagepub.com

Sage Publications Ltd.
1 Oliver's Yard
55 City Road
London EC1Y 1SP
United Kingdom

Sage Publications India Pvt. Ltd.
B-42, Panchsheel Enclave
Post Box 4109
New Delhi 110 017  India

Printed in the United States of America

*Library of Congress Cataloging-in-Publication Data*

Handbook of feminist research : theory and praxis / edited by Sharlene Nagy Hesse-Biber.
    p. cm.
Includes bibliographical references and index.
ISBN 1-4129-0545-1 or 978-1-4129-0545-9 (cloth)
    1. Women—Research—Methodology.  2.  Women's studies—Methodology.
3.  Social sciences—Research—Methodology.  4.  Feminist theory.  I. Hesse-Biber, Sharlene Nagy.
HQ1180.H35 2007
305.42072—dc22                                        2006011641


This book is printed on acid-free paper.

06   07   08   09   10    10  9  8  7  6  5  4  3  2  1

| | |
|---|---|
| *Acquisitions Editor:* | Lisa Cuevas Shaw |
| *Associate Editor:* | Margo Beth Crouppen |
| *Editorial Assistant:* | Karen Greene |
| *Production Editor:* | Laureen A. Shea |
| *Typesetter:* | C&M Digitals (P) Ltd. |
| *Cover Designer:* | Michelle Kenny |

# CONTENTS

**Acknowledgments**      ix

1. Feminist Research: Exploring the Interconnections
   of Epistemology, Methodology, and Method    1
   *Sharlene Nagy Hesse-Biber*

**PART I. Feminist Perspectives on Knowledge Building**

2. Feminist Empiricism    29
   *Catherine Hundleby*

3. Feminist Standpoints    45
   *Sandra Harding*

4. Postmodern, Poststructural, and Critical Theories    71
   *Susanne Gannon and Bronwyn Davies*

5. The Politics of Border Crossings: Black, Postcolonial,
   and Transnational Feminist Perspectives    107
   *Hyun Sook Kim*

6. Feminist Interdisciplinary Approaches to Knowledge Building    123
   *Sally L. Kitch*

**PART II. Feminist Research Praxis**

7. From Theory to Method and Back Again:
   The Synergistic Praxis of Theory and Method    143
   *Sharlene Nagy Hesse-Biber and Deborah Piatelli*

8. Toward Understandings of Feminist Ethnography    155
   *Wanda S. Pillow and Cris Mayo*

9. Feminist Interviewing: Experience, Talk, and Knowledge    173
   *Marjorie L. DeVault and Glenda Gross*

10. Using Survey Research as a
    Quantitative Method for Feminist Social Change    199
    *Kathi Miner-Rubino, Toby Epstein Jayaratne, and Julie Konik*

11. The Link Between Theory and Methods:
Feminist Experimental Research    223
*Sue V. Rosser*

12. Reading Between the Lines: Feminist Content
Analysis Into the Second Millennium    257
*Shulamit Reinharz and Rachel Kulick*

13. Feminist Evaluation Research    277
*Sharon Brisolara and Denise Seigart*

14. Participatory and Action Research and Feminisms:
Toward Transformative Praxis    297
*M. Brinton Lykes and Erzulie Coquillon*

15. Narratives and Numbers:
Feminist Multiple Methods Research    327
*Abigail J. Stewart and Elizabeth R. Cole*

16. Feminisms, Grounded Theory, and Situational Analysis    345
*Adele E. Clarke*

17. Emergent Methods in Feminist Research    371
*Pamela Moss*

18. Feminist Perspectives on Social Movement Research    391
*Sarah Maddison*

19. Institutional Ethnography: From a
Sociology for Women to a Sociology for People    409
*Dorothy E. Smith*

**PART III. Feminist Perspectives on the Research Process:
Issues and Insights**

20. Core Feminist Insights and Strategies on Authority,
Representations, Truths, Reflexivity, and Ethics
Across the Research Process    419
*Sharlene Nagy Hesse-Biber and Abigail Brooks*

21. Authority and Representation in Feminist Research    425
*Judith Roof*

22. What's Good Writing in Feminist Research? What
Can Feminist Researchers Learn About Good Writing?    443
*Kathy Charmaz*

23. Reading for Another: A Method for Addressing Some
Feminist Research Dilemmas    459
*Laurel Richardson*

24. Truth and Truths in Feminist Knowledge Production    469
*Mary Hawkesworth*

25. Holistic Reflexivity: The Feminist Practice of Reflexivity    493
*Sharlene Nagy Hesse-Biber and Deborah Piatelli*

26. Feminist Research Ethics                                                    515
    *Judith Preissle*

**PART IV. Commentaries on Future Directions
in Feminist Theory, Research, and Pedagogy**

27. Dialoguing About Future Directions in Feminist
    Theory, Research, and Pedagogy                                             535
    *Sharlene Nagy Hesse-Biber*

28. Reason, Truth, and Experience: Tyrannies or Liberation?                    547
    *Helen E. Longino*

29. Critical Perspectives on Feminist Epistemology                             553
    *Noretta Koertge*

30. The Feminism Question in Science: What Does It
    Mean to "Do Social Science as a Feminist"?                                 567
    *Alison Wylie*

31. Standpoint Epistemology and Beyond                                         579
    *Nancy A. Naples*

32. Commentary: Using Feminist Fractured Foundationalism
    in Researching Children in the Concentration Camps
    of the South African War (1899–1902)                                       591
    *Liz Stanley and Sue Wise*

33. Future Directions in Difference Research:
    Recognising and Responding to Difference                                   605
    *Diane Reay*

34. Feminist Designs for Difference                                            613
    *Michelle Fine*

35. Decolonizing Approaches to Feminist Research:
    The Case of Feminist Ethnography                                           621
    *Katherine Borland*

36. Future Directions of Feminist Research: Intersectionality                  629
    *Bonnie Thornton Dill, Amy E. McLaughlin, and Angel David Nieves*

37. Interconnections and Configurations:
    Toward a Global Feminist Ethnography                                       639
    *Kum-Kum Bhavnani*

38. Feminizing Global Research/Globalizing Feminist
    Research: Methods and Practice Under Globalization                         651
    *Jennifer Bickham Mendez and Diane L. Wolf*

39. A Global Feminist Perspective on Research                                  663
    *Maria Mies*

40. Future Directions of Feminist Research: New Directions
    in Social Policy—The Case of Women's Health                                669
    *Lynn Weber*

41.  From Course to Discourse:
     Mainstreaming Feminist Methodology                          681
     *Debra Renee Kaufman*

42.  Feminist Pedagogy Reconsidered                              689
     *Daphne Patai*

43.  A Passion for Knowledge:
     The Teaching of Feminist Methodology                        705
     *Judith A. Cook and Mary Margaret Fonow*

**Author Index**                                                 **713**

**Subject Index**                                                **733**

**About the Editor**                                             **749**

**About the Contributors**                                       **749**

# ACKNOWLEDGMENTS

This *Handbook* would not be possible without the assistance and support of many members within the feminist community. First, I want to express a heartfelt "thank you!" to the authors of this *Handbook* for providing stellar, state-of-the-art *Handbook* chapters.

I am deeply grateful to each of the amazing members of the editorial board for their support, guidance, and hard work in assisting with reviewing chapter drafts, as well as providing me with intellectual and emotional support.

I want to especially thank several graduate students at Boston College, Department of Sociology, two of whom are members of our editorial board, Deborah Piatelli and Abigail Brooks. In addition, I want to thank Denise Leckenby, whose research assistance was invaluable in the early stages of this project. My gratitude also to my research assistants, Emily Barko, Cooley Horner, and Melissa Ricker.

I want to thank the Graduate Consortium in Women's Studies at the Massachusetts Institute of Technology for the opportunity to learn and teach feminist perspectives on theory and research in an interdisciplinary environment. I am especially grateful to my consortium colleagues and graduate students there from whom I have learned so much.

The *Handbook* would not be possible without the vision, wisdom, and support of some outstanding people at Sage Publications. I especially want to thank Alison Mudditt, Executive Vice President, Higher Education, at Sage and my senior editor at Sage, Lisa Cuevas Shaw. I want to express my heartfelt thanks to Laureen Shea, project editor at Sage Publications.

I want to express my love and deepest appreciation to my family, in particular my daughters, Julia Ariel and Sarah Alexandra, for their patience, love, and forbearance. I especially value the friendship, love, and support of my husband, Michael Peter Biber, MD.

In addition, I want to thank Jodi Wigren for providing me with encouragement and advice. My gratitude also to Kira Stokes for reminding me how important it is for women to keep a strong mind and body.

I dedicate this *Handbook* to all whose knowledge remains subjugated, and I hope this *Handbook* serves as a stepping-stone to emancipation for those who seek to gather new perspectives on the knowledge-building process and those who seek to use new research tools and refashion old ones—I hope that this *Handbook* will nurture as well as encourage dialogue about our differences.

I also dedicate this volume to my dearest sister, Janet Green Fisher, whose youthful life was cut short by breast cancer. Her humor, courage, love, and compassion remain to sustain and inspire those whose lives she touched.

Sharlene Nagy Hesse-Biber
*Boston College*
*Chestnut Hill, Massachusetts*

# 1

# FEMINIST RESEARCH

## *Exploring the Interconnections of Epistemology, Methodology, and Method*

SHARLENE NAGY HESSE-BIBER

## FEMINIST VOICES AND VISIONS ACROSS THE CENTURIES

I do earnestly desire to arouse the women of the North to a realizing sense of the condition of two millions of women at the South, still in bondage, suffering what I suffered, and most of them far worse. I want to add my testimony to that of abler pens to convince the people of the Free States what Slavery really is. Only by experience can anyone realize how deep, and dark, and foul is that pit of abominations. May the blessing of God rest on this imperfect effort in behalf of my persecuted people!

—*Harriet Jacobs (1861/1987, pp. 1–2)*

It was thus that I found myself walking with extreme rapidity across a grass plot. Instantly a man's figure rose to intercept me. Nor did I at first understand that the gesticulations of a curious-looking object, in a cut-away coat and evening shirt, were aimed at me. His face expressed horror and indignation. Instinct rather than reason came to my help: he was a Beadle; I was a woman. Thus was the turf; there was the path. Only the Fellows and Scholars are allowed here; the gravel is the place for me.

—*Virginia Woolf (1929/1999, p. 258)*

Thus humanity is male and man defines woman not in herself but as relative to him; she is not regarded as an autonomous being. . . . For him she is sex—absolute sex, no less. She is defined and differentiated with reference to man and not he with reference to her; she is the incidental, the inessential as opposed to the essential. He is the Subject, he is the Absolute—she is the other.

—*Simone de Beauvoir (1952, pp. xviii, xxiii)*

Author's Note: Much appreciation and gratitude to Abigail Brooks, who contributed her insights and provided skillful editorial advice. My many thanks also to Deborah Piatelli for her wisdom as this chapter evolved.

The problem lay buried, unspoken, for many years in the minds of American women. It was a strange stirring, a sense of dissatisfaction, a yearning that women suffered in the middle of the twentieth century in the United States. Each suburban wife struggled with it alone. . . . she was afraid to ask even of herself the silent question—"Is this all"? For over fifteen years there was no word of this yearning in the millions of words written about women, for women, in all the columns, books and articles by experts telling women their role was to seek fulfillment as wives and mothers. . . . We can no longer ignore within women that voice that says: "I want something more than my husband, my children and my home."

—*Betty Friedan (1963, pp. 15, 32)*

Women [were] largely excluded from the work of producing the forms of thought and the images and symbols in which thought is expressed and ordered. . . . The circle of men whose writing and talk was significant to each other extends backwards in time as far as our records reach. What men were doing was relevant to men, was written by men about men for men. Men listened to what one another said.

—*Dorothy Smith (1978, p. 281)*

The tensions between opposing theories and political stances vitalize the feminist dialogue. But it may only be combined with respect, partial understanding, love, and friendship that keeps us together in the long run. So mujeres think about the carnalas you want to be in your space, those whose spaces you want to have overlapping yours.

—*Gloria Anzaldúa (1990, p. 229)*

Working right at the limits of several categories and approaches means that one is neither entirely inside or outside. One has to push one's work as far as one can go: to the borderlines, where one never stops, walking on the edges, incurring constantly the risk of falling off one side or the other side of the limit while undoing, redoing, modifying this limit.

—*Trinh T. Minh-ha (1991, p. 218)*

I continue to be amazed that there is so much feminist writing produced and yet so little feminist theory that strives to speak to women, men and children about ways we might transform our lives via a conversion to feminist practice.

—*bell hooks (1994, pp. 70–71)*

Advocating the mere tolerance of difference between women is the grossest reformism. It is a total denial of the creative function of difference in our lives. Difference must be not merely tolerated, but seen as a fund of necessary polarities between which our creativity can spark like a dialectic. Only then does the necessity for interdependency become unthreatening. Only within that interdependency of different strengths, acknowledged and equal, can the power to seek new ways of being in the world generate, as well as the courage and sustenance to act where there are no charters.

—*Audre Lorde (1996, p. 159)*

The history of research from many indigenous perspectives is so deeply embedded in colonization that it has been regarded as a tool only of colonization and not as a potential tool for self-determination and development. For indigenous peoples, research has a significance that is embedded in our history as natives under the gaze of Western science and colonialism.

—*Linda Tuhiwai Smith (2005, p. 87)*

This *Handbook* begins with voices, visions, and experiences of feminist activists, scholars, and researchers, speaking to us across the decades of the 19th, 20th, and 21st centuries. They provide a legacy of feminist research, praxis, and activism. There lies within these voices a feminist consciousness that opens up intellectual and emotional space for all women to articulate their relations to one another and the wider society—spaces where the personal transforms into the political. Harriet Jacobs calls for the alignment of women across their racial, class, and geographical differences to fight the abomination of slavery. Through her words, Jacobs demonstrates how the concrete lived experience is a key place from which to build knowledge and foment social change. Virginia Woolf, Simone de Beauvoir, Betty Friedan, and Dorothy Smith, speaking many decades later, express their deep feelings of exclusion from the dominant avenues of knowledge building, seeing their own experiences, concerns, and worth diminished and invalidated by the dominant powers of their society.

In some ways, the origins of feminist research's epistemological and methodological focus draws on these insights and struggles; feminist empiricism, standpoint theories, postmodernism, and transnational perspectives all recognize the importance of women's lived experiences with the goal of unearthing subjugated knowledge. Each perspective forges links between feminism and activism, between the academy and women's everyday lives.

Feminist perspectives also carry messages of empowerment that challenge the encircling of knowledge claims by those who occupy privileged positions. Feminist thinking and practice requires taking steps from the "margins to the center" while eliminating boundaries of division that privilege dominant forms of knowledge building, boundaries that mark who can be a knower and what can be known. For Virginia Woolf, it is the demarcation between the "turf" and the "path"; for Simone de Beauvoir, it is the line between the "inessential" and the "essential"; and for Dorothy Smith, it is the path that encircles dominant knowledge, where women's lived experiences lie outside its circumference or huddled at the margins.

To engage in feminist theory and praxis means to challenge knowledge that excludes, while seeming to include—assuming that when we speak of the generic term *men,* we also mean women, assuming that what is true for dominant groups must also be true for women and other oppressed groups. Feminists ask "new" questions that place women's lives and those of "other" marginalized groups at the center of social inquiry. Feminist research *disrupts* traditional ways of knowing to create rich new meanings, a process that Trinh T. Minh-ha (1991) terms becoming "both/and"—insider and outsider—taking on a multitude of different standpoints and negotiating these identities simultaneously. Feminists bob and weave their threads of understanding, listening to the experiences of "the other/s" as legitimate knowledge. Feminist research is mindful of hierarchies of power and authority in the research process that are so well voiced by Linda Tuhiwai Smith (2005), including those power differentials that lie within research practices that can reinforce the status quo, creating divisions between colonizer and colonized.

A quality of agency is contained within the preceding quotations that challenges dominant discourses of knowledge building, words that urge women to live and invite in differences, to embrace the creativity and knowledge building that lies within the tensions of difference. Difference matters. Author bell hooks (1994) implores feminists to root their scholarship in "transformative politics and practice," pointing out that "in this capitalist culture, feminism and feminist theory are fast becoming a commodity that only the privileged can afford" (p. 71). Audre Lorde (1996) provides a path to empowerment by urging an embrace of difference through an "interdependency of different strengths, acknowledged and equal" (p. 159). Indeed, it is our acknowledgment and appreciation of difference that sustains our ability to navigate uncharted terrain toward meaningful social change. Gloria Anzaldúa (1990) employs a "sandbar" metaphor to capture traversals of the difference divide:

> Being a sandbar means getting a breather from being a perpetual bridge without having to withdraw completely. The high tides and low tides of your life are factors which help decide whether or where you're a sandbar today, tomorrow. . . . A sandbar is more fluid and shifts locations, allowing for more mobility and more freedom. Of course there are sandbars called shoals, where boats run amuck. (p. 224)

Although Anzaldúa now envisions herself turning into a sandbar, her own stance on difference fluctuates between a "persistent bridge," a "drawbridge," or even "an island." For Anzaldúa (1990), traversing the difference divide becomes a process with its own range of connections and disconnections—"each option comes with its own dangers" (p. 224).

Feminist research shares some common angles of vision that are "connected in principle to feminist struggle" (Sprague & Zimmerman, 1993, p. 266), often with the intent of changing the basic structures of oppression. But there is no single feminist epistemology or methodology. Instead, multiple feminist lenses wake us up to layers of sexist, racist, homophobic, and colonialist points of view. Some lenses provide radical insights into knowledge building that upends traditional epistemologies and methodologies, offering more complex understandings and solutions toward reclaiming subjugated knowledge.

Feminists engage both the theory and practice of research—beginning with the formulation of the research question and ending with the reporting of research findings. Feminist research encompasses the full range of knowledge building that includes epistemology, methodology, and method. An *epistemology* is "a theory of knowledge" (Harding, 1987b, p. 3) that delineates a set of assumptions about the social world—who can be a knower and what can be known. These assumptions influence the decisions a researcher makes, including what to study (based on what *can* be studied) and how to conduct a study. A *methodology* is "a theory of how research is done or should proceed" (p. 3). A *method* is "a technique for (or way of proceeding in) gathering evidence" (p. 2). Very often, the term *method* is used as an umbrella term to refer to these three different components of the research process, which can make the use of the term method somewhat confusing.

Feminist research takes many twists and turns as a mode of social inquiry. In this introduction, we provide a brief overview of some of the "critical moments" in the legacy of feminist theory and praxis. We take up the dialogues surrounding issues of epistemology, methodology, and method. Feminist research begins with questioning and critiquing androcentric bias

within the disciplines, challenging traditional researchers to include gender as a category of analysis. Subsequently, through this shift in perspective, we can observe the beginnings of an overall challenge to the scientific method itself and the emergence of new paradigms of thinking about basic foundational questions such as What is Truth? Who can be a knower? and What can be known?

## FEMINIST RESEARCHERS CHALLENGE ANDROCENTRIC BIAS ACROSS THE DISCIPLINES

In the 1960s through to the 1980s, feminist scholars and researchers called attention to examples of androcentric bias within the sciences and social sciences. These feminist scholars and researchers, known as feminist empiricists, embarked on projects to "correct" these biases by adding women into research samples and asking new questions that enable women's experiences and perspectives to gain a hearing. Margrit Eichler and Jeanne Lapointe's (1985), research primer, *On the Treatment of the Sexes in Research*, provides a critique of empirical research as well as a checklist for inclusion of gender as a category of analysis in social research. Their work provides many important nuggets of advice concerning what *not* to do (p. 9). Some of these include the following:

- Treating Western sex roles as universal
- Transforming statistical differences into innate differences
- Difference does not mean inferiority

Feminist empiricist researchers did much to "deconstruct" what they perceived as errors, or examples of androcentrism, across a range of academic disciplines and professional fields. Feminist empiricists' insights on androcentrism, and their goals of eradicating sexist research, cascaded across the disciplines of psychology, philosophy, history, sociology, education, and anthropology and the fields of law, medicine, language, and communications. The 1970s and 1980s saw the publication of many different pathbreaking anthologies critical of andro-centric research. In 1975, Marcia Millman and Rosabeth Moss Kanter coedited the volume *Another Voice: Feminist Perspectives on Social Life and Social Science*. In their editorial introduction, they compare traditional knowledge building with the story of "The Emperor's New Clothes." They note,

> Everyone knows the story about the Emperor and his fine clothes; although the townspeople persuaded themselves that the Emperor was elegantly costumed, a child, possessing an unspoiled vision, showed the citizenry that the Emperor was really naked. . . . The story also reminds us that collective delusions can be undone by introducing fresh perspectives. (p. vii)

Sociologists Millman and Kanter (1975) criticize the androcentric bias of sociology by noting how sociology uses certain "field-defining models" that prevent the asking of new questions. They note, for example, that the Weberian concept of rationality used to understand an individual's motivations and social organization "defines out of existence, from the start, the equally important element of emotion in social life and structure" (p. ix). Their edited volume presents a range of new feminist perspectives on social reality to "reassess the basic theories, paradigms, substantive concerns, and methodologies of sociology and the social sciences to see what changes are needed to make social theory and research reflect the multitude of both female and male realities and interests" (p. viii). The works in this volume also point out how sociology emphasizes the "public sphere" of society and "leaves out the private, supportive, informal, local social structures in which women participate most frequently" (p. xi). A stark example of this comes from a research article in their volume by Arlie Hochschild (1975), "The Sociology of Feeling and Emotion: Selected Possibilities." Hochschild demonstrates how the frequency of specific emotions is not distributed evenly across social structures. She explores the gendered, raced, and classed aspects of emotional expression. She notes, for example, that anger tends to flow down the social structure, while love flows up the social

hierarchy. In effect, those at the bottom of the social ladder become "the complaint clerks of society, and . . . for the dwellers at the top, the world is more often experienced as a benign place" (p. 296). She notes in particular the role of gender in emotional expression whereby women "receive not only their husband's frustration displaced from the office to home, but also the anger of other women who are dissimilarly displaced upon" (p. 296). In a later work, Hochschild (1983), a prime mover in establishing the field known as "the sociology of emotions," demonstrates how emotions are often co-opted for commercial benefit. For example, those women employed in female-dominated clerical, service, and sales occupations often find that "emotional work" is a part of their job in addition to their more formal job description. They are expected to keep things functioning smoothly by managing the emotional climate at work—by smiling and creating an upbeat and friendly attitude.

Dale Spender's (1981) anthology *Men's Studies Modified: The Impact of Feminism on the Academic Disciplines* focuses on gender and knowledge building across the disciplines. Spender notes,

> Most of the knowledge produced in our society has been produced by men. . . . They have created men's studies (the academic curriculum), for, by not acknowledging that they are presenting only the explanation of men, they have "passed off" this knowledge as human knowledge. (p. 1)

In writing this volume, Spender hoped to draw attention to cutting-edge research across the disciplines that began to "alter the power configurations in the construction of knowledge in society" (p. 8).

Many anthologies quickly followed, including Sandra Harding's (1987a) edited volume, *Feminism and Methodology*. In the preface to this volume, Harding raises a central issue, namely, "Is there a unique feminist method of inquiry?" She suggests that at the heart of feminist inquiry are the emergent questions and issues that feminists raise about the social reality and the practices of traditional research. She asserts,

A closer examination of the full range of feminist social analyses reveals that often it is not exactly alternative methods that are responsible for what is significant about this research. Instead, we can see in this work alternative origins of problematics, explanatory hypotheses and evidence, alternative purposes of inquiry, and a new prescription for the appropriate relationship between the inquirer and his/her subject of inquiry. (p. vii)

If we look inside Harding's volume, we find several chapters that interrogate the relationship between gender and the social sciences. Carolyn Wood Sherif's (1987) article calls attention to androcentric research being conducted in the field of psychology. Sherif begins her analysis of bias by quoting Weisstein's thesis of the 1960s that "psychology has nothing to say about what women are really like, what they need and what they want, essentially because psychology does not know" (p. 38). In seeking to raise the status of their discipline, psychologists began to emulate the theories and practices of the more prestigious hard sciences. This reliance on biological and physical science models of inquiry invariably led to biased theories about women and gender. Bonnie Thornton Dill's (1987) chapter in this same volume points to the tendency of researchers, including some feminist researchers, to generalize women's social situation, leaving out differences of race, class, and cultural context. She uses the example of "femininity" and explains how the concept has been dominated by images of white middle- and upper-middle-class conceptions of womanhood. She provides alternative frameworks for analyzing the concept by taking women's race, class, and cultural context-bound differences into account. Joan Kelly-Gadol's (1987) chapter in Harding's edited volume provides a critique of the androcentrism of historical method by illustrating the myriad ways in which feminist research questions historical work. Kelly-Gadol focuses on historians' use of field-defining concepts such as "periodization," a particular set of events historians chose to focus on (usually those activities men were engaged in, such as diplomatic and constitutional history, as well as political, economic, and cultural history). She troubles the concept of periodization by including gender as a category of analysis that opens

the possibility of asking new questions: Was the period of *Renaissance* beneficial for women? While the Renaissance brought dramatic changes in social and cultural life that benefited many men, a growing division between the private and the public life meant that most women, even those of the upper class, experienced increasing segregation from men and a loss of power and freedom in the public sphere. Kelly-Gadol's vision of including women in history changes the fundamental way historians visualize historical periods. In addition, our understanding of social change also shifts when we conceive of women as *agents* of historical change. Kelly-Gadol does not include a specific discussion of other differences such as race, class, and sexual preference in her vision of historical method. However, by decentering white male concerns and activities as the central focal point of historical inquiry and by making gender a category fundamental to historical analysis, the way is paved for alternative viewpoints to enter the historical landscape. Including gender as a category of analysis also provides historians with a more complex understanding of history's influence on both genders.

Nancy Tuana's edited volume *Feminism & Science* (1989a) contains a range of readings that critique the gendered nature of the sciences. In the preface to her volume, Tuana notes, "Although feminists were not the first to reject the traditional image of science, we were the first to carefully explore the myriad ways in which sexist biases affected the nature and practice of science" (p. xi). Nancy Tuana's own research article in this volume reveals the extent to which "scientists work within and through the worldview of their time" (Tuana, 1989b, p. 147). Tuana examines theories of reproduction from Aristotle to the preformationists, and shows how these theories justify women's inferiority. She notes, "Aristotle set the basic orientation for the next 2000 years of embryological thought . . . the gender/science system is woven tightly into the fabric of science" (p. 169).

Emily Martin's (1987) monograph, *The Woman in the Body*, published around the same time as Nancy Tuana's book, also provides a feminist analysis of science but through an examination of medical discourse. Martin exposes the range of sex-biased assumptions embedded within reproductive medical texts that serve to disempower women and compares these images to women's perceptions of their reproductive lives. She discovers that medical texts employ an image of birth as "production," with the uterus likened to a "machine." Within this framework, menstruation and menopause become "failed production." Martin also finds that white middle-class women are most apt to accept these dominant images. Like Tuana's, Martin's research underscores the androcentrism embedded in scientific literature and research and demonstrates the extent to which the "hard" sciences exist within value-laden social contexts that affect their practices and findings.

## TURN TOWARD FEMINIST EPISTEMOLOGIES AND METHODOLOGIES: THE SHIFTING OF TECTONIC PLATES

Although we have barely touched on the range of contributions of feminist scholarship, it is clear that the decades of the 1970s and 1980s contributed to the deconstruction of traditional knowledge frameworks—taken-for-granted knowledge across several disciplines. In contrast to this endeavor, the 1980s and 1990s saw feminists launching other important challenges to knowledge building, starting with a basic foundational question:

- What is the nature of the social reality?

*Positivism* is a traditional research paradigm based on "the scientific method"; a form of knowledge building in which "there is only *one* logic of science, to which any intellectual activity aspiring to the title of 'science' should follow" (Keat & Urry, cited in Neuman, 2000, p. 66). Positivism's model of inquiry is based on logic and empiricism. It holds out a specific epistemology of knowing—that truth lies "out there," in the social reality waiting to be discovered, if only the scientist is "objective" and "value-free," in the pursuit of knowledge building. It posits "causal relationships" between variables that depend on the testing of specific hypotheses deduced from a general theory. The

goal is to generalize research findings to a wider population and even to find causal laws that predict human behavior. Positivists present their results in the form of quantified patterns of behaviors reported in the form of statistical results. Early on, the social sciences wanted to establish themselves as a "science" in consort with the "natural sciences." Auguste Comte (1798–1857), known as the father of French positivism, sought to incorporate the primary tenets of positivism, into the discipline of sociology. Comte envisioned knowledge building passing through the "law of three stages": the "theological" or "fictitious" stage, characterized by beliefs in the supernatural; "the metaphysical" or "abstract" stage, a transitional state of knowledge building where nature and its abstract forces are at work; and, finally, the "positivist" or "scientific stage," the pinnacle of knowledge, through which we seek to uncover the laws that govern social behavior (Comte, 1896/2000, p. 27).

Émile Durkheim also aspired to make sociology more scientific. In *The Rules of Sociological Method*, Durkheim (1938) asserts that the discipline of sociology can create the same objective conditions that existed in the natural sciences. He codifies positivism by providing social scientists with specific rules and guidelines that will enable them to conduct value-free research, to separate facts from values, and to discover what he terms "social facts"—facts that "have an independent existence outside the individual consciousness" (p. 20). According to Durkheim, discarding sensation (feelings, values, and emotion) is an imperative aspect of knowledge building:

> It is a rule in the natural sciences to discard those data of sensation that are too subjective, in order to retain exclusively those presenting a sufficient degree of objectivity. Thus the physicist substitutes, for the vague impressions of temperature and electricity, the visual registrations of the thermometer or the electrometer. The sociologist must take the same precautions. (p. 44)

Feminist researchers do not necessarily embrace or eschew the practice of a positivist mode of inquiry. Some feminist researchers warn that the practice of positivism can lead to "bad science." This was the very motivation of *feminist empiricists* who urged scholars and researchers across the disciplines to be mindful of who is *left out* of research models in attempts to claim generalizations and to tend to issues of difference in the research process (see, e.g., the preceding critique of androcentrism and Hundleby, this volume). Other feminist scholars and researchers have critiqued positivism's tendency toward dualisms—between quantitative and qualitative research, between the subject and object of research, and between rationality and emotion. Sprague and Zimmerman (1993) argue, for example, that by setting up a subject-object split, whereby the researcher is removed from the research process and placed on a different plane, the practice of positivism promotes a hierarchy between the researcher and the researched that mimics patriarchy. Sprague and Zimmerman also challenge the positivist exclusion of emotions and values from the research process and call for an integration of quantitative and qualitative research.

On the other hand, positivism per se is not the enemy of all feminist inquiry; rather, the problem is with certain practices arising from how the method is carried out by some mainstream social researchers. Some feminist researchers see positivism as having merit, especially by adding validity to feminist research projects. Feminist empiricists continue to draw on positivists' traditions (see the chapters in this volume by Miner-Rubino, Jayaratne, & Konik; Rosser; and Stewart & Cole), and some research questions may call forth a positivistic framework, especially if the goal of the research project requires the testing of a specific research hypothesis on a broad spectrum of data with the goal of generalizing to a wider population. Some feminist social policy advocates have also argued for its inclusion. For example, Roberta Spalter-Roth and Heidi Hartmann, in their social policy work on women and welfare, call for the "strategic" use of a quantitative paradigm in conjunction with a qualitative one to "heighten consciousness and to provide credible numbers that can help advocates to mobilize political support" (Spalter-Roth & Hartmann, 1996, p. 221).

Finally, sociologist Janet Saltzman Chafetz (2004) objects to the confounding of positivism with terms such as "instrument of social control" and "masculine knowledge building." She attributes these misrepresentations to the confusion surrounding the meaning of the term:

> In part this has happened because of the erroneous confusion of this term with the kind of mindless empiricism that has marked so much sociological research. I believe that theory development and well-crafted, theoretically oriented research go hand-in-hand, and that this is in fact what "positivism" is all about. (p. 327)

According to Chafetz (2004), there is "nothing in the view that patterned behaviors and processes exist, can be measured, and can be explained in substantial measure cross-culturally and pan-historically that *automatically* denigrates or controls people" (p. 328). Instead, Chafetz sees the positivistic perspective working for feminist ends.

*Feminist empiricism* made important contributions toward uncovering androcentric bias in social research by encouraging the practice of good science. A more radical set of feminist epistemologies and methodologies was to come, as feminist researchers began to interrogate, disrupt, modify, and at times radically challenge existing ways of knowing within and across their disciplines, creating a shift in the tectonic plates of mainstream knowledge building. Beginning with a critique of positivism's concept of scientific objectivity—and from the idea of a "value-free" science with its stress on the detachment of the researcher from the researched—the feminist movement toward alternative epistemologies began to take shape. Feminists went to the heart of some basic foundational questions, namely, Who can know? What can be known?

Instead of working to improve the accuracy, objectivity, and universality of mainstream research by including women, feminists started to challenge the viability and utility of concepts like objectivity and universality altogether. Knowledge is achieved, not through "correcting" mainstream research studies by adding women, but through paying attention to the specificity and uniqueness of women's lives and experiences.

Donna Haraway (1988), Sandra Harding (1993), and Kum-Kum Bhavnani (1993) argue, for example, that objectivity needs to be transformed into "feminist objectivity." Donna

Haraway defines feminist objectivity as "situated knowledges." Feminist objectivity asserts that *knowledge and truth are partial, situated, subjective, power imbued, and relational.* The denial of values, biases, and politics is seen as unrealistic and undesirable (see also Bhavnani, 1993, p. 96; Harding, 1993, p. 49). Historian Joan Scott (1999) disputes the positivist notion of a one-to-one correspondence between experience and social reality. Instead, she asserts that experience is shaped by one's particular context—specific circumstances, conditions, values, and relations of power. Each influences how one articulates "experience." Scott ushered in a "linguistic turn" in our understanding of social reality by pointing out how experience is discursively constructed by dominant ideological structures. Tracing the discourse surrounding experience provides a method for examining the underlying mechanisms of oppression within society that in fact may provide new avenues of resistance and transformation.

In addition to valuing women's unique and situated experiences as knowledge (Bowles & Duelli-Klein, 1983; Smith, 1987, 1990; Stanley & Wise, 1983), some feminists make the case for validating the importance of emotions and values as a critical lens in research endeavors (Jaggar, 1997; Sprague & Zimmerman, 1993). Alison Jaggar recognizes emotion as a central aspect of knowledge building. According to Jaggar (1997), it is unrealistic to assume emotions and values do not surface during the research process. Our emotions, in fact, are an integral part of why a given topic or set of research questions is studied and how it is studied. The positivistic dualism between the rational and the emotional becomes a false dichotomy:

> Values and emotions enter into the science of the past and the present not only on the level of scientific practice but also on the metascientific level, as answers to various questions: What is Science? How should it be practiced? And what is the status of scientific investigation versus nonscientific modes of enquiry? (p. 393)

Sandra Harding's (1993) concept of "*strong objectivity*" is a specific example of how to practice the basic premise of "feminist objectivity."

Harding critiques the traditional, or positivist, concept of objectivity because its focus resides only on the "context of justification," of the research process—how the research is carried out and making sure that the researcher's values and attitudes do not enter into this process. What is left out of consideration is the extent to which values and attitudes of the researcher also enter into the "context of discovery," that part of the research process that asks questions and formulates specific research hypotheses. Donna Haraway (1988) characterizes this positivist tendency as the "god trick," and notes that it is "that mode of seeing that pretends to offer a vision that is from everywhere and nowhere, equally and fully" (p. 584). By contrast, Harding (1993) argues that throughout the research process, subjective judgments on the part of the researcher are always made "in the selection of problems, the formation of hypotheses, the design of research (including the organization of research communities), the collection of data, the interpretation and sorting of data, decisions about when to stop research, the way results of research are reported, and so on." And to practice strong objectivity requires researchers to self-reflect on what values, attitudes, and agenda they bring to the research process—strong objectivity requires that "the subjects of knowledge be placed on the same critical causal plane as the objects of knowledge" (p. 69). How does a researcher's own history and positionality influence, for example, the questions she or he asks? It is in the practice of strong self-reflexivity that the researcher becomes more objective.

Feminist philosopher Lorraine Code (1991), in her book *What Can She Know? Feminist Theory and the Construction of Knowledge,* offers yet another viewpoint regarding positivism's "objectivity" claim. She argues for a "mitigated relativism" that avoids charges of "objectivism" and "relativism."

> I prefer to characterize the position I advocate as a *mitigated relativism*, however, or the freedom it offers from the homogenizing effects of traditional objectivism, in which differences, discrepancies, and deviations are smoothed out for the sake of achieving a unified theory. With its commitment to difference, critical relativism is able to resist reductivism and to accommodate divergent

perspectives. Mitigated in its constraints by "the facts" of material objects and social/political artifacts, yet read to account for the mechanisms of power (in a Foucauldian sense) and prejudice (in a Gadamerian sense) that produce knowledge of these facts, and committed to the self-critical stance that its mitigation requires, such relativism is a resourceful epistemological position. (pp. 320–321)

Through disclosing their values, attitudes, and biases in their approach to particular research questions and in engaging in strong reflexivity throughout the research process, feminist researchers can actually improve objectivity of the research. Feminists have forged new epistemologies of knowledge by incorporating women's lived experiences, emotions, and feelings into the knowledge building process. We now turn to take a more in-depth look at the branch of feminist epistemology that centers on women's experience as a primary source of knowledge.

## FEMINIST STANDPOINT EPISTEMOLOGY: FEMINIST RESEARCH GROUNDED IN THE EXPERIENCE OF THE OPPRESSED

Feminist standpoint epistemology borrows from the Marxist and Hegelian idea that individuals' daily activities or material, lived experience structures their understanding of the social world. Karl Marx viewed knowledge as historically constructed and relative because it is based on a given "mode of production." Elites (owners of the "means of production") shape knowledge and ideology to justify social inequality. For both Marx and Hegel, the master's perspective is partial and distorted, whereas the worker/slave's is more complete because the worker/slave must comprehend her or his own world and the master's—the worker/slave must know both worlds to survive. Feminist standpoint scholars argue that it is a woman's oppressed location within society that provides fuller insights into society as a whole; women have access to an enhanced and more nuanced understanding of social reality than men do precisely because of their structurally oppressed location vis-à-vis the dominant group, or men. Dorothy Smith (1987), an early proponent of the standpoint perspective, stresses the necessity

of starting research from women's lives, taking into account women's everyday experiences through paying particular attention to and finding and analyzing the gaps that occur when women try to fit their lives into the dominant culture's way of conceptualizing women's situation. By looking at the difference between the two perspectives, the researcher gains a more accurate and theoretically richer set of explanations of the lives of the oppressors and the oppressed.

Early critics of standpoint epistemology argued that it collapses all women's experiences into a single defining experience, with little attention paid to the diversity of women's lives, especially those women who differ by race, class, sexual preference, and so on. Still others raised questions such as the following: If knowledge starts out from the oppressed, how does one ascertain who is the most oppressed? Feminist standpoint scholars and researchers have responded to these concerns, and standpoint epistemology has undergone many different iterations over time. The concept of multiple standpoints has been introduced. Later versions of standpoint are open to comparing and understanding the interlocking relationships between racism, sexism, heterosexism, and class oppression as additional starting points into understanding the social reality (see the chapters in this volume by Harding, Naples, and Wylie). The current dialogue (Harding, 2004), ongoing development, and diversity of approaches to feminist standpoint epistemology notwithstanding, by calling attention to women's lived experiences of oppression as the starting point for building knowledge, feminist standpoint scholars and researchers provided a new way to answer two epistemological questions: Who can know? and What can be known?

## FEMINIST EPISTEMOLOGIES AND METHODOLOGIES: THE CHALLENGE AND POSSIBILITIES OF THE POSTMODERN TURN

We can think of postmodernism as a theoretical paradigm that serves as an "umbrella term" for a variety of perspectives from critical theory to poststructural theory to postmodern theories. What creates unity among these perspectives is their concern for highlighting the importance of researching difference—there is an emphasis on including the "other" in the process of research (Hesse-Biber, Leavy, & Yaiser, 2004, p. 18). The perspectives contained within this umbrella term call for, in a range of degrees, the transformative practices of research that lead toward challenging dominant forms of knowledge building and empowering of subjected understandings. But there is also variation and contestation among and between perspectives within this umbrella term. For example, critical theory is especially cognizant of the role that power plays in producing hegemonic knowledge. Critical theorists seek to expose dominant power relationships and knowledge that oppresses with the goal of "critical emancipation"—creating an environment where oppressed groups "gain the power to control their own lives in solidarity with a justice-oriented community" (see Kincheloe & McLaren, 2000, p. 282). However, some might consider critical theory's emphasis on emancipation to be inconsistent with the tendency of postmodern and poststructural theories to deconstruct dominant discourse. These variations in postmodern perspectives are compared and contrasted in more detail by Gannon and Davies (this volume). Gannon and Davies point out how labels such as postmodernism, poststructuralism, and critical theory are often confusing, and how practitioners of these perspectives don't always agree on what these terms mean. They note,

> What each of these names refers to is not an orderly, agreed on, and internally consistent set of ideas. What they mean depends on the vantage point from which the speaking or writing is being done. Among those who wear each of these labels there are many interesting and productive divisions, which are ignored when they are lumped together under one collective noun.

In the volume *Feminist Perspectives on Social Research* (Hesse-Biber et al., 2004), Patricia Leavy, Michelle Yaiser, and I point out the affinity of postmodernism with feminist research pursuits. We note that postmodernism's emphasis on bringing the "other" into the research process

> meshes well with the general currents within the feminist project itself. Feminists from all

traditions have always been concerned with including women in their research in order to rectify the historic reliance on men as research subjects. This is a general feminist concern. (Hesse-Biber et al., 2004, p. 18)

In addition, the postmodernist emphasis on empowerment of oppressed groups is congruent with the feminist emphasis on social change and social justice. This is also particularly the case with postmodern feminists including postcolonial feminists who seek to explore "political cultural resistance to hierarchical modes of structuring social life by being attentive to the dynamics of power and knowledge" (Hesse-Biber et al., 2004, p. 18).

Although postmodern and poststructural perspectives invigorate feminist theory and praxis, there is also a tendency for them to destabilize it (Barrett & Phillips, 1992). For example, poststructural theorists have challenged essentialist categories: women, sex, gender, and the body. Michèle Barrett and Anne Phillips (1992), in *Destablizing Theory: Contemporary Feminist Debates,* note,

> The fear now expressed by many feminists is that the changing theoretical fashions will lead us towards abdicating the goal of accurate and systematic knowledge; and that in legitimate critique of some of the earlier assumptions, we may stray too far from feminism's original project. (p. 6)

Gilmartin, Lydenberg, and I point out in our book *Feminist Approaches to Theory and Methodology* (Hesse-Biber, Gilmartin, & Lydenberg, 1999) how the destabilizing of these binary categories served to polarize feminist theory:

> French feminists like Hélène Cixous (1986), Luce Irigaray (1991), and Julia Kristeva (1986) were accused by social constructionists of biological essentialism, of establishing the female body and maternity as foundational and symbolic sources of woman's psychic and sexual difference. . . . poststructuralist critics, like Judith Butler, expose even the materiality of the body as "already gendered, already constructed." Extending her argument that gender and sex are the result of the "ritualized repetition" of certain behaviors designed to render

the body either "intelligible" (normative, heterosexual) or abject (unthinkable, homosexual), Judith Butler asserts that the body itself is "forcibly produced" by power and discourse (Butler, 1993, p. xi). (Hesse-Biber et al., 1999, p. 4)

The challenge for feminism is to dialogue around these tensions, and to be open to different points of view. Gannon and Davies (this volume) examine the opportunities that open up for feminist theory and research when the postmodern meets the feminist terrain of theory and praxis.

## FEMINIST EPISTEMOLOGIES AND METHODOLOGIES: THE TURN TOWARD DIFFERENCE IN FEMINIST THEORY AND PRACTICE

The positivist paradigm assumes the viability of the *value-neutral and objective* researcher, who, by applying value-neutral and objective research methods, can obtain generalized findings or universal truths. Based on these assumptions, positivism has very specific answers to epistemological questions. Certain types of "knowledge" are not considered scientific knowledge, certain ways of obtaining knowledge are not valid, and certain people may not possess knowledge. Because positivism was the dominant paradigm in social science for many years, certain people, knowledge, and methods have been excluded from social science research. These "others" and the knowledge they possess are not considered valid or valuable.

Feminists initiated their critique of positivism by (1) calling attention to the fact that women had been left out of much mainstream research and (2) valuing the perspectives, feelings, and lived experiences of women as knowledge. In the 1980s and 1990s, however, some feminists warned against the tendency to reduce all women to one category with shared characteristics. Yes, it was important to give voice to women who had been left out of mainstream research models and to recognize women's life stories as knowledge. But which women's stories were being told—whose life experiences were included and whose were left out?

Through feminism's interaction with postcolonialism, poststructuralism, and postmodernism, there occurred a turn toward difference research. Feminists became increasingly conscious of the diversity of women's experiences. They argued against the idea of one essential experience of women and began to recognize a plurality of women's lived experiences.

Feminist research on difference stressed issues of difference regarding race, class, and gender. Feminists of color critiqued the shortcomings of early feminist research to explore the important interconnections among categories of difference in terms of gender, ethnicity, and class (see, e.g., Anzaldúa, 1987; hooks, 1990; Mohanty, 1988). As Hirsch and Keller (1990) observed, "Feminists of color have revealed to white middle-class feminists the extent of their own racism" (p. 379). Sociologist Patricia Hill Collins (1990) stresses the significance of Black feminist thought—"the ideas produced by black women that clarify a standpoint of and for Black women" (p. 37). Listening to the experiences of the "other" leads to a more complete understanding of knowledge. Black women, argues Hill Collins, are "outsiders within." To socially navigate within white society, black women have to cope with the rules of the privileged white world but at the same time, they are constantly aware of their marginalized position in terms of their race and gender. In contrast, sociological insiders, because of their privileged positionality, are "in no position to notice the specific anomalies apparent to Afro-American women, because these same sociological insiders produced them" (p. 53). Along with this epistemology, Patricia Hill Collins develops a "matrix of domination" framework for conceptualizing difference along a range of interlocking inequalities of race, class, and gender. These factors inflect each other and are socially constructed. It is only through collectively examining the intricately connected matrix of difference that we can truly understand a given individual's life experience. Feminists of color challenged and changed white feminist scholarly research and the conceptualization of feminist standpoint epistemology by asking the question Which women? For example, Patricia Hill Collins's conception of "standpoint" as relational, and including multiple systems of oppression, forced white feminists to examine white privilege as an element of oppression (see McIntosh, 1995).

Bonnie Thornton Dill, Amy McLaughlin, and Angel David Nieves expand and elaborate on the early work of scholars like Hill Collins whose focus lies in analyzing the interconnections of differences among race, class, and gender. They employ the term *intersectionality* to describe the idea that "people live multiple, layered identities and can simultaneously experience oppression and privilege." Their chapter traces the impact of diversity on disciplinary and interdisciplinary scholarship over the past several decades and charts some future directions for knowledge building that embody a vision of intersectionality within academic institutions.

## FEMINIST EPISTEMOLOGIES AND METHODOLOGIES: THE TURN TOWARD GLOBALIZATION

Feminist scholars and researchers continue to engage issues of difference across gender, ethnicity, and class. As Bonnie Thornton Dill (1987) reminds us, "Our analysis must include critical accounts of women's situation in every race, class, and culture—we must work to provide resources so that every woman can define problematics, generate concepts and theories" (Dill, 1987, p. 97). In the first decade of the 21st century, feminists are expanding their focus on difference to include issues of sexual preference and disability, as well as nationality and geographical region. There is also a growing awareness among feminist researchers of the importance of women's experiences in a global context with respect to issues of imperialism, colonialism, and national identity (see the chapters in this volume by Bhavnani; Bickham Mendez & Wolf; Dill, McLaughlin, & Nieves; and Kim). Frequently, analyses that incorporate race, class, and gender differences ignore the diversity among women with regard to their particular geographical/cultural placement across the globe.

- How do we conceptualize and study difference in a global context?

- What research frameworks serve to empower and promote social change for women?

Feminists doing international research, who attempt to speak for "the other/s" in a global context, should be particularly mindful of the inherent power dynamics in doing so. In what sense does the researcher give voice to the other and to what extent is that privilege one that is taken or granted by "the other/s"? Postcolonial feminist Spivak (1994) notes:

> On the other side of the international division of labor, the subject of exploitation cannot know and speak the text of female exploitation even if the absurdity of the nonrepresenting intellectual making space for them to speak is achieved. The woman is doubly in shadow.

Historian Deniz Kandiyoti (1999) discusses the tendency of some Western feminist researchers to "universalize" disciplinary concepts, ignoring the ethnocentrism that lies deep within constructs such as patriarchy. Kandiyoti also calls for the employment of a historical-comparative lens to strengthen our understanding of the cross-cultural context of conceptual meaning across Western and non-Western societies (Mohanty, 1988).

Feminists working in a global context call for a heightened attention to power and difference. But what about the potential for women to come together across difference and forge social change? Some feminist researchers call for employing a type of "strategic essentialism" in their research projects (Spivak, 1994). Susan Bordo (1990) encourages the strategic use of essentialism for women to promote their political agenda (see also Spivak, 1990, p. 10). She argues that "too relentless a focus on historical heterogeneity . . . can obscure the transhistorical hierarchical patterns of white, male privilege that have informed the creation of the Western intellectual tradition" (Bordo, 1990, p. 149). Chandra Talpade Mohanty (1999) also employs the strategic use of essentialism, using three case studies of Third World women involved in the global division of labor. Mohanty shows how ideologies of domesticity, femininity, and race are employed by capitalists to socially construct the "domesticated woman worker"—the dominant perception of the women as "dependent housewives" allows the capitalist to pay them low wages. By having women identify with each other as "women" and through their shared material interests as "workers," they are able to overcome differences in nationality, race, and social class background. These identifications across difference provide a rethinking of Third World women as agents rather than victims. Mohanty argues for political solidarity among women workers as a potential "revolutionary basis for struggles against capitalist re-colonization" (p. 385; see also Hesse-Biber, 2002).

Locating the intersections where women's differences cross is a way that some feminists have begun to research difference in a global context and to empower women's voices. Kum-Kum Bhavnani (this volume) suggests the need to look for *interconnections* between women and does not believe that using an "intersecting" metaphor works well to empower women's lives. In fact, the concept of an "intersection" implies the image of a crossroad, whereby those who meet are coming from and going to given locations, which are determined by the route that these roads take. This metaphor does not provide a way for a new road to be charted; instead the roads are fixed. A race-d/gender-ed person stands at the crossroad (that point where race and gender routes intersect), yet as Bhavnani notes,

> the meeting point of those crossroads . . . directs the gaze to the intersections of the roads and the directions in which they travel and meet. . . . This matters because if we are not only to analyze the world but also to change it, then the easiest way to imagine the shifts in the relationships between "race"/ethnicity and gender is to imagine the roads being moved to form new intersections.

Bhavnani suggests that a more empowering metaphor might be to think of these roads as

> "interconnections" that configure each other—because *interconnections that configure* connotes more movement and fluidity than lies in the metaphor of intersection, as well as offering a way of thinking about how not only race and gender but also nation, sexuality, and wealth all interconnect, configure, and reshape each other.

Much of the theorizing and research studies on the concerns of women in a global context, however, remain fragmented. Black feminists, Third World feminists, and global/postcolonial/transnational feminists often remain uninformed about each other's theories/perspectives and research (see especially Kim's comments, this volume). What remains a challenge for feminist research is the creation of links between these strands of knowledge building to gather a more complex understanding of the workings of racism, imperialism, and neocolonialism across historical and cultural contexts. What are the models of knowledge building that will allow feminist researchers to study these interconnections? To do this requires an understanding of how feminists carry out their research and what overarching principles guide their work.

The journey we have only briefly outlined thus far opens a window into feminist thinking on issues of epistemology and methodology. Feminists have employed new ways of thinking and modified our understanding of the nature of the social world—providing new questions and angles of vision with which to understand women's issues and concerns. Feminist epistemology and methodology directly affects feminist praxis.

## FEMINIST PRAXIS: SYNERGISTIC PERSPECTIVE ON THE PRACTICE OF FEMINIST RESEARCH

Feminist praxis refers to the varied ways feminist research proceeds. Feminist perspectives challenge the traditional research paradigm of positivism, which assumes a unified truth with the idea of testing out hypotheses. There is little room for the exploration of personal feelings and experiences, given the strict observance of objectivity as a basic tenet of positivism. Yet as we have seen, new theoretical contributions from feminist standpoint theory (see the chapters in this volume by Harding, Naples, and Wylie), postcolonial theory (Kim, this volume; Mohanty, 1999), and postmodernism (Gannon & Davies, this volume), for example, ask *new* questions that call forth getting at subjugated knowledge, particularly as this relates to issues of difference. Early on, feminists saw the need to make a radical break in positivism's traditional research paradigm. Helen Roberts's (1981) edited volume *Doing Feminist Research* asks the question "What is Feminist Research?" Roberts's pathbreaking volume puts a feminist sociological lens onto the research process, and notes, "The accounts in this collection point to the theoretical, methodological, practical and ethical issues raised in projects in which the investigator has adopted, or has at least become aware of a feminist perspective" (p. 2). Ann Oakley's (1981) now classic article "Interviewing Women: A Contradiction in Terms" demonstrates the importance of breaking down the hierarchical power relationship between the interviewer and the researched that she views as characteristic of a positivist research paradigm and antithetical to the view of women as agents of social change with their own set of experiences. In her introduction to Oakley's article, Helen Roberts notes that for Ann Oakley interviewing is *not* "a one-way process where the interviewer elicits and receives, but does not give information" (p. 30).

Liz Stanley and Sue Wise's (1983) visionary volume *Breaking Out: Feminist Consciousness and Feminist Research* calls for feminist researchers to "upgrade the personal as an object of study." They argue for a "naturalist" as opposed to a "positivistic model" of research to study women's experiences, or what they term "feminist consciousness" in which "feeling and experience" are the primary guideposts for feminist research (p. 178). For Stanley and Wise, there is no demarcation between "doing feminism" and "doing feminist research." Patti Lather's (1991) book *Getting Smart: Feminist Research and Pedagogy With/in the Postmodern* takes up the issue of power in research and teaching practices. She combines insights from feminism and postmodernism with the goal of "emancipatory" knowledge building, where the researcher and researched cocreate meaning through "reciprocity and negotiation." She is interested in what research designs, teaching practices, and curricula produce "liberatory knowledge" and "empower" the researched and the pedagogical process.

Other works on the intersection of feminism and methods quickly followed and spanned the next several decades. Some of the most notable volumes, to name only a few, are Patricia Hill Collins's (1990) *Black Feminist Thought: Knowledge, Consciousness, and the Politics of Empowerment;* Joyce McCarl Nielson's (1990) *Feminist Research Methods: Exemplary Readings in the Social Sciences;* bell hooks's works, *Feminist Theory: From Margin to Center* (1984) and *Yearning: Race, Gender, and Cultural Politics* (1990); Liz Stanley's (1990) *Feminist Praxis: Research, Theory, and Epistemology in Feminist Sociology;* Mary Margaret Fonow and Judith A. Cook's (1991) *Beyond Methodology: Feminist Scholarship as Lived Research;* Sherna Berger Gluck and Daphne Patai's (1991) *Women's Words: The Feminist Practice of Oral History;* Shulamit Reinharz's (1992) *Feminist Methods in Social Research;* Liz Stanley and Sue Wise's follow-up edition to their classic 1983 volume (1993) *Breaking Out Again: Feminist Ontology and Epistemology;* Mary Maynard and June Purvis's (1994) *Researching Women's Lives From a Feminist Perspective;* Sandra Burt and Lorraine Code's (1995) *Changing Methods: Feminists Transforming Practice;* Diane L. Wolf's (1996) *Feminist Dilemmas in Fieldwork;* Louise Lamphere, Helena Ragone, and Patricia Zavella's (1997) *Situated Lives: Gender and Culture in Everyday Life;* Marjorie L. DeVault's (1999) *Liberating Method: Feminism and Social Research;* Linda Tuhiwai Smith's (1999) *Decolonizing Methodologies: Research and Indigenous Peoples;* Elizabeth A. St. Pierre and Wanda S. Pillow's (2000) *Working the Ruins: Feminist Poststructural Theory and Methods in Education;* Caroline Ramazanoğlu's (2002) work *Feminist Methodology: Challenges and Choices;* and Nancy A. Naples's (2003) *Feminism and Method: Ethnography, Discourse Analysis and Activist Research.* Each volume highlights how feminist researchers create a tight link between the elements of the research process—epistemology, methodology, and method. We see this linkage unfolding by looking at how feminists engage with the research process—starting with the research questions they devise, how research methods are practiced, and the special attention given to issues of power, authority, reflexivity, ethics, and difference in the practice, writing, and reading of feminist research.

In all these volumes, feminist epistemologies and methodologies inform research practices. A feminist empiricist perspective on knowledge building informs the practice of survey methods by interrogating the male bias of some survey questions as well as the power differentials between the researcher and the researched in the survey interview. A feminist standpoint epistemologist questions whether the research sample and research questions of a particular method are responsive to issues of difference; whether the findings are interpreted in a way that includes the experiences of marginalized populations. Increasingly, feminists are tweaking old methods and inventing new methods to get at women's experience. We see this most vividly in how feminists practice interview methods. In Marjorie DeVault's (1990, 1999) works on feminist research and methodology as well as in her coauthored chapter with Glenda Gross (this volume), "Feminist Interviewing: Experience, Talk, and Knowledge," there is an awareness of the importance of listening during the interview process:

> One of feminism's central claims is that women's perspectives have often been silenced or ignored; as a result, feminist researchers have been interested in listening for gaps and absences in women's talk, and considering what meanings might lie beyond explicit speech.

By listening through the gaps in talking and by attending to what is not stated, but present—such as the hidden meanings in terms like "you know?"—DeVault (1990) suggests one can get at "subjugated knowledge." What each of these books also demonstrates is that feminists use a range of methods and some even employ multiple methods within the same, concurrent, or follow-up research project to answer complex and often novel questions. Feminist research then becomes qualitative or quantitative or a combination of both.

Shulamit Reinharz (1992), in her classic text *Feminist Methods in Social Research,* notes that "feminism supplies the perspective and the disciplines supply the method. The feminist researcher exists at their intersection" (p. 243). Although feminist research is multiple, complex, quantitative, and qualitative, nevertheless, if we were to *inductively* examine the range of research studies and topics cited in these works and within this volume, which are not exhaustive of the population of feminist research, we can discern some common themes regarding the nature of feminist research that run through it.

## Feminists Ask New Questions

The women's movement of the 1960s, as well as increasing globalization, forged new feminist theoretical perspectives (see Part I of this *Handbook*). Feminist standpoint theory (see the chapters in this volume by Harding, Naples, and Wylie), postcolonialism (Kim, this volume), postmodernism, ethnic studies, queer studies, critical theory, and critical race theory (see the chapters in this volume by Gannon & Davies and Kim) serve to upend traditional knowledge by asking new questions that expose the power dynamics of knowledge building. "Subjugated" knowledge is unearthed, and issues of race, class, sexuality, nationality, and gender are taken into account. These types of questions are different from those questions feminist empiricists ask in that they go beyond correcting gender bias in dominant research studies. In asking new questions, feminist research maintains a close link between epistemology, methodology, and methods.

## Feminist Research Takes Up Issues of Power, Authority, Ethics, and Reflexivity in the Practice of Research

Feminist praxis builds on the understanding of difference and translates these insights by emphasizing the importance of taking issues of power, authority, ethics, and reflexivity into the practice of social research. Feminist researchers are particularly keen on getting at issues of power and authority in the research process, from question formulation to carrying out and writing up research findings (see especially the chapters in this volume by Borland and Roof). Focusing on our positionality within the research process helps to break down the idea that research is the "view from nowhere."

Feminist research practitioners pay attention to reflexivity, a process whereby researchers recognize, examine, and understand how their social background, location, and assumptions affect their research practice. Practicing reflexivity also includes paying attention to the specific ways in which our own agendas affect the research at all points in the research process—from the selection of the research problem to the selection of method and ways in which we analyze and interpret our findings (see Hesse-Biber & Piatelli, this volume). Hesse-Biber and Leckenby (2004), in their work on the importance of self-reflexivity on the part of the researcher, note,

> Feminist researchers are continually and cyclically interrogating their locations as both researcher and as feminist. They engage the boundaries of their multiple identities and multiple research aims through conscientious reflection. This engagement with their identities and roles impacts the earliest stages of research design. Much of feminist research design is marked by an openness to the shifting contexts and fluid intentions of the research questions. (p. 211)

Ethical discussions usually remain detached from a discussion of the research process; some researchers consider this aspect of research as an afterthought. Yet, the ethical standpoint or *moral integrity* of the researcher is a critically important aspect of ensuring that the research process and a researcher's findings are "trustworthy" and valid. The term *ethics* derives from the Greek word *ethos,* which means "character." A feminist ethical perspective provides insights into how ethical issues enter into the selection of a research problem, how one conducts research, the design of one's study, one's sampling procedure, and one's responsibility toward research participants. Feminist ethical issues also come into play in deciding what research findings get published (see Preissle, this volume).

## Feminist Researchers Work at the Margins of Their Disciplines

Feminist research, while breaking out of the traditional circle of knowledge building, remains on the margins of discussion within mainstream methods texts. In 1962, Thomas Kuhn published *The Structure of Scientific Revolutions* (Kuhn, 1962). Kuhn argues that science is enmeshed in a particular mode of thinking—a paradigm, or worldview—that tends to dominate a given field of science. Those insiders who practice within a reigning paradigm do get recognition, and gain legitimacy for their work, through a range of institutional structures—from promotions and tenure committees within the academy and mainstream journals within their field, to monetary rewards from granting agencies and foundations. For feminist epistemologies and methodologies to gain greater recognition and rewards in and outside the academy, and to harness these gains into social policy changes for women, feminists must work at multiple levels. Work must be done within and outside the circle to ensure that women's scholarship is recognized and rewarded as legitimate scholarship within their disciplines and within the social policy initiatives of funding agencies:

> Feminist researchers may need to be strategic about their mission and goals concerning how to organize as a research movement toward social change for women. Issues of difference in the research process need to be carefully addressed as this discussion proceeds. Issues dealing with power and control both within the research process and discussions of differences and similarities among different/competing feminist epistemologies and methodologies would be productive and energetic beginnings toward raising the consciousness of the feminist research communities. (Hesse-Biber & Leckenby, 2004, p. 225)

## ORGANIZATION AND VISION OF THE *HANDBOOK OF FEMINIST RESEARCH*

The *Handbook of Feminist Research* is both a theoretical and a practical approach to conducting social science research on, for, and about women. A goal of this *Handbook* is to help readers develop an understanding of feminist research by introducing a range of feminist epistemologies, theories, methodologies, and methods that have had a significant impact on feminist research practice and on the teaching of women's studies scholarship. This *Handbook* materialized after many semesters of my own involvement as a teacher of undergraduate and graduate methods courses where I found that the topic of feminist research was too often neglected in standard research methods books. This *Handbook* is meant to be a distinctive break from that tradition and to represent instead the establishment and legitimization of new perspectives on the theory and practice of research.

As a teacher at the Graduate Consortium in Women's Studies at Radcliffe College in the mid-1990s, I came to appreciate the importance of taking an interdisciplinary approach to the study and teaching of feminist perspectives on theory and methods. The mission of this program, which began in 1992, was to bring faculty from various disciplines "to discuss ways of consolidating and increasing the availability of feminist research and teaching across the disciplines and across institutions" (Hesse-Biber, Gilmartin, & Lydenberg, 1999, p. 5). I co-taught a course titled "Feminist Perspectives in Research: Interdisciplinary Practice in the Study of Gender" with historian Christina Gilmartin and literary critic Robin Lydenberg. This course became the basis for our coedited book titled *Feminist Approaches to Theory and Methodology* (Hesse-Biber et al., 1999), which brings together a range of interdisciplinary scholarship at the intersection with feminist research and activism. As Christina Gilmartin, Robin Lydenberg, and I note in our introduction to the book, teaching within an interdisciplinary environment was not what we had expected:

> Over the three years during which the editors of this volume revised and team taught this course, we were surprised to discover that as contested as the terrain of feminism has become, the interdisciplinary aspects of the course proved equally if not more problematic. While we eventually reached some shared understandings about feminism—that although its methodologies were rooted in social activism, it could not be reduced to an easily defined set of propositions, theoretical claims, or research methods—the nature and practice of interdisciplinarity remained more elusive. (Hesse-Biber et al., 1999, pp. 5–6)

In a second coedited anthology, *Feminist Perspectives on Social Research* (Hesse-Biber & Yaiser, 2004), I sought to take my experiences of teaching and learning in an interdisciplinary environment and apply them more broadly to all aspects of the research process, paying particular attention to the linkages between epistemology, methodology, and methods. The discussion of a method is followed with research examples, using that method. Thus, my coedited volume, with Michelle Yaiser, became both the theory and praxis of feminist perspectives on research. This volume also underscored for us the critical difference between *acknowledging and practicing difference* within our research endeavors:

> Feminist research has taught us that it is not enough to merely acknowledge the importance of difference. Difference is critical to all aspects of the research process. It is important to incorporate difference into our views of reality, truth, and knowledge. We must examine the difference that difference makes. (Hesse-Biber & Yaiser, 2004, p. 117)

The *Handbook* is directed at two primary audiences: The first group is made up of researchers, practitioners, and students within and outside the academy who conduct a variety of research projects and who are interested in consulting "cutting-edge" research methods and gaining insights into the overall research process. This group includes policymakers and activists who are interested in how to conduct research for social change. The second audience consists of academics who will use the *Handbook* in their scholarship, as well as in courses, primarily at the upper undergraduate and graduate levels as a main or supplementary text.

The variety of use of this *Handbook* required careful consideration in the organization and writing process. For practitioners, the *Handbook* was written in as little technical language as is possible. The authors point to the ongoing debates in the field as well as the practical applications and issues for those whose research affects social policy and social change. For academics, the *Handbook* reflects the most current thinking about feminist research emerging within and across the disciplines and geographical regions. For professors and students who will use the *Handbook* in their courses, the content (concepts/ideas) is well-grounded and, wherever possible, includes specific examples from the literature. The *Handbook* content reflects a diversity of scholarship with respect to race, class, and sexual preference as well as geographic region (e.g., Western and Third World societies). For practitioners and activists, the content is reflective of the ongoing power relationships in which research is practiced.

## Part I. Feminist Perspectives on Knowledge Building

This section traces the historical rise of feminist research and begins with the early links between feminist theory and research practice. We trace the contours of early feminist inquiry and introduce the reader to the history of, and historical debates within, feminist scholarship. We explore the political process of knowledge building by introducing the reader to the link between knowledge and power relations. A series of questions guide our selection of theoretical and research articles for this section:

- How have feminist scholars redefined traditional paradigms in the social sciences and humanities?
- What new theoretical and research models guide their work?

Here we will explore the nature of methodologies, frameworks, and presumptions dominant within the social sciences and humanities. We will point out what we think are the critical turning points in feminist research–"adding women and stirring," feminist standpoint theory, the inclusion of difference, and the debates surrounding method, methodology, and epistemology. Feminist research endeavors often began by pointing out the androcentrism in the sciences. This is often referred to as feminist empiricism, as we shall see in "Feminist Empiricism." Philosopher Catherine Hundleby explores the specific challenges feminists pose for traditional models of knowledge building. She investigates the concept of "objectivity" in the research process and how some feminist researchers have developed alternatives to traditional objectivity. Feminist empiricists work within a positivistic model of knowledge building with the goal of creating "better" science. This better and more objective science is achieved through the application of more

rigorous practices, incorporating difference into the research process, and more strictly following the basic tenets of positivism.

Sandra Harding's chapter "Feminist Standpoints" looks at the origins of standpoint theories that grew out of feminist activism of the 1960s and 1970s and examines the antipositivist "histories, sociologies and philosophies of science" emerging in Europe and the United States. Harding provides us with a history of the development of the standpoint perspective. Feminist standpoint theorists begin with research questions (methodologies) rooted in women's lives—their everyday existence. Drawing on the Marxist theory of the master-slave relationship, Nancy Hartsock (1983), for example, argues that because of women's location within the sexual division of labor, and because of their experience of oppression, women have greater insights as researchers into the lives of other women. Dorothy Smith (1987) stresses the importance of women's own standpoint and experience in creating knowledge. Harding also takes up the critiques against a standpoint perspective. Some critics are uncomfortable with giving up positivism's claim of universal truth. If, as standpoint theory suggests, there are multiple subjectivities, there is the fear that such a perspective leads to chaos. Others charge standpoint theory as too essentialist and Eurocentric in that it distills all women's experience (Western, white women's) into a single vision. Although Harding notes that early examples of standpoint theory, in practice, do give this impression, she states,

> It took the flourishing of writing by women of color, and the delineation of "intersectionality" and of "matrices of oppression," for standpoint theorists to learn to insist on the multiple and often conflicting experiences, lives, and claims of women and of feminists.

The following three chapters address a range of issues including understanding the diversity of women's experiences and the commitment to the empowerment of women and other oppressed groups. Susanne Gannon and Bronwyn Davies discuss postmodern, poststructural, and critical perspectives regarding cultural theory. They look at how some feminist theorists such as

Butler, Grosz, and Briadotti (as cited by Gannon & Davies) incorporate the insights of these perspectives into their own theoretical work and research. Gannon and Davies also illuminate several feminist critiques of these perspectives, such as relativism, a lack of a political vision, and the tendency of some of these perspectives to reinforce the status quo.

Hyun Sook Kim's chapter, "The Politics of Border Crossings: Black, Postcolonial, and Transnational Feminist Perspectives," specifically highlights those epistemologies and methodologies that address issues of political and social difference. Kim discusses the prospects and problems of black feminist and Afrocentric theories of knowledge building. She suggests that although these theories have done a great deal to bring issues of difference to our understanding of knowledge building, each

> uncritically assumes a particular (African American) women's experience as being representative of all black women, not unlike the way Euro-American middle-class Western women assumed theirs to be universally shared by all women. Hence, the critiques of black feminist standpoint theory correctly point to the fissures, fragmentations, and differences between women who differ by race, class, gender, sexuality, nationality, culture, and so on.

Postcolonial and transnational feminist perspectives are particularly aware of the issues knowledge building comes up against as researchers cross over cultural and geographical boundaries. Transnational feminists are interested in examining issues of the "interconnectedness" of gender, race, class, sexuality, ethnicity, and national origin. Kim notes,

> Transnational feminist methodologies attend to the diverse ways in which women and men in particular places and spaces produce and transmit knowledge (and local forms of feminist thought). . . . Feminists working in their specific locations need to reflect on how feminist theories and methodologies travel transversely across cultural and geographical borders and reconsider what happens when and as they do so. . . . How do (and must) feminist researchers and activists address and respond to the uneven and completing flows of ideas and practices?

Kim directly addresses these concerns and questions by zeroing in on the specific power relations in knowledge production, especially those created by the growing power of global capitalism and (neo-imperial) forces. She provides a range of perspectives in the study of difference as well as tools for praxis that meaningfully engage with subjugated knowledge. She notes, "Feminist scholars and activists must constantly ask where the questions and concepts we frame capture the fluid, situated and varied contexts, and whether our analysis adequately attends to the voices and consciousness of marginalized groups."

In her chapter "Feminist Interdisciplinary Approaches to Knowledge Building," Sally Kitch notes that there is little agreement on exactly what the term *interdisciplinary* means as it is used among scholars. Instead, she suggests using the term as an umbrella that includes concepts such as "multidisciplinarity" and "cross-disciplinarity," as well as "transdisciplinarity." She argues that the pursuit of knowledge within a traditional discipline can create "knowledge silos" or boundaries between the terminology, frameworks, methods, and focus areas of participating disciplines.

Although "multidisciplinarity" and "cross-disciplinarity" would seem to break down the boundaries of knowledge silos through collaboration and the borrowing of ideas and concepts, Kitch notes that these efforts are more or less "weak or additive," with little integration of ideas. She argues,

> Participants in such an exchange may borrow tools, data, results, and methods from one another, but that borrowing is not intended to transform existing disciplinary frameworks or boundaries. Indeed, a likely result of cross-disciplinary collaboration is the appropriation of borrowed data or methods into the borrowing discipline. . . . The result tends to be what Diane Elam calls an "interdisciplinary handshake" rather than true disciplinary integration.

What is truly needed, Kitch suggests, is a less prevalent form of interdisciplinarity, known as transdisciplinarity. Transdisciplinarity occurs when researchers working on similar issues or problems engage in a "transformative interaction"—an interaction that is character-ized by integration and reciprocity. According to Kitch, "integrative, reciprocal interdisciplinar-ity, or transdisciplinarity," has "twin feminist epistemological goals: the development of both inclusivity and transnational perspectives in knowledge formation." The goals of feminist transdisciplinary research must never close the circle of knowledge building. As Kitch notes,

> rather, the goal of feminist transdisciplinary research to produce comprehensive, inclusive, appropriately synthesized knowledge about women and gender, which encompasses both synchronies and contradictions and continues to investigate and redefine its own processes, must find its data, theories, and analyses wherever they exist. Without a commitment to this kind of scholarly openness, transdisciplinary femi-nist research might stagnate and succumb to the traditional disciplinary pitfalls it was designed to avoid.

Kitch provides several in-depth examples of the practice of transdisciplinarity within the women's studies curriculum from her home institution, Ohio State University, and the Comparative Gender Studies PhD program at Central European University in Budapest, Hungary.

Feminist perspectives on knowledge build-ing have pushed against the dominant circles of knowledge, cautious about re-creating hege-monic knowledge of the past, sometimes stum-bling, but committed to pushing past the boundaries of traditional knowledge. Feminists do not always agree on the specific paths to travel, and there remain significant tensions among feminists concerning how best to research and represent women's issues and concerns, as well as how to confront the power dynamics that continue to reinforce hegemonic forces that serve the status quo. What is clearly needed from examining the range of perspec-tives feminists offer onto the landscape of knowledge building is a dialogue among feminists. Where are the points of agreement? Disagreement? How can we foster a more transdisciplinary approach to knowledge build-ing? How do we construct a climate where feminist theorists and researchers listen to each other? How tolerant are feminists of each other's points of view? These are the issues that we address in Part I of this *Handbook*. A longer summary of Part I is provided above, because we will launch directly into this section next. But before doing so, I want to give you a peek at what is to follow in Parts II through IV.

## Part II. Feminist Research Praxis

Part II of this *Handbook* debates the issue of whether or not there is a unique feminist method. What makes a method feminist? What are the unique characteristics feminists bring to the practice of this method? What are the strengths and challenges in practicing feminist research? What is gained and what is risked? This section looks at how feminists use a range of research methods in both conventional and unconventional research studies. Many feminist research projects have used survey methods and quantitative data analysis—two tradition-ally androcentric methods—to produce very women-centered results. Methods such as inten-sive interviewing, the collection of oral histories, and qualitative data analysis are often labeled feminist methods by traditional sociolo-gists; however, these methods in the hands of feminists have been tweaked and modified to uncover women's issues and concerns. The labeling of certain methods as traditional or feminist by social scientists, and the use of spe-cific methods by feminist researchers, are the focus of Part II.

This section also stresses the idea that femi-nist researchers come from a variety of episte-mological positions. Feminist researchers use multiple tools to gain access to and understand-ing of the world around them and may use mul-tiple methods within the same study. The selections chosen for this section are not exhaustive of all feminist research or all the methods feminists use. These selections do, however, provide a broad context within which to examine feminist research. Deborah Piatelli and I provide a detailed introduction and theo-retical and research context for Part II in our chapter, "From Theory to Method and Back Again: The Synergistic Praxis of Theory and Method."

## Part III. Feminist Perspectives on the Research Process: Issues and Insights

In Part II of this *Handbook*, we observed how feminist research fosters a tight link between epistemology, methodology, and method. Each of these aspects of knowledge building influences the others. Feminist epistemologies and methodologies stress the importance of starting research from women's lives, and call for examining the lived experience as a mode of truth seeking. These aspects of feminist research, in particular, have important implications for feminist theory and praxis, independent of any particular method feminists may employ. In Part III, "Feminist Perspectives on the Research Process: Issues and Insights," we look at several "key" theory and praxis issues for feminist researchers.

Judith Roof's chapter, "Authority and Representation in Feminist Research," provides a historical context for looking at how feminist researchers have framed issues of power and authority and argues that feminists are "trading between the authority of science and the power of experience." In particular, she notes the tensions between "the impersonal practices of generalization and the more problematic questions of rhetoric and representation." Kathy Charmaz's chapter, "What's Good Writing in Feminist Research? What Can Feminist Researchers Learn About Good Writing?" and Laurel Richardson's "Reading for Another: A Method for Addressing Some Feminist Research Dilemmas" speak to issues of how feminists tackle the process of representation. Both scholars provide specific strategies of representation, especially as this pertains to difference. Kathy Charmaz gives specific advice on what makes for good writing and provides researchers with specific writing advice, from how to title a research paper to how to represent the experiences of those we study. She suggests, for example, that the use of metaphor and specific rhetorical devices as well as tending to the respondents' particular use of language are all important writing strategies. Laurel Richardson provides a "feminist-poststructural method of reading/writing." Both Charmaz and Richardson provide powerful reading and writing techniques that allow for the emergence of subjugated knowledge within the research process.

Mary Hawkesworth's chapter, "Truth and Truths in Feminist Knowledge Production," takes up a central theoretical issue feminists have grappled with, namely, "the nature of and possibilities of truth in feminist research." Sharlene Nagy Hesse-Biber and Deborah Piatelli's chapter stresses the need for a holistic approach to the process of reflexivity that runs "from the formulation of the research problem, to the shifting positionalities of the researcher and participants, through interpretation and writing." They provide specific research examples and strategies for implementing "holistic reflexivity" in the research process. Judith Preissle's chapter, "Feminist Research Ethics," examines feminist challenges to traditional Western approaches to ethics. She conceptualizes feminist ethics as an "ethics of care," and discusses the implications of a feminist ethical approach for the practice of social research. What are the specific ethical practices feminist researchers employ across the research process? Preissle notes that a feminist perspective on ethics is a double-edged endeavor, which will "likely generate as many issues as they may help either avoid or address. This is particularly evident in trading a detached, distant, and hierarchical stance for an intimate, close, and equitable position. Distance and intimacy create their own problems" (Preissle, this volume). Abigail Brooks and I provide a fuller context and discussion of these articles in our introductory chapter to Part III, "Core Feminist Insights and Strategies on Authority, Representations, Truths, Reflexivity, and Ethics Across the Research Process."

## Part IV. Commentaries on Future Directions in Feminist Theory, Research, and Pedagogy

This section is not intended to be an overview of feminist research in a particular discipline or subject matter, but instead, a place for cutting-edge feminist researchers, policymakers, and teachers of feminism to present their visions for the theory, practice, and teaching of feminist research and its implications for creating new research paradigms. This section examines the current tensions within feminist research and the positioning of feminist research within the dominant research paradigms and emerging research practices. I provide a more detailed picture on the range of feminist "conundrums" regarding knowledge building that deal with issues of truth, reason, and logic; how difference is and should be conceptualized and practiced in the research process; how feminists can develop an empowered feminist community of researchers across transnational space; and finally, how feminists can or should convey the range of women's scholarship that refutes the charge that women's studies scholarship conveys only ideology, not knowledge.

## A Parting Reflection

It is my hope that this *Handbook* provides you with a set of unique knowledge frameworks to enhance your understanding of the social world, especially the range of women's lived experiences. The *Handbook* contributors explored a range of feminist issues, themes, and questions including the emphasis on understanding the diversity of women's experiences and the feminist commitment to the empowerment of women and other oppressed groups. Although by no means exhaustive, the *Handbook* examines a broad spectrum of some of the most important feminist perspectives in taking an in-depth look at how a given methodology intersects with epistemology and method to produce a set of research practices. Our thesis is that any given feminist perspective does not preclude the use of specific methods, but serves to guide how a given method is practiced. Whereas each perspective is distinct, it sometimes shares elements with other perspectives.

The ground underneath the theory and practice of feminist research is ever evolving, and it is the shifting of these tectonic plates of knowledge that provides us with an opportunity for what Teresa de Lauretis (1988) suggests as "not merely an expansion or reconfiguration of boundaries, but a qualitative shift in political and historical consciousness" (pp. 138–139).

## References

Anzaldúa, Gloria. (1987). *Borderlands/la frontera: The new mestiza.* San Francisco: Spinsters/Aunt Lute.

Anzaldúa, Gloria. (1990). *Bridge, drawbridge, sandbar or island.* In Lisa Albrecht & Rose M. Brewer (Eds.), *Bridges of power: Women's multicultural alliances* (pp. 216–231). Philadelphia: New Society Publishers.

Barrett, Michèle, & Phillips, Anne. (1992). *Destabilizing theory: Contemporary feminist debates.* Stanford, CA: Stanford University Press.

Bhavnani, Kum-Kum. (1993). Tracing the contours: Feminist research and feminist objectivity. *Women's Studies International Forum, 16,* 95–104.

Bordo, Susan. (1990). Feminism, postmodernism, and gender-skepticism. In Linda Nicholson (Ed.), *Feminism/postmodernism* (pp. 133–156). London: Routledge.

Bowles, G., & Duelli-Klein, R. D. (Eds.). (1983). *Theories of women's studies.* London: Routledge & Kegan Paul.

Burt, Sandra, & Code, Lorraine. (Eds.). (1995). *Changing methods: Feminists transforming practice.* Ontario, Canada: Broadview Press.

Butler, Judith. (1993). *Bodies that matter: On the discursive limits of "sex."* New York: Routledge.

Chafetz, Janet Saltzman. (2004). Some thoughts by an unrepentant "positivist" who considers herself a feminist nonetheless. In Sharlene Hesse-Biber & Michelle L. Yaiser (Eds.), *Feminist perspectives on social research* (pp. 320–329). New York: Oxford University Press.

Code, Lorraine. (1991). *What can she know? Feminist theory and the construction of knowledge.* Ithaca, NY: Cornell University Press.

Collins, Patricia Hill. (1990). *Black feminist thought: Knowledge, consciousness, and the politics of empowerment.* New York: Routledge.

Collins, Patricia Hill. (1999). Learning from the outsider within: The sociological significance of black feminist thought. In Sharlene Hesse-Biber, Christina Gilmartin, & Robin Lydenberg (Eds.), *Feminist approaches to theory and methodology* (pp. 135–178). New York: Oxford University Press.

Comte, Auguste. (2000). *The positive philosophy of Auguste Comte* (Harriet Martineau, Trans., Vol. 1). Kitchener, Canada: Batoche Books. (Original work published 1896)

de Beauvoir, Simone. (1952). *The second sex*. New York: Vintage Books.

de Lauretis, Teresa. (1988). Displacing hegemonic discourses: Reflections on feminist theory in the 1980s. *Inscriptions, 3*(4), 127–145.

DeVault, Marjorie L. (1990). Talking and listening from women's standpoint: Feminist strategies for interviewing and analysis. *Social Problems, 37,* 96–116.

DeVault, Marjorie L. (1999). *Liberating method: Feminism and social research*. Philadelphia: Temple University Press.

Dill, Bonnie Thornton. (1987). The dialectics of black womanhood. In Sandra Harding (Ed.), *Feminism and methodology* (pp. 97–108). Bloomington: Indiana University Press.

Durkheim, Émile. (1938). *The rules of sociological method*. Glencoe, IL: Free Press.

Eichler, Margrit, & Lapointe, Jeanne. (1985). *On the treatment of the sexes in research*. Ottawa, Canada: Social Sciences and Humanities Council.

Fonow, Mary Margaret, & Cook, Judith A. (Eds.). (1991). *Beyond methodology: Feminist scholarship as lived research*. Bloomington: Indiana University Press.

Friedan, Betty. (1963). *The feminine mystique*. New York: W. W. Norton.

Gluck, Sherna Berger, & Patai, Daphne. (Eds.). (1991). *Women's words: The feminist practice of oral history*. New York: Routledge.

Haraway, Donna. (1988). Situated knowledges: The science question in feminism and the privilege of partial perspective. *Feminist Studies, 14*(13), 575–599.

Harding, Sandra. (Ed.). (1987a). *Feminism and methodology*. Bloomington: Indiana University Press.

Harding, Sandra. (1987b). Introduction. In Sandra Harding (Ed.), *Feminism and methodology* (pp. 1–14). Bloomington: Indiana University Press.

Harding, Sandra. (1993). Rethinking standpoint epistemology: What is "strong objectivity"? In Linda Alcoff & Elizabeth Potter (Eds.), *Feminist epistemologies* (pp. 49–82). New York: Routledge.

Harding, Sandra. (Ed.). (2004). *The feminist standpoint theory reader: Intellectual and political controversies*. New York: Routledge.

Hartsock, Nancy. (1983). The feminist standpoint: Developing the ground for a specifically feminist historical materialism. In Sandra Harding & Merrill Hintikka (Eds.), *Discovering reality* (pp. 283–310). Dordrecht, the Netherlands: Kluwer Academic.

Hesse-Biber, Sharlene. (2002). Feminism and interdisciplinarity. In JoAnn DiGeorgio-Lutz (Ed.), *Women in higher education* (pp. 57–66). Westport, CT: Praeger.

Hesse-Biber, Sharlene, Gilmartin, Christina, & Lydenberg, Robin. (Eds.). (1999). *Feminist approaches to theory and methodology: An interdisciplinary reader*. New York: Oxford University Press.

Hesse-Biber, Sharlene Nagy, Leavy, Patricia, & Yaiser, Michelle L. (2004). Feminist Approaches to research as a process: Reconceptualizing epistemology, methodology, and method. In Sharlene Nagy Hesse-Biber & Michelle L. Yaiser (Eds.), *Feminist perspectives on social research* (pp. 3–26). New York: Oxford University Press.

Hesse-Biber, Sharlene Nagy, & Leckenby, Denise. (2004). How feminists practice social research. In Sharlene Nagy Hesse-Biber & Michelle L. Yaiser (Eds.), *Feminist perspectives on social research* (pp. 209–226). New York: Oxford University Press.

Hesse-Biber, Sharlene Nagy, & Yaiser, Michelle L. (2004). Difference matters: Studying across race, class, gender, and sexuality. In Sharlene Nagy Hesse-Biber & Michelle L. Yaiser (Eds.), *Feminist perspectives on social research* (pp. 101–120). New York: Oxford University Press.

Hirsch, Marianne, & Keller, Evelyn Fox. (1990). Practicing conflict in feminist theory. In Marianne Hirsch & Evelyn Fox Keller (Eds.), *Conflicts in feminism* (pp. 370–385). New York: Routledge.

Hochschild, Arlie Russell. (1975). The sociology of feeling and emotion: Selected possibilities. In Marcia Millman & Rosabeth Moss Kanter (Eds.), *Another voice: Feminist perspectives on social life and social science* (pp. 280–307). New York: Anchor Press/Doubleday.

Hochschild, Arlie Russell. (1983). *The managed heart: Commercialization of human feeling*. Berkeley: University of California Press.

hooks, bell. (1984). *Feminist theory: From margin to center*. Boston: South End Press.

hooks, bell. (1990). *Yearning: Race, gender, and cultural politics*. Boston: South End Press.

hooks, bell. (1994). *Teaching to transgress: Education as the practice of freedom*. New York: Routledge.

Jacobs, Harriet A. (1987). *Incidents in the life of a slave girl, written by herself*. Cambridge, MA: Harvard University Press. (Original work published 1861)

Jaggar, Alison. (1997). Love and knowledge: Emotion in feminist epistemology. In Diana Tietjens Meyers (Ed.), *Feminist social thought: A reader* (pp. 385–405). New York: Routledge.

Kandiyoti, Deniz. (1999). Islam and patriarchy: A comparative perspective. In Sharlene Hesse-Biber, Christina Gilmartin, & Robin Lydenberg (Eds.), *Feminist approaches to theory and methodology: An interdisciplinary reader* (pp. 236–256). New York: Oxford University Press.

Kelly-Gadol, Joan. (1987). The social relation of the sexes: Methodological implications of women's history. In Sandra Harding (Ed.), *Feminism and methodology* (pp. 15–28). Bloomington: Indiana University Press.

Kincheloe, Joe L., & McLaren, Peter. (2000). Rethinking critical theory and qualitative research. In Norman K. Denzin & Yvonna S. Lincoln (Eds.), *Handbook of qualitative research* (2nd ed., pp. 279–313). Thousand Oaks, CA: Sage.

Kuhn, Thomas. (1962). *The structure of scientific revolutions*. Chicago: University of Chicago Press.

Lamphere, Louise, Ragone, Helena, & Zavella, Patricia. (Eds.). (1997). *Situated lives: Gender and culture in everyday life*. New York: Routledge.

Lather, Patty. (1991). *Getting smart: Feminist research and pedagogy with/in the postmodern*. New York: Routledge.

Lorde, Audre. (1984). *Sister outsider*. Trumansburg, NY: Crossing Press.

Lorde, Audre. (1996). The master's tools will never dismantle the master's house. In Audre Lorde (Ed.), *The Audre Lorde compendium: Essays, speeches and journals* (pp. 158–171). London: HarperCollins.

Martin, Emily. (1987). *The woman in the body: A cultural analysis of reproduction*. Boston: Beacon Press.

Maynard, Mary, & Purvis, June. (Eds.). (1994). *Researching women's lives from a feminist perspective*. London: Taylor & Francis.

McCarl Nielsen, Joyce. (Ed.). (1990). *Feminist research methods: Exemplary readings in the social sciences*. Boulder, CO: Westview Press.

McIntosh, Patricia. (1995). White privilege and male privilege: A personal account of coming to see correspondences through work in women's studies. In Margaret Andersen & Patricia Hill Collins (Eds.), *Race, class, and gender: An anthology* (pp. 76–86). Belmont, CA: Wadsworth.

Millman, Marcia, & Kanter, Rosabeth Moss. (Eds.). (1975). *Another voice: Feminist perspectives on social life and social science*. New York: Anchor Press/Doubleday.

Mohanty, Chandra. (1988). Under Western eyes: Feminist scholarship and colonial discourses. *Feminist Review, 30,* 61–88.

Mohanty, Chandra. (1999). Women workers and capitalist scripts: Ideologies of domination, common interests, and the politics of solidarity. In Sharlene Hesse-Biber, Christina Gilmartin, & Robin Lydenberg (Eds.), *Feminist approaches to theory and methodology* (pp. 362–388). New York: Oxford University Press.

Naples, Nancy A. (2003). *Feminism and method: Ethnography, discourse analysis and activist research*. New York: Routledge.

Neuman, W. Lawrence. (2000). *Social research method*. Boston: Allyn & Bacon.

Nielson, Joyce McCarl. (Ed.). (1990). *Feminist research methods: Exemplary readings in the social sciences*. Boulder, CO: Westview Press.

Oakley, Ann. (1981). Interviewing women: A contradiction in terms. In H. Roberts (Ed.), *Doing feminist research* (pp. 30–61). London: Routledge & Kegan Paul.

Ramazanoğlu, Caroline (with Janet Holland). (2002). *Feminist methodology: Challenges and choices*. London: Sage.

Reinharz, Shulamit. (1992). *Feminist methods in social research*. New York: Oxford University Press.

Roberts, Helen. (Ed.). (1981). *Doing feminist research*. London: Routledge & Kegan Paul.

Scott, Joan. (1999). The evidence of experience. In Christina Gilmartin & Robin Lydenberg (Eds.), *Feminist approaches to theory and methodology* (pp. 79–99). New York: Oxford University Press.

Sherif, Carolyn Wood. (1987). Bias in psychology. In Sandra Harding (Ed.), *Feminism and methodology* (pp. 37–56). Bloomington: Indiana University Press.

Smith, Dorothy E. (1978). A peculiar eclipsing: Women's exclusion from man's culture. *Women's Studies International Quarterly, 1*(4), 281–296.

Smith, Dorothy E. (1987). *The everyday world as problematic: A feminist sociology.* Boston: Northeastern University Press.

Smith, Dorothy E. (1990). *The conceptual practices of power: A feminist sociology of knowledge.* Boston: Northeastern University Press.

Smith, Linda Tuhiwai. (1999). *Decolonizing methodologies: Research and indigenous peoples.* London: Zed Books.

Smith, Linda Tuhiwai. (2005). On tricky ground: Researching the native in the age of uncertainty. In Norman K. Denzin & Yvonna S. Lincoln (Eds.), *The SAGE handbook of qualitative research* (3rd ed., pp. 85–107). Thousand Oaks, CA: Sage.

Spalter-Roth, Roberta, & Hartmann, Heidi. (1996). Small happiness: The feminist struggle to integrate social research with social activism. In Heidi Gottfried (Ed.), *Feminism and social change: Bridging theory and practice* (pp. 206–224). Urbana: University of Illinois Press.

Spender, Dale. (Ed.). (1981). *Men's studies modified: The impact of feminism on the academic disciplines.* Oxford, UK: Pergamon Press.

Spivak, Gayatri Chakravorty. (1990). *The postcolonial critic: Interviews, strategies, dialogue.* New York: Routledge.

Spivak, Gayatri Chakravorty. (1994). Can the subaltern speak? In Patrick Williams & Laura Chrismen (Eds.), *Colonial discourse and postcolonial theory: A reader.* New York: Columbia University Press.

Sprague, Joey, & Zimmerman, Mark. (1993). Overcoming dualisms: A feminist agenda for sociological methodology. In Paula England (Ed.), *Theory on gender/feminism on theory* (pp. 255–280). New York: Aldine de Gruyter.

Stanley, Liz. (Ed.). (1990). *Feminist praxis: Research, theory, and epistemology in feminist sociology.* London: Routledge.

Stanley, Liz, & Wise, Sue. (1983). *Breaking out: Feminist consciousness and feminist research.* London: Routledge & Kegan Paul.

Stanley, Liz, & Wise, Sue. (1993). *Breaking out again: Feminist ontology and epistemology* (2nd ed.). London: Routledge.

St. Pierre, Elizabeth, & Pillow, Wanda S. (Eds.). (2000). *Working the ruins: Feminist poststructural theory and methods in education.* New York: Routledge.

Trinh, Minh-ha T. (1991). *Framer framed.* New York: Routledge.

Tuana, Nancy. (Ed.). (1989a). *Feminism & science.* Bloomington: Indiana University Press.

Tuana, Nancy. (1989b). The weaker seed: The sexist bias of reproductive theory. In Nancy Tuana (Ed.), *Feminism & Science* (pp. 147–171). Bloomington: Indiana University Press.

Wolf, Diane L. (Ed.). (1996). *Feminist dilemmas in fieldwork.* Boulder, CO: Westview Press.

Woolf, Virginia. (1929). *A room of one's own.* New York: Harcourt Brace Jovanovich.

Woolf, Virginia. (1999). A room of one's own. In Charles Lemert (Ed.), *Social theory: The multicultural and classic readings* (2nd ed., pp. 257–258). Boulder, CO: Westview Press. (Original work published 1929)

# PART I

## FEMINIST PERSPECTIVES ON KNOWLEDGE BUILDING

# 2

# FEMINIST EMPIRICISM

CATHERINE HUNDLEBY

Feminist empiricism draws in various ways on the philosophical tradition of empiricism in epistemology that appeals to experience as the basis for knowledge. Because experience involves engagement with nature, empiricism seems to capture well the sort of knowledge sought by science. Yet feminist critiques of science reveal inadequacies in traditional forms of empiricism, and so feminist empiricists substantially revise the empiricist tradition.

Although empiricists' appeal to experiential evidence remains important, many feminists emphasize the significance of "the underdetermination of theory by data." That no amount of experiential data is complete grounding for any isolated belief or theory explains how there is always room for sexism in science. Treating the play of social values in science as inevitable because of underdetermination also leads many feminist empiricists toward naturalized epistemology, which studies the gap between evidence and theory by using science itself.

Whether or not feminists embrace naturalism, the implication of underdetermination that all sorts of science carries sociopolitical values— both desirable and undesirable—raises a number of further issues for empiricism. The empirical value that beliefs may have—for instance, theoretical fecundity and simplicity—may not be purely epistemological or cognitive;[1] it can also be political and therefore either sexist or feminist, among other possibilities. Furthermore, for envisioning how sexism might be eliminated from science, considering the subject or agent of empirical knowledge, the knower, to be an individual person seems inadequate. So, many feminists, empiricists among them, reject the traditional empiricist distinction of epistemology from political considerations and, within epistemology, the view of knowers as isolated individuals.[2]

Empiricism is conservative in the sense of drawing on the Anglo-American tradition in epistemology and philosophy of science, and this may seem problematic from a feminist perspective. This theoretical conservatism is especially a risk for those who embrace naturalism, because they risk taking on board and reinforcing sexism in existing science. Yet, feminist naturalists demonstrate how revolutionary empiricism can be, including questioning its own foundations. Ultimately, feminist empiricism has a flexibility that encourages engagement with various methodologies, which suggests new radical possibilities.

Author's Note: Thanks to Bob Pinto, Sandra Harding, Phyllis Rooney, and an anonymous reviewer for their very constructive advice on an early draft of this chapter, and to Alex Leferman and the University of Windsor Outstanding Scholars Program for assistance in compiling the research.

## FEMINIST ATTRACTION TO EMPIRICISM

Empiricism can be found in the history of "northern" philosophy as far back as Aristotle, but it is classically associated with the 18th-century British philosophers John Locke, George Berkeley, and David Hume. Most recently, the noteworthy empiricists include the logical empiricists as well as Willard Van Orman Quine and his naturalist followers. All empiricists emphasize the role of sensory experience in knowledge and downplay the role of innate ideas and inborn mental capacities that "rationalists" champion. The role of sensory evidence is also central to contemporary philosophy of science, and so feminists often turn to empiricist epistemologies when they look for resources in the philosophical canon to account for observations of sexism in science.

Traditional understandings of empirical inquiry suggest ways that science might be remedied of sexism. Feminist empiricists draw on case studies of sexism in science and invoke the empiricist tradition in the same way that other feminists invoke other theoretical traditions, such as liberalism, Marxism, and postmodernism. In contrast with at least some postmodern feminist projects, feminist empiricism along with feminist standpoint theories is a "successor science project," aiming to correct science rather than abandon it (Harding, 1986).

The specific attractions of empiricism include its traditional concern with directing science toward the development of a better society. Representing progressive values in the empiricist language, which is familiar to scientists and Anglo-American philosophers of science, also provides strategic advantage. Furthermore, both the emancipatory potential of science and its regressive history are explained by the empiricist account of the underdetermination of theory by data. Finally, naturalist versions of empiricism recognize that science is dynamic and that it may transform in accord with changes, not only in physical resources but also in history, people, and problems.

## The Problem of Sexism in Science

Scientific knowledge is popularly considered the best of human empirical inquiry, yet it can appear inadequate in light of a number of clearly defined case studies of gender prejudice in institutionalized science. To illustrate sexism in the general context of scientific knowledge claims, I'll first outline one of the problems identified in cellular biology. Cellular biologists have uniformly described the egg in passive and the sperm in active terms, and perpetuated gender ideology through various other forms of description.

A common description of the relationship between egg and sperm is like fairy tale or romantic courtship, but images of the egg also variously include whoring, dutiful wifehood (Biology and Gender Study Group, 1988), and even hunted prey (Martin, 1991). At the same time, in both scientific and popular accounts of fertilization, the sperm appears as a victorious hero reminiscent of characters in the *Odyssey* or the *Aeneid* (Biology and Gender Study Group, 1988). Even using the term *fertilization* to name the process that can be more accurately described as "cellular fusion" assumes an asymmetry in activity (Longino, 1997).

Eliminating the ubiquity of sexist assumptions in research through feminist critique is needed as a form of experimental control, feminist empiricists argue, and neglecting to pursue feminist critique has serious implications. We may laugh at the sexist anthropomorphism, but it obscures much of the real activity of the egg. Moreover, the assumed hierarchy echoes throughout cellular biology in that the nucleus of any cell tends to be understood as the masculine dominator of the whole cell. Likewise, genetic inheritance through cellular cytoplasm is described as "maternal" (Biology and Gender Study Group, 1988).

The egg's activity should not be conceived instead in aggressive terms that will also play into stereotypes of femme fatales and devouring mothers. Even equalitarian metaphors may be problematic insofar as they encourage us to anthropomorphize cells, argues Emily Martin (1991).

Although the scientific convention is to call such metaphors "dead," they are not so much dead as sleeping, hidden within the scientific content of texts—and all the more powerful for it. Waking up such metaphors, by becoming aware of when we are projecting cultural imagery onto what we study, will improve our ability to investigate and understand nature. Waking up such metaphors, by becoming aware of their implications, will rob them of their power to naturalize our social conventions about gender. (p. 501)

For instance, we must beware of how anthropomorphizing gametes grants intentionality to the egg and sperm. Intervening in defense of such "persons" on the basis of metaphorical understanding might include technological and legal interventions against the will or interest of the very *real* people who produce these cells (Martin, 1991). A range of social and moral views and actions that science informs can end up loaded with undesirable social assumptions and projected images.

## Empiricism as a Traditional Resource

A traditional remedy for sexism in science may mean either more rigorous application of existing scientific standards or appeal to traditional philosophies of science. Both have been described as "feminist empiricism," but this tends to conflate them. Feminist appeals to empiricism do seek out generalized accounts of how knowledge is based on experience that will explain how a range of values—including sexism, feminism, political values in general, and recognized epistemological values—operate in science. Appealing to the traditional empirical valuation of experience and logic provides a strategic advantage for feminism. Yet along with not specifically feminist inheritors of the empiricist tradition, feminists must rework empiricism to account for the role of sociopolitical values.

Deferring to existing scientific practices to weed out sexism is a strategy recently defended by Sharyn Clough (2003). She argues that feminists should attend to the local empirical standards of specific sciences—that is, in Harding's (1986) terms, to become "spontaneous" feminist empiricists. Attending to the standards local to particular debates keeps feminists from vain attempts to specify the general roles values have in science, Clough argues. To ask general questions about justification and to seek a universal methodology opens the door to questions that lead to global skepticism.

Part of what inspires Clough's concern is that epistemologies of science and so many proper or full-fledged versions of feminist empiricism develop a systematic general account of what makes science provide valuable beliefs. Moreover, institutionalized science is only one source of knowledge that concerns feminist empiricists, because the bulk of common sense may be empirical knowledge—and empiricists traditionally argue that all knowledge is empirical. Whether or not the lessons are to be applied in science or in the humanities or other forms of human inquiry, feminist empiricism draws on empiricist traditions especially from philosophy of science. Science not only seems to be the best example of empirical knowledge, but also provides dramatic case studies, such as "fertilization."

Harding (1986) argues that the earliest forms of spontaneous feminist empiricism inevitably crumble under their contradictory view that social values both matter and don't matter in science, an incoherence described by Louise Antony (2003) as "the bias paradox." This tension can arise from generalizing about sexism in science relative to the logical empiricism out of which philosophy of science emerged as a distinct subdiscipline. This intellectual movement aimed to account for scientific knowledge purely as a combination of necessary (e.g., logical and mathematical) truths with sensory evidence. These together provided an account of the meaningfulness of scientific theories and beliefs that dominated how many people understood science, even how scientists understood it, for most of the 20th century. So, appealing to scientific standards in many contexts can involve invoking the standards of logical empiricism.

Feminists' rejection of empiricism tends to focus on how logical empiricists isolated scientific value from political concerns. Some feminist appropriation of logical empiricism is, however, possible, as Kathleen Okruhlik (2003) argues. She explains that one of the founding and most influential members of the famous "Vienna Circle" was Otto Neurath, who maintained the necessity of "conative" as well as cognitive aspects of science. Although Neurath considered ethical and sociopolitical considerations to be immune from rational scrutiny, he recognized that such "auxiliary motives" must play a role in even the best science. This admission suggests a possibly fruitful commonality between feminists and the frequently reviled logical empiricists. Not only Neurath, but many of the early logical empiricists, aimed to develop a science that would serve social purposes, including sociopolitical emancipation of various sorts; and so, Okruhlik argues, the goal of providing an emancipatory science is part of the empiricist heritage.

Because of its mainstream Western heritage, feminist empiricism is analogous to liberal feminism. Each employs the most traditionally accepted approaches to the issues at hand: empiricist accounts of scientific knowledge and liberal accounts of democratic politics, respectively.[3] Mainstream language and concepts give these theories a purchase in the dominant culture and in the culture of science (Harding, 1989) that may not be available to more contested socialist, poststructuralist, and postcolonial approaches. The conservative language can convey radical ideas, and when it does it can be far more powerful than the more obviously revolutionary approaches. Therefore, as Sandra Harding (1986) recognizes, a radical future can emerge from feminist empiricism just as Zillah Eisenstein argued it does from liberal feminism.

Harding's suggestion that feminist empiricism has a rhetorical advantage might seem to be a thin compliment. Yet that advantage is strategically essential according to some self-proclaimed feminist empiricists, such as Lynn Hankinson Nelson (1990), because it allows feminists to transform the power of science.

> The point of feminist science criticism must, in the end, be to change science, and changing science requires changing the practices of scientists. Hence, scientists must be brought into the dialogue. Since scientists are empiricists, that dialogue will have to make room, at least in the beginning, for empiricists and for, at least as a topic of discussion, empiricism. (pp. 6–7)

Nelson (1990) explains further that changing science is crucial for feminist progress. "Science as currently practiced is too entrenched, too pervasive, and too successful to be simply abandoned" (p. 7). Science not only is a source of power, and great power, but also is inescapable and demands confrontation.

## Employing Underdetermination

Neurath recognized the need for conative values because he accepted what is now known as "the Duhem-Quine thesis" or "the underdetermination thesis." Underdetermination explains why the activity of the egg wasn't observed until women entered molecular biology. In this case, the observations themselves are beliefs about the world that were different for the earlier men than for the later women, although based on essentially the same sensory data. In addition, however, larger, consciously developed, and thoroughly scrutinized theoretical beliefs are equally subject to underdetermination, which helps feminists to explain how sexism takes different forms in science. Underdetermination is also central to postpositivist empiricist philosophies of science, especially those developed by Thomas Kuhn and by Quine.

To say that theory is underdetermined by data, or observational evidence, is to say that no statements or theories are meaningful on their own or can face the tribunal of experience on their own, even combined with logic.[4] "If we had to rely on nothing but logic and the contingencies of sensory experience, we could never get anywhere in the process of forming an opinion" (Antony, 2003, p. 132). For Quine (1969), the theories that are underdetermined by data include our commonsense theory of physical objects. No particular theory or claim provides the only possible way to project our future sense experiences based on our past sense experiences. "[A] typical statement about bodies has no fund of experiential implications to call its own" (p. 79). Any of our empirical understandings could be altered on the basis of future discoveries.

Feminists employ the underdetermination thesis in many different ways. It implies that inquirers are logically free when accommodating experience contrary to their expectations to hold on to any particular hypothesis by altering other beliefs that are part of our current theories. The recalcitrance of the experience may be interpreted with regard to a number and range of aspects of the overarching account, and even discipline. We ultimately appeal to background beliefs for deciding which particular beliefs to revise, because the available evidence underdetermines that decision. Likewise, for determining whether data support a theory and which particular claims they support, "the relation between hypotheses and evidence is mediated by background assumptions" (Longino, 1990, p. 75).

The social ideologies are deeply hidden in the background as auxiliary hypotheses in biology, and so their operation is more difficult to detect than in the social sciences. Thus, biology provides more surprising cases of underdetermination and more challenging grist for the mill of feminist empiricism. Likewise, politics has more direct influence on the content of claims from the life sciences than from the physical sciences, for which underdetermination has less clear political implications (Okruhlik, 1994).

How extensively data underdetermine scientific approaches is clear in the case of the "man-the-hunter" view that dominated the history of evolutionary anthropology and the emergence of the alternative "woman-the-gatherer" theory. Anatomical evolution goes hand in hand with the evolution of individual behaviors, capacities, and dispositions. These include the intelligence and sociability that seem to distinguish humans. Human upright posture, bipedalism, dietary habits, and tool use emerge as features in relation to anatomical developments. Unfortunately, very few fossils remain of the earliest hominids, and this provides little evidence for either theory. So, as Helen Longino and Ruth Doell (1983) argue, such evidence is always subject to reinterpretation, according to the underdetermination thesis. Furthermore, the significance of evidence is especially tenuous regarding the development of social features, such as intellectual capacity, because of substantial physiological variation among primate populations.

Anthropologically, one critical behavioral change is the development of tool use, and likewise the bipedalism and upright posture that support the use of tools that are especially effective for survival. The development of tool use depends in the man-the-hunter account on male hunting behavior. In turn, the availability of these tools eliminates the need for defensive and aggressive male displays of the canine teeth, and hence there is no need for the teeth to be large, which allowed for dietary pressures to select for smaller-sized male canines. Diet enters the picture earlier in evolution for the woman-the-gatherer account of tools as an innovation to meet women's greater nutritional needs during pregnancy. Thus, the first tools for digging, carrying, and defense favored intelligence and flexibility. In turn, female choice selected for smaller male canines because they indicate less aggression and therefore greater sociability (Longino & Doell, 1983).

Deciding between the man-the-hunter and woman-the-gatherer theories is immensely complex. To begin with, discovered fragments of rock may or may not be ancient tools, and they may or may not be intended for hunting, digging, or a variety of other tasks. Moreover, organic tools that decayed, and now cannot serve as evidence, may have preceded stone tools.

Such examples of underdetermination, from feminists among others, challenge the logical positivist view that empirical confirmation substantiates particular beliefs,[5] and also Karl Popper's argument[6] that empirical disconfirmation rather than confirmation distinguishes scientific practice. On Popper's view, the potential for testing makes a theory scientific, and surviving testing provides scientific support for a belief, although never a proof. Decisive testing that could lead to abandoning a theory demarcates science from other forms of belief. Yet decisive tests are not possible at all given the ubiquity of underdetermination.

Moreover, rarely in fact do investigators completely abandon theories; instead they revise them. Thus, Kuhn (1962, 1977) argued that puzzle solving within theories distinguishes scientific practice. Overarching theoretical and practical paradigms, under which scientists work, provide models of the world for scientific practice that are particular to a given science at a given period of time. Observations that conflict with the current theory are not sufficient reason to overthrow the theory and search for another one, as Popper maintained, but only provide puzzles that demand the theory be adjusted.

In Kuhn's (1962) view, the culture of a paradigm constitutes scientific understanding, and so scientific validity becomes largely a matter of operating in a tradition, at least so he seemed to say in *The Structure of Scientific Revolutions*. This sociological definition of science marks a profound challenge not only to positivism but also to the epistemology of science in general. Most philosophical disagreements in

Anglo-American epistemology concern the criteria that qualify beliefs as knowledge claims, for example, why I only *believe* that it rained recently based on observing a wet sidewalk, but I *know* that water is $H_2O$. Such distinctions may be made in terms of logic, or subjective certainty, or experience; but the *methods* for defining such distinctions—traditionally armchair philosophizing, conceptual analysis, or "rational reconstruction"— receive only the rarest scrutiny.

The notable exceptions, in addition to Kuhn and post-Kuhnian philosophers of science who attend to the history of science, are self-proclaimed naturalists who argue for viewing human cognitive practices as a part of nature and, as such, subject to empirical investigation of their effectiveness. Science, as our most successful method of empirical investigation, can inform epistemology and methodology about how inquirers determine which beliefs are relevant to which data. Epistemological naturalism gives a central role to the sciences of cognition, as does Kuhn to the history of science.

## Feminist Naturalism

Interest in underdetermination as an explanation for the role of sociopolitical values in science leads feminists to take up available epistemological accounts that address it, especially the naturalized epistemology proposed by Quine. Naturalized epistemologists begin with the assumption that people actually have knowledge, and hence with an implicit rejection of global skepticism, which is the worry that knowledge is not at all possible. The means for rejecting skepticism, according to Quine, is using our science itself to provide the explanation of how some beliefs are justified, or warranted, over others. Final answers regarding standards for inquiry are not the goal, however, for thoroughgoing naturalists. That would beg the question about the assumptions underpinning the sciences of cognition and ignore that scientific investigation continues to develop.

The relevant sciences for Quine are the sciences of individual cognition, behaviorism, and neuroscience, which some feminist naturalists, such as Jane Duran (1993) and Louise Antony (2003), also take up. Even on Quine's account, however, other forms of science may

shed light on how people's experiences can justify their beliefs; and thus his reformed empiricism complements Kuhn's historicism. Making use of all our available resources to scrutinize our understanding reflects naturalism's historical origins in the empiricism of David Hume, which Annette Baier (2002) argues has a distinctly social cast that suits it for feminism.

More specifically, feminists appreciate naturalists' attention to the situation of human physical and cultural embodiment, abandoning abstract ideals of knowledge that assume a god's-eye view. The same approaches that naturalists reject on empiricist grounds, feminists reject for being implicitly masculine: Disassociating from the material realities of human existence is not typically or traditionally part of women's way of engaging the world. Attention to the material aspects of knowledge not only affirms women's knowledge claims, it suggests new resources for addressing and redressing the traditional Western discounting of these claims.

Indeed, feminist epistemologists—whether they consider themselves naturalists or even empiricists—demonstrate the use of empirical data to scrutinize science, for which naturalists argue. Feminist naturalism involves more than appropriating science to provide accounts of knowledge, as Phyllis Rooney (2003) argues; it extends to examining the underlying motivations and worldviews of the social and individual cognitive sciences. Background assumptions, for instance, about the nature of gender taken from biology and psychology, are not merely noted but subject to contention (Rooney, 2003, pp. 226–227).

Thus, feminists critically scrutinize the methodologies and basic concepts of the contemporary cognitive sciences that inform their naturalism—whether individual cognitive science favored by Quine, or Kuhnian and post-Kuhnian social studies of knowledge. And so, feminist naturalists recognize that the scientific resources for epistemology themselves are subject to *improvement*. After all, science is open-ended in several different ways due to the open-endedness of the future, natural human ingenuity and creativity, and even human differences (Rooney, 2003). This dynamism provides the *verb-sense* of science:

A diversity of dynamic disciplines, the concepts, questions, and methods of which respond to changing conditions, including the changing conditions of empirical investigation and the changing social and political worlds within which such investigations are situated. (p. 219)

Feminist treatment of the scientific resources for theorizing about knowledge as dynamic in turn produces a verb-sense of epistemology. This contrasts with the usual epistemological pursuit of a "final" view, epistemology as a noun: coherentism, positivism, empiricism, and so on. Such static treatments of knowledge may be involved in feminist methodologies, but the accounts must be made defeasible, subject to change over time. In the face of potentially transforming claims about what counts as knowledge, all that remains continuous and distinctive in feminist epistemology, and feminist naturalism in particular, is its reliance on feminism and on science, in whatever ways these may change (Rooney, 2003).

## THEMES IN FEMINIST EMPIRICISM

Feminists have developed new versions of empiricism that reflect two related considerations. The first is a reassessment of the nature of cognitive values, which feminist empiricists consider to also have political significance. This suggests the converse, that sociopolitical values have cognitive or epistemic significances and help warrant beliefs and theories. Second, this tangle of cognitive and social forms of evaluation implies that knowledge is not an individual concern and can be best understood by considering ways in which communities are agents of knowledge.

### Theoretical Values

Following Kuhn (1977), contemporary empiricists generally recognize a range of cognitive values operating in science that include simplicity, precision, and explanatory power as well as predictive accuracy or testability. Of these, predictive accuracy is especially important and recognized as a general overarching value in contemporary empiricist philosophy of science, and when combined with retrodictive power is sometimes described simply as *empirical adequacy* or *accuracy*. Moving beyond the limited scope for

sociopolitical values admitted by the logical empiricists, feminist empiricists recognize these values as necessary to science, and some insist that they can be subject to empirical scrutiny. A provisional list of feminist empirical virtues competes with those that echo Kuhn, agreeing only in the primacy of empirical adequacy.

Many feminist empiricists, explicitly Helen Longino and Miriam Solomon,[7] hope to steer a middle course between traditional empiricism and the social constructivism of the Strong Program in the sociology of science that is sometimes read into early Kuhn. The logical empiricists recognized that political matters influence how theories are generated, along with any subjective or social inspiration. The processes of testing or rational theory choice that employ values constitutive or internal to science were supposed to eliminate political, subjective, and social influences, thus rendering a purely epistemologically authorized result. That sociopolitical neutrality never actually results does not, however, imply that observation and logic are insufficient for knowledge (Longino, 2004, p. 133).

The most generally accepted of the cognitive or epistemological values is of course *truth*, which carries realist metaphysical implications. To avoid metaphysical connotations, most philosophers of science speak instead in terms of *empirical adequacy,* and sometimes *objectivity* or *rationality*. These general cognitive values are accommodated or articulated as part of scientific practice in terms of some of the following more specific qualities of theories or beliefs: ontological simplicity (Ockham's razor), modesty, internal coherence, external consistency (including theoretical conservatism), predictability, explanatory power (also described as unifying power, generality, or breadth of scope), testability (also described as refutability), and theoretical fruitfulness (or fertility).

Feminist empiricists argue that whether or not scientific methods of testing are neutral, the nonepistemological influences from the context of theory generation remain in those theories that succeed. Testing only shows a claim to be epistemically superior among the available and contending possibilities. So, considering the familiar case of testing under patriarchy, Okruhlik (1994) argues:

If [the available] theories have been generated by males operating in a deeply sexist culture, then it is likely that they will all be contaminated by sexism. Non-sexist rivals will never even be generated. Hence the theory which is selected by the canons of scientific appraisal will simply be the best of the sexist rivals; and the very *content* of science will be sexist, no matter how rigorously we apply objective standards of assessment in the context of justification. In fact, the best of the sexist theories will emerge more and more highly *confirmed* after successive tests. (pp. 34–35)

Scientific method and rational theory choice—articulated in terms of predictive success, observation independence, and explanatory power, by Richmond Campbell (1998, pp. 25–27)—are not sufficient to eliminate and instead entrench sociopolitical influences. Moreover, noncognitive values must play a role in scientific results because science always operates in a communal historical context.

Social ideology and sociopolitical values play as substantial a role as "stereotypically scientific issues of evidence and logic" in all scientific knowledge (Longino, 1990, p. 3). Both science in general or "as usual" and particular cases of incompetent or "bad" science involve more than purely cognitive concerns.

There are standards of rational acceptability that are independent of particular interests and values but . . . satisfaction of these standards by a theory or hypothesis does not guarantee that the theory or hypothesis in question is value- or interest-free. (p. 12)

Indeed, the moral and sociopolitical values dismissed by Quine for being the result of natural selection can be vindicated by those origins, according to Nelson. She argues that their evolutionary success provides scientific reason to consider the values cognitively *good*: They meet the common practical needs of societies and of humanity (Nelson, 1990, p. 133).

Although accepting the place of sociopolitical values in science implies that nastier—sexist, racist, and so on—sociopolitical values could be justified, it also subjects them to the ordinary standards of criticism by which people customarily dismiss them. For instance, Quine's

broad notion of science provides a buffer of commonsense reasoning that can be used as a basis for criticism (Nelson, 1990). Perhaps the most general value that requires attention from naturalists is the value of human survival, because that is the value that evolutionary biology suggests underpins human nature. Yet survival only receives direct attention in Lorraine Code's argument (1996)[8] that accounting for survival requires developing ecological models of knowledge.

Whichever of the cognitive values make up the basis for criticism, the list is never intended to be exhaustive, nor can the individual values be applied in a straightforward algorithmic manner. Indeed, rarely is there consensus about how to apply them, and they don't have the immediate cognitive or epistemic effect philosophers project. Not only can theoretical fertility, for instance, be interpreted in different ways by different investigators and different research programs—we may ask "fruitful for what?"—but fruitfulness may also be weighted in various ways relative to the other cognitive values (Rooney, 1992).

In addition to such individual or programmatic contingencies, opposition among cognitive values occurs even in the abstract, as both Kuhn and Quine recognize. For instance, the detailed focus necessary for an accurate account clearly conflicts with how well that account applies over a range of phenomena in a range of situations that constitutes breadth of scope (Longino, 1997).

How we identify, interpret, and weigh cognitive values may reflect political commitments. Consider, for instance, Longino's feminist defense of a social-cognitive model over the linear-hormonal or "biological determinist" model for gendered differences in human physical and cognitive behavior. No "cognitive" decision between the two models seems available in Longino's (1990) original analysis, but the values of theoretical unification and simplicity that support the social-cognitive model cannot be treated only in cognitive terms, as Rooney (1992) argues: "Part of the constitutive force of 'simplicity' on this model is due to the fact that in it gender dimorphism is motivating in part the very understanding of biological determinism itself, rather than the other way round" (p. 18).

Gender dimorphism offers the valued "simplicity" in this case because of its resonance with existing social hierarchies; it is preferable because it was already preferred. Furthermore, historically, all sorts of androcentric biases have informed what psychologists count as higher cognitive functioning (Fausto-Sterling, 1985).

Likewise, feminist interests support certain cognitive values over others, and empiricism can support feminist politics as part of good scientific practice (Campbell, 1998). Exactly how to develop specific methodologies is unclear, and Longino (1990) argues against searching for definitive general criteria for evaluating the content of science. Instead of viewing science as a product, she suggests we treat it as a practice, and reach a feminist science through "doing science as a feminist" (p. 188). "We can . . . fashion and favor research programs that are consistent with the values and commitments we express in the rest of our lives" (p. 191).

Longino (1997) does not intend that feminist research practice be completely ad hoc, and she recognizes that feminists embrace an alternative set of theoretical values that she has started to catalog. Like the traditional values, the feminist set begins with empirical adequacy or accuracy, which she argues supports a specific feminist value: "to reveal both gender in the phenomena and gender bias in the accounting of them" (p. 45). Furthermore, revealing gender is served by *novelty*, *ontological heterogeneity*, and *mutuality of interaction* in theories and research programs. Beyond these empirically oriented matters, other considerations that serve feminist goals include *applying science to meet current human needs,* such as those traditionally ministered by women, and *diffusing scientific power* by encouraging general access and participation in science. Yet these values only contingently serve feminism, being neither uniquely nor intrinsically feminist (pp. 50–51).

## Social Agency

Moving beyond viewing sociopolitical influences on science as a matter of values, three feminist empiricists argue that scientific rationality and objectivity rest primarily, if not wholly, on communities. Addressing these three accounts in order of the degree to which they move away from individual agency in science, I begin with Longino's (1990) "contextual empiricism," then address the more exclusive priority of the community in Nelson's (1990) Quinean empiricism. Longino (1990) and Nelson (1990) argue that the practices of people coordinated in their communal relationships allow individual experiences to become significant, qualify individual beliefs as objective, and count individual observations as evidence. Individuals fall completely out of the picture of scientific reasoning for the third approach, Miriam Solomon's (2001) *social empiricism*. Solomon maintains that scientific rationality occurs only in relationships among competing theories, and so only at the level of communities.

Longino sets a social standard for assessing the objectivity of scientific discourse by suggesting four criteria of critical interpersonal engagement. An objective community has the following: (1) avenues for the expression and diffusion of criticism; (2) uptake of, and response to, criticism; (3) public standards by reference to which theories and the like are assessed; and (4) equality of intellectual authority (Longino, 1990, 1993). Communities that meet these criteria, to the *extent* that they meet the criteria, produce objective views.

Such objective communities provide objectivity to the beliefs of Longino's (1990) individual community members by providing constraining values. "Individual values are held in check not by a methodology but by social values" (p. 102). No individual strategies motivate scientific methods, yet Longino implies that individuals may work toward building the appropriate communities, which is to say those that engage a maximal number of different points of view.

As inquirers, we can also choose our cultures, within limits; so feminists can choose to whom we are accountable, and even choose combinations of communities. "The feminist scientist is responsive to the ideals of a political community as well as to some subset of the standards endorsed in her or his scientific community" (Longino, 1990, p. 192). Longino's advice to choose a feminist community does not entail adopting any particular methodology. Nevertheless "doing science as a feminist" requires interpreting empirical adequacy in terms of the concerns of one's chosen community, as described in the previous section on theoretical values.

Similarly, for Nelson, individuals acquire their scientific values from communities, but for her the community plays a more comprehensive role. The communal quality of the standards necessary for a person to be said to know any particular thing entails that some community to which that person belongs must also know. Individual people do not have knowledge or evidence at all except insofar as we participate in knowing communities. People share background beliefs and standards—for example, regarding the techniques for collecting evidence and how to make inferences from data—that provide varying degrees of support for our theories. Nelson's (1990) communal view of knowledge follows from her arguments that social values play an important role in science. Sociopolitical criteria are among our tools for justifying knowledge claims, again as outlined in the previous section, which Nelson further argues demonstrates that the society or community is the primary epistemic agent. If any one member of a community knows something, then some other member could also know it. As common sense indicates, "we know" doesn't mean "I and you and . . . you," that each of us knows. Moreover, "acceptable answers to the question 'Who knows?' include 'Everyone,' 'All of us,' 'Lots of people,' 'Many of us,' but only very problematically 'Only me'" (p. 255).

Solomon's (2001) social empiricism is still more radically social and so has less intuitive appeal than Nelson's or Longino's social views of cognitive agency. Unlike both Nelson and Longino, Solomon does not base her position on the interdependence of cognitive or epistemological and sociopolitical values, but rather on the rejection of this distinction in favor of another. In place of the traditional epistemological distinction between cognitive, or rational ("cold"), and noncognitive, or biasing ("hot"), factors in how scientists decide among theories, Solomon develops a distinction between empirical and nonempirical decision vectors. Empirical decision vectors include salience of data, availability of data, egocentric bias toward one's own data (noncognitive—but driven by data!), and preference for a theory that generates novel predictions. Nonempirical decision vectors include ideology, pride, conservativeness,

radicalism, elegance, competitiveness, peer pressure; the list goes on and includes more than the sociopolitical values addressed by other feminist empiricists. Social and idiosyncratic personal values can interfere with scientific rationality, but Solomon argues that they can also be part of the motivation behind states of science that are justified. It is the appropriate *distribution* of decision vectors that makes a scientific decision rational, not whether any particular vectors are present. This justification is visible, however, only at the social level, whether in consensus or in dissent.

Whereas the notion of communal knowledge tends to bring to mind the importance of social consensus, Solomon (2001) bucks intuition and argues that dissent is the scientific norm, in the sense of being the more common and general state of science. *Rational dissent* occurs under the following circumstances:

1. All theories under consideration have *some* empirical success (explain some observations).

2. All empirical vectors are distributed *proportionately* to the empirical success of each theory (productive scientific methods fall under theories proportional to their empirical success).

3. The nonempirical vectors are equally *distributed*.

Dissent occurs more frequently than consensus partly because only a very specific configuration of the decision vectors can justify consensus. When there is consensus, dissent approaches zero, and the conditions (1–3) are met as follows:

1. One theory has *all* the empirical successes (explains all the different observations).

2. *All* the empirical vectors support that theory (productive scientific methods all fall under the theory).

3. With maintained consensus, nonempirical decision vectors *all* begin to support the one theory.

Because forming consensus is only appropriate when all the empirical success supports one theory, it is the *limiting case* of dissent.

Methodologically, for Solomon (2001), as individuals neither can we expect nor should we desire to be free from bias, even to a degree, although we should aim to pursue theories that have empirical success. More specifically, the role of nonempirical decision vectors can only be understood in social terms. For individuals to recognize, assess, and redistribute the nonempirical vectors to justify the state of science requires a range of techniques.

> The identification of decision vectors and improvement of their distribution . . . typically require expertise, and, often, multidisciplinary knowledge and skills. The critical training required to identify presuppositions about gender, for example, is quite different from the psychological training and methods required to detect cognitive bias. And the statistical techniques needed to assess the role of birth order are quite different from scientific and philosophical knowledge of theoretical constraints such as simplicity. (p. 140)

Identifying decision vectors requires substantial and various skills, so that methodological considerations must be multidisciplinary.

Just as broad representation from the disciplines benefits the identification and reconfiguration of decision vectors, so Solomon (2001) suggests that the social democratization that Longino recommends may benefit the identification of political decision vectors. Yet at best, only political decision vectors will gain improved attention, and even that remains to be demonstrated empirically. In this way, Solomon's naturalism restrains her endorsement of Longino's recommendation to join or develop an egalitarian community for the sake of improving one's investigations.

## CONTROVERSIES ABOUT FEMINIST EMPIRICISM

Feminist empiricism rarely receives complimentary treatment in overviews of feminist science studies, in large part because it has been misunderstood. The theoretical conservativeness of empiricism does not entail a political conservativeness that is adverse to feminism. The most potentially regressive movement in feminist empiricism is naturalism because it defers to scientific input, and so is inevitably influenced by the status quo. Yet naturalism also has a revolutionary spirit that brings into question even its own empiricist precepts.

## The Conservative Quality of Empiricism

Naturalism may seem to resist progress in several different ways. Some concern the critical potential of naturalism, and others concern the patriarchal content of the science it relies on. Still others suggest that empirical understanding, naturalized or not, can never be sufficient for political analysis. Feminist naturalists do recognize that there is always a prior epistemology, and other prior ways to evaluate beliefs, and demand continuous scrutiny of these values. This critical process may seem to halt with Lynn Hankinson Nelson's view that communities are the ultimate arbiters of knowledge, except that she too insists on a dynamic relationship between the theory provided by communities and the experiences of individuals.

In the first place, relying on science, as naturalists do, seems to at least limit and perhaps exclude the possibility of establishing new ideals for human reasoning. Describing scientifically how people reason doesn't account for whether or not people reason well, an inadequacy that discourages some feminist empiricists, including Longino (1993), from naturalism. Furthermore, naturalism's tendency toward scientism may be inherently quietist. In practice many of the central tenets of science are beyond scrutiny, although in some ideal form science may be self-revising to an extent (Linker, 2003).

Scientistic conservatism poses a special problem for feminists because the patriarchal social system produces almost all the science available that might provide standards for evaluating knowledge claims. As a practical political resource, science has a history of resisting social accounts of gendered differences and seeking instead accounts based on biology that portray the differences as relatively immutable. The tendency in the scientific study of knowledge to accept gender as given and ahistorical is especially likely when women's capacities are judged to be inferior. For instance, some significant gendered difference has been found with spatial ability, but still the differences are so small as to be easily explained by differences in socialization. Yet researchers persist in looking for biological reasons for gendered differences in understanding, as Anne Fausto-Sterling (1985) argues, such that cognitive science seems bent on justifying women's low social status. Indeed, psychologists resolutely search for differences, even in verbal ability, although empirical results consistently reveal gender parity. So, taking up scientific accounts of gender can be regressive, and epistemologically dubious, especially when it comes to cognition. Thus, scientific accounts of cognition support claims made by Jane Duran (2001) that women benefit from an especially "relational" view of themselves and the world.[9] Admittedly, Duran's is among the most thorough versions of naturalism, both feminist and not specifically feminist, because she engages deeply in empirical research in both cognitive science (Duran, 1993) and contemporary cultural studies (Duran, 2001). That depth is, however, at the expense of considering other empirical factors, including socialization, that address how gender dichotomies in cognition can be symptoms of oppression.

A different kind of conservatism, about feminist empiricism in general, concerns Sandra Harding (1986). She argues that despite its rhetorical advantage, adherence to the empiricist tradition rules out the relevance of social liberation movements to fostering advances in science (pp. 25–26). Its future is only radical insofar as the internal conflicts spark a move away from the empiricism itself. Furthermore, empirical evidence doesn't seem involved in the normative correction of many forms of human knowledge, such as those assessed in terms of logical, linguistic, and moral truths, as Maureen Linker (2003) argues.

Yet accounting for the relationship between issues not traditionally considered cognitive and their cognitive counterparts, such as empirical adequacy, is part of feminist empiricism. Appealing to experience is only part of the process of developing knowledge, including developing methodology. Cultural resources, including some rudimentary prior epistemology, must inform all epistemologies and methodologies in whatever ways these accounts of knowledge employ our current knowledge. Our

investigations in psychology and the history of science, for instance, cannot move ahead without some notion of what needs examination, a functional ontology or account of the nature of the world that supports the possibility of meaningful inquiry. For instance, cognitive sciences generally assume that discrete propositional beliefs are the form knowledge takes, that individuals are the agents of knowledge, and that science is the best example of knowledge. However, "stipulation . . . simply begs the question against more robust forms of naturalizing epistemology where questions about the cognitive demarcation and delineation of beliefs are open to question" (Rooney, 2003, p. 216). No authority absolves the need to scrutinize background concepts and values, whether they include the sexism of cognitive science or the empirical adequacy of psychoanalysis.

Background epistemologies belong to the communal resources that Nelson (1990) argues are necessary for individual knowledge of any kind. So, her picture of communities as *prior* to individual knowledge seems to entail that what can be known is static and individual knowledge is passive. To the contrary, Edrie Sobstyl (2004) argues, science and common sense are in a constant flux and in dynamic interaction with individual experience.

> This creates opportunities for knowledge to grow and change—or it could, if Nelson is willing to give up epistemic privilege for the community. The fact that women alter their behavior in order to avoid being targets of sexual assault shows that they recognize the prevailing beliefs of a patriarchal community. But the fact that women *resist* such constraints on their behavior and demand freedom from sexual predation shows that our common sense, and gendered social and political experiences have a concrete impact on what we know. It is not helpful to say that this resistance is entirely derived from the community, because our community has not been particularly willing to warrant such ideals. (p. 131)

Sobstyl (2004) suggests that we revise and complete Nelson's (1990) approach to allow for a symmetrical relationship between embodied individuals and communities rather than giving complete priority to communities. Individual knowledge may be derived from communal knowledge as Nelson argues or it may be situated in or interdependent with communal knowledge. Viewing knowledge as having so many facets allows for the generation of different sets of evidence on a given issue, for the generation of recalcitrant evidence, and for choice among beliefs for those that best suit our sociopolitical goals. Such choice may be especially useful if our goals include eliminating or mitigating asymmetries in social power among different individuals in a community or among different communities.

> With respect to any question under investigation, the world may look very different from the perspective of a particular individual than it does from the community's, and different again from the perspective of other individuals and their communities. As an individual, I may want a safe vaccine for a dangerous virus. My community may share in this desire, but other individuals in my community may wish to test this vaccine in a developing nation where restrictions on human subjects experiments are more lax. I will not be reassured that the standards of my community for informed consent and provision of health care have been met. I want to know how the situation looks to the community that will be affected by such tests, and to individuals marginalized within that community. (Sobstyl, 2004, p. 138)

Sobstyl's multiaspect approach maintains Nelson's view of the dynamic interdependence between experience and theory, without Nelson's restricted view of who can have knowledge that restricts the possibilities for change (p. 139).

## Naturalism Supporting Rationalism

The self-critical impulse in naturalist epistemology takes the general form of requiring empiricism to be based itself on empirical investigation. The scientific evidence concerning human inquiry may turn out to support a nonempiricist view of knowledge, to make available "genuinely novel and transformative philosophical strategies" (Antony, 2003, p. 142), which explain how bias can play a positive role in reasoning. Indeed, some evidence does support the view that people have native intellectual capacities, such as for

language, and that in this way what people can know is independent of their past experience. Thus, empiricism may not follow from naturalism, and, as Louise Antony (2003) argues, what follows may be rationalism. The classic rationalist epistemology of René Descartes suggests that the mind involves innate structures or ideas that guide what people learn from the world. These directions are productive because of the need to order the chaotic input from our senses. Limitations in perspective are understood as forms of bias by Antony, which she argues makes sense of how some sociopolitical biases may be epistemologically preferable to others.

However, on the basis of this view of innate mental capacities, Antony adopts the further rationalist view that knowers are interchangeable, which most feminists find objectionable because it denies the impact on knowledge of social situation and different forms of embodiment. Moreover, the bodies that do play a role in Antony's work and provide for perspective on the world are not "biased" in the usual sense, but at best are only analogous to the forms of prejudgment that are properly called biases. How fruitful this analogy can be is an open question. The empirical evidence Antony employs in favor of Noam Chomksy's (1969) view that people have innate linguistic capacities is itself debatable.

There are many reasons to believe the program of naturalizing epistemology will change substantially in the future. To begin with, naturalizing epistemology is currently in its very early stages. Even those who are sympathetic to naturalism or describe themselves as naturalists are "slow to renounce the old modes of legitimation" (Roth, 2003, p. 296), and what exactly will be the new scientific modes remains unclear. In addition, the development of naturalism is slow because it is neglected in favor of arguing for the importance or viability of naturalist techniques, as Phyllis Rooney (2003) argues. Furthermore, naturalism is a continuous process. New ways of viewing knowledge constantly emerge from the open texture of science.

> Science is a diversity of dynamic disciplines, the concepts, questions and methods of which respond to changing conditions, including the changing conditions of empirical investigation and the changing social and political worlds within which

such investigations are situated. (Rooney, 2003, pp. 218–219)

New scientific tools may emerge not just as science progresses in addressing people's existing concerns, but as it responds to new questions we have about knowledge.

Admittedly, as Antony's argument demonstrates, changes in scientific accounts of cognition could go so far that feminist naturalist accounts of knowledge would not at all support the traditional empiricist view of the mind and the entailed epistemology (Campbell, 1998, p. 33). Such a turnabout can arise because developing scientific perspectives on knowledge is an ongoing activity, and this is one reason to view naturalism in a "verb-sense" (Rooney, 2003). Naturalizing is never complete but a perpetual activity. One may practice epistemological naturalism on an ongoing basis, such that epistemology is never *finally, ultimately* naturalized. The constant revision entails that feminist empiricists may find themselves engaging in quite different forms of theorizing than those with which they started.

Yet empiricism remains at the moment viable for naturalists. Antony's argument does not clearly succeed so far as it attempts in trying to turn naturalism toward rationalism. Admittedly, Chomsky's rationalist view of the mind may now or at some time reflect the evidence better than the behaviorism that Quine favored. Yet even Quine considers behaviorist psychology useful only for individuating belief states. It is not sufficient to support epistemology because behaviors are neither the same as beliefs nor sufficient to explain them, for which he suggests biology, especially neurophysiology (Nelson, 1990, pp. 126–128). Explaining beliefs must involve the impact of different social situations and different bodies. These nonbehavioral factors affect neurophysiology, including language development (pp. 286–287), and so have implications not only for Quinean empiricism but also for Antony's Chomskyan rationalism. Quine's own naturalism is inspired by the need to account for how the social world affects evidence (Nelson, 1990, p. 288; Quine, 1960). So to ignore social influences, as the rationalist move does, is to depart from the basic spirit of naturalism, rather than to defeat it in its own terms.

## THE STILL RADICAL FUTURE OF FEMINIST EMPIRICISM

Employing empiricism provides feminists with valuable purchase in the dominant culture and access to existing scientific resources, providing a radical potential both critics (Harding, 1986) and defenders (Campbell, 1998; Nelson, 1990) of feminist empiricism recognize as going far beyond a merely strategic use of language. Other supporters, notably Nancy Tuana (1992), argue that feminist naturalism demonstrates the radical future of feminist empiricism because it holds all the strengths of the commonly recognized competing approaches known as feminist standpoint theory and feminist postmodernism. Her analysis is specific to Nelson's naturalism, but more generally significant is Tuana's argument that feminist naturalism provides clear grounds for evaluating not only beliefs, but also values and practices that include political views. That is part of the reason that Antony can find in it a door toward rationalism. Whether we follow her through it or not, naturalism clearly has revolutionary potential in feminist hands.

Naturalism's open-endedness suggests how feminist empiricism may be mutually complementary with other feminist methodologies, and it encourages treating methodological choices as provisional, according to the problem at hand, rather than definitive. Methodologies may be taken up as guerilla strategies based on shared oppositional consciousness that "operates like the clutch of an automobile: the mechanism that permits the driver to select, engage, and disengage gears in a system for the transmission of power" (Sandoval, 1991, p. 14). This U.S. Third World feminist strategy encourages flexibility in taking up the competing political tactics of liberal, Marxist, radical, and socialist feminism that denies the need to commit to a final strategy. Likewise, shifting among empiricist and other methodologies keeps inquirers free from the stagnation of any overarching epistemology. So, feminist empiricism continues its radical progression by transforming from a hegemonic strategy into a "processual relationship" (Sandoval, 1991).

Such flexibility is recommended in feminist empiricism's own terms. Solomon would advise methodological dissent because different methodologies and epistemologies, including rationalism, have some empirical support. Keeping different options at hand also serves Rooney's verb-sense of epistemology that recognizes the open-endedness of human inquiry. Finally, this pluralism can be endorsed without assuming naturalism. Longino's (1990, 2004) requirement of ongoing critical engagement among divergent perspectives can apply to feminist methodology as much as it does to science itself.

## NOTES

1. For the purposes of this chapter, epistemological value is the same as cognitive value.

2. For a detailed account of the feminists' critiques of empiricism, see Nelson (2000).

3. The connections between empiricism and liberalism may be deeper than a mere analogy, as Steven Shapin and Simon Schaffer suggest in *Leviathan and the Air-Pump* (1989).

4. Related to underdetermination is indeterminacy about the truthfulness of claims made in the object language, and about our epistemological views including the theory of sense experience (Nelson & Nelson, 2003).

5. Because our beliefs cannot be fully verified, Quine denied the viability of Rudolph Carnap's logical positivist project of providing a rational reconstruction for beliefs.

6. Popper is a logical empiricist but not a positivist.

7. Solomon does not present a specifically feminist epistemology, but she does engage and promote feminist concerns, especially in Chapter 8 of *Social Empiricism* (2001).

8. This is also the subject of her forthcoming book.

9. Duran bases this on object-relations theory, which generally falls under feminist standpoint theory (Harding, 1986), but she aims to develop a naturalist version.

## REFERENCES

Antony, L. M. (2003). Quine as feminist: The radical import of naturalized epistemology. In L. H. Hankinson Nelson & J. Nelson (Eds.), *Feminist interpretations of W. V. Quine* (pp. 95–149). University Park: Pennsylvania State University Press.

Baier, A. (2002). Hume: The reflective women's epistemologist? In L. Antony & C. Witt (Eds.), *A mind of one's own* (2nd ed., pp. 38–52). Boulder, CO: Westview Press.

Biology and Gender Study Group. (1988). The importance of feminist critique for contemporary cell biology. *Hypatia, 3*(1), 172–187.

Campbell, R. (1998). *Illusions of paradox: A feminist naturalized epistemology.* New York: Rowman & Littlefield.

Chomsky, N. (1969). Quine's empirical assumptions. In D. Davidson & J. Hintikka (Eds.), *Words and objections: Essays on the work of W. V. Quine* (pp. 53–68). Dordrecht, the Netherlands: Reidel.

Clough, S. (2003). *Beyond epistemology: A pragmatist approach to feminist science studies.* New York: Rowman & Littlefield.

Code, L. (1996). What is natural about epistemology naturalized? *American Philosophical Quarterly, 33*(1), 1–22.

Duran, J. (1993). *Knowledge in context.* New York: Rowman & Littlefield.

Duran, J. (2001). *Worlds of knowing: Global feminist epistemologies.* New York: Routledge.

Fausto-Sterling, A. (1985). *Myths of gender: Biological theories about men and women.* New York: Basic Books.

Harding, S. (1986). *The science question in feminism.* Ithaca, NY: Cornell University Press.

Harding, S. (1989). How the women's movement benefits science: Two views. *Women's Studies International Forum, 12*(3), 271–283.

Kuhn, T. (1962). *The structure of scientific revolutions.* Chicago: University of Chicago Press.

Kuhn, T. (1977). *The essential tension.* Chicago: University of Chicago Press.

Linker, M. (2003). A case for responsibly rationalized feminist epistemology. In L. H. Hankinson Nelson & J. Nelson (Eds.), *Feminist interpretations of Quine* (pp. 153–171). University Park: Pennsylvania State University Press.

Longino, H. E. (1990). *Science as social knowledge: Values and objectivity in scientific inquiry.* Princeton, NJ: Princeton University Press.

Longino, H. E. (1993). Subjects, power and knowledge: Description and prescription in feminist philosophies of science. In Linda Alcoff & Elizabeth Potter (Eds.), *Feminist epistemologies* (pp. 101–120). New York: Routledge.

Longino, H. E. (1997). Cognitive and noncognitive values in science: Rethinking the dichotomy. In L. H. Hankinson Nelson & J. Nelson (Eds.), *Feminism, science and the philosophy of science* (pp. 39–58). Boston: Kluwer.

Longino, H. E. (2004). How values can be good for science. In P. Machamer & G. Wolters (Eds.), *Science, values and objectivity* (pp. 127–142). Pittsburgh, PA: University of Pittsburgh Press.

Longino, H., & Doell, R. (1983). Body, bias and behaviour: A comparative analysis of reasoning in two areas of biological science. *Signs, 9,* 206–227.

Martin, E. (1991). The egg and the sperm: How science has constructed a romance based on stereotypical male-female roles. *Signs, 16,* 485–501.

Nelson, L. H. (1990). *Who knows: From Quine to a feminist empiricism.* Philadelphia: Temple University Press.

Nelson, L. H. (2000). Empiricism. In A. M. Jaggar & I. M. Young (Eds.), *A companion to feminist philosophy* (pp. 30–38). Malden, MA: Blackwell.

Nelson, L. H., & Nelson, J. (2003). Introduction. In L. H. Hankinson Nelson & J. Nelson (Eds.), *Feminist interpretations of Quine* (pp. 1–55). University Park: Pennsylvania State University Press.

Okruhlik, K. (1994). Gender and the biological sciences. *Biology and Society, Canadian Journal of Philosophy, 20*(Suppl.), 21–42.

Okruhlik, K. (2003). Logical empiricism, feminism, and Neurath's auxiliary motive. *Hypatia, 19*(1), 48–72.

Quine, W. V. O. (1960). *Word and object.* Cambridge: MIT Press.

Quine, W. V. O. (1969). *Ontological relativity and other essays.* New York: Columbia University Press.

Rooney, P. (1992). On values in science: Is the epistemic/non-epistemic distinction useful? *PSA, 1992,* 13–22.

Rooney, P. (2003). Feminist epistemology and naturalized epistemology: An uneasy alliance. In L. H. Hankinson Nelson & J. Nelson (Eds.), *Feminist interpretations of Quine* (pp. 205–239). University Park: Pennsylvania State University Press.

Roth, P. (2003). Feminism and naturalism: If asked for theories, just say "no." In L. H. Hankinson Nelson & J. Nelson (Eds.), *Feminist interpretations of Quine* (pp. 269–305). University Park: Pennsylvania State University Press.

Sandoval, C. (1991). U.S. third-world feminism: The theory and method of oppositional consciousness in the postmodern world. *Genders, 10.*

Shapin, S., & Schaffer, S. (1989). *Leviathan and the air-pump: Hobbes, Boyle and the experimental life.* Princeton, NJ: Princeton University Press.

Sobstyl, E. (2004). Re-radicalizing Nelson's feminist empiricism. *Hypatia, 19*(1), 119–141.

Solomon, M. (2001). *Social empiricism.* Cambridge: MIT Press.

Tuana, N. (1992). The radical future of feminist empiricism. *Hypatia, 7*(1), 100–113.

# 3

# FEMINIST STANDPOINTS

SANDRA HARDING

Feminist standpoint theories emerged in the 1970s and 1980s. Four goals are expressed in these early writings: (1) to explain in a more accurate way relations between androcentric institutional power and the production of sexist and androcentric knowledge claims, (2) to account for the surprising successes of research in the social sciences and biology that were overtly guided by feminist politics, (3) to provide guidelines for future research, and (4) to provide a resource for the empowerment of oppressed groups. Such projects have remained controversial at the same time as they have become ever more widely used in the natural and social sciences and in public policy. This chapter first indicates the sources of standpoint theory and then outlines the distinctive standpoint "logic of inquiry" and its contributions to decolonizing research processes. It closes by reviewing the main criticisms of standpoint theory.

## ORIGINS[1]

Feminist standpoint theories are deeply indebted to the women's political movements of the 1960s and 1970s and also to the antipositivist histories, sociologies, and philosophies of science then emerging in Europe and the United States. Canadian sociologist Dorothy Smith (1987, 1990a, 1990b, 1999) and then U.S. political philosopher Nancy Hartsock (1983, 1998) argued that the existing relations between politics and the production of knowledge were far from the scientifically and socially progressive ones claimed by research disciplines or by the economic, legal, medical, health, education, welfare, scientific, and other institutions that made public policies based on such research. When it came to accounting for gender relations, the prevailing philosophies of science and the research projects they legitimated were politically regressive, philosophically weak, and scientifically less than maximally effective. British sociologist of science Hilary Rose (1983), philosopher Alison Jaggar (1983), historian of science Donna Haraway (1978, 1981, 1989), and Harding (1983, 2003) had all contributed to the development of standpoint accounts by 1983.

Evidence for these claims appeared in the increasing documentation of sexist and androcentric results of research in biology and the social sciences. Standpoint theorists analyzed causes of the gaps between actual and ideal relations between knowledge and power, and reflected on causes of the successes of feminist research in the social sciences and biology. Such work led to prescriptions in some of these writings for how to produce empirically and theoretically more successful research. These writers focused also on how standpoint approaches to research could empower oppressed groups. Moreover, they argued that it was precisely the guidance of such research by feminist political goals that enabled the production of empirically better supported knowledge claims. Epistemic and scientific successes were possible because certain kinds of "good politics" in themselves had the potential to advance the growth of scientific knowledge: Some kinds of politics could be productive of knowledge.

This feminist argument drew on older sources. Marx and Engels had argued for a proletarian standpoint. How the class system actually worked could not be detected if one started off thought from the activities of beneficiaries of that system, such as factory owners and the bankers who invested in industries. Instead, one should start off from the lives of the workers. Only from such a standpoint could one accurately explain how misery accumulated in the lives of workers as wealth accumulated in the lives of factory owners. Marx and Engels's accounts of how class hierarchy works followed this prescription. The Hungarian theorist Georg Lukacs developed the Marxian standpoint arguments further in the 1930s and 1940s. But these arguments were plagued with apparently unsolvable problems and abandoned by Marxist social scientists and philosophers. Fredric Jameson (1988) points out that it was not until the work of feminist theorists that the logic of Marxian arguments was again pursued.[2] Jameson argues that the feminists solved problems that the Marxian tradition had not through their distinctive challenge to the natural sciences and in their innovative account of how an oppressed group could come to consciousness "for itself," not just as the object of the gaze of others (Jameson, 1988; Lukacs, 1971).[3]

Yet this "logic of inquiry" has other sources in which such a legacy is not directly visible. Moreover, echoes of its themes appear in other writings. The sociologists also cite powerful themes in Mannheim (1954), Merton (1972), and Simmel (1921) about the resources provided by the "stranger's" social position. Collins (1986, 1991) develops this into the "outsider within" position of disciplinary researchers from marginalized social groups, such as a black woman sociologist. In such a contradictory social location as an insider in one respect and an outsider in others, a researcher can learn to detect aspects of social relations not accessible by those who are only outsiders or only insiders.[4] The writings of Paulo Freire (1970) and the participatory action researchers also echo standpoint themes (Maguire, 1987; McTaggart, 1997; Petras & Porpora, 1993).[5] Other feminist writers at least partially independently developed standpoint arguments.[6] From a perspective in post-Kuhnian science and technology studies and the history of primatology, Donna Haraway (1981, 1991) demonstrated the social situatedness of the field of primatology, and engaged with standpoint authors on their ambivalence toward their own insistence on the situatedness of knowledge. Thomas Kuhn's (1970) project "to display the historical integrity of . . . science in its own time" (p. 1), as he famously put the point, opened the way for thinking about the "historical integrity" of social and natural science conceptual frameworks, methods, and practices with the gender relations of their day.[7] Sara Ruddick (1989/2004) looked at the institution of mothering from the standpoint of everyday mothering concerns. Author bell hooks (1983, 1990) argued that the very marginalization of black people's lives created "a space of radical openness" from which race relations could be seen with a kind of clarity unavailable from the perspective of those who, intentionally or not, benefit from white supremacy. Meanwhile, a standpoint logic can now be seen to structure much recent work in the multicultural and postcolonial studies, as well as in their science and technology studies' movements. Twenty-five years of these studies have revealed how Western natural sciences and technologies, no less than those from other cultures, are "local knowledge systems" even though they are far more powerful in many respects than other cultures' knowledge systems. Western sciences have a "historical integrity" with powerful global social relations of their eras that they in turn helped to constitute and maintain (Figueroa & Harding, 2003; Harding, 1998; Hess, 1995; Selin, 1997).

In the interests of full disclosure, I should confess my own role in this history. I became aware of Dorothy Smith's early essays by the late 1970s.[8] Meanwhile, I was working closely with Nancy Hartsock as she developed her 1983 accounts (we were in a reading group together), and reflecting on the work of early feminist critics of the natural sciences such as Ruth Hubbard (1983/2003), Evelyn Fox Keller (1983/2003), and Donna Haraway (1978, 1989), with whom I occasionally shared conference sessions. One of Hartsock's influential essays appeared in a collection that I coedited with Hintikka (Hartsock, 1983), along with my essay suggesting the material historical conditions for the emergence of the new feminist research. Distinctive social formations both enable and limit what a culture can know, I was arguing (Harding, 1983, 2003). I subsequently discussed standpoint theory as a class of epistemologies in *The Science Question in Feminism* (Harding, 1986) and then included one of Dorothy Smith's early essays (as well as Hartsock's) in a feminist methodology reader (Harding, 1987).

Smith (1997) argues that it was I who invented this class of epistemologies. She is not comfortable that her work is included under such a category. She sees her work as methodological, not epistemological. She rightly (in my view) points out that amalgamating arguments developed in the context of specific disciplinary discussions decontextualizes them, thereby losing the important disciplinary particularity of these writings—for example, how her work has always specifically been engaged with ongoing disputes and discussions in sociology. Smith's comment is an illuminating clue to why standpoint theory looks different in the hands of theorists in different disciplines, and why theorists in one discipline tend to ignore those in another. Yet I was looking at the more or less simultaneous appearance of similar kinds of antiempiricist arguments by Smith, Hartsock, Rose, Jaggar, and Haraway and the flourishing of distinctively feminist standpoint projects in biology and the social sciences, though the latter were not so named by those researchers.

I do know that I named "feminist empiricism" as the feminist philosophy of science to which I saw the standpoint approaches as opposed. In the late 1970s and early 1980s, I was looking at feminist empiricist empirical work in biology and the social sciences. Philosophers such as Helen Longino (1990), Lynn Hankinson Nelson (1990), and Lorraine Code (1991) subsequently developed feminist empiricism into a full-fledged philosophy of knowledge that pushed the horizons of mainstream empiricist philosophy in ways that the early accounts by biologists and social scientists had not.[9]

Two more "confessions." I consciously used a standpoint research approach in a series of publications that look at Western science "from the lives" of peoples in Third World cultures who have borne a disproportionate share of the costs and received few of the benefits of Western imperialism and colonialism, both of which were intimately involved with the growth of European sciences (Harding, 1998). As a person of European descent, I started off my research project from literatures reporting a very different story about the value of Western sciences and technologies than the kinds of triumphalist and exceptionalist accounts that have been standard in mainstream Western cultures. And I have written essays arguing that men can make important contributions to feminist research and scholarship by starting off from their own lives as these have been framed by feminist accounts, to explore topics female feminists frequently ignore—such as the meanings of masculinity and of male bodies to men (Harding, 1991b). I return to both issues. Thus, I have interrogated and developed standpoint research possibilities in a variety of ways. In the next section, I will outline the concept of "strong objectivity" through which I have tried to transform and strengthen a central concept in mainstream philosophy of science in ways that respond to standpoint insights.

What was this abandoned "logic of inquiry" that the feminist standpoint theorists took up?

## A STANDPOINT LOGIC OF INQUIRY

In the Marxian accounts, bourgeois understandings of class relations were articulated in specific claims about such matters as the inferiority of workers and the superiority of the educated classes. But they were expressed also in the abstract conceptual frameworks within which research was organized and conducted on such topics as human evolution, reproductive practices, the distinguishing features and distribution of intelligence, social deviance, the appropriate organization of work and of the economy, and the thought and behavior of "masses" (Sohn-Rethel, 1978). Bourgeois politics shaped the most abstract elements of social and scientific theories such as conceptions of the natural and the social, objectivity, rationality, and good method, and a host of other elements of such theories. Thus, abstractions are not in fact immune from cultural values and interests, contrary to the assumptions of standard Enlightenment philosophies of science. Feminist theorists made a similar claim about the way sexist and androcentric understandings of gender relations appeared in the most abstract conceptual practices. They noted, as had Marx himself, that the social relations between women and men in significant respects resembled those between workers and their bosses: Gender and class relations had parallel structures. Men, in their double capacity as designers and managers of social institutions and as heads of households, intentionally or not, exploited women's reproductive and productive labor. They benefited as men, as well as in the capacity of some of them as managers, administrators, and capitalists, from the perception that male control of women's bodies was natural. They benefited also from the conceptualization of women's unpaid domestic labor as an extension of women's "natures" or as "done for love," and from the discrimination against and exploitation of women's work in wage labor, conceptualized as reasonable because women were first and foremost mothers, not wage workers. The exploitation of women in the spheres of domestic and wage labor were causally linked, for each undermined women's power in the other domain.[10] Such exploitation, domination, and oppression were legitimated through the conceptual frameworks of research disciplines and social institutions.

Feminist sociologists, political scientists, legal theorists, anthropologists, psychologists, economists, and biologists were often active participants in the emerging women's movements. They began to provide accounts of how gender relations were articulated not only in explicit claims about women and men and their appropriate social roles but also in the apparently value-neutral abstract conceptual frameworks of the dominant institutions and of the disciplines that serviced them. They began to look at the "conceptual practices of power," in Dorothy Smith's phrase (Smith, 1990a). They did so, the theorists argued, by starting off research from women's concerns and practices in everyday life rather than from the concerns of those institutions and disciplines. For example, Carol Gilligan's analyses (1982) started off thinking about the absence in moral theory of attention to the distinctive kinds of moral decisions women faced as mothers and caretakers. Moral theory elevated to the highest ethical categories only the kinds of decisions that men made as managers, administrators, lawyers, and the like—decision making from which women had long been excluded. Why was it that the most influential authors on morality and moral development (such as Kant, Freud, Piaget, Rawls, and Kohlberg) could not perceive the kinds of moral decisions with which women were faced as also exemplifying the highest categories of moral thought? Similarly, Catherine MacKinnon (1982, 1983) identified how what counted as rape and what counted as objectivity had a distressingly close fit with only men's conceptions of such matters—conceptions that reasonably arose from men's kinds of social experiences with women and in institutionalized public thinking, such as in law courts. Thus, these researchers and scholars began their projects not from the dominant conceptual frameworks of their disciplines and institutions but rather from women's everyday lives. They did so in order to reveal and challenge dominant institutional understandings of women, men, and social relations between them. Note that although they began their projects from women's lives, they went on to "study up," to critically reveal the principles and practices of dominant institutions, including research disciplines. Ethnographies of women's lives can be useful to standpoint projects, but the latter insist on looking at how women's lives are constrained by the assumptions and practices of dominant institutions, including research disciplines.

Natural and social science disciplines lacked both the will and the effective mechanisms to examine critically how their own conceptual frameworks served hierarchical power relations in the larger society. A major problem was that traditional philosophy of science held that the "context of discovery" should be left free of methodological controls. Yet this stance blocked from critical scrutiny a major route for the entrance of social values and interests into the research process. Some such values and interests, namely those that differed between researchers, would be detected by subsequent methodological controls. But those that were shared by virtually an entire research community and the larger society, as has been characteristic of androcentric, white supremacist, and Eurocentric values, for instance, could not be detected by standard research methods. If the community of qualified researchers and critics systematically excludes, for example, all African Americans and women of all races, and if the larger culture is stratified by race and gender and lacks powerful critiques of this stratification, it is not plausible to imagine that racist and sexist interests and values would be identified within a community of scientists composed entirely of people who benefit—intentionally or not—from institutionalized racism and sexism. The restriction of scientific method, where technical expertise is required, to the context of justification reinforces the conventional belief that the truly scientific part of knowledge seeking occurs only in the context of justification. The methods of science are restricted to procedures for the testing of already formulated hypotheses. Untouched by such methods are those values and interests entrenched in the very statement of what problem is to be researched and in the concepts favored in the hypotheses that are to be tested. Recent histories of science are full of cases in which broad social assumptions stood little chance of identification or elimination through the very best research procedures of the day.

Such "objectivism" operationalizes the notion of objectivity in much too narrow a way to permit the achievement of the value-free research that is supposed to be its outcome. Scientific method could come into play only in the "context of justification," after researchers (and their funders) had selected the social or natural phenomena to be examined, what they identified as problematic about them, and the hypotheses and concepts they favored to examine such problems and had designed a research process. It was only in the research design that the methods of research were specified; obviously, these could not exercise any control over the processes that led up to their very designation, a point to which we return.[11] In directing research to start off not from the dominant disciplinary conceptual frameworks but rather from the lives of oppressed peoples, standpoint theory in effect extended the benefits of methodological controls back to the beginning of research so as to include the "context of discovery." It makes a difference to the results of research whose questions get to count as ones worth pursuing and how these questions are to be conceptualized and research designed to answer them.

But objectivism also conceptualizes the desired value-neutrality of objectivity too broadly. Objectivists claim that objectivity requires the elimination of all social values and interests from the research process and the results of research. It is clear, however, that not all social values and interests have the same bad effects on the results of research. Democracy-advancing values, such as feminist concerns for social justice, have systematically (though not invariably) generated less partial and distorted beliefs. To be sure, some values, interests, and other cultural influences can block the growth of knowledge. Yet some other aspects of culture evidently are productive of knowledge.

Articulating the "logic" of standpoint research in terms of conventional scientific goals such as good method and the objectivity of research enables the strengths of this approach to be grasped more clearly. In starting off inquiry from women's lives, feminist research projects appeared to violate the norms of good research in the disciplines in several ways. They failed to respect the rule that protected the "context of discovery" from the possibility of methodological controls. They were claimed to be adding to research feminist political agendas when they revealed the androcentric commitments of highly regarded social theories and empirical studies and the norms that guided them. Because most of these researchers were women who began research from lives that were at least something like their own, they were perceived to fail to respect the importance of impartiality, separation, distance in the researcher's relation to the researched—a challenge that, mysteriously, men did not seem to think arose when they studied other men. Moreover, they proposed something that appeared outrageous to conventional philosophies of science, namely, that the purportedly culturally neutral conceptual frameworks of research disciplines, including standards for objectivity and good method, were not in fact culturally neutral. Yet in spite of such violations of research norms, it was hard to deny that substantive feminist research in the social sciences and biology that did start off from women's lives often produced empirically more accurate and theoretically more comprehensive accounts of nature and social life, as an inspection of any feminist introduction to the issues of a discipline will reveal (Andersen, 2006; Barker & Feiner, 2004; Reiter, 1975). Indeed, the achievements of such substantive research tended to be systematically ignored by critics of standpoint epistemology and philosophy of science.[12]

How was this kind of apparently illicit feminist research practice to be understood? Standpoint epistemology seemed to provide resources that traditional epistemologies lacked for responding thoughtfully to such a question. Several central themes in the standpoint accounts provide a fuller picture of such resources.[13] First, how societies are structured has epistemological consequences. Knowledge and power are internally linked; they co-constitute and co-maintain each other. What people do—what kinds of interactions they have in social relations and relations to the natural world—both enables and limits what they can know.[14] Yet what people typically can "do" depends in part on their locations in social structures—whether or not they are assigned the work of taking care of children, and of people's bodies and the spaces they inhabit, or of administering large agencies, corporations, or research institutes. Material life both enables and limits what people can come to know about themselves and the worlds around them. So the social structures of societies provide a kind of laboratory within which we can explore how different kinds of assigned or chosen activities enable some insights and block others.

Second, when material life is hierarchically organized, as in societies structured by class, gender, race, ethnic, religious, or other forms of oppression and discrimination, the understandings of such hierarchical relations that are available to "rulers" and "ruled" will tend to be opposed in certain respects. The understandings available to the dominant group tend to support the legitimacy of its dominating position, whereas the understandings available to the dominated tend to delegitimate such domination. The slave owner can see his slaves' actions only as (unwilled) "behavior" caused by slaves' inferior nature or obedience to the master's will: He commands and they obey. Slaves don't appear to be fully human to their masters. However, following around the slaves in their everyday life, one could see their purportedly natural laziness as the only kind of political protest that they reasonably think that they can get away with, or their smiling at the master as a subterfuge to obscure that they are secretly planning to run away or perhaps even to kill him. One can see them struggling to make their own human history in conditions not of their choosing. Similarly, the women's movement of the 1970s revealed how women's work was both socially necessary and exploited labor, not just an expression of their natural inclinations or only a "labor of love," as men and public institutions saw it. To take another example, feminists pointed out that women never "asked for" or "deserved" rape or physical violence, contrary to the view of their abusers and the legal system. Rather, as MacKinnon (1982) argued, the state is male in its insistence on regarding as objective and rational a perception of violence against women that could look reasonable only from the perspective of men's position in social relations between the genders. Feminists revealed many more inversions and, from the standpoint of women's lives, perverse understandings of nature and social relations in the conceptual frameworks of dominant institutions.

Thus, third, the oppressors' false and perverse perceptions are nevertheless made "real" and operative, for all are forced to live in social structures and institutions designed to serve the oppressors' understandings of self and society. These hierarchical structures and institutions engage in conceptual practices that solidify and disseminate their continued power as natural, inevitable, and desirable. Social and natural sciences play an important role in developing and maintaining such ideologies, involuntarily or not.[15] If women are not permitted training in Latin, logic, science, or public speaking, they will appear less rational than their brothers. If they are discouraged from physical exercise and sports, they will appear naturally weaker than their brothers. If they are not permitted legal or other training in sound argument, they will appear less capable of reasoned moral judgments in the eyes of legal systems and religious institutions. If they are encouraged to pitch their voices at the high end of their natural register and always to smile or look pleasant, whereas their brothers are encouraged to pitch their voices at the low end of their natural register and in public appearances to look serious or even on occasion angry, women speakers will appear less authoritative. Dominant social relations can make real many aspects of the worlds they desire.

Fourth, consequently, it takes both science and politics to see the world "behind," "beneath," or "from outside" the oppressors' institutionalized vision. Of course, no one's understanding can completely escape its historical moment; that was the positivist dream that standpoint approaches deny. All understanding is socially located or situated. The success of standpoint research requires only a degree of freedom from the dominant understanding, not complete freedom from it. And it requires collective effort. Thus, a standpoint is an achievement, not an ascription. Women do not automatically have access to a standpoint of women or a feminist standpoint. Such a standpoint must be struggled for against the apparent realities made to appear natural and obvious by dominant institutions, and against the ongoing political disempowerment of oppressed groups. Dominant groups do not want to reveal either the falsity or the unjust political consequences of their material and conceptual practices. They usually do not know that their assumptions are false (that slaves are fully human, that poverty is not necessary, that men are not the only model of the ideal human), and do not want to confront the claim that unjust political conditions are the consequence of their views and practices. It takes "strong objectivity" methods to locate the practices of power that appear only in the apparently abstract, value-neutral conceptual frameworks favored by dominant social institutions and the disciplines that service them (to be discussed further below) (Harding, 1992a, 1992b, 1998). Importantly, the standpoint claim is that these political struggles that are necessary to reveal such institutional and disciplinary practices are themselves systematically knowledge producing.[16]

Thus, such liberatory research "starts off" from the everyday lives of oppressed groups rather than from the conceptual frameworks of the dominant social institutions and the disciplines that provide them with the resources they need for administration and management of the oppressed. However, such research doesn't stop there, in the lives of oppressed groups, as do conventional hermeneutic and ethnographic approaches. Rather it "studies up" to identify the "conceptual practices of power," in the words of Dorothy Smith (1990a). Standpoint theory is part of post-Marxian critical theories that regard ideology critique as crucial to the growth of knowledge and to liberation. The causes of the conditions of the lives of the oppressed cannot be detected by only observing those lives. Instead, one must critically examine how the Supreme Court, Pentagon, transnational corporations, and welfare, health, and educational systems "think" in order to understand why women, racial minorities, and the poor in the United States have only the limited life choices that are available to them. Because the maintenance and legitimacy of these institutions depend on the services of research disciplines, one must critically examine the conceptual frameworks of sociology, economics, and other social (and natural) sciences to understand the thinking of dominant institutions.

Fifth, the achievement of a standpoint brings the possibility of liberation.[17] An oppressed group must become a group "for itself," not just "in itself"—as others observe it—in order for it to see the importance of engaging in political and scientific struggles to see the world from the perspective of its own lives. Women have always been an identifiable category for social thought—an object conceptualized from outside the group—namely, from the perspective of men. But it took women's movements for women to recognize their shared interests and transform themselves into groups "for women"—defining themselves, their lives, their needs, and desires for themselves. They learned together to recognize that it was not just "their man" (father, husband, boss) who was mean or misbehaving. Rather cultural meanings and institutional practices encouraged and legitimated men's treatment of women in such ways at home, in workplaces, and in public life.

Women's movements created a group consciousness (or, rather, many different group consciousnesses in different groups of women) in those that participated in them (and many who only watched) that enabled feminist struggles and then further feminist perceptions. As Fredric Jameson points out, feminist standpoint theorists opened "a space of a different kind for polemics about the epistemological priority of the experience of various groups or collectivities (most immediately, in this case, the experience of women as opposed to the experience of the industrial working class)" (Jameson, cited in Harding, 2004a, p. 144). Similarly, it took civil rights struggles and black nationalist movements of the 1960s to mobilize African Americans into collective political actions that could, it was hoped, end racial inequities. The Chicano/a movement developed to mobilize Mexican Americans to a group consciousness capable of advancing an end to the injustices visited on them. The Lesbian and Gay Pride movement had a similar goal and effect. New group consciousnesses were created through these processes, consciousnesses that could produce new understandings of social relations, past and present.

Let us turn to consider standpoint theory as a philosophy of method—as a methodology. In particular, let us consider it as a counter to the charge that social research intrinsically is structured in a way that ensures that it will replicate the "colonial relation." Whatever the social inequalities the researcher and the researched bring to a social research project, this charge goes—the research process itself increases the oppression of the already oppressed peoples who are usually its topics of research. Standpoint theorists have tried to design a research process that itself provides resources for oppressed peoples.

## Against Intrinsically "Colonial" Research Processes

Of course, researchers often bring to the research situation a higher social status than those they study. There is a long history of men studying women, professional researchers studying poor people, whites studying blacks, Westerners studying people in Third World countries, and heterosexuals studying "sexual deviants." In addition to this source of inequality between the researcher and the researched, the structurally designated relation between the researcher and the researched appears to be intrinsically socially unequal, even a "colonial" relation. Of course, feminists are certainly not the first group to be concerned about the intellectual and political effects of this structural inequality in the research situation itself (Blauner & Wellman, 1973).

Conventionally, it is the researcher, influenced by the assumptions of her discipline and her culture—not to mention of her potential funders—who decides on what social conditions, peoples, events, or processes the research project will focus and how it will be organized, conducted, interpreted, and, to a large extent, disseminated. With the assistance of peer review committees she decides which social situations to study; what is problematic about them; which hypothesis to pursue; upon which concepts and background literatures to rely; what constitutes an appropriate research design, including the choice of methods; how to interpret, sort, analyze, and write up data into evidence; and how and to whom the results of research will be disseminated (to the extent that she can control this last). Conventionally, the researched are allotted little say in this process. Through self-discipline plus rigorous attention to disciplinary methodological rules, the researcher is to secure her own disinterest, impartiality, and distance from the concerns of those she studies—control of the research process is to belong entirely to her, the researcher. If this were not the case, according to conventional thinking, the project would not be sufficiently objective and scientific.

Yet emancipatory movements have two kinds of reasons to criticize this level of researchers' control of research. One is political. It is the behaviors of the less powerful—workers, union activists, militaries, prisoners, students, potential consumers, women, welfare users, voters, already economically and politically disadvantaged races and classes, plus actual or soon-to-be colonized groups—that the institutions funding social research have wanted to discover how to manage more effectively for their own purposes. Thus, whatever disempowerment the researched bring to the research project is further added to the disempowerment by research that is designed to enable powerful social institutions to manage them and their lives more effectively. Reflection on such disempowerment also illuminates reasons for the resistance of dominant groups to becoming the object of study of social scientists. "Studying up" is politically offensive to those studied.

However, the other reason is scientific: The disempowerment of the researched in the research process (as well as outside it) tends to nourish distorted accounts of their beliefs and behaviors. Left to their own devices, researchers, like the rest of us, will tend to impose on what they observe, and how they interpret it, the conceptual frameworks valued in their cultures and disciplines, which all too often are those valued by the already powerful groups in the larger society. Moreover, as is well-known, such a colonial situation simultaneously nourishes distorted accounts of the researchers themselves and of the social groups to which they belong and that their work services. The dominant groups' perverse understandings of themselves, too, are reinforced by research that further disempowers the groups likely to be most critical of their dominance. The purportedly natural talents and abilities, good intentions, moral virtue, intelligence, and rightful authority of the dominant groups appear far less impressive from the standpoint of the lives of those they dominate.

This is not to imply that researchers do not seek to block such conceptual imposition; they often do so in response to both consequences of conventional research practices. The history of ethnography, sociology, and other disciplines shows constant attempts to control the cultural impulses of inquirers—attempts that have been successful in many respects. Nor is it to imply that all such imposed conceptual frameworks are unreliable; many are valuable because "the stranger" often can detect patterns and causes of behavior that are difficult for "the natives" to see. Rather, the issue is that even the most well-intentioned researchers lack some of the resources that the researched possess— resources that can be used critically to evaluate researchers' own taken-for-granted conceptual frameworks. This is the case regardless of the relative social status of the researcher and the researched. However, the chances that the researchers' conceptual frameworks are unreliable increase the greater the difference in social power between the observers and the observed. So the disempowerment of already politically disadvantaged research subjects not only tends to further disempower them but also tends to produce "bad science"—or, rather, the false results of what is generally considered to be "good science" (L. T. Smith, 1999; Wolf, 1996).

How can the kind of disempowering and distorting power of the researcher, apparently inherent in the research process, be blocked to prevent such colonialization of research? How can this be accomplished without losing the valuable "powers of the stranger"?

## Futile Strategies

First of all, the futility of several widely practiced strategies requires recognition. For example, it should be recognized that the social statuses that the researcher and the researched bring to the research processes are for the most part permanent. No amount of empathy, careful listening, or "going native," valuable as such strategies may be for various reasons, will erase the fact that the Western, white, masculine, university educated, or international-agency-funded researcher is going to leave the research process with no less than the economic, political, and cultural resources with which he or she arrived. And the researched will leave with, for the most part, whatever such resources they brought to the research process. Of course, research processes frequently do enlarge the vision, invite self-reflection, and in other ways contribute to ongoing personal growth in both the researcher and the researched. For example, each can become inspired to experience more of the resources available in the other's lifeworld. Yet the fundamental economic, political, and social structural inequalities that positioned the researcher and the researched in their social relation initially will not be changed by the research process alone (Blauner & Wellman, 1973).

Another inevitably unsuccessful strategy for equalizing the power between the researcher and the researched—a strategy that young (and, alas, not so young) researchers attempt—is for the researcher to try to disempower herself personally by "confessing" to the reader her particular social location: "I, the author, am a woman of European descent, a middle-class academic, trained as a philosopher, who has lived all her life in the U.S." Some such information can be useful to the reader, but for the researcher to stop her analysis of her social location here, with just the confession, is to leave all the work up to the reader. It is the reader who must figure out just how such a location has shaped the disciplinary and other conceptual frameworks used, the questions asked, how they are pursued, and so forth. Moreover, such a strategy makes the familiar faulty liberal assumption that individuals are capable of voluntarily identifying all the relevant cultural assumptions that shape their research practices; yet Marx, Freud, and historians have taught us how self-deluding that assumption is.

Yet another futile strategy researchers attempt, or at least think their methods courses have directed them to pursue, is to try to forego any theoretical or conceptual input into the research process itself. Researchers sometimes think the most useful procedure they can undertake is simply to "record the voices" of their subjects. Critics (and even misguided defenders) of standpoint approaches have often thought that this was the standpoint project. To be sure, there are good reasons to want to record the voices of all kinds of subjects. Moreover, it is valuable to recommend that researchers try to set aside their own assumptions when approaching a research situation, whether or not it is familiar. Yet to restrict research in such ways would be to reduce the researcher to a kind of (inevitably inaccurate) transcription machine. This strategy has the effect of discarding some of the most valuable political and scientific resources of the researcher. These include precisely the often higher social status carried by the researcher that instead of enacting a colonial destiny can be deployed on behalf of the researched. It includes the expertise and resources to conceptualize and articulate social relations in, paradoxically, the kinds of disciplinary and institutional languages that can be heard by public policymakers and the disciplines and institutions on which they depend.

So what contributions can standpoint approaches make to block the inherently colonial relations of social research? And how do they raise new philosophic and scientific questions that conventional philosophies of science ignored or disallowed? The research process can be divided into four sites where such "colonial" relations between the observer and the observed can flourish. The first is the selection of the research problem and the design of the research project: the "context of discovery." The second is the conduct of the research—the way the particular research design is carried out in field work, survey, interview, observational, archival, or quantitative work associated with any of such designs, or other kinds of research. The third is the writing up of the research findings—the interpretation and theorization of the data. The last is the dissemination procedures, intended or not by the researcher. Standpoint methodology is valuable in every part of research. Here I focus on the first stage because it is standpoint theories that have made a distinctive contribution to methodology in insisting that this stage can valuably be brought under the control of research methods, contrary to conventional disciplinary assumptions.

## The Context of Discovery: Whose Questions?

Standpoint approaches innovatively recommend that the "context of discovery" be brought under methodological controls. The dominant group's values and interests perhaps most powerfully shape research projects at this stage of inquiry in ways identified earlier. Yet it is only the "context of justification" that is regarded as legitimately controllable by method. The "logic" of scientific research does indeed begin with bold conjectures, yet the sciences have designed their methods to focus only on the process of seeking the severe refutations of primarily those hypotheses that manage to get thought up by people who can get research funded. Not everyone's "bold conjectures" are counted as equally valuable when it comes to sponsoring and funding research projects. Yet in fields where research is expensive, it is only the hypotheses favored by funders that reach the starting line to face the trials of attempted refutation. The issues that oppressed groups raise or might want to pursue frequently seem outlandish—outside "the realm of the true"—to conventional researchers. Consider, for example, the resistance to considering feminist proposals that it is social arrangements, not biological traits, that account for men's greater achievements in mathematics and the sciences (Fausto-Sterling, 1992); that assumptions underlying the dominant economic theory, political philosophy, and international relations are not universally valid but rather are distinctively gendered (Tickner, 2001); or that what counts as rationality and objectivity in U.S. judicial systems and philosophies of science similarly is also distinctively gendered (Jaggar, 1989; Lloyd, 1984). Thus, a new question arises: Which are the politically and scientifically valuable ones and which are the problematic ways to bring the context of discovery under methodological controls? Pursuing such a question deploys a stronger kind of reflexivity: a robust attempt critically to evaluate the selection of research problems and their conceptual frameworks and methods.

One justification for seeking out standpoints available from the lives of oppressed peoples is thus that such understandings balance and can serve as important critical views on the values and interests of the funders and sponsors of research and the professional communities whose disciplinary values and interests have shaped the standards for what counts as "good research." Because feminist researchers are both trained into such communities and members of at least one oppressed group, they are in a particularly good position to locate such critical standpoints. Of course, as members of professional communities they are also in a privileged group (whatever their class, race, or ethnicity of origin); so they have often designed research projects that start off from women's lives different from their own. The point here is not to rank oppressions but rather to seek analyses that take account of the kinds of oppression that can produce valuable questions and insights in a particular research context. The kinds of standpoints useful in studying obstacles to women's leadership in international organizations may be in part different from those important for understanding the needs of women in U.S. prisons, or of women refugees in Eastern Europe.

But how can useful standpoints be identified? Recollect that contrary to conventional methodological prescriptions, standpoint methods are engaged. They are not dispassionate, disinterested, distanced, and value-free. It takes politics as well as science to see beneath, behind, or through the institutional rules and practices that have been designed to serve primarily the already most economically and politically advantaged groups. Standpoint methods recognize that some kinds of passions, interests, values, and politics advance the growth of knowledge and that other kinds block or limit it. Politics can be productive of the growth of knowledge as well as an obstacle to it as, to be sure, it often is. Which such political engagements promote and which limit the growth of knowledge? The hypothesis standpoint analyses make plausible is that vigorous commitments to democratic inclusiveness, fairness, and accountability to the "worst off" can also advance the growth of knowledge. Such commitments do not automatically do so, but neither should they automatically be excluded from playing a possibly productive role in research processes.

Thus, such considerations require reevaluation of the conventional conception of objectivity, which requires maximizing value-neutrality. Such a requirement blocks the deployment of politics that increase the inclusiveness, fairness, and accountability of research. If research is to be accountable only to disciplinary conceptual frameworks and methodological requirements that in fact often service ruling institutions but not the "ruled," more research will succeed in further entrenching such ruling conceptual frameworks and increasing the gap between the "haves" and the "have-nots." The solution here is not to abandon the project of maximizing objectivity but rather to cease to require the maximization of complete social neutrality in order to achieve it (Harding, 1992a; 1998, chap. 8).

## Strong Objectivity

There is no single, fixed, eternal meaning of "objectivity." Indeed, historians have shown how it is an essentially contested concept. In modern societies, it is persistently a site for controversies over conflicting knowledge claims (Novick, 1988; Proctor, 1991). It also has no fixed referent. Objectivity, or the incapacity for it, has been attributed to individuals or groups of them, knowledge communities, the results of research, and methods of research—our focus here. Claims to objectivity sometimes are used to advance and sometimes to retard the growth of knowledge. Such claims can be made on behalf of or against democratic research tendencies.

Maximizing objectivity has usually been taken to require maximizing the social neutrality of research methods. This is how the goal of objectivity is "operationalized," as philosophers of science used to put forth the point. Good methods are supposed to be able to identify social values, interests, and assumptions that researchers bring to the research process. If a different researcher or group of them repeats the procedures first used to support a claim, and if they come up with different results of research, the cause of this difference may well be found in the values, interests, and assumptions that each group brings to its research. This procedure of different scientists or groups of them repeating each others' observations works relatively well to detect those values, interests, and assumptions that differ between individual researchers or groups of them such as research teams. But in cases where social values, interests, and assumptions are shared by all or virtually all the researchers in a given field, even in a discipline, or in the larger society, as has been the case for androcentrism, white supremacy, Eurocentrism, bourgeois values, and heterosexism, repeating observations within such a field, discipline, or society will not bring into focus such shared social commitments. Starting off research from "outside" such a field, discipline, or society— even from just a little bit outside, such as on the margins—can enable the detection of the dominant values, interests, and assumptions in existing knowledge claims. Of course, one can never completely get "outside" one's cultural group to float freely completely above historical and cultural specificity, as the conventional epistemologies and philosophies of science have assumed. But finding or creating even just a little critical distance from "the normal" can be sufficient to enable new critical perspectives to come to light. Thus standpoint theory enables us to see that the conventional notions of objectivity have been too weak to achieve their goals.

However, in another respect this notion has been too broadly understood to maximize the objectivity of research. The value-neutrality requirement has called for eliminating all social values, interests, and assumptions from the research process. Yet standpoint theorists (and other postcolonial and science studies scholars) have argued that some such values, interests, and assumptions can be productive of knowledge. In many contexts feminist social commitments have contributed to the recognition of regularities of nature and social relations that were not detected or documented before. To be sure, social commitments can often block the growth of knowledge. But at least some kinds of democratic or social justice commitments offer resources for expanding our knowledge.

Thus standpoint approaches call for "strong objectivity" to replace the only weak and excessively broad "objectivist" notion characteristic of mainstream methodology and philosophy of science. The intrinsically "colonial" character of the research process can be diminished through requiring such stronger standards for maximizing the objectivity of research.[18]

Let us turn now to consider responses to criticisms and questions about standpoint theory and methodology that were raised in the opening section.

## RESPONSES TO CRITICISMS

First I take up the most common charge against standpoint theory and the one that seems to express the deepest anxieties, namely, the purported relativism of standpoint epistemology and approaches to research. Then, I address other familiar criticisms in brief.[19]

### Relativism

Critics often accuse standpoint theory of committing or even embracing a damaging methodological and epistemological relativism because standpoint theorists argue that all knowledge claims are socially located. The purportedly culturally neutral conceptual frameworks of research disciplines and the main social institutions (science research foundations and agencies, the law, social welfare, health care, "the family") are not neutral at all, standpoint theorists argued. Instead, they represent their worlds as these tend to be understood by men of European descent in the dominant classes, races, and ethnicities who have designed and maintain the standards of these disciplines and social institutions. Standpoint theory is sometimes said to share this relativist flaw with the field of the social studies of science and technology and with postmodernism more generally.[20] What is and is not an issue here?

Let us begin by noting that although ethical relativism is a very old issue for Western thinkers, the possibility of epistemological relativism is relatively new. Anthropologists and philosophers have long pondered the fact that different cultures seem to have not just different moral practices, but different standards—different ethical principles—for what counts as a desirable kind of moral practice. So on what culture-neutral grounds could one decide between competing moral or ethical claims? Attempts to identify a universally valid standard that could fairly adjudicate between competing local practices seem invariably to be confronted with the challenge that the standard proposed—egoism or altruism, utilitarianism, Kantian or Rawlsian rationalism—is not in fact culturally neutral. So the issues of moral and ethical relativism are not new. But until the emergence of the field of the social studies of science and technology in the 1960s and 1970s (see Kuhn, 1962; Lakatos & Musgrave, 1970), claims to knowledge about nature and about science itself appeared to escape such relativist charges.

Knowledge claims certified by modern Western sciences were assumed to be grounded in reality in ways that claims without such a pedigree were not. Non-Western cultures' knowledge systems were, at best, merely technologies, speculative claims, or prescientific elements of traditional thought. At worst, they were dogma, magic, superstition, and even the "products of the savage mind," in the early 20th century anthropologists' judgment (Harding, 1998). However, with the appearance of Thomas S. Kuhn's (1962) *The Structure of Scientific Revolutions,* the horrifying possibility of epistemological relativism emerged. Kuhn had argued that moments in the history of modern science had an "integrity with their era"; that is, they were somehow permeated by historically and culturally local values and interests. Progress in science was not a matter of linear addition of observations and explanations but rather revolutionary upheavals in which a scientific community suddenly seemed to move into a different conceptual and research world—a different paradigm, as he put it. The subsequent four decades of the history, philosophy, and social studies of science and technology have had to struggle continuously against charges of a damaging epistemological relativism, which, the critics say, threatens to undermine the rationality of preferring modern sciences to other knowledge systems, as well as the legitimacy of these new fields themselves.[21]

Standpoint theory, along with postmodern and some postcolonial approaches, can seem to share this debilitating relativism because it, too, acknowledges that all knowledge claims and the standards for legitimating them are socially situated. Worse, standpoint approaches argue that some kinds of social values can advance the growth of knowledge. The anxieties generated by such perceptions require more extended attention than can be given to them here. Yet perhaps relativist fears can be set aside by consideration of the following four points.

First, there are familiar research areas where cultural assumptions, values, and interests clearly shape the direction, conceptual frameworks, research methods, and content of research, and yet this characteristic is not considered to deteriorate the empirical or theoretical quality of such research. For example, medical and health research are directed to preserving life, finding a cure for cancer, relieving pain, and other such social values. We can easily forget that these are indeed particular cultural values. They are not shared, for example, by some ethnic and religious groups who think either that this life is a misery to be got through so that believers can get to the better afterlife or that one should trust God's mysterious ways rather than modern medical interventions. Yet we do not disqualify the results of searches for a pain reliever because the research was shaped by such a value. Rather, the standard is the ability of the knowledge claim emerging from research to predict and control nature's regularities. Does the pill reduce pain? Does the treatment cause cancers to disappear? Again, much scientific research has been directed by national security needs. There certainly are reasons to object to expenditure of scarce resources on the funding of such research or to object to it for other reasons, but the fact that it is directed by such needs has not in itself been considered a reason to doubt its objectivity. Rather the adequacy of the research is judged by whether the knowledge claims that emerge will in fact predict and control nature's regularities. Can the missile hit its target? Will the vest deflect bullets? Considered in this light, the adequacy of feminist standpoint claims should be judged on the basis of the efficacy of their consequent practices. Does starting from some particular group of women's lives in a particular context raise new questions and thus expand the horizons of knowledge? Does it highlight previously undetected androcentric cultural assumptions?

Second, claims of any sort have meaning only in some particular cultural context; that is, relative to some set of cultural practices through which the meaning of the claim is learned and subsequently understood. Claims thus have meaning "relative" to that context of practices.[22] We are often surprised when our communication goes astray in another culture because our words are understood through some other set of assumptions than we intended. Indeed, this is a familiar experience in our own culture, and even in our own households. But this kind of semantic relativity does not remove grounds for evaluating the empirical adequacy of the claims. In daily life, as in science, meanings of terms and claims are negotiated so that some degree of agreement can be reached. Contrary to the fears of absolutists, complete incommensurability between individuals' or cultures' meanings is absolutely never encountered, I would dare to say. Neither does the fact that standpoint projects are designed to produce knowledge that is for women, instead of for the effective management of dominant institutions, remove grounds for evaluating the empirical adequacy of the results of standpoint research. Does it or doesn't it produce a reliable account of some part of reality, and an account of what women need to know?

Third, in everyday life we often have to make choices in conditions of great urgency as well as insufficient evidence to feel completely certain about the choices made. For example, we must choose between the value-laden and interested claims by pharmaceutical companies, physicians, insurance companies, the Internet sources, and our kin and friends when faced with a health crisis. Yet we gather all the information we can from every source available, weigh it, and tentatively choose, standing ready to revise our decision if the patient doesn't improve. We would regard as mentally disturbed someone who let herself be paralyzed by relativist considerations in such circumstances, or who felt completely certain of the efficacy of one such value-laden and interested recommendation though aware of what look to us to be other reasonably competing choices. Thus, the loss of an absolute standard certainly can feel like an inconvenience, but we generally manage to struggle forward making well-considered, tentative judgments, and standing ready to revise our opinions should evidence for other judgments appear. We are here behaving no differently than do scientists in their everyday practices. Good science is not stopped by the unavailability of a standard known to be eternally reliable. Indeed, the whole value of science is to carry on in the absence of such a standard. For cultures that think they have such a standard—the Bible, Koran, or teachings of The Prophet—science can appear unnecessary. Exegeticists are needed, but not scientists. Of course, religious traditions can provide other valuable resources for scientific projects such as useful conceptual frameworks and valuable motivations, as historians of Western sciences have pointed out (Needham, 1969). But the point here is a different one.

Last but not least, if in fact all knowledge claims are necessarily socially located, including those of modern sciences, and thus permeated by local values and interests, then it should seem a poor strategy to continue to insist that one particular set of such claims—those credentialed by modern science—are not. Instead, we need to work out an epistemology that can account for both this reality that our best knowledge is socially constructed, and also that it is empirically accurate. As Donna Haraway (1991) put the point in an oft-quoted remark, social justice movements need "to have *simultaneously* an account of radical historical contingency for all knowledge claims and knowing subjects, a critical practice for recognizing our own 'semiotic technologies' for making meanings, *and* a no nonsense commitment to faithful accounts of a 'real' world" (p. 187). The first three remarks above are intended to direct us to such a project.

No doubt these considerations will not convince some readers. But sometimes we just have to live with uncertainty and anxiety about our belief-choices. Contrary to the claims of some philosophic tendencies, learning to live with cognitive dissonance can be a sign of maturity and creativity. That may be the best one can hope for with respect to defeating fears of relativism. At any rate, let us turn to other criticisms of standpoint approaches to research.

## Challenges to Rationalist, Empiricist, and Positivist Assumptions

Standpoint theory does indeed challenge and in some cases undermine conventional rationalist, empiricist, and positivist assumptions and claims.[23] Those assumptions and claims looked reasonable and desirable in social worlds very different from our own. We need philosophies of research that enable the growth of knowledge in our worlds, where it is not the institutions and practices of feudalism, monarchy, the Catholic Church, or the early European industrial order that are the problem. In our world, those rationalist, empiricist, and positivist assumptions, and the social and intellectual institutions and practices they have enabled, have become part of our problem. Yet standpoint approaches do not completely reject standards for objectivity, rationality, and "good method," to mention three such conventional notions. Rather, they revise and strengthen these so that they can function more effectively in research contexts today.

## Modern or Postmodern?

A related question is whether standpoint theory is grounded in modern or postmodern assumptions. This has been a vexing question to both fans and critics of feminist standpoint theory. On the one hand, virtually every feminist standpoint theorist has critically engaged explicitly or implicitly with the still widespread Enlightenment epistemology and philosophy of

science and the methodological procedures they seem to require, as do the post-Kuhnian social studies of science and technology and postcolonial science and technology studies (Biagioli, 1999; Harding, 1988; Hirschmann, 1997). On the other hand, standpoint theorists and their projects seem to follow and even strengthen central Enlightenment concepts, values, and interests, such as the commitment to objectivity, rationality, good research, and the possibility and social value of increased knowledge, as do most of the post-Kuhnian and postcolonial science and technology studies scholars. Feminist standpoint theorists have often been criticized for being far too modern for contemporary feminist needs. This is much too rich and complex a topic to fully explicate in a few paragraphs.[24] Yet one can get a taste of the postmodernist charge in a well-known passage from an essay by Jane Flax (1990) where she also raises related criticisms to which we shortly turn:

> The notion of *a* feminist standpoint that is truer than previous (male) ones seems to rest upon many problematic and unexamined assumptions. These include an optimistic belief that people act rationally in their own interests and that reality has a structure that perfect reason (once perfected) can discover. Both of these assumptions in turn depend upon an uncritical appropriation of . . . Enlightenment ideas. . . . Furthermore, the notion of such a standpoint also assumes that the oppressed are not in fundamental ways damaged by their social experience. On the contrary, this position assumes that the oppressed have a privileged (and not just different) relation and ability to comprehend a reality that is "out there" waiting for our representation. It also presupposes gendered social relations in which there is a category of beings who are fundamentally like each other by virtue of their sex—that is, it assumes the otherness men assign to women. Such a standpoint also assumes that women, unlike men, can be free of determination from their own participation in relations of domination such as those rooted in the social relations of race, class, or homophobia. (p. 56)

Other feminist theorists argue that to the contrary, feminism needs modernist assumptions (DiStefano, 1990; Hartsock, 1987). Standpoint theorists themselves have sometimes taken firm positions on one side or the other of this contemporary debate. Indeed, I explicitly claimed a modernist project in developing more powerful notions of objectivity and good method than those that characterize contemporary philosophies of science. The debate is itself one that has shaped contemporary feminism more generally, not just considerations of standpoint theory, in that feminism seems committed to escaping Enlightenment restrictions and yet needs both better sciences and a kind of political solidarity characteristic of modernist politics, neither of which postmodernism seems able to provide. Perhaps most illuminating with respect to research and knowledge issues are those who reject the choice between modernism and postmodernism itself. For example, Kathi Weeks has argued that this choice obscures important issues that standpoint theory can effectively address (Weeks, 1998). And we saw Donna Haraway insisting in the earlier quotation on both postmodern and modern commitments for feminist science projects. My own development of standpoint theory and use of it has sought even more effective ways for social justice movements to negotiate a path through both these grand contemporary discourses while refusing to be contained by either.

## Essentialist? Eurocentric?

The passage from Flax (1990) also raises other frequently appearing criticisms of standpoint projects. Are this theory and its practices essentialist, assuming that all women (or men) share some kind of common experience? The appeal to start research projects from women's lives has often been read this way. This tendency was reinforced by the fact that in spite of their gestures to the race and class differences between women, the examples given in early standpoint writings tended to call up images of white women. Moreover, the borrowed Marxian standpoint theory, like the liberal Enlightenment theory of which it was so critical, had little ontological space for thinking about differences between its would-be knowers or between those who controlled knowledge projects. Workers and factory owners were treated each as homogeneous groups in working out the "logic" of the proletarian standpoint. Early feminist

standpoint accounts, though they usually asserted that different groups of women lived in different conditions of oppression and had different experiences, nevertheless did write about "women's experiences" and "women's knowledge." Even accounts that focused on one kind of difference, though acknowledging others, tended to be concerned with what was common to their group of interest. Thus, writings focused on "black women," for example, frequently had much to say about racism, poverty, and sexism, but little to say about sexual differences or ethnic and cultural differences between "black women" (e.g., in Africa or the United States, in Haiti, Brazil, or Puerto Rico—settings in which colonizers from different European languages and cultures have dominated). It took the flourishing of writing by women of color, and the delineation of "intersectionality" and of "matrices of oppression," for standpoint theorists to learn to insist on the multiple and often conflicting experiences, lives, and claims of women and of feminists. Standpoint theory has had to transform assumptions it inherited about the binary structure of oppression in order to do justice to differences among the oppressed and among oppressing groups. The conditions of women that will be relevant to any particular research project depend on the setting and goal of that particular project. Of course, standpoint approaches, like most others, can be and no doubt have been used in essentialist ways. My point is that they need not be. Essentialist readings of "women's lives" are not necessary in taking standpoint approaches.

## Automatic Privilege for "Women's Ways of Knowing"?

Flax (1990) also points to the assumption that standpoint theorists seem to automatically privilege "women's ways of knowing."[25] All feminisms certainly value the role of women's experiences in the production of feminist knowledge, though just what such experiences are, how they should be interpreted, and how they should be "processed" to achieve the status of knowledge are valuably contested issues. Experience is not knowledge, for the latter requires kinds of critical reflection and collective legitimation that are not characteristic of women's or anyone else's experiences. As noted earlier, standpoint knowledge requires collective intellectual as well as political struggles, as Nancy Hartsock put the point. As Jameson pointed out (noted above), feminist development of standpoint theory opened the way for new "polemics" about the role of collective experience in the production of knowledge (Jameson, 1988).

## Useful for Anti-Eurocentric and Postcolonial Projects?

Next, is feminist standpoint theory useful for anti-Eurocentric and postcolonial projects? On the one hand, it has overtly been used by feminist standpoint theorists themselves for such projects (Collins, 1986, 1991; Harding, 1998). Moreover, its "logic of inquiry" was inherited from the Marxian analysis of class and knowledge, which in itself has illuminated issues about the West's exploitation of Third World peoples. Additionally, a particular development of the Marxian account, "world systems theory" and its analysis of how the "center" exploits, dominates, and oppresses the "periphery" in the global political economy (Frank, 1969; Wallerstein, 1974) continues to play an important role in postcolonial studies today, including in postcolonial science and technology studies (Sachs, 1992). Furthermore, one could argue that feminist standpoint theory implicitly structures the arguments of many feminist scholars of color in the United States and from the Third World, such as bell hooks, Maria Mies, Vandana Shiva, and Chela Sandoval (Harding, 2004a). Indeed, unless one holds to the essentialist charge against standpoint theory, it seems obvious that anti-Eurocentric and postcolonial projects will find useful an approach that recommends starting off research from the lives of the oppressed instead of from the conceptual frameworks of the disciplines that peoples of European descent have traditionally used to study the oppressed.

Yet one feature of standpoint theory seems to this observer to limit its usefulness to anti-Eurocentric and postcolonial projects. This is that its intellectual legacy, at least in the West, comes from a distinctively Western tradition: the Enlightenment, Marxism, and Western feminist oppositions to and revisions of this legacy in the context of the 20th-century women's movements and of post-Kuhnian social studies of science and technology. This feature makes it especially valuable to Westerners who can locate it within that particular legacy of theories, protests and counterclaims, revisions, and so on. But it may make it less valuable to researchers from other cultures where, for example, positivism is not the reigning epistemology, as Indian American philosopher Uma Narayan (1989) has pointed out, or where modern sciences and their philosophies are not yet vividly present, let alone the target of widespread social analysis. There are probably additional substantive aspects of feminist standpoint theory that may bear distinctively Western fingerprints.

## Relevant to Natural Sciences?

Finally, is standpoint theory relevant to the natural sciences or only to the social sciences? What does it mean to start off research from women's lives in biology, let alone in physics or chemistry? The science studies movement to which standpoint theory owes a debt has largely kept standpoint theory at arm's length, to put the issue politely! Its own politics and intellectual status has been compromised, in my opinion, by this antipathy. For example, with important exceptions,[26] it has also rarely made use of the rich postcolonial science and technology studies literature to inform its own analyses, a shortcoming I attribute to its resistance to start off thought about Western sciences and technologies from the lives of those who have borne its costs in the Third World. This question about standpoint theory deserves an essay of its own. Yet we can note here that feminists working on women's health issues, environmental issues, primatology, molecular biology, the history of chemistry, and evolutionary theory, to mention just a few areas, as well as feminist intellectual historians and philosophers, have indeed started off from women's lives to challenge conventional claims, standards, and procedures in the sciences.[27] The natural sciences are also social phenomena and their understandings of nature are also shaped by the cultural assumptions, values, and interests of their era no less than is the case in the social sciences. Moreover, standpoint theorists challenge the philosophies of the natural sciences that much social science research has itself adopted. It is these projects that Jameson had in mind when he noted the innovative features of standpoint theory in feminist hands.

There are many other criticisms of standpoint theory, some of which have already been taken up in earlier parts of this chapter.[28] In my view, this theory should be controversial, because it addresses and tries to resolve some of the most puzzling and anxiety-producing issues confronting thoughtful people in today's world.

## DIFFERENCE, DEMOCRACY, AND THE PRODUCTION OF KNOWLEDGE

In their almost three-decade history, feminist standpoint theories have learned to exploit economic, social, psychological, and cultural heterogeneity. Bringing into focus accounts of nature and social relations as these emerge from the lives of many different subjugated groups creates a broader horizon of understanding of how nature and social relations work. As we have noted, it is not that these subjugated understandings are automatically the best ones on sound empirical and theoretical grounds, but sometimes they are. Additionally, they can lead to the identification of undetected problematic or just interesting natural and social phenomena, suggest different hypotheses and conceptual frameworks for investigating them, suggest different lines of evidence and challenges to favored evidence practices, uncover unnoticed cultural tendencies in the writing up of data, and make strong arguments for dissemination practices that differ from those favored by contemporary research property rights systems.

The ideal conditions for exploiting heterogeneity require genuinely democratic societies in which inequality has already disappeared and no group is or can legitimately be silenced through formal or informal means. All citizens then could be equally articulate and effective in the selection of problems to research, the specification of what is problematic about them, the selection of a conceptual framework and methods of research, and so on. Of course, we do not have such a situation. My point—and the

argument of standpoint theorists—is that standpoint epistemologies, philosophies of science, sociologies of knowledge, methodologies, and their political resources can help move toward such a goal. There is no sure formula for ensuring that subjugated groups will become empowered in research processes and that what counts as knowledge will not be identical to what the powerful want to be the case. One contribution standpoint theory can offer to such struggles is to help those of us who do occupy relatively powerful social locations to see ourselves and our conceptual practices as others see us.

Some reasons for standpoint theory's contentiousness are immediately apparent: it challenges or, worse, undermines still widely held dogmas of rationalism, empiricism, and positivism. Some of these, such as the commitment to the exclusion of politics from and selection of value-neutral methods of research, have been retained even in some forms of postpositivism, so this feminist work challenges even some other progressive intellectual projects.[29] Disputes have arisen also over whether standpoint theory is an epistemology, a philosophy of science, a sociology of knowledge, a methodology, a social theory, or just a political project. Moreover, critics persist in attributing to standpoint writings three positions that standpoint theorists mostly never held or perpetrated, and have subsequently again and again denied and countered. These are essentialist assumptions about women (and men), assumptions that standpoint theory is arguing for the automatic privileging of "women's ways of knowing," and that this approach either intentionally commits or unintentionally perpetrates a damaging epistemological relativism.[30]

Yet other sources of standpoint theory's contentiousness may be less obvious. For example, the histories of its independent development and subsequent debate within several distinct disciplinary contexts, with their different histories and preoccupations, have produced emphases on different aspects of it. This is clear if one examines the concerns of theorists and researchers working in the sociology of knowledge, political philosophy, and the philosophy of science and epistemology, to mention three central sites of standpoint development. More generally, standpoint approaches can reasonably appear to be multidisciplinary, antidisciplinary, transdisciplinary, and, paradoxically, deeply disciplinary. Additionally, the theory has served as a site for debate about more general intriguing or troubling contemporary intellectual and political issues that are only partially about rethinking the positivist legacy. Is it postmodernist or antipostmodernist, stuck in modernity or creatively updating modernity's problematics? Is it relevant to the natural sciences, including physics, chemistry, and mathematics? Is it part of post-Kuhnian science and technology studies or a critique of it? Finally (for this chapter), what are its uses for anti-Eurocentric and postcolonial projects, or does it further promote Eurocentrism and neocolonialism?

After all this controversy, what is surprising is that standpoint theory appears not only to have survived, but to be flourishing anew after more than two decades of contention. In the last few years, a flurry of reappraisals has begun to chart its recent history and its still promising potential (Campbell & Manicom, 1995; Harding, 2004a; Hekman, 1997; Kenney & Kinsella, 1997). Moreover, other authors hyperbolically do it the honor of claiming it to be a serious threat to feminism, science, and civilization more generally (Gross & Levitt, 1994; Nanda, 2004; Walby, 2001). Disturbing though virtually everyone may find some or other of its claims and projects, standpoint theory apparently is destined to persist at least for a while as a seductively volatile site for reflection and debate about persistent research dilemmas as well as contemporary social anxieties more generally.

## NOTES

1. I have written at least 19 essays and chapters of books focused mainly on standpoint theory over the last two decades. Parts of this chapter borrow from earlier versions of Harding (2003) and a section of the introduction (on relativism) from Harding (2004b).

2. Jameson's examples were the work of Hartsock, Jaggar, and Harding.

3. Hartsock (1983), Jaggar (1983), and Pels (2004) also review the Marxian history of this approach. The feminist theorists have generally avoided Lukacs's Hegelian machinery. While its internal problems did discourage Marxist social scientists

from appealing to standpoint epistemology in support of their research procedures, there were also other, topical reasons for its abandonment. Given the prevailing political climate of McCarthyism and the Cold War, it is understandable that researchers and philosophers distanced their work from an epistemology/methodology that wore both its political engagement and its specifically Marxian origins on its sleeve, so to speak. In the United States, Marxian social scientists in the 1960s, 1970s, and later tended to appeal to the Popperian form of a positivist philosophy of science to justify their research strategies (Popper, 1972).

4. Representations of similar researcher positions appear in Anzaldúa's (1987) "borderlands" consciousness, hooks's (1983) "theory from margin to center," and Dorothy Smith's (1987) "bifurcated consciousness" of the woman sociology graduate student. W. E. B. DuBois's "double consciousness" of African Americans is one precursor of this kind of representation.

5. See also Cooke and Kothari (2001) and Kesby (2005) for debates about participatory action research, some of which are relevant to standpoint approaches.

6. Hartsock (1998), Hirschmann (1997), and Pels (2004) review some of these accounts.

7. In philosophy, W. V. O. Quine's work on how scientific "networks of belief" seamlessly link everyday and scientific thought, and other aspects of his criticisms of logical positivism, directly influenced at least some standpoint theorists (Harding, 1976; Quine, 1953).

8. See Marcia Westkott's (1979) discussion of them in her review of feminist criticism of the social sciences.

9. Empiricism is a distinctive philosophy of science with origins in Hume and early modern science. Empirical research is what those who observe nature and/or social relations do. It can be contrasted with archival, mathematical, and theoretical or philosophic research.

10. Such an analysis did not usually illuminate the lives of women domestic workers, as feminist scholars of color pointed out (Collins, 1991).

11. I have discussed this problem in a number of papers on "strong objectivity." See, for example, Harding (1992a; 1998, chap. 8).

12. Indeed, some disciplines are still immensely resistant to feminist work. See, for example, recent analyses of international relations (Tickner, 2005) and economics (Barker, 2005; Barker & Feiner, 2004).

13.  As indicated earlier, such theories were developed within a number of different disciplines with diverse histories and preoccupations, and by theorists with commitments of varying strength to Marxian and to Enlightenment projects. Consequently, it is risky to try to summarize this approach in any way that attributes to it a unified set of claims. Nevertheless, theorists from these different disciplines do share important assumptions and projects that differ from conventional understandings of what makes good science, including, I propose, the following. (I articulate them in a form that stays close to Hartsock's [1983] account.) Of course, not every theorist equally prioritizes or emphasizes each of these, because what is perceived to be important in the context of sociology may be less important to political philosophers or philosophers of science and vice versa. Nor are disciplinary concerns, themselves heterogeneous, the only ones that lead to divergence in how standpoint approaches have been developed.

14.  Note that this theme echoes standard beliefs about the effectiveness of scientific methods: Which interactions with, or kinds of observations of, natural and social worlds are pursued both enables and limits what one can know.

15.  I use the term *ideology* here to mean systems of false interested beliefs, not just of any interested beliefs.

16.  A motto of the early days of the women's movements of the 1970's said, "The degree of his resistance is the measure of your oppression." If this point is lost, and even some standpoint defenders sometimes lose it, *standpoint* seems like just another term for a perspective or viewpoint. Yet the standpoint claim about the epistemic value of some kinds of political struggle—the epistemic value of the engagement of the researcher—is thereby made obscure when its technical use, which I retain here, is abandoned.

17.  I shall refer to standpoint approaches as inherently progressive since that is the way they have been understood today through the Marxian legacy inherited by leading movements for social justice. Yet it is useful to recall that Nazi ideology also (ambivalently) opposed modern science on standpoint grounds and, indeed, conceptualized its murderous program as one of advancing social justice. See Pels (2004). Religious fundamentalist, geographically based ethnic, and patriot or neo-Nazi social movements usually are not reasonably characterized as dominant groups. Nevertheless, they too are threatened by modernity's political values and interests. They often make something close to politically regressive standpoint arguments. So theories about which kinds of social movements are liberatory, and for whom, must be articulated to justify research projects in the natural and social sciences. See Castells (1997) for an interesting discussion of the different political potentialities of various identity-based social movements around the world today and Castells (2000) for an overview of the project within which this discussion is set.

Of course there is nothing new about natural and social science research *assuming* political theories; conventional philosophies of natural and social science always assumed—consciously or not— liberal political philosophies and their understandings of relations between knowledge, politics, and social emancipation (see, e.g., Shapin & Schaffer, 1985). Sciences and their philosophies are always at least partially integrated into their larger economic, political, and social formation, to put Kuhn's (1970) point another way. Thus, it is not standpoint theory that introduces the conjunction of social theory (or political philosophy) and epistemology, let alone their 'integrity" with actual historical features of a society.

18.  Other valuable feminist revisions of the notion of objectivity may be found in the work of two physicists, Evelyn Fox Keller (1983/2003) and Karen Barad (1996, 2003).

19.  For other rebuttals of these and other criticisms of standpoint theory see the responses by Hartsock (1997), Collins (1997), Harding (1997), and Smith (1997) to Hekman (1997), which are all reprinted or excerpted in Harding (2004a), and by Sprague (2001) and Harding (2001) to Walby (2001). See also Hartsock (1998), Hirschmann (1997), and Wylie (2003) (all reprinted or excerpted in Harding 2004a).

20.  Examples of this criticism may be found in Gross and Levitt (1994), Longino (1993), Nanda (2004), and Walby (2001).

21.  This kind of issue is at the base of the recent "science wars" (e.g., see Gross & Levitt, 1994).

22.  One important discussion of this issue appears in Ian Hacking's (1983) and Joseph Rouse's (1996) call for conceptualizing scientific activity as fundamentally intervention in, rather than representation of, nature.

23.  See, for example, the critics cited in Note 20.

24.  One place where I have discussed this already is "Feminist Epistemology in and After the Enlightenment" (Harding, 1991a).

25. See also Grant (1987), Walby (2001), and the discussion in Wylie (2003).

26. Such as all the work of Donna Haraway, as well as David Hess (1995) and Sharon Traweek (1988).

27. See, for example, Fausto-Sterling (1992), Haraway (1989), Keller (1983/2003), Potter (2001), Rose (1983), and Seager (1993, 2003).

28. Virtually all these criticisms may be found in Harding (2004a).

29. Some of these projects are shared with feminist science studies more generally. See Rouse's (1996) account of the way feminist science studies, in contrast to contemporary (postpositivist) sociologies of science and traditional philosophies of science, take what Rouse calls a "post epistemological" stance toward the production of scientific knowledge.

30. All three of these attributed positions are excessive versions, or perhaps the only imaginable alternatives in the eyes of critics, of standpoint rejections of conventional positions. Thus, critics assume that someone who claims that women are a political group, rather than only the individuals of liberal political philosophy, must have an essentialist understanding of women. They suppose that if a standpoint theorist thinks that women's claims about their own or others' lives have any authority at all, standpoint theory must be giving women automatic epistemic privilege. If someone claims that women or feminists can have a distinctively different epistemic position than that held by dominant institutions, standpoint theory must be committing epistemic relativism, they say. See Hartsock (1998) and Wylie (2003) for two reviews of responses to such charges.

## REFERENCES

Andersen, Margaret. (2006). *Thinking about women.* New York: Macmillan.

Anzaldúa, Gloria. (1987). *Borderlands/la frontera: The new mestiza.* San Francisco: Spinsters/Aunt Lute.

Barad, Karen. (1996). Meeting the universe halfway: Realism and social constructivism without contradiction. In Jack Nelson & Lynn Hankinson Nelson (Eds.), *Feminism, science and the philosophy of science* (pp. 161–194). Dordrecht, the Netherlands: Kluwer.

Barad, Karen. (2003). Posthumanist performativity: Toward an understanding of how matter comes to matter. *Signs: Journal of Women in Culture and Society, 28*(3), 801–832.

Barker, Drucilla. (2005). Beyond women and economics: Rereading women's work. *Signs: Journal of Women in Culture and Society, 30*(4), 2189–2209.

Barker, Drucilla, & Feiner, Susan F. (2004). *Liberating economics: Feminist perspectives on families, work, and globalization.* Ann Arbor: University of Michigan Press.

Biagioli, Mario. (1999). *The science studies reader.* New York: Routledge.

Blauner, Robert, & Wellman, David. (1973). Toward the decolonization of social research. In Joyce A. Ladner (Ed.), *The death of white sociology* (pp. 310–330). New York: Random House.

Campbell, Marie, & Manicom, Ann. (Eds.). (1995). *Knowledge, experience, and ruling relations: Studies in the social organization of knowledge.* Toronto, Ontario, Canada: University of Toronto Press.

Castells, Manuel. (1997). *The information age: Economy, society and culture: Vol. II. The power of identity.* Oxford: Blackwell.

Castells, Manuel. (2000). Materials for an exploratory theory of the network society. *British Journal of Sociology, 51*(1), 5–24.

Code, Lorraine. (1991). *What can she know?* Ithaca, NY: Cornell University Press.

Collins, Patricia Hill. (1986). Learning from the outsider within: The sociological significance of black feminist thought. *Social Problems, 33*(6), S14–S32. (Reprinted in Harding, 2004a)

Collins, Patricia Hill. (1991). *Black feminist thought: Knowledge, consciousness, and the politics of empowerment.* New York: Routledge.

Collins, Patricia Hill. (1997). Comments on Hekman's "Truth and method: Feminist standpoint theory revisited": Where's the power? *Signs: Journal of Women in Culture and Society, 22*(2), 375–381.

Cooke, Bill, & Kothari, Uma. (Eds.). (2001). *Participation: The new tyranny?* New York: Zed Press.

DiStefano, Christine. (1990). Dilemmas of difference. In L. J. Nicholson (Ed.), *Feminism/postmodernism* (pp. 63–82). New York: Routledge.

Fausto-Sterling, Anne. (1992). *Myths of gender: Biological theories about women and men.* New York: Basic Books.

Figueroa, Robert, & Harding, Sandra. (Eds.). (2003). *Science and other cultures: Issues in the philosophies of science and technology.* New York: Routledge.

Flax, Jane. (1990). Postmodernism and gender relations in feminist theory. In Linda J. Nicholson (Ed.), *Feminism/postmodernism* (pp. 39–62). New York: Routledge.

Frank, Andre Gunder. (1969). *Capitalism and underdevelopment in Latin America.* New York: Monthly Review Press.

Freire, Paulo. (1970). *Pedagogy of the oppressed.* New York: Herder & Herder.

Gilligan, Carol. (1982). *In a different voice: Psychological theory and women's development.* Cambridge, MA: Harvard University Press.

Grant, Judith. (1987). I feel, therefore I am: A critique of female experience as the basis for a feminist epistemology. *Women and Politics, 7, 3.*

Gross, Paul R., & Levitt, Norman. (1994). *Higher superstition: The academic left and its quarrels with science.* Baltimore: Johns Hopkins University Press.

Hacking, Ian. (1983). *Representing and intervening.* Cambridge, UK: Cambridge University Press.

Haraway, Donna. (1978). Animal sociology and a natural economy of the body politic, Pts. 1 and 2. *Signs: Journal of Women in Culture and Society, 4*(1), 21–36, 37–60.

Haraway, Donna. (1981). In the beginning was the word: The genesis of biological theory. *Signs: Journal of Women in Culture and Society, 6*(3), 469–481.

Haraway, Donna. (1989). *Primate visions: Gender, race and nature in the world of modern science.* New York: Routledge.

Haraway, Donna. (1991). Situated knowledges: The science question in feminism and the privilege of partial perspectives. In *Simians, cyborgs, and women.* New York: Routledge. (Reprinted in Harding, 2004a)

Harding, Sandra. (Ed.). (1976). *Can theories be refuted? Essays on the Duhem-Quine thesis.* Dordrecht, the Netherlands: Reidel.

Harding, Sandra. (1983). Why has the sex/gender system become visible only now? In Sandra Harding & Merrill B. Hintikka (Eds.), *Discovering reality: Feminist perspectives on epistemology, metaphysics, methodology, and philosophy of science* (pp. 311–324). Dordrecht, the Netherlands: Kluwer Academic.

Harding, Sandra. (1986). *The science question in feminism.* Ithaca, NY: Cornell University Press.

Harding, Sandra. (Ed.). (1987). *Feminism and methodology: Social science issues.* Bloomington: Indiana University Press.

Harding, Sandra. (1988). Feminism, science and the anti-Enlightenment critiques. In Linda Nicholson (Ed.), *Feminism/postmodernism* (pp. 83–106). New York: Methuen/Routledge & Kegan Paul.

Harding, Sandra. (1991a). Feminist epistemology in and after the Enlightenment. In *Whose science? Whose knowledge? Thinking from women's lives* (pp. 164–187). Ithaca, NY: Cornell University Press.

Harding, Sandra. (1991b). *Whose science? Whose knowledge? Thinking from women's lives.* Ithaca, NY: Cornell University Press.

Harding, Sandra. (1992a). After the neutrality ideal: Politics, science, and "strong objectivity." In Margaret Jacob (Ed.), *The politics of Western science, 1640–1990* (pp. 81–101). Atlantic Highlands, NJ: Humanities Press.

Harding, Sandra. (1992b). Rethinking standpoint epistemology. In L. Alcoff & E. Potter (Eds.), *Feminist epistemologies.* New York: Routledge. (Reprinted in Harding, 2004a).

Harding, Sandra. (1997). Can men be the subjects of feminist thought. In Tom Digby (Ed.), *Men doing feminism* (pp. 171–195). New York: Routledge.

Harding, Sandra. (1998). *Is science multicultural? Postcolonialisms, feminisms, and epistemologies.* Bloomington: Indiana University Press.

Harding, Sandra. (2001). Comment on Walby's "Against epistemological chasms: The science question in feminism revisited": Can democratic values and interests ever play a rationally justifiable role in the evaluation of scientific work? *Signs: Journal of Women in Culture and Society, 26*(2), 511–525.

Harding, Sandra. (2003). How standpoint methodology informs philosophy of social science. In S. P. Turner & P. A. Roth (Eds.), *The Blackwell guide to the philosophy of the social sciences* (pp. 291–310). New York: Blackwell.

Harding, Sandra. (2004a). *The feminist standpoint theory reader: Intellectual and political controversies.* New York: Routledge.

Harding, Sandra. (2004b). Introduction: Standpoint theory as a site of political, philosophic, and scientific debate. In *The Feminist standpoint theory reader: Intellectual and political controversies* (pp. 1–15). New York: Routledge.

Hartsock, Nancy. (1983). The feminist standpoint: Developing the ground for a specifically feminist historical materialism. In Sandra Harding & Merrill Hintikka (Eds.), *Discovering reality* (pp. 283–310). Dordrecht, the Netherlands: Reidel/Kluwer. (Reprinted in Harding, 2004a)

Hartsock, Nancy. (1987). Epistemology and politics: Minority vs. majority theories. *Cultural Critique, 7,* 187–206.

Hartsock, Nancy. (1997). Comments on Hekman's "Truth and method: Feminist standpoint theory revisited": Truth or justice? *Signs: Journal of Women in Culture and Society, 22*(2), 367–374.

Hartsock, Nancy. (1998). *The feminist standpoint revisited and other essays.* Boulder, CO: Westview Press.

Hekman, Susan. (1997). Truth and method: Feminist standpoint theory revisited. *Signs: Journal of Women in Culture and Society, 22*(2), 341–365 (see also responses by Patricia Hill Collins, Sandra Harding, Nancy Hartsock, & Dorothy Smith and Hekman's reply, in the same issue, pp. 367–402). (Reprinted in Harding, 2004a)

Hess, David J. (1995). *Science and technology in a multicultural world: The cultural politics of facts and artifacts.* New York: Columbia University Press.

Hirschmann, Nancy. (1997). Feminist standpoint as postmodern strategy. In Sally J. Kenney & Helen Kinsella (Eds.), *Politics and feminist standpoint theories* (pp. 73–92). New York: Haworth Press. (Reprinted in Harding, 2004a)

hooks, bell. (1983). *Feminist theory: From margin to center.* Boston: South End Press.

hooks, bell. (1990). Choosing the margin as a space of radical openness. In *Yearnings: Race, gender, and cultural politics* (pp. 145–153). Boston: South End Press.

Hubbard, Ruth. (2003). Have only men evolved? In Sandra Harding & Merrill B. Hintikka (Eds.), *Discovering reality: Feminist perspectives on epistemology, metaphysics, methodology and philosophy of science* (pp. 45–69). Dordrecht, the Netherlands: Reidel/Kluwer. (Original work published 1983)

Jaggar, Alison. (1983). Feminist politics and epistemology: The standpoint of women. In *Feminist politics and human nature* (pp. 353–393). Totowa, NJ: Rowman & Allenheld. (Excerpted in Harding, 2004a)

Jaggar, Alison. (1989). Love and knowledge: Emotion in feminist epistemology. In Alison Jaggar & Susan Bordo (Eds.), *Gender/body/knowledge: Feminist reconstructions of being*

*and knowing* (pp. 145–171). New Brunswick, NJ: Rutgers University Press.

Jameson, Fredric. (1988). "History and class consciousness" as an unfinished project. *Rethinking Marxism, 1,* 49–72. (Excerpted and revised in Harding, 2004a)

Keller, Evelyn Fox. (2003). Gender and science. In Sandra Harding & Merrill Hintikka (Eds.), *Discovering reality* (pp. 187–205). Dordrecht, the Netherlands: Kluwer. (Original work published 1983)

Kenney, Sally J., & Kinsella, Helen. (Eds.). (1997). *Politics and feminist standpoint theories.* Haworth Press: New York. (Published simultaneously as a special issue of *Women and Politics, 18,* 3)

Kesby, Mike. (2005). Retheorising empowerment-through-participation as a performance in space: Beyond tyranny to transformation. *Signs: Journal of Women in Culture and Society, 30*(4), 2037–2067.

Kuhn, Thomas S. (1962). *The structure of scientific revolutions.* Chicago: University of Chicago Press.

Kuhn, Thomas S. (1970). *The structure of scientific revolutions* (2nd ed.). Chicago: University of Chicago Press.

Lakatos, Imre, & Musgrave, Alan. (Eds.). (1970). *Criticism and the growth of knowledge.* New York: Cambridge University Press.

Lloyd, Genevieve. (1984). *The man of reason: "Male" and "female" in Western philosophy.* Minneapolis: University of Minnesota Press.

Longino, Helen. (1990). *Science as social knowledge.* Princeton, NJ: Princeton University Press.

Longino, Helen. (1993). Feminist standpoint theory and the problems of knowledge: Review essay. *Signs: Journal of Women in Culture and Society, 19*(1), 201–212.

Lukacs, Georg. (1971). *History and class consciousness* (R. Livingstone, Trans.). Cambridge: MIT Press.

MacKinnon, Catherine A. (1982). Feminism, Marxism, method, and the state: Part 1. An agenda for theory. *Signs: Journal of Women in Culture and Society, 7*(3), 515–544.

MacKinnon, Catherine A. (1983). Feminism, Marxism, method, and the state: Part 2. Toward feminist jurisprudence. *Signs: Journal of Women in Culture and Society, 8*(4), 635–658.

Maguire, Patricia. (1987). *Doing participatory research: A feminist approach.* Amherst, MA: University of Massachusetts, Center for International Education.

Mannheim, Karl. (1954). *Ideology and Utopia: An introduction to the sociology of knowledge.* New York: Harcourt, Brace.

McTaggart, Robin. (Ed.). (1997). *Participatory action research: International contexts and consequences.* Albany, NY: State University of New York Press.

Merton, Robert. (1972). Insiders and outsiders: A chapter in the sociology of knowledge. *American Journal of Sociology, 78*(1), 9–47.

Nanda, Meera. (2004). *Prophets facing backwards: Postmodern critiques of science and Hindu nationalism in India.* New Brunswick, NJ: Rutgers University Press.

Narayan, Uma. (1989). The project of a feminist epistemology: Perspectives for a non-Western feminist. In Susan Bordo & Alison Jaggar (Eds.), *Gender/body/knowledge: Feminist reconstructions of being and knowing* (pp. 256–269). New Brunswick, NJ: Rutgers University Press.

Needham, Joseph. (1969). *The grand titration: Science and society in East and West.* Toronto, Ontario, Canada: University of Toronto Press.

Nelson, Lynn Hankinson. (1990). *Who knows? From Quine to a feminist empiricism.* Philadelphia: Temple University Press.

Novick, Peter. (1988). *That noble dream: The "objectivity question" and the American historical profession.* Cambridge, UK: Cambridge University Press.

Pels, Dick. (2004). Strange standpoints, or how to define the situation for situated knowledge. In Sandra Harding (Ed.), *The feminist standpoint theory reader* (pp. 273–289). New York: Routledge.

Petras, E. M., & Porpora, D. V. (1993). Participatory research: Three models and an analysis. *American Sociologist, 23*(1), 107–126.

Popper, Karl. (1972). *Conjectures and refutations: The growth of scientific knowledge* (4th rev. ed.). London: Routledge & Kegan Paul.

Potter, Elizabeth. (2001). *Gender and Boyle's law of gases.* Bloomington: Indiana University Press.

Proctor, Robert. (1991). *Value-free science? Purity and power in modern knowledge.* Cambridge, MA: Harvard University Press.

Quine, Willard Van Orman. (1953). Two dogmas of empiricism. In *From a logical point of view.* Cambridge, MA: Harvard University Press.

Reiter (Rapp), Rayna. (1975). *Toward an anthropology of women.* New York: Monthly Review Press.

Rose, Hilary. (1983). Hand, brain, and heart: A feminist epistemology for the natural sciences. *Signs: Journal of Women in Culture and Society, 9,* 1.

Rouse, Joseph. (1996). Feminism and the social construction of scientific knowledge. In Lynn Hankinson Nelson & Jack Nelson (Eds.), *Feminism, science, and the philosophy of science* (pp. 192–215). Dordrecht, the Netherlands: Kluwer Academic.

Ruddick, Sara. (2004). Maternal thinking as a feminist standpoint. In Sandra Harding (Ed.), *The feminist standpoint theory reader* (pp. 161–169). New York: Routledge. (Original work published 1989)

Sachs, Wolfgang. (Ed.). (1992). *The development dictionary: A guide to knowledge as power.* Atlantic Highlands, NJ: Zed Press.

Seager, Joni. (1993). *Earth follies: Coming to feminist terms with the global environmental crisis.* New York: Routledge.

Seager, Joni. (2003). Rachel Carson died of breast cancer: The coming of age of feminist environmentalism. *Signs: Journal of Women in Culture and Society, 28*(3), 945–972.

Selin, Helaine. (Ed.). (1997). *Encyclopedia of the history of science, technology, and medicine in non-Western cultures.* Dordrecht, the Netherlands: Kluwer.

Shapin, Steven, & Schaffer, Simon. (1985). *Leviathan and the air-pump.* Princeton, NJ: Princeton University Press.

Simmel, Georg. (1921). The sociological significance of the "stranger." In Robert E. Park & Ernest W. Burgess (Eds.), *Introduction to the science of sociology.* Chicago: University of Chicago Press.

Smith, Dorothy E. (1987). *The everyday world as problematic: A sociology for women.* Boston: Northeastern University Press.

Smith, Dorothy E. (1990a). *The conceptual practices of power: A feminist sociology of knowledge.* Boston: Northeastern University Press.

Smith, Dorothy E. (1990b). *Texts, facts, and femininity: Exploring the relations of ruling.* New York: Routledge.

Smith, Dorothy E. (1997). Comment on Hekman's "Truth and method: feminist standpoint theory revisited." *Signs: Journal of Women in Culture and Society, 22*(2), 392–398.

Smith, Dorothy E. (1999). *Writing the social: Critique, theory, and investigations.* Toronto, Ontario, Canada: University of Toronto Press.

Smith, Linda Tuhiwahi. (1999). *Decolonizing methodologies: Research and indigenous peoples.* Atlantic Highlands, NJ: Zed Press.

Sohn-Rethel, Alfred. (1978). *Intellectual and manual labor.* London: Macmillan.

Sprague, Joey. (2001). Comment on Walby's "Against epistemological chasms: The science question in feminism revisited": Structured knowledge and strategic methodology. *Signs: Journal of Women in Culture and Society,* 26(2), 527–536.

Tickner, J. Ann. (2001). *Gendering world politics: Issues and approaches in the post-Cold War era.* New York: Columbia University Press.

Tickner, J. Ann. (2005). Gendering a discipline: Some feminist methodological contributions to international relations. *Signs: Journal of Women in Culture and Society,* 30(4), 2173–2188.

Traweek, Sharon. (1988). *Beamtimes and life times.* Cambridge: MIT Press.

Walby, Sylvia. (2001). Against epistemological chasms: The science question in feminism revisited. *Signs: Journal of Women in Culture and Society,* 26(2), 485–510. (See also responses in the same issue by Joey Sprague and Sandra Harding, and Walby's reply, pp. 511–540.)

Wallerstein, Immanuel. (1974). *The modern world-system* (Vol. 1). New York: Academic Press.

Weasel, Lisa. (2000). Laboratories without walls: The science shop as a model for feminist community science in action. In Maralee Mayberry, Banu Subramaniam, & Lisa Weasel (Eds.), *Feminist science studies* (pp. 305–320). New York: Routledge.

Weeks, Kathi. (1998). *Constituting feminist subjects.* Ithaca, NY: Cornell University Press.

Westkott, Marcia. (1979). Feminist criticism of the social sciences. *Harvard Educational Review,* 49(4), 422–430.

Wolf, Diane L. (Ed.). (1996). *Feminist dilemmas in fieldwork.* Boulder, CO: Westview Press.

Wylie, Alison. (2003). Why standpoint matters. In Robert Figueroa & Sandra Harding (Eds.), *Science and other cultures* (pp. 26–48). New York: Routledge. (A revised version appears in Harding, 2004a)

# 4

# Postmodern, Poststructural, and Critical Theories

Susanne Gannon
Bronwyn Davies

## What Are the Principles of Postmodern, Poststructural, and Critical Theories?

In this chapter, we explore postmodern, poststructural, and critical theories and discuss how they affect feminist research. These labels are sometimes taken to refer to the same thing and are sometimes taken up in oppositional ways. Further, what each of these names refers to is not an orderly, agreed on, and internally consistent set of ideas. What they mean depends on the vantage point from which the speaking or writing is being done. Among those who wear each of these labels there are many interesting and productive divisions, which are ignored when they are lumped together under one collective noun. Butler (1992) points out,

> A number of positions are ascribed to postmodernism, as if it were the kind of thing that could be the bearer of a set of positions: discourse is all there is, as if discourse were some kind of monistic stuff out of which all things are composed; the subject is dead, I can never say "I" again; there is

no reality, only representations. These characterizations are variously imputed to postmodernism or poststructuralism, which are conflated with each other and sometimes understood as an indiscriminate assemblage of French feminism, deconstruction, Lacanian psychoanalysis, Foucaultian analysis, Rorty's conversationalism and cultural studies. (p. 4)

*Postmodernism* is a term often used by critics who believe postmodernism is undermining the most fundamental assumptions necessary for social science and feminist research. Against this monster they try "to shore up the primary premises, to establish in advance that any theory of politics requires a subject, needs from the start to presume its subject, the referentiality of language, the integrity of the institutional description it provides" (Butler, 1992, p. 3).

Through exploring these commonalities and oppositionalities, we will make visible some of the ideas and practices that emerge in the writing and research to which these names are given. We will extract a set of principles that characterize these paradigms and set them apart from different understandings of research and the world. Our account of these perspectives is written neither from a distance, informed by a positivist ideal of objectivity, nor as if they can be defined once and for all. Every definition creates exclusions that might (and should) be contested. Among feminist concepts, for example, sisterhood was an important concept for feminist activism for much of the 20th century, but it underpinned the policing of behavior and the exclusion of those who did not display appropriate sisterhood: "As bad as it is for a woman to be bullied into submission by a patriarch's unitary truth, it is even worse for her to be judged as not a real feminist by a matriarch's unitary truth" (Tong, 1998, p. 279). We will, with this caveat on categorizing, attempt to create some coherent storying of the interconnections of postmodern, poststructural, and critical theories as they are taken up by feminist researchers. *It is a principle of critical, poststructural, and postmodern approaches to feminism that objectivity must be carefully rethought. An account, from these perspectives, is always situated. It is an account from somewhere, and some time, and some one (or two in this case), written for some purpose and with a particular audience in mind. It is always therefore a partial and particular account, an account that has its own power to produce new ways of seeing and that should always be open to contestation.* In this view of feminism, we do not rely on objective truth but on "being accountable for what and how we have the power to see" (Castor, 1991, p. 64). The particular position from which we write this chapter is as feminist poststructuralists looking back, as we trace the emergence of that field and its influences on feminist work, and looking forward,

simultaneously, to the possibilities that such work opens up.

Like many other feminist researchers in the 1980s and early 1990s, Patti Lather (1991) combined what she called a critical approach with postmodern and poststructural approaches. In envisaging the task she was undertaking, she located these three approaches along with feminism within the overarching social science framework in terms of the analytic work that social scientists took themselves to be doing in their analyses (p. 7). (See the table below.)

In this representation, earlier forms of research characterized as positivist and interpretive adopted a naturalistic or realist approach in which the researcher is understood as separate from the research and the social world as independent of the researcher's gaze. This is in marked contrast to work that sets out to make a difference to that social world, to emancipate subordinated groups from oppressive versions of reality.

The deconstructive or poststructuralist/ postmodern movement will be the main topic of this chapter. In this section, we will adopt the shorthand "deconstructive" to refer to postmodern and poststructural approaches and we will subsume the "critical," for the moment, inside that term. Our account is not offered as a grand narrative of the progress of feminist theory from one approach to another. Such grand narratives exclude other ways of seeing, privilege accounts from those with power, and promote falsely linear versions of history. In what follows, we will point out how, and on what grounds, some feminists have been alarmed by the effects of

Postpositivist Inquiry

| Predict | Understand | Emancipate | Deconstruct |
|---------|------------|------------|-------------|
| Positivism | Interpretive<br>Naturalistic<br>Constructivist<br>Phenomenological<br>Hermeneutic | Critical<br>Neo-Marxist<br>Feminist<br>Praxis oriented<br>Educative<br>Freirian Participatory<br>Action research | Poststructural<br>Postmodern<br>Postparadigmatic Diaspora |

"deconstructive" ways of thinking on feminist action and on our research and writing practices. We will provide some responses to these critiques, while reminding readers that neither the criticisms nor our responses to them are intended to be taken as the final word.

This chapter—and indeed the practices of the research to be discussed here—can be read as a simultaneous and constant weaving and unweaving of how we think and what we do and say in feminist research. *This is a second principle. Particular attention must be paid to the mode of writing, to the discursive strategies through which particular versions of the world are accomplished, especially in the present moment of writing.* In the figure of the weaver, simultaneously weaving and unweaving who she is, we ask you to consider the stuff of her weaving as the discursive threads of what is possible (nameable, seeable, doable, speakable, writeable) at any particular moment in time and place, and from a particular situated position. Feminist writers such as Laurel Richardson (1997) and Trinh T. Minh-ha (1989, 1991, 1992) draw attention to the weft and weave of research texts and the subjectivities realized within them. Acute reflexivity—especially at the very moment of writing—is necessary for researchers working within critical, postmodern, and poststructural frameworks.

A further principle of these theoretical frameworks has to do with questions of power, emancipation, freedom, and agency. *Our third principle is that relations of power are understood as established and maintained through discourse and through positions taken up and made possible within particular discourses* (Davies & Harré, 2000). Power is seen as complex and unstable and possibilities for agency, resistance, "freedom," and emancipation as contingent and limited. These concepts are treated differently within critical, postmodern, and poststructural theories: Indeed, their different takes on power, freedom, and agency act as distinguishing features between them. Furthermore, feminist poststructuralism insists on a particular position on agency that tends to differ from the works of other poststructuralists (Davies, 2000a; Davies & Gannon, 2005, 2006;

Weedon, 1997). Feminists working in poststructural paradigms seek to reconfigure agency so that we still might claim it as a possibility, albeit contingent and situated, that will assist us to conceptualize and bring about change.

You will notice that some of the theorists we mention in this chapter are men, who do not position themselves (and are not offered the position) as "feminist." Their positioning in the world as "men" may be seen by some radical feminists as negating their value for feminism because male theorists cannot know how one would think when positioned as a woman. From a deconstructive point of view, one can, rather, examine the nature of the "binary" division being discursively constructed in this concern: "Identity categories are never merely descriptive, but always normative, and as such exclusionary" (Butler, 1992, p. 16). Binary modes of thought limit and constrain thinking in ways that are oppositional and hierarchical. These binary categories—such as man/woman and good/evil—are implicated in dividing and constraining the world in ways that may be violent in their effects. So too, the category feminist, if understood in binary terms, implies the existence of an imagined and oppositional category that contains those items, people, or ideas that are "not-feminist" or even "antifeminist" (mobilizing the divisive logic of "if you are not with us you are against us"). Detecting these binary or oppositional and hierarchical modes of thinking, where categories emerge to structure thought on axes of this/not-this and good/bad, is of particular interest to researchers working within deconstructive frameworks. The binaries are implicated in relations of power and in maintaining the status quo. Despite the apparent orderliness of binary thought, categories tend to slip around and to glue themselves onto other binaries, conflating one with another. For example, feminist may be conflated with "woman" (and, conversely, not-feminist with "man"). The conflation of not-feminist with misogyny or patriarchy is a further binary move. Some of the binaries found glued to each other in Western traditions of mythology and that continue to inform our cultures and social practices are as follows (Wilshire, 1989, pp. 95–96):

KNOWLEDGE (accepted wisdom)/IGNORANCE (the occult and taboo)

higher (up)/lower (down)

good, positive/negative, bad

mind (ideas), head, spirit/body (flesh), womb (blood), Nature (Earth)

reason (the rational)/emotions and feelings (the irrational)

cool/hot

order/chaos

control/letting be, allowing, spontaneity

objective (outside, "out there")/subjective (inside, immanent)

literal truth, fact/poetic truth, metaphor, art

goals/process

light/darkness

written text, Logos/oral tradition, enactment, Myth

Apollo as sky-sun/Sophia as earth-cave-moon

public sphere/private sphere

seeing, detached/listening, attached

secular/holy and sacred

linear/cyclical

permanence, ideal (fixed) forms/change, fluctuations, evolution

"changeless and immortal"/process, ephemera (performance)

hard/soft

independent, individual, isolated/dependent, social, interconnected, shared

dualistic/whole

MALE/FEMALE

---

SOURCE: From Wilshire, D., The uses of myth, image, and the female body in revisioning knowledge. In A. M. Jagger & S. R. Bordo (Eds.), *Gender/body/knowledge: Feminist constructions of being and knowing,* copyright © 1989, Rutgers University Press.

The binary metaphors through which our narratives and storylines are constructed and our identities as men and women are made real are recognizable here. It is possible to recognize one's gendered identity (who you are or believe you should be or are seen to be) by looking at the appropriate side of the table (the one you have been "assigned" to). But it is also possible to claim characteristics from the other side. Nevertheless, the binaries act as an ordering device, defining what is appropriately "male" or "female" in terms of their opposition from one another. They rule out multiplicity and differences to create order, social coherence, and predictability around the idea of two opposite hierarchical categories (Davies, 1994).

By drawing attention to the way binaries insert themselves into thought, deconstructive writers provoke us to think differently and more carefully about the nuances and the possibilities of meaning in the language and the ideas that we might use. In pondering the nature of deconstructive thinking and the concern that it might not be useful for feminists because it has been produced by men, it is fascinating to run down the female side of Wilshire's table. Most of these metaphors can be used to characterize the theorizing that is done by deconstructive writers whether male or female. We might ask, then: Is poststructural and postmodern theorizing female even when it is produced by men? We can use such questions and observations to begin the work of deconstructing the male/female binary. We can ask: How are such categories constructed and maintained? What exclusions and inclusions mark such sites? How are social identities, the iterations of sex/gender, performed and sedimented in the particularities of people's lives? How are they lodged in their bodies? How are the unstable borders of these sites policed by individuals and institutions through oppositional and moralistic discourses and regimes of truth? As Cixous (1986) writes,

> Men and women are caught up in a web of age-old cultural determinations that are almost unanalyzable in their complexity. One can no more speak of "woman" than of "man" without being trapped within an ideological theatre where the proliferation of representations, images, reflections, myths, identifications transform, deform, constantly change everyone's Imaginary and invalidate in advance any conceptualization. (p. 83)

Feminist deconstructive writing searches for ways to disrupt the grip that binaries have on thought and on identity. Such deconstructive writing draws not only on rational argument but also on poetic writing, on fiction, on music, and on the performing arts. Sometimes it rewrites figures from the past (e.g., Cixous, 1991; Clément, 1989). Through play with language and alternative forms of narrative and representation such writing can blur the gender binaries, making a deconstructive move from either/or to both/and, disrupting, deconstructing, and troubling the clichés and stereotypes of everyday thought and practice in which we are enmeshed. *This is a fourth principle: The binaries within discourse limit and constrain modes of thought and the possibilities of identity. They disguise them as natural and give us only one option—of mimicking one part and abjecting the other. It is vital, life-giving work to play with and find ways of disrupting those linguistic forms, the binary oppositions, and the identities and meanings they hold in place. The power of language must be understood and language itself opened up for revision.*

It is here that we run into one of the deepest divisions within the approaches we are writing about in this chapter. The disruptive and deconstructive work on the categories through which we know ourselves and through which we argue

for change is read by some who work within the critical framework to destroy the categories and to make them unusable for the work of changing society. Others do not see deconstructive play as destruction. Butler (2004a), for example, suggests that calling terms into question doesn't mean debunking them but leads, rather, to their revitalization (p. 178). From a deconstructive perspective it is clear that we must work within the language we have. The terms and the categories that we wish to question are nonetheless powerful categories that have a great deal of political purchase. They can and do accomplish a great deal within our personal and social worlds whether we choose to mobilize them for political ends or not. In drawing attention to their constitutive power, a deconstructive approach does not foreclose the use of constituted categories on behalf of those who are subordinated by them. In a double move characteristic of deconstructive writing, we continue to use particular categories, like feminist, but work to destabilize some of the category's certainties. We put them "sous rature," or "under erasure," following Derrida (1976), using a textual reminder— ~~feminist~~ —to stand as a permanent reminder that we continue to need the concept but are also wary of some of its dangers. *A fifth and important principle of thought is this deep skepticism toward assumed truths and taken-for-granted knowledges, because they are generated through language, combined with a pragmatic understanding of the power of those categories to effect powerful positionalities and actions within the social world.*

The history of feminism can be read as a series of moments in which wins against patriarchal structures and practices have been achieved, and then subtly undermined by a shifting ground of resistance that negates the wins that have been made and keeps women's subordinate status carefully locked in place. Deconstructive approaches to feminism eschew simple recipes and actions in favor of a complex and continuous reflection on the ways in which identities, realities, and desires are established and maintained. This does not mean that they are prevented from action. Feminists are capable of working within multiple discourses, depending on the social and interactive contexts in which they find themselves, the particular moment in history, and the particular task in hand.

## How Have Critical Theory, Postmodernism, and Poststructuralism Been Taken Up Within Feminist Research?

In this section, we will separate critical, postmodern, and poststructural theories and elaborate some of the key concepts within them. We then elaborate the ways in which approaches, concepts, and strategies derived from each theoretical framework have been taken up and developed within feminist research.

### Critical Theory, Postmodernism, and Poststructuralism: Their Emergence and Interconnections

*Critical Theory*

Many poststructural and postmodern feminist writers began as critical theorists and maintain a strong critical edge in their writing (e.g., Haug et al., 1987; Henriques, Hollway, Urwin, Venn, & Walkerdine, 1998; Lather, 1991; Walkerdine, 1990). Critical theory, as a formal description of a particular mode of research and analysis, first emerged in the Frankfurt School of Social Research in Germany in the 1920s and 1930s through the work of Adorno, Horkheimer, Marcuse, and, later, Habermas. These philosopher-sociologists rejected fixed notions of hierarchies of social domination, such as might be found in Marxism, although Marxism was an important influence. They disrupted disciplinary authority by critiquing the supposedly objective "view from nowhere" of a positivist social science that had been modeled on the natural sciences and that had emerged from Enlightenment beliefs in universal reason and objective thought. Critical theorists brought philosophical questions into the arena of empirical social research. They developed a reflexive and critical social inquiry that saw social scientific knowledge itself as implicated in complex modes of production and regimes of truth. In so doing, they historicized and contextualized social science for the first time. Their work highlighted the logocentrism of Western rationalist and liberal humanist thought—questioning the belief that reason is universal, disinterested, and dispassionate and that it can set us free. However,

they did not abandon the tenets of Enlightenment thought—the belief in reason and the rational subject. Rather than dismantle them, they reconstructed them as sociocultural forms. In contrast to some of their successors, they resisted the lure of relativism and remained committed to the belief that truth is possible and can ground social action (McCarthy, 1994, pp. 7–30; Zima, 2002, pp. 194–198). For the critical social theorists of the Frankfurt School emancipation was part of their goal. This aspect of their work has threaded through into the liberatory discourses of contemporary critical theory.

Critical theorists continue to be influential in qualitative research in diverse disciplines and in different geographic locations. Current critical theory uses discourses of equity, inclusion, and social justice that are familiar and compatible with feminist agendas. Lincoln and Denzin (2003) note,

> The critique and concern of the critical theorists has been an effort to design a pedagogy of resistance within communities of difference. The pedagogy of resistance, of taking back "voice," of reclaiming narrative for one's own rather than adapting to the narratives of a dominant majority . . . [aims at] overturning oppression and achieving social justice through empowerment of the marginalized, the poor, the nameless, the voiceless. (pp. 625–626)

Critical theorists make grand claims for the potential of such work to change the world. Kincheloe and McLaren (2003), for instance, claim that critical theory produces "dangerous knowledge, the kind of information and insight that upsets institutions and threatens to overturn sovereign regimes of truth" (p. 433). They characterize the current "criticalist" as any researcher who believes

> that all thought is fundamentally mediated by power relations that are social and historically constituted, [that] facts can never be isolated from the domain of values or removed from ideological inscription, [that the] relationship between concept and object and between signifier and signified is never stable or fixed and is often mediated by social relations of capitalist production/ consumption; that language is central to the

formation of subjectivity; . . . that certain groups in society are privileged over others. (p. 453)

This description could also include many theorists who are called postmodernists or poststructuralists. With language like "ideological" and "social relations of capitalist production/ consumption," the authors also reference the traces of Marxism in current critical theory. However, their claim that "institutions" and "sovereign regimes of truth" might be overturned implies a more rigid and hierarchical conception of power and its operations than that to be found in poststructural theory (e.g., Butler, 1997b; Foucault, 1980).

Although few feminists overtly cling to the founding fathers of critical theory, there is much sympathy with these positions, particularly in our longing for emancipatory agendas. Indeed, recent critical theory is sometimes called new left theory or neo-Marxism,[1] and it informs critical race theory, critical multiculturalism, critical psychology, critical feminist theory, and critical pedagogy. In *Getting Smart: Feminist Research and Pedagogy With/in the Postmodern,* Lather's (1991) early synthesis of feminist and critical pedagogies, she articulates her indebtedness to critical theory and continuing affinity with its emancipatory objectives, but she critiques aspects of critical theory from a postmodern perspective. Although it can also be claimed that critical theory has "largely mutated into poststructuralism" (Boler, 2000, p. 362), authors and areas of study that thematize the "critical" tend to insist that, unlike those working with postmodern and poststructural approaches, the outcome they envisage is "real" social change, with the implication that this must entail subjects who have agency in the world. As we will argue later, these agendas are not as absent from the work of postmodern and poststructural feminists as some critical theorists claim, though the concept of agency is carefully revised by these feminists as a "radically conditioned" form of agency (Butler, 1997b, p. 15). In Judith Butler's view, for example, the social subject is a site of ambivalence where power acts to constitute these subjects (who might elsewhere be called "individuals") in certain limiting ways but where, at the same time, and through the same effects of power, possibilities to act (albeit constrained

and limited) also emerge. Critical theorists are committed to a more straightforward concept of emancipation, and of the freedom of individuals to strive toward it, as a necessary and permanent possibility. Power tends to be seen within critical theory as oppressive and unilinear, and it is enacted by certain groups on other groups. Emancipatory potential lies in the radical overturning of those hierarchical relations of power. Freedom from oppression is a central goal of critical theorists. In pursuit of this outcome, discursive analyses of sexism, homophobia, racism, and religious and cultural oppressions in everyday life and institutional practices are part of their methodological arsenal though they may not take up postmodern or poststructural positions on truth or subjectivity.

Two prominent feminist exponents of critical theory have been philosophers Seyla Benhabib and Nancy Fraser. In their influential and polemical collection *Feminist Contentions* (Benhabib, Butler, Cornell, & Fraser, 1995), they defend the tenets of critical social feminist theory against the effects of poststructuralism, represented in the collection in two papers by Butler.[2] Benhabib and Fraser see value in some postmodernist ideas, but they are wary of theories that they see as radical and dangerously relativist. Benhabib grounds her critique in three principles that she argues must not be abandoned by feminism and that, she claims, are weakened within a deconstructive approach. First, feminists must be able to assume an autonomous feminist subject who remains capable of self-reflection and agency. Second, she argues that large-scale narratives have their purposes, and feminists need to maintain some distance from social contexts they critique to develop objective perspectives and contribute to new narratives. Third, she insists that utopian ideals, abandoned by postmodernism, are necessary for feminist ethics and social and political activism (Benhabib, 1995, p. 30). In *Feminist Contentions*, Fraser is less resistant than Benhabib to postmodern feminism. She argues that feminism can benefit from incorporation of "weak" versions of postmodern ideas, but that feminist work must enable political action (Fraser, 1995a, 1995b). Benhabib and Fraser acknowledge some of the contributions of postmodernism to feminism, including the constitutive effects of language and the rejection of abstract (and masculine) universal reason. Their commitment remains, however, with critical theory, which they read as emancipatory and as enabling political activism in a way that they perceive postmodernism does not. The goal of critical theorists, they say, is not only to interpret social life but also to transform it. This transformation, like any theory of liberation, they argue, is dependent on a notion of subjectivity that allows some agency and incorporates possibilities for choice and for freedom to act in the world.

Within postmodern and poststructural approaches to feminist research, in contrast, "liberation" is made problematic, because one can never stand outside of discourse, agency is always radically conditioned by the positions made available to the acting, agentic subject, and subjectivity is always also subjection to the available ways of being. Further, absolute moral or ethical truth claims are regarded with a measure of skepticism, though that does not prevent feminists who take up these approaches from passionate attachments to both morality and action. Nevertheless, critical theorists are wary of postmodernism and poststructuralism because of the obstacles they see in such positions for political, social, or economic transformation. If critiquing the foundations of radical thought and activism leads to their collapse, then how are we to move on? How might we, they ask, effect change in the world? How might we "work the ruins" of what we had and knew (St. Pierre & Pillow, 2000)? Accusations of ethical paralysis and apoliticism as the inevitable consequences of poststructuralist thought are common, but they rest on an assumption that criticism and transformation are binary, irreconcilable opposites that cannot work together in a "both/and" kind of way. In such feminist dismissals of poststructuralism, criticism is allied with "theory," transformation with "praxis," and each side of the pair is positioned as oppositional; that is, as mutually exclusive. Michel Foucault (2000a) argued, in contrast, that critique and transformation are necessarily implicated in each others' operations, indeed that radical transformation can only emerge from radical critique:

> I don't think that criticism can be set against transformation, "ideal" criticism against "real" transformation.

A critique does not consist in saying that things aren't good the way they are. It consists in seeing on what type of assumptions, of familiar notions, of established, unexamined ways of thinking the accepted practices are based. . . .

There is always a little thought occurring even in the most stupid institutions; there is always thought even in silent habits.

Criticism consists in uncovering that thought and trying to change it; showing that things are not as obvious as people believe, making it so that what is taken for granted is no longer taken for granted. To do criticism is to make harder those acts which are now too easy.

Understood in these terms, criticism (and radical criticism) is utterly indispensable for any transformation. For a transformation that would remain within the same mode of thought, a transformation that would only be a certain way of better adjusting the same thought to the reality of things, would only be a superficial transformation.

On the other hand, as soon as people begin to have trouble thinking things the way they have been thought, transformation becomes at the same time very urgent, very difficult, and entirely possible. (pp. 456–457)

The project for any critical theory, Foucault argues, is to make it possible to think differently and thus to open the possibility for acting differently. This has profound implications for social practice and for social research. In this sense, critical theory, poststructural theory, and postmodern theory can work together rather than in antagonism with each other.

### Postmodern Theory

The terms *postmodern* and *poststructural* have at times been used interchangeably in the United States, both terms signaling a "crisis of confidence in western conceptual systems" (Lather, 1991, p. 159). Postmodernism is "an American term" (St. Pierre, 2004, p. 348) that has been used in diverse arenas of social and cultural life and that was in the early 1990s inclusive of poststructuralism. In a recent anthology of postmodernism, Bertens and Natoli (2002) trace three aggregations of this "protean" term: first, as a set of literary and artistic practices; second, as "a set of philosophical traditions centered on the rejection of realist epistemology and the Enlightenment project" mostly associated with French poststructural thought (p. xii); and third, in its most "ambitious" form, as a term that seeks to describe "a new sociocultural formation and/or economic dispensation . . . an aggressive entrepreneurialist capitalism" (pp. xiii–xv).

In architecture and the arts, in general, postmodern aesthetics are marked by the collapse of distinctions between high and popular culture, by self-referential reflexivity, by irony, parody, pastiche, appropriation, and surprising juxtapositions of images and ideas. Postmodernism is often viewed with alarm in other domains, such as economics. It sometimes stands as a synonym for "post-Fordist," "late," or "fast" capitalism, signaling the rise of Western consumer culture, multinationalism, and the globalization of corporate culture, capital, and labor. The postmodern logic underpinning the movement of global capital challenges the work of feminists who have fought long and hard for more equitable distribution of income, labor, and other resources. Global corporate culture can be understood as a new form of colonialism. Neoliberal approaches to management emphasizing the flexibility of workforces and workplaces—and thus the instability of subjects and the relations of power and knowledge within which they are located—are underpinned by these versions of postmodern culture. Regardless of the context or ideological intent, discourses that deploy postmodernism "seek to distance us from and make us skeptical about beliefs concerning truth, knowledge, power, the self and language that are often taken for granted within and serve as legitimation for contemporary western culture" (Flax, 1990, p. 41). The turn from critical theory to postmodernism is thus marked by a profound skepticism toward taken-for-granted foundational concepts, including those that underpin emancipatory agendas.

In its very naming, postmodernism is produced both in opposition to and as a continuation of some aspects of modernism. While gurus of postmodernity, like Lyotard (1984) and Bauman (2004), have claimed that postmodernity was very modernist, postmodernity is more usually characterized as replacing modernity, which was the era of social and cultural life and

aesthetics that spanned the latter half of the 20th century in the West. Modernity—emerging from the Enlightenment overturning of church and king as the origins of truth—validates reason, logic, and universal truth as the foundation for action in the world. The emancipatory impulses of liberal humanism and Marxism, both of which have influenced feminist movements, are rooted in the modernist project. Critique of the institutions and social practices that routinely excluded women became possible because of modernist thought. Yet many feminists have noted that the tenets of modernism have not been friendly to women. They argue that the modernist subject, able to act autonomously in the world, his actions driven by scientific, objective knowledge and by will, is always already a masculine subject, an individual subject more or less separate from the social world and free to act on it. As Hekman (1990) notes, the feminist position on "the modernist-postmodernist debate" is "anomalous" (p. 2). Modernism is part of our legacy, and as the humanist ideals of social justice and equity that remain important for feminism emerge from modernism, its vocabulary and politics continue, inevitably, to work through us (St. Pierre, 2000a, p. 478). Nevertheless, both feminists and postmodernists have been critical of the modernist project, and these critiques signaled a shift toward different conceptions of the subject and of society and its signifying systems. Postmodern approaches in art and social analysis "privileged aesthetics, language and singularity over the analysis of social institutions and social structures, and in their more extreme and polemical form declared the social to be dead" (Baudrillard, 1983, cited in Gane, 2004, p. 4). Postmodernists argue that knowledge is contextual, historically situated, and discursively produced; that subjects are constituted within networks of power and knowledge. Yet postmodernism, like feminism, is not uncontested. Bauman (2004) explains why he gave up the term:

> "The postmodern" was flawed from the beginning: all disclaimers notwithstanding, it did suggest that modernity was over. . . . In time more flaws became clearer to me—I'll mention but two of them. One was, so to speak, objective: "postmodern" barred the much needed break or

rupture. . . . "Postmodern thinking" could not but adhere to the "modernity grid." . . . The second was subjective. I prefer to select my bedfellows and affinities myself. Ascription to the "postmodernist" camp grew more and more unsavory and unpalatable by the day as the "postmodern" writings went further and further astray and "postmodernism" came to mean, more than anything else, singing praise of the brave new world of ultimate liberation rather than subjecting it to critical scrutiny. (p. 18)

Foucault (1998) also drew attention to categorical problems when he asked, "What are we calling postmodernity? I'm not up to date" (p. 447), and, he continued, "I've never clearly understood what was meant in France by modernity . . . I do not grasp clearly what that might mean, though the word itself is unimportant; we can always use any arbitrary label" (p. 448). He goes on, nevertheless, to name the "recasting of the subject" as the central problem that allied those who had been working in what might be called postmodern theory up to that time. Of his own work he says,

The goal of my work during the last twenty years . . . has not been to analyze the phenomena of power, nor to elaborate the foundations of such an analysis. My objective, instead, has been to create a history of the different modes by which, in our culture, human beings are made subjects. (Foucault, 2000b, p. 326)

It is this task of resituating the human subject not as the central heroic and active agent who shapes her own destiny but as the subject who is constituted through particular discourses in particular historical moments that is central to the postmodern approach to research. Butler also traces the splits and contradictions that are elided by the abstract collective noun postmodernism. Like Foucault, Butler (1992) rejects the name: "I don't know about the term 'postmodern' but . . . [I know that] power pervades the very conceptual apparatus that seeks to negotiate its terms, including the subject position of the critic" (p. 6), and again, "I don't know what postmodernism is, but I do have some sense of what it might mean to subject notions of the body and materiality to a deconstructive critique" (p. 17). The subject, power, and the body—and deconstruction as a strategy for critique—are issues that they both signal and that are at the core of our theoretical conversations in this chapter.

Although categories are useful in academic work, and we use them and are here engaged in their perpetuation, we are less concerned with policing their borders than with exploring the work that might be done with ideas emanating from these modes of thought. The semantic puzzles prompted by the naming of theoretical positions—and the seductions of theoretical progress narratives and successor regimes—have led us to a moment when we are variously faced with "post-postmodern theory," "posthumanist theory," "postfeminist theory," and even "post-theory theory." Rather than becoming entangled in these confabulations, and having alerted readers to some of the problems with such labels, we go on to explore in more detail poststructuralism and what that might be said to entail. Because many feminist authors who originally used the term postmodern have since vacated the term and moved toward poststructural, we will devote the remainder of this section to an exploration of poststructural theory and the concepts that have been taken up within it by feminist researchers.

### Poststructural Theory

While the postmodern label was initially used to cover both the postmodern and the poststructural, the term poststructural has subsequently become more common. The poststructural label signals in particular the "linguistic turn," although many theorists who would see themselves as responding to this turn would not describe themselves as poststructuralists and may or may not see themselves as postmodernists or critical theorists. The turn to language marked by poststructuralism is a recognition of the constitutive power of language and of discourse, particularly as introduced through the work of Michel Foucault (1997b), where discourses are seen to "articulate what we think, say and do" and to be historically contingent. The subject is discursively produced and the very body and its desires are materialized through discourse. Thus, the linguistic turn of poststructuralism is, more accurately, a "discursive" turn. Poststructural theory turns to discourse as the primary site for analysis and brings a deep skepticism to realist approaches where the task of social science is to discover and describe real worlds, which are taken to exist independent of their observations and their subjects. It troubles the individualism of humanist approaches, seeing the humanist individual as a (sometimes) troubling and fictional accomplishment of social and discursive practices (Davies & Gannon, 2005, 2006). In this sense, poststructuralism, in marked contrast to postmodernism, might be seen as the antithesis of global capitalism and of neoliberalism in which the individual is emphasized and the social is proclaimed as dead. Humanist psychology and some aspects of psychoanalysis are among the metanarratives that have been brought into question by poststructuralism, though many feminist poststructural researchers find aspects of psychoanalysis useful (e.g., Britzman, 1998; Butler, 1997b, 2004b; Clément, 1989, 1994; Flax, 1990, 1993; Grosz, 1990, 1994a; Ussher, 1997; Walkerdine, 1990). These theorists use psychoanalysis to theorize desire and to explore the changes individual subjects must engage in to bring about new patterns of desire and thus new ways of being.

The focus of poststructural thinking is on cultural life as the production and reading of texts and on the deconstruction of those texts. Its work is in marked contrast to the realist and naturalistic modes of thought in which the task was to "understand" or to make predictions about what was already there (Lather, 1991, p. 7). This poststructural work, which Butler (2003) describes as the work of critical intellectuals, is often a difficult and painful process of making strange that which we take for granted:

> I believe it has to be the case (certainly since Marx it has been the case) that becoming a critical intellectual involves working hard on difficult texts. From Marx through Adorno, we learned that capitalism is an extremely difficult text: it does not show itself as transparent; it gives itself in enigmatic ways; it calls for interpretive hermeneutic effort. There is no question about it. We think things are the way they must be because they've become naturalized. The life of the commodity structures our world in ways that we take for granted. And what was Marx's point? Precisely to make the taken-for-granted world seem spectral, strange. And how does that work?

> It only works by taking received opinion and received doxa and really working through it. It means undergoing something painful and difficult: an estrangement from what is most familiar. (p. 46)

Though poststructuralism does not provide a clear set of practices that might be taken up and ossified as a "method," it does provide a new set of approaches that might be made use of in analysis to provoke the sort of estrangement that Butler speaks of and to allow for new thought. In addition, methodologies themselves are made strange as "thinking technologies" that are also, always, subject to critical scrutiny (Haraway, 2000). Within a poststructural research paradigm it becomes difficult to define discrete methods for research. Indeed, Barthes (1989) suggests that we need to "turn against Method . . . regard it without any founding privilege, as one of the voices of plurality: as a *view* . . . a spectacle, mounted within the text" (p. 319). It is more useful to think of strategies, approaches, and tactics that defy definition or closure. Poststructuralism promotes close textual analysis as a central strategy, but the idea of a text encompasses far more than conventional written or spoken data. It allows for macrotexts like "capitalism" (or Marxism, humanism, feminism, postmodernism), and it allows for more familiar "micro" level texts like interview transcripts or literary texts. Strategies for poststructural analysis have nomadic tendencies and cross over disciplinary boundaries. Texts go beyond the conventional perceptions of literary or linguistic texts and might include bodies in space, spaces without bodies, or texts comprising nonlinguistic semiotic systems.

In poststructural research, the shift of interpretive focus is from language as a tool for describing real worlds to discourse, as constitutive of those worlds. There are no "right" research methods that will produce a reality that lies outside of the texts produced in the research process because reality does not preexist the discursive and constitutive work that is of interest to poststructural writers. This is important for feminist researchers in that it makes visible the historical, cultural, social, and discursive patterns through which current oppressive or dominant realities are held in place. What might have been taken for granted as natural, even essential to the human condition, and therefore unable to be questioned in any systematic way, is no longer taken to be inevitable, no longer left invisible. The structures and practices of every-day life are opened to scrutiny. Inevitabilities are reviewed as constituted realities (which have the possibility within themselves of their own reconstitution or collapse). In its focus on dis-course and discursive and regulatory practices, poststructural analysis seeks to transcend the individual or social divide and to find the ways in which the social worlds we inhabit, and the possibilities for existence within them, are actively spoken into existence by individuals and collectives. The individual in this way of thinking is not separate from the social land-scape, but continuous with it (Davies, 2000b).

An important focus of feminist poststructural theorizing is on the processes of *subjectification* and the discursive regimes through which we become gendered subjects. In this way it breaks with theoretical frameworks in which gender and sexuality are understood as inevitable, as *determined* through structures of language, social structure, cognition, or biology. It rejects the essentialism that attributes the experiences of women to "an underlying essence of woman-ness, an essence contained in bodies and expressed in culture," or that universalizes women's experiences (Ferguson, 1993, p. 81). Thus, it rejects conventional elements of radical and liberal feminisms. It also breaks with theo-retical frameworks that define *power* as that which is held in hierarchical and institutional frameworks by certain groups and individuals (Foucault, 1980). The question for poststruc-tural feminism then becomes that of *agency* and what possibilities there are for us to act. This agency does not presume freedom from discur-sive constitution and regulation of self (Davies, 2000a, 2000b) but rather lies in the capacity to recognize that constitution as historically spe-cific and socially regulated through particular games of truth, and thus as able to be called into question and changed. Meaning and intention are not stable across times, places, interactive contexts, and discourses. Individual subjects take up their existence in specific moments and are always located historically, politically, and discursively in contexts from which they are not separate (Davies, 2000b). In what follows we will elaborate each of these concepts of dis-course, subjectivity, agency, power, and truth.

## Poststructural Concepts

*Discourses* are complex interconnected webs of modes of being, thinking, and acting. They are in constant flux and often contradictory. They are always located on temporal and spatial axes; thus they are historically and culturally specific. We are always already constituted within discourse, and discourses operate on and in us simultaneously at the levels of desire and reason. The concept of discourse is used by post-structuralists to bring language into the material world where what can be understood and what can be said and done is seen as historically, socially, and culturally constituted. The range of possible ways of thinking are encompassed within (in)finite discursive possibilities that open thought up to us and close thought down. Discourse "can never be just linguistic since it organizes a way of thinking into a way of acting in the world" (St. Pierre, 2000a, p. 485). We do not have a prediscursive rational self, existing outside of or apart from discourse; we are our-selves constituted within discursive regimes, some of which are more powerful and more readily available than others. Discourses are not fixed but subject to constant revision and contes-tation to flux and flow. The concept of discourse serves to denaturalize what seems "natural," and to interrupt essentialist thought. It links together "power, knowledge, institutions, intellectuals, the control of populations, and the modern state as these intersect in the functions of systems of thought" (Bové, 1990, pp. 54–55). Influential discourses related to femininity, heterosexuality, fertility, and maternity have structured the con-ditions of women's lives. Feminists have worked to reform these structures. That reformation became possible through rethinking discursive regimes of truth about the essential qualities of women at particular moments in time. The suf-fragettes worked to make it possible to think about women differently—as rational and intel-ligent beings—at a time when women were excluded from citizenry. As it became possible to think differently, discourses about democracy and the institutions within which these dis-courses of citizenry were regulated and dissemi-nated shifted until, quite rapidly, it became impossible to think that women were not capa-ble of voting. The discourses of equity and women's rights that came to be called feminism in the West did not arise independently—outside of space and time—but from an intersection of historically situated discourses relating to emancipation and revolutionary changes in France and the United States that questioned what it is to be a human subject in a democracy. They arose in part from the new thinking that became possible at these intersections for individual subjects and from the strategic alliances that these women made with others who had begun this deconstructive thinking. Poststructuralists, however, are suspicious of successor regimes and victory narratives. They prefer to trace how a certain mode of thought became possible at a particular juncture, and how it became a dominant discourse or regime of truth that can itself be subjected to retracings and retellings. Butler (1992) sees such questioning of democracy as central to radical, deconstructive politics:

> A social theory committed to democratic contestation within a postcolonial horizon needs to find a way to bring into question the foundations it is compelled to lay down. It is this movement of interrogating that ruse of authority that seeks to close itself off from contest that is, in my view, at the heart of any radical political project. (p. 8)

Possibilities for shifting discourses, for taking up new ways of thinking and being, that is, for *agency* in the world, become possible in the contradictions and mo(ve)ments[3] within discursive regimes (Davies & Gannon, 2006). In contrast to the humanist essentialist, more or less fixed version of identity, poststructuralism proposes a *subjectivity* that is "precarious, contradictory and in process, constantly being reconstituted in discourse each time we speak" (Weedon, 1997, p. 32). Some feminists have worried that the idea of doing away with the subject (i.e., the humanist, essentialized subject) has meant an abandoning of the possibility of agency and so of social change. Theorizing agency has thus become one of the most important tasks for feminists working within poststructural perspectives (Butler, 1997b; Davies, 2000a). In "Contingent Foundations," Butler (1992) makes a strong argument for subjection being a precondition of agency:

> The constituted character of the subject is the very precondition of its agency. For what is it that

enables a purposive and significant reconfiguration of cultural and political relations, if not a relation that can be turned against itself, reworked, resisted. . . . In a sense, the epistemological model that offers us a pregiven subject or agent is one that refuses to acknowledge that agency is always and only a political prerogative. As such it seems crucial to question the conditions of its possibility, not to take it for granted as an a priori guarantee. (p. 13)

Subjectivity is an ongoing construction taking place through an ongoing process of subjectification, in which one is both subjected to available regimes of truth and regulatory frameworks and at the same time and through the same processes becomes an active subject. As we are imbricated within discourse, we become complicit in our own subjection, simultaneously seeking submission and mastery (Butler, 1997b).

In contrast to the poststructural interest in subjectification, both radical and liberal feminisms relied on a humanist conception of the individual subject as separate from and outside of language, as autonomous and capable of rationality. However, because individualism and realism have been opened up to question by critical theory and the wider effects of postmodern and poststructural thinking, many of the strong claims made from within liberal feminist and radical feminist frameworks can no longer be counted as absolute certainties (Clough, 1994; Davies, 2000a; Moi, 1985; Tong, 1998). These essentializing claims were already under challenge because feminists of color (other than white) queried their invisibility—or their objectification—and these so-called third world women challenged the common sense of Western feminism.

The question of the ongoing formation of the subject in everyday practices draws attention to the poststructuralist concepts of *power/knowledge*. Foucault (2000b) attended very closely to the micropractices of power relations and their effects in the creation of subjects:

> This form of power that applies itself to immediate everyday life categorizes the individual, marks him by his own individuality, attaches him to his own identity, imposes a law of truth on him that he must recognize and others have to recognize in him. It is a form of power that makes individuals subjects. There are two meanings of the word

"subject": subject to someone else by control and dependence, and tied to his own identity by a conscience or self knowledge. Both meanings suggest a form of power that subjugates and makes subject to. (p. 331)

Power is not hierarchical, for Foucault (1980), but it proceeds in every direction at once: It is capillary. It is not a possession that we have (or do not have) and that we can deploy to oppress (or to liberate) ourselves or others. Power is productive rather than oppressive, productive of subjects and of nets of domination and subjection within which subjects are always in motion. Subjects are constituted within power relations: They are not prior to or apart from them, nor can they be delivered from them. The rational, autonomous subject of some critical theory is a subject generated with a masculinist discourse. Foucault talks more often about power relations, that is, about how power is operationalized in interactions between individuals and institutions, than about power as something apart or prior to the discursive regimes within which power is in continual circulation. Indeed, we are always within relations of power, because we are always within discourse. In his work on power, beginning with his early work on asylums and prisons through to his later work on the care of the self, Foucault explored how the disciplinary power that was exercised in institutions became part of the humanist subject. Disciplinary power shifted from something brought on the individual, from outside the self, to a form of power relations taken up and internalized by individuals as their own responsibility. Similarly, women have sometimes been seen within feminism as complicit in their own oppression, though those feminisms assumed that once "false consciousness" was revealed, women would be free. Within poststructuralist conceptions of power, and the knowledge that power produces, there is no freedom from power relations, nor is there any place outside discourse. But just as within discourse we might find the possibilities for deploying new discourses, power relations also contain their own possibilities for resistance, albeit resistance that is "local, unpredictable and constant" (St. Pierre, 2000a, p. 492).

The concept of power in Foucault's (2000c) work then circles back, inevitably to the concept of discourse that he developed in his early work as he struggled to analyze power and its quotidian operations. Political thought from neither the Right nor the Left gave him the tools with which to think about power:

> The way power was exercised—concretely and in detail—with its specificity, its techniques and tactics, was something that no one attempted to ascertain; they contented themselves with denouncing it in a polemical or global fashion . . . the mechanics of power in themselves were never analyzed. This task could only begin after 1968, that is to say, on the basis of daily struggles at grass-roots levels, among those whose fight was located in the fine meshes of the web of power. This is where the concrete nature of power became visible. (p. 117)

The concrete nature of power is materialized in women's desires, in their bodies, and in social relations and institutional structures, and these areas remain the focus of much feminist poststructural empirical research (Davies & Gannon, 2005, 2006; St. Pierre & Pillow, 2000).

Foucault's work provides concepts with which we might think differently through what we still call "data" (though that term belongs squarely in positivist regimes of thought), about the *truth games* within which disciplinary and other knowledge is produced and reified. He provides us with a toolbox of strategies: *archaeology*, *genealogy,* and *technologies of the self.* Rather than distinct methods for analysis, these are intertwined modes of thought that make possible particular inquiries into games of truth, as sets of possibilities that we might take up because they are useful to us. Foucault's initial strategy of archaeology studies the conditions of possibility through which disciplinary knowledge is formed and becomes sedimented. It looks at discursive formations, at historical archives; it searches for subjugated knowledges. Rather than the human subject as the source of knowledge, which Foucault called "anthropological" history, archaeology works in the labyrinth of the archive, in "the domain of things said" (Foucault, cited in Eribon, 1992, p. 191). Archaeology interrogates the edifices of the disciplines, tracing how knowledge has come to define a particular domain, and to underpin its associated regimes of truth. It analyzes groups of statements to ascertain how they achieved "unity as a science, a theory or a text"; beneath the surface continuities we find "discontinuities, displacements and transformations" (Smart, 2002, p. 38). Foucault (1984) is interested in the modes of transformation of discursive practices, and his strategy of genealogy is directed at interrogating knowledge and power relations particularly as they operate at the level of the body, where the body is the object of the operations and technologies of power. The body is understood as

> the inscribed surface of events (traced by language and dissolved by ideas), the locus of a dissociated self (adopting the illusion of a substantial unity), and a volume in perpetual disintegration. Genealogy as an analysis of descent is thus situated within the articulation of the body and history. (p. 83)

Foucault (1984) talks about genealogy as "gray, meticulous and patiently documentary" (p. 76). It has been taken up by researchers in many different ways—including as a contemporary catchall phrase for any sort of historical analysis—thus, how the subject is treated within genealogical studies differs greatly (Hekman, 1990). But it is in his final work on the care of the self that Foucault (1985, 1997b, 1997c, 1997d, 1999, 2005) turns his attention most explicitly to individual subjects rather than larger systems of thought and relations of power.

Although we sketch out some component parts of what Foucault called his "little toolboxes" (Foucault, cited in Mills, 2003, p. 7), it is important to note that Foucault was not dogmatic. His whole corpus was dedicated to the dismantling of dogma, of received and sedimented "truth." This included others' use of his own work: "A discourse is a reality which can be transformed infinitely. Thus, he who writes has not the right to give orders as to the use of his writings" (Foucault, cited in Carrette, 1999, p. 111). Mills (2003) suggests that "we should draw on his work as a resource for thinking, without slavish adherence, and we should be very aware of Foucault's weaknesses and blind

spots" (p. 7). Deleuze (1988) argued that we should see Foucault not as a guru but as someone whose work might be useful in our everyday lives. Following Foucault, feminists might work with the cracks and fissures of dominant discourses, and the contradictory detail of the everyday, to multiply and enable alternative discourses. We might keep in mind, as we take up those aspects of Foucauldian thought that might be useful to us, that "a truly Foucauldian reading or method is one that moves beyond Foucault's writing and thinking" (Mills, 2003, p. 31). The potent pleasures for feminists in poststructural deconstructive work lies in the potential for finding the means to undo sedimented truths through which they might otherwise be held captive.

## Poststructural Analytic and Textual Strategies

In our discussion of the work of Foucault, whose troubling of concepts—including truth, power, knowledge, discourse, and the subject— underpinned the emergence of poststructural thinking, we have already introduced some of the analytic strategies that feminist poststructuralists have found useful. The generic term *discourse analysis* is sometimes used to signal the close textual work that researchers are engaged in, and it reflects the turn to language as a constitutive force that underpins poststructuralism; however, it is imprecise and applied within a wide range of theoretically incompatible paradigms. In the remainder of this section, we will focus on explicitly poststructural approaches and strategies that have been important in feminist work.

### Deconstruction

The term *deconstruction* has also migrated into populist discourse but, more precisely, it emerged from the work of Jacques Derrida. His analytic strategies work into the inconsistencies and weaknesses in meaning that are inherent within any text. Deconstruction was rapidly popularized in American literary studies partly because of its complementarity with the work of the Yale New Critics (Royle, 2000, p. 5). Meaning is to be found within the text for literary deconstructionists, but that meaning will always be multiple, shifting, and deferred. The text can be provoked to reveal its own contradictions and (im)possibilities through deconstructive analysis. Analysis does not produce definitive new readings of a text but is oriented toward the continuous deferral and displacement of meaning, which Derrida (1976) calls *différance*. Derrida's work began from the linguist Saussure's separation of the signified (the concept) from the signifier (the word representing the concept). Derrida argued that the relationship between word and meaning is arbitrary. Rather than being fixed or transcendental, meaning emerges in specific temporal and discursive contexts. As we suggested in the first section of this chapter, deconstruction pays particular attention to detecting and displacing binary pairs. In its narrowest application, deconstruction is a strategy for identifying and disrupting binary pairs. As Royle (2000) describes it, this form "took hold (like a virus or parasite)" and could be "stupidly formalistic" (p. 5). On the other hand, in its widest context, deconstruction has come to mean almost any analytical operation on any sort of text. McQuillan (2001) defines deconstruction as "an act of reading which allows the other to speak"; that is, as a practice that resists closure, a "situation or event of reading" rather than a method applied to a text (p. 6). Derrida prefers to consider "deconstructions," and he stresses that this term has "never named a project, a method, or a system" (Derrida & Ewald, 1995, p. 283). Although Derrida's work can be usefully applied to specific texts, which may be its most prolific application, deconstruction is applicable to social institutions and discursive regimes that exceed a single text or set of texts. Deconstruction as it is useful for feminist poststructural research can be applied as an everyday everywhere practice, something we might use in our lives, something active that might help us "make sense" of lived experience but that is most likely to trouble our sense making, even to reach "into the bare bones" of who we see ourselves to be (Lenz-Taguchi, 2004).

Whatever its object or its scope, or its particular strategy, deconstructive work aims to unfix meaning so that it remains incessantly at play, mobile, fluid, unable to come to rest or ossify into any rigid structures of meaning. Derridean deconstruction opens language to différance, a principle that captures both "difference" and "deferral." Deconstruction attends to the spectral logic of absences that haunt the text. It is productive, inventive, and creative, concerned with excess and ceaseless iteration. It "opens a passageway, it marches ahead and leaves a trail" (Derrida, 1989, p. 42), and the trails crisscross to create new trails and surprising openings and closings. Deconstruction can, perhaps, be anything: "and indeed, one starts laughing, and I'm tempted to add 'deconstruction and me, and me, and me . . . ,' to parody the parody of a famous French song—'50 million Chinese and me and me and me'" (Derrida, 2000, p. 283). Parody is one of numerous strategies that Derrida—and those who have found his work useful—have taken up to dislodge the fixity of meaning in a text (see Kamuf, 1981; Spivak, 1976). Gayatri Spivak (1976), translator of *Of Grammatology*, describes the difficulties of capturing Derrida's work in language:

> The movement of "difference-itself," precariously saved by its resident "contradiction" has many nicknames . . . trace, différance, reserve, supplement, dissemination, hymen, . . . and so on. They form a chain where each may be substituted for the other, but not exactly (of course, even two uses of the same word would not be exactly the same): "no concept overlaps with any other." . . . Each substitution is also a displacement and carries a metaphoric change. (p. lxx)

Although Derrida has used particular figures to work as "hinges"—as analytic devices to double and displace meaning—in particular texts under analysis, the figures available to feminist researchers for this sort of work are limited only by our imaginations and the texts we take up. Along with Spivak, who has used deconstruction to take on the fields of cultural studies (2000) and politics (2001), literary theorists Diane Elam and Peggy Kamuf have found Derridean strategies particularly fruitful for deconstructing "feminism" (Elam, 2000), "sexual difference" (Elam, 2001), "love" (Kamuf, 2000), and "critique" itself (Kamuf, 2001). Yet deconstruction as an analytic approach exceeds its origins and its originator. Judith Butler (1990, 1993, 1997a, 2004b), for instance, makes only passing reference to Derrida in the articulation of her radically deconstructive theory of gender performativity.

## Rhizoanalysis and Nomadism

The rhizoanalytic work of Deleuze and Guattari (1972, 1987) has also been of great interest to feminists working within poststructural paradigms. In contrast with the linear, systematic branching of tree roots, the rhizome is a secret, unseen, underground, creeping, multiplying growth that can strangle the tree or the root of conventional thought, that "plots a point, fixes an order" from beneath (Deleuze & Guattari, 1987, p. 7). Rhizomatic plants, such as heliconias, are knobbly, unpredictable, unstable, vigorous, prolific, extending in multiple directions at once, moving underground, splitting off, and springing up anew in unexpected places. Thought modeled on the rhizome links unexpected texts and events to make surprising new connections and unpredictable, unreplicable insights. Such analysis is also concerned with the dissolution of the transcendental and unitary rational subject, of he who "knows." Deleuze and Guattari modeled many strategies—cartography, rhizomatic analysis, assemblages, figurations, becomings, flows, and intensities—that have been taken up and extended in interesting and provocative work by feminists (Braidotti, 1991, 1994, 2002; Colebrook, 2002; Gatens, 2000; Grosz, 1994a, 1994b; Probyn, 2000; St. Pierre, 1997a, 1997b, 1997c). This provocative philosophical shift has also been critiqued by feminist scholars. For example, provocative concepts, such as "bodies without organs" (BwO), emphasizing the corporeal as "non-stratified, unformed, intense matter" (Deleuze & Guattari, 1987, p. 153), as intensity and energy rather than matter, have been both vehemently rejected by feminists concerned about the erasure of the materiality of embodied experience (Irigaray, 1977, cited in Braidotti, 2002, p. 76) and taken up by other feminists as productive ways to rethink female corporeality. Rosi Braidotti (1994, 2002) has used the figuration of the nomad to generate a feminist nomadic subjectivity that emphasizes "flows of connection" and "becomings" that rely on "affinities and the capacity both to sustain and generate interconnectedness" (Braidotti, 2002, p. 8). The

feminist nomadic subject "critiques liberal individualism and promotes instead the positivity of multiple connections"; it emphasizes "the role of passions, empathy and desire as non-self-aggrandizing modes of relation to one's social and human habitat" (p. 266). The sort of feminist subjectivity that Braidotti theorizes emerges from an "empathic proximity and intensive interconnectedness" (p. 8) rather than from any independent, separate, or selfish mode of being human. In contrast to theories of the self that emphasize individualism, subjectivity is always already a "socially mediated process" (p. 7). Feminists who think through Deleuze and Guattari also attend to questions about imagination and creativity in their search for ways to think differently, and playfully, against the grain of dominant discourses and sedimented truths. Another feminist figuration, analogous to Braidotti's nomad, is Donna Haraway's (1991) cyborg, a type of nonsentimental Deleuzean BwO, neither girl nor woman, human nor animal, nature nor culture, corporeal nor technological but composite of all of them, becoming all of them. Yet the cyborg is a material and political figure as well, representing the human exploitation of underpaid workers, the invisible underclass of white capitalist production. Haraway brings Deleuzian thought together with an update of Foucault's conception of bio-power, showing that "contemporary power does not work by normalized heterogeneity any more, but rather by networking, communication redesigns and by multiple interconnections" (Braidotti, 2002, p. 242). Haraway's dissolution of the binary of subject/object through the figuration of the cyborg is a call for a feminist poststructuralism that entails both pleasure and responsibility. In *Volatile Bodies*, Elizabeth Grosz (1994a) also brings Deleuzian and Foucauldian concepts together to develop a deconstructive corporeal feminism. The body is the inscribed surface of events—as Foucault theorized—but in her cartography of the female body she theorizes a fleshy volatile body, subject to flows and intensities of desire and of substances, particularly fluids (e.g., blood, milk, vomit). She deconstructs inside/outside to show that the female body is "an assemblage of organs, processes, pleasures, passions, activities, behaviors linked by fine lines and unpredictable networks to other elements, segments and assemblages" (p. 120). Where poststructural philosophy had been accused of abstraction and elision of bodies, Grosz writes the fleshy carnality of the body back into that domain and addresses both the "somatophobia" of Western philosophy (p. 5) and the "universal, innate, nonhistoric" subject of biology (p. 187). All the feminists we have discussed here have appropriated and furthered the ideas generated by Deleuze and Guattari to open up new ways to think through the body in feminist theory.

### Deconstructive Writing

The feminist poststructuralists we have discussed thus far take up theoretical concepts creatively and put them to new uses but, for the most part, their writing remains clearly on the side of theory. Other feminist writers take the deconstructive challenge into radical play with form and genre, defying binaries that organize writing into either analytical or creative writing and disregarding categories like theory, prose, poetry, drama, and film. As we have suggested earlier in this chapter, critical, postmodern, and particularly poststructural paradigms bring with them a hypervigilance to the politics, effects, and rhetorical tropes of language. Language is not a transparent tool for transmitting some truth that exists elsewhere, apart from the text. A text is never innocent but is constitutive of certain truths and exclusive of others, and thus must always be placed under interrogation. Language within poststructural frameworks tends to draw attention to its constructedness and to its multiplicity. The writers whose work we explore in the following paragraphs push language to the brink, using its creative possibilities to do highly original feminist textual work that is authorized by postmodern or poststructural paradigms.

Writing itself is a method of inquiry, as Laurel Richardson (1997) has demonstrated, rather than a transparent medium for re-presenting data. Richardson re-presents interview transcripts and other research "data" in poetic form, shifting the epistemological and ontological terrain in the process. With Richardson, Elizabeth St. Pierre theorizes writing as a "nomadic" practice, as a Deleuzian "line of flight" that asks, *"What else might writing do except mean?"*

(St. Pierre, cited in Richardson & St. Pierre, 2005). With this shift, writing is no longer "a tracing of thought already thought" but a provocation to différance (St. Pierre, cited in Richardson & St. Pierre, 2005). Trinh T. Minh-ha is a filmmaker whose writing has been particularly important for postcolonial and feminist poststructural scholars. Her films problematize the Eurocentric ethnographic gaze on the Other as "native" and as "woman" and her writing enacts a textual practice where Otherness is retained and given voice. Writing itself is the site of theorizing, and of interrogating theory through displacement and disintegration of the subject writing, the reader, of writing. Trinh (1989) claims a "hyphenated" textual space, a space where writing is both one thing and another, as the site for women's writing: "So where do you go from here? where do I go? and where does a committed woman writer go? Finding a voice, searching for words and sentences: say some thing, one thing, or no thing; tie/untie, read/unread" (p. 20).

Her writing brings together theory and fiction, analysis and creativity. Trinh (1992) develops a "politics of form" of "irrespectfully mixing . . . theoretical, militant and poetical modes of writing" (p. 154). She provokes a collision where "theorizing and practices of representation [are brought] into the same space each to bring the other into crisis" (Clough, 1994, p. 118). Trinh (1999) refuses the separation of theoretical and creative linguistic practice:

> Word as idea and word as word. These two movements of language are interdependent and always at work in the space of writing. When the telling and the told remain inseparable, the dichotomy between form and content radically loses its pertinence. That is the way I would try to describe the way I proceed in writing. The way a thought, a feeling, an argument, a theory, or a story takes shape on paper is at the same time "accidental" and very precise, very situated, just like a throw of the dice . . . if language is subjected to being a vehicle for thought and feeling, or if the focus is only laid on the told, the message, or the object of analysis, then the work will never resonate. And without resonance, writing becomes primarily a form of information retrieval or of administrative inquisition. (p. 35)

Trinh's work plays with the aesthetics and effects of language, and is simultaneously intensely and provocatively political.

Hélène Cixous, likewise, works in another highly original textual location. Although she has been positioned for English readers as a theorist, she refuses that name. She writes fiction, criticism, psychoanalysis, and philosophy "without enclosing herself in any of them" (Conley, 1991, p. 12) and often within the same texts. In conversation with Conley, she locates her work in relation to "theory":

> I am obviously not without a minimum of philosophical and analytical knowledge, simply because I am part of a historical period. I cannot act as if I were not a contemporary of myself. Neither do I think that I must wage a mortal war against a certain type of discourse . . . I do have knowledge of theoretical discourses. Yet the part that represses women is a part which I quickly learned to detect and from which I keep my distance. One leaves these parts aside. (Cixous, in Conley, 1991, p. 147)

Cixous's (1981, 1986) explication and practice of *écriture féminine*, of a feminine writing that exceeds the phallogocentrism of rational thought, has influenced diverse feminists, including Trinh. Écriture féminine is a practice of writing that Cixous (1986) says "will never be able to be theorized, enclosed, coded, which does not mean it does not exist" (p. 92). Nevertheless, Cixous's work can be understood within a theoretical landscape. Cixous's texts are dense, enigmatic, intensely lyrical texts of desire and of loss that might be understood as texts of bliss (Barthes, 1975).

Cixous's (1991) writing is deeply metaphorical. Her writing shimmers with "signifiers that flash with a thousand meanings" (p. 46). Her writing entails careful attention to the possibilities of language, sensitivity to the multiplicity, and excess of language. Like Trinh she shows that the simple truth (if such a thing can be said to exist) is neither desirable nor possible. She attends to other sources of language beyond the conscious, beyond reason. She locates her imagery and understanding of the corporeal effects of language in dreams, in the unconscious, and in what she calls *zones in(terre)conscious*

(Cixous & Calle-Gruber, 1997, p. 88). Language emerges in zones between earth and consciousness, deep in the body and memory (Davies, 2000b).

Cixous (1991) reads her body as a text. She sources the "truths" of life and of writing within the body, which always mediates every experience and which is itself the ultimate text (of life):

> History, love, violence, time, work, desire inscribe [life] in my body. I go where the "fundamental language" is spoken, the body language into which all the tongues of things, acts and beings, translate themselves, in my own breast, the whole of reality worked upon in my flesh, intercepted by my nerves, by my sense, by the labor of all my cells, projected, analyzed, recomposed into a book. (p. 52)

The body is the fundament of writing, and the poetic writing practice that Cixous developed derives from the body and reverberates with the body and with other bodies. It resonates in and with the body—like music or like blood. Bodies are texts of lives and can be written within an embodied writing practice of écriture féminine, a writing that seeks to preserve Otherness. It was in theater that Cixous found the medium where the writer, as ego, could let go and make space for the multiplicity of the other: "In the theater one can only work with a self that has almost evaporated, that has transformed itself into space" (Cixous, cited in Sellers, 1996, p. xiv). In the space of theater, the writer must imagine and create and *be* everyone. She can encounter and inscribe the other, and in writing the other she puts herself under erasure. It is in writing for theater that the self will "consent to erase itself and to make space, to become, not the hero of the scene, but the scene itself: the site, the occasion of the other" (Cixous, cited in Sellers, 1996, p. xv). She sees her writing for theater as a critical component of her scholarly practice and as the place where an ethics of writing becomes possible.

These authors, as well as ourselves, have also been influenced by Roland Barthes, who, like other French "founding fathers" of contemporary theory, marked the movement from structuralism into poststructuralism through his body of work. Barthes (1989) explicitly rejected the binary of science and literature in academia:

Science will become literature, insofar as literature—subject moreover to a growing collapse of traditional genres (poem, narrative, criticism, essay)—is already, has always been, science; for what the human sciences are discovering today, in whatever realm: sociological, psychological, psychiatric, linguistic, etc., literature has always known; the only difference is that literature has not *said* what it knows, it has *written* it. (p. 10)

In his later works, Barthes (1977, 1978) troubled the category of the individual writer and the practices of writing the self. His work, with that of the other writers in this section, has been inspirational in our own writing, provoking Gannon (2001, 2002, 2004a, 2004b, 2004c, 2005, in press) to develop a poststructural practice of autoethnography, and to (re)work data as fiction, drama, and poetry in a range of feminist textual interventions. This work has also been concerned to disrupt the binary of academia and the world, so that a text that began as a research project in a feminist academic context reemerges as a fictional play on a public stage and vice versa (Gannon, 2004b, 2005), and memory becomes the site for collectively theorizing a feminist poststructuralism (Davies, 2000a, 2000b; Davies & Gannon, 2005, 2006).

The writers we discuss in this section aim to bring language into crisis, to push at the boundaries of understanding so that multiple meanings can be provoked and multiple readings invited through a politics of form that disrespects generic integrity and disciplinary boundaries. They work at the limits of language where, as Trinh (1991) says, the aim is

to listen, to see like a stranger in one's own land; to fare like a foreigner across one's own language. . . . It is, to borrow a metaphor by Toni Morrison "what the nerves and the skin remember as well as how it appeared. And a rush of imagination is our flooding." What she wishes to leave the reader/viewer with, finally, is not so much a strong message, nor a singular story, but "the fire and the song." (p. 199)

## Controversies and Gaps, Critiques

The intersection of feminist and poststructural theories has been a vehemently contested but productive site. Although some readings of the debates suggest that poststructuralism has closed off possibilities for feminist work, vigorous new fields such as queer theory and feminist postcolonial theory have emerged in part from this collision. We have already explored some of the new work done by feminists and have discussed some of the concerns. In this final section of the chapter, we will further delineate feminist criticisms of these paradigms. Many of the accusations with which poststructural and postmodernist work have been charged by feminists hinge on their apparent *relativism*, explicitly their rejection of fixed truths and certainties. In contrast, researchers who locate their work as "critical theory," who claim emancipatory agendas and privilege praxis over (or alongside) theory, are not generally subjected to this critique. Accusations of relativism work along various axes in critiques of poststructural theorizing. Each axis rests on a binary way of thinking that asserts particular possibilities and impossibilities entailed in poststructuralism.

### Relativism and Social Action

The first axis relates to *action*. The history of the feminist movement, as "women's liberation," was characterized by individual and collective action directed at political and social change. The relativism of poststructural feminism is seen by some critics as incapable of provoking any action to improve the lives of women. If "women" as a coherent category has been deconstructed, and "power" is seen as a capillary and localized operation, then how and where can feminists work to improve social worlds? And who is a feminist anyway in these times? According to Delmar,

At the very least a feminist is someone who holds that women suffer discrimination because of their sex, that they have specific needs which remain negated and unsatisfied, and that the satisfaction of these needs would require a radical change . . . in the social, economic and political order. (Delmar, 1986, cited in Beasley, 1999, pp. 27–28)

Appropriate feminisms, and feminists, are driven by the imperative for social critique and the possibility of radical social change. Social theory that does not foreground radical social action is suspect for feminist purposes. This position is evident in critiques of postmodern or poststructural feminism, where the focus on discourse is seen as inconsistent with an orientation to social change. Waugh (1998), for example, parodies this:

> Rather than searching for scientific proof or metaphysical certainty, or a structural analysis of economic or social inequality, we should now recognize that the way to understand and to change our world is through the artificial mutation and manipulation of vocabularies. (p. 183)

Not surprisingly, she goes on to claim that (her version of) what she calls a "strong" postmodern position "raises enormous difficulties for any emancipatory collective movement concerned with profound economic and social inequalities" (p. 183). This "emancipatory collective movement" stands in for "feminism" in the sentence and in her argument. Differences between and within feminism(s) are elided to allow feminism—as a collective and unitary movement—to right the wrongs of patriarchy. Feminism is equated with and defined by its action orientation, much as an orientation to praxis and social transformation is definitive of Marxist, socialist, and critical theories. The argument rests on a set of binary oppositions whereby postmodernism or poststructuralism is set on one side of a binary against feminism, and the former is associated primarily with language and the latter with action. Each side of the binary excludes the other and is defined by that exclusion.

Taking a similar line through the axis of social action, Francis (1999) critiques deconstructive paradigms in educational research by imagining what she calls a "pure poststructuralism" that might be set against the sort of "applied poststructuralism" that she sees in Davies's deconstructive work with children and gendered identities (Davies, 1989, 2003; Davies & Kasama, 2003). The binary that Francis constructs does not hold, in our view, within poststructuralism where *thinking* differently necessarily and inevitably leads to *acting* differently in the world. Her argument seems to be that if it can be applied in social worlds, then theory isn't "pure" or "true." Thus, deconstructive paradigms

are seen to be forever and necessarily precluded from social action. As we have previewed in our earlier discussions of Foucault, Derrida, and Butler, we do not see this to be the case. The problem, rather, if there is a problem, lies in how we might bring postmodernism and poststructuralism with all that they entail (including a deconstructive stance toward language and the social world) together with the action orientation of feminist politics.

Of course, the dismissal of postmodern and poststructural thought from the arena of "action" in the critique we have just discussed relies on the definitions of social activism and of emancipation that are used and on the scale on which they are imagined. Waugh and Francis assert that worthwhile social action is underpinned by grand narratives (such as the relentless oppression of women by patriarchy) that imply large-scale social action as the ideal goal for feminists. We do not see this as the only possibility. Neither do we see a necessary dilution of the "purity" of the paradigm—an idea that we find antithetical to these paradigms—as resulting from moments of social critique, action, or agency. Although it does not provide broad or simple answers to social problems, poststructural critique does enable close analysis of the operations of power. It enables us to examine how power operates to construct our desires, our thoughts, our ways of being in the world—our subjectivities—in ways that can make us unconsciously complicit in our own oppression. Poststructural analysis of subjectification—that is, of how power works on bodies to produce us as subjects—enables individuals and groups to undertake close readings of lived experience (Davies & Gannon, 2005, 2006). With subjectification, we focus on the *processes* through which the subject is produced, on subjectivities that are "precarious, contradictory and in process, constantly being reconstituted in discourse each time we speak" (Weedon, 1997, pp. 32–33). The poststructural research and writing strategy of collective biography that we have developed from the memory work of Haug et al. (1987) works at this level to map the operations of power on bodies (Davies, 1994, 2000b; Davies & Gannon, 2005, 2006).

As critics like Waugh have noted, the dislodging of habitual ways of thinking and being that underpins poststructural work also entails the dislodging of fixed notions of the subject. This abandonment of the stable subject as the foundation for agency is seen as detrimental to action, as potentially paralyzing for feminists. However, the contrary has been the case for some feminists working with poststructuralist notions of the subject. For example, one woman tells how poststructuralist thought provides "a map through a crisis" when she discovers that her fiancé has sexually abused her daughter (in Davies, 1994). In the subsequent weeks, intersecting discourses of "legality, brotherhood, childhood, sexuality and psychology" work against each other to construct the woman and her daughter in ways that are disempowering. The analysis enables her to see by "pulling out the discursive frameworks why [she feels] so crazy and [how she is] being pulled to pieces" (p. 34). Reconstructing the way she thinks about the event is itself a powerful action and provides a clearer way forward into further action. She is able to move more easily between those discourses within which she felt trapped and can better "judge when she could resist and when she had little realistic choice but to comply" (p. 34). Feminist work that takes deconstruction seriously puts it to use in everyday social life.

Social change cannot be held apart from transformation that becomes possible at the levels of individuals and groups. Yet the social and personal transformation that might be possible in these paradigms is an ongoing and continuous process of self and societal critique and engagement rather than a step forward in a linear progress narrative toward something we might recognize as "emancipation," into which we might relax with satisfaction as though we have achieved the social changes we desired. As we suggested earlier in this chapter, at the beginning of this millennium the achievements of second-wave liberal feminism are proving remarkably fragile in the face of neoconservative discursive regimes. We do not see that an interest in deconstructive philosophies of the subject prevent us from participating in large-scale social activism, nor from seeking social justice in all the arenas of our lives. Nevertheless, within this paradigm, the claims we (and others) make about our projects, the language we (and others) use, and the actions we

(and others) take will be subjected to rigorous and continual reflexive examination rather than accepted as taken-for-granted truths or emancipatory programs. The social transformation of gender relations remains the focus of feminism and, as Butler (2004b) has recently argued, though "theory is itself transformative," it is not "sufficient for social and political transformation" (p. 205).

## Relativism and Politics

Obviously then, related to the charge that the supposed relativism of poststructuralism is detrimental to social action is the charge that poststructuralism is apolitical, or politically conservative. Braidotti (2000) argues that rather than being apolititical, "post-structuralists are politically to the far Left of the spectrum. They deconstruct, build genealogical approaches that clash with the dogma of historical materialism" though they emphasize the continuous "process of 'becoming,' that is the social, political and personal *pursuit* [italics added] of radical change and transformation" rather than any utopian achievement of transformation (p. 717). The subject is always in motion, and it is in this movement, these mo(ve)ments of becoming, that the imperatives of political activism will call us into action. Braidotti sees that the radicalism of poststructuralism lies in the very qualities that some feminist critics have claimed make it useless for political activism: "This radicality consists in unhinging the very foundations of the subject, freeing him/her from the linearity of a *telos* where reason, justice and revolution always end up playing the last hand" (p. 717).

Nevertheless, no theory can be purely "left" or "right" or any other category. Nor is sophisticated theoretical work necessarily distant from praxis. Foucault's (1977) analysis of prisons in *Discipline and Punish* was accompanied by his active involvement in the establishment of a prison reform movement (Mills, 2003, p. 76). Nevertheless, it is imaginable that fragments of Foucault's work could be used to justify fascism or deny the Holocaust (p. 7). This is not to suggest that theory can be inherently good or evil. Rather, we should ceaselessly interrogate the political use to which theory is put, we must situate our own with care and continuous attention. For example, the radically disruptive works of Butler (1990, 1993) have influenced diverse fields. In her early works, she unhinged the sex/gender distinction and theorized the performativity of gender in ways that have been useful for queer politics. The questions she raises in *Undoing Gender* (Butler, 2004b) about the conditions of normativity that produce unintelligible and unviable subjects, precluding some from the very category of the human, reverberate across current neoconservative domains of social and political life. In the different spheres of global politics, beginning with her discussion of the first war in Iraq (Butler, 1992) through to *Precarious Life* (Butler, 2004a), she has continued her relentless interrogation of the practices of Othering that underpin Western neocolonialism as it plays out from the bloody arena of the Middle East to the indefinite detention of prisoners held by the U.S. military in Guantanamo Bay. In an earlier work, Butler (1995) describes the work of herself and her fellow philosophers as though it was removed from the world:

> We toil in the domain of philosophy and its critique, and in that way dwell within a presupposed sense that theoretical reflection matters. As a result, though, the important questions raised concerning the rarefied status of theoretical language, the place of narrative in or as theory, the possibility of a theoretical activism, the tension between theory and empiricism . . . are not interrogated. (p. 132)

Nevertheless, we believe that it is necessary to have different thoughts to work the world differently, and, as an exemplar, the work of Butler has been useful for particular domains of social life. This highlights another issue for feminists who are working in densely theoretical arenas. Academic intellectual thought is marginalized in the English-speaking world. If we see the role of "public intellectuals" as part of our responsibility as feminists, then how are we to cross back and forth between the academy and the world? How might we increase our communicative repertoires without sliding into a simplistic reductionism of complex ideas? How are we to act and speak in the world, as well as work to think it differently? How might we be "specific intellectuals" (Foucault, 2000d, p. 384) who

might critique repressive systems of thought and collaborate with practitioners to change institutional practices? The work of the specific intellectual who talks about an area of specific knowledge is also a form of "action" that might have a transformative effect in the social world. Theory and praxis cannot be understood as mutually exclusive binaries; indeed they might rather be understood as mutually constitutive.

## Relativism, Morality, and Ethics

Another axis for critiques of postmodern and poststructural theories rests on the question of *morality*. Although these paradigms—like any theoretical model—are not in themselves "moral" or "immoral," they do question the absolutist foundations of any system of morality. This is the work that postmodern and poststructural researchers set out to do. Entangled with the idea of morality are questions of ethics, what makes some behavior more moral or ethical than other behavior.[4] In humanist philosophy, ethics operates as an appeal to autonomous, rational subjects who are able to act impartially to choose their actions. Rather than relying on an autonomous subject or promoting any set of absolute rules, approaches to ethics or morality within a poststructural framework will shift to analysis of the forms of thought and action that are made possible in any particular context. Multiple readings of a particular event might elaborate different discursive effects and operations within that event. If feminist morality and ethics are contingent on absolutisms, then poststructuralist approaches are problematic for feminism. But if feminists take up and further poststructural interrogations of these concepts, then inventive and radical work becomes possible. Early feminist work in this field theorized an ethics that was based on "mothering" and was characterized by "caring and interpersonal relations" (see McNay, 1992, p. 93). In this framework, characterized by the work of Carol Gilligan (1982), morality and questions of right behavior are relativized within a network of relationships and responsibilities, but they tend to rest on ahistorical and acultural essentialist notions of the feminine that are incompatible with the antifoundationalism of poststructural thinking. The work of reconfiguring ethics for feminists within poststructuralism entails insisting on responsibility and on judgment, but at the same time destabilizing the subject and the social contexts within which she is constituted and constitutes herself. In a poststructural feminist ethics, the subject is "neither sovereign nor autonomous but always caught up in a network of responsibility to others" (Elam, 1994, p. 105).

Ethics and morality are necessarily closely entwined in poststructural analyses. Foucault attempts to disentangle them by describing morality as having two elements—prescriptive codes of moral behavior that are externally imposed (though they may be taken up as our own desires) and ethical projects of the self on the self (Foucault, 1985). The second form of morality is intimately connected with the "biographical project of self-realization" (Rose, 1991, p. 12). Rather than a revelation (or an imposition) of right thought, poststructural conceptions of morality imply that we must engage constantly in the project of "self-reflection, self-knowledge, self-examination . . . the decipherment of the self by oneself, . . . the transformations that one seeks to accomplish with oneself as object" (Foucault, 1985, p. 29). The process of seeking to behave "morally" entails the intersection and effects of both of these sets of moral practices. The poststructural interest in morality lies particularly in these reflexive processes, unconscious as well as conscious, which Foucault calls "technologies of the self." These are the everyday practices through which we shape our bodies into particular bodies, historically and culturally specific bodies. Thus, we are simultaneously governed and govern ourselves. We are individualized and totalized through the same processes. Through continuous reflection and adjustment—unconscious and conscious—we shape ourselves appropriately for our contexts. In his examination of the history of sexuality, Foucault (1980, 1997b, 1997c, 1997d) traced technologies of the self through two conflicting imperatives—the obligation to "care for the self" and the obligation to "know the self." Morality lies in "the kind of relationship you ought to have with yourself, *rapport à soi*, which I call ethics, and which determines how the individual is supposed to constitute himself as a moral subject of his own actions" (Foucault, 1997b, p. 263).

Foucault's (1978, 1985, 1997b, 1997c, 1997d, 1999, 2005) work on the technologies of the self looked at how journal and letter writing, verbal self-criticism, and confession were taken up as reflexive and ethical strategies that contributed to the constitution of subjects in classical societies. However, his work set out to explore the formation of men as subjects in classical and premodern Western societies. Women (as well as children, slaves, and others) were explicitly excluded from the processes of subjectification that would have made them free and ethical subjects. In its implication that "questions of moral self-regulation were not relevant to women" (Grosz, 1994a, p. 159), feminists might have been tempted to reject this work as patriarchal or exclusionary. However, it has been more productive for feminists to view these gaps and omissions as invitations for feminist interventions and reconfigurations. St. Pierre (2004), for example, uses Foucault's work to interrogate the category "older woman" in ethnographic fieldwork in her hometown in the rural American south. She uses his theories on the care of the self to examine how through their daily lives the women she interviewed enact "a particular aesthetics of existence in ethical relations with oneself and others" (p. 333). The subject of women, she theorized (of these women in this place), is constituted *in practice*, realized in the details of everyday interactions, through friendships that are played out in intimate neighborhood spaces and in each others' homes. These private spaces act as "loopholes . . . that encourage subversive citation and the disruption of the fierce moral codes that aim to keep women in their place . . . Christianity, patriarchy, racism and . . . the 'white southern woman's code'" (p. 342). St. Pierre describes the practices she examines in Foucauldian terms as representing "the mode of subjection—the way in which one is invited to become ethical . . . to have a beautiful existence" and as manifesting in attention to detail and in a particular "care for others" (p. 343). In poststructural practice, morality is manifest in part through these arts of existence and practices of the self.

From the perspective of Derridean deconstruction, Bennington (2000) claims that "ethics" is impossible. As a metaphysical concept—one of those which has been put under erasure by poststructuralism—ethics must be "a theme and object of deconstruction" rather than something that can "simply be assumed or affirmed" (p. 64). He warns against any illusion that sharp-eyed deconstruction might deliver us "into the clear light of ethical felicity and self-righteousness" (p. 64). Nevertheless, he argues that "deconstructive thought will have *specific* interventions to make in the traditional metaphysical vocabulary of ethics, around concepts such as responsibility, decision, law and duty" (p. 65). The core of any system of ethics, in philosophy as in the small southern U.S. town where St. Pierre did her research, is located in relations to others. Bennington differentiates between ethic and duty:

> Simply following one's duty, looking up the appropriate action in a book of laws or rules, as it were, is anything but ethical—at best this is an *administration* of right and duties, a *bureaucracy* of ethics. In this sense an ethical act worthy of its name is always *inventive*, not at all in expressing the "subjective" freedom of the agent, but in response and responsibility to the other." (p. 68)

Rather than poststructural thought having abandoned ethical practice, Derrida's work locates it within social relations:

> The other has a radical prior claim on me, or even allows "me" to exist as essentially responsible to and for the other. I do not exist first, and then encounter the other: rather the (always singular) other calls me into being as always already responsible for him. (Bennington, 2000, p. 69)

Feminist poststructuralists have also found the work of Deleuze productive in reconceptualizing questions of ethics within the social. Bray and Colebrook (1998), for instance, argue that appropriation of his work opens the possibility for positive, active, and affirmative ethics with the potential to vitalize feminism. Braidotti (2002) describes the Deleuzean reconceptualization of the self as

> a relay-point for many sets of intensive intersections and encounters with multiple others, a self that "can envisage forms of resistance and political agency that are multilayered and complex . . . an empirical transcendental site of becoming . . . [that] actively desires processes of metamorphosis

of the self, society and its modes of cultural representation . . . [that] results in a radical new ethics of enfleshed, sustainable subjects. (p. 75)

The work of reconfiguring ethics in which feminist poststructuralists are interested destabilizes both the subject—who is always already caught up in networks of responsibility to others—and the social world. It rejects essentialist categories and foundational assumptions and attends to the constant work of becoming that an ethical life entails. As Elam (1994) points out, this can seem paralyzing because "the words that the patriarchy have left us for this are anarchy and chaos" (p. 109). For feminist ethics, poststructuralism offers the possibility of a "groundless solidarity" with the "possibility of a community which is not grounded in the truth of a presocial identity" but in a contingent, precarious, and vital solidarity that "forms the basis, although not the foundation, for political action and ethical responsibility" (p. 108). Thus, in community, we "try to do the right thing, here, now, where we are . . . in our pragmatic context" with no "transcendental alibi to save us" (p. 108).

## Male Theory/Patriarchal Theory

Some feminists claim that postmodern and poststructural theories are patriarchal white male theories (e.g., Brodribb, 1992). The influence of male theorists on contemporary feminist theory is clear throughout this chapter, but we have argued that this is irrelevant to the uses to which feminists might put their ideas to critique gender. Critiques of the canonical "French feminists" also assert the primacy of sex in policing what can be considered feminist. Kristeva, Irigaray, and Cixous—packaged in the early 1980s for English readers as the triumvirate of feminist poststructural theorists (Marks & de Coutrivon, 1981; Moi, 1985)—rely primarily on male theorists—Lacan, Foucault, and Derrida. Cixous (1981) insists that the poetic practices of écriture féminine are as available to men as they are to women. Kristeva's (1984) avant-garde poetic writers are all men. But, as happens with poststructural thought, categories slip about, become unstable, canons tend to topple over. The French feminists are not feminists, according to

Moses's (1998) history of French feminism; nor are they French, but "Belgian, Algerian and Bulgarian-born," as Rosi Braidotti (2000, p. 720) reminds us, nor are they necessarily poststructuralist. Moses and Braidotti each produce a careful rereading of their emergence and commodification for the English-speaking world illustrating the use to which feminists might put their skepticism of familiar stories and the attention to detail that characterizes genealogical work. They draw attention to the discursive regimes of consumption and circulation within which knowledge and power are produced and commodified in postmodern times. Retracing histories for cracks and ruptures is important work, but what matters most is not the origin of an idea but the use to which it might be put and the resonance it has with your own work. Whether we turn to Foucault, Deleuze, or Butler—or any other theorist—is determined by the moment and creative potential that we find in a concept and that provokes us to think differently about our data.

Feminists have taken Derrida to task for his appropriation of figures from women's bodies to use as deconstructive tools, such as "hymen" and "invagination." Derrida has been characterized as misogynistic and overtly antifeminist. Yet Derrida has claimed that feminism that remains committed to Enlightenment ideals and positivist paradigms is implicated in phallogocentric thought: "Feminism . . . is the operation through which a woman desires to be like a man, like a dogmatic philosopher, demanding truth, science, objectivity; that is to say, with all masculine illusions" (Derrida, 1978, cited in Elam, 1994, pp. 15–16). Elam carefully evaluates the charges and finds that, despite cautions, there are diverse points of intersection between them, indeed "there is a sense in which feminism already 'is' deconstruction, and deconstruction already 'is' feminism" (p. 19). Nevertheless, it is true that "if Derrida is positioned 'as a woman' in philosophy, he is still *not* a woman" (p. 64). The question, then, for feminists, is to what extent does this matter? Derrida might even be applauded for his figurative use of the materiality of the body to achieve the displacements and deferral of meanings that characterize textual deconstruction. In "Circumfession" (Bennington & Derrida, 1993) and "A silkworm of one's own" (Cixous &

Derrida, 2001), he uses male circumcision as the figure that defers and displaces the integrity of the text and the speaking self. The sex of the figure is less important than the work to which it might be put to displace the truth claims in a text. Nevertheless, it is relevant here to note that the poststructural theories and theorists we have discussed in this chapter also tend to be "Western" and "white." Although categories of cultural and geographic location are themselves complex and contradictory, feminist postcolonial theory emerges in part from the work of important poststructuralist thinkers (e.g., Spivak) and is discussed in detail elsewhere in this volume.

## Lack of Relevance

Poststructural feminists have been accused of irrelevance, as though *relevance* is some pure state of moral value. Some critics claim that these ivory tower feminists—spinning language renowned more for its opacity than for its sense—rarely leave "their blissful surroundings, and as time passes their sayings become increasingly irrelevant to the majority of women" (Tong, 1998, p. 207). Of course, such criticisms are predicated on the existence of a cohesive "majority of women" who can be neatly positioned in opposition to the academic feminists. Who are these women and who decides what is relevant or irrelevant, or what these terms mean, what discursive regimes of truth they re-present?

A similar criticism of poststructuralist feminist theory in terms of irrelevance or relevance harnesses the Other women of the world to construct a sort of moral hierarchy. The final paragraph of a recent book on feminist methodology states that "for many women around the world, caught up in struggles to survive, raise children, cope with poverty, natural disasters, corrupt regimes or varieties of social exclusion, resources for thinking are irrelevant luxuries" (Ramazanoğlu, 2002, p. 169). The work of postcolonial feminist theorists (e.g., Alexander & Mohanty, Trinh, Spivak) alerts us to the dangers of assuming that any women in the privileged West might be able to speak for these "many women" who are placed as abject others to those of us who peddle the "irrelevant luxuries" of critical thought. Although Ramazanoğlu's criticism rests on an unsustainable essentialist view of all non-white and non-Western women as too poor and too busy to theorize, it implies the more important critique that these theories are grounded in assumptions of the white, non-indigenous subject as the unmarked subject of feminism. Postcolonial feminists are ambivalent about the effects of postmodern thought for women other than those in the hegemonic West. Although liberal humanist feminism simultaneously appropriated and marginalized women of color, postmodernism generates "epistemological confusions regarding the interconnections between location, identity and the construction of knowledge," according to Jacqui Alexander and Chandra Mohanty (1997, p. xvii). They explain how global realignments and fluid movements of capital in postmodernity have led to "processes of recolonization" (1997, p. xvii) that have been particularly destructive in the lives of women.[5]

The charge of irrelevance is implied in the metaphor of the "garden of intellectual delights" as a retreat from the world for feminist poststructuralists (Tong, 1998, p. 207). Dense language, replete with language games and strategies intended to destabilize and displace meaning, is an irritant to many critics. Calls for "clarity" assume that transparency is possible and that simplicity is desirable (Lather, 1996; St. Pierre, 2000b). Lather (1996) claims that clarity forecloses thought:

> Rather than resolution, our task is to live out the ambivalent limits of research as we move towards something more productive of an enabling violation of its disciplining effects. Inhabiting the practices of its rearticulation, "citing, twisting, queering" to use Judith Butler's words (1993, p. 237), we occupy the very space opened up by the (im)possibilities of ethnographic representation. (p. 541)

Thus, poststructural work entails a politics and practice of writing differently. It is through writing differently that thinking differently becomes possible. Neither comes prior to the other, but they are simultaneously realized through the folds and hinges of language. Poststructural theory can be "of use in a time when the old stories will not do" (Lather, 1996,

p. 541). Familiar research practices in the social sciences, such as ethnographic research, become sites of doubt rather than certainty (Britzman, 2000; St. Pierre, 1997a, 1997b, 1997c).

Another criticism locates poststructural thought as an exclusionary mechanism within the power/knowledge regimes of the academy. Ramazanoğlu (2002) claims that these paradigms are intellectually elitist and disadvantage many feminists: "The difficulties and abstractions of so much postmodern thought have coincided with a period of competitive career pressures in higher education so that only certain kinds of feminist thought are deemed worthy of respect, funding or promotion" (p. 166). She describes scenarios where "terms such as 'empiricist,' 'essentialist,' 'foundationalist' . . . are fashionable weapons for trashing traces of modern thinking . . . (Pity the unsuspecting empiricist caught in a circle of contemptuous postmodern thinkers—and vice versa)" (p. 166). Apart from its implicit denigration of the intellectual capacities and flexibilities of women, and its assumptions that different feminisms must necessarily be combative, this claim rests on a rhetorical strategy of generalization that is difficult to uphold within deconstructive paradigms. It assumes a monolithic, even conspiratorial, new feminist oppression that disregards the specificity and capillary operations of power/knowledge. Poststructural analysis would seek out the particularities and specificities of social sites—faculty meetings, interview panels, corridor conversations—to interrogate and to challenge the local practices shaping academic feminism.

## Erasure of Body and Materiality

Another criticism of philosophically oriented theoretical frameworks is that they valorize discourse at the expense of the carnal body. How can postmodern or poststructural theory account for the corporeal enfleshed events that impact on women's lives? How can theory help to explain menstruation, birth, rape, breast cancer and how these are lived in the flesh of women's bodies? Does this theoretical work inevitably entail a degree of "somatophobia" (Grosz, 1994a; Kirby, 1991) that is unhelpful for feminists? Although for Foucault (1984) "the body is the inscribed surface of events" (p. 83), it is feminist poststructuralists who have brought the corporeal sexed body into poststructural theory. This can be a risky strategy for poststructural work in that sex, gender, and desire are put under erasure and troubled by deconstructive work (e.g., Butler, 1990, 2004b). Feminists who attend to the body can risk slippage into an essentialism that would be disavowed within poststructuralist paradigms. Yet some of the most sophisticated and subtle poststructuralist work has come from feminists rethinking the body theoretically within poststructural philosophical paradigms. For example, Susan Bordo (1993) uses Foucauldian language and ideas to refine her readings of women's bodies in Western culture. Moira Gatens (1991) deconstructs the sex/gender distinction of liberal feminism that served to separate biological and social dimensions of women's lives, and centers a corporeal feminism in her feminist approach to ethics (Gatens, 1996). Vicki Kirby (1991, 1997) interrogates essentialist thinking and further disrupts the nature/culture binary as she theorizes the material body at the (as the) scene of writing. Elizabeth Grosz, in particular, has been influential in her theorizing of a corporeal feminism.

Grosz (1994a) argues that there has been "a conceptual blind spot" in both philosophy and feminism and argues that feminism is "complicit in the misogyny that characterizes Western reason" (p. 3) in uncritically adopting philosophical assumptions about the implicitly masculine rational body of Enlightenment thought. The female body is abject and expelled from (male) normativity as "unruly, disruptive, in need of direction and judgement" (p. 3). Grosz's project is feminist because that universal body has, she suggests, always functioned as "a veiled representation and projection of a masculine which takes itself as the unquestioned norm, the ideal representative without any idea of the violence that this representational positioning does to its others" (p. 188). Although Grosz admits that her program is a preliminary one and does not neatly provide "materials directly useful for women's self-representation" outside of patriarchy (p. 188), she does begin the hard work of rethinking what has been impossible to think in ways that other feminists have been able to work with. Prior to this work, feminist philosophy had generally been "uninterested

in or unconvinced about the relevance of refocusing on bodies in accounts of subjectivity" (p. vii). Her work on inverting the inside/outside dichotomy to characterize female bodies as corporeal flows and intensities began to move poststructural feminists beyond this impasse. Elspeth Probyn (1991, 1993, 2000) has also brought the lived body to the foreground to explore the nexus of body and theory. She describes how reconfiguring her (anorexic) body with theory made "postmodernists nervous" and "feminists angry" (Probyn, 1991, p. 113). Vicki Kirby (1997) describes how poststructural feminists, despite their disavowals of binary thought, have inadvertently reified the central Cartesian binary:

> Perhaps commerce with the body is considered risky business because the split between mind and body, the border across which interpretations of the body might be negotiated, just cannot be secured. This fear of being discovered unwittingly behind enemy lines, caught in the suffocating embrace of that carnal envelope, menaces all conciliatory efforts. (p. 73)

Indeed, it has been argued that the body is only glimpsed, in much feminist poststructural work, just as it is disappearing from view (Somerville, 2004). Nevertheless, we suggest that it is here that much potential exists for feminism. The works of Grosz and others enable a theoretical engagement with the messiness of the lived corporeal body. The fleshy body is neither separate from nor inferior to a discursive poststructural body, but is the inscribed surface of discourse, the material effect of discursive practices made manifest in the flesh. The body for Grosz (1995) is "concrete, material, animate organization of flesh, organs, nerves, and skeletal structure, which are given a unity, cohesiveness, and form through the psychical and social inscription of the body's surface" (p. 104). Rather than absented through poststructural theory, the body might be privileged by it. Bell (1994), for example, claims that the body is the "only irreducible in Foucault's theorizing ... simultaneously a biophysical given and a cultural construct" (p. 12). Bodies are also critical to Judith Butler's theorizing because "discourses do actually live in bodies. They lodge in bodies; bodies in fact carry discourses as part of their own lifeblood" (Butler, cited in Meijer & Prins, 1998, p. 282). Butler (1997a) rejects the binary opposition between discursive construction and the lived body in part by emphasizing the "fundamentally dramatic"; the body is not

> merely matter but a continual and incessant *materializing* of possibilities. One is not simply a body, but, in some very key sense, one does one's body and indeed, one does one's body differently from one's contemporaries and from one's embodied predecessors and successors as well. (p. 404)

Despite claims that these paradigms elide the body, work that foregrounds and simultaneously deconstructs the body as the foundation for knowledge can be found in much critical and poststructurally oriented feminist research. The work of Haug et al. (1987), using memories of lived experience to unpack how the female body is materially inscribed by discourses of appropriate feminine deportment, demonstrates how critical theory can be held to account by female corporeality. In our own adaptations of this work (Davies, 1994; Davies & Gannon, 2005, 2006; Gannon, 2001, 2004c), we generate texts of the body to interrupt poststructural theory with our own flesh and expand theory in directions that are amenable to feminist readings of bodies and the world. Lather and Smithies (1997) conduct poststructurally inflected ethnographic research in a community of women who are HIV positive, producing a textual mosaic that is concerned to retain "the weight and density" of the women and to resist the allure of the "comfort text" by using a range of disruptive textual strategies to trouble any easy reading (Lather, 2001, p. 212). Sedgwick (1999) takes what she calls an "adventure in applied deconstruction" in writing of her own experience with breast cancer within a poststructural analytical framework. Acknowledging the astonishment that some readers might have at the possibility "that deconstruction can offer critical resources of thought for survival under duress," Sedgwick responds that she encountered breast cancer "as someone who needed all the cognitive skills she could get," including "some good and relevant ones from my deconstructive training" (p. 156). At the ethnographic "coalface," many feminist researchers working with girls and women use corporeal feminism and poststructural approaches to female bodies to think their data differently. In turn, their work, theoretically informed and politically oriented, feeds back into theory. A sampling of recent feminist empirical research shows how poststructural research interrogates the fleshy subjectivities of girls and women. Working with preteens, Gonick (2003) analyzes the discourses and practices of feminine sexuality, embodiment, desire, and relationship to others through which these girls imaginatively and corporeally construct femininity. Pillow (2000, 2004) takes up the body as a "deconstructive practice" in her study of teenage mothers and schooling. In a study of Danish university students, Søndergaard (2002) examines enactments of desire in the "signs on the body" inscribed by sexual and romantic storylines. Malson (1998) deconstructs the ideal of "the thin woman" underpinning anorexia nervosa. Each of these empirical investigations thinks back into theory from enfleshed female bodies.

Feminist theoretical and empirical work must engage with sexed bodies in one way or another. We are inclined to agree with Grosz (1994a) that corporeal interventions into theory—across the mind and body split—will bring theory toward new and productive horizons because, after all, "bodies have all the explanatory power of minds" (p. vii) and vice versa. We might go further in deconstructing this split by claiming that "theory-making is a labor of the body" (Zita, 1998, p. 204). Feminist appropriations of critical, postmodern, and poststructural theories foreground the body and make use of it as the volatile, unstable, and inventive ground for theorizing around the discursive production of sexed corporeal subjects.

## Conclusion

In closing, we would like to reiterate the strengths of feminist postmodern, poststructuralist, and critical discourses. Rather than conceive of this work as nihilistic, excessively relativist, amoral, or apolitical, we hold that poststructuralist thought opens us into new futures. When dominant discourses that hold us in place and lock us into sedimented ways of thinking and being are dislodged, then we might shift into other—more hopeful and often more radical—modes of thought and existence. How we might relate this work to feminist research in other paradigms is an ongoing and irresolvable question. We might argue, in contrast to the implications of the critics, that feminism and critical, postmodern, and poststructural paradigms have much in common to begin with in that they share a "hermeneutics of suspicion" (Braidotti, 2002, p. 68). Feminist work has been characterized as celebrating interdisciplinarity; indeed, it is likely that a "disciplinary approach to feminist theorizing is untenable" (Clough, 1994, p. 168). Beasley (1999) describes contemporary feminism "as a kind of empty shell into which may be poured any number of different concerns, details and explanations" (p. 28). In the academy, despite the academic institutionalization of women's studies, "contemporary feminist scholarship is not [engaged] in mass group conversation but is, rather, engaged with respective disciplines, or bodies of theory, that are themselves rarely engaged with each other" (Brown, 2001, p. 33). We suggest, as savvy bricoleurs, that disciplinary borders should be treated by feminists with some disdain. They are not pure states or bodies of knowledge but, as archaeological analysis would demonstrate, they are inventions of the commodification of knowledge and of thought emanating from the Enlightenment. It is in the interstices between disciplines, as between discourses, that new thought might fruitfully be generated. Additionally, we would stress that we do not intend to locate critical, postmodern, and poststructural paradigms as successor regimes within a history of feminist ideas. Rather than abandoning discourses emanating from liberal or radical feminisms—those allied with humanist Enlightenment ideals—we would hold on to what we can of the "ruins" of such thought. There are many discourses of feminism in circulation, and we need, at times, to deploy them all. We cannot abandon discourses, like humanism, that have shaped how we know and live in the world (Foucault, 1997a; St. Pierre, 2000a). Rather than rejecting them we need to become adept at mobilizing these discourses alongside and within a poststructural postpositivist skepticism, aiming to become able to think different,

even contradictory, thoughts simultaneously. Taking up the poststructuralist dissolution of the subject as our project, what feminist poststructuralism allows for is a "new" subject of feminism who is "not Woman as the complementary and specular other of man but rather a complex and multi-layered embodied subject who has taken her distance from the institution of femininity . . . a subject-in-process" (Braidotti, 2002, p. 11).

How might we conclude this chapter on postmodern, poststructural, and critical theories and their sometimes uneasy relation to feminism? Early in this chapter, we introduced the figure of the woman weaver, engaged in the constant and simultaneous processes of weaving and unweaving herself in the discursive texts of the wor(l)d. This figure recalls Penelope, the wife of Odysseus, from Greek mythology, who for 20 years wove in daylight and unpicked her work by moonlight.[6] Through this tactic she was able to fend off the suitors who would replace the missing king in her bed and on the throne. Resolution of her work—completion of the cloth she wove—was stalled, deferred, postponed, undone. In the endless iteration of her daily and nightly work, she came to it each time anew. Each time, no doubt, it changed. She changed. The threads would fade and thin and twist, as did her fingers. One day the light would draw to her attention a tiny part of the design that might be better. Another day the particular blue of the sky, the dark of clouds, or her own longings would provoke a subtle variation. The themes of the work would change as time passed, or would change in response to the company she kept. There may have been as many versions as there were days. Penelope is usually read as the quintessential devoted wife; indeed, her story is shaped by her responsibility to this other, her husband. But she managed the estates and the nation in his absence. She was trapped in a patriarchal system, the wife whose only likely option was a change in husbands, a woman trapped in a tale told by a man. Not even a central character. Yet she found the possibility to make something her own, something new, something that was not an answer, not freedom, not escape, not truth, but a way to live in the place and time where she found herself, a way to live that had integrity, which was hers.

## NOTES

1. Or "neonmarxism" in Lather (1998, p. 487).

2. Butler's chapter "Contingent Foundations" appears in both Butler and Scott (1992) and in Benhabib et al. (1995). Butler's "For a Careful Reading" appears only in the 1995 edition, along with the essays by Fraser and Benhabib that we refer to in this chapter.

3. The formulation "mo(ve)ments" brings together "movement" and "moment" to stress that opportunities for agency, for ways of moving into different discursive frameworks, open and close in unexpected and transitory spaces. We use "mo(ve)ment" also to signify the simultaneity of memory and movement in the methodology of collective biography through which we shift analysis of lived experience from individual biography toward collective readings of discursive regimes, and through which we aim to dislodge habitual ways of thinking (Davies & Gannon, 2006).

4. Hoffmann (2003) suggests that while in everyday language morals and ethics are used interchangeably, in philosophy they differ slightly:

> moral is typically used to refer to specific, prescriptive rules, principles or behaviours, whereas "ethics" is used in a more general sense to describe entire theories, codes and systems of conduct, both prescriptive and descriptive. But this distinction is not absolutely hard and fast, and little turns on demarcating strictly between these two words. (p. 104)

5. See, for example, *The Globalised Woman* (Wichterich, 2000).

6. It also recalls and appropriates the trope of weaving that Derrida uses in "A Silkworm of One's Own" (Cixous & Derrida, 2001). The weaving he talks of here is within a male ordered system of Jewish law where the silk tallith, the men's prayer shawl, is the text that he unravels or ravels. It references also Barthes's (1989) view of text as "tissue" where "lost in this tissue—this texture—the subject unmakes himself, like a spider dissolving in the constructive secretions of its web" (p. 64).

## REFERENCES

Alexander, M. J., & Mohanty, C. T. (1997). Introduction: Genealogies, legacies, movements. In M. J. Alexander & C. T. Mohanty (Eds.), *Feminist genealogies, colonial legacies, democratic futures* (pp. xiii–xlii). New York: Routledge.

Barthes, R. (1975). *The pleasure of the text* (R. Miller, Trans.). New York: Noonday Press. (Original work published 1973)

Barthes, R. (1977). *Roland Barthes* (R. Howard, Trans.). Berkeley: University of California Press. (Original work published 1975)

Barthes, R. (1978). *A lover's discourse: Fragments* (R. Howard, Trans.). London: Penguin. (Original work published 1977)

Barthes, R. (1989). *The rustle of language* (R. Howard, Trans.). Berkeley: University of California Press. (Original work published 1984)

Bauman, Z. (2004). Liquid sociality. In N. Gane (Ed.), *The future of social theory* (pp. 17–46). London: Continuum.

Beasley, C. (1999). *What is feminism, anyway? Understanding contemporary feminist thought.* St. Leonards, New South Wales, Australia: Allen & Unwin.

Bell, S. (1994). *Reading, writing and rewriting the prostitute body.* Bloomington: Indiana University Press.

Benhabib, S. (1995). Feminism and postmodernism. In S. Benhabib, J. Butler, D. Cornell, & N. Fraser (Eds.), *Feminist contentions: A philosophical exchange* (pp. 17–34). New York: Routledge.

Benhabib, S., Butler, J., Cornell, D., & Fraser, N. (1995). *Feminist contentions: A philosophical exchange.* New York: Routledge.

Bennington, G. (2000). Deconstruction and ethics. In N. Royle (Ed.), *Deconstructions: A user's guide* (pp. 64–82). New York: Palgrave.

Bennington, G., & Derrida, J. (1993). *Jacques Derrida* (G. Bennington, Trans.). Chicago: University of Chicago Press. (Original work published 1991)

Bertens, H., & Natoli, J. (Eds.). (2002). *Postmodernism: The key figures.* Martens, MA: Blackwell.

Boler, M. (2000). An epoch of difference: Hearing voices in the 90s. *Educational Theory, 50*(3), 357–381.

Bordo, S. (1993). *Unbearable weight: Feminism, western culture and the body.* Berkeley: University of California Press.

Bové, Paul A. (1990). Discourse. In F. Lentricchia & T. McLaughlin (Eds.), *Critical terms for literary study* (pp. 50–65). Chicago: University of Chicago Press.

Braidotti, R. (1991). *Patterns of dissonance.* New York: Routledge.

Braidotti, R. (1994). *Nomadic subjects.* New York: Columbia University Press.

Braidotti, R. (2000). The way we were: Some poststructuralist memoirs. *Women's Studies International Forum, 23*(6), 715–728.

Braidotti, R. (2002). *Metamorphoses: Towards a materialist theory of becoming.* Cambridge, UK: Polity Press.

Bray, A., & Colebrook, C. (1998). The haunted flesh: Corporeal feminism and the politics of (dis)embodiment. *Signs: Journal of Women in Culture and Society, 24*(1), 35–67.

Britzman, D. (1998). *Lost subjects, contested objects: Toward a psychoanalytic inquiry of learning.* Albany: State University of New York Press.

Britzman, D. (2000). "The question of belief": Writing poststructural ethnography. In E. A. St. Pierre & W. Pillow (Eds.), *Working the ruins: Feminist poststructural theory and methods in education* (pp. 27–40). New York: Routledge.

Brodribb, S. (1992). *Nothing mat(t)ers: A feminist critique of postmodernism.* Melbourne, Victoria, Australia: Spinifex.

Brown, W. (2001). *Politics out of history.* Princeton, NJ: Princeton University Press.

Butler, J. (1990). *Gender trouble: Feminism and the subversion of identity.* New York: Routledge.

Butler, J. (1992). Contingent foundations. In J. Butler & J. W. Scott (Eds.), *Feminists theorize the political* (pp. 3–21). New York: Routledge.

Butler, J. (1993). *Bodies that matter: On the discursive limits of sex.* New York: Routledge.

Butler, J. (1995). For a careful reading. In S. Benhabib, J. Butler, D. Cornell, & N. Fraser (Eds.), *Feminist contentions: A philosophical exchange* (pp. 127–144). New York: Routledge.

Butler, J. (1997a). Performative acts and gender constitution: An essay in phenomenology and feminist theory. In K. Conboy, N. Medina, & S. Stanbury (Eds.), *Writing on the body: Female embodiment and feminist theory* (pp. 401–417). New York: Columbia University Press.

Butler, J. (1997b). *The psychic life of power: Theories in subjection.* Stanford, CA: Stanford University Press.

Butler, J. (2003). Judith Butler [Interview]. In G. A. Olsen & L. Worsham (Eds.), *Critical intellectuals on writing* (pp. 42–52). Albany: State University of New York Press.

Butler, J. (2004a). *Precarious life: The powers of mourning and violence.* London: Verso.

Butler, J. (2004b). *Undoing gender.* New York: Routledge.

Butler, J., & Scott, J. W. (Eds.). (1992). *Feminists theorize the political.* New York: Routledge.

Carrette, J. R. (1999). *Religion and culture.* New York: Routledge.

Castor, L. (1991). Did she or didn't she? The discourse of scandal in the 1988 US Presidential campaign. *Genders, 12,* 62–76.

Cixous, H. (1981). The laugh of the medusa. In E. Marks & I. de Courtivron (Eds.), *New French feminisms: An introduction* (pp. 245–264). Brighton, UK: Harvester Press.

Cixous, H. (1986). Sorties: Out and out: Attacks/ways out/forays (B. Wing, Trans.). In H. Cixous & C. Clément (Eds.), *The newly born woman* (pp. 63–134). Manchester, UK: Manchester University Press. (Original work published 1975)

Cixous, H. (1991). *"Coming to writing" and other essays* (S. Cornell, D. Jenson, A. Liddle, & S. Sellers, Trans.). Cambridge, MA: Harvard University Press.

Cixous, H., & Calle-Gruber, M. (1997). *Rootprints: Memory and life writing.* London: Routledge.

Cixous, H., & Derrida, J. (2001). *Veils: Cultural memory in the present* (G. Bennington, Trans.). Stanford, CA: Stanford University Press. (Original work published 1998)

Clément, C. (1989). *Opera or the undoing of women* (B. Wing, Trans). Minneapolis: University of Minnesota Press. (Original work published 1988)

Clément, C. (1994). *Syncope: The philosophy of rapture* (S. O'Driscoll & D. M. Mahoney, Trans.). Minneapolis: University of Minnesota Press.

Clough, P. T. (1994). *Feminist thought: Desire, power and academic discourse.* Cambridge, MA: Blackwell.

Colebrook, C. (2002). *Understanding Deleuze.* Crow's Nest, New South Wales, Australia: Allen & Unwin.

Conley, V. A. (1991). *Hélène Cixous: Writing the feminine.* Lincoln: University of Nebraska Press.

Davies, B. (1989). *Frogs and snails and feminist tales: Preschool children and gender.* St. Leonards, New South Wales, Australia: Allen & Unwin.

Davies, B. (1994). *Poststructuralist theory and classroom practice.* Geelong, Victoria, Australia: Deakin University Press.

Davies, B. (2000a). *A body of writing.* Walnut Creek, CA: AltaMira Press.

Davies, B. (2000b). *(In)scribing body/landscape relations.* Walnut Creek, CA: AltaMira Press.

Davies, B. (2003). *Shards of glass: Children reading and writing beyond gendered identities* (2nd ed.). Cresskill, NJ: Hampton Press.

Davies, B., & Gannon, S. (2005). Feminism/poststructuralism. In C. Lewin & B. Somekh (Eds.), *Research methods in the social sciences* (pp. 318–325). London: Sage.

Davies, B., & Gannon, S. (Eds.). (2006). *Doing collective biography: Investigating the production of subjectivity.* Berkshire, UK: Open University Press/McGraw-Hill.

Davies, B., & Harré, R. (2000). Positioning: The discursive production of selves. In B. Davies (Ed.), *A body of writing* (pp. 87–106). Walnut Creek, CA: AltaMira Press.

Davies, B., & Kasama, H. (2003). *Japanese preschool children and gender: Frogs and snails and feminist tales in Japan.* Creskill, NJ: Hampton Press.

Deleuze, G. (1988). *Foucault.* London: Athlone Press.

Deleuze, G., & Guattari, F. (1972). *Anti-Oedipus: Capitalism and schizophrenia.* London: Athlone Press.

Deleuze, G., & Guattari, F. (1987). *A thousand plateaus: Capitalism and schizophrenia.* London: Athlone Press.

Derrida, J. (1976). *Of grammatology* (G. Spivak, Trans.). Baltimore: Johns Hopkins University Press. (Original work published 1967)

Derrida, J. (1978). *Spurs: Nietzsche's styles/Éperons: les styles de Nietzsche* (B. Harlow, Trans.). Chicago: University of Chicago Press. (Original work published 1976)

Derrida, J. (1989). Psyche: Inventions of the other (C. Porter, Trans.). In L. Waters & W. Godzich (Eds.), *Reading de Man reading.* Minneapolis: University of Minnesota Press. (Original work published 1987)

Derrida, J. (2000). Et cetera. In N. Royle (Ed.), *Deconstructions: A user's guide* (pp. 282–305). New York: Palgrave.

Derrida, J., & Ewald, F. (1995). A certain "madness" must watch over thinking. *Educational Theory, 45*(3), 273–291.

Elam, D. (1994). *Feminism and deconstruction: Ms. en abyme.* London: Routledge.

Elam, D. (2000). Deconstruction and feminism. In N. Royle (Ed.), *Deconstructions: A user's guide* (pp. 83–104). Basingstoke, UK: Palgrave.

Elam, D. (2001). Unnecessary introductions. In M. McQuillan (Ed.), *Deconstruction: A reader* (pp. 275–282). New York: Routledge.

Eribon, D. (1992). *Michel Foucault* (B. Wing, Trans.). London: Faber & Faber. (Original work published 1989)

Ferguson, K. (1993). *The man question: Visions of subjectivity in feminist theory.* Berkeley: University of California Press.

Flax, J. (1990). *Thinking fragments: Psychoanalysis, feminism and postmodernism in the contemporary west.* Berkeley: University of California Press.

Flax, J. (1993). *Disputed subjects: Essays on psychoanalysis, politics, and philosophy.* New York: Routledge.

Foucault, M. (1977). *Discipline and punish: The birth of the prison.* New York: Pantheon.

Foucault, M. (1978). *The history of sexuality: Vol. 1. An introduction* (R. Hurley, Trans.). London: Penguin. (Original work published 1976)

Foucault, M. (1980). *Power/knowledge: Selected interviews and other writings.* Brighton, UK: Harvester Press.

Foucault, M. (1984). Nietzsche, genealogy, history. In P. Rabinow (Ed.), *The Foucault reader* (pp. 76–120). New York: Pantheon.

Foucault, M. (1985). *The history of sexuality: Vol. 2. The use of pleasure* (R. Hurley, Trans.). London: Penguin. (Original work published 1984)

Foucault, M. (1997a). What is enlightenment? In P. Rabinow (Ed.), *Michel Foucault: Ethics: Essential works of Foucault 1954–1984* (C. Porter, Trans., Vol. 1, pp. 303–320). London: Penguin.

Foucault, M. (1997b). On the genealogy of ethics: An overview of work in progress. In P. Rabinow (Ed.), *Michel Foucault: Ethics: Essential works of Foucault 1954–1984* (Vol. 1). London: Penguin.

Foucault, M. (1997c). Technologies of the self. In P. Rabinow (Ed.), *Michel Foucault: Ethics: Essential works of Foucault 1954–1984* (Vol. 1, pp. 223–252). London: Penguin.

Foucault, M. (1997d). The ethics of the concern for the self as a practice of freedom (P. Aranov & D. McGrawth, Trans.). In P. Rabinow (Ed.),

*Michel Foucault: Ethics: Essential works of Foucault 1954–1984* (Vol. 1, pp. 281–301). London: Penguin. (Original work published 1994)

Foucault, M. (1998). Structuralism and poststructuralism. In P. Rabinow (Ed.). *Michel Foucault: Aesthetics: Essential works of Foucault 1954–1984* (Vol. 2, pp. 433–458). New York: New Press.

Foucault, M. (1999). About the beginnings of the hermeneutics of the self (T. Keenan & M. Blasius, Trans.). In J. R. Carrette (Ed.), *Religion and culture* (pp. 158–181). New York: Routledge. (Original work published 1978)

Foucault, M. (2000a). So is it important to think? In J. D. Faubion (Ed.), *Michel Foucault: Power: Essential works of Foucault 1954–1984* (Vol. 3, pp. 454–458). New York: New Press.

Foucault, M. (2000b). The subject and power. In J. D. Faubion (Ed.), *Michel Foucault: Power: Essential works of Foucault 1954–1984* (Vol. 3, pp. 326–348). New York: New Press.

Foucault, M. (2000c). Truth and power. In J. D. Faubion (Ed.), *Michel Foucault: Power: Essential works of Foucault 1954–1984* (Vol. 3, pp. 111–133). New York: New Press.

Foucault, M. (2000d). What is called punishing? In J. D. Faubion (Ed.), *Michel Foucault: Power: Essential works of Foucault 1954–1984* (Vol. 3, pp. 382–393). New York: New Press.

Foucault, M. (2005). *The hermeneutics of the subject: Lectures at the College de France 1981–1982* (G. Burchell, Trans.). New York: Palgrave Macmillan.

Francis, B. (1999). Modernist reductionism or poststructural relativism: Can we move on? An evaluation of the arguments in relation to feminist educational research. *Gender and Education, 11*(4), 381–393.

Fraser, N. (1995a). False antitheses. In S. Benhabib, J. Butler, D. Cornell, & N. Fraser (Eds.), *Feminist contentions: A philosophical exchange* (pp. 59–74). New York: Routledge.

Fraser, N. (1995b). Pragmatism, feminism and the linguistic turn. In S. Benhabib, J. Butler, D. Cornell, & N. Fraser (Eds.). *Feminist contentions: A philosophical exchange* (pp. 157–172). New York: Routledge.

Gane, N. (2004). Introduction: Rethinking social theory. In N. Gane (Ed.), *The future of social theory* (pp. 1–16). London: Continuum.

Gannon, S. (2001). (Re)presenting the collective girl. *Qualitative Inquiry, 7*(6), 787–800.

Gannon, S. (2002). "Picking at the scabs": A poststructuralist/feminist writing project. *Qualitative Inquiry, 8*(5), 670–682.

Gannon, S. (2004a). Dream(e)scapes: A poetic experiment in writing a self. *Auto/Biography, 12,* 107–125.

Gannon, S. (2004b). Out/performing in the academy: Writing "The Breast Project." *International Journal of Qualitative Studies in Education, 17*(1), 65–81.

Gannon, S. (2004c). Crossing "boundaries" with the collective girl: A poetic intervention into sex education. *Sex Education, 4*(1), 81–99.

Gannon, S. (2005). "The tumbler": Writing an/other in fiction and ethnography. *Qualitative Inquiry, 11,* 622–627.

Gannon, S. (in press). The (im)possibilities of writing the self: French poststructural theory and autoethnography. *Cultural Studies: Critical Methodologies.*

Gatens, M. (1991). A critique of the sex/gender distinction. In S. Gunew (Ed.), *A reader in feminist knowledge* (pp. 139–157). London: Routledge.

Gatens, M. (1996). *Imaginary bodies: Ethics, power and corporeality.* London: Routledge.

Gatens, M. (2000). Feminism as "password": Rethinking the "possible" with Spinoza and Deleuze. *Hypatia, 15*(2), 59–75.

Gilligan, C. (1982). *In a different voice.* Cambridge, MA: Harvard University Press.

Gonick, M. (2003). *Between femininities: Ambivalence, identity and the education of girls.* Albany: State University of New York Press.

Grosz, E. (1990). *Jacques Lacan: A feminist introduction.* Sydney, New South Wales, Australia: Allen & Unwin.

Grosz, E. (1994a). *Volatile bodies: Towards a corporeal feminism.* Bloomington: Indiana University Press.

Grosz, E. (1994b). A thousand tiny sexes: Feminism and rhizomatics. In C. V. Boundas & D. Olkowski (Eds.), *Gilles Deleuze and the theatre of philosophy* (pp. 187–210). London: Routledge.

Grosz, E. (1995). *Space, time and perversion: The politics of bodies.* Sydney, New South Wales, Australia: Allen & Unwin.

Haraway, D. (1991). *Simians, cyborgs and women: The reinvention of nature.* New York: Routledge.

Haraway, D. (2000). "There are always more things going on than you thought!" Methodologies as thinking technologies. *Kvinder, Køn & Forskning, 4,* 53–60.

Haug, F., et al. (1987). *Female sexualization: A collective work of memory* (E. Carter, Trans.). London: Verso. (Original work published 1983)

Hekman, S. J. (1990). *Gender and knowledge: Elements of a postmodern feminism.* Boston: Northeastern University Press.

Henriques, J., Hollway, W., Urwin, C., Venn, C., & Walkerdine, V. (1998). *Changing the subject: Psychology, social regulation and subjectivity.* London: Methuen.

Hoffmann, P. (2003). *Nothing so absurd: An invitation to philosophy.* Peterborough, Ontario, Canada: Broadview Press.

Kamuf, P. (Ed.). (1981). *A Derrida reader: Between the blinds.* New York: Columbia University Press.

Kamuf, P. (2000). Deconstruction and love. In N. Royle (Ed.), *Deconstructions: A user's guide* (pp. 151–170). Basingstoke, UK: Palgrave.

Kamuf, P. (2001). The ghosts of critique and deconstruction. In M. McQuillan (Ed.), *Deconstruction: A reader* (pp. 198–213). New York: Routledge.

Kincheloe, J., & McLaren, P. (2003). Rethinking critical theory and qualitative research. In N. K. Denzin & Y. S. Lincoln (Eds.), *The landscape of qualitative research* (2nd ed., pp. 433–488). Thousand Oaks, CA: Sage.

Kirby, V. (1991). Corporeal habits: Addressing essentialism differently. *Hypatia, 6*(3), 4–24.

Kirby, V. (1997). *Telling flesh: The substance of the corporeal.* New York: Routledge.

Kristeva, J. (1984). *Revolution in poetic language* (M. Waller, Trans.). New York: Columbia University Press. (Original work published 1974)

Lather, P. (1991). *Getting smart: Feminist research and pedagogy with/in the postmodern.* New York: Routledge.

Lather, P. (1996). Troubling clarity: The politics of accessible language. *Harvard Educational Review, 66*(3), 525–545.

Lather, P. (1998). Critical pedagogy and its complicities: A praxis of stuck places. *Educational Theory, 48*(4), 487–497.

Lather, P. (2001). Postbook: Working the ruins of feminist ethnography. *Signs: Journal of Women in Culture and Society, 27*(1), 199–227.

Lather, P., & Smithies, C. (1997). *Troubling the angels: Women living with HIV/AIDS.* Boulder, CO: Westview.

Lenz-Taguchi, H. (2004). *In på bara benet.* [Into the bare bones. Introduction to feminist poststructuralism]. Stockholm: HLS Forlag.

Lincoln, Y. S., & Denzin, N. K. (2003). The seventh moment: Out of the past. In N. K. Denzin & Y. S. Lincoln (Eds.), *The landscape of qualitative research* (2nd ed., pp. 611–640). Thousand Oaks, CA: Sage.

Lyotard, J. F. (1984). *The postmodern condition.* Manchester, UK: Manchester University Press.

Malson, H. (1998). *The thin woman: Feminism, poststructuralism and the social psychology of anorexia nervosa.* London: Routledge.

Marks, E., & de Coutrivon, I. (Eds.). (1981). *New French feminisms: An introduction.* New York: Schocken Books.

McCarthy, T. (1994). Philosophy and critical theory: A reprise. In D. Couzens Hoy & T. McCarthy (Eds.), *Critical theory* (pp. 5–100). Oxford, UK: Blackwell.

McNay, L. (1992). *Foucault and feminism.* Cambridge, UK: Polity Press.

McQuillan, M. (2001). Introduction: Five strategies for deconstruction. In M. McQuillan (Ed.), *Deconstruction: A reader* (pp. 1–43). New York: Routledge.

Meijer, I. C., & Prins, B. (1998). How bodies come to matter: An interview with Judith Butler. *Signs: Journal of Women in Culture and Society, 23*(2), 275–286.

Mills, S. (2003). *Michel Foucault.* London: Routledge.

Moi, T. (1985). *Sexual/textual politics: Feminist literary theory.* London: Methuen.

Moses, C. Goldberg. (1998). Made in America: French feminism in academia. *Feminist Studies, 24*(2), 241–274.

Pillow, W. (2000). Exposed methodology: The body as a deconstructive practice. In E. St. Pierre & W. Pillow (Eds.), *Working the ruins: Feminist poststructural theory and method in education* (pp. 199–219). New York: Routledge.

Pillow, W. (2004). *Unfit subjects: Educational policy and the teen mother.* New York: Routledge Falmer.

Probyn, E. (1991). This body which is not one: Speaking an embodied self. *Hypatia, 6*(3), 111–124.

Probyn, E. (1993). *Sexing the self: Gendered positions in cultural studies.* London: Routledge.

Probyn, E. (2000). *Carnal appetites: FoodSexIdentities*. London: Routledge.

Ramazanoğlu, C. (with Holland, J.). (2002). *Feminist methodology: Challenges and choices*. London: Sage.

Richardson, L. (1997). *Fields of play: Constructing an academic life*. New Brunswick, NJ: Rutgers University Press.

Richardson, L., & St. Pierre, E. A. (2005). Writing: A method of inquiry. In N. K. Denzin & Y. S. Lincoln (Eds.), *Handbook of qualitative research* (3rd ed., pp. 959–978). Thousand Oaks, CA: Sage.

Rose, N. (1991). *Governing the soul: The shaping of the private self*. London: Routledge.

Royle, N. (2000). What is deconstruction? In N. Royle (Ed.), *Deconstructions: A user's guide* (pp. 1–13). New York: Palgrave.

Sedgwick, E. Kosofky. (1999). Breast cancer: An adventure in applied deconstruction. In J. Price & M. Shildrick (Eds.), *Feminist theory and the body: A reader* (pp. 153–156). New York: Routledge.

Sellers, S. (1996). *Hélène Cixous: Authorship, autobiography and love*. Cambridge, UK: Polity Press.

Smart, B. (2002). *Michel Foucault* (Rev. ed.). London: Routledge.

Somerville, M. (2004). Tracing bodylines: The body in feminist poststructuralist research. *International Journal of Qualitative Studies in Education, 17*(1), 47–63.

Søndergaard, D. M. (2002). Poststructuralist approaches to empirical analysis. *International Journal of Qualitative Studies in Education, 15*(2), 187–204.

Spivak, G. C. (1976). Translator's preface. In J. Derrida (Ed.), *Of grammatology*. Baltimore: Johns Hopkins University Press.

Spivak, G. C. (2000). Deconstruction and cultural studies: Arguments for a deconstructive cultural studies. In N. Royle (Ed.), *Deconstructions: A user's guide* (pp. 14–43). New York: Palgrave.

Spivak, G. C. (2001). Practical politics of the open end. In M. McQuillan (Ed.), *Deconstruction: A reader* (pp. 397–404). New York: Routledge.

St. Pierre, E. A. (1997a). Circling the text: Nomadic writing practices. *Qualitative Inquiry, 3*(4), 403–417.

St. Pierre, E. A. (1997b). Methodology in the fold and the irruption of data. *Qualitative Studies in Education, 10*(2), 175–189.

St. Pierre, E. A. (1997c). An introduction to figurations: A poststructural practice of inquiry. *Qualitative Studies in Education, 10*(3), 279–284.

St. Pierre, E. (2000a). Poststructural feminism in education: An overview. *Qualitative Studies in Education, 13*(5), 477–515.

St. Pierre, E. (2000b). The call for intelligibility. *Educational Researcher, 29*(5), 25–28.

St. Pierre, E. A. (2004). Care of the self: The subject and freedom. In B. Baker & K. Heyning (Eds.), *Dangerous coagulations? The use of Foucault in the study of education* (pp. 325–358). New York: Peter Lang.

St. Pierre, E. A., & Pillow, W. S. (Eds.). (2000). *Working the ruin: Feminist poststructural theory and methods in education*. New York: Routledge.

Tong, R. P. (1998). *Feminist thought: A more comprehensive introduction* (2nd ed.). New York: Westview Press.

Trinh, Minh-ha. (1989). *Woman, native, other*. Bloomington: University of Indiana Press.

Trinh, Minh-ha. (1991). *When the moon waxes red*. New York: Routledge.

Trinh, Minh-ha. (1992). *Framer framed*. New York: Routledge.

Trinh, Minh-ha. (1999). *Cinema-interval*. London: Routledge.

Ussher, J. M. (1997). *Body talk: The material and discursive regulation of sexuality, madness and reproduction*. London: Routledge.

Walkerdine, V. (1990). *Schoolgirl fictions*. London: Verso.

Waugh, P. (1998). Postmodernism and feminism. In S. Jackson & J. Jones (Eds.), *Contemporary feminist theories* (pp. 177–193). New York: New York University Press.

Weedon, C. (1997). *Feminist practice and poststructural theory* (2nd ed.). Oxford, UK: Blackwell.

Wichterich, C. (2000). *The globalised woman*. New York: Zed Books.

Wilshire, D. (1989). The uses of myth, image and the female body in revisioning knowledge. In A. M. Jagger & S. R. Bordo (Eds.), *Gender/body/knowledge: Feminist reconstructions of being and knowing* (pp. 92–114). New Brunswick, NJ: Rutgers University Press.

Zima, P. V. (2002). *Deconstruction and critical theory*. London: Continuum.

Zita, J. (1998). *Body talk: Philosophical reflections on sex and gender*. New York: Columbia University Press.

# 5

# THE POLITICS OF BORDER CROSSINGS

*Black, Postcolonial, and Transnational Feminist Perspectives*

HYUN SOOK KIM

Feminist scholarship in the past three decades has continued to theorize about the politics of various borders, or about how divisions and inequalities across race, culture, sexuality, class, and nationality create tensions and fragmentation. Theoretically and politically, feminist researchers and activists working across various sociocultural divides have critiqued the notions of universal patriarchy and global sisterhood (womanhood) and have analyzed how multiple forms of hegemonies are configured unevenly in "scattered," fragmented, conflicting, and contradictory ways (Grewal & Kaplan, 1994; Mirza, 1997; Mohanty, 2005). These tensions, however, appear to have deepened with the increasing inequalities and polarizations caused by globalization—namely, of capitalist free trade and corporate market economy, or economic liberalism. Given this backdrop, how do feminist researchers produce critical knowledge about domination and subordination, power and privilege, and geopolitical and institutional rule that is historically salient today? What are the ways in which feminist

scholars contribute to knowledge production without reinforcing or legitimating their interests and agendas, or those of privileged groups and places? How is feminist production of knowledge made more explicitly tied to material and cultural politics, so that the less privileged groups, communities, and places are made visible and integrated into analysis?[1]

Some strands of feminist scholarship have been more explicit than others in grappling with these questions about epistemology and praxis—about how feminists speak about, frame, and engage across multiple divides and putative borders without privileging the interests of dominant groups. I consider these questions, which have been similarly raised elsewhere by feminist geographers Staeheli and Nagar (2002), to examine epistemological and methodological issues facing feminist scholarship. This chapter focuses, in particular, on black feminist thought, postcolonial feminist theory and, transnational feminist perspectives. These feminist trajectories have developed in parallel movements, and while they may reflect uneasy relations with each other, their mutual concerns deal with issues of voice, authority, and subjectivity of groups (or women) in subjugation.

My working premise is that in the current context of globalization, it is necessary to draw important lessons about feminist epistemology and methodology that will enable making connections and linkages across variously polarized communities and places. Such analytical and political linkages are necessary for several reasons. One is that the issues of race, empire, imperialism, colonialism, and nations/states are particularly salient today in light of globalization, but they remain overlooked and undertheorized in feminist scholarship. When these questions are probed, more often feminist analyses tend not to study them in relation to gender, sexuality, class, patriarchy, and feminist epistemology.[2] Partially, this is due to the blind spots that exist in our feminist approaches to studying these questions, and partially also because the different strands of feminist scholarship (of black and "Third World" feminist approaches, postcolonial feminist studies, and transnational feminist analyses) remain separated from each other and on the "margins" of academic disciplines. In this chapter, I not only examine such conceptual limits but also review the important contributions offered by them. Although different in their epistemic positions, black, Third World, postcolonial, and transnational feminists have been attentive to the problems of racism, imperialism, and neocolonialism found in knowledge production and have offered critiques and insights on the complex matrix of power and representation. They have articulated the complexities and specificities of material and cultural practices across historical and cultural contexts, as well as exposing the intricate workings of power dynamics in knowledge production. These particular feminist trajectories offer necessary insights on how we can unravel these matrixes of power.

Furthermore, given the realignments of nation-states and the reconfiguration of empires today, feminist scholars and activists now face new challenges and opportunities. Concerns of (neo)colonialism and imperialism, with the United States extending its military, political, and economic power globally, are as relevant today to feminist scholars working in metropolitan centers in the global North as they are for those residing in the Third World or the global South. Decolonization, or a resistance against forces of imperial domination, is a political and theoretical project not only pertinent to the Third World communities and peoples, but also equally, if not more, urgent for feminist scholars working in Anglo-American academia. This is the case because neocolonial structures fostered through the latest political and economic liberalization—otherwise referred to as globalization—continue to impose (and extend) cultural, social, economic, and political practices of the Anglo-European powers elsewhere. We need to be aware that feminist knowledge production is not innocent or value-free in this context; rather, as in other forms of knowledge construction, feminist knowledge is produced within the matrix of power. In this age of global and multinational capital, feminist scholarship is embedded in the patterns of unequal exchange and transfer of hegemonic notions and ideas (Grewal & Kaplan, 1994; Kim-Puri, 2005; Mani, 1990; Mohanty, 2005; Ong, 1988, 1999; Radcliffe, 1994). Feminist theories, concepts, and methods continue to travel in one direction, typically from the Anglo-European academy to its "peripheral" sites and places (Bulbeck, 1997; Collins, 1990, 1998; Grewal & Kaplan, 1994; Massey, 1994; Narayan, 1997; Sandoval, 1991, 2000; Spivak, 1988, 1990). In other words, presumptions made about the boundaries and borders between the First World and Third World (women) in the Anglo-American feminist scholarship is not innocent, and decentering its hegemony in knowledge construction is necessary. This means, as so aptly described by Sarah Radcliffe (1994), that in process of knowledge production and communication, "Western feminists are engaged in fissiparous and highly complex gendered and racialized relations of power at global and regional levels" (p. 31).

Similarly, concerning the process of knowledge production on Africa, Mojúbàolú Olúfúnké Okome (2001) problematizes the politics of appropriation of "Western" concepts and issues in/to African studies in the contemporary context of globalization. Okome argues that it has now become fashionable for African scholars to write about the issues of hybridity and cosmopolitanism. The engagements with these ideas have suddenly become the new and dominant—though not the only—ideologies shaping the field of African studies. In Okome's view, the knowledge produced about hybridity and cosmopolitanism is defined by and within the Anglo-European academy, and African scholars now appropriate these notions because they are fashionable. When "Western" and African scholars apply such categories and concepts to Africa, they "explain not very much." Okome laments that with the circulation of such discourses of hybridity and cosmopolitanism, Africa is seen as "even more of an enigma" to the West and African cultural philosophies are made effectively irrelevant or erased from the "cosmopolitan" imagination.[3]

In a different context, recent feminist research has documented the gendering of globalization and its pernicious effects on women in various places (Gibson-Graham, 1996; Marchand & Runyan, 2000; Ong, 1999). Feminist scholars point out that local socioeconomic and cultural production (and consumption) cannot be adequately understood without looking at how globalization discourses and practices also inject power in various sites via the circulation of finance, capital, labor, and information technology. The globalization processes and practices pose new challenges for feminist scholars and activists.

Given this political terrain, some key questions—theoretical, epistemological, and methodological[4]—need to be reexamined and are hence explored in this chapter:

- Against the backdrop of global capitalism, how do feminists theorize about differences and borders that are central to feminist research and praxes?
- How do feminist scholars conceptualize political, material, and geographical borders (and communities) without reifying the world through binarisms and dualisms? (i.e., self/other, center/margin, First World/Third World, Western/non-Western, West/East, North/South, global/local, modern/traditional, black/white, religious/secular).
- As cultures and groups become multiply fragmented, oppositional, and heterogeneous (and homogenized in other ways as well) under global capitalism, what feminist knowledge helps to make analytic and political *linkages across disparately marginalized and unequal* places, groups, and relations?
- How do feminist researchers produce knowledge that is tied explicitly to the cultural and material politics of social change that challenge the matrix of domination and subordination without reinforcing the interests, agendas, and priorities of privileged groups and places?

This chapter examines these questions from black, postcolonial, and transnational feminist perspectives. It seeks to identify the distinct methodologies that have been conceived in feminist scholarship that aim to destabilize a series of naturalized categories: to question the boundaries presumed in our imaginaries about borders, to decolonize our conceptions of self and other, and to cross multiple boundaries (i.e., conceptual, cultural, geographical, and political) by forging transnational linkages. As critical methodologies, these feminist approaches can be viewed as "analytic weapons" applied to unravel the fracturing dualisms and binarisms that have been drawn around the notions of "self" and "other" (Collins, 1990, 1998; Grewal & Kaplan, 1994; Narayan, 1997; Sandoval, 2000; Spivak, 1990).[5]

## BLACK FEMINIST THOUGHT: TRIPLE OPPRESSION, AFROCENTRIC STANDPOINT THEORY, AND THE U.S. HEGEMONY

At the heart of black feminist theory in the United States are concepts that speak to African American women's historical and collective experiences: of triple oppression; of subjugated knowledge; of black feminist standpoint; of Afrocentric epistemology; of voice, authority, and authenticity. The notion of triple oppression captures the critical and reflexive thinking about the cumulative experiences of black women and people of color who are subjugated and discriminated against on the basis of race, class, and gender (Carby, 1985; Collins, 1990; hooks, 1991; James & Busia, 1993; King, 1988; Lorde, 1984; Lugones & Spelman, 1983). For black women, history is embedded in experience, one that creates a specialized knowledge about their collective struggle, pain, and marginalization, which are direct outcomes of the cumulative effects of slavery, colonialism, and ongoing discrimination they face in the global labor market as cheap and reserve labor. The historical evolution of black feminist thought in the United States emerges not only out of black women's antagonistic and dialectical engagement with Euro-American women but more significantly out of this recognition of the need for self and group empowerment. Black feminism can be viewed as "a process of self-conscious struggle that empowers women and men to actualize a humanist vision of community" (Collins, 1989).

As Naples (1996) and Collins (1990) highlight, black women have mobilized against the myriad practices of discrimination and subjugation in their everyday working lives. Black women's resistance and social movements in the United States and elsewhere reflect struggles to collectively voice and organize themselves against the forces of discrimination based on race, class, and gender. This recognition has led feminist scholars to articulate a concept of intersectionality, which describes the co-dependence and co-constitution of race, class, gender, and sexuality as axes of power. The axes of this interlocking system of oppression and domination cannot be analytically or politically separated (Crenshaw, 1991; King, 1988).

While these notions center on the common experience rooted in racism, classism, sexism, and heterosexism, Amos and Parmar (1984) and Mama (1995) contest that the difference and diversity between black women cannot be ignored. They argue that it is problematic to valorize a global discourse on triple oppression that somehow binds black women together in a collective identity and struggle. Similarly, Mirza (1997) suggests that the framework of triple oppression is an outmoded way of understanding the diverse and different histories of black women's lives. Implicated in this concept of oppression is the assumption of the common notion of universal black womanhood, which masks heterogeneity of women's voices and forms of authority. While struggles against the interlocking forms of domination and marginalization are still central to black women, Mirza suggests a need for more inclusive and nuanced modes of analysis that capture the different voices among black women across cultural contexts.

Her study of black women in Britain shows, for example, that they challenge the discourses of black womanhood that are specific to and dominant in local sites—such as about motherhood, family, education, employment, and community activism—rather than against a global discourse.

In contrast to the British black feminist call for specificity and diversity, Collins (1989, 1990) developed an Afrocentric black feminist standpoint theory that theorized the commonness of black women's experiences. Collins's articulation of black feminist epistemology emphasizes four essential points. First, she argues that black women empower themselves by creating self-definitions and self-valuations that help them to establish positive, multiple images and to repel negative, controlling representations of black womanhood. Second, black women confront and dismantle the "overarching" and "interlocking" structure of domination in terms of race, class, and gender oppression. Third, black women do not disconnect but combine intellectual thought and political activism. Fourth, in Collins's view, the black women recognize a distinct cultural heritage that gives them the energy and skills to resist and transform daily discrimination. In this sense, Collins describes a "subjugated knowledge" that runs counter to the dominant ideology (that privileges heteronormative male, middle-class, and Euro-American feminist), which she argues has not been accepted as a valid form of knowledge by the dominant groups in the United States.

Black feminist standpoint theory traces its roots to the distinct Afrocentric philosophical episteme, and it not only enables the possibility of black women's "ways of knowing the world" but also "measure[s] knowledge against concrete experience, test[s] [it] through dialogue, and judge[s] it in relation to an ethic of personal accountability" (DeVault, 1996, p. 42). The black feminist standpoint is, therefore, an important political and analytical tool for articulating black women's voices, struggles, and histories. Parallel to the emergence of Third World feminist critiques offered in the United States and elsewhere, black feminist perspectives rose out of the matrix of the very discourses that have denied, suppressed, and produced differences. As a subjugated knowledge determined by the "other" or marginal structural location of black women, this feminist standpoint theory creates a discursive space within which a "new politics of resistance and critique" may be possible (Hall, 1992). In the past two decades, however, black feminist standpoint theory and Afrocentric epistemology have been critiqued for overhomogenizing black women as a group and for erasing their heterogeneity. The criticisms raise the following concerns: The first point, as already mentioned, is that diversity and differences among black women are effectively ruled out in black feminist Afrocentric standpoint theory in order to insist on black women's communality and common interests. Critics argued that the black feminist Afrocentric standpoint mirrors, in this sense, all standpoint theories (e.g., Dorothy Smith, who developed early the standpoint that all women constitute a "group"). It uncritically assumes a particular (African American) women's experience as being representative of all black women, not unlike the way Euro-American middle-class Western women assumed theirs to be universally shared by all women. Hence, the critiques of black feminist standpoint theory correctly point to the fissures, fragmentations, and differences between women who differ by race, class, gender, sexuality, nationality, culture, and so on. The criticisms resonate with similar challenges directed at Western, Euro-American feminists who have been criticized too often for falsely generalizing and universalizing a particular group of women's lives across history and cultures.

The second point centers on the limitations of black feminist standpoint theory in its constraining and essentialist deployment of the notion of black womanhood and black women's voice and authority. By privileging "experience" and promoting images of authentic and essential black women, the Afro- or black-centric epistemology assumes the idea that their experience is primordial. This "authenticized" and "valorized" view of black women's experience, as Reynolds (2002) tells us, is based on the recognition of their suffering, dysfunction, and marginalization, but black women are fixed into particular positions of oppression (and subjugation) where they are victims without agency. This perspective has been criticized for its presumptions of universalization and essentialization of black womanhood, which

masks differences in black women's lives while also ignoring the complexity in cultural, social, economic, and political variations in black communities throughout history. For these reasons, some feminists have concluded that the conceptual framework of black feminist standpoint theory is reductionist (Reynolds, 2002; Sylvester, 1995).

The third point concerns the issue of U.S.-centrism. Some British black and African feminist writers have argued that Afrocentric black feminist standpoint theory is, in fact, "Americocentric"; it represents the application of a particular U.S. black feminist knowledge and worldview to interpret the diverse histories and lives of black women everywhere, and in the process cultural and political differences are erased (Nzegwu, 2001; Oyewumi, 1997, 2002; Reynolds, 2002; Sylvester, 1995). Even more problematic, according to Reynolds (2002), who writes from a British context, is that black women's experiences that do not fit with this particular U.S.-based worldview are effectively *silenced*. In spite of the differences and diversity among black women, the U.S. black feminists valorize a discourse of global similarity based on notions of a black women's collective history presumably involving a common racial struggle, common suffering, and common experience of marginalization (Amos & Parmar, 1984; Mama, 1995; Mirza, 1997).

Fourth, these U.S.-centric black feminist theories that ironically emerged from marginality produce hegemonic concepts and impose U.S. dominance in knowledge production. As mentioned, the recent criticisms and challenges offered by African, British black, and Third World feminists are worthy of reflection. Writing about the perspectives of Third World women inside and outside of the United States (or of Western nations), feminist thinkers such as Amos and Parmar (1984), Chandra Mohanty (2005), Oyeronke Oyewumi (2001, 2002), and Uma Narayan (1997) have commented that black feminists within the First World (and in the United States in particular) have ignored the specific geographical, cultural, and historical context that underpins black women's experiences. Raising the problem of cultural imperialism in knowledge production, Oyewumi (2001) asks, "On what basis are feminist concepts, developed from

Western social categories, transferable or exportable to other cultures that display a different social organization and cultural logic?" (p. 7). The concepts of "gender" and "sisterhood," Oyewumi (2001) argues, are grounded in Anglo-European feminist somatocentric interpretations of their particular histories and are based on the model of Anglo-American nuclear family structures; they are, nonetheless, uncritically applied to *Africa,* whose dynamic cultures and histories and varying forms of households, family relations, and social organizations are made invisible. Such misconstrued rendering of Africa and African cultures is, however, also reflected in Afro-American imagination. Oyewumi (2001) argues that the quest of Africa is articulated as a theme of "paradise demonized" for some black feminists. For example, Alice Walker represents Africa as "the ultimate fountainhead of misogyny" and villagizes it as a culture where lesbianism is presumably not accepted and female genital mutilation is widely practiced.

Similarly, Mojúbàolú Olúfúnké Okome (2001) also notes these problems inherent in the assumptions made by First World black women when they speak on behalf of black women globally and when African scholars mimic or appropriate theories and concepts produced by U.S. scholars. The U.S.-dominated feminist knowledge, for example, can mask black women's voices from elsewhere in the world that receive limited theoretical consideration in the production of a black feminist standpoint. These practices hinder an understanding of the differing cultural and social contexts in which other black women live and the way their cultural and gendered identities are situated within specific historical and geographical locations (Hall, 1992). This U.S.-centered black feminist standpoint differs from its counterpart in Britain where the distinctive struggles and patterns of black women from Africa, the Caribbean, and the Indian subcontinent are openly acknowledged in feminist engagements (Mirza, 1997).

In sum, the politics and negotiation of black Afrocentric feminist standpoints reveal ongoing epistemological dilemmas. They suggest that power is connected to the process of knowledge production. As Harding and Haraway rightly suggest, all knowledge (including the claim of a black feminist knowledge) is *socially constructed* and is representative of a partial perspective. Postcolonial feminists have similarly noted that interpretations and applications of concepts need to be situated in specific historical and cultural contexts. In other words, all knowledge production is context and time bound.

Taking these criticisms seriously, black feminist theories that are produced in a U.S. hegemonic context need to consider a more contextual, more reflexive, and more fluid, approach to understanding black women's lives. Such decentering is necessary so that the scope, complexities, and diversity of black women's lives in the transnational world can be successfully captured. A theoretical and political decentering, however, requires a different methodology. Which methodologies enable flexible and mobile border crossings and capture differences across histories and cultures? The postcolonial and transnational feminist theories address precisely these questions, which are discussed below.

## POSTCOLONIAL FEMINIST THEORIES: THE INESSENTIAL WOMEN AND DECOLONIZATION

Sunder Rajan and Park (2000) have stated that, in their view, a postcolonial feminism that addresses the concerns of "the most 'backward' parts of the world" may be a theoretical paradigm that offers "the most advanced understanding of the contemporary 'reality'" (p. 66). Postcolonial feminism examines issues of subjectivities (often subaltern) and "scattered hegemonies" composed in and through patriarchies, nations, states, empires, political economy, and (neo)colonialism. Postcolonial feminists typically rely on "a rigorously historical and dialectical approach" to understand the imbrication of gender, nation, class, caste, race, culture, and sexualities in the different but historically specific contexts of women's lives (p. 66).

Moreover, "Western" feminist notions of the family, patriarchy, and the state have been critically decentered and sufficiently analyzed in the contexts of racism and colonialism. Postcolonial and Third World feminist studies have been guided by twin goals: to situate feminist theory in the politics of racial relations and to offer gendered conceptualization of colonialism and postcolonialism

(Bulbeck, 1997; Hurtado, 1989; Lewis & Mills, 2003; Mohanty, 2005; Okome, 2001; Suleri, 1992; Sylvester, 1995). While the aim here is not one of offering an extensive summary of postcoloniality and postcolonial feminism, this section discusses some of the key insights found in postcolonial feminist theory that deal with questions of difference and decolonization.

Drawing on the insights of Edward Said, Homi Bhabha, Abdul JanMohammed, and Gayatri Spivak, among others, postcolonial feminists aim to heal the discursive and "epistemic violence" (in Spivak's words) of imperialism and posit that "politics at this moment of history are [still] about decolonization" (Emberley, 1993, p. 5; Grewal & Kaplan, 1994; Mohanty, 2005; Schutte, 1998; Spivak, 1988). In this sense, postcolonial feminism is not simply a subset of postcolonial studies, or another variant of feminism, as explained by Sunder Rajan and Park (2000), but rather a political and theoretical intervention that aims to reconfigure both postcolonial *and* feminist studies.

First and foremost, postcolonial feminist theories analyze the limits of modernist paradigms and deconstruct the naturalized boundaries that are presumed to be normative (De Lauretis, 1988; Grewal & Kaplan, 1994; Haraway, 1988; Narayan, 1997; Sandoval, 2000). Parallel to postmodern and poststructuralist feminist engagements, postcolonial feminists directly challenge and unravel the modernist frames, essentialist categories, and androcentric politics; this includes representations of women and cultures in binary terms and attributions of Western notions of enlightenment, rationalism, and individualism applied to all peoples and cultures (Bulbeck, 1997; Nash, 2002).

From a poststructuralist critique, the category of "women" is not reduced to an effect of discourse because its referent is, as it should be, constantly shifting. Similarly, as in poststructuralist and postmodern feminisms, postcolonial feminists have pointed to the problems of ahistorical universalist frames of reference and the essentialist fixing of subject's positionality when the privileged individuals and groups study the "other"—that is, when Western Euro-American middle-class feminist scholars study "Third World women," or when U.S. black feminists speak for African women, or when "women of color" or nationalist feminists speak for the

"oppressed" peoples. Instead, what is highlighted is the need to shift our attention (and analysis) to the fragmented and situated forms of knowledge, not generalizing about the uniformity and homogeneity as a group (of women, sexuality, race, nationality, culture, religion, etc.).

In this regard, postcolonial feminist delineations also echo those provided by black feminists regarding the falsely universalized Western/feminist frames of reference about world cultures and people/women of color, as was discussed in the previous section. But postcolonial feminism offers a distinct alternative to feminist standpoint theories and goes beyond other "post" theories to consider the continuing legacy of gendered colonialisms.

Second, the questions of agency, subjectivity, and representations (of Third World women in Western feminism and of women in nationalist and colonialist discourses, for example) are central in postcolonial feminist theories. Similar to black and Third World feminist writers, postcolonial feminist critics focus on the ways racism, sexism, and colonialism shape representations. As Sarah Radcliffe aptly describes, "white women" have depicted "Third World women as static loci of eternal suffering, a privileged recipient of First World concern" (1994, p. 26). This point has been well analyzed by Mohanty (2005), Trinh (1989), and Ong (1988). As these feminist writers have shown, these condescending depictions lock Third World women in a distinct temporal, spatial, and historical frame as people who are assumed to have little agency or differentiation and who are cast as being "special" others (Radcliffe, 1994, p. 27; Trinh, 1989).

Mohanty's (1988) "Under Western Eyes," published almost 2 decades ago, asserted a thesis of discursive colonialism; that is, Mohanty examined and analyzed the institutionalization of Western feminist discourses that produce a reductive and homogeneous notion of Third World women and deny their agency. She showed that such discursive practices are akin to colonialism within which the complexities that characterize the lives of women of different classes, religions, cultures, races, and castes are effectively erased. Mohanty challenged Western feminists to situate themselves and their discourses in global economic, political, and historical contexts and to address the complex interconnections between First and Third World nations. Although influential, Mohanty's own way of framing and identifying "Western feminists" in the status of "true subjects" and Third World women as objects has invited legitimate criticism. Suleri (1992), for example, argues that Mohanty's own position is not free of binarism (that she herself problematizes), and that her analysis treats gender as history and gender as culture as being irreconcilable. According to Suleri, the recuperation of the "ethnic" voice of womanhood (in oppositional terms of West vs. Third World) cannot replace or counteract the cultural articulation found in the exegesis of Western feminism.

Third, the contentious issue concerning epistemology is, hence, also central to postcolonial feminist theory. As related to Suleri's points above, others have charged that Mohanty is beholden to an epistemological position of championing the experiences of the oppressed (Third World women) that purportedly cannot be understood by Western feminists because the latter could not really speak about Third World women without assuming a cultural imperialist stance (Nagel, 2004). Mohanty counters and clarifies that her criticism of Eurocentric feminist analyses does not mean that cross-cultural analysis is impossible or that North/South solidarity is futile. But she insists that feminists need to take seriously the limits of ahistorical universalist theories and about their own positionality in knowledge production.

Fourth, if the issue of epistemology is crucial in feminist theorizing, so is the related question of voice and authority. As Spivak, Mohanty, Grewal, Narayan, and other postcolonial feminist scholars have shown, Third World women are perceived and represented as victims or members of a minority, both authorially and politically, and are allowed to speak only to give evidence of the "Third World difference." In discursive representations, subaltern women (Western/feminist, nationalist/feminist, and colonialist) are excluded from having their voice and subjectivity.

But can the "objectification" of Third World women be countered by allowing the "authentic" subaltern to speak? Spivak (1988, 1990) answered this question in her seminal articles, including "Can the Subaltern Speak?" Spivak (1990) rejects the alternatives of letting

"subalterns" speak for themselves and at the same time also discounts the strategy of having the "radical critic" speaking for them. Instead, she advocates for necessary changes in the process of academic knowledge production so that "the postcolonial critic" learns to speak in a form that is, and can be, taken seriously by disenfranchised subaltern women. She theorizes about the possibilities of border crossings and addresses the tensions and contradictions across the academic-nonacademic divide. Spivak pushes for the unlearning of "our privileges" as academics and theorists in the North and the recognition that feminist representations of the "gendered subaltern" do not produce necessary communication with Third World women. Spivak's and other postcolonial feminist theorists' strategies of intervention are enabling, and they advocate for an analytical shift away from the "difference" impasse and a move beyond the binary hierarchy and across various borders to forge a dialogue among women.

Fifth, the issue of border crossings (analytical and political), therefore, raises important questions about differences and possibilities of how to decolonize self and other. The postcolonial theorist JanMohammed (1986) had already stated that "a Manichean opposition between colonizer and colonized is based on absolute moral and metaphysical differences, rather than relative and qualitative differences" (p. 89). He convincingly argued that such a binary framing of self and other (the colonizer and the colonized) reinforces "an empty gulf" between reductionist oppositions. Similarly, feminist scholars pointed to such problematic binary categories that do not foster imageries of decolonization: of self and other, mind and body, reason and emotion, First World/Third World, West/Orient, male/female, white/black, modernity/traditional, West/East, active/passive, civilized/primitive, secular/religious, universal/local, culture/nature, intellect/instinct, and so on (Bulbeck, 1997, p. 45; duCille, 1994).

Postcolonial feminist scholars are grappling with this question of how Third World and First World women can work together in ways that are authorized by dialogue with Third World subjects, as advocated by Spivak, rather than engaging solely with the First World academy and audiences (Nagar, 2003; Peake &

Trotz, 1999). Radcliffe (1994) explains, for example, that "the processes of producing representations of women (whether Third World, Western, or both) could be relocated, mapped out across the patriarchal priorities, rather than as appropriations" (p. 31). She further suggests,

> Rather than representing Third World women in political and authorial ways, "we" [feminists] would self-consciously contribute to jointly-produced authorial representations of relations of local and global patriarchies, racisms, and (post)colonialisms, and only claim to politically represent the coalition that is (provisionally) "ourselves." (p. 31)

These postcolonial feminist thinkers advocate for and foreground the many and different ways in which subjectivity and identity are constructed in any given historical moment.[6] They also underscore the charge Sangari (1987) offered already two decades ago: "The history of the West and the history of the non-West are by now irrevocably different and irrevocably shared. . . . The cultural projects of both the West and the non-West are implicated in a larger history" (cited in Chanda, 2000, p. 486). Echoing Sangari, postcolonial feminists have pushed for "a genuinely dialogic and dialectical history that can account for the formation of different selves and the construction of different epistemologies" (Chanda, 2000, p. 486).

## TRANSNATIONAL FEMINIST PERSPECTIVES: FORGING ANALYTICAL AND POLITICAL LINKAGES

What feminist methodologies are then needed if we are to forge analytical and political spaces of collaborative engagements? To chart new possibilities for crossing cultural borders and epistemological divides, various feminist "trans-" studies have emerged recently in a number of disciplines, including geography, sociology, and women's studies (Basch, Schiller, & Blanc, 1994; Kaplan, Alarcón, & Moallem, 1999; Katz, 2001; Kim-Puri, 2005; Mohanty, 2005; Nagar, 2003; Pratt & Yeoh, 2003; Radcliffe, 1994; Tambe, 2005). Seeking to develop new theoretical frameworks and

languages, some feminist research from "trans-" perspectives focuses on making linkages across social relations and places on multiple scales—such as neighborhood, community, city, region, nation. They shift the analytical focus away from issues of representation, reflexivity, and positionality embedded in texts and move toward comparing localized places and relations that are simultaneously affected by the same global processes.

## Geographies of Power

Feminist geographers have offered insights on the direction of the kind of theories and methodologies that might be considered for transnational feminist praxis (Katz, 2001; Massey, 1994; Mitchell, 1997; Nagar, 2002, 2003; Pratt & Yeoh, 2003; Raju, 2002; Rose, 1997). Pointing to the limits of postcolonial feminist analyses that tend to center on issues of representation and discourse, they emphasize the need to connect issues of subjectivity and identity with institutional, geopolitical, material, and cultural practices of power and privilege. Nagar (2002) states, for example, that "in the last decade, reflexivity, positionality and identity have become keywords in feminist fieldwork in much of anglophone academia," which has led to "an impasse" (pp. 179–180, 182). The challenge is, as Nagar reminds us, "the epistemological dilemma" of whether and how women's struggles in "Third World contexts" can be represented "accurately" and through which theoretical frameworks. She further notes that feminist scholarship in the United States has contributed to this "in/ability to talk across worlds" by avoiding these vexing questions (p. 179).

Drawing her fieldwork on marginalized, poor, rural women in Tanzania and North India, Nagar (2000, 2002) examines the sociospatial strategies that they develop to curb caste- and class-based inequalities and gendered violence facing local communities. Her ethnographic study of "local feminism" facing the Chitrakoot district of Uttar Pradesh highlights the concrete ways in which local women theorize both empowerment and disempowerment in their everyday lives, and how they develop strategic sociopolitical acts that are "inherently geographic" practices

(Nagar, 2000, p. 344). The women situate their struggles and subjectivities in "the geographical spaces from *and* within which they derive their resources, meanings, visions, and limitations (Nagar, 2000, p. 344). The socially and politically "peripheralized women" successfully organize campaigns to address domestic and patriarchal violence and to forge self and collective identities through street plays and theater. The two women's organizations—*Mehila Samakkhya* (Education for Women's Equality) and *Vanangana* (Daughter of the Forest)—resort to street campaigns to challenge spatial demarcations between home, body, and community, or about marriage, gender violence, and caste and class oppression.

Theoretically and methodologically, such analysis enables "discursive geographies" of women's resistance—in other words, it situates "local" women's activism in "place-specific" contexts and identifies the strategies such subjects develop to critique and transform "the hegemonic views of empowerment and violence, masculinity and femininity, crime and justice" (Nagar, 2000, p. 360). This type of feminist empirical research and methodology emphasize a grounded, collaborative study, one that incorporates perspectives of the global South and the global North and sheds light on the importance of place, space, and the local in global processes (Nagar, Lawson, McDowell, & Hanson, 2002). This methodology of feminist geography also maps social relations and inequalities that are found across multiple geographic scales, such as household, community, body, and nation-state, as well as paying attention to the intersecting hierarchies of gender, caste, and class. Pratt (1999), for example, analyzes "geographies of power" that operate in local and transnational scales; she does this by looking at the global labor market segmentation and transnational migration circuits that shape Filipinas' discourses of survival and resistance in Vancouver. The analytical focus here centers on women's political responses to power at various geographic scales and places.

Similarly, to further the study of gender in transnational social spaces, Mahler and Pessar (2001) have developed a conceptual model called "gendered geographies of power" (p. 445). With this, they delineate the term *geographies* to understand how "gender operates simultaneously on multiple *spatial and social* scales (e.g., the body, the family, the state) across transnational terrains" (Mahler & Pessar, 2001, p. 445). By "transnational," they refer to processes that occur in particular places and histories, while "connecting collectivities located in more than one national territory" (Mahler & Pessar, 2001, p. 444). Hence, their model is applied to examine how power and privilege are differentiated on race, ethnicity, class, nationality, and other identities in conjunction with gender. Examples include Guatemalan women's struggle for citizenship claims beyond the nation for human and women's rights, while they are displaced to Mexican refugee camps, and rural Salvadoran and Haitian migrant women in the United States working to send transnational remittances despite the fact that the intertwining of gender, class, race, and ethnicity conspires to make them vulnerable.

## Place Making

Recent scholarship by feminist geographers on space and place making illustrates the nuanced ways in which neocolonial relations of power and political economic structures of domination and subordination combine to shape gender politics of inequality, difference, and resistance in specific communities (Nagar, 2000). In line with this, transnational feminist studies have recast their analyses on the lives and voices of marginalized subjects situated in particular places rather than on the general processes of economic globalization.

For example, Cindi Katz (2001) uses a methodology of critical *topography* to show the material effects of globalization "on particular grounds" or to examine in detail "some part of the material world" in a particular place (p. 1214). By considering topography as a distinct research method, Katz aims to reveal "a local that is constitutively global," within which knowledge is situated (p. 1214). She examines how the socioeconomic, demographic, and personal information that is compiled and fed to global databases, such as geographical information systems (GIS), actually facilitate resource extraction, surveillance, and domination. Topographical knowledge, she argues, is used to foster globalization and is "integrally important to capitalists and other agents of domination" to maintain uneven global development (p. 1215).

Her analysis of the effects of capitalism, imperialism, and state power on the local population of Howa, Sudan, looks at both the global capitalist relations of production and reproduction and their intersections with the history of volatile political circumstances and racialized religious and ethnic conflicts shaping particular locales. By applying topography as a research method, Katz (2001) reexamines the historical and material transformation of central eastern Sudan where the Howa pastoralists and their rural economies become commoditized as cash relations through structural adjustment policies and state-sponsored and international agricultural development projects. She shows that displacement and de-skilling of children in Howa, as well as conscriptions of young boys into militias in Sudan, have to do with both local and international political economies—of structural adjustment policies, the international embargo, and the enduring civil war.

This method of topography enables us to understand globalization as both a script and process of differentiation and fragmentation of the world, which is much like scattered hegemonies described by Inderpal Grewal and Caren Kaplan (1994). According to Katz (2001), we need to better understand the specific and concrete ways that globalization processes play out on "particular grounds" and to "work out a situated, but at the same time scale-jumping and geography-crossing, political response to it" (p. 1216). By scrutinizing local details and analyzing larger politics shaping particular locales, Katz sheds light on the intertwined structural consequences of globalizing capitalist production. She further compares the impact of divestments in social reproduction in Harlem, a section of New York City, and Howa, Sudan, and argues that in both places young people are affected by a common set of political and economic processes. While a different kind of politics is necessary for each particular place, a detailed topographical analysis reveals that the young generation in these disparate geographical settings is similarly deprived of formal education and "warehoused" in prisons or armies instead of being empowered.

## Beyond National Borders

A similar analysis of *geographical* border crossings is offered in Ashwini Tambe's analysis of international trafficking in women. In keeping with a transnational feminist understanding of subject formation, Tambe (2005) explains that racial and sexual categories do not have fixed, pregiven meanings, but rather, they are produced in contextually specific ways. She employs a transnational feminist lens to illustrate that emphasis on national borders can mask the ways power and coercion are reproduced in local and regional places. Tambe (2005) does this by critiquing the discourse of antitrafficking that unduly located the problem of prostitution on European women's crossing of national borders while ignoring regional and local trafficking in the sex trade. She uses transnational analytical frameworks that typically problematize nationalist and state-bound definitions of social problems and offers instead a historically grounded empirical analysis of colonial state power. When international antitrafficking campaigns emerged in the 1910s and 1920s that regulated national/international borders, Tambe shows that the colonial state in Bombay (now called Mumbai) protected and fostered trafficking in European women while also marking them as sexually potent, foreign outsiders. Through a detailed historical analysis, Tambe demonstrates that the global discourse on the international sex trade in the Anglo-European colonial metropoles was connected to the ways colonial state agents promoted and coercively regulated sex trafficking locally in Bombay. As Tambe (2005) shows, the enclave of European brothels in Kamathipura, Bombay, became "the site of pervasive relations of coercive protection between police and prostitutes" (p. 175) and entirely bypassed the antitrafficking conventions that emphasized international movements.

## Bringing Nations/States Back In

From a transnational feminist sociological approach, there is a renewed interest in bringing the nations/states back into analysis. This methodology involves probing and questioning the naturalization of nations/states (as well as empires and imperialism) as the fixed and stable order of social/material life. Related to this, a number of feminist scholars have recently called into question the popular view of social relations as taking place inside the boundaries of contemporary nations/states, or as being defined by nationalized societies or cultures (Kim-Puri, 2005; Mitchell, 1997). As Mitchell (1997) explains, geopolitical research typically defines states as "containers" of the nation and are also conceived of as completely circumscribed entities (p. 105). By foregrounding "transnational spatial geographies," critical scholars instead conceive of nation-state borders as being differentially porous—that is, borders varying not just by nation or by political regime, but depending on "historical relations of unequal exchange" (Mitchell, 1997, p. 111).

In this vein, feminist sociologists Kim-Puri (2005) offer a new methodology to *reframe* issues of gender and sexuality in direct relation to states and nations. The concerns of nations/ states are, in their view, salient to the sociological analyses, especially given contemporary trajectories of global capitalism, and they need to be brought back into feminist sociology. They consider the analytical categories of gender, sexuality, states, and nations to be co-constituted in particular historical and social contexts. Drawing on the work of feminist social scientists who have studied nationalisms as profoundly gendered phenomena, the analyses of the fault lines of nationhood, they aruge, need to be deepened and extended.

Writing against the dominant approach in social science that implicitly and explicitly treats the national and international as a dichotomy, they emphasize that such binaries are not only limiting but also misleading with the national falsely homogenized as the "local" and the international distanced as the "foreign." Like feminist geographers, Kim-Puri (2005) call for a methodology that better illuminates the cultural, material, and political interconnections *across* geographical borders without relying on the nation-to-nation comparisons. This methodology of "transnational feminist sociology" focuses on understanding social processes that shape various spatial settings in a contradictory and unequal manner. Extending transnational feminist cultural studies to materialist analysis, this methodology of transnational feminist sociology emphasizes four dimensions:

1. An approach that *bridges discursive and material* analyses to understand how unequal economic, political, and social relations are mediated and (re)produced through cultural representations and discourses. Sociological analyses of power, structures, relations, processes, organizations, identities, subjectivity, and movements need to attend to material/cultural meanings and conditions that jointly produce inequalities and exclusions.

2. An approach that highlights the importance of *social structures and the state*. This emphasis on social structures and especially the attention to state institutions and relations is necessary to contend with empires, imperialisms, colonialism, and nationalisms that are shaped through gendered, sexualized, and racialized imageries.

3. An approach that shifts analyses to linkages refers to various forms of *border crossings,* including conceptual, temporal, bureaucratic, geopolitical, geographical, economic, cultural, and so on. This focus on linkages eschews nation-to-nation comparisons and treats scale or geographic unit of analysis as historically and culturally contingent.

4. An approach that stresses the role of *empirical research* for shredding light on cultural, material, structural, and historical forces, which in turn shape social relations, hierarchies, identities, and conflicts in distinct ways. (Kim-Puri, 2005, p. 143)

Through such a methodology and approaches, transnational feminist sociology seeks to avoid binary reductionism and generalizations about power/resistance, dominance/subordination, modernity/tradition, East/West, national/ international, and feminism/patriarchy. The key focus is to recognize the possibilities of building transnational feminist alliances that link fragmented groups and places and to understand how material and cultural inequalities affect places unevenly. This methodology also emphasizes the study of the material and the cultural within a transnational feminist framework. This means that in contrast to the transnational feminist cultural studies such as those offered by Inderpal Grewal and Caren Kaplan (1994), the materiality of social structures and historical analysis of institutions such as nations and states are also examined in relation to cultural representations of gender and sexuality.

Kim-Puri also point out that U.S. feminist sociology has not sufficiently engaged with transnational methodologies or with feminist research on gender and sexuality that is produced outside of the Anglo-European contexts. Aside from the obvious problems of not taking seriously other cultural and geographical contexts into consideration, Kim-Puri (2005) argue that this neglect reveals a theoretical and methodological oversight in Euro-American feminist research on gender, sexuality, and nation-states. Through transnational feminist methodology, they emphasize the value in connecting locales and places across transversal borders and suggest that the United States not be considered the sole site of feminist knowledge production. This theoretical framework and methodology are spelled out in the April 2005 special issue of *Gender & Society*, which provides critical feminist analysis of global and transnational discourses and processes.

## CONCLUSION

This chapter examined distinctive feminist epistemologies and methodologies that deal with the questions of political and social difference. How do (and must) feminist researchers and activists address and respond to the uneven and competing flows of ideas and practices? It is this question concerning power relations in knowledge production (and politics) that has motivated feminist scholars to look for new theoretical directions in (and methods for) research and praxis. But with the contemporary force of global capitalism and (neo)imperial impulses shaping realigning communities, feminist scholars need to keep constant vigilance on power and develop research and praxis that meaningfully engage with marginalized subjects. Such meaningful feminist research and praxis would also involve more than the application of the most current theories or concepts. Instead, feminist scholars and activists must constantly ask whether the questions and concepts we frame capture the fluid, situated, and varied contexts, and whether our analysis adequately attends to

the voices and consciousness of marginalized groups.

The feminist theories and methodologies discussed in this chapter grapple with these questions, albeit in different ways. In particular, postcolonial and transnational feminist approaches invite us to question what is an adequate way of theorizing various borders and boundaries, and through which methodologies. Transnational feminist methodologies discussed in the chapter further point to the importance of understanding the interconnectedness of issues that are often separated analytically and politically, such as gender, class, sexuality, race, ethnicity, nationality, nations/states, imperialism, and so on. Instead of simplifying or obfuscating these linkages, transnational feminist methodologies attend to the diverse ways in which women and men in particular places and spaces produce and transmit knowledge (and local forms of feminist thought). Our feminist analyses need to reflect on the heterogeneous locations, relations, and identities that not only affect the processes of knowledge production but also shape the form and content of feminist research. Feminists working in their specific locations need to reflect on how feminist theories and methodologies travel transversely across cultural and geographical borders and reconsider what happens when and as they do so.

## NOTES

1. Recently, feminist geographers have engaged with these questions and offered new insights. Particularly noteworthy are the works of Geraldine Pratt (1999), Katharyne Mitchell (1997), Richa Nagar (2000, 2002, 2003), Cindi Katz (2001), and Doreen Massey (1994). Some theoretical and methodological questions about border crossings raised in the 2002 special issue of *Gender, Place and Culture* are very similar to the ones I raise in this chapter.

2. Exceptions are the following: Antoinette Burton (1998), Inderpal Grewal and Caren Kaplan (1994), Anne McClintock (1995), and Ann Stoler (1997).

3. On these points, see Okome's (2001) article, "African Women and Power: Reflections on the Perils of Unwarranted Cosmopolitanism," *Jenda: A Journal of Culture and African Women Studies*. For other provocative discussions on discursive forms of colonialism (and Westernization) in knowledge

production, see African feminist scholars' perspectives in the online journal *Jenda*.

4. Following Sandra Harding (1987) and Liz Stanley (1990), I distinguish "methodology" to mean theorizing about research practice and "epistemology" to mean the study of how we create knowledge and of what can be known.

5. The chapter does not, however, aim to offer a comprehensive survey of these feminist paradigms.

6. This is similar to the discussion about the term *feminisms* that emerged in the late 1980s as a politically strategic term.

> It is intended to deny the claiming of feminism by any one group of feminists and to signify the multiplicity of ways in which those who share a feminist critique may come together to address issues. Feminism acknowledges that specific historical and cultural experiences will differently construct understandings of gender at different times and places. Feminism is meant to create discursive space in a fraught arena. It is quintessentially historical, resisting homogenization, generalization, nostalgia. (Miller, 1998, p. 569)

## REFERENCES

Amos, Valerie, & Parmar, Pratibha. (1984). Challenging imperialist feminism. *Feminist Review, 17*(July), 3–19.

Basch, Linda, Schiller, Nina Glick, & Blanc, Cristina Szanton. (1994). *Nations unbound: Transnational projects, postcolonial predicaments, and deterritorialized nation-states*. Langhorne, PA: Gordon & Breach.

Bulbeck, Chilla. (1997). *Re-orienting Western feminisms: Women's diversity in a postcolonial world*. Cambridge, UK: Cambridge University Press.

Burton, Antoinette. (1998). Some trajectories of "feminism" and "imperialism." *Gender & History, 10*(3), 558–568.

Carby, Hazel V. (1985). On the threshold of woman's era: Lynching, empire and sexuality in black feminist theory. *Critical Inquiry, 12*, 262–277.

Chanda, Ipshita. (2000). Feminist theory in perspective. In Henry Schwarz & Sangeeta Ray (Eds.), *A companion to postcolonial studies* (pp. 486–507). Oxford, UK: Blackwell.

Collins, Patricia Hill. (1989). The social construction of black feminist thought. *Signs, 14*.

Collins, Patricia Hill. (1990). *Black feminist thought: Knowledge, consciousness and the politics of empowerment*. Boston: Unwin Hyman.

Collins, Patricia Hill. (1998). It's all in the family: Intersections of gender, race and nation. *Hypatia, 13*(3), 62–82.

Crenshaw, Kimberle W. (1991). Mapping the margins: Intersectionality, identity politics and violence against women of color. *Stanford Law Review, 43*(6), 1241–1299.

De Lauretis, Teresa. (1988). Displacing hegemonic discourses: Reflections on feminist theory in the 1980s. *Inscriptions, 3–4*, 127–144.

DeVault, Marjorie L. (1996). Talking back to sociology: Distinctive contributions of feminist methodology. *Annual Review of Sociology, 22*, 29–50.

duCille, Ann. (1994). Postcolonialism and Afrocentricity: Discourse and dat course. In Werner Sollors & Maria Diedrich (Eds.), *The black Columbiad*. Cambridge, MA: Harvard University Press.

Emberley, Julie V. (1993). *Thresholds of difference: Feminist critique, native women's writings, postcolonial theory*. Toronto, Canada: University of Toronto Press.

Gibson-Graham, J. K. (1996). *The end of capitalism (as we knew it): A feminist critique of political economy*. Oxford, UK: Blackwell.

Grewal, Inderpal, & Kaplan, Caren. (Eds.). (1994). *Scattered hegemonies: Postmodernities and transnational feminist practices*. Minneapolis: University of Minnesota Press.

Hall, Stuart. (1992). New ethnicities. In James Donald & Ali Rattansi (Eds.), *Race, culture and difference*. London: Sage.

Haraway, Donna J. (1988). Situated knowledges: The science question in feminism as a site of discourse on the privilege of partial perspective. *Feminist Studies, 14*(3), 575–599.

Harding, Sandra. (Ed.). (1987). *Feminism and methodology*. Bloomington: Indiana University Press.

hooks, bell. (1991). *Yearning: Race, gender, and cultural politics*. Boston: South End Press.

Hurtado, Aida. (1989). Relating to privilege: Seduction and rejection in the subordination of white women and women of color. *Signs, 14*, 833–855.

James, Stanlie M., & Busia, Abena P. (1993). *Theorizing black feminisms: The visionary pragmatism of black women*. New York: Routledge.

JanMohammed, Abdul. (1986). The economy of Manichean allegory: The function of racial difference in colonialist literature. In Henry Louis Gates, Jr. (Ed.), *"Race," writing and difference* (pp. 78–106). Chicago: University of Chicago Press.

Kaplan, Caren, Alarcón, Norma, & Moallem, Minoo. (Eds.). (1999). *Between woman and nation: Nationalisms, transnational feminisms, and the state.* Durham, NC: Duke University Press.

Katz, Cindi. (2001). On the grounds of globalization: A topography for feminist political engagement. *Signs, 26*(4), 1213–1234.

Kim-Puri, H. J. (2005). Conceptualizing gender-sexuality-state-nation: An introduction. *Gender & Society, 19*(2), 137–159.

King, Deborah. (1988). Multiple jeopardy, multiple consciousness: The context of black feminist ideology. *Signs, 14*, 42–72.

Lewis, Reina, & Mills, Sara. (Eds.). (2003). *Feminist postcolonial theories: A reader.* New York: Routledge.

Lorde, Audre. (1984). The master's tools will never dismantle the master's house. In *Sister outsider* (pp. 110–113). Freedom, CA: Crossing Press.

Lugones, M., & Spelman, Elizabeth. (1983). Have we got a theory for you! Feminist theory, cultural imperialism and the demand for "the woman's voice." *Women's Studies International Forum, 6*, 573–581.

Mahler, Sarah, & Pessar, Patricia. (2001). Gendered geographies of power: Analyzing gender across transnational spaces. *Identities: Global Studies in Culture and Power, 7*, 441–459.

Mama, Amina. (1995). *Beyond the mask: Race, gender and subjectivity.* London: Routledge.

Mani, Lata. (1990). Multiple mediations: Feminist scholarship in the age of multinational reception. *Feminist Review, 35*, 24–41.

Marchand, Marianne, & Runyan, Anne Sisson. (Eds.). (2000). *Gender and global restructuring: Sighting, sites, and resistances.* New York: Routledge.

Massey, Doreen. (1994). *Space, place and gender.* Minneapolis: University of Minnesota Press.

McClintock, Anne. (1995). *Imperial leather: Race, gender and sexuality in the colonial context.* New York: Routledge.

Miller, Francesca. (1998). Feminisms and transnationalism. *Gender & History, 10*(3), 569–580.

Mirza, Heidi Safia. (1997). Introduction: Mapping a genealogy of Black British feminism. In Heidi Safia Mirza (Ed.), *Black British feminism: A reader* (pp. 1–30). London: Routledge.

Mitchell, Katharyne. (1997). Transnational discourse: Bringing geography back in. *Antipode, 29*(2), 101–114.

Mohanty, Chandra Talpade. (1988). Under Western eyes: Feminist scholarship and colonial discourses. *Feminist Review, 30*, 61–88.

Mohanty, Chandra Talpade. (2005). *Feminism without borders: Decolonizing theory, practicing solidarity.* Durham, NC: Duke University Press.

Nagar, Richa. (2000). Mujhe jawab do! (Answer me!): Women's grass-roots activism and social spaces in Chitrakoot (India). *Gender, Place and Culture, 7*(4).

Nagar, Richa. (2002). Footloose researchers, traveling theories and the politics of transnational feminist praxis. *Gender, Place and Culture, 9*(2), 179–186.

Nagar, Richa. (2003). Collaboration across borders: Moving beyond positionality. *Singapore Journal of Tropical Geography, 24*(3), 356–372.

Nagar, Richa, Lawson, Victoria, McDowell, Linda, & Hanson, Susan. (2002). Locating globalization: Feminist (re)readings of the subjects and spaces of globalization. *Economic Geography, 78*(3), 285–306.

Nagel, Mechthild. (Ed.). (2004). Editorial: Feminists confront empire [Special issue]. *Wagadu, 1*(1), 1–3.

Naples, Nancy. (1996). Activist mothering: Cross generational continuity in the community work of women from low-income urban neighborhoods. In Esther Chow, Doris Wilkinson, & Maxine Baca Zinn (Eds.), *Race, class and gender: Common bonds, different voices.* London: Sage.

Narayan, Uma. (1997). *Dislocating cultures: Identities, traditions, and Third World feminism.* New York: Routledge.

Nash, Kate. (2002). Human rights for women: An argument for "deconstructive equality." *Economy and Society, 31*(3), 414–433.

Nzegwu, Nkiru. (2001). Globalization and the Jenda journal. *Jenda: A Journal of Culture and African Women Studies, 1*(1). Retrieved August 18, 2004, from www.jendajournal.com

Okome, Mojúbàolú Olúfúnké. (2001). African women and power: Reflections on the perils of unwarranted cosmopolitanism. *Jenda: A Journal of Culture and African Women Studies.*

Retrieved August 18, 2004, from www.jenda journal.com

Ong, Aiwha. (1988). Colonialism and modernity: Feminist representations of women in non-Western societies. *Inscriptions, 3–4,* 79–93.

Ong, Aiwha. (1999). *Flexible citizenship: The cultural logics of transnationality.* Durham, NC: Duke University Press.

Oyewumi, Oyeronke. (1997). *The invention of women: Making an African sense of Western gender discourses.* Minneapolis: University of Minnesota Press.

Oyewumi, Oyeronke. (2001). Ties that (un)bind: Feminism, sisterhood and other foreign relations. *Jenda: A Journal of Culture and African Women Studies, 1*(1). Retrieved August 18, 2004, from www.jendajournal.com

Oyeronke, Oyewumi. (2002). Conceptualizing gender: The Eurocentric foundations of feminist concepts and the challenge of African epistemologies. *Jenda: A Journal of Culture and African Women Studies, 2*(1). Retrieved August 18, 2004, from www.jendajournal.com

Peake, L., & Trotz, D. A. (1999). *Gender, ethnicity and place: Women and identity in Guyana.* New York: Routledge.

Pratt, Geraldine. (1999). From registered nurse to registered nanny: Discursive geographies of Filipina domestic workers in Vancouver, BC. *Economic Geography, 75,* 215–236.

Pratt, Geraldine, & Yeoh, Brenda. (2003). Transnational (counter) topographies. *Gender, Place and Culture, 10*(2), 159–166.

Radcliffe, Sarah. (1994). (Representing) post-colonial women: Authority, difference and feminisms. *Area, 26*(1), 25–32.

Raju, Saraswati. (2002). We are different, but can we talk? *Gender, Place and Culture, 9*(2), 173–177.

Reynolds, Tracey. (2002). Re-thinking a black feminist standpoint. *Ethnic and Racial Studies, 25*(4), 591–606.

Rose, Gillian. (1997). Situating knowledges: Positionality, reflexivities and other tactics. *Progress in Human Geography, 21*(3), 305–320.

Sandoval, Chela. (1991). U.S. Third World feminism: The theory and method of oppositional consciousness in the postmodern world. *Genders, 10,* 1–24.

Sandoval, Chela. (2000). *Methodology of the oppressed.* Minneapolis: University of Minnesota Press.

Sangari, Kumkum. (1987). Politics of the possible. *Cultural Critique, 7,* 157–186.

Schutte, Ofelio. (1998). Cultural alterity: Cross-cultural communication and feminist thought in North-South dialogue. *Hypatia: A Journal of Feminist Philosophy, 13*(2), 53–72.

Sharp, Joanne P. (2004). Feminism and cultural geography. In James Duncan, N. Johnson, & R. Schein (Eds.), *The handbook of cultural geography.* Oxford, UK: Blackwell.

Spivak, Gayatri. (1988). Can the subaltern speak? In C. Nelson & L. Grossberg (Eds.), *Marxism and the interpretation of culture* (pp. 271–313). Urbana: University of Illinois Press.

Spivak, Gayatri. (1990). *The postcolonial critic: Interviews, strategies, dialogues.* New York: Routledge.

Staeheli, Lynn, & Nagar, Richa. (2002). Feminists talking across worlds. *Gender, Place and Culture, 9*(2), 167–172.

Stanley, Liz. (1990). Feminist auto/biography and feminist epistemology. In J. Aaron & S. Walby (Eds.), *Out of the margins: Women's studies in the nineties* (pp. 204–209). London: Falmer Press.

Stoler, Ann. (1997). Sexual affronts and racial frontiers: European identities and the cultural politics of exclusion in colonial Southeast Asia. In Frederick Cooper & Ann Stoler (Eds.), *Tensions of empire: Colonial cultures in a bourgeois world* (pp. 198–237). Berkeley: University of California Press.

Suleri, Sara. (1992). Woman skin deep: Feminism and the postcolonial condition. *Critical Inquiry, 18,* 756–769.

Sunder Rajan, Rajeswari, & Park, You-me. (2000). Postcolonial feminism/postcolonialism and feminism. In H. Swartz & S. Ray (Eds.), *A companion to postcolonial studies* (pp. 53–71). Malden, MA: Blackwell.

Sylvester, Christine. (1995). African and Western feminisms: World-traveling, the tendencies and possibilities. *Signs, 20*(4), 941–969.

Tambe, Ashwini. (2005). The elusive ingenue: A transnational feminist analysis of European prostitution in colonial Bombay. *Gender & Society, 19*(2), 160–179.

Trinh, Minh-ha T. (1989). *Woman, native, other.* Bloomington: Indiana University Press.

# 6

# FEMINIST INTERDISCIPLINARY APPROACHES TO KNOWLEDGE BUILDING

SALLY L. KITCH

Fewer words are more used and less understood in today's academy than "interdisciplinarity." Almost every plan for the future of higher education in general, or a single college or university in particular, touts the importance of interdisciplinary research or fields of study. This ubiquity should come as good news to feminist scholars who consider interdisciplinarity the hallmark of women's studies and feminist research. Support for interdisciplinarity seems to validate feminist criticism of the structures and methodologies of conventional disciplines for promoting gender bias. Moreover, it appears to signify widespread acceptance of the new forms and sources of knowledge that are most likely to generate significant and inclusive scholarship about women, gender, and traditionally marginalized human groups.

Unbridled celebration of the apparent validation of interdisciplinarity would be premature, however. Glee must be tempered by a simultaneous awareness of the hidden disagreements and debates obscured by the frequent lip service paid to interdisciplinarity. In truth, there is little consensus about the meaning and significance of interdisciplinarity or its relationship to other forms of scholarship. Even among feminist scholars, significant conflicts remain over the definition of interdisciplinarity and its relationship to discipline-based feminist research. Scholars in traditional disciplines often resent what they regard as undue attention to the value of interdisciplinarity, as they recall their own struggles to restructure disciplinary scholarship in their fields to counter long-standing gender distortions and omissions.

Such reservations complicate any effort to understand the role of interdisciplinarity in feminist research. Nevertheless, it will be the task of this chapter to investigate feminist approaches to interdisciplinarity in the construction of knowledge about women and gender. In the course of this analysis, the chapter will parse the term *interdisciplinarity* as it is used by feminist scholars and explore both its multiple meanings and the doubts some feminist scholars have expressed about it. Then it will consider what kinds of interdisciplinary approaches are most useful for feminist scholarship and discuss the reasons why. The chapter will conclude with examples and case studies that illustrate the role of integrative, reciprocal interdisciplinarity, or transdisciplinarity, in achieving twin feminist epistemological goals: the development of both inclusivity and transnational perspectives in knowledge formation.

On the way to analyzing feminist interdisciplinary approaches to knowledge, this chapter will also consider the multiple and sometimes contradictory forms of scholarship that huddle beneath the academy's "interdisciplinary" umbrella and compare them to prevailing concepts of disciplinarity. It will discuss the importance of striking a balance between disciplinary and interdisciplinary research, demonstrating, as Peter Weingart explains, that "they are complementary rather than contradictory. . . . innovations on the one hand, and rigour and control for error on the other" (Weingart, 2000, p. 29). Also along the way, this chapter will consider the benefits and risks entailed in the production of interdisciplinary research.

## THE INTERDISCIPLINARY "BUZZ"

Proponents of interdisciplinary scholarship throughout the academy emphasize its role in rejuvenating research for a changing, unstable world. They explain that contemporary social, scientific, and political events and discoveries require fluid, flexible, and dynamic research processes that allow scholars to think outside the box. They assume that increased complexity in the world requires increasingly comprehensive methodologies to chart and spearhead innovative knowledge. Conceding that traditional disciplines are themselves engaged in a "permanent search for knowledge," as Michael Finkenthal (2001) writes, they still worry that disciplinary scholars typically temper their search for novelty with a simultaneous desire to conserve meaning and to ensure consistency in the handling of concepts (pp. 3–5).

While traditional disciplines, such as mathematics, continue to provide essential tools for interdisciplinary inquiry, according to Julie Klein (2000), the persistence of "older forms and images" in academic pursuits creates resistance to changing concepts of knowledge that have moved from "a static logic of a foundation and a structure to the dynamic properties of a network, a web, a system, and a field" (p. 21) as well as to scholarship that follows suit (Klein, 2000). Only a commitment to interdisciplinarity can counter the older forms, according to Michael Finkenthal (2001) and Joe Moran (2002), by reinvigorating the disciplines and requiring scholars to be more self-aware about both their methods and the intellectual and institutional constraints affecting their disciplines. In this way, interdisciplinarity can keep scholars from "becoming stupid and insensitive" and protect them from "the excesses of [their] own minds" which have built "huge dialectic edifices, pompous systems of thought (or of lack of it)" (Finkenthal, 2001, p. 136) in the form of static disciplinary empires. Thus, one important contribution of interdisciplinarity is its role in making disciplinary scholars more receptive to new ways of structuring and representing their knowledge of the world. Interdisciplinarity encourages communication between disciplines and strives "to create new intellectual configurations or alliances" (Moran, 2002, p. 187).

At its best, interdisciplinary scholarship creates new meaning "out of what first appears to be noise as the exchange of codes and information across boundaries is occurring, whether the activity is borrowing, solving technical problems, developing hybrid interests, or disrupting and restructuring traditional practices" (Klein, 2000, p. 22). Specializations work well for problems that can be conceptualized in the terms of those specializations, but complex new issues and problems, such as identity, globalism, and racism, require more than expertise within single disciplines (Weiss & Wodak, 2003, pp. 18–19). Among the feminist issues that cannot be fully conceptualized within existing disciplinary terms are motherhood, violence against women, and rape (Allen & Kitch, 1998, pp. 278–279).

What remains unclear, however, is exactly what such scholars mean by interdisciplinarity. For some, the term's obvious value resides in its "flexibility and indeterminacy" (Moran, 2002, p. 15). Thus, it can connote everything from "weak" interdisciplinary activities, such as borrowing methods or common metaphors across disciplines that do not disrupt existing disciplinary frameworks or boundaries, to the development of full-blown hybrid "interdisciplines." For other scholars, the flexibility of interdisciplinarity signifies its inadequacy. Loose interdisciplinarity can even do damage, some claim, if disciplinary scholars believe they understand one another in knowledge exchanges when they really do not (Finkenthal, 2001, p. 12).

Even scholars who support the concept of interdisciplinarity do not necessarily agree on its meaning. It connotes an array of possible variations, from multidisciplinarity or cross-disciplinarity to transdisciplinarity. Each of those forms has the capacity to rejuvenate disciplinary knowledge, in the ways that Klein and Moran discuss, but they differ in their potential for transforming knowledge or for integrating or synthesizing knowledge around particular problems or questions. By the same token, all forms of interdisciplinarity do not entail the same potential for creating new intellectual niches or knowledge domains. Only transdisciplinarity can produce a new knowledge niche. The field of geography exemplifies such a niche. Its investigation of space via a range of interdependent agents and practices both requires and transcends disciplinary insights (Moran, 2002, p. 165). Key to the different effects these interdisciplinary variants have on new knowledge creation is the degree to which they either challenge or maintain what we might call knowledge "silos" or boundaries between the terminology, frameworks, methods, and focus areas or domains of participating disciplines.

Multidisciplinarity and cross-disciplinarity are most likely to maintain boundaries between knowledge silos, even though both forms of interdisciplinary may involve scholarly collaboration. They are also the most prevalent variants connoted by the term *interdisciplinarity,* as my own recent survey of more than 500 examples of self-identified interdisciplinary publications has revealed. A large majority of those publications uses multidisciplinarity as a synonym for interdisciplinarity. In many cases, a collection of discipline-based articles in a single volume constitutes the interdisciplinary project.

Multidisciplinarity is a relatively weak or additive form of interdisciplinarity because it represents "the simple juxtaposition of two or more disciplines" (Klein, 1990, cited in Moran, 2002, p. 16), as Moran and Klein explain. Multidisciplinarity, therefore, involves a relationship of proximity rather than of integration,

even if accomplished by an individual scholar. The juxtaposition of literary and historical material to illuminate the "frontier mentality" exemplifies such a multidisciplinary project. In that case, among others, the scholarship neither challenges the epistemological origins of the juxtaposed disciplines nor questions their compatibility (Weiss & Wodak, 2003, p. 20).

Cross-disciplinarity, a close relative of multidisciplinarity, typically involves collaboration among specialists around a particular problem or issue in which each speaks from the standpoint of his or her field. Both the specialists' individual mind-sets and assumptions and the approaches and foci of their fields typically remain unchanged by the interaction, however. Participants in such an exchange may borrow tools, data, results, and methods from one another, but that borrowing is not intended to transform existing disciplinary frameworks or boundaries. Indeed, a likely result of cross-disciplinary collaboration is the appropriation of borrowed data or methods into the borrowing discipline. While some of these appropriations can fruitfully link fields through concepts and terminology—as *text, discourse, interpretation,* and *culture* now link the humanities and social sciences, and as the concepts *role, status,* and *area* cross-fertilize the social sciences—the result tends to be what Diane Elam calls an "interdisciplinary handshake" rather than true disciplinary integration (Elam, 1994, p. 12; Klein, 2000, pp. 11, 13).

C. P. Snow's suggestion in the 1950s that the sciences and humanities could be linked via biology illustrates the cross-disciplinary process. Snow saw humanistic possibilities in biology, because that particular science did not require advanced mathematics and invited people to consider the questions that dominate humanistic inquiry, such as the origin of life, human beings' relationship with other species, and the nature of the self (Moran, 2002, p. 159). While Snow's proposal identified an important site for translating concerns between disciplines, it did not offer a fundamental change in either humanistic or scientific inquiry. Rather, Snow thought that the borrowed vocabularies and information across scholarly domains would advance mutual understanding, a goal that reflects both the potential and the limitations of most cross- and multidisciplinary projects.

Creating new knowledge species, variations, mutations, or niches (to continue the biological metaphor) requires transdisciplinary scholarship that transcends disciplinary silos, possibly by creating a "hybrid" interdiscipline, such as neuroscience, peace studies, and women's studies, through the cross-breeding of heterogeneous elements (Klein, 2000, pp. 9, 19). Transdisciplinary research can link disciplines through concepts that emerge from overlapping disciplinary domains, as in the interconnection of physics and chemistry via thermodynamics, which ultimately alter the course of each discipline. Transdisciplinarity can also result in the absorption of one discipline into another, as in the incorporation of astronomy into physics, or the amalgamation of disciplines into new conglomerates via shared fundamental principles, as in the joining of geometric and arithmetic sciences into mathematical science (Klein, 2000, pp. 18–19). Transdisciplinary mechanisms also include the collaborative development of new paradigms, discourses, generative grammars, collective mentalities, and definitions of relationships between power and knowledge (Goldman, 1995, cited in Klein, 2000, p. 23).

Sometimes transdisciplinary initiatives emerge from interests that fall between disciplines. These initiatives require the modeling of more complex phenomena than the current state of knowledge allows (Klein, 2000, p. 16). Participants in such initiatives work over time toward the development of common terminology, as well as common or compatible theories and perspectives, as Weiss and Wodak (2003) explain. Inevitably, some of these integrative collaborations based on shared research questions and problems produce new theory and practices and generate new knowledge niches (p. 20).

The development of women's and gender studies illustrates both aspects of transdisciplinarity. Scholars in the field began with the "problem" of women's exclusion from both the contents and the structural processes of academic curricula and research agendas, and they developed integrative strategies that made women's experience and gender constructs central rather than peripheral or invisible in knowledge production. At the time, no existing discipline addressed motherhood as a psychological, political, religious, cultural, and historical phenomenon, for example, let alone as an institution shaped by the social construction of gender, race, and class. If addressed at all, motherhood was typically seen as a personal experience of individual women. By the same token, no science dealt with the possibility that a scientist's standpoint as a gendered, classed, and raced human being might constitute a hidden element of scientific inquiry. Having identified such gaps in knowledge and methodology, the field's emphasis evolved from the simple inclusion of women within existing knowledge bases and paradigms to the creation of new paradigms and analytical frameworks that required their own new knowledge niche.

For some pioneers in the field, this niche equated to a new *interdiscipline*, or an intellectually coherent entity that identified persistent themes and problems as well as disciplinary gaps, fissures, and "unsolved mysteries that [could] form the basis of new research questions and projects" (Allen & Kitch, 1998, p. 278). Only an integrative, reciprocal transdisciplinarity would do, in which the "often hidden 'gendered' dimension of various disciplinary missions [could be] revealed," and a "discipline-transcendent command of the full array of knowledges that have shaped conventional understandings of women, gender, and sexuality" (p. 278) could be pursued. This process, in turn, would provide a foundation for new investigation that would entail specialized research unfettered by conservative disciplinary constraints.

As the field progressed over many years, scholars turned their attention to developing and critiquing its generative grammars, terminologies, mind-sets, and paradigms. (Such critiquing continues into the present, keeping some feminist scholars more focused on the use and misuse of gender analyses, terms, and basic concepts by other feminists than on the exclusion of women or gender issues from nonfeminist scholarship.) For example, developing methodologies and frameworks for transnationalizing the study of women and gender has recently become a high transdisciplinary priority in the field. Scholars like Chandra Mohanty, Caren Kaplan, Inderpal Grewal, and Gayatri Spivak are leaders in that effort, urging all feminist scholars to go beyond amassing information about a plurality of women and isolating their status and experience in the separate realms of economics or politics. Instead, they recommend transcending existing categories by analyzing "how women become 'women' (or other kinds of gendered subjects) around the world" (Kaplan & Grewal, 2002, p. 79) and identifying the transnational forces that produce uneven, unequal, and complex relationships among women in diverse parts of the globe. There is no universal patriarchy, they argue, but rather "specific and historicized gendering practices that create inequalities and asymmetries" (p. 79) via particular global and local processes. By the same token, feminist scholars must recognize that nations and governments are no longer the most salient actors within these processes. Multinational corporations, media producers, and religious movements now shape economic, political, and cultural institutions in ways that transcend both traditional nation-states and disciplines. Only institutionalized transdisciplinarity will allow for the necessary investigation of such practices and inequities.

## FEMINIST PERSPECTIVES ON INTERDISCIPLINARITY

From the field's beginnings, then, practitioners of women's studies have identified interdisciplinarity as a basic scholarly mission. Feminist scholars in many fields felt "impatience with the power arrangements of the university as an institution, and the way that the experience of women [was] devalued or excluded" (Moran, 2002, pp. 102–103) in existing disciplinary frameworks. From the multidisciplinary handshakes around issues such as sexual harassment, the feminization of poverty, and women's health, to the construction of entirely new, transdisciplinary epistemological categories for the study of gender such as "visual and narrative cultures" instead of art, film, and literature, interdisciplinarity has long been the hallmark of feminist research problems, questions, and theoretical debates across the academy.

Equally important in the early decades of women's studies were sometimes scathing critiques of traditional disciplines. Dale Spender's (1981) influential edited volume, *Men's Studies*

*Modified: The Impact of Feminism on the Academic Disciplines*, for example, critiqued numerous fields, including linguistics, philosophy, history, sociology, political science, anthropology, medicine, biology, and law. The anthology's authors routinely identified disciplinary structures built by men as responsible for excluding women from the knowledge base, valorizing male subjectivity as objectivity, and reinforcing "the 'authority' of men and the 'deficiency' of women" in society at large (Spender, 1981, p. 2). Even when women were somehow allowed into the knowledge base or literary canon, Spender (1981) observed, it was always on men's terms. Women had little to do with the construction of religious, philosophical, literary, or political thought. Spender believed that the infusion of women's knowledge and experience into the curriculum would have far-reaching effects beyond the classroom. She predicted that it would cause a reevaluation of subjectivity, a new appreciation for complexity, and a reevaluation of the research methods that then characterized "men's studies," which she defined as everything except women's studies (pp. 3, 8).[1]

Such disciplinary critiques have not eliminated the value of discipline-based feminist research, of course. No one would argue that discipline-based paradigms, terminology, and generative grammars have been unimportant to feminist scholars in multiple fields or in women's studies itself. From political science has come "the gender gap" in voting patterns, as well as Carol Pateman's "sexual contract." From law has come Kimberlé Crenshaw's "intersectionality" of identity markers, a term that has dominated many feminist analyses of the relationship between gender and race in a variety of fields. Nancy Chodorow's "reproduction of motherhood," Carol Gilligan's "different voice" and "ethic of care," Patricia Hill Collins's "outsider within," Brackette Williams's (1996) "inappropriate genders," Judith Butler's "performativity," Donna Haraway's "situated knowledges," and Nancy Cott's "bonds of womanhood" represent just a few of the concepts and paradigms that have emerged from discipline-based research to influence feminist scholarship, albeit in a somewhat fragmentary and haphazard way (Allen & Kitch, 1998, p. 286).

It is equally important to recognize, however, that just as many, if not more, significant insights have emerged from work done outside conventional disciplines: Alice Walker's "womanism," Audre Lorde's "sister outsider," Gloria Anzaldúa's "la conciencia de la mestiza" and "borderlands," Laura Mulvey's "male gaze," and Adrienne Rich's "lesbian continuum." Conceptual frameworks and analyses have also emerged from deliberately interdisciplinary endeavors, such as Inderpal Grewal and Chandra Mohanty's "scattered hegemonies" and the new interdiscipline called critical race feminism (CRF), which has recently expanded to the global level.

CRF began with a disciplinary critique of the study and practice of law but evolved into a demand for transdisciplinary scholarship and analysis as the only appropriate "fix" for the problem it was designed to address—inherent disadvantages to women of color in existing antidiscrimination law. To correct this endemic discrimination, critical race feminists observed that "sometimes a little mortar will suffice" to repair the cracks in the legal regime through which women of color fall in the United States and around the world, but "in other instances an entire wall of a legal edifice must come down" (Wing, 2000, p. 2). Erasing the inherent injustice within the law requires a transdisciplinary integration of scholarship from fields such as history, sociology, African American studies, and women's studies (p. 6).

There is also evidence that transdisciplinary feminist conceptual frameworks, terminology, and "generative grammars" have transformed research and curriculum development in traditional disciplines. The insistence by pioneers of women's studies that women's lost contributions to history and literature be recovered and that the historical and literary canons and critical schools of thought be redesigned in light of this recovery has been replicated in other fields, such as art and music. These developments may "add women and stir," but they still represent important new data points for disciplinary revision. In psychology, for example, transdisciplinary gender considerations have infused definitions of individual identity and mental health with a social analysis. Feminist transdisciplinary discoveries and analyses have also promoted or furthered the generation of numerous

other interdisciplines, such as sexuality studies, disability studies, popular culture studies, and lesbian/gay studies. The transnationalization of gender studies has contributed to several disciplines and fields such concepts as the "global sex trade" and the key idea that women's rights are human rights (see Lay, Monk, & Rosenfelt, 2002).

Without transdisciplinary work on women, disciplinary scholars would lack the concept of women's "second shift" or "double day" of work with which to analyze labor and the economy (McVicker, 2002). Important disciplinary analyses of heterosexism, racism, and postcolonialism can also trace their origins to transdisciplinary gender scholarship.

Some feminist scholars continue to resist transdisciplinarity, however, for a variety of reasons. For some, the promise of integrative interdisciplinary innovation sounds hollow. They can accept transdisciplinarity in the curriculum, but they wonder how it works in a single person's research. How could anyone possibly know enough to master more than one field? How could interdisciplinary scholarship not lead to dilettantism? Others believe that traditional disciplinary research is the only source of truly rigorous scholarship. Using that rationale, such scholars may object to the development of transdisciplinary women's and/or gender studies PhD programs. Still others argue that efforts to codify interdisciplinarity will co-opt women's studies into "the system" (Allen & Kitch, 1998, p. 287).[2] Fearing such appropriation, they warn against interdisciplinary rigidity and obsession with interdisciplinary purity (Kaplan & Grewal, 2002, p. 69).

For still other feminist scholars, resistance to transdisciplinarity entails issues of affiliation. Their scholarly identities and research agendas were honed within their disciplines of training. Few programs in women's studies can provide an equivalent academic home because only a minority of programs can grant tenure. Such scholars may develop their feminist research agendas in the context of the women's or feminist "wing" of their disciplinary professional organizations, such as the American Psychological Association or the Modern Language Association, partly because their universities may be more willing to fund attendance at discipline-based conferences.

Postmodern, antipositivist objections have also entered the debate about transdisciplinary feminist research, especially in a field called "women's studies," which scholars like Wendy Brown have argued depends on a falsely coherent definition of "women" as the object of study. Using that premise, Brown argued "the impossibility of women's studies" in an article published in 1997. She claimed that gender never exists apart from equally embedded categories, such as race, class, sexuality, and geographical location. Even linking those categories—as in "middle-class Tejana lesbian"—oversimplifies models of social power and excludes people who "feel misdescribed by such descriptions even as they officially 'fit' them" (Brown, 1997). Brown called for the dissolution of women's studies as an interdiscipline in favor of incorporating nonunified definitions of gender into scholarship conducted in traditional disciplines.

Brown's objections echo general critics of transdisciplinarity who protest the creation of interdisciplines. Speaking of women's studies in particular, Stanley Fish offers two familiar reasons for his objections: transdisciplinary entities will suffer from their own ingrown codes and practices, much like traditional disciplines; and the incommensurability of the disciplines prohibits their integration in any meaningful way in a single enterprise. Attempts at such integration will simply result in the disappearance of one discipline into another, an idea Fish resists (Moran, 2002, p. 111).

Supporters of transdisciplinarity in feminist scholarship point out that critiques like Brown's and Fish's are too sanguine about the integrity, coherence, and distinctiveness of traditional disciplines. Moreover, they argue, such critiques disregard the continued marginalization of women and gender concepts in traditional disciplines, as well as the contributions to knowledge made by transdisciplinary women's and gender studies in the past 30 years. Dynamic change within disciplines and even the amalgamation of traditional disciplines can be positive for knowledge production, they argue. If objections are based on fears that transdisciplinary feminist scholarship will ultimately reduce everything to gender, they are misguided. Feminist scholars are unlikely to follow the lead of, say, sociobiologists who reduce everything, including

literature and art, to a genetic cause (Moran, 2002, pp. 111, 177–179).

Proponents of transdisciplinarity as a staple of feminist scholarship further argue that this form of interdisciplinarity rests on the reality of permeable boundaries between disciplines, as well as on the many overlaps and commonalities shared among fields of inquiry. Transdisciplinarity does not require knowledge of every field but rather an understanding of the ways in which various fields conduct inquiry and produce knowledge. It requires comprehension of the levels of and relationship between aspects of scholarly work: knowing, for example, what kinds of detailed evidence from a range of epistemological domains are necessary to construct concepts and theoretical claims that transcend a particular field. The transdisciplinary researcher can be compared to an orchestra conductor who is not expert on every instrument but, rather, on the way the instruments work together to produce various sounds and effects.

## What Is Feminist About Interdisciplinarity?

Feminist researchers have a particular stake in transdisciplinarity, supporters argue, for a variety of reasons. For openers, it is only through the validation of gender as a methodological and epistemological foundation for knowledge that feminist research in any field acquires its validity. Integrative interdisciplinarity promotes that foundation, even in light of postmodern objections like Brown's (1997). There is no need to consider gender a natural category in order to analyze the way it functions in social life and structures. Nuanced gender analyses incorporate such complexities as genderized race and racialized gender without necessarily oversimplifying either structural gender or lived experience.

In addition, there is little doubt that a range of integrative and reciprocal interdisciplinary research efforts over the past three decades has been crucial to developing comprehensive knowledge about all those included in the category *women* and has provided the foundation for action to promote gender equity and other goals of feminist research. Often these efforts have evolved from discipline-based research, which provides the detailed data and analysis that transdisciplinary scholars require. But without transdisciplinary syntheses and generative grammars, the root metaphors for gender analysis within and across disciplines, the comparisons of conclusions and methodologies that inspire new research, and constructions of theory that guide social action would not have occurred. Those goals require dialogue among scholars and discoveries of points of convergence and conflict that produce conclusions, on the one hand, and urgent new research projects, on the other. Transdisciplinary scholarship helps link the sources, terminologies, and processes of justification for gender research.

Kaplan and Grewal (2002) provide an example. In detailing their call for transnational feminist analyses, theories, and practices, they call for "generative grammars" that transcend single disciplines, using such concepts as "complicity and conflict, alliance and commonality," boundaries, and "institutionalized discourses," as well as precedents in analytical protocols, such as measuring the impact of dominant knowledge frameworks on the construction of individual choice and on what passes for "common sense," and the role of technology and media in the creation of culture (pp. 79–80).

Exposing sexual harassment as a structural feature of the work world provides another example of transdisciplinary generative grammar. Without an integrative analytical process, there would have been no vocabulary and no syntax to link cause and effect in challenging conventional definitions of unwanted sexual advances in the workplace as simply isolated, individual experiences attributable to particular women's sexual allure. Once generated, such transdisciplinary grammars reveal phenomena that were previously obscured. New transdisciplinary paradigms can, in turn, shape disciplinary and cross-disciplinary inquiry.

Within the feminist research community, various forms of integrative interdisciplinary research have generated debates about such underlying theoretical precepts as the relationship between experience and knowledge, identity and knowledge, and theory and activism. Transdisciplinary work provides critical opportunities to redesign the nature and processes of inquiry itself, according to the most novel

insights about women and gender wherever they occur. It creates opportunities to share research results, to explain the relationship of theoretical work to more practical concerns, to connect scholarship across disparate objects of study (from film to labor unions, and from novels to historical events and trends), and to synthesize as well as problematize research results and recommendations. In short, transdisciplinarity is an important mechanism for compiling, comparing, critiquing, and conveying feminist research results (Allen & Kitch, 1998, p. 281).

The work of feminist transdisciplinary research is not finished, of course. Although much progress has been made in developing a broad transdisciplinary knowledge base about women and gender, some disciplinary boundaries have proven less permeable than others. Some social science and scientific fields have resisted gender incursions on the grounds that research in their fields has little to do with gender. Despite epistemological work by feminist scholars such as Sandra Harding and Donna Haraway, scientists may ask, for example, what an analysis of gendered racial standpoint can reveal about thermodynamics. That question overlooks many things, including gender's role in the formulation of scientific research questions as well as in the interpretation of research results.

Even within feminist scholarship itself, transgressions across disciplinary boundaries have occurred more often in curricular design than in research agendas. Discipline-based feminist scholars have seen the advantages of at least multidisciplinarity in the curriculum of women's studies, if not in their individual classrooms, because they understand that the most salient and intransigent gender issues and problems require knowledge from across disciplinary, theoretical, and methodological boundaries. But as we have seen, they may continue to resist the idea that their own research can or should transcend those boundaries and remain rigorous.

## METHODOLOGY AS EPISTEMOLOGY AND POLITICS

Transdisciplinary research is most likely to occur as scholars become persuaded that their own epistemological and political goals depend on it. Feminist scholars who most support trans-disciplinary research believe that it offers the best opportunity for them to construct knowledge that promotes their purposes—however defined—in the academy and/or society. These purposes are "political" in that they concern the distribution of power, opportunities, and resources along gen-dered, racial, ethnic, class, and other "marked" lines. It is in this sense that feminist research, whether empirical, textual, or theoretical (or any combination thereof) typically has the political goal of exposing, analyzing, and/or transforming actual or perceived power relationships and gen-dered social and cultural material or conceptual structures in the world. This goal is typically shared even among feminist scholars who agree on little else.

I am among the scholars who claim that such feminist political and epistemological goals can be best achieved through integrative and recipro-cal interdisciplinarity, or transdisciplinarity. In making this claim, I agree with Renate Klein's (1991) description more than a decade ago of the "interconnections, continuity and interrelation-ships" among pieces of information and analyses that would both expose and counteract the com-partmentalization of knowledge inherent in tradi-tional disciplines and thereby avoid limiting the construction of knowledge about women and gen-der to what she called "glass wombs." The kind of transdisciplinarity I advocate goes beyond mere self-reflexive contemplation of research methods and practices to the integration of methods and knowledge in a new epistemology that rebuilds prevailing structures of knowledge, and creates new organizing concepts, methodologies, and/or skills. Such work seeks "reciprocal assim-ilation" among disciplines, in which all partici-pants are changed because of their interaction (Klein, 1993). At its best, such transdisciplinarity carves out new territory, fills in gaps between existing knowledge domains, creates new intellec-tually coherent entities that both emerge from the fusion of fields and transcend them, and expands the opportunities for new knowledge to transform the actual conditions of women's lives.[3]

I (and others) argue that transdisciplinarity has always been important to the production of the most nuanced and complex knowledge about women and gender. It was from transdisciplinary research that feminist scholars came ultimately to understand the constructed nature of gender identities, the inextricable interconnection of race, sexuality, class, and gender in social, famil-ial, economic, and political status, and the impact of such categories on social structures that regu-late access to resources and opportunities and produce unequal material benefits for different individuals and groups.

Such transformative transdisciplinarity should not be mistaken for the simple synthesis of knowl-edge. Rather, it should be seen as a foundation for analyzing both convergences and contradictions within a framework that accounts for both. New epistemological categories that emerge from such an analysis are key to its transformative potential. Through them, researchers are equipped to unearth the deepest evidence, avoid misinterpreta-tions of data, and craft the most comprehensive explanations for and antidotes to the intransigent and complex gendered racial, class, sexual, and ethnic distinctions, hierarchies, and mechanisms of control that still structure human experience around the globe. Traditional disciplinary and multidisciplinary "handshake" scholarship can play a vital role in the transdisciplinary process, but multidisciplinarity alone cannot typically provide the new mechanisms necessary for rear-ranging and renaming observations and data that transdisciplinarity offers.

Transcending disciplinary constraints, rebuild-ing structures of knowledge, and creating new organizing concepts are more necessary than ever for analyzing and tackling local and global gender issues—from the glass ceiling to the gendered implications of terrorism. Rather than promoting the oversimplified universalization of women, as Brown feared and transnational scholars warn against, transdisciplinarity offers the best critical tools for conceptualizing the complexities of the category *women*, and for linking feminist epistemological and political goals. At the same time, transdisciplinarity pro-vides a platform from which to scrutinize, cri-tique, and revise feminist political perspectives.

## FEMINIST TRANSDISCIPLINARITY: THE OHIO STATE UNIVERSITY EXAMPLE

Those are large claims, and I would like to offer two examples to illustrate them in more detail.

The first comes from my own Department of Women's Studies at Ohio State University (OSU). In the early 1990s, the faculty undertook an internal graduate curriculum transformation project designed to detach the study of women and gender from traditional disciplines and theoretical schools of thought.[4] The point was not to banish discipline-based data, analyses, theories, and insights from the curriculum; after all, more than half our faculty at the time had joint appointments in other fields and conducted their research within the parameters of those fields. Rather, we intended to reanalyze such disciplinary or traditional knowledge from the perspective of an epistemological structure that best reflected the social and cultural construction of gender difference and inequality, both conceptually and materially, in men's and women's lives in the United States and around the world. We intended for this epistemological structure to reflect our commitments to inclusion and the structural analysis of gender and to generate both curriculum and research.

Over the course of a year, we wrestled with the kinds of knowledge about women and gender produced in the humanities, arts, social sciences, and medical sciences—the provinces of our faculty and curriculum. Disciplinary and divisional boundaries in the academy increasingly seemed to form barriers rather than pathways to the comprehensive framework we sought. To transcend them, we identified both meaningful distinctions between conventional knowledge bases and promising overlaps among disciplinary domains. We were determined not to divide, during the process of inquiry, the information and insights that must be united to produce both comprehensive knowledge about women and gender and the foundations for meaningful social and conceptual transformation. By defining, analyzing, and addressing feminist theory and purposes, including their contradictions and disagreements, we hoped to link our epistemological and political frameworks. After months of work, we identified three epistemological categories that seemed most promising for the transdisciplinary work we envisioned: *gender representation*; *difference/diversity*; and *gender, power, and social change*.

The category of *gender representation* incorporates the analysis of visual and narrative images and depictions of women, men, gender

relationships, racialized gender, sexuality, class, ability, and so on in all representational forms, including popular culture, literature, art, film, and advertising. It incorporates both traditional and feminist methodologies related to those representational forms, including feminist film theory and numerous theoretical approaches to literature and art. But the real focus of the category *representation* is the process itself, the way in which the media and texts produce rather than simply mimic gender, racial, and class inequality, difference, and identities. Moreover, representation entails both the history of and the possibility for challenging and reconstructing these representations to produce equity and agency, for example, where discrimination, subordination, and passivity once prevailed. In addition, *representation* includes the study of nonliterary narratives, such as historical texts, scientific rhetoric, government documents, medical research, and "legal fictions" that produce raced, gendered, and classed political subjects. Some scholars of representation explore the ways in which those fictions define identities and frame public discourse, regardless of their accuracy.

Representation intersects with *gender, power, and social change*, because social opportunities and resources are inevitably shaped by media and texts in both local and global cultures. The imbricated nature of representation ensures that its study will center on the concept of difference/diversity, including racial difference and sexualities, in local, national, and transnational contexts.

When we formulated our PhD curriculum in 2000, we identified *visual and narrative cultures* (VNC) as a specialization within *gender representation*. VNC both links a wide variety of representational forms and analyzes their relationship to social power structures and mechanisms for change. Thus, the VNC research focus involves the study of texts and visual representations, both individually and in relationship to one another, as well as of the gendered/racialized/sexualized processes of construction and distribution of representations via production companies, corporate sponsors, media outlets, and policymakers.

Siobhan Somerville's (2000) *Queering the Color Line: Race and the Invention of Homosexuality in American Culture* exemplifies transdisciplinary representation research. Somerville traces the representation of homosexuality in early 20th-century American culture via racialized images and associations in film, autobiography, and literature, as well as in the cultural and material conditions that produced and promoted those representations. The book's first chapter, for example, analyzes the varying content and the production processes involved in, first, a stage play and, then, a 1914 film titled *A Florida Enchantment*. Both were based on an 1891 novel of the same name, which fantasized both racial and sexual transformations via a magic seed. The story's relationship to slavery in Florida, to the racist structures of Florida's Vitagraph movie studios, to the history of the film industry as a whole, and to the evolving gendered and racialized audience for cinema in the United States in the early 1900s all figure prominently in Somerville's analysis of the story's varied messages about genderized race and sexuality across its several manifestations.

In particular, Somerville's analysis of the film version of *A Florida Enchantment* reveals the limitations of a purely textual or aesthetic analysis, which might conclude that the film's apparently "sexually transgressive aspects" and "unusually sustained and unambiguous display of female homoeroticism" make it a "proto-gay" film. Somerville's transdisciplinary gendered racial analysis of the film, however, which includes the detailed study of the economic and social context in which it was produced, clearly undermines such transgressive possibilities. She reveals the film's gendered racist and homophobic implications through the interconnection of its narrative and aesthetic qualities with its historical context (Somerville, 2000, pp. 41, 43).[5]

As evident from my discussion of representation, the category *difference/diversity* is the centerpiece of our department's transdisciplinary structure. This category provides a framework for feminist debates about the gendered meaning of sexual, class, and cultural/geographic differences that serves as a launching pad for all definitions and analyses of women and gender. The category's "slashed" form deliberately keeps the two terms in tension. Their juxtaposition suggests the complexity and supercharged political terrain of inclusion. "Difference" signifies both the recognition and critique of the normative aspects it implies: difference *from* some standard for

gender, race, ethnicity, sexuality, and ability. It implies that one must always ask, "Different from what?" "Diversity" alone suggests a nonhierarchical pluralism: "let a hundred flowers bloom" multiculturalism. But linked to "difference," the combination implies that all analyses of diversity must consider the power inequities built into racial, ethnic, sexual, and other categories. The juxtaposed terms also invite the simultaneous exploration of both specific groups and identities and their historical and political interconnections. This theoretical work, in turn, promotes the interrogation of the identity categories themselves as they are experienced by or attributed to individuals and groups.

*Sexualities* and *Latina/Black Women's Studies* are the PhD specialties that have emerged so far from the *difference/diversity* epistemological category. Work in these specialties connects the study of particular gendered, raced, sexualized, and/or ethnicized political groups, literatures, representations, and histories with analyses of groups' differences from one another and relationships to social and cultural structures of power and opportunity.

David Eng's (2001) *Racial Castration: Managing Masculinity in Asian America* provides an example of transdisciplinary difference/diversity research. The book integrates representational and political/historical analyses to illuminate the way that issues of gender and sexuality inflect Asian American social status and identity. Eng observes that Asian American men have been constructed as the "oriental-antithesis" of manhood and masculinity. His book provides a transdisciplinary analysis of that construction in both historical events and trends—such as the building of the transcontinental railroad, the wartime internment of Japanese Americans, and immigration laws—and in literary texts, by such writers as Frank Chin, Maxine Hong Kingston, Lonny Kaneko, and Ang Lee.

Because of his transdisciplinary approach, Eng's project does not lead him to what he considers the typical false conclusion, reached by Frank Chin and others, which predicates the elevation of the Asian population as a whole on reestablishing conventional heterosexual masculine credentials for Asian men and suppressing or derogating Asian women. Rather, Eng's perspective allows him to see that temptation as a capitulation to the stereotypes that have dogged Asians since at least the 19th century, including today's gendered stereotype of Asians as the "model minority." His title, *Racial Castration*, suggests the book's transdisciplinary generative grammar for both defining and counteracting the queering of Asian men. Using cultural/psychoanalytic theories of Freud, Lacan, and Fanon, as well as feminist, queer, postcolonial, and critical race theories, Eng explores Asian American men's sexualized as well as genderized struggles for identity in U.S. society. He acknowledges the racial insults experienced by Asian men through decades of immigration, labor discrimination, and cultural isolation, but his broad understanding of the full historical, cultural, and psychological origins and impact of those insults, as well as the relationship between Asian American male subjectivity and the larger transnational Asian diaspora, leads him to conclude that "it is this turning to queerness and diaspora that provides us with a new set of images for a different type of Asian American male subjectivity in the twenty-first century" (Eng, 2001, p. 228).

The category *gender, power, and social change* in the OSU Women's Studies graduate curriculum investigates historical, transnational, and contemporary social and political processes, policies, and practices. This rubric goes beyond looking for gender implications in politics or economics or analyzing "gender roles" to the study of gender, race, class, ability, and sexuality as they intersect in the construction of social and political institutions and rationales for (typically inequitable) allocations of resources and power across social domains. Objects of study in this rubric include everything from the economics of family life to Congressional elections, from the glass ceiling for female professionals to political activism, and from labor unions to global consumerism. This category entails the study of processes of historical, contemporary, and future social change and transformation via a complexly gendered lens. Both *representation* and *difference/ diversity* are crucial to this study, as feminist researchers increasingly discover the interconnection of racialized gender representations with public policy formation, economic opportunities, electoral politics, and legal practices. It is within this rubric that the intersection of "legal fictions"

with the material conditions of people's lives becomes most apparent.

One specialization that has emerged from this epistemological category is *states, economies, and social action*. Although grounded in social science methodologies and material concerns, research in this focus area transcends the traditional methods and knowledge domains of the social sciences by including the investigation of culture and representation and by engaging with theories of social construction, such as psychoanalysis, Marxism, and socialist/materialist feminism. Explorations of empirical data and the material conditions of women's lives serve the larger investigation of power, governments, social and political institutions, economic forces, and social change.

Anne McClintock's (1995) *Imperial Leather: Race, Gender, and Sexuality in the Colonial Conquest* exemplifies research in *states, economies, and social action*. Although some feminist anthropologists have faulted it for homogenizing colonialism and relying a bit too heavily on psychoanalytic theory, McClintock's book about Britain's colonial empire is an innovative transdisciplinary reconstruction of socioeconomic history via intersecting gender, race, class, and sexuality discourses seen through a psychoanalytic lens (Midgley, 1998, p. 9). Specifically, McClintock exposes both the gender differences in attitude and behavior among colonial agents and subjects and the gendered foundations of the imperial impulse by rethinking "the circulation of notions . . . between the family, sexuality and fantasy (the traditional realm of psychoanalysis) and the categories of labor, money and market (the traditional realm of political and economic history)" (McClintock, 1995, p. 8). Moreover, like other transnational scholars, McClintock identifies a series of transdisciplinary categories that guide her investigation: a "dense web of relations between coercion, negotiation, complicity, refusal, dissembling, mimicry, compromise, affiliation and revolt" (p. 15).

A pivotal theme in McClintock's (1995) book is the construction of nationalism via discourses that "cannot be understood without a theory of gender power." She offers various examples of gendered national discourses in several nation-states that depend on gendered symbolism. Particularly stunning is the development of Afrikaner national identity after the Boer War of 1899 to 1902. Before the war, the Boers did not share a historic identity or even a language, so they consciously invented both in an effort to redefine their defeat by the British. As they created a language through the publication of news magazines and other print media (which resulted in the legal recognition of Afrikaans as a language in 1918), as well as by cultural events fabricated by clever "spin doctors," would-be Afrikaners circulated a "male national narrative figured as an imperial journey into empty lands," whose virginity was being impugned by "degenerate Africans." According to that narrative, a white nation emerged from a male birthing ritual, which (ironically) produced a *volksmoeder*, or mother of the nation (McClintock, 1995, pp. 355, 357–358, 368–369).

Afrikaners fabricated another gendered nationalist narrative in 1938 as a means of transforming the Boers' 1838 humiliation by the British into a virtue. According to that gendered neo-narrative, the Dutch historical mutiny was an epic trek, a reconstruction that allowed Afrikaners to celebrate its centennial by staging a second journey, or *Tweede Trek*, designed to reinforce both the validity and the nobility of white rule in South Africa. Nine replica *Voortrekker* wagons were built, and each became a microcosm of colonial society. A central figure in each wagon was a "whip-wielding white patriarch prancing on horseback, [with] black servants toiling alongside, [and] white mother and children sequestered in the wagon." The women's starched, white bonnets symbolized white racial purity, which was analogous to the "decorous surrender of their sexuality to the patriarch and the invisibility of white female labor." The Tweede Trek lasted for 4 months and wound its way along different routes from Cape Town to Pretoria, arousing nationalist (and racial) pride. It culminated in a pageant with Nazi overtones (from whose fetish symbolism and cultural persuasion it was borrowed), with Afrikaner boy scouts carrying flaming torches. The spectacle "invented white nationalist traditions and celebrated unity where none had existed before" (McClintock, 1995, pp. 371–373, 385).

McClintock's consideration of gender power across the knowledge domains of history, politics, economics, and anthropology (with its emphasis on cultural symbolism) exemplifies the potential of transdisciplinarity. Studies of social forces alone might validate existing frameworks and structures and allow "the nation-state [to] remain a repository of male hopes, male aspirations and male privilege" (McClintock, 1995, p. 385). But studies that recognize the imbrication of social forces by cultural influences, especially as seen through the highly gendered theoretical perspective of psychoanalysis, can expose another level of "truth" about nationalism that has the power to transform the knowledge base.

The categories created by the OSU transdisciplinary graduate curriculum serve both epistemological and political goals. As they interconnect and transcend knowledge domains, the categories also demonstrate the social constructedness rather than the "naturalness" of gender and promote intersectional analyses of race, class, sexuality, ethnicity, and other identity and status markers. Another specialization in our PhD program, *sexuality studies*, provides a final example of those interconnected goals. That subfield integrates the representational and political/material aspects of sexuality and sexual identity formation, just as *visual and narrative cultures* combines the study of specific artistic or literary forms or genres with the analysis of material and political contexts and the constraints of production processes.

## FEMINIST TRANSDISCIPLINARITY: CENTRAL EUROPEAN UNIVERSITY'S COMPARATIVE GENDER STUDIES PHD PROGRAM

The PhD program in Comparative Gender Studies at Central European University (CEU), established in 2002 in Budapest, Hungary, offers a somewhat different example of transdisciplinary research in which feminist epistemology and politics converge.[6] The stated purpose of the CEU program is to "intertwine theoretical and empirical inquiry into gender . . . with inquiry into diversified patterns of social and cultural change." Founders of the program based their rationale on the epistemological significance of women's and gender studies over the previous 30 years, specifically the ways in which the field has challenged "both traditional concepts of the objectivity of academic knowledge and of the relation between the social and the symbolic order" (Proposal, p. 4). From the outset, they recognized the importance of transdisciplinary analyses and research to overcoming gender biases in social, theoretical, and cultural scholarship throughout the humanities and social sciences, as well as to breaking down barriers between studies of individuals and the social structures within which they form their identities and perspectives on the world. Thus, the founders saw transdisciplinarity as the best way to overcome "the tendency to study gender in a seemingly a-historical, unsituated, and fragmented manner, with insufficient grounding in analyses of institutions, social processes, and the material conditions of life" (Proposal, p. 6).[7]

To overcome the historical isolation, fragmentation, and insufficiency in traditional forms of knowledge production, CEU's program both deconstructs "unexamined norms and pre-suppositions underlying much scholarship" (Proposal, p. 6) and requires a comparative framework among case studies. Scholars analyze similarities, differences, and relationships among compared "cases" that range from geographic regions to themes, such as labor and larger systemic patterns of asymmetric influence and dependency. They compose "comparative-integrative perspectives" by negotiating between each case and its larger historical and political context (Proposal, p. 8). The program also encourages collaborative research, in which multiple scholars draw insight from and reflect on one another's transdisciplinary research projects and consider the complex interaction between analysis and data.

While identifying their transdisciplinary epistemological goals, the CEU Gender Studies faculty also identified a pressing political agenda for their PhD program, with "political" again understood as the power component of social structures and relationships. The faculty wanted their program to focus on "diversified patterns of social and cultural change in general and on Central-Eastern Europe in particular" (Proposal, p. 5) because their own region is a unique crucible of social change and reconstruction in the post-Soviet era. They specifically

wanted knowledge production in their program to have an impact on their region's unprecedented opportunity to re-create the very concept of national identity and the nation-state. They hoped their program would facilitate the creation of critically aware citizens who can relate local experiences to global processes and structures and of understanding the gendered foundations of state structures in Eastern Europe as well as around the world (Purpose, p. 14).

Such transnational citizens, in Kaplan and Grewal's terms, must necessarily be transdisciplinary subjects, because creating new political citizens requires destabilizing classical disciplines; that is, disrupting and replacing taken-for-granted categories and disciplinary boundaries, interrogating subject fields to establish new basic metaphors and paradigms, and exposing "important 'missing linkages' among aspects of human life, social structures and motivations" (Purpose, p. 7). The transnational subject's epistemological goals must therefore entail a simultaneous critique of both androcentrism and "Eurocentric perspectives and epistemologies" (Proposal, p. 6).

These transdisciplinary goals, in turn, promote political goals. Primary among them is establishing gender awareness in understanding "the often unequal entangling, intertwining transfer between global and local forces" (Proposal, p. 6) and in pursuing a new democratic state. Such gender awareness could result from analyses of the ways in which the traditional sexual division of labor and men's and women's subject positions within this structure shape individuals' relationship to the state and degree of social agency. It could also result from analyzing how the separation of production from reproduction devalues women's cultural and social status. New knowledge in those areas could empower states to prevent discrimination and disadvantage to one sex through policies related to the reproduction of households and individuals, as well as to production (Purpose, pp. 13–14).

The CEU program's transnational subject avoids the "cosmopolitanism" that Kaplan and Grewal warn against in the nomad or "world subject" whose diasporic identity is made possible by her elite economic status. The CEU transnational subject, by contrast, is rooted in her region while remaining unattached to existing nation-state configurations and notions of sovereignty. The CEU transnational subject is also well-positioned to critique local variations of patriarchy in relationship to the state and to interrogate state-sponsored remedies, such as police intervention in "domestic violence," from multiple perspectives (Kaplan & Grewal, 2002, pp. 72, 73, 75).

The other primary political goal of the transdisciplinary CEU PhD program is to revalue and reinvigorate women's cultural and social status. Its transdisciplinary epistemological and political design is intended not only to analyze gender's role in defining citizens and the state but also to promote gender equity and the revaluation of women as cultural agents in new post-Soviet states (Purpose, pp. 5–6).

## CALLING FOR FEMINIST TRANSDISCIPLINARITY

The feminist theory implicit in the OSU and CEU programs, transnational scholarship, and CRF takes interdisciplinarity in feminist research to a new level. It suggests that multidisciplinary and cross-disciplinary "handshakes" fall short of transformative scholarship, just as earlier efforts to supply "lost" women, identify gender components in the study of politics, anthropology, psychology, and other disciplines, and analyze the sometimes hidden sexist agendas in neutral-sounding scholarship are necessary but no longer sufficient for accomplishing the ultimate goals of feminist research.

Young "new wave" feminists, such as Daisy Hernández and Bushra Rehman, state this case quite clearly when they note that the multicultural and multidisciplinary women's studies classes they have taken, which bring diverse women's texts and critiques together but do not integrate or grapple with their implications or contradictions, keep feminist perspectives "xenophobic," much like American society "that pretends to be racially integrated but remains racially profiled" (Hernández & Rehman, 2002, p. xxiv). Carole McCann and Seung-Kyung Kim (2003) echo that combined epistemological and political concern in their introduction to *Feminist Theory Reader: Local and Global*

*Perspectives.* They suggest that destabilizing normative "white, Northern, middle-class, and heterosexual women's experiences as *the* experience of women" and rethinking feminist constructs in light of non-Western interpretations of difference require collaborative, reciprocal comparativism and integrative, reciprocal interdisciplinarity—that is, transdisciplinarity—in feminist research (p. 5).

At the same time, however, support for transdisciplinarity in feminist research entails some caveats. First, transdisciplinarity in and of itself does not necessarily achieve feminist aims. It, too, can reflect androcentric biases and exclude women and gender from scholarly inquiry. Second, by the same token, even nonfeminist, discipline-based, and theoretical scholarship can be useful to feminist research. Feminist scholars should remain receptive to insights and methodologies that lie outside the overtly feminist purview and utilize useful theoretical or empirical work by "dead white males" or other unlikely sources in creating transformative transdisciplinary feminist scholarship. This means the transdisciplinary project of feminist research must not become a closed culture that focuses its attention only on itself. Rather, the goal of feminist transdisciplinary research to produce comprehensive, inclusive, appropriately synthesized knowledge about women and gender, which encompasses both synchronies and contradictions and continues to investigate and redefine its own processes, must find its data, theories, and analyses wherever they exist. Without a commitment to this kind of scholarly openness, transdisciplinary feminist research might stagnate and succumb to the traditional disciplinary pitfalls it was designed to avoid.

## NOTES

1. All the chapters in Spender's anthology also describe the impact of feminism on research in these fields.

2. For a full discussion of this debate, see the entire issue *Feminist Studies, 24*(2).

3. For further discussion of the ideas in this section, see Judith A. Allen and Sally L. Kitch (1998).

4. At the time of this graduate curriculum revision, our department offered only the MA degree. As of 2002, we have also offered the PhD. The epistemological foundation we established in the early 1990s is still in effect for the entire graduate program.

5. For more on *A Florida Enchantment*, see Somerville (2000, pp. 39–76).

6. I became familiar with the CEU program both as an outside reviewer for their PhD proposal and as a keynote speaker on the field of women's and gender studies in their Zero Week (preterm) lecture series in September 2002.

7. All quotations in this discussion of the CEU PhD program in Comparative Gender Studies come from either the Proposal for the program, which was submitted to the Board of Regents of the New York State Education Department in 2002, or the Statement of Purpose for the Department of Gender Studies at CEU, written in 2001. Sources are identified in parentheses in the text.

## References

Allen, Judith A., & Kitch, Sally L. (1998). Disciplined by disciplines? The need for an interdisciplinary research mission in women's studies. *Feminist Studies, 24*(2), 275–299.

Brown, Wendy. (1997). The impossibility of women's studies. *Differences, 9*(3).

Elam, Diane. (1994). *Feminism and deconstruction: Ms. en abyme.* London: Routledge.

Eng, David. (2001). *Racial castration: Managing masculinity in Asian America* (Perverse Modernities, J. Halberstam & L. Lowe, Eds.). Durham, NC: Duke University Press.

Finkenthal, Michael. (2001). *Interdisciplinarity: Toward the definition of a metadiscipline?* (American University Studies, Series V, Philosophy Vol. 187). New York: Peter Lang.

Hernández, Daisy, & Rehman, Bushra. (Eds.). (2002). *Colonize this! Young women of color on today's feminism.* New York: Seal Press.

Kaplan, Caren, & Grewal, Inderpal. (2002). Transnational practices and interdisciplinary feminist scholarship: Refiguring women's and gender studies. In Robyn Wiegman (Ed.), *Women's studies on its own: A next wave reader in institutional change* (pp. 66–81). Durham, NC: Duke University Press.

Klein, Julie Thompson. (1993). Blurring, cracking, and crossing: Permeation and the fracturing of discipline. In Ellen Messer-Davidow, David R. Shumway, & David J. Sylvan (Eds.), *Knowledges: Historical and critical studies in disciplinarity* (pp. 95–96). Charlottesville: University Press of Virginia.

Klein, Julie Thompson. (2000). A conceptual vocabulary of interdisciplinary science. In Peter Weingart & Nico Stehr (Eds.), *Practising interdisciplinarity* (pp. 3–24). Toronto, Canada: University of Toronto Press.

Klein, Renate D. (1991). Passion and politics in women's studies in the 1990s. In Jane Aaron & Sylvia Walby (Eds.), *Out of the margins* (p. 76). London: Falmer Press.

Lay, Mary M., Monk, Janice, & Rosenfelt, Deborah S. (Eds.). (2002). *Encompassing gender: Integrating international studies and women's studies.* New York: Feminist Press at the City University of New York.

McCann, Carole R., & Kim, Seung-Kyung. (Eds.). (2003). *Feminist theory reader: Local and global perspectives.* New York: Routledge.

McClintock, Anne. (1995). *Imperial leather: Race, gender and sexuality in the colonial conquest.* New York: Routledge.

McVicker, Jeanette. (2002). The politics of "Excellence." In Robyn Weigman (Ed.), *Women's studies on its own: A next wave reader in institutional change* (pp. 233–242). Durham, NC: Duke University Press.

Midgley, Clare. (1998). Gender and imperialism: Mapping the connections. In Clare Midgley (Ed.), *Gender and imperialism* (pp. 1–11). Manchester, UK: Manchester University Press.

Moran, J. (2002). *Interdisciplinarity* (The New Critical Idiom, John Drakakis, Ed.). London: Routledge.

Somerville, Siobhan B. (2000). *Queering the color line: Race and the invention of homosexuality in American culture.* Durham, NC: Duke University Press.

Spender, Dale. (1981). Introduction. In Dale Spender (Ed.), *Men's studies modified: The impact of feminism on the academic disciplines* (pp. 1–8). Oxford, UK: Pergamon Press.

Weingart, Peter. (2000). Interdisciplinarity: The paradoxical discourse. In Peter Weingart & Nico

Stehr (Eds.), *Practising interdisciplinarity* (pp. 25–41). Toronto, Canada: University of Toronto Press.

Weiss, Gilbert, & Wodak, Ruth. (2003). Introduction: Theory, interdisciplinarity, and critical discourse analysis. In Gilbert Weiss & Ruth Wodak (Eds.), *Critical discourse analysis: Theory and interdisciplinarity* (pp. 1–32). New York: Palgrave Macmillan.

Williams, Brackette F. (1996). Introduction: Mannish women and gender after the act. In Brackette F.

Williams (Ed.), *Women out of place: The gender of agency and the race of nationality* (pp. 1–33). New York: Routledge.

Wing, Adrien Katherine. (2000). Introduction: Global critical race feminism for the twenty-first century. In Adrien Katherine Wing (Ed.), *Global critical race feminism: An international reader* (pp. 1–23). New York: New York University Press.

# PART II

## FEMINIST RESEARCH PRAXIS

# 7

# FROM THEORY TO METHOD AND BACK AGAIN

*The Synergistic Praxis of Theory and Method*

SHARLENE NAGY HESSE-BIBER

DEBORAH PIATELLI

In the introduction to *Feminism and Methodology,* Sandra Harding (1987) asked, "Is there a distinctive feminist method of inquiry?" (p. 1). Harding responded "no" and instead discussed the contributions of feminism to the practice of research, calling attention to the interrelatedness of epistemology, methodology, and method. Methods are simply research techniques, tools that get at the research problem, whereas epistemology shapes our research questions and the theories we hold about the social world. Methodology can be thought of as a bridge between epistemology and method, shaping *how* we approach and conduct research. Whether one's epistemology is rooted in empiricism, standpoint, postmodernism, or postcolonial critique, a feminist methodology challenges status quo forms of research by linking theory and method in a synergistic relationship that brings epistemology, methodology, and method into dynamic interaction across the research process. A feminist methodology can spawn the development of new methodological tools that in turn can offer new angles of vision, reshaping both our research questions and the way we build knowledge.

Feminist scholars have long argued that conventional science operates within a male-dominated paradigm (Harding, 1991, 1993; Hartsock, 1998; Reinharz, 1992; Smith, 1987). The scientific model of research subscribes to the tenets of verification, generalization, objectivity, value-neutrality, and the unity of science or the belief that the logic of scientific inquiry is the same for all fields. Feminists have challenged these principles and argued that they are rooted in a historical, positivist, androcentric paradigm that produces biased research and supports an objective, hierarchical approach to knowledge building (Harding, 1986, 1991, 1993; Hartsock, 1998; Longino, 1990; Oakley, 1998; Reinharz, 1992; Smith, 1987). In Part II of this book, Sue Rosser discusses in her chapter "The Link Between Theory and Methods: Feminist Experimental Research" how, historically, this model has produced flawed research by focusing only on male-centered problems; omitting females in experimental research—both as researchers and as subjects; and interpreting data in a patriarchal context. Moreover, this model has made neutral and universal scientific claims based on distorted data. Through the lens of several feminist perspectives, Rosser cites a number of examples and shows how feminist research has challenged "science as usual" (Harding, 1991) and produced less biased and more valid scientific research. Rosser demonstrates how the scientific model has been challenged across disciplines in the natural, physical, and social sciences and, to some degree, engineering—specifically in "choice and definition of problems chosen, approaches used, and theories and conclusions drawn from the research." For instance, by placing women in the center of analysis, feminist experimental research has made ground-breaking discoveries into many health-related problems such as cardiovascular disease, various cancers, and AIDS. Hence, feminists have called for a decentering of the white, male subject in research, allowing for a multiplicity of voices and diverse research issues to be brought to the forefront—producing more complete and trustworthy research.

Feminists not only question androcentric bias, but also critique the hierarchical, deductive approach to knowledge building often found in conventional models of research. These approaches are laden with power and treat knowledge as something to be discovered rather than created (Collins, 2000; Haraway, 1991; Harding, 1991; Hartsock, 1998; Reinharz, 1992; Smith, 1987). Feminist researchers call attention to the partiality, fluidity, and situatedness of knowledge and seek new ways to approach knowledge building. *Who* can know, *what* can be known, and *how* we can construct the most authentic view of the social world are at the center of feminist concerns. Feminists advocate positioning the researcher "in the same critical plane" (Harding, 1987, p. 184) as their participants, rejecting the separation of object and subject, and call for more participatory, reflexive approaches to knowledge construction. Knowledge building becomes a relational process, rather than an objective product, that demands critical self-reflection, dialogue, and interaction (Collins, 2000; DeVault, 1990; Mies, 1983). This requires the researcher to make continuous shifts and negotiations in positionality

and a commitment to address power imbalances along the entire research process, engaging participants in the telling and interpreting of their own lives and experiences (DeVault, 1990; Reinharz, 1992; Smith, 1987; Wolf, 1996). Dorothy Smith (1974, 1987, 1999) has written at length on the inadequacies of the scientific model in studying "the social," because research questions have negated the problems of women and marginalized people, thereby silencing their voices and experiences from public discourse. Most important to Smith is the failure of conventional research to place people's experiences at the center of its inquiry rather than appropriating experience to advance its own theoretical frameworks. Although feminists advocate the privileging of lived experience, they also acknowledge that experience is relational and mediated and that all knowledge claims must be interrogated and decentered (Collins, 2000; Haraway, 1991; Harding, 1991; Smith, 1987, 1999). Through continuous reflection about how biography and historical social context shape the research process, the situatedness of both the researcher and the participants are integrated into the process of knowledge building. This requires an active and collaborative, rather than passive, role on the part of the researcher.

An inductive approach to knowledge building is the essence of grounded theory. Grounded theory as a mode of analysis emerged in the mid-1960s as a response to a myriad of critiques of qualitative research (Charmaz, 1995, 2000). Rather than taking a deductive approach to knowledge building where researchers impose theories on the data, grounded theory turns interpretation and analysis on its head by generating theory from, rather than imposing theory on, the lives and experiences of those we research. Most importantly, grounded theory revitalized the importance of the interplay between theory and method, data collection and analysis, which conventional modes of research neglected (Charmaz, 1995, 2000; Coffey & Atkinson, 1996; Glaser & Strauss, 1967; Strauss & Corbin, 2000). In her chapter "Feminisms, Grounded Theory, and Situational Analysis," Adele Clarke draws our attention to the implicit feminist assumptions of grounded theory in that it draws on and is grounded in the voices of participants and their experiences, values and acknowledges the multiplicity of interpretation and meaning, and facilitates the interaction and reflexivity of the researcher with the data. Clarke highlights the work of a number of feminist researchers who have made grounded theory more explicitly feminist. By choosing research topics that place gender at the center of analysis, feminist researchers are able to uncover silenced discourse and generate better knowledge that displaces inadequate theories and false stereotypes about women's lives.

In the spirit of grounded theory, the themes in this introduction were derived inductively by examining the writings in Part II. When reading the chapters in this section, we found that although the contributors come from a variety of disciplines and hold varying epistemologies, they do share a common ground in terms of what constitutes a feminist perspective on research. A feminist perspective on research offers new angles of vision that can create opportunities for raising new questions, engaging in new kinds of relationships, discovering innovative research techniques, and organizing different kinds of social relations. The research questions feminists ask are often rooted in issues of social justice, social change, and social policy for women and other marginalized groups. By raising new questions, feminists push the boundaries on traditional theoretical paradigms and conventional methodological techniques and create spaces for innovative knowledge building and research practice. By focusing on the lives and experiences of those who are often silenced in public discourse, a feminist perspective can illuminate new ways of knowing that can challenge conventional assumptions that shape social policy and our lives.

The authors in this section attempt to initiate dialogue across disciplines, epistemologies, and methodologies to facilitate more inclusive and egalitarian research practices and processes. Through their writings, they demonstrate how they, as feminist researchers, challenge conventional views on power and knowledge as they select research questions, engage their participants, choose, invent, and practice research techniques, and address social inequality. By engaging feminism and challenging status quo approaches to research, the authors in this *Handbook* demonstrate the synergistic relationship

between epistemology, methodology, and method and bring subjugated knowledge into the forefront of public discourse.

## FEMINIST PERSPECTIVES ON THE RESEARCH PROCESS

### Asking New Questions

The chapters in this section of the *Handbook* provide an array of insights into how a feminist perspective on research allows us to see features of the world that remain invisible to conventional research. Starting from the lives of marginalized people can provide new angles of vision and reveal new research questions (Collins, 2000; Harding, 1991; Smith, 1987). Focusing on marginalized knowledge has long been a priority within feminist discourse. In their chapter, "Participatory and Action Research and Feminisms: Toward Transformative Praxis," Brinton Lykes and Erzulie Coquillon discuss the impact feminism has had on generating new forms of participatory and action research—"feminist-infused action and participatory research." Although conventional participatory action research prioritizes local knowledge, fosters empowerment, and seeks transformation of social structures that promote inequality, Lykes and Coquillon argue that traditionally it has "failed to either include women as independent actors in their local projects or to problematize gender oppression and heterosexism." Sharon Brisolara and Denise Seigart, in their chapter "Feminist Evaluation Research," present a similar argument regarding conventional approaches to evaluation research. For these women, research is a political project. For Lykes and Coquillon, a feminist-infused action research approach addresses the absence of women and other marginalized people in traditional studies, values the multiplicity of experience and knowledge, and reinforces the strengths that vulnerable populations bring to social change work in their communities. By placing the focus on women and marginalized communities, new questions are raised, silenced voices are brought into public discourse, and social change is facilitated. One of the many examples that Lykes and Coquillon offer of how feminist-infused action research uncovers and brings forth subjugated knowledge in a project includes the research that Lykes and her colleague Jean Williams conducted in collaboration with Mayan women. Lykes and Williams worked in partnership with these women on a project documenting the history of violence this community had suffered over long periods of war. Weaving in multiple voices, this "collective history," written by women about their experiences of violence, has challenged conventional assumptions about who gets to write history and how it is documented and told. This project has also raised new questions about the impact of war on women. Moreover, through the process of telling, these women were able to reflect on and find ways to overcome barriers of difference and oppression in their community.

For Brisolara and Seigart, evaluation research that focuses on the concerns of underrepresented stakeholders, such as women and people of color, can raise new questions for the field around the purpose, processes, and outcome of the evaluation project—questions concerning positionality, bias, plurality, and ethics. In their piece, Brisolara and Seigart offer an example of a feminist evaluation that demonstrates how feminist researchers were able to draw attention to the inadequacy of theories that correlate poverty with self-esteem issues and ignore the structural inequalities that contribute to the low self-esteem of many women. By engaging women in the evaluation, these researchers uncovered new lines of inquiry around the needs of poor women, such as family planning and affordable housing. Although they have produced exemplary works, both Lykes and Coquillon and Brisolara and Seigart point to the difficulties in *naming* this work feminist. Their concerns around this issue, along with those of other authors, are discussed in the latter section of this introduction.

Bringing a gendered lens to research and examining the ways in which gender is constructed and reconstructed within relations of power is emphasized in Wanda Pillow and Cris Mayo's chapter, "Toward Understandings of Feminist Ethnography." Pillow and Mayo argue that feminist ethnography, unlike conventional forms, uncovers new knowledge by "studying the lived experiences of gender and its

intersectionalities" and then building theory from these lived experiences. Feminist ethnographies look at "what is missing, what is passed over, and what is avoided." By applying a gendered lens and interrogating the "continued interplay of race [class, sexuality] and gender in the structure of power," new questions are raised about both conventional and unconventional topics.

Dorothy Smith, in her chapter "Institutional Ethnography: From a Sociology for Women to a Sociology for People," shares her personal thoughts on the influence feminism has had on her own biography and the practice of sociology. Drawing from feminism's attention to consciousness-raising, empowerment, and embodied experience, Smith challenges us to take people's lives as the starting point of our investigations rather than as a particular discipline's conceptual practices, and to problematize the social relations and organization that extend beyond people and their experiences. By engaging in what Smith terms *institutional ethnography*, researchers can begin to fuse micro- and macrosocial levels of inquiry, thereby uncovering how extra-local relations shape our everyday world. Institutional ethnography transforms the practice of research by revealing what is beyond the scope of observable experience and expands the process of knowledge building by examining the broader social relations in which local experience is embedded. Unlike conventional ethnography, which treats the localized social world of the individual or group as an end in itself, institutional ethnography explores how that world is organized by using the experience of some particular person or persons as the entry point into forms of social organization that shape local settings but originate outside them. *How things work,* rather than simply describing *how things are*, becomes the focus of investigation. Along with this work, Smith and her colleagues have written numerous pieces demonstrating the significance and contributions of the institutional ethnographic approach (Campbell & Gregor, 2002; Campbell & Manicom, 1995; DeVault & McCoy, 2002; Smith, 1987, 1999, 2002; Smith, 1990).

Everyday experience as an entry point for investigation is emphasized in many of the writings in this section. For instance, Sarah Maddison, in her chapter "Feminist Perspectives on Social

Movement Research," urges researchers to begin their inquiry with lived experience. Drawing parallels between feminist standpoint theory and the study of the processes of collective identity formation, Maddison discusses her approach to research that "begins by acknowledging and privileging an activist standpoint." In her work with two submerged networks of contemporary young feminist activists in Australia, Maddison privileges the activist standpoint by giving activists "a voice in articulating their commitment, highlighting their strategic and fluid engagement with a differential consciousness and revealing the processes by which they construct their collective identities." Like other feminist social movement scholars, Maddison critiques certain theoretical approaches to social movement research, which have failed to acknowledge not only gender but also its intersection with other identities such as race, class, and ethnicity. By placing these concerns at the center of social analyses, researchers can attend to unresolved questions and better contribute to advancing the aims of social activists. Using a constructivist approach, Maddison considers her participants' multiple standpoints and the impact this has on both creating and sustaining a collective understanding of *who they are.* Her analyses focus not on the product of collective identity but rather on the process of how these women construct and reconstruct understandings of themselves and their place in the contemporary Australian women's movement.

Like Smith, Shulamit Reinharz and Rachel Kulick, in their chapter "Reading Between the Lines: Feminist Content Analysis Into the Second Millennium," are interested in exploring how local and extra-local symbols, discourse, and images influence our everyday lives. Reinharz and Kulick point to the need for novel approaches to content analysis due to the ever increasing computer-mediated flow of images and texts that "transmit a wide range of norms and values regarding gender, sexuality, and social relations" around the globe. Feminist content analyses aim to uncover the "multilayered politics of gendered and sexualized representation" and examine not only texts and images, but also the context in which they were produced. Content is not neutral, Reinharz and

Kulick say, and feminist content analyses must pay particular attention to the power dynamics and politics of production. Moreover, as with other feminist practices of methods, feminist content analyses are attentive to what has been silenced or omitted. Hence, feminist content analyses "read between the lines" and consider not only *existing* texts and images both in virtual and in *real* space but also those that are absent.

## Engaging in New Kinds of Relationships

Raising new questions can bring feminist researchers into dialogue with new conversational partners. By focusing on inequalities that lead to social injustices, feminists are often drawn to working with vulnerable populations (Lather & Smithies, 1997), while others choose to *study up* and strive to uncover the hidden discourse of privileged populations and how it shapes daily social interaction (Frankenberg, 1993). Although relationships become more complicated as one ventures into conversations across multiple differences, the project of deconstructing power relations within the research context is important in all researcher and participant relationships. Feminists have long questioned the canon of objectivity and argue that a detached relationship exercises control and power over the participants and can run the risk of exploitation and abuse (Reinharz, 1992; Smith, 1987; Wolf, 1992). To minimize harm and control over both the process and the product, feminists have devised innovative research strategies that cultivate collaboration and emphasize reflexivity to lessen and make visible the power inherent in the research process.

At the root of feminist inquiry is attention to power and *how* knowledge is built. Feminist research takes people as active, knowing subjects rather than passive objects of study. Knowledge is produced and mediated through lived experience and communicated through interaction in the form of face-to-face encounters, textual discourse, or visual mediums. Tapping into lived experience is the key to feminist inquiry and requires innovative practices in developing relationships and building knowledge. Through collaborative, reflexive practices, researchers and participants work to eliminate hierarchies of knowledge construction, and marginalized knowers are able to name themselves, speak for themselves, and construct a better understanding of the structures and forces that influence their experience (Dodson, 1998). The power of a feminist perspective is that it enables us to bring into view how our everyday lives are affected by social institutions and uncover possibilities for change (Smith, 1987). A feminist perspective argues that without empathic, interpersonal relationships, researchers will be unable to gain insight into the meaning people give to their lives (Collins, 2000; DeVault, 1990). Through collaborative inquiry and reflexive knowledge building, researchers can deconstruct hierarchical relationships and produce research that is useful and meaningful to participants and the larger society.

Embracing a participatory research strategy is the epitome of collaborative inquiry. Participatory inquiry incorporates collaboration across the research process from the development of the research question, to the conduct of research, through the interpretation and treatment of the data. In their respective chapters, Brisolara and Seigart and Lykes and Coquillon emphasize how collaborative inquiry holds the potential to shift positionalities, moving research participants from objects of study to agents over the research process. The role of the researcher is engaging and interactive, working with participants to promote dialogue, foster relationships, and collectively develop greater understanding about the social structures that oppress people on a daily basis. Other authors, such as Smith and Maddison, discuss in their respective chapters how they bring collaborative practices into their research processes by placing their subjects at the center of their inquiry, generating their research questions directly from their lived experience.

Integral to this collaborative process is a commitment to reflexive knowledge building. Polyvocality is central to a feminist understanding of how knowledge is built. Feminists of color have drawn our attention to the multiplicity of knowledge and have asked us to consider the cultural, social, national, racial, and gendered composition of historically different and specific forms of knowledge. These situated knowledges are partial knowledges located in a particular time and space, the knowledges of specific cultures and peoples. These knowledges express a multiple reality; they are not fixed but are ever changing. They are both critical of and vulnerable to the dominant culture, separated from it as well as opposed to it but also contained within it. Reflexive knowledge building occurs through the dialogical practice of sharing with others. It is only by reflexively considering the relationality between varying positionalities through dialogue that we are able to build knowledge. Reflexive knowledge building requires interrogation of social biographies and historical context, examination of the intersectionality of privilege and power, and the decentering of knowledge claims around interpretation and representation.

Listening, interacting, sharing, and translating are some of the techniques feminists have developed to foster greater connectedness, understanding, and self-empowerment (DeVault, 1990; Mies, 1983; Oakley, 1981; Smith, 1987). Marjorie DeVault and Glenda Gross, in their chapter "Feminist Interviewing: Experience, Talk, and Knowledge," state that a feminist approach to interviewing can lessen power dynamics and create research that is more accountable and applicable to participants' lives. Sustained engagement in the field, personal disclosure on the part of the researcher, and contextualizing discourse are some of the ways feminist researchers have attempted to deconstruct power imbalances and allow for greater trust and rapport. Dorothy Smith begins her inquiry from where she is situated and makes her experience of the everyday world not a barrier to knowledge building but, rather, an asset or point of entry. Smith problematizes lived experience by contextualizing it within its historical and social bounds and is attentive to how it is mediated. Similarly, a feminist-infused participatory and action research approach problematizes both the researcher's and the participants' positionalities and how they interact within the context of the research project. Lykes and Coquillon draw attention to the many ways feminist researchers "work the hyphen" (see Fine, 1998) by "challenging static, boundaried notions of 'insider' and 'outsider'" and clarifying "the mediated nature of all knowledge construction and exemplify[ing] ways of knowing that are frequently absent from mainstream, top-down theory building."

## Discovering Innovative Research Techniques

By generating new questions and exploring new forms of knowledge, have feminists radically altered the terrain of research methods? In her chapter "Emergent Methods in Feminist Research," Pamela Moss offers a glimpse into her journey of inquiry around these questions and asks us to consider the contexts in which emergent methods arise. Moss explores the field of feminist research and, using a typology of four different approaches, finds that researchers, who choose a conventional method, whether they are addressing mainstream questions or brand new questions, tweak, revise, or transform the technique. In addition, Moss observes that many feminists across disciplines are devising and choosing more unconventional techniques. Although many factors influence the choice of method, Moss argues that innovative forms emerge as a result of "the constitutive combination of a specific topic with a specific question with a specific data collection technique with a specific analysis in a specific context."

A feminist perspective can transform the most conventional of methodological techniques. Feminists have criticized traditional quantitative research on various grounds, and many have called for the dissolution of the dualism of quantitative and qualitative methods in an effort to build an emancipatory social science. They have agreed that quantitative methods can be useful, but that they are in need of reformulation to avoid bias and objectification of research participants, reduce the hierarchical nature of research relationships, and eliminate the reproduction of dominance (DeVault, 1999; Eichler, 1997; Harding, 1987, 1991; Jayaratne & Stewart, 1991; Mertens, 2003; Oakley, 1998; Sprague & Zimmerman, 1993; Stanley & Wise, 1993). Kathi Miner-Rubino, Toby Epstein Jayaratne, and Julie Konik, in their chapter "Using Survey Research as a Quantitative Method for Feminist Social Change," and Abigail J. Stewart and Elizabeth R. Cole, in "Narratives and Numbers: Feminist Multiple Methods Research," discuss how traditional *quantitative* methods have been influenced by the feminist perspective. Because feminists are more likely to focus on questions relevant to social change and ensure that vulnerable voices

are translated and represented accurately, Miner-Rubino et al. argue that a feminist perspective can uniquely contribute to the survey process in the development of research questions and in the interpretation of findings. Several examples of survey research that reflects a feminist perspective are discussed, illustrating the transformative potential of the survey method in supporting social change. By proposing new lines of inquiry and examining data through multiple theoretical and social lenses, a feminist perspective on survey research can advocate for women and marginalized groups in the areas of education, legislation, and public policy.

Stewart and Cole address the dilemmas of combining quantitative and qualitative methods in a single study and demonstrate how quantitative methods can support, contextualize, or broaden data analyses and research questions. Moreover, in the hands of feminists, quantitative methods and analyses have been used to study different levels of inquiry; increase the researcher's potential for insight, understanding, and knowledge building; and most important, influence public policy. Through their presentation of seven different models of integrating *narratives and numbers*, Stewart and Cole demonstrate how the principles of polyvocality, contextualization, authenticity of voice, and the commitment to improving the lives of women and marginalized people inherent in a feminist perspective influence how quantitative methods are collected, interpreted, and applied.

Several chapters in this section illustrate how feminist researchers have also transformed conventional *qualitative* methods as well as generated new forms of methodological inquiry, such as institutional ethnography, feminist-infused participatory and action research, and feminist evaluation research. Marjorie DeVault and Glenda Gross discuss the necessary augmentations feminists have made to the practice of interviewing in order to excavate meaning and experience. DeVault and Gross explore the idea of "radical, active listening" as a key component of feminist interviewing. Radical, active listening involves a fully engaged relationship, whereby the researcher listens for gaps and silences and considers "what meanings might lie beyond explicit speech." Being an active listener is being attentive to "the complexity of human talk," the pauses and patterns of speech and emotion that appear in everyday talk, and placing talk into historical and situational context. Radical, active listening helps create "knowledge that challenges rather than supports ruling regimes." While Lykes and Coquillon use conventional methods, such as focus groups, and observation, their feminist orientations influence the practice of these techniques. Attention to avoiding exploitation, consciousness-raising, and avoiding decontextualization shape their interactions and conversations with their participants. When crossing boundaries of culture, language, and difference, feminists are required to invent new techniques to excavate experience and foster greater understandings. Lykes and Coquillon use more creative techniques such as photography, drawings, storytelling, and drama to engage a diverse array of participants.

As mentioned previously, Dorothy Smith, in her chapter, discusses the integral role feminism has played in shaping institutional ethnography's approach to social inquiry. While revolutionary in its own right as a methodological practice, institutional ethnography questions conventional ways of thinking about and analyzing texts and discourse. By viewing texts as both material objects and vehicles of knowledge building across time and space, Smith states that we can better understand their role in organizing and regulating our everyday life. Through mapping the interrelationship between lived experience, texts, and institutional structures, institutional ethnography can reveal opportunities for social action.

Emergent methods are not solely restricted to data collection techniques. Clarke offers her "postmodern extension of grounded theory," which she calls "situational analysis." Similar to institutional ethnography, situational analysis uses mapping techniques to uncover the connections between material reality and discourse. Situational analysis builds on grounded theory in that it takes "the situation of inquiry itself" as the problematic versus "the main social processes–human action." In other words, situational analysis seeks to make the connections and disconnections visible between discursive positions and actors across time and space to uncover the voices of "implicated actors" (actors who are left out of public discourse on issues that affect their lives), and reveals the ways in which public discourse and social policy are shaped by the more privileged and powerful in society.

Lykes and Coquillon draw not only on conventional forms but also on nuanced forms of interpretive processes to re-present data. For instance in community-based research, researchers often seek out and cultivate relationships with "cultural interpreters" to assist in the difficult process of translating experiential meaning and ensure that indigenous knowledge is appropriately represented. These "interpreters" or "translators" become "the experts" because the researcher takes a back stage in the interpretive process. Similarly, Pillow and Mayo not only support active engagement by participants in the interpretative phase as well as throughout the research process but also draw attention to the political implications of choosing to write in the voice of oneself or "the other." In their chapter, Pillow and Mayo offer many examples of how feminists are grappling with this issue and creating innovative strategies and styles for re-presenting narratives.

## Fostering Social Justice and Social Change

Feminist research is committed to challenging power and oppression and producing research that is useful and contributes to social justice. It provides space for the exploration of broader questions of social justice because of the ways in which feminists have sought to address multiple forms of structural inequality, such as race, ethnicity, class, and sexuality, as well as gender. Research is political work and knowledge building is aimed at empowerment, action, and ultimately social transformation. Feminist research creates democratic spaces within the research process for cultivating solidarity and action. Feminist research "goes beyond documenting what is to proposing an alternative and imaginative vision of what should be" (Maguire, 1987, p. 104). For some, such as Lykes and Coquillon, this work translates into full, participatory studies that value local knowledge systems and support collective, community-based solutions to systems of inequality and oppression. For others, such as Smith, inquiry begins with people's everyday lives and experiences, reaches out and beyond the local, revealing the social processes that organize experience, and then comes full circle back to the origin of inquiry expanding local knowledge with a view toward change. Or for social movetment researchers such as Maddison, inquiry begins as they place the voices of activists at the center of research and provide space for the development of tools and strategies that can support social change. And for many others, such as Brisolara and Seigart, this work generates research that influences public discourse and challenges conventional assumptions that shape social policy. While diverse in approaches and aims, feminists are socially engaged, committed activists in their own disciplines and in society at large.

Creating safe spaces where counter hegemonic knowledge can be produced is the focus of Reinharz and Kulick's discussion on the emergence of "virtual, feminist communities." Advances in technology and an increase in cyber communication has created unique opportunities for feminists to "claim public spaces" and "disseminate knowledge," thereby generating places for building community and dialogue across borders. In these feminist communities, women are brought together across differences and national boundaries. Women can converse when their local public mediums have been heavily constricted, make connections, and exchange and develop resources. Cyber communication allows the quick transport of communications across the globe from sources that might not otherwise be heard. By building shared understandings and trust, this process can help foster identity building and a sense of solidarity. Reinharz and Kulick provide several examples of innovative feminist research that examines the possibilities and limits of knowledge building and activism in virtual feminist communities.

## THE POLITICS OF PRACTICING A FEMINIST PERSPECTIVE IN RESEARCH

Are there risks in labeling your project "feminist"? While DeVault and Gross find that feminist research is a well-accepted approach in their discipline, other authors in this section point to dilemmas feminist researchers have encountered in getting their work published or in obtaining funding. "Calling an evaluation a feminist evaluation is a political act," and Brisolara and Seigart argue that feminist evaluation researchers continue to have to defend their research on the grounds of such positivist ideals as objectivity, generalizability, and value-free bias. In many disciplines, feminist research continues to be criticized for its action and advocacy agenda, its attention to emotionality and participatory methods. Brisolara and Seigart state that funders do not want to be "construed as too radical" and worry about "maintaining a particular image in the community" so as not to jeopardize future financial support by more conservative donors. Funders sometimes choose concerns that more closely match their needs than the needs of the community. This raises important ethical questions about who has control over the research project, process, and outcomes. DeVault and Gross, along with Pillow and Mayo, caution researchers not only to consider the danger of "appropriation" and how material is disseminated and interpreted by various audiences but also to consider whether the data serve the population involved in the study. Although in most cases, the researcher has the ultimate authority over how and what data are collected, processed, and distributed, researchers can undertake reflexive practices to share interpretive authority with participants to ensure better representation. However, as Pillow and Mayo point out, reflexivity cannot eliminate authority and privilege because "there is no resolution to the problem of speaking for others" (Richardson, 1997, p. 58). Recognizing and balancing the tension between writing for and writing with is a measure of accountable research.

Risks to the researcher are not the only concerns in embarking on a feminist research project. Lykes and Coquillon express concern that feminist participatory action research runs the danger of exploitation and urges researchers to critically examine their roles in this process. It is the very bonds that are created in collaborative inquiry that can present dilemmas for feminist researchers (Lal, 1996; Stacey, 1991; Wasserfall, 1993). Examining one's social privileges and biases, overcoming cultural and language barriers, and shifting the center of power from researcher to community are some of the many tasks of the reflexive researcher. Lykes and Coquillon warn that researchers who engage in close, interactive relationships should be aware of the potential for participants to feel misunderstood, disappointed, or exploited if the research effort fails to meet their expectations. It requires great effort on the part of the researcher to continuously find ways to reflexively examine her or his positionality, relationships, and the research process to ensure that confidentiality and trust are upheld.

Feminist research, although gaining recognition in some disciplines, still remains at the margins of mainstream research. Debates continue as to the legitimacy of feminist research that is deemed "too subjective" or "not scientific." What is not recognized fully is that getting at subjugated knowledge oftentimes requires going beyond traditional methods, reaching out across the quantitative and qualitative divide as well as our own disciplinary boundaries. Feminist researchers embrace the full terrain of research techniques, incorporate new disciplinary tools in their work, and as needed forge emergent tools to gain a fuller picture of reality. To move feminist research from the "margins to the center," feminist scholars must push on the boundaries of what is considered "legitimate" (read "positivistic only") research. This will require the creation of a feminist research community of knowledge building that has as one of its goals the legitimizing of women's scholarship and research. As part of this process of community building, there also needs to be an internal dialogue, not debate, among the different and sometimes competing feminist epistemologies and methodologies. Where are the differences and similarities within this community? How do feminists deal with difference across their range of epistemologies and methodologies? What is/are the most productive way/s to raise the consciousness of the feminist research community as a whole in creating a viable force for contending with dominant research structures (see also Hesse-Biber & Leckenby, 2004)? This is the challenge, and we take up this challenge in Parts III and IV of the *Handbook*.

## REFERENCES

Campbell, Marie, & Gregor, Frances. (2002). *Mapping social relations: A primer in doing institutional ethnography.* Aurora, Ontario, Canada: Garamond.

Campbell, Marie, & Manicom, Ann. (Eds.). (1995). *Knowledge, experience, and ruling relations: Studies in the social organization of knowledge.* Toronto, Ontario, Canada: University of Toronto Press.

Charmaz, Kathy. (1995). Grounded theory. In Jonathan Smith, Rom Harre, & L. Van Langenhove (Eds.), *Rethinking methods in psychology* (pp. 27–49). Thousand Oaks, CA: Sage.

Charmaz, Kathy. (2000). Grounded theory: Objectivist and constructivist methods. In Norman K. Denzin & Yvonna S. Lincoln (Eds.), *Handbook of qualitative research* (pp. 509–535). Thousand Oaks, CA: Sage.

Coffey, Amanda, & Atkinson, Paul. (1996). *Making sense of qualitative data: Complementary research strategies.* Thousand Oaks, CA: Sage.

Collins, Patricia Hill. (2000). *Black feminist thought* (2nd ed.). New York: Routledge.

DeVault, Marjorie L. (1990). Talking and listening from women's standpoint. *Social Problems, 37,* 96–116.

DeVault, Marjorie L. (1999). *Liberating method: Feminism and social research.* Philadelphia: Temple University Press.

DeVault, Marjorie L., & McCoy, Liza. (2002). Institutional ethnography: Using interviews to investigate ruling relations. In Jaber Gubrium & James Holstein (Eds.), *Handbook of interview research* (pp. 751–776). Thousand Oaks, CA: Sage.

Dodson, Lisa. (1998). *Don't call us out of name: The untold lives of women and girls in poor America.* Boston: Beacon Press.

Eichler, Margrit. (1997). Feminist methodology. *Current Sociology, 45,* 9–36.

Fine, Michelle. (1998). Working the hyphens: Reinventing self and other in qualitative research. In Norman K. Denzin & Yvonna S. Lincoln (Eds.), *The landscape of qualitative research* (pp. 130–155). Thousand Oaks, CA: Sage.

Frankenberg, R. (1993). *White women, race matters: The social construction of Whiteness.* Minneapolis: University of Minnesota Press.

Glaser, Barney G., & Strauss, Anselm L. (1967). *The discovery of grounded theory: Strategies for qualitative research.* Chicago: Aldine.

Haraway, Donna. (1991). *Simians, cyborgs, and women.* New York: Routledge.

Harding, Sandra. (1986). *The science question.* New York: Cornell Press.

Harding, Sandra. (1987). *Feminism and methodology*. Bloomington: Indiana University Press.

Harding, Sandra. (1991). *Whose science, whose knowledge? Thinking from women's lives*. New York: Cornell Press.

Harding, Sandra. (Ed.). (1993). Rethinking standpoint epistemology: What is strong objectivity? In Linda Alcoff & Elizabeth Potter (Eds.), *Feminist epistemologies* (pp. 49–82). New York: Routledge.

Hartsock, Nancy. (1998). *The feminist standpoint revisited*. Boulder, CO: Westview.

Hesse-Biber, Sharlene Nagy, & Leckenby, Denise. (2004). How feminists practice social research. In Sharlene Nagy Hesse-Biber & Michelle L. Yaiser (Eds.), *Feminist perspectives on social research* (pp. 209–226). New York: Oxford University Press.

Jayaratne, Toby Epstein, & Stewart, Abigail J. (1991). Quantitative and qualitative methods in the social sciences: Current feminist issues and practical strategies. In Mary Margaret Fonow & Judith A. Cook (Eds.), *Beyond methodology* (pp. 85–106). Bloomington: Indiana University Press.

Lal, Jayati. (1996). Situating locations: The politics of self, identity, and other in living and writing the text. In Diane Wolf (Ed.), *Feminist dilemmas in fieldwork* (pp. 185–214). Boulder, CO: Westview.

Lather, Peggy, & Smithies, Chris. (1997). *Troubling the angels: Women living with HIV/AIDS*. Boulder, CO: Westview.

Longino, Helen. (1990). *Science as social knowledge: Values and objectivity in scientific inquiry*. Princeton, NJ: Princeton University Press.

Maguire, Patricia. (1987). *Doing participatory research*. Amherst: University of Massachusetts.

Mertens, Donna M. (2003). Mixed methods and the politics of human research: The transformative-emancipatory perspective. In Abbas Tashakkori & Charles Teddlie (Eds.), *Handbook of mixed methods in social and behavioral research* (pp. 297–319). Thousand Oaks, CA: Sage.

Mies, Maria. (1983). Towards a methodology for a feminist research. In G. Bowles & R. Duelli Klien (Eds.), *Theories of women's studies* (pp. 173–191). Boston: Routledge.

Oakley, Ann. (1981). Interviewing women: A contradiction in terms. In Helen Roberts (Ed.), *Doing feminist research* (pp. 30–61). London: Routledge & Kegan Paul.

Oakley, Ann. (1998). Gender, methodology and people's way of knowing: Some problems with feminism and the paradigm debate in social science. *Sociology, 32*(4), 707–731.

Reinharz, Shulamit. (1992). *Feminist methods in social research*. New York: Oxford University Press.

Richardson, Laurel. (1997). *Fields of play (constructing an academic life)*. New Brunswick, NJ: Rutgers University Press.

Smith, Dorothy. (1974). Women's perspective as a radical critique of sociology. *Sociological Inquiry, 44,* 7–13.

Smith, Dorothy. (1987). *The everyday world as problematic: A feminist sociology*. Boston: Northeastern University Press.

Smith, Dorothy. (1999). *Writing the social: Critique, theory, and investigations*. Toronto, Ontario, Canada: University of Toronto Press.

Smith, Dorothy. (2002). Institutional ethnography. In Tim May (Ed.), *Qualitative methods in action* (pp. 150–161). Thousand Oaks, CA: Sage.

Smith, George W. (1990). Political activist as ethnographer. *Social Problems, 37*(4), 629–648.

Sprague, Joey, & Zimmerman, Mary K. (1993). Overcoming dualisms: A feminist agenda for sociological methodology. In Paula England (Ed.), *Theory on gender* (pp. 255–280). New York: Aldine de Gruyter.

Stacey, Judith. (1991). Can there be a feminist ethnography? In Daphne Patai & Sherna B. Gluck (Eds.), *Women's words: The feminist practice of oral history* (pp. 111–120). New York: Routledge.

Stanley, Liz, & Wise, Sue. (1993). *Breaking out again: Feminist ontology and epistemology*. New York: Routledge.

Strauss, Anselm, & Corbin, Juliet. (2000). Grounded theory methodology: An overview. In Norman K. Denzin & Yvonna S. Lincoln (Eds.), *Handbook of qualitative research* (pp. 273–285). Thousand Oaks, CA: Sage.

Wasserfall, Rahel R. (1993). Reflexivity, feminism, and difference. *Qualitative Sociology, 16*(1), 23–50.

Wolf, Diane. (1996). Situating feminist dilemmas in fieldwork. In Diane Wolf (Ed.), *Feminist dilemmas in fieldwork* (pp. 1–55). Boulder, CO: Westview.

Wolf, Margery. (1992). *A thrice told tale: Feminism, postmodernism, and ethnographic responsibility*. Stanford, CA: Stanford University Press.

# 8

# Toward Understandings of Feminist Ethnography

Wanda S. Pillow
Cris Mayo

The task of defining feminist ethnography is daunting not only because attempting to define a field within a chapter feels inadequate but also because of the unique and unstable place of feminism and feminist theory today. Indeed some have declared that feminism is obsolete while others feel that feminism is irrelevant or too problematic in today's world. Is feminism still relevant? Does gender matter? Even those who respond to these questions affirmatively acknowledge that feminism and particularly what is presented as a Western feminist movement have come under heated debate and attacks—from within, for its own essentialism, nationalism, perpetuation of race and class inequities, and generational differences and from without, for its role in the national decline of moral values and breakdown of societal structures, including the "traditional" two-parent, male head of household family unit. Furthermore, many question the viability of feminism in today's increasingly global world, asking how feminism is possible when we acknowledge the range of differences among women. How does feminism hold up as a theoretical and political theory for women when the category of "woman" is necessarily complex because of the range of experiences of women?

How can there be a feminism that accounts for the myriad of ways women experience being woman differently across varying cultures and histories, and across markers of race, class, sexuality, and language?

Calls for feminism to be attentive to intersections of race, class, ethnicity, sexuality, disability, and gender have been around since feminism's beginnings, although certainly not always well manifested in dominant feminist groups. However, if we are not to retain feminism for its usefulness in naming and identifying the unique experiences of women, then what are we saying? While the challenges facing feminism in theory and praxis seem overwhelming, are we ready or able to *not* talk about gender? As Zillah Eisenstein (1994) succinctly states, "however differentiated gender may be, gender oppression exists" (p. 8), and until gender ceases to matter, feminism is necessary and correspondingly feminist research, including feminist ethnography, is necessary.

As we think about what it means to do feminist research, we assume that feminism entails a complex examination of the identity positions and community and cultural associations that structure the lives of variously gendered people. We take it as axiomatic that the vectors of difference mean that gender is constituted differently and differently understood and experienced according to context. As feminists, we also understand that while gender bias continues, in all its varied forms, so too gender advocacy needs to continue. In our examination of feminist methods of ethnography, we draw on an understanding that all forms of oppression operate simultaneously and that to address gender bias, all forms of bias must also be examined and challenged. We also understand that the intersectionality of identity means that women of color and/or of nondominant sexuality and/or with disabilities will experience gender as outsiders within, simultaneously understanding their gendered identity and also knowing that gender is imbricated in all other forms of identity.

Here, then, we use the term *feminist*, with an acknowledgment of its troublesome history and usages, because we need it. At present, feminism and feminist theory remains the only lens that specifically names and is reflexive about the politics and problematics of gender and that offers a means of analysis of the complicated ways gender, race, sexuality, class, and embodiment are distinct yet intertwined in dominant structures of power. While holding on to the term *feminist* to describe trends in feminist research, here specifically ethnography, we assume that such research attends to the processes and problems entailed by the concept of gender, foregrounding, for example, questions such as the following: How do we keep open the question not of what gender is but how it operates? How do we remain attentive to the complex interactions of identities that constitute gender? How do we understand gender as not necessarily inhering in "appropriate" bodies?

Thus, the feminist theory we speak of in this chapter is a feminism that recognizes the existence of a "racialized patriarchy" and points to the "continued interplay of race [class, sexuality] and gender in the structure of power" (Eisenstein, 1994, p. 3). As Patricia Hill Collins (1990) explains it,

> Intersectionality . . . highlights how African American women and other social groups are positioned within unjust power relations, but it does so in a way that introduces added complexity to formerly race-, class-, and gender-only approaches to social phenomena. The fluidity that accompanies intersectionality does not mean that groups themselves disappear, to be replaced instead by decontextualized, unique individuals whose personal complexity makes group-based identities . . . that emerge from group constructions impossible. Instead, the fluidity of boundaries operates as a new lens that potentially deepens understanding of how the actual mechanisms of institutional power can change dramatically even while they reproduce long-standing group inequalities of race, class, and gender. (p. 68)

While we argue that ethnography needs to be attentive to intersectionality and processes of gender constitution, we also emphasize that identity categories continue to have meaning for people, even as they critically understand how these categories operate. As de Beauvoir (1953) argues, if identities do not have essential characteristics, they also do not all simply melt into one another. For example, one is hard-pressed to explain that women are men. Identity categories, even when ascribed, do construct the lived experiences of those who inhabit those identities. De Beauvoir (1953) notes, "To decline to accept such notions as the eternal feminine, the black soul, the Jewish character does not represent a liberation for those concerned, but rather a flight from reality" (p. 12). In other words, there are aspects of ascribed identities that are pushed on groups and are oppressive, but there are other aspects of those identities that are useful to the groups themselves and may even be oppositional or opposed to oppression. Furthermore, when we think about intersectionality, we stress that all aspects of identity and community are not similarly arrayed along a leveled list: in a racist context, race will have more weight of meaning, experience, and politics; in a homophobic context, sexuality may trump gender, even though we might see that homophobia is constituted through gender bias.

Highlighting feminism's and feminist theory's necessary intersectionality both historically and at present, we explore the arena of feminist ethnography considering what makes feminist ethnography unique. We raise questions such as the following: Is there a feminist ethnography? What does it mean to call ethnography feminist? What does a feminist ethnography look like? Does feminist ethnography study different issues or study issues differently? Who can do feminist ethnography? While this chapter cannot or would not purport to provide answers to these questions (as the real work is in the asking and debating the above questions), we ask the reader to keep these questions in mind when reading the remainder of this chapter.[1] The above questions provide a basis for considering how feminist ethnography operates across what we here characterize as four stages of research: choosing, doing, analyzing/writing, and endings.[2] Using reflective notes and experiences from the ethnographic research of one of the authors, we explore what is uniquely feminist across each of these stages.[3]

To situate the discussion of the stages and data examples, we begin with a brief overview of the history, shifts, and debates in feminist ethnography and then take up these shifts and debates within each of the above stages. We conclude with consideration of where feminist ethnography is now poised and where it might be heading. As this chapter makes evident, it is one thing to say one will do a feminist ethnography and another to actually do it. We hope that the challenges involved in actually doing feminist ethnography are ones that will be taken up by those readers who are engaging with feminist theory and research and those who believe they will themselves be doing feminist ethnography.

## Introducing Feminist Ethnography

Defining what feminist research is cannot be separated from feminist theory's ontology and epistemology. Even the brief overview presented here of feminist ethnography's history reveals that issues that were key to feminist research in the 1970s—including relationships with subjects, and the politics of representation, reflexivity, and power—remain pertinent and foremost today. When considering how and why it is that these issues have remained pressing for feminist researchers, it is helpful to return to Sandra Harding's (1987) question, "Is there a feminist method?" Harding's response to this question is "no." Rather she argues that while methods (the way we collect our data, i.e., observations, interviews, surveys) are limited in scope (there are only so many tools we can use

to collect our data), our methodologies (lens of doing our research) and epistemologies (our knowledge base) are multiple. Feminism thus provides a methodological and epistemological lens for the carrying out of research methods. While there may not be distinct feminist methods, there are feminist methodologies and epistemologies that affect our use of methods. That is, the method may be changed or altered by the lens with which the researcher approaches the methods, as in the case of, for example, feminist interviewing. In short, how we do our methods is influenced by feminist methodologies and epistemologies, and which methodologies and epistemologies we use matters when we do research (Pillow, 2003a). This is an acknowledgement that what we study, analyze, and write, and how we study, analyze, and write is integrally connected to our methodological and theoretical lens.[4]

Shulamit Reinharz (1992) provides an excellent and thorough overview of feminist research in the social sciences in which she states that feminist theory and research is about "questions of identity (what are feminist research methods?) and of *difference* (what is the difference between feminist research methods and other research methods; how do feminist research methods differ from one another?)" (p. 3). Reinharz reviews a variety of methods feminist researchers use and how their use is altered by feminist theory and practice. Or using Harding's definitions above, Reinharz considers how methods of research are changed by encounters with feminist methodologies and epistemologies. Reinharz notes that research methods are always conducted within and against past and present methods and includes a review of feminist uses of interviewing, ethnography, oral history, content analysis, case studies, action research, survey and statistical research, and mixed/multiple methods. Reinharz's review and Harding's negative response to the question of whether there is a feminist method widens the arena of what is typically thought of as feminist methods. Whereas early feminist researchers argued that interviewing is the only method of feminist research, Reinharz and Harding make the case that feminists may engage in and use multiple methods for their research. What is important is *how* research is conducted and to what purpose.

For example, feminist research according to Reinharz is focused on analyzing and understanding gender within the context of lived experiences, is committed to social change, and is committed to challenging thinking about researcher subjectivity and the relationship between the researcher and the researched. Applying Reinharz's characterization of feminist research, in general, to ethnography identifies several trends in feminist ethnography. To understand the relationship between feminist theory and ethnography, it is helpful to review the climate in which the work of feminist ethnography has been conducted.

Similar to waves of feminist thought and action (Nicholson, 1997), feminist ethnography has developed and changed through key shifts in social theory and political social action. Furthermore, the field and arena of qualitative research and ethnography as a whole have affected thinking about feminist ethnography. For instance, Denzin and Lincoln (2005) identify what they describe as "eight moments" of qualitative research delineating a history of key shifts, key "moments," in the arena of qualitative research, including ethnography. These moments include traditional, modernist, blurred genres, crisis of representation, and postmodern period, with postexperimental, methodologically contested present and future moments representing the sixth, seventh, and eighth moments.

In Denzin and Lincoln's model, feminist research and ethnography rises in importance in the third moment of blurred genres, a moment that "blurs" lines between the humanities and social sciences and science and ethnography. Feminist research is also integral to the fourth moment marked by a perceived crisis of representation in qualitative research and ethnography—a moment that calls into question the ability of the researcher to represent raising critical questions about researcher authority, identity, and the ethics of representation. This moment is highlighted by attentiveness, which some find paralyzing, to the politics of the gaze in ethnographic research. Who is recording whom, why, and how became integral to ethnographic writings and led to a rise of researcher confessionals and practices of reflexivity in ethnographic writing. Questions of representation and practices of reflexivity are integral to

feminist ethnography where attentions to the specificities of identity and power relations are primary to the research methodologically and epistemologically.

Similarly, feminist research and ethnography have been integral to shifts and debates within what Denzin and Lincoln describe as the postmodern and future moments of research. As is apparent in the above description of feminist research, feminist ethnography begins from a different place than traditional ethnography; a place that questions the power, authority, and subjectivity of the researcher as it questions the purposes of the research (Oakley, 1981). Feminist ethnography has thus often initiated and influenced new ways of thinking about engaging in research and ethnographic writing. The specific contributions and questions raised by feminist ethnographers in postmodern research and future moments of research are raised at the end of this chapter, but it is important to highlight again here that consistent across feminist ethnography is a focus on gender and its intersectionalities as central to the praxis and theory of research. This emphasis is evident precisely because a history of ethnographic traditions left out, ignored, or essentialized gender, both in terms of those who produce feminist ethnography and in terms of the study of gender.

The absence of feminist productions of ethnography was made apparent by a 1986 volume, *Writing Culture: The Poetics and Politics of Ethnography,* edited by two well-known anthropologists, James Clifford and George Marcus. *Writing Culture* signaled a crisis in representation in ethnographic writing and called for a new self-awareness to the discipline, but the volume excluded and ignored feminist ethnographic writing, including only one feminist writer—a literary critic, not an ethnographer. Although calling for a "new ethnography" that would investigate and make visible power and truth relations through the writing of ethnographies that are more dialogical, experimental, and reflexive, *Writing Culture* did not acknowledge the work and contributions of feminist writers to this agenda. Justifying this exclusion, Clifford and Marcus (1986) declared that the absence of feminist writing in the volume was because those women anthropologists who they determined had made contributions to ethnographic writing "had not done so on feminist grounds," while feminist ethnographers who had worked to challenge the canon of ethnography had not "produced either unconventional forms of writing or a developed reflection on ethnographic textuality as such" (pp. 21–22).

As Ruth Behar and Deborah Gordon (1995) note, "To be a woman writing culture became a contradiction in terms: Women who write experimentally are not feminist enough, while women who write as feminists write in ignorance of the textual theory that underpins their own texts" (p. 5). Furthermore, Behar and Gordon note that the "innovative" practices written of in *Writing Culture*—reflexivity, use of personal voice, attention to textuality of the written text—were "undermined when used by women" yet "given the seal of approval in men's ethnographic accounts" (p. 4). Behar and Gordon's (1995) edited volume, *Women Writing Culture*, can be read as a feminist response to *Writing Culture*, but the authors were also influenced by the initial 1981 publication of *This Bridge Called My Back*, edited by Cherrie Moraga and Gloria Anzaldúa. *This Bridge* challenged and opened up what feminist issues, subjects, and writings are, and as Behar and Gordon (1995) state, "*This Bridge* thrust a different kind of arrow into the heart of feminist anthropology—it made us rethink the ways in which First World women had unself-consciously created a cultural other in their images of 'Third World' or 'minority' women" (p. 6). In this way, Behar and Gordon point out that feminist ethnography was forced to "come home," to focus on its own assumptions, its own agendas. *This Bridge* further signified a shift/crisis for ethnography and feminist ethnography questioning who has the right to write culture for whom and grappling with what it means to write and write ethnography from a "native" perspective. The issues, questions, and crisis raised by *Writing Culture*, *Women Writing Culture*, and *This Bridge* have shaped feminist ethnography, and the challenges raised in these publications remain key to ethnography today.

Similar to the above brief review of anthropology's tense relationship with feminist productions of ethnography, the ethnographic study of gender also is a history of absences, tensions, and shifts. For example, the 1960s and 1970s experienced a growing momentum of interest in the study of cultural perspectives in education. This new perspective, often termed the *new sociology,* worked against traditional positivistic education theory and questioned the accepted hierarchical structure of knowledge (Acker, 1992). Both Freire's (1970) and Willis's (1977) work focused on studying the "underprivileged" and the working class. While such theorists introduced issues of patriarchy and agency, gender differences were not considered of major importance and, therefore, were not explicitly explored. When gender was included as a unit of analysis, it was often as an add-on to a list of other social indicators. Much of the existing research on women centered on a female as a deficit model—research that studied women from the perspective of men as the norm.

Feminist research seeking to refute the prevailing woman as deficit model placed women at the center, emphasized the "personal as political," and sought to improve the situation of women by giving voice to women's experiences focusing on women's own interpretations of their experiences (Belenky, Clinchy, Goldberger, & Tarule, 1986; Gilligan, 1982; Leck, 1987; Statham, Richardson, & Cook, 1991). This research worked from and further reinforced the necessity of feminist theory and practice and sought to identify "women's ways of knowing"—finding, naming, and reclaiming common characteristics across women's experiences and ways of being. Much of this research affirmed and "proved" what was already believed about women—that women are, for example, more relational, more empathetic in their relationships, personal or professional, with others. However, feminist theorists soon found that such markers of womanhood could continue to oppress women (e.g., if women are innately more caring, then they are best suited for careers in the caring professions and not for technical or tactical careers). Facing this problematic, a new wave of feminist researchers sought to resist binary, essentialized notions of understanding gender while still placing women at the center of their research. For example, Barrie Thorne's research complicated the recovery of "women's ways of knowing," by showing the processes by which "children act, resist, rework, and create" gender (Thorne, 1993, p. 3). By shifting from an analysis that assumes the salience of gender to one that examines the where and when of gender salience, Thorne gives us a way to understand when gender is open to contestation, when it recedes from importance, and when it is a crucial site for meaning making.

This shift from the purpose of feminist research being to identify a set of characteristics common to the category of women to research that seeks to understand gender as performative and further understand this performativity as altered by intersections with race, sexuality, class, and embodiment has led to a wealth of feminist ethnography exploring and rethinking the intersections of gender, race, class, and embodiment (Davies, 1989; Evans-Winters, 2005; Miranda, 2003; Moraga, 1997; Patai, 1988; Walkerdine, 1990). Angela McRobbie's (2000) *Feminism and Youth Culture* raises an interesting methodological example. While McRobbie initially situated her work within a cultural studies framework that emphasized social class, she later came to understand gender as operating separately from, though overlapping with, class. Her reanalysis of her work also raises nondominant sexuality as an initially underexamined part of her findings, and her critical engagement with her own work provides a model for research reflexivity and shows how reworking one's lens of analysis raises the complexities already immanent in the experiences of the young women she studied.

For example, of three young women who were crucially important to her work on punk subculture, McRobbie (2000) says, "They were drawn to lesbianism but disliked radical feminism and separatism, nor were they keen on the way in which feminism appeared to dictate on how women should look, and on the antifashion ethos of that moment in feminist politics" (pp. 6–7). In other words, her research subjects were already enacting a gender/sexuality critique of feminist ideology, but because her work was not centrally involved in gender, she did not initially highlight the gendered components of the punk subculture in the same way she might have had her lens included gender. Even in the context of discussing class, her work does challenge expectations about gender. Countering prevailing beliefs about the dominance of heterosexuality to young girls' lives, she argues that researchers have been mistaken in assuming that all girl spaces are spaces of last resort. She

notes, in a discussion of girls at a youth center organizing discos that only attracted girls, that this practice of single-gender dancing—even for part of the evening—has a long history. From the dance halls of the 1920s, where according to historians the disappointed, unchosen girls would dance with one another as a last resort, to the high school dances of contemporary times where girls begin dancing with one another and then have boys cut in, girls are often more comfortable with one another. Or at least they find comfort in one another, failing in their ability to attract a man. The distinction is important, but one problem with research on girls is that it is clear that researchers often assume that when girls are together, they are disappointed.

In contrast, McRobbie (2000) points to the ways in which single-gender spaces allow girls more room to engage in cultural production. For instance, McRobbie describes girls at a disco, noting, "They did not feel self-conscious about dancing, nor did they need to adopt their more usual defensive strategies. In fact this was the one occasion when all the barriers were down. The girls were immersed in what was a thoroughly enjoyable activity" (p. 62). Still, they are also thinking about what it would be like if there were boys present, knowing that boys would think dancing was "cissy" or would need to "be drunk before they'd dance" (p. 63). At the very least, the girls are of two minds—or two desires—about the boys. As she explains it, "The features mentioned above point to a series of anomalies or contradictions within girls' culture. While many of their concerns and interests were focused on boys and sexuality, in practice, they set themselves apart from the boys. The reality of boys belonged to a later stage. This might be only a matter of months, but in the meantime a much more cohesive female culture based on friendship groups prevailed" (p. 64). McRobbie's reflections on her earlier work points to how even feminist ethnography can unknowingly replicate dominant constructions of gender, race, sexuality, and class.

McRobbie's reexamination and critical reflection on her own earlier writing represents a continued attentiveness to methodology in feminist ethnography. Despite shifts in moments or waves of feminist research and ethnography, the characteristics of feminist research that Reinharz describes remain prevalent and present in current ethnographic practices and writings. Recall that what is key across feminist research and feminist ethnography is a commitment to studying the "lived experiences" of gender and its intersectionalities resulting in theory that is built from these lived experiences. This changed relationship with research in addition to a commitment to doing research responsibly and doing research that will be beneficial for women breaks down binaries between theory and praxis, the researcher and the researched, and objectivity and subjectivity. The importance of such challenges to the dualities of research will become apparent as we turn to discussion of the unique purposes and practices of feminist ethnography through four "stages" of research: choosing, doing, analysis/writing, and endings. Specifically, issues of representation, voice, and power as manifested in the interplay of research relationships and reflexivity are situated as key across all the presented stages of ethnography.

## PURPOSES AND PRACTICES OF FEMINIST ETHNOGRAPHY: CHOOSING

The first decision the ethnographer faces is what to research. This first step raises questions of what is a feminist topic. Or rather, what is not a feminist topic? Can any issue be studied as a feminist ethnography? The above discussion of common characteristics of feminist research and the necessary intersectionality of feminist research situates the topic of the research perhaps as less important than how one approaches and does research. Yet despite the idea that any topic or issue can be a feminist issue of study, most feminist ethnographers are doing what may be thought of as "women's work"—asking and investigating questions about what is typically and normatively assigned as being a women's issue. This work in addition to attempting to fill in the gaps and silences surrounding the dailiness of women's lives and experiences is often reclaiming work—work that focused on making visible the experiences of women and rethinking these experiences through critical analyses of gendered power relations. For example, Mary Leach's (1997) reclamation of gossip, an "activity in which we all engage, an activity where women have been historically and

particularly implicated," speaks to a "*female feminist specificity*" that while working toward a redefining of the subject of feminism adds a "specific gender inflection resulting in the political and epistemological project of asserting difference in a nonhierarchical manner, refusing to disembody and therefore desexualize a vision of the subject."

There is a move in this work not only to pay attention to gender but also again, as Leach (1997) notes, to work through and validate a "female feminist specificity" while working to "interrupt a singular version" of identity (MacLure, 1997, p. 316). Feminist ethnography also moves into private spaces and seemingly trivial topics to upset the usual regime of spectacularity that may guide research. In her ethnography, Valerie Hey (1997) notes that "girls 'being rather personal' was treated with indifference except when girls' absorption with each other erupted into passionate fallouts. Then girls were viewed as 'dangerous'" (p. 5). Hey's ruminations on what it means to do research on intimate relations among girls also problematizes her entrance into their private spaces. As she points out, the spaces of her research were often places organized by girls to keep adults and other outsiders at bay. In other words, while feminism does push us to examine and research the dailiness of everyday life, following the common refrain of "the personal is political," the very ways in which we do research alter the character of these spaces. Not only do we as researchers change the interactions of our subjects by our presence, but we also change the character of the spaces: Our presence makes private spaces public or, at the very least, highlights the political and public character of seemingly private spaces, an issue we discuss further in the following section on "doing" ethnography.

Fonow and Cook (1991) note that key to feminist ethnography is a "tendency to use already given situations both as the focus of investigation and as a means of collecting data" (p. 11). Fonow and Cook argue that feminist approaches to research are thus necessarily more creative, spontaneous, and open to improvisation, stumbling across the unexpected and being willing to follow where the unexpected leads. Such an approach yields research with a focus on the everyday world, on the lived experiences close at hand to us as researchers, and often results in the researcher feeling like the research found her or him rather than the researcher choosing the research.

Researching in this way often means that the research will be changed from what the researcher expected (Delgado-Gaitan, 1993; Pillow, 2004) and has also resulted in an opening of researchers studying what is close to them, in terms of identity or interest, and discussing their own role and subjectivity as outsiders/within in such research. Traditionally, it was not viewed as valid to study a topic "too close" to one's identity or interest; being too similar to one's research subjects was assumed to invalidate the research. Feminist research challenged this mode of thinking, pointing out how much under such a model goes unresearched, unwritten. Now, it is quite common to find that researchers are studying subjects like themselves, and indeed we may be facing the opposite problem now in terms of expecting that we now have to look like our research subjects (Pillow, 2003a).

Researchers who study community or identity groups they "come from," "belong to," or "identify with" are often referred to as "outsiders/within" (Collins, 1991; Johnson-Bailey, 1999)—researchers who seemingly have access to a setting or subjects because of their own identity (e.g., an African American woman interviewing African American teen girls or a lesbian woman interviewing other lesbian women) or because of their own shared experiences (a former teen mother interviewing a young teen mother). While such researchers often refer to and use what Delgado Bernal (1998) terms a shared "cultural intuition," these researchers also note the unique challenges, and limits of researching on one's own identity/community. For example, Sofia Villenas (1996, 2000) critically reflects on her role as a researcher of Latina mothers, noting that while her own identity as a Latina mother should have seemingly situated her as in "insider," her role as a graduate student and her access to the privilege and power associated with access to higher education situated her as an outsider and colonizer of these women.

The lived status as outsiders/within also, however, provides a unique lens of analysis. Ethnographers who find themselves to be "insiders/outsiders" or "outsider/within" in their research face unique, conflicting, and productive issues; issues faced by all researchers—issues of relationships, reciprocity, representation, and power—are heightened in research settings where one identifies with or is perceived to be a part of the research site or subjects (Chaudhry, 2000; Delgado Bernal, 1998; Kondo, 1990; Talburt, 2000; Villenas, 2000; Visweswaran, 1994). For example, Villenas's own understandings and lived experiences as a racialized Latina likely allow her to gain the level of critically reflexive insight that she brings to her work. Similarly, Collins (1991) argues that the history of race and power in the United States has provided "a special standpoint on self, family, and society for Afro-American women" (p. 35). The writings of women who experience and live under and with the intersections of simultaneous oppression of race, gender, class, and sexuality lend vital understandings of political reality and provide a vital theoretical lens of analysis for feminist ethnography (Anzaldúa, 1987; Collins, 1990; Davis, 1981; hooks, 1981, 1984; Lorde, 1984; Moraga & Anzaldúa, 1983; Smith, 1983; Walker, 1974). How researchers change and are changed when faced with these conditions is further addressed below. Regardless of whether we choose our research or feel that our research chooses us, the choosing of research is closely related to how we actually "do" research.

## PURPOSES AND PRACTICES OF FEMINIST ETHNOGRAPHY: DOING

Is there something uniquely different that occurs when one is doing feminist ethnography? Recall that Reinharz (1992) and Fonow and Cook (1991) note that commitment to action/change and attention to relationships with subjects is key to feminist research. Further practices of reflexivity—of researchers reflecting, critically examining, and exploring the nature of the research process—is key to feminist methodology. In this section we focus on these two issues—relationships and reflexivity—considering the contributions and practices of feminist theory to the doing of feminist ethnography.

What does it mean to have a "feminist" relationship with research subjects? While feminist theory would suggest that feminist research should be reciprocal, another response to this question is that thinking, reflecting, and writing about relationships with subjects is a feminist task. In other words, the attention to and concern about relationships with subjects—including concerns about issues of reciprocity, representation, and voice—is uniquely feminist. Writing and sharing how ethnographers experience their research, how ethnographers do their work—with all the good and the bad—works against naming the relational aspects of research as illogical or invalid, and makes visible the questions, complexities, and processes of doing research. Fortunately, several feminist ethnographers have taken up this task, exploring the complexities of their own and their subjects' identities and positionings (Abu-Lughod, 1992; Chaudhry, 2000; Delgado-Gaitan, 1993; Kondo, 1990; Trinh, 1989; Villenas, 1996, 2000; Visweswaran, 1994).

Reading the above examples reveals that there is not one response to what a feminist relationship with research subjects should be because feminist ethnography may range from the researcher being an observer, to a participant observer, to full collaborator. Finding a balance as an observer and a participant—when to wear the researcher hat and when to become involved by giving your opinion, providing help, or actively leading a project—is difficult and specific to each research context. Furthermore, as Wax (1971) argues, having successful or unsuccessful relationships with subjects is not something that can be taught, instructed, rehearsed, or measured— rather the relationships must be experienced, and we may often find we are unprepared for what we experience in the research setting.

For example, Delgado-Gaitan (1993) discusses how she became more involved with her research subjects than she ever imagined or ever thought was "right." As Delgado-Gaitan entered her research setting, she found that her research protocol did not fit the needs of the subjects she met. The longer she was in the field, the more the design and intent of her study became less important and shifted according to the subjects' needs. For Delgado-Gaitan, these shifts were impossible for her to avoid—she came to feel that ethically she had to change her research as she questioned her privilege and the doing of her research over the explicit needs of the

people she was studying. Delgado-Gaitan further notes that as much as the research question and process changed, she too was changed by the changing nature of her research. Her relationships to subjects, her relationships to research, and her relationships to methods were all affected and changed by the changing of the research. Delgado-Gaitan's experiences acknowledge that research relationships can be reciprocal and not simply one-way; that indeed the researcher may find herself more "changed" by the research than the subjects themselves.

Yet how much involvement with subjects is too much? What is ethical here? As we move from research to advocacy, are we still doing research? In the midst of working with Latina/o parents seeking work with school personnel to improve the educational conditions for their children, my colleagues and I began attending parent-teacher conferences at parents' request (Mayo, Candela, Matusov, & Smith, in press). Initially, we were engaged in taking field notes and engaging in discussions with parents and children afterward, but as school personnel began to use disrespectful language, we increasingly engaged with parents directly before meetings, making sure that our interventions were discussed ahead of time and responded to parental concerns. As our experience with parents grew and we learned from experienced parents to watch for particular maneuvers from school personnel (principals who couldn't be found at the scheduled time of the meeting, teachers who would address only weaknesses of students, personnel who refused to make appointments that didn't involve parents' missing work, etc.), parents and researchers all knew how to forestall the problematics encountered in other meetings. In other words, our collaboration and education about advocacy from parents enabled us to change the character of our research setting as well as ensure that positive outcomes for children were part of our research goal. Rather than taking detailed notes of school disrespect of Latina/o parents and students, we worked together with parents to prevent it. At the same time, we also recognized that it was largely our presence as researchers that was effecting the change.

While race, ethnicity, and language issues were the dominant vectors of oppression and disrespect, there were gendered components to the schools' relationship with the students. Teachers tended to criticize young Latinas for having too many friends or spending too much time with their cousins. Essentially, girls were characterized as too social or too family oriented to take school seriously. Latino boys, in contrast, were accused by teachers of being violent and/or too disrespectful of teachers' authority to be good students. As a result of these distinctions, boys' failure was considered to be a problem that needed intervention from school personnel (moving to special classes, expulsion, and then shifting to programs for students at risk), whereas girls' failure was largely ignored. In one case, a Latina's ability to pass as male further complicated all the overlapping biases we had encountered, and parents began important conversations on the need to respect all genders and sexualities in their community, a situation made easier because of the ethnocentric bias of the school that was subtending the school's homophobic/transphobic response to the problems the passing girl was having (while she did pass as male, her preferred pronoun was female). The reciprocity between researchers and researched, then, opened all our understandings to the complexity of the research situation and also pushed us to be sure that our research had a positive effect on the school experiences of the children involved.

In addition to researchers who note how their research focus and emphasis is changed according to the relational needs of those in the research setting, a review of feminist ethnography also identifies a concerted focus on methodology—the hows and whys of the research. Many feminist ethnographers engage in continual negotiations of and explicit reflections about power relations and the specific ways gender and power work in our research. Such authors engage in a continual reflexive critique of their own gaze. This "draw(s) into view unarticulated assumptions and expectations that operate silently within one's theories" (Ferguson, 1993, p. ix); Ferguson goes on to argue that "poking and prodding" around within our theories and our positionalities are "significant feminist tasks" (p. ix).

For instance, in Mayo's (2005) research on gay-straight alliances, it became less than clear exactly who was gay and who was straight in these groups. As researchers somewhat used to particular generationally specific definitions of sexual orientation, visits to school dances troubled our understandings of what counts as gayness or straightness. Having noted that we saw no more than the usual same-gender flirting and slow dancing, we wondered what the usual amount of same gender attraction was. The research question began to shift from "who are queer people in high school and what kinds of spaces do they make" to "how straight are 'straight' girls?" (p. 2). On the one hand, we found substantial same-gender flirting among girls, but not as much among boys (and most of the boys doing same-gender flirting were out as young gay men already). On the other hand, we also found a lack of imagination about what it would be like to be a young queer person—some of the same girls flirting with one another had no sense of same-sex attraction as a possibility prior to high school and no clear idea about how young queer people might organize their lives in the face of "default" heterosexuality. In other words, while student activities challenged our understandings of the relationship between straightness and queerness, the girls nonetheless evinced a lack of understanding of queer experiences of coming out, forming oppositional communities, being in the closet, and so on.

Part of feminist research, then, is looking at what is missing, what is passed over, and what is avoided. In a gay-straight alliance beginning to discuss sexualities, we observed a young black woman attempt to raise race as an issue for the group to consider. First, she suggested a T-shirt design that would advocate for diversity. A white group member, citing her anger at an administration attempt to change the group's name from "gay straight alliance" to "diversity club," argued it would be against the group's decision to decide its own name. The next time the young black woman suggested that the group think about race was in a suggestion that they also attend an alliance that discussed African American culture and literature. She was met with silence. Although the group had just been sharing racial and ethnic family stories, she was the only African American engaged in the conversation and the only person whose comment went unanswered.

What is the role and responsibility of the researcher in this situation? Should the researcher intervene and direct conversation or allow the "natural" group dynamics to continue. Again, there is no one right feminist response to such questions. Feminist researchers have written about both the necessity and the dangers of being involved in proactive ways in the research setting (Fonow & Cook, 1991; Stacey, 1988). Reflexivity then becomes necessary as a way to think through the problematics of attempting to do feminist research. Reflexivity under feminism is not only about investigating the power embedded in one's research but also about doing research differently. The need to do research differently arises from the ethical and political problems and questions raised by feminists about traditional research methods (Oakley, 1981). These questions include the following: How to be a nonexploitative researcher? How to produce research that is useful and empowering to women? How to make research that is linked with political action? Feminist research points out that there are multiple places for reflexivity to work and work differently in the research process. We discuss reflexivity further in the following section.

## PURPOSES AND PRACTICES OF FEMINIST ETHNOGRAPHY: ANALYZING AND WRITING

Is there a feminist method of analyzing data? Of writing? Analyzing data cannot be separate from data collection and writing. Feminists have claimed that writing and choosing how to tell the stories of our research are political acts as well as places of responsibility—as we code, theme, and imagine our data chapter, we are in essence writing and constructing our text (Richardson, 1994). As Richardson (1997) explains, "deciding on my narrative voice was more than a literary and theoretical problem. It was a political issue" (p. 21).

A review of ethnographies finds that feminist researchers are paying attention to *how* they write as well as what they write. *Women Writing Culture* makes apparent the "particular challenges that ethnographic writing has posed for women authors" (Behar & Gordon, 1995, p. 12), and since that publication, many women writers

have taken up theses challenges and explored and experimented with a variety of writing and narrative styles as well as a variety of textual styles. Ranging from ethnography written as fiction, as poetry, as play to texts that are interrupted with split texts and visual elements to disrupt the eye and mind, these works seek not simply to perform something different but to "better understand the politics of representation, how different narrative strategies may be authorized at specific moments in history by complex negotiations of community, identity, and accountability" (Visweswaran, 1994, p. 15).

Michelle Fine (1991) provides her reader with storylike thick descriptions at the introduction of her ethnography "*Framing Dropouts*"; Laurel Richardson (1997) writes of her research as "fields of play" (but she also turns the phrase to "play the field"); Kamala Visweswaran (1994) makes the nuances of her writing visible in her texts to expose the politics of representation and impossibilities of representation; Patti Lather and Chris Smithies (1997) embrace the split text interspersed with angel artifacts in their book on women living with HIV/AIDS; St. Pierre (1997) writes of being a nomadic armchair ethnographer deterritorializing data through "asides" (p. 370) and "stopovers" (p. 371); James Sanders (1999) writes his data as a play with characters, backdrops, sound effects, and props. These writers are pushing the edges and boundaries of what ethnographic writing is, looks like, and yields. In a different vein, reading some ethnographies can leave the reader feeling as if she or he has learned more about the researcher than about the subjects or topic at hand. For example, in Ruth Linden's (1992) and Dorinne Kondo's (1990) work we learn as much about these women as researchers as we do their subjects. Other ethnographies become ethnographies of the self (Moraga, 1997), while others explore their own hybridity and identities in the writing of their research (Abu-Lughod, 1992; Chaudhry, 2000; Villenas, 1996; Visweswaran, 1994).

Yet it is not simply textual styles or formats that mark certain ethnographic writing as feminist, but rather the methodology behind the method. As Visweswaran (1994) reminds us, "fiction, as we know, is political" (p. 15). No textual experimentation removes the fact that we are writing "about"—whether it is about others or ourselves or ourselves/others. As Richardson (1997) argues, "Whoever writes for/about/of whatever is using authority and privilege," and there is "no resolution to the problem of speaking for others" (p. 58) even in the speaking of ourselves.

One way feminist ethnographers approach issues of representation, authority, and power in their research is reflexivity. According to Anderson (1989), reflexivity involves a dialectical process consisting of the researcher's constructs, the informants' commonsense constructs, the research data, the researcher's ideological biases, and the structural and historical forces that shaped the social construction under study. Denzin (1997) identifies five types of reflexivity in use in qualitative research: methodological, intertextual, standpoint, queer, and feminist reflexivity (pp. 218–223). Fonow and Cook (1991) define the "role of reflexivity as a source of insight" defining relflexivity as the "tendency . . . to reflect upon, examine critically, and explore analytically the nature of the research process" (p. 2). While reflexivity necessarily occurs through the research process, reflexivity remains integral to feminist practices of writing ethnography.

Pillow (2003b), however, cautions against using reflexivity as simply a validated strategy to have "better data" and better ethnographic accounts. She traces how as reflexivity has moved into the mainstream of ethnography it is often used as a tool to demonstrate the validity and truthfulness of research instead of committing to, as Fonow and Cook describe, critical analysis of the "nature of the research process." Reviewing four practices of reflexivity that can be problematic—reflexivity as recognition of self, reflexivity as recognition of other, reflexivity as truth, and reflexivity as transcendence—Pillow argues for what she calls a "reflexivity of discomfort" (p. 187). Reflexivity of discomfort makes the work of reflexivity visible and interrupts the ethnographer's desire to know, to name, to claim, asserting that not knowing is often as powerful as knowing.

Reflexive accounts by "native" ethnographers have further challenged processes of writing ethnography. As *This Bridge* powerfully made apparent, analysis and writing are often changed when produced by those who were

once or remain the colonized and those who were once or remain the objects of the ethnographic gaze. Villenas (2000) explores the complexities of doing feminist ethnography noting,

> As a Xicana and indigenous woman, I cannot escape my own experiences of marginalization and dislocation . . . at the same time, I cannot escape the privilege afforded to me as a university professor. Yet precisely because we are not the same "we" anthropologists, our interrogations, revelations, and vulnerabilities in a feminist praxis generate intriguing insights and creations. (pp. 75–76)

Ethnographers like Villenas and Visweswaran note that "insider" status is never truly insider, yet they are also not "insiders" to the historical production of knowledge in the academy and to the construction of ethnographic writing. The tension that exists when those who were/are objects of the gaze not only return but also rewrite this gaze is central to feminist research and feminist ethnography and changes the types of conversations, discussions, and theories produced in ethnographic texts.

## PURPOSES AND PRACTICES OF FEMINIST ETHNOGRAPHY: ENDINGS

Given how feminist researchers engage in their research—with attention to relationships, reciprocity, representation, and voice—how does one "end" the research? When is our research concluded—when we leave the field; when we write; when we complete the article, dissertation, or book? Perhaps as the previous example from McRobbie's (2000) work demonstrates, we do not ever leave our research; perhaps it is never ended as we continue to reflect on our actions and interpretations. Thus, the question becomes *can one end* rather than *how one ends* the research.

These questions have both pragmatic and methodological/theoretical implications, and an overview of feminist ethnographies finds researchers struggling with these questions (Evans-Winters, 2005; Fine, 1991; Kondo, 1990; Miranda, 2003; Villenas, 2000; Visweswaran, 1994). Making the often invisible and taken-for-granted process of completing one's fieldwork visible as ethical and methodological issues arising from feminist understandings of power, relationships, and responsibility in qualitative research is a feminist act.

Thus, while an overview of ethnographies that talk about "endings" will provide examples of continuing relationships with subjects past the official research time to provision of some service or product to those who were subjects, most researchers remark that ending our research is as complex and problematic as the doing of it. Is there a way to "end" research responsibly? There is not a set answer to this question—each researcher needs to find her or his own way through the process of endings. The endings will be based on how one was "doing" research and how connected and involved the researcher was with subjects in the research.

However, this focus on endings should not overinflate the role and importance of the researcher. While the researcher may feel deeply embedded in and a part of the research setting, the fact is this place and people were operating without the researcher before she or he arrived and will continue to function without the researcher. Rosalie Wax (1971) found that not even an extended length of time in the field can be an assumption of intimacy. After publishing a book based on her and her husband's many years living in and studying an American Indian community, Wax was informed that the consensus among the community readers of her book was, "If we had known this was the kind of book those white people were going to write, we would *really* have talked to you" (p. 248).

Thus, while we can talk about practices of responsible ethnographic endings (easing out of the researcher relationship over time, providing continued support as desired by subjects, sharing writing with subjects or cowriting with subjects), what again remains key is the researcher's own awareness and reflexivity about power relations in the research setting and the researcher's own acknowledgment of her or his own positionalities in the research and research setting.

## FEMINIST RESEARCH SITUATED AT THE "RUINS OF FEMINIST ETHNOGRAPHY"

What is the state and place of feminist ethnography today? Where are the possible futures of feminist ethnography? Some of the most interesting work in feminist ethnography is situated, as Lather and Smithies (1997) state, "in a feminist poststructural problematic of accountability to stories that belong to others . . . and how to tell such stories in a way that attends to the crisis of representation" (p. 286). Echoing Judith Stacey, they find that feminist researchers are working out of and with "the ruins of feminist ethnography" (p. 286)—that is, working out of the ruins of interpretive and postmodern turns that no-longer allow us to situate feminist ethnography as "innocent in its desire to give voice to the voiceless" (p. 286). Feminist researchers take on the methodological and epistemological paradoxes of "knowing through not knowing, knowing both too little and too much" (p. 286) and attempt to address Kamala Visweswaran's (1994) question, "How does one act knowing what one does?" (p. 80).

Furthermore, as Visweswaran notes, "with the loss of ethnographic authority, the subjects about whom we write now write back, and in so doing pose us as anthropological fictions" (p. 9). Such critiques have led some to question whether there is or even can or should be such a thing as feminist ethnography (Abu-Lughod, 1990; Stacey, 1988; Visweswaran, 1994). While some feminist researchers have been loath to attend the critiques that postmodernism, in particular, raises for feminist theorists and doggedly stick to telling *the* feminist story and capturing the essence of their subjects' voices, other feminist researchers have found that there is much work to do among the ruins. As Lather (Lather & Smithies, 1997; Lather, 2000) reading Judith Butler (1993) points out, this failure, this ruin, of our theories and methodologies produces a site from which to ask different sorts of questions, to open contestatory possibilities, and to only now closely examine in their unsustainability what beliefs made concepts such as, for example, a linear unfolding of history sustainable. Lather and Smithies (1997) further point out that "terms understood as no longer fulfilling their promise do not become useless. On the contrary, their very failures become provisional grounds and new uses are derived" (p. 300).

For example, Visweswaran (1994) turns to a "feminist practice invested in decolonizing" and "one that rests on the recognition of certain impossibilities" (p. 13). The "impossibility" that must be deconstructed, decolonized, and acknowledged is in this case representation of the subject, in what Visweswaran refers to as a "refusal of subject" (p. 60). Taking up what has been central to feminist theory and practice—centering of female subjectivity—and now reworking that category of subjectivity as a refusal is a move to retain the subject yet acknowledge the problematics with any attempt to claim, or know, the subject. This, then, is a feminist subject who cannot be contained by a researcher/writer who actively and reflexively "refuses" to contain her.

Perhaps, then, futures for feminist ethnography continue a commitment to uncovering, revealing, or responding to inequities in theory and practice and continue a commitment to analyzing and deconstructing our own research, discursive, and textual practices while at the same time findings ways to think, write, and live with unknowability. This does not mean that we stop asking questions, but rather that we ask questions differently. If, as Jane Flax (1990) states, the "fundamental purpose" of feminism remains to analyze "how we think, or do not think, or avoid thinking about gender" (p. 43), then feminist ethnography remains a ripe vehicle for doing and unpacking this thinking in all its intricacies, intersectionalities, nuances, and ruins.

## NOTES

1. For further discussion and exploration of these questions see Abu-Lughod (1990); Collins (1990); Ferguson (1993); hooks (1984); Jardine and Smith (1987); Johnson-Bailey (1999); Lingard and Douglas (1999); Mohanty, Russo, and Torres (1991); Moraga and Anzaldúa (1983); Nicholson (1990); Paker, Dehyle, and Villenas (1999); Patai (1991); Porter (1992); Pillow (2002); Reinharz (1992); and St. Pierre and Pillow (2000).

2. The organization of this chapter through these "stages" of research is not an assumption that the process of research is easily experienced as stages. We recognize that the stages of research cross over into and influence each other. See Van Maanen (1989).

3. The data stories used in this chapter are from Cris Mayo's research with the Latino/a parental involvement project and will be published in Cris Mayo, Maria Alburquerque Candela, Eugene Matusov, and Mark Smith (in press).

4. For discussion of how feminist theory affects methodology see Collins (1990), Fine (1994), Fonow and Cook (1991), Lather (1991), and Reinharz (1992). Certainly, researchers may use multiple theoretical lenses, including feminism and postmodernism, feminism and race theory, and feminism and queer theory (see Collins, 1990; Johnson-Bailey, 1999; Lather, 1991; Nicholson, 1990; Sanders, 1999; St. Pierre & Pillow, 2000; Walkerdine, 1990). While in this chapter we are not advocating for a particular approach, we assume, as does Harding, that all feminist research is about social critique.

## References

Abu-Lughod, L. (1990). Can there be a feminist ethnography? *Women and Performance: A Journal of Feminist Theory, 5*(1), 7–27.

Abu-Lughod, L. (1992). *Writing women's worlds: Bedouin stories.* Berkeley: University of California Press.

Acker, J. (1992). Gendered institutions: From sex roles to gendered institutions. *Contemporary Sociology, 21,* 565–569.

Anderson, G. (1989). Critical ethnography in education: Origins, current status, and new directions. *Review of Educational Research, 59*(3), 249–270.

Anzaldúa, G. (1987). *Borderlands/la frontera: The new mestiza.* San Francisco: Aunt Lute Books.

Behar, R., & Gordon, D. (Eds.). (1995). *Women writing culture.* Berkeley: University of California Press.

Belenky, M., Clinchy, B., Goldberger, N., & Tarule, J. (1986). *Women's ways of knowing.* New York: Basic Books.

Butler, J. (1993). Poststructuralism and postmarxism. *Diacritics, 23*(4), 3–11.

Chaudhry, L. N. (2000). Researching "my people," researching myself: Fragments of a reflexive tale. In E. St. Pierre & W. Pillow (Eds.), *Working the ruins/feminist poststructural theory and methods in education* (pp. 96–113). New York: Routledge.

Clifford, J., & Marcus, G. (Eds.). (1986). *Writing culture: The poetics and politics of ethnography.* Berkeley: University of California Press.

Collins, P. H. (1990). *Black feminist thought/knowledge, consciousness and the politics of empowerment.* London: HarperCollins Academic.

Collins, P. H. (1991). Learning from the outsider within: The sociological significance of Black feminist thought. In M. Fonow & J. Cook (Eds.), *Beyond methodology/feminist scholarship as lived research* (pp. 35–59). Bloomington: Indiana University Press.

Davies, B. (1989). *Frogs and snails and feminist tales: Preschool children.* St. Leonards, Australia: Allen & Unwin.

Davis, A. (1981). *Women, race, and class.* New York: Random House.

de Beauvoir, S. (1953). *The second sex.* New York: Pantheon Books.

Delgado Bernal, D. (1998). Using a Chicana feminist epistemology in educational research. *Harvard Educational Review, 68*(4), 555–582.

Delgado-Gaitan, C. (1993). Researching change and changing the researcher. *Harvard Educational Review, 63*(4), 389–411.

Denzin, N. (1997). *Interpretive ethnography: Ethnographic practices for the 21st century.* Thousand Oaks, CA: Sage.

Denzin, N., & Lincoln, Y. (2005). *The Sage handbook of qualitative research.* Thousand Oaks, CA: Sage.

Eisenstein, Z. (1994). *The color of gender: Reimaging democracy.* Berkeley: University of California Press.

Evans-Winters, V. (2005). *Teaching black girls: Resiliency in urban classrooms.* New York: Peter Lang.

Ferguson, K. (1993). *The man question: Visions of subjectivity in feminist theory.* Berkeley: University of California Press.

Fine, M. (1991). *Framing dropouts: Notes on the politics of an urban high school.* Albany: State University of New York Press.

Fine, M. (1994). Dis-tance and other stances: Negotiations of power inside feminist research. In A. Gitlin (Ed.), *Power and method* (pp. 13–35). New York: Routledge.

Flax, J. (1990). Postmodernism and gender relations in feminist theory. In L. Nicholson (Ed.), *Feminism/postmodernism* (pp. 39–62). New York: Routledge.

Fonow, M. M., & Cook, J. (Eds.). (1991). *Beyond methodology/feminist scholarship as lived research.* Bloomington: Indiana University Press.

Freire, P. (1970). *Pedagogy of the oppressed.* New York: Herder and Herder.

Gilligan, C. (1982). *In a different voice: Psychological theory and women's development.* Cambridge, MA: Harvard University Press.

Harding, S. (1987). Introduction: Is there a feminist method? In S. Harding (Ed.), *Feminism & methodology* (pp. 1–14). Bloomington: Indiana University Press.

Hey, V. (1997). *The company she keeps: An ethnography of girls' friendships.* Buckingham, UK: Open University Press.

hooks, b. (1981). *Ain't I a woman: Black women and feminism.* Boston: South End Press.

hooks, b. (1984). *Feminist theory: From margin to center.* Boston: South End Press.

Jardine, A., & Smith, P. (Eds.). (1987). *Men in feminism.* New York: Routledge.

Johnson-Bailey, J. (1999). The ties that bind and the shackles that separate: Race, gender, class, and color in a research process. *International Journal of Qualitative Studies in Education, 12*(6), 659–670.

Kondo, D. (1990). *Crafting selves.* Chicago: University of Chicago Press.

Lather, P. (1991). *Getting smart: Feminist research and pedagogy with/in the postmodern.* New York: Routledge.

Lather, P. (2000). Drawing the lines at angels: Working the ruins of feminist ethnography. In E. St. Pierre & W. Pillow (Eds.), *Working the ruins/feminist poststructural theory and methods in education* (pp. 284–311). New York: Routledge Press.

Lather, P., & Smithies, C. (1997). *Troubling the angels: Women living with HIV/AIDS.* Boulder, CO: Westview Press.

Leach, M. (1997). Feminist figurations: Gossip as a counterdiscourse. *International Journal of Qualitative Studies in Education, 10*(3).

Leck, G. M. (1987). Review article—feminist pedagogy, liberation theory, and the traditional schooling paradigm. *Educational Theory, 37*(3), 343–354.

Linden, R. (1992). *Making stories, making selves: Feminist reflections on the holocaust.* Columbus: Ohio State University Press.

Lingard, B., & Douglas, P. (1999). *Men engaging feminism.* Philadelphia: Open University Press.

Lorde, A. (1984). *Sister outsider.* Trumansburg, NY: Crossing Press.

MacLure, M. (1997). Eccentric subject, impossible object: A poststructural reading of Hannah

Cullwick. *International Journal of Qualitative Studies in Education, 10*(3), 315–332.

Mayo, C. (2005, November). *Complex subjectivity in student associational groups: How straight are the straight girls in GSAs?* Paper presented at the Wisconsin Center for Educational Research, University of Wisconsin at Madison.

Mayo, C., Candela, M. A., Matusov, E., & Smith, M. (in press). Families and schools apart: University experience to assist Latina/o parents' activism. In F. Peterman (Ed.), *Urban schools and democratic challenges.* Washington, DC: AACTE Press.

McRobbie, A. (2000). *Feminism and youth culture* (2nd ed.). New York: Routledge.

Miranda, M. K. (2003). *Homegirls in the public sphere.* Austin: University of Texas Press.

Mohanty, C. T., Russo, A., & Torres, L. (Eds.). (1991). *Third world women and the politics of feminism.* Bloomington: Indiana University Press.

Moraga, C. (1997). *Waiting in the wings: Portrait of a queer motherhood.* Ithaca, NY: Firebrand Books.

Moraga, C., & Anzaldúa, G. (Eds.). (1981). *This bridge called my back: Writings by radical women of color.* Watertown, MA: Persephone Press.

Nicholson, L. (Ed.). (1990). *Feminism/postmodernism.* New York: Routledge.

Nicholson, L. (Ed.). (1997). *The second wave/a reader in feminist theory.* New York: Routledge.

Oakley, A. (1981). Interviewing women: A contradiction in terms? In H. Roberts (Ed.), *Doing feminist research* (pp. 30–62). London: Routledge.

Parker, L., Dehyle, D., & Villenas, S. (Eds.). (1999). *Race is . . . race isn't: Critical race theory and qualitative studies in education.* Boulder, CO: Westview Press.

Patai, D. (1988). Constructing a self: A Brazilian life story. *Feminist Studies, 14,* 143–160.

Patai, D. (1991). U.S. academic women and third world feminism: Is ethical research possible? In S. Gluck & D. Patia (Eds.), *Women's words* (pp. 137–154). New York: Routledge.

Pillow, W. S. (2002). When a man does feminism should he dress in drag? *International Journal of Qualitative Studies in Education, 15*(5), 545–554.

Pillow, W. S. (2003a). Race-based methodologies: Multicultural methods or epistemological shifts?

In Geraldo Lopez & Laurence Parker (Eds.), *Interrogating racism in qualitative research methodology* (pp. 181–202). New York: Peter Lang.

Pillow, W. S. (2003b). Confession, catharsis, or cure: The use of reflexivity as methodological power in qualitative research. *International Journal of Qualitative Studies in Education, 16*(2), 175–196.

Pillow, W. S. (2004). *Unfit bodies: Educational policy and the teen mother.* New York: Routledge.

Porter, D. (Ed.). (1992). *Between men and feminism.* New York: Routledge.

Reinharz, S. (1992). *Feminist methods in social research.* New York: Oxford University Press.

Richardson, L. (1994). Writing: A method of inquiry. In N. K. Denzin & Y. S. Lincoln (Eds.), *Handbook of qualitative research* (pp. 516–529). Thousand Oaks, CA: Sage.

Richardson, L. (1997). *Fields of play (constructing an academic life).* New Brunswick, NJ: Rutgers University Press.

Sanders, J. (1999). Dissertation as performance [Art Script] (Take Three). *International Journal of Qualitative Studies in Education, 12*(5), 541–562.

Smith, B. (1983). *Home girls: A black feminist anthology.* New York: Kitchen Table, Women of Color Press.

Stacey, J. (1988). Can there be a feminist ethnography? *Women's Studies International Forum, 11*(1), 21–27.

Statham, A., Richardson, L., & Cook, J. A. (1991). *Gender and university teaching: A negotiated difference.* Albany: State University of New York Press.

St. Pierre, E. (1997). Nomadic inquiry in the smooth space of the field: A preface. *International Journal of Qualitative Studies in Education, 10*(3), 365–383.

St. Pierre, E., & Pillow, W. (Eds.). (2000). *Working the ruins: Feminist poststructural theory and methods in educational research.* New York: Routledge.

Talburt, S. (2000). *Subject to identity: Knowledge, sexuality, and academic practices in higher education.* Albany: State University of New York Press.

Thorne, B. (1993). *Gender play/girls and boys in school.* New Brunswick, NJ: Rutgers University Press.

Trinh, M. T. (1989). *Women, native, other*. New York: Routledge.

Van Maanen, J. (1989). *Tales of the field: On writing ethnography*. Chicago: University of Chicago Press.

Villenas, S. (1996). The colonizer/colonized Chicana ethnographer: Identity, marginalization, and co-optation in the field. *Harvard Educational Review, 66,* 711–731.

Villenas, S. (2000). This ethnography called my back: Writings of the exotic gaze, "othering" Latina, and recuperating Xicanisma. In E. St. Pierre & W. Pillow (Eds.), *Working the ruins/feminist poststructural theory and methods in education* (pp. 74–95). New York: Routledge Press.

Visweswaran, K. (1994). *Fictions of feminist ethnography*. Minneapolis: University of Minnesota Press.

Walker, A. (1974). *In search of our mothers' gardens*. New York: Harcourt Brace Jovanovich.

Walkerdine, V. (1990). *Schoolgirl fictions*. New York: Verso.

Wax, R. (1971). *Doing fieldwork: Warnings and advice*. Chicago: University of Chicago Press.

Willis, P. (1977). *Learning to labour*. Farnborough, UK: Saxon House.

# FEMINIST INTERVIEWING

## *Experience, Talk, and Knowledge*

Marjorie L. DeVault
Glenda Gross

The simple thing to say is that interview research is research conducted by talking with people. It involves gathering informants' reports and stories, learning about their perspectives, and giving them voice in academic and other public discourse. Talking with others is a fundamental human activity, and research talk simply systematizes that activity.

While true, this simple view neglects the fascinating complexity of human talk—the flexibility and productive powers of language; the subtle shades of meaning conveyed through the nuances of speech, gesture, and expression; issues of translation; the ineluctable locatedness of any moment or stretch of talk; the specialized vocabularies of particular settings and groups; the organizing effects of format and genre; the injuries and uses of silence; the challenges inherent in listening; and so on. The simple view also neglects the dynamics of power involved in any empirical research: the hierarchical, often charged relations between researcher and informants, the politics of interpretation and representation, and the social consequences of making claims on the basis of science. Add to this picture a political commitment to feminism, and one begins to see the terrain of feminist interview research.

Much qualitative and feminist research has been based on a relatively straightforward commitment to collecting and representing the perspectives of informants, and those projects have often had powerfully liberatory effects. Drawing on the political traditions of testimony and consciousness-raising and the research traditions of life history and open-ended interviewing, feminists have brought forward a wealth of previously untold stories—those of marginalized peoples, and also those that the more privileged may have kept hidden, awaiting a receptive audience (or a skillful interlocutor). But another essential aspect of feminist interview research interrogates the challenges of communication and the inherent contradictions in the desire to give voice to others. This strand of thinking has produced a variety of feminist studies that use interview data in complex and nuanced ways, often to explore language and discourse itself.

Feminist scholars operate reflexively and relationally, so we begin by considering our own intellectual biographies and contexts and our relations with each other and the concerns of this chapter. We are feminist scholars of different generations—Marj coming to feminism and the early days of women's studies in the mid-1970s, and Glenda entering well-established fields of feminist sociology and women's studies in the mid-1990s. When Marj took "Introduction to Women's Studies" in Madison, Wisconsin, in 1975, there was a dearth of feminist writing in the academy; texts for the course included the Bible and the novels of writers like D. H. Lawrence—works awaiting our critique. At that time, talking together about sexual harassment or lesbianism was startlingly illuminating. By the time Glenda took a first women's studies course in upstate New York, we had textbooks and readers, which drew on a rich feminist literature, as well as official policies and procedures on sexual harassment. When Marj began a study of housework as a graduate student in the early 1980s, she had to justify focusing interviews on such a "trivial" matter; yet she was inspired by a lively political literature, including that from a "wages for housework" movement. When Glenda formulated her doctoral research project in 2001, she set out to interview "feminist pedagogues," a group who had come into existence as a result of two decades of feminist theory and practice; yet her interest in their practice arose in part from the ways their practice was organized by a conservative response to academic feminism.

These histories and our reflections on the politics of feminism, especially its institutionalization in the academy, form the backdrop for our approach here. We recognize Sandra Harding's (1987) distinction between "methods" (i.e., particular research tools and practices), "methodology" (theorizing about research practices and their implications for people and communities), and "epistemology" (the study of how one comes to know); we would suggest that feminist researchers have mostly used standard methods, and that distinctive feminist insights have come in our strategic theorizing about the research process and knowledge production more generally. We see that feminist research has become an established enterprise, and that "feminist interviewing" is widely accepted and taught as an approach that any scholar should know and appreciate. Yet we worry that the label may travel more easily than the politics, and we yearn for ways to renew continually the political force of feminist scholarship. These observations frame our approach to this chapter. In keeping with the aims of a handbook, we hope to provide guidance for new and experienced researchers conducting feminist interview research; at the same time, our understanding of feminism leads us away from any settled codification of tools and techniques.

## ARTICULATING A CONCEPTION OF FEMINIST METHODOLOGY

Researchers who claim the label *feminist* for their methodological projects must be prepared to reply to questions about the meaning and distinctiveness of "feminist" methodology and research. Because interviewing always has, to some degree, the quality of "going to the people" (Taylor & Bogdan, 1998)—located either outside or within structures of power—this definitional task is especially important for scholars who wish to claim a distinctiveness for feminist interview methodology. The range and variety of feminist theories in the social sciences are beyond the scope of our discussion here; for the purposes of this chapter, we define feminism broadly as a set of practices and perspectives that affirm differences among women and promote women's interests, health, and safety, locally and abroad. It is a diverse and differentiated social and scholarly movement; for most adherents, it includes the aspiration to live and act in ways that embody feminist thought and promote justice and the well-being of all women. This formulation reflects our desire to contribute to an inclusive and multicultural feminism, and it draws on lessons we have learned from scholarly work of "women of color feminists" such as Patricia Hill Collins (1990), María Lugones (1990), and many others.

We understand feminism as one of several related and intersecting social justice projects, linked to critical social theory (Collins, 1998), that have gathered new or renewed momentum in the second half of the 20th century (others include anticolonialist struggles, antiracist projects, and liberation movements undertaken by people of color, queer activists, and people with disabilities). Feminism, as distinct from its allied movements, problematizes gender and brings women and their concerns to the center of attention. It challenges the allied movements to attend to women and gender, and it challenges feminists to learn and attend to others' liberation and justice struggles. We would also define feminism, along with these other movements, as activity that crosses the (blurred) boundaries between academic and other activist sites. Feminist and other critical academics continually draw on the insights produced by activism outside the university; we also can sometimes create relatively protected spaces for the development and dissemination of activist perspectives. Sometimes, feminist researchers are engaged in activism, either in or outside the academy. Scholars may also at times co-opt activist ideas, "taming" them for wider consumption, and we wish to keep those risks in mind. While the academy can be a "space for imagining opposition, for producing multiple subjectivities that are capable of critical thinking and resistant action against the institution itself," it is also "an institutional structure that is part of capitalist relations of rule within the nation state as well as internationally" (Mohanty, cited in Dua & Trotz, 2002, p. 74). So, as feminists in the academy, we feel it is important to emphasize the importance of grassroots organizing, as well as political teaching and research work, in bringing about change.

Two features of contemporary feminist scholarship have important implications for those who wish to approach the research process as a feminist practice. First (and as reflected in our definition of feminism), feminists' internal critiques have dismantled the notion of "woman" as the unified and foundational subject of feminism. Arguing that women are diversely situated in history, culture, and class; that genders are multiple; and that gender itself is a discursive production, theorists of gender and sexuality (and their intersections with race, class, ability, age, and nation) now resist any simple reliance on this categorical identity. This strand of thought has traveled much further in theory than in empirical study, and another important feature of contemporary feminist scholarship is its strongly theoretical character, at least in its interdisciplinary formations. There has been a rich conversation taking place among feminists in the academy about the connection between our practice as researchers and educators and the implications of that practice for

people's daily lives. But this conversation does not easily translate into specific techniques for gathering and analyzing data. We do not mean to suggest that such theories have no relevance to practice; on the contrary, they continue to inform research practice in numerous, invaluable ways. But the theories of power and knowledge emerging from this conversation tend to emphasize historicity and ambiguity, rather than codification. Furthermore, such developments have proceeded unevenly through the disciplines: In those fields tied more closely to positivist epistemologies, scholars continue to treat gender as a relatively unproblematic variable (though with increasing attention to how it is crosscut by other identities), and those in applied fields and working in activist community settings (women's shelters, women's prisons, women's entrepreneurship programs, for instance) may find that their fields of activity remain tied to cultural and political assumptions about gender, even as scholars subject those assumptions to increasingly sophisticated critique.

These developments produce two challenges for feminist interview researchers. The first is to construct a rationale for labeling research feminist, without reproducing the false homogenization and separations of historical feminisms. That is, we need to be cognizant of the differences that exist among women and be sure that when we speak on behalf of women, we are not really only speaking on behalf of some women (e.g., North American, Anglo, able-bodied, middle-class women). We need to locate the "historically specific differences and similarities between [ourselves] in diverse and asymmetrical relations" so that we are able to create "alternative histories, identities, and possibilities for alliances" (Kaplan, 1994, p. 139). The history of feminism, much like any history, is characterized by conflict, struggle, and resistance. And feminism owes much of its history to the political organizing of women of color, poor women, lesbian women, and women with disabilities. The work of these groups of women was instrumental in dismantling the idea that all women are the same and positioned evenly in the social landscape. The second challenge is to adapt new theorizations of feminism so that they serve empirical projects—understood in our discussion quite broadly, as projects in which researchers engage with others (in the flesh, or less directly) to produce new knowledge. In other words, researchers need to take up the writings of feminist theorists, learn from those writings, and consider their implications for research practices.

## Aspects of Interview Research

With this background in mind, we explore below the central idea of interviewing, that knowledge can be produced in structured encounters organized around "telling about experience." We consider feminist thinking about how to organize and conduct such encounters, and then discuss several aspects of interview research with which feminists have been especially concerned: active listening; the opportunities afforded by a focus on language, narrative, and discourse; interviewing ethics and the risks of "discursive colonization" (Mohanty, 1991); and feminist strategies in quantitative survey research. We conclude with a discussion of the accountability of the feminist interviewer to research participants and other audiences and the importance of continual reflection on the intellectual and institutional context in which we do scholarship. Our approach is broadly "postpositivist": that is, we reject the idea that social realities are simply "there" for researchers to find. Instead, we understand the social contexts of people's lives as historically situated and constituted through people's activities, and the research process itself as an integral aspect of the construction of knowledge about society. While we identify a number of practices that (in our view) make interview research feminist, we would also suggest that these are never matters solely related to collecting, analyzing, or presenting data, but instead are modes of thought and action that continually inform these mutually constitutive stages of the research process.

### Telling About "Experience"

Various forms of interviewing have long been used to bring people's experiences forward and make those experiences visible in more public discussions, and such projects have often been conducted with the aim of social reform. In the progressive era, British and U.S. social reformers conducted "social surveys" in immigrant neighborhoods and racially segregated communities: Beatrice and Sidney Webb, Jane Addams and the women of Hull House, and African American researchers and reformers such as W. E. B. Dubois and Zora Neale Hurston all spent time meeting and talking with people in such communities, and they recorded those encounters systematically to bring neglected voices into a civic conversation. Interviews are not always conducted with marginalized peoples, of course—as the social sciences have matured, interviews have also been used to explore the lives and actions of the powerful (e.g., Ostrander, 1984), to display or uncover experiences of "ourselves" (e.g., DeVault, 1991), and to map discursive contexts and "regimes" of ruling (e.g., Chase, 1995; Griffith & Smith, 2005). Interviewing has also become a central element in such regimes—the way we get jobs, apply for social assistance, talk through the media, prove that we are good parents, and so on. Indeed, interviews have become so central to contemporary life and governance that Gubrium and Holstein (2002) suggest that we live in an "interview society." Still, the traditions of research interviewing have been strongly linked to social justice concerns and projects and the idea of bringing forward neglected voices—and these traditions have been especially important for feminist projects.

The practice of open-ended, semistructured interviewing favored by feminist researchers is discussed in every textbook of qualitative research methods and many general methods texts in the social sciences; recent editions of such texts generally include attention to feminist research and writing about interviewing (e.g., Bogdan & Biklen, 1998; Esterberg, 2002; May, 2002; Taylor & Bogdan, 1998; Warren & Karner, 2005). There are also a number of excellent book-length treatments of social science interviewing (e.g., Gubrium & Holstein, 2002; Mishler, 1986; Weiss, 1994; for focus groups, see Morgan, 1997; for narrative approaches, see Riessman, 1993), and we recommend these to feminist researchers as useful sources for basic background and technique. As women's studies and feminist research in the disciplines began to develop, in the 1970s and early 1980s, feminist scholars took up these methods enthusiastically and also began to fashion distinctively feminist ways of conducting interview research.

The notion of "experience" was central to the resurgence of Western feminist activism in the 1960s and 1970s: The insights of the women's movement of that period came from women's collective talk, which was emerging from women's wartime participation in work and labor union settings, the state and federal women's commissions of the time, the civil rights and antiwar movements, and also in structured consciousness-raising groups.[1] The practice of feminist consciousness-raising was borrowed (via civil rights and other radical organizing of the time) from the revolutionary Chinese practice of "speaking bitterness," a grassroots method for empowering peasant communities (Hinton, 1966; see also McLaren, 2000); Kathie Sarachild's (1978) talks to radical groups, Pamela Allen's (1973) booklet, and the statement of the Combahee River Collective (1982) outline U.S. feminist adaptations of the practice. In a sense, women who were part of these developments were "interviewing" themselves and others like them, and then working together to make sense of experiences that were both "personal" and "political" (Hainisch, 1970, cited in Mansbridge, 1995, p. 28). Looking back, we can see that these efforts were sometimes flawed by a failure to work out the broader politics of the "personal"; that is, the institutions, processes, and interactions shaping women's experiences were sometimes overlooked, and the unequal relations among different groups of women (and the extent to which the privileges of some women were contingent on the dehumanizing treatment of others) were often unaddressed. Still, these were conversations that allowed groups of women to begin theorizing their relations to one another, and to introduce into public discussion ideas like "sexism," "battering," and "woman identification."

Feminist theorists and researchers of the 1970s and 1980s followed these activists in their reliance on experience. Feminist theorists urged scholars to "start thought" or "begin with experience" (Harding, 1991; Smith, 1987) and to rely on "the authority of experience" (Diamond & Edwards, 1977), and researchers embraced interviewing as a method of making experience hearable and subjecting it to systematic analysis. These early moves were radical, because they suggested locating authority and "truth" somewhere other than the received wisdom of the Euro- and androcentric disciplines—in the realities of Black women's lives, for instance, or in detailed historical analyses of struggle, resistance, and everyday living. They produced studies that told "truths" about women's lives, in contrast to often distorted representations produced in scholarly networks made up of predominantly white or Anglo, middle- to upper-class men. African American feminists produced interview studies that portrayed Black women as strong and competent in the face of oppression, writing against sexist scholarship of the era that charged Black women with responsibility for supposed "flaws" of African American families: Joyce Ladner (1971) used interviewing and participant observation to produce an influential sympathetic study of African American teenaged girls living in poverty, *Tomorrow's Tomorrow*, and Inez Smith Reid (1972), responding to a call for information about "militant" women, wrote instead about *"Together" Black Women*. Ann Oakley (1974) and Helena Lopata (1971), in Britain and the United States, respectively, interviewed working-class women and middle-class women about housework and their lives as housewives—exploring the contours of the "problem with no name" (Friedan, 1963). Pauline Bart (1971) interviewed midlife Jewish women hospitalized for depression when their children left home and produced an account of their situation that located the problem in the culturally constructed mothering role that engulfed them, rather than their "overinvolvement." Such studies used women's stories in a collective project of ideological critique. These scholars set women's own words against the ideological constructions of a racist and "sexist society" (Gornick & Moran, 1971): African American women's words against cultural stereotypes, middle-class women's words against the culture's simultaneous romanticization and trivialization of household labor, and depressed women's own stories against individualizing psychiatric diagnoses of their pain.

As these studies went forward, feminist researchers became more attentive to the dynamics of the interview process, and began to write about distinctively feminist issues and approaches to interviewing. Ann Oakley's (1981) article, "Interviewing Women: A Contradiction in Terms," challenged the prevailing "rules" of distanced objectivity in social research; she argued that the social science pretense of neutrality (the requirement, e.g., that a woman interviewing other women about pregnancy should feign ignorance of the subject in order not to contaminate the data) was in conflict with the principles of feminism. Rather than viewing women informants as objects of the researcher's gaze, feminists should develop ways of conceptualizing the interview as an encounter between women with common interests, who would share knowledge. Joan Acker, Kate Barry, and Joke Esseveld (1983)—interested in how feminism was affecting their own lives—interviewed women who had been housewives about the process of making changes in their lives, and then wrote about the challenges of analyzing the women's reports. They wrote reflexively, looking critically at their attempts to involve participants in the research, considering how they heard and interpreted the women's accounts, and acknowledging their own concerns echoing through their analyses. Sherry Gorelick (1989) reported on her interviews with Jewish feminists, troubling the feminist idea that women's stories were straightforwardly a source of truth. She emphasized the contradictions in women's reports of their experiences, and suggested that interview researchers must develop interactive methods that allow them to challenge and explore contradictory accounts. Dorothy Smith (1987) developed the idea that one would discover "lines of fault" in women's experience, because their activities and perspectives are tied both to an everyday world of mundane caring and support work and also to a more ideologically structured realm in which those everyday concerns are relatively invisible. Her method of inquiry—"institutional ethnography" (discussed in more detail below)—was built on the notion that women could report on their everyday work, and the researcher could examine their reports and map the lines of fault they reveal.

Historian Joan Scott's (1991) landmark article, "The Evidence of Experience," crystallized these observations about women's "own stories" and opened a series of debates about the relation of experience and language that continue to the present. She argued that "experience" is always discursively structured—that what a person sees and understands is always shaped by what one already knows and can articulate. This argument presented a fundamental challenge to historians and empirical social science researchers who took as their charge finding out "what happened." Scott (1992) suggests that to understand experience as natural, inherent, or "uncontestable evidence" (p. 24) is too simple. Such a naturalist view takes for granted categories like "man, woman, black, white, heterosexual or homosexual by treating them as given characteristics of individuals" (p. 27) and ignores the constructed and historically situated character of any experience. "Questions about . . . how subjects are constituted as different in the first place, about how one's vision is structured—about language (or discourse) and history—are left aside" (p. 25). Instead of telling what happened, researchers should examine the discourses at play and the subject "positions" constructed by those discourses. One might, for example, conduct a kind of Foucauldian genealogical study (tracing the historical emergence of various categories and representations with an interest in how they organize consciousness and social institutions; e.g., Foucault, 1977, 1978) or use people's accounts of experience to investigate how such discursive formations appear in their talk, but it would be naïve to take their accounts as straightforward reports of some "actual" experience. Scott's article poses a challenge to positivism by suggesting that reality is not out there to be "discovered" but rather that realities are produced out of varying geopolitical contexts and social discourses.

Feminist researchers continue to explore and debate the implications of these ideas. Some have suggested that they signal the impossibility of any representation of others untainted by the researcher's own need and desire (Clough, 1992). But other scholars have been reluctant to abandon some grounding notion of experience (Dalmiya & Alcoff, 1993; Moya, 2000), emphasizing experience as a "resource for critical reflection" (Stone-Mediatore, 1998, p. 121), and some have noted that the argument that there is no fixed truth seemed to have arisen just as women and other "outsiders" began to make their own truth claims (Christian, 1990; Mascia-Lees, Sharpe, & Cohen, 1989). Moreover, Shari Stone-Mediatore (2003) notes that "despite academic critiques of experience, many social struggles, from welfare rights campaigns to fair trade coalitions . . . continue to rely on stories of experience to bring public attention to their concerns" (p. 1). Certainly, these debates have produced more sophisticated understandings of experience. Smith (1999, chap. 6), for example, in an essay on "Telling the Truth After Postmodernism," makes an argument that recognizes and draws on the central ideas of poststructuralist theory and also preserves the significance of embodied existence. She points to the groundedness of language in social interaction; in her approach language is critically important, but it cannot be separated from activity.

For interview researchers, we believe that these theoretical perspectives point to the necessity for a critical approach to informants' accounts. A critical approach does not have to be a dismissive or "debunking" approach; indeed, we have tried to illustrate above the potential uses of interview studies founded on a relatively straightforward notion of experiential authority. But the strongest feminist research brings along with that idea a complementary awareness that researchers are always working with accounts constructed linguistically, that experience recounted is always emergent in the moment, that telling requires a listener and that the listening shapes the account as well as the telling, that both telling and listening are shaped by discursive histories (so that fragments of many other tellings are carried in any embodied conversation), and so on. In the next section, we consider relations between teller and listener in the feminist interview.

## Conditions and Conduct of the Interview

Interview researchers have long been concerned with the identities and social locations of parties to the interview, worrying that differences will produce failures of rapport that limit disclosure and that similarities may lead to "over-rapport" and bias. Standard practice has typically involved "matching" interviewer and interviewees to the extent possible; especially in large-scale survey and collaborative research, team members may divide interviewing labor so as to achieve this kind of fit between researcher and participants. Feminist researchers share these concerns and practices, but they have developed more complex, more thoroughly reflexive views of identity and its effects in the interview. Much feminist research has been conducted by women researchers with women participants, and, typically, feminist researchers have been committed to finding and acknowledging common ground with participants. That commitment, we suggest, has—perhaps unexpectedly—helped to bring differences into view, because feminist researchers have explored and debated what actually happens when women interview women.

White feminists' early writings on interview research often began with the assumption of an automatically direct and comfortable relationship between the feminist researcher and her woman interviewee (like Black feminist writers on their research with Black women), but the dynamics of interviews, as they actually happen, brought more complex formulations. Catherine Kohler Riessman's (1987) influential article, "When Gender Is Not Enough," displayed her initial assumption that she would find common ground with women interviewees and then critiqued that too-simple desire by rereading interview material she appeared to have misunderstood in the moment of interviewing. Her article has been especially useful, because it not only cautions researchers against taking rapport for granted, but also models a strategy for working with the awkward moments of difficulty in talking with others. Josephine Beoku-Betts (1994) wrote about similar challenges related to differences among women of African descent, concluding that there are also times "When Black Is Not Enough." And Patricia Zavella (1993) added an important idea to this strand of thought, with an analysis of how her own Mexican American identity was crosscut by other dimensions (age, education, marital and family status) so that her relation to informants who shared her racial or ethnic identity was nuanced and constantly shifting—researcher and participants were both "similar" and "different," in different contexts.

Despite a preponderance of research by women with women, feminist researchers have not wanted to be limited to "cozy" interviews with participants who are comfortably similar; some have wanted to conduct research on and with men, or with women who have had very different experiences and points of view (e.g., Blee, 1991; Klatch, 1987). Terry Arendell (1997) reports that interviewing men about their divorce experiences was more challenging than her previous research with women: The men who participated in her study responded in various ways to the interview situation, but often tried to take charge of the situation, challenge the terms of the study, assert a masculinist superiority, and so on. Her account displays some men's remarkably explicit readings of her—they chastised her, as if she were the former wife; assumed from her interest in the topic that she was angry and bitter; and addressed her as "one of those feminists." She discusses the challenge of managing these conversations and also points out that telling such stories, and thus opening these encounters to "analytic scrutiny," allows researchers to examine the dynamics of gender in the research relation. We would add that, while these men's readings of the research are particularly obvious, research participants no doubt always make assumptions about the interviewer, and feminist researchers would be wise to consider those assumptions, and their effects, even when they are not so evident. For example, informants may assume that the interviewer does not care about the informant, despite a shared gender status, or assume—particularly if the interviewer and informant are positioned differently with respect to race, gender, ability, sexuality, or age—that the interviewer will judge or misunderstand the informant.

There is relatively little writing on disability issues in feminist research, no doubt because people with disabilities have been so absent, until quite recently, from most of the disciplines. Yet ability structures interview encounters in powerful ways: Communication difficulties make it less likely that some will even be included in research, leading some disability advocates to argue for a "right to be researched"

(Robert Bogdan, personal communication), and when people with disabilities are included, able-bodied researchers may rely on false assumptions or slip too easily into stereotypical ways of thinking about their lives and capacities. Most scholarship on interviewing presumes an able-bodied researcher and is geared toward an able-bodied audience. Interview techniques are designed with particular verbal and cognitive capacities in mind, assuming a relatively easy back-and-forth between interviewer and interviewee; able-bodied researchers (and researchers with disabilities) who interview elderly people with cognitive difficulties, or people with sensory, intellectual, or other impairments, for example, must adjust styles of interviewing, and in most cases must plan on spending more time with each participant in order to produce useful data. Recognition and discussion of the additional work researchers studying people with disabilities carry out is missing from most scholarship related to interviewing and feminist research.

For feminist (and other) interviewers, we suggest that debates about who can research what (and which researchers should interview which participants) raise important issues, but ultimately suggest that the more important question is how to organize interviews so as to produce more truly collaborative encounters, whatever the identities and commitments of participants. One strategy feminists have adopted is based on the basic fieldwork principle of sustained immersion: For example, projects based on life history interviewing, such as Ruth Behar's (1993) work with her Mexican informant Esperanza, usually involve sustained contact over long periods of time. Behar's account of her relationship with Esperanza provides illuminating details about the give-and-take of their research relations—on both emotional and material levels—and her text, *Translated Woman*,[2] uses a collage technique that combines reporting on the interviews with "confessional" and autobiographical writing to display reflexively how the data were produced and analyzed over time. A somewhat different strategy of immersion might involve seeking data in multiple ways, as in Christine Bigby's (2000) study of older women with intellectual (or developmental) disabilities.[3] Recognizing that some of the women might not be able to provide all the information she wished to collect (and discovering that a few women were willing to participate in the study, but couldn't or didn't want to be interviewed), Bigby sought additional information about each woman's situation from relatives, advocates, social workers, and other caregivers; thus, she was able to produce case studies that included the women's own perspectives, and to fill out their stories with supplementary information from others. Such a strategy has the drawback of relying on others to interpret for the people with disabilities, but in some cases providing alternative modes of inclusion in the research may allow the researcher to explore experiences and issues that would otherwise be neglected.

Another dimension of reflexive interviewing that feminists have experimented with involves strategic disclosure on the part of the interviewer, whether that means sharing personal information or a willingness to reveal research interests and political commitments. Rosalind Edwards (1990), for example, suggests that white researchers interviewing Black participants should address racial identities and issues explicitly; she found that the best rapport with participants in her study came not when she asserted their similarities as women but rather when she acknowledged explicitly that her own social location differed from that of the interviewees. Marianne Paget (1983) argues that interviewing can produce a "science of subjectivity"—that is, a rigorous account of another's perspective—and that this is accomplished most successfully when the interviewer approaches the interview as a "search procedure"—a process of seeking meanings together. She suggests that the researcher share with the interviewee the concerns that animate the research, so that the conversation can unfold as a collaborative moment of making knowledge, and she illustrates that kind of sharing and unfolding with excerpts from her interview with a woman artist. In some projects, it may be appropriate not only to share thoughts but to press informants, challenging their taken-for-granted constructions. Sometimes, such a strategy might run through a set of interviews, as in Ruth Frankenberg's (1993) study of white women's racism; she asked open-ended questions, but

given the relatively subtle ways that racism may be expressed (especially in a culture of "color-blindness" that Frankenberg labels "color- and power-evasive"), she sought throughout the interviews to intervene "dialogically" in ways that would open up discussion of race and racism. In other instances, challenges to informants' taken-for-granted constructions may be more improvisational, arising in a moment of listening. For example, after several working-class informants had rejected feminism, explaining that they wanted their husbands to "open the car door and light my cigarette," Lillian Rubin (1976) thought to ask one of them about the last time her husband had done that. Her interviewee, a bit taken aback, had to laugh and admit that she didn't even smoke (pp. 131–132). The moment is enlightening because it shows how this woman's perspective on feminism is rooted in cultural discourses as well as in her experience.

In the conduct of any interview research, feminists must maintain a reflexive awareness that research relations are never simple encounters, innocent of identities and lines of power, but, rather, are always embedded in and shaped by cultural constructions of similarity, difference, and significance. When Susan Chase (1995) interviewed women school superintendents with her research collaborator Colleen Bell, for example, they realized that the position of these powerful women shaped even the questions it was possible to ask: It was reasonable to ask them to spend time in research on their careers and achievements, while they likely would not have agreed to spend time answering questions about hobbies. Chase's treatment of those interviews makes such concerns central to the analysis: She examines the interviews with an eye to the stories that can be easily told and those that emerge only haltingly. Her reflexive approach gives us new knowledge about white and racial-minority women in a male-dominated profession, and also about "realms of discourse" and the difficulties of speaking about gender- and race-based discrimination. Her book *Ambiguous Empowerment* is an extremely useful source for feminist researchers because it illustrates how constructions of similarity and difference influence every aspect of the interview project: shaping the questions researchers ask and don't ask, the ease or difficulty of recruiting informants, the kinds of rapport that develop in the encounter, and the lenses through which researchers produce and analyze interview data.

It is our impression that feminist ideas about reflexivity have traveled through the disciplines more successfully than any other feminist insights. We have observed that most scholars in the social sciences now recognize the ways that a researcher's background and commitments can influence his or her thought, and it is no longer unusual for audiences to demand some accounting of the researcher's personal stake in a project. We attribute the successful dissemination of this feminist idea to the clarity and strength with which feminist scholars have spoken of the androcentric and ethnocentric biases that so often mark research conducted as if "from nowhere." And we attribute that clarity and strength to feminists' passionate and engaged desire for scholarly coalitions that will produce research that can speak to women in many different locations and circumstances.

The desire for an inclusivity that acknowledges and values difference has also led feminist thinkers to key insights about the challenges of listening to others. Listening actively and well is such an important part of the conduct of interviews that we treat it in a separate section.

## Listening

> Listening can be a radical activity. . . . For any listener, at risk are not only a sense of self, place and society, but also knowledge of one's own complicity with oppression. (Lester C. Olson, 1998, p. 448)

Listening is not as simple as it sounds, and failures of listening are often part of our interactions with others. Active listening means more than just physically hearing or reading; rather, it is a fully engaged practice that involves not only taking in information via speech, written words, or signs, but also actively processing it—allowing that information to affect you, baffle you, haunt you, make you uncomfortable, and take you on unexpected detours, "away from abstract . . . bloodless, professionalized questions," toward peoples, knowledges, and experiences that have been disavowed, overlooked, and forgotten (Gordon, 1997, p. 40).

Antiracist feminists have long theorized the transformative potential of active listening. Audre Lorde (1984), for instance, has written on the troubling consequences of Anglo women's inability to listen actively to women of color's experiences with racism, (hetero)sexism, and economic exploitation. When white women use women of color's anger as an excuse to ignore and dismiss women of color's concerns, she argues, the possibilities for meaningful, systemic change are significantly weakened. While Lorde acknowledges that "the history of white women who are unable to hear Black women's words, or to maintain dialogue with [Black women], is long and discouraging" (p. 66), she hopes more and more white women will hold themselves accountable to recognize the various forms of violence and oppression that characterize the realities and experiences of women of color. As Bernice Johnson Reagon (1983) explains in "Coalition Politics: Turning the Century," moving outside one's cozy "barred room" into situations or spaces that are uncomfortable is not easy, but is certainly necessary if any coalition work is to be successful. Active listening, she suggests, is about survival. "There is no chance that you can survive by staying *inside* the barred room" (p. 358). Feminist researchers can learn from these activist writings: If we wish to create knowledge that challenges rather than supports ruling regimes, we must constantly be attentive to histories, experiences, and perspectives that are unnoticed, unfamiliar, or too easily neglected or misrepresented.

A researcher's practice of listening deeply affects the data and knowledge she or he produces. The feminist researcher who takes the work of active listening for granted risks producing data, writing up her or his findings, and responding in ways that are colonizing rather than liberating because they reproduce dominant perspectives. For instance, a researcher who enters a research encounter assuming she or he is a naturally good listener, without consciously acknowledging the work that active listening entails, may end up hearing only what she or he wants or expects to hear. Furthermore, while it may seem plausible to assume that our status as women or feminists prevents us from reproducing power relations during and after an interview, such an assumption is problematic.

As researchers, we must be cognizant of the fact that feminists may be divided by relations of power and privilege, and that listening may require that we acknowledge the ignorance our own privileges may have produced before we can hear what others wish to tell us.

It is difficult, of course, to know from published reports about a researcher's practice of listening, but some feminist scholars have written in ways that open a window onto listening as an element of interview research. DeVault (1990), for example, in "Talking and Listening from Women's Standpoint," adopts an analytic approach influenced by ethnomethodology that entails close examination of the interview talk—a kind of textual representation of listening, constructed retrospectively. She suggests that this kind of approach allows the researcher to attend to silences and difficulties of communication produced by the lines of fault in women's lives: Noticing when women speak haltingly, or circuitously, for instance, can provide an opening for analysis of a misfit between women's own experiential perspectives and the languages or ideological constructions of their cultures. Amy Best (2003) adopts a related approach to "hear" and bring forward the ways that she and the participants in her study were producing "whiteness" as they managed and negotiated their racial identities through their interview talk.

Some researchers bring forward particular instances of listening (often highlighting difficulties) and discuss what they reveal. Alison Griffith and Dorothy Smith (1987, 2005), for example, report noticing the discomfort they experienced as they interviewed mothers about their children's schooling; recognizing that some of the mothers' reports elicited intense guilt about their own mothering, they developed an analysis of a mothering discourse that produces such feelings. Similarly, Sari Knopp Biklen (1995) reports on a series of interviews with an African American schoolteacher in which she wanted to focus on the teacher's professional work, while her informant seemed to want to share talk about their children and family lives; in retrospect, and noticing that they were the only two "working mothers" of young children in the school, Biklen believes she failed to hear the woman's attempt to share perspectives with someone in a similar circumstance.

Listening may also become an explicit topic when it is especially challenging. Rebecca Klatch (1987), who interviewed "right-wing women," describes her "non-argumentative approach": "If asked, of course I would state my own doubts or disagreements, but generally I defined my own role entirely in terms of listening and absorbing the other world view" (p. 17). Kathleen Blee (1991) conducted oral history interviews with women who had been members of the white-supremacist Ku Klux Klan in Indiana during the 1920s, when the group was quite active. As an antiracist sociologist, she reports that she was "prepared to hate and fear" her informants, but instead forged more complex and ultimately more disturbing relations: She was able to speak easily with the women, so long as she didn't denounce the Klan, and could identify shared cultural backgrounds and values. Listening carefully allowed her to see that the Klan of the 1920s expressed a racism that was exaggerated, but not unrelated to the white culture of its time and place. Sometimes, this kind of challenging listening, across differences, may serve as the basis for an interview project, as in Faye Ginsburg's (1989) study of grassroots activists on both sides of the abortion debate.

One of feminism's central claims is that women's perspectives have often been silenced or ignored; as a result, feminist researchers have been interested in listening for gaps and absences in women's talk, and considering what meanings might lie beyond explicit speech. DeVault (1990, 1991) attempts this kind of analysis through close attention to speech, focusing interpretation on the moments when speech seems to falter. Wendy Luttrell (1997), who conducted life-story interviews with working-class women that focused on their experiences with schooling, reflects not only on the content of the interviews but on moments when she believes she caught unspoken meanings in her exchanges with informants (see, e.g., pp. 16–17). In a more recent project (Luttrell, 2003), she worked with African American teens continuing their schooling during pregnancy. The young women had to confront negative social stereotypes in talking about themselves, and Luttrell developed an innovative methodology to explore their self-perspectives: The girls made collage art pieces, and Luttrell interviewed them, as a group, about the images they had chosen for these representations.

Some experiences are more obdurate, and feminist researchers must sometimes be content simply to point toward silences. R. Ruth Linden (1993), for example, in a reflexive analysis of Holocaust survivors' attempts to narrate their experiences, draws on Hannah Arendt's notion of unassimilable "sheer happenings." She suggests that gaps and silences in their narratives may point to events they experience as simply so horrific that they cannot be narrativized. Another intriguing example comes from Rannveig Traustadóttir's (2000) ethnographic study of the friendship between two young women, one with an intellectual disability and the other a "typical" student preparing for a career in special education. Traustadóttir spends time with the two girls, interviewing them informally along the way; she also conducts more formal interviews with the young student, but cannot elicit a clear statement of the other girl's perspective through formal interviewing. Despite this silence, the researcher provides a tentative interpretation of the disabled girl's (possibly) increasing dissatisfaction with the relationship, "read" through clues that Traustadóttir could observe in her behavior. As in Bigby's (2000) study (discussed above), there are risks of misinterpretation in such a strategy, but we would suggest that the value of bringing forward, however tentatively, a perspective that might otherwise simply fall out of view outweighs those risks. We assume, of course, that researchers' readings of informants' views in such cases will be based on extensive and systematic observation, as well as knowledge about informants' circumstances and contexts, and we recommend such "readings" be put forward "lightly" (DeVault, 1999, chap. 5), with explicit acknowledgement that readers should consider alternative interpretations.

In summary, we argue that if feminist researchers are interested in creating knowledge that is for rather than about the people they study, then they must be active listeners. Like the playful "world" traveler that María Lugones (1990) imagines, the active listener must interrogate her or his deep-seated assumptions about various worlds and her or his arrogant perceptions of others in those worlds. Both playful "world" traveling and active listening operate as means to identify with and love people living in alternate, unfamiliar worlds without (ab)using them. We have learned what it means to be active listeners not only from second-wave feminists in the social sciences, but also from women of color like Audre Lorde and others whose writings and edited collections continue to call our attention to and nourish us with stories of oppression, resistance, and survival (Alexander, Albrecht, Day, & Segrest, 2003; Anzaldúa, 1990; Anzaldúa & Keating, 2002; Bulkin, Pratt, & Smith, 1984; Jordan, 1985; Lorde, 1984; Moraga & Anzaldúa, 1981). These writers and writings fuel many feminists' investigations of the social world. They remind feminist researchers to be self-reflective and critical of deeply disciplined research practices by offering "imaginative access to what is, for some, an unimaginable experience" (Code, 2001, p. 273). The insights of women of color feminists and Anglo feminists continue to cultivate the transformation of scholars from arrogant perceivers to empathetic, decolonizing researchers and foreground the importance of active listening in all stages of the research process.

## Structures of Talk and Discourse

Perhaps because of the significance of listening, feminist researchers have been especially attentive to one recent trend in interview research, which involves a heightened attention to the structures and organization of language, talk, and discourse. Throughout the social sciences, scholars refer to an interdisciplinary stream of thought focused on narrative and representation as a linguistic or narrative "turn" (Behar & Gordon, 1995; Clifford & Marcus, 1986), which has gathered momentum since the 1980s. One central idea is that narratives are fundamental to identity and to the ways that people make sense of their worlds. People are constantly telling stories, to themselves and to others. Elliot Mishler's (1986) influential book on interviewing pointed to the pervasiveness of stories in most interview data, and suggested that conventional approaches to analysis, which extract thematic bits of those stories, are likely to disrupt the coherence of informants' perspectives. By contrast, looking at longer stretches of talk (referred to by some as "discourse analysis"), and especially the stories people tell, and how they tell them (typically labeled "narrative analysis"), offers distinctive possibilities for maintaining the coherence of a person's perspective. Feminist scholars such as Catherine Kohler Riessman (1990, 2002) and Susan Bell (1999) have developed these insights and applied them in studies of women's experiences of divorce, infertility, and reproductive health. Some studies of this sort focus extensively on the structures of people's stories, so that the content of their talk becomes secondary, but feminists using narrative analysis generally want to examine the structures of storytelling in order to enhance their interpretations of women's reports. Riessman's (1987) analysis of the form of her Latina interviewee's story, for example, provides a way for her to hear more fully what is being said. Riessman expected a linear narrative of the informant's divorce and at first felt that she didn't understand the woman's perspective; but through careful study of the interview transcript, she recognized a different kind of narrative that built meaning by circling around its main themes.

Another important idea is that how stories are told is not just an individual matter; people's stories are shaped by the formats available to them and reflect the perspectives and values of their communities. Thus, a narrative may be a place to see human agency in play with social structures, expressive activity that is shaped by its social context. The narrative turn brought a new consciousness of such issues to the practice of oral history and life history interviewing, and feminist scholars began to write much more reflexively about how such interviews are negotiated between the parties and how the researcher produces a representation of the encounter. One excellent source on such issues is the collection produced by the interdisciplinary Personal Narratives Group (1989); their title, *Interpreting Women's Lives*, puts the emphasis on interpretation, signaling the shift from an approach that emphasized collecting material as if that were a simple and straightforward process (see also Gluck & Patai, 1991).

Judy Long's (1999) book, *Telling Women's Lives*, provides a more theoretical and epistemological discussion of these issues, formulating an interpretive prism of sorts with four facets: subject, narrator, reader, and text. She includes in her discussion not only life history interview

studies, but also the production of biography and autobiography; and drawing from feminist scholars in literary studies, such as Carolyn Heilbrun (1998), she explores the intersections of gender with genre, or the ways that typical or expected narratives may constrain what women can easily tell (and what listeners or readers can easily grasp) about their experience.

Dorothy Smith's (1987) development of a "sociology for women," based on a mode of inquiry she calls "institutional ethnography" or "IE" research (Smith, 2002), provides a method explicitly focused on the ideological practices of "ruling" that shape women's experiences and how they recount them (in interviews and elsewhere). Smith has formulated IE as a "feminist method" arising from the change in women's consciousness associated with the women's movement of the 1970s, and more broadly as a "sociology for people" or "alternative sociology," and her writing about the approach touches on much more than just interview research. However, interviews are often quite important in feminist IE studies (see DeVault & McCoy, 2002), and Smith's writings on the theoretical foundations of IE research have broad implications for interview research of many sorts.

Briefly, the IE approach takes up some "standpoint" as a point of entry to inquiry. Interviews are often used to explore activities of a particular group and to produce a full picture of their experiences at that point of entry. However, IE researchers are committed to looking beyond local experience, and the next step in the research is to examine local activities to see how they are connected with or "hooked into" activities occurring elsewhere. This "hooking in" or alignment is typically accomplished in contemporary societies through various texts, such as time cards and job descriptions, mission statements and strategic plans, databases and the statistics compiled from them, media portrayals and the conceptual framings they employ, and so on. These texts allow for coordinated action in the complex and interlocking institutional formations that coordinate contemporary societies, putting in place "ruling relations" that reach into people's daily (and nightly) activities. The "problematic," or question, posed in an IE study is how a particular piece of "everyday life" is organized, extralocally. Often, IE researchers find that institutional practices produce difficulties in everyday life, because institutional ideologies fragment "what's actually happening" for the person. It may be, for example, that only part of a battered woman's story is written up in the police report (Pence, 2001) or that only part of what the clerical or health care worker does is recognized in her job description (Diamond, 1992; Reimer, 1995). Thus, only part of that experience is accountable in other places—in the sentencing or probation hearing, for example, or in the calculation of wages, or promotion and managerial policy.

Smith (1987, 1990a, 1990b, 1999) has developed these ideas in a series of essays on women's perspective as a critique of conventional sociology, and on text-mediated social organization and what she calls "conceptual practices of power." Many of her arguments rest on a distinction between "primary narratives"—told by an embodied narrator, from an experiential point of view—and various institutional narratives produced from the "raw materials" of primary storytelling: how a single observer's account of a political demonstration compares with the official account in the voice of the authorities, for example; how a woman's behavior is worked up by acquaintances as "mental illness"; how a death becomes an officially warranted "suicide"; or how Virginia Woolf's state of mind before she killed herself is read as insanity. The logic of these essays suggests an approach to interview data, based on the idea that one can find social organization "in talk." At some points, people will narrate what they do, specifically and straightforwardly; a researcher can encourage that kind of reporting through the questions she or he asks. At other points, the interviewee's talk will draw on institutional categories and concepts, as when teachers refer to "ADHD kids" or make reference to organizational texts, such as grade-specific curricula, or the "IEP" (or Individualized Education Plan) used in U.S. schools to spell out accommodations to be made for students identified as having disabilities. The IE researcher can use both kinds of talk to explore the textual "leap" from experience to "documentary reality"—that is, how the organization "works up" the activities of teachers and students, and how the coordinative texts of the educational system recruit them into relations they may not intend.

Researchers using the IE approach often conduct interviews with people working in several different sites, rather than designing studies limited to one particular group. Because IE researchers are seeking connections across sites, their research designs focus on translocal "regimes" of social organization. Once the researcher has identified significant texts, she may want to interview those who produce or work with that text. Ellen Pence's (2001) "audit" studies of the processing of domestic violence cases, for example, involve extensive interviews with 911 operators, police dispatchers and responding officers, advocates, judges, and probation officers; each contributes a locally grounded piece of the "processing" picture, and seeing how each works with a particular case shows how a woman's experience gets transformed as it becomes a "case." In addition, IE researchers often combine interviewing with textual analysis, as Kamini Maraj Grahame (1998) does in a study of a feminist community organization's "outreach" to women of color, and Rosamund Stooke (2003, 2004) does in her study of the gendered work of children's librarians. And sometimes, they may use interviews to explore how people use visual texts, as in Liza McCoy's (1995) study of the interpretation of wedding pictures. More on the IE approach can be found in Campbell and Gregor's (2002) "primer," Smith (2005), and DeVault and McCoy's (2002) discussion focused specifically on interview research.

Feminist anthropologists have also adopted innovative "multisited" approaches that involve interviewing to investigate cultural discourses. Emily Martin (1994), for instance, interviewed scientists and laypeople to explore the common social metaphors that appear in their talk. And Catherine Lutz and Jane Collins (1993) used observation and interviewing to examine the production of *National Geographic* images and then interviewed lay readers about how they saw those images.

## Appropriation and the Ethics of Interview Research

What analytical and strategic knowledges and conceptual tools do we need to not relive the violence of our inherited histories? (Chandra Talpade Mohanty, 2003, p. 187)

All qualitative researchers are, of course, bound by the codes of ethics of their disciplines: Those conducting interviews are required to secure informed consent from participants, to conduct the interview in ways that are sensitive to participants' concerns and feelings, and to protect the identity of interviewees by using pseudonyms and, if necessary, changing some details when representing them in research reports. The costs of participation in the research, for informants, are to be weighed against potential benefits of the research for participants and others. Feminist researchers, acutely aware of the harms produced by generations of male-centered research that distorted women's realities, have set themselves an even higher ethical standard. In some cases, they have challenged disciplinary codes of ethics.

A group of feminist scholars who called themselves the Nebraska Feminist Collective (1983) developed an early statement of feminist research ethics, arguing that from a feminist point of view ethical conduct is not just a procedural matter, but also a matter of content and, ultimately, allegiance. They insisted on an allegiance to women first, even if that sometimes puts feminist researchers in conflict with their disciplinary standards. Confidentiality, for instance, does not always seem to serve feminist goals. Linden (1993) provides a provocative discussion of routine procedures for protecting subjects' identities, suggesting that such practices may not be appropriate for her participants, whose survival through the Holocaust is itself a testimony. Given their history and its meaning, assigning pseudonyms (or worse, numbers) to these people, in the name of protection, may seem more like another erasure of their existence. Such discussions have encouraged feminist researchers to be flexible about confidentiality and to negotiate procedures for identifying participants individually, respecting each participant's wishes.

As feminists have become increasingly concerned with building knowledge inclusive of all perspectives, and attentive to differences of power and privilege among women, they have developed constructions of ethics that address how interview material is used—issues of "appropriation." The question here is whether the interview is a one-way or reciprocal exchange: When the participant offers up her story, does the researcher simply take it and disappear? To what use does she put the data—does it serve only the researcher's career, or also people in the informant's group or community? These concerns might perhaps be construed in the "cost-benefit" terms of the ethical review board, but these institutionalized procedures have not historically emphasized such concerns, focusing instead on rights and harms as individual matters. Feminist constructions of research ethics are sharpened by an acute sensitivity to a "matrix of domination" (Collins, 1990) within which research is conducted and by an awareness of collective interests in researchers' representations.

Feminist theorists have contributed to methodologists' heightened sense of the stakes in research ethics. Calling attention to the politics of any representation, they remind us that writing responsibly calls for a cautious and careful approach: Researchers must be continually mindful of the power relations organizing our actions at every stage of the research process. The participants in our scientific investigations must be understood as "subjects in their own right," instead of being made "into mere bearers of unexplained categories" who have no existence outside those categories (Lazreg, 1988, p. 94). They must not be violently abstracted into categories that presume a universal, ahistorical reality. Instead, women must be acknowledged as agents actively located in history—as makers of the worlds around them rather than mere victims of an overarching patriarchy.

Antiracist feminists, particularly women of color, have critiqued and continue to challenge knowledge that presumes to be outside history, beyond the contexts and workings of actual people (Bannerji, 1995a; Collins, 2000; Mohanty, 2003; Narayan, 1997). These writers suggest that analyses of the experiences of non-white and Third World women are often problematic because they are organized around stereotypes and assumptions, for example, that Third World women are victims of backward, uncivilized traditions and cultures (the same assumption that has been and is being used to justify imperialism and the violent colonization and appropriation of seemingly untamed bodies and territories). For instance, Uma Narayan (1997) has argued that white Western feminist representations of sati as an uncivilized Indian practice replicate what she terms a "colonialist stance" toward Third World cultures and communities (p. 43). These representations suggest that "Third-World contexts are uniform and monolithic spaces [unaffected by historical change] with no important internal cultural differentiations, complexities and variations" and falsely homogenize Indian women as "victims of their culture" (p. 58). Representations emanating from this "colonialist stance," she argues, erase the work and agency of women and others involved in the transformation of their worlds, legitimize efforts to economically exploit and politically dominate India, and stifle transnational feminist coalitions and cross-cultural communities of resistance (p. 126).

Practically, such critiques suggest that, too often, well-meaning feminist researchers embark on projects involving other women without a thorough and grounded knowledge of their contexts and the histories that have produced those contexts. They suggest that feminist researchers should carefully think through the purpose of interviewing; that they must study and learn as much as possible before approaching others. In particular, feminist researchers should avoid using interviews—especially with women in vulnerable or marginalized social locations—as a way to learn things that could be gleaned from available sources. Taking care in that respect is one way that researchers can display respect for the time, effort, and, often, pain involved in sharing experiences. In a critique of the continued tokenist treatment of women of color, Lynet Uttal (1990) argues that researchers should not presume a monolithic experience of racism. Rather, she suggests, "Anglo feminists and feminists of color who are concerned about women of color from different racial/ethnic groups than their own need to more actively seek out information about women of color and relate it to their particular interest" (p. 44). Researchers should go to the library, search through online databases and periodicals, and become better informed "about different groups and their critiques" (p. 44), Uttal argues, before recruiting women of color to fill the gaps in our understanding. Only by doing such "homework" (p. 44) will the process of inclusion of women of color in feminist scholarship be more productive.

Another strategy for avoiding discursive colonization (Mohanty, 1991) is to analyze and present interview material with an eye to its historical context. What is often lacking in colonizing social scientific analyses is a presentation of women research participants as agents active in transforming their surroundings and shaping their experiences. Says Marnia Lazreg (1988, p. 98): "To take intersubjectivity into consideration when studying Algerian women or other Third World women means seeing their lives as meaningful, coherent, and understandable instead of being infused 'by us' with doom and sorrow." Often, such a goal may be achieved by combining interview data with other kinds of material, as in Lisa Law's (1997) study of women's entry into sex work in the Philippines; setting the women's stories against a political-economic history of U.S. military presence and state sponsorship of tourism, she challenges conventional, dichotomous thinking about choice or coercion, agency, and structure. Studies of paid domestic workers in the United States (e.g., Hondagneu-Sotela, 2001; Rollins, 1985; Romero, 1992) have also fruitfully set women's accounts of that work within a broader historical context.

It is also useful to be mindful of women interviewees as agents in their own lives. Sometimes, feminist researchers accomplish this goal by seeking out women who are challenging oppressive conditions, either individually or collectively. Two volumes that include such studies—some based on interview research— are Kimberly Springer's (1999) *Still Lifting, Still Climbing: African American Women's Contemporary Activism,* which includes studies of African American women's activism, and Nancy Naples and Manisha Desai's (2002) collection *Women's Activism and Globalization,* which deals with the activist efforts of transnational feminist organizations. In other studies, treating women as agents is more a matter of how the researcher interprets their struggles. For example, Ellen Scott, Andrew London, and Nancy Myers (2002) look searchingly at interview accounts from welfare-reliant women in the recent period of U.S. welfare "reform" and find that, as benefits are withdrawn, some of them are drawn into "dangerous dependencies" on violent partners; despite the women's circumstances, the researchers do not see them only as vulnerable victims, but rather treat their actions as decisions they make about how to survive.

Finally, feminist interview researchers often strive to share or negotiate interpretive authority with research participants. Ultimately, the researcher makes decisions about producing the final text, but feminists have involved interviewees in decision making about representation in various ways, primarily by asking for commentary on developing analyses or feedback on representational decisions. While such practices parallel qualitative researchers' traditional reliance on "member checks," the feminist emphasis is not only on "getting it right," but also on the politics of representation. Oral history researchers, who address such issues frequently by virtue of their sustained contact with informants, and those using narrative methods, by virtue of their sustained attention to particular stories, have produced a large and fascinating literature on dilemmas and strategies (Gluck & Patai, 1991; Personal Narratives Group, 1989; Riessman, 1987). Some feminists adopt participatory research methods to share research decision making more fully (Campbell, Copeland, & Tate, 1998; Naples, 1996), but their discussions frequently point to practical barriers and often question whether full sharing is always desirable.

Feminist theorists have shown us that texts produce and carry ideology (Bannerji, 1995b), and the research texts we produce do so no less than the texts we critique. As researchers, therefore, we must be cognizant of how our representations of other women will operate and travel as ideology. Interview researchers can use an emergent corpus of critical writing on scholarly textual production (Clough, 1992; McCloskey, 1990; Richardson, 1997; Smith, 1999) to develop an awareness of the politics carried in research texts; we urge interview researchers to continue such reflective consideration and to devote more attention to the reception and uses of interview research, an area that has been less explored.

## Feminist Perspectives on Survey Research

We are researchers trained and primarily interested in relatively unstructured interview techniques and in qualitative, interpretive analysis of interview material; these are also the approaches that feminist scholars have taken up most enthusiastically—to such an extent that many associate feminist with qualitative research and some practitioners insist explicitly on that linkage. We do not: We have emphasized qualitative interviewing here, but we also recognize the possibility and, more important, the desirability of developing more structured feminist interviewing methods that will contribute to quantitative research and analysis.

Historically, writing on feminist methodology has emphasized qualitative interview techniques. Some have asserted that open-ended interviews, involving relatively intimate face-to-face relations, fit best with feminist commitments because they allow women to speak more freely than in structured interview situations. Yet any interview is an artificial, constructed encounter. Despite a relative paucity of writing on feminist uses of quantitative, survey-type interview data, many feminist researchers do take up those techniques. They argue that feminist scholars and policymakers need various kinds of data, and that often quantitative results carry more weight in public discourse. Certainly, survey techniques are superior when one needs to know about the prevalence of some condition or perspective in a population.

The challenges facing feminist survey-interview researchers are quite different from those that arise in open-ended interviewing. Qualitative interviewing is often improvisational: The researcher can adapt the agenda and questions asked to a particular informant, and adjust the interview strategy over time as she or he begins to develop an analysis. But quantitative analysis depends on uniformity in the conditions and conduct of a large number of interviews. The analyst needs a reasonable confidence[4] that a particular question was asked of each participant in the same way. Because of the need for uniformity, quantitative researchers must make sure they know ahead of time what they wish to learn from interviews and how best to achieve that—they devote a great deal of time and effort to planning the interview and standardizing a protocol for administering it. Because surveys require large numbers of participants, they may be administered by an interviewing staff, and researchers must train interviewers so as to ensure consistency.

In addition, surveying a large sample of some population is an enormous endeavor, and, as a result, many quantitative researchers use data produced by others in large collaborative surveys mounted by various government agencies and other groups. For feminist researchers, these data sets provide both challenges and opportunities. From a feminist point of view, there are several problems with producing large survey data sets: Issues and questions are limited by the concerns of those who design the survey, and the exclusivity of the discipline is reflected in the composition of such committees. For surveys that are administered regularly to allow analysis of trends over time, there may be conflicts between the need to maintain consistency over time and the need to reflect and incorporate new issues or language. Thus, large surveys may be marked by a kind of cultural lag—a gap between the questions on the page and the pressing issues at the time when the researcher begins to work with the data. As feminists have moved into positions of power and influence within the discipline, they have had more opportunities to introduce women's issues and perspectives into decisions about survey design. The effects of this work can be seen in areas such as women's health, sexual assault, work-family issues, and so on.

Early on in the development of feminist methodology, Margrit Eichler (1988) examined a range of social science journals and identified particular forms of sexist error that were often built into the wording of survey interviews (e.g., asymmetries in the way questions were asked) or the analysis of data (e.g., universalizing claims made on the basis of investigations with one group). Her discussion is mostly based on the straightforward assumption that scholars should treat men and women research participants similarly, and some might now question or trouble that assumption, but it is still illuminating to discover the kinds of unexamined gender truisms that were (and in many cases, continue to be) routinely built into data collection. Eichler's discussion is shaped by its moment in feminist studies, but it remains a useful tool for bringing sexist assumptions (and by analogy other discriminatory practices) to light.

In a more recent discussion, Assata Zerai and Rae Banks (2002) consider how one might analyze existing survey data through an "intersectional" feminist lens. Noting that race, class, and gender intersectionality is properly a "heuristic device" that means more than simply including these variables, they explain how, in a study of social policy on maternal drug use, they built contextual variables from a "data set which focuses almost solely on the individual woman" (p. 25). Including analyses of income inequality and the "hostile climate" produced by some state policies allowed them to discuss the contexts that shape women's behaviors and the outcomes of their drug use. They also analyzed interactions between class and hostile climate, and those analyses allowed them to discuss women's agency, showing that women with more resources were able to buffer the effects of a harsh social context. These creative analytic techniques illustrate the possibilities for feminist analysis of existing survey data; they also suggest that survey research would be stronger and more useful if interview data were more frequently produced so as to include material that would facilitate analyses of contextual circumstances.

## Accountability

Are my hands clean? (Sweet Honey in the Rock)

Feminist interview research is often characterized by a desire to make change or produce material results. That is to say, most feminist researchers aim to do more than merely stimulate contemplation about women's status locally and abroad. The challenge, then, is to make the knowledge produced through interviewing applicable to the worlds that women live in. Some interview studies are designed so as to lead to quite specific modifications of institutional practice. For example, Ellen Pence's (2001) institutional audits of domestic violence case processing are designed to discover how changes in institutional practice might enhance women's safety; she works with a team of community responders and finds that they not only have the expert knowledge of those actually doing the work of processing, but are often quite interested in discussing modifications of their practice. In other projects, researchers develop ways of disseminating information gleaned from interviews to nonacademic audiences who might have use for it. After interviewing paid domestic workers in Los Angeles, Pierrette Hondagneu-Sotela (2001) worked with an advocacy organization to produce materials about these workers' rights and how they might address exploitative situations, distributing them in an accessible graphic format modeled after the culturally familiar *novela*. It is important to note that these explicit efforts at social change require a phase of activity not typically considered part of the research process; these researchers not only speak and write about what they have learned from others, but also commit time and energy to activities that will carry research results beyond the academy. Such efforts are relatively rare, because they are not so consistently rewarded as more academic forms of disseminating results.

Another goal shared by many feminist researchers is that of producing "relational knowledge"—that is, showing how the varied circumstances of women (and others) are related through the web of social organization that connects us all. It is not only our status as "women" that matters, but understanding the unequal, uneven, complex relationships between women—locally and abroad—and our relationships to histories of colonialisms, patriarchies, imperialisms, and racisms that is key to any liberatory feminist project (Grewal & Kaplan, 1994, 2000; Mohanty, 2003). Power is multifaceted and complex; therefore, if our aim is to understand how power works, we need to make a concerted effort to map the relations among people's activities, experiences, struggles, histories, and broader geopolitical and economic systems. Such mapping might entail illuminating Third World women's engagement with feminism and resistance to oppressive regimes in relation to states and histories of colonization, as Chandra Talpade Mohanty (2003) did in "Cartographies of Struggle," or taking on a more technical approach, meticulously detailing how the everyday lives of people and the textually mediated activities of organizations and institutions are "connected into the extended relations of ruling and the economy" (Smith, 1987, p. 188), as evidenced in Gillian Walker's (1990) *Family Violence and the Women's Movement*. Mapping is fundamental to any project seeking to explicate relationships

among groups, histories, and contexts. As a methodological tool, it brings the social (i.e., historicity, activity, and agency) back to the knowledge we produce. We cannot understand the worlds we live in, comprehend how power works, or create meaningful change without making our connectedness to people and economic, geopolitical, and historical processes clear. Moreover, because we are always located (in terms of our race, class, nation, ability, sexuality, and age, and as employees of institutions of higher learning), we must also map the political, intellectual, and institutional context in which we write (Mohanty, 2003, p. 224). In our interview studies, it is our responsibility not only to report back on what our respondents said, but also to locate our informants' responses in a particular historical context and to recognize each response as emerging from a very complex set of local and global raced, classed, and gendered relationships. Our emphasis should not only be the "micropolitics of context, subjectivity, and struggle," but "the macropolitics of global economic and political systems and processes" as well (p. 223).

As universities and colleges become more and more corporatized, the challenges to antiracist feminism and oppositional knowledge production grow. Feminists in the academy continue working to transform dominant ways of thinking and acting, confronting processes of administration and governance designed to manage difference-affirming efforts and "dialogic spaces of dissent and transformation" (Mohanty, 2003, p. 185). Like educators elsewhere, we are also required to be more accountable to a production-oriented administrative regime; and our heightened accountability to these institutional concerns makes holding ourselves accountable to the communities and people we write about all the more difficult. Still, to succumb to the bureaucracy of the academy, to shortchange our hopes of changing the world around us, and to forget the brutal realities and histories of subaltern peoples is to become the colonizers we've been so adamant to critique. When we write for, rather than about, the people we study, we begin to redefine the relationship between our work in the academy and the world we live in, reorienting the knowledge we produce to attend to "the needs and interests of . . . people" rather than "the needs and interests of ruling" (Smith, 1999, p. 16). As feminist researchers, we need to use interviews to facilitate our participants' and their communities' understanding of the social world and their efforts to change it.

## CONCLUSION

Interviewing is a powerful research tool for feminist researchers interested in exploring women's experiences and the contexts that organize their experiences. Interviewing is powerful in part because it involves relatively direct exchanges of views and perspectives among researchers, participants, and readers. Because those exchanges are mediated by the language and discourses that shape experience and knowledge, interviews can also be seen as occasions that put those discursive operations in view. Feminist scholars have used interviewing, in various ways, to challenge received knowledge about women's and other lives, and we have no doubt that interviewing will continue to be significant for creative, critical feminist work.

We have tried to consider interview research as part of an "apparatus of knowledge production," a site where women's oppression is "constructed and sustained," but also resisted (DeVault, 1999, p. 30). Dorothy Smith (1996) argues: "Knowledge is socially organized; its characteristic textual forms bear and replicate social relations. Hence, knowledge must be differently written and differently designed if it is to bear other social relations than those of ruling" (p. 187). Feminist research is a process that is situated and carried out in a larger historical context. Like knowledge, it, too, is socially organized. If we acknowledge that the "cognitive domain of social science is itself a social relation" (Smith, 1987, p. 72) and that "knowledge is a social accomplishment," then as social scientists we are also responsible for continually questioning the methods we use to establish our findings and develop our analyses.

We would also insist that, given our "historical and positional differences" (Mohanty, 1990, p. 180), there is no commonality of gender experience across "race and national lines"; our experiences as women are ineluctably complex and varied. Assuming that there is a unified common experience among all women violates and ignores women's differences. Ignoring or dismissing rather than affirming women's differences produces divisions and hinders coalition efforts. Thus, while making generalizations about groups of women can be useful (particularly in the social sciences where one goal is to identify domestic and cross-cultural trends in human behavior), such generalizations can also be used to reinforce the very power structures feminists in the academy have sought to dismantle. Indeed, it was the critique of abstract, generalized forms of knowledge as lacking the complexity and contradictions that characterize women's lives that pushed feminists to acknowledge that representing others is no objective, benign process; therefore, understanding how we represent others, who has the power to represent others, and the implications of our representations of others is imperative to any feminist research project. We suggest that it is in continuing to work out the implications of these ideas that scholars will sustain the political force of feminist interview research.

## NOTES

1. On the history of U.S. feminism, see Freeman (1975), Rosen (2001), and Springer (1999).

2. This book is also very useful as a source on life history methods, both traditional and experimental.

3. Bigby, an Australian scholar, uses the term "intellectual disabilities," whereas U.S. scholars would likely use "developmental disabilities."

4. Of course, what is "reasonable" is a collective construction. Opening up the "black box" of survey interviewing, as in Cicourel (1964, chap. 3), reveals a great deal of undesirable inconsistency as a routine feature of data collection. Specialists recognize this fact and adopt various safeguards to minimize its effects on findings. The requirement for consistency, then, is not absolute, but rather reflects the shared standards of a research community. Feminists might want to debate some of those shared standards, to the extent that routine practices

introduce androcentric biases (Eichler, 1988). But in other contexts, feminist researchers may accept the messiness of survey research as the price of deploying its social power.

## REFERENCES

Acker, Joan, Barry, Kate, & Esseveld, Joke. (1983). Objectivity and truth: Problems in doing feminist research. *Women's Studies International Forum, 6,* 423–435. (Reprinted, with an "Afterword," in Heidi Gottfried (Ed.), *Feminism and social change* (pp. 60–87). Urbana: University of Illinois Press)

Alexander, M. Jacqui, Albrecht, Lisa, Day, Sharon, & Segrest, Mab. (Eds.). (2003). *Sing, whisper, shout, pray! Feminist visions for a just world.* Fort Bragg, CA: EdgeWork Books.

Allen, Pamela. (1973). Free space. In Anne Koedt, Ellen Levine, & Anita Rapone (Eds.), *Radical feminism* (pp. 271–279). New York: Quadrangle. (Reprinted from *Free Space*, by Pam Allen, Times Change Press, 1970)

Anzaldúa, Gloria. (Ed.). (1990). *Making face, making soul: Haciendo Caras: Creative and critical perspectives by feminists of color.* San Francisco: Aunt Lute Books.

Anzaldúa, Gloria, & Keating, Analouise. (Eds.). (2002). *This bridge we call home: Radical visions for transformation.* New York: Routledge.

Arendell, Terry. (1997). Reflections on the researcher-researched relationship: A woman interviewing men. *Qualitative Sociology, 20,* 341–368.

Bannerji, Himani. (1995a). *Thinking through: Essays on feminism, Marxism, and anti-racism.* Toronto, Ontario, Canada: Women's Press.

Bannerji, Himani. (1995b). Beyond the ruling category to what actually happens: Notes on James Mill's historiography in *The history of British India.* In Marie Campbell & Ann Manicom (Eds.), *Knowledge, experience, and ruling relations: Studies in the social organization of knowledge* (pp. 49–64). Toronto, Ontario, Canada: University of Toronto Press.

Bart, Pauline B. (1971). Depression in middle-aged women. In Vivian Gornick & Barbara K. Moran (Eds.), *Woman in sexist society: Studies in power and powerlessness* (pp. 163–186). New York: Basic Books.

Behar, Ruth. (1993). *Translated woman: Crossing the border with Esperanza's story.* Boston: Beacon Press.

Behar, Ruth, & Gordon, Deborah A. (1995). *Women writing culture.* Berkeley: University of California Press.

Bell, Susan E. (1999). Narratives and lives: Women's health politics and the diagnosis of cancer for DES daughters. *Narrative Inquiry, 9,* 1–43.

Beoku-Betts, Josephine. (1994). When black is not enough: Doing field research among Gullah women. *NWSA Journal, 6,* 413–433.

Best, Amy. (2003). Doing race in the context of feminist interviewing: Constructing whiteness through talk. *Qualitative Inquiry, 9,* 895–914.

Bigby, Christine. (2000). Life without parents: Experiences of older women with intellectual disabilities. In Rannveig Traustadóttir & Kelley Johnson (Eds.), *Women with intellectual disabilities: Finding a place in the world* (pp. 69–85). London: Jessica Kingsley.

Biklen, Sari Knopp. (1995). *School work: Gender and the cultural construction of teaching.* New York: Teacher's College Press.

Blee, Kathleen M. (1991). *Women of the Klan: Racism and gender in the 1920s.* Berkeley: University of California Press.

Bogdan, Robert C., & Biklen, Sari Knopp. (1998). *Qualitative research for education: An introduction to theory and method.* Boston: Allyn & Bacon.

Bulkin, Elly, Pratt, Minnie Bruce, & Smith, Barbara. (1984). *Yours in struggle: Three feminist perspectives on anti-Semitism and racism.* Ithaca, NY: Firebrand Books.

Campbell, Marie, Copeland, Brenda, & Tate, Betty. (1998). Taking the standpoint of people with disabilities in research: Experiences with participation. *Canadian Journal of Rehabilitation, 12,* 95–104.

Campbell, Marie, & Gregor, Frances. (2002). *Mapping social relations: A primer in doing institutional ethnography.* Aurora, Ontario, Canada: Garamond.

Chase, Susan E. (1995). *Ambiguous empowerment: The work narratives of women school superintendents.* Amherst: University of Massachusetts Press.

Christian, Barbara. (1990). The race for theory. In Karen V. Hansen & Ilene J. Phillipson (Eds.),

*Women, class, and the feminist imagination: A socialist-feminist reader* (pp. 568–579). Philadelphia: Temple University Press.

Cicourel, Aaron V. (1964). *Method and measurement in sociology*. New York: Free Press.

Clifford, James, & Marcus, George E. (Eds.). (1986). *Writing culture: The poetics and politics of ethnography*. Berkeley: University of California Press.

Clough, Patricia Ticiento. (1992). *The end(s) of ethnography: From realism to social criticism*. Newbury Park, CA: Sage.

Code, Lorraine. (2001). Rational imaginings, responsible knowings: How far can you see from here? In Nancy Tuana & Sandra Morgen (Eds.), *Engendering rationalities* (pp. 261–282). Albany: State University of New York Press.

Collins, Patricia Hill. (1990). *Black feminist thought: Knowledge, consciousness, and the politics of empowerment*. Boston: Unwin Hyman.

Collins, Patricia Hill. (1998). *Fighting words: Black women and the search for justice*. Minneapolis: University of Minnesota Press.

Collins, Patricia Hill. (2000). *Black feminist thought: Knowledge, consciousness, and the politics of empowerment* (Rev. 10th anniversary ed.). New York: Routledge.

Combahee River Collective. (1982). A black feminist statement. In Gloria T. Hull, Patricia Bell Scott, & Barbara Smith (Eds.), *All the women are white, all the blacks are men, but some of us are brave* (pp. 13–22). Old Westbury, NY: Feminist Press.

Dalmiya, Vrinda, & Alcoff, Linda. (1993). Are "old wives tales" justified? In Linda Alcoff & Elizabeth Potter (Eds.), *Feminist epistemologies* (pp. 217–244). New York: Routledge.

DeVault, Marjorie L. (1990). Talking and listening from women's standpoint: Feminist strategies for interviewing and analysis. *Social Problems, 37,* 96–116.

DeVault, Marjorie L. (1991). *Feeding the family: The social organization of caring as gendered work*. Chicago: University of Chicago Press.

DeVault, Marjorie L. (1999). *Liberating method: Feminism and social research*. Philadelphia: Temple University Press.

DeVault, Marjorie L., & McCoy, Liza. (2002). Institutional ethnography: Using interviews to investigate ruling relations. In Jaber Gubrium & James A. Holstein (Eds.), *Handbook of interview research* (pp. 751–776). Thousand Oaks, CA: Sage.

Diamond, Arlyn, & Edwards, Lee R. (1977). *The authority of experience: Essays in feminist criticism*. Amherst: University of Massachusetts Press.

Diamond, Timothy. (1992). *Making gray gold: Narratives of nursing home care*. Chicago: University of Chicago Press.

Dua, Ena, & Trotz, Alissa. (Eds.). (2002). Transnational pedagogy: Doing political work in women's studies: An interview with Chandra Talpade Mohanty. *Atlantis, 26*(2), 66–77.

Edwards, Rosalind. (1990). Connecting method and epistemology: A white woman interviewing black women. *Women's Studies International Forum, 13,* 477–490.

Eichler, Margrit. (1988). *Nonsexist research methods: A practical guide*. Boston: Unwin Hyman.

Esterberg, Kristin G. (2002). *Qualitative methods in social research*. Boston: McGraw-Hill.

Foucault, Michel. (1977). *Discipline and punish: The birth of the prison* (Alan Sheridan, Trans.). New York: Pantheon Books.

Foucault, Michel. (1978). *The history of sexuality* (Robert Hurley, Trans.). New York: Pantheon Books.

Frankenberg, Ruth. (1993). *White women, race matters: The social construction of whiteness*. Minneapolis: University of Minnesota Press.

Freeman, Jo. (1975). *The politics of women's liberation: A case study of an emerging social movement and its relation to the policy process*. New York: McKay.

Friedan, Betty. (1963). *The feminine mystique*. New York: Norton.

Ginsburg, Faye D. (1989). *Contested lives: The abortion debate in an American community*. Berkeley: University of California Press.

Gluck, Sherna Berger, & Patai, Daphne. (1991). *Women's words: The feminist practice of oral history*. New York: Routledge.

Gordon, Avery F. (1997). *Ghostly matters: Haunting and the sociological imagination*. Minneapolis: University of Minnesota Press.

Gorelick, Sherry. (1989). The changer and the changed: Methodological reflections on studying Jewish feminists. In Alison M. Jaggar & Susan R. Bordo (Eds.), *Gender/body/knowledge: Feminist reconstructions of being and knowing* (pp. 336–358). New Brunswick, NJ: Rutgers University Press.

Gornick, Vivian, & Moran, Barbara K. (Eds.). (1971). *Woman in sexist society: Studies in power and powerlessness*. New York: Basic Books.

Grahame, Kamini Maraj. (1998). Feminist organizing and the politics of inclusion. *Human Studies, 21,* 377–393.

Grewal, Inderpal, & Kaplan, Caren. (Eds.). (1994). *Scattered hegemonies: Postmodernity and transnational feminist practices.* Minneapolis: University of Minnesota Press.

Grewal, Inderpal, & Kaplan, Caren. (2000). Postcolonial studies and transnational feminist practices. *Jouvert: A Journal of Postcolonial Studies, 5*(1). Retrieved from http://social.chass.ncsu.edu/jouvert/v5i1/grewal.htm

Griffith, Alison I., & Smith, Dorothy E. (1987). Constructing cultural knowledge: Mothering as discourse. In Jane Gaskell & Arlene McLaren (Eds.), *Women in education: A Canadian perspective* (pp. 87–103). Calgary, Alberta, Canada: Detselig.

Griffith, Alison I., & Smith, Dorothy E. (2005). *Mothering for schooling.* New York: Routledge/Falmer Press.

Gubrium, Jaber F., & Holstein, James A. (Eds.). (2002). *Handbook of interview research: Context and method.* Thousand Oaks, CA: Sage.

Harding, Sandra. (1987). Introduction: Is there a feminist method? In Sandra Harding (Ed.), *Feminism and methodology* (pp. 1–14). Indianapolis: Indiana University Press.

Harding, Sandra. (1991). *Whose science? Whose knowledge: Thinking from women's lives.* Ithaca, NY: Cornell University Press.

Heilbrun, Carolyn G. (1998). *Writing a woman's life.* New York: Norton.

Hinton, William. (1966). *Fanshen: A documentary of revolution in a Chinese village.* New York: Vintage Books.

Hondagneu-Sotela, Pierrette. (2001). *Doméstica: Immigrant workers cleaning and caring in the shadows of affluence.* Berkeley: University of California Press.

Jordan, June. (1985). *On call: Political essays.* Boston: South End Press.

Kaplan, Caren. (1994). The politics of location as transnational feminist critical practice. In Inderpal Grewal & Caren Kaplan (Eds.), *Scattered hegemonies: Postmodernity and transnational feminist practices* (pp. 137–152). Minneapolis: University of Minnesota Press.

Klatch, Rebecca E. (1987). *Women of the new right.* Philadelphia: Temple University Press.

Ladner, Joyce A. (1971). *Tomorrow's tomorrow: The black woman.* Garden City, NY: Doubleday.

Law, Lisa. (1997). A matter of "choice": Discourses on prostitution in the Philippines. In Lenore Manderson & Margaret Jolly (Eds.), *Sites of desire, economies of pleasure: Sexualities in Asia and the Pacific* (pp. 233–261). Chicago: University of Chicago Press.

Lazreg, Marnia. (1988). Feminism and difference: The perils of writing as a woman on women in Algeria. *Feminist Studies, 14*(1), 81–107.

Linden, R. Ruth. (1993). *Making stories, making selves: Feminist reflections on the Holocaust.* Columbus: Ohio University Press.

Long, Judy. (1999). *Telling women's lives: Subject/narrator/reader/text.* New York: New York University Press.

Lopata, Helena Z. (1971). *Occupation housewife.* New York: Oxford University Press.

Lorde, Audre. (1984). *Sister outsider: Essays and speeches.* Freedom, CA: Crossing Press.

Lugones, María. (1990). Playfulness, "world"-traveling, and loving perception. In Gloria Anzaldúa (Ed.), *Making face, making soul: Haciendo Caras: Creative and critical perspectives by feminists of color* (pp. 390–402). San Francisco: Aunt Lute Books.

Luttrell, Wendy. (1997). *Schoolsmart and motherwise: Working-class women's identity and schooling.* New York: Routledge.

Luttrell, Wendy. (2003). *Pregnant bodies, fertile minds: Gender, race, and the schooling of pregnant teens.* New York: Routledge.

Lutz, Catherine A., & Collins, Jane L. (1993). *Reading National Geographic.* Chicago: University of Chicago Press.

Mansbridge, Jane. (1995). What is the feminist movement? In Myra Marx Ferree & Patricia Yancey Martin (Eds.), *Feminist organizations: Harvest of the new women's movement* (pp. 27–34). Philadelphia: Temple University Press.

Martin, Emily. (1994). *Flexible bodies: The role of immunity in American culture from the days of polio to the age of AIDS.* Boston: Beacon Press.

Mascia-Lees, Frances E., Sharpe, Patricia, & Cohen, Coleen Ballerino. (1989). The postmodernist turn in anthropology: Cautions from a feminist perspective. *Signs, 15,* 7–33.

May, Tim. (2002). *Qualitative research in action.* London: Sage.

McCloskey, Dierdre N. (1990). *If you're so smart: The narrative of economic expertise.* Chicago: University of Chicago Press.

McCoy, Liza. (1995). Activating the photographic text. In Marie Campbell & Ann Manicom (Eds.), *Knowledge, experience, and ruling relations: Studies in the social organization of knowledge* (pp. 181–192). Toronto, Ontario, Canada: University of Toronto Press.

McLaren, Anne E. (2000, September). The grievance rhetoric of Chinese women: From lamentation to revolution. *Intersections: Gender, history and culture in the Asian context.* Retrieved February 5, 2005, from http://wwwsshe.murdoch.edu.au/intersections/issue4/mclaren.html

Mishler, Elliot G. (1986). *Research interviewing: Context and narrative.* Cambridge, MA: Harvard University Press.

Mohanty, Chandra Talpade. (1990). On race and voice: Challenges for liberal education in the 1990s. *Cultural Critique, 14,* 179–208.

Mohanty, Chandra Talpade. (1991). Under Western eyes: Feminist scholarship and colonial discourses. In Chandra Talpade Mohanty, Ann Russo, & Lourdes Torres (Eds.), *Third World women and the politics of feminism* (pp. 51–80). Bloomington: Indiana University Press.

Mohanty, Chandra Talpade. (2003). *Feminism without borders: Decolonizing theory, practicing solidarity.* Durham, NC: Duke University Press.

Moraga, Cherríe, & Anzaldúa, Gloria. (Eds.). (1981). *This bridge called my back: Writings by radical women of color.* Watertown, MA: Persephone.

Morgan, David L. (1997). *Focus groups as qualitative research* (2nd ed.). Thousand Oaks, CA: Sage.

Moya, Paula M. L. (2000). Introduction: Reclaiming identity. In Paula M. L. Moya & Michael R. Hames-García (Eds.), *Reclaiming identity: Realist theory and the predicament of postmodernism* (pp. 1–26). Berkeley: University of California Press.

Naples, Nancy A. (with Emily Clark). (1996). Feminist participatory research and empowerment: Going public as survivors of childhood sexual abuse. In Heidi Gottfried (Ed.), *Feminism and social change: Bridging theory and practice* (pp. 160–183). Urbana: University of Illinois Press.

Naples, Nancy A., & Desai, Manisha. (Eds.). (2002). *Women's activism and globalization: Linking local struggles and transnational politics.* New York: Routledge.

Narayan, Uma. (1997). *Dislocating cultures: Identities, traditions, and Third-World feminisms.* New York: Routledge.

Nebraska Feminist Collective. (1983). A feminist ethic for social science research. *Women's Studies International Forum, 6,* 535–543.

Oakley, Ann. (1974). *The sociology of housework.* New York: Pantheon Books.

Oakley, Ann. (1981). Interviewing women: A contradiction in terms. In Helen Roberts (Ed.), *Doing feminist research* (pp. 30–61). London: Routledge & Kegan Paul.

Olson, Lester C. (1998). Liabilities of language: Audre Lorde reclaiming difference. *Quarterly Journal of Speech, 84,* 448–470.

Ostrander, Susan A. (1984). *Women of the upper class.* Philadelphia: Temple University Press.

Paget, Marianne A. (1983). Experience and knowledge. *Human Studies, 6,* 67–90.

Pence, Ellen. (2001). Safety for battered women in a textually mediated legal system. *Studies in Cultures, Organizations and Societies, 7,* 199–229.

Personal Narratives Group. (1989). *Interpreting women's lives: Feminist theory and personal narratives.* Bloomington: Indiana University Press.

Reagon, Bernice Johnson. (1983). Coalition politics: Turning the century. In Barbara Smith (Ed.), *Home girls: A black feminist anthology* (pp. 356–368). New York: Kitchen Table Press.

Reid, Inez Smith. (1972). *"Together" black women.* New York: Emerson Hall.

Reimer, Marilee. (1995). Downgrading clerical work in a textually mediated labour process. In Marie Campbell & Ann Manicom (Eds.), *Knowledge, experience, and ruling relations: Studies in the social organization of knowledge* (pp. 193–208). Toronto, Ontario, Canada: University of Toronto Press.

Richardson, Laurel. (1997). *Fields of play: Constructing an academic life.* New Brunswick, NJ: Rutgers University Press.

Riessman, Catherine Kohler. (1987). When gender is not enough: Women interviewing women. *Gender and Society, 1,* 172–207.

Riessman, Catherine Kohler. (1990). *Divorce talk: Women and men make sense of personal relationships.* New Brunswick, NJ: Rutgers University Press.

Riessman, Catherine Kohler. (1993). *Narrative analysis.* Newbury Park, CA: Sage.

Riessman, Catherine Kohler. (2002). Analysis of personal narratives. In Jaber Gubrium & James A. Holstein (Eds.), *Handbook of interview research* (pp. 695–710). Thousand Oaks, CA: Sage.

Rollins, Judith. (1985). *Between women: Domestics and their employers*. Philadelphia: Temple University Press.

Romero, Mary. (1992). *Maid in the U.S.A.* New York: Routledge.

Rosen, Ruth. (2001). *The world split open: How the modern women's movement changed America.* New York: Penguin.

Rubin, Lillian B. (1976). *Worlds of pain: Life in the working-class family*. New York: Basic Books.

Sarachild, Kathie. (1978). Consciousness-raising: A radical weapon. *Documents from the women's liberation movement: An on-line archival collection*, Special Collections Library, Duke University Libraries. Retrieved February 5, 2005, from http://scriptorium.lib.duke.edu/wlm/fem/sarachild.html

Scott, Ellen K., London, Andrew S., & Myers, Nancy A. (2002). Dangerous dependencies: The intersection of welfare reform and domestic violence. *Gender & Society, 16*(6), 878–897.

Scott, Joan W. (1991). The evidence of experience. *Critical Inquiry, 17,* 773–797.

Scott, Joan W. (1992). Experience. In Judith Butler & Joan W. Scott (Eds.), *Feminists theorize the political* (pp. 22–40). New York: Routledge.

Smith, Dorothy E. (1987). *The everyday world as problematic: A feminist sociology*. Boston: Northeastern University Press.

Smith, Dorothy E. (1990a). *Conceptual practices of power: A feminist sociology of knowledge.* Boston: Northeastern University Press.

Smith, Dorothy E. (1990b). *Texts, facts, and femininity: Exploring the relations of ruling.* New York: Routledge.

Smith, Dorothy E. (1996). The relations of ruling: A feminist inquiry. *Studies in Cultures, Organizations and Societies, 2,* 171–190.

Smith, Dorothy E. (1999). *Writing the social: Critique, theory, and investigations.* Toronto, Ontario, Canada: University of Toronto Press.

Smith, Dorothy E. (2002). Institutional ethnography. In Tim May (Ed.), *Qualitative research in action* (pp. 17–52). Thousand Oaks, CA: Sage.

Smith, Dorothy E. (2005). *Institutional ethnography: A sociology for people.* Lanham, MD: AltaMira.

Springer, Kimberly A. (Ed.). (1999). *Still lifting, still climbing: African American women's contemporary activism.* New York: New York University Press.

Stone-Mediatore, Shari. (1998). Chandra Mohanty and the revaluing of "experience." *Hypatia, 13*(2), 116–134.

Stone-Mediatore, Shari. (2003). *Reading across borders: Storytelling and knowledges of resistance.* New York: Palgrave Macmillan.

Stooke, Rosamund. (2003). (Re)visioning the Ontario early years study: Almost a fairy tale—but not quite. *Journal of Curriculum Theorizing, 19*(2), 91–101.

Stooke, Rosamund. (2004). *Healthy, wealthy, and ready for school: Supporting young children's education and development in the era of the national children's agenda.* PhD dissertation, University of Western Ontario, London, Ontario, Canada.

Taylor, Steven J., & Bogdan, Robert. (1998). *Introduction to qualitative research methods* (3rd ed.). New York: Wiley.

Traustadóttir, Rannveig. (2000). Friendship: Love or work? In Rannveig Traustadóttir & Kelley Johnson (Eds.), *Women with intellectual disabilities: Finding a place in the world* (pp. 118–131). London: Jessica Kingsley.

Uttal, Lynet. (1990). Inclusion without influence: The continuing tokenism of women of color. In Gloria Anzaldúa (Ed.), *Making face, making soul: Haciendo Caras: Creative and critical perspectives by feminists of color* (pp. 42–45). San Francisco: Aunt Lute Books.

Walker, Gillian. (1990). *Family violence and the women's movement: The conceptual politics of struggle.* Toronto, Ontario, Canada: University of Toronto Press.

Warren, Carol A. B., & Karner, Tracy X. (2005). *Discovering qualitative methods: Field research, interviews, and analysis.* Los Angeles: Roxbury.

Weiss, Robert S. (1994). *Learning from strangers: The art and method of qualitative interview studies.* New York: Free Press.

Zavella, Patricia. (1993). Feminist insider dilemmas: Constructing ethnic identity with "Chicana" informants. *Frontiers, 13,* 53–76.

Zerai, Assata, & Banks, Rae. (2002). *Dehumanizing discourse, anti-drug law, and policy in America: A "crack mother's" nightmare.* Aldershot, UK: Ashgate.

# 10

# Using Survey Research as a Quantitative Method for Feminist Social Change

Kathi Miner-Rubino

Toby Epstein Jayaratne

Julie Konik

*The point is not merely to describe the world but also to change it.*

—Gorelick (1996)

Conducting research with a feminist perspective means exploring issues of feminist relevance with an awareness of difference, social power, and scientific oppression that is in service of political and social activism (Hesse-Biber, Leavy, & Yaiser, 2004). Feminist research, then, is one avenue to advance social change. Like most researchers, those who engage in feminist research select from a diverse array of investigative methods, and therefore they can allow their questions, rather than one particular method, to guide their work. Of course, the methods that feminist researchers are most apt to use are influenced by their feminist perspective and the disciplinary norms from which they come. As psychologists, we (the authors) use the quantitative survey research method almost exclusively.[1] Thus, we approach this chapter schooled in the standards of mainstream social science research and with an appreciation of the utility of quantitative survey research. Bridging the disciplines of women's studies and psychology, we see ourselves as social justice scholars who hold a feminist perspective and strive to use survey research as a vehicle for improving the lives of women.

Although we use survey research methods to achieve feminist goals, we acknowledge that some feminists have been critical of these methods. They argue that as a quantitative method, survey research is antithetical to feminist aims. We disagree. We believe that the use of this method has the potential for concrete social change in alignment with feminist values. With many feminist researchers seeking new ways to extend their research into practical action and social transformation for women (however these goals may be conceived), we advocate survey research as a valuable strategy for achieving these objectives, particularly though legislation and public policy reform. We contend that survey research can be one of the most effective tools for social change and can be wholly consistent with feminist goals and philosophies. Consequently, we believe that survey research is one method which, when conducted properly, can facilitate our understanding of women's and other marginalized groups' lived experiences.

Over the past few decades, criticism of survey research and other quantitative research techniques has emanated not only from the feminist community (and other researchers who do work on marginalized peoples) but also from mainstream survey researchers themselves. This has led to discussions, usually within these groups, about how survey research might be improved and developed. In fact, these criticisms of and suggestions for improving survey research from the feminist and the mainstream perspectives have actually been quite parallel. One objective in this chapter, therefore, is to explicitly link these two perspectives and demonstrate their compatibility. We point out how current mainstream survey researchers and feminist survey researchers both seek one common goal: high-quality research that helps us to understand social phenomena. Such research is work that is reliable, valid, respectful, ethical, and reported honestly. In addition, as has generally been the case for feminist researchers, many current mainstream survey researchers emphasize the importance of social change particularly with regard to marginalized social groups. We will cite examples of such research throughout this chapter.

Another objective, as a way to address feminist concerns, is to give the reader a clearer understanding of how we actually go about doing survey research with a feminist perspective. We will describe the major components of this method and point out how each is fully compatible with feminist principles, again offering examples to demonstrate this correspondence. Knowing how survey research is conducted may be particularly useful for feminist scholars who are unfamiliar with such techniques but who have an interest in adding them to their methodological toolbox.

In this chapter, then, we promote survey research as a useful investigative strategy and explain how it can be effectively applied in the exploration of feminist issues. In the first section of the chapter, we define the concepts that are central to our subsequent discussion of feminist survey research and present an overview of (1) the historical development of survey research; (2) the major feminist criticisms of quantitative methods, including the epistemological issues surrounding survey research; (3) the similarities between feminist and mainstream survey research; and (4) the ways a feminist perspective uniquely contributes to the survey research process. In the second section, we introduce the major components of this method, highlighting significant issues that should be addressed in conducting high-quality feminist survey research. Although this chapter offers feminist scholars a general introduction to survey research, it is critical to acquire a more comprehensive understanding of survey techniques before engaging in such research. We refer the reader to several excellent sources of additional information on this topic (e.g., Alreck & Settle, 1995; Czaja & Blair, 1996; Dillman, 1978, 2000; Groves, 1989; Groves et al., 2004; Tourangeau, Rips, & Rasinski, 2000).

## OVERVIEW OF ISSUES

### Definitions of Key Concepts

In order to understand fully the various issues that are addressed in this chapter, it is helpful to review a few basic concepts undergirding our discussion. Following Harding (1987), the term *research methodology* refers to "a theory and analysis of how research does or should proceed" (p. 3). Feminist researchers generally employ a *feminist research methodology* in their research. That is, they believe that research should be predicated on feminist principles and the unique feminist vision of social change for women (Hesse-Biber et al., 2004; Sprague & Zimmerman, 1993). Additionally, Acker, Barry, and Esseveld (1983/1996) described feminist methodology as encompassing three components: (1) a goal of social change for women through the production of knowledge that is for, rather than on, women; (2) the use of methods in the attainment of this goal that are not oppressive; and (3) a continuous questioning of dominant intellectual paradigms and their development.

In contrast, "a *research method* [italics added] is a technique used for gathering evidence" (Harding, 1987, p. 2). Thus, the *survey research method* is one technique used for acquiring information. Within this specific technique, there are a number of components, including the design, collection, processing, and analysis of survey data (Groves et al., 2004). A *survey* (as a specific component of the survey research method) is a way of obtaining "information from (a sample of) entities for the purpose of constructing *quantitative* [italics added] descriptors of the attributes of the larger population of which the entities are members" (Groves et al., 2004, p. 2).[2] The entities are usually individual people, but they can be any source of information (e.g., organizations or media articles). The quantifiers are called *statistics*, which are "summaries of observations on a set of elements" (Groves et al., 2004, p. 2). The general goal of statistics is to describe the characteristics and experiences of a population or to test specific hypotheses. Typically, a standardized set of questions in a survey is called a *questionnaire*, and a survey that is read to a respondent either over the phone or in person is called an *interview*. Having reviewed these key terms, we now turn to a brief history of survey research.

## Historical Outline of the Survey Research Method

The history of survey research reflects a field of inquiry that has evolved in response to social and technological change. We will briefly highlight a few of the major historical developments but suggest other sources (e.g., Converse, 1987; Groves et al., 2004) for more detailed coverage of this subject. The earliest and most well-known type of survey is the census, which began in the United States in 1790 and is conducted each decade by the federal government (U.S. Census Bureau, 1989). The census seeks to describe the characteristics (e.g., gender, race, average number of people per household) of an entire population (e.g., people in the United States). Another purpose of surveys in their early development was to gain an understanding of social problems (e.g., see http://booth .lse.ac.uk), and indeed, even feminists employed such methods at that time. For example, during

the late 1800s and early 1900s, feminists at the University of Chicago designed surveys and developed statistical techniques to assist social reform efforts (Deegan, 1988, as cited in Spalter-Roth & Hartmann, 1996). This first generation of feminist survey researchers used the results of their surveys to educate the public and influence legislation supporting a host of progressive causes, such as reducing poverty, unemployment, and child labor.

A significant impetus for mainstream survey research development was World War II, because the federal government was interested in assessing Americans' opinions and attitudes regarding the war and other social issues (Groves et al., 2004). This was a critical period in the evolution of survey research, as survey researchers began to learn the importance of question wording, data collection techniques, interviewer training, and sampling procedures (Converse, 1987; Groves et al., 2004). Since that time, opinion surveys have been conducted in the areas of journalism and market research to gain understanding of the "typical" American's views, including preferences for political candidates in upcoming elections and for various products and services (Groves et al., 2004). Perhaps the most important development in survey research was the use of computers in the research process, starting in the 1960s. Survey researchers first employed computers only for statistical analyses, but computers quickly became indispensable for all aspects of the research process, including survey design, sampling, data collection, and data analysis.

A second generation of feminist survey researchers, who received their training during the 1960s and 1970s, was, like the earlier generation, committed to using surveys to advance social policy. Although they were passionate activists in the quest for social change for women (Spalter-Roth & Hartmann, 1996), this later generation was generally critical of positivist methodology (i.e., the belief that truth is based on empirical observation), as exemplified by scientific investigation. These feminists employed the survey research method but also acknowledged some limits of quantitative methods. While their critiques still resonate today, they have been refined and responded to by feminist scholars in subsequent decades. This discourse resulted in more general acceptance of survey research among many feminists, although some are still wary about the use of quantitative methods. Thus, while there has been rapid growth in the use and sophistication of survey techniques, and some feminists have used such methods, others in the feminist community continue to be cautious with regard to quantitative research.

## Feminist Criticisms of Quantitative Research and the Survey Research Method

### Epistemological Issues

In the past few decades, much scholarship has addressed the epistemological groundings of survey research. Discussions of these issues have come from many disciplines, have been inherently philosophical, and have often been filled with technical jargon (Campbell & Wasco, 2000). The major criticism of survey research focuses on its roots in the tradition of positivism, which embraces a pursuit of knowledge that is objective and value-free. Numerous feminist scholars (e.g., Crawford & Marecek, 1989; Eichler, 1988; Harding, 1987, 1998; Haraway, 1991; Hartsock, 1998; Keller, 1978; Peplau & Conrad, 1989; Sherif, 1979) have challenged the positivist feature of science and argue that the ideal of objectivity and neutrality, on which the survey research method is primarily based, is necessarily masculine. Science is purported to be impersonal, unemotional, and detached—attributes that are central to the traditional male gender norm. The culmination is a science that is built on a foundation of masculinity and male perspectives, while femininity and female perspectives become antithetical to science. Consequently, what is considered to be objective and neutral can only be seen as masculine because these aspects are at the core of traditional masculinity. The opposite of these scientific attributes (e.g., emotionality, subjectivity, compassion) is thought to be associated with the feminine and to have no place in science. As a result, women are not perceived as being objective and are often excluded from traditional scientific discourse. Not only are women's voices stifled by traditional science in this way, but women have been discouraged from pursuing scientific careers because they are not seen as legitimate researchers (e.g., as unbiased investigators).

Advocates of feminist standpoint epistemology (e.g., Harding, 1987, 1998; Hartsock, 1998) argue that to rectify the problems associated with conventional objectivity, we should focus on women's unique experiences, because knowledge gained from conventional objectivity represents only a partial understanding of human behavior and social life. The premise of this theory is that the perspective of people in subordinated positions provides for a more complete understanding of human behavior and experiences. Because each subordinate social group is in a position that those with power do not occupy, they come to know a world that remains invisible for other, more powerful groups. Therefore, each unique social position has a perspective that other groups do not share.

As a related issue, feminist scholars (e.g., Crawford & Marecek, 1989; Harding, 1987, 1998; Haraway, 1991; Hartsock, 1998; Peplau & Conrad, 1989; Sherif, 1979; Wittig, 1985) have criticized traditional science's goal of establishing universal laws of behavior and experience. For example, standpoint theorists argue that because people live in different social locations, attempting to establish general laws of behavior and experience is futile. They point out that such an approach ignores individuals' unique experiences, especially as they are influenced by the interlocking systems of gender, race, class, sexual orientation, and other social identities. Moreover, they observe that even though the goal of traditional, mainstream science has been to determine laws that can apply to all people, women have largely been excluded as research participants. For example, it is not uncommon for research findings based exclusively on samples of men (usually white) to be used to represent the experiences of both men and women. Further, even when women are included as participants in the research, their experiences are sometimes folded into those of men, masking women's unique voice and any important differences between men and women (Crawford & Marecek, 1989; Eichler, 1988; Lykes & Stewart, 1986). This practice is obviously problematic because women's unique experiences, perspectives, and voices are overlooked, resulting in research findings that are ultimately biased and inaccurate (even though they are often purported to be objective and applicable to all human beings).

Although many feminist scholars have criticized the notion of objectivity and neutrality, some feminist researchers have actually advocated closer adherence to the scientific method as a way of incorporating feminist principles into their research. This strategy has been labeled *feminist empiricism* (Harding, 1987, 1998). In contrast to the criticisms outlined above, feminist empiricists actually promote conventional objectivity and argue that male-centered bias can be eliminated from the research process *only if* the positivist principle of objectivity is rigorously upheld. However, feminist empiricists differ from traditional scientists in that they consciously examine both the *context of discovery* (i.e., the process through which researchers develop research questions) and the *context of justification* (i.e., the process of selecting the research questions, data collection, testing of hypotheses, etc.). In other words, feminist empiricists discuss both *why* and *how* they study a particular topic; this *why* aspect of research is typically absent from traditional science. In disclosing this information, feminist empiricists generally address the decisions that influenced the design of the research, power relations pertaining to the topic, and how they can continue to be reflexive about the research process (Hesse-Biber et al., 2004). Thus, feminist empiricists, like other feminist researchers, view their research as a holistic process, attending to the relationship between the context of discovery and the context of justification. However, feminist empiricists do not question the primary epistemological tenets of the scientific method, especially the value of conventional objectivity. It is this aspect that continues to be a factor in discussions of feminist research, because some feminists contend that objective, bias-free research is impossible and, thus, should not form a basis for inquiry. Given the central role that these disagreements have played in feminist discourse, we discuss the issue of objectivity in research and the epistemological underpinnings of feminist survey research more broadly in coming sections.

Despite these disagreements, the current consensus among many feminist scholars is that positivism is not necessarily intrinsic to the survey research method, and in fact, surveys are frequently used by feminist social scientists (Maynard, 1994). Indeed, feminist survey researchers have integrated feminist beliefs into their research and often question the core assumptions of conventional science (Peplau & Conrad, 1989). Many have reshaped traditional approaches to research so they are more in line with feminist goals (Harding, 1987; Peplau & Conrad, 1989). We will offer concrete examples of feminist survey research in subsequent sections.

## Narratives and Numbers

The epistemological issues reviewed above often serve as the foundation in discussions regarding a preference for qualitative or quantitative research methods. In these debates, some of the most vigorous in feminist studies, some scholars have claimed that applying a feminist perspective may necessitate the use of qualitative methods (e.g., Condor, 1986; Landrine, Klonoff, & Brown-Collins, 1992; Marecek, Fine, & Kidder, 1997; Sherif, 1979; Smith, 1987). Alternatively, we posit that both qualitative and quantitative methods are useful in feminist research, but in different ways. Before discussing the specific benefits of quantitative research, we will describe the major differences between quantitative and qualitative research methods.

When a researcher collects quantitative data, individuals' experiences are translated into numerical categories, usually predefined by the researcher and then evaluated using statistical analyses. Often, the categories defined are very narrow in scope (e.g., for race, there may only be the categories of white and nonwhite), with most researchers deciding beforehand what specific aspects of people's experiences or attitudes they will examine. In this situation, research participants have little influence on what information is subjected to analysis (Jayaratne & Stewart, 1991). Moreover, because the categories are defined beforehand, researchers assume they know enough about the phenomena to construct relevant categories. However, not all quantitative research proceeds in this way. Sometimes researchers collect data without confining them to predetermined categories (e.g., asking for race as a free-response, fill-in-the-blank question), and they later transform these responses into quantitative data (e.g., collapsing responses of "white" and "Euro-American" into the same category). Whichever data collection method is used, once the data are categorized into numerical codes, they are subjected to statistical analysis, based on those codes. Statistics has been a major topic of feminist debate because it quantifies people's experiences as a "true reality" (Reinharz, 1992), limiting, to some extent, our understanding of that reality. One statistical procedure that has been heavily criticized in this way is the removal or "control" of the effects of particular factors, such as gender, race, or social class, to rule them out as explanations in hypothesis testing. These factors are treated as error rather than as important sources of information, and this confines the interpretation of data. However, this practice is rarely used by feminist survey researchers who consider these factors important social categories of analysis.

In contrast to quantification, qualitative data (e.g., nonnumeric data from semistructured or unstructured interviews) are generally evaluated through the use of themes or categories that emerge *after* data collection (although this practice is not universal in all qualitative methods). Because the themes or categories are not narrowly defined a priori by the researcher, participants often have the freedom to respond to research questions in ways that make sense to them. As a result, these data typically include information that participants themselves think is important. Proponents of qualitative research methods argue that this aspect of qualitative research is extremely important because participants should be able to describe their experiences as they perceive them, not through the researcher's preconceived notions about what their world is like (Landrine et al., 1992; Marecek et al., 1997; Wallston & Grady, 1992). Additionally, the fact that the data are analyzed in a contextual form allows the researcher to understand the responses more broadly, with the potential for an in-depth understanding of phenomena. This is not to say that qualitative data are not prone to bias; indeed, qualitative research is also subject to the researcher's perspective, as Gorelick (1996) points out:

After all, it is I who asked the questions, I who read the transcript, I who selected the materials to be placed in the text. . . . It is when I am trying to be most faithful to their meaning . . . that I am most painfully aware that simply "giving voice" is not so simple after all. . . . It is fraught with interpretation. (p. 38)

### Benefits of Quantitative Methods

Quantitative research methods, including survey research, can serve as an effective tool for supporting feminist goals and philosophies and can offer a number of advantages not found in qualitative work. First, quantitative research methods provide a vehicle for feminists to introduce issues of sexism, racism, classism, heterosexism, and other social justice concerns into mainstream discourses. This is perhaps the biggest benefit of quantitative research methods. Because science (including much of social science) is built on the ideal of stringent objectivity, mainstream researchers and the general public may be uncomfortable with alternative epistemologies and may be more apt to listen to and consider valid research that is quantitative (Spalter-Roth & Hartmann, 1996). Maynard (1994) points out that "feminist work needs to be rigorous if it is to be regarded as intellectually compelling, politically persuasive, policy-relevant, and meaningful to anyone other than feminists themselves" (p. 24). In describing her experiences as a feminist advocacy researcher, Steinberg (1996) recalls the necessity of "conducting defensible studies of publishable quality" (p. 247) so that her research would be positively received. "We followed, to the letter, mainstream social science quantitative techniques, conducting . . . a pilot test of our questionnaire, validating each question included, conducting tests of reliability and validity . . . and using rigorous sample selection procedures" (p. 236).

Second, the use of statistics may facilitate disseminating findings to nonfeminists, the lay public, and policymakers. Specifically, the brevity of numerical information makes it easy to report (e.g., women earn 70 cents for every dollar men earn for comparable work) and allows greater recall and comprehension (Reinharz, 1992) than other methods. This advantage of statistical research can be particularly beneficial for feminist advocates, because its relative simplicity can be readily translated into policy (Jayaratne, 1983; Jayaratne & Stewart, 1991).

Finally, quantitative research techniques can be helpful for understanding how particular attitudes, behaviors, or experiences are distributed or associated in a population, which can then determine the best course of action in implementing social change for women. For example, Chafetz (2004) has argued that finding similarities among women is a particularly useful way to proceed in understanding and alleviating gender oppression. While acknowledging that these commonalities "take different values in different times, places, and among subpopulations in a given time and place" (p. 322), she emphasizes that unless a researcher's aim is to develop a *deep* level of understanding about a phenomenon, identifying and connecting overarching patterns of experience (e.g., via survey research and the testing of quantitative models) are appropriate and necessary to examine the validity of and advance theories about gender. She concludes that rigorous quantitative-data-based research methods should be retained as a tool to promote a feminist agenda.

In sum, qualitative and quantitative research procedures are simply specific methods, and both have a well-founded place in the broader theory of how to do feminist research (Harding, 1987). Indeed, many claim that there is no particular method that is consistent with feminist values (Riger, 1992; Stanley & Wise, 1983), and rather than relying on one method, we should employ multiple methods (Reinharz, 1992). "Feminists no longer argue for a single procedure that produces one true story . . . the terrain has moved from singularity to plurality" (Gottfried, 1996, p. 14). Such *triangulation* (Jick, 1979) helps confirm that our findings are not an artifact of the specific method used; consequently, we can be more confident of findings and conclusions. By using multiple methods, feminist researchers can balance the drawbacks and benefits of different methods (see the chapter by Stewart & Cole, this volume). Triangulation also allows interpretations about the complexities of human behavior that may not be possible with other methods. In sum, qualitative and quantitative research methods

can be congruent with feminist values, and many contemporary feminist researchers embrace both these techniques. In this chapter, we focus specifically on the use of quantitative methods in survey research because, as outlined above, we believe there are clear benefits to using the survey research method to advocate for feminist social change.

## Similarities Between Feminist and Mainstream Survey Research

In the past few decades, many of the changes that feminist scholars have incorporated into their research have also been implemented by mainstream survey researchers. In fact, most current mainstream survey method texts (e.g., Groves et al., 2004) explicitly discuss the importance of issues raised by feminists and how to address them actively. Thus, there has been a parallel evolution of the work of feminist survey researchers and those doing mainstream survey research. Although these changes developed somewhat independently, the advances in both domains are compatible, because both emphasize the importance of high-quality research that provides valid and useful data.

A major concern of both mainstream and feminist survey researchers (and all scientists) is minimizing error in research. Error occurs when the information that is collected deviates from a "true" value—that is, the intended meaning of a response to a survey question given by a participant. Of course, we acknowledge that we can never know or assess that true value perfectly, but the point in survey research is to measure it as accurately (i.e., objectively, without bias) as possible. The more precise the information, the better our understanding of social phenomena and, thus, the more effective we can be in changing social conditions to benefit women.

There are two types of error, systematic and random. *Systematic error* refers to particular aspects of the researcher (e.g., her or his gender), the research participants (e.g., their understanding of English), the survey (e.g., questions that are very embarrassing), and the context (e.g., a shopping mall) that consistently influence the findings in such a way that the results are biased in a particular direction. For example, a male interviewer asking women about their sexual history might make women feel uncomfortable so that they do not report particular sexual experiences; this would influence the results in terms of underestimating the frequency of such experiences. Following accepted survey research methods can minimize this type of error (e.g., using female interviewers who are trained to be sensitive to sexual issues). In contrast, *random error* refers to all other fluctuations in measurement that might distort the data. For example, women who are asked how many hours per week they do housework are likely to interpret the term *housework* somewhat dissimilarly (e.g., either including food shopping or excluding food shopping). But which way a particular woman interprets the meaning of the question should be random; therefore, it does not bias the data. Thus, random error is less of a concern among researchers than systematic error.

Most mainstream survey research is also aligned with feminist research in that both emphasize the respectful treatment of participants, the use of ethical research questions, and the importance of dissemination of findings, topics we will explain and discuss more fully elsewhere in the chapter. Both traditions also generally have the ultimate goal of social transformation, although the specific types of social change may differ. As with feminists, many mainstream survey researchers are deeply committed to improving the human condition through their work. Because of these parallels, and because survey research is a mainstream method that can garner wide respect compared with alternative research methods, we argue that it can and, when appropriate, should be used as a vehicle to achieve feminist goals. However, there are important differences between feminist and mainstream survey researchers. What, then, distinguishes these two approaches to research?

## Feminist Methodology and the Survey Research Process

Feminist survey researchers differ from mainstream survey researchers in that they employ a *feminist methodology* in their research. In other words, the progression of their work is based on feminist principles (e.g., doing research "for" rather than "on" women) and a feminist vision of social change. What most distinguishes

feminist research from other types of scholarship, then, is the particular social change perspective that feminists bring to their work, specifically a focus on advancing social justice for women as a group. This perspective is critical in contributing to some, but not necessarily all, aspects of the survey research process. In line with Kelly (1978), we contend that the feminist perspective is most applicable during two specific points in the research process: the development of research questions (i.e., the context of discovery) and the interpretation of findings. These two points occur at the beginning and end stages of the survey research process, respectively. This applicability of the feminist perspective can best be conceptualized as the "bookends" of the survey research process; it holds the core of the research together (i.e., the "books") and gives individual components of the research process shape, structure, and meaning.

The components of the survey research method that come after the development of research questions and before the interpretation of findings (i.e., the middle stage, or books) involve decisions about how to implement the research—that is, choosing specific survey research techniques. According to Kelly (1978), the decisions in this middle stage must be made so that the research is unbiased and impartial rather than influenced by the perspective of the researcher. This is the case because the primary purpose of this phase of the research is to answer the research question. The middle stage of the survey research process, then, should be the least influenced by the feminist perspective, because it is during this stage that accepted survey research protocol should be followed so that bias is minimized. To be clear, we are not arguing that incorporating a feminist methodology into the survey research process does not or should not affect the other intermediary steps of the research, but rather that the feminist perspective is most applicable during the beginning and end stages of the process. Moreover, we maintain that the progression of feminist survey research in the middle stage is not necessarily feminist, because good survey research incorporates the same principles inherent in a feminist methodology.

We agree with Kelly's recommendation, then, while at the same time, we acknowledge and concur with the feminist criticisms that science (in any stage of the research process) cannot be *entirely* value neutral. Thus, while we contend that research is never completely impartial, we also recognize the importance of conducting research (the middle stage) in such a way as to reduce bias (error) as much as possible, whether that bias emanates from a sexist or a feminist perspective (or any other ideology). This approach was recently termed *strong objectivity* by Harding (2004) and earlier was called *feminist objectivity* by Haraway (1988). Hesse-Biber et al. (2004) summarize feminist objectivity as

> knowledge and truth that is partial, situated, subjective, power imbued, and relational. . . . [It] combines the goal of conventional objectivity—to conduct research completely free of social influence and or personal beliefs—with the reality that no one can achieve this goal . . . and recognizes that objectivity can only operate within the limitations of the scientists' personal beliefs and experiences. (p. 13)

In this view, by recognizing that knowledge is situated, objectivity is actually maximized. In other words, by becoming aware of and acknowledging the factors that influence the research process (including their own perspectives) while at the same time attempting to minimize such influences, researchers are better able to understand the true meaning of the information obtained.

Additionally, some have argued that for feminist research to make a real difference in women's lives, women's voices must be translated and linked with the social world via the researcher's interpretation of the experiences of research participants (Acker et al., 1983/1996; Gottfried, 1996). Gorelick (1996) maintains that this link between the researcher and the researched is necessary for substantive social change. The researcher, then, acts as an interpreter of the experiences of the researched by tracing and connecting the commonalities among participants and linking them with the social world and the structure of oppression. In this way, the researcher attempts to uncover "hidden oppressions both as they are felt and as they are obscured" (Gorelick, 1996, p. 38),

leading to a more complete understanding of women's lives. This translation is similar to the final stage (i.e., the interpretation stage) of the survey research process.

Although we emphasize that the feminist perspective is most critical at the start and end of a research project, as noted above, we do not mean to imply that feminist principles and values should never impact other aspects of the research. Indeed, we believe that the feminist values of inclusiveness, sensitivity, comprehensiveness, and respect are necessary elements of each phase of the research process (particularly during the middle stage), because these are all aspects of a feminist methodology. However, as another way in which feminist and mainstream survey research methods are parallel, good mainstream survey researchers are concerned with the same values. Thus, these values do not represent the feminist perspective alone, but they are shared by researchers who follow the standards of the survey research method, regardless of their overarching research orientation.

In sum, we recommend that if the survey method is selected as a research strategy, the unique feminist perspective should be emphatically employed at the beginning (development of research questions) and end (interpretation of findings) stages of the research endeavor. All subsequent decisions during the research process, including which type of survey to use; who to interview; how to design the survey instrument; how to collect the data; and how to prepare, analyze, and interpret data, should be based on the general principles of survey research and feminist objectivity. Below we present a brief overview of these components of survey research and highlight issues of particular relevance to feminist researchers.

## MAJOR COMPONENTS OF SURVEY RESEARCH

### Research Questions and Hypotheses

The first steps in the typical research process are to formulate research questions and develop hypotheses (the researcher's predictors about what the data will show), based on the analysis of previous research, theory, and the need for social change. The investigator then conducts the research to answer the questions and test the hypotheses. In some mainstream research, questions derive from an interest in advancing theory, without direct application to solving social problems. However, feminists are more likely to ask questions and develop hypotheses in a manner such that the research findings will have direct relevance to feminist social change. For example, feminist researchers interested in decreasing violence against women might ask, "What influences this violence?" The hypotheses researchers put forth will reflect not only their knowledge of previous research (e.g., that gender roles contribute to this violence) but also their interest, as feminists, in applying the findings of the research to ultimately decrease violence toward women. In this way, a feminist perspective directly influences the formulation of research questions as well as the way the hypotheses are articulated. A good illustration of how the feminist perspective affects and informs the context of discovery is the work of Spalter-Roth and Hartmann (1996). In their research, they set out to challenge the discourse of dependency surrounding single mothers on welfare. Thus, from the beginning, they sought to conduct and disseminate statistical findings from survey research to help destigmatize these women and reform public policy. By starting their research with the ultimate goal of social change, these researchers were able to gain "situated knowledge" (Haraway, 1991) about women on welfare and, thus, make concrete "real-world" progress for these women.

Only after the research questions and hypotheses are formulated should one consider which specific research method to use. What factors influence the decision to employ the survey research method? In general, if the goal of the research is to generalize the findings, to influence policymakers and public opinion, or to test hypotheses or complex theoretical models, the survey method may be an appropriate choice. For example, Jayaratne, Thomas, and Trautmann (2003) employed the survey method to evaluate an intervention program designed to keep middle school girls involved in science. The specific goal of the research was to determine the effectiveness of various aspects of the program among minority and nonminority girls. The survey research method was chosen for this project because it allowed the researchers to (1) gather the opinions of a large number of girls, (2) generalize the findings to middle school girls in general, (3) influence policymakers on the importance of science interventions for girls, and (4) statistically test hypotheses about outcome differences between girls who participated in the intervention and those who did not. Although qualitative interviews were initially considered because they would have yielded more in-depth understanding of the girls' opinions of the program, the main goals of the study were better addressed with the use of surveys than with other strategies. This use of survey research reflects a feminist perspective in that the ultimate objective was to generate information that would be used in the development of programs to increase both minority and nonminority girls' participation in science.

The discussion above assumes that the research process is deductive (i.e., starts with a theory or research hypothesis). While this is the traditional method of conducting survey research and the primary focus of this chapter, we acknowledge the value of using survey research techniques in inductive (i.e., exploratory) research. Such research starts with observations without a clear theoretical framework, with the goal of developing theory based on those observations. Most exploratory research tends to be qualitative in nature, partly because it is perceived as providing a more in-depth understanding of the data than quantitative methods. Because established theories have tended to reflect only the male perspective, many feminists have promoted the use of exploratory research to generate theory more consistent with women's viewpoints. Consequently, this is one reason why feminists have long called for greater use of qualitative methods. However, both qualitative and quantitative data can be a rich source of information, and thus, both can be used to generate and test theory. Therefore, survey research, while primarily considered a quantitative method, can be effectively employed for either inductive or deductive purposes. Feminist researchers, then, should be open to using the survey research method whether their research is inductive or deductive, or whether their preference is to collect qualitative or quantitative data. Indeed, using survey research as part of a mixed method research design may be an important addition to the qualitative researcher's toolbox because using many different methods can ultimately lead to data that are seen as both rich and objective.

## Types of Surveys

Surveys are typically categorized by how they are administered—that is, how the data are collected. Traditional methods include face-to-face interviewing (questions asked by an interviewer in person, also termed *personal interviewing*), telephone interviewing (questions asked by an interviewer over the phone), and paper-and-pencil or mailed questionnaires (typically when respondents fill in answers on paper and return the questionnaire to the researcher, usually by mail). Newer methods of survey administration employ computers in the data collection process. The fastest growing application of computers is the development of Web surveys, which many survey researchers are now using to replace traditional paper-and-pencil questionnaires (Groves et al., 2004).

Each of these survey techniques has various benefits and drawbacks. Factors such as availability of funding, privacy issues, interaction between interviewer and respondent, question format, experience with technology, sampling, and response bias are all relevant aspects that should be taken into account. Many researchers employ multiple methods or combine methods to balance these factors. In some situations, the optimal type of survey will be determined by a single overriding factor, such as strict funding limitations. Below we briefly outline some of the major advantages and disadvantages of each type of survey.

Face-to-face interviews tend to be very costly, but they allow more direct involvement of the interviewer. This method is most appropriate for surveys that require extensive probing and clarification. However, when the topic of investigation is particularly sensitive, face-to-face interviews may yield data that are influenced by social desirability, because the presence of an interviewer may cause respondents to reply with answers that they believe the interviewer prefers (see Campbell, 1982; Rogers,

1971). This is important to consider when conducting research on gender, race, or sexuality, which may involve sensitive and controversial matters. However, high-quality feminist research on very sensitive issues has been conducted using such interviewing techniques. Stewart and Dottolo's (2005) research provides a good example. In their work, diverse groups of faculty were interviewed regarding their experiences of sexism, racism, and heterosexism in academia, and the researchers appeared to receive quite thoughtful and honest responses. If done respectfully and ethically, face-to-face interviews can provide a wealth of information.

Telephone interviewing has been shown to produce results generally similar to those obtained with face-to-face interviewing methods (Groves & Kahn, 1979). Although telephone interviews are considerably less expensive and seem less intrusive, results can also be affected by the interview process, often by what the interviewer says (or does not say) during the interview. In recent years, the development of devices or services for screening telephone calls has resulted in lower rates of response for telephone surveys. Research shows that in general, these lower rates have not affected the types of individuals who answer telephone surveys (Pew Research Center, 2004). However, researchers should be aware of this issue and how it might affect data collection.

Paper-and-pencil or mailed surveys and Web surveys are typically less expensive than either telephone or face-to-face surveys, but there tends to be less control over how they are administered because respondents often fill them out in unknown circumstances. In addition, they may have lower response rates because people can easily refuse to participate. Incentives can help enormously with this problem (as detailed in Dillman, 1978). However, an advantage of these surveys is that they typically allow more privacy and, thus, are helpful when investigating sensitive issues. This setting can create an important advantage for feminist researchers, because research participants are likely to feel comfortable with the research situation and give voice to their true opinions or experiences. Obviously, the decision about which type of survey to employ is multifaceted, but it is significant in that it affects all other aspects of the research and has major implications for the quality of the data collected.

## Sampling

Sampling refers to the selection of people from a population to whom the survey instrument will be administered (Stangor, 2004). A *population* is defined as the larger group of individuals the researcher wants to study, and a *sample* is the smaller subset of individuals that actually participates in the research. Sampling is important in survey research because it determines if it is appropriate to generalize the research findings from a sample to a population.

There are two main types of sampling techniques, probability and nonprobability. Each has its own set of advantages and disadvantages, and both are prone to sample bias. In nonprobability sampling, respondents are selected using some nonrandom procedure. One type of nonprobability sampling is *convenience sampling.* Convenience sampling consists of recruiting participants from places where they are easily accessible. For example, much research in feminist social psychology uses samples of college students (e.g., Smith & Frieze, 2003). While convenience sampling can provide insights into the sampled population (e.g., college students), researchers who use this method of selection need to be cautious about generalizing their findings beyond the characteristics of their sample (e.g., to middle-aged individuals). A variation of convenience sampling is *snowball sampling*, in which participants invite others in their social network to join the sample. The work of Konik and Stewart (2004) provides a good example of snowball sampling. This research was rooted in the feminist goal of illuminating the psychological strengths of sexual minorities, who have often been stigmatized by both mainstream psychology and the general public. This sampling method was used because minority group members (i.e., sexual minorities) can be difficult to identify in the larger population. By using this sampling technique, these researchers were able to increase the number of people included in their study because participants were encouraged to recruit their friends, acquaintances, and so on to also participate. However, a major drawback of snowball sampling

is that it can create systematic sources of sampling error, because participants are likely to recruit others who share similar characteristics. Overall, the primary benefits of nonprobability sampling are that it is relatively inexpensive and can usually generate a large sample more quickly than probability sampling strategies (Biemer & Lyberg, 2003). This sampling method can also be ideal for preliminary tests of hypotheses before validating them with a more representative sample, as in exploratory research. The major disadvantage of nonprobability sampling is that is does not permit researchers to make broad generalizations about their findings.

Probability samples (also called random samples) are those in which every individual in a target population has a known (nonzero) chance of selection, and the selection process is random (Czaja & Blair, 1996). This sampling strategy has the distinct advantage of producing findings that can be generalized to the population of interest. Because probability sampling techniques allow the researcher to collect information from a wider spectrum of people, compared with nonrandom techniques, the findings will be inclusive of many viewpoints. This should be important to feminist researchers. Additionally, if the goal of the research is to inform public policy regarding women's issues, probability sampling may be preferable, because such research will be more persuasive if it is generalizable. A major disadvantage is the monetary cost associated with obtaining probability samples. The choice of whether to use probability or nonprobability sampling, however, ultimately depends on the resources available to the researcher and the need to apply the results broadly. Researchers should carefully choose the sampling method by weighing the advantages and disadvantages associated with various sampling techniques.

## Survey Construction

Survey construction concerns issues of length and format of the overall survey, as well as the design, order, and format of the specific questions that will be included. The main prerequisites for designing a good survey are deciding exactly what is important to *measure* (i.e., what questions will be asked) and *how* questions will be asked (Fowler, 1984). For feminists, some of those decisions come in the context of discovery and should be based on what information is needed to evaluate the stated hypotheses. This process of translating a hypothesis into a specific, testable, and measurable procedure is called *operationalization* (Vogt, 1999), and exactly which questions are asked will depend on how concepts are operationalized.

In the beginning stage of survey construction, it can be beneficial to conduct in-depth discussions with individuals who are representative of the population of interest (e.g., *focus groups*). This can help the researcher understand the way people talk about the issues the survey will address and choose the appropriate vocabulary and phrasing of questions. This can also suggest issues, concerns, and ways of looking at the topic that the researcher has not considered (Fowler, 1984). Thus, these discussions can be a valuable tool to gain situated knowledge about a subordinated group. For example, in their study of AIDS-related behaviors and attitudes, Quina et al. (1999) conducted focus groups with two community samples of low-educated women who gave feedback about readability, length, format, content, emotional responses, and truthfulness in responding to their survey. This allowed the population of interest (i.e., low-educated women) to participate in the research process and have a voice in the research; these are aspects that are central to feminist methodology.

## Survey Organization

The organization of the survey—that is, the layout and format of the questions—should make the tasks of the respondent (and the interviewer if doing survey interviews) as easy as possible. Alreck and Settle (1995) recommend that surveys be organized into three main sections: introduction, body, and conclusion. The survey should flow smoothly and easily from section to section. Unless there is good reason to administer different questions or survey formats to different groups of respondents, all respondents should get the same set of questions in the same order (Fowler, 1984). Any differences in the surveys will likely create differences in responses and, thus, will make it harder to compare responses from one individual and another.

The survey should avoid employing questions that might be threatening, particularly sensitive, or very difficult to answer. If possible, it should begin with the most general questions. However, because the order of questions can profoundly affect responses, the dependent measures (i.e., the outcome variable[3] of interest) should come before the independent measures (i.e., the cause of the variable of interest). Respondents should also be assured early in the survey that honest rather than favorable answers are the most helpful (Fowler, 1984). If possible, questions in the body of the survey should be grouped together by topic (e.g., questions about work) and response categories (e.g., agree/disagree) so respondents have to focus on only one issue or set of response options at a time (Alreck & Settle, 1995). The survey should conclude with the most sensitive and intrusive questions, when rapport and trust are likely greatest—important components of the feminist research process.

## Designing Questions

It is preferable to use measures already shown to be valid and reliable (Fowler, 1984). Valid measures are those that actually assess what they are supposed to access; reliable measures consistently measure the same construct. If such measures are not available, or their exact format is not practical, the researcher will need to design questions or adapt existing measures suited to the population of interest. One significant problem with early survey research was that measures that were validated on men were often given to women without being validated with samples of women (Eichler, 1988). Because these measures were based on the male perspective, they may not have been appropriate or meaningful for use with women. Thus, in researching any specific group of individuals, it is important, if possible, to use measures that have been validated on individuals in that group. If an existing measure has not been appropriately validated, or if the researcher is unsure of the validation history of the measure, the validation of the measure should be incorporated into the research.

The major issues to address in designing questions are comprehension (the ease with which the respondent interprets and understands the question), retrieval (the degree to which the respondent can recall the information needed to answer the question), and reporting (the ability to formulate a response and put it in the format required by the questionnaire) (Groves et al., 2004). Clearly, if questions are not understood by the respondent, retrieval and reporting will be inaccurate. An excellent example of feminist research that adapted a survey for increased comprehension is Quina et al.'s (1999) work on AIDS behavior and attitudes. In the process of modifying their survey to make it more appropriate for the population of interest, they brought the readability level of the survey from the 12th-grade level (for which it was originally designed) to the 6th-grade level. They accomplished this with comments and feedback from groups of women who were similar to those that would be completing the survey (women with low literacy skills). This strategy allowed women in the population of interest to "be on the same plane" as the researchers and incorporate their voice into research that was ultimately about and for them—this is an important aspect of employing feminist methodology. Of course, when questions are rewritten to improve readability for use with diverse samples, they can still sustain rigorous psychometric properties and, thus, maximize feminist objectivity.

Empirical research shows that respondents can and do have different interpretations of the same questions, especially when those questions are vague or contain technical terms (Groves et al., 2004; Schwarz, Groves, & Schuman, 1998). As a result, it is important to word questions so that all respondents are likely to interpret them similarly (Fowler, 1984). To minimize the likelihood of different interpretations, it is helpful to use everyday, nontechnical, unambiguous language when designing questions. Additionally, following the principles of feminist research, it is important to take into account differences between various social groups (e.g., different ethnicities, social classes, or cultures) (Fowler, 1984) and to use nonoppressive (i.e., nonsexist, nonracist) language (Eichler, 1988). Landrine et al. (1992) examined black and white women's interpretations of gender-related words and phrases (e.g., "I am feminine," "I am passive," and "I am assertive") and found that women associated very different meanings with the words, which influenced their responses to how well the words characterized themselves. For example, while black women defined the word *passive* as not saying what one really thinks, white women defined it as laid-back or easygoing, suggesting differences in question meaning and interpretation.

### Types of Questions

There are two different types of questions used in survey research: *closed-ended* questions and *open-ended* questions. Closed-ended questions present participants with a list of specific response options, while open-ended questions allow participants to provide their own answers. In survey research, open-ended questions are similar to fill-in-the-blank or short-answer questions, and closed-ended questions are more like multiple-choice questions (Groves et al., 2004). For example, if researchers are interested in assessing feelings about gay men and lesbians serving in the military, they might ask respondents to choose between two alternatives in describing their views on this issue (e.g., "They should not be allowed to serve." and "They should be allowed to serve."). The researcher could also ask this as an open-ended question (such as "What are your views on gay men and lesbians in the military?").

It is important to consider carefully answer categories when designing closed-ended questions. Researchers should provide a broad range of response options so that they do not exclude those an individual might want to offer. Eichler (1988) describes how this was a major problem with early survey research. Results often were androcentrically biased, as closed-ended questions in surveys would routinely only provide response options for the answers that men were more likely to supply.

Mainstream survey researchers provide recommendations for designing questions pertaining to feelings, behaviors, and attitudes about sensitive and highly charged issues. Because feminist researchers often conduct research on these types of issues, outlining these recommendations here might be helpful. When constructing a survey on sensitive issues, Sudman and Bradburn (1982, as described in Groves et al., 2004) suggest it is better to use open-ended questions for eliciting the frequency of behaviors and experiences, because closed-ended questions suggest general norms, which may be outside the respondents' experiences. These authors also suggest asking respondents about their experiences over a long time period (e.g., "your life" vs. "the last year"), which can help minimize embarrassment associated with some issues, and using familiar nontechnical terms for describing sensitive behavior because it may make respondents more comfortable (e.g., "sex" rather than "coitus"). Finally, with extremely sensitive issues, these authors recommend that researchers consider collecting data in diary form. These mainstream strategies for constructing survey questions with respect parallel the principles of feminist research.

One example that illustrates the use of both open- and closed-ended questions is the research on violence against women conducted by Smith (1994). He found that including open-ended questions and asking about the prevalence of violence over their lifetime aided tremendously in interviewer-respondent rapport, and this practice ultimately led to a more nuanced understanding of victims' experiences. He suggests that both closed- and open-ended questions should be included when assessing sensitive experiences in a survey. Although closed-ended questions can limit richness and variety because they do not allow respondents to answer in their own words, they can also be beneficial because they are quicker and easier to answer, making individuals more likely to respond (Fowler, 1984). Whether one uses closed-ended or open-ended questions, the format should be short and specific, resulting in less error on the part of both the respondent and, in the case of survey interviews, the interviewer (Fowler, 1984).

*Pretesting*

After the survey instrument is initially designed, it is helpful to pretest it, that is, to administer it to a small group of individuals (similar to those who will be included in the final sample) in order to determine if it requires further revision. In a pretest, the researcher typically asks individuals not only to respond to questions, but also to articulate their thoughts about the wording of the questions (e.g., if the questions were clear) and the overall design of the survey. This process can provide insights into interpretations of question meanings (Schwarz et al., 1998) and, therefore, may enhance the quality of the survey instrument. A similar technique for improving surveys prior to their administration is cognitive interviewing, in which respondents report in-depth understanding of questions (e.g., verbalize their thoughts while they are answering a question).

## Data Collection

Although the term *data collection* tends to imply that respondents' opinions exist independently of how they are assessed, it is critical to recognize that the *process* of data collection is an integral part of what constitutes data (Groves et al., 2004). For example, the interviewer, the interview setting, and the answer options, as well as extraneous conditions, can all influence the information that is obtained. Early survey research tended to ignore the effect of some of these elements, resulting in data that were often biased in favor of the researcher's viewpoint or the prevailing social discourse. This aspect of traditional survey research was a major focus of much feminist criticism, because it meant that a woman's viewpoint was frequently distorted. Riessman (1987), for example, has documented how both ethnicity and social class affect the interview process, and ultimately how the data are interpreted. In her research, an Anglo, middle-class woman conducted an interview with both a middle-class Anglo woman and a working-class Puerto Rican woman on the topic of marital separation and divorce. In describing their experiences, the narratives of the two women interviewees differed dramatically, representing dissimilar backgrounds. From an evaluation of the transcripts of these interviews, Riessman found that the interviewer's comments (reflecting the interviewer's own middle-class background) influenced the interview process. In this way, Riessman showed how being from a different social class (despite being of the same gender) can alter the meaning of the respondent's narrative, thus potentially increasing error in the data. Current survey techniques emphasize the value of minimizing such error effects during data collection (see Groves et al., 2004) and promoting awareness of how cultural factors (e.g., ethnicity, gender, and class) and interviewer attributes affect the quality of the research. As such, both mainstream and feminist survey researchers see interviewing as an exchange rather than as a one-way process. They are distinguished, however, by their emphasis on the role that this two-way exchange plays in the research process. Feminist researchers are more likely to employ unstructured interviews in their research, whereas mainstream researchers are more likely to use structured or semistructured interviews as a way to lessen bias and to find consistencies in the data (if the research participants respond to different questions, it may be difficult to find overarching themes). The point is that both groups of researchers are aware of and committed to taking into account the various perspectives of the participants and minimizing the effects of extraneous factors that might unduly influence the data during the interviewing process.

### Ethical Treatment of Participants

Numerous aspects of the research process are subject to ethical evaluation (e.g., truthful reporting of data, giving credit to those contributing to the research), that is, the assessment of how well the research conforms to culturally accepted ethical principles. However, most discussions of research ethics have tended to focus on how the participants in research are treated by the researcher. This is likely a result of serious abuses of research participants that have occurred in the not too distant past. Perhaps the most notorious examples are Milgram's (1974) obedience studies and the Tuskegee syphilis study (see Jones, 1981). Milgram led participants to believe they were administering shocks to another person for purposes of "teaching," a procedure that greatly distressed many of the participants. In the Tuskegee experiment, the government studied the progress of syphilis in African American males without informing these men of their disease and without treating them, despite the existence of penicillin as an effective remedy. Although these are not examples of survey research, per se, an awareness of such exploitation resulted in a broad effort to prevent mistreatment of participants in all research on human subjects.

Among the voices included in this movement to enact strict standards for the ethical treatment of research participants were those of feminist scholars. In fact, many initial feminist critiques of research targeted this particular aspect of the research process, because exploitation of research participants conflicted with basic humanistic values that are fundamental to feminism. These critiques often advocated decreasing or eliminating the power differential between the researcher and the researched (Du Bois, 1983; Fee, 1983). For example, Reinharz (1979) suggested that an equal relationship would likely yield information that reflects the participant's reality rather than the researcher's reality. She characterized this collaboration as "non-hierarchical, non-authoritarian, non-manipulative" (p. 181), terms that reflect core feminist principles. Other feminists called for the need to redefine the process as "research with" or "research for" rather than "research on" (Stanley & Wise, 1983). As Harding (1987) explained, "the best feminist analysis . . . insists that the inquirer her/himself be placed in the same critical plane as the overt subject matter" (p. 9). Thus, feminists sought to appreciate and value research participants rather than consider them as "objects" of study.

One result of this effort was the establishment of Institutional Review Boards (now commonplace in most research organizations), which set mandatory standards for the conduct of research, such as the protection of privacy and protection from harm. These standards are clearly laid out in The Belmont Report, written by the National Commission for the Protection of Human Subjects of Biomedical and Behavioral Research (1998). The Belmont Report specifies three principles for the conduct of research on human research participants: (1) respect for persons (informed consent and protection from the risk of harm), (2) beneficence (maximizing benefits and minimizing risks to subjects), and (3) justice (fairness in the distribution of the benefits of research and equal treatment). In addition to these formal standards, most current research texts, including those focusing on the survey research method, explicitly address these issues and emphasize both the ethical and the legal basis for conducting research ethically (e.g., Dooley, 1990; Groves et al., 2004; Rubin & Babbie, 1993). While these guidelines cannot guarantee that all research involving humans will follow these principles, they do go a long way in promoting such standards. Certainly, these principles are central to feminist methodology and have long been advocated among feminist researchers.

One major change resulting from these guidelines is that individuals who currently participate in research must give informed consent—that is, they must indicate that they understand the nature of their research participation and freely agree to be involved. Previously, individuals could show passive consent by not refusing a request to participate. Informed consent, thus, makes explicit the importance of respect for those taking part in the research. Although it is heartening that science has come so far in attempting to protect individuals who are susceptible to exploitation in the name of science, it is imperative that we, as feminists, continue to be vigilant in maintaining and applying those safeguards. Furthermore, while these standards promote the ethical treatment of subjects, they do not eliminate the power differential between the researcher and the researched, a theme of central importance among feminists. Despite the unconventionality of conceptualizing respondents as "collaborators" in survey research (as in all research methods), thinking of respondents in this way not only will help to minimize the power differential but, as Reinharz (1979) suggests, will also allow us to gather information that more accurately describes the reality of respondents' lives.

## Preparing, Analyzing, and Interpreting Data

### Processing of Data

Once the data are collected, a series of procedures are frequently required before they can be analyzed. These involve data entry (entering the raw numeric data into computer files), codebook construction (variable documentation), and coding (translating nonnumeric data into numerical categories). A codebook is a record (typically in printed form) of the variables in the survey and includes the variable name, a number assigned to the variable (required in many statistical analysis programs), the question wording, and the numeric code value for and meaning of each of the answer options (e.g., the value of "1" could be assigned to represent "women" in the gender variable). Most of these procedures are routine and serve to minimize errors in the data while increasing the efficiency of the data analysis; therefore, they have little direct relevance to feminist values. One exception is when open-ended questions are coded. In this case, the interpretation and classification of responses can be influenced by the particular perspective of the coder and are thus especially relevant to the issue of feminist objectivity. Below, we briefly discuss the coding of open-ended data, because of the popularity of these types of questions among many feminist researchers. Open-ended questions are often favored among feminist researchers because they allow the individuals to respond in their own voices (Landrine et al., 1992; Marecek et al., 1997; Wallston & Grady, 1992).

Typically, answers to closed-ended questions (e.g., agree/disagree) are precoded, in that each answer is associated with a particular numeric value prior to the coding process. Open-ended questions with relatively few answer options or with short, simple answers that are clearly interpreted (e.g., employment status) can be coded in a straightforward manner by assigning a number code to each category. For more complex open-ended answers, such as political opinions expressed in participants' own words, it is necessary to interpret the meaning of the response as well as to assign the response to a particular numeric category. Because data in survey research are not presented verbatim, but rather are aggregated into categories, the interpretation and coding of those responses is significant. One the one hand, because the interpretive process can be highly subjective, applying a feminist perspective (or any other particular perspective) when coding can distort the *intended* meaning of the response (and may increase error). On the other hand, such interpretation may be seen as using a feminist lens through which to view the data and articulating a feminist viewpoint (which may otherwise be suppressed). This dialectical aspect of feminist survey research (i.e., translating open-ended data into categories for statistical analysis) can be an important issue in feminist scholarship, because the researcher attempts to maintain conventional objectivity while at the same time giving voice to women or any subjugated group. To help ease this tension, various methods can be used to minimize or estimate bias during coding, such as conducting extensive coder training, using more than one coder and calculating the interrater reliability of coding, obtaining feedback from the coders during the coding process, and asking for input from respondents regarding the "correct" interpretation of their words. However, none of these methods ensures accuracy of the intended meaning of the response, and thus, researchers who engage in coding of qualitative data should use caution and reflexivity during this process.

### Data Analysis

As quantitative information, survey data are analyzed using a broad and complex array of statistical techniques, which are continually evolving and expanding to meet the needs of survey researchers. Given the large number of possible ways in which data can be analyzed, a subject that is covered thoroughly in statistical courses and texts (e.g., Pedhazur & Schmelkin, 1991), we will focus here on more general issues regarding both the function of statistical analysis and the appropriate use of statistics for answering the research question. In discussing the uses of statistics, we will briefly address feminist concerns that statistics are tools that objectify and distort women's voices, a view expressed in some early feminist scholarship.

*Purpose of Statistical Analysis.* Statistical analysis is a technique used to summarize data, that is, to aggregate individual items of data. This is necessary in survey research because the information that is collected cannot be easily understood, interpreted, or disseminated in its raw form, as it is composed of multiple elements representing the opinions or beliefs of many individuals. Without statistical analysis, determining the meaning of this information would be unwieldy and subject to a wide range of interpretations. Because statistics allow us to better understand the data, they can offer a way

to more "objectively" judge various hypotheses, compared with other analytic methods (Jayaratne, 1983). For example, if two different but equally plausible strategies are proposed by feminists for persuading voters to support legislation upholding women's right to choose, a statistical analysis of data on voter attitudes should demonstrate which method is likely to be the most effective in accomplishing this goal.

Statistics have been the target of feminist criticism because feminists have linked them with the quantification of subjective personal experiences. However, as feminist methodology has evolved, some feminist scholars (e.g., Jayaratne & Stewart, 1991) have tempered this criticism by pointing out that it is not statistics, per se, that are objectionable, but rather how they are used within the broader context of research that determines whether they violate feminist principles. For example, sexist or racist theories have often been supported by supposedly objective statistical analyses (e.g., Buss, 1989; Herrnstein & Murray, 1994). Despite the use of statistics to buttress such research, the evaluation of data based on mathematical standards and statistical principles is not inherently consistent with either feminist or sexist values. We contend that rather than seeing statistical methods as a violation of feminist values, as mentioned in earlier critiques, the appropriate use of statistics in feminist research can actually increase the likelihood that the findings are interpreted as valid (Jayaratne, 1983; Reinharz, 1992). Because of this, we argue that the use of statistics can advance feminist research goals of achieving social justice and change for women.

*Appropriate Use of Statistical Techniques and Knowledge of Statistics.* Knowing which statistical techniques should be used to answer a specific research question is a significant issue, because conducting inappropriate statistical analyses can not only distort the findings of a study, but, in the worst-case scenario, can actually produce results that are opposite from those that accurately reflect the collected data. Therefore, we emphasize the importance of a comprehensive understanding of statistics before embarking on any survey research study. However, it is also critical to recognize that no matter how well one applies statistical principles during data analysis, if other aspects of the research are in violation of accepted standards of methodology, the results of the statistical analysis will be invalid; as it is commonly phrased, "garbage in, garbage out." For example, when a survey question does not capture the intended construct, then statistical procedures will produce results that are not valid in testing the hypothesis.

*Evaluating Hypotheses Using Statistical Results.* When statistical analyses are complete, researchers must judge the statistical results based on their experience and training and then apply that judgment to the evaluation of the hypotheses. If the research components (e.g., sampling, question wording, data analysis) are appropriately chosen and implemented, then this interpretation should be clear. However, this is rarely as straightforward as it sounds. For example, it is not uncommon for statistical analyses to produce equivocal findings. Sometimes, one set of results contradicts other results. It might also be the case that the research findings appear to conflict with feminist ideals and interests. In this situation, it may be worthwhile to reevaluate the research to explore the possibility that such findings result from a deviation in accepted research protocol (e.g., misinterpretations of question wording or sampling bias). However, it may additionally be helpful to ask why a particular finding appears to conflict with feminist principles. This might lead to alternative understandings of the phenomena of interest that were previously not considered. For the novice feminist researcher, who is likely to expect clear-cut answers, this can be frustrating. Nevertheless, because social behavior is subject to multiple, interacting influences, which frequently cannot be accounted for, our attempt to understand or predict human behavior is inexact. For many investigators, studying complex phenomena without definitive answers is a valuable and rich part of research. Science is an iterative process with numerous attempts to establish a knowledge framework that is then subject to modification with the next set of findings (Kuhn, 1970).

# Interpretation and Dissemination of Results

The final component of survey research is the interpretation and dissemination of findings,

following the evaluation of the hypotheses. We consider the feminist perspective to be particularly applicable and necessary in this phase of the survey research process. We believe that this stage (or bookend) can be most amenable to influencing real social change for women and other marginalized groups.

## Interpretation of Results

How a researcher interprets the overall results is the culmination of the investigation in the sense that it involves the evaluation of findings as they pertain to the research question, which was articulated in the initial steps of the research process. Unlike the evaluation of the hypotheses using statistical information (a process that should follow accepted survey research practice), interpreting the meaning of the research results, as it applies to the research question, should especially be subject to a feminist perspective. In other words, giving feminist significance to the results is a critical aspect of feminist survey research. For example, if a statistic indicates that there is a significant difference between men and women on some characteristic (such as mathematical ability), there are myriad interpretations of what that means. One could see this finding as indicating support for the "deficit hypothesis," that is, that women are naturally inferior to men—an orientation seen frequently in earlier (and sometimes current) psychological and social research and much criticized by feminist scholars (Eichler, 1988; Jayaratne & Kaczala, 1983). Alternatively, one could interpret this difference as reflecting the oppression of women (e.g., due to unequal educational experiences) and pointing to the need for social change. Therefore, the feminist meanings we give our results are what mark the research endeavor as a significant feminist enterprise.

*Evaluating the Findings in Relation to the Literature.* As noted above, the purpose of social research is to advance incrementally our understanding of the interplay among human behaviors, attributes, and social and environmental conditions. To attain this goal, it is imperative to interpret the overall findings as they relate to the larger body of empirical and theoretical literature. This can mean supporting previous research by presenting findings that are consistent with prevailing work or, as in the case of much feminist scholarship, challenging the dominant paradigm. Revisionist activity (i.e., the reinterpretation of traditional, male-oriented research by infusing new findings that are consistent with feminist perspectives) has been a major function of feminist scholarship and continues to be a central aspect of feminist methodology.

### The Dissemination of Research Findings

The final step of the entire research process can be an exceptionally gratifying part of the research journey, not only because there is anticipated closure, but also because this step addresses the most fundamental goal of feminist research—to enact real-world social change for women. This step is the dissemination of findings, and it acts as a catalyst for that change. For feminists, this means reporting the results to scholars, the public, the media, or policymakers by linking the results back to women's lives with a clear understanding of how the findings can benefit women. As we have argued, survey research can be particularly effective in advocating for women and other marginalized groups in public policy arenas, because it is both mainstream and feminist. Spalter-Roth and Hartmann (1996) called the synthesis between conducting research that meets the standards of mainstream social science and the feminist goal of doing research "for" rather than "on" women "the dual vision of feminist policy research" (p. 207). In applying this dual vision in their work for women who combine paid employment and welfare, they placed women at the center of their research and also provided credible evidence that welfare policies stigmatized the survival efforts of single mothers. Spalter-Roth and Hartmann distributed their findings through a number of public and media outlets.

Another excellent example of how survey research can be applied to real-world social change for women is the Supreme Court's rulings on affirmative action at the University of Michigan. In 2003, the American Psychological Association submitted an amicus curiae brief to the Supreme Court, which supported the University of Michigan's policy of race- and gender-aware admissions in higher education in two court cases (*Gratz v. Bollinger*, 2003; *Grutter v. Bollinger*, 2003). This brief drew heavily from feminist psychologist Patricia Gurin's survey research on the value of diversity in academia, which demonstrated the benefits of such environments for students (as summarized in Gurin, Dey, & Hurtado, 2002). The Court's decision to uphold the principle of considering race and gender in college admissions illustrates the effective use of survey data in contributing to social change efforts.

We strongly advocate the dissemination of findings from survey research to effect social change for women and as part of feminist methodology. However, Jayaratne and Kaczala (1983) caution that misinterpretations of findings are frequently used to advance nonfeminist agendas. These authors, as well as McCall and Stocking (1982), suggest that feminist researchers take steps to minimize and correct any misunderstandings of their own or others' research that may arise.

A final important aspect of disseminating results is acknowledging the limitations of the research. This is one way of employing feminist objectivity. Indeed, no research is perfect; all research includes some unintended error. Because error decreases the validity of the findings, this aspect of research must be acknowledged up front, as the results are disseminated. Specifically, it is important to indicate major limitations that are likely to affect the findings or their generalizability. It is helpful when doing this to identify particular sources of error explicitly, such as those found in sampling, in measurement, or as a result of misspecification of the model (e.g., not including important variables in the analyses). This aspect of the research is imperative for those whose goals include feminist social change, because of the possibility that this research will generate skepticism from those with a more traditional perspective. Stating the limitations of one's research lends methodological credibility to the entire research process, because it diminishes the likelihood that the findings will appear as ideologically influenced, which is a major criticism some mainstream researchers have directed toward feminist research. Although it might seem counterintuitive that by admitting error the data can seem more error free, we posit that by recognizing the limitations of the research the results appear more objective and, thus, are more likely to be accepted as valid.

## CONCLUSION

Feminist research includes a multitude of methods for investigation, each of which can uniquely influence the social change effort to improve the lives of women and attain greater gender equity. In this chapter, we focused on one particular method, survey research, and the important role it can play in this endeavor. This method can be a potent tool for social change because it is a respected research strategy among nonfeminists and can suggest effective ways to challenge the existing power structure. But more important, it is wholly consistent with feminist values and goals. Our perspective derives directly from our personal experiences as feminists and as social science researchers who have employed survey methods to examine issues of significance to women and minority groups. We have seen how our work and that of other survey researchers has promoted a progressive agenda and has influenced public opinion and legislative policy. Although our work in survey research occurs primarily in the social sciences, this research strategy has application across many academic and nonacademic domains. Survey research is thus an appropriate method of study for a wide array of feminist topics that remain ripe for investigation. As feminist scholars explore the various research methods available, it is important that they select those that can best address their research goals. We hope that the survey research method, which we have outlined in this chapter, is among the many options considered.

## NOTES

1. This is not to say that psychologists use only quantitative survey research methods. Indeed, psychologists use a number of different methods to conduct their studies.

2. Although traditionally, survey research studies involve the quantitative analysis of data, some survey researchers employ qualitative analyses. This issue is addressed elsewhere in the chapter.

3. A variable is any concept that can assume different values among people, such as age, gender, income, or attitudes.

## REFERENCES

Acker, J., Barry, K., & Esseveld, J. (1996). Objectivity and truth: Problems in doing feminist research. In H. Gottfried (Ed.), *Feminism and social change: Bridging theory and practice* (pp. 60–87). Urbana: University of Illinois Press. (Reprinted from *Women's Studies International Forum, 4,* 423–435, by Elsevier Science, 1983, Oxford, UK: Pergamon Press)

Alreck, P. L., & Settle, R. B. (1995). *The survey research handbook: Guidelines and strategies for conducting a survey.* Burr Ridge, IL: Irwin.

Biemer, P. P., & Lyberg, L. E. (2003). *Introduction to survey quality.* Hoboken, NJ: Wiley.

Buss, D. M. (1989). Sex differences in human mate preferences: Evolutionary hypotheses tested in 37 cultures. *Behavioral and Brain Sciences, 12,* 1–49.

Campbell, P. B. (1982). Racism and sexism in research. In H. Mitzel (Ed.), *Encyclopedia of educational research* (5th ed., pp. 1515–1520). New York: Free Press.

Campbell, R., & Wasco, S. M. (2000). Feminist approaches to social science: Epistemological and methodological tenets. *American Journal of Community Psychology, 28,* 733–791.

Chafetz, J. S. (2004). Some thoughts by an unrepentant "positivist" who considers herself a feminist nonetheless. In S. N. Hesse-Biber & M. L. Yaiser (Eds.), *Feminist perspectives on social research* (pp. 320–329). New York: Oxford University Press.

Condor, S. (1986). Sex role beliefs and "traditional" women: Feminist and intergroup perspectives. In S. Wilkinson (Ed.), *Feminist social psychology: Developing theory and practice* (pp. 97–118). Philadelphia: Open University Press.

Converse, J. (1987). *Survey research in the United States.* Berkeley: University of California Press.

Crawford, M., & Marecek, J. (1989). Psychology reconstructs the female, 1968–1988. *Psychology of Women Quarterly, 13,* 147–165.

Czaja, R., & Blair, J. (1996). *Designing surveys: A guide to decisions and procedures.* Thousand Oaks, CA: Pine Forge Press.

Dillman, D. A. (1978). *Mail and telephone surveys: The total design method.* New York: Wiley-Interscience.

Dillman, D. A. (2000). *Mail and internet surveys: The tailored design method.* New York: Wiley.

Dooley, D. (1990). *Social research methods.* Englewood Cliffs, NJ: Prentice Hall.

Du Bois, B. (1983). Passionate scholarship: Notes on values, knowing and method in feminist social science. In G. Bowles & R. Duelli Klein (Eds.), *Theories of women's studies* (pp. 105–116). Boston: Routledge & Kegan Paul.

Eichler, M. (1988). *Nonsexist research methods: A practical guide.* New York: Routledge.

Fee, E. (1983). Women's nature and scientific objectivity. In M. Lowe & R. Hubbard (Eds.), *Woman's nature: Rationalizations of inequality* (pp. 9–27). New York: Pergamon Press.

Fowler, F. J. (1984). *Survey research methods.* Beverly Hills, CA: Sage.

Gorelick, S. (1996). Contradictions of feminist methodology. In H. Gottfried (Ed.), *Feminism and social change: Bridging theory and practice* (pp. 23–45). Urbana: University of Illinois Press.

Gottfried, H. (1996). Engaging women's communities: Dilemmas and contradictions in feminist research. In H. Gottfried (Ed.), *Feminism and social change: Bridging theory and practice* (pp. 1–20). Urbana: University of Illinois Press.

Gratz v. Bollinger, 539 U.S. 244 (2003).

Groves, R. (1989). *Survey errors and survey costs.* New York: Wiley.

Groves, R., Fowler, F. J., Couper, M. P., Lepkowski, J. M., Singer, E., & Tourangeau, R. (2004). *Survey methodology.* Hoboken, NJ: Wiley.

Groves, R., & Kahn, R. (1979). *Surveys by telephone: A national comparison with personal interviews.* New York: Academic Press.

Grutter v. Bollinger, 539 U.S. 306 (2003).

Gurin, P., Dey, E. L., & Hurtado, S. (2002). Diversity and higher education: Theory and impact on educational outcomes. *Harvard Educational Review, 72,* 330–366.

Haraway, D. (1988). Situated knowledges: The science question in feminism and the privilege of partial perspective. *Feminist Studies, 14,* 575–599.

Haraway, D. (1991). *Simians, cyborgs, and women: The reinvention of nature.* New York: Routledge.

Harding, S. (1987). Is there a feminist method? In S. Harding (Ed.), *Feminism and methodology* (pp. 1–14). Bloomington: Indiana University Press.

Harding, S. (1998). *Is science multicultural? Postcolonialisms, feminisms, and epistemologies.* Bloomington: Indiana University Press.

Harding, S. (2004). Rethinking standpoint epistemology: What is "strong objectivity"? In S. N. Hesse-Biber & M. L. Yaiser (Eds.), *Feminist perspectives on social research* (pp. 39–64). New York: Oxford University Press.

Hartsock, N. C. M. (1998). *The feminist standpoint revisited and other essays.* Boulder, CO: Westview Press.

Herrnstein, R. J., & Murray, C. (1994). *The bell curve: Intelligence and class structure in American life.* New York: Simon and Schuster.

Hesse-Biber, S. N., Leavy, P., & Yaiser, M. L. (2004). Feminist approaches to research as a process: Reconceptualizing epistemology, methodology, and method. In S. N. Hesse-Biber & M. L. Yaiser (Eds.), *Feminist perspectives on social research* (pp. 3–26). New York: Oxford University Press.

Jayaratne, T. E. (1983). The value of quantitative methodology for feminist research. In G. Bowles & R. Duelli Klein (Eds.), *Theories of women's studies* (pp. 140–161). Boston: Routledge & Kegan Paul.

Jayaratne, T. E., & Kaczala, C. M. (1983). Social responsibility in sex difference research. *Journal of Educational Equity and Leadership, 3,* 305–316.

Jayaratne, T. E., & Stewart, A. J. (1991). Quantitative and qualitative methods in the social sciences: Current feminist issues and practical strategies. In M. M. Fonow & J. A. Cook (Eds.), *Beyond methodology: Feminist scholarship as lived research* (pp. 85–106). Bloomington: Indiana University Press.

Jayaratne, T. E., Thomas, N. G., & Trautmann, M. T. (2003). An intervention program to keep girls in the science pipeline: Outcome differences by ethnic status. *Journal of Research in Science Teaching, 40,* 393–414.

Jick, T. D. (1979). Mixing qualitative and quantitative methods: Triangulation in action. *Administrative Science Quarterly, 24,* 602–610.

Jones, J. (1981). *Bad blood: The Tuskegee syphilis experiment.* New York: Free Press.

Keller, E. F. (1978). Gender and science. *Psychoanalysis and Contemporary Thought: A*

*Quarterly of Integrative and Interdisciplinary Studies, 1,* 409–433.

Kelly, A. (1978). Feminism and research. *Women's Studies International Quarterly, 1,* 225–232.

Konik, J., & Stewart, A. J. (2004). Sexual identity development in the context of compulsory heterosexuality. *Journal of Personality, 72*(4), 815–844.

Kuhn, T. S. (1970). *The structure of scientific revolutions.* Chicago: University of Chicago Press.

Landrine, H., Klonoff, E. A., & Brown-Collins, A. (1992). Cultural diversity and methodology in feminist psychology. *Psychology of Women Quarterly, 16,* 145–163.

Lykes, M. B., & Stewart, A. J. (1986). Evaluating the feminist challenge to research in personality and social psychology: 1963–1983. *Psychology of Women Quarterly, 10,* 393–412.

Marecek, J., Fine, M., & Kidder, L. (1997). Working between worlds: Qualitative methods and social psychology. *Journal of Social Issues, 53,* 631–644.

Maynard, M. (1994). Methods, practice and epistemology: The debate about feminism and research. In M. Maynard & J. Purvis (Eds.), *Researching women's lives from a feminist perspective* (pp. 10–26). Bristol, PA: Taylor & Francis.

McCall, R. B., & Stocking, S. H. (1982). Between scientists and public. *American Psychologist, 37,* 985–995.

Milgram, S. (1974). *Obedience to authority.* New York: Harper & Row.

National Commission for the Protection of Human Subjects of Biomedical and Behavioral Research. (1998). *The Belmont report.* Retrieved October 15, 2004, from www.fda.gov/oc/ohrt/IRBS/belmont.html

Pedhazur, E. J., & Schmelkin, L. P. (1991). *Measurement, design, and analysis: An integrated approach.* Hillsdale, NJ: Lawrence Erlbaum.

Peplau, L. A., & Conrad, E. (1989). Beyond nonsexist research: The perils of feminist methods in psychology. *Psychology of Women Quarterly, 13,* 379–400.

Pew Research Center. (2004). *Polls face growing resistance, but still representative survey experiment shows.* Retrieved on April 14, 2005, from http://people-press.org/reports

Quina, K., Rose, J. S., Harlow, L. L., Morokoff, P. J., Deiter, P. J., Whitmire, L. E., et al. (1999). Focusing on participants: Feminist process

model for survey modification. *Psychology of Women Quarterly, 23,* 459–493.

Reinharz, S. (1979). *On becoming a social scientist.* San Francisco: Jossey-Bass.

Reinharz, S. (1992). *Feminist methods in social research.* New York: Oxford University Press.

Riessman, C. K. (1987). When gender is not enough: Women interviewing women. *Gender & Society, 1,* 172–207.

Riger, S. (1992). Epistemological debates, feminist voices: Science, social values, and the story of women. *American Psychologist, 47,* 730–740.

Rogers, T. F. (1971). Interviews by telephone and in person: Quality of responses and field performance. In E. Singer & S. Presser (Eds.), *Survey research methods: Scheduling telephone interviews.* Chicago: University of Chicago Press.

Rubin, A., & Babbie, E. (1993). *Research methods for social work.* Pacific Grove, CA: Brooks/Cole.

Schwarz, N., Groves, R. M., & Schuman, H. (1998). Survey methods. In D. T. Gilbert, S. T. Fiske, & G. Lindzey (Eds.), *The handbook of social psychology* (Vol. 1, pp. 143–179). New York: McGraw-Hill.

Sherif, C. W. (1979). Bias in psychology. In J. Sherman & E. T. Back (Eds.), *The prism of sex: Essays in the sociology of knowledge* (pp. 93–133). Madison: University of Wisconsin Press.

Smith, C. A., & Frieze, I. H. (2003). Examining rape empathy from the perspective of the victim and the assailant. *Journal of Applied Social Psychology, 33,* 476–498.

Smith, D. E. (1987). *The everyday world as problematic: A sociology for women.* Boston: Northeastern University Press.

Smith, M. D. (1994). Enhancing the quality of survey data on violence against women: A feminist approach. *Gender & Society, 8,* 109–127.

Spalter-Roth, R., & Hartmann, H. (1996). Small happinesses: The feminist struggle to integrate social research and social activism. In H. Gottfried (Ed.), *Feminism and social change: Bridging theory and practice* (pp. 206–224). Urbana: University of Illinois Press.

Sprague, J., & Zimmerman, M. (1993). Overcoming dualisms: A feminist agenda for sociological methodology. In P. England (Ed.), *Theory on gender/feminism on theory* (pp. 255–280). New York: Aldine de Gruyter.

Stangor, C. (2004). *Research methods for the behavioral sciences.* Boston: Houghton Mifflin.

Stanley, L., & Wise, S. (1983). *Breaking out: Feminist consciousness and feminist research.* London: Routledge & Kegan Paul.

Steinberg, R. J. (1996). Advocacy research for feminist policy objectives: Experiences with comparable worth. In H. Gottfried (Ed.), *Feminism and social change: Bridging theory and practice* (pp. 225–255). Urbana: University of Illinois Press.

Stewart, A. J., & Dottolo, A. L. (2005). Socialization to the academy: Coping with competing social identities. In G. Downey, J. Eccles, & C. Chatman (Eds.), *Navigating the future: Social identity, coping and life tasks* (pp. 167–187). New York: Russell Sage.

Tourangeau, R., Rips, L., & Rasinski, K. (2000). *The psychology of survey response.* Cambridge, UK: Cambridge University Press.

U.S. Census Bureau. (1989). *A century of population growth, from the first census of the United States to the twelfth, 1790–1900.* Baltimore: Genealogical Publishing.

Vogt, W. P. (1999). *Dictionary of statistics and methodology: A nontechnical guide for the social sciences.* Thousand Oaks, CA: Sage.

Wallston, B. S., & Grady, K. E. (1992). Integrating the feminist critique and the crisis in social psychology: Another look at research methods. In J. S. Bohan (Ed.), *Seldom seen, rarely heard: Women's place in psychology* (pp. 307–336). Boulder, CO: Westview Press.

Wittig, M. (1985). Metatheoretical dilemmas in the psychology of gender. *American Psychologist, 40,* 800–812.

# 11

# THE LINK BETWEEN THEORY AND METHODS

## Feminist Experimental Research

SUE V. ROSSER

At the beginning of the 21st century, as the wave of feminism and women's studies marks its third decade, the cross-fertilization of the interaction among science, technology, medicine, and feminism has begun to blossom and bear fruit. Unlike the humanities, where much of the impetus for women's studies originated and where feminist scholarship has become mainstream in most disciplines, and even the social sciences, where gender analyses and questioning of positivist approaches have become routine, science, technology, and medicine have come to accept feminist perspectives and gender analyses, and particularly their extension to experimental methods, more slowly. Those of us who had one foot in science and the other in women's studies worked hard to build the two-way streets between science and feminism articulated by Anne Fausto-Sterling (1992).

Most researchers in the behavioral, biomedical, and physical sciences are trained in the scientific method and believe in its power. Few, however, are aware of its historical and philosophical roots in logical positivism and objectivity. Positivism implies that "all knowledge is

constructed by inference from immediate sensory experiences" (Jaggar, 1983, pp. 355–356). It is premised on the assumption that human beings are highly individualistic and obtain knowledge in a rational manner that may be separated from their social conditions. This leads to the belief in the possibilities of obtaining knowledge that is both objective and value free, the cornerstone of the scientific method.

Longino (1990) has explored the extent to which methods employed by scientists can be objective and lead to repeatable, verifiable results while contributing to hypotheses or theories that are congruent with nonobjective institutions and ideologies of the society. "Background assumptions are the means by which contextual values and ideology are incorporated into scientific inquiry" (p. 216). The institutions and beliefs of our society reflect the fact that the society is patriarchal. Even female scientists have only recently become aware of the influence of patriarchal bias in the paradigms of science (Rose & Rose, 1980; Rosser, 1992). For example, in his early primatology work, Yerkes (1943) chose the baboon and the chimpanzee as species for study primarily because their social organization was seen by the human observers to closely resemble that of human primates because of male dominance. It was not until a significant number of women entered primatology that the concepts of the universality and male leadership of dominance hierarchies among primates (Lancaster, 1975; Leavitt, 1975; Leibowitz, 1975; Rowell, 1974) were questioned and shown to be inaccurate for many primate species.

A first step for feminist scientists was recognizing the possibility that androcentric bias would result from having virtually all theoretical and decision-making positions in science held by men (Keller, 1983). Not until a substantial number of women had entered the profession (Rosser, 1986) could this androcentrism be exposed. As long as only a few women were scientists, they had to demonstrate or conform to the male view of the world to be successful and have their research meet the criteria for "objectivity."

In the past two decades, feminist historians and philosophers of science (Fee, 1982, 1983; Haraway, 1978, 1989, 1997; Harding, 1986, 1993, 1998; Longino, 1990; Tuana, 1993, 1995), anthropologists (Martin, 1987, 1994, 1999; Rapp, 1999), and feminist scientists (Birke, 1986; Bleier, 1984, 1986; Fausto-Sterling, 1992; Keller, 1983, 1985, 1992; Rosser, 1988, 1994, 1997; Spanier, 1995) have pointed out the bias and absence of value neutrality in science, particularly biology. By excluding females as experimental subjects, focusing on problems of primary interest to males, using faulty experimental designs, and interpreting data based on language or ideas constricted by patriarchal parameters, scientists have introduced bias or flaws into their experimental results in several areas. These flaws and biases were permitted to become part of the mainstream of scientific thought and were perpetuated in the scientific literature for decades. Because most scientists were men, values held by them as males were not distinguished as biasing; rather they were congruent with the values of all scientists and thus became synonymous with the "objective" view of the world (Chodorow, 1978; Keller, 1982, 1985) and the aspects of it studied.

The demonstration that contextual values, including gender, bias not only the scientific research of individuals but also what is accepted as valid science by the entire scientific community represents one of the major contributions that feminism has made to science. In *Feminism in Twentieth-Century Science, Technology, and Medicine* (Creager, Lunbeck, & Schiebinger, 2001), the contributing authors responded to the question of what difference feminism has made to the fields of science, technology, and medicine. It built on coeditor Londa Schiebinger's (1999) book *Has Feminism Changed Science?* In that volume, Schiebinger examined how the presence of women in traditionally male disciplines has altered scientific thinking and awareness, concluding that feminist perspectives have had little effect on mathematics and the physical sciences but more impact on biology, including medicine, archaeology, reproductive and evolutionary biology, and primatology. For example, Schiebinger describes impacts on primatology as follows: "Feminist interventions have remade foundational paradigms in the field. Nonhuman females are no longer seen as docile creatures who trade sex and reproduction for protection and food, but are studied for their own unique contributions to primate society" (p. 3).

Although the degree and the specifics of the impact of feminism on science, medicine, and technology vary from one subdiscipline to another, as the coeditors of that volume state, "Feminism connects gender to other systems that structure our lives and individual identities" (Creager et al., 2001, p. viii). Linking methods for experimental research with feminist theories provides a framework for understanding this connection. In this chapter, I use different feminist theories to explore feminist impact in the various stages of the scientific method—in choice and definition of problems chosen, approaches used, and theories and conclusions drawn from the research.

Feminisms and feminist perspectives have increased in variety and complexity over time. All feminist theories place women and gender in central focus, but each theory brings a specific angle or perspective to that focus. Many feminist theories evolved in response to correct a deficiency or add a dimension missing from previous theories. The particular theories I have chosen to discuss here represent those I find most influential in understanding the impact of feminism on experimental methods in the natural, physical, and social sciences. Although feminist analyses have had greatest exploration and impact in biology and health-related fields where gender applies directly to experimental subjects and results, I will also attempt to include examples from the physical sciences and engineering under each feminist theory.

## LIBERAL FEMINISM

Beginning in the 18th century, political scientists, philosophers, and feminists (Friedan, 1974; Jaggar, 1983; Mill, 1970; Wollstonecraft, 1975) have described the parameters of liberal feminism. The differences between 19th- and 20th-century liberal feminists have varied from libertarian to egalitarian, and numerous complexities exist among definitions of liberal feminists today. A general definition of liberal feminism is the belief that women are suppressed in contemporary society because they suffer unjust discrimination (Jaggar, 1983). Liberal feminists seek no special privileges for women and simply demand that everyone receive equal consideration without discrimination on the basis of sex.

Most scientists would assume that the implications of liberal feminism for biology and other disciplines within the sciences are that scientists should work to remove the documented overt and covert barriers (National Science Foundation [NSF], 2002; Rosser, 2004; Rossiter, 1982; Vetter, 1988) that have prevented women from entering and succeeding in science. Although they might hold individual opinions as to whether or not women deserve equal pay for equal work, access to research resources, and equal opportunities for advancement, most scientists do not recognize that the implications of liberal feminism extend beyond employment, access, and discrimination to the acceptance of positivism as the theory of knowledge and belief in the ability to obtain knowledge that is both objective and value free (Jaggar, 1983).

Given the high costs of sophisticated equipment, maintenance of laboratory animals and facilities, and salaries for qualified technicians and researchers, virtually no experimental research is undertaken today without governmental or foundation support. The choice of problems for study in research is substantially determined by a national agenda that defines what is worthy of study (i.e., worth funding). As Marxist (Zimmerman et al., 1980), African American (Campbell, Deanes, & Morrison, 2000), and feminist (Harding, 1998) critics of scientific research have pointed out, the scientific research undertaken in the United States reflects the societal bias toward the powerful, who are overwhelmingly white, middle- or upper-class, and male. Members of Congress and the individuals in the theoretical and decision-making positions within the medical and scientific establishments that set priorities and allocate funds for research exemplify these descriptors. The lack of diversity among Congressional and scientific leaders may allow unintentional, undetected flaws to bias the research in terms of what we study and how we study it. Examples from research studies demonstrate that unintentional bias may be reflected in at least three stages of application of the scientific method: (1) choice and definition of problems to be studied; (2) methods and approaches used in data gathering, including whom we choose as subjects; and (3) theories and conclusions drawn from the data.

## Choice and Definition of Problems to Be Studied

Feminist critiques revealed the impact of distinct gender bias in choice and definition of health research problems. For example, many diseases that occur in both sexes have been studied in males only or with a male-as-norm approach. Cardiovascular diseases serve as a case in point. Research protocols for large-scale studies (Grobbee et al., 1990; Multiple Risk Factor Intervention Trial Research Group [MRFIT], 1990; Steering Committee of the Physicians' Health Study Group, 1989) of cardiovascular diseases failed to assess gender differences. Women were excluded from clinical trials of drugs because of fear of litigation from possible teratogenic effects on fetuses. Exclusion of women from clinical drug trials was so pervasive that a meta-analysis surveying the literature from 1960 to 1991 on clinical trials of medications used to treat acute myocardial infarction found that women were included in less than 20% and the elderly in less than 40% of those studies (Gurwitz, Nananda, & Avorn, 1992).

The choice of development of particular technologies from basic research may also reflect male priorities. Having large numbers of male engineers and creators of technologies also often results in technologies that are useful from a male perspective (i.e., these technologies fail to address important issues for women users). In addition to the military origins for the development and funding of much technology (Barnaby, 1981; Norman, 1979), which makes its civilian application less useful for women's lives (Cockburn, 1983), men designing technology for the home frequently focus on issues less important to women users. For example, Berg's (1999) analysis of "smart houses" reveals that such houses do not include new technologies; instead, they focus on "integration, centralised control and regulation of all functions in the home" (p. 306). "Housework is no part of what this house will 'do' for you" (p. 307). Knowledge of housework appears to be overlooked by the designers of smart houses. As Ruth Schwartz Cowan's (1976/1985) work suggests, the improved household technologies developed in the first half of the 20th century actually increased the amount of time housewives spent on housework and reduced their role from general managers of servants, maiden aunts, grandmothers, children, and others to an individual who worked alone doing manual labor aided by household appliances.

## Approaches and Methods Used in Data Gathering

Using the white, middle-aged, heterosexual male as the "basic experimental subject" ignores the fact that females may respond differently to the variable tested; it also may lead to less accurate models even for many men. For example, the standard dosage of certain medications is not only inappropriate for many women and the elderly, but also for most Asian men, because of their smaller body size and weight. Certain surgical procedures such as angioplasty and cardiac bypass initially resulted in higher death rates for women (Kelsey et al., 1993) and Asian men and required modification for the same reason (Chinese Hospital Medical Staff and

University of California School of Medicine, 1982; Lin-Fu, 1984).

Male dominance in engineering and the creative decision-making sectors of the IT workforce may result in similar bias, particularly design and user bias. Shirley Malcom (personal communication, October 1997) suggested that the air bag fiasco suffered by the U.S. auto industry serves as an excellent example of gender bias reflected in design; this fiasco would have been much less likely had a woman engineer been on the design team. Because, on the average, women tend to be smaller than men, women on the design team might have recognized that a bag that implicitly used the larger male body as a norm would be flawed when applied to smaller individuals, killing, rather than protecting, children and small women.

## Theories and Conclusions Drawn From the Data

Theories may be presented in androcentric, ethnocentric, or class-biased language. An awareness of language should aid experimenters in avoiding the use of terms such as *tomboyism* (Money & Erhardt, 1972), *aggression*, and "*hysteria*, which reflect assumptions about sex-appropriate behavior (Hamilton, 1985). Researchers should use evaluative terms such as *prostitute* with caution. Often the important fact for AIDS research is that a woman has multiple sex partners or is an IV drug user, rather than that she has received money for sex. The use of such terms as *prostitute* in analyzing data may induce bias by promoting the idea that women are vectors for transmission to men when, in fact, the men may have an equal or greater number of sex partners to whom they are transmitting the disease.

Many studies have explored the overt and covert links between the military, whose origins and current directions conjoin with masculinity in our culture, and the theories for applications drawn from the research funded for the military. For example, Janet Abbate (1999) studied the origins of the Internet in ARPANET (Advanced Research Projects Agency Network), funded by the Department of Defense. The unique improvement of the Internet was that it was a network, overcoming the vulnerability to nuclear attack of the previous star configuration computer network.

Although liberal feminism suggests that true equity of women in the science and technology workforce would lead to inclusion of women in clinical trials and correct bias in design to better serve women's interests, by definition, liberal feminism does not address the potential of gender to affect "fundamentals" (i.e., Do women scientists define, approach, or discover different fundamentals such as string theory?). Liberal feminism accepts positivism as the theory of knowledge and assumes that human beings are highly individualistic and obtain knowledge in a rational manner that may be separated from their social conditions, including conditions of race, class, and gender. Because liberal feminism reaffirms, rather than challenges, positivism, it suggests that "fundamentals" would always remain the same. Now that they have become aware of potential bias, both male and female scientists and engineers can correct for such biases previously resulting from failure to include women and their needs and interests.

## SOCIALIST FEMINISM

In contrast to liberal feminism, socialist feminism rejects individualism and positivism. Although socialist feminists argue that women's oppression predated the development of class societies, Marxist critiques form the historical precursors and foundations for socialist feminist critiques and define all knowledge, including science, as socially constructed and emerging from practical human involvement in production. Because knowledge is a productive activity of human beings, it cannot be objective and value free because the basic categories of knowledge are shaped by human purposes and values. In the early-21st-century United States, capitalism, the prevailing mode of production, determines science and technology and favors the interests of the dominant class.

This Marxist or socialist theory undergirds the work of numerous scholars of science and technology who have used this framework for their studies, producing a large body of research commonly known as "the social shaping of science and technology" (MacKenzie & Wajcman, 1999). Different societies construct their material worlds, including the artifacts created and used, in different ways. The culture of a certain society may use the artifacts or attach particular meanings to them differently at different times or historical periods. Thus, particular technology and science are situated in place, time, and culture (Lerman, Oldenziel, & Mohun, 2003).

Feminist scholars rightly point out that science and technology and the social shaping of technology (Wajcman, 1991; Webster, 1995) and science (Rose, 1994) have often been conceptualized in terms of men, excluding women at all levels. Socialist feminist critiques include women and place gender on equal footing with class in shaping science and technology. In this dual-systems approach (Eisenstein, 1984; Hartmann, 1981), capitalism and patriarchy function as mutually reinforcing parts of a system where the sexual division of labor stands with wage labor as a central feature of capitalism, and where gender differences in wages, along with failing to count contributions of women to reproduction and child rearing as "productivity" in a capitalist economy, reinforce patriarchy and power differentials in the home. The social and technological shape each other. This so-called mutual shaping at times of technological change leads to contests over social categories such as gender being reflected in new interactions with the material world (Lerman et al., 2003). Some scholars (Fox, Johnson, & Rosser, in press) have also called this "mutual shaping" of the social and technological aspects as the "co-evolution of gender and technology."

### Choice and Definition

Considerable research focus and dollars target diseases, such as cardiovascular disease, especially problematic for middle- and upper-class men in their prime earning years. Although women die from cardiovascular disease with the same frequency as men, on average women die at later ages. Hence, until recently most cardiovascular disease research targeted white, middle-class men. Many of these studies, including the Physicians' Health Study, were flawed not only by the factors of gender and age but also by factors of race and class. Susceptibility to cardiovascular disease is known to be affected by lifestyle factors such as diet, exercise level, and stress, which are correlated with race and class. Because physicians in the United States are not representative of the overall male population with regard to lifestyle, the results may not be applicable even to most men.

Understandings of class relations emerging under capitalism and gender relations under patriarchy help to explain the intertwining of military and masculinity (Enloe, 1983, 1989; MacKenzie & Wajcman, 1999), which drives much technological innovation in this country and elsewhere. These understandings also explain the choices made to develop technologies in a certain way. This exemplifies engineering decisions that favor fewer rich people over relatively less expensive technologies such as devices for the home to aid many people, especially women.

Caro's (1974) work revealed that Robert Moses, the master builder of New York's roads, parks, bridges, and other public works from the 1920s to the 1970s, had overpasses built to specifications to discourage buses on parkways. White upper- and middle-class car owners could use the parkways, such as Wantagh Parkway, for commuting and for accessing recreation sites, including Jones Beach. Because the 12-foot height of public transit buses prohibited their fitting under the overpass, blacks and poor people dependent on public transit did not have access to Jones Beach (Winner, 1980).

## Approaches

Designation of certain diseases as particular to one gender, race, or sexual orientation leads to overuse of that group for research protocols and the neglect of other groups. This not only cultivates ignorance in the general public about transmission or frequency of the disease but also results in research that does not adequately explore the parameters of the disease. Most of the funding for heart disease has been appropriated for research on predisposing factors for the disease (such as cholesterol level, lack of exercise, stress, smoking, and weight) using white, middle-aged, middle-class males. Much less research has been directed toward elderly

women, African American women who have had several children, and other high-risk groups of women. Virtually no research has explored predisposing factors for these groups, who fall outside the disease definition established from the dominant perspective.

Class and gender analyses document women's occupation of the worst paid, most tedious, and health-destroying segment of the labor market in electronics assembly (Office of Population Censuses and Surveys, 1991)—etching circuits onto wafers of silicon, dipping circuits into vats of carcinogenic solvents, and peering through microscopes for 7 to 10 hours per day to bond wires to silicon chips (Fuentes & Ehrenreich, 1983). Socialist feminist analyses reveal that the extremely low wages paid to women in these jobs, along with women's geographic immobility, may lead to work done by men, despite its being less menial and more difficult to automate, being automated more quickly to keep wages low or destroy unions (Cockburn, 1981). Socialist feminist approaches also suggest why men dominate the creation of new technologies: Access to venture capital, geographic mobility, and ability to work long hours may be as critical as is technological expertise for the success of start-ups.

## Theories and Conclusions

Biases in populations sampled and choice and definition of problems raise ethical issues. Health care practitioners treat the majority of the population, which consists of females, minorities, and the elderly, based on information gathered from clinical research in which women and minorities are undersampled or not included. Bias in research thus leads to further injustice in health care diagnosis and treatment.

Current intellectual property rights agreements and laws provide opportunities for choices in technology development that further exacerbate class differences by transferring technologies developed using public moneys to the private realm through patents. The decisions regarding which products are developed fall under the influence of capitalist interests in profit margins. Such intellectual property rights function as a form of privatization (Mohanty, 1997). They permit decisions of which products will be developed to occur in the private, rather than the public, realm. This results in capitalist interests in the bottom line, rather than public needs and interests, dictating which "products" are developed. In the patenting of intellectual property, rights (and profits) get transferred from the public who paid for the research with their tax dollars to the private company, institution, or individual who controls the patent. Socialist feminists might view this as a transfer from the pockets of the working class, who pay the taxes to underwrite federal research, to the patent holders in the private sector who will reap massive profits, as serving the interests of bourgeois capitalists. New technologies in computer science and engineering are often developed using federal grants (paid for by taxes).

## African American/ Womanist Feminism

African American or black/womanist (Collins, 1990; hooks, 1992) feminism also rejects individualism and positivism for social construction as an approach to knowledge. It is based on African American critiques of Eurocentric approaches to knowledge (Harding, 1998). In addition to rejecting objectivity and value neutrality associated with positivist approaches accepted by liberal feminism, African American approaches critique dichotomization of knowledge or at least the identification of science with the first half and African American with the latter half of the following dichotomies: culture/ nature; rational/feeling; objective/subjective; quantitative/qualitative; active/passive; focused/ diffuse; independent/dependent; mind/body; self/others; knowing/being. Like socialist critiques, African American critiques question methods that distance the observer from the object of study, thereby denying a facet of the social construction of knowledge.

Whereas socialism posits class as the organizing principle around which the struggle for power exists, African American critiques maintain that race is the primary oppression. African Americans critical of the scientific enterprise may view it as a function of white Eurocentric interests with the methodology a reflection of those interests.

Just as socialist feminist theory provided insights into the gender and class distributions of science experiments and technological innovation, African American feminism critiques uncover the place or role of race in combination with gender. Racism intertwines and reinforces differing aspects of capitalism and patriarchy. African American feminists have examined the respective intersection of race and gender to provide a more complex, comprehensive view of reality. Many African American women are also uncomfortable with the word *feminism*, because of its historical association with white women and ignoring racial/ethnic diversity. Womanist (Steady, 1982), critical race theory (Williams, 1991, 1998) and black feminism (Collins, 1990), while all placing race in central focus, provide slightly differing critiques. Just as their African American sisters have done, Latina, Asian American, and American Indian women and women from other racial or ethnic perspectives have developed critiques that place race/ethnicity and gender in central focus.

## Choice and Definition

Data indicate that the initial designation of AIDS as a disease of male homosexuals, drug users, and Haitian immigrants not only has resulted in homophobic and racist stereotypes but also has particular implications for women of color. In 1981, the first official case of AIDS in a woman was reported to the Center for Disease Control and Prevention (CDC). By 1991, $80 million had been spent since the inception of the Multicenter AIDS Cohort Study (MACS), designed to follow the natural history of HIV among gay and bisexual males (Faden, Kass, & McGraw, 1996). Although by 1988 the case reports for women were higher than the number for men in 1983, the year the MACS began (Chu, Buehler, & Berelman, 1990), it was not until the final quarter of 1994 that the first study on the natural history of HIV infection in women began. In 1998, the CDC reported that AIDS remains the leading cause of death among black females aged 25 to 44, and the second leading cause of death overall among those aged 25 to 44 (CDC, 1998). In the 21st century, the majority of women diagnosed with AIDS are black or Hispanic.

Because technology generally reflects and reinforces race relations, socialist feminist and African American feminist theories imply that women engineers, computer scientists, and technology designers, through a collective process of political and scientific struggle (Jaggar, 1983), might produce technologies different from those produced by men of any race or class. These technologies might reflect the priorities of more people and be user-accessible and user-friendly for more people because they would be based on the experience of women, whose standpoint as the nondominant group in engineering provides them with a more comprehensive view of reality because of their race, class, and gender. For example, one could imagine that if the National Academy of Engineers (NAE) contained more women and men of color, it might have different priorities and make different recommendations. Women of color in a sexist, racist society are likely to have had very different experiences than members of the NAE. Their experiences and perspectives might in turn lead them to hold differing priorities and to propose different technologies.

## Approaches

When women of color are used as experimental subjects, clinicians often hold stereotypical and racist views that limit accurate diagnosis. For example, numerous research studies have focused on sexually transmitted diseases in prostitutes in general (CDC, 1987; Cohen, Alexander, & Woofsey, 1988; Rosser, 1994), and African American women prostitutes in particular. Several studies have also revealed that practitioners recognize and report at higher rates crack-cocaine abuse in African American women and alcohol abuse in American Indian women, compared with white women seeking prenatal care. In many cases, the women lost their children after they were born or had to serve jail time for detoxification. An American Civil Liberties Union study revealed that in 47 out of 53 cases brought against women for drug use during pregnancy in which the race of the woman was identifiable, 80% were brought against women of color (Pattrow, 1990).

Like socialist-feminism, African American/ womanist or racial/ethnic feminism, based on African American critiques of a Eurocentric approach to knowledge, also rejects individualism and positivism for social construction as an approach to knowledge. African American critiques also question methods that distance the observer from the object of study. Because technology, for the most part, involves practical application of more abstract, basic scientific research, the problem of the distance between engineer (researcher) and the technology (object of study) needs to be understood, discussed, and addressed to make technological research methodologies clearer to both developers and users. Unlike theoretical scientific projects, which do not necessarily have immediate practical outcomes, projects in computer science or engineering must accommodate the impact of the uses of technology with particular attention to the users of technology. When designing technologies, engineers, designers, and computer scientists not only would ask how and under what conditions the technology would be used, but would also have to allow the potential consumer to shape the design of the product. Potentially, gender, class, and race, along with other factors such as age and ability status, should be considered in defining who the user will be. For example, the Blacksburg Electronic Village, an online community network, "routes around" race and relies on the "digital default" of white, heterosexual, middle-aged, middle- to upper-class male (Silver, 2000, p. 143). Does this normative "default" position help to explain the digital divide and African Americans' lower use of the Internet and computers?

A growing recognition has evolved of the strength and necessity for diversity on teams (Knights, 2004). Diversity in gender and race are beginning to be understood to be critical, along with the long-established recognition of the importance of having an engineering team representing varied intellectual and technical backgrounds, for designing complex technologies. Because knowledge and consideration of the user, client, or customer are central to the technology design, a design team with racial and gender diversity coupled with surveys of demographically diverse customers will increase diversity in technology design.

## Theories and Conclusions

Frequently it is difficult to determine whether women are treated disrespectfully and unethically due to their gender or whether race and class are more significant variables. From the Tuskegee syphilis experiment (1932–1972), in which the effects of untreated syphilis were studied in 399 men over a period of 40 years (Jones, 1981), it is clear that men who are black and poor may not receive appropriate treatment or information about the experiment in which they are participating. Scholars (Clarke & Olesen, 1999) now explore the extent to which gender, race, and class become complex, interlocking variables that may affect access to and quality of health care.

African Americans and Hispanics are underrepresented in engineering and in the upper end of the technology workforce, relative to their percentage in the overall U.S. population (22.4%) (NSF, 1999). In 1998, African Americans constituted 3% of engineers and 4% of computer and mathematical scientists (p. 106); 2.5% to 3% of engineers and mathematical and computer scientists identified as Hispanic (p. 109). Although engineering has been traditionally defined as a career path for mobility from the working to middle class, engineering is pursued by disproportionately fewer blacks and Latinos than whites. Even fewer African American women and Latinas than their male counterparts become engineers or scientists, despite the higher percentage of African American women (compared with African American men) in college (p. 113).

In stark contrast, women of color are disproportionately represented in the lowest paying and highest health risk portions of the technology labor force. Studies demonstrate that women of color occupy the ghettos in the cities where the electronic assembly occurs (Fuentes & Ehrenreich, 1983; Hesse-Biber & Carter, 2005; Women Working Worldwide, 1991). Outside the technology production workforce, women of color also represent the group most likely to be replaced by technology when automation takes over the work formerly done by their hands. Although technology has not resulted in the extreme reductions in female clerical workers once feared, increasing automation has forced some women of color

from higher paying assembly line factory work into lower paying service sector jobs (Hesse-Biber & Carter, 2005; Mitter, 1986).

## ESSENTIALIST FEMINISM

African American and socialist feminist critiques emphasize race and class as sources of oppression that combine with gender in shaping and being shaped by science and technology. In contrast, essentialist feminist theory posits that all women are united by their biology. Women are also different from men because of their biology, specifically their secondary sex characteristics and their reproductive systems. Frequently, essentialist feminism may extend to include gender differences in visuospatial and verbal ability, aggression and other behaviors, and other physical and mental traits based on prenatal or pubertal hormone exposure. For example, some sociobiological research such as that by Wilson (1975), Trivers (1972), and Dawkins (1976) and some hormone and brain lateralization research seem to provide biological evidence for differences in mental and behavioral characteristics in males and females.

## Choice and Definition

The biomedical model, although too restricted for an approach to most diseases, remains especially inadequate for women's health, particularly for exploring causes, treatments, and prevention of diseases such as breast cancer. Many critics of breast cancer research (Altman, 1996; Love, 1990) have pointed out that the overreliance on the biomedical model (or a narrowly defined version of the biomedical model) has focused attention on the cellular, hormonal, and genetic causes of the disease at the expense of attention to behavioral, social, and environmental causes. This model, because it explores cancer cells, leads to an emphasis on treatment, rather than prevention (Batt, 1994). Biomedicine has a tradition of researching disease and how to cure it rather than studying health and how to prevent disease (Bailar & Smith, 1986). This tradition places responsibility at the level of the individual rather than the society as a whole.

Essentialist feminism suggests that men, because of their biology and inability to conceive, also develop technologies to dominate, control, and exploit the natural world, women, and other peoples (Easlea, 1983). Women, in contrast, because of our biology, not only have less testosterone, but also have the ability to give birth. Giving birth gives us less direct control over our bodies and connects us more closely with nature, other animals, and life (King, 1989; Merchant, 1979). In its most simplistic extreme form, essentialism implies that men use technologies to bring death and control to other people, women, and the environment, while (or because) women give birth and nurture life in all its forms. In his study of the discovery and development of nuclear weapons and the atomic bomb, Easlea (1983) examines the language and behavior of the scientists. Analyzing the aggressive sexual and birth metaphors the scientists use to describe their work, he argues that men "give birth" to science and weapons to compensate for their inability to give birth to babies.

## Approaches

Using only the methods traditional to a particular discipline may result in limited approaches that fail to reveal sufficient information about the problem being explored.

The Human Genome Era has produced a particularly reductionistic version of the biomedical model, in which extreme attention is drawn to genetic causes for diseases. This genetic focus became necessary to justify the huge amount of resources diverted from epidemiology and public health measures to prevent disease, and studies of other causes for disease, to pour them into the $3 billion Human Genome Initiative. For breast cancer research, this helps to explain the focus on the isolation of BRCA1 and BRCA2 genes. The media attention surrounding the isolation and copying of the breast cancer genes fueled the public perception that the overwhelming cause of breast cancer is hereditary and that a cure for the genetic cause would soon be found; the reality is that only 5% to 10% of breast cancer is inherited and that the BRCA1 and BRCA2 genes are responsible for only half of the inherited cases (King, Rowell, & Love, 1993). This leaves 90% or 95% of

breast cancer cases unaccounted for by the BRCA1 and BRCA2 genes and points to the role caused by social, behavioral, and environmental factors.

Both ecofeminism and essentialism suggest that because of our biology, women would design different technologies and use them differently. Indeed, the studies done of inventions by women and surveys of patents obtained by women (Macdonald, 1992) suggest that many women develop technologies related to reproduction (e.g., Nystatin to prevent vaginal yeast infections), secondary sex characteristics (backless bra), or babies or children (folding crib). An essentialist feminist theoretical approach to these invention and patent data studies implies that differences in women's, compared with men's, biology—differences such as hormone levels, menstruation, giving birth, and ability to lactate to nourish offspring—leads to women designing different technologies and using technologies differently from men.

## Theories and Conclusions

Focusing basic research at the level of the cell and below also has consequences for the types of treatments developed. Susan Love's (1990) characterization of "Slash, burn, and poison" as the treatment methods for breast cancer highlights the cellular approach. The theory of cancer as cells growing out of control leads to treatments that attempt to limit the cell growth by surgically removing the cells (slash), killing the cancer cells that divide more rapidly than nonmalignant cells (burn through radiation therapy), or changing the cellular environment to one that is less favorable for the growth of cancer cells (poisoning through chemotherapy). These treatments center on individual responsibility rather than overall societal responsibility for addressing environmental pollution, advertising to promote tobacco and alcohol, and calling attention to food additives, fat content, and preservatives.

Essentialism can be used to support either superiority or inferiority of women compared with men, as long as the source of difference remains rooted in biology. Essentialism and the sociobiology research supporting it were critiqued by feminist scientists (Bleier, 1979; Fausto-Sterling, 1992; Hubbard, 1979; Rosser,

1982) as not providing sufficient biological evidence to justify differences in mental and behavioral characteristics between males and females. Essentialism was seen as a tool for conservatives who wished to keep women in the home and out of the workplace. Eventually, feminists reexamined essentialism from perspectives ranging from conservative to radical (Corea, 1985; Dworkin, 1983; MacKinnon, 1982, 1987; O'Brien, 1981; Rich, 1976) with a recognition that biologically based differences between the sexes might imply superiority and power for women in some arenas.

Girls said they use computers to communicate and perform specific tasks, while boys have underdeveloped social skills and use computers to play games and "fool around." Turkle said, "Instead of trying to make girls fit into the existing computer culture, the computer culture must become more inviting for girls." The report said girls and women cannot settle for being consumers of technology. They must be prepared to become designers and creators if they are going to fully participate and shape the new computer age (Association of American University Women, 2000).

## EXISTENTIALIST FEMINISM

Existentialist feminism, first described by Simone de Beauvoir (1949/1989), suggests that women's "otherness" and the social construction of gender rest on society's interpretation of biological differences. Existentialists see "women's and men's lives as concretely situated" and emphasize concepts like "freedom, interpersonal relations, and experience of lived body" (Larrabee, 2000, p. 187). In contrast to essentialist feminism, existentialist feminism purports that it is not the biological differences themselves, but the value that society assigns to biological differences between males and females that has led woman to play the role of the Other (Tong, 1989). The philosophical origins of existentialist feminism emphasize that it is man's conception of woman as "other" that has led to his willingness to dominate and exploit her (de Beauvoir, 1949/1989). Because of their emphasis on freedom, interpersonal relations, and experience of the lived body,

many existentialist feminists attempt to resist culturalist feminist notions of socially imposed gender roles, implying that through nature or nurture, women have developed feminine or female characteristics.

## Choice and Definition

Research on conditions specific to females receives low priority, funding, and prestige, although women make up half of the population and receive more than half of the health care. In 1988, the National Institutes of Health (NIH) allocated only 13.5% of its total budget to research on illnesses of major consequence for women (Narrigan, 1991). The Women's Health Initiative launched by NIH in 1991 to study cardiovascular diseases, cancers, and osteoporosis attempted to raise the priority of women's health and provide baseline data on previously understudied causes of death in women (Pinn & LaRosa, 1992). Cardiovascular diseases (Healy, 1991) and AIDS (Norwood, 1988; Rosser, 1994) stand as classic examples of diseases studied using a male-as-norm approach. Aspects of this approach included research designs that failed to assess gender differences in cardiovascular disease (Grobbee et al., 1990; MRFIT, 1990; Steering Committee of the Physicians' Health Study Group, 1989), case definitions that failed to include gynecologic conditions and other symptoms of AIDS in women until 1993 (Rosser, 1994), and exclusive use of males as research subjects in clinical trials. This male focus results in an accumulation of data and methods that work for exploring health and disease in the male body against which to compare new data from research on cancer; a similar accumulation of data does not exist for the female body against which to assess new research in breast cancer.

An existentialist feminism framework might be used to explain the higher frequency of inventions by women of technologies useful for menstruation, childbirth, lactation, and hormones. In contrast to essentialism, rather than placing the emphasis for the origin of the technology on the biology itself, existentialism would suggest that it is value assigned by society to women as other that leads to the technology. Women serve as the predominant caretakers of babies and children, perhaps because they give birth to them and nurse them. Existentialist feminism would suggest that this assignment of the role as other, based on the biological reasons, would lead to women having more experience caring for babies and children. In turn, this experience would lead them to invent more technologies useful for child care, such as the pull-down–from–the–wall baby changing stations found in public bathrooms, disposable diapers, and folding cribs (Macdonald, 1997).

## Approaches

Significant amounts of time and money are expended on clinical research on women's bodies in connection with other aspects of reproduction. In the 20th century up until the 1970s, considerable attention was devoted to the development of contraceptive devices for females rather than for males (Cowan, 1983; Dreifus, 1977). Furthermore, substantial clinical research has resulted in increasing medicalization and control of pregnancy, labor, and childbirth. Feminists have critiqued (Ehrenreich & English, 1978; Holmes, 1981) the conversion of a normal, natural process controlled by women into a clinical, and often surgical, procedure controlled by men. More recently, the new reproductive technologies such as amniocentesis, in vitro fertilization, and artificial insemination have become a major focus as means are sought to overcome infertility. Feminists (Klein, 1989; Rothman, 2001) have warned of the extent to which these technologies place pressure on women to produce the "perfect" child while placing control in the hands of the male medical establishment.

In direct ways, the use of the male norm excludes women as the users of technology. Military regulations often apply Military Standard 1472 of anthropometric data so that systems dimensions use the 95th and 5th percentile of male dimensions in designing weapons systems. This led to the cockpits of airplanes being designed to fit the dimensions of 90% of male military recruits (Weber, 1997). This worked relatively well as long as the military was entirely male. In the case of the Joint Primary Aircraft Training System, used by both the Navy and Air Force to train its pilots, the application of the standard accommodated the 5th through 95th percentile (90%) of males, but only approximately the 65th through 95th percentile (30%) of

females. The policy decision by Secretary of Defense Les Aspin (1993, p. 1) to increase the percentage of women pilots uncovered the gender bias in the cockpit design. Designed to exclude only 10% of male recruits by dimensions, the cockpit excluded 70% of women recruits. Exclusion of such large numbers of women by dimensions alone made it extremely difficult to meet the military's policy goal of increasing the number of women pilots. The officers initially reacted by assuming that the technology reflected the best or only design possible and that the goal for the percentage of women pilots would have to be lowered or the number of tall women recruits would have to be increased. This initial reaction, which represented the world viewpoint of men, changed (de Beauvoir, 1949/1989). When political coalitions, the Tailhook scandal, and feminist groups reinforced the policy goal, a new cockpit design emerged, which reduced the minimum sitting height from 34 to 32.8 inches, thereby increasing the percentage of eligible women (Weber, 1999, p. 379).

## Theories and Conclusions

The examples of reproductive technologies suggest that considerable resources and attention are devoted to women's health issues when those issues are directly related to men's interest in controlling production of children. Contraceptive research may permit men to have sexual pleasure without the production of children; research on infertility, pregnancy, and childbirth has allowed men to assert more control over the production of more "perfect" children and over an aspect of women's lives over which they previously held less power.

In similar fashion, the computing industry in its language, as well as hardware, reflects the world of the designers. That world reflects the world of men who spend less time in child care and have relatively more time to "crack the code."

> And once you've done that [spent hours in front of screens] ... you'd know there were things you could exchange, a level of hints and tips, but more deeply a level of understanding, shared language ... but they [those men] don't look around and see the absence of women, they don't perhaps

think that they are creating a language, and perhaps, as it's expressed at work, a power-base which is exclusive. And they don't realise that they are where they are because the computing industry is designed for them. It's designed for people who *have* got hours to spare: in the garage, or the shed, or the attic, cracking the code. (Male library research officer, quoted in Green, Owen, & Pain, 1993, pp. 145–146)

## PSYCHOANALYTIC FEMINISM

Based on the Freudian prejudice that anatomy is destiny, psychoanalytic theory assumes that biological sex will lead to different ways for boys and girls to resolve the Oedipus and castration complexes that arise during the phallic stage of normal sexual development. Rejecting the biological determinism in Freud, Dinnerstein (1977) and Chodorow (1978) in particular have used an aspect of psychoanalytic theory known as object relations theory to examine the construction of gender and sexuality during the Oedipal stage of psychosexual development, which usually results in male dominance. In contrast to Lacanian feminists who emphasize the symbolic role of the father in formation of masculinity and femininity, using language and signifiers (Ferrell, 1996), Dinnerstein and Chodorow conclude that the gender differences resulting in male dominance can be traced to the fact that in our society women are the primary caretakers for most infants and children. Accepting most Freudian ideas about the Oedipus complex, Chodorow and Dinnerstein conclude that boys are pushed to be independent, distant, and autonomous from their female caretakers, whereas girls are permitted to be more dependent, intimate, and less individuated from their mothers or female caretakers.

Keller (1982, 1985), in particular, applied the work of Chodorow and Dinnerstein to suggest how science, populated mostly by men, has become a masculine province in its choice of experimental topics, use of male subjects for experimentation, and interpretation and theorizing from data, as well as the practice and applications of science undertaken by the scientists. Keller suggests that because the scientific method stresses objectivity, rationality, distance,

and autonomy of the observer from the object of study (i.e., the positivist neutral observer), individuals who feel comfortable with independence, autonomy, and distance will be most likely to become scientists. Feminists have suggested that the objectivity and rationality of science are synonymous with a male approach to the physical, natural world.

## Choice and Definition

The particularly reductionistic version of the biomedical model currently in vogue, in which extreme attention is drawn to genetic causes for diseases, has been critiqued by feminists as positivist and enforcing distance and autonomy between the observer and object of study. Interdisciplinary approaches might most effectively target women's health issues, including dysmenorrhea, incontinence in older women, nutrition in postmenopausal women, and effects of exercise level and duration on alleviation of menstrual discomfort. Although these issues would not require high tech or expensive drug testing as solutions, effective research would include methods, such as interviews and case studies, from the social and natural sciences that shorten the distance between the observer and the object of study.

A psychoanalytic feminist framework might provide the theoretical backdrop for Cockburn's (1981, 1983, 1985) work documenting the intertwining of masculinity and technology. Encouraged to be independent, autonomous, and distant, male engineers and computer scientists design technologies and IT systems reflecting those characteristics. As Bodker and Greenbaum (1993) suggest, the "hard-systems" approach to computer systems developments follows the positivist, linear, and technicist approach compatible with Western scientific thought. The technical capabilities, constraints of the machines, and rational data flow become the focus and driver of the technology design.

This "hard-systems" design approach used by developers (mostly male) of computer systems assumes separation, distance, and independence on several levels: (1) between the abstract systems development and the concrete real world of work—separation ignores the often circular and interconnected forces of organization, assuming that they remain linear and unaffected by other hierarchical power relations; and (2) between the developers and users—because users do not contribute to the design of the system, their needs and suggestions that might make the system function more smoothly in the real world of work are ignored. The problems caused by this abstraction, objectivity, autonomy, and separation have spawned new methods such as "soft-systems" human factors approaches to solving the problems and mediating the gap.

## Approaches

The distant, autonomous approaches of science become reflected in tests that do little to connect with the realities for women susceptible to breast cancer. As a result of the isolation and copying of the BRCA1 and BRCA2 genes, several biotech firms and at least one academic medical center now market tests to detect genetic susceptibilities to breast cancer. Ignoring the fact that this again takes attention from social, behavioral, and environmental factors and prevention to focus on inherited susceptibilities, which account for between 5% and 10% of those who will get breast cancer, the test raises numerous other problems and ethical dilemmas: Marketed as laboratory services rather than products, the tests do not fall under FDA regulation. Thus, the tests have not undergone standardization before coming on the market, resulting in variation in the data on the effectiveness, safety, and implications of the tests. For example, two laboratories differed in the estimates by age of the chance of getting breast cancer if the test is positive (National Breast Cancer Coalition, 1997). Second, there is no "cure" or definitive treatment for a positive test. When an individual learns she has the BRCA1 or BRCA2 gene, she cannot "remove" the gene to prevent the development of cancer. Third, some indicators suggest that insurance companies might view positive results as a basis for a preexisting condition (based on what happened with the gene for sickle cell) and cancel coverage (Andrews, Fullarton, Holtzman, & Mutulsky, 1993).

The gender constellation predicted by psychoanalytic feminism also becomes transparent in technology: The men who design hardware systems design them in ways reflective of their perspective on the world with which they feel comfortable. Such system designs tend to place priority on data and ignore relationships between people. Women, socialized to value connections and relationships, tend to feel uncomfortable with the hard-systems approach. As users, they find that the technology fails to aid much of the real-world work. The design inhibits or fails to foster good teamwork and other relationships among coworkers. Because the design does not reflect their view of priorities in the organization and work, and actively ignores the reality of power and gender relations, women tend to be excluded, and exclude themselves, from hard-systems design.

## Theories and Conclusions

The BRCA1 and BRCA2 gene sequencing may represent an exciting breakthrough in basic research. Yet its implications for future collaborative and open research may be problematic because of patenting and its immediate impact on testing and treatment. An unfortunate fallout from the work is the misperception by some women that the BRCA1 and BRCA2 genes are the exclusive cause of breast cancer and that, consequently, they might as well stop doing breast self-examination, because cancer will be inevitable if they have the gene and not occur if they lack the gene.

Critiques of information technologies from a psychoanalytic feminist perspective raise the very interesting question of how systems design might change if more feminine values and connection became priorities. Sorenson (1992) explored whether male and female computer scientists worked differently. He found that men tended to focus on mathematical models and computer programming while women spent more time running experiments, reading scientific literature, and plotting data. After studying the technological and political values of men and women engineering students, graduate students, and junior R&D scientists at the Norwegian Institute of Technology, Sorenson found that women brought "caring values" to research in computer science. "Caring values" included empathy and rationale of responsibility. "In computer science, this means that women have a caring, other-oriented relationship to nature and to people, an integrated, more holistic and less hierarchical world-view, a less competitive way of relating to colleagues and a greater affinity to users" (p. 10).

Understanding the importance of relationships and power, some women computer systems designers (Microsysters, 1988; Suchman, 1994) have attempted to link users with systems design as an explicit attempt to empower women. Although some might view this as an example of Harding's "strong objectivity," this shortening of distance between the user and the system design mimics Keller's (1983) description of McClintock's work in "A Feeling for the Organism." In the shortening of the distance between the observer and the object of study, Keller describes less autonomy, independence, and separation as classic hallmarks of psychoanalytic feminism when applied to the work of women scientists.

## RADICAL FEMINISM

Radical feminism, in contrast to psychoanalytic feminism and liberal feminism, rejects the possibility of a gender-free science or a science developed from a neutral, objective perspective. Radical feminism maintains that women's oppression is the first, most widespread, and deepest oppression (Jaggar & Rothenberg, 1994). Because men dominate and control most institutions, politics, and knowledge in our society, they reflect a male perspective and are effective in oppressing women. Scientific institutions, practice, and knowledge are particularly male dominated and have been documented by many feminists (Bleier, 1984; Fee, 1983; Griffin, 1978; Haraway, 1978, 1989; Hubbard, 1990; Keller, 1985; Merchant, 1979; Rosser, 1990) to be especially effective patriarchal tools to control and harm women. Radical feminism rejects most scientific theories, data, and experiments precisely because they not only exclude women but also are not women centered.

The theory that radical feminism proposes is evolving (Tong, 1989) and is not as well developed as some of the other feminist theories previously discussed. The reasons that its theory is less developed spring fairly directly from the nature of radical feminism itself. First, it is

radical. That means that it rejects most currently accepted ideas about scientific epistemology—what kinds of things can be known, who can be a knower, and how beliefs are legitimated as knowledge. Radical feminism also rejects the current methodology—the general structure of how theory finds its application in particular scientific disciplines. Second, unlike the feminisms previously discussed, radical feminism does not have its basis in a theory such as Marxism, positivism, psychoanalysis, or existentialism, already developed for decades by men. Because radical feminism is based in women's experience, it rejects feminisms rooted in theories developed by men based on their experience and worldview. Third, the theory of radical feminism must be developed by women and based in women's experience (MacKinnon, 1987).

Because radical feminism maintains that the oppression of women is the deepest, most widespread, and historically first oppression, women have had few opportunities to come together, understand their experiences collectively, and develop theories based on those experiences. Perhaps because of this dearth of opportunities, radical-libertarian feminists (Firestone, 1970; Rubin, 1984) view sexuality as a powerful force that society seeks to control and encourage women to violate sexual taboos and use artificial means to control reproduction. In contrast, radical-cultural feminists (Dworkin, 1983; Ferguson, 1984) view heterosexual relations as forms of male domination as evidenced in pornography, prostitution, rape, and sexual harassment; they encourage elimination of patriarchal institutions and care in using artificial intervention in reproduction, which they see as a source of power for women.

The implications of radical feminism for science and experimental methods are much more far-reaching than those of other feminist theories. Radical feminism implies rejection of much of the standard epistemology of science. It perceives reality as an inseparable whole, always alive and in motion, both spiritual and material (Capra, 1973), so that connections between humans and other parts of the natural and physical world constitute part of what can be known (Jaggar, 1983) and should be investigated. Radical feminism posits that it is women, not men, who can be the knowers. Because women have been oppressed, they know more than men. They must see the world from the male perspective to survive, but their double vision from their experience as an oppressed group allows them to see more than men.

However, radical feminism deviates considerably from other feminisms in its view of how beliefs are legitimated as knowledge.

Because radical feminists believe in a connection with and a conception of the world as an organized whole, they reject dualistic and hierarchical approaches. Dichotomies such as rational/feeling, objective/subjective, mind/body, culture/nature, and theory/practice are viewed as patriarchal conceptions that fragment the organic whole of reality. Linear conceptions of time and what is considered to be "logical" thinking in the Western traditions are frequently rejected by radical feminists. Cyclicity as a conception of time and thinking as an upward spiral seem more appropriate approaches to studying a world in which everything is connected in a process of constant change (Daly, 1978, 1984). Radical feminists view all human beings, and most particularly themselves, as connected to the living and nonliving worlds. Consequently, radical feminists view themselves as "participators" (Jaggar, 1983) connected in the same plane with, rather than distanced from, their object of study. Many radical feminists also believe that because of this connection, women can know things by relying on intuition or spiritual powers.

## Choice and Definition

How does the male bias in research—male-as-norm approach and exclusion of women from clinical trials—which has had negative effects for women for diseases that occur in both sexes, affect a disease such as breast cancer? Because more than 90% of cases of breast cancer occur in women, the male has not usually been perceived as the norm for the disease in the way that he often is in diseases, such as AIDS and cardiovascular diseases, which occur in both sexes. Still the male-as-norm approaches have created a history of general medical research, including cancer research, which has accumulated significant data and methods that work for exploring health and disease in the male body. Only now as a result of the Women's Health Initiative and other forces for change are data comparable with data for the male body being collected on the effects of reproductive cycles to fill this dearth of information for the female body.

Some might define the work of Bratteteig (2002) and her coworkers as radical feminism, because it originates from women's discourse on computer science problems and methods. Indeed, they insist on prioritizing applicability of systems and putting users and developers in the same plane as collaborators in systems development. This starting from the understanding of a woman worker and her abilities and then focusing on how her professional competence can be augmented by the use of a system does begin with women's experience. This focus on women (Hacker, 1989; Thoresen, 1989) is consistent with feminist principles.

## Approaches

For breast cancer research, this missing information would appear critical to understanding causes and treatments of a disease where hormone levels and reproductive history have documented, critical roles. Differing estrogen levels among women and changing levels associated with pregnancy, breast-feeding, and menopause within a woman have been correlated with different risks, treatment success, and mortality outcomes in breast cancer. A long history of understanding changes in hormone levels over the life cycle in women of diverse races, ages, and social classes with differing reproductive backgrounds in many different diseases would appear crucial for breast cancer research. The very cyclicity of the female body and interaction between estrogen and other drugs may serve as keys to breast cancer breakthroughs. For example, the differential survival rate of women receiving surgery for tumor removal in the follicular compared with the luteal phase of the cycle (Hrushesky, 1996; Hrushesky, Bluming, Gruber, & Sothern, 1989; Senie, Rosen, Rhondes, & Lesser, 1991) suggests that stage of the ovulatory cycle—that is, hormone levels—significantly influences disease progress. The substitution of a history of female-as-norm approaches, where phases of the menstrual cycle and hormone levels and their interactions with drugs and surgery had been well studied, might have led to this "discovery" before 1989. Some of the current controversies in screening and treatment, such as mammography for premenopausal women and use of tamoxifen for prevention, might be understood better if decades of research had focused on pre- and postmenopausal women, their cycles, and hormonal interactions.

In addition to the focus on women and seeking to empower women, MacKinnon (1987) adds a further criterion to radical feminism. She suggests that the consciousness-raising group provides a methodology for radical feminism. Because patriarchy pervades and dominates all institutions, ideologies, and technologies, women have difficulty placing their experiences, lives, and needs in central focus in everyday life and environments. A successful strategy that women use to obtain reliable knowledge and correct patriarchal ideology is the consciousness-raising group (Jaggar, 1983). Using their personal experiences as a basis, women meet together in communal, nonhierarchical groups to examine their experiences to determine what counts as knowledge (MacKinnon, 1987). Suchman in her work at Xerox PARC uses this approach in her view that knowledge held by users is central to the design process. They are "taking computerization as an occasion to articulate unacknowledged forms of expertise and to take that knowledge seriously as a basis for design" (Suchman & Jordan, 1989, p. 158). In recognizing the gap between technologies created by experts and their use in real working environments, they have produced a "radical reconceptualisation of the computer systems development process which recognises the innovatory character of the implementation process and places the local expertise of users at the centre" (Webster, 1995, p. 165).

The interplay between designing and use, or designer and user, described in the Suchman example, also might be seen to demonstrate the cyclicity, often associated with radical feminism: Because of the belief of radical feminists in connection and a conception of the world as an organic whole, they reject dualistic, hierarchical approaches, and dichotomies that fragment the organic whole of reality. Cyclicity as a conception of time and thinking as an upward spiral seem more appropriate ways to study a world where everything is connected in a process of constant change (Daly, 1978, 1984).

## Theories and Conclusions

Another aspect of hierarchy appears in the organization of the specialties within medicine, which may contribute to the dearth of research and lack of focus on breast cancer. The breast does not "fit" into the territory of any particular specialty. The breast fails to fit the traditional location of obstetrics or gynecology, usually considered to be a woman's reproductive system below the waist—the ovaries, oviduct, uterus, vagina, urethra, and their associated glands; even its involvement in sexual activity has not resulted in its being claimed as the province of obstetrics or gynecology. After birth, during lactation, the breast may briefly fit under pediatrics. For palpation to detect changes or lumps, it may fall into the territory of the obstetrician or gynecologist, general practitioner, or internist during the course of a physical examination. Radiologists claim the breast for mammography screening.

Only after the breast becomes cancerous does it intersect with the territory of other specialists—the surgeon for lumpectomy or mastectomy, the pathologist for determination of malignancy, the oncologist to oversee chemotherapy, and the radiologist who delivers radiation to kill cancerous cells. Eventually, a plastic surgeon may undertake reconstruction using implants. In brief, the breast is the territory of virtually all specialists and of none. Although the notion of a team of specialists now enjoys recognition as the favored approach for patient treatment, the typical breast cancer research project does not routinely use such a large, interdisciplinary team of researchers. Because the organization of NIH correlates with the medical specialties, it is not remarkable that breast cancer research has fallen through the cracks until recently.

Radical feminists examining information technologies might interpret the binary 0,1 foundation of computers and computing as based on the primary dichotomy/dualism of male-female. The "switchers," "controls," and "operations" language of computing fit the patriarchal mode of control. The dichotomy receives reinforcement by the domination of men and relative absence of women from the design process. "So, the domination of men and the absence of women from the design process is *one* factor which creates technologies which are closely geared to the needs of men and which are inappropriate to women's requirements" (Webster, 1995, p. 179).

## LESBIAN SEPARATISM

To understand the complete, comprehensive influence of patriarchy and begin to imagine alternative technologies, lesbian separatism would suggest that women must separate entirely from men (Frye, 1983; Hoagland, 1988). Lesbian separatism, often seen as an offshoot of radical feminism, would suggest that separation from men is necessary in a patriarchal society for females to understand their experiences and explore the potential of science and the impact of technologies. Although some lesbian separatists also now identify with queer theory, because queer theory also embraces gay men (Butler, 1990; de Lauretis, 1991), some lesbians prefer to retain a more separate stance.

Lesbians may be at higher risk for certain diseases such as breast and uterine cancer. Haynes estimates that one in three lesbians may develop breast cancer during her lifetime because lesbians are more likely than other women to fall into high-risk categories for the disease (Campbell, 1992). Many lesbians do not have children, have higher body fat, and limit their access to regular health care checkups relative to heterosexual women because of fear of discrimination. Very few studies have focused on lesbians as a separate population for health studies.

Cockburn (1983) advocates women-only organizations in information technology:

> In my view, by far the most effective principle evolved to date is separate, woman-only organisation. It enables us to learn (teach each other) without being put down. Provide schoolgirls with separate facilities and the boys won't be able to grab the computer and bully the girls off the console. Provide young women with all-women courses so that they can gain the experience to make an informed choice about an engineering career. We need to demand a massive increase in resources from the state, from industry, from industrial training boards, for women-run, women-only, initiatives. Everywhere we have tried it, from women's caucuses to Greenham Common (the women's peace camp at a cruise missile base), autonomy works wonders for our feelings and our strength. We need, before all else, a great expansion of the autonomous sphere in technology. (p. 132)

The establishment of engineering at Smith College, a women's college, may provide a site where ideas, curriculum, and pedagogy in technology can be explored in an environment somewhat separate from men.

Radical feminism would suggest that the reason no truly feminist alternative to technology exists is that men, masculinity, and patriarchy have become completely intertwined with technology and computer systems in our society. Imagining technology from a woman-centered perspective in the absence of patriarchy becomes extremely difficult, if not impossible. Because engineering and technology development in the West/North foreground control—control over nature, over people, and over machines—imagining a technology premised on cooperation, collaboration, and working with nature, people, and machines runs contrary to our image of the technology that evolved in a patriarchal, heterosexist society. Brun (1994) suggests that the creation and protection of human life should be the point of departure for technological development for women:

> Women's ethics . . . is not sentimental. It is practical. It implies a concrete and holistic consideration of people's need for a sustainable environment and that basic security which is the precondition of common responsible action. . . . A step by step process . . . makes the protection of the weak its highest priority: creating social solidarity and collective security in a sustainable manner from below. This must go hand in hand with a gradual reduction of the importance of wage labour in the shape of a collective re-appropriate of control over the means of subsistence. . . . In the

context of such a process new technology must be invented, old technologies transformed or abandoned. (p. 79)

## Queer and Transgender Theories

Queer and transgender theories, seen by some as successors to theories of radical feminism and lesbian separatism, question links between sex, gender, and sexual orientation (Butler, 1990; de Lauretis, 1991; Stryker, 1998). They raise additional challenges about the links between economic, racial, and dominance factors with gender in our society. As Judith Butler (1990, 1992, 1994) argues, the very act of defining a gender identity excludes or devalues some bodies and practices, while simultaneously obscuring the constructed character of gender identity; describing gender identity creates a norm.

When lesbians are lumped together with heterosexual women in studies of incidence or cause of sexually transmitted diseases or other gynecological problems from which they are exempt or for which they are at low risk because they do not engage in heterosexual intercourse, both lesbians and nonlesbians suffer. Defining such studies generally as research on "women's health issues" rather than on "health issues for women engaging in heterosexual sex" leads the general population and some health care workers to think that lesbians are at risk for diseases that they are unlikely to contract, while obscuring the true risk behavior for heterosexual women.

The creators of *The Turing Game,* a computer game modification of Alan Turing's suggestion of ways to differentiate machines from people and men from women, explain their goals and methodologies in the following terms:

Do men and women behave differently online? Can you tell who is a man and who is a woman based on how they communicate and interact with others on the Internet? Can you tell how old someone is, or determine their race or national origin? In the online world as in the real world, these issues of personal identity affect how we relate to others. Societies are created and destroyed by these understandings and misunderstandings in the real world. Yet, as the online world becomes increasingly a part of our lives, identity in this new medium is still poorly understood. At the Georgia Institute of Technology, we have created an online game to help us explore and teach about these issues. This environment, called The Turing Game, is a game of identity deception, expression, and discovery. Available on the Internet, it has been played by more than 9000 people. Players from seventy-six countries on all seven continents have used the game to learn about issues of identity and diversity online through direct experience. At the same time, they have created communities of their own, and explore the boundaries of electronic communication. (Berman & Bruckman, 2000)

This *Turing Game* explores the creations of these norms and how the Internet opens possibilities for identity changes or deception.

## Postmodern or Poststructural Feminism

Liberal feminism suggests that women have a unified voice and can be universally addressed (Gunew, 1990). Poststructuralists (Derrida, 2000; Foucault, 1978; Lacan, 1977, 1998) have challenged some of the fundamental assumptions about knowledge, subjectivity, and power through transforming the theory of meaning and the assumptions about subjectivity found in structural linguistics. Feminist poststructuralists (Irigaray, 1985; Kristeva, 1986) critiqued the absence of women and the feminine in these assumptions.

Like poststructuralists, postmodernists (Jameson, 1981; Lyotard, 1986) question fundamental assumptions of the Enlightenment, with postmodern feminists critiquing the absence of women. In postmodernism, the self is no longer regarded as "masterful, universal, integrated, autonomous, and self-constructed; rather it is socially constructed by ideology, discourse, the structure of the unconscious, and/or language" (Rothfield, 1990, p. 132). Postmodernism dissolves the universal subject and postmodern feminism dissolves the possibility that women speak in a unified voice or that they can be universally addressed. Postmodern perspectives stress that due to her situatedness—the result of her specific national, class, and cultural identities—the category of woman can no longer be regarded as smooth, uniform, and homogeneous. Although postmodern feminists (Grosz, 1994; Irigaray, 1985) see the material body as significant and a site of resistance to patriarchy, postmodern feminist theories imply that no universal health research agenda or application of technologies will be appropriate and that various women will have different reactions to science and technologies depending on their own class, race, sexuality, country, and other factors.

## Choice and Definition

A limitation of the biomedical model with its cellular, hormonal, and genetic approaches becomes its tendency to center on the individual and her body, while bringing less attention to surrounding social, economic, and political factors that may contribute to disease and its progress. The incidence of breast cancer has increased 1% per year since 1940 (Harris, Lippman, Veronesi, & Willett, 1992). This fact, coupled with studies from the 1970s, which documented a fivefold variation in breast cancer rates around the world (Armstrong & Doll, 1975) and showed that the incidence of breast cancer in Japanese women who migrate from their low-incidence home country to the United States becomes that of U.S. women, suggests that factors besides genetics are significant for the disease.

As postmodern feminist theory recognizes limitations with perceiving women as a universal group, so have deeper, more complex studies of technology industries revealed limitations of simplistic assumptions in technology designs. For example, Webster (1995) suggests that critiquing the absence of understanding of women's needs is easier than identifying what women's needs and priorities really are.

> First of all, they are of course not uniform across all women or across all social classes, nationalities and cultures. Then, making the link between women's needs and the consequently desirable features of an IT [information technology] system is a vexed question, and one that is too often dealt with in an essentialist manner by reference to the supposedly universal characteristics of women IT users (for example, as lacking in confidence with computers, as disinterested in computers except as tools, as caring and sociable rather than rational and technical). Feminist design initiatives have often encountered this difficulty. Most have addressed it by focusing away from the eventual characteristics of the IT *products* which they shape, and towards the *processes* of shaping which offer scope for permanently redefining the role of female users in systems design. (p. 178)

## Approaches

Inclusion of social, psychological, and public health perspectives is needed for a more comprehensive research base to explore why poor women and women of color have higher death rates from breast cancer than middle-class white U.S. women. Epidemiological approaches include these perspectives; they reveal factors important for disease prevention. Because "the poor, in general, have a 10 to 15 percent lower cancer survival rate regardless of race" (Altman, 1996, p. 37), research that relies on biology alone and ignores socioeconomic factors will be unlikely to uncover the best way to remove this survival differential. Similarly, the fact that "the five-year survival rate is 75 percent in white women compared to 63 percent for African American women" (p. 38) is likely to be most fully explored when methods from social sciences are coupled with those from biomedicine. Such interdisciplinary approaches may tease apart the relative effects that more exposure to workplace and environmental carcinogens and less access to high-quality medical care, nutritious food, and decent living conditions have on the higher incidence and lower survival rates experienced by African Americans with regard to breast cancer.

Studies focused on women in the technology workforce have tended to imply a universalist stance that all women have similar needs for uses of technology and that the employment categories and effects within technology industries affect women uniformly. The "flexibility" and "casualization" of the workforce, which telecommuting permits, may hurt wages, benefits, and long-term stability overall. Although it creates or increases the double burden for women who can mind children while working at home, some women prefer this option to no work at all.

Women have always needed to find ways of managing their domestic responsibilities while in employment, and ICT-supported (Information Communication Technologies–supported) forms of working, such as teleworking, as well as other "contingent" forms of employment, such as part-time work, offer them the means to do this. To the extent that ICTs provide the wherewithal for carrying these casual forms of employment to new heights of sophistication, they are an important mechanism in the confirmation of women's marginal relationship to the labor market.

> But ICTs can also directly allow women to handle paid and unpaid work simultaneously. A simple example is the cell phone. Frissen (1995) suggests that it allows working women to transform the double burden of home and work into a parallel burden, allowing them to multitask and manage their domestic responsibilities better (from a distance). (Webster, 1995, pp. 184–185)

This quotation suggests why women may react differently to technologies, depending on their race, class, age, ability status, parental status, urban-rural location, or other factors. Coupled with the rapid and changing pace of technology, postmodern feminism suggests why universal theories fail to fit the reality of women's lives. The lack of universalism may inhibit gender-based coalitions and organizing, making it also easier to understand the political inactivism of which individuals who articulate postmodern perspectives may be accused (Butler, 1992).

## Theories and Conclusions

Epidemiological studies do attempt to consider or at least control for social, psychological, economic, and environmental factors through using matched cohorts (individuals who are the same for all variables except the risk factor under study) or case studies (individuals who differ only by whether they have the disease or not). Use of epidemiology in breast cancer research has begun to elucidate potential contributions of diet, lifestyle, and environmental factors to breast cancer such as dietary fat content, smoking, environmental contaminants, and exercise. Because of the complexity of breast cancer, different epidemiological studies often

yield conflicting results; sample size, failure to control for all variables, and length of study contribute to these conflicting results. Increased funding of epidemiological studies might not only lead to improved studies but also shift the focus to prevention.

Just as women's needs for IT or technology designs differ and vary, depending on class, nationality, culture, age, and other factors, employment of women in technology industries also does not fit a universal or uniform pattern. Innovations in technology have not led to overall restructuring of established sexual divisions of labor, or unequal gender or race relations (Kirkup, 1992). Some groups of women have improved or lost ground in their employment in technology industries. For example, some women have benefited from programs designed to increase female representation in IT and other technology industries. These equity and access programs (based in liberal feminist theories) have benefited some professional middle-class women whose educational backgrounds position them to capitalize on better employment opportunities (Wickham & Murray, 1987).

Although relocation and temporization of work have tended to hurt employees in general and women in particular, the effects may depend on urban location. For example, closing offices in city centers and metropolitan areas has tended to hurt urban women, more likely to be of lower socioeconomic status and of color, while creating employment for women in the suburbs (Greenbaum, 1995). In contrast, development of offshore information processing has improved employment for women in poorer countries. Information and data processing functions, once performed by women in the First World, have now been exported to low-cost economies because telecommunications and satellite technologies make this possible (Webster, 1995, p. 182).

### Postcolonial Feminism

Beginning in 1947, following various campaigns of anticolonial resistance, often with an explicitly nationalist basis, many colonial empires formally dissolved and previously colonized countries gained independence (Williams & Crissman, 1994). Although the end of colonial rule created high hope for a proper postcolonial era, the extent to which the West had not relinquished control became clear quickly. The continuing Western influence, particularly in the economic arena, but also in the political, ideological, and military sectors, became known as neocolonialism by Marxists (Williams & Crissman, 1994). Feminists have suggested that patriarchy dominates postcolonial and neocolonial, much as it dominated colonial, everyday life.

Not surprisingly, science and technology reflect the varying complex aspects of the interrelationships among developed and developing countries in general and between the particular cultures of the colonized and colonizing countries. General themes include the underdevelopment of the southern continents by Europe and other northern continents (Harding, 1993); ignoring, obscuring, or misappropriating earlier scientific achievements and history of countries in southern continents; the fascination with so-called indigenous science (Harding, 1998); the idea that the culture, science, and technology of the colonizer or former colonizing country remains superior to that of the colony or postcolonial country; and the insistence that developing countries must restructure their local economies, to become scientifically and technologically literate to join and compete in a global economy (Mohanty, 1997). In northern, former colonizing countries, the concurrent restructuring effects of multinational corporations and other forces of globalization are evidenced in downsizing, privatization, and widening economic gaps between the poor and very wealthy. The particular forms and ways that these general themes take shape and play out vary, depending on the history, culture, geography, and length of colonization for both the colonized and colonizing countries.

Both postcolonialist and feminist discourses center on otherness or "alterity." Postcolonial feminism has focused generally around issues of cultural identity, language, nationalism, and the position of women in formerly colonized countries as they become nation-states (Mehta, 2000). As the new nation-states are constructed, women in formerly colonized countries experience discrimination along race, class, and gender lines due to the entanglement of patriarchy with colonialism (Grewal, 1996). The new nation-states such as India often provide access to law and authority for men only, thereby depriving women, characterized as "subaltern" (Spivak, 1988), of a voice. In contrast, some women from new African countries have extended definitions of motherhood beyond the biological to the communal. Including community and culture and providing new models of femininity independent of patriarchal and western definitions (Ogunyemi, 1996; Steady, 1982) makes these women exemplify the survival and integrity of their culture and people.

## Choice and Definition

The implementation and use of reproductive technologies demonstrate quite vividly the significance of diversity among women surrounding health issues. The use of low-technology techniques such as cesarean section and high-technology processes such as in vitro fertilization and rented uteri varies within countries and among countries. Pressures to make women conform to the norms of the patriarchal culture and class within which they are located provide similarities for women in the use of these technologies. Different cultures, classes, races, and nationalities provide the parameters for differences of use between women within a culture and among cultures.

Although differences and complexities among cultures represent one type of diversity, class differences represent another. Women in developed countries experience more use of such technologies than women in developing countries, possibly because of socioeconomic differences between less- and more-developed countries. Sometimes class serves as the most reliable predictor of the use of technologies on women across cultures. Substantial abuses resulting from the refusal to remove the contraceptive Norplant in Bangladesh, first revealed in the 1980s, continued in 1998 (Gillespie, 1998). Because of government policies seeking to decrease fertility, health practitioners refused to remove the Norplant transdermal sticks when women complained of side effects ranging from continual bleeding, through migraines and dizziness, to ectopic pregnancies. Similar coercion occurs in U.S. inner cities, where Norplant is implanted in welfare mothers, primarily African Americans, as a condition for receipt of checks, and in Native American women who receive health care from the Indian Health Service on reservations (Washburn, 1996). The diffractions of reproductive health in modern global society define infertility as the health problem for women of certain races and classes in developed countries, while overpopulation is defined as the problem for women of other races and lower socioeconomic status in developing countries.

Many women in the so-called Third World or developing countries receive employment in technology industries or because of technological developments such as satellites that permit rapid data transmission over large geographic distances. The United States, Western Europe, and Japan house the corporate headquarters, owners, and decision makers of these global, multinational corporations; technological developments permit these companies to roam the globe and use women in offshore, formerly colonized, or developing nations as cheap sources of labor. Because new technologies transcend boundaries of time and space, they facilitate corporations in dispersing work around the globe to exploit sexual and racial divisions of labor.

## Approaches

Using observation, trial and error, and sharing of information across generations, women in developing countries used methods of cleaning and cooking and fed their families food to maximize health and minimize disease; women learned which plants held medicinal properties. Part of their indigenous scientific knowledge included recognition of herbal remedies to enhance fertility, prevent conception, and cause abortion. The major efforts made by pharmaceutical companies to identify the plants used in traditional healing in indigenous cultures today constitute some recognition of the women's knowledge. However, just as when doctors obtained herbal remedies from midwives and witches in the 19th-century United States (Ehrenreich & English, 1978), the modern pharmaceutical companies award the patent to

the scientist who does the "work" of synthesizing the compound based on the extract from the medicinal plant, thereby defining the indigenous women's knowledge as nonscience and nonwork.

Information technology, satellites, and computerization become the glue that holds the global networks within a company together and permits them to function smoothly and efficiently. Benetton exemplifies this:

> At the Italian headquarters is a computer that is linked to an electronic cash register in every Benetton shop; those which are far away, like Tokyo and Washington are linked via satellite. Every outlet transmits detailed information on sales daily, and production is continuously and flexibly adjusted to meet the preferences revealed in the market. (Elson, 1989, p. 103)

## Theories and Conclusions

As the results of the 1991 National Council for International Health Conference on Women's Health, The Action Agenda (Koblinsky, Timyan, & Gay, 1993), and the 1995 Beijing Conference (Basch, 1996) underline, poverty causes two thirds of the world's women to have poor health. Six of the twelve items of a list of "What We Want—Voices from the South" focus on health, contraception, and family planning issues (Jacobson, 1993).

In many developing countries, cultural mores encourage adoption of only part of the health care practices from developed countries; mores prevent adoption of other practices. In overpopulated parts of Latin America, such as the favelas in the Nordest of Brazil, the culture of breast-feeding has been lost, because the father's provision of milk symbolizes paternity. To breast-feed her baby signifies that the woman has been abandoned by the baby's father. The adoption of some "modern" health practices such as bottle-feeding simultaneously with nonadoption of others such as contraception demonstrates the role of culture in mediating these diffracted reproductive health practices.

The IT industry uses subcontracted female labor in developing countries, particularly for software development. Western managements control the conduct of software development projects, relying on women from India, China,

Mexico, Hungary, and Israel as programmers. Telecommunications technologies ease the transmission of specifications and completed work between the workers in developing countries and client companies in the West. Women from these developing countries are preferred as workers over those in developed countries because of their technical skills and English proficiency, relatively high roles of productivity, and relatively low costs of labor.

These examples clearly demonstrate aspects of postcolonialism in that control of the economy of developing countries remains in the hands of developed countries. They demonstrate patriarchal control because women, not men, in the developing countries become the sources of cheap labor. Language becomes an interesting feature that continues to tie former colony with colonizer. Theoretically, satellites and telecommunications transcend geographical barriers and permit any developed country to use labor in any developing country. Practically, the former ties developed between colony and colonizer, as well as the language of the colonizer learned by the colonized during the period of colonization, means that former relationships continue in the neocolonial modern world. Does the conversion of some Indian universities to software factories exemplify this language connection in the IT world, where English dominates?

## CYBERFEMINISM

Cyberfeminism stands not only as the most recent feminist theory but also as the theory that overtly fuses modern science and technology with gender. As the name suggests, cyberfeminism explores the ways that information technologies and the Internet provide avenues to liberate (or oppress) women. In the early 1990s, the term *cyberfeminism* first began to be used in various parts of the world (Hawthorne & Klein, 1999), with VNS Matrix, an Australian-based group of media-based artists being one of the first groups to use the term.

The individuals who defined cyberfeminism (Hawthorne & Klein, 1999; Millar, 1998) saw the potential of the Internet and computer science as technologies to level the playing field and open new avenues for job opportunities and creativity for women. They describe cyberfeminism as

> a woman-centered perspective that advocates women's use of new information and communications technologies of empowerment. Some cyberfeminists see these technologies as inherently liberatory and argue that their development will lead to an end to male superiority because women are uniquely suited to life in the digital age. (Millar, 1998, p. 200)

Absence of sexism, racism, and other oppression would serve as a major contrast between the virtual world and the real world:

> Cyberfeminism as a philosophy has the potential to create a poetic, passionate, political identity and unity without relying on a logic and language of exclusion. It offers a route for reconstructing feminist politics through theory and practice with a focus on the implications of new technology rather than on factors which are divisive. (Paterson, 1994)

## Choices and Definitions

Biomedicine fuses technology with the biological human body in the forms of artificial hips, heart valves, pacemakers, and implants to deliver drugs, creating the cyborgs discussed by Donna Haraway (1997). Simultaneously, new media technologies explore the reciprocity between science and media, where in this age of genetics as the life code, culture may become biology. Analyses of metaphors in genome research suggest that because researchers transpose literature on to biology, it is not possible to critique science without critiquing culture.

In 1980, women represented 37% of computer science majors. The early history of computing reveals that Ada Lovelace contributed to the development of the protocomputer, and Grace Hopper created the first computer language composed of words and invented virtual storage (Stanley, 1995). Women performed calculations and wired hardware for the first digital electronic computer, ENIAC (Electronic Numerical Integrator and Computer). In the late 1980s, a drastic change began to occur. The numbers of women majoring in computer science plummeted; this plunge coincided with the restructuring of the capitalist system on a global scale and with the rise of financial speculation permitted by the nonproductive economic investment in the new information technologies (Millar, 1998).

## Approaches

Haraway moves beyond the use of computers to sequence the Human Genome to explore how the image of the cyborg embodies the extent to which technoscience interventions have become part of us and of women's health. She uses the image of the "virtual speculum" in *Modest_Witness@Second_Millennium. FemaleMan©_Meets_OncoMouse™: Feminism and Technoscience* to "open up observation into the orifices of the technoscientific body politic to address these kinds of questions about knowledge projects" (1997, p. 67). As the pioneer of feminist science studies, Haraway focuses on interdependencies and interrelationships among bodies, technologies, and cultures.

As Millar and other cyberfeminist critics point out, the existing elites have struggled to seize control and stabilize the commercial potential of digital technologies, as well as their research and development. Discontinuity, speed, symbolic and linguistic spectacle, and constant change characterize information technology and digital discourse. Although these characteristics of instability and indeterminacy because of the changing technology open the possibility for other changes in the social realm and power relations, it is very unclear that information technologies and cyberculture will result in such social changes.

## Theories and Conclusions

Technologies, particularly visual or imaging technologies of science or medicine, allow mapping of the human body. These maps and images in the forms of X rays, MRIs, CAT scans, and ultrasounds are now common parts of popular culture that appear not only in medical settings but also in the movies and on the nightly news. The media coverage of people's reaction to each not only entrenches it in popular culture, but also affects the evolution and use of the visual

technology itself. The *Visible Human Project*, which exists in the form of globally standardized data that integrates physical, biochemical, and informational worlds (Reiche, 2004), is also described as facilitating an information "revolution" in medicine by providing the "first digital description of an entire human being" (National Library of Medicine, 1990).

Some critics suggest that the current information technology revolution has resulted in a rigidifying and reifying of current power relations along previously existing gender, race, and class lines. The Internet becomes a tool making women more vulnerable to men using it for ordering brides from developing countries, prostitution, cybersex, assumption of false identities, and pornography (Hawthorne & Klein, 1999).

Despite their postmodern veneer of fragmentation, shifting identities, and speed, information technologies rest on the power of science and technology to emancipate humans and a faith in abstract reason. Millar (1998) defines this situation as "hypermodern." Hypermodern describes the packaging of modernity power relations that are universally patriarchal, racist, and bourgeois in a postmodern discourse of discontinuity, spectacle, and speed.

This raises the question of whether cyberfeminism is really a feminist theory. In *Cyberfeminism: Next Protocols,* the Old Boys Network (2004) claims that "CYBERFEMINISM is not simply an evolution of historical feminism created as a more adequate answer to meet the changed conditions of the Information Age" (p. 14). After describing cyberfeminism as a feminist intervention into the information age to explore how the conditions of the information age challenge political and social conditions of feminism, the authors raise questions about the parameters of cyberfeminism. These parameters range from "if CYBERFEMINISM is a powerful label for some vague ideas" (p. 14) through "ELSE IF CYBERFEMINISM is not a teleology" (p. 16), to "ELSE IF CYBERFEMINISM is a monster" (p. 17).

Could cyberfeminism merely represent an attempt to see information technology as the latest venue for women's liberation, much as Shulamith Firestone (1970) envisioned such liberation resulting from reproductive technologies? Although reproductive technologies have resulted in significant feminist critiques, theorizing, and discussion, no one considers them to be a feminist theory or method.

## Conclusion

This chapter has used several feminist theoretical perspectives to examine the relationships among women, gender, science, and technology. Taken together, the spectrum of feminist theories provides different, new insights to explore these relationships. All of these perspectives have affected experimental methods by placing women in central focus. Each of the theories discussed here (and some not included) has contributed at least one new perspective or emphasis overlooked in other theories. Because many feminist theories emerged in response to critiques of a preceding theory or theories, successor theories tend to be more comprehensive and compensatory for factors or groups overlooked by previous theories.

Knowledge of the range of theories and the particular factors each emphasizes allows one to better understand the context in which each may be most useful. For example, in providing testimony before Congress or other legislative bodies, a liberal feminist approach remains the theoretical venue most likely to resonate successfully with the audience, because despite the failure to pass the Equal Rights Amendment (ERA), the universal equity and access underlined in liberal feminism are acceptable and familiar to those enmeshed in our judicial and legislative systems. Although raising issues of class (socialist feminism) or race (African American feminism), particularly if the testimony centers on health care or other issues known to be affected by income or ethnicity, may be successful, using radical feminist approaches would be unlikely to work in the Congressional setting.

Just as the composition of the audience and the context of the setting make different feminist theoretical approaches more useful in some settings than others, the impact of feminism on experimental methods also varies with different disciplines. Feminism appears to affect experimental methods more significantly in fields such as the social sciences and biology, where sex or gender is prominent and evident. Feminism seems to have less effect in areas of basic research in the physical sciences and mathematics on fundamentals such as string theory.

In addition to the fact that sex and gender in the forms of males or females and associated masculinity and femininity are not overt in the physical sciences and technology, the disciplines in these fields also have significantly smaller percentages of women than the biological and social sciences (National Science Board, 2004), where women now receive half of undergraduate degrees. In the humanities and many areas of the social sciences, increases in the numbers and percentages of women correlated with increases in emphases on women and gender in research and scholarship (Boxer, 2000; Rosser, 2002). A critical mass of women physicians was needed to push for medicine to provide increased attention to women's health (Dan & Rosser, 2003) and basic research on gendered medicine (Sarto, 2005). When the percentage of women in physics, computer science, and engineering exceeds 30%, perhaps women may begin to explore the gendered nature of the questions asked, approaches, and theories and conclusions drawn from the data in those disciplines.

In the technological and applied areas of physics, math, and the natural sciences such as engineering, computer science, and medicine, the very powerful fusion of biology and computer science has created a new technoscience. Technoscience has facilitated sequencing the Human Genome and amazing advances in biomedical engineering, as well as cyberfeminism. Feminist theories must be used to place gender in central focus to critically evaluate the social and political implications of these new technosciences. Although I question whether cyberfeminism is a theory or an experimental approach, it raises once again the significance of linking feminist theories with research methods to critique this new fusion of feminism and technology. As the editor of *Cyberfeminism: Next Protocols* concludes, "has cyberfeminism already become a cultural practice, reflected by its own academic theory, history, and art? [If] . . . [else]—what will be [next]?" (Kuni, 2004, p. 327).

# REFERENCES

Abbate, Janet. (1999). Cold war and white heat: The origins and meanings of packet switching. In Donald MacKenzie & Judy Wacjman (Eds.), *The social shaping of technology* (2nd ed., pp. 351–371). Philadelphia: Open University Press.

Altman, Roberta. (1996). *Waking up/fighting back: The politics of breast cancer.* Boston: Little, Brown & Company.

Andrews, Lori B., Fullarton, Jane E., Holtzman, Neil A., & Mutulsky, Arno G. (Eds.). (1993). *Assessing genetic risks: Implications for health and social policy.* Institute of Medicine Report. Washington, DC: National Academy of Medicine.

Armstrong, B., & Doll, R. (1975). Environmental factors and cancer incidence and mortality in different countries, with special reference to dietary practice. *International Journal of Cancer, 15,* 617–631.

Aspin, Les. (1993, April). *Policy on the assignment of women in the armed forces.* Washington, DC: Department of Defense.

Association of American University Women. (2000). *Tech-savvy: Educating girls in the new computer age.* Washington, DC: AAUW Educational Foundation.

Bailar, John C., & Smith, Elaine. (1986). Progress against cancer? *New England Journal of Medicine, 314*(19), 1226–1232.

Barnaby, F. (1981). Social and economic reverberations of military research. *Impact of Science on Society, 31,* 73–83.

Basch, Linda. (1996). Beyond Beijing. *Issues Quarterly, 2*(1), 2–52.

Batt, Sharon. (1994). *The politics of breast cancer.* Charlottetown, Canada: Gynergy Books.

Berg, Anne-Jorunn. (1999). A gendered socio-technical construction: The smart house. In Donald MacKenzie & Judy Wacjman (Eds.), *The social shaping of technology* (2nd ed., pp. 301–313). Philadelphia: Open University Press.

Berman, Joshua, & Bruckman, Amy. (2000). The Turing game: A participatory exploration of identity in online environments. *Proceedings of Directions and Implications of Advanced Computing (DIAC) 2000.* Seattle, WA: Computer Professionals for Social Responsibility.

Birke, Lynda. (1986). *Women, feminism, and biology: The feminist challenge.* New York: Methuen.

Bleier, Ruth. (1979). Social and political bias in science: An examination of animal studies and their generalizations to human behavior and evolution. In Ruth Hubbard & Marian Lowe (Eds.), *Genes and gender II: Pitfalls in research on sex and gender* (pp. 49–70). New York: Gordian Press.

Bleier, Ruth. (1984). *Science and gender. A critique of biology and its theories on women.* New York: Pergamon Press.

Bleier, Ruth. (1986). Sex differences research: Science or belief? In Ruth Bleier (Ed.), *Feminist approaches to science* (pp. 147–164). New York: Pergamon Press.

Bodker, S., & Greenbaum, J. (1993). Design of information systems: Things versus people. In J. Owen Green & D. Pain (Eds.), *Gendered by design: Information technology and office systems* (pp. 53–63). London: Taylor & Francis.

Boxer, Marilyn. (2000). Unruly knowledge: Women's Studies and the problem of disciplinarity. *NWSA Journal, 12*(2), 119–129.

Bratteteig, Tone. (2002). Bringing gender issues to technology design. In C. Floyd, G. Kelkar, S. Klein-Franke, & C. P. Limpangog (Eds.), *Feminist challenges in the information age* (pp. 91–105). Opladen, Germany: Leske & Budrich.

Brun, E. (1994). Technology appropriate for women? In E. Gunnarsson & L. Trojer (Eds.), *Feminist voices on gender, technology, and ethics.* Lulea, Sweden: University of Technology Centre for Women's Studies.

Butler, Judith. (1990). *Gender trouble: Feminism and the subversion of identity.* New York: Routledge.

Butler, Judith. (1992). Introduction. In J. Butler & J. Scott (Eds.), *Feminists theorize the political* (pp. xii–xvii). New York: Routledge.

Butler, Judith. (1994). *Bodies that matter: On the discursive limits of "sex."* New York: Routledge.

Campbell, George, Jr., Deanes, Ronni, & Morrison, Catherine. (Eds.). (2000). *Access denied: Race, ethnicity and the scientific enterprise.* Oxford, UK: Oxford University Press.

Campbell, Kristina. (1992, October 2). 1 in 3 lesbians may get breast cancer, expert theorizes. *Washington Blade,* pp. 1, 23.

Capra, Frank. (1973). *The Tao of physics.* New York: Bantam Books.

Caro, Robert. (1974). *The power broker: Robert Moses and the fall of New York.* New York: Random House.

Centers for Disease Control. (1987). Antibody to human immunodeficiency virus in female prostitutes. *Morbidity and Mortality Weekly Report, 36,* 157–161.

Centers for Disease Control. (1998). Guidelines for evaluating surveillance systems. *Morbidity and Mortality Weekly Report, 37,* 1–18.

Chinese Hospital Medical Staff and University of California School of Medicine. (1982, May). *Conference on health problems related to the Chinese in America,* San Francisco: Author.

Chodorow, Nancy. (1978). *The reproduction of mothering: Psychoanalysis and the sociology of gender.* Berkeley: University of California Press.

Chu, S. Y., Buehler, J. W., & Berelman, R. L. (1990). Impact of the human immunodeficiency virus epidemic on mortality in women of reproductive age, United States. *Journal of the American Medical Association, 264,* 225–229.

Clarke, Adele E., & Olesen, Virginia L. (Eds.). (1999). *Revisioning women, health, and healing: Feminist, cultural, and technoscience perspectives.* New York: Routledge.

Cockburn, Cynthia. (1981). The material of male power. *Feminist Review, 9,* 41–58.

Cockburn, Cynthia. (1983). *Brothers: Male dominance and technological change.* London: Pluto Press.

Cockburn, Cynthia. (1985). *Machinery of dominance: Women, men and technical know-how.* London: Pluto Press.

Cohen, Judith, Alexander, Priscilla, & Woofsey, Constance. (1988). Prostitutes and AIDS: Public policy issues. *AIDS and Public Policy Journal, 3,* 16–22.

Collins, Patricia Hill. (1990). *Black feminist thought.* New York: Routledge.

Corea, Gena. (1985). *The mother machine: Reproductive technologies from artificial insemination to artificial wombs.* New York: Harper & Row.

Cowan, Ruth S. (1983). *More work for mother: The ironies of household technology from the open hearth to the microwave.* New York: Basic Books.

Cowan, Ruth S. (1985). The industrial revolution in the home. In D. MacKenzie & J. Wajcman (Eds.), *The social shaping of technology* (pp. 181–201). Milton Keynes, UK: Open University Press. (Reprinted from The industrial revolution: In the home: Household technology

and social change in the twentieth century, 1976. *Technology and Culture, 17,* 1–23)

Creager, Angela N. H., Lunbeck, Elizabeth, & Schiebinger, Londa. (Eds.). (2001). *Feminism in twentieth-century science, technology, and medicine.* Chicago: University of Chicago Press.

Daly, Mary. (1978). *Gyn/ecology: The metaethics of radical feminism.* Boston: Beacon Press.

Daly, Mary. (1984). *Pure lust: Elemental feminist philosophy.* Boston: Beacon Press.

Dan, Alice, & Rosser, Sue. (2003). Editorial. *Women's Studies Quarterly, 31*(1–2), 6–24.

Dawkins, Richard. (1976). *The selfish gene.* New York: Oxford University Press.

de Beauvoir, Simone. (1989). *The second sex* (H. M. Parshley, Trans. & Ed.). New York: Vintage Books. (Original work published 1949)

de Lauretis, Teresa. (1991). Queer theory: Lesbian and gay sexualities. *Differences: A Journal of Feminist Cultural Studies, 3*(2), iii–xvii.

Derrida, Jacques. (2000). *Limited, Inc.* Evanston, IL: Northwestern University Press.

Dinnerstein, Dorothy. (1977). *The mermaid and the minotaur: Sexual arrangements and human malaise.* New York: Harper Colophon Books.

Dreifus, Claudia. (Ed.). (1977). *Seizing our bodies: The politics of women's health.* New York: Vintage Books.

Dworkin, Andrea. (1983). *Right-wing women.* New York: Coward-McCann.

Easlea, Brian. (1983). *Fathering the unthinkable: Masculinity, scientists and the nuclear arms race.* London: Pluto Press.

Ehrenreich, Barbara, & English, Deirdre. (1978). *For her own good: 150 years of the experts' advice to women.* New York: Anchor Press, Doubleday.

Eisenstein, Hester. (1984). *Contemporary feminist thought.* London: Allen and Unwin.

Elson, D. (1989). The cutting edge: Multinationals in the EEC textiles and clothing industry. In D. Elson & R. Pearson (Eds.), *Women's employment and multinationals in Europe* (pp. 80–110). Basingstoke, UK: Macmillan.

Enloe, Cynthia. (1983). *Does khaki become you? The militarisation of women's lives.* London: Pluto Press.

Enloe, Cynthia. (1989). *Bananas, beaches and bases.* Berkeley: University of California Press.

Faden, R., Kass, N., & McGraw, D. (1996). Women as vessels and vectors: Lessons from the HIV epidemic. In S. M. Wolf (Ed.), *Feminism and bioethics: Beyond reproduction* (pp. 252–281). New York: Oxford University Press.

Fausto-Sterling, Anne. (1992). *Myths of gender.* New York: Basic Books.

Fee, Elizabeth. (1982). A feminist critique of scientific objectivity. *Science for the People, 14*(4), 8.

Fee, Elizabeth. (1983). Women's nature and scientific objectivity. In Marian Lowe & Ruth Hubbard (Eds.), *Women's nature: Rationalizations of inequality* (pp. 9–27). New York: Pergamon Press.

Ferguson, Anne. (1984). Sex wars: The debate between radical and liberation feminists. *Signs: Journal of Women in Culture and Society, 10*(1), 15–31.

Ferrell, R. (1996). *Passion in theory: Conceptions of Freud and Lacan.* London: Routledge.

Firestone, Shulamith. (1970). *The dialectic of sex.* New York: Bantam Books.

Foucault, Michel. (1978). *The history of sexuality: Vol. 1. Introduction* (R. Hurley, Trans.). New York: Pantheon Books. (Original work published 1976)

Fox, Mary, Johnson, Deborah, & Rosser, Sue. (Eds.). (in press). *Women, gender and technology.* Champaign: University of Illinois Press.

Friedan, Betty. (1974). *The feminine mystique.* New York: Dell.

Frissen, V. (1995). Gender is calling: Some reflections on past, present and future uses of the telephone. In K. Grint & R. Gill (Eds.), *The gender-technology relation: Contemporary theory and research* (pp. 79–94). London: Taylor & Francis.

Frye, Marilyn. (1983). *The politics of reality.* Trumansburg, NY: Crossing Press.

Fuentes, A., & Ehrenreich, B. (1983). *Women in the global factory.* Boston: South End Press.

Gillespie, Marcia Ann. (1998). Norplant is back in Bangladesh. *MS, 9*(1), 32.

Green, E., Owen, J., & Pain, D. (1993). "City libraries": Human-centred opportunities for women? In E. Green, J. Owen, & D. Pain (Eds.), *Gendered by design: Information technology and office systems* (pp. 127–152). London: Taylor & Francis.

Greenbaum, J. (1995). *Windows on the workplace: Computers, jobs and the organization of office work in the late twentieth century.* New York: Monthly Review Press.

Grewal, I. (1996). *Home and harem.* Durham, NC: Duke University Press.

Griffin, Susan. (1978). *The death of nature.* New York: Harper & Row.

Grobbee, D. E., Rimm, E. B., Giovannucci, E., Colditz, G., Stampfer, M., & Willett, W. (1990). Coffee, caffeine, and cardiovascular disease in men. *New England Journal of Medicine, 321,* 1026–1032.

Grosz, Elizabeth. (1994). *Volatile bodies: Towards a corporeal feminism.* Bloomington: Indiana University Press.

Gunew, Sneja. (1990). *Feminist knowledge: Critique and construct.* New York: Routledge.

Gurwitz, J. H., Nananda, F. C., & Avorn, J. (1992). The exclusion of the elderly and women from clinical trials in acute myocardial infarction. *Journal of the American Medical Association, 268*(2), 1417–1422.

Hacker, Sally. (1989). *Pleasure, power and technology.* Boston: Unwin Hyman.

Hamilton, Jean. (1985). Avoiding methodological biases and policy-making biases in gender-related health research. In Ruth L. Kirschstein & Doris H. Merritt (Eds.), *Women's health: Report of the public health service task force on women's health issues* (pp. 54–64). Washington, DC: U.S. Department of Health and Human Services, Public Health Service.

Haraway, Donna. (1978). Animal sociology and a natural economy of the body politic. *Signs: Journal of Women in Culture and Society, 4*(1), 21–60.

Haraway, Donna. (1989). *Primate visions: Gender, race, and nature in the world of modern science.* New York: Routledge.

Haraway, Donna. (1997). *Modest_Witness@Second_ Millenium. FemaleMan©_Meets_OncoMouse™: Feminism and technoscience.* New York: Routledge.

Haraway, Donna. (1999). The virtual speculum in the new world order. In Adele Clarke & Virginia Olesen (Eds.), *Revisioning women, health, and healing* (pp. 49–96). New York: Routledge.

Harding, Sandra. (1986). *The science question in feminism.* Ithaca, NY: Cornell University Press.

Harding, Sandra. (1993). Introduction. In Sandra Harding (Ed.), *The racial economy of science* (pp. 1–22). Bloomington: Indiana University Press.

Harding, Sandra. (1998). *Is science multicultural? Postcolonialisms, feminisms, and epistemologies.* Bloomington: Indiana University Press.

Harris, J. R., Lippman, M. E., Veronesi, U., & Willett, W. (1992). Breast cancer. *New England Journal of Medicine, 327,* 319–328.

Hartmann, Heidi. (1981). The unhappy marriage of Marxism and feminism: Towards a more progressive union. In L. Sargent (Ed.), *Women and revolution: A discussion of the unhappy marriage of Marxism and feminism* (pp. 1–42). Boston: South End Press.

Hawthorne, Susan, & Klein, Renate. (1999). *Cyberfeminism.* Melbourne, Victoria, Australia: Spinifex.

Healy, Bernadine. (1991). Women's health, public welfare. *Journal of the American Medical Association, 266,* 566–568.

Hesse-Biber, Sharlene Nagy, & Carter, Gregg Lee. (2005). *Working women in American: Split dreams.* Oxford, UK: Oxford University Press.

Hoagland, S. L. (1988). *Lesbian ethics.* Chicago: Institute of Lesbian Studies.

Holmes, Helen B. (1981). Reproductive technologies: The birth of women-centered analysis. In Helen B. Holmes, B. B. Hoskins, & M. Gross (Eds.), *The custom-made child* (pp. 1–18). Clifton, NJ: Humana Press.

hooks, bell. (1992). *Race and representation.* London: Turnaround Press.

Hrushesky, William. (1996). Breast cancer, timing of surgery, and the menstrual cycle: Call for prospective trial. *Journal of Women's Health, 5*(6), 555–566.

Hrushesky, W. J. M., Bluming, A. Z., Gruber, S. A., & Sothern, R. B. (1989). Menstrual influence on surgical cure of breast cancer. *Lancet, 2,* 949.

Hubbard, Ruth. (1979). Introduction. In Ruth Hubbard & Marian Lowe (Eds.), *Genes and gender II: Pitfalls in research on sex and gender* (pp. 9–34). New York: Gordian Press.

Hubbard, Ruth. (1990). *The politics of women's biology.* New Brunswick, NJ: Rutgers University Press.

Irigaray, L. (1985). *This sex which is not one* (C. Porter & C. Burke, Trans.). Ithaca, NY: Cornell University Press. (Original work published 1977)

Jacobson, Jodi. (1993). Women's health: The price of poverty. In Marge Koblinsky, Judith Timyan, & Jill Gay (Eds.), *The health of women: A global perspective* (pp. 3–32). Boulder, CO: Westview Press.

Jaggar, Alison. (1983). *Feminist politics and human nature.* Totowa, NJ: Rowman & Allanheld.

Jaggar, Alison, & Rothenberg, Paula. (Eds.). (1994). *Feminist frameworks.* New York: McGraw-Hill.

Jameson, Fredric. (1981). *The political unconscious: The narrative as a socially symbolic act.* Ithaca, NY: Cornell University Press.

Jones, James H. (1981). *Bad blood: The Tuskegee syphilis experiment: A tragedy of race and medicine.* New York: Free Press.

Keller, Evelyn Fox. (1982). Feminism and science. *Signs: Journal of Women in Culture and Society, 7*(3), 589–602.

Keller, Evelyn Fox. (1983). *A feeling for the organism.* San Francisco: Freeman.

Keller, Evelyn Fox. (1985). *Reflections on gender and science.* New Haven, CT: Yale University Press.

Keller, Evelyn Fox. (1992). *Secrets of life, secrets of death.* New York: Routledge.

Kelsey, Sheryl F., James, M., Holubkov, A. L., Holubkov, R., Cowley, M. J., Detre, K. M., & Investigators from the National Heart, Lung, and Blood Institute Percutaneous Transluminal Coronary Angioplasty Registry. (1993). Results of percutaneous transluminal coronary angioplasty in women: 1985–1986. *Circulation, 87*(3), 720–727.

King, Mary-Claire, Rowell, Sara, & Love, Susan M. (1993). Inherited breast and ovarian cancer: What are the risks? What are the choices? *Journal of the American Medical Association, 269,* 1975–1980.

King, Ynestra. (1989). The ecology of feminism and the feminism of ecology. In J. Plant (Ed.), *Healing the wounds: The promise of ecofeminism* (pp. 18–28). Philadelphia: New Society.

Kirkup, G. (1992). The social construction of computers: Hammers or harpsichords? In G. Kirkup & L. S. Keller (Eds.), *Inventing women: Science, technology and gender.* Cambridge, UK: Polity Press.

Klein, Renate. (1989). Resistance: From the exploitation of infertility to the exploration of in-fertility. In Renate Klein (Ed.), *Infertility* (pp. 229–295). London: Pandora Press.

Knights, James J. (2004). Why the FBI seeks more women as special agents. *Women in Higher Education, 13*(3), 30–31.

Koblinsky, Marge, Timyan, Judith, & Gay, Jill. (1993). *The health of women: A global perspective.* Boulder, CO: Westview Press.

Kristeva, Julia. (1986). *The Kristeva reader* (Toril Moi, Ed.). Oxford, UK: Blackwell.

Kuni, Verena. (2004). Frame/work. In Claudia Reiche & Verena Kuni (Eds.), *Cyberfeminism: Next protocols*. Brooklyn, NY: Automedia.

Lacan, Jacques. (1977). The agency of the letter in the unconscious or reason since Freud. In *Ecrits: A selection* (Alan Sheridan, Trans.). New York: W. W. Norton. (Original work published 1957)

Lacan, Jacques. (1998). *The four fundamental concepts of psychoanalysis*. New York: W. W. Norton.

Lancaster, Jane. (1975). *Primate behavior and the emergence of human culture*. New York: Holt, Reinhart & Winston.

Larrabee, Mary Jeanne. (2000). Existentialist feminism. In Lorraine Code (Ed.), *Encyclopedia of feminist theories* (pp. 186–187). New York: Routledge.

Leavitt, Ruth. (1975). *Peaceable primate and gentle people: Anthropological approaches to women's studies*. New York: Harper & Row.

Leibowitz, Lila. (1975). Perspectives in the evolution of sex differences. In R. R. Reiter (Ed.), *Toward an anthropology of women* (pp. 20–35). New York: Monthly Review Press.

Lerman, Nina, Oldenziel, Ruth, & Mohun, Arwen. (2003). *Gender & technology*. Baltimore: Johns Hopkins University Press.

Lin-Fu, J. S. (1984, July/August). The need for sensitivity to Asian and Pacific Americans' health problems and concerns. *Organization of Chinese American Women Speaks*, pp. 1–2.

Longino, Helen. (1990). *Science as social knowledge: Values and objectivity in scientific inquiry*. Princeton, NJ: Princeton University Press.

Love, Susan M. (1990). *Dr. Susan Love's breast book*. New York: Addison-Wesley.

Lyotard, Jean-Francois. (1986). *The postmodern condition*. Manchester, UK: Manchester University Press.

Macdonald, Anne L. (1992). *Feminine ingenuity: Women and invention in America*. New York: Ballantine Books.

MacKenzie, D., & Wajcman, J. (1999). *The social shaping of technology* (2nd ed.). Milton Keynes, UK: Open University Press.

MacKinnon, Catharine. (1982). Feminism, marxism, and the state: An agenda for theory. *Signs: Journal of Women in Culture and Society, 7*(3), 515–544.

MacKinnon, Catharine. (1987). *Feminism unmodified: Discourses on life and law*. Cambridge, MA: Harvard University Press.

Martin, Emily. (1987). *The woman in the body*. Boston: Beacon Press.

Martin, Emily. (1994). *Flexible bodies: Tracking immunity in American culture from the days of polio to the days of AIDS*. Boston: Beacon Press.

Martin, Emily. (1999). The woman in the flexible body. In Adele Clarke & Virginia Olesen (Eds.), *Revisioning women, health, and healing* (pp. 97–115). New York: Routledge.

Mehta, Brinda J. (2000). Postcolonial feminism. In Lorraine Code (Ed.), *Encyclopedia of feminist theories* (pp. 395–397). New York: Routledge.

Merchant, Carolyn. (1979). *The death of nature*. New York: Harper & Row.

Microsysters. (1988). *Not over our heads: Women and computers in the office*. London: Author.

Mill, J. S. (1970). The subjection of women. In A. S. Rossi (Ed.), *Essays on sex equality* (pp. 123–242). Chicago: Chicago University Press.

Millar, Melanie. (1998). *Cracking the gender code: Who rules the wired world?* Toronto, Ontario, Canada: Second Story Press.

Mitter, S. (1986). *Common fate, common bond*. London: Pluto.

Mohanty, Chandra T. (1997). Women workers and capitalist scripts: Ideologies of domination, common interests, and the politics of solidarity. In M. Jacqui Alexander & Chandra T. Mohanty (Eds.), *Feminist genealogies, colonial legacies, democratic futures* (pp. 3–29). New York: Routledge.

Money, John, & Erhardt, Anke. (1972). *Man and woman, boy and girl*. Baltimore: Johns Hopkins University Press.

Multiple Risk Factor Intervention Trial Research Group. (1990). Mortality rates after 10.5 years for participants in the multiple risk factor intervention trial: Findings related to a prior hypothesis of the trial. *Journal of the American Medical Association, 263,* 1795.

Narrigan, Deborah. (1991, March/April/May). Research to improve women's health: An agenda for equity. *The Network News: National Women's Health Network,* pp. 3, 9.

National Breast Cancer Coalition. (1997). Legislative update. Fall/Winter. *Call to Action, 4*(3–4).

National Library of Medicine. (1990). *Electronic imaging* (Report of the Board of Regents, U.S. Department of Health and Human Sciences, Public Health Service, National Institutes of Health, NIH Publication 90-2197). Bethesda, MD: Author.

National Science Board. (2004). *Science and engineering indicators—2004* (NSBB 04-01). Arlington, VA: Author.

National Science Foundation. (1999). *Women, minorities, and persons with disabilities in science and engineering: 1998* (NSF 99-338). Arlington, VA: Author.

National Science Foundation. (2002). *Women, minorities, and persons with disabilities in science and engineering: 2002* (NSF 03-312). Arlington, VA: Author.

Norman, C. (1979, July 26). Global research: Who spends what? *New Scientist,* pp. 279–281.

Norwood, Chris. (1988, July). Alarming rise in deaths. *MS,* pp. 65–67.

O'Brien, Mary. (1981). *The politics of reproduction.* Boston: Routledge & Kegan Paul.

Office of Population Censuses and Surveys. (1991). *Census of population.* London: HMSO.

Ogunyemi, C. (1996). *Africa, wo/man, Palava: The Nigerian novel by women.* Chicago: University of Chicago Press.

Old Boys Network. (2004). Call for contributions. In Claudia Reiche & Verena Kuni (Eds.), *Cyberfeminism: Next protocols.* Brooklyn, NY: Autonomedia.

Paterson, Nancy. (1994). *Cyberfeminism.* http://echonyc.com.70/0/Cul/Cyber/paterson

Pattrow, Lynn M. (1990, Winter/Spring). When becoming pregnant is a crime. *Criminal Justice Ethics.*

Pinn, Vivian, & LaRosa, Judith. (1992). *Overview: Office of research on women's health.* Bethesda, MD: National Institutes of Health.

Rapp, Rayna. (1999). One new reproductive technology, multiple sites: How feminist methodology bleeds into everyday life. In Adele Clarke & Virginia Olesen (Eds.), *Revisioning women, health, and healing* (pp. 119–135). New York: Routledge.

Reiche, Claudia. (2004). On/off-scenity: Medical and erotic couplings in the context of the visible human project. In Claudia Reiche & Verena Kuni (Eds.), *Cyberfeminism: Next protocols* (pp. 159–184). Brooklyn, NY: Autonomedia.

Rich, Adrienne. (1976). *Of woman born: Motherhood as experience.* New York: Norton.

Rose, Hilary. (1994). *Love, power, and knowledge: Towards a feminist transformation of the sciences.* Bloomington: Indiana University Press.

Rose, Hilary, & Rose, Steven. (1980). The myth of the neutrality of science. In Rita Arditti, Pat Brennan, & Steve Cavrak (Eds.), *Science and liberation* (pp. 17–32). Boston: South End Press.

Rosser, Sue V. (1982). Androgyny and sociobiology. *International Journal of Women's Studies, 5*(5), 435–444.

Rosser, Sue V. (1986). *Teaching science and health from a feminist perspective: A practical guide.* Elmsford, NY: Pergamon Press.

Rosser, Sue V. (1988). Women in science and health care: A gender at risk. In Sue V. Rosser (Ed.), *Feminism within the science and health care professions: Overcoming resistance* (pp. 3–15). New York: Pergamon Press.

Rosser, Sue V. (1990). *Female friendly science.* New York: Pergamon Press.

Rosser, Sue V. (1992). *Feminism and biology.* New York: Twayne/Macmillan.

Rosser, Sue V. (1994). *Women's health: Missing from U.S. medicine.* Bloomington: Indiana University Press.

Rosser, Sue V. (1997). *Re-engineering female friendly science.* New York: Teachers College Press.

Rosser, Sue V. (2002). Twenty-five years of NWSA: Have we built the two way streets between women's studies and women in science and technology? *NWSA Journal Special 25th Anniversary Issue, 14*(1), 103–123.

Rosser, Sue V. (2004). *The science glass ceiling: Academic women scientists and the struggle to succeed.* New York: Routledge.

Rossiter, Margaret. (1982). *Women scientists in America: Struggles and strategies to 1940.* Baltimore: Johns Hopkins University Press.

Rothfield, Philipa. (1990). Feminism, subjectivity, and sexual difference. In Sneja Gunew (Ed.), *Feminist knowledge: Critique and construct* (pp. 121–144). New York: Routledge.

Rothman, Barbara Katz. (2001). *The book of life: A personal and ethical guide to race, normality and the implications of the Human Genome Project.* Boston: Beacon Press.

Rowell, Thelma. (1974). The concept of social dominance. *Behavioral Biology, 11,* 131–154.

Rubin, Gayle. (1984). Thinking sex: Notes for a radical theory of the politics of sexuality. In C. Vance (Ed.), *Pleasure and danger* (pp. 267–319). Boston: Routledge & Kegan Paul.

Sarto, Gloria. (2005). Women's health: A woman's issue. In Londa Schiebinger (Ed.), *Gendered innovations in science and engineering conference proceedings*, April 15–16, Stanford University.

Schiebinger, Londa. (1999). *Has feminism changed science?* Cambridge, MA: Harvard University Press.

Senie, R., Rosen, P., Rhondes, P., & Lesser, M. (1991). Timing of breast cancer excision during the menstrual cycle influences duration of disease-free survival. *Annals of Internal Medicine, 115,* 337.

Silver, David. (2000). Margins in the wires: Looking for race, gender, and sexuality in the Blacksburg Electronic Village. In Martha McCaughey & Michael Ayers (Eds.), *Cyberactivism* (pp. 133–150). New York: Routledge.

Sorenson, K. (1992). Towards a feminized technology? Gendered values in the construction of technology. *Social Studies of Science, 22*(1), 5–31.

Spanier, Bonnie. (1995). *Im/partial science: Gender ideology in molecular biology.* Bloomington: Indiana University Press.

Spivak, Gayatri. (1988). Can the subaltern speak? In Carey Nelson & Leon Grossberg (Eds.), *Marxism and the interpretation of culture* (pp. 271–313). Urbana: University of Illinois Press.

Stanley, Autumn. (1995). *Mothers and daughters of invention: Notes for a revised history of technology.* New Brunswick, NJ: Rutgers University Press.

Steady, Filomena. (1982). *The black woman culturally.* Cambridge, MA: Schenkman Publishing.

Steering Committee of the Physicians' Health Study Group. (1989). Final report on the aspirin component of the ongoing physician's health study. *New England Journal of Medicine, 321,* 129–135.

Stryker, S. (1998). The transgender issue: An introduction. *glq: A Journal of Lesbian and Gay Studies, 4*(2), 145–158.

Suchman, L. (1994). Supporting articulation work: Aspects of a feminist practice of technology production. In A. Adam, J. Emms, E. Green, & J. Owen (Eds.), *Women, work and computerization: Breaking old boundaries—Building new forms* (pp. 7–21). Amsterdam: North Holland.

Suchman, L., & Jordan, B. (1989). Computerization and women's knowledge. In K. Tijdens, M. Jennings, I. Wagner, & M. Weggelaar (Eds.), *Women, work and computerization: Forming new alliances* (pp. 13–160). Amsterdam: North Holland.

Thoresen, K. (1989). Systems development: Alternative design strategies. In K. Tijdens, M. Jennings, I. Wagner, & M. Weggelaar (Eds.), *Women, work and computerization: Forming new alliances* (pp. 123–130). Amsterdam: North Holland.

Tong, Rosemarie. (1989). *Feminist thought: A comprehensive introduction.* Boulder, CO: Westview Press.

Trivers, R. L. (1972). Parental investment and sexual selection. In B. Campbell (Ed.), *Sexual selection and the descent of man, 1871–1971* (pp. 136–179). Chicago: Aldine.

Tuana, Nancy. (1993). *Feminism and science.* Bloomington: Indiana University Press.

Tuana, Nancy. (1995). The values of science: Empiricism from a feminist perspective. *Synthese, 104*(3), 441–461.

Vetter, Betty. (1988). Where are the women in the physical sciences? In Sue V. Rosser (Ed.), *Feminism within the science and health care professions: Overcoming resistance* (pp. 19–32). New York: Pergamon Press.

Wajcman, Judy. (1991). *Feminism confronts technology.* University Park: Pennsylvania State University Press.

Washburn, Jennifer. (1996, November/December). The misuses of Norplant: Who gets stuck? *MS,* pp. 32–36.

Weber, Rachel. (1999). Manufacturing gender in commercial and military cockpit design. *Science, Technology and Human Values, 22,* 235–253.

Webster, Juliet. (1995). *Shaping women's work: Gender, employment and information technology.* New York: Longman.

Wickham, J., & Murray, P. (1987). *Women in the Irish electronic industry.* Dublin: Employment Equality Agency.

Williams, Patricia. (1991). *The alchemy of race and rights.* Cambridge, MA: Harvard University Press.

Williams, Patricia. (1998). *Seeing a color-blind future.* New York: Noonday Press.

Williams, Patrick, & Crissman, Laura. (1994). Colonial discourse and post-colonial theory: An introduction. In Patrick Williams & Laura

Crissman (Eds.), *Colonial discourse and post-colonial theory* (pp. 1–20). New York: Columbia University Press.

Wilson, Edward O. (1975). *Sociobiology: The new synthesis.* Cambridge, MA: Harvard University Press.

Winner, Langdon. (1980). Do artifacts have politics? *Daedalus, 109,* 121–136.

Wollstonecraft, Mary. (1975). *A vindication of the rights of woman* (C. H. Poston, Ed.). New York: W. W. Norton.

Women Working Worldwide. (1991). *Common interests: Women organising in global electronics.* London: Author.

Yerkes, R. M. (1943). *Chimpanzees.* New Haven, CT: Yale University Press.

Zimmerman, Bill, et al. (1980). People's science. In Rita Arditti, Pat Brennan, & Steve Cavrak (Eds.), *Science and liberation* (pp. 299–319). Boston: South End Press.

# 12

# Reading Between the Lines

## *Feminist Content Analysis Into the Second Millennium*

Shulamit Reinharz

Rachel Kulick

In 1992, one of us published *Feminist Methods in Social Research,* a review and analysis of various feminist approaches to the major forms of research up to that point. Thirteen years later, the chapter devoted to content analysis is the one that needs most updating because the nature of "content" itself has changed so much in the intervening period (Reinharz, 1992a). In 1992 the information highway did not have off-ramps into everyone's computer; e-mail addresses were not part of everyone's business cards; and blogs, e-zines, instant messaging, and the myriad other forms of communication were still in the future. Today, information and imagery saturate contemporary Western society—and to a certain extent all societies, with the prospect of even deeper saturation to come with transnational flows of information in the form of television, music, Web sites, advertising, and print media; the sheer scope and range of content produced and consumed is almost incomprehensible. Developing methods for probing these forms and formats is a key challenge for feminist research. It should not come as a surprise, therefore, that a search on Google using the phrase "feminist content analysis" produces more than 2,000,000 entries.

Despite the upsurge in new communication formats, however, older media forms remain significant for feminist analysis, as well. Mainstream magazines are filled with sexualized imagery of young women, usually scantily clad, thin to an unhealthy degree, and highly concerned with appearance, beauty, and sexual abilities. These are the everyday images of silent women available to us for scrutiny. Movies and television portray popularized narratives of men as hypermasculine, active, heroic, violent, and often devoid of emotion other than rage or stoicism. Some independent films attempt to depict alternative constructions of gender and sexuality. People surf the Internet, cybershopping or cyberproducing their own content and counternarratives through blogs, Web sites, chat rooms, and other virtual devices. People are out there communicating, viewing, buying, writing, working, learning, cooking, selling, dating—in other words, living. These discourses and the meanings embedded in them reflect and transmit a wide range of norms and values regarding gender, sexuality, and social relations.

As mentioned above, given the wide expanse of easily accessible or produced information and the ubiquitous, yet diverse, messages about gender and sexuality, feminist scholarship in the area of content analysis is imperative. Fortunately, some work has begun. Feminist researchers seek to understand not only the meanings infused in cultural materials but also the contextual and social processes of cultural production and reader reception.

In this chapter, we examine the dynamic array of approaches to feminist content analysis at the start of the 21st century, with an eye toward analyses of systems of representation, interpretation, and identity construction. To accomplish this, we first explore what is "feminist" about feminist content analysis. Second, we examine the role of feminist content analyses in revealing the multilayered politics of gendered and sexualized representation in print media and imagery, as well as online forms. We then look to the online feminist communities in which feminist knowledge is being produced and studied.

## What Is *Feminist* About Feminist Content Analysis?

Sociologists, historians, literary analysts, anthropologists, and archeologists, among others—whether feminist or not—employ content analysis to study cultural materials as something produced by people. These products stem from every aspect of human life, including relatively private worlds, "high" culture, popular culture (Goldsen, 1974; Haskell, 1973; Mellon, 1973; Newcomb, 1974; Tuchman, Daniels, & Benet, 1978), and organizational life. Cultural artifacts are the products of individual activity, social organization, technology, and cultural patterns. The only limit to what can be considered a cultural artifact—and thus used as a "text" for research—is the researcher's imagination. People who study cultural materials or artifacts employ a systematic approach by counting, coding, or interpreting a set of identified themes contained in the content.

There is no general consensus for the terminology of this type of work. Sociologists tend to use the term *content analysis*; historians, the term *archival research*; and philosophers and students of literature, the terms *text analysis* or *literary criticism* (Millet, 1970; Petraka & Tilly, 1983). Different disciplines also apply a variety of interpretive frameworks to the analysis of cultural artifacts. Discourse analysis, rhetoric analysis, and deconstruction are additional terms that refer to the examination of texts.

With respect to feminist content analysis, by and large, studies focus both on the interpretation of the content and on its juxtaposition in the larger sociopolitical context. Nineteenth-century Harriet Martineau (1838/1988)—arguably the first sociologist—and 20th-century Rose Weitz (1977) extol the value of studying "things" or "cultural products" as a promising approach for understanding social arrangements:

> To arrive at the facts of the condition of a people through the discourse of individuals, is a hopeless enterprise. . . . The grand secret of wise inquiry into Morals and Manners is to begin with the study of THINGS, using the DISCOURSE OF PERSONS as a commentary upon them. (Martineau, 1838/1988, p. 73)

The cultural products of any given society at any given time reverberate with the themes of that society and that era (Weitz, 1977, p. 194).

Onboard a ship preparing to study the United States in 1834, Harriet Martineau wrote:

> The eloquence of Institutions and Records, in which the action of the nation is embodied . . . , is more comprehensive and more faithful than that of any variety of individual voices. The voice of a whole people goes up in the silent workings of an institution; the condition of the masses is reflected from the surface of a record. . . . The records of any society . . . whether architectural remains, epitaphs, civic registers, national music, or any other of the thousand manifestations of the common mind which may be found among every people, afford more information on Morals in a day than converse with individuals in a year. (1838/1998, pp. 73–74)

Harriet Martineau was stressing the value of nonreactive data or "unobtrusive measures" (Webb, Campbell, Schwartz, & Sechrest, 1966). Although the value of unobtrusive measures is still recognized today, her idea of "reflection" is challenged. Some texts may, in fact, "reflect" conditions, but others (e.g., television and movies) are thought to "mediate" experience, that is, to reflect those who produced it, such as culture industries.

## Historical Roots

Harriet Martineau's enthusiastic endorsement of the examination of documents for sociological research has echoes in the work of teacher, journalist, lecturer, researcher, and activist Ida B. Wells (1862–1929),[1] a daughter of freed slaves. In 1891, Ida Wells investigated the circumstances surrounding the lynching of blacks in the South, questioning the ubiquitous assumption that black men were lynched for raping white women. Was that, in fact, the crime of which the lynched person was accused? To conduct her study, Wells culled newspaper reports for accounts of lynchings, went to the scenes of the crimes, and interviewed eyewitnesses. Women's studies scholar Paula Giddings (1984) described Ida B. Wells's work as follows:

> All in all, she researched the circumstances of 728 lynchings that had taken place during the last decade. . . . Only a third of the murdered Blacks were even accused of rape, much less guilty of it. . . . Most were killed for crimes like "incendiarism," "race prejudice," "quarreling with whites," and "making threats." Furthermore, not only men but women and even children were lynched. . . . In the course of her investigations, Wells uncovered a significant number of interracial liaisons. She dared to print not only that such relationships existed, but that in many cases white women had actually taken the initiative. Black men were being killed for being "weak enough," in Wells's words, to "accept" white women's favors. (pp. 28–31)

Ida Wells concluded that black men were lynched because of whites' racial hatred and sense of threat, rather than for a particular wrongdoing. On June 5, 1892, she published the landmark results of her study in newspaper article form. In response, a large group of New York black women held an unprecedented, successful fund-raiser to support the publication of her findings as a pamphlet, seeing in her research a defense of their own moral integrity as well as that of black men. This reaction forged a path for the next stage of black women's political development and their involvement (Giddings, 1984; Thompson, 1990). Ida Wells stressed that her research relied on the collection and analysis of documents written by whites. She knew that only such data would make her findings credible in white society. As she predicted, her methods forced whites to confront ugly truths and challenged them to alter their stereotypes, a process most heartily resisted.

## Contemporary Feminist Content Analysis

Contemporary feminist scholars of cultural texts see "meaning" as mediated and, therefore, examine both the text and the processes of its production. In other words, interpretative practices involve analyzing not only the content but also the assumptions of the producers and readers. Of course, interpretations of these materials, such as this very chapter, are cultural artifacts, too. In considering the wide array of cultural materials, four types predominate as objects of feminist study. They are *written records* (e.g., diaries,[2] scientific journals, town names,[3] science fiction,[4] and graffiti); *narratives and visual texts* (e.g., movies,[5] television shows,[6] advertisements, greeting cards, and the Internet[7]); *material culture* (e.g., music,[8] technology,[9] contents of children's rooms,[10] and ownership of books[11]); and *behavioral residues* (e.g., patterns of wear in pavement).

Feminist researchers also examine the processes that prevent texts from being produced. Similarly, there has been a strong impetus to identify information missing about particular women and about women in general. Interest in pointing out what is missing is different from mainstream scholarship's practice of delineating "lacunae" to stake out a research turf that can be "filled in." Rather, in the identification of exclusions, erasures (Karon, 1992), and missing information (Reinharz, 1988) of interest, feminist researchers seek to understand the ways certain topics came to be missing and the implications of these gaps. Thus, feminist content analysis is a study both of texts that exist and of texts that do not.

Typically, studying cultural products through the lens of feminist theory involves examining gender at the intersection of such interlocking social forces as sexuality, race, ethnicity, class, religion, ability, and so forth. To a large extent, these studies yield findings that expose a pervasive patriarchal and even misogynist culture (Negrey, 1988, p. 21). Sometimes these cultural themes are found even when feminist literature is the object, as was the case in Nancy Chodorow and Susan Contratto's study of feminist treatments of the topic of mothering (Chodorow & Contratto, 1982; Contratto, 1984).[12] Similarly, Judith Dilorio's (1980) content analysis of scholarly articles about gender role research concluded that the methods used serve to reify social facts and are a conservative force. On the other hand, some cultural artifacts *oppose* the dominant culture. Popular culture created or chosen by women may express resistance to male domination. Feminist scholars are likely to interpret these in terms of counterhegemonic narratives or resilience of "women's culture" without, however, making the claim that there is a single women's culture.

Given the wide breadth of feminist content analyses, this chapter illustrates ways in which feminists have applied a form of this method to study the gendered and sexualized discourses inherent in cultural content, including the conditions of production and systems of interpretation. These new understandings challenge and destabilize the notion that our actions are simply "human nature" because "boys will be boys" and "girls will be girls." In the language of sociologist Michael Kimmel (1994), "from the materials we find around us in our culture—other people, ideas, objects—we actively create our worlds, our identities" (p. 120).

## THE POLITICS OF REPRESENTATION

How is the meaning of femaleness created and sustained in society? And how is this set of options pervasive even when gender is not the explicit topic? To a large extent, feminist research recognizes the gendered and sexualized politics of representation as a prevailing locus of female and gender subordination and liberation. In the watershed article "Is Female to

Male as Nature Is to Culture?" anthropologist Sherry Ortner (1974) aptly reveals the complexities and deeply engrained nature of female subordination:

> The universality of female subordination, the fact that it exists within every type of social and economic arrangement and in societies of every degree of complexity, indicates to me that we are up against something very profound, very stubborn, something we cannot rout out simply by rearranging a few tasks and roles in the social system, or even by reordering the whole economic structure. (p. 68)

Ortner (1974) suggests that the concept of female subordination can be divided into three theoretical frameworks: (1) ideologies and statements that *explicitly* devalue women, attributing them, their roles, their work, their products, and their social circles less prestige than those attributed to men; (2) symbolic mechanisms that *implicitly* indicate female inferiority; and (3) social and structural arrangements that *exclude* women from participation or powerful roles (p. 69). Symbolic mechanisms embodied in texts and imagery of gendered and sexualized representations subtly and insidiously inform social arrangements and systems of power. They are ubiquitous and inescapable.

## Uncovering Gendered Messages: From Women's Magazines to Teen Magazines: A Case Study

Contemporary cultural representations transmit messages of patriarchy, sexism, homophobia, ageism, and racism. They transmit messages about the able-bodied and the beautiful, as cultural ideals tied to gender as well. A common practice in content analyses is to examine how gender and other interlocking social forces are embedded in mainstream texts and imagery. Betty Friedan's early study of women's magazine fiction was devoted to this purpose. In Chapter 2, "The Happy Housewife Heroine," of her classic *The Feminine Mystique,* Betty Friedan (1963) explains the childish themes that dominate women's magazine fiction, and then plaintively expresses her guilt:

I helped create this image. I have watched American women for fifteen years try to conform to it. But I can no longer deny my own knowledge of its terrible implications. It is not a harmless image. There may be no psychological terms for the harm it is doing. But what happens when women try to live according to an image that makes them deny their minds? What happens when women grow up in an image that makes them deny the reality of the changing world? (p. 38)[13]

The idealized image of the "happy housewife heroine" portrayed in these magazines negates other important aspects of the women of the 1950s because they detract from the project of socializing and promoting the domestic woman—for men and for the state.

Feminist scholars theorize the majority of feature stories, articles, and advertisements of women's magazines as instruments of female socialization into subordinate roles. Angela McRobbie (2000), in her semiotic study of the weekly British teen magazine *Jackie,* asserts that the magazine connotes a "class-less, race-less sameness, a kind of false unity which assumes a common experience of womanhood or girlhood" (p. 70). In effect, these types of magazines embody ideological meanings and a "consensual totality of feminine adolescence" by which "all girls want to know is how to catch a boy, lose weight, look their best, and be able to cook" (p. 70). By encapsulating individuals into age and/or other interest categories, mainstream magazines obfuscate interlocking social forces such as race, class, and sexuality for the sake of underscoring points of commonality. Although these studies are powerful, they do not study the readers, and thus, we do not know how girls respond to these messages—a response we can only surmise.

In her content analysis of fiction articles in *Teen* and *Seventeen* magazines, Kate Pierce found that the majority of the female characters were portrayed as dependent (Schlenker, Caron, & Halteman, 1998). Working females filled traditionally female-specific occupations. In an extension of Pierce's analysis, Schlenker et al. (1998) at the University of Maine systematically examined selected editions of *Seventeen* magazine from 1945 through to 1995 to see if the content of the editorial pages reflected the

changing agendas and goals of the feminist movement. They found that during 3 years (1945, 1975, and 1995) that they define as key years for feminist activism, there were higher percentages of feminist content in the editorials. Nevertheless, at least half of these magazine issues were still dedicated to traditional content (Schlenker et al., 1998).

On the other hand, some feminist scholars contend that mainstream teen magazines offer a social construct of pleasure and resistance anchored in a female-centric space. Some perceive these social texts as female-focused enjoyment: the "simple act of taking pleasure through a female-centered venue itself resists patriarchal prescriptions of a self-abnegating and passive femininity" (Currie, 1999, p. 9). The female gaze, so to speak, may be honored in these magazines. Laura Carpenter (1998) examined sexual scripts in *Seventeen* from 1974 to 1994 and found "new scripts" of female desire, homosexuality, oral sex, masturbation, and female sexual ambivalence. The incorporation of progressive or nonnormative discourses of sexuality may encourage young women to choose safer sexual practices, resist gender and sexual subordination, and validate their own understandings and experiences of sexuality. At the same time, Carpenter found these benefits to be limited. Editors, she found, legitimize dominant sexual scripts over alternative scripts such as homosexuality, fellatio, or recreational orientations of sexuality. Overwhelming countervailing capitalist sexist messages found in the advertisements also diminish the power of these scripts.

Most of this research, based solely on the content in women's and teen magazines, presumes that the text has a uniform impact on its readership. Suzanna Danuta Walters (1995) looks at the multiple faces and expressions of the performer Madonna to illustrate the complexity of content in popular culture:

> The figure of Madonna is emblematic of the confused way women are represented in popular culture. We must reckon with the complicated and contradictory nature of images in our culture. It is too simplistic to state that there are "bad" images that produce "bad" attitudes and behaviors; unfortunately, the situation is more complex than that. Different audiences may interpret the same

images in different ways. One group's "negative" image may be another's source of empowerment. (pp. 2–3)

Walters underscores an important distinction. Gender and sexuality imagery is not necessarily understood by researchers and readers in the same way. Feminist scholars have contributed significantly to cultural analyses by examining the position of women in imagery and narratives. These scholars have illuminated how patriarchy informs the structure of content and the gaze. They have illustrated the constructed nature of imagery and texts. Yet Walters (1995) identifies three problems with most of this research—an absence of "real" women, social relations, and politics and history (pp. 145–147). To get beyond this methodological impasse, Walters suggests research with an intersubjective emphasis that flows from the researcher's analysis of the text and also includes interpretations from real women.[14]

Dorothy E. Smith (1990) develops a framework for analyzing the social relations embodied in and mediated by texts in which women are both the subjects and the readers. She insists that women are not simply passive receptacles of socialization processes; they are active constructors of their identities. Yet the market and advertising for clothing, makeup, shoes, accessories, and so on through print and film play a significant role in their self-creation and the choices available to them for work and leisure. Thus, Smith (1990) asserts, "The relations organizing this dialectic between the active and creative subject and the market and productive organization of capital are those of a textually mediated discourse" (p. 161). In other words, the meanings attached to femininity are interpretative practices mediated by social texts and the commercial and patriarchal objectives embedded within them. Accordingly, the discourse extends beyond the text. It involves "the talk" women do in association with social texts, and "the work" of creating oneself to actualize the textual imagery, the skills and actual effort involved in shopping, wearing makeup, and putting oneself together in a way that will gain approval from other women and appeal to men (Smith, 1990, p. 163).

In her study of teen magazines, sociologist Dawn Currie (1997) replaces herself as the interpreter with 48 girls, "real" and "active"

readers of the text aged 13 to 17 years. By bringing the real readers into the fore, Currie (1999) forges an empirical path for examining social subjectivity, the ways in which texts are mediated, interpreted, internalized, contested, and rearticulated through "the struggles of competing accounts of the 'social'" (p. 247). In contrast to traditional approaches to content analyses, Currie implements a grounded intersubjective analysis that focuses on what girls, the real readers of teen magazines, have to say about the role of cultural imagery and narratives in their lived experience of becoming a woman. Her team of researchers conducted focus groups and interviews with female teens regarding magazine reading preferences and habits, interpretations of advertising images, and topics of interest, as well as more general teenage topics. Strangely, her research is similar to the market research that drives the publication policies of these for-profit publications.

For many of the female teenage informants in Currie's study, magazines were one of the few social spaces where they were acknowledged as both teenagers and women. Currie (1999) notes that the magazines did not simply "fill a discursive void" (p. 247). Rather, the girls were discerning in their likes and dislikes of teen-zines, expressing predilections for articles that explored the realities of teenage life. Despite this, many of the informants were aware of the ideological messages imbued in these magazines that girls are expected to "always look good and that guys' opinions and preferences are important" (p. 247). While the magazines "reassure girls that their experiences fall within the boundaries of 'normal' teenage life," many of these girls mentioned that "it is difficult 'to be a girl,' especially to pursue the cultural mandate to 'look good'" (p. 19).

By connecting the dots from these social texts of fashion, beauty, and consumption to the industries advertising in these magazines to the large publishing industries themselves, Currie (1999) renders transparent the economic motives and patriarchal values lurking behind the glossy imagery of airbrushed women and their accompanying messages of beauty and consumption. In other words, idealized notions of beauty and advice around sexual practice produce strong profit for the fashion and beauty industry. Magazines are money, whether they are teenmags or pornography. If the profit-making advertising and readership decline, the magazine folds.

Currie's intersubjective approach to cultural materials charts an empirical course that breaks down the sociological dichotomy between structure and agency. Currie redefines "gender scripts" magazines as "textually mediated discourses," thereby illustrating how the gendered ideologies infused in magazine content do not destroy agency. This method breaks the social silence by unveiling unacknowledged dimensions of the magazine content, including the commercial context and the interpretations of readers. Her work exposes how we actively create ourselves as women, and how we are influenced by the commercial conditions of production that are not of our making.

## Looking to the General Mediascape: Overt and Not So Overt Stereotypes

Whereas the cultural analyses discussed above focus on media tailored for women, this next section looks at the broader media landscape where feminist scholars examine stereotypes of gender, race, and sexuality in newspaper articles, photojournalism, and advertisements (Fox, 1990). These analyses reveal gender relations not only between men and women but also among women of differing social locations. By challenging assumptions about gender, feminist researchers expose the political nature of mainstream content, prying open embedded social mythologies that many are committed to concealing (Fine, 1992, p. 221).

Sociologists Linda Blum and Nena Stracuzzi's (2004) content analysis of "Gender in the Prozac Nation" reveals a subtle presentation of gendered norms. Looking at 83 major newspaper articles on Prozac between 1987 and 2000, Blum and Stracuzzi developed coding categories based on theoretical concerns and multiple close readings. They identified explicit and subtle gendered cues of depressed people, including the traits attributed to Prozac users, their occupations, bodily concerns, and everyday obsessions (p. 274). Their analysis indicates that the overarching presentation of Prozac was fairly gender neutral. Yet the articles were replete with covert gendered messages of the elite productive female body:

> Our in-depth analysis suggests that this worthy user, with an enhanced and productive body, is gendered female. . . . New Scientist was most direct, observing that it "seems to be a drug of our times" that "helps produce ambitious, extrovert go getters," particularly among the women who are "most" likely to use it: "it may help take them to the success that society expects of them." (p. 279)

As such, the degendered guise of popular Prozac talk was often contradicted by gendered vignettes and imagery endowed with messages about disciplining, improving, and strengthening the female body. In addition, there was a "pronounced absence of race" in the articles that seemed to privilege "whiteness," as the unmarked or assumed position of "feminine fitness or new body ideals" (Blum & Stracuzzi, 2004, p. 283). This multilayered approach culled out explicit and implicit expressions of gender, moving us from a superficial gender-neutral read of these articles to an important feminist critique of the subtle ways in which popular media generalize, mythologize, and commodify particular brands of women by decontextualizing them from the fabric of their everyday lives.

Feminist content analyses are also useful in investigating the role of gendered and sexualized texts and imagery in public policy. Sociologist Karen Booth (2000) analyzed 108 "Baby AIDS" news stories published in New York newspapers. Her goal was to question if racist, heterosexist, and sexist assumptions informed HIV surveillance during the 1993 Baby AIDS debates in New York. At the time, HIV infection and cases of AIDS among women of childbearing age were expected to triple in New York. Despite this danger, many women were not finding out that they were at risk for the disease because mandatory HIV newborn tests were confidential and doctors were barred from disclosing their patients' HIV status to the sexual partners.

Booth's (2000) analysis of the stories reveals a blaming discourse toward women of color. For example, in 1993, the *New York Times* ran a front-page report, "Testing Newborns for AIDS Virus Raises Issues of Mothers' Privacy," on the emerging Baby AIDS issue. The story begins by asserting without explanation that "most infected women who give birth each year are black or Hispanic." Booth notes that in this story, women of color are defined as a category that is more likely to infect children, thus legitimating the question of whether their privacy should be invaded by mandatory newborn testing. White women, it seems, would not be affected by this testing policy (Booth, 2000, pp. 653–654). Booth also identifies an "anti-gay hostility" in many of the newspaper stories (p. 651). Her findings suggest a binary representation of who is and who is not affected by HIV and AIDS. As such, the general public of invisibly privileged people—by implication, white female heterosexual nondrug injectors—receive a "false and extremely dangerous illusion of safety," while drug users, women of color, sex workers, and homosexual men are discursively dislodged from the general public to the marginalized periphery of "groups at risk" (p. 658).

In her content analysis of news stories and images in Israeli popular media between 1994 and 1997, Dafna Lemish (2000) shows that the press depicts female immigrants from the former Soviet Union as hypersexualized, marginalized, and estranged. Lemish asks, "What cultural forces perpetuate these images and grant them discriminatory meaning?" Her descriptive categories included the type of newspaper and the article's salience; main themes discussed with regard to women immigrants and stance provided; and main themes intimated in the headline, in the sub-headline, or more subtly conveyed. Three major images or typologies emerged from the analysis: (1) "the whore," supplier of sexual services; (2) "the other," an explicit questioning of the "women's Jewishness . . . deviation from expected norms of a functioning wife and mother . . . or relating the immigrants to crime and poverty—at the social periphery of normative society"; and (3) "the exceptional immigrant"— a few articles were success stories about women immigrants "who against all odds, overcame obstacles and made it in Israeli society" (pp. 339–343).

According to Lemish, limited contextualization of these stories blurs reality and conflates portrayals of immigration, prostitution, and marginalization. These stereotypical misrepresentations and representations of female

immigration speak volumes about the cultural mechanisms at play. Lemish notes that minimizing individual characteristics and emphasizing appearance and sexuality expels these women from the mainstream of Israeli society:

> Polarized binary forms of representation, such as deviant whores and unfit mothers versus the expected definition of Jewish femininity and motherhood, are used to signify otherness. Such a symbolic marking of difference serves to maintain the symbolic boundaries by which the absorbing culture defines its identity. (p. 345)

Such a polarized view presents a challenging situation for both women in Israel who are *not* immigrants from the former USSR and female immigrants who come from the former USSR. Lemish exposes the media's deployment of divisive measures to reinforce relational systems not only between men and women but also among women of differing social locations.

In more recent content analyses, feminists are operationalizing the category of "woman" in new ways. Instead of lumping all women together, researchers systematically differentiate representations of women. Attention to multiple social forces allows feminists to frame their research in ways that highlight gender justice issues between men and women and among women of various races and classes.

## Researching Online Pornography: The Male Gaze in Virtual Reality

So far we have discussed the politics of representation in print media. But 21st-century analyses must address the Internet with its wide and fast circulation of text and imagery. The Internet is a major distributor of pornography, and thus it is no surprise that feminist scholarship is focusing on online pornography. Studies have begun by asking, What is different and unique about the online experience of pornography? In a study comparing the extent of sexual violence in magazines, videos, and an Internet user group, Martin Barron and Michael Kimmel (2000) found the content of pornography to be more violent on the Internet. They attribute the increased violence in online pornography to the growing "democratization of pornographic media" (p. 165) and decreases in production costs and control of content on new technologies.

Despite the myriad studies of pornography that differentiate between violent and nonviolent imagery, there has been little discussion of what constitutes violent pornographic representations. Addressing this problem, Jennifer Gossett and Sarah Byrne (2002) conduct an online content analysis to determine how "social inequities and power differentials—particularly with regard to race and age—play into the construction of violent pornographic images" (p. 705). To identify rape sites on the Internet, Gossett and Byrne employed a variety of Internet search engines (Yahoo! Altavista, and Excite) to search terms evoking violent pornography such as *rape, gang rape, forced sex, torture, bondage, rapist, forced fuck, bitch*, and so forth (p. 694). They sought Web sites with female rape victims. Thirty-one free Web sites of this type were linked predominantly to advertisement sites for pay-per-view sites. Gossett and Byrne coded the sites as a whole in terms of their structural elements (e.g., graphic techniques, navigational headings) as well as in terms of the narrative and visual elements, including the presence of violent words, the total number of real images, and descriptions of imagery, including the number of victims and perpetrators, kinds of weapons, scenes of bondage, types of locations, and race of perpetrators and victims (p. 696). Through this careful analysis of content and structure, they found that the Web sites comprise graphic imagery and narratives of female victims with more attention to race and age and less to individual attributes (p. 701). They found an overrepresentation of Asian women on the Web sites vending rape pornography and attribute this in part to their faces being more easily recognizable. In addition, they identified the sites through the search term *torture*, a term associated with imagery of Asian women in other forms of pornography (Bell, 1987; Gossett & Byrne, 2002). Gossett and Byrne draw on the concepts of sociologist Patricia Hill Collins (1991), who has reconceptualized contemporary pornography as a "series of icons or representations that focus the viewer's attention on the relationship between the portrayed individual and the general qualities ascribed to that class of individuals"

(p. 168). Pornographic images are iconographic because they reflect the realities of the social context from which they surface. Her complex view contrasts with the views of some feminists, who use a broad-brush definition of pornography as a way that "men oppress women" (p. 180). While many feminists contend that pornography affects all women, deploying the sweeping categories of men and women without reference to race or ethnicity tends to underestimate the way that race marks and shapes pornography (Gossett & Byrne, 2002, p. 703).

This reconceptualization of pornography poses the question, how does the social context of the Internet shape the way female victims are represented on "rape" Web sites? Gossett and Byrne (2002) suggest that the *global* reach of the Internet might be shaping the pornography market through different social dimensions than what we might observe if the pornography was targeted solely to an American audience of consumers (p. 701). They contend that a racialized discourse underlies the representation of rape on the Internet.

These sites also depict violent pornography as a sexualized representation of the uneven power relations between men and women. Drawing from Mulvey's conception of the male gaze, Gossett and Byrne (2002) reveal its pervasiveness on these sites:

> In Internet rape, the gaze of the man is the privileged point of view. This is implied by the relative absence of perpetrator images or descriptions of the perpetrator and is made explicit in the site he advertises, "Through the Eyes of the Rapist." The viewer of these sites is given not only the power of the gaze but also the power to choose which representations of inequality he or she prefers to see. This exemplified by the presence of jukeboxes describing categories of women who can be selected for victimization. . . . The perpetrators are given great power over the women by tying them up, strangling them, or not being shown at all. (p. 704)

The interactive capabilities of the Internet introduce new dimensions of power over women and manipulative choices for the pornographic seeker. By clicking an icon or navigational heading, these viewers virtually acquire the power to see "through the eyes of a rapist." The Internet allows the viewer to select a story, adjust the size of the image, decide to move to a more violent image, or toggle between a few stories.

Given the accessibility, interactivity, and male dominance of these sites, the Gossett and Byrne (2002) study propels us to expand feminist stances toward pornography from simple censorship to global concerns of dissemination and interpretation. Their analysis of violent pornographic content on the Internet underscores its complexity, its integration of gender and race, and the ability of rape Web site users to experience the virtual power of violence against women. How this translates to real life remains a difficult question. Gossett and Byrne (2002) hope that the emergence of new technologies such as the Internet will spur debate about the availability, content, and implications of pornography for the purpose of stopping "sexual violence against women and understand(ing) ways racism and sexism are expressed and reinforced through cultural representations, such as pornography" (p. 706).

While content analyses of the male dominant and misogynistic dimensions of the Internet such as the rape Web sites could have resulted in a feminist avoidance of the Internet, this has not been the case. On the contrary, feminist scholarship is tackling the complexity and contradictory character of the Internet. Some feminist research demonstrates how the Internet functions as a male-dominated space that continues to subordinate women (Herring, Johnson, & DiBenedetto, 1995; Kendall, 1996, 2000; Kramarae, 1995). In the article "This Discussion Is Going Too Far! Male Resistance to Female Participation on the Internet," Herring et al. (1995) reveal how males participating in mixed-sex online discussion groups employ numerous strategies to silence women, including "threats to the group and cries of 'this is too much'" when female participation exceeds 30% (p. 92). It is no surprise that to a large extent, women feel safer and more comfortable on women-centered and women-only sites in which they establish the terms of discourse. The progressive and democratizing potential of the Internet as a new and safe medium for women to network, strategize, and share knowledge has been recognized in some feminist studies, as long as the sites constitute a separate space (Cherny & Weise, 1996; Pearce, 1999; Sinclair, 1996; Spender, 1995b).

## STRETCHING THE BOUNDARIES OF KNOWLEDGE PRODUCTION

Because women are claiming new terrain, cultivating networks, and producing and exchanging knowledge, we believe there is cautious optimism about the Internet among feminists. Gillian Youngs (2004), for one, enthusiastically describes this new feminist frontier as a site that enables women to interact and strategize across geographic borders:

> Access to the Internet has heralded a new stage of feminism with regard to the international reach of women and the NGOs that represent their interests. Virtual technologies are facilitating women's collective endeavors in diverse ways, including consciousness-raising, intervention in policy processes, and project-driven innovations. . . . Those I have learned from have enhanced and made more complex my initial feminist sense that part of the problem with the "information society" is that what counts as knowledge is too readily assumed; and furthermore, that the international reach of the internet could be much more actively used to share and discover new and established knowledge, including knowledge about technology and its potential applications. (p. 203)

Youngs characterizes the feminist frontier in cyberspace as a base to produce new forms of "knowledge."

Feminists point to women's historical absence from public enterprises of knowledge production. To a large extent, this absence has meant exclusion from power. In the article "The Man of Reason," Genevieve Lloyd (1989) challenges the "natural order" of knowledge production by proposing an inclusive framework that expands membership to women. Lloyd asserts that the thin facade of impartiality in "objective," "neutral" knowledge masks the inherent bias and privilege of male knowledge producers and the social location from which they generate knowledge. Women sometimes adopt the male stance, so some men of reason may, in fact, be women. This reinvention of who can be a knower, in turn, leads to the question, what constitutes reason? While one could simply accommodate other knowers into an already existing rubric, Lloyd chooses to expand our notion of knowledge. She advocates documenting, analyzing, and including the "contingencies and vicissitudes of interactions with individuals" as a means to identify knowledge beyond delimiting "what is common to all" (p. 119).

For feminist historians, personal documents have been a key source for understanding the knowledge produced by women of the past. Historically ignored women are made visible when relevant artifacts are located and studied (Brown, 1986). At the same time, analysis of this type of material illuminates the forces that shape the lives of the vast majority, in contrast to the elite minority (Bushman, 1981; Springer & Springer, 1986). Historians looking through a feminist lens at the materials women have produced often challenge conventional knowledge. Just as feminist historians have rescued shards of evidence from the lives of *anonymous* women, they have also resuscitated the record of *literate* or *powerful* women.[15] It is important to remember that some women were not powerless or voiceless even if their power was exerted on the interpersonal rather than the international stage. Some women did have access to education, some were inspired, and some were able to produce important work; key examples in sociology are Harriet Martineau, Jane Addams, and Charlotte Perkins Gilman in the early history of sociology. Some have reputations that have little to do with their major accomplishments; key examples are Florence Nightingale and many female scientists. Examining both the anonymous majority and the later ignored minority is an important methodological perspective in feminist historical research. This interwoven interpretation understands women whose voices were heard in the context of women whose voices were muted or silenced. The "extraordinary" woman and the "ordinary" woman may not be as different from one another as they seem at first glance; to fully understand each, we need to understand both.

## Emerging Cyberfeminisms: A Case Study of Virtual Feminist Communities

Feminist historians use personal documents to examine the lives of women in the past, just as contemporary feminists use the Internet to link with women in other communities and cultures. The virtual public space of the Internet has opened up important possibilities for feminists to claim public spaces online and to disseminate knowledge that might otherwise go unseen. In the words of Dale Spender (1995a), "Women have to take part in making and shaping that cyber-society, or else they risk becoming outsiders." Sociologist Ann Travers (2003) reminds us that cyberspace is not unique. She argues that all public spaces are socially constructed. Nevertheless, the Internet offers feminists "unique opportunities for establishing visible feminist publics, for creating feminist spaces without 'going away' from the 'general' public space" (p. 231). Travers's words connote an interesting connection between current feminist virtual publics and feminist consciousness-raising groups of the late 1960s and early 1970s in the United States. While educated white women were likely to populate the consciousness-raising groups, feminist virtual communities seem more diverse in participation and broader in function (Weiler, 1991).

Some analyses of virtual feminist communities suggest that the Internet moves beyond the constraints of face-to-face communication. It creates unique spaces for community development and dialogue across difference. Sibylle Gruber (2001) explains:

> Various women's activists groups have started to "recast" their positions online. In doing so, they do not intend to create a virtual image remote from real causes; instead, they desire to increase their visibility and broaden their appeal to those who would otherwise be restricted to localized borders, barbed wire, and religious or political persecution, while at the same time keeping their local concerns in mind. (p. 79)

Gruber analyzes the discourse strategies on three feminist Web sites: Bat Shalom in Jerusalem—a feminist peace organization of Israeli women, NEWW—Network of East-West Women, and UNIFEM—United Nations Development Fund for Women. She titles her conclusion "Silent No More" and discusses the combination of alternative and traditional rhetorical devices these sites employ. The interface of alternative rhetorics of peace, cooperation, equity, and empowerment with traditional assertive, authoritative, male-oriented vocabularies encourages women to engage in local issues as well as in larger goals such as women's equal representation in global economic and political endeavors. The online participation of these three organizations extends their offline partnerships. The rhetorical strategies of active involvement, participatory change, and networking cultivate a strong sense of community to work toward creating a world that resists violence, oppression, and hatred (Gruber, 2001, pp. 88–89).

Building an online feminist community involves the development of a collective identity. Joyce Nip (2004) analyzes the identity building capacity of the Internet in social movements by focusing on the Queer Sisters, the women's group in Hong Kong, and the online bulletin they produce. Nip uses a multidimensional design, including content analysis, online surveys, interview, and observation on the Queer Sisters Web site. Nip indicates that the Queer Sisters face a number of challenges in cultivating a collective identity. Verta Taylor and Nancy Whittier (1992) define "collective identity" as individuals who share a sense of solidarity, internalize a collective consciousness (political interpretative frameworks, relational networks, and goals), and create a culture of direct opposition to the dominant order. The Internet adds a wrinkle to this definition as online collective identity processes are not face-to-face interactions for interpreting grievances and debating political opportunities. Rather, they are interactions mediated by the conventions of the Internet (Nip, 2004, p. 27).

As the Queer Sisters draw from queer theory grounded in postmodernism and poststructuralism, the possibility of a collective consciousness is further complicated. As such, participants on the Queer Sisters Web site confront the "contradictory task of consolidating a sense of identity among supporters" while advocating the deconstruction of a stable identity (Nip, 2004, p. 28). In addition, the Queer Sisters home page privileges inclusivity over political perspectives:

> Although the home page of the Queer Sisters did introduce the group's aims and goals, visitors with a lesbian inclination would still find themselves accommodated within the fluid sexual values advocated by the group. Neither the Queer Sisters home page nor the bulletin board suggested any expectation for board participants to be politically aware of their social conditions. Thus, the Queer Sisters were faced with an aggregate of people whose values and aspirations differ substantially. This made the project of collective identity building much more difficult. (p. 44)

In considering identity building on the Queer Sisters bulletin, Nip finds that the participants develop a sense of solidarity and share a sense of opposition toward the dominant order while they do not identify or internalize a sense of collective consciousness. Her findings reflect an important distinction between strategy- and identity-oriented social movements. The participants on the Queer Sisters' bulletin board convey less interest in building consciousness and more focus on creating a space for dialogue. Instead of using the bulletin board to build a collective queer identity, the board provides the Queer Sisters with a site to express and exchange their differing views and experiences, thus destabilizing a monolithic or stable notion of identity.

Other studies of feminist communities and content on the Internet punctuate the tremendous possibilities and challenges of cyberfeminism. Yisook Choi, Linda Steiner, and Sooah Kim (2005) analyze two feminist cyberspaces, Dalara Talsepo (Moon World and Cells of Daughters) and Unninet (Sisters' Village and Network) to examine the ways in which Korean feminists are and are not successfully carving out spaces for feminism in cyberspace. Their multidimensional research design brings into relief the social architecture and content of online feminist media. In effect, Choi and her colleagues interweave these two dimensions to examine the continuities and discontinuities of cyberfeminism:

> As the two zines' demonstrate, the advantage of the Internet in bringing together people who share neither temporal nor spatial co-presence also means that their bonds may be attenuated to the point of fracture. Time, energy: these are crucially limited resources, even for online feminists. Money remains an even more intractable issue. . . . The flexibility and easy access of the Internet predict that many sites will inevitably come and go.

But the ocean of ever-proliferating voices on the Internet suggests that if feminists are to find one another and together to form a mutually supportive activist community on and offline, this short-lived nature of webzines will be problematic. That is, sustaining and expanding online feminist media is itself important to the social and political impact of the feminist movement. (p. 24)

By interfacing the ways in which daily organizational issues affected the production of content, Choi and her colleagues clearly demonstrate the need for sustainable infrastructures to support feminist knowledge production. While both these feminist Web communities shared commonality in the desire to cultivate a safe platform to talk freely and experiment with alternative definitions of womanhood, the ephemerality of the Internet and ongoing issues of limited resources in the form of revenue, time, and energy have significantly affected their ability to sustain their organizations. Taking into account the dimensions of social production—in particular, organizational sustainability—adds an important layer to the discussion of online feminist communities.

## Virtual Possibilities and Shortcomings

What distinguishes feminist knowledge production on the Internet from other modes of production? Sherry Turkle (1995), professor in the MIT Program of Science, Technology, and Society, identifies the Internet as a space for experimentation and risk. Turkle, drawing from Robert Jay Lifton's book *The Protean Self,* indicates that there is room online for multiple identities. Akin to "Proteus, of fluid transformations," online identities can be multiple, yet integrated and anchored in coherence and a moral outlook (Turkle, 1995, p. 261). Turkle suggests that one can have a sense of self without being limited to one self. By experimenting with multiple identities, self-awareness of "our inner diversity" can also expose our limitations:

When identity was defined as unitary and solid it was relatively easy to recognize and censure deviation from a norm. A more fluid sense of self allows a greater capacity for acknowledging diversity. It makes it easier to accept the array of

our (and others') inconsistent personae—perhaps with humor, perhaps with irony. We do not feel compelled to rank or judge the elements of our multiplicity. We do not feel compelled to exclude what does not fit in. (p. 262)

While the threshold for trying on new identities and ways of being is low on the Internet, facilitating endless possibilities for bending gender, age, race, sexuality, or religion, this fluid sense of self does not live in a vacuum; it emerges from how one connects and communicates in a constructed virtual space (p. 258).

Experiences on the Internet involve cycling and toggling back and forth between virtual windows. Producing and drawing knowledge from these windows is partial and ever changing as people and Web communities continuously modify and add new content to their sites. The historian and theorist Donna Haraway (1991) asserts that people cannot fully see themselves because their perspectives are mediated by technology. The expectation that all aspects of self, community, state, nation, and planet will seamlessly fit together silences those who do not possess the "right" piece. In the language of Haraway (1991), "The knowing self is partial in all its guises, never finished, whole, simply there and original; it is always constructed and stitched together imperfectly; and therefore able to join with another, to see together without claiming another."

Feminist online communities embody this notion of partial situated knowledge as they manufacture spaces where different perspectives are presented but not subsumed with a totalizing notion of knowledge. Life on these virtual communities can expand the ways in which knowledge is produced and interpreted. Nevertheless, these feminist communities are not immune to systems of power and informal hierarchies because access to the Internet and resources vary significantly and subtly among participating men and women.

In contrast to other groups using the Internet for political mobilizing, women develop safe, personalized spaces for communication, strategic planning, and networking. For many women, the relative anonymity of going online offers the possibilities for new and unexplored forms of expression. Nicole Constable (2003), anthropologist at the University of Pittsburgh, differentiates Internet conversations, asynchronous communications, from face-to-face, synchronous communications, indicating that Internet conversations involve a lapse in time between posting a statement and receiving a response. Akin to telephone conversations, "Internet conversations lack the facial cues and body language that accompany most face-to-face conversations" (p. 36). As a result of these Internet conventions, Constable contends that people are less inhibited online. Wendy Harcourt (2000) also notes that women find virtual encounters to be easier than face-to-face interactions as the element of appearance is removed. Women virtually communicating on feminist Web sites might be more inclined to reveal their negotiations with identity and gender than they would offline in a social space with their colleagues and families where they perceive a greater risk of vulnerability or alienation. In particular, women speaking about issues of violence against women are more likely to express their experiences, including their emotions. The relatively anonymous nature of the Internet provides a safety net for women to break down barriers between private and public knowledge.

In cyberspace, feminist academics and activists cross paths on online communities from which they look for words to understand one another. Harcourt (2000) notes that online politics differ from those in the classroom or at political protests:

> In cyberspace there is no actual classroom, no trade union hall, no ancestral ground to defend, no government office to lobby. These remain virtual points of reference that are imagined not actually embraced or shared. Those who would not meet with professors or high-level policy makers find themselves in correspondence with them through e-mail. Papers that would never have reached an African NGO in rural Senegal are translated and sent in a few days of delivery at a scientific or intergovernmental event. . . . Women engrossed in their own battles for survival suddenly find groups living in other countries [who] share the same concerns and exchange valuable strategic knowledge. (p. 27)

As previously closed lines of connection and conversation begin to open, the Internet lends itself to overcoming traditional barriers of communication between and within communities. These new lines of communication and increased networking between communities, to some extent, expand the boundaries and possibilities of knowledge production, thus enabling new forms of social action. According to Harcourt (2000), "a more women designed webweaving could reflect women's sense of community and move us away from the consumer focused alienated individual interaction that characterizes most interaction on the Web today" (p. 29).

Despite these possibilities, there are limitations to this virtual mode of feminist knowledge production. While many feminist cyberspaces extol inclusivity, many people live in places that are not technically set up for online participation. In addition, there are many who are marginalized or without access to the Internet:

> the non-English speaking nations, "irrelevant" nations and peoples, national, religious, and ideological minorities, poor in poor countries and poor in rich countries (the majority of whom are women), most old and disabled, and all children (although certainly not Western screenagers). (Harcourt, 2000, p. 29)

The questions emerge: To what extent are these virtual modes generating new insiders and outsiders, and are these boundaries more or less fluid than other forms of communication? Generally speaking, the Internet as a public sphere is not a fixed space. Given the imperfect and changing characteristics of the Internet, feminist counterpublics need to both accept this incompleteness and commit to ongoing critical reflexivity (Travers, 2003, p. 234).

The question of how online dialogue translates into real life is critical for those engaged in cyberfeminist communities. Although the Internet provides an open space for ongoing conversations, Harcourt inquires, "Where do all these cyber dialogues go?" Some feminists who participate online experience virtual overload as they are inundated with never-ending e-mails and information. Most agree that differentiating between what is and what is not relevant on a long list of e-mail messages is time-consuming. But there is disagreement about whether e-mail and discussion boards are impersonal or are an efficient means for communication. E-mail carries the risks of endless conversations, messages sent in haste, and tempers escalating (Harcourt, 2000, p. 28). Although these risks could be perceived as generative tensions, they distract feminists from the "real" work of confronting gender injustices. Offline extensions of online feminist communities bring a live dimension to cyberfeminists. They can create face-to-face events and initiatives.

When we look to those who are engineering the Web, where are the women? While women create and inhabit political spaces on the Internet, these spaces are frequently not controlled and designed by women. The policy- and decision-making realm of telecommunications includes very few women (Harcourt, 2000, p. 28). And for those women in high positions in the telecommunications industry, voicing an alternative agenda, a feminist agenda within this arena is no small feat. Infiltrating the field of telecommunications is a particularly charged area as it is often intensely male coded and circumscribed for expert systems of computer scientists and government authorities with a limited opening for feminist participation.

## CONCLUSION

The preceding overview of feminist content analysis demonstrates that it is increasing with the development of new forms of content and virtual media. Despite the varying contexts and media, however, feminist content analysis retains a basic approach of examining the underlying political message of this content, even if the producers attempt to conceal or are unaware of these aspects. It is important to remember that content is not neutral. And as Marshall McLuhan and Quentin Fiore (1967) wrote, *The Medium Is the Message.* The subtle (and not so subtle) political aspects of content in the form of text, images, film, magazines, newspapers, academic journals, and Web sites are a primary vehicle of power.

For this reason there are many organizations and Web sites devoted to unpacking, tracing, promoting, and undermining the media vehicles. For example, Probe Ministries is a nonprofit corporation whose mission is to reclaim the primacy of Christian thought and values in

Western culture through media, education, and literature. In seeking to accomplish this mission, Probe provides perspective on the integration of the academic disciplines and historic Christianity. Another example is the Committee for Accuracy in Middle East Reporting in America (CAMERA), a media-monitoring, research and membership organization founded in 1982 and devoted to promoting accurate and balanced coverage of Israel and the Middle East. CAMERA fosters rigorous reporting while educating news consumers about Middle East issues and the role of the media. Because public opinion ultimately shapes public policy, distorted news coverage that misleads the public can be detrimental to sound policymaking. A nonpartisan organization, CAMERA takes no position with regard to American or Israeli political issues or with regard to ultimate solutions to the Arab-Israeli conflict. Organizations such as these underscore the point that cultural forms are socializing tools that instruct us with text and imagery of how we should live and look (Smith, 1987).

Many feminist researchers examine cultural forms to open a political analysis about content and form that convey sexist, homophobic, racist, and other oppressive messages. Moreover, those who study texts point to the significance of expanding our understanding of gender beyond the totalizing categories of woman and man. In this way, a more complex analysis of gendered representations and relations between women and between men emerges, revealing the multiple political layers of representation. Finally, feminist researchers focus not only on mainstream expressions of content but also on content produced by feminists. Reclaiming public spaces to produce feminist knowledge does not necessarily imply one feminist perspective. Cyberfeminism and online communities created by women are an evolving space for multiple expressions of feminisms. The generative, participatory forms of virtual feminist communities dispel the illusion of uniformity in feminism through the exposure and politicization of intersecting social forces, including gender, sexuality, race, class, education, and geographic location. Content generated by feminists needs to be viewed through a cross-cultural and social lens that reveals issues of both oppression and liberation.

To a large extent, feminist research in all these areas warrants a multidimensional approach that includes the analysis of content as well as interviews with those who are producing and consuming content. Importantly, integrating these dimensions brings into view the political and interpretative aspects of cultural production and reception.

## NOTES

1. Kay Richards Broschart discusses Ida Bell Wells-Barnett as a sociologist (Broschart, 1986). See Ida Wells, *Southern Horrors, Lynch Law in All Its Phases* (1892); *The Reason Why the Colored American Is Not in the World's Columbian Exposition* (1893); *A Red Record: Tabulated Statistics and Alleged Causes of Lynchings in the United States* (1895); *Mob Rule in New Orleans* (1900) (see also Duster, 1970).

2. See Karen V. Hansen (1987).

3. See Shulamit Reinharz (2003).

4. See Karen Keller (1980).

5. See Annette Kuhn (1982) and Kathi Maio (1988).

6. See Nancy Grant-Colson (1981), Barbara Hollands Peevers (1979), and Joseph Dominick (1979).

7. See C. Adams and R. Laurikietis (1980) and Micaela di Leonardo (1987).

8. See Sheila M. Krueger (1981).

9. See Judith A. McGaw (1982).

10. See H. L. Rheingold and K. V. Cook (1975).

11. See Susan Groag Bell (1982).

12. Nancy Chodorow and Susan Contratto discuss, among others, Judith Arcana (1979), Phyllis Chesler (1981), Dorothy Dinnerstein (1976), Jane Flax (1978), Nancy Friday (1981), Jane Lazarre (1986), Adrienne Rich (1976), and Alice Rossi (1972).

13. See H. H. Franzwa (1975).

14. One of the most engaging such analyses is by Susan J. Douglas (1994).

15. See Shulamit Reinharz, numerous articles on Manya Wilbushewitz Shohat (Reinharz, 1984, 1992b).

## REFERENCES

Adams, C., & Laurikietis, R. (Eds.). (1980). *The gender trap, a closer look at sex roles: Book 3. Messages and images.* London: Virago.

Arcana, Judith. (1979). *Our mothers' daughters.* Berkeley, CA: Shameless Hussy Press.

Barron, Martin, & Kimmel, Michael. (2000). Sexual violence in three pornographic media: Toward a sociological explanation. *Journal of Sex Research, 37*(2), 161–168.

Bell, Laurie. (Ed.). (1987). *Good girls/bad girls: Feminists and sex trade workers face to face.* Toronto, Ontario, Canada: Seal Press.

Bell, Susan Groag. (1982). Medieval women book owners: Arbiters of lay piety and ambassadors of culture. *Signs: Journal of Women in Culture and Society, 7*(4), 742–768.

Blum, Linda, & Stracuzzi, Nena. (2004). Gender in the Prozac nation: Popular discourse and productive femininity. *Gender & Society, 18*(3), 269–286.

Booth, Karen. (2000). "Just testing": Race, sex, and media in New York's "Baby AIDS" debate. *Gender & Society, 14*(5), 644–661.

Broschart, Kay Richards. (1986, August). *In search of our mothers' gardens: The process and consequences of discovering our foremothers.* Paper presented at the American Sociological Association/Sociologists for Women in Society Annual Meeting, New York.

Brown, Judith C. (1986). *Immodest acts: The life of a lesbian nun in renaissance Italy.* New York: Oxford University Press.

Bushman, Claudia. (1981). *A good poor man's wife: Being a chronicle of Harriet Hanson Robinson and her family in nineteenth-century New England.* Hanover, NH: University Press of New England.

Carpenter, Laura. (1998). From girls to women: Scripts for sexuality and romance in *Seventeen* magazine, 1974–1994. *Journal of Sex Research, 35*(2), 158–169.

Cherny, Lynn, & Weise, Elizabeth Reba. (1996). *Wired women: Gender and new realities in cyberspace.* Seattle, WA: Seal Press.

Chesler, Phyllis. (1981). *With child: A diary of motherhood.* New York: Berkley.

Chodorow, Nancy, & Contratto, Susan. (1982). The fantasy of the perfect mother. In Barrie Thorne & Marilyn Yalom (Eds.), *Rethinking the family: Some feminist questions* (pp. 54–75). New York: Longman.

Choi, Yisook, Steiner, Linda, & Kim, Sooah. (2005, August). *Claiming feminist space in Korean cyber territory.* Presented at the Association for Education in Journalism and Mass Communication Conference, San Antonio, TX.

Collins, Patricia Hill. (1991). *Black feminist thought: Knowledge, consciousness, and the politics of empowerment.* New York: Routledge.

Constable, Nicole. (2003). *Pen pals, virtual ethnography, and "mail order" marriages: Romance on the global stage.* Berkeley: University of California Press.

Contratto, Susan. (1984). Mother: Social sculptor and trustee of the faith. In Miriam Lewin (Ed.), *In the shadow of the past: Psychology portrays the sexes* (pp. 226–255). New York: Columbia University Press.

Currie, Dawn. (1997). Decoding femininity: Advertisements and their teenage readers. *Gender & Society, 11*(4), 453–477.

Currie, Dawn. (1999). *Girl talk: Adolescent magazines and their readers.* Buffalo, NY: University of Toronto Press.

di Leonardo, Micaela. (1987). The female world of cards and holidays: Women, families and the work of kinship. *Signs: Journal of Women in Culture and Society, 12*(3), 440–453.

Dilorio, Judith. (1980, June). *Toward a phenomenological feminism: A critique of gender role research.* Paper presented at the National Women's Studies Association Annual Meetings, Bloomington, IN.

Dinnerstein, Dorothy. (1976). *The mermaid and the minotaur: Sexual arrangements and human malaise.* New York: Harper & Row.

Dominick, Joseph. (1979). The portrayal of women in prime time, 1953–1977. *Sex Roles, 5*(4), 405–411.

Douglas, Susan J. (1994). *Where the girls are: Growing up female with the mass media.* New York: Times Books.

Duster, Alfreda. (Ed.). (1970). *Crusade for justice: The autobiography of Ida B. Wells.* Chicago: University of Chicago Press.

Fine, Michelle. (1992). *Disruptive voices: The possibilities of feminist research.* Ann Arbor: University of Michigan Press.

Flax, Jane. (1978). The conflict between nurturance and autonomy in mother-daughter relationships and within feminism. *Feminist Studies, 4*(2), 171–189.

Fox, Bonnie J. (1990). Selling the mechanized household: 70 years of ads in *Ladies Home Journal. Gender & Society, 4*(1), 25–40.

Franzwa, H. H. (1975). Female roles in women's magazine fiction. In Rhoda K. Unger & Florence L. Denmark (Eds.), *Woman: Dependent or independent variable* (pp. 42–53). New York: Psychological Dimensions.

Friday, Nancy. (1981). *My mother/myself.* New York: Dell.

Friedan, Betty. (1963). *The feminine mystique.* New York: Dell.

Giddings, Paula. (1984). *When and where I enter: The impact of black women on race and sex in America.* New York: Morrow.

Goldsen, Rose. (1974). *The show and tell machine.* New York: Dell.

Gossett, Jennifer Lynn, & Byrne, Sarah. (2002). "Click here": A content analysis of Internet rape sites. *Gender & Society, 16*(5), 689–709.

Grant-Colson, Nancy. (1981). Women in sitcoms: "I Love Lucy." In Terry Nygren & Mary Jo Deegan (Eds.), *Wimmin in the mass media* (pp. 21–30). Lincoln: University of Nebraska Press.

Gruber, Sibylle. (2001). The rhetorics of three women activist groups on the web. In Laura Gray-Rosendal & Sibylle Gruber (Eds.), *Alternative rhetorics: Challenges to the rhetorical tradition* (pp. 77–92). Albany: State University of New York Press.

Hansen, Karen V. (1987). Feminist conceptions of public and private: A critical analysis. *Berkeley Journal of Sociology, 32,* 105–128.

Haraway, Donna. (1991). The geography is elsewhere: Postscript to "cyborgs at large." In Constance Penley & Andrew Ross (Eds.), *Technoculture.* Minneapolis: University of Minnesota Press.

Harcourt, Wendy. (2000). Women's empowerment through the Internet. *Asian Women, 10,* 19–31.

Haskell, Molly. (1973). *From reverence to rape: The treatment of women in the movies.* Baltimore: Penguin.

Herring, Susan, Johnson, Deborah, & DiBenedetto, Tamra. (1995). This discussion is going too far! Male resistance to female participation on the Internet. In Kira Hall & Mary Bucholtz (Eds.), *Gender articulated: Language and the socially constructed self* (pp. 67–96). New York: Routledge.

Karon, Sarita. (1992). The politics of naming: Lesbian erasure in a feminist context. In Shulamit Reinharz & Ellen Stone (Eds.), *Looking at invisible women: An exercise in feminist pedagogy.* Washington, DC: University Press of America.

Keller, Karen. (1980). Freudian tradition versus feminism in science fiction. In Terry Nygren & Mary Jo Deegan (Eds.), *Wimmin in the mass media* (pp. 41–52). Lincoln: University of Nebraska Press.

Kendall, Lori. (1996). MUDer? I hardly know 'er! Adventures of a feminist MUDer. In Lynn Cherny & Elizabeth Reba Weise (Eds.), *Wired women: Gender and new realities in cyberspace* (pp. 207–223). Toronto, Ontario, Canada: Seal Press.

Kendall, Lori. (2000). "Oh no! I'm a nerd!" Hegemonic masculinity on an online forum. *Gender & Society, 14,* 256–274.

Kimmel, Michael. (1994). Masculinity as homophobia: Fear, shame, and silence in the construction of gender identity. In Harry Brod & Michael Kaufman (Eds.), *Theorizing masculinity* (pp. 119–141). Thousand Oaks, CA: Sage.

Kramarae, Cheris. (1995). A backstage critique of virtual reality. In Steven Jones (Ed.), *Cybersociety: Computer-mediated communication and community* (pp. 36–56). Thousand Oaks, CA: Sage.

Krueger, Sheila M. (1981). Images of women in rock music: Analysis of B-52's and Black Rose. In Terry Nygren & Mary Jo Deegan (Eds.), *Wimmin in the mass media* (pp. 11–20). Lincoln: University of Nebraska Press.

Kuhn, Annette. (1982). *Women's pictures: Feminism and cinema.* London: Routledge & Kegan Paul.

Lazarre, Jane. (1986). *The mother knot.* Boston: Beacon Press.

Lemish, Dafna. (2000). The whore and the other: Israeli images of female immigrants from the former USSR. *Gender & Society, 14*(2).

Lloyd, Genevieve. (1989). The man of reason. In Ann Garry & Marilyn Pearsall (Eds.), *Women, knowledge, and reality: Explorations in feminist philosophy* (pp. 111–128). Boston: Unwin Hyman.

Maio, Kathi. (1988). *Feminist in the dark: Reviewing the movies.* Freedom, CA: Crossing Press.

Martineau, Harriet. (1988). *How to observe morals and manners, 1838* (Michael R. Hill, Ed.). New Brunswick, NJ: Transaction Books. (Original work published 1838)

McGaw, Judith A. (1982). Women and the history of American technology. *Signs: Journal of Women in Culture and Society, 7*(4), 798–828.

McLuhan, Marshall, & Fiore, Quentin. (1967). *The medium is the message: An inventory of effects.* New York: Bantam Books.

McRobbie, Angela. (2000). *Jackie* magazine: Romantic individualism and the teenage girl. In Angela McRobbie (Ed.), *Feminism and youth culture* (pp. 67–117). New York: Routledge.

Mellon, Joan. (1973). *Women and sexuality in the new film.* New York: Dell.

Millet, Kate. (1970). *Sexual politics.* Garden City, NY: Doubleday.

Negrey, Cynthia. (1988, October). Film review of "Still Killing Us Softly." *SWS Network News, 6*(1).

Newcomb, Horace. (1974). *TV: The most popular art.* New York: Anchor Books.

Nip, Joyce. (2004). The Queer Sisters and its electronic bulletin board: A study of the Internet for social movement mobilization. *Information, Communication, & Society, 7*(1), 23–49.

Ortner, Sherry. (1974). Is female to male as nature is to culture? In Michelle Rosaldo & Louise Lamphere (Eds.), *Women, culture, and society* (pp. 67–87). Stanford, CA: Stanford University Press.

Pearce, Kimber Charles. (1999). Third wave feminism and cybersexuality: The cultural backlash of the new girl order. In Meta Carstarphen & Susan Zavoina (Eds.), *Sexual rhetoric: Media perspectives on sexuality, gender, and identity* (pp. 271–281). Westport, CT: Greenwood.

Peevers, Barbara Hollands. (1979). Androgyny on the TV screen? An analysis of sex-roles portrayal. *Sex Roles, 5*(6), 797–809.

Pemberton, Jane. (1981). Examining the top ten or why those songs make the charts. In Terry Nygren & Mary Jo Deegan (Eds.), *Wimmin in the mass media* (pp. 1–10). Lincoln: University of Nebraska Press.

Petraka, Vivian, & Tilly, Louise. (Eds.). (1983). *Feminist re-visions: What has been and might be.* Ann Arbor: University of Michigan (Women's Studies Program).

Reinharz, Shulamit. (1984). Toward a model of female political action: The case of Manya Shohat, founder of the first kibbutz. *Women's Studies International Forum, 7*(4), 275–287.

Reinharz, Shulamit. (1988). What's missing in miscarriage? *Journal of Community Psychology, 16*(1), 84–103.

Reinharz, Shulamit. (1992a). *Feminist methods in social research.* New York: Oxford University Press.

Reinharz, Shulamit. (1992b). Manya Wilbushewitz-Shohat and the winding road to Sejera. In Deborah Bernstein (Ed.), *Pioneers and Homemakers in Pre-State Israel* (pp. 95–118). Albany, NY: SUNY Press.

Reinharz, Shulamit. (2003). Women's names and place(s): Exploring the map of Israel. In Judith Tydor Baumel & Tova Cohen (Eds.), *Gender, place and memory in the modern Jewish experience* (pp. 240–251). Edgware, Middlesex, UK: Vallentine Mitchell.

Rheingold, H. L., & Cook, K. V. (1975). The contents of boys' and girls' rooms as an index of parent's behavior. *Child Development, 46*(2), 459–463.

Rich, Adrienne. (1976). *Of women born.* New York: Norton.

Rossi, Alice. (1972). Sexuality, maternalism and the new feminism. In Joseph Zubin & John Money (Eds.), *Contemporary sexual behavior: Critical issues in the 1970's* (pp. 145–174). Baltimore: Johns Hopkins Press.

Schlenker, Jennifer, Caron, Sandra, & Halteman, William. (1998). A feminist analysis of *Seventeen* magazine: Content analysis from 1945 to 1995. *Sex Roles, 38*(1–2), 135–149.

Sinclair, Carla. (1996). *Net-chick: A smart girl guide to the wired world.* New York: Holt.

Smith, Dorothy. (1987). *The everyday world as problematic: A feminist sociology.* Boston: Northeastern University Press.

Smith, Dorothy. (1990). *Texts, facts, and femininity: Exploring the relations of ruling.* New York: Routledge.

Spender, Dale. (1995a). Electronic scholarship: Perform or perish. In Cheris Kramarae & Maureen Ebben (Eds.), *Women, information technology and scholarship.* Urbana, IL: Center for Advanced Study.

Spender, Dale. (1995b). *Nattering on the net: Women, power, and cyberspace.* Melbourne, Victoria, Australia: Spinifex Press.

Springer, Marlene, & Springer, Haskell. (Eds.). (1986). *Plains woman: The diary of Martha Fransworth, 1882–1922.* Bloomington: Indiana University Press.

Taylor, Verta, & Whittier, Nancy. (1992). Collective identity in social movement communities:

Lesbian feminist mobilization. In Aldon Morris & Carol McClurg Mueller (Eds.), *Frontiers in social movement theory* (pp. 104–129). New Haven, CT: Yale University Press.

Thompson, Mildred. (1990). *Ida B. Wells-Barnett: An exploratory study of an American black woman, 1893–1930.* New York: Carlson.

Travers, Ann. (2003). Parallel subaltern feminist counterpublics in cyberspace. *Sociological Perspectives, 46*(2), 223–237.

Tuchman, Gaye. (1989). *Edging women out: Victorian novelists, publishers, and social change.* New Haven, CT: Yale University Press.

Tuchman, Gaye, Daniels, Arlene Kaplan, & Benet, James. (1978). *Hearth and home: Images of women in the mass media.* New York: Oxford University Press.

Turkle, Sherry. (1995). *Life on the screen: Identity in the age of the Internet.* New York: Simon & Schuster.

Walters, Suzanna Danuta. (1995). *Material girls: Making sense of feminist cultural theory.* Berkeley: University of California Press.

Webb, Eugene, Campbell, Donald, T. Schwartz, Richard D., & Sechrest, Lee. (1966). *Unobtrusive measures: Nonreactive research in the social sciences.* Chicago: Rand McNally.

Weiler, Kathleen. (1991). Freire and a feminist pedagogy of difference. *Harvard Educational Review, 61*(4), 462.

Weitz, Rose. (1977). *Sex roles.* New York: Oxford University Press.

Wells-Barnett, Ida B. (1991). *On lynchings, southern horrors, a red record, mob rule in New Orleans.* Salem, NH: Ayer Company. (Original work published 1892)

Youngs, Gillian. (2004). Cyberspace: The new feminist frontier? In Karen Ross & Carolyn M. Byerly (Eds.), *Essays in feminism and media* (pp. 185–208). Oxford, UK: Blackwell.

# 13

# FEMINIST EVALUATION RESEARCH

SHARON BRISOLARA
DENISE SEIGART

## THE EVALUATION ENTERPRISE

Program evaluation emerged as a professional field in the United States during the 1960s with the expansion of social programs during that period. Although evaluation is a discipline in its own right, practitioners often receive training in other fields before embarking on a career in program evaluation. Program evaluation makes use of a range of social science research methods but is much more focused than social research. Essentially, social research methods and procedures are applied to assess "the conceptualization, design, implementation, and utility of . . . social intervention programs" (Rossi & Freeman, 1993, p. 5).

Many evaluators choose to design their work in adherence with a particular evaluation model. By *model,* we mean an approach to program evaluation that espouses particular theoretical values and methodologies; a model, therefore, provides guidelines to designing and conducting evaluations and to ways of thinking about evaluation practice and utilization. Despite the relatively short history of the profession, numerous evaluation models have been developed and gained legitimacy. Responsive evaluation, utilization evaluation, and stakeholder evaluation are a few of the models that have gained a wide following and the respect of the profession.

During the past 15 years, several models have emerged that have challenged the core beliefs and practices of the evaluation profession. Initially, the challenges were epistemological, continuing a move from the positivist beginnings of the profession to a belief, for some, that reality cannot be fully known. Soon, however, these newer models were vigorously posing ontological and methodological challenges as well, questioning what can be known, what is reality and truth, and what are the most ethical and effective ways of understanding a program, its outcomes, and program dynamics. Among the most successful in pushing the parameters of the profession by inciting dialogue and debate have been participatory evaluation, empowerment evaluation, and fourth generation evaluation. Such models have provided fodder for what Donald Campbell, one of the earliest evaluation theorists and practitioners, termed the contentious community of truth seekers. Feminist evaluation is one of the more recent challenger models to receive attention within the field.

Evaluation practitioners who espoused feminist beliefs were engaged in what they had begun to call *feminist evaluation* long before the term was recognized in the field as an emerging model. There were limited papers or articles on feminist evaluation before an attempt was made in the mid-1990s to propose a *New Directions for Evaluation* volume on feminist evaluation (Seigart & Brisolara, 2002). The project initially met with resistance and considerable requests for revisions. New editors were found, and the project was completed in 2002. It was also in 1995 that the American Evaluation Association first provisionally included feminist issues as a topical interest group (TIG) within the association; the TIG was formally recognized as active in 1997. Feminist evaluation is still being forged as more projects are implemented, as the model gains legitimacy, and as involved practitioners share their experience and expertise.

## VISIONING FEMINISM

Feminism is not any more inclined than other philosophies or positions to be defined and categorized—perhaps even less so, given the critique at the heart of feminist theory about the essentializing tendency of male-dominated theories or disciplines, the caution against claiming to speak for all women, even all feminists, and the revolutionary nature of the feminist project (Fox-Genovese, 1992). Women's movements in the United States and Britain, for example, have been charged in the past with privileging the concerns and priorities of white, middle-class women. In many Latin American nations, the concerns of middle- to upper-class women more obviously of European heritage have often been privileged. Much attention (and more resources for gaining that attention) has been given to feminist theory developed by Western scholars, many of whom are white, middle- to upper-class, and highly educated. In fact, there exist groups of women who have chosen not to identify themselves with the term *feminist,* choosing instead other names and titles to describe their particular women-centered ideological positions. This variety of concerns, priorities, and perspectives about what are the aims and tenets of feminist inquiry (shaped as they are by race, culture, and class) result in *feminisms.*

The fact that there are feminisms, however, does not preclude a definition of some of the elements that unite these various forms. For us, feminism is a practical and ideological position arising from social and intellectual movements that deeply values and acts in keeping with women's perspectives and experiences with the greater aim of fostering greater social justice and equality. Feminism acknowledges that most contemporary cultures are organized around patriarchal values and institutions and that, consequently, greater equality and justice for all persons often requires greater attention to the social, economic, physical, spiritual, and political needs of women, people of color, and individuals of all ages and sexual orientations or preferences. Among the themes that have prevailed in feminist inquiry is an interest in remedying the unfair distribution of material, political, social, cultural, and psychic rewards across individuals, a distribution that adversely affects women.

Contemporary forms of feminist inquiry contend that inquiry, and the knowledge that emerges from inquiry, should contribute to the removal or alleviation of such distortions. Feminist evaluation is an evaluation-specific form of inquiry espousing methods, methodology, and theory informed by feminist theory and values in the service of greater equity for women and greater social justice for all people. As an evaluation-specific model, feminist evaluation also seeks to inform and guide the development of evaluation practice more broadly, with the aim of encouraging attention to the ontological and epistemological challenges raised by feminist theory and the ethical and practical implications of these challenges for the field. Central to feminist evaluation are the key feminist values that guide the questions, structure, and process of the evaluation and that one commits to some form of action as a critical element of the evaluation project. These values are addressed in a later section of the chapter.

### Apertures

One is often on shaky ground in attempting to define contemporary or recent trends in feminist thought, much like the attempt to describe the landscape from a fast-moving train. Recent feminist-related movements have included ecofeminism, racial or cultural identity-based collectives (such as the Latina or Chicana movement), and theoretical or philosophical stances (e.g., postmodernist, poststructuralist, and psychoanalytic feminism). Feminist and women's movements in recent years have been shaped by responses to conservative backlashes in the 1980s and early 1990s, the scaling back of abortion rights, attention to domestic and wartime violence against women, and the effect of the global assembly line on women workers. Feminist literary theorists have raised the importance of voice as a conceptual category. They, and others, have revisited Freud, Foucault, Lacan, and Derrida to invite the heuristic possibilities that their work offers feminist thought. More recently, some have urged a return to feminist theory to find inspiration and resources for understanding concepts such as power, empowerment, representation, and the like. Feminist postmodernism suggested that there is no truth about reality, that all views are partial (Hawkesworth, 1989). However it may be defined in retrospect, this stage of feminist thought will be partly characterized by a search to recognize, embrace, and celebrate diversity; to achieve balance; and to recognize and promote solutions to pressing ecological concerns that threaten the sustainability of all life-forms.

Along with diversity there has been a focus on multiplicity and the best ways of addressing multiplicity within the research project. There has certainly been a focus on multiplicity of methods (mixed-method designs), competing values, stakeholders, and even realities within feminist theories and models as well as within other models that have challenged traditional scientific practice (Brisolara, 1998). Furthermore, the idea that individuals operate from a position that is informed by and straddles multiple social identities is a key feminist concept. Our divergent identities construct each other and are inextricably linked: Our sex and gender cannot be isolated from our class, age, sexual orientation or preference, and physical ability. Oppression is recognized as being structural, socially constructed, externally imposed, and both consciously and unconsciously internalized. Forms of oppression that focus on one of these identities (e.g., homophobia, classism, ageism) inevitably oppress women who are members of these groups as well and generally do so in a disproportional manner. At the heart of many forms of feminist inquiry and feminist

evaluation lies a belief in the importance of working to overcome, to the extent that this is possible, one particular form of oppression, sexism and gender inequality, as one strand in a web of oppressions, none of which can be ignored.

In recent decades, there has been within the social sciences a new and stronger focus on action research models and participatory forms of inquiry. Evaluation models that valued democratic decision making and stakeholder participation, including responsive evaluations, stakeholder evaluation, democratic evaluation, and Stufflebeam's decision-making approach (Brisolara, 1998), were already in place. More recently, explicitly collaborative and participatory models that combine participation with action in evaluation have emerged and gained a significant following: Key examples include participatory evaluation (Weiss & Greene, 1992; Whitmore, 1998, among others), morally engaged evaluation (Schwandt, 1991), empowerment evaluation (Fetterman, 1992), and emancipatory and critical action research (McTaggart, 1991; Noffke, 1994). Evaluation models such as these have developed alongside feminist evaluation, and the contributions made through dialogue and sharing have been mutually beneficial.

## KEY FEMINIST EVALUATION CONCEPTS, EMERGING GUIDELINES, AND THEIR THEORETICAL GROUNDING

As is true of other models, feminist evaluation has emerged from theoretical developments in a number of disciplines and has been brought into evaluation in response to pressing needs within evaluation practice. Proponents have also spoken of contributions that feminist evaluation can make, given the profession's growing interest in utilization of evaluation results, including traditionally underrepresented stakeholders, addressing pluralism, grounding evaluation practice in theory and evaluation theory in practice, and recognizing and responding to the play of power and politics in an ethically sound manner. Challenger or alternative models such as feminist evaluation have raised new questions for the field and have continued to press for responses to some of the questions with which the larger evaluation community is also struggling. How do we respond to the fact that "objectivity" cannot be achieved? How do we position ourselves (or our work) given that the subject matter, programs, and products of our work are political in nature? Which voices are not being heard (who and what important data are missing from our work), and what does this mean for our clients (or our integrity)? If we maintain a commitment to social justice and pluralism, what is the evaluator's role vis-à-vis our primary clients, other stakeholders, and members of the larger community? How is the role of the evaluator shaped and bounded by her or his personal experiences and characteristics? What constitutes ethical evaluation practices, particularly regarding our interaction with the people most likely affected by our work? What assumptions are we bringing to our work, and how does this affect what we "know"? Feminist evaluation offers many contributions to evaluation practice, theory, and methodology, including its own responses to such questions based on a rich and varied theoretical history that focuses specifically on how to conduct feminist inquiry.

In our recent volume on feminist evaluation, we proposed six key ideas from which feminist evaluations emerge and that feminist evaluators have used in selecting and designing their efforts (Bowen, Brisolara, Seigart, Tischler, & Whitmore, 2002). The list that appears below has been expanded since the volume was published and is not intended to be the definitive statement on what constitutes key feminist evaluation concepts. (A more complete discussion of the ideas behind these concepts follows.) It has been our intention to engage in continued dialogue and discussion surrounding an articulation of guidelines that remains sensitive to changing times. Rather, the following guidelines have informed feminist evaluation to date and form the basis of what makes feminist evaluation unique.

## Key Feminist Evaluation Concepts

1. Feminist evaluation is in part a response to the fact that evaluation and research methods, institutions, and practices are all social constructs and have been strongly influenced by a dominant male or patriarchal ideology.

2. Feminist evaluation has as a central focus the gender inequities that lead to social injustice. A central moral premise is that gender inequities are one manifestation of social injustice and are an important starting point given that gender issues have long been and are frequently overlooked.

3. Discrimination based on gender is systemic and structural. Although it may manifest differently, it cuts across and is inextricably linked to race, class, and culture.

4. Evaluation is a political activity. The contexts in which evaluation operates are politicized and imbued with asymmetrical power relationships. The personal experiences, perspectives, and characteristics evaluators bring to evaluations (and with which we interact) both come from and lead to a particular political stance. Evaluation projects and their contexts are imbued with asymmetrical power relationships.

5. Knowledge is a powerful resource that serves an explicit or implicit purpose. Knowledge should be a resource of and for the people who create, hold, and share that knowledge.

6. Action and advocacy are morally and ethically appropriate responses of an engaged feminist evaluator. The purpose of knowledge is action.

7. There are multiple ways of knowing; some ways are privileged over others (e.g., within the social sciences or evaluation) by those with the power to sanction or privilege certain ways of knowing. Consequently, engaging a range of stakeholders in a participatory manner is important to feminist evaluation practice.

8. Knowledge is culturally, socially, and temporally contingent. Knowledge is also filtered through the knower.

Feminist evaluation theory has been developed within and has influenced the development of many disciplines, each of which has made unique and important contributions to feminist thought. Those scholars who engaged in the development of feminist theory and practice have generally been provided with the opportunity to refine their work in the fire of heated debates and challenges, sometimes from the sharpest critics in diverse fields. The responses, which have been open to criticism and scholarly debate since, have encouraged theoretical and methodological development outside feminist circles. The following section describes some of the key feminist contributions from various disciplines that have influenced the creation of these feminist evaluation values. We frame this discussion in terms of our eight key concepts.

*Feminist Evaluation as a Response to "Traditional," Postpositivist, Male-Dominated Practice*

An early focus of feminist theorists[1] was to critique practices within the social and natural sciences that had been developed exclusively, or nearly exclusively, by a relatively homogeneous scientific community: predominantly white, privileged men. They challenged the appropriateness and validity of knowledge that was devoid of the input and perspectives of women and of questions and priorities that reflected male middle- and upper-class concerns. Moreover, feminists charged that the experiences and concerns of women and people of color were rarely reflected in scientific work. They reminded the scientific community that methods and methodology as well as what constitutes important questions and knowledge are constantly in flux, being influenced by a number of historical, societal, and disciplinary concerns (Reinharz, 1989). The acceptance of particular methods and theories within a discipline depends on the attention and interest that they attract to a greater extent than their unique (and/or improved) ability to ferret out truth. The work of these scholars often emphasized the contributions that women's perspectives could make to knowledge acquisition and the ethical and practical issues involved with including or excluding women. A conservative perspective was posited by feminist empiricists who held on to many tenets of positivism while critiquing misogynist bias as an important obstacle to obtaining objective knowledge (Harding, 1983; Hawkesworth, 1989). For feminist empiricists, objectivity remained a possibility once prejudice was removed: One remedy these feminists recommended was to promote more women to important positions within scientific institutions, to encourage more women to choose careers in science, and to make women the focus of more studies. Later, feminist writers working within the field of international development, among others, were quick to point out the inefficacy of an "add women and stir" approach. Such a response, they argued, merely extended the authority of the existing paradigm (Smith, 1972).

Although feminist theorists contend that there is no one Truth (capital T) or Reality (capital R), there are, as Sandra Harding (1991) states, underlying regularities. Bringing multiple and diverse perspectives to a social situation to unearth these underlying regularities is one of the tasks of feminist inquiry (Harding, 1990). Truman draws from Harding and others in positing that feminist objectivity is not neutral but that it can be achieved through the use of reflexive processes. Feminist objectivity criteria include accountability (to those being researched and to feminist values), positioning (acknowledging one's social positions and identities), and a conscious partiality of the limits of research (Bhavnani, 1993; Harding, 1990; Truman, 2002). Such a position invites greater participation in research or evaluation dynamics and promotes democratic principles. Illuminating these underlying tendencies and the forces that constrain or promote them is one of the gifts of feminist inquiry and evaluation. As Hawkesworth (1989) has noted, "In the absence of claims of universal validity, feminist accounts derive their justificatory force from their capacity to illuminate existing social relations, to demonstrate the deficiencies of alternate interpretations, and to debunk opposing views."

*Feminist Evaluation Has as a Central Focus the Gender Inequities That Lead to Social Injustice*

This, perhaps, is the central concept that distinguishes feminist evaluation from other participatory, action models. Sexism (like racism and classism) is an issue that has long affected our world, including the contexts in which we work and the theories produced within our field. Recognizing and minimizing the effects of discrimination requires a concentrated and intentional focus. A woman-centered perspective is the lens through which feminist evaluators approach discrimination. As others have noted, "by emphasizing the suppression of all women as women, feminists are attempting to understand the advantage and prerogative of some women by race, class, and nationality" (Fox-Genovese, 1992, p. 230). Historically, women have been adversely affected by gender equities to a greater degree than have men. However, feminist evaluation is also interested in gender inequity experienced by men, who may also be feminist evaluators. Gender, Hood and Cassaro (2002) remind us, is a relational concept: An identity as woman is interdependent with an identity as man. Gender cannot be abstracted; rather it is one position that must be negotiated among other positions (Hurtado, 1996). Hood and Cassaro further highlight the attention of some feminist researchers in questioning the existence of only two sexes, in recognizing the biological gradations from female to male that occur, in recognizing new categories that include transgendered individuals, and in developing an awareness of the intersexed body (Fausto-Sterling, 1993).

Ward (2002) suggests a guideline for creating and developing feminist evaluations that are related to this concept. She suggests that we place women and their material realities at the center of evaluation planning and analysis. Ward posits that this guideline is what defines feminist evaluation and separates it from other forms of evaluation. Other feminist evaluators would suggest that putting gender (issues) and the material realities of those being considered in the evaluation project at the center of evaluation planning and analysis is an alternative articulation of this guideline that is closer to the spirit of feminist theory. Truman's (2002) needs assessment of the sexual health needs of men who have sex with men is a clear example of a feminist evaluation project that illustrates this difference.

### Discrimination Based on Gender Is Systemic and Structural

Gender discrimination is shaped and bounded by race and class; it is historically and culturally situated. For feminist evaluators, it is critical that we realize the ways in which discrimination is deeply embedded within society—how key institutions (such as churches, temples, mosques, schools, and governmental programs), popular media, and culture reinforce the dominant patriarchal paradigm. Divergent forms of oppression are related: They support and reinforce each other, as previously discussed. The stakes of continued oppression (societal and domestic violence, poverty, sexual violence as a tool of war, and addiction are a few examples) are exceedingly high.

Ward (2002) suggests a second guideline appropriate to this concept: Understand the problem context from a feminist perspective. Understanding the structural and systemic nature of gender discrimination is, perforce, to use a feminist lens. But beyond the initial recognition, Ward reminds us to not forget the obvious, the need to center and re-center our questions and approaches within feminist thought and to clarify the feminist perspective from which activities are developed.

### Evaluation and Evaluation Contexts Are Political and Imbued With Asymmetrical Power Relationships

The idea that evaluation is political is no longer a radical notion. There is greater agreement that our work offers a particular response from a particular position to the questions of whose interests are served, what agendas are being promoted, what will be the consequences for people involved, and what or who is being neglected, even when we address these issues indirectly. For feminist evaluators, the evaluation process, the role played by the evaluator, and the products and learning that issue forth from a project are politicized expressions of feminist tenets and assumptions.

From the women's liberation movement in the 1970s came the well-known phrase "the personal is political." From a feminist scientific perspective, this phrase signified the need to value the lived experiences of others (particularly of women) as legitimate and important subjects of study and to recognize the importance of daily, often discounted experiences (Stanley & Wise, 1989). Writers such as these were quick to note the explicit and implicit political agendas promoted via the construction of research communities and projects. They began asking for what purpose(s) knowledge is being generated and for whom. Maria Mies (1991) and others began their critique by pointing out that positivists and postpositivist paradigms were political in the very claim to be "objective" and "value-free." Feminist thinkers responded, in part, to criticism regarding the political nature of their work by countering that all research, all science, was political in motivation and in use. Many took the stance that the ethical choice, given this situation, was to make one's political stance apparent and to challenge existing power structures, opening these structures to greater participation by people who are not normally "heard." With time, feminist writers spent less time in countering challenges, because such debates implicitly acknowledged that the current state of affairs was the standard by which all practice should be judged, and invested greater effort in developing their own theories.

Recognizing power dynamics and asymmetrical relationships in which power comes to play is a central theme of many underlying key feminist evaluation concepts. Feminist evaluators have drawn from the work of critical theorists and others in developing a textured understanding of the power dynamics interacting within relationships, cultures, institutions, academia, and the world of science. Power differentials lead to gender inequities; the exercise of "power over others" has created systemic and structural discrimination, including the legitimizing of particular scientific paradigms or agendas. We know that power is exerted in many overt and covert ways and that powerlessness can be internalized and perpetuated by the very groups who are being oppressed by the messages they believe. Feminist evaluators are keenly aware that language is a constitutive force that creates reality. It legitimizes particular evaluation practices, how we see ourselves, how others come to see us, the relationship between individuals and groups, and what is valued (Bierema & Cseh, 2003; Patton, 2002; Richardson, 1994).

> The power to define is the power to control, to include and exclude. . . . This root problem is the power of the dominant few to define what constitutes legitimate activity and real knowledge, and these dominant few not only define themselves as

the inclusive kind of whatever is being defined, in this case evaluator, but also as the norm and the ideal. (Patton, 2002, p. 99)

Examples of feminist research into power issues include the work of feminist economists and those writing within the field of international development. These scholars have made great strides in understanding differential labor processes, including the sexual division of labor and the shifting role of production under structural adjustment (see, e.g., Beneria & Roldan, 1987; Hartsock, 1983; Moser, 1989). These scholars have helped promote shifts in our understanding of economic theory (Blank, 1992), exploitation within the capitalist system and within the family (Bwyer & Bruce, 1988; Folbre, 1982), individual and household economic decision-making (Sen, 1990; Stitcher & Papart, 1990), and the intersection of the patriarchal state with the patriarchal family (Safa, 1995).

Centering an evaluation analysis in key gender issues, understanding the project from a feminist perspective or with a feminist lens, and engaging a wide variety of individuals as real participants in a critical discussion of the evaluation and related issues are all guidelines suggested by Ward (2002) that can be implemented to keep the evaluation true to its feminist ideals.

### Knowledge Is an Important Resource and Should Be Used for Action

Knowledge is a powerful resource within the fields of power and politics. It has immediate and long-term effects. It serves a purpose. Ethically and morally, for the feminist evaluator, knowledge should serve pressing human (social, political, and economic) needs. Knowledge is for action in the service of greater equity.

Within a feminist framework, furthermore, knowledge should be placed in service of those who have generated such knowledge: the people studied or evaluated. In particular, feminists purport that knowledge should be enacted in service of those who are most affected by structural inequities by shifting the balance of power in favor of those currently disadvantaged. Furthermore, to "know reality" requires action because reality is a process, something that is encountered and enacted in a relationship

(Reason & Rowan, 1981); or, as Marx argued, reality consists of "sensuous human activity, practice" (quoted in Hartsock, 1983). Action on research or evaluation issues may occur throughout the project, is overt, and is informed by multiple perspectives. Thus, a focus on action requires participant involvement in problem formulation, at the very least, to make possible such collaboration (Reinharz, 1989). How action is envisioned and expressed differs according to different theories. At the heart of this urge to action is Mies's (1991) explanation:

> In calling for the integration of research and science in an emancipatory process, I do not have in mind a particular action or action research model. . . . It is much more a matter of the reunification of life and thought, action and knowledge, change and research. (p. 68)

Feminist values, social justice aims, and the needs and desires of the people involved in the projects guide action strategies.

Ward (2002) suggests that feminist evaluators should exhibit a willingness to challenge the status quo. Feminist evaluators in our volume agreed that their work necessarily challenged the status quo on a number of fronts. Feminist evaluators speak of challenging academic and other institutions, programs, conventional ideas of how and which methods should be implemented, the role of the evaluator, and the field of evaluation, among other areas.

*Multiple Ways of Knowing*

Feminists have also challenged the predominantly rationally based thinking that characterizes research practices. There are many ways of knowing and many sources of knowledge: Hawkesworth (1989), for example, has mentioned "perception, intuition, conceptualization, inference, representation, reflection, imagination, remembrance," among other forms of knowing. Knowing, for feminists, is an interactive process that occurs within relationships. Emotions, intuition, and relationships themselves serve as legitimate sources of knowledge. Jane Goodall, who worked with chimpanzees, and Barbara McClintock, who worked with grains of maize, have both acknowledged the significant role that empathy, love, and affection played in leading them to make the significant contributions that they made (in Keller, 1985). Within a rationally based view of knowledge, emotions are separated from sense. Jaggar (1989) has described emotions as intentional as well as socially constructed "ways in which we engage actively, even construct the world" (pp. 152–153). Others, espousing concerns and interests similar to those of ethnographers and anthropologists, urge feminist researchers to explicitly identify the self as data source and instrument (Stanley & Wise, 1989).

In addition to focusing on who is generating the defining questions of science and of scientific studies, feminists began to ask who, or what sorts of individuals, were legitimated as "knowers." They enjoined their colleagues to consider the wisdom possessed by others not typically "sanctioned" by science as individuals capable of generating knowledge: ordinary people, nonscientists, and scientists from different racial, cultural, and socioeconomic backgrounds who possessed ideas shaped by their very different experiences in the world. Feminist social scientists within sociology, among others, rejected the idea that scientists, or feminists, could become experts in the lives of others (Stanley & Wise, 1989) and thus emphasized the importance of individuals' participation in the construction of meaning surrounding issues of significance to them. Furthermore, feminist sociologists and those within the philosophy of science criticized the tendency to usurp the knowledge of others and urged a greater emphasis on the people who are the foci of the studies conducted (Harding, 1991). Another guideline to feminist evaluation recommended by Ward is related to multiple ways of knowing. Ward exhorts us to use mixed methods to enhance our ability to "see" in different ways. We agree and would further suggest that using mixed methods has gained wider acceptance and is often simply good evaluation. Gender, of course, is a category of analysis, and feminist concepts and guidelines are used in the design, selection, and implementation of methods and in the analysis of data.

## Knowledge Is Culturally, Socially, and Temporally Contingent

Knowledge is inevitably from a perspective, colored by the social and personal experiences and characteristics of the individual. Feminist standpoint theorists posited that knowledge is always mediated by a particular (engaged and interested) position. Other feminists have been instrumental in acknowledging that knowledge is historically, culturally, and socially contingent, based on the judgments of a community of inquirers (Hawkesworth, 1989) who are, like all of us, limited in their ability to understand reality (Harding, 1991). From this perception comes the feminist concern with location and being situated.

> If we begin from the world as we actually experience it, it is at least possible to see that we are located and that what we know of the other is conditional upon that location as part of a relation comprehending the other's location also. (Smith, 1972, p. 93)

Feminists suggest that certain social positions, such as that of the oppressed, offer a unique perspective from which existing ideologies can be pierced or deconstructed (Hawkesworth, 1989). Rather than claiming or attempting to approximate objectivity, many feminist theorists recommend revealing their particular histories and characteristics, attitudes, and values for the reader to better detect where an author might favor or espouse a particular political or philosophical position. For the same reason, others urge transparency: an accounting of the research process and a clarification of the relationship between the researcher and the researched. There can be no, and it is not desirable that there be any, dispassionate research; individuals approach research questions with particular interests in the questions, people, or issues involved. Indeed, the notion of objectivity as criticized by feminists and others relies on a radical separation between self and the object of study, an idea that relies heavily on the concept of a separative self (England, 1989; Keller, 1985). Many feminist theorists suggest that it is more appropriate to consider a subjective-objectivity, a full, textured understanding of pluralistic values, beliefs, and knowledge systems of others (Lather, 1991; Reason & Rowan, 1981).

To say that knowledge is situated does not mean that nothing can be known. It does mean that to know something we are obliged to recognize and explore the unique conditions and characteristics of the issue under study. We must also be clear about the particular values, experiences, and histories through which we are filtering our understanding so that we do not essentialize the people who will ultimately be affected by our work. We must also allow for critical review of our work. Another implication of this principle is that, although we learn from our work and contribute to the knowledge that is brought to bear on similar issues, generalizability is a concept of limited usefulness for many feminist evaluators.

Ward (2002) offers as a guideline the entreaty to ensure participant input. How participation is negotiated and in what areas of an evaluation design depend on a given context. However, feminist evaluation shares a deep affinity with participatory evaluation ideas and for many of the same reasons. Not all feminist evaluators design participatory projects; however, having participant input beyond that of the subjects of data collection is an important feminist evaluation response.

## Action and Advocacy Are Morally and Ethically Appropriate Responses of an Engaged Feminist Evaluator

The role of action within feminist inquiry is predicated on an understanding of power and politics that is structural and systematic. Knowledge is described as an important resource in the move toward action. And the language we use and the dialogues we create are also constitutive elements of reality. Feminist evaluation is also committed to broader, more explicit action, including advocacy, if appropriate, and other forms of social action. Feminist evaluators join empowerment evaluation (Fetterman, 2000), diversity inclusive evaluation (Mertens, 1998), transformative participatory evaluation (see Cousins & Whitmore, 1998), and elements of democratic evaluation (House & Howe, 2000) in using critical change criteria as a means of judging the credibility of feminist evaluation (Patton, 2002).

Ward (2002) offers two guidelines related to action: (1) collaborate with advocates and activists and actively disseminate findings and (2) advocate for and with female participants.

## AN EXAMPLE OF A FEMINIST EVALUATION

Detailed examples of feminist evaluations are limited, partially because evaluators who have completed these evaluations have not yet published and partially because some feminist evaluators do not label their evaluation approaches as feminist.

In a recent evaluation conducted in upstate New York by K. Bowen (personal communication, November 2004) and others, the word *feminist* was not used, although the evaluators were working from a feminist perspective and for a foundation that often considers itself feminist in its orientation toward meeting the needs of women. This was decided in keeping with the concerns of the foundation that their public image not be construed as too radical and is not surprising considering the challenges this foundation faced early on when trying to begin a philanthropic organization that would focus on the needs of women and girls.

The challenges and successes of implementing an evaluation with a feminist approach are many. In the following section, we share a few challenges and successes using this example as illustrations.

## INCORPORATING KEY FEMINIST EVALUATION CONCEPTS

### Feminist Evaluation as a Response to "Traditional," Postpositivist, Male-Dominated Practice

Recognizing that evaluations of programs often begin from a postpositivist and male perspective, the evaluators in this project determined to pay careful attention to their own biases and the biases of those they were working with. Bowen and other members of the evaluation team were all female, well versed in feminist theory, and committed to the ideal of a feminist evaluation process. They were able to approach the evaluation with a perspective that often is not present in more traditional evaluations, and they were frequently able to challenge each other when nonfeminist biases worked their way into the design, methods, analysis, and other evaluation processes.

### Feminist Evaluation Has as a Central Focus the Gender Inequities That Lead to Social Injustice

In this evaluation project, Bowen and coworkers were intently interested in evaluating the needs of poor women in upstate New York. They understood the structural inequalities present in our society and desired to approach the evaluation attending not only to the needs of the foundation (by which they had been hired), but also reflectively to the needs of the women in the community, using a feminist perspective. For example, when program staff frequently expressed the belief that women in the community suffered from poverty due to low self-esteem, the evaluators questioned this underlying assumption and asked the poor women themselves what they thought about the relationship between self-esteem and poverty. Not surprisingly, poor women stated that though they often did suffer from low self-esteem, they believed that this was more a result than a cause of their poverty. Thus, Bowen and coworkers found that the many programs that target poor women for self-esteem–raising workshops to improve their economic situation are in a sense "putting the cart before the horse." Gender assumptions that equate women's low self-esteem with their lack of success ignore the structural inequalities that contribute to the low self-esteem of many women. The poor women interviewed for this evaluation frequently described those factors that contributed to their low self-esteem (lack of interesting jobs that pay a living wage, inadequate housing, poor health care, lack of child care, domestic violence, etc.).

### Discrimination Based on Gender Is Systemic and Structural

In this evaluation, much of the poverty suffered by these women in upstate New York was related to race, class, educational levels, and correlates with single motherhood. As our larger society continues to deal ineffectively with the needs of poor women and children, we continue to see the effects of structural inequalities throughout our country, and upstate New York does not escape these realities. It is not necessarily easy for a women-focused foundation to escape systemic practices, for example those common in the world of nonprofit programs, that assume women's experiences or capacities to be much more limited that they are.

## Evaluation and Evaluation Contexts Are Political and Imbued With Asymmetrical Power Relationships

In spite of our desire to implement a feminist evaluation and in spite of the fact that we were working with a foundation known to be sensitive to feminist ideas and the needs of women, the political realities of identifying oneself as feminist quickly surfaced. Foundation board members who participated in the evaluation objected to any language associated with feminist theory in the evaluation reports. They kept a strong hold on the progress of the evaluation and frequently denied the evaluators opportunities to move in directions that seemed important from a feminist perspective and in keeping with feminist ideals. The board members were very concerned with maintaining a particular image in the community that would foster continued financial contributions by powerful (and often conservative) local donors. Family planning, for example, was not an issue open to exploration, in spite of the fact that during interviews many women had mentioned early or frequent childbearing or both as a contributor to their current financial difficulties. This was a continual frustration for the evaluators in the process of conducting the evaluation and became an insurmountable barrier.

## Knowledge Is an Important Resource and Should Be Used for Action

It was an important criterion of the evaluators that the results of the evaluation be widely shared, not only with powerful foundation groups and program staff but also with the local woman who participated in the study. The results of the evaluation were widely disseminated both through foundation reports and in the mass media. Program staff and women being served by various programs were given access to evaluation results, and the report was also published on the Internet. In common with other feminist evaluation projects we have studied is the importance placed on disseminating results to the people actually served by the projects being evaluated.

## Multiple Ways of Knowing

The design of the evaluation included focus groups with a wide representation of program staff, participants, and foundation members. Individual interviews and surveys were also conducted, and foundation members participated at a high level in all parts of the evaluation process. In attending to the needs of the women being served, the evaluators also frequently negotiated the investigation of new questions as they emerged from the data. Bowen et al. (2002) reported not always being successful in incorporating these new questions into the evaluation as the foundation members frequently invalidated questions that arose from the perspectives of poor women and inserted new questions that arose from their own interests. Again, the evaluators attempted to include as many questions as possible that arose from those who were most in need in the community but were also careful (in a pragmatic sense) to address the concerns and interests of the foundation members who had hired them. Multiple methods were utilized to address questions of interest to the foundation members, program staff, program recipients, and the evaluators themselves. As mentioned previously, interviews, surveys, focus groups, document analysis, statistical analysis of federal and state census data, and frequent participatory meetings with foundation members were all part of the evaluation process. In keeping with their concern about their image, foundation members often valued quantitative data more highly than qualitative data, and frequent negotiation and explanation of the benefits of various methods and evaluation approaches were necessary.

## Knowledge Is Culturally, Socially, and Temporally Contingent. Knowledge Is Also Filtered Through the Knower

What was valued at the end of this project's evaluation was not necessarily what evaluators would have considered to be the most important findings. In the end, the foundation members picked through the evaluation findings cafeteria style and chose to address those concerns that matched most closely their own ideas about what were the most important needs in the community. Though the evaluators believed they had presented a comprehensive summary of the needs of poor women in the upstate New York community, it was the prerogative of the foundation to select those needs they felt most able to address. For example, although access to family planning and adequate, affordable housing may have been identified as the two greatest needs by poor women, the foundation chose instead to focus on education, development of job skills, and better referral networks between programs, areas commonly supported by local wealthy donors and perhaps more easily achieved through bounded social programs. As feminist evaluators, Bowen and coworkers also realized that what we choose to focus on in what we see (even affordable housing and family planning) are in part a product of what those of us asking the questions have experienced, where we have lived, the range of theoretical possibilities we have allowed into our consciousness, and the currents of the time in which we live.

## Action and Advocacy Are Morally and Ethically Appropriate Responses of an Engaged Feminist Evaluator

The power to promote action and change through feminist evaluation is a complicated and labor-intensive task. In this particular example, Bowen and coworkers were not residents of the community in which they conducted the evaluation. Foundation members who reside in the community and who participated in the study will be the ones to carry forth the results and implement change in ways that seem most appropriate to them. The wide publication of the evaluation report in various mediums, including the Internet, increases the potential for action. The lessons learned from this evaluation will likely also be carried forth by the feminist evaluators who participated in this process as advocates for the evaluation recommendations personally as well as professionally. Feminist evaluators are also committed to promoting the contributions of feminist evaluation to the field.

## CHALLENGES TO FEMINIST EVALUATION AND THE RESULTING DEBATE

In the short term, feminist evaluators find themselves in the position of having to respond to criticism and challenges posed by evaluation practitioners and theorists not inclined to be open to feminist principles; all models that have challenged the status quo have engaged in discussions surrounding these questions. Many of these challenges arise in a context of beliefs and assumptions that have been long held as inviolable truth, often accepted without critical reflection. Because feminist evaluation challenges the assumptions on which these questions are based, theorists have begun to respond to the spirit of the questions posed as understood from within a feminist inquiry perspective. Some of the most common questions raised by critics, and the feminist reframing of these issues, appear below. The foregoing discussion and the discussion that follows provide some responses to these questions.

## Challenges to Feminist Evaluation as a Legitimate Evaluation Model

1. How does feminist evaluation ensure objectivity? Feminist reframing: What procedures and stances do we introduce to ensure that we are making the best effort to know or assess what is happening? Who is asking the questions and from what position?

2. Of what use are your findings if they are not generalizable (or extendable) to other similar situations? Feminist reframing: For whom are we producing "knowledge"? What constitutes knowledge? How open are we to other ways of knowing?

3. Doesn't a focus on action compromise the center of evaluation practice, making of evaluation, advocacy? Feminist reframing: How (and to what extent) should an evaluator be involved in social action aimed at meeting the needs of those involved in the evaluation project? What

is the role of action in evaluation practice and how do we define action?

4. Doesn't the action agenda and involvement of the evaluator compromise, if not prevent, validity? Feminist reframing: What constitutes validity, and what is needed in order to create meaningful and credible results? Who is being affected by our work and in what ways? How should we orient ourselves to the cultural and social challenges of changing demographics and economic trends?

## Challenges to the Practical Implementation of Feminist Evaluation

1. Does it matter whether or not an evaluation is named a feminist evaluation? When and with whom should that naming occur? How important is the naming, and in what cases should an evaluator call herself or himself a feminist evaluator?

2. In what cases and under what circumstances is a feminist evaluation possible? Desirable?

3. What expectations should we realistically have of those implementing feminist evaluations?

Challenges to feminist evaluation as a legitimate evaluation practice are largely addressed in the section on feminist theory. We discussed the use of mixed methods and participation as means of insuring that we are better positioned to recognize the underlying regularities that are "reality." Feminist theory encourages us to disclose who we are, to engage in self-reflexive practices and dialogue with others as we focus and refocus on key feminist concepts and guidelines. We have discussed the idea that knowledge is primarily a resource for the people who have generated that knowledge, that there are multiple ways of knowing and forms of knowledge (including emotions and intuition, for example), and that knowledge is not only a powerful resource for action; its final end is action.

However, it is important that we say a few more words about the role of action and advocacy in evaluation. Feminist evaluation, as previously mentioned, is not the only evaluation model that proposes action as an important,

even necessary, element of the evaluation enterprise. Whether or not action and advocacy are appropriate roles for the evaluator is one of several contemporary debates hotly contested among evaluation professionals. Most evaluators, however, would agree that evaluation findings should be useful, that building capacity through evaluation is a positive outcome, and that evaluators are well-positioned to facilitate how findings may be used to improve social programs.

Critics like Scriven suggest that truth and objectivity, although not understood in the same manner as they were understood under a positivist paradigm, remain critical to the evaluation enterprise and that critiques of truth and objectivity levied by empowerment models and others go too far in their distancing from these terms and from traditional evaluation practice (see Scriven, 1997). Indeed, not all feminist evaluators or participatory evaluation practitioners reframe the notion of truth and objectivity as described in the foregoing for the reasons that Scriven describes as well as because of a need to convince particular audiences of the legitimacy of their claims (Truman, 2002). Scriven has spoken strongly against the idea that the evaluator serve as an advocate; the evaluator's role is to be an empiricist and logician. Few feminist evaluators, regardless of how wedded they are to objectivity, would see their role as so narrowly defined, even if they were uncomfortable with a more engaged advocacy position. Stake has written that evaluators should resist and minimize advocacy even if engaged in helping others recognize the kinds of advocacies present. He suggests that some types of advocacy are acceptable whereas others are not and that a key issue of concern for the profession should be the lack of rigorous debate and holding each other to standards. "Advocacy for educational reform, curricular remediation, and pedagogical change . . . are fundamental to our work. . . . But we seem to be moving further and further into advocacy of little-agreed-upon values. And of course we know that some advocacies are not acceptable" (Stake, 1997, p. 475). On the other side of the fence, Stake names Jennifer Greene (1995), who has written that advocacy, like politics, is inherent in evaluation and so the decision becomes for whom we advocate and in what ways. Greene suggests that we advocate for the program participants.

There is no one feminist evaluation position on action and advocacy. However, the continuum is shaped by an interest in the welfare of the individuals who are the subject of study, in ensuring that the evaluation findings are used and correctly understood, particularly when the stakes are high, and in conducting evaluations and dissemination of findings that will be put to use in the service of achieving greater social justice with respect to gender inequities. Many feminist evaluators would find themselves strongly aligned with Greene.

Some of the challenges to the practical implementation of feminist evaluation will be addressed in the following section. However, language is an important issue that requires attention. Patton (2002) wrote on the role of language in feminist evaluation in preparation for his chapter in the *New Directions* feminist evaluation volume. In a section not included in the final volume he writes that language, like gender, matters and that, furthermore, "calling an evaluation a 'feminist evaluation' is a political act, one hopefully taken with intentionality and knowledge. However, the primary elements of feminist evaluation can be manifest in a design without attaching the feminist label." What is important to consider, he suggests, is what may be gained and what may be lost in the naming or not naming.

Among feminist evaluators, this is not an easily resolved matter. For some, self-reflexive practice and disclosure require us to be up front and honest about who we are, our values, and our agendas. In such cases, a key concern may be how we present ourselves as feminists and how we present feminist evaluation—as the sole model or as one of two or more models or as supporting ideology. Where a feminist evaluation can be called a feminist evaluation, it should be. However, others take the position that social change, particularly with respect to gender inequity, will not happen if we only speak to those sympathetic to and comfortable with feminist ideals. Taking this position raises many questions: Are we suggesting that a relationship must be formed before feminist evaluation can be a possibility? If the key feminist concepts are employed and other stakeholder evaluation needs and interests are met, are we accomplishing the goals of feminist evaluation?

Is it more in keeping with feminist ideas to work for a greater awareness of these issues in an evaluation that uses another model as the dominant guiding force? Can such feminist concerns be advanced if we do not promote feminist evaluation as legitimate?

Feminist evaluation (like participatory evaluation) has been criticized for being idealist, promoting romantic unrealistic notions of what the evaluator practitioner should achieve, and what she or he must be. Perhaps this is related to the passionate nature of the proponents of feminist evaluation who are deeply committed in their personal lives to social change. Perhaps we, as evaluation practitioners, are not used to discussing personal standards outside the ethical standards of our profession. Perhaps we would be better served by presenting expectations in more practical language: Instead of urging practitioners to be self-reflexive, we could speak of the methods by which other ways of knowing and awareness of biases may be documented; instead of encouraging participation, we could provide guidelines of various circumstances and show how feminist theory helps in the selection of participation; we could clarify levels of action and advocacy and give guidance as to making choices between levels of involvement.

Other questions such as "How should we orient ourselves to the cultural and social challenges of changing demographics and economic trends?" are the subject of ongoing debate and dialogue. Indeed, many of the how questions raised by feminist evaluators and others may be answered: Reflexively, in dialogue, and with a constant revisiting of the feminist guidelines and theoretical ideas we have chosen to follow in the focusing of the feminist lens.

## Implementing Feminist Evaluation

The implementation of feminist evaluation, like other models, can be more challenging than the theoretical discussion. In fact, Roy (2004) has suggested that

> what the feminist inquiry does . . . is to ask the scientist to uncover the social and political forces driving their research questions as well as establish a relationship with their research subject(s).

Perhaps the real problem that traditional scientists have with feminism is that they are not up to the intellectual challenge presented by the feminist inquiry. (p. 276)

Questions such as who can do feminist evaluation, when or in what circumstances can feminist evaluation be done, and what methods are appropriate within a feminist evaluation are all debated in the evaluation field. Some evaluators will argue that feminist evaluation can only be done by evaluators with a feminist orientation. Others will argue that feminist issues and concerns can be addressed by including feminist viewpoints in the design and implementation of evaluation studies. Although many examples of feminist research exist, few studies using a feminist evaluation approach have been published to date. Recent examples can be found in the *New Directions for Evaluation* issue edited by Seigart and Brisolara (2002).

Just as there is no orthodox feminism and the set of guidelines that define feminist evaluation are emerging, there are multiple ways of implementing feminist evaluation. In the brief discussion that follows, we address the key elements of implementation, sharing our perspective on the parameters of implementation from a feminist evaluation perspective. These elements include who can be a feminist evaluator, what methods are legitimate within a feminist evaluation, in what circumstances one can implement a feminist evaluation, and how feminist evaluations are implemented.

Although many evaluation practitioners would argue that women are better suited to conduct feminist evaluation, given their social positions and, hence, ability to identify with gender discrimination and develop a feminist perspective, most would agree that not sex but ideology and theory are the most important criteria determining who might be a feminist evaluator. What is critical is that an evaluator be well-versed in feminist theory, hold key feminist values, and actively express and engage these values within her or his evaluation practice. A feminist evaluator should be willing to explore and adhere to feminist values in the design, implementation, and analysis stages of evaluation and must be prepared to be self-reflexive and to willingly disclose potential conflicts of interest, sources of privilege, and other areas where who she or he is may obfuscate or distort what participants or the subjects of the evaluation project experience or articulate. She or he must be able and willing to engage in and reflect the lived experiences of women or other evaluation subjects.

Not only women are feminist evaluators and not only women are the subjects of feminist evaluation. Truman (2002) provides us with an example of a feminist evaluation conducted with gay and bisexual men with the end being policy development. For the most part, the experiences of women are the focus of feminist evaluations. However, the central concern of feminist evaluation is structural, systematic discrimination that perpetuates gender inequality and in some cases, for example, those affected by such discrimination are gay men or transgendered individuals.

Earlier in the development of feminist inquiry, qualitative methods, particularly the unstructured interview, were seen as being the feminist inquiry method of choice. It is true that qualitative methods do provide a greater opportunity for the subject-based expression of lived experiences and allow for the emergence of unanticipated thoughts and understandings. However, individuals engaged in feminist evaluation have often found themselves in need of quantitative data and most are proponents of mixed-method evaluation designs for the same reasons that other evaluators use mixed-method designs. Ward (2002) suggests that one of the guidelines for conducting a feminist evaluation is the use of mixed methods and describes the value of using mixed methods in her analysis of an adolescent gender violence prevention program. Beardsley and Miller (2002) administered surveys that collected quantitative and qualitative information in their three-phase study of a women's substance abuse program. Bamberger and Podems (2002) discuss the value of implementing mixed-method evaluation designs, noting that evaluations conducted in the context of international development experience several constraints but could benefit from such a mixing of methods and that new guidelines in the field recommend the use of multiple methods. Feminist evaluators concur with Harding: Methods are not feminist or nonfeminist. What is important is the methodology that one selects in applying particular mixed methods and the way in which methods are chosen and implemented (Hood & Cassaro, 2002; Reinharz, 1992).

It is more difficult for feminist evaluators to come to a consensus regarding in what circumstances a feminist evaluation can or should be implemented. Earlier in this chapter we discussed the significance of whether or not we call an evaluation a feminist evaluation. But what are the parameters under which a feminist evaluation should be implemented, regardless of what it is called? There are many questions that arise in this regard. For example, how much resistance to a feminist approach is too much resistance? To what extent should concerns about the legitimacy of the project to external agencies determine whether or not a feminist evaluation model should be used? In other words, are the feminist aims of the project or evaluation better served by bringing a feminist perspective to a different evaluation model and sacrificing other elements of a feminist evaluation? To what extent should the economic environment determine whether or not one uses more traditional evaluation models?

Contributors to the feminist evaluation model did not address these questions directly. However, their work provides us with some clues as to the direction(s) feminist evaluators may take. To force a feminist evaluation model is antithetical to the nature of the feminist evaluation project, and, depending on the political context, pushing a feminist evaluation can seriously jeopardize the feminist and other aims of the evaluation project. Bamberger and Podems (2002) note that, given the importance of cultural sensitivity to feminist evaluation and to evaluations in the international development context, rather than assuming a feminist agenda, creating a space in which a range of issues can be discussed is important. Truman (2002) writes that an evaluator's legitimacy and credibility to the audience(s) contracting the evaluation are an important primary factor that, ostensibly, helps to legitimize the evaluation model chosen. Finally, Patton (2002) reminds us that in the world of praxis, models and criteria from different evaluation frameworks are often mixed, suggesting that a feminist evaluation model can contribute significantly to an evaluation without being implemented in its "pure" form and without making feminist evaluation the dominant evaluation model.

Feminist evaluators, as is true of other challenger models, tend to be imbued in theory but pragmatic in implementation, seeking an engaged praxis. A few guidelines in making a decision about a circumstance include the following. The evaluator leading a feminist evaluation should either be a feminist evaluator or identify strongly with the key values of feminist evaluation. The lead evaluator should not operate in isolation, even if participatory methods are implemented; continued dialogue and reflection should be the manner in which the lead evaluator operates. We would suggest that an initial resistance to feminist evaluation does not preclude a feminist evaluation from emerging, through dialogue and discussion. However, strong resistance to such an approach limits the effectiveness of the evaluation or any action that may occur as a result. Feminist evaluation values would also suggest that a feminist evaluation not be implemented if the risk of doing so will be borne by participants in the project who are those ostensibly served by the program.

How feminist evaluations are implemented may vary widely; however, there are some key role responsibilities for the feminist evaluator. The feminist evaluator should engage in dialogue with key stakeholders of the project, immerse herself or himself as much as possible in the evaluation context, reflexively engage with others to understand and check out emerging ideas and analyses, and self-disclose (to others but also by documenting one's own reflections) regarding any biases or identities that might lead to limits in perspective. Reflexivity and keeping feminist evaluation guidelines in the forefront of one's work and thought can aid in paying attention to language and power dynamics within the evaluation; once observed or once such issues are raised, the feminist evaluator is called on to work toward restoring power balance within the evaluation setting. Finally, it is important that the feminist evaluator keep in mind that the purpose of the evaluation is action and specific use of the evaluation findings.

## The Future of Feminist Evaluation

Feminist evaluation, like other evaluation models, will face various challenges in the coming years. Some of those challenges are ones that will affect the profession as a whole. Technological changes bring new methods and change the ways in which we implement old methods. One simple example is the way we might design and calculate error for telephone surveys, given the effect of cell phone-only households, caller ID, call blocking, and the tendency to screen calls. Current legislation (such as the No Child Left Behind Act, welfare reform measures, and the Patriot Act) might have profound effects on families, in particular female-headed households, and on activism. Changing demographics in the United States and increasingly diverse communities will not only change the face of how we do evaluation but also the methods that we choose. Increasing diversity will inevitably change the face of feminism as well as the context in which feminism operates. New voices will emerge from new arenas.

Feminist evaluation will likely continue to struggle with some of the same questions that it has attempted to influence since its inception. There is a continuing debate, for example, on what the role of the evaluator should be (partner, critical friend, advocate, or objective assessor of facts), what the purpose of evaluation should be (action, use, knowledge, program improvement, accountability, or what measure of each), what practitioners think about current and emerging evaluation theories and their methods, and what can be learned from and by emerging evaluation fields in countries around the globe. Feminist evaluation will likely, given the divergent interests of its practitioners, continue simultaneously to push for legitimacy and to work from outside officially sanctioned models, continually pressing for changes its adherents believe are needed in the field. We believe that the field will be richer for its contributions.

## Note

1. In this section, we use *feminist theorists* as a convenient means of describing those scholars and practitioners who contributed directly or indirectly to the development of feminist thought, recognizing that their definitions of feminism or of feminist priorities may differ significantly.

## References

Bamberger, M., & Podems, D. (2002). Feminist evaluation in the international development context. In D. Seigart & S. Brisolara (Eds.), *New directions for evaluation: Vol. 96. Feminist evaluation: Explorations and experiences* (pp. 83–96). San Francisco: Jossey-Bass.

Beardsley, R., & Miller, M. (2002). Revisioning the process: A case study in feminist program evaluation. In D. Seigart & S. Brisolara (Eds.), *New directions for evaluation: Vol. 96. Feminist evaluation: Explorations and experiences* (pp. 57–70). San Francisco: Jossey-Bass.

Beneria, L., & Roldan, M. (1987). *The crossroads of class and gender: Industrial homework, subcontracting, and households dynamics in Mexico City*. Chicago: University of Chicago Press.

Bhavnani, K.-K. (1993). Tracing the contours: Feminist research and feminist objectivity. *Women's Studies International Forum, 16*(2), 95–104.

Bierema, L., & Cseh, M. (2003). Evaluating AHRD research using a feminist research framework. *Human Resource Development Quarterly, 14*(1), 5–26.

Blank, R. M. (1992). A female perspective on economic man? In S. Rosenberg Salk & J. Gordon-Kelter (Eds.), *Revolutions in knowledge: Feminism in the social sciences* (pp. 111–124). Boulder, CO: Westview Press.

Bowen, K., Brisolara, S., Seigart, D., Tischler, C., & Whitmore, E. (2002). Exploring feminist evaluation: the ground from which we rise. In D. Seigart & S. Brisolara (Eds.), *New directions for evaluation: Vol. 96. Feminist evaluation: Explorations and experiences* (pp. 3–8). San Francisco: Jossey-Bass.

Brisolara, S. (1998). The history of participatory evaluation and current debates in the field. In B. Cousins & E. Whitmore (Eds.), *New directions for evaluation: Vol. 80. Understanding and practicing participatory evaluation* (pp. 25–42). San Francisco: Jossey-Bass.

Bwyer, D., & Bruce, J. (1988). *A home divided: Women and income in the Third World*. Stanford, CA: Stanford University Press.

Cousins, B., & Whitmore, E. (1998). Framing participatory evaluation. In E. Whitmore (Ed.), *New directions for evaluation: Vol. 80. Understanding and practicing participatory evaluation* (pp. 5–24). San Francisco: Jossey-Bass.

England, P. (1989). A feminist critique of rational choice theories: Implications for sociology. *American Sociologist, 20*(1), 14–28.

Fausto-Sterling, A. (1993). The five sexes: Why female and male are not enough. *Sciences, 33*(2), 20–25.

Fetterman, D. (1992). In response to Lee Sechrest's 1991 AEA presidential address: "Roots: Back to Our First Generations." *Evaluation Practice, 13*(3), 171–172.

Fetterman, D. M. (2000). *Foundations of empowerment evaluation: Step by step.* Thousand Oaks, CA: Sage.

Folbre, N. (1982). Exploitation comes home: A critique of the Marxian theory of family labour. *Cambridge Journal of Economics, 6,* 317–329.

Fox-Genovese, E. (1992). *Feminism without illusions: A critique of individualism.* Chapel Hill: University of North Carolina Press.

Greene, J. (1995, November). *Evaluators as advocates.* Paper presented at the annual meeting of the American Evaluation Association, Vancouver, Canada.

Harding, S. (1983). Why has the sex/gender system become visible only now? In S. Harding & M. Hintikka (Eds.), *Discovering reality: Feminist perspectives on epistemology, metaphysics, methodology, and philosophy of science* (pp. 311–325). Dordrecht, the Netherlands: Reidel.

Harding, S. (1990). Feminism, science and the anti-enlightenment critiques. In L. J. Nicholson (Ed.), *Feminism/postmodernism* (pp. 83–106). New York: Routledge.

Harding, S. (1991). *Whose science? Whose knowledge?* Ithaca, NY: Cornell University Press.

Hartsock, N. (1983). The feminist standpoint: Developing a ground for a specifically feminist historical materialism. In S. Harding & M. Hintikka (Eds.), *Discovering reality: Feminist perspectives on epistemology, metaphysics, methodology and philosophy of science* (pp. 283–310). Dordrecht, The Netherlands: D. Reidel.

Hawkesworth, M. E. (1989). Knowers, knowing, known: Feminist theory and the claims of truth. *Signs: Journal of Women in Culture and Society, 14*(31).

Hood, D., & Cassaro, D. (2002). Feminist evaluation and the inclusion of difference. In D. Seigart & S. Brisolara (Eds.), *New directions for evaluation: Vol. 96. Feminist evaluation: Explorations and experiences* (pp. 27–40). San Francisco: Jossey-Bass

House, E. R., & Howe, K. R. (2000). Deliberative democratic evaluation. In K. E. Ryan & L. De Stephano (Eds.), *New directions for evaluation: Vol. 85. Evaluation as a democratic process: Promoting inclusion, dialogue and deliberation* (pp. 3–12). San Francisco: Jossey-Bass.

Hurtado, A. (1996). Strategic suspensions: Feminists of color theorize the production of knowledge. In N. R. Goldberger, J. M. Tarule, B. M. Clinchy, & B. Belenky (Eds.), *Knowledge, difference and power: Essays inspired by women's ways of knowing* (pp. 372–392). New York: Basic Books.

Jaggar, A. M. (1989). Love and knowledge: Emotion in feminist epistemology. In A. M. Jaggar & S. R. Bordo (Eds.), *Gender/body/knowledge: Feminist reconstructions of being and knowledge* (pp. 145–171). New Brunswick, NJ: Rutgers University Press.

Keller, E. F. (1985). *Reflections on gender and science.* New Haven, CT: Yale University Press.

Lather, P. (1991). *Getting smart: Feminist research and pedagogy with/in the postmodern.* New York: Routledge.

McTaggart, R. (1991). *Action research: A short modern history.* Geelong, Victoria, Australia: Deakin University Press.

Mertens, D. M. (1998). *Research methods in education and psychology: Integrating diversity with quantitative and qualitative approaches.* Thousand Oaks, CA: Sage.

Mies, M. (1991). Women's research or feminist research? The debate surrounding feminist science and methodology (A. Spencer, Trans.). In M. M. Fonow & J. A. Cook (Eds.), *Beyond methodology: Feminist scholarship as lived research* (pp. 60–84). Bloomington: Indiana University Press.

Moser, C. (1989). The impact of recession and adjustment policies at the micro-level: Low income women and their households in Guayaquil, Ecuador. In UNICEF (Ed.), *The invisible adjustment: Poor women and the economic crisis* (pp. 137–166). Santiago, Chile: UNICEF.

Noffke, S. (1994). Action research: Towards the next generation. *Educational Action Research, 2*(1), 9–21.

Patton, M. Q. (2002). Feminist, yes, but is it evaluation? In D. Seigart & S. Brisolara (Eds.), *New directions for evaluation: Vol. 96. Feminist evaluation: Explorations and experiences* (pp. 97–108). San Francisco: Jossey-Bass.

Reason, P., & Rowan, J. (Eds.). (1981). *Human inquiry: A sourcebook of new paradigm research*. New York: Wiley.

Reinharz, S. (1989). Experiential analysis: A contribution to feminist research. In S. Bowles & R. D. Klein (Eds.), *Theories of women's studies* (pp. 162–191). London: Routledge & Kegan Paul.

Reinharz, S. (1992). *Feminist methods in social research*. New York: Oxford University Press.

Richardson, L. (1994). Writing: A method of inquiry. In N. K. Denzin & Y. S. Lincoln (Eds.), *Handbook of qualitative research* (pp. 516–529). Thousand Oaks, CA: Sage.

Rossi, P. H., & Freeman, H. E. (1993). *Evaluation: A systematic approach* (5th ed.). Newbury Park, CA: Sage.

Roy, D. (2004). Feminist theory in science: Working toward a practical transformation. *Hypatia, 19*(1), 255–279.

Safa, H. I. (1995). Economic restructuring and gender subordination. *Latin American Perspectives, 22*(2), 32–50.

Schwandt, T. (1991). Evaluation as moral critique. In C. L. Larson & H. Preskill (Eds.), *New directions for evaluation: Vol. 49. Organizations in transition: Opportunities and challenges for evaluation*. San Francisco: Jossey-Bass.

Scriven, M. (1997). Truth and objectivity in evaluation. In E. Chelimsky & W. Shadish (Eds.), *Evaluation for the 21st century: A handbook* (pp. 477–500). Thousand Oaks, CA: Sage.

Seigart, D., & Brisolara, S. (Eds.). (2002). *New directions for evaluation: Vol. 96. Feminist evaluation: Explorations and experiences*. San Francisco: Jossey-Bass.

Sen, A. K. (1990). Gender and cooperative conflicts. In I. Tinker (Ed.), *Persistent inequalities: Women and world development*. New York: Oxford University Press.

Smith, D. E. (1972, June). Presentation at the meeting of the American Academy for the Advancement of Science (Pacific Division), Eugene, OR.

Stake, R. (1997). Advocacy in evaluation: A necessary evil? In E. Chelimsky & W. Shadish (Eds.), *Evaluation for the 21st century: A handbook* (pp. 470–476). Thousand Oaks, CA: Sage.

Stanley, L., & Wise, S. (1989). "Back into the personal" or: Our attempt to construct "feminist research." In S. Bowles & R. D. Klein (Eds.), *Theories of women's studies* (pp. 192–209). London: Routledge & Kegan Paul.

Stitcher, S., & Papart, J. L. (1990). *Women, employment and the family in the international division of labor*. Philadelphia: Temple University Press.

Truman, C. (2002). Doing feminist evaluation with men: Achieving objectivity in a sexual health needs assessment. In D. Seigart & S. Brisolara (Eds.), *New directions for evaluation: Vol. 96. Feminist evaluation: Explorations and experiences* (pp. 71–82). San Francisco: Jossey-Bass.

Ward, K. (2002). Reflections of a job done: Well? In D. Seigart & S. Brisolara (Eds.), *New directions for evaluation: Vol. 96. Feminist evaluation: Explorations and experiences* (pp. 41–56). San Francisco: Jossey-Bass.

Weiss, H. B., & Greene, J. (1992). An empowerment partnership for family support and education programs and evaluation. *Family and Science Review, 5,* 131–149.

Whitmore, E. (Ed.). (1998). *New directions for evaluation: Vol. 80. Understanding and practicing participatory evaluation* (pp. 5–24). San Francisco: Jossey-Bass.

# 14

# PARTICIPATORY AND ACTION RESEARCH AND FEMINISMS

## Toward Transformative Praxis

M. BRINTON LYKES

ERZULIE COQUILLON

Community- or organization-based research projects by local participants and university-based researchers seeking to transform social inequalities have been described as action research (AR), participatory research (PR), or participatory action research (PAR). Some have argued that these approaches to knowledge generation and social change can be traced back to early Greek philosophers or to indigenous communities (see, e.g., Eikeland, 2001). Others trace their beginnings to 20th-century social scientific research, more specifically to the work of Kurt Lewin in the 1940s and the experiential learning and inquiry communities of the 1960s (see Adelman, 1993; Greenwood and Levin, 1998; Gustavsen, 2001). Moreover, action research contributed significantly to the fields of organizational behavior and development, introducing strategies for enhancing communication and cooperation as well as system changes. Lewin and his students developed such practices in industry and business (Whyte, 1991).

Adelman (1993) defined action research as a "means of systematic enquiry for all participants in the quest for greater effectiveness through democratic participation" (p. 7). This approach was later extended into the fields of sociology, psychology, and education. In the latter arena, Zeichner (2001) identified five major traditions in the English-speaking world and argued that some of these draw on the emancipatory practices developed in Asia, Africa, and Latin America, extending their focus beyond the school to the local community (see also Brydon-Miller & Greenwood, 2003, for a brief historical overview). This emancipatory perspective moved well beyond Lewin's work, which did not include a critique of the wider society or consider "power bases that define social roles and strongly influence the process of any change" (Adelman, 1993, p. 10).

Those who live and work in Latin America, Africa, and Asia and engage in PAR, AR, and PR are more likely to trace the origin of their praxis to the work of Paulo Freire (1970) or the early

PAR of Orlando Fals-Borda and Mohammad Anisur Rahman (Fals-Borda, 1985; Fals-Borda & Rahman, 1991). In the late 1960s and 1970s in India and Latin America, liberation educators and social change advocates were influenced by Paolo Freire's understanding of critical consciousness, that is, *conscientização* (conscientization). These educators and community activists sought to create participatory processes that tap into and engage local knowledge systems toward emancipatory practices. Participatory rural appraisal (PRA) within the context of community development and humanitarian aid initiatives in rural communities of Africa and Asia embraces similar values.

## SHARED VALUES AND GOALS: APPROXIMATING AN UNDERSTANDING

Despite many differences in context, origin, and specific methods, the theoretical assumptions underlying most forms of participatory and action research draw on systems theory, humanistic values and the development of human potential, democratic participation and decision making, and action or change. Action researchers seek to promote collective processes of inquiry that expose the ideological, political, and social processes underlying and permeating systems of inequality. They seek solutions to everyday problems and—to a greater or lesser extent— to transform the social inequalities exposed through research by facilitating and engaging in specific actions that contribute to human well-being and a more just and equitable world. PAR, AR, and PR are approaches to research wherein collaborations or partnerships are formed between those directly affected by an issue or problem that becomes the focus of the project (often called insiders, participants, community members) and others with technical skills and formal knowledge (often called outsiders, researchers, facilitators, catalysts) that complement indigenous knowledge systems and expertise to facilitate knowledge construction, education, collaborative learning, and transformative action. Participatory and action research, thus, emphasizes the processes as well as the outcomes of research and the sharing of results within and beyond the participant communities.

PAR, AR, and PR projects seek to generate knowledge and practice that is of genuine interest to all coresearchers.[1] Thus, they necessitate the development of "mutually dependent and cooperative relationships" (Martin, 1996, p. 88). Participants engaged in PAR, AR, and PR transform themselves at a very personal level, and the process typically politicizes them with respect to relationships and to the desired outcomes (Khanna, 1996). The generation of shared spaces wherein the various knowledge systems and skill levels of all research participants can be valued, shared, and exchanged is critical to this work. These spaces facilitate the development of shared procedures for generating, appraising, and reflecting on the data gathered during the research process.

Participatory and action research as methodology and epistemology challenges the myth of neutrality and objectivity that exists in much empirical social scientific and educational research. It emphasizes subjectivity and involvement throughout the research process and strives for consensual validation through data collection and analysis formulated around local priorities. Institutional, professional, or personal interests and choices are negotiated within a primary commitment to generate knowledge and action toward addressing immediate social issues or problems.

An understanding of knowledge as socially constructed in particular social, cultural, and linguistic communities, which is characteristic of most participatory and action research, has contributed to Peter Reason and Hilary Bradbury's (2001) argument that action researchers have embraced the mid-20th-century postmodern linguistic and cognitive turn within social science. Moreover, the problem-posing methods inherent in these methodologies presume that there is a "real" reality that facilitates and constrains all social relations, thus confirming that participatory and action researchers embrace at least the basic assumption of positivism that there is a real and material social world. The turn toward action, characteristic of all action research, enriches the interface of the modern and postmodern and creates a synergy that is shared by the diversities of practice emergent among participatory and action researchers. Finally, although individual researchers distinguish among PAR, AR, and PR, we use the phrase *participatory and action research* when referring to this research tradition as a whole and use specific abbreviations (AR, PR, PAR, PRA, etc.) as reflective of their usage by specific researchers whose work we discuss.

## FEMINISMS AND THE RESEARCH PROCESS

Although early participatory and action researchers criticized power inequalities and sought to redress social injustice, they failed either to include women as independent actors in their local projects or to problematize gender oppression and heterosexism. Women and, more specifically, feminists were marginal(ized) in the early articulations of these research processes as well as in professional gatherings (see, e.g., Maguire, 2001, for details). Yet during this same time, feminists were making important contributions to social movement building (see, e.g., Evans, 1979; Freeman, 1975; Friedan, 1963; Rosen, 2000) and to university-based scholarship (see, e.g., Personal Narratives Group, 1989; Roberts, 1981).

Despite the importance of this work, the second wave of the U.S.-based women's movement (see, e.g., Firestone, 1970; Millet, 1969; Rosen, 2000), from whence feminism within the academy drew its early energy and critical edge, was criticized by women of color for its oversimplified and universalizing tendency to essentialize women's oppression and ignore diversities of race and social class (see, e.g., Davis, 1981; Moraga & Anzaldúa, 1983; Spelman, 1988). Ignoring the particularities and specificities of women's experiences, the women's movements and early feminist scholarship failed to analyze critically racism and class oppression within and among its adherents and to create spaces wherein the diversities of women's experiences were analyzed and coalitions formed across those diversities to redress gendered, racial, and class-based inequalities of power (see, e.g., Collins, 1998; hooks, 1981; Lorde, 1982, 1984; among many others). More recent feminist discourse and organizing, particularly the work of women of color within the United States (hooks, 1984) and of postcolonial theorists of color (Mohanty, 2003; Trinh, 1989; Williams &

Chrisman, 1994), challenge the white privilege characteristic of much second-wave feminist organizing and scholarship and contribute to the development of an increasingly diverse critical feminist theory, research, and practice.

Early contributions to an emerging field of feminist research methodology include Barbara Du Bois (1983), Sherna Gluck and Daphne Patai (1991), Sandra Harding (1986), and the Personal Narratives Group (1989). This work has been significantly complemented and extended by the work of postcolonial theorists (e.g., Sandoval, 2000), which informs contemporary theory and activist research, particularly work that crosses national, linguistic, and cultural borders (see, e.g., Mitchell & Reid-Walsh, 2002; Mohanty, 2003). Working at the interface of feminist movements, theory, and research is challenging. Feminist academics or scholars who infuse their work with feminist values and ideals seek, minimally, to design research that looks for what has been left out of previous research and to use gender as an analytic tool (see Stewart, 1998). Others argue that feminist research is not (only) about gender differences but critically explores aspects of social status and the participants' positionalities (see Collins, 1990; Naples, 2003; Smith, 1987, 1991). Thus, many feminist researchers focus their work on raising awareness or generating consciousness (their own and that of others with whom they work) about gendered oppression and how it constrains women's lives.

The sociologist Shulamit Reinharz (1992) summarized the dramatically diverse range of feminist research practices in *Feminist Methods in Social Research.* She argued that feminism is a perspective, not a research method, and identified seven themes characteristic of feminist research, including being guided by feminist theory, involving an ongoing criticism of nonfeminist scholarship, being trans- or interdisciplinary, aiming to create social change, and striving to represent human diversity. Feminist research is not, according to Reinharz, methodologically rigid but, rather, uses a multiplicity of research methods. The diversity of feminist research and a parallel diversity of methods published over the past 20 years (see, e.g., *Feminism & Psychology* [1991 to date] or *Signs* [1975 to date]) confirms Reinharz's plea for flexibility in defining this body of work.

This flexibility in feminist research methodology is reflected, for example, in the following studies, which contribute to understanding and organizing within and among low-income women workers, that is, those who have been typically "left out of" the researcher's gaze. The sociologist Heidi Gottfried, at Purdue University, offered her expertise to labor unions as a pro bono consultant and used, among other methods, a demographic study of clerical workers to help in organizing drives (Gottfried, 1996). Using an activist research methodology that included interviews and participant observations, Pierrette Hondagneu-Sotelo (1996) worked with illegal immigrant women in paid domestic work in California. She engaged with the women as a *servidora,* or informal social worker, to gain entry into this community, to better understand their lives as immigrants, and to develop novellas, "booklets with captioned photographs" (p. 106), that tell a story and serve as organizing resources.

In addition to this diversity of methods, feminists using a single research method do so from different epistemological stances or frameworks. For example, constructivist or critical theorist feminists may distribute surveys or engage other, more positivist research methods to gain understanding of or develop a critique of existing relations for the purpose of transforming them rather than for the purposes of explanation, prediction, or control characteristic of more positivist and postpositivist research designs (Denzin & Lincoln, 2000). Similarly, researchers who position themselves within positivist or postpositivist epistemologies may use methods that are more typically associated with a constructivist or interpretivist epistemology, such as oral history narratives or ethnographic observation. Thus, epistemologies differentially inform the methodologies and the methods that feminists employ and deploy in their work, that is, how the research is conceptualized; what is considered valid data and how they are gathered; the subjectivity, positionality, and reflexivity of the coresearchers; the way in which the data are analyzed or interpreted; and how the data are applied and disseminated.

Feminist critical scholarship informs contemporary feminist participatory and action researchers. For example, Patricia Hill Collins's (1990) and Dorothy Smith's (1987, 1991) discussions of how power shapes gender relations within and across racial, class, and sexual diversities are reflected in the work of Fine, Maguire, Lykes, McIntyre, and others who work at the interface of feminism and participatory and action research. These researchers' practices reflect the critical feminist epistemologies wherein women's work is problematized and women's agency tapped toward activism and social change. They use a diverse range of research methods to facilitate distinct processes of knowledge construction, engagement with women, political activity, and social change work. They are representative of a much wider group of feminist researchers who have contributed significantly to theory and practice within participatory and action-engaged research.

The remainder of this chapter will focus on women and men who engage in research at the interface of feminisms and participatory and action research. We begin with a brief attempt to characterize, if not define, the parameters of this interface. We present selected research examples in a variety of settings where women live and work, with a focus on education, health, and community development. This praxis is presented and participatory and then discussed to identify a set of cross-cutting issues that, we argue, frame research at the interface of feminisms and participatory and action research. Finally, we identify challenges facing those who seek to engage with communities and their indigenous knowledge systems and suggest that despite the best intentions, researchers nonetheless sometimes recapitulate systems of hierarchical power and inequality in their interventions. We further explore both the possibilities and the limitations of feminist-infused participatory and action research.

## PARTICIPATORY ACTION RESEARCH AND FEMINISMS: SITES OF PRAXIS

As suggested above, despite the diversities within participatory and action research processes that sought to transform educational, community development, and organizational theory and practice and the goals that overlap or intersect with those of feminist and womanist social movements, research, and scholarship, there has been—and some would argue, continues to be—relatively little visibility of work at the interface of these traditions. One example of an effort to redress this apparent disconnect was a workshop convened in the summer of 2001, wherein Mary Brydon-Miller, Patricia Maguire, and Alice McIntyre invited a group of feminists and action and participatory researchers to "meet at the crossroads" and critically explore the intersection of what some perceived to be overlapping circles of the feminist and the participatory and action research communities. The resulting coedited volume (Brydon-Miller, Maguire, & McIntyre, 2004) explores a range of critical issues among women and men working at this interface and the equally challenging dynamics between those working from the academy and those working from the community.

Today, as participatory and action research methods have become increasingly visible in universities, in the work of governments, international organizations (e.g., the World Bank), and nongovernmental organizations, in schools, and in the research literature (see, e.g., Dick, 2004, for a review), there is a growing concern that PAR, AR, and PR risk becoming depoliticized tools for improving practice. Similar concerns have been raised repeatedly by communities of color and women vis-à-vis the theory and research generated by feminist and race theorists in the academy. In 2003, Cornell University brought together academic and community feminists and activists who engage participatory and action research methods to, among other things, explore the possibility that the interface of feminisms and action research might facilitate the revitalization of all, at least for those whose praxis is based in or emerges from the academy (see www.einaudi.cornell.edu/parfem/parfem.htm). There, Patricia Maguire argued for the importance of reenergizing and repoliticizing participatory work. She suggested that participatory and action research bring to feminist theory a challenge to act, while feminism has significantly challenged action researchers to turn their critical lens toward women's experiences of oppression and marginalization as well as to the important strengths women bring to social change work (see Fine, 1994, for similar arguments and Patai, 1994, for a contrasting position).

## Approximating an Understanding of Work at the Interface

Drawing on Maguire's (1987, 1996, 2001, 2004) work, as well as that reviewed in this chapter, we argue that researchers who work at the interface of feminisms, participation, and action embrace a continuous and iterative process or approach to life, an attitude toward being and doing "in the world" rather than a single research method. This approach seeks to recognize and value the multiple intelligences, diverse ways of knowing, and frequently contradictory and sometimes silent or silenced voices among us toward developing "just enough" trust to initiate a coresearch process. It requires creating "safe enough" spaces that strive to be inclusive and supportive of these developing relationships, valuing our strengths and capacities while being sufficiently challenging to engage us in reflective critical practices that problematize the matrices of power, privilege, and domination that circulate among us and in our social worlds.

## Selecting Research Strategies

Methods are selected, therefore, for their appropriateness to these processes, to focus on problems or issues, and to gather diverse types of information or data that serve the iterative discovery, colearning, and action goals. As suggested above, the inclusion of participants with a wide range of abilities, languages, and skills demands a diversity of methods that facilitate engagement among all. Some examples of such participatory methods include focus group discussions; observational strategies, for instance, ethnographic and participant observation; visual texts, including collages, collective drawings, photography, and photovoice (see www.photovoice.com); oral histories, life stories, narratives, and testimony; embodied movement, including dramatization, dramatic multiplication, sculptures; and community- and asset-based mapping exercises. These strategies have been used individually or in combination to facilitate active engagement among all coresearchers and others within their organizations or communities with whom they seek to collaborate. Equally significant, researchers who enter a community or organization "from outside" its linguistic, cultural, racial, gender, sexual, or ability borders have used these methods to generate processes of discovery whereby potential participants can clarify their traditional knowledge systems.

Strategies for appraising, reflecting on, and analyzing shared experiences used in the exemplars presented below and by others engaged in similar work include content analysis, grounded theory analysis, narrative analysis, and a range of techniques for analyzing or re-presenting collages and other visual resources. In addition to these participatory methods, techniques that require more advanced technical skills, inaccessible to some participants, are reserved for specific tasks that have been identified by all coresearchers as serving the goals of their shared work. Otherwise, as has been reported by many academically trained researchers, only a subgroup of community participants engages in the analysis and interpretation of data.

Moreover, nonformally educated community groups with no statistical experience might contract with a coresearcher or external consultant with this technical expertise when the group itself agrees that these resources will advance their goals. For example, epidemiological data about their community have sometimes been critical to local HIV/AIDS groups' activist goals. Large volumes of survey data may need to be reduced and interpreted to complement other knowledge sources generated by more participatory strategies. A university-based technical consultant who works at the behest of the group or community may facilitate the group's achieving its research goals. Alternatively, a university-based researcher's assertion of her or his academic expertise in the absence of a collective request may be experienced as a threat (for further discussion, see www.incommunityresearch.org/research/paresearch.htm).

## Discussion

Faithful to its diverse geographical roots in Latin America, Asia, and Africa, as well as in the English-speaking world, work at the interface of feminisms and participatory and action research can be found throughout the world. The work described below was selected to illustrate the diversities of work at the interface of feminist and participatory and action research processes as well as to help clarify similarities or shared characteristics across projects. This work can most frequently be found in and with women and children (and some men) in educational and health-related organizations or institutions and, to a lesser extent, in private sector business or industry or in governmental or multinational agencies, and, increasingly, in and with nongovernmental community-based organizations. Within these sites of engagement and, quite frequently, in local communities or neighborhoods, collaborations have been initiated with particularly vulnerable or marginalized women (e.g., the elderly, youth, war survivors, domestic workers, victims of domestic violence and child abuse). The studies discussed below were selected as exemplars of the issues discussed above and to elucidate cross-cutting issues characteristic of feminist-infused participatory and action research and its challenges. They are organized in terms of the sites in which they were developed, that is, within education, health, and local communities.

## PARTICIPATORY AND ACTION RESEARCH AND EDUCATION

Action research in schools emerged in the 1970s in England during the teacher-as-researcher movement, which was characterized by school-based curriculum reforms. This movement was a reaction to an exclusive focus on measurable learning outcomes, and it emphasized the importance of process values as a basis for redesigning the curriculum. Since then, there has been a virtual explosion of AR processes in the English-speaking educational world. Action research has, for example, been used by educators in preservice and in-service teacher training, to improve the quality of instruction in classrooms and whole school districts, to measure the effectiveness of curricula and instructional changes, to transform particular classroom settings and educational systems, and to develop and disseminate knowledge about issues of particular relevance to schools (see Zeichner, 2001, for a review of this literature). Inquiry practitioners argue that educators are likely to make better decisions and engage in more effective practices if they are participants in their own research activities or, conversely, if they engage in research about their teaching practices.

## Action Research in Schools

A compelling example of the reach of this work is seen in Madison, Wisconsin, where one AR project aimed at helping elementary school teachers explore issues related to developing new instructional strategies for students from diverse ethnic and socioeconomic backgrounds. While the project began in classrooms, AR was later extended throughout the district (Caro-Bruce & McCreadie, 1995). More than 400 AR studies have been conducted in this school district since 1990, investigating a variety of issues and questions ranging from teacher and class-room practice to efforts to influence the social conditions of practice (e.g., reallocation of resources) (Zeichner, 2001). Thus, in the context of improving education, AR methods have been used to draw out problems in education at all levels (classrooms, schools, and school systems) as well as collaboratively to produce contextually appropriate advocacy and change methods.

In an Australian English-language AR educational project, teachers discovered that undertaking classroom AR, when done in a coordinated fashion in an entire school, encouraged them to engage more closely with their curriculum through processes of reflection, provided an opportunity to collaborate with other teachers, stimulated a sense of personal and professional growth, clarified the needs for an institution-wide curriculum, encouraged the recognition and translation of evolving ideas into action, and encouraged flexibility in school or classroom improvement efforts (Burns, 1999). The participating teachers also described an increased capacity to more confidently and effectively evaluate curriculum policy decisions, which in turn affirmed their roles as teachers (Burns, 1999).

This seeming explosion of work supports Maguire's (2004) suggestion that educational action research has become a "cottage industry." Moreover, it has been marketed to educators as a set of resources for improving practice, through the development of school-based curriculum, teachers' in-service education or professional development, and projects to improve an individual school or school systems. Parents have also engaged in participatory or action inquiry processes to collaborate in improving school-based educational practices or organization and administration. However, despite their contributions, much of these researchers' work has lacked an explicit political or feminist underpinning and has failed to question the broader goals of improving education practice (i.e., to what ends is this work directed?). For example, one recent U.S. educational policy, No Child Left Behind, emphasizes accountability, high-stakes testing, and outcomes-based education. In efforts to "address the achievement gap" in this environment, school-based AR to improve practice is frequently focused on "teaching to the test" rather than to the needs of each child, or on systemic change.

## Freirian Pedagogical Practice, Participatory Action Research, and Education

In contrast to much of this work, most explicitly political forms of participatory and action research in education—feminist or otherwise—are situated within the legacy of the Brazilian educator, activist, and political leader Paulo Freire (1970; see www.paulofreire.org for a sense of the breadth and depth of Freire's work and influence on education and beyond). Freire's liberatory and popular educational praxis informed literacy campaigns in the majority world,[2] for example, in his home country, Brazil, and in Nicaragua (Miller, 1985). Feminists working in educational contexts from a Freirian perspective have sought to develop praxis that raises consciousness about, for example, the gendered, racialized, and class-based dimensions of the achievement gap reflected in, for example, high-stakes test outcomes. This educationally focused work has been extended to include prisons, urban and rural barrios, and beyond. Specifically, Freirian pedagogical practices, including problem posing, decoding, and conscientization inform participatory and action research in schools and in community- or organization-based educational settings.

## Participatory Education, Women, and Research for Social Change

The Highlander Research and Education Center in New Market, Tennessee, is one of the best examples of how participatory and action research methods have been engaged with political purposes to educate and activate within and among marginalized communities of women and men in the United States. The Highlander Center was founded during the Depression era, to redress injustices and inequalities within Appalachian communities. Women have always been at the forefront as organizers, educators, and coresearchers at Highlander, problematizing the matrix of domination at the interface of race, gender, and class that frames the experiences of low-income communities in the South. Participatory research became an explicit part of the work of the Center in the 1970s, when John Gaventa and Juliet Merrifield organized participatory workshops and created a resource center to assist community groups and citizens to educate and organize themselves more effectively to participate in public policy decision making. As a result, community groups were able to study the local effects of, for example, coal companies' policies, and to educate about (1) the health hazards they faced as a result of irresponsible toxic waste disposal and (2) the local economic impact of exploitative industrial land ownership practices and taxation (Lewis, 2001).

An urban base from which another group of women and men is organizing to challenge opportunity gaps in education across the life span is the Graduate Center of the City University of New York, particularly through work facilitated by Michelle Fine. Recently, Fine and her colleagues (2004) engaged urban and suburban youth in a series of PAR projects organized around what the youth themselves renamed the "opportunity gap." University researchers and more than 50 high school students who represent the diversities of U.S. adolescents formed a Youth Research Community and participated in research camps where they learned participatory skills to explore their own and other high school students' perceptions of social class, race, ethnicity, and opportunity in local schools, communities, and, more broadly, the United States (Torre & Fine, 2003). In

participatory workshops, they designed a survey that was later completed by 9,174 youth from 15 New York and New Jersey urban and suburban districts and analyzed by a team of youth- and university-based coresearchers. Focus groups, observations, and archival research complemented the surveys, and the findings, represented through youth and adult coresearchers' creative writing, songs, and dramatizations, were performed, recorded on DVD, and published (Fine et al., 2004). The research process created a variety of "safe spaces" where youth and adults could, according to Torre, work together "to go deeper" and analyses of experiences of racism and oppression (Fine et al., 2004). Diversity and difference were embraced, and each participant's knowledge was valued. Conflicts were opportunities for developing a more critical understanding of the macrostructures that create access for privileged youth—primarily white and with economic resources—and deny it to others—primarily "of color" and poor. Storying and analyzing the micropractices of injustice in daily school and community-based experiences richly complemented structural analyses and are threaded through the multiple actions that commemorate, celebrate, and challenge U.S. educators and communities 50 years after *Brown v. Board of Education*. This highly politicized PAR process was deeply participatory and critically situated within and challenging of the matrix of domination that continues to marginalize the majority of U.S. youth from educational opportunity (Collins, 1990). The projects briefly summarized here are explicitly activist and, we argue, deeply infused by the feminist stance Fine so clearly articulated in her earlier work (see, e.g., Fine, 1992, 1994).

## Teaching Feminist-Infused Participatory Action Research in the Academy

As the number of participatory and action research projects has expanded, the demand to teach and to learn about the design and implementation of action research has increased. A Web-based search revealed 11 such courses in universities across the United States and Canada. Most syllabi for courses on PAR, AR, and PR assign readings related to feminism or give space for critical reflection on the implications of power in the research process, including power differentials associated with gender. This suggests a growing recognition of work at this interface.

Examples of this pedagogy are described by Christine Sleeter, Myriam Torres, and Peggy Laughlin (2004). They discuss different course contexts in which they have used teacher inquiry to scaffold conscientization processes for and with preservice teachers. Working in different contexts with varying diversities of students and in different courses, they demonstrate how reflexivity, scaffolded inquiry, and Freire's problem-posing pedagogy have been deployed in educating students about the sociocultural foundations of schooling, institutional discrimination, and privilege; how they themselves have been the victims of propaganda, deception, and lies; and how they can develop their own critical inquiries.

Alice McIntyre (1997) developed a feminist-infused PAR project with a group of white middle- and upper-middle-class female student teachers who examined their "whiteness" and developed ways of thinking critically about race and racism in educational practice. Through self-reflective journaling and creative exercises they explored their own racial identities and how they are implicated in the formation and implementation of their teaching practices. The project sought to better understand how whiteness is sustained and reproduced within and among those seeking change and to better equip this small group of future teachers to disrupt and eliminate systems of discrimination and white privilege in their future classrooms.

Patricia Maguire (2004) explicitly inserted feminism in a required AR course for graduate students at the Western New Mexico University School of Education. Based on her conviction that we grow and thrive in relationships, she argued that this was a context where as "traveling companions on a journey of how to do collaborative action research in service to social justice . . . we are challenged to take action, however imperfect. When all is said and done, feminism is about action: collective politicized action" (pp. 131–132). The students in Maguire's course were challenged to critically examine their multiple identities and the implications that these have for their work as teachers

with diverse student populations. Each student designed an AR project on-site, that is, where they were teaching, in order to clarify where and how feminisms were implicated. The assumption underlying Maguire's pedagogical praxis was that integrating feminism into AR is critical to developing its transformative potential.

## Discussion

Each of these examples demonstrates how through a problem-posing, reflexive, critical, and self-critical teaching and learning process, feminisms encourage examination of self that facilitates and sustains perspective change and action for social justice. The processes are not linear, or without conflict, but each example demonstrates how the coresearchers are moving roughly forward toward developing critical consciousness about oppression, the coresearchers' roles in maintaining it, and possibilities for actions for liberatory transformation. Moreover, educational participatory and action research processes in the absence of feminism risk making change that sustains rather than challenges the broader sociopolitical status quo, and feminist research within the academy without participation and action risks confusing method with power.[3]

## PARTICIPATORY ACTION RESEARCH AND HEALTH

Public health initiatives and participatory and action research methodologies most often meet purposes in the form of community-based research projects, of which there is a flourishing body in Europe, the United States, and Canada, and a growing number in the majority world. In epidemiology in particular, there has been growing recognition of the need for more participatory and action-oriented approaches to public health issues (Minkler & Wallerstein, 2003, p. 4). Issues of sexual health (e.g., sexually transmitted diseases and reproductive health), given the oftentimes socially circumscribed nature of their discussion and evaluation, as well as the implications they may have for communities as a whole, tend to be among the most commonly addressed by community-based research in health. HIV/AIDS in particular is a common subject of community-based participatory research (CBPR), as are the health needs of women and, primarily in the United States, the lesbian, gay, bisexual, and transgender communities (Minkler & Wallerstein, 2003).

Equally significant, at least since the publication of the first edition of *Our Bodies, Ourselves* (Boston Women's Health Book Collective, 1973), women and, more particularly, feminists have organized to criticize sexism throughout the health care delivery system, in research, and in the increasingly market-driven health care industry. They have challenged all women to reclaim their bodies and demand that research and practice be marshaled to create quality prevention and treatment for all women. These two independent but overlapping social forces situate work at the interface of feminist and participatory and action research described below.

## Participatory Research Processes, Cultural Knowledge, and Health Care

Nurses and public health practitioners have used participatory and action research strategies to critically examine medical practices and the health profession in a variety of health care settings, from traditional, hierarchical hospitals to grassroots community health centers (see, e.g., Minkler & Wallerstein, 2003). In countries of the majority world, participatory and action research has been used by public health workers in conjunction with community members and with individuals and communities affected by the problems or issues being studied, to assess community needs and implement educational initiatives regarding, for example, HIV and AIDS (see, e.g., McTaggart, 1997). These initiatives discourage top-down mandates and draw up from the community the challenges that could create barriers to effective health provision. They are more flexible than top-down strategies at incorporating and providing for cultural particularities in solution generation. Care is taken not to transgress implicit or explicit community communication codes that limit the people with whom one can safely discuss such issues, for example, in discussions of HIV and AIDS prevention. Such discussion is grounded in an understanding of acceptable and taboo topics

within a community vis-à-vis "talk about sex" (see, e.g., Welbourne, 1998). Participatory approaches are more likely to ensure that solutions are sustainable in the context for which they are generated. Action research has also been used to help a group or community set policy goals and to develop strategies to influence policymakers, thus equipping local residents with the power to make change (Themba & Minkler, 2003).

## Feminist Perspectives and the Health Care Profession

Nursing researchers and practitioners, in particular, have taken up forms of participatory and action research methods to address the changing nature of the field, to enhance pedagogy, and to contest nurses' marginalization in hierarchical hospital settings and health care structures. Angie Titchen (1997) and a senior ward nurse at John Radcliffe Hospital in Oxford undertook an AR project to help nurses facilitate a cultural change within their workplace, from a hierarchical, task-focused system of care to a more patient-centered system. Ultimately, the project facilitated nurses' increased sense of agency in aspects of their own professional development, helped to break down personal barriers to constructive criticism, and fostered an environment of engaged, collaborative inquiry.

Susan Smith (1995) sought to understand how Canadian public health nurses' (PHNs) engagement with PAR served as "a form of collective, self-reflective inquiry that supports the implementation of democratic, empowering health care practices" (p. 48). Smith recognized that Canadian PHNs were navigating changes within the health care system that had an impact on how they saw their roles and their perceptions thereof. Challenges facing them included a need to enhance role clarity, a need to heighten government and public recognition of the importance of preventive health services, a need to gain recognition as a unique subspecialty within nursing, a need to increase nurses' political involvement, and a need for an adequate supply of well-prepared nurse-administrators. Among the PHNs with whom Smith worked, engagement in the "spiraling moments" of reflection, connection seeking, education analysis, action, and conscientization helped them positively change their environment and create more spaces for control by individual nurses.

Arphorn Chuaprapaisilp (1997) facilitated a study among nurses in Thailand wherein experiential learning theory, critical theory, and action research were enhanced by a local "consciousness-raising" technique from Buddhist teaching, *Satipatthana*, which culturally situated the PAR process. Participants indicated that the inclusion of *Satipatthana* helped them to work more effectively with the model, and they described a positive change in their attitudes and behaviors toward the use of reflective practice.

These three research processes sought to raise critical consciousness among participants and to mobilize them to challenge dominant, patriarchal structures in order to improve both their own work environments and the care that they provide to the public. They thus demonstrate the interweaving of feminist epistemology with participatory and action research methodologies toward concrete change.

## Cultural Community-Based Health Education and Women

Participatory and action research has also been used in community-based health education. Working in southern Africa, Ambreena Manji (1999) found that the techniques of participatory and action research are well suited to the study of the HIV/AIDS epidemic because they address the broader effects of the pandemic, including its economic impact, which have been neglected by the biomedical model that dominates research in this area. According to Manji (1999), a more accurate account of the consequences of HIV/AIDS emerges from a process that is grounded in the real lives of those experiencing it.

Similarly, Welbourne (1998) encourages the use of participatory and action processes to assess community needs, educate communities about HIV, and mobilize intracommunity support around the issue rather than relying on top-down lectures from prevention workers or one-on-one counseling from aid workers. In a participatory initiative in Buwenda, Uganda, in 1998, she aimed to educate participants regarding HIV, with the goal of improving prevention measures among members of the community

where HIV was spreading at a significant rate. The work was framed around a "Stepping Stones" approach, wherein similar participants met in peer groups for periods of self-reflection and action planning. The peer group meetings were periodically interchanged with "mixed sessions," where members from different peer groups would meet together. These discussions allowed for examination of similarities, differences, and solutions among participants. Community participants reported outcomes that included greater awareness of the causes of HIV, sustained increase in condom use, improved relations among others in the community who had learned about the workshop, increased ability to communicate positively (particularly between men and women), and a greater sense of well-being and respect for others (Welbourne, 1998).

In Panchmahals, a district of Gujarat in western India, Renu Khanna (1996) collaborated with SARTHI, a local volunteer organization, to develop a PAR project for women's health. They organized to create a space for sharing their stories and then began to research traditional remedies for women's health. Based on these experiences they developed self-help workshops to train women in socially embedded and gender-sensitive gynecology. Khanna (1996) identified evidence of women's empowerment and health activism at multiple levels, including the intra- and interpersonal, the group, and the community. In the first instance, women moved beyond *sharam* (shame) and began to talk about their bodies. In small group discussions they identified characteristics of daily living that impeded or facilitated health and well-being. At the community level, participants organized for collective action, mobilizing for quality health care and addressing health issues women of their community faced, including domestic violence (Khanna, 1996).

## Discussion

Although the language of feminism is explicit in some of these projects while implicit in others, they share a common concern with engaging women (and some men) in raising awareness about their bodies and the social conditions that impede well-being in health care institutions and in local communities. As in the examples drawn from educational environments, a problem-posing, reflexive, critical, and self-critical teaching-learning process is central to all the projects. They encourage a critical examination of self that facilitates and sustains perspective change and collective action for change. The changes described enable women more fully to articulate their values and beliefs, incorporating and reflecting their cultural and gendered positions better to serve themselves and their organizations or communities.

## PARTICIPATORY ACTION RESEARCH IN AND WITH LOCAL COMMUNITIES

In contrast to the previously discussed examples of research at the interface of participatory and action research and feminisms wherein much of the action-reflection described was carried out in or through educational and health organizations or institutions, the community is a more frequent locus for participatory and action research within the majority world. Much of the participatory and action research within the context of local communities has been carried out as part of community economic or participatory development processes. In Latin America, the work has been and continues to be strongly influenced by Paulo Freire's liberatory pedagogy and his theories of critical consciousness and empowerment. Similar approaches that assume that knowledge generates power and that people's knowledge is central to social change emerged in Asia (Fals-Borda & Rahman, 1991) and in Africa (see Hope & Timmel, 1984–2000). These efforts emphasize full and active participation of people historically marginalized from power, decision making, and knowledge construction. They stress the ideological, political, and economic dimensions of social relations in and through which all knowledge is generated. They frequently involve international collaborations wherein external catalysts engage with local farmers (see, e.g., Debbink & Ornelas, 1997) or cooperatives (see, e.g., Arriata & de la Maza, 1997) to improve the quality of life for residents through participatory processes that are designed to generate change. Some of these participatory and action strategies have been extended to humanitarian aid and interventions with survivors of war and state-sponsored violence to inform collaborative approaches to rethreading social life in the context of structural economic poverty or in the wake of violence. Although an extensive discussion of these two literatures is beyond the scope of this chapter, we discuss below some of the multiple challenges facing researchers and activists seeking to better understand these realities and accompany communities in responding to them.

## Women, Community Development, and Change

Participatory and action research strategies have been significantly constitutive of community development efforts over many years. PRA and farmer participatory research (FPR), as well as people-centered development movements (see, e.g., Korten, 1990, cited in Roodt, 1996) were developed to facilitate change in rural communities, many of which lack basic survival resources such as water and land. Because women produce as much as 80% of the food crops grown in sub-Saharan Africa, the Indian subcontinent, and Latin America (Jacobsen, 2005; see also Seager, 2003); have a central role in the economic survival of themselves and their families in the majority world; and are protagonists in many of these efforts, the methods warrant at least brief attention here.

### Participatory Practices in Rural Communities

Similar to other participatory approaches, FPR was developed as an alternative to the traditional top-down transfer of technology approach to agricultural work and PRA, as a critique of top-down strategies in much rapid rural appraisal. Major assumptions underlying these approaches include an emphasis on farmers' indigenous knowledge and farmers' capacity for experimentation and an appreciation of interdisciplinary collaboration between researchers and farmers. Villagers analyze their local situations, document local knowledge, and develop agricultural and natural research management experiments and actions. Although much of early PRA research neither incorporated a gender perspective nor focused on women, at least since the identification of women as "low risks" for small loans in Muhammad Yunus's Grameen bank initiative in the early 1980s (see Yunus, 1999), women have become an increasingly important focus in economic development initiatives and participatory field research. Yet despite this growing involvement of women as participants, Heaven Crawley (1998) argues that "for many involved in participatory research or action, gender is a footnote, rather than a place from which to begin the analysis" (p. 25) and that gender as a critical aspect of power relations is ignored in this work.

## Participatory Processes, Development, and Gender

Although the feminist-infused participatory work being done in development is not widely read by teachers or health workers in the northern hemisphere, it contributes importantly to a critical analysis of participatory and action research processes as they inform feminist analysis and vice versa. Anne Hope and Sally Timmel's (1984–2000) creative and contextually infused adaptation of Freire's theories to the African context is presented in their four-volume series of popular education resources, *Training for Transformation*. This work with women in rural communities of Tanzania, Kenya, and, more recently, South Africa focuses on local communities' indigenous knowledge and relies heavily on Freire's pedagogical decoding practices through which local residents can better understand, and then critically evaluate, their social realities. Unlike some previous liberatory praxis, this work is particularly attentive to local spiritualities and to the role that belief systems play in people's personal and social understanding. Most recently, their work at the interface of development, education, and organizing focuses more explicitly on gender and how gender inequalities constrain women's lives (see especially, Hope & Timmel, 1984–2000, Vol. 4).

Irene Guijt and Meera Kaul Shah's (1998) edited volume, *The Myth of Community: Gender Issues in Participatory Development*, reports on a wide range of field experiences particularly in the English-speaking majority world and, more specifically, in parts of Africa and India. These case studies are preceded by seven theoretical chapters that discuss a range of challenges confronting researchers who seek to destabilize gender assumptions in a diverse

range of participatory projects toward facilitating local communities' interrogation of the causes of power inequalities that impede development processes. The editors challenge those engaged in participatory processes who are committed to redressing power inequalities to deconstruct the local community functions of maleness and femaleness and to extend their focus on consciousness raising to include transformation of structural or institutional systems of oppression (see, e.g., Cornwall, 1998; see also, Cornwall, 2000, 2003).

Andrea Cornwall (2003) cautions community-based development researchers who assume women's solidarity, arguing that in local communities, women may rather see their interests as aligned with those of their sons or kin. Significantly, institutional or structural barriers to women's participation in decision making and social constraints, including a lack of education, of public speaking experience, or of their critical mass in public spaces, conspire to make significant changes in power difficult to achieve. Many participatory projects may offer women the "tactics to grapple with" these realities but not real "strategies for change because they [these women] lack the power and agency to do so" (p. 1331). Cornwall cautions that the essentialist axes of difference (e.g., gender) that characterize much of "women in development" (WID), "women and development" (WAD), "women and sustainable development" (WED), and "gender and development" (GAD) (Currie, 1999) research and activism obscure complex and deeply contextualized constructions of power and powerlessness within local communities.

Dawn Currie (1999) challenges development theoreticians and practitioners to transform or "indigenize" knowledge. Her goal is to "develop a methodology that links social change to the experiences and needs of women as defined by women, and for social justice for women." She draws on the work of Kate Young (1993), who differentiated our practical needs as women from our strategic interests in political and social struggles for equality. This work echoes earlier theoretical work by the feminist Shulamith Firestone (1970) that distinguished women's reproductive and productive labor and focused importantly on women's empowerment as involving both individual change and collective action. Young (1993) situates the construct of "women's needs" within a framework often overlooked by many, that is, cultural and social realities in which women lack a sense of having rights or needs. She suggests further that "women's lack of access to information about their own societies, and the range of debate about political and economic matters is often a key element in their hesitancy about change" (p. 157). Her work is an important contribution for participatory and action researchers who seek to develop a community-based process wherein participants develop their capacities to identify and share their needs and from that base begin to develop change processes.

### Extending Participatory Community Development to Policy

Caroline Wang and her colleagues sought to equip rural Chinese women with the resources to identify their needs through the innovative combination of local and national government structures and their own creativity (Wang, Burris, & Xiang, 1996). Through a PAR strategy that yokes photography and the analysis of pictures as text about women's lives (see www.photovoice.com), rural Chinese women were able to develop a photo-text exhibit and book that informed local, regional, and provincial policymakers about the risks of rural labor practices to women's and children's safety and well-being. The inclusion of photography, a non-literacy-dependent research strategy, extended opportunities for participation to a wider group of women, many of whom have heretofore been excluded from collaboration as coresearchers. The work generated significant social change, improving child care and health care in the participating provinces. Ironically, perhaps, the highly centralized and hierarchical Chinese service delivery system and sponsorship of this project by regional officials facilitated greater access to decision making and change than is typically available to rural women.

## Women, War, and Participatory Action Research

Contemporary communities are increasingly established and reconstituted by immigrants and displaced populations fleeing poverty and violence. Although war has historically been fought by armed men in conflict, who were its primary victims and survivors, the majority of the victims of contemporary warfare are civilians and, increasingly, women and children. The United Nations Children's Fund (UNICEF) estimates that 90% of those killed in today's wars are civilians, and half of those are children; 80% of refugees are estimated to be women and children (UNICEF, 2005). Violence against women and gender inequalities in war are extreme manifestations of discrimination and gender violence under conditions of peace. In war, women, including young girls, are victims of incest, rape, pornography, battering, harassment, and sexual slavery. Members of militaries or paramilitary forces frequently rape women as part of war's booty (Swiss & Giller, 1993) or, as human rights observers in the former Yugoslavia suggest, as one dimension of a strategy of ethnic cleansing (Ecumenical Women's Team Visit, 1992; Mazowiecki, 1993).

### Gendered Identities, Ethnic Conflict, and Women's Organizing

Feminists and participatory and action researchers have been engaged with local communities in ongoing war and subsequent transitions. In contemporary intrastate conflict, ethnic violence is a prominent dimension wherein difference is mobilized for political purposes and targeted as a basis for transgression. This creates fear among and places in opposition those who once existed in solidarity and community, thereby undermining social relationships and polarizing identities. Cynthia Cockburn (1998) has explored multiple sites of nationalist or ethnic conflict, including Northern Ireland, Israel, and Bosnia-Herzegovina. To understand some of the ways in which women activists negotiate gender and their national identities in situations of conflict, Cockburn identified a wide range of women's organizations and worked alongside them, documenting their approaches and interviewing participants. In Cyprus, Cockburn (2004) collaborated with a Greek and Cypriot women's organization formed specifically to explore women's contributions to the divided society. Her participatory-action-infused research with and for them became an opportunity to collaborate in exploring multiple lines—ethnic, sexual, national, economic—within the categories "woman" and "feminist" and what these mean "to those who have power to operationalize them, what they imply of those who are named, shaped, differentiated, and excluded by them" (pp. 204–205).

### Community Survival, Voice, and Women's Lives

In a participatory action project in rural Guatemala, Lykes, in collaboration with 20 Maya women in Chajul (Women of Photovoice/ADMI & Lykes, 2000), addressed the challenges they faced in organizing as women in the midst of civil war in a context of ongoing ethnic- and gender-based discrimination and violence. The research emerged from and was embedded in the work of a local women's organization that fostered economic development (through several animal husbandry projects and a revolving load fund), education (through a community after-school program for children and a community library), leadership development, and psychosocial healing (see Lykes, 1999, for details). Society-wide initiatives to end the war, including the 1996 Peace Accords signed by the government and the revolutionary movements, and the initiation of two commissions to document gross violations of human rights (Commission for Historical Clarification, 1999; Office of Human Rights of the Archdiocese of Guatemala, 1998) created some of the conditions necessary for this work. Drawing on a "talking pictures" methodology developed by the Chilean anthropologist Ximena Bunster (Bunster & Chaney, 1989) and Caroline Wang's work in rural China (see above and Wang et al., 1996), the coresearchers developed a process through which to construct the community's stories of war, its effects, and how one small group of women were rethreading their lives and creating alternatives for their children.

The project was undertaken in Spanish and Ixil and culminated in the production of a bilingual photoessay, *Voices and Images: Mayan Ixil Women of Chajul* (Women of Photovoice/ADMI & Lykes, 2000). Their research with women of villages surrounding their town contributed to deepening their understanding of the diverse consequences of the 36-year war there and in more remote contexts and facilitated action processes through which they organized women's groups with participants whose stories they had recorded in the more remote communities. Equally significant, these participatory workshops and the community narrative they produced offered contexts for self-discovery and critical analysis as well as for engaging chronic conflicts while facilitating a process of breaking silences to speak the truth in a context of ongoing impunity.

## Discussion

Each of the projects described here engaged women across significant ethnic, political, religious, racial, class, age, and sexual diversities in processes that required a level of support from outsiders to forge ahead in complex contexts fraught with ongoing violence and oppression. The participatory and action research processes described engaged women at the level of their individual lives, within local communities, and through national-level public processes. All the projects described here implicitly or explicitly challenged dominant gender hierarchies, with the result that men frequently responded negatively, ranging from expressions of disbelief, to disruption of women's work, to discrimination and violence. Thus, this feminist-infused participatory and action research offered a resource to women surviving war, yet similar to the examples from contexts of economic injustice and extreme inequality, wider social conditions of gendered inequalities and ongoing poverty and oppression deeply constrained what could be achieved through any single project.

Many of the examples discussed document processes through which women begin to name their individual and collective needs and desires as well as their social realities. According to Young (1993) this process implies conflict— "Empowerment is not just about women acquiring something, but about those holding power relinquishing it" (p. 159). The examples presented in this chapter suggest processes by which women in diverse contexts facing inequality, marginalization, and social oppression struggle for survival, for the right to name who they are, and to promote change. Specifically, this work entails, in the words of Dorothy Smith (1987, cited in Currie, 1999), an analysis of a "'complex of organizational practices, including government, law, business and financial management, professional organization, and educational institutions, as well as discourses in texts that interpenetrate the multiple sites of power.'" Currie (1999) challenges those working with and for women in marginalized communities to situate themselves at the interstices of participatory and grassroots activism and theoretical critical feminisms. She makes explicit the critical importance of infusing feminism, particularly a feminist critique of power, with participatory and action research processes.

## CROSS-CUTTING ISSUES: PERFORMING POWER, DESIGNING FEMINIST PARTICIPATORY ACTION RESEARCH

Feminist-infused PAR, AR, and PR and activist-infused feminist research are complex processes. Many have argued that it is more likely for participatory and action researchers in educational, health, and community contexts to ignore gender or recapitulate traditional gendered community relations than to enact transformative praxis alongside women in ways that help them move from the margin to the center. Many of the initiatives designed to facilitate change fail to equip women with the resources necessary to engage in the complex new relations that are envisioned. To sustain a developing transformative collaboration, feminist, participatory, and action researchers must challenge themselves to think critically about their roles in the research endeavor. By explicitly shifting the role of research participants from objects of study to agents or actors, feminist and participatory and action researchers implicitly concern themselves with issues of power and relationship. The work discussed here suggests just a few of the risks faced in engaging traditional dynamics of domination or control that, at a broader social level, constitute the situations that coresearchers aim to change.

In the feminist-infused participatory and action research projects described herein, participants as coresearchers, through reflexivity and in relationship, discover the limits and constraints of their own personal and interpersonal power. Through processes of conscientization within local matrices of power and powerlessness they contest social oppression and sometimes collectively mobilize resources on behalf of themselves, their families, and their communities. Below we explore five processes that cut across the examples presented, that is, insider-outsider dichotomy, reflexivity, voice, relationality, and community. These processes both emerge from and constitute feminist-infused PAR, AR, and PR. They are defined and redefined through a dialectical and iterative process of action and reflection.

### "Insiders" and "Outsiders"

As argued above, the researchers' theories of being (ontology) and knowing (epistemology) influence who they are, the positions they assume, the roles they play, and the methodologies they engage during the research process. Participatory and action research challenge participants to think critically about their own identities, as well as the ways in which the multiple identities of all participants, that is, all coresearchers, interact within the context of the research process. Some participatory and action researchers argue that presumed power inequities between "insiders" and "outsiders" need to be examined, critiqued, and deconstructed in all research (see, e.g., Bartunek & Louis, 1996; Fine, 1994; Merton, 1972). These critiques challenge feminist-infused participatory and action researchers to stretch the boundaries of the hypothesized insider-outsider dichotomy or, in the words of Michelle Fine (1994), "work the hyphen."

Many participatory and action research processes are collaborations between researchers with technical skills who live outside of the community of praxis and insiders or participants who are members of the "target" community. In examining feminist methodology, Sherry Gorelick (1996) cautions all who hope to do feminist-infused participatory and action research beyond their communities of origin, suggesting that the external researcher's "relationship to oppression, as either privileged or oppressed . . . is contradictory, complex, and, to some degree, up to us" (p. 40). In a CBPR project working with public health professionals in low-income communities of color in the United States, Chavez, Duran, Baker, Avila, and Wallerstein (2003) suggested that for "professionally trained researchers who are white or otherwise advantaged, privilege is one of the most important and difficult arenas . . . to address, as it in part defines who [the researchers] understand [themselves] to be" (p. 91).

The work of the independent researcher-activist Susan Stern exemplifies some of these challenges "at the hyphen." Stern undertook a conversation-based research project in a predominantly black suburban neighborhood near Washington, D.C., in the early 1980s, being appalled at the poor quality of the teaching and the low academic expectations rampant in the local elementary school in which her daughter had enrolled. As a white woman, her activism required continual conversation with other predominantly black parents and teachers about the implications of race and racism for their collaboration. As Stern (1998) explains,

> At the personal level, our different racial backgrounds threatened to maintain a barrier between us. At the social level, racial differences and race-based policies and procedures were at the core of the problem at hand—[in the] children's school. (p. 115)

Although Stern was an insider in the school community because of her status as the parent of a student, as a white Euro-American in an almost exclusively black community she was an outsider. Each of her multiple identities held different implications and challenges for her position and the relationships she formed and actions in which she engaged in and through the research process.

Stern's example demonstrates the matrix of interlocking interactions between researchers and participants that both conceal and illuminate continuities and discontinuities in participatory processes of meaning making and change. By challenging static, boundaried notions of insider and outsider or researcher and participant, feminist-infused participatory and action research clarifies the mediated nature of all knowledge construction and exemplifies "ways of knowing" that are frequently absent from mainstream, top-down theory building.

Furthermore, Rahman (2004) suggests that the "desired relation between external activists and people is best expressed by the term *uglolana*," meaning "sharpening each other" and a "companion concept . . . *uakana*, meaning 'to build each other.'" He suggests that these two South African Bantu terms are "the profoundest articulation of the participatory development paradigm" (p. 17). We suggest that they not only redefine the insider-outsider dialectic of coresearchers but also refashion the discourse of power at the interface of feminisms and participatory and action research that seeks transformation.

## Reflexivity: Self as a Vehicle for Reflection and Action

Nancy Naples (2003) argues that collaboration is possible only if coresearchers can create a space of engagement where participants can assert themselves through reflective strategies and dialogic processes. She argues that reflective strategies are tools to "make visible what is privileged as . . . data" (p. 38). By adopting reflective strategies, feminist researchers "work to reveal the inequalities and processes of domination that shape the 'field'" (p. 38). Although Naples was referring explicitly to the ethnographic research with which she was engaged, these methodological considerations are informative for the feminist-infused participatory and action research discussed in this chapter.

Some authors (see, e.g., Fine, 1992; Williams & Lykes, 2003) have extended these ideas, suggesting that *reflexivity*, namely, the ways in which researchers and participants use themselves and their critical reflections about themselves and their positionality and praxis to generate knowledge and collective action, rather than reflectivity, is critical in feminist-infused participatory and action research processes. Through critical and self-critical reflections on one's standpoint as a participant or researcher, one accesses different kinds of knowledge about the observable processes in which one is engaged, and this in turn enables one to deploy one's particular "selves" within the collective processes of action research. Moreover, the recognition and acknowledgement of reflexivity facilitates the possibility for self-criticism, that is, when one is inadequate to the task at hand.

For example, in 1996, Williams joined Lykes and 20 Maya Ixil women in Guatemala engaged in the photovoice project described briefly above. Lykes and Williams sought to collaborate with Maya Ixil women as they storied their lives through words and photographs to, among other things, "strengthen their individual and organizational capacities and resources" (Williams & Lykes, 2003, p. 288). On reconvening 1 month after a series of successful and enthusiastic meetings through which the project had been launched and the participants had received training in the use of cameras, the Mayan women revealed that only a few of them had even attempted to take photographs, despite their earlier agreement to do so. Williams and Lykes's (2003) disappointment notwithstanding, they facilitated a "participatory process of reflection and action" using their own disappointment, doubts, and self-questioning about what had happened as a starting point. To explore their own responses through participation, they invited the Ixil women to role-play what had occurred when they set off to take their first photographs, and then to identify and analyze the barriers they had experienced. The material and psychological challenges were enacted through dramatizations and re-enacted through dramatic multiplication techniques (Lykes, 1994). This praxis facilitated the participants' clarification of the emotional responses that had contributed to their inaction as well as reconnected them to the thoughts and feelings they had experienced as a consequence of war and organized violence.

Thus, Williams and Lykes's (2003) reflexive practices generated a process through which participants engaged in self-reflective actions. The project's impasse was transformed; women engaged the process as photographers while increasing in self-knowledge. Other similar participatory problem-solving processes provided a forum for the group's discussion of family and community conflicts, gender relations, and Mayan traditions, serving as awareness-raising functions among the participants. Significantly, the "external researchers" became more integrated within the PAR process as they better understood the powerful tool of reflexively engaging their own emotional responses to the research process and using them as entry into strengthened relationships with the participants and as resources for data generation and analysis.

## Multiplicity of Voices

### Language Barriers

A systemic barrier to the full expression of participants' "voices" in some participatory and action research projects is language. Literal translation within and across native languages sometimes complicates the research process. The impossibility of communicating many culturally situated and embedded linguistic constructs and social expressions serves to dilute further the messages of participants or confuse their meanings. Questions of translation may also emphasize or reinforce existing racial dynamics. Cultural interpreters and translators are frequently essential players in a community-based research process, yet as Chavez et al. (2003) noted in their work with public health workers in low-income communities of color, researchers of color are often not the primary researchers but translators or interpreters, bridging the gap between communities of color and institutions of research yet relegated to less powerful roles in some participatory and action processes.

Moreover, the language and the assumptions of the academy also "often clash with the majority of people in the communities where research is conducted" (Chavez et al., 2003, p. 89). Indeed, the institutional/academic-community divide has been felt by many participatory and action researchers. Researchers based in the academic community "face many difficulties in balancing the social worlds of academia, policymakers, and the public, and the 'community'" (Cancian, 1996, p. 188).

### Balancing the Input of Coresearchers

Qualitative research methods are more generally designed to encourage the preservation of participants' individual input and particular context than many deindividualizing positivist methods. What is at stake is how the voices of participants, that is, their lived experiences, their indigenous knowledge, their perceptions, and their words, are accepted as data and how and for what purpose those data are appropriated.

Yet as Marecek, Fine, and Kidder (2001) note, "As researchers become witnesses, bringing their knowledge of theory and their interpretive methods to participants' stories, they . . . become active agents" (p. 34). The researcher, thus, becomes a variable in the research being done, regardless of the methods used, and co-constructive processes may obscure or distort insiders' voices (Stacey, 1996, pp. 91–92).

Michelle Fine (1992) cautioned strongly that the researcher who serves as a "ventriloquist," that is, who speaks over or for participants, often contributes disinformation, obscuring the respective and varied roles and voices of the participants. She urges researchers to situate themselves as facilitators of the voices of the community participants with whom they work by creating opportunities through which they are enabled to tell their stories and where there is a public to both hear these stories and be held accountable to the storytellers.

### Cocreating a "Third Voice"

Although an important cautionary tale, Fine's analysis implies a "self" and "other" who are independent, wherein one holds power and the other is less powerful or powerless. Lykes, Terre Blanche, and Hamber (2003) have suggested that participatory collaborations that seek to be transformative are constitutive of a new or "third voice" through which the voices of researcher and researched together transgress traditional representational forms. They worked with two women's groups, one in Guatemala and the other in South Africa, both of which are situated in moments of larger ongoing political struggles to overcome externally imposed repressive practices that censor the voices of marginalized communities. The authors, thus, joined historically marginalized women of color in transforming and deploying representational tools (photography and press releases) to "speak out" about experiences of political and military repression. In both cases the groups' agendas evolved over time, so that what emerged was not so much a particular account of themselves, or even the development of a particular voice for speaking about themselves, but an unfolding process—for the groups and for the researchers who accompanied them—of becoming active

players in the postmodern, mediated world of self-representational politics and social struggle (Lykes et al., 2003).

Although many projects describe themselves as processes wherein outsider researchers "give voice" to the "voiceless" or marginalized, we suggest here that feminist-infused participatory and action research seeks to interrogate and contest these ideas by problematizing voice and transforming the binaries of power and powerlessness, voice and voicelessness, situating the work within representational and transformational politics.

## Research Relationality: Building and Sustaining Relationships

Establishing collaborative research relationships is central to many qualitative approaches to research and is a basic goal of critical theorist and constructivist feminist researchers. Researchers committed to democratic participation and emancipation seek to raise individual and collective awareness of oppressive practices in the world and organize for change. Feminist-infused participatory and action research is, thus, built on the development of relationships; it is through relationships that participants are transformed (McIntyre & Lykes, 2004). Hierarchical research models are antithetical to this value system because, as Joyce Lander notes,

> the [traditional] relationship between researcher and his (sic) subjects, by definition, resembles that of the oppressor and the oppressed, because it is the oppressor who defines the problem, the nature of the research, and to some extent, the quality of interaction between him and his subjects. (Lander, 1971, cited in Tolman & Brydon-Miller, 2001, p. 36)

In contrast to this model, human beings undergoing a shared process of personal and collective change through feminist-infused participatory and action research naturally form bonds and attachments. McIntyre and Lykes (2004) argue, on the basis of years of collaboration with women in the north of Ireland and in Guatemala, that personal relationships constructed over time through PAR and collaborative activism stretch the boundaries of the presumed dichotomy between researchers and participants. They suggest that friendships formed through long-term commitments may be more accurately descriptive of feminist-infused PAR. Indeed, it has been argued here that such bonds are the stuff of transformation.

However, the practical requirements of those bonds beyond the boundaries and goals of participatory and action research processes raise challenging questions for some participatory and action researchers. While a bond may exist among researchers and participants, developing that bond into a working friendship requiring continual, mutual self-disclosure, reciprocity, and sustainability may not be an appropriate or productive extension of the experience of the research process. Some researchers have found that the expectations of reciprocity in feminist-infused participatory and action research limit them. For example, in reevaluating a 1983 qualitative study of white, mostly middle-class, women "at the end of their intense period of mothering," Acker, Barry, and Esseveld (1996) reflected on the burden that they as researchers experienced in not being able to meet the expectations of friendship that participants developed during the project. In addition, they felt that negative self-comparisons of the female interviewees to one of the external researchers of the same age resulted in self-editing that might not have occurred in a traditionally hierarchical research relationship (Acker et al., 1996).

Participants' expectations of relationality within feminist-infused participatory and action research are frequently intertwined with issues of researcher self-disclosure. Reflecting on a feminist PR project educating immigrant women in Canada regarding their legal rights, Susan McDonald (2003) urged that external researchers fully consider the implications of self-disclosure prior to embarking on a feminist-infused research project, opining that they hold a level of responsibility to attend to participant needs for "appropriate support" (identified as emotional and logistical support, among other forms). Patricia Maguire (1987) discussed similar challenges in her feminist PAR among Native American survivors of domestic abuse.

In part because of the complexities involved, these deeply contextualized experiences defy formulas and require fluidity and ongoing negotiation. A research conversation between and among coresearchers and communities requires interconnected and overlapping dialogue, wherein the relationships themselves are interrogated and the role of difference and power at work on both interpersonal and larger systems levels are explored.

## Encountering or Crafting Community(ies)

Most of the projects described in this chapter are carried out "in" or "with" communities, yet few of the coresearchers involved define what they mean by the term *community* or who is included when they use it. Community psychologists (see, e.g., Chavis & Newbrough, 1986; Sarason, 1974, among many others) have written extensively about community, distinguishing between objective and subjective communities. The former refers to a locality, place, or neighborhood and implies interactions among members who share interests and goals and, frequently in participatory and action research, are able to mobilize collective social and political power. However, in today's increasingly global world, more and more people use the term *community* to refer to a psychological sense of belonging, a perception of similarity to others, or a feeling that one is part of a larger whole—all sentiments that do not necessarily require geographical proximity. Many communities that are sites of participatory and action research entail shared membership, influence, integration, and emotional connection (McMillan & Chavis, 1986).

External researchers or catalysts encounter multiple challenges as they enter the objective and subjective communities wherein they seek to engage in collaborative participatory and action research processes. According to Baker Collins (2005, citing Cleaver, 2001), "Participatory research has a tendency to stress the solidarity of communities and to picture community as a natural social entity" (p. 15). Feminist theorists have problematized representations of "the other" in terms of similarity or sameness (see, e.g., Hurd & McIntyre, 1996) and difference (see Spelman, 1988, among many others). Similarly, researchers in feminist-infused participatory and action research projects are challenged to understand the similarities and differences within the community they enter *from the perspective of the community(ies)*, to the extent possible. Participatory and action researchers working in community development in the more collectivist societies of the majority world have discovered, for example, that women's alliances may not lie with other women but rather with male kin (Cornwall, 2003). Thus, communities are characterized by "both solidarity and conflict, shifting alliances, power and social structures" (Cleaver, 2001, p. 45).

For some women's groups, such as the Serbian Women in Black who protested the Balkan conflicts of the early 1990s, acknowledging and embracing difference serve as a method of establishing gender solidarity or women's community. The Women in Black proudly claimed,

> "We foster and further differences." . . . [They set] the most divisive difference, ethnicity/nationality, in a context of other, less threatening, differences . . . [and] say of themselves, "We are a heterogeneous group. The age of our members ranges from eighteen to seventy-five. Their backgrounds and lifestyles differ greatly. Some of them have been active feminists for a long time, while others participate in the feminist discourse for the first time." (Cockburn, 1998, pp. 171–172)

Thus, Cockburn encountered a complexly varied group of women wherein gender served as the definitional parameter that fostered their sense of belonging and where diversity or difference within similarity served a unifying role.

These experiences challenge feminist participatory and action researchers to interrogate assumptions about and definitions of community. *Community* is thus fluid of necessity, typically experienced affectively as a "sense of belonging" by those "on the inside" but defined through descriptive categories most typically by those "outside," who seek to "study it" or engage "with it" for political purposes that are often, again, defined from the "outside" (Naples, 2003). Women's experiences of community include, therefore, not only "the internal dynamics of 'communities,' [but also] the relationships between those who take part in[, for example,] a PRA exercise; those who stand up to present or make a case and those who watch from the sidelines" (Cornwall, 1998, p. 48). As suggested above, coresearchers develop relationships and facilitate a multiplicity of voices as they are informed by existing communities and create new ones within the research process. Accessing indigenous knowledge and generating alternative or transformative knowledge and action require all coresearchers to navigate not only the complex interpersonal relationships of any given community but also the contrasting and sometimes conflicting groups and subgroups within which these relationships develop.

## FEMINIST-INFUSED PARTICIPATORY ACTION RESEARCH: TOWARD THE POSSIBILITY OF TRANSFORMATIONAL PRAXIS

Feminist-infused participatory and action research and activist feminist research are, as argued here, theoretical and methodological orientations whereby researchers and groups of women, men, and children engage in cross-community knowledge construction and action. They are also, at least in part, focused on redressing inequality and facilitating social change. Such claims do not negate the potential contribution toward solving social problems claimed by those who engage in more traditional, hierarchical, positivist research. For example, Cancian (1996) argues that survey research by demographers and sociologists regarding the widening income gap between the rich and the poor in the United States had an impact on legislators' and voters' willingness to redistribute resources within the United States in the mid-1990s (pp. 202–203).

However, in contrast to positivist and post-positivist forms of research, participatory and action researchers seek to "mobilize oppressed people to act on their own behalf" rather than to act for them (Maguire, 1996, p. 29). Feminisms introduce a number of critical questions into this movement-building agenda, including, for example, whether a feminist perspective on participatory and action research challenges researchers to rethink the organizational and community-building aspects of these research methodologies. These questions, and others summarized in our discussion of cross-cutting issues, are fundamentally about power and the need not only to redistribute power but also to interrogate traditional understandings of power and to transform the praxis of power. We argue here, as suggested by Maguire (1996), that feminist-infused participatory and action research "re-conceptualize[s] the very notion of power" (p. 29).

Specifically, power, a term of relationality, is typically conceptualized as "power over" or possessing the resources and authority to impose one's will on individuals or groups with fewer resources. Power is typically associated with domination and vested in the state, religion, rulers, and so forth. However, feminist-infused participatory and action research suggests alternative formulations, focusing frequently on power as the "capacity to." Many social scientists, feminists, and development workers embrace the language of "empowerment." Yet the term *empowerment*, about which there is now a significant body of theory and research (see, e.g., Rappaport, 1987; Zimmerman, 1995, 2000), suggests that someone is handing power over to a less powerful person or group. Yet if power is the potential for an increased sense of an individual's or a community's capacity or ability to act for themselves that is the result of their involvement in participatory or action research projects, then it cannot be given but must be appropriated or taken. Thus, greater equity among coresearchers, a principle of participatory and action research processes, translates through shared action to enhanced or transformed equality within the research process and beyond—that is, in the wider community or in the world at large. From this perspective, "a popular people's organization [could be] a necessary prerequisite or a hoped-for outcome of participatory research" (Maguire, 1996, p. 29). Despite these critically important goals, many of the programs and projects described above fall short of transforming power or building a movement.

In this final section, we explore the ways in which, despite transformative goals and a discourse of change, feminist-infused participatory and action researchers sometimes reify rather than redress existing systems of power and control and fail to reduce the social injustices that are so carefully and critically described and analyzed through their work. We offer these concluding remarks both as cautionary tales and also to reflect through praxis the underlying assumptions of feminist-infused participatory and action research, that is, that they are continually iterative processes, not end points.

## Interrogating Power: Status, Functions, and Ideology

The issues of power described above hold particular resonance for feminist researchers in the academy, who, once among the population of the oppressed, now increasingly find themselves in positions of relative power and "gatekeeping." Social mobility may thus allow them vantage points as insiders *and* outsiders, challenging them "to continue to question the sources of [their] power, [and] how it cannot be separated from the politics and the ideological position of the user, and how power [over] functions even within communities committed to social justice" (Unger, 2004, p. 177).

External researchers often serve as "catalysts" asked to perform multiple roles as technical adviser, participant, and link to power sources, depending on the context. This role as catalyst or "external change agent" can cause tensions in movement building, especially when a project becomes a group undertaking or a collective process rather than one housed in the world of the catalyst (Martin, 1996; McDonald, 2003). McDonald (2003) discusses this tension in feminist-infused participatory and action research between demands that leadership be a driving force behind a project and feminist ideals of collaboration. Specifically, she discusses challenges in shifting or transforming the collective understanding of the project from "her project" to "our project" (McDonald, 2003, p. 77).

The researcher may struggle with navigating group dynamics and encouraging equitable participation by all while acknowledging that she is being treated as an expert, being deferred to by the group but also, in many ways, excluded from the group process. Yet she may also yield to a desire to use her status as a tool, exercising control or "power over" in order to keep the research project "on a comfortable course" progressing toward "her goals." Her "expert status" may also complicate basic decision making in participatory and action research endeavors, where the researcher may hold important knowledge regarding the suitability of specific methods, while the ideals of the project dictate that such a decision be made collectively rather than executively by the researcher (Martin, 1996). Ospina et al. (2004) argue that "for groups to function both effectively and democratically each member must feel authorized by the group and they must take up their own authority in the service of the group" (p. 65). Attention should be paid to understanding multiple forms of leadership, different leadership styles, and strategies for transferring control of a project to the participants or the community prior to the beginning of any project. Moreover, researchers are challenged to be transparent about these processes, each of which is frequently negotiated with partners external to the research process (e.g., funding agents, universities) that nonetheless exercise powerful influence at different points in the process.

## Participation and Empowerment: New Forms of Colonial Power?

Despite the reflexive self-awareness described above, and the commitments toward transformation, many participatory development practitioners and researchers have been criticized as only involving "local people taking part in other people's projects, according to agendas set by external interests" (Cornwall, 1996, p. 95). Participation, a sine qua non of participatory and action research, is highly structured, frequently yoked to democratic group processes, and often described as in the service of empowerment. Thus, participation carries with it expectations of public speech or group sharing, activities with varied meanings for women in the majority world. Participatory and action researchers rarely interrogate the values underlying norms of participation, or the parameters that define and characterize what constitutes participation. Cooke and Kothari (2001) have argued that it is critical to interrogate the discourse of participation itself, what they describe, somewhat provocatively, as the "tyranny of participation." Among other cautions, they suggest that the particular forms of "democratic participation" championed by action researchers working in development projects and, we would argue, by feminists shape particular identities that facilitate engagement in "the modern sector of developing societies" (p. 13), mapping and codifying local knowledge, thereby marginalizing indigenous ways of knowing that might

challenge a newly developing status quo or be "messy" or unmanageable.

### Exposing Difference

Moreover, as Andrea Cornwall (1998) notes, "there may be aspects of women's lives and livelihoods which are especially important to conceal from fellow traders, worshippers or from family members that might be shared with others" (p. 55) through a participatory methodology. In southwestern Nigeria, for example, women meet in various fora, including market associations, prayer groups, and lineage groups, all of which have different communication dynamics and goals that are specific to the women involved and to the nature of the meeting group (Cornwall, 1998). Moreover, Parpart (2000) argues that in Java, women's ability to control their speech and public behavior is equated with empowerment. This local understanding reflects a concept of empowerment that, in its implementation, may be at odds with Euro-American conceptualizations and action research goals.

Of equal concern are the possible risks to participants of exposing differences or private concerns in group or public fora, strategies endorsed by participatory and action research. Moreover, "care needs . . . to be taken to ensure that the use of group fora, which emphasize group consensus, do not mask intra-group differences" (Kindon, 1998, p. 160). For example, at a discussion group meeting of a men's *dusun* (the smallest administrative unit of a government village in Bali), facilitated as part of a CBPR process, the researcher Sara Kindon (1998) noted that because of the presence of a high-caste (Brahmin) man in a group of middle- to lower-caste men, the lower-caste men did not openly challenge the Brahmin's statements "for fear of losing face." Kindon concluded that "the group's consensus to follow such status-related codes of conduct masked considerable disagreement with this particular man's views" (p. 160). Others (see, e.g., Baker Collins, 2005; Guijt & Shah, 1998) have suggested that participatory tools or techniques are sometimes used as devices to achieve technical outcomes rather than as principles that inform or transform political or social realities.

These experiences underscore the ways in which cultural specificities significantly inform and transform feminist discourse and praxis. Also important, they suggest that conflict management and facilitation may be important resources for increasing the likelihood for the best representation of the less powerful in participatory and action research projects undertaken from a feminist or gender-analytical perspective.

### Inter- and Cross-Cultural Feminist Dialogue?

Feminist researchers are often based in Euro-American academic circles and grounded in modes of discourse and analysis that may not be considered relevant to the individuals in or culture of the communities with whom they work, both in the West and abroad. As suggested in many of the examples described in this chapter, this is particularly true for feminist discourse, ideology, and activism. For example, in a PR project with black and white women in a Michigan drug treatment program, Dorothy Jo Henderson (1994) found that activism was not necessarily a method of change to which the participants could relate. Or, at the Medica Women's Centre established in Central Bosnia following the Balkan conflicts, Cockburn (1998) found that women held varied perspectives on feminism, some scoffing at Euro-American theories of feminism and International Women's Day—the former considered a luxury of women without families, the latter a disingenuous display of "flowers and flattery." Moreover, women in many majority world societies place great value on their opportunities for social and political influence that exist because of their roles as wives and mothers. Euro-American feminism's emphasis on challenging patriarchy and traditional gender roles may be seen as threatening to such women's cultural traditions and as devaluing their contributions within their traditional gender roles.

More locally, sociologist Nancy Naples's (2003) attempts to develop a feminist-based dialogue with a fellow survivor of childhood incest led her to the realization that "Emily [her coresearcher, a native Iowan, mother, and community activist] does not see the immediate relevance of academic discourse and feminist methodology for her goals [of empowering victims of sexual violence to tell their stories]"

(pp. 192–193). Despite Naples's expectations of the ability of feminist participatory research to "[generate] survivor-centered discourses that could broaden our understanding of the myriad forces contributing to violence against women" (p. 187) through dialogue and community outreach with adult survivors of sexual abuse and other survivors of violence, "the final product [of the efforts] was inevitably more an extension of [her] concerns than of [her coresearcher] Emily's" (pp. 192–193).

## Discussion

Explicitly feminist praxis, with its critique of power and gender asymmetries, sometimes sits uneasily within the participatory norms of action research. Others have argued that these participatory norms fail to challenge gendered hierarchies or to transform traditional relations that oppress women. Much of participatory and action research emphasizes local issues, dynamics, and change and does not directly address larger political and economic structures. Participants may choose not to work on social change at the level of state or national power structures—either because it is not a priority or because they are not confident that they have the power to achieve that change. Who *does* participate is in many cases who *can* participate. Specifically, the duration of a participatory or action project (i.e., more hours than a participant can spare from minimum-wage work or day work), its location at a distance from the duties of participants (e.g., away from the field or one's children), and the participant's lack of skills to contribute to report writing and analyses required of some participatory and action research are all obstacles that may have a negative impact on the ability of community members to participate (Parpart, 2000).

## Toward the Possibility of Transformational Praxis

Participatory and action researchers working from a feminist standpoint articulate a commitment to challenge systems of power and to redress social injustice. Thus, at least implicitly, they have committed to challenging national and global power structures that maintain local systems of inequality and oppression, and despite multiple challenges, feminist-infused participatory and action research processes and outcomes have transformative potential. In a report written for the Centre of African Studies at the University of Copenhagen, Jane Parpart (2000) articulates certain requirements for rethinking and implementing anew participation and empowerment techniques for participatory and action researchers and participatory development projects. She challenges such researchers and feminists

> to develop a more nuanced and sophisticated analysis of power . . . [that] incorporate[s] an analysis of the way global and national power structures impact on the local, the character and resilience of local power structures, the link between knowledge/discourse and power; and the complex ways people seek to ensure their well-being in the world. . . . Participatory empowerment techniques will have to pay more attention to the way national and global power structures constrain and define the possibilities for change at the local level. (p. 18)

Many of the projects described in this chapter share a desire for change that supports movement building and social transformation. The group and community processes are designed to open spaces wherein women and men address gender relations and to consider new approaches to struggles that they face in their ever-widening circles of relationality. The liberatory aspects of feminist, participatory, and action research seek to raise awareness regarding oppressive forces at work in daily life. Through this, and the equitable power dynamic of the research process itself, the collaborative project identifies and works to transform power imbalances that contribute to the maintenance of systems of oppression. When coresearchers take the knowledge and momentum of these collective and community-based processes forward into the society at large for the purpose of addressing other, larger power imbalances, feminist-infused participatory and action research processes reach toward the creation of social and transformative change.

## Notes

1. In this chapter we use the term *core-searchers* to capture the collaborative relationships among researcher-catalyst-outsider-facilitator and participant-insider-community member. In reporting some studies, we distinguish among researchers and participants for clarity and consistency. However, this terminology is not meant to distract from the primary aims of participatory and action research, that is, to de-emphasize these distinctions and to recognize collaborative contributions to knowledge construction through the processes described herein.

2. Rather than the terms *Third World* or *developing world*, we use the term *majority world* to refer to countries outside the United States and Europe. These countries have a majority of the world's population and occupy a majority of the earth's land surface or geographical space, excluding China.

3. This idea was informed by Daphne Patai's (1994) response to Michelle Fine's and Patti Lather's feminist perspective on power and method, which appears in Andrew Gitlin's *Power and Method: Political Activism and Educational Research.*

## References

Acker, J., Barry, K., & Esseveld, J. (1996). Objectivity and truth: Problems in doing feminist research. In H. Gottfried (Ed.), *Feminism and social change: Bridging theory and practice* (pp. 60–87). Urbana: University of Illinois Press.

Adelman, C. (1993). Kurt Lewin and the origins of action research. *Educational Action Research, 1*(1), 7–24.

Arriata, M., & de la Maza, I. (1997). Grounding a long-term deal: Working with the Aymara for community development. In S. E. Smith & D. G. Willms (with N. A. Johnson) (Eds.), *Nurtured by knowledge: Learning to do participatory action-research* (pp. 111–137). New York: Apex Press.

Baker Collins, S. (2005). An understanding of poverty from those who are poor. *Action Research, 3*(1), 9–31.

Bartunek, J. M., & Louis, M. R. (1996). *Insider/outsider team research* (Qualitative Research Methods, Series 40). Thousand Oaks, CA: Sage.

Boston Women's Health Book Collective. (1973). *Our bodies, ourselves: A book by and for women.* New York: Simon & Schuster.

Brydon-Miller, M., & Greenwood, D. (2003). Why action research? *Action Research, 1*(1), 9–28.

Brydon-Miller, M., Maguire, P., & McIntyre, A. (2004). *Traveling companions: Feminism, teaching, and action research.* Westport, CT: Praeger.

Bunster, X., & Chaney, E. M. (1989). Epilogue. In X. Bunster & E. M. Chaney (Eds.), *Sellers & servants: Working women in Lima, Peru* (pp. 217–233). Granby, MA: Bergin & Garvey.

Burns, A. (1999). *Collaborative action research for English language teachers.* New York: Cambridge University Press.

Cancian, F. (1996). Participatory research and alternative strategies for activist sociology. In H. Gottfried (Ed.), *Feminism and social change: Bridging theory and practice* (pp. 187–205). Urbana: University of Illinois Press.

Caro-Bruce, C., & McCreadie, J. (1995). What happens when a school district supports action research? In S. E. Noffke & R. B. Stevenson (Eds.), *Educational action research: Becoming practically critical* (pp. 154–164). New York: Columbia University, Teachers College.

Chavez, V., Duran, B., Baker, Q., Avila, M., & Wallerstein, N. (2003). The dance of race and privilege in community-based participatory research. In M. Minkler & N. Wallerstein (Eds.), *Community-based participatory research for health* (pp. 81–97). San Francisco: Jossey-Bass.

Chavis, D., & Newbrough, J. R. (1986). The meaning of "community" in community psychology. *Journal of Community Psychology. Special Psychological Sense of Community: II. Research and Applications, 14*(4), 335–340.

Chuaprapaisilp, A. (1997). Action research: Improving learning from experience in nurse education in Thailand. In R. Taggart (Ed.), *Participatory action research: International contexts and consequences* (pp. 247–261). Albany: State University of New York Press.

Cleaver, F. (2001). Institutions, agency and the limitations of participatory approaches to development. In B. Cooke & U. Kothari (Eds.), *Participation: The new tyranny?* (pp. 36–55). London: Zed Books.

Cockburn, C. (1998). *The space between us: Negotiating gender and national identities in conflict.* London: Zed Books.

Cockburn, C. (2004). *The line.* London: Zed Books.

Collins, P. H. (1990). *Black feminist thought: Knowledge, consciousness, and the politics of empowerment.* Boston: Unwin Hyman.

Collins, P. H. (1998). *Fighting words: Black women and the search for justice.* Minneapolis: University of Minnesota Press.

Commission for Historical Clarification. (1999). *Guatemala: Memory of silence* (Report of the Commission for Historical Clarification). Retrieved May 10, 2005, from http://shr.aaas .org/guatemala/ceh/report/english/recs1.html

Cooke, B., & Kothari, U. (Eds.). (2001). *Participation: The new tyranny?* London: Zed Books.

Cornwall, A. (1996). Towards participatory practice: participatory rural appraisal (PRA) and the participatory process. In K. de Koning & M. Martin (Eds.), *Participatory research in health: Issues and experiences* (pp. 95–107). Johannesburg, South Africa: Zed Books.

Cornwall, A. (1998). Gender, participation and the politics of difference. In I. Guijt & M. K. Shah (Eds.), *The myth of community: Gender issues in participatory development* (pp. 46–57). London: Intermediate Technology.

Cornwall, A. (2000). *Making a difference? Gender and participatory development* (IDS Discussion Paper No. 378). Sussex, UK: Institute of Development Studies.

Cornwall, A. (2003). Whose voices? Whose choices? Reflections on gender and participatory development. *World Development, 31*(8), 1325–1342.

Crawley, H. (1998). Living up to the empowerment claim? The potential of PRA. In I. Guijt & M. K. Shah (Eds.), *The myth of community: Gender issues in participatory development* (pp. 24–34). London: Intermediate Technology.

Currie, D. (1999). Gender analysis from the standpoint of women: The radical potential of women's studies in development. *Asian Journal of Women's Studies, 5*(3).

Davis, A. (1981). *Women, race and class.* New York: Vintage Books.

Debbink, G., & Ornelas, A. (1997). Cows for campesinos. In S. E. Smith, D. G. Willms, & N. A. Johnson (Eds.), *Nurtured by knowledge: Learning to do participatory action research* (pp. 13–33). New York: Apex Press.

Denzin, N. K., & Lincoln, Y. S. (Eds.). (2000). *Handbook of qualitative research* (2nd ed.). Thousand Oaks, CA: Sage.

Dick, B. (2004). Action research literature: Themes and trends. *Action Research, 2*(4), 425–444.

Du Bois, B. (1983). Passionate scholarship: Notes on value, knowing, and method in feminist social science. In G. Bowles & R. D. Klein (Eds.), *Theories of women's studies* (pp. 105–116). London: Routledge & Kegan Paul.

Ecumenical Women's Team Visit. (1992). *Rape of women in war.* Geneva, Switzerland: Author.

Eikeland, O. (2001). Action research as the hidden curriculum of the Western tradition. In P. Reason & H. Bradbury (Eds.), *Handbook of action research: Participative inquiry and practice* (pp. 145–156). Thousand Oaks, CA: Sage.

Evans, S. M. (1979). *Personal politics: The roots of women's liberation in the civil rights movement and the New Left.* New York: Vintage Books.

Fals-Borda, O. (1985). *Knowledge and people's power: Lessons with peasants in Nicaragua, Mexico, and Colombia.* New Delhi: Indian Social Institute.

Fals-Borda, O. R., & Rahman, M. A. (Eds.). (1991). *Action and knowledge: Breaking the monopoly with participatory action research.* New York: Apex Press/London: Intermediate Technology.

Fine, M. (1992). *Disruptive voices: The possibilities of feminist research.* Ann Arbor: University of Michigan Press.

Fine, M. (1994). Dis-stance and other stances: Negotiation of power inside feminist research. In A. Gitlin (Ed.), *Power and method: Political activism and educational research* (pp. 13–35). New York: Routledge.

Fine, M., Roberts, R. A., Torre, M. E., Bloom, J., Burns, A., Chajet, L., et al. (2004). *Echoes of Brown: Youth documenting and performing the legacy of Brown v. Board of Education.* New York: Teachers College Press.

Firestone, S. (1970). *The dialectics of sex: The case for a feminist revolution.* New York: Bantam Books.

Freeman, J. (Ed.). (1975). *Women: A feminist perspective.* Oxford, UK: Mayfield.

Freire, P. (1970). *Pedagogy of the oppressed* (M. B. Ramos, Trans.). New York: Continuum.

Friedan, B. (1963). *The feminine mystique.* New York: W. W. Norton.

Gluck, S. B., & Patai, D. (Ed.). (1991). *Women's words: The feminist practice of oral history.* New York: Routledge.

Gorelick, S. (1996). Contradictions of feminist methodology. In H. Gottfried (Ed.), *Feminism and social change: Bridging theory and practice* (pp. 23–45). Urbana: University of Illinois Press.

Gottfried, H. (Ed.). (1996). *Feminism and social change: Bridging theory and practice.* Urbana: University of Illinois Press.

Greenwood, D., & Levin, M. (1998). *Introduction to action research: Social research for social change.* Thousand Oaks, CA: Sage.

Guijt, I., & Shah, M. K. (Eds.). (1998). *The myth of community: Gender issues in participatory development.* London: Intermediate Technology.

Gustavsen, B. (2001). Theory and practice: The mediating discourse. In P. Reason & H. Bradbury (Eds.), *Handbook of action research: Participative inquiry and practice* (pp. 17–26). Thousand Oaks, CA: Sage.

Harding, S. (1986). *The science question in feminism.* Ithaca, NY: Cornell University Press.

Henderson, D. J. (1994). *Feminist nursing participatory research with black and white women in drug treatment.* Unpublished doctoral dissertation, University of Michigan School of Nursing.

Hondagneu-Sotelo, P. (1996). Immigrant women and paid domestic work: Research, theory and activism. In H. Gottfried (Ed.), *Feminism and social change: Bridging theory and practice* (pp. 105–122). Urbana: University of Illinois Press.

hooks, b. (1981). *Ain't I a woman: Black women and feminism.* Boston: South End Press.

hooks, b. (1984). Black women: Shaping feminist theory. In *Feminist theory: From margin to center* (pp. 1–15). Boston: South End Press.

Hope, A., & Timmel, S. (1984–2000). *Training for transformation: A handbook for community workers* (Vols. 1–4). London: Intermediate Technology.

Hurd, T., & McIntyre, A. (1996). The seduction of sameness: Similarity and representing the other. *Feminism & Psychology, 6*(1), 86–92.

Jacobsen, J. L. (2005). *Gender bias: Roadblock to sustainable development.* Washington, DC: WorldWatch Institute. Retrieved April 19, 2005, from http://feminism.eserver.org/gender/cyberspace/gender-bias-causes-poverty.html

Khanna, R. (1996). Participatory action research (PAR) in women's health: SARTHI, India. In K. de Koning & M. Martin (Eds.), *Participatory research in health: Issues and experiences* (pp. 62–71). Johannesburg, South Africa: Zed Books.

Kindon, S. (1998). Of mothers and men: Questioning gender and community myths in Bali. In I. Guijt & M. K. Shah (Eds.), *The myth of community: Gender issues in development* (pp. 152–164). London: Intermediate Technology.

Lewis, H. M. (2001). Participatory research and education for social change: Highlander Research and Education Center. In P. Reason & H. Bradbury

(Eds.), *Handbook of action research: Participative inquiry & practice* (pp. 356–362). London: Sage.

Lorde, A. (1982). *Zami: A new spelling of my name.* Berkeley, CA: Crossing Press.

Lorde, A. (1984). *Sister outsider: Essays and speeches.* Berkeley, CA: Crossing Press.

Lykes, M. B. (1994). Terror, silencing and children: International, multidisciplinary collaboration with Guatemalan Maya communities. *Social Science and Medicine, 38*(4), 543–552.

Lykes, M. B. (with Mateo, A. C., Anay, J. C., Caba, A. L., Ruiz, U., & Williams, J. W.). (1999). Telling stories—rethreading lives: Community education, women's development, and social change among the Maya Ixil. *International Journal of Leadership in Education: Theory and Practice, 2*(3), 207–227.

Lykes, M. B., Terre Blanche, M., & Hamber, B. (2003). Narrating survival and change in Guatemala and South Africa: The politics of representation and a liberatory community psychology. *American Journal of Community Psychology, 31*(1/2), 79–90.

Maguire, P. (1987). *Doing participatory research: A feminist approach.* Amherst: University of Massachusetts, Massachusetts Center for International Education.

Maguire, P. (1996). Proposing a more feminist participatory research: Knowing and being embraced more openly. In K. de Koning & M. Martin (Eds.), *Participatory research in health: Issues and experiences* (pp. 27–29). Johannesburg, South Africa: Zed Books.

Maguire, P. (2001). Uneven ground: Feminism and action research. In P. Reason & H. Bradbury (Eds.), *Handbook of action research: Participative inquiry and practice* (pp. 59–69). Thousand Oaks, CA: Sage.

Maguire, P. (2004). Reclaiming the F-word: Emerging lessons from teaching and feminist-informed action research. In M. Brydon-Miller, P. Maguire, & A. McIntyre (Eds.), *Traveling companions: Feminisms, teaching, and action research* (pp. 117–136). Westport, CT: Praeger.

Manji, A. (1999). Feminism and methodology: Studying the impact of AIDS using participatory research. *Southern African Feminist Review, 3*(2), 1–18.

Marecek, J., Fine, M., & Kidder, L. (2001). Working between two worlds: Qualitative methods and psychology. In D. L. Tolman & M. Brydon-Miller (Eds.), *From subjects to subjectivities: A handbook of interpretive and participatory methods* (pp. 29–44). New York: New York University Press.

Martin, M. (1996). Issues of power in the participatory research process. In K. de Koning & M. Martin (Eds.), *Participatory research in health: Issues and experiences* (pp. 82–93). London: Zed Books.

Mazowiecki, T. (1993). *United Nations Commission on Human Rights: Situation of human rights in the territory of the former Yugoslavia.* New York: United Nations.

McDonald, S. (2003). Answering questions and asking more: Reflections on feminist participatory research. *Resources for Feminist Research, 30*(2), 77.

McIntyre, A. (1997). *Making meaning of whiteness: Exploring racial identity with white teachers.* Albany: State University of New York Press.

McIntyre, A., & Lykes, M. B. (2004). Weaving words and pictures in/through feminist participatory action research. In M. Brydon-Miller, P. Maguire, & A. McIntyre (Eds.), *Traveling companions: Feminism, teaching, and action research* (pp. 57–77). Westport, CT: Praeger.

McMillan, D. W., & Chavis, D. M. (1986). Sense of community: A definition and theory. *Journal of Community Psychology. Special Psychological Sense of Community, I: Theory and Concepts, 14*(1), 6–23.

McTaggart, R. (Ed.). (1997). *Participatory action research: International contexts and consequences.* Albany: State University of New York Press.

Merton, R. K. (1972). Insiders and outsiders: A chapter in the sociology of knowledge. *American Journal of Sociology, 78,* 9–47.

Miller, V. (1985). *Between struggle and hope: The Nicaraguan literacy crusade.* Boulder, CO: Westview Press.

Millet, K. (1969). *Sexual politics.* New York: Doubleday.

Minkler, M., & Wallerstein, N. (2003). Introduction to community based participatory research. In M. Minkler & N. Wallerstein (Eds.), *Community based participatory research for health* (pp. 3–26). San Francisco: Jossey-Bass.

Mitchell, C., & Reid-Walsh, J. (2002). *Researching children's popular culture: The cultural spaces of childhood.* New York: Routledge.

Mohanty, C. T. (2003). *Feminism without borders: Decolonizing theory, practicing solidarity.* Durham, NC: Duke University Press.

Moraga, C., & Anzaldúa, G. (1983). *This bridge called my back: Writings by radical women of color.* New York: Kitchen Table, Women of Color Press.

Naples, N. A. (2003). *Feminism and method: Ethnography, discourse analysis, and activist research.* New York: Routledge.

Office of Human Rights of the Archdiocese of Guatemala [Oficina de Derechos Humanos del Arzobispado de Guatemala]. (1998). Never again: Report of the inter-diocescan project on the recovery of historic memory [*Nunca más: Informe proyecto interdiocesano de recuperación de la memoria histórica*] (Vols. 1–5). Guatemala: Author.

Ospina, S., Dodge, J., Godsoe, B., Minieri, J., Reza, S., & Schall, E. (2004). From consent to mutual inquiry: Balancing democracy and authority in action research. *Action Research, 2*(1), 47–69.

Parpart, J. L. (2000). *The participatory empowerment approach to gender and development in Africa: Panacea or illusion?* Occasional paper. Copenhagen, Denmark: University of Copenhagen, Centre of African Studies.

Patai, D. (1994). When method becomes power [Response]. In A. Gitlin (Ed.), *Power and method: Political activism and educational research* (pp. 61–73). New York: Routledge.

Personal Narratives Group. (1989). *Interpreting women's lives: Feminist theory and personal narratives.* Bloomington: Indiana University Press.

Rahman, A. (2004). Globalization: The emerging ideology in the popular protests and grassroots action research. *Action Research, 2*(1), 9–23.

Rappaport, J. (1987). Terms of empowerment/exemplars of prevention: Toward a theory for community psychology. *American Journal of Community Psychology, 15*(2), 121–148.

Reason, P., & Bradbury, H. (2001). Introduction: Inquiry and participation in search of a world worthy of human aspiration. In P. Reason & H. Bradbury (Eds.), *Handbook of action research: Participative inquiry and practice* (pp. 1–14). Thousand Oaks, CA: Sage.

Reinharz, S. (1992). *Feminist methods in social research.* New York: Oxford University Press.

Roberts, H. (1981). *Doing feminist research.* Boston: Routledge & Kegan Paul.

Roodt, M. J. (1996). "Participatory development": A jargon concept? In J. K. Coetzee & J. Graaff (Eds.), *Reconstruction, development and people* (pp. 312–323). Halfway House, South Africa: International Thomson.

Rosen, R. (2000). *The world split open: How the modern women's movement changed America.* New York: Penguin Putnam.

Sandoval, C. (2000). *Methodology of the oppressed.* Minneapolis: University of Minnesota Press.

Sarason, S. (1974). *The psychological sense of community: Prospects for a community psychology.* Oxford, UK: Jossey-Bass.

Seager, J. (2003). *The Penguin atlas of women in the world.* New York: Penguin Books.

Sleeter, C., Torres, M. N., & Laughlin, P. (2004). Scaffolding conscientization through inquiry in teacher education. *Teacher Education Quarterly, 31*(1), 81–96.

Smith, D. E. (1987). *The everyday world as problematic: A feminist sociology.* Boston: Northeastern University Press.

Smith, D. E. (1991). *The conceptual practices of power: A feminist sociology of knowledge.* Boston: Northeastern University Press.

Smith, S. (1995). *Dancing with conflict: Public health nurses in participatory action research.* Unpublished doctoral dissertation, University of Calgary, Department of Educational Policy and Administrative Studies.

Spelman, E. V. (1988). Gender in the context of race and class: Notes on Chodorow's "Reproduction of mothering." In *Inessential woman: Problems of exclusion in feminist thought* (pp. 80–113). Boston: Beacon.

Stacey, J. (1996). Can there be a feminist ethnography? In H. Gottfried (Ed.), *Feminism and social change: Bridging theory and practice* (pp. 88–101). Urbana: University of Illinois Press.

Stern, S. P. (1998). Struggle over schooling in an African American community. In N. Naples (Ed.), *Community activism and feminist politics: Organizing across race, class, and gender* (pp. 107–127). New York: Routledge.

Stewart, A. J. (1998). Doing personality research: How can feminist theories help? In B. M. Clinchy & J. K. Norem (Eds.), *Gender and psychology reader* (pp. 54–68). New York: New York University Press.

Swiss, S., & Giller, J. E. (1993). Rape as a crime of war: A medical perspective. *Journal of the American Medical Association, 270,* 612–615.

Themba, M. N., & Minkler, M. (2003). Influencing policy through community based participatory research. In M. Minkler & N. Wallerstein (Eds.), *Community-based participatory research for health* (pp. 349–370). San Francisco: Jossey-Bass.

Titchen, A. (1997). Creating a learning culture: A story of change in hospital nursing. In S. Hollingsworth (Ed.), *International action research: A casebook for educational reform* (pp. 244–260). London: Falmer Press.

Tolman, D. L., & Brydon-Miller, M. (Eds.). (2001). *From subjects to subjectivities: A handbook of interpretive and participatory methods.* New York: New York University Press.

Torre, M. E., & Fine, M. (2003). Youth reframe questions of educational justice through participatory action research. *Evaluation Exchange, 9*(2), 6.

Trinh, M. T. (1989). *Woman, native, other: Writing post-coloniality and feminism.* Bloomington: Indiana University Press.

Unger, R. K. (2004). Dilemmas of power: Questions for all of us. In M. Brydon-Miller, P. Maguire, & A. McIntyre (Eds.), *Traveling companions: Feminism, teaching, and action research* (pp. 169–178). Westport, CT: Praeger.

United Nations Children's Fund. (2005). Patterns in conflict: Civilians are now the target. In *Information: Impact of armed conflict on children.* Retrieved May 25, 2005, from www.unicef.org/graca/patterns.htm

Wang, C., Burris, M., & Xiang, Y. (1996). Chinese village women as visual anthropologists: A participatory approach to reaching policymakers. *Social Science & Medicine, 42*(10), 1391–1400.

Welbourne, A. (1998). Gender, participation and HIV: A positive force for change. In I. Guijt & M. K. Shah (Eds.), *The myth of community: Gender issues in participatory development* (pp. 131–140). London: Intermediate Technology.

Whyte, W. F. (Ed.). (1991). *Participatory action research.* Newbury Park, CA: Sage.

Williams, J. W., & Lykes, M. B. (2003). Bridging theory and practice: Using reflexive cycles in feminist participatory action research. *Feminism & Psychology, 13*(3), 287–294.

Williams, P., & Chrisman, L. (Eds.). (1994). *Colonial discourse/political theory.* New York: Columbia University Press.

Women of Photovoice/ADMI & Lykes, M. B. (2000). *Voces e imagenes: Mujeres mayas ixiles de Chajul* [Voices and images: Mayan Ixil women of Chajul]. Guatemala: MagnaTerra.

Young, K. (1993). *Planning with women: Making a world of difference.* London: Macmillan.

Yunus, M. (with Jolis, A.). (1999). *Banker to the poor: Micro-lending and the battle against world poverty.* New York: Public Affairs.

Zeichner, K. (2001). Educational action research. In P. Reason & H. Bradbury (Eds.), *Handbook of action research: Participative inquiry and practice* (pp. 273–284). Thousand Oaks, CA: Sage.

Zimmerman, M. A. (1995). Psychological empowerment: Issues and illustrations. *American Journal of Community Psychology. Special Empowerment Theory, Research, and Application, 23*(5), 581–599.

Zimmerman, M. A. (2000). Empowerment theory: Psychological, organizational, and community levels of analysis. In J. Rappaport & E. Seidman (Eds.), *Handbook of community psychology* (pp. 43–63). Dordrecht, the Netherlands: Kluwer Academic.

# 15

# NARRATIVES AND NUMBERS

## *Feminist Multiple Methods Research*

ABIGAIL J. STEWART

ELIZABETH R. COLE

S everal years ago, along with our colleague David Featherman, we were fortunate to have the opportunity to coteach a yearlong graduate seminar introducing students to feminist social science research that integrates both qualitative and quantitative methods. The goal of the seminar was to move beyond a conflict about the value of these two approaches that has been characterized as a debate (sometimes known as the QQD; Rabinowitz & Weseen, 1997) or even a war (Tashakkori & Teddlie, 1998). Without advocating any particular methods, we aimed to examine the obstacles and benefits associated with combining and integrating qualitative and quantitative methods and to encourage students to become skilled in the use of both approaches.

Our syllabus began with readings that outlined ideal approaches for combining methodologies (Newman & Benz, 1998; Tashakkori & Teddlie, 1998, 2002); with these as a backdrop, the remainder of the course was a series of invited lectures by researchers whose research programs used both qualitative and quantitative methods. Over the academic year, we learned a great deal about how researchers called on these two approaches to address their research questions; the combinations both reflected a wish to gain knowledge about a phenomenon unconstrained by methodological preconceptions and at the same time were almost always pragmatic, often innovative, and even occasionally based on serendipity or the resources at hand.

In this chapter, our goal is to distill some of what we learned from this teaching experience, thereby sharing it with a broader audience. Our reflections have led us to generate a typology of approaches based not on ideal types but on

Authors' Note: We are grateful to the Rackham Graduate School at the University of Michigan for a Rackham Interdisciplinary Seminar Grant to develop and teach a graduate course on Narratives and Numbers with our colleague David Featherman. We owe a great deal to David Featherman, to the guest visitors to the course, and to the students in the seminar for providing such a stimulating opportunity to think about these issues. Thanks are also due to Amal Fadlalla for her suggestions about combining qualitative and quantitative methods in the field of anthropology. Finally, we appreciate the thoughtful and helpful feedback on an early draft of this manuscript from Christa McDermott, Perry Silverschanz, Cynthia Torges, and the editor.

combinations of strategies actually used by researchers whose work addresses women, gender, and sexuality. To cast our net widely, we have used a broad definition of feminist research in this chapter: We are interested in work that takes gender and/or sexuality as a central focus or category of analysis. But this endeavor, as we have defined it, begs two larger questions. First, is feminist mixed method research different from that undertaken by any other researcher, and if so, how? Here, we are in agreement with Harding (1987): Feminist research is distinguished not so much by its methods, that is, the procedures through which information or observations are collected, but by its methodology, that is, the underlying theory about how research should be conducted and what its aims should be. Harding argues that feminist researchers typically ground their research questions in the experience of women, with the goal of understanding women's experience and improving women's lives, and in doing so, many attempt to equalize the hierarchy in the traditional relationship between "researchers" and "subjects."

The second question is why any social scientist should attempt to combine these methods, methods that some would argue are based on fundamentally different assumptions about epistemology and ontology (Guba & Lincoln, 1994).[1] Perhaps the most commonly offered answer to this question is that different methods suit different questions or aspects of questions. Courses in research methods typically represent the research process as composed of two sequential phases: the context of discovery, in which hypotheses are generated, and the context of justification, in which they are tested. In this tradition, qualitative methods are often presented as subjective, unsystematic, and inherently unreliable and, thus, only appropriate for the context of discovery.[2] In contrast, the strengths of quantitative methods are held to be reliability, replicability, and generalizability. They, therefore, hold sway over the context of justification. However, Lin (1998) cogently challenged this binary, arguing that although many believe qualitative and quantitative approaches are divided by an underlying divergence in their epistemological assumptions (which she termed *interpretivist* and *positivist,* respectively), this characterization is misleading. Lin argued that positivist approaches aim to identify relationships between variables that are generalizable to different contexts; in contrast, interpretivist methods are designed to reveal the mechanisms that underlie these relationships in particular cases or contexts. She argued that qualitative methods can be used in research with both types of epistemological aims and demonstrated this with examples from public policy research.

For example, both Stack (1974) and Edin (1991) used qualitative methods to study how poor women survive on very limited incomes. Stack's project, an interpretivist one, demonstrated how women shared resources within social networks even when doing so came at personal costs to individuals. Stack studied the norms and sense of obligation among women in one kin network, richly documenting the particularity of this social context. In contrast, Edin used qualitative methods of in-depth interviews and ethnography to construct a detailed accounting of her respondents' household budgets, finding that women often used family gifts and undocumented work to make ends meet. Because the gap between the cost of living and welfare payments was similar in different parts of the country, Edin argued that it was appropriate to generalize these findings. Thus, Lin's (1998) insights suggest that one of the most commonly given justifications for combining qualitative and quantitative methods in a single project may unnecessarily constrain researchers; a researcher with both interpretivist and positivist aims could also choose to design a pair of qualitative studies to address these research questions. Proponents of mixing qualitative and quantitative methods also argue that this approach can increase our confidence in the robustness of a finding when the relationship appears to hold using a variety of research approaches (this represents a form of replication or cross-validation, and is often termed triangulation). However, as Lin's work reminds us, this particular strength of the multimethods approach could be accomplished using any combination of methods and does not necessitate the combination of quantitative and qualitative approaches.

Among social scientists, feminist scholars have been particularly vocal in arguing for the value of mixed methods research approaches, although for a variety of different reasons (see especially Fine & Gordon, 1989; Jayaratne & Stewart, 1991; Peplau & Conrad,

1989; Reinharz, 1992). First, because feminist scholars often begin from a posture of critique of existing social science findings, and recognize that social science research has often "left out" or ignored aspects of phenomena that they care about, they are much less inclined to believe that a single method is the "royal road" to understanding. Thus, feminist scholars have often embraced pluralism partly as a strategy that might be less likely to produce such a narrow and selective picture of human experience (Jayaratne & Stewart, 1991; Rabinowitz & Weseen, 1997; Sherif, 1987; Unger, 1981; Weisstein, 1971).

Feminist scholars are wary of the dangers of false generalization in formulating research questions. For example, Sapiro (1995) noted, of political science, that "in the early days most work was of the 'add women and stir' or compensatory variety, taking conventional questions in different fields, but especially political behavior and political theory, and asking, 'what about the women?'" (p. 291). Smith (1987) made a parallel argument about sociological studies of the family and education—that they began from the standpoint of men, even when they included attention to women and children. Similarly, feminist scholars commented that much of psychology was in fact a generalization from research on male college sophomores until the late 1960s (Lykes & Stewart, 1986; Wallston, 1981; Weisstein, 1971). Because of their recognition of this early false generalization from men, or even male college sophomores, to "people," feminist scholars were sensitive to the importance of care in defining and describing samples, as well as specific measures (Morawski, 1994).

For example, one early target of feminist critique was the notion of "achievement motivation," which was based on a model of male-male competition that was clearly too narrow to cover all kinds of achievement even for men, much less women (see, e.g., Horner, 1972)! To many feminist scholars, multiple measures help ensure greater sampling of the phenomenon (with different definitions and techniques of assessment), and that increase in sampling of the phenomenon seems likely to increase the likelihood of legitimate generalizability (see, e.g., Ÿllo, 1988, on studying marital rape).

Alternatively, of course, a deeper reflection on the nature of generalizability can be an outgrowth of this preoccupation. Instead of worrying about ensuring generalizability, many feminist scholars urged greater specificity about the nature of the generalizability that could be claimed (Morawski, 1994). For example, Fine and Weis (1998) showed that women of different ethnic backgrounds viewed and responded to domestic violence differently because of the different relationships of each ethnic group with social institutions such as the police. Such differences are not only systematic; they also mean that one cannot make broad generalizations about how women—even poor women—respond to domestic violence.

Because feminist scholars are often particularly interested in phenomena that are studied in many different social science disciplines (women's labor market experience, breastfeeding, sexual harassment, etc.), they tend to read across fields. This exposure to interdisciplinary theory and evidence inevitably exposes feminist scholars to alternative habits about methods. Thus, for example, feminist psychologists may be drawn to ethnographic or historical methods (Stewart, 2003), while feminist sociologists may consider interpreting psychological tests (Martin, 1996), and political scientists may decide to include experimental treatments in their surveys (Huddy et al., 1997). In short, exposure to a wider range of methods in the literatures that feminist scholars study nearly inevitably produces an increased temptation to borrow methods from neighboring disciplines.

Equally, because feminist scholars are generally reading across disciplinary boundaries, they are also inclined to theorize about problems that are new to their own disciplines. Thus, for example, feminist psychologists are increasingly interested in studying issues that arise in the "workplace" (such as sexual harassment and incivility), historically the province of sociologists (see, e.g., Cortina, Magley, & Williams, 2001; Ragins, 2004), while feminist political scientists increasingly notice that people's family lives (traditionally the domain of sociology and psychology) have implications for their political behavior (see, e.g., Burns, Schlozman, & Verba, 1997). Anthropologists who study culturally based conceptualizations of health and fertility may use the tools of demography to complement ethnographic methods (Bledsoe, 2002). There is an intellectual energy and excitement that occurs as feminist scholars identify and theorize these new questions, and their new theories demand methods that are often new to the field of study.

This wish to study phenomena that may or may not fit within traditional boundaries, and the need to study them with unfamiliar tools, often result in a desire to speak to new and different audiences, audiences who may find different methods persuasive. Thus, feminist scholars may find that because they want to use a concept like "intersectionality" to study multiple social identities (e.g., gender and race or class at the same time), they want not only to address audiences across disciplines and methods but also to address scholars of race and class and gender, and not just one of these. The need to address different audiences in turn often reinforces the use of multiple methods, because different audiences are likely to be persuaded by different kinds of evidence—evidence that is familiar within "their" paradigm and not someone else's.

Finally, feminist scholars' intellectual commitments may lend themselves to combine methods in improvisational or nonsystematic ways—ways that are quite different from the traditional ways advocated by texts touting the virtues of "multiple methods" (e.g., Newman & Benz, 1998; Tashakkori & Teddlie, 1998). For example, an interest in postmodern and poststructuralist theory is likely to lead researchers to a much greater comfort with paradox and complexity, with seeming contradiction, even with "messiness" (Gergen, 2001; Stewart, 1994).

Alternatively, the habit of reflexivity—of continually revisiting and reframing questions in light of knowledge produced or insight gained—may support an iterative rather than a linear process. Studies based on this kind of process may deviate radically from conventional notions that separate contexts of discovery from contexts of justification. Instead, they may seem to circle around a phenomenon, clarifying (it is hoped) its nature and features as they do so (Tolman & Szalacha, 1999).

Thus, we argue that there can be no prescriptive typology for combining qualitative and quantitative methods (although some methods texts have aimed to develop them; see, e.g., Morgan, 1998; Newman & Benz, 1998). Instead, in the following sections we turn to a review of the research literature to identify projects that we feel have fruitfully combined "narratives and numbers" and, in this way, we generate a necessarily partial and preliminary list of suggested approaches for those considering mixing these approaches.

## MODELS FOR INTEGRATING "NARRATIVES AND NUMBERS"

There are several different ways to integrate "narratives," or qualitative data, with "numbers," or quantitative data, in a single study. Each approach requires different resources and assets of a research project and offers different benefits to a study or a researcher. In this section, we will examine different strategies for combining these two kinds of data in a single project. In most cases we refer to studies conducted by researchers who explicitly identify themselves as having feminist perspectives or aims; however, in some cases we will discuss research that may not have an explicitly feminist perspective but focuses on women's or girls' experiences, or gendered phenomena.

### Systematic Transformation of Qualitative Data Into Quantitative Data

Perhaps the most common and the least controversial approach is to gather narrative or qualitative data in the course of a research project and then to transform it (usually via systematic content analysis) into quantitative data that can be analyzed (see, e.g., Boyatzis, 1998; Smith, 1992). Feminist scholars who have developed longitudinal studies of women's lives have often adopted this strategy (see Hulbert & Schuster, 1993, for a compendium of such studies), often arguing that including material that is articulated freely by women in their own terms enables a larger, generally quantitative project to represent women's experience more adequately (Hulbert & Schuster, 1993, pp. 12–13; see also, e.g., Helson, 1993; Stewart & Vandewater,

1993; Tangri & Jenkins, 1993). Often, researchers adopting this strategy develop systematic content analysis strategies—reflecting either a priori themes or emergent themes from the data gathered—to transform the qualitative data gathered into presence/absence codes or ratings, both of which can be treated as numbers in data analysis. Thus, for example, the Ginzberg-Yohalem study (see Yohalem, 1993, for a summary) included an open-ended question about whether "there were any attractive opportunities for career or other long range activities which you did not pursue? Why did you not pursue them? Any regrets?" (Ginzberg & Yohalem, 1966, p. 206). Yohalem (1993) quoted one woman from their study of women who earned graduate degrees at Columbia in the late 1940s:

> Having children before finishing a Ph.D. made the pursuit of the highest degree impractical for me. Not getting a Ph.D. has made the salary range I command smaller. I regret not having had the opportunity to finish that work as a younger woman. The competing demands of family and career can make a woman's choice very difficult, especially if she marries after 30 as I did. (p. 149)

Data like these enriched the project's ability to represent not only the choices women made but also the ways in which those choices felt constrained, and reverberated over the years of their lives. In addition, by collecting such data, researchers were able to develop "codes" that turned these data into numbers. This kind of quantification is not particularly valued by some qualitative researchers (see, e.g., Mishler, 1990), but we believe that it permits some kinds of analyses that are otherwise impossible.

Stewart and Vandewater (1999) developed a measure of regrets about career and family decisions, which they used to code data collected in two different longitudinal studies that asked the same question (and some different ones) that Ginzberg and Yohalem had. By categorizing women's responses to capture the nature of their regrets, they were able to show that women who expressed regrets about making more "traditional" role choices (not to acquire education or pursue careers) were lower in well-being in middle age, but if they made life changes in the direction of remedying those regrets, their

subsequent well-being was equivalent to that of women who had no regrets of that sort. In more recent research, Torges, Stewart, and Miner-Rubino (2005) looked at related issues in an older sample and found that it was possible to code qualitative data to capture whether individuals have "come to terms" with their regrets internally or not. They found that not coming to terms at that later age was associated—as was regret itself—with poorer health outcomes. Collecting the qualitative data (as Ginzberg did in 1951) and recognizing the important and variable life experiences it might be capturing (as later scholars could) allowed researchers to assess an aspect of these people's lives for which no standard measures exist.

Duncan and Agronick (1995) were interested in the differential impact of social experiences occurring at different life stages in women's lives for different cohorts. Stewart and Healy (1989) had gathered quantitative ratings of the impact of a list of social events on women in that study; Helson had asked an open-ended question along these lines, but there were no ratings available in her sample from a slightly—and crucially—different birth cohort (see Helson, 1993, for an overview). In a creative and imaginative study, Duncan and Agronick (1995) were able to explore the same question in both data sets by coding qualitative data in one data set to render it roughly equivalent to the quantitative data in another. They coded Helson's data and conceptually replicated their findings from one sample of college-educated women in another, strengthening our confidence in the finding's validity both because it was robust in two different samples and cohorts and because it held up when assessments were made in such different ways. This kind of approach—in which a phenomenon is assessed with multiple measures, and its relations with other phenomena are also multiply assessed—is sometimes referred to as "triangulation" (see, e.g., Tashakkori & Teddlie, 1998).

In these examples, qualitative data are used to address questions that can be addressed—if they are recognized and assessed—with quantitative data. Tolman and Szalacha (1999) provided an example of a study in which qualitative data may be the only way actually to assess the phenomenon under study—adolescent girls' experience of sexual desire. Tolman and Szalacha (1999) argued that collecting "in-depth narrative and descriptive data from girls on their thoughts about and subjective experiences of sexuality, including sexual desire, sexual pleasure, feeling sexy and sexual fantasies, during private, one-on-one, semi-structured clinical interviews" (pp. 12–13) itself constitutes a feminist intervention, because "one of the primary tools of oppression of women is the maintenance of silence about their experiences and perspectives." Using an iterative process, they used the data they collected to address three different research questions.

First, they used the qualitative data simply to describe girls' experiences of sexual desire. Despite social pressures to the contrary, most girls described an intense, urgent, and powerful experience of sexual desire. At the same time, they also expressed doubt and confusion about what their feelings implied. The qualitative analysis indicated that girls from urban versus suburban backgrounds articulated very different reasons that desire must be countered by self-control. Urban girls felt that sexual expression carried many practical risks or dangers; in contrast, suburban girls viewed the issue as one of internal self-image, for example, "I don't like to think of myself as feeling really sexual" (Tolman & Szalacha, 1999, p. 16).

Once they had generated this distinction in the qualitative analysis, Tolman and Szalacha were interested in assessing the degree to which this distinction characterized girls' experiences. They coded the 128 narratives (produced by 30 girls) for expressions of vulnerability and of pleasure. They found that there was a modest difference between urban and suburban girls' narratives in expressions of vulnerability (with urban girls expressing more such themes), but a larger difference in expressions of pleasure (with suburban girls expressing more of the pleasure theme). They further considered the role of sexual abuse in association with these themes and found that suburban girls who had experienced abuse expressed similar themes to urban girls (whose narratives did not differ as a function of their sexual abuse experience).

In a third iteration, the researchers returned to the original qualitative data to explore in detail the different sexual experiences of these four groups of girls (suburban or urban; survivors of abuse or not). This study demonstrates how readily qualitative data can be pressed into service to provide richer understanding of a phenomenon or to test a relatively narrowly specified hypothesis. In the hands of flexible and creative researchers they can be used to do both, allowing a single study with a relatively small sample to provide a solid base for further research on adolescent girls' sexuality.

In an ongoing program of research, Diamond (1998, 2000, 2003) has examined the development and relinquishment of different sexual identities among women, using systematic content analysis of interview data. Those data revealed, contrary to expectation, that women who had relinquished their sexual minority identity during the 5 years under study were significantly *less* likely than women who maintained their identities to view sexuality as fluid. Diamond pointed out that perhaps this apparent paradox makes sense. She noted that "acknowledging and accepting one's capacity for diverse, fluctuating desires and experiences might actually promote stability in sexual identification by eliminating the implicit pressure to jettison one's identity label once it is contradicted by novel feelings or behaviors" (Diamond, 2003, p. 361).

We have seen, then, that generating quantitative indicators out of qualitative data allows researchers to create new measures for previously unmeasured variables (as in the case of types of regrets and responses to regret), to replicate findings with other measures (as in the study of the impact of political events), and to assess the frequency of newly identified features of phenomena (as in the study of adolescent girls' sexual experiences).

## Using Quantitative Data to Contextualize or Frame Issues Raised by Qualitative Data

One approach taken by multimethods scholars is to employ quantitative data as a way to frame and contextualize findings from a qualitative study. Researchers who do qualitative studies with interpretive or constructivist aims may be hesitant to generalize those findings to other settings or populations (Lin, 1998). In these cases, findings from a more positivist-based quantitative study can provide a context in which the qualitative findings may be understood.

Raffaelli and Ontai's (2004) study of gender socialization in Latino/a families provides a paradigmatic case. They conducted in-depth interviews with a small sample of adult Latinas regarding their experiences of socialization about sexuality within their families of origin, as well as their early sexual and romantic experiences. They used multiple coders to identify emergent themes in the interview transcripts. This process revealed three main themes of parental behavior: differential treatment of boys and girls, enforcement of feminine behavior among girls, and restriction of girls' freedom of activity. Based on these interviews, survey items were developed tapping each of these themes, and a larger sample of both women and men were asked to rate the extent to which their mothers and fathers had encouraged these behaviors. These survey data confirmed the qualitative analysis, because men and women reported the expected differences in their gender socialization. Quantitative analyses also revealed reliable patterns of gender socialization for parents with different backgrounds; for example, mothers who were more acculturated to the United States were more likely to encourage tomboy behavior in their daughters. The use of both qualitative and quantitative approaches within this study allowed the researchers to gauge how typical the results from the qualitative study were and to develop a quantitative measure that is likely to have a high degree of ecological validity.

The work of Patillo-McCoy (1998) represents a slightly different approach to this type of multi-method strategy. She conducted an in-depth ethnography of a black middle-class neighborhood, involving several years of participation in the social networks of the community, as well as interviews with community leaders and residents. Much of the interpretive power of her analysis of these interviews, however, came from the way she contextualized this community using census data. She demonstrated that this neighborhood was surrounded by neighborhoods with higher rates of poverty and crime. She contrasted this geographical proximity of the black middle class with white neighborhoods of comparable socioeconomic status. Her ethnography confirmed that spatial proximity fosters a social proximity as well, which engenders both costs and benefits: links between gang members and more stable members of the community provided a form of social control while simultaneously making it impossible to eradicate gangs and drugs from the community. This work suggests that combining qualitative and quantitative data in this way is a means of understanding a phenomenon at multiple levels of causality.

Similarly, Cohen's award-winning book, *The Boundaries of Blackness* (1999), combined qualitative and quantitative methods to understand the African American community's limited and late response to the HIV/AIDS crisis at multiple levels. She used content coding to chart the incidence of coverage of HIV/AIDS stories in both mainstream and black media. Her analysis of coverage in the *New York Times* between 1983 and 1994 is a good example. During this period, the rate of AIDS cases among African Americans grew steeply, as did the coverage of AIDS stories in general, but stories concerning HIV among blacks were scarce until a sharp uptick in 1991, when Magic Johnson announced his diagnosis. Indeed, only 38% of the reporting on African Americans and HIV/AIDS during this time concerned anyone other than Johnson and Arthur Ashe. This discrepancy in media coverage was made even more stark by Cohen's finding that African Americans composed 32% of all AIDS cases during this time, while only 5% of *Times* stories were devoted to this group. Cohen asserted that these analyses revealed a pattern of marginalization, a contention that was bolstered by her more finely grained analysis of the way the AIDS crisis and the black community's response to it were framed in these stories. Importantly, she argued that practices of marginalization take place at multiple levels and change over time. Later chapters used interviews to explore the ways black political and religious leaders chose not to define AIDS as a threat to African Americans because they did not want to acknowledge gay people and users of intravenous drugs as part of the black community, framing AIDS instead as a problem caused by the "bad behavior" of individuals. Taken together, these multiple levels of analysis, employing both qualitative and quantitative techniques as appropriate, painted a picture of how narrow identity politics led to social conservatism, exclusion of certain segments of the black community, and ultimately a public health crisis.

Finally, Hodson (2004) used quantitative analyses to generalize from qualitative research in a very unusual way, conducting a meta-analysis of ethnographies aimed at understanding the role played by gender and race in shaping experience in workplaces. Rather than averaging effect sizes, as the traditional meta-analysis would, Hodson systematically coded 120 book-length ethnographies. This method allowed him to capitalize on the strengths of the ethnographic method—the opportunity to draw on many observations of a social system and to analyze these observations in great depth—while avoiding its greatest drawback, which is that the ethnographer brings this depth and range to only a very small number of social systems, often only one. Hodson noted that several ethnographies had characterized women as dutiful, acquiescent, and, thus, relatively complacent workers (particularly in contrast to men). Thus, he expected the meta-analysis to confirm this with women having higher job satisfaction; however, the opposite was true. Nevertheless, in the United States, men were more likely to express their dissatisfaction by engaging in confrontational behavior such as infighting and strikes. However, among people of color and workers outside the United States, men were actually more acquiescent. Clearly, the breadth of these findings was beyond the scope of a single ethnography to address.

These examples of using quantitative data to frame qualitative findings suggest that this approach offers a way to magnify the strengths of qualitative methods, including depth, validity, and descriptive and interpretive power, either by leveraging the qualitative findings into a more generalizable set of findings or by helping to understand them as one piece of a complex system working at many levels.

## Use of Ethnographic or Interview Narratives to Illuminate Issues Raised by Quantitative Findings

Another way quantitative and qualitative methods are often combined is to use a qualitative study as a follow-up to clarify or explain findings from the quantitative analysis. This approach is consistent with Lin's (1998) distinction between the epistemological standing of *positivist methods*, which can establish relationships among variables, and *constructivist methods*, which can demonstrate causal mechanisms. The approach of using qualitative methods to illuminate issues raised by quantitative findings is one of the more commonly used forms of combining them; this is noteworthy because it challenges the wisdom so often received in traditional research methods courses (Bernard, 1865/1927; Hempel, 1965) that qualitative methods are most appropriate for the context of discovery. Findings revealed in such a (discovery-oriented qualitative) study, so the classical argument goes, should be validated through the context of justification, usually involving a more positivist and usually quantitative study.

Carr's (2004) research on the retrospective career reflections of midlife women who came of age in the 1950s provides a prototypical example of a study in which qualitative analysis was used to help illuminate quantitative findings. Based on a large-scale longitudinal survey of mostly white mothers of daughters, Carr found that mothers who felt that their daughters were more occupationally successful than they themselves had been suffered no decrement in self-acceptance if the mothers took a great deal of credit for their daughters' success. Because this outcome contradicted the predictions made by social comparison theory, Carr turned to qualitative data to understand how mothers could maintain self-esteem even when making an upward comparison between themselves and their daughters. Interviews with a subsample of original respondents revealed that mothers who rated their daughters as more successful often explained their attainment in terms of social changes that gave their daughters more choices, but many also cited the additional stress that combining roles contributed to their daughters' lives. She concluded that these attributions protected mothers' self-esteem. Interestingly, Carr argued that this part of the project sought "to explore and generate hypotheses—not to test hypotheses—about the ways social comparisons are made, explained and interpreted" (p. 138). Thus, she carefully framed her project within the traditional parameters of the contexts of discovery and justification—an interesting move given that her qualitative analysis was subsequent to her quantitative analyses.

Guinier, Fine, Balin, Bartow, and Stachel (1997) similarly designed their qualitative inquiry to illuminate the findings of their quantitative analysis. Interestingly, they wrote that the initial survey emerged from Bartow's desire to make a film documenting her personal experiences of gender bias in law school. She approached Guinier to supervise the project, who suggested that she begin by surveying her classmates to learn whether her experiences were typical. The original impetus for the project was thus the desire to learn whether the personal was indeed reflective of a larger political context. The research team began by examining student records obtained from the law school. They learned that although women entered with qualifications comparable to those of their male peers, women's grades were consistently lower through all 3 years, and women were much less likely to achieve honors. Results of Bartow's survey revealed other, perhaps more disturbing, patterns: First-year women students reported a systematic pattern of bias against women, including exclusion, disregard, and even sexist comments in the classroom. By the third year, it appeared that either such experiences had decreased or women had become more tolerant of such behaviors, because fewer were reported. At the same time, this cross-sectional comparison indicated that women entered with greater enthusiasm for public interest law, but by the third year, they were no more interested in pursuing this area than were men. The authors argued that in these ways, law schools force women to "become gentlemen." The qualitative data, based on open-ended survey questions and interviews, suggested the cost of this transformation. Women students reported feeling alienated, outraged, and silenced in law school. Sadly, many internalized these feelings, looking for counseling and support from women peers to address what they felt were personal shortcomings. Most reported that to overcome these feelings, and the obstacles they posed to success in law school, they had to suppress and repress their feelings.

Thus, although women have been allowed access to legal education, these results indicate that women have not truly won equality in this setting. Instead, first-year law students enter an environment in which "a gender system is established, legitimated, and subtly internalized" (Guinier et al., 1997, p. 61). This analysis would not have been possible based only on the data from the registrar and the survey; indeed, the findings generated from such methods might have been plausibly explained in terms of women students' inadequacies. The qualitative data enabled Guinier et al. (1997) to understand the context in which the outcomes described in the quantitative data emerged. This example clearly illustrates Lin's distinction between the strength of positivist methods to demonstrate relationships among variables and that of interpretivist methods to demonstrate causal processes.

## Using Quantitative and Qualitative Methods in "Parallel"

Some researchers find that quantitative and qualitative methods enable them to address *different* research questions, not to explore the same ones in different ways. In these cases, the particular constraints on interpretation or inference imposed by different methods can be offset by parallel use of both approaches. Most often, qualitative methods are used in these research programs to unearth or identify issues or themes, while quantitative methods are used to answer questions about frequency and association that often cannot be addressed by qualitative methods.

Cortina, in the context of a larger program of research on gender in the workplace, provides us one model in her research on Latinas' experiences of sexual harassment. The goal of this research was to develop a fuller understanding of how the phenomenon of "sexual harassment" (defined in terms of white women's experience in the United States) might be different for Latinas—both because of differences in the way people treat them and because of differences in the social context or cultures they bring to their experience.

In the first study, Cortina (2001) began by conducting focus groups with 45 Latinas recruited through a public adult vocational school in San Diego. The focus group facilitator was "a native Spanish-speaking Mexican American woman who understood the culture and life experiences of the participants, spoke both English and Spanish fluently, and possessed the skills necessary to guide focus group discussions" (p. 167). Focus group transcripts were transcribed by a bilingual researcher, and Cortina examined the transcripts in both languages twice and noted "specific behavioral examples of harassing behaviors" and "references to categories of harassing behaviors." She then compared the terms generated in this way from the focus group discussions with a standard measure developed and based on the experiences of white women. This comparison yielded six items, of which two covered unique verbal behavior not covered (or not covered in the same way) in the standard measure. For example, one item was "addressed you informally when a more formal manner of address was more appropriate (e.g., used *tu* rather than *usted*)." In addition, four of the new items addressed nonverbal behaviors, such as "gave you a sexual 'look' that made you feel uncomfortable or dirty." Finally, five new items addressed a sense of the intersection of sexual harassment with ethnic or racial harassment; Cortina (2001) termed this "sexual racism." Examples of these items include the following behaviors: "called you insulting names that referred to your gender and ethnicity (e.g., 'Mexican bitch')," and "said they expected you to behave in certain ways because you are a Latina woman (e.g., expecting you as a Latina woman to wear sexy clothes)."

Cortina (2001) then used these new items, along with the "standard" ones with a large sample of Latinas recruited in a similar way. Using a process of double translation of items, she gave participants the option to complete the survey in Spanish or English. Analyses of these data aimed at identifying the common and unique features of sexual harassment experiences of Latinas and white women. This strategy yielded some important insights: Both the focus group and the survey data suggested that Latinas were more inclined than more heterogeneous, predominantly white samples of women to infer sexual intentions from behavior that was not explicitly sexual. She quoted one woman as saying,

What I've seen is that [white women] are more open . . . if it's something sexual they'll laugh and giggle about it, and I would take that offensively. And they wouldn't, because they're like more open to sexual stuff than Mexican or Hispanic ladies are. (p. 176)

Interestingly, although there were clear examples of sexual racism reported in the focus groups, the quantitative study provided little support for the importance of this construct. Nevertheless, Cortina (2001) pointed out that the likely explanation is not that sexual racism is unimportant but "the relative absence of racial harassment in participants' workplaces. . . . the great majority of participants did *not* work in environments dominated by non-Latinos—who would be most likely to racially harass Latinos" (p. 177). Thus, she weighted the qualitative data fully equally with the quantitative and concluded by advocating for more research on Latinas' workplace experiences in environments dominated by Anglos. In subsequent research, Cortina and her colleagues (Cortina, 2004; Cortina, Fitzgerald, & Drasgow, 2002) used the revised version of the standard measure created for Latinas (the Sexual Experiences Questionnaire–Latina) to study the effect of sexual harassment on Latinas while paying close attention to features of Latino culture and processes of acculturation.

Sigel, a political scientist, offered another version of a parallel model in her study *Ambition and Accommodation: How Women View Gender Relations* (1996). Like Cortina, Sigel employed both focus groups and surveys; however, rather than developing a scale, Sigel aimed to understand both "what the population-at-large (or a given segment of the population) thinks about an important issue" and also "a great deal about each individual and how she or he comes to hold these thoughts or sentiments" (p. 24). Thus, she was interested both in the generalizability of findings and in the depth and complexity of the material that could be obtained. Sigel conceded that although her initial expectation was that the focus groups would be mainly "guides to questionnaire construction, it soon became obvious that they had an independent contribution to make" (p. 34). She stressed that the focus group data did in fact guide the development of the survey protocol and that they also were used to help interpret the survey findings. She said,

> Listening to men and women in the groups actually helped shape my sensitivity to the role the topic [gender] played in the daily lives of the public. I felt as though I became privy to some of their frustrations as well as gratifications, and most of all, I learned what mattered to them and what did not when they thought about gender. (p. 35)

## Diversity of Materials as Data

Often those who wish to describe the challenge posed by multiple methods research are particularly concerned about the difficulty of combining qualitative and quantitative data due to the opposing epistemological assumptions underlying each approach (see Lin, 1998; Tashakkori & Teddlie, 2002). However, the work of some feminist researchers transcends this simple dichotomy to incorporate data from unusual sources, such as photographs or other visual media, material from historical archives, or even literature, often combining these less often used types of data with more commonly used sources, such as responses to interviews or surveys. Some who employ these creative data sources also draw on innovative methods to analyze these data.

To begin with an example that represents a fairly common approach, scholars within communications studies often pair a close reading of a media text with an audience reception study of that same text. One such example is Press and Cole's (1999) examination of the way social class and position on abortion as a political issue shape women's readings of prime-time entertainment television depictions of women facing abortion decisions. Drawing on the work of Condit (1994), they reviewed entertainment television depictions of abortion decisions, arguing that television offers a limited pro-choice position in which legal abortion is seen as necessary but undesirable unless the woman faces extreme hardship, including extreme financial hardship or blocked opportunities for moving up out of poverty. Focus group interviews showed that pro-choice women viewed these narratives very differently. Although

middle-class women often claimed to be critical of television as a medium, they were very accepting of the rationales proffered by the working-class heroines seeking abortions in the shows. In contrast, many working-class women did not accept the heroines' protests that they had no option but abortion; many working-class viewers could offer stories in which they had faced similar obstacles and had overcome them. By pairing the textual analysis of television shows with the qualitative analysis of women's responses to them, Press and Cole were able to identify an important rift within the pro-choice movement.

Metzl, a psychiatrist and cultural critic, has similarly employed methods from both the humanities and the social sciences in his attempt to understand how the gendered meanings associated with clinical depression have shifted over time in relation to changes in psychiatric opinion on how the disease is best treated. In his book *Prozac on the Couch* (2003), he conducted a close interpretive reading of news and fashion periodicals and popular literature (such as memoirs and novels) dealing with psychotropic drugs and, more recently, the selective serotonin reuptake inhibitors (SSRIs, such as Prozac and Zoloft). Through the methods commonly employed in the humanities, Metzl persuasively demonstrated that notions of gender informed by psychoanalysis are pervasive even within the realm of scientific, biologically based psychiatry. In a subsequent paper, Metzl and Angel (2004) adopted standard social science methods to approach the same research question in a very different way: systematic content analysis of a random sample of popular representations of depression appearing between 1985 and 2000. These data showed that as the SSRIs gained in social acceptance and visibility, conditions that had previously been viewed as normative for women (such as emotional disturbances associated with menstruation, childbirth, or menopause) became conceptualized as biologically based, pathological, and treatable. Side by side, these two projects could be viewed simply as the triangulation of methods, long recommended even in mainstream thinking on methodology (e.g., see Jick, 1979). Yet by freely drawing on two very disparate traditions of scholarship, Metzl's important contribution to current thinking about medicine and mental health and illness continued a tradition of ardent conversation between the humanities and the social sciences that has been taking place in women's studies programs since their inception in the early 1970s.

Clearly, this approach to combining qualitative and quantitative approaches is particularly fruitful for those who are interested in popular culture and visual imagery. Moreover, by expanding traditional social science notions of what constitutes "data," this approach could open new avenues of inquiry and may be a particularly promising approach for the study of individuals and groups that are not literate (for innovative examples of such qualitative work, see Killion & Wang, 2000; Painter, 1994).

## Bringing Together Qualitative and Quantitative Researchers in a Team

Some projects address the issue of bringing together qualitative and quantitative research methods by bringing together teams of researchers with different dispositions, backgrounds, and talents. (Obviously, these researchers do not, and cannot, view the epistemological barriers to this kind of collaboration as insurmountable.) Most often, studies using this approach have fairly substantial resources, which permit them to involve researchers who will impose quite different design and measurement constraints and who may operate both independently and collaboratively within the study. The teams may include feminist scholars (as do the ones discussed here), but because the studies tend to be designed to be broad and inclusive in their reach, the scholars are unlikely to take an exclusively feminist perspective throughout the project.

One study that deliberately set out to draw on both types of methods is the New Hope Project, an evaluation study of a large-scale poverty intervention program (Huston et al., 2001). The intervention employed a truly experimental design and aimed to assess the relative benefits for working poor families of a comprehensive support package, including a wage supplement, subsidies for health insurance, child care vouchers, and a job opportunity program (Huston et al., 2004). Of course, many of the key outcomes for the program were quantitative (actual income, assessed performance of all family members in many social arenas, etc.), and many of the collaborators on the project were primarily quantitative researchers (e.g., psychologists Huston and McLoyd and economist Duncan). However, the project also included an anthropologist (Weisner), who set up a fieldwork team of seven ethnographers who worked in the Milwaukee, Wisconsin, area of the project. The aim was to use ethnographic data collected from a stratified random sample of cases

> to assist in gaining a richer, more detailed understanding of the impact of New Hope on participating families than could be gained from the . . . survey alone. The ethnographic study was also linked closely to the quantitative data from the surveys and child assessment data, with ongoing conversations among the group. (Lieber, Weisner, & Presley, 2003, p. 411)

Several New Hope Project collaborators were impressed by the power of the qualitative data to reveal things that could be confirmed with the larger quantitative survey but had not been guessed at the outset of the study. In their valuable consideration of these issues, Gibson and Duncan (2005) reported that Gibson and Weisner (2002) found, using the qualitative data, that the family participants in the study valued the elements of the program in vastly different ways (e.g., some in cost-benefit terms and others because it served some personal preferences; see also Romich & Weisner, 2000). These different values in turn guided service use. Basing her analyses on these insights, Gibson used the survey data to confirm the importance of this heterogeneity in shaping the program's effect on families.

In a more complicated example of the iterative relationship between the qualitative and the quantitative findings, quantitative researchers noted that the boys in the experiment, but not the girls, were rated as significantly higher achieving than the controls (see Gibson & Duncan, 2005). The qualitative data helped researchers recognize that in fact parents tended to view their male children as more "at-risk" than the females and to channel more of the program's resources to their sons than their daughters. Armed with this insight, quantitative researchers were able to examine other aspects of national survey data and to show that parents with both sons and daughters who live in impoverished neighborhoods systematically direct time and other resources toward boys rather than girls (Romich, 2000).

On a project like this, it was critical, then, for the dialogue between qualitative and quantitative researchers to be continual and respectful. It is clear that in this context the New Hope Project benefited greatly from its own successful mixed-method collaborative environment. Attempting this kind of collaboration does not, though, guarantee its success: One can easily imagine a project in which insights and findings would be on parallel tracks and would never meet. Moreover, even when successful, this sort of effort exacts a high cost in communication labor.

The Fragile Families and Child Wellbeing Study is another umbrella project involving many collaborators and including both qualitative and quantitative researchers on a variety of narrower subprojects. In fact, two feminist sociologists with different backgrounds (England, a quantitative researcher, and Edin, a qualitative researcher) have joined forces with each other and several other collaborators (including the economist McLanahan) on a subproject within that study that aims to understand "why some couples with very young children break up while others remain together, and why some fathers remain actively involved with their families" (Institute for Policy Research Web site www.northwestern .edu/ipr/.). The Time, Love, Cash, Care and Children Study (TLC3) was set up to examine a subsample of 75 low- to moderate-income couples drawn from the larger Fragile Families Study (of nearly 5,000 families). In this project, qualitative and quantitative researchers actually joined together to examine qualitative findings in the context of quantitative data and quantitative findings in the context of qualitative data. For example, Gibson-Davis, Edin, and McLanahan (2005) began by noting that quantitative data suggested that the Fragile Families couples who were unmarried had positive views of marriage and said they planned to marry. Yet few did. Gibson-Davis, Edin, and McLanahan used qualitative data from the TLC3 data to explore this contradiction and argued that the qualitative data suggest that actually the views these couples hold

of marriage were so positive that they felt their relationships did not warrant it. There are a variety of economic and achievement milestones they believed they must reach in order to justify marriage. In another paper, England, Edin, and Linnenberg (2003) found that the women struggled in relatively unsatisfying nonmarital relationships with their children's fathers because they believed that financial independence and stability are prerequisites for marriage they have not yet achieved.

It is clear that this kind of collaborative project has remarkable potential to leverage insight from both quantitative and qualitative data to account for, enrich, and validate one other. That potential is only realized, though, to the extent that these projects engage researchers with both kinds of gifts and training, who are willing and able to collaborate. Feminist research—which often aims to excavate key voices and perspectives that are relatively silent, powerless, or subordinated—is particularly likely to benefit from this sort of collaboration.

## Building a Narrative Account From a Quantitative Description

The final strategy we have encountered for combining quantitative and qualitative methods is perhaps the least common. It involves researchers taking quantitative indicators—for an individual or group of individuals—and constructing a qualitative analysis on the basis of those indicators. There is no doubt room for more inventive efforts along these lines. Perhaps the most straightforward example of this approach involves identifying an individual outlier or a group of people who score very high (or low) on some dimension and then conducting a case study of those individuals or that group. Helson, Mitchell, and Hart (1985) did this when they studied the "lives of women who became autonomous," by selecting the seven women in Helson's longitudinal study who scored at the autonomous stage on Loevinger's (1976) measure of ego development at middle age. By conducting a group "case study," they hoped to identify the personality and life experiences that might underlie successful personality achievement and specifically to evaluate both Levinson's (1978) model of male development and Gilligan's (1982) model of female development. They found that the theories were uneven in their applicability and that different paths led to successful ego development. They were struck, though, that "to an unusual degree, the seven sought out the challenges and suffered the hardships particular to their time in history" (Helson et al., 1985, p. 283). They concluded that

> it may still be true that *autonomous* ways of thinking and behaving are so much discouraged in women that only those who have known pain or marginality develop a high ego-level, and those who have a high ego-level are unlikely to live a conventional life. (p. 284)

This emphasis on both suffering and unconventionality offered new insight into the pathway toward the highest levels of ego development.

Peterson (1998) used a similar strategy in his study of women who were high in different forms of midlife generativity. He aimed to identify the characteristics of women who are high (and low) in generativity realization or generativity motivation or both. He selected 12 women who scored high on both measures, on one measure, or on neither measure. With 3 women in each group, he hoped to avoid being distracted by highly idiosyncratic details and instead to identify some patterns across the 3 women within each cell that differentiated them from the women in the other three cells. His analysis pointed to the centrality of life's disappointments and ongoing preoccupations (rather than specific personality qualities or life experiences) as differentiating the groups from each other. Thus, the women who were high on both forms of generativity were currently engaged in generative activities, but (unlike the group low in realization but high in motivation) they did not report frustration or disappointment with past generative efforts. The group with the reverse pattern (high in realization and low in motivation) was not actively focused on generative activities in the present at all, although they also reported no frustrations or disappointments in that domain. Finally, the group low in both was also low in well-being, and quite distressed. These midlife portraits certainly "fit" the pattern of scores (and Peterson's account is of course much richer than this one!), but they also extend our understanding of how two related but separate personality characteristics may interact to produce distinctive patterns.

Finally, Singer and Ryff (2001; see also Singer, Ryff, Carr, & Magee, 1998) pioneered a person-centered method that goes further. They actually prepared a narrative account of the individuals in their studies, based on the quantitative data about their lives. They then used this narrative as data, constructing taxonomies of life histories or profiles that reflect different pathways to a range of health outcomes.

## Drawing Conclusions

Our hope in presenting alternative models to our students, and to the readers of this chapter, is that it is both stimulating and empowering to consider a range of alternative ways to conduct research. Our view, then, is frankly pragmatic and thereby finesses one of the key debates among some feminist scholars. Tashakkori and Teddlie (1998) outlined in detail the ways in which positivism and postpositivism (normally philosophical positions promoted by quantitative methodologists), on the one hand, and constructivism (a position often promoted by qualitative methodologists), on the other, have resisted reconciliation. They detailed six important differences in the assumptions made by researchers adopting one or the other position (assumptions about the nature of reality, the relationship of the knower to the known, the role of values in inquiry, the nature of generalizations, the possibility of establishing cause and effect, and the importance of induction or deduction). This polarized debate has been reproduced in a slightly different form among feminist scholars, among whom an additional issue is added: which kind of method produces knowledge compatible with feminists' goals (Jayaratne & Stewart, 1991; Peplau & Conrad, 1989). Even to consider combining narrative and numbers in a single study, one must refuse this binary framing and proceed instead from something like the assumption associated with pragmatism, that there is no essential link between epistemology and method (see Tashakorri & Teddlie's exposition, 1998, pp. 11–13).

Because social scientists and feminist researchers have been so preoccupied with the incompatibilities between these kinds of methods, certain developments have been quite uneven. For example, we have well-developed criteria for evaluating validity in quantitative research. Although there have been increasing efforts along these lines with regard to qualitative methods, a consensus on criteria has not yet emerged among qualitative researchers, much less been widely disseminated among all researchers. Even more, we have virtually no established criteria for assessing the success of any given combined or integrated use of both kinds of methods. Such criteria can be successfully developed only if we have more models of successful combinations and integrations. We will all benefit—in our own research and in our efforts to equip students for the future—when there are many more models of individuals and projects that have brought narratives and numbers together in a fruitful way on many different topics.

## NOTES

1. Epistemology is concerned with the study of knowledge and how it is possible to make knowledge claims. Sprague and Zimmerman (1993) argue that positivism, which holds that definitive knowledge can be obtained only through the systematic and objective observation of observable phenomena, has been the dominant epistemology since the mid-19th century. Ontology refers to the metaphysical study of existence.

2. The context of discovery refers to the creative or even intuitive phase of the research process in which ideas are generated; in contrast, the context of justification involves testing these ideas using the stringent and objective principles of the scientific methods.

## REFERENCES

Bernard, C. (1927). *An introduction to the study of experimental medicine.* New York: Macmillan. (Original work published 1865)

Bledsoe, C. H. (2002). *Contingent lives: Fertility, time, and aging in West Africa.* Chicago: University of Chicago Press.

Boyatzis, R. E. (1998). *Transforming qualitative information: Thematic analysis and code development.* Thousand Oaks, CA: Sage.

Burns, N., Schlozman, K., & Verba, S. (1997). The public consequences of private inequality: Family life and citizen participation. *American Political Science Review, 9,* 373–389.

Carr, D. (2004). "My daughter has a career; I just raised babies": The psychological consequences of women's intergenerational social comparisons. *Social Psychology Quarterly, 67,* 132–154.

Cohen, C. J. (1999). *The boundaries of blackness: AIDS and the breakdown of black politics.* Chicago: University of Chicago Press.

Condit, C. (1994). *Decoding abortion rhetoric: Communicating social change.* Urbana: University of Illinois Press.

Cortina, L. (2001). Assessing sexual harassment among Latinas: Development of an instrument. *Cultural Diversity and Ethnic Minority Psychology, 7,* 164–181.

Cortina, L. M. (2004). Hispanic perspectives on sexual harassment and social support. *Personality and Social Psychology Bulletin, 30,* 570–584.

Cortina, L. M., Fitzgerald, L. F., & Dragsow, F. (2002). Contextualizing Latina experiences of sexual harassment: Preliminary tests of a structural model. *Basic and Applied Social Psychology, 24,* 295–311.

Cortina, L. M., Magley, V. J., & Williams, J. H. (2001). Incivility in the workplace: Incidence and impact. *Journal of Occupational Health Psychology, 6*(1), 64–80.

Diamond, L. (1998). Development of sexual orientation among adolescent and young adult women. *Developmental Psychology, 34,* 1085–1095.

Diamond, L. (2000). Sexual identity, attractions and behavior among young sexual-minority women over a two-year period. *Developmental Psychology, 36,* 241–250.

Diamond, L. (2003). Was it a phase? Young women's relinquishment of lesbian/bisexual identities over a 5-year period. *Journal of Personality and Social Psychology, 84,* 352–364.

Duncan, L., & Agronick, G. (1995). The intersection of life stage and social events: Personality and life outcomes. *Journal of Personality and Social Psychology, 69,* 558–568.

Edin, K. (1991). Surviving the welfare system: How AFDC recipients make ends meet in Chicago. *Social Problems, 38,* 462–474.

England, P., Edin, K., & Linnenberg, K. (2003, September). *Love and distrust among unmarried parents.* Paper presented at the National Poverty

Center Conference on Marriage and Family Formation among Low-Income Couples, Washington, DC.

Fine, M., & Gordon, S. M. (1989). Feminist transformations of/despite psychology. In M. Crawford & M. Gentry (Eds.), *Gender and thought* (pp. 146–174). New York: Springer-Verlag.

Fine, M., & Weis, L. (1998). *The unknown city: Lives of poor and working-class young adults.* Boston: Beacon.

Gergen, M. (2001). *Feminist reconstructions in psychology: Narrative, gender, and performance.* Thousand Oaks, CA: Sage.

Gibson, C. M., & Weisner, T. (2002). "Rational" and ecocultural circumstances of program take-up among low-income working parents. *Human Organization, 61,* 154–167.

Gibson, C. M., & Duncan, G. J. (2005). Qualitative/quantitative synergies in a random-assignment program evaluation. In T. S. Weisner (Ed.), *Discovering successful pathways in children's development: New methods in the study of childhood and family life* (pp. 283–303). Chicago: University of Chicago Press.

Gibson-Davis, C. M., Edin, K., & McLanahan, S. (2005). High hopes but even higher expectations: The retreat from marriage among low-income couples. *Journal of Marriage and the Family, 67,* 1301–1312.

Gilligan, C. (1982). *In a different voice.* Cambridge, MA: Harvard University Press.

Ginzberg, E., & Yohalem, A. M. (1966). *Educated American women: Life styles and self-portraits.* New York: Columbia University Press.

Guba, E. G., & Lincoln, Y. S. (1994). Competing paradigms in qualitative methods. In N. Denzin & Y. Lincoln (Eds.), *Handbook of qualitative research* (pp. 105–117). Thousand Oaks, CA: Sage.

Guinier, L., Fine, M., Balin, J., Bartow, A., & Stachel, D. L. (1997). Becoming gentlemen: Women's experiences at one ivy league law school. In L. Guiner, M. Fine, & J. Balin (Eds.), *Becoming gentlemen: Women, law school and institutional change.* Boston: Beacon Press.

Harding, S. (1987). Is there a feminist method? In S. Harding (Ed.), *Feminism and methodology: Social science issues* (pp. 1–14). Bloomington: Indiana University Press.

Helson, R. (1993). The Mills classes of 1958 and 1960: College in the fifties, young adulthood in the sixties. In K. D. Hulbert & D. T. Schuster (Eds.), *Women's lives through time: Educated American women of the twentieth century* (pp. 190–210). San Francisco: Jossey-Bass.

Helson, R., Mitchell, V., & Hart, B. (1985). Lives of women who became autonomous. *Journal of Personality, 53,* 257–285.

Hempel, C. (1965). *Aspects of scientific explanation.* New York: Free Press.

Hodson, R. (2004). A meta-analysis of workplace ethnographies: Race, gender and employee attitudes and behaviors. *Journal of Contemporary Ethnography, 33,* 4–38.

Horner, M. S. (1972). Toward an understanding of achievement-related conflicts in women. *Journal of Social Issues, 28,* 157–176.

Huddy, L., Billig, J., Bracciodieta, J., Heoffler, L., Moynihan, P. J., & Pugliani, P. (1997). The effect of interviewer gender on the survey response. *Political Behavior, 19,* 197–220.

Hulbert, K. D., & Schuster, D. T. (Eds.). (1993). *Women's lives through time: Educated American women of the twentieth century.* San Francisco: Jossey-Bass.

Huston, A. C., Duncan, G. J., Granger, R., Bos, J., McLoyd, V. C., Mistry, R., et al. (2001). Work-based anti-poverty programs for parents can enhance the school performance and social behavior of children. *Child Development, 72,* 318–336.

Huston, A. C., Miller, C., Richburg-Hayes, L., Duncan, G. J., Eldred, C. A., Weisner, T. S., et al. (2004). *New hope for families and children: Five-year results of a program to reduce poverty and reform welfare.* New York: MDRC.

Jayaratne, T. E., & Stewart, A. J. (1991). Quantitative and qualitative methods in the social sciences: Current feminist issues and practical strategies. In M. M. Fonow & J. A. Cook (Eds.), *Beyond methodology: Feminist scholarship as lived research* (pp. 85–106). Bloomington: Indiana University Press.

Jick, T. D. (1979). Mixing qualitative and quantitative methods: Triangulation in action. *Administrative Science Quarterly, 24,* 602–611.

Killion, C. M., & Wang, C. C. (2000). Linking African American mothers across lifestage and station through photovoice. *Journal of Health Care for the Poor and Underserved, 11,* 310–325.

Levinson, D. J. (1978). *The seasons of a man's life.* New York: Knopf.

Lieber, E., Weisner, T. S., & Presley, M. (2003). EthnoNotes: An Internet-based field note management tool. *Field Methods, 15,* 405–425.

Lin, A. C. (1998). Bridging positivist and interpretivist approaches to qualitative methods. *Policy Studies Journal, 26,* 162–179.

Loevinger, J. (1976). *Ego development.* San Francisco: Jossey-Bass.

Lykes, M. B., & Stewart, A. J. (1986). Evaluating the feminist challenge to research in personality and social psychology: 1963–1983. *Psychology of Women Quarterly, 10,* 393–412.

Martin, K. A. (1996). *Puberty, sexuality, and the self: Girls and boys at adolescence.* New York: Routledge.

Metzl, J. M. (2003). *Prozac on the couch: Prescribing gender in the era of wonder drugs.* Durham, NC: Duke University Press.

Metzl, J. M., & Angel, J. (2004). Assessing the impact of SSRI antidepressants on popular notions of women's depressive illness. *Social Science and Medicine, 58,* 577–584.

Mishler, E. G. (1990). Validation in inquiry-guided research: The role of exemplars in narrative studies. *Harvard Educational Review, 60,* 415–442.

Morawski, J. G. (1994). *Practicing feminisms, reconstructing psychology.* Ann Arbor: University of Michigan Press.

Morgan, D. L. (1998). Practical strategies for combining qualitative and quantitative methods: Applications to health research. *Qualitative Health Research, 8,* 362–376.

Newman, I., & Benz, C. (1998). *Qualitative-quantitative research methodology: Exploring the interactive continuum.* Carbondale, IL: Southern Illinois Press.

Painter, N. I. (1994). Representing Truth: Sojourner Truth's knowing and becoming known. *Journal of American History, 81,* 461–492.

Patillo-McCoy, M. E. (1998). Sweet mothers and gangbangers: Managing crime in a black middle-class neighborhood. *Social Forces, 76,* 747–774.

Peplau, L. A., & Conrad, E. (1989). Beyond nonsexist research: The perils of feminist methods in psychology. *Psychology of Women Quarterly, 13,* 379–400.

Peterson, B. E. (1998). Case studies of midlife generativity: Analyzing motivation and realization. In D. P. McAdams & E. de St. Aubin (Eds.), *Generativity and adult development* (pp. 101–131). Washington, DC: American Psychological Association.

Press, A. L., & Cole, E. R. (1999). *Speaking of abortion: Television and authority in the lives of women.* Chicago: University of Chicago Press.

Rabinowitz, V. C., & Weseen, S. (1997). Elu(ci)d(at)ing impasses: Re-viewing the qualitative/quantitative debates in psychology. *Journal of Social Issues, 53*(4), 605–630.

Raffaelli, M., & Ontai, L. L. (2004). Gender socialization in Latino/a families: Results from two retrospective studies. *Sex Roles, 50,* 287–299.

Ragins, B. R. (2004). Sexual orientation in the workplace: The unique work and career experiences of gay, lesbian and bisexual workers. *Research and Human Resources Management, 23,* 35–120.

Reinharz, S. (1992). *Feminist methods in social research.* New York: Oxford University Press.

Romich, J. (2000, March). *To sons and daughters: Gender, neighborhood quality and resource allocation in families.* Paper presented at the 2000 Annual Meeting, Population Association of America, Los Angeles.

Romich, J., & Weisner, T. (2000). How families view and use the EITC: Advance payment versus lump sum delivery. *National Tax Journal, 53,* 1245–1265.

Sapiro, V. (1995). Feminist studies and political science: And vice versa. In D. Stanton & A. J. Stewart (Eds.), *Feminisms in the academy* (pp. 291–310). Ann Arbor: University of Michigan Press.

Sherif, C. W. (1987). Bias in psychology. In S. Harding (Ed.), *Feminism and methodology* (pp. 37–56). Bloomington: Indiana University Press.

Sigel, R. (1996). *Ambition and accommodation: How women view gender relations.* Chicago: University of Chicago Press.

Singer, B., & Ryff, C. D. (2001). Person-centered methods for understanding aging: The integration of numbers and narratives. In R. H. Binstock (Ed.), *Handbook of aging and the social sciences* (pp. 44–65). San Diego, CA: Academic Press.

Singer, B., Ryff, C. D., Carr, D., & Magee, W. J. (1998). Linking life histories and mental health: A person-centered strategy. In A. Raftery (Ed.), *Sociological methodology* (pp. 1–51). Washington, DC: American Sociological Association.

Smith, C. P. (1992). *Motivation and personality: Handbook of thematic content analysis.* New York: Cambridge University Press.

Smith, D. E. (1987). *The everyday world as problematic: A feminist sociology.* Toronto, Canada: University of Toronto Press.

Sprague, J., & Zimmerman, M. K. (1993). Overcoming dualisms: A feminist agenda. In P. England (Ed.), *Theory on gender; feminism on theory* (pp. 255–280). New York: Aldine de Gruyter.

Stack, C. (1974). *All our kin: Strategies for survival in a black community.* New York: Harper and Row.

Stewart, A. J. (1994). Toward a feminist strategy for studying women's lives. In C. Franz & A. J. Stewart (Eds.), *Women creating lives: Identities, resilience and resistance* (pp. 11–35). Boulder, CO: Westview Press.

Stewart, A. J. (2003). 2002 Carolyn Wood Sherif Award Address: Gender, race and generation in a Midwest high school: Using ethnographically informed methods in psychology. *Psychology of Women Quarterly, 27,* 1–11.

Stewart, A. J., & Healy, J. M. (1989). Linking individual development and social changes. *American Psychologist, 44,* 30–42.

Stewart, A. J., & Vandewater, E. A. (1993). The Radcliffe class of 1964: Career and family social clock projects in a transitional cohort. In K. D. Hulbert & D. T. Schuster (Eds.), *Women's lives through time: Educated American women of the twentieth century* (pp. 235–258). San Francisco: Jossey-Bass.

Stewart, A. J., & Vandewater, E. A. (1999). "If I had it to do over again . . .": Midlife review, midcourse corrections, and women's well-being in midlife. *Journal of Personality and Social Psychology, 76,* 270–283.

Tangri, S. S., & Jenkins, S. R. (1993). The University of Michigan class of 1967: The women's life paths study. In K. D. Hulbert & D. T. Schuster (Eds.), *Women's lives through time: Educated American women of the twentieth century* (pp. 259–281). San Francisco: Jossey-Bass.

Tashakkori, A., & Teddlie, C. (1998). *Mixed methodology: Combining qualitative and quantitative approaches.* Thousand Oaks, CA: Sage.

Tashakkori, A., & Teddlie, C. (Eds.). (2002). *Handbook of mixed methods social and behavioral research.* Thousand Oaks, CA: Sage.

Tolman, D. L., & Szalacha, L. A. (1999). Dimensions of desire: Bridging qualitative and quantitative methods in a study of female adolescent sexuality. *Psychology of Women Quarterly, 23,* 7–39.

Torges, C., Stewart, A. J., & Miner-Rubino, K. (2005). Personality after the prime of life: Men and women coming to terms with regrets. *Journal of Research on Personality, 39,* 148–165.

Unger, R. K. (1981). Sex as a social reality: Field and laboratory research. *Psychology of Women Quarterly, 5,* 645–653.

Wallston, B. (1981). What are the questions in the psychology of women? A feminist approach to research. *Psychology of Women Quarterly, 5,* 597–617.

Weisstein, N. (1971). *Psychology constructs the female or, the fantasy life of the male psychologist.* Boston: New England Free Press.

Ÿllo, K. (1988). Political and methodological debates in wife abuse research. In K. Ÿllo (Ed.), *Feminist perspectives on wife abuse* (pp. 28–50). Newbury Park, CA: Sage.

Yohalem, A. (1993). Columbia University graduate students: The vanguard of professional women. In K. D. Hulbert & D. T. Schuster (Eds.), *Women's lives through time: Educated American women of the twentieth century* (pp. 140–157). San Francisco: Jossey-Bass.

# 16

# FEMINISMS, GROUNDED THEORY, AND SITUATIONAL ANALYSIS

ADELE E. CLARKE

Since its inception in 1967 (Glaser & Strauss, 1967), grounded theory (hereafter GT) has become a leading method used in qualitative research globally,[1] not only in sociology (e.g., Strauss & Corbin, 1997) and nursing (e.g., Benoliel, 1996, 2001; Schreiber & Stern, 2001), where it was originally taught, but also in organization and management studies (Locke, 2001); education (Cresswell, 2002); cultural studies (e.g., Gelder & Thornton, 1997); computer and information science (Bryant, 2002; Star & Strauss, 1998); social work (e.g., Riessman, 1994); science, technology, and medicine studies (e.g., Clarke & Star, 2003, 2007); and queer studies (Gamson, 2000; Hausman, 2001).

GT has also been quite well elaborated over the years by a number of scholars,[2] and I have very recently developed an updated postmodern extension of GT called situational analysis (hereafter SA) (Clarke, 2003, 2005). In terms of feminism(s) and GT, we also found vast numbers of citations from sites across multiple disciplines.[3] Thus, examining GT and SA in terms of their

past, present, and future usefulness in feminist research seems most appropriate.

In this chapter, I will not elaborate much on what I and others in general conceive as (good) feminist research (past, present, and future) in the abstract. Such concerns have long been addressed and this volume both exemplifies and sustains them.[4] We have come a long way since Stacey's (1988) lament about the impossibility of feminist ethnography. Responses to it such as Wheatley's (1994) have emphasized not only that those problems are endemic to all ethnographic work— feminist and not—but also that no one method can do everything that feminists might want to do methodologically. Haraway (1999), for example, insists that different problems feminists seek to address can demand radically different methodological approaches, and that all knowledges are partial regardless (Haraway, 1997). Fonow and Cook (2005) assert that "there has never been one correct feminist epistemology generating one correct feminist methodology" (p. 213), and I would add that there never will be.

---

Author's Note: I want to thank Leigh Star, Monica Casper, Virginia Olesen, and Jennifer Fosket for helpful comments on this chapter. Carrie Friese provided superb research and bibliographic assistance. I am citing the GT literature somewhat lightly here for reasons of space, usually offering one citation per scholar. Please see also the bibliography posted at www.situationalanalysis.com for extended citations.

Rather, my project for this chapter is to elucidate first what GT is and to specify the ways in which GT has always already been *implicitly* feminist in its pragmatist epistemology/ontology. I then turn to the feminist GT literature and demonstrate how scholars have to date made GT more *explicitly* feminist through using it in feminist projects—how pragmatism is alive and well in feminism. Next I discuss what SA is, how it is also always already implicitly feminist, and some feminist research using it to date. In conclusion, I elucidate my hopes for the feminist futures of both GT and SA.

## What Is Grounded Theory?

> Social phenomena are complex. Thus they require complex grounded theory. (Strauss, 1987, p. 1)

GT and SA are both first and foremost modes of *analysis* of qualitative research data. That is, neither claims to offer a fully elaborated methodology from soup to nuts—from project design to data collection to final write-up. Many elements of a full-blown methodology are offered by both, and situational maps can be especially useful for design stages. But analysis is the core goal of both. Building on traditional GT usually used with field data and/or in-depth interviews, SA explicitly extends analysis to discursive data, including narrative, historical, and visual materials. The trend toward multisite research is thus supported.

GT and SA are both deeply *empirical* approaches to the study of social life through qualitative research and analysis. The very term *grounded theory* means data-grounded theorizing. In the words of Atkinson, Coffey, and Delamont (2003), "Grounded theory is not a description of a kind of theory. Rather it represents a general way of generating theory (or, even more generically, a way of having ideas on the basis of empirical research)" (p. 150). The theorizing is generated abductively by tacking back and forth between the nitty-gritty specificities of empirical data and more abstract ways of thinking about them. In doing SA too the analyst relentlessly returns to the crudest of the maps to remind her- or himself of the palpability and heterogeneity of the data.

In using/doing GT, the analyst initially codes the qualitative data (open coding)—word by word, segment by segment—and gives temporary labels (codes) to particular phenomena. Over time, the analyst determines whether codes generated through one data source also appear elsewhere, and elaborates their properties. Related codes that seem robust through the ongoing coding process are then densified into more enduring and analytically ambitious "categories." Analytic memos are written about each designated category—what does it mean; what are the instances of it; what is the range of variation within it found in the data to date; what does and doesn't it seem to "take into account"? These categories are ultimately integrated into a theoretical analysis of the substantive area that is the immediate focus of the current research project. Thus, a "grounded theory" of a particular phenomenon of concern is composed of the analytic codes and categories generated abductively in the analysis and explicitly integrated to form a theory of the substantive area that is the focus of the research project: The analyst generates an empirically based "substantive theory." In traditional GT, over time, after the researcher(s) have generated multiple substantive theories of a particular broad area of interest through an array of empirical research projects, so the argument went, more "formal theory" could be developed (see especially Strauss, 1995). Formal theory was originally used here in the modernist sense of social theory, aiming at "Truth," and I return to this point below.

What remains relatively unique and very special to this approach was first GT's requiring that analysis begin as soon as there are data. Coding begins immediately, and theorizing based on that coding does as well, however provisionally (Glaser, 1978). Second, "sampling" is driven not necessarily (or not only) by attempts to be "representative" of some social body or population or its heterogeneities but especially and explicitly by *theoretical* concerns that have emerged in the provisional analysis to date. Such "theoretical sampling" focuses on finding *new data sources* (persons or things—and *not* theories) that can best explicitly address specific theoretically interesting facets of the emergent analysis. Theoretical sampling has been integral to GT from the outset, remains a fundamental strength of this analytic approach, and is also crucial for SA.[5]

In fact, it can certainly be argued that precisely what is to be studied *emerges* from the analytic process over time, rather than being designated a priori: "The true legacy of Glaser and Strauss is a collective awareness of the heuristic value of developmental research designs [through theoretical sampling] and exploratory data analytic strategies, not a 'system' for conducting and analyzing research" (Atkinson et al., 2003, p. 163). I would argue that this emergence is itself implicitly feminist in that it tries to build an adequate "database" for a project *through* expanding the data to be collected "as needed" through the researcher's mining their reflexivity. This is a much more modest than arrogant approach to the production of new knowledge, and one that takes "experience" into account in all its densities and complexities (Scott, 1992)—especially the experiences of the researcher with the project and the researcher's reflexivity about it.

Most research using GT has relied on fieldwork to generate interview and/or ethnographic data through which to analyze human action (e.g., Glaser, 1993; Strauss & Corbin, 1997). Conventional GT has focused on generating the "basic social process" occurring in the data concerning the phenomenon of concern—the basic form of human action. Studies have been done, for example, on *living with* chronic illness (Charmaz, 1991), *disciplining* the scientific study of reproduction (Clarke, 1998), *classifying* and its consequences (Bowker & Star, 1999), *making* CPR the main emergency response to sudden death (Timmermans, 1999), and *creating* a new social actor—the unborn patient— via fetal surgery (Casper, 1998).

In a traditional GT study, the key or basic social process is typically articulated in gerund form connoting ongoing action, and at an abstract level. Around this basic process, the analyst then constellates the particular and distinctive conditions, strategies, actions, and practices engaged in by human and nonhuman actors involved with/in the process and their consequences. For example, subprocesses of disciplining the scientific study of reproduction include *formalizing* a scientific discipline, *establishing* stable access to research materials, *gleaning* fiscal support for research, *producing* contraceptives and other technoscientific products, and *handling* the social controversies the science provokes (e.g., regarding use of contraceptives) (Clarke, 1998). Many excellent projects have been done using basic GT, and this action-centered approach will continue to be fundamentally important analytically.

## GROUNDED THEORY AS ALWAYS ALREADY IMPLICITLY FEMINIST

There are several ways in which I and others such as Susan Leigh Star[6] have long understood GT to have been always already implicitly feminist: (1) its roots in American symbolic interactionist sociology and pragmatist philosophy emphasizing actual experiences and practices— the lived doingness of social life; (2) its use of George Herbert Mead's concept of perspective that emphasizes partiality, situatedness, and multiplicity; (3) its assumption of a materialist social constructionism; (4) its foregrounding deconstructive analysis and multiple simultaneous readings; and (5) its attention to range of variation as featuring of difference(s).

First and foremost here is what I and other feminists see as the roots of GT in symbolic interactionist sociology and pragmatist philosophy. This was not always the case. Historically, Glaser and Strauss (1967), Glaser (1978), and Schatzman and Strauss (1973) argued that GT as a methodological approach could be effectively used by people from a variety of theoretical as well as disciplinary perspectives. That is, they initially took a "mix and match" approach. Their challenge—which they ably met—was to articulate a new qualitative methodology in the belly of the haute positivist quantitative sociological beast of the 1960s. They sought to do so through a systematic approach to analyzing qualitative research data.[7] Their emphases in the early works cited were on taking a *naturalistic* approach to research, having initially *modest* (read substantively focused) theoretical goals, and being *systematic* in what we might today call the interrogation of qualitative research data in order to work against what they and others then saw as the "distorting subjectivities" of the researcher in the concrete processes of interpretive analysis.

In considerable contrast, it can be argued that GT is rooted in American pragmatist philosophy and the approach to sociology generated through it—symbolic interactionism (Blumer, 1969). That is, grounded theory/symbolic interactionism can be seen as constituting a theory/methods package that is implicitly feminist. Star (1989) framed such theory/methods packages as including a set of epistemological and ontological assumptions along with concrete practices through which a set of practitioners go about their work, including relating to/with one another and the various nonhuman entities involved in the situation. This concept of theory-methods package focuses on the integral—and ultimately nonfungible—aspects of ontology and epistemology as these are co-constitutive. And, vis-à-vis symbolic interactionism, this features researching the meanings held by the actors themselves—an implicitly feminist stance.

Specifically, I and others have argued that GT is a methodology inherently predicated on a symbolic interactionist theoretical and philosophical ontology (e.g., Charmaz, 2006; Clarke, 2003, 2005; Crooks, 2001). GT is thus one method among many of "performing" (Butler, 1993; Goffman, 1963) or "doing" (Fenstermaker & West, 2002) interactionism. "Method, then, is not the servant of theory: method actually grounds theory" (Jenks, 1995, p. 12).[8]

Historically, as GT grew in stature and began to be used more and more widely, and as the implications of Berger and Luckmann's (1966) *The Social Construction of Reality* began to be taken up more explicitly, more and more practitioners of GT began tugging GT in constructionist and postmodernist directions. Charmaz (1995, 2000, 2005, 2006) has written about this, and both she and Locke (1996, 2001) view Strauss but certainly not Glaser as moving in such directions. I agree and would argue further that such directions are requisite if GT is to continue to be a useful method for feminist research.[9]

The second way in which GT has been always already implicitly feminist is its rootedness in George Herbert Mead's concept of perspective. Much of symbolic interactionism has always been distinctly perspectival in ways fully compatible with producing through research what are today understood as situated knowledges (Haraway, 1991, 1997). This involves the commitment to representing those we study on their own terms/through their own perspectives. That is, the groundedness of good traditional grounded theorizing is not only in the data per se but, I would argue, most deeply in the seriousness of the analyst's commitment to representing *all* understandings, all knowledge(s) and action(s) of those studied—as well as their own—as perspectival. Feminists have often come to grasp such partialities through considerable pain.

That is, the interactionist concept of perspective can be deployed to complicate—to make analyses more radical, democratic, and transgressive. Representing the full multiplicity of perspectives in a given situation, from the heterogeneous "powers that be" to the various prisoners of various kinds of panopticons, "minority" views, "marginal" positions, and/or the "other(s)"/alterity, disrupts the *representational* hegemony that usually privileges some and erases others. Representing *is* intervening (Hacking, 1983). This, of course, has been at the heart of many feminist projects (Lather & Smithies, 1997). (It also links to the concept of implicated actors, discussed below.)

Third, I would argue that GT is always already feminist (at least vis-à-vis my grasp of feminisms) because an interactionist constructionism is a *materialist* social constructionism (Law & Mol, 1995; Seigfried, 2001; Tuana, 2001). That is, many people (mis)interpret social constructionism as concerned only with the ephemeral or ideological or symbolic. But the material world is itself constructed—materially produced, interpreted, and given meaning(s)—by us and by those whom we study. This *is* what we study—our own constructions of our research problems, including human and nonhuman material aspects. The material world, including our own embodiment, is present and to be accounted for in our interpretations and analyses. This materialism, this importance of things, this sociality of things was also argued by Mead (1934/1962, p. 373), as McCarthy (1984) has most elegantly demonstrated (see also Barad, 2003). We routinely make meaning about, within, through, and as embodied parts of the material world—human, nonhuman, and hybrid. The social is relentlessly material *and* constructed—not "merely" epiphenomenal.

The fourth way in which GT can be viewed as always already feminist lies in its foregrounding of a deconstructive mode of analysis via open coding. Open coding connotes just that—data are open to multiple simultaneous readings/codes. Many different phenomena and many different properties can be named, tracked, and traced through reams of all different kinds of data. There is no one right reading. All readings are temporary, partial, provisional, and perspectival—themselves situated historically and geographically.

As analysts we can ourselves attempt to read the data from different perspectives and for different purposes. In fact, Strauss developed a concrete practice approach to producing multiple readings: Working data analysis groups that take up individual members' project data. Multiple readings are routinely and explicitly sought and produced through group effort. This is also the usual pedagogical tradition for teaching/learning GT—to bring multiple perspectives together so that you can more easily produce multiple readings, multiple possible codes. In this way of working, the analyst is constantly banging into and bouncing off the interpretations of others. This also ultimately legitimates and enhances the capacity of the analyst her/himself to come up with multiple possible readings on their own and to abandon ideas about "right" and "wrong" readings.[10] I would go so far as to call such analytic working groups "consciousness raising"!

The fifth way in which GT is always already tacitly feminist concerns difference as range of variation. Variation has always been attended to in GT, but the attention has, I argue, been too scant. Strauss (1993) returned to this point in his capstone book and emphasized it as follows:

> [Social science activity] is directed at understanding the entire range of human actions, of which there are so many that the dictionary can scarcely refer to them all. That is, an interactionist theory of action should address action generally and be applicable to specific types of action, so that in effect the theory can also help us understand the incredibly variegated panorama of human living. (p. 49)

Through SA, discussed later, I seek to further shift the emphasis in GT from attending primarily to commonalities to attending to this "incredibly variegated panorama of human living," to mapping and analyzing differences of all kinds. Making differences more visible and making silences speak (also often about difference) are two of the explicit goals of SA.

I want to end this section by clearly stating that for all its implicit feminisms, there were and remain serious problems for feminists with traditional forms of GT. These include a lack of reflexivity, tendencies toward oversimplification, interpretation of data variation as "negative cases" rather than differences worthy of understanding, and, for some, a search for fundamental(ist) "purity" and "Truth" through GT (Clarke, 2005, pp. 11–18).

## Making Grounded Theory More Explicitly Feminist

Over the years, a huge number of scholars have forged GT into explicitly feminist tools for qualitative research (see Note 4). I use the plural because the range of feminist usages of GT is broad. While it is truly impossible to review this vast literature here, I will highlight several clusters of contributors who have made GT explicitly feminist in important and enduringly valuable ways: nurse researchers; sociologists; and science, technology, and medicine scholars. I also note feminist GT contributions from social work, clinical psychology, and related fields.

It should come as no surprise that the first grouping of scholars here are nurse researchers—usually nurses working in academia rather than health care provision. Strauss and Glaser were faculty in the School of Nursing at UC San Francisco (UCSF) in 1967 when they conceived the GT method and published their book, and Strauss remained on the faculty until his death in 1996. Virginia Olesen was also on the faculty and introduced both feminist theory and feminist social science perspectives on women's health to the sociology and nursing curricula beginning in 1973.[11]

The earliest wave of feminist nursing GT scholarship was undertaken by Holly Wilson, Sally Hutchinson, Phyllis Noerager Stern, Ellen O'Shaughnessy, June Lowenberg, Barbara Bowers, Susan Kools, and others.[12] I would characterize it as usually more tacitly rather than explicitly feminist. That is, while the research topics themselves often featured women and/or concerns particular to girls and women, and often centered on giving voice to ill people and their families noting gender, they did not pursue explicitly gendered analyses (the problematization, production, and/or performance of gendered identities), nor did they pursue the intersectionalities of gender with race and class issues as feminist research often does. Jeanne Quint Benoliel (1996, pp. 419–421) analyzed GT nursing research published from 1980 to 1994 and found the following topics: family processes/adaptations, health-seeking practices (weight and contraception), infertility, individual adaptations to chronic illnesses, family processes in chronic illnesses, the illness experience, processes and practices of nurses, interventions and interactional processes by nurses, contextual/ environmental influences, institutional/interactional processes and practices, and passages and processes of vulnerable people.

More recently, Benoliel (2001) also edited a special issue of *Health Care for Women International* on "Expanding Knowledge About Women Through Grounded Theory," which offers an array of both substantive and more theoretically oriented work (e.g., Crooks, 2001). Other, more recent feminist-informed GT work in nursing has focused on children with terminal illnesses and their families, including siblings and fathers (Davies, 1995, 1999), nursing interventions for domestic violence (Ford-Gilboe, Wuest, & Merritt-Gray, 2005), and foster care (Kools & Kennedy, 2003). Marcellus (2005) offers a current review of the use of GT in maternal-infant research and practice. Much, if not most, of this work has clear advocacy, intervention, and policy aims, and all would be of interest to feminists focusing on such topics.

Nurses also have written extensively on GT (Benoliel, 1996, 2001; Kools, McCarthy, Durham, & Robrecht, 1996; Olshansky, 1996), including on debates between Straussian and Glaserian approaches to it (Annells, 1996; Corbin, 1998; Crooks, 2001; Melia, 1996; Stern, 1994), on issues of developing formal theory (Kearney, 1998, 2001; Wuest, 2001), on GT and postmodern theory (MacDonald & Schreiber, 2001; Wuest & Merritt-Gray, 2001), and on

feminism and GT (Keddy, Sims, & Stern, 1996; Kushner & Morrow, 2003; Wuest, 1995; Wuest & Merritt-Gray, 2001; see also the 2001 special double issue on grounded theory of *Health Care for Women International, 22*[1–2]). As Susan Kools (personal communication, September 2005) noted, many of the early generation of GT nurse scholars were "trained before the postmodern turn by the white men at UCSF," and I can personally attest to the problems that Strauss, Glaser, and Schatzman had with explicit feminist approaches.

For example, at the request of several nurse scholars, Glaser (2002b) explicitly took up issues of "Grounded Theory and Gender Relevance." He reasserted the theme that gender, race, and other "face sheet data" need to "earn their way into" a GT analysis (p. 789) rather than "forcing" their way in. He argued about domestic violence and rape, for example, that GT should be used to develop a general theory of domination that would be capable of explaining such phenomena via "abstraction from time, place and people." He does not grasp that there already exist general theories of gender, that gender (like domination) is learned, performative, variegated, enculturated, and situated social action much less in the forms of *both* masculinities and femininities (see also Bryant, 2002, 2003; Glaser, 2002a).

In contrast, I would argue that focused feminist GT and SA research need to engage the intersectionalities of theories of gender and of domination, along with class, race, and other identity issues in their local, situated, contextualized specificities. One example is the stunning GT work of sociologist Beth Richie (1996) on "gender entrapment." Richie analyzes how battered African American women's gender identities can position them to pursue illegal activities "for" their male abusers, including going to prison. Richie uses the legal notion of "entrapment" to emphasize the gendered vulnerabilities of these women that lure them into compromising acts, vulnerabilities in part distinctive to particularly racialized and classed African American masculine and feminine gender identities in the United States today.

Recently, feminist nurse scholars have both sustained and extended their GT efforts in more explicitly feminist directions.[13] Among these is

Margaret Kearney, whose research on pregnant women using crack cocaine was groundbreaking. On her own and with colleagues (Kearney, 1998; Kearney, Murphy, Irwin, & Rosenbaum, 1995; Kearney, Murphy, & Rosenbaum, 1994), Kearney analyzed how women protected their children by keeping them and their drug taking apart and "running between the rooms." This was also a strategy for these women to salvage shreds of a valued self. Kearney then pursued an array of further studies leading to her GT-based *Understanding Women's Recovery From Illness and Trauma* (1999; see also Kearney, 2001). Ingram and Hutchison (1999) also studied "defensive mothering," focusing on HIV-positive mothers.

Other feminist GT nursing studies include Suellen Miller's (1996) research on how new mothers developed career reentry strategies—by questioning, resisting, acquiescing, balancing, and most of all by improvising. Her and Kearney's GT diagrams are among the best in print, vividly encapsulating actions and conditions that may shape them. Debora Bone studied dilemmas of emotion work in nursing under managed health care. As part of feminist revelations of "invisible work," Bone sought to preserve knowledge of the broader caregiving culture of nursing. She focused on how nurses are "getting squeezed" (an "in vivo" code)—and how they understood and felt about the consequences for themselves, for nursing work, and for nursing as a profession (Bone, 2002; Olesen & Bone, 1998).

Looking to the future of GT in nursing research, Kushner and Morrow (2003) recently elucidated its current and exciting potential future relations with interactionist, feminist, and critical theories. They found several commonalities of GT with feminist and critical theories useful in nursing and beyond, including special focus on vulnerable groups, explication of researchers' standpoints, respect for participant expertise within the research process, and emancipatory intent. In a paper titled "Feminist Grounded Theory Revisited," Wuest and Merritt-Gray (2001) emphasize how enhanced researcher reflexivity needs to attend with care to the potential of the research to do harm or oppress; develop strategies to make research more respectful, useful, and transformative;

include differences more; and consider participant review of results.

Feminist sociologists have also used GT most effectively for decades, both in classic GT studies of lived experiences and in taking GT in new feminist directions such as science, technology, and medicine studies (Clarke & Star, 2003, 2007). A classic GT study of lived experience was undertaken by Lora Lempert (1996, 1997) to understand how women succeeded in leaving abusive relationships (rather than study why they stayed). She found that women needed to redefine their situations through dialogues with their abusers, others, and themselves in order to develop the agency and sense of autonomy necessary to move on. Parr (1998) found that while patriarchal theories were explanatorily crucial, they were also insufficient to fully understand the mature women students she had studied who were recovering from abuse and making new lives.

Taking GT into feminist queer studies, Laura Mamo (2005, 2006) used GT at the intersection of lived experience and technology studies to explore how both cultural discourses and assisted reproduction are used by lesbian-identified women seeking pregnancy through technoscientific means. Mamo argues that lesbians both follow given technological scripts and create their own interpretations of the technologies, thus subverting the expectations of developers, marketers, and service providers. Ekins (1997) offered one of the earliest studies of transgender. Calling it "male femaling," Elkins found three major modes—body femaling, erotic femaling, and gender femaling—set within overarching femaling career paths, or what Strauss (1993) would have called trajectories.

Taking GT in new feminist directions by using it with discursive materials, Mamo and Fishman (2001) analyzed promotional materials for Viagra, arguing that such ads perform cultural and ideological work through discursive scripts that reinforce and augment the inscription of dominant cultural narratives onto material bodies, particularly hegemonic masculinity and heterosexuality. At the same time, through both subtexts and imaged signals, advertising strategies also seek an open market for heterogeneous (off label) users, including gay men and (any and all) women. Fishman (2004) uses GT in science, technology, and medicine studies to examine the biomedical construction of "male and female sexual dysfunction" currently being produced in conjunction with the availability of new pharmaceutical technologies to treat them such as Viagra and testosterone therapies. Lisa Jean Moore's (in press) new book, *Sperm Tales: Social, Cultural and Scientific Representations of Human Semen*, examines such representations from reproductive scientists, the Internet, children's "facts of life" books, forensic transcripts, sex workers' narratives, and personal expertise. Semen representations, she finds, are distinctively related to changing social positions of men, masculinities, and constructions of male differences (see also Moore & Schmidt, 1998, 1999).

Also going in new science and technology studies directions is Fosket's (2002) study of the emergence of tamoxifen and raloxifene as powerful hormonal breast cancer *prevention* drugs. She examines the processes of biomedical and epidemiological construction of appropriate users of such chemoprevention drugs as "high-risk women," a technoscientific identity (Clarke, Shim, Mamo, Fosket, & Fishman, 2003) determined by a set of calculations called the "Gail model" (Fosket, 2004). This model works as a "risk assessment technology" that women can use themselves—by going online. Pitts (2004) studied "Illness and Internet Empowerment" using GT to analyze writing and reading about breast cancer in cyberspace, especially on personal Web sites.

Janet Shim's (2000, 2002, 2005) ambitious research combines the lived experiences tradition with the emergent feminist science, technology, and medicine studies approaches in GT research. Shim focused on two different sets of people concerned with cardiovascular diseases (CVDs) in the United States today: epidemiologists and related researchers who study the racial, ethnic, sex/gender, social class, and other distributions of CVDs in populations, and people of color diagnosed as having CVDs. Shim's explicitly comparative approach centers on the *meanings* of race, class, and sex vis-à-vis CVDs constructed by the epidemiologists on the one hand and by the people of color diagnosed and living with CVDs on the other (see also Bowker & Star, 1999; Schwalbe, Goodwin, Schrock, Thompson,

& Wolkomir, 2000). Shim's work demonstrates the fruitfulness of doing feminist GT with a comparative design and then teasing out comparisons both within and between her emerging categories (Kathy Charmaz, personal communication, October 2005).

Family studies scholars also use GT to examine feminist issues. Ramona Oswald's (2000) award-winning paper focused on what happened to friendships and family relations when young women came out as bisexual or lesbian by interviewing the women, their families, and their friends. She found a period of intense focus on and negotiation around how this "new" homosexuality would be handled relationally. Kerry Daly (2001) works on deconstructing family time, contrasting discursive ideologies with lived experience in the "doing" of family life amid a deeply work-oriented culture—an area of concern to many feminists.[14] Kushner and Harrison (2002) used a feminist and critical GT approach to study family health decision making among working-class women negotiating meanings of motherhood, work, health, family, and so on. Another exemplar of interesting feminist GT was Gustafsson-Larsson and Hammarstrom's (2005) project, which offers a theoretical model of how flows of energy and spaces of action generate health and ill health in the doing of rural community work. The multiple meanings the women had of participation and the multiple possible outcomes were emphasized.

Feminist economists have challenged traditional economic theory by developing a gendered reconceptualization of social indicators based on the use of GT with focus group data (Austen, Jefferson, & Thein, 2003). Such new indicators can be used to reorganize how economic analyses are done in ways that, quite radically even today, include gender! Feminist social workers have also put GT to good use. For example, Judith Ivy Fiene (1993) sought to "add to the store of knowledge about rural Appalachian families, particularly low-income women and children" (p. 1), from their own perspectives. She sought to displace stereotypes with deeply situated accounts of lived experience that capture dilemmas and contradictions in women's lives at the intersection of gender and class issues (see also Schulz & Mullings, 2006). Feminist psychotherapists also draw on GT (Fassinger, 2005; Parker, 1998), as do physiotherapists (Ohman & Hagg, 1998) and occupational therapists (Gutman & Napier-Klemic, 1996).

My favorite titles, after scanning close to 1,000, were "Cinderella Was a Wuss: A Young Girl's Responses to Feminist and Patriarchal Folktales" (Trousdale & McMillan, 2003), "To Prove Them Wrong Syndrome: Voices From Unheard African American Males in Engineering Disciplines" (Smith, 2003), "A Grounded Theory of the Flow Experiences of Web Users" (Pace, 2004), and "Do Promise Keepers Dream of Feminist Sheep?" (to which the answer is no) (Silverstein, Auerbach, & Grieco, 1999).

Let me end this section with an apology. While I discuss some works pursued in "faraway places," my "lite" review here of necessity emphasizes work done by nurses and sociologists who trained at UCSF. I certainly do not mean to imply that I consider these works in any way "better" than others. Rather, I merely know them better myself.

## WHAT IS SITUATIONAL ANALYSIS?

Doyle McCarthy (1996) has asserted that "all aspects of human being and knowing are *situated*" (p. 107). In the extension of GT I developed called situational analysis (Clarke, 2003, 2005), *the situation of inquiry itself broadly conceived is the key unit of analysis.*[15] This is radically different from traditional GT, which focuses on the main social processes—human action—in the area of inquiry. In SA, the situation of inquiry is empirically constructed through the making of three kinds of maps and following through with analytic work and memos of various kinds. The first maps are *situational maps* that lay out the major human, nonhuman, discursive, historical, symbolic, cultural, political, and other elements in the research situation of concern and provoke analysis of relations among them. They intentionally work *against* the usual simplifications so characteristic of scientific work (Star, 1983) in particularly postmodern and feminist ways. Specifically, these maps are intended to capture and provoke discussion of the many and heterogeneous elements and the messy complexities of the situation in their dense relations and permutations.

Second, the *social worlds/arenas maps* lay out all of the *collective* actors, key nonhuman elements, and the arena(s) of commitment within which they are engaged in ongoing discourse and negotiations. Such maps offer mesolevel interpretations of the situation, taking up its social organizational, institutional, and discursive dimensions. They are distinctively postmodern in their assumptions: We cannot assume directionalities of influence; boundaries are open and porous; negotiations are fluid; discourses are multiple and potentially contradictory. *Negotiations* of many kinds from coercion to bargaining are the "basic social processes" that construct and constantly destabilize the social worlds/arenas maps (Strauss, 1993). Things could always be otherwise—not only individually but also collectively/organizationally/institutionally/discursively, and these maps portray such postmodern possibilities.

Third, *positional maps* lay out the major positions taken, and *not* taken, in the data vis-à-vis particular axes of variation and difference, focus, and controversy found in the situation of concern. Perhaps most significantly, positional maps are *not* articulated with persons or groups but rather seek to represent the full range of *discursive* positions on particular issues—fully allowing multiple positions and even contradictions within both individuals and collectivities to be articulated. Complexities are themselves heterogeneous, and we need improved means of representing them.

All three kinds of maps are keyed to taking the nonhuman in the situation of inquiry—including discourses—seriously. In doing initial situational maps, the analyst is asked to specify the nonhuman elements in the situation, thus making pertinent materialities and discourses visible from the outset. The flip side of the second kind of maps, the social worlds/arenas maps, are discourse/arenas maps. Social worlds are "universes of discourse" routinely producing discourses about elements of concern in the situation. Such discourses can be mapped and analyzed. Last, positional maps seek to open up the discourses per se by analyzing positions taken on key axes. Discourses can thereby be disarticulated from their sites of production, decentering them and making further analytic complexities visible.

## SITUATIONAL ANALYSIS AS ALWAYS ALREADY IMPLICITLY FEMINIST

I would assert that SA is always already feminist in both the ways discussed above as characteristic of GT (since SA is an extension of GT after the postmodern turn) and additionally in (at least) the following ways:

1. Acknowledging researchers' embodiment and situatedness

2. Grounding analysis in the lived material and symbolic situation itself

3. Conceptually foregrounding complexities and differences in the data

4. Mapping *all* the actors and discourses in the situation regardless of their power in that situation

First, while GT historically and today may have a foot (and sometimes two) in the positivist domain that assumes the possibility of "scientific objectivity" and "Truth," SA does not. Instead, SA not only assumes but explicitly acknowledges the embodiment and situatedness of knowledge producers—both us (the researchers) and them (who and what we are studying)—as we collaborate in the production of new knowledge. SA also accepts the partialities of knowing. These issues have long been part of feminist research concerns (Haraway, 1991, 1997; Harding & Norberg, 2005; Visweswaran, 1994), and are also at the heart of recent postmodern scholarship on qualitative methods (Fine, 1994; Lather, 1991, in press). Embodiment is inscribed on/in the knowledge produced.

A second way in which I view SA as always already feminist lies in its overall analytic focus on the situation itself as the unit of analysis—actually transforming what are often seen as "objects of study" and their "contexts" into a single ultimately nonfungible unit by refusing the object/context binary. The important so-called contextual elements are not constellated somehow *around* the objects of study, but instead are actually *inside the situation itself.* They are *constitutive* of it, including structural and power elements, and we can map and analyze them as such. Figure 16.1 illustrates this point.

The term *situation* signals for me several scholarly contributions of which I am intellectually inordinately fond. In William I. Thomas's and Dorothy Swayne Thomas's (Thomas, 1923/1978; Thomas & Thomas, 1928/1970) conception of "the definition of the situation," they argued that *situations defined as real are real in their consequences.* Or perspective dominates the interpretation on which action is based. In C. Wright Mills's (1940) classic and deeply pragmatist paper on "Situated Actions and Vocabularies of Motive," Mills asserted: "Most researches on the verbal level merely ask abstract questions of individuals, but *if we can tentatively delimit the situations* [italics added] in which certain motives may be verbalized, *we can use that delimitation in the construction of situational questions* [italics added]." *Situational questions* then become a focus of data gathering for situational analyses. SA thus embraces the limitations of analyzing a particular situation rather than (over)generalizing.

Another key text on the concept of situation is Donna Haraway's (1991) classic feminist theory paper on "Situated Knowledges," in which she asserts that all knowledges are situated—historical, geographic, culturally infused, and produced by embodied human beings: "Feminist objectivity means quite simply *situated knowledges.* . . . In this way we might become answerable for what we learn how to see" (p. 188). Here, Haraway points to the moral importance of researchers' reflexivity, how we are accountable for our work in the world.

The concept situation is also important in terms of its *gestalt*—how a situation is always greater than the sum of its parts because it includes their relationality in a particular temporal and spatial moment. A gestalt understanding of situations as generating "a life of their own" offers a very poststructuralist reading, granting a kind of agency to the situation per se similar to the agency discourses have/are in Foucauldian terms, most important in understanding SA. Last, today the situation is being taken up more broadly in social theory in new ways. For example, Massumi (2002) builds on this gestalt of situations, arguing that the "excess"—that which makes a situation greater than the sum of its parts—"*belongs to their joint situation.* More

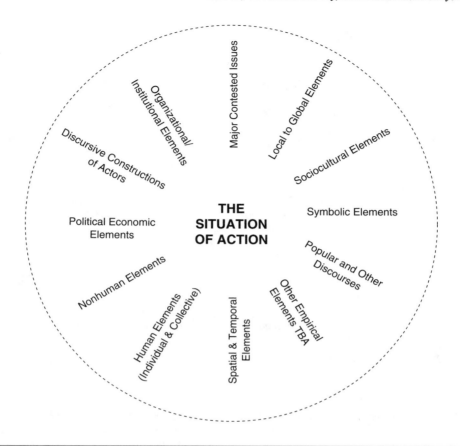

**Figure 16.1**    The Situational Matrix

precisely, it enters their situation" (p. 211). It becomes part of that situation and deserves analysis as such.

The third way in which I would argue that SA is always already feminist concerns the assumption and representational strategies of focusing on normativity/homogeneity versus differences/complexities/heterogeneities. The capacity of GT techniques to fracture data and permit multiple analyses is its key contribution to the capacity to represent difference(s), complexities, multiplicities. But to empower this capacity of grounded theorizing—to feature it— involves an array of efforts embodied in SA. Most foundationally, it involves analyzing *against* the assumptions of the normal curve that are implicit throughout the social sciences. The normal curve is the implanted default drive of Western science, black-boxed inside the hardwares of knowledge production and inside the

softwares of social science training. It is today, I would argue, a *cultural* assumption of the Western educated mind/person and deeply embedded in a wide array of discourses. It is one of the ways in which a distinctively functionalist positivism and scientism have become culturally and transnationally taken for granted—that is, naturalized (Foucault, 1965, 1975). Once naturalized, its dominance is rendered invisible as part of intellectual colonization processes that Gramsci (1949/1971) described as hegemonic.

### NORMAL CURVE
Imagine a drawing of the normal curve here
[It won't be hard]

The normal curve is a measure of central tendency. The foundational assumption is that frequencies of "x" phenomenon will distribute

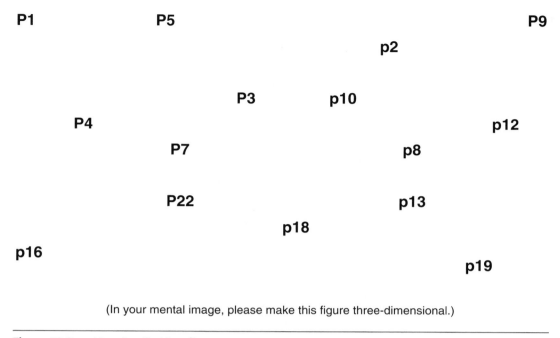

(In your mental image, please make this figure three-dimensional.)

**Figure 16.2**     Mapping Positionality

themselves in a patterned way with most of the variation falling at two "opposite" "ends" of a binary continuum. The "nonvariation"—"normal"—or majority will fall in the "middle." Again, this is frequency based and also commonly appears as a bar graph. Representationally, it is as if the blanket of inquiry has been thrown over the data points and pushed them down and forward into a single dimension at the bottom of the page/figure, carefully containing them within their "natural" classificatory slots. The normal curve is clearly a high modern concept that embodies Enlightenment thinking and thereby produces knowledge that fits its ordered and orderly classificatory preconceptions (see also Bowker & Star, 1999).

The normal curve operates both graphically and metaphorically: While the fringes or margins are literally contiguous with the center, we are led to assume they are not constitutive of the "normal." Certainly Canguilhem (1978), Foucault (1965, 1975), symbolic interactionists (e.g., Becker, 1963, 1970; Blumer, 1969), and others have argued otherwise. In sharp contrast, it is the boundaries/margins that *produce* the center, the peripheries/colonies that constitute

the core/metropole (Said, 1978). Moreover, in narrowly focusing on what is construed as "the normal," the broader situation in which the phenomenon has been historically and otherwise located recedes to the point of invisibility.

Instead, SA seeks to replace metaphors of normal curves and normativity with relational metaphors of ecology and cartography (see Figure 16.2). We need to conceptually replace modernist unidimensional normal curves with postmodern multidimensional mappings in order to represent lived situations and the variety of positionalities and human and nonhuman activities and discourses within them. Otherwise we merely continue performing recursive classifications that ignore the empirical world.

This alternative relational modality of representation does not concern itself particularly with frequency but instead with positions and their distribution across some kinds of situational or topographical maps that do the work of helping us to "see" the range of positions. This alternative draws maps to help make known, understand, and represent the heterogeneity of positions taken in the situation under study and/or within given (historical and/or visual and/or narrative) discourses in that situation.

The main goal of SA vis-à-vis differences is to enhance their *empirical* study. That is, we cannot assume what any kinds of differences mean to those in a given situation, and need more and better methods to explore those meanings and their consequences in concrete social practices, including the production and consumption of discourses as practices (Schwalbe et al., 2000). Differences need to be de-reified and de-essentialized through empirical research. We need to grasp variation *within* data categories, range of variation within data, complexities, contradictions, multiplicities, and ambivalence(s) manifest individually, collectively, and discursively. The situational maps are each and all designed to do precisely this work.

The fourth and last way I would argue that SA is always already feminist is that it requires mapping of *all* the actors and discourses in the situation regardless of their power in that situation. This can be both a feminist and a democratizing move. Many contemporary modes of analysis, including those of Foucault (e.g., 1965, 1975) and Latourian actor-network theory (e.g., Law & Hassard, 1999), center on the analysis of (those in/discourses in) power. In sharp contrast, SA goes beyond what could be called "the master discourse" (Hughes, 1971). By *not* analytically recapitulating the power relations of domination, analyses that represent the full array of actors and discourses turn up the volume on lesser but still present discourses, lesser but still present participants, the quiet, the silent, and the silenced. Such analyses can amplify not only differences but also resistances, recalcitrance, and sites of rejection. The concept of *implicated actors* is important here. These are actors explicitly constructed and/or addressed by a social world and for whom the actions of that world may be highly consequential but who are either not present or not fully agentic in the actual doings of that world. The actions taken on behalf of implicated actors are often supposedly for the implicated actors' own good. Individuals and social groups with less power in situations tend to be implicated rather than fully agentic actors (Clarke, 2005, pp. 46–48; Clarke & Montini, 1993). They often tend to be female or otherwise "othered."

In sum, the goal of SA is not prediction but vivid descriptions and strong analytic insights. Theorizing should make thick description and thick interpretation possible, what Fosket (2002, pp. 40–41) called "thick analysis." SA studies also seek to specify what has gone and goes unstudied—what Evelynn Hammonds (1994) calls "black (w)holes"—sites of particular tensions of omission. What goes unstudied may not be seen or perceived, or may be refused—and is worthy of note regardless (Star, 1991). Thus, making the heretofore invisible visible is a goal, congruent with ongoing feminist analytics.

## MAKING SITUATIONAL ANALYSIS MORE EXPLICITLY FEMINIST

The form of SA I have developed has not as yet been widely taken up by anyone, feminist or not; it first appeared as a whole only in 2005 (Clarke, 2005). This section is therefore brief! It begins with the few feminist SA studies to date, all of which used the social worlds/arenas maps that Strauss developed and I elaborated prior to making them part of SA (Clarke, 1991; Strauss, 1978, 1993). I then turn to my hopes for feminist implementations.

Social worlds are groups with shared commitments to certain activities, sharing resources of many kinds to achieve their goals, and building shared ideologies about how to go about their business. They are interactive units, worlds of discourse, bounded not by geography or formal membership "but by the limits of effective communication" (Shibutani, 1955, p. 566). Social worlds are fundamental "building blocks" of collective action and the main units of analysis in such studies. In arenas, all the social worlds come together that focus on a given issue and are prepared to act in some way. In science, technology, and medicine studies, a major thrust of social worlds/arenas research centers on relations among scientific and nonscientific worlds in broader substantive arenas, especially in studies of discipline formation. Disciplines, specialties, and research traditions are conceived as social worlds. The major processes of social world

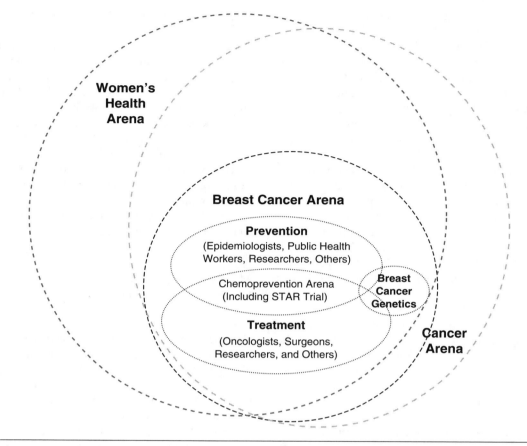

**Figure 16.3**    Fosket's Social Worlds/Arenas Map Locating the Star Trial

formation and development (segmentation, inter-section, and legitimation) characterize scientific social worlds as they do others.

Clarke and Montini (1993) provide an especially accessible exemplar of this mode of analysis, focusing on the multiple social worlds concerned with the abortifacient RU486, also known as "the French abortion pill." The article analytically places RU486 in the center and then moves through the specific perspectives taken on it by each of the major social worlds involved in the broader abortion and reproduction arena: reproductive and other scientists, birth control and population control organizations, pharma-ceutical companies, medical groups, anti-abortion groups, pro-choice groups, women's health movement groups, politicians, Congress, the FDA, and, last but not least, women users of RU486 who were (except when rarely objects of research downstream in terms of "acceptance" of the method) "implicated actors" in this situation. Significantly, Clarke and Montini demonstrate that social worlds themselves are not at all monolithic but commonly contain extensive differences of perspective that may be more or less contentious.

Fosket (2002, 2006) offers a fuller situational analysis of the STAR trial of tamoxifen and raloxifene as powerful hormonal breast cancer *prevention* drugs, including the role of Big Pharma (multinational pharmaceutical corpora-tions) and the discourses and rhetorics used in recruitment and retention in a large-scale, mul-tisited clinical trial. As she uncovered the layers of experience, action, and meaning that consti-tuted the trial, it became increasingly evident that, while ultimately producing what appeared to be a coherent set of knowledges defined as objective, the knowledge being produced was fragmented, partial, and very situated. To frame her work, see Figures 16.3 and 16.4. Here, we can see that the small arena of chemoprevention,

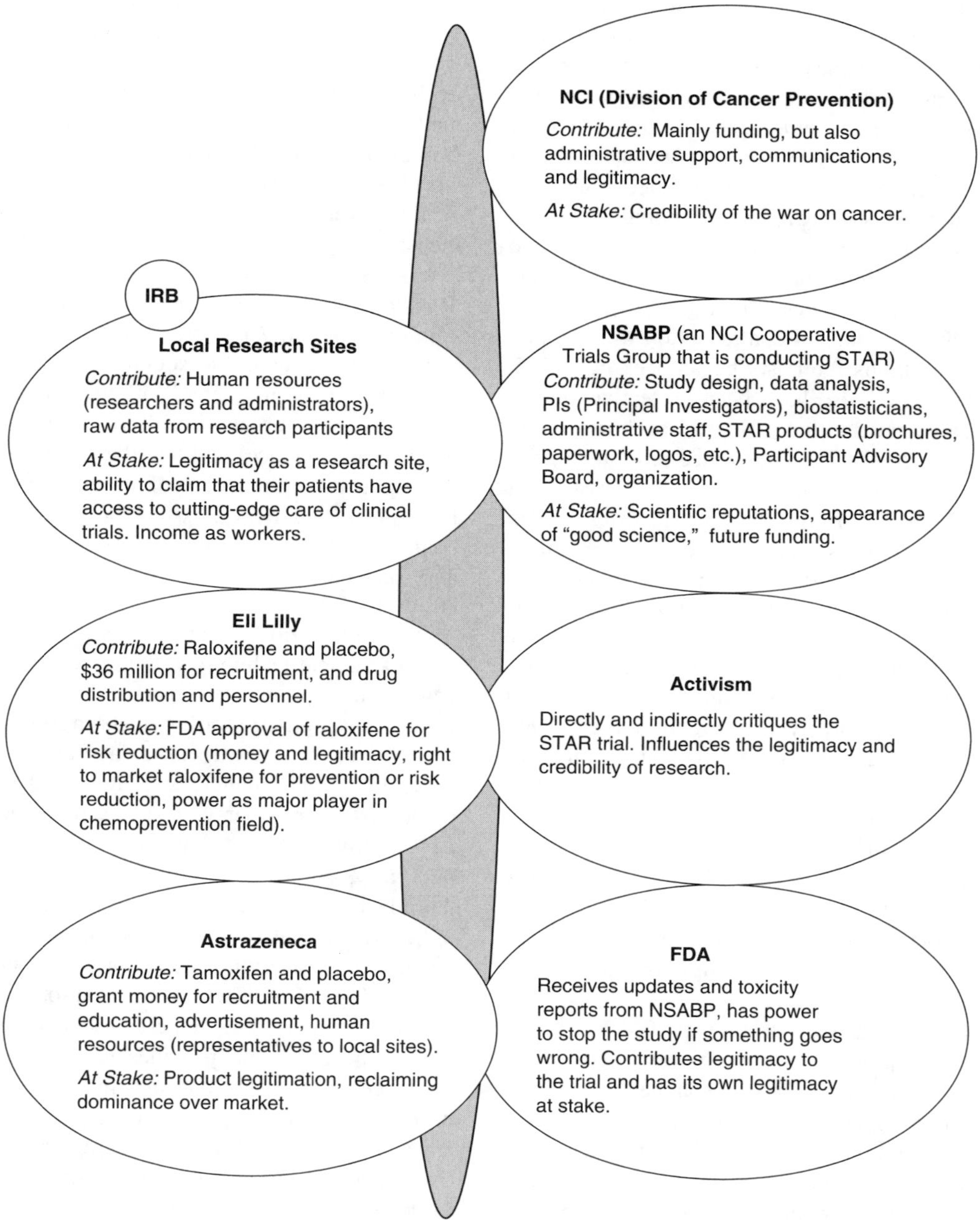

**NCI (Division of Cancer Prevention)**

*Contribute:* Mainly funding, but also administrative support, communications, and legitimacy.

*At Stake:* Credibility of the war on cancer.

**IRB**

**Local Research Sites**

*Contribute:* Human resources (researchers and administrators), raw data from research participants

*At Stake:* Legitimacy as a research site, ability to claim that their patients have access to cutting-edge care of clinical trials. Income as workers.

**NSABP** (an NCI Cooperative Trials Group that is conducting STAR)
*Contribute:* Study design, data analysis, PIs (Principal Investigators), biostatisticians, administrative staff, STAR products (brochures, paperwork, logos, etc.), Participant Advisory Board, organization.

*At Stake:* Scientific reputations, appearance of "good science," future funding.

**Eli Lilly**

*Contribute:* Raloxifene and placebo, $36 million for recruitment, and drug distribution and personnel.

*At Stake:* FDA approval of raloxifene for risk reduction (money and legitimacy, right to market raloxifene for prevention or risk reduction, power as major player in chemoprevention field).

**Activism**

Directly and indirectly critiques the STAR trial. Influences the legitimacy and credibility of research.

**Astrazeneca**

*Contribute:* Tamoxifen and placebo, grant money for recruitment and education, advertisement, human resources (representatives to local sites).

*At Stake:* Product legitimation, reclaiming dominance over market.

**FDA**

Receives updates and toxicity reports from NSABP, has power to stop the study if something goes wrong. Contributes legitimacy to the trial and has its own legitimacy at stake.

**Figure 16.4**    Fosket's Star Trial Social Worlds Map

which includes the Star Trial, is located within much larger women's health and cancer arenas, at the intersectional overlap between the "Treatment" and "Prevention" arenas, and it also intersects with breast cancer genetics. The Star Trial is thus located in a very dense and contested site. Figure 16.4 portrays the multiple social worlds involved, what each contributes to

the clinical trial, and what is at stake for them. Through these maps we can vividly see how widely distributed the Star Trial in fact is. (Fosket also offers situational and positional maps in the paper, not reproduced here.)

My own work includes a major study of the emergence and coalescence of the American reproductive sciences across the 20th century

(Clarke, 1998). Thanks to social worlds theory, I was able to grasp this enterprise as an intersectional discipline dwelling in three professional domains: biology, medicine, and agriculture. I also grasped the emergence of this scientific social world within the larger sociocultural reproductive arena, which included other key social worlds—birth control, population control, eugenics movements, religious groups, and strong philanthropic sponsors. I studied the reproductive sciences in part to understand why we have the kinds of contraception we do rather than the kinds feminists began seeking c1915, which would also have been protective against sexually transmitted diseases such as AIDS (Clarke, 2000). The emergence of fetal surgery, a more rarefied specialty, was studied by Casper (1997, 1998), offering detailed histories of both the laboratory science and clinical practices. Like Clarke, she found that links to other social worlds, specifically anti-abortion movements, were characteristic and deeply important. She analyzes the relations (sometimes cooperative, sometimes vituperative) among the different practitioners involved in fetal surgery who struggle with who is the patient—mother or fetus. Casper also takes up the significance of animal experimentation, the limitations of ethical oversight on clinical trials, and the experiences of pregnant women, significantly framing fetal surgery as a women's health issue rather than solely a pediatric issue. This book won one of sociology's most prestigious honors, the C. Wright Mills Award.

Prenatal genetic testing is fast becoming standard practice in the highly medicalized arena of pregnancy in American health care provision. Karlberg (2000) offers a highly accessible description of the provision of genetic care by caregivers themselves, using empirical data from providers trained in heterogeneous professional worlds (genetic counselors, geneticists, perinatologists, and obstetricians). She pays close attention to how they deal with the inherent uncertainties and ambiguities omnipresent in medical genetics, especially prenatal genetic testing. Rarely are test results able to be interpreted with clear, straightforward descriptions. Karlberg found that two major work ideologies were implemented to handle these ambiguities and uncertainties: assessing the patient and

tailoring the information to the patient. These work ideologies are examined through social worlds/arenas theory, as providers themselves explicated their own (re)constructions of genetic medical knowledge for patients through the frameworks of the particular professional worlds in which they had been trained.

Controversies about the construction of premenstrual syndrome (PMS) as a psychiatric disease classification in the *Diagnostic and Statistical Manual of Mental Disorders*, third edition (*DSM-III-R*), were examined by Ann Figert (1996) using a social worlds/arenas analysis. She found that PMS was salient in three different arenas (health/mental health, women, and science) and that the controversies were quite different in each of these arenas (centered, respectively, on issues of professional control, the definition of a "healthy" woman, and the nature and adequacy of scientific "truth").

The redemption of an absolutely disastrous pharmaceutical technology, thalidomide, which was taken by pregnant women in the 1960s and which caused severe birth defects in more than 10,000 babies, is the focus of a social worlds study by Timmermans and Leiter (2000) that emphasizes controversy. They examine how a new, highly controlled, standardized drug *distribution* system was built that could allow the therapeutic and symbolic makeover of thalidomide by normalizing the risk of fetal birth defects and preserving the autonomy of health care professionals. The new distribution system for this particular drug centers on female reproductive behavior and provides very close surveillance of female (but not male) patients/users, constructing females as requiring close supervision because of their inherent reproductive capacities, for which they cannot be trusted to be responsible. The distribution system thus crystallizes yet again traditionally gendered patterns of social inequality, including professional powers over patients. Such patterns of finding "old wine in new [technological] bottles" are all too common (Forsythe, 2001).

Finding "old wine in new [technological] bottles" was also characteristic of Moore and Clarke's (1995, 2001) studies of sex/gender/sexualities in print and digital visual cultures of anatomy from 1900 to 2000 using GT and an early incarnation of SA positional mapping. We focused on representations of human genitalia, especially on what (if anything) counted as "the clitoris," and found that narratives and images often work together to render a discourse of *external* genital size as synonymous with physical superiority. In terms of images and/or labeling, the female may or may not have a clitoris, while the male always has a penis. Clitoral agency or purpose (capacity for sensation and action such as engorgement) is rarely addressed, while the capacities and actions of the penis form lively central narratives. Orgasm is a phenomenon experienced solely in the penis, except in the few explicitly feminist anatomies. Last, in most anatomies, conventions of heterosexualization inextricably link if not actually replace sexual function with reproductive function in the female in narratives and often through visual representation of pregnancy as well.

Further feminist SA will be produced through its concrete use. Some ideas about this are discussed next.

## CONCLUSIONS

With Lather (in press), I am seeking "a fertile space and ethical practice in asking how research based knowledge remains possible after so much questioning of the very ground of science . . . gesturing toward the science possible after the critique of science" (Preface). I believe that in feminist hands both GT and SA can help provide such fertile spaces and ethical practices.

In terms of future feminist research using grounded theory, my hopes and dreams are for more explicitly feminist projects, and especially for projects that question the very grounds of traditional disciplinary categories and conventions and open up possible new avenues for enhancing social justice. Here, I am thinking of Austen et al.'s (2003) exciting deconstruction of "social indicators" in the discipline of economics, which for decades remained relatively impenetrable by feminist perspectives. Another exemplar is Shim's (2000, 2002, 2005) study of the meanings of "race," "class," and "gender" to epidemiologists and people of color with CVDs. Further, the entire third edition of Denzin and

Lincoln's (2005) *Handbook of Qualitative Research* is specifically oriented toward using qualitative inquiry to enhance social justice. Charmaz's (2005) paper in that volume powerfully details how GT can be used toward these important ends, as does Olesen's (2005) paper on feminist research.

I highly recommend using SA in feminist studies where import is placed on elucidating differences, making silences speak, and revealing contradictions within positions and within groups. Furthermore, Samik-Ibrahim (2000) has argued that GT methodology is especially useful in less developed countries and settings. I would assert the same for SA, hence their potential utility in feminist postcolonial studies. SA would be especially valuable where infrastructural elements of situations are quite different (availability of roads, water, health care, traditional and changing gender arrangements, and divisions of labor) and researchers want to take these differences into *explicit* account for policy recommendations and programmatic interventions. An example here is local needs assessment research where the desire is to grasp both the specifics of the local situation *and* the perspectives of local people on their own needs—remembering that these may be multivocal, gendered, and contradictory. Thus, SA should be helpful in feminist postcolonial studies and studies of globalization wherein the particularities of situatedness are of especial import (e.g., Adams & Pigg, 2005).

I also hope for feminist research using GT and SA in the study of discourses—historical, visual, and narrative—and in multisite research that combines studies of discursive data with that from interviews and ethnographic work. I have framed how this can be pursued via integrative mapping (all data sources analyzed together) and/or comparative mapping (data sources analyzed separately) (Clarke, 2005, pp. 176–177). I would argue that the time has come for more comparative work, explicitly contrasting the positions articulated in public discourses with those produced by the various sets of actors active in and implicated by those discourses (Collins, 1999; Lather & Smithies, 1997; Press & Cole, 1999).

I also want to follow in Anselm Strauss's (1987) footsteps and advocate researchers' participation in working groups of various kinds to provoke analysis by having to come to grips with other perspectives, other interpretations of data, commentary on preliminary incarnations of integrated analyses, and so on. Strauss believed so strongly in the working group process that in his 1987 GT book, he actually provides transcripts of sessions of such groups. Groups focused on feminist research would also echo consciousness raising and would further provoke discussions of feminist theoretical developments and needs (e.g., Lather, 1999). Using GT and SA in such groups can be done in actual collaborative research (e.g., Finch & Mason, 1990; Lather & Smithies, 1997) or with independent research projects using such groups as analytic worksites (e.g., Lessor, 2000).

Beyond actually using GT and SA in feminist research, my major recommendation for making them—or any other approach—more explicitly feminist is to engage with the work of exciting feminist and other theorists, methodologists, and researchers. Feminist qualitative research is itself what Marge DeVault[16] called a "community of ongoing discourse"—a widely distributed and very heterogeneous social world that can be a source of wondrous provocation. It exceeds "conversations" and "collaborations," and it too has a gestalt that is greater than the sum of it parts. I think here, for example, of reading Lather (e.g., 1991, 1999, in press), who I see as a theorist of feminist methodologies, dwelling on dilemmas, conundrums, partialities, contradictions, ethics. She vividly portrays the agonies and ecstasies of research, *trying* to be feminist, "getting lost" along the way, knowing we grasp and acknowledge only a few of the shortfalls of our work. I think also of recent powerful work by Bhavani (2004) on historicization of research; Naples (2003) on combining ethnography, discourse analysis, and activism; Smith (2005) and Campbell and Gregor (2004) on doing institutional ethnography; Smith (1999), Twine and Warren (2000), Collins (2004), and Schulz and Mullings (2006) on issues of race, indigeneity, intersectionality, and identity; Lewis and Mills (2003) on feminist postcolonial theory; and Thompson (2006) and Adams and Pigg (2005) on feminist transnational perspectives, among many others. As much as I believe in and "do" GT and SA, reading and

teaching much more widely in our feminist "community of ongoing discourse" nurtures and sustains me deeply both intellectually and as a feminist. This volume will be a major resource for such practices.

## NOTES

1. Samik-Ibrahim (2000) views GT methodology as a key research strategy for developing countries (see www.qualitative-research.net/fqs/fqs-eng.htm). Online searches performed on September 22, 2005, found the following: 94 books with GT in the title and 95 books with GT as a keyword (Melville—the UC Systemwide Library); 1,811 references in ISI Web of Knowledge—Web of Science; in Sociological Abstracts, there were 1,146 total listings (861 in journals, 722 in peer-reviewed journals, 95 in conferences, and 16 Web sites). A Current Contents database search on GT done May 25, 2004, found 1,353 citations, 435 of which were after 2002.

2. See especially Glaser (1978, 1992, 2002a), Glaser and Holton (2004), Strauss (1987, 1995), Strauss and Corbin (1990, 1994, 1998), Charmaz (1995, 2000, 2006), Bryant and Charmaz (2007), Clarke (2003, 2005, in press), and Locke (2001). A third edition of Strauss and Corbin's *The Basics of Qualitative Analysis* is expected in 2007.

3. On July 6, 2005, a search of ERIC (including Sociological Abstracts, PAIS, PsychInfo, social sciences and services) found 95 citations on "GT and feminist," 40 on "GT and feminism," 238 on "GT and gender," 46 on "GT and women," 226 on "GT and men," and 10 on "GT and sexism." ISI Web of Knowledge found 34 cites on "GT and sexism," 3 on "GT and feminism," 83 on "GT and gender," 142 on "GT and women," 88 on "GT and men," 19 on "GT and females," and 20 on "GT and males." PubMed had 84 cites on "GT and gender," 315 on "GT and women," 106 on "GT and men," 45 on "GT and male," and 51 on "GT and female." GenderWatch offered 26 cites in the above categories. Popline located 47 records. The Cumulative Index to Nursing and Allied Health Literature (CINAHL) had 466 listings under "GT and feminist," 1,801 listings under "GT and female," 1,201 under "GT and male," 21 under "GT and feminism," 19 under "GT and gender," and 23 under "GT and men."

4. On feminist research, see, for example, the introduction to this volume, Hesse-Biber and Yaiser

(2004), Delamont (2003), Harding and Norberg (2005), Olesen (1994, 2000, 2005), Sprague (2005), and Lather (1991, in press).

5. See, on theoretical sampling, Glaser and Strauss (1967, pp. 45–77), Glaser (1978, pp. 36–54), Strauss (1987, pp. 38–39), and Strauss and Corbin (1998, pp. 201–215).

6. At an early National Women's Studies Association conference, held in Bloomington, Indiana, in 1980, there was a panel on "Qualitative Methods and Feminism" (www.nwsaconference.org/archives .html). On the panel, according to Star, were Sandra Harding, Pauline Bart, and herself. Star's presentation was predicated on the dissertation research of Barbara DuBois at Harvard in clinical psychology, which used GT to analyze women's experiences. See, for example, DuBois (1983).

7. See also Atkinson et al. (2003, pp. 148–152). Glaser (1978, 2002a) and Glaser and Holton (2004) argue that GT could also be used with quantitative research.

8. There are, of course, many symbolic interactionisms and many related interpretive empirical approaches all situated and grounded somehow in contrast to most scientist positivisms. See, for example, Tuana (2001) and Seigfried (2001).

9. On the debate between Glaser and Strauss, and Corbin, which has implications for feminist research, see Charmaz (1995, 2000, 2005, 2006), Locke (1996, 2001), Bryant (2002, 2003), Atkinson et al. (2003), Corbin (1998), and Clarke (2005, pp. 12–18).

10. Strauss so much believed in this process that he incorporated transcripts of group analysis sessions into one of his major methods books (Strauss, 1987). Yet the idea of deconstruction is even stronger here. Recently, GT and other *analytic* approaches have been criticized for "fracturing" data, for "violating" the integrity of participants' narratives, for "pulling apart" stories, and so on (e.g., Mattingly & Garro, 2000; Riessman, 1993). To me, this is not a weakness or problem but instead the key to GT's *analytic*, rather than (re)representational, strength. Analysis and (re)representation are two deeply different qualitative research approaches, both valuable and both of which I support. Rerepresentation usually centers on experiences of individuals (occasionally on collectivities). Analysis usually centers on elucidating processes of social phenomena—action.

11. See the Anselm Strauss Web site at www.ucsf.edu/anselmstrauss. See Glaser's Web site at www.groundedtheory.com. On Virginia Olesen

(1994, 2000, 2005), see http://nurseweb.ucsf.edu/ www/ffolesv.htm.

12. See the bibliography at http://nurseweb.ucsf .edu/www/ix-fd.shtml#fpr, and www.son.wisc.edu/ directories/faculty/bowers/bowers.htm.

13. The Cumulative Index to Nursing and Allied Health Literature (CINAHL) had 466 listings under "GT and feminist," 1,801 listings under "GT and female," 1,201 under "GT and male," 21 under "GT and feminism," 19 under "GT and gender," and 23 under "GT and men." See also the journal *Qualitative Health Research* and www.uofaweb.ualberta.ca/iiqm.

14. See www.uoguelph.ca/research/publications/ Assets/HTML_MAGS/health/page66.html and www .vifamily.ca/newsroom/press_sep_7_04.html.

15. After the publication of my book, I discovered several other methods also called "situational analysis." Annan's (2005) version had just appeared in school psychology, Matzner and Jarvie (1998) had recently edited a special issue of a journal focusing on Karl Popper's idea of "situational analysis," and Goldfried and D'Zurilla's (1969) version dwells in psychology. Mine has wholly different origins. What this means in terms of electronic searching for my version of "situational analysis" is that it needs to be done with "AND grounded theory."

16. Marge DeVault made the comment at a session on feminist methods and research at the 2005 meetings of the American Sociological Association in Philadelphia.

## REFERENCES

Adams, V., & Pigg, S. L. (Eds.). (2005). *Sex in development: Science, sexuality and morality in global perspective*. Durham, NC: Duke University Press.

Annan, J. (2005). Situational analysis: A framework for evidence-based practice. *School Psychology International, 26*(2), 131–146.

Annells, M. (1996). Grounded theory method: Philosophical perspectives, paradigm of inquiry and postmodernism. *Qualitative Health Research, 6*(3), 379–393.

Atkinson, P., Coffey, A., & Delamont, S. (2003). *Key themes in qualitative research: Continuities and change*. Walnut Creek, CA: AltaMira Press/ Rowman and Littlefield.

Austen, S., Jefferson, T., & Thein, V. (2003). Gendered social indicators and grounded theory. *Feminist Economics, 9*(1), 1–18.

Barad, K. (2003). Posthumanist performativity: Toward an understanding of how matter comes to matter. *Signs: Journal of Women in Culture and Society, 28*(3), 801–831.

Becker, H. S. (1963). *Outsiders: Studies in the sociology of deviance*. New York: Free Press.

Becker, H. S. (1970). Whose side are we on? In *Sociological work: Method and substance* (pp. 123–134). New Brunswick, NJ: Transaction Books.

Benoliel, J. Q. (1996). Grounded theory and nursing knowledge. *Qualitative Health Research, 6*(3), 406–428.

Benoliel, J. Q. (2001). Expanding knowledge about women through grounded theory: Introduction to the collection. *Health Care for Women International, 22*(1–2), 7–9.

Berger, P., & Luckmann, T. (1966). *The social construction of reality: A treatise in the sociology of knowledge*. Garden City, NJ: Doubleday.

Bhavani, K. K. (2004). Tracing the contours: Feminist research and feminist objectivity. In S. Hesse-Biber & M. L. Yaiser (Eds.), *Feminist perspectives on social research* (pp. 65–77). New York: Oxford University Press.

Blumer, H. (1969). *Symbolic interactionism: Perspective and method*. Englewood Cliffs, NJ: Prentice Hall.

Bone, D. (2002). Dilemmas of emotion work in nursing under market-driven health care. *International Journal of Public Sector Management, 15*(2), 140–150.

Bowker, G., & Star, S. L. (1999). *Sorting things out: Classification and its consequences*. Cambridge: MIT Press.

Bryant, A. (2002). Re-grounding grounded theory. *Journal of Information Technology Theory and Application, 4*(1), 25–42.

Bryant, A. (2003). A constructive/ist response to Glaser. *FQS: Forum for Qualitative Social Research, 4*(1). Retrieved December 2003 from www.qualitative-research.net/fqs

Bryant, A., & Charmaz, K. (Eds.). (2007). *The handbook of grounded theory*. London: Sage.

Butler, J. (1993). *Bodies that matter*. New York: Routledge.

Campbell, M., & Gregor, F. (2004). *Mapping social relations: A primer in doing institutional ethnography*. Walnut Creek, CA: AltaMira Press.

Canguilhem, G. (1978). *On the normal and pathological*. Dordrecht, the Netherlands: Reidel.

Casper, M. J. (1997). Feminist politics and fetal surgery: Adventures of a research cowgirl on the reproductive frontier. *Feminist Studies, 23*(2), 233–262.

Casper, M. J. (1998). *The making of the unborn patient: A social anatomy of fetal surgery*. New Brunswick, NJ: Rutgers University Press.

Charmaz, K. (1991). *Good days, bad days: The self in chronic illness and time*. New Brunswick, NJ: Rutgers University Press.

Charmaz, K. (1995). Between positivism and postmodernism: Implications for methods. *Studies in Symbolic Interaction, 17*, 43–72.

Charmaz, K. (2000). Grounded theory: Objectivist and constructivist methods. In N. Denzin & Y. Lincoln (Eds.), *Handbook of qualitative research* (2nd ed., pp. 509–536). Thousand Oaks, CA: Sage.

Charmaz, K. (2005). Grounded theory in the 21st century: Applications for advancing social justice studies. In N. K. Denzin & Y. Lincoln (Eds.), *The Sage handbook of qualitative research* (3rd ed., pp. 507–536). Thousand Oaks, CA: Sage.

Charmaz, K. (2006). *Constructing grounded theory: A practical guide through qualitative analysis*. London: Sage.

Clarke, A. E. (1991). Social worlds theory as organization theory. In D. Maines (Ed.), *Social organization and social process: Essays in honor of Anselm Strauss* (pp. 17–42). Hawthorne, NY: Aldine de Gruyter.

Clarke, A. E. (1998). *Disciplining reproduction: Modernity, American life sciences and the "problem of sex."* Berkeley: University of California Press.

Clarke, A. E. (2000). Maverick reproductive scientists and the production of contraceptives c1915–2000. In A. Saetmam, N. Oudshoorn, & M. Kirejczyk (Eds.), *Bodies of technology: Women's involvement with reproductive medicine* (pp. 37–89). Columbus: Ohio State University Press.

Clarke, A. E. (2003). Situational analyses: Grounded theory mapping after the postmodern turn. *Symbolic Interaction, 26*(4), 553–576.

Clarke, A. E. (2005). *Situational analysis: Grounded theory after the postmodern turn*. Thousand Oaks, CA: Sage.

Clarke, A. E. (in press). Grounded theory. In W. Outhwaite & S. P. Turner (Eds.), *The SAGE handbook of social science methodology*. London: Sage.

Clarke, A. E., & Montini, T. (1993). The many faces of RU486: Tales of situated knowledges and technological contestations. *Science, Technology and Human Values, 18*(1), 42–78.

Clarke, A. E., Shim, J. K., Mamo, L., Fosket, J. R., & Fishman, J. R. (2003). Biomedicalization: Technoscientific transformations of health, illness, and U.S. biomedicine. *American Sociological Review, 68*, 161–194.

Clarke, A. E., & Star, S. L. (2003). Symbolic interactionist studies of science, technology and medicine. In L. Reynolds & N. Herman (Eds.), *Symbolic interactionism* (pp. 539–574). Walnut Creek, CA: AltaMira Press.

Clarke, A. E., & Star, S. L. (2007). Social worlds/ arenas analysis: A theory/methods package. In M. Lynch, O. Amsterdamska, E. J. Hackett, & J. Wajcman (Eds.), *The new handbook of science and technology studies*. Cambridge: MIT Press.

Collins, P. H. (1999). Will the "real" mother please stand up? The logic of eugenics and American national family planning. In A. E. Clarke & V. L. Olesen (Eds.), *Revisioning women, health and healing: Feminist, cultural and technoscience perspectives* (pp. 266–282). New York: Routledge.

Collins, P. H. (2004). *Black sexual politics: African Americans, gender, and the new racism.* New York: Routledge.

Corbin, J. (1998). Comment: Alternative interpretations—valid or not? *Theory and Psychology, 8*(1), 121–128.

Cresswell, J. W. (2002). *Educational research: Planning, conducting, and evaluating quantitative and qualitative research.* Upper Saddle River, NJ: Merrill/Prentice Hall.

Crooks, D. L. (2001). The importance of symbolic interaction in grounded theory research on women's health. *Health Care for Women International, 22*(1–2), 11–27.

Daly, K. (2001). Deconstructing family time: From ideology to lived experience. *Journal of Marriage and Family, 63*(2), 283–294.

Davies, B. (1995). *Fading away: The experience of transition in families with terminal illness.* Amityville, NY: Baywood.

Davies, B. (1999). *Shadows in the sun: Experiences of sibling bereavement in childhood.* Philadelphia: Brunner/Mazel.

Delamont, S. (2003). *Feminist sociology.* London: Sage.

Denzin, N. K., & Lincoln, Y. (Eds.). (2005). *The Sage handbook of qualitative research* (3rd ed.). Thousand Oaks, CA: Sage.

DuBois, B. (1983). Passionate scholarship: Notes on values, knowing and method in feminist social sciences. In G. D. K. Bowles & R. Duelli-Klein (Eds.), *Theories of women's studies* (pp. 105–117). London: Routledge & Kegan Paul.

Ekins, R. (1997). *Male femaling: A grounded theory approach to cross-dressing and sex changing.* London: Routledge.

Fassinger, R. E. (2005). Paradigms, praxis, problems, and promise: Grounded theory in counseling psychology research. *Journal of Counseling Psychology, 52*(2), 156–166.

Fenstermaker, S., & West, C. (Eds.). (2002). *Doing gender, doing difference: Inequality, power, and institutional change.* New York: Routledge.

Fiene, J. I. (1993). *The social reality of a group of rural, low-status, Appalachian women: A grounded theory study.* New York: Garland.

Figert, A. (1996). *Women and the ownership of PMS: The structuring of a psychiatric disorder.* New York: Aldine de Gruyter.

Finch, J., & Mason, J. (1990). Decision taking in the fieldwork process: Theoretical sampling and collaborative working. In R. G. Burgess (Ed.), *Studies in qualitative methodology II: Reflections on field experience* (pp. 25–50). Greenwich, CT: JAI Press.

Fine, M. (1994). Working the hyphens: Reinventing self and other in qualitative research. In N. Denzin & Y. Lincoln (Eds.), *Handbook of qualitative research* (pp. 70–82). Thousand Oaks, CA: Sage.

Fishman, J. R. (2004). Manufacturing desire: The commodification of female sexual dysfunction. *Social Studies of Science, 34*(2), 187–218.

Fonow, M. M., & Cook, J. A. (2005). Feminist methodology: New applications in the academy and public policy. *Signs: Journal of Women in Culture and Society, 30*(4), 211–236.

Ford-Gilboe, M., Wuest, J., & Merritt-Gray, M. (2005). Strengthening capacity to limit intrusion: Theorizing family health promotion in the aftermath of woman abuse. *Qualitative Health Research, 15*(4), 477–501.

Forsythe, D. E. (2001). *Studying those who study us: An anthropologist in the world of artificial intelligence.* Stanford, CA: Stanford University Press.

Fosket, J. R. (2002). *Breast cancer risk and the politics of prevention: Analysis of a clinical trial.* Unpublished doctoral dissertation, University of California, San Francisco.

Fosket, J. R. (2004). Constructing "high risk" women: The development and standardization of a breast cancer risk assessment tool. *Science, Technology & Human Values, 29*(3), 291–313.

Fosket, J. R. (2006). *"Situating knowledge": Analyzing a clinical trial.* Manuscript submitted for publication.

Foucault, M. (1965). *Madness and civilization.* New York: Random House.

Foucault, M. (1975). *The birth of the clinic: An archeology of medical perception.* New York: Vintage/Random House.

Gamson, J. (2000). Sexualities, queer theory and qualitative research. In N. Denzin & Y. Lincoln (Eds.), *Handbook of qualitative research* (2nd ed., pp. 347–365). Thousand Oaks, CA: Sage.

Gelder, K., & Thornton, S. (1997). *The subcultures reader.* London: Routledge.

Glaser, B. G. (1978). *Theoretical sensitivity: Advances in the methodology of grounded theory.* Mill Valley, CA: Sociology Press.

Glaser, B. G. (1992). *Emergence versus forcing: Basics of grounded theory analysis.* Mill Valley, CA: Sociology Press.

Glaser, B. G. (Ed.). (1993). *Examples of grounded theory: A reader.* Mill Valley, CA: Sociology Press.

Glaser, B. G. (2002a). Constructivist grounded theory? *FQS Forum: Qualitative Social Research, 3*(3). Retrieved September 2005 from www.qualitative-research.net/fqs-texte/3-02/3-02glaser-e.htm

Glaser, B. G. (2002b). Grounded theory and gender relevance. *Health Care for Women International, 23*(8), 786–793.

Glaser, B. G., & Holton, J. (2004). Remodeling grounded theory. *Forum for Qualitative Social Research, 5*(2). Retrieved September 2005 from http://www.qualitative-research.net/fqs-texte/2-04/2-04glaser-e.htm

Glaser, B. G., & Strauss, A. L. (1967). *The discovery of grounded theory: Strategies for qualitative research.* Chicago: Aldine.

Goffman, E. (1963). *Behavior in public places: Notes on the sociology of gatherings.* New York: Free Press.

Goldfried, M. R., & D'Zurilla, T. J. (1969). A behavioral-analytic model for assessing competence. In C. D. Spielberger (Ed.), *Current topics in clinical and community psychology* (pp. 151–195). New York: Academic Press.

Gramsci, A. (1971). *Selections from the prison notebooks* (Q. Hoare & G. N. Smith, Trans.). New York: International Publishers. (Original work published 1949)

Gustafsson-Larsson, S., & Hammarstrom, A. (2005). Health perceptions of local community works: Network women describe how flows of energy and space of action generate health and ill health. *Work, 24*(3), 215–227.

Gutman, S. A., & Napier-Klemic, J. (1996). The experience of head injury on the impairment of gender identity and gender role. *American Journal of Occupational Therapy, 50*(7), 535–544.

Hacking, I. (1983). *Representing and intervening: Introductory topics in the philosophy of natural science.* Cambridge, UK: Cambridge University Press.

Hammonds, E. M. (1994). Black (w)holes and the geometry of black female sexuality. *Differences: A Journal of Feminist Cultural Studies, 6*(2+3), 126–145.

Haraway, D. (1991). Situated knowledges: The science question in feminism and the privilege of partial perspectives. In *Simians, cyborgs, and women: The reinvention of nature* (pp. 183–202). New York: Routledge.

Haraway, D. (1997). Modest_witness@second_millennium. In *Modest_Witness@Second_Millennium.FemaleMan©_Meets_OncoMouse™: Feminism and technoscience* (pp. 23–39). New York: Routledge.

Haraway, D. (1999). The virtual speculum in the new world order. In A. E. Clarke & V. L. Olesen (Eds.), *Revisioning women, health, and healing: Feminist, cultural, and technoscience perspectives* (pp. 49–96). New York: Routledge.

Harding, S., & Norberg, K. (2005). New feminist approaches to social science methodologies: An introduction. *Signs: Journal of Women in Culture and Society, 30*(4).

Hausman, B. L. (2001). Recent trans-gender theory. *Feminist Studies, 27*(2), 465–490.

Hesse-Biber, S., & Yaiser, M. L. (Eds.). (2004). *Feminist perspectives on social research.* New York: Oxford University Press.

Hughes, E. C. (1971). *The sociological eye.* Chicago: Aldine Atherton.

Ingram, D., & Hutchison, S. A. (1999). Defensive mothering in HIV-positive mothers. *Qualitative Health Research, 9*(2), 243–258.

Jenks, C. (1995). The centrality of the eye in Western culture: An introduction. In *Visual culture: An introduction* (pp. 1–16). London: Routledge.

Karlberg, K. (2000). The work of genetic care providers: Managing uncertainty and ambiguity. *Research in the Sociology of Health Care, 17,* 81–97.

Kearney, M. H. (1998). Ready to wear: Discovering grounded formal theory. *Research in Nursing and Health, 21,* 179–186.

Kearney, M. H. (1999). *Understanding women's recovery from illness and trauma.* Thousand Oaks, CA: Sage.

Kearney, M. H. (2001). New directions in grounded formal theory. In R. S. Schreiber & P. N. Stern (Eds.), *Using grounded theory in nursing* (pp. 227–246). New York: Springer.

Kearney, M. H., Murphy, S., Irwin, K., & Rosenbaum, M. (1995). Salvaging self: A grounded theory of pregnancy on crack cocaine. *Nursing Research, 44*(4), 208–213.

Kearney, M. H., Murphy, S., & Rosenbaum, M. (1994). Mothering on crack cocaine: A grounded theory analysis. *Social Science & Medicine, 38*(2), 351–361.

Keddy, B., Sims, S., & Stern, P. N. (1996). Grounded theory and feminist research methodology. *Journal of Advanced Nursing, 23,* 448–453.

Kools, S., McCarthy, M., Durham, R., & Robrecht, L. (1996). Dimensional analysis: Broadening the concept of grounded theory. *Qualitative Health Research, 6*(3), 312–330.

Kools, S. B., & Kennedy, C. (2003). Foster child health and development: Implications for primary care. *Pediatric Nursing, 29*(1), 39–46.

Kushner, K. E., & Harrison, M. J. (2002). Employed mothers: Stress and balance—focused coping. *Canadian Journal of Nursing Research, 34,* 47–65.

Kushner, K. E., & Morrow, R. (2003). Grounded theory, feminist theory, critical theory: Toward theoretical triangulation. *Advances in Nursing Science, 26*(1), 30–43.

Lather, P. (1991). *Getting smart: Feminist research and pedagogy with/in the postmodern.* New York: Routledge.

Lather, P. (1999). Naked methodology: Researching lives of women with HIV/AIDS. In A. E. Clarke & V. L. Olesen (Eds.), *Revisioning women, health and healing: Feminist, cultural and technoscience perspectives* (pp. 136–154). New York: Routledge.

Lather, P. (in press). *Getting lost: Feminist efforts toward a double(d) science.* Albany: State University of New York Press.

Lather, P., & Smithies, C. (1997). *Troubling the angels: Women living with HIV/AIDS.* Boulder, CO: Westview Press.

Law, J., & Hassard, J. (Eds.). (1999). *Actor-network theory and after.* Malden, MA: Blackwell.

Law, J., & Mol, A. (1995). Notes on materiality and sociality. *The Sociological Review, 43*(2), 274–294.

Lempert, L. B. (1996). Women's strategies for survival: Developing agency in abusive relationships. *Journal of Family Violence, 11*(3), 269–289.

Lempert, L. B. (1997). The line in the sand: Definitional dialogues in abusive relationships. In A. Strauss & J. M. Corbin (Eds.), *Grounded theory in practice* (pp. 147–170). Thousand Oaks, CA: Sage.

Lessor, R. (2000). Using the team approach of Anselm Strauss in action research: Consulting on a project on global education. *Sociological Perspectives, 43*(4), S133–S147.

Lewis, R., & Mills, S. (Eds.). (2003). *Feminist postcolonial theory: A reader.* New York: Routledge.

Locke, K. (1996). Rewriting the discovery of grounded theory after 25 years? *Journal of Management Inquiry, 5*(1), 239–245.

Locke, K. (2001). *Grounded theory in management research.* Thousand Oaks, CA: Sage.

MacDonald, M., & Schreiber, R. S. (2001). Constructing and deconstructing: Grounded theory in the postmodern world. In R. S. Schreiber & P. N. Stern (Eds.), *Using grounded theory in nursing* (pp. 33–54). New York: Springer.

Mamo, L. (2005). Biomedicalizing kinship: Sperm banks and the creation of affinity-ties. *Science as Culture, 14*(3), 237–264.

Mamo, L. (2006). *Queering reproduction: Achieving pregnancy in the age of technoscience.* Durham, NC: Duke University Press.

Mamo, L., & Fishman, J. R. (2001). Potency in all the right places: Viagra as a technology of the gendered body. *Body and Society, 7,* 13–35.

Marcellus, L. (2005). The grounded theory method and maternal-infant research and practice. *Journal of Obstetrical, Gynecological and Neonatal Nursing, 34*(3), 349–357.

Massumi, B. (2002). *Parables for the virtual: Movement, affect, sensation.* Durham, NC: Duke University Press.

Mattingly, C., & Garro, L. C. (Eds.). (2000). *Narrative and the cultural construction of illness and healing.* Berkeley: University of California Press.

Matzner, E., & Jarvie, I. C. (1998). Introduction to the special issues on situational analysis. *Philosophy of the Social Sciences, 28*(3), 333–338.

McCarthy, D. (1984). Towards a sociology of the physical world: George Herbert Mead on physical objects. *Studies in Symbolic Interaction, 5,* 105–121.

McCarthy, D. (1996). *Knowledge as culture: The new sociology of knowledge.* New York: Routledge.

Mead, G. H. (1962). *Mind, self and society* (C. W. Morris, Ed.). Chicago: University of Chicago. (Original work published 1934)

Melia, K. M. (1996). Rediscovering Glaser. *Qualitative Health Research, 6*(3), 368–378.

Miller, S. (1996). Questioning, resisting, acquiescing, balancing: New mothers' career reentry strategies. *Health Care for Women International, 17,* 109–131.

Mills, C. W. (1940). Situated actions and vocabularies of motive. *American Sociological Review, 6.*

Moore, L. J. (in press). *Sperm tales: Social, cultural and scientific representations of human semen.* New York: Routledge.

Moore, L. J., & Clarke, A. E. (1995). Genital conventions and trangressions: Graphic representations in anatomy texts, c1900–1991. *Feminist Studies, 22*(1), 255–301.

Moore, L. J., & Clarke, A. E. (2001). The traffic in cyberanatomies: Sex/gender/sexuality in local and global formations. *Body and Society, 7*(1), 57–96.

Moore, L. J., & Schmidt, M. (1998). Constructing a good catch, picking a winner: The development of technosemen and the deconstruction of the monolithic male. In R. Davis-Floyd & J. Dumit (Eds.), *Cyborg babies: From techno-sex to techno-tots* (pp. 17–39). New York: Routledge.

Moore, L. J., & Schmidt, M. (1999). On the construction of male differences: Marketing variations in technosemen, *Men and Masculinities, 1*(4), 339–359.

Naples, N. A. (2003). *Feminism and method: Ethnography, discourse analysis and activist research.* New York: Routledge.

Ohman, A., & Hagg, K. (1998). Attitudes of novice physiotherapists to their professional role: A gender perspective. *Physiotherapy Theory and Practice, 14*(1), 23–32.

Olesen, V. L. (1994). Feminisms and models of qualitative research. In N. Denzin & Y. Lincoln (Eds.), *Handbook of qualitative research* (pp. 158–174). Thousand Oaks, CA: Sage.

Olesen, V. L. (2000). Feminisms and qualitative research at and into the millennium. In N. Denzin & Y. Lincoln (Eds.), *Handbook of qualitative research* (2nd ed., pp. 215–256). Thousand Oaks, CA: Sage.

Olesen, V. L. (2005). Early millennial feminist qualitative research: Challenges and contours. In N. K. Denzin & Y. S. Lincoln (Eds.), *The Sage handbook of qualitative research* (3rd ed., pp. 235–278). Thousand Oaks, CA: Sage.

Olesen, V. L., & Bone, D. (1998). Emotions in the rationalizing organizations: Conceptual notes for professional nursing in the USA. In G. Bendelow & S. J. Williams (Eds.), *Emotions in social life: Critical themes and contemporary issues* (pp. 313–329). London: Routledge.

Olshansky, E. F. (1996). Theoretical issues in building a grounded theory: Application of an example of research on infertility. *Qualitative Health Research, 6,* 394–405.

Oswald, R. F. (2000). Friendship and family relations after young women come out as bisexual or lesbian. *Journal of Homosexuality, 38*(3), 65–83.

Pace, S. (2004). A grounded theory of the flow experiences of web users. *International Journal of Human-Computer Studies, 60*(3), 327–363.

Parker, L. (1998). Keeping power issues on the table in couples work. *Journal of Feminist Family Therapy, 10*(3), 17–38.

Parr, J. (1998). Theoretical voices and women's own voices: The stories of mature women students. In J. Ribbens & R. Edwards (Eds.), *Feminist dilemmas in qualitative research: Public knowledge and private lives* (pp. 87–102). London: Sage.

Pitts, V. (2004). Illness and Internet empowerment: Writing and reading breast cancer in cyberspace. *Health, 8*(1), 33–59.

Press, A. L., & Cole, E. R. (1999). *Speaking of abortion: Television and authority in the lives of women.* Chicago: University of Chicago Press.

Richie, B. E. (1996). *Compelled to crime: The gender entrapment of battered black women.* New York: Routledge.

Riessman, C. K. (1993). *Narrative analysis.* Newbury Park, CA: Sage.

Riessman, C. K. (Ed.). (1994). *Qualitative studies in social work research.* Thousand Oaks, CA: Sage.

Said, E. (1978). *Orientalism.* New York: Random House.

Samik-Ibrahim, R. M. (2000). Grounded theory methodology as the research strategy for a developing country. *Forum: Qualitative Social Research, 1*(1). Retrieved September 2005 from www.qualitative-research.net/fqs-texte/1-00/1-00samik-e.htm

Schatzman, L., & Strauss, A. (1973). *Field research.* Englewood Cliffs, NJ: Prentice Hall.

Schreiber, R. S., & Stern, P. N. (Eds.). (2001). *Using grounded theory in nursing.* New York: Springer.

Schulz, A. J., & Mullings, L. (Eds.). (2006). *Gender, race, class, and health: Intersectional approaches.* San Francisco: Jossey-Bass.

Schwalbe, M., Goodwin, D. H., Schrock, S., Thompson, S., & Wolkomir, M. (2000). Generic processes in the reproduction of inequality: An interactionist analysis. *Social Forces, 79,* 419–452.

Scott, J. W. (1992). Experience. In J. Butler & J. W. Scott (Eds.), *Feminists theorize the political* (pp. 22–40). New York: Routledge.

Seigfried, C. H. (2001). Beyond epistemology: From a pragmatist feminist experiential standpoint. In N. Tuana & S. Morgen (Eds.), *Engendering rationalities* (pp. 99–124). Albany: State University of New York Press.

Shibutani, T. (1955). Reference groups as perspectives. *American Journal of Sociology, 60,* 562–569.

Shim, J. K. (2000). Biopower and racial, class, and gender formation in biomedical knowledge production. In J. J. Kronenfield (Ed.), *Research in the sociology of health care* (Vol. 17, pp. 173–195). Stamford, CT: JAI Press.

Shim, J. K. (2002). Understanding the routinised inclusion of race, socioeconomic status and sex in epidemiology: The utility of concepts from technoscience studies. *Sociology of Health and Illness, 24,* 129–150.

Shim, J. K. (2005). Constructing "race" across the science-lay divide: Racial projects in the epidemiology and experience of cardiovascular disease. *Social Studies of Science, 35*(3), 405–436.

Silverstein, L. B., Auerbach, C. F., & Grieco, L. (1999). Do promise keepers dream of feminist sheep? *Sex Roles, 40*(9–10), 665–688.

Smith, D. (2003). To prove them wrong syndrome: Voices from unheard African American males in engineering disciplines. *Journal of Men's Studies, 12*(1), 61–73.

Smith, D. E. (2005). *Institutional ethnography: A sociology for people.* Lanham, MD: Rowman & Littlefield.

Smith, L. T. (1999). *Decolonizing methodologies: Research and indigenous peoples.* New York: St. Martin's Press.

Sprague, J. (2005). *Feminist methodologies for critical researchers: Bridging differences.* Lanham, MD: Rowman & Littlefield.

Stacey, J. (1988). Can there be a feminist ethnography? *Women's Studies International Forum, 11*(1), 21–27.

Star, S. L. (1983). Simplification in scientific work: An example from neuroscience research. *Social Studies of Science, 13,* 208–226.

Star, S. L. (1989). *Regions of the mind: Brain research and the quest for scientific certainty.* Stanford, CA: Stanford University Press.

Star, S. L. (1991). Power, technologies and the phenomenology of conventions: On being allergic to onions. In J. Law (Ed.), *A sociology of monsters: Essays on power, technology and domination* (pp. 25–56). New York: Routledge.

Star, S. L., & Strauss, A. L. (1998). Layers of silence, arenas of voice: The ecology of visible and invisible work. *Computer Supported Cooperative Work: The Journal of Collaborative Computing, 8,* 9–30.

Stern, P. N. (1994). Eroding grounded theory. In J. Morse (Ed.), *Critical issues in qualitative research methods* (pp. 212–223). Thousand Oaks, CA: Sage.

Strauss, A. L. (1978). A social world perspective. *Studies in Symbolic Interaction, 1,* 119–128.

Strauss, A. L. (1987). *Qualitative analysis for social scientists.* Cambridge, UK: Cambridge University Press.

Strauss, A. L. (1993). *Continual permutation of action.* New York: Aldine de Gruyter.

Strauss, A. L. (1995). Notes on the nature and development of general theories. *Qualitative Inquiry, 1*(1), 7–18.

Strauss, A. L., & Corbin, J. (1990). *Basics of qualitative research: Grounded theory, procedures and techniques.* Newbury Park, CA: Sage.

Strauss, A. L., & Corbin, J. (1994). Grounded theory methodology: An overview. In N. Denzin & Y. Lincoln (Eds.), *Handbook of qualitative research* (pp. 273–285). Thousand Oaks, CA: Sage.

Strauss, A. L., & Corbin, J. (Eds.). (1997). *Grounded theory in practice*. Thousand Oaks, CA: Sage.

Strauss, A. L., & Corbin, J. (1998). *The basics of qualitative analysis: Grounded theory procedures and techniques* (2nd ed.). Thousand Oaks, CA: Sage.

Thomas, W. I. (1978). The definition of the situation. In R. Farrell & V. Swigert (Eds.), *Social deviance* (pp. 54–57). Philadelphia: Lippincott. (Original work published 1923)

Thomas, W. I., & Thomas, D. S. (1970). Situations defined as real are real in their consequences. In G. P. Stone & H. A. Farberman (Eds.), *Social psychology through symbolic interaction* (pp. 154–155). Waltham, MA: Xerox College Publishing. (Original work published 1928)

Thompson, C. (2006). *Charismatic megafauna and miracle babies: Essays in selective pronatalism.* Manuscript submitted for publication.

Timmermans, S. (1999). *Sudden death and the myth of CPR*. Philadelphia: Temple University Press.

Timmermans, S., & Leiter, V. (2000). The redemption of thalidomide: Standardizing risk and responsibility. *Social Studies of Science, 30*(1), 41–72.

Trousdale, A. M., & McMillan, S. (2003). Cinderella was a wuss: A young girl's responses to feminist and patriarchal folktales. *Children's Literature in Education, 34*(1), 1–28.

Tuana, N. (2001). Material locations: An interactionist alternative to realism/social constructivism. In N. Tuana & S. Morgen (Eds.), *Engendering rationalities* (pp. 221–244). Albany: State University of New York Press.

Twine, F., & Warren, J. W. (Eds.). (2000). *Racing research, researching race: Methodological dilemmas in critical race studies*. New York: New York University Press.

Visweswaran, K. (1994). *Fictions of feminist ethnography*. Minneapolis: University of Minnesota Press.

Wheatley, E. (1994). How can we engender ethnography with a feminist imagination? A rejoinder to Judith Stacey. *Women's Studies International Forum, 17,* 403–416.

Wuest, J. (1995). Feminist grounded theory: An exploration of the congruency and tensions between two traditions in knowledge discovery. *Qualitative Health Research, 5*(1), 125–137.

Wuest, J. (2001). Precarious ordering: Toward a formal theory of women's caring. *Health Care for Women International, 22*(1–2), 167–178.

Wuest, J., & Merritt-Gray, M. (2001). Feminist grounded theory revisited. In R. S. Schreiber & P. N. Stern (Eds.), *Using grounded theory in nursing* (pp. 159–176). New York: Springer.

# 17

# Emergent Methods in Feminist Research

## Pamela Moss

## Feminist Questions About Feminist Methods

For some time now, feminists have been discussing what it is about research methods that make them feminist. Some feminists follow Harding's (1987) lead and maintain that it is not the method that makes feminist research feminist; rather, feminist research is feminist because it draws on women's experiences, investigates issues that women want and need to address (i.e., the research is *for* women), and offers up the research process as a site of scrutiny (i.e., research is reflexive). Some feminists follow Reinharz's (1992) claim that feminist research is about using various feminist perspectives to understand and explain social phenomena. For her, feminist research is a complex amalgam of perspectives arising both from the location of the researcher (i.e., the researcher has identified as a feminist) and from multiple feminist theories that employ different techniques to collect data, bring the researcher into the research process, and effect social change. Some feminists take up these particular

themes, in addition to developing others, in their own attempts to create approaches to research that are feminist (see Bloom, 1998; Bondi et al., 2002; DeVault, 1999; Moss, 2002; Naples, 2003; Ramazanoğlu, 2002).

One of the key arguments feminists seem to be drawn to in figuring out the link between theory and method (including both data collection and analysis) is the argument that techniques are not intrinsically feminist; it is the theorizations of research itself that make research feminist. This argument is quite appealing because pretty much any method can be made feminist. And yet feminist research cannot be configured so simply, for as Gailey (1998) notes, "Theory informs method and method shapes theory" (p. 204). Particular methods may fit more snugly with certain types of feminist work because choices of method arise out of unique combinations of epistemological (regarding knowledge) and ontological (regarding existence) orientations within feminist theories. Working from a premise that theory and method are constitutive of each other, one could argue that what makes research

Author's Note: Thanks to Stephanie Abel, who assisted with the literature review. I also thank Martha McMahon, Margo Matwychuk, and Sharlene Hesse-Biber for comments on a long, rough first draft. I thank Sharlene, too, for challenging me to make my arguments clearer.

feminist are the research designs, the interpretations and analyses of data using feminist theory, and the uses of the results of the research (see arguments in Dyck, 1993; Wolf, 1996). Indeed, a history of theory and method in feminist research could be written from this viewpoint. It might read like this: Because of the social positionings of feminist researchers throughout the past four decades as wanting both to disrupt the status quo and to be taken seriously by those in positions of power, it is not surprising that feminist research strategies vary between being highly innovative and tamely conventional. What this means is that feminists use a wide range of methods because there are many reasons for feminists to do research. Some feminists wanted to make some disruptive headway in long-standing disciplines by using conventional methods that were specific to a discipline itself so that their arguments would be taken seriously more widely. At the same time, there were feminists similarly located interested in integrating feminist political principles into their research (cf. Mies, 1983) and in contributing to disrupting the staidness of disciplinary knowledge more generally within the academy. Doing research based on a set of radical premises gave rise to an unconventional practice where data collection and analytical methods were *not* at the forefront of the decision making. Rather, principles favoring grassroots and full participant participation were front and center— sometimes resulting in the use of conventional methods and sometimes resulting in new, innovative ways of designing research and asking questions. Thus, because of the desire both to be disruptive and to be taken seriously, *a* feminist method did not arrive neatly on the academic scene to define feminist research as, for example, a challenge to the conventionality of research methods; rather, what emerged was the idea that what matters in defining feminist methods is how feminists actually theorize, characterize, and depict research as a feminist activity and how they make the methods themselves integral to the research.

Yet even with a history of long-term use of both conventional and unconventional methods, feminists from a variety of disciplines are using even more unconventional methods of research in their inquiries. One recent trend within feminist research is integrating visual representations into the research process. Photos are increasingly popular as a way of initiating discussion of sensitive topics like body image (Clarke, 2003), heightening awareness about environmental hazards in the home (Dobscha & Ozanne, 2001), and observing governance practices in situ (Riley & Manias, 2003). Furthermore, there are several attempts to incorporate video into data collection, analysis, and the presentation of research findings: videotaping the inside of homes for studies about the home as a place for long-term care (Dyck, Kontos, Angus, & McKeever, 2005); using a combination of picture taking, debriefing sessions, and storytelling (known as "photovoice") for community organizing (Wang & Redwood-Jones, 2001); using video making as a liberatory method for understanding place, identity, and social cohesion in community (Kindon, 2003); and presenting video clips in the write-up of an analysis of the politics of representation of community theater (Pratt & Kirby, 2003). Visual representation is not the only trend; it is just one of many unconventional methods being used and developed: some use counter-storytelling (e.g., Solórzano & Yosso, 2002), some use dance (e.g., Ylönen, 2003), some resist traditional modes of writing (e.g., Brossard, 2000), some use queer forms of material processes (e.g., Sullivan, 2002), and some apply innovative concepts to bring together diverse literatures (e.g., Probyn, 2004).

As a response to this proliferation of unconventional methods, I wondered if feminists were asking different questions than the ones they asked before that would prompt somehow the use of more unconventional methods. Were the methods that feminists were using linked to the types of questions they were asking? Would it matter if the questions feminists were asking were the ones they had been regularly asking for a couple of decades? Would visual material, dance, or new concepts provide more interesting data for analysis, interpretation, or reading? Some of the questions feminists were asking didn't readily appear to be different. Mapping women's lives, for example, had been of interest to feminist geographers for some time; engaging more visual methods seemed to draw on conventional types of methods from the discipline of geography. These mappings emphasize the spatial dimensions of women's lives in areas such as community development, time–space paths of everyday living, and reading material bodies through technologies (e.g., Johnston, Ved, Lyall, & Agarwal, 2003; Kwan, 2002; Kwan & Moss, 2003). To make matters more complicated, I had anticipated some of the questions these researchers asked: That is, what constitutes women's lives and what is the experience of oppression? But some of the questions I hadn't anticipated, as for example, how can a feminist rethink the relationship between the material and the political outside patriarchal politics and remain feminist, and what concepts are useful to bridge disciplinary thinking so as to form a different language through which to communicate similar sets of ideas?

As I worked through my quandary, I found myself rethinking the basis on which a feminist researcher chooses a method and designs a project. I asked myself, Had feminist research interests shifted so much that conventional methods were no longer useful in gathering data? Had feminist researchers changed the questions they asked? Had they found different ways to get the necessary information to answer their questions? After reviewing Harding, Reinharz, and other feminist literature, my thinking shifted a bit. I had come to the point where I had almost accepted the notion that feminists had different interests, asked different questions, and found different methods. But I remained unsettled. What was it about these new, unconventional methods emerging that I was interested in? Fostering curiosity for different feminist interests? Pioneering unusual, imaginative questions? Searching for quirky techniques? In my quest for understanding, I came to an interim resolution, one that frames my discussion in this chapter. I realized that my questions as I had posed them really did not address the environment within which feminist interests, questions, and methods emerge. What was at issue, it seemed, was that the connection between feminist theory and method was being reconceptualized in more adventurous ways. Once I grasped this notion, I started thinking in terms of methods emerging in the literature being more complex than simply a research fad or trend and involving more than just either data collection or data analysis. Finally, I began to recognize that

there were no clear links between the type of question asked and the type of method used. What seemed to be happening was that feminists were posing questions (ones that could be anticipated and ones that couldn't) and were drawing on lots of different types of methods (ones that were familiar and ones that weren't). I realized I needed a different framework to understand the notion of emergent methods in feminist research.

In the rest of this chapter, I work through a way to conceptualize the connections between theory and method in feminist research to account for emergent methods. To this end, I first define emergent methods and then present a framework that focuses on the processes through which research questions and choices of research techniques emerge. I next present a heuristic typology through which to discuss detailed examples of emergent methods in feminist research. I organize the discussion around my initial foray into this inquiry of looking at emergent methods in feminist research, focusing on works that pose either anticipated or unanticipated questions with regard to feminist issues that use either familiar or unfamiliar research methods. I close by reiterating my argument in the context of Scott's (2002) concept of *reverberation* as a venue for opening possibilities among emergent methods in feminist research.

## EMERGENT METHODS

Reconceptualizing the link between theory and method assists in making sense of the spate of unconventional methods emerging in feminist research in the recent past.[1] Conceiving emerging methods as part of a process instead of presuming them an entity is useful because it draws attention to *how* various dimensions of feminist research are taken up in specific research settings. In holding on to the notion of process in describing emergent methods as part of a feminist methodological orientation, one can actually account for shifts, adaptations, or changes in (1) the nature, form, or combination of the choice of topic; the research question; the form of data collection; the analysis; and the presentation of the research; and (2) the approach to the research itself without having to attribute adjectives such as new, innovative, or novel to the method or to lay out an argument to make claims that a particular method is uniquely, in and of itself, feminist. If one conceives of emergent methods as a process, what become important are the contexts through which emergent methods arise.

Following from the argument that "theory informs method and method shapes theory" (Gailey, 1998, p. 204), specific emergent methods depend on a number of elements interacting that then produce something we come to recognize as emerging in feminist research. Emergent methods as a process include assorted combinations of methods and feminist methodologies. By methods I mean those techniques used to gather and analyze information, data, and evidence. Data collection methods are the specific ways of gathering information, including, for example, numbers, words, noises, statistics, pictures, experiences, sensations, visual images, or landscapes. The analysis (comprising specific analytical techniques) is the explicit path through which the researcher links specific data, information, or evidence with theoretical or conceptual arguments. By methodology I mean the theory or analysis as to how the research should proceed; it is the glue that holds a specific research project together.

Clarifying what constitutes emergent methods in this way affects how one makes sense of how theory and method link in any particular context. One context that can be used to illustrate this point is the disciplinary context. Take, for instance, the disciplinary debates in feminist geography. There was an implicit assumption in the English-speaking debates among feminist geographers throughout the 1980s and 1990s that qualitative methods were better than quantitative methods. This led to extensive debate over what constitutes feminism, what is feminist about a methodology, and what methods are in sync with feminist values (see, e.g., *Antipode*, 1995; *Canadian Geographer*, 1993; McDowell, 1992; *Professional Geographer*, 1995; Rose, 1997). Although feminist geographers draw on feminist methodological works from other disciplines, this set of issues still frames the way in which feminist geographers make arguments about feminist methodology—they still locate their works within debates about

reflexivity, collaboration, and the construction of knowledge (see, e.g., *ACME*, 2003; Browne, 2003; Schuurman & Pratt, 2002). Feminist geographers mediated the contexts within which they had to make arguments about feminist methods and feminist methodologies. Their emergent methods arose, and still arise, out of these contexts, which are part of their own configuration. Emergent methods in feminist research in particular disciplines are partially a result of what conventional topics are taken up within a discipline as well as the way in which disciplinary feminisms have developed alongside their interaction with feminists in other disciplines.

The specifics of the example of feminist geography do not apply to all disciplinary settings; however, being sensitive to the variation in the way feminists take up issues about feminist method within a disciplinary setting may be useful. Such sensitivity highlights the importance of treating the *process* through which methods emerge as the crux of the discussion, rather than homing in on any one dimension of an emergent method, that is, a method, a methodology, or some combination of both. If the discussion slips from a focus on process to any particular method or methodology, then depictions of feminist research can become monolithic, and, in turn, particular forms of feminist methods (and by extension feminist theory) can become hegemonic. Various discipline-based discussions about feminist research take up different issues—Harding (1987), in philosophy, is interested in defining feminism; Lather (1991), in education, is interested in emancipatory ways of doing research; and Ferber and Nelson (2003), in economics, are interested in what constitutes economic actors and acts. In sociology and anthropology, where feminist methodological discussions are well developed, emergent methods are integral to the ongoing engagement by feminist researchers with theory and method in their home disciplines, and they contribute to discussions in others as well (see, e.g., Eadie, 2001, and collections edited by Behar & Gordon, 1995; Greenhouse & Mertz, 2002; Ribbens & Edwards, 1998). In spite of relatively little direct discussion about methodology by feminists in social work, political science, law, and policy studies, emergent methods as a process are central to the development of feminist thinking in these fields (see Dominelli, 1991; Grosfoguel & Cervantes-Rodríguez, 2002; Lopez, 2000; Pillow, 2003).

Granted, the bases of variation lie within particular research topics: the specific questions feminists pose as part of the research plan; the tweaking, development, and use of data collection techniques; the innovative analyses of data, information, or evidence vis-à-vis a theory or set of concepts; and the contexts of disciplinary debates. And this is the point. What is significant is not any one topic, question, data collection method, analysis, or context; what is significant is the constitutive combination of a *specific* topic with a *specific* question with a *specific* data collection technique with a *specific* analysis in a *specific* context.

## FRAMEWORK FOR UNDERSTANDING EMERGENT METHODS

To understand how emergent methods as a process can account for shifts and changes within feminist research more widely, it is important to focus on specific configurations of research methods arising out of multiple research contexts. Specific configurations include combinations of methods and methodologies, and multiple contexts include disciplinary debates (as discussed in the previous section) as well as political environments, research relations, ethical considerations, feminist thinking outside the academy, and technological availability, to name but a few. The ways through which these combinations and contexts interact to produce *specific* methods and approaches to feminist research are contingent on the relations within and between the various elements of the research, including, for example, the familiarity of a method and the anticipated nature of the question being asked.

These notions about how to understand emergent methods as a process can be sorted into three concepts: contingency, context, and specificity. To illustrate what I mean by each, I discuss each in terms of producing knowledge. By "knowledge" here I mean specific types of knowledge, not knowledge as an undifferentiated entity. There are different knowledges (e.g., women's, local, collective, feminist methodological, racialized), just as there are different ways of knowing (e.g., experiential, theoretical, hypothetical, imaginary). The

ideas underlying these concepts are common topics within feminist literatures and are important conceptual tools used to figure out how social relations involved in the research process matter in figuring out what is going on in a specific research setting.

*Contingency* refers to the situatedness of knowledge, especially in the sense that difference emerges as a temporarily fixed moment (as identity) via engagement through ongoing and fluctuating social processes (see Haraway, 1988, on situated knowledges; Mouffe, 1992, on fixity and identity). *Context* is also part of the situatedness of knowledge, especially in the sense that differentiation (or the process of creating difference) among what is knowable, what is known, and who is a knower is enmeshed in and constitutive of multiple sets of relations imbued with power (see Sandoval, 2000, on differential politics; Young, 1990, on power and social relations; Hawkesworth, 1990, on feminist epistemology). *Specificity* serves as the descriptor for the process through which temporal and spatial moments of contingency and context are made explicit (see Moss, 2005, p. 44). What specificity can do conceptually is describe the momentary fixity of various sets of contingent relations coming together in a particular combination of social processes (in context) for the production of knowledge. For feminist research, this means that there are various contexts interacting (e.g., disciplinary, political, historical, social, intellectual, institutional, personal, cultural) that are locally mediated by contingent sets of relations (e.g., place, intensity, networks, language, subjectivities, politics, identities) and producing specific renditions of feminist methods and methodologies. For example, because of the contingent nature of the relations involved in the production of knowledge, including, for example, access to intellectual and financial resources as well as tasks associated with research positions (i.e., activism, teaching, administration, household, child rearing, elder care), feminist methodological innovations emerging in the English-speaking academy can become privileged in international and global discussions of feminism and feminist research. Or, because cartography and mapmaking are located in geography as a discipline, feminist geographers may choose to engage in discussion of how data about the restrictiveness of women's travel patterns can be used to demonstrate women's oppression spatially. In contrast, feminist sociologists may be more interested in taking up the discussion of women's oppression in terms of employment opportunities and household tasks. The choice of survey questionnaires, maps, or in-depth interviews, when taken up in a different research setting, can appear new, innovative, and insightful—depending on the context.

Locating the discussion of emergent methods as a process in terms arising from discussion about the production of knowledge—contingency, context, specificity—is useful because it highlights the variation of methods across feminisms, disciplines, and fields of study. The contingent nature of social relations constituting disciplinary, intellectual, and academic contexts shapes choices about methods. Specific research methods emerge as feminist research in different places at different times. For example, feminists using poststructural thought may use discourse analysis as a means of scrutinizing text (e.g., Harding, 1997), whereas feminists working from a global critical race feminist perspective might use interpretations of legal codes and agreements to document women's oppression (e.g., Knapp, 2000). Both these analyses use text as a data source, and both are feminist. Yet the methods differ because the interests and specific questions of the researchers differ: The former uses text to get at discourse as a set of discursive strategies and practices associated with hormone replacement therapy as a particular social phenomenon, and the latter uses text as a way of plotting the legal challenges facing Japanese women in national and international arenas.

Although this framework accounts for variation in the ways feminists take up research, at the same time it focuses discussion on *emergence* as a process (or as flux, or as fixity, or as difference). Viewed this way, debates and discussions within feminist research move away from marking emergent methods in feminist research with identifiable characteristics toward emphasizing the notion that feminist research has within it numerous possibilities, ones that continuously seek to address challenging questions and provoke innovative, groundbreaking ways to go about thinking and doing feminist research. Emergent methods as a process, then,

is a contingent notion, one that is made specific only through undertaking research in concrete research settings, wherein the research is then made real by the social relations existing on the ground, in a particular locale. By refusing fixed links between feminism and any one, or set of, particular method(s), feminist research can foster an openness to multiple feminist practices based on feminist research questions and feminist theory. Parallel to the argument that Gailey (1998) makes about the constitutive nature of the relationship between theory and method, emergent methods are not uniquely or solely feminist. Emergent methods are constitutive of a process through which configurations of ideas about and practices within research contexts and settings manifest that already have within them a feminist ethic, politic, or principle. How feminists engage with emergent methods matters because if there is an understanding of how (process and contingency) and why (context and specificity) particular configurations of methods and methodologies emerge and are taken up, then feminist researchers can learn from each other. Making space for an understanding of emergent methods in feminist research means coming to terms with what may be possible as feminist research.

## SPACES FOR EMERGENT METHODS

I sit here poised to write about the examples of emergent methods I have found to be interesting, innovative, and challenging. But I am filled with trepidation. I am not sure what fills these spaces. I am not sure what provokes one to think in such a space. How can I be sure if a piece of research reports on, uses, or engages with an emergent method? Although Diprose (2000) was writing about shifting from one set of ideas to another, the catalyst initiating her process was similar to my dilemma here: "Something has got under my skin. Something has disturbed me, made me think in a direction that was not altogether different from what I thought initially, but different all the same" (p. 116). Intuitively, I know what an emergent method is, and I think I can articulate what an emergent method is, but I don't know (and can't know) thoroughly any one, let alone all, of a method's multiple dimensions. So, I am not sure. I wonder if this impediment blocks access to the space for emergent methods (arising through emergence as a process). Diprose does not seem to think so. She works with the notion that thinking is affective and reasoned at the same time to try to understand the teaching of another's set of viewpoints, ones differing from her own (pp. 116–117). Part of her argument involves the claim that connections made to another's alterity are primarily affective (e.g., sympathy, outrage, anger, pain, joy), and through these connections, meaning as a process is initiated. These connections do not mean that the other's ideas are accepted without question; what is suggested is merely to think again.

Diprose's argument about thinking again resonates with my grasp of emergent methods constitutive of a process. The concepts of contingency, context, and specificity describe what is involved with the process and together provide an account of how methods emerge in feminist research. Being sensitive to the *specificity* of each emergent method makes an engagement with *any* method—specific combination of topic, question, data collection method, analysis, presentation of findings, approach to research, and context—a possibility. To take up any specific emergent method wholeheartedly without critical reflection undermines the notion of emergence as a process. Treating emergent methods as a process seriously entails looking for spaces that have been created through complex sets of contingent relations arising from numerous contexts that make *specific* a particular method. These spaces permit one to think again.

The remainder of this chapter, then, is just that: a space to permit one to think again. Such spaces are important because they provide room to begin an inquiry, reflect on what has gone on before, and figure out what to do next. For the most part, the constitutive contingent relations and mediation of their multiple contexts are not part of the review because they have not been recorded in the write-up of the research results of process. The rest of the chapter looks as if what I have written is "not altogether different from what I thought initially" about emergent methods seeming to be new, unconventional, or novel methods. Yet because I "thought again" about emergent methods as a process in the

context of defining emergent methods, I can offer a typology as a space to read the literature that makes it "different all the same."

## QUESTIONS AND METHODS: ANTICIPATION AND FAMILIARITY

Against this backdrop of understanding the link between theory and method by conceiving emergent methods as a process, I found it useful to sort through the pieces of work in terms of my initial quandary of thinking about emergent methods, that is, in terms of anticipated and unanticipated questions alongside familiar and unfamiliar methods (see Figure 17.1). By anticipated questions, I mean those questions that feminists have been asking for some time, and by unanticipated, those questions feminists are beginning to ask or are resurrecting from other points in time or place. By familiar methods, I mean those methods that feminists have been using for some time, and by unfamiliar, those methods feminists are beginning to use or are resurrecting from other points in time or place. Although neatly boxed, the boundaries of course are porous and leaky. Some pieces fit easily within a "box." Some fit awkwardly at the juncture between two. Still others appear not to fit at all. I am uneasy offering such a well-defined typology, with fixed categories for thinking about possibilities for emergent methods in feminist research. Such fixity compromises my commitment to be sensitive to the contingent nature of social relations constituting the contexts within which research takes place that shape the specific configuration of what we come to recognize as an emergent method. I want to pass some of this unease to the reader—either in the sense that my arguments about contingency, context, and specificity need to be rejected in whole or in part, or that they resonate with one's experience of doing and reading about feminist research.

The typology proposed here, based on anticipated and unanticipated questions alongside familiar and unfamiliar methods, is a constructive categorization to sort through what it is about a particular study, project, or piece of writing that makes it an emergent method. The examples cited in all four categories fall within

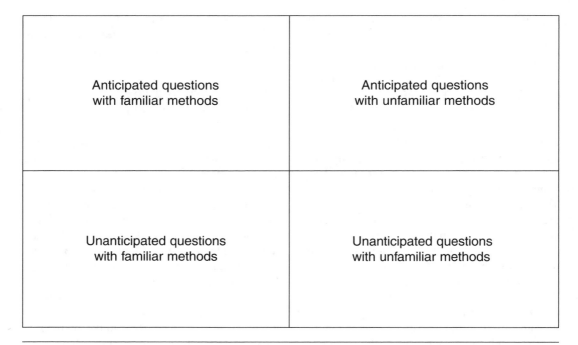

| Anticipated questions with familiar methods | Anticipated questions with unfamiliar methods |
| --- | --- |
| Unanticipated questions with familiar methods | Unanticipated questions with unfamiliar methods |

**Figure 17.1**    Heuristic Device With Categories to Initiate Discussion About Emergent Methods in Feminist Research

the expanded view of what emergent methods are—ones that *contingently* arise from multiple *contexts* that bring together various dimensions of research in *specific* ways as part of a reconceptualization of the link between theory and method. Parallel to the argument about the emergence of methods within feminist research, this typology is a specific product of constitutive contingent relations involved in feminist methodological discussions. It is exhaustive of neither these specific categories of emergent methods (for there are many other examples of works that could have been part of the discussion) nor the types of emergent methods themselves (for a typology could have been developed using other dimensions of emergent methods). It is only a device that assists in sorting pieces of information, which then contributes to the production of feminist knowledge about emergent methods in feminist methodology. In short, I offer this categorization as a heuristic device, one developed to suggest—simply—that one think again.

## Anticipated Questions With Familiar Methods

Focus groups are a familiar method that has been taken up widely by feminists in some disciplines, especially those with participatory approaches to research (see Wilkinson, 1999). Although focus groups are used to draw out opinions on a particular issue, they can be useful in addressing limitations of analysis, collective experience, and silence. Van Steveren (1997) used focus groups to talk with women as economic empowerment activists in Nairobi, Kenya. She argues that the focus groups were useful in providing insight into her own limiting moral dimensions that threatened to impose a particular (and judgmental) reading of the link between economic independence and feeling empowered. With regard to collective experiences, as a member of a group of women housing activists, I worked on an exploratory project on social housing cooperatives. We conducted four focus groups as the basis for information gathering (Moss, 2003). These focus groups were different from conventional focus groups because they were collectively conducted, collectively interpreted, and collectively edited— first by members of each of the four groups, resulting in four documents, and then by all participants in the project, resulting in one document with four parts. The documents at the end of the process constitute the data source for the project: The focus of the analysis is not on what was said in the discussions; rather, the analysis is about the information produced through the four focus groups about access to housing and support services for women in transition. Hyams (2004) also uses focus groups a little differently. She is concerned about giving voice to minority groups through focus group discussion and interaction. What is innovative about Hyams's project is that she is more interested in the silences present in the formation of girls' Latina gender identities. She argues that a feminist group discussion method (a cross between feminist consciousness-raising and a focus group) needs to make space for a politics of voice that includes silence as part of the group interaction. These examples show how feminists use focus groups differently. Although the questions are conventional for feminist research (i.e., questions are posed about economic participation in the household, women's housing needs, and young women's identity) and the focus group as a method is familiar, these works provide insight into questions that feminists across disciplines are asking about reflexivity in the context of limits to analysis, collectivity in the sense of whose experiences are driving the research design, and what type of politics need to inform feminist research with the implication that a feminist politics is not only about voice but also about silence.

A specific method, such as focus groups, is not the only *specificity* apparent in these types of emergent methods. For example, feminists using the familiar method of depth interviews are querying the construction of the narrative itself and how a self-reflexive reading of one's own participation can have an impact on the topic of inquiry, as for example, whiteness and sexuality (Byrne, 2003; Valentine, 2002). Feminist researchers also make known their own methodological specificity (institutional,

intellectual, political, cultural contexts) while using familiar methods through contributions to existing feminist literature about, for example, action research (e.g., Gatenby & Humphries, 2000; Humble & Morgaine, 2002; Lynch, 2000), globalization and international justice (e.g., Adam, 2002; Barandun, 2000), rhetorical and theoretical strategies (e.g., Collins, 1999; Squire, 2002), and feminist institutional politics (e.g., Koikari & Hippensteele, 2000; Teghtsoonian, 2003). Although each addresses questions that the discipline or field of study warrants (e.g., the expected, the usual, the conventional as questions in terms of what constitutes action research) and each uses familiar methods within each one's discipline or field of study (e.g., reading text, contextualizing ideas, introducing useful concepts), there is some different configuration emerging that makes the research different (e.g., using a successful implementation of a policy to show that such a success is, in these times, woefully inadequate and demonstrating the precariousness of how state institutions take up feminist concerns). Each of these works has emerged as a result of *thinking again* about the topic, the question, the data collection, the analysis, or the context. They are reengaging similar terrain in different ways, ways that are sensitive to the contingent nature of research milieus. Although seemingly tame and not trendy, these kinds of emergent methods, the ones that ask anticipated questions and use familiar methods, assist in forging feminist knowledges that sustain feminist research as an area of intellectual inquiry.

## Anticipated Questions With Unfamiliar Methods

Several works dealing with long-standing feminist interests are using less conventional methods to address questions that have come to be associated with feminist research, for example, historically comparative popular writing and feminism, presentation of public selves and sexuality, and conversation analysis and gender (Broad & Joos, 2004; Stokoe & Weatherall, 2002; Walls, 2002). This combination of anticipated feminist research questions with unfamiliar methods often reinvigorates a long-standing substantive interest and, as a result, sparks feminists to ask different questions and generate different analyses.

There are works, however, that *literally* ask the same question of the same set of data, observations, texts, and evidence while using a different method of analysis. For example, Lanser (1999) published a piece that calls into question a standard feminist interpretation of a canonized work. She makes the case that feminist literary critics (between 1973 and 1986) developed, reproduced, and reified a unified feminist interpretation of Gilman's *The Yellow Wallpaper*: The only sane response to women's patriarchal oppression is insanity. Having been left troubled by the singularity of the interpretation of Gilman's work, Lanser posed to herself the question left unasked: What does the *yellow* wallpaper mean? She revisited the political and cultural contexts at the turn of the 20th century and found classist, racist, and nationalist assumptions in the text that had up to that time been ignored. She convincingly argues that the fear and mass anxiety about Chinese immigration in California, where Gilman lived when she wrote *The Yellow Wallpaper,* are embedded in the text. She further supports her self-professed "disturbing" (p. 205) reading by looking at Gilman's later work and her nonsocialist political activities in her own life—both of which indicate that Gilman supported a Protestant, White, American, nonimmigrant society. By reengaging with earlier texts and textual interpretations, Lanser produces an amazing, and quite distressing, *specific* analysis that puts into practice—both methodologically and analytically—a sensitivity to constitutive contingent relations constituting the contexts through which feminist knowledge is produced.

This type of critical reengagement of texts is not limited to literary criticism. Feminist social scientists also have the opportunity to reenter previously published works and produce, with critical engagement, different analyses. The act of revisiting one's own published work does not in itself spawn a critical reengagement. Reentering a previously published analysis of data could generate a more critical, a more rigorous, or some type of "better" analysis just as it could produce a less insightful, a less precise, or some type of "worse" analysis. What makes this kind of feminist work exceptional is the vigilant attention to both reflexive and critical approaches within the analysis. Roulston (2001) takes up this challenge. She reengages some of her previous research, work that was part of her first research project. Roulston uses "analysis as theorizing ideology" (from Smith, 1974) to describe how novice researchers move from data to meaning by molding transcribed words in pursuit of answering a question. In the article, she compares her original approach to interpreting data from a particular interview with music teachers through themes analysis with a new approach to the same data through conversation analysis. Because of the detail left out of the original transcriptions needed for conversation analysis, she retranscribed the original audio-recording of the interview.[2] She then turns to conversation analysis to demonstrate the shortcomings of her original write-up and provides a different reading that she claims is less "naïve" and more reflexive.

With the advent of engaging with poststructural accounts of knowledge construction, especially those that emphasized words and texts, methods accessing meaning and discourse became more popular. Conversation analysis, providing an inroad into an inquiry of the relationship between the researcher and participants in the research project, is emerging in various feminist fields of study, particularly in feminist social psychology and feminist communication studies. For example, Speer (2002) argues that although feminists acknowledge and write about the impact of the researcher on the research process, most feminists do not include these reflexive moments in their analysis. She thinks that conversation analysis is a way of interrogating the interactional contexts within which researchers and the researched socially construct the phenomenon under scrutiny (e.g., gender, illness, politics). Such an approach could conceivably actually trace the production of feminist knowledge. Yet conversation analysis is not only used for the analysis of interviews; it can also be used in nonresearch settings. Cook (2000), in her analysis of talk from a radio talk-back show host, extends the strengths of conversation analysis, particularly its ability to discern relational aspects of the construction of talk. Talk-back radio focuses on the interaction between the radio host and the caller. Cook makes the point that the conversation eventually aired is mediated through the radio production team, which involves a vetting process. In this sense, the talk is not natural talk; it is constructed for show. She goes on analytically to make the case that by politicizing (and contextualizing) the talk of the host and the caller, discourses that continue to sustain the talk show itself can be accessed, thus moving beyond a microscale of analysis. Cook maintains that through this type of analysis, even in (or perhaps especially in) situations where the purpose of the engagement of the talk is to be antagonistic, spaces of resistance emerge, spaces where talk can be challenged.

All these examples show how thinking again about a topic and using methods usually not used in a particular context can bring out a configuration of an emergent method that can enhance, challenge, or sustain conventional takes on issues of interest to feminists. Feminist researchers in training often use this combination of anticipated questions and unfamiliar methods as an approach to feminist research, by chance or design, because innovation in methods of data collection, analysis, or presentation style usually takes root when there already exists a solid, topical foundation on which one can build, paving the way for such innovation to be more readily accepted by other feminists.

## Unanticipated Questions With Familiar Methods

Autobiographical writing is a relatively familiar method that can address unanticipated questions because of its versatility. Autobiography is a resourceful analytical method used by feminists for over a decade and has been gaining favor among feminists in nonliterary disciplines just as it is a source of data for interpretation, a methodological choice, and sometimes both (e.g., Baker, 2001; Larson, 1999; Rivera-Fuentes, 2000; Ryan, 2004). The complexity of autobiographical writing provides plenty of fodder for asking unexpected questions. For example, Lentin (2000), in a write-up of her study of herself and other women as daughters of Shoah survivors,[3] asks several questions, both substantive and methodological, throughout her piece. Why do families whisper life stories?

What gives voice to autobiography? Does dual subjectivity capture my life as a first generation Israeli taught to despise the Jewish diaspora and a member of a family of Shoah survivors? How is self constructed? Through her questioning, she reconfigures the boundaries of the possibilities for autobiographical writing. Henderson (2002) notes that autobiography itself is about crisis, epistemological instability, and representation. In reading texts of Australian activist feminists, Henderson asks how these memoirs regulate the history of feminist activism and the feminist subject in the Australian women's movement. She proposes a counterautobiography, as an emergent method, that reenters the discussion by siting, sighting, or citing parts of the "revolution" not included in the privileged texts. Magarey and Round (2004, p. 87) are writing a biography of Roma Flinders Mitchell, "Queen's Counsel, Judge, Founding Chair of the Human Rights Commission, Chancellor of the University of Adelaide, Governor of South Australia." Their piece begins and ends with a set of questions that they seek to address while using the authorized version of Mitchell's life, ranging from asking what her daily life was like when so few people had reached her esteemed position, especially as a woman, to querying the manifestations of the feminine unsettling of the masculine notion of law in her own life. These examples demonstrate that autobiography as a familiar method provides ample room to ask a range of questions without shoving aside the purpose of the writing or undermining the research question itself.

Familiar methods also shift a bit when researchers ask unanticipated questions. With regard to the research process, Deem (2002), in her work on and with feminist manager-academics, writes about the challenges feminism poses to research teams during projects. From her experiences, she observed that nonfeminist members of the research team she was involved with found that feminist input into the research was important and that many of the research team practices were commensurate with feminist methodologies. Sometimes, feminists approach multiperspective research teams as places of conflict; Deem turns this around by asking about points of consensus. In connection with asking unanticipated questions about a topic itself, Horne, Mathews, Detrie, Burke, and Cook (2001) address feminist identity formation. They use grounded theory to investigate what constitutes a feminist identity among emergent feminists (those younger women coming to feminism) and experienced feminists (those older women who have self-identified as feminist for a long time). Grounded theory is an empirically rich approach whereby the researcher pulls themes from data collected during the intensely reflexive research process. This approach differs from many of the theory-driven accounts of identity formation. Two of their key findings contribute to the overall debate about feminist identity—younger women have been exposed to lots of negative characterizations of feminism (in part via the excessive backlash in the early 1990s), and the methods for raising consciousness differ from the methods more experienced feminists used in their own consciousness-raising (that is, the process of feminist politicization is contingent on its context and takes a specific form). Finally, with regard to finding space for a feminist politics, Murphy (2001) uses feminist theory as a departure point for asking what self-help literature can contribute to feminism. Her work shows that self-help literature, while simple, can still be moved to feminist ends. In asking this unexpected question, she is able to identify a space between the text in the self-help book and the audience the self-help book seeks to help. She maintains that in this space there is room for feminist political engagements.

Surprising theoretical queries about any of the elements that make up a project can kindle the process of thinking again about how to approach feminist research. As each of these examples suggests, the unanticipated aspect of the questions a method addresses lies not (only or necessarily) in the content of the questions; rather, it is the multiple combinations of endless questions that make up the unanticipated aspect of questions with familiar methods: ones that lead to emergent methods—as data collection, analysis, and presentation.

## Unanticipated Questions With Unfamiliar Methods

Addressing unanticipated questions with unfamiliar methods within feminist research can be read as the introduction of a methodological approach largely not taken up by feminists. Portraiture, for example, is a well-established method outside feminism that developed through methodological debates in critical race theory (see Lawrence-Lightfoot & Davis, 1997). Portraiture is a flexible methodological approach that is a combination of storytelling, knowledge creation, mutual autobiographical construction, artistic expression, scientific endeavor, individual reflexivity, and community building. Portraitists approach a research topic either with a single method or with multiple methods. Harding (2005), for example, accesses the articulation of race and gender in the classroom between teacher and student through portraiture. She uses portraiture to document the process through which narratives are co-constructed by the researcher and the participants in the research project in everyday life settings, which double as research settings. Chapman (2005) examines the numerous ways in which voice is conceptualized and expressed in and through portraiture. She pulls out six forms of voice used in portraiture as part of the emancipatory research process: voice as autobiography, voice as preoccupation, voice in dialogue, voice as witness, voice as interpretation, and voice discerning other voices. This analytically rich work could be especially useful in discussion of the construction of (feminist) knowledge(s). Dixson (2005), also working with portraiture, develops jazz as an epistemological positioning and a methodological approach. Through identifying and then marking the points of articulation among multiple aspects of a set of experiences, of teaching in her work, she seeks to draw attention to the intricacies of the interconnectedness of Black experience. Jazz as a method, she argues, is pertinent and appropriate for African American communities, classrooms, and education practitioners. Lawrence-Lightfoot (2005) makes an argument about the usefulness of portraiture as a method in documentation, analysis, and narrative development. She takes up issues of interdisciplinarity, authenticity, legitimacy, and identity in the context of methodology at the intersection between science and art. Some of these critical race theory scholars are also engaged with feminist theory. Just as the contributions of critical race theory have not been fully articulated by many feminists, portraiture, too, lacks adaptation and integration into feminist research. Portraiture has tremendous potential to contribute to enriching feminist research if done sensitively through a recognition of contingency, context, and specificity.

Another approach not popular among feminists is Deleuzean-inspired inquiries. Theoretically, Deleuze is becoming an influence in feminist theory (see Buchanan & Colebrook, 2000). Notions of becoming-woman, deterritorialization, body without organs, war machines, assemblages, and rhizomatic thinking are but a few of the concepts Deleuze develops in his theoretical work (see Deleuze & Guattari, 1987). For feminists using his conceptually rich framework, there are implications for both the choice of topic and the linking together of the data and theory (analysis). In one example, Potts (2004) shows how effective a Deleuzean-inspired approach can be. She uses Deleuze's notions of molar lines, molecular lines, and lines of flight that together describe a range of possible relationships between individuals and society. Molar lines are macroforces that reinforce social norms; molecular lines are microsocial processes that are related to molar lines but not as structured; and lines of flight are activities that break with both macro- and microprocesses to effect some sort of shift or change. Potts uses these concepts to critique the biomedical model of reading men's uneven or inconsistent sexual response in terms of erectile dysfunction syndrome. Potts's query of men's socially constructed sexual dysfunction is not a question feminists would typically be interested in; nor is her methodological approach of employing unfamiliar, abstract concepts to analyze interview data. Using a different concept from Deleuze, Bray and Colebrook (1999) draw on positive ontology to think again about anorexia nervosa. They argue that by beginning with the conceptualization of the sensation of hunger as desire, rather than of starvation as denial, the activities that women diagnosed with anorexia nervosa engage in—measuring food, monitoring weight, counting calories—can be reinterpreted as self-formative rather than self-destructive. For them, the illness is not a matter of embodying the notion of a lack in the constitution of self; rather, anorexia nervosa as a construct is a matter of looking at events, acts,

and connections that positively produce an entity with a strong ontological sense. Their query around positive ontology dramatically shifts thinking about a woman diagnosed with anorexia nervosa. Instead of being ill as a result of not having a thin body, the woman participates in a set of activities positively producing herself as a woman with anorexia nervosa. What may happen as a result of this rethinking is that therapeutic intervention techniques may change. These are but two examples of the many possibilities of Deleuzean-inspired feminist research projects. Although a major stumbling block has been the obscure language Deleuze uses to describe his framework, feminists are increasingly engaging with his work in exciting new ways (see, e.g., Braidotti, 1994, 2003; Colebrook, 2002, 2004; Shildrick, 1997, 2002).

Addressing unanticipated questions with unfamiliar methods can also be read as taking up feminist topics and interests in light of methodological challenges, especially in areas of study where feminism has not yet taken hold. For example, Lock (2004) talks about living cadavers and the notion of what constitutes death. Living cadavers are people who have been pronounced brain-dead and are kept living with machines and advanced medicalized technology. She draws on concepts in the literatures on technology, biomedicine, ethics, and public discourse to explore what brain death means, what feeds those definitions, and what problems arise when doing research with living cadavers. Mountz, Miyares, Wright, and Bailey (2003) turn a *collective* reflexive eye on the collective practices of the research team. Their recognition that methodologies are not fixed conceptually or in practice is an insight not always acted on either when in the field or in the write-up. They use the notion of methodologically becoming to describe the dilemmas they faced together and individually. Collective analyses of collective research processes are unique, indeed. Their work signals a movement toward a collaborative postresearch process that could provide insight into how feminist research "should" be undertaken. Gibbs (2003) provides readings of psychoanalysis that treat theory as fiction and emphasize textuality over truth. She defines her approach, fictocriticism, as a methodological approach to criticism (primarily literary criticism) that sets up theoretical engagements through fiction and engages theory through rhetorical strategies. Moss and McMahon (2000) use a similar approach without naming it fictocriticism. We were interested in writing about our struggles within university settings over (not) being valued because we do qualitative research. We create a series of fictionalized encounters between ourselves and some feminist colleagues about specific institutional practices (e.g., tenure) that affect feminist academic careers. Visweswaran (1994), too, uses this type of approach in her work in fictional ethnography. She uses the topic of fictional ethnographic accounts to explore theoretical and methodological issues about truth, fieldwork, and knowledge.

These examples demonstrate that, in their various forms, asking unanticipated questions while using unfamiliar methods has tremendous potential to break open the topics feminists choose to investigate, the discussions feminists have about methodology, the choices feminists make about research techniques, and the presentations of feminists' research. It is here, with surprising twists emerging from *thinking again,* that emergent method as a process is most clearly articulated because the diversity of the specificity draws out the contingent nature of context, especially with respect to issues of power, reflexivity, and authority.

## CONCLUDING REMARKS AS FEMINIST REVERBERATIONS

A metaphor used by Scott (2002) gets at another aspect of thinking again, an aspect that describes both how emergent methods arise and what impact they have in feminist research. In describing difference, Scott uses *reverberations* to denote the echoing characteristic of a relationship between feminist politics and feminist action. Through the notion of a feminist analytics of power, she demonstrates how a particular set of acts emerges collectively in similar ways in different contexts. She writes about Women in Black as a global phenomenon with no central organizing body. Each unit engages in the same set of acts—wearing black, standing silently in a public place at a regularly scheduled time, peacefully protesting war and violence. Their political goals differ because they arise from the contexts within which each woman in black lives. Traces of ideas that circulate over the globe from one place and time to another generate feminist acts here and there, loosely aligned, yet politically distinct.

Reverberations, too, can work as a descriptor of emergent methods as a way of creating a venue for discussion about possibilities. Changes in feminist research are not always momentous or earth-shattering; they can be incremental and supportive, sometimes overlooked, or even disregarded. Traces of ideas, acts, and concepts echo and resonate loudly in some places, softly in others. There are ongoing articulations, engagements, activities, attempts, innovations, failures, entrenchments, questions, dismissals, assertions, statements, inquiries, mistakes, answers, discussions, introductions, successes, disagreements . . . shaping how a feminist researcher takes up issues around research topics, questions, data, analyses, and contexts within a field of study. The sheer number of innovative, noteworthy combinations of theory and method emerging during the last decade demonstrates that feminist research is indeed thriving. The textured character of emergent methods in feminist research arises out of the lush array of the adventurous links between theory and method feminists are now engaging with, ricocheting back and forth, catalyzing thought and action. As feminists continue to do research, *specific* research methods will emerge—some anticipated, some unanticipated, some familiar, some not so familiar. Yet oddly enough, with such diversity enhancing feminist research, what constitutes feminist research is still up for grabs. Within a milieu of contingency and context, one of the debates is still going to be what it is about research methods that make them feminist. It will remain so because challenges made to feminist research arise from the spaces through which feminist researchers are invited and permitted to think again. These thoughts reverberate, strengthening feminist researchers' resolve to remain feminist.

## NOTES

1. The discussion of what constitutes feminist theory, too, matters in figuring out how the links

between theory and method are conceptualized. For a glimpse into the larger debate, see the exchanges in *Feminist Theory* (*Feminist Theory*, 2001; Stanley & Wise, 2000) and in *Sociology* (Letherby, 2004a, 2004b; Oakley, 2004).

2. Many university ethics vetting processes prevent keeping original audio-recorded data after transcription. So, unfortunately, this type of analysis cannot always take place unless expressly planned for in the original research design.

3. Lentin (2000) defines *Shoah* and says why she uses the term: "I use the term 'Shoah' which means, in Hebrew, calamity or cataclysm, rather than the English term 'Holocaust' which derives from the Greek 'holocauston' meaning 'burnt offering,' because of the latter's implication of the Jews being sacrificed" (p. 248).

# References

*ACME: An International E-Journal for Critical Geographies*. (2003). Symposium: Practices in feminist research. *ACME: An International E-Journal for Critical Geographies, 2*(1), 57–111.

Adam, B. (2002). The gendered time politics of globalization: Of shadow lands and elusive justice. *Feminist Review, 70*, 3–29.

*Antipode*. (1995). Discussion and debate: Symposium on feminist participatory research. *Antipode, 27*, 71–101.

Baker, D. G. (2001). Future homemakers and feminist awakenings: Autoethnography as a method in theological education and research. *Religious Education, 96*(3), 395–407.

Barandun, P. (2000). *A gender perspective on conflict resolution: The development of the Northern Ireland Women's Coalition (NIWC) and its role in the multi-party peace talks (1996–1998)*. Bern, Switzerland: Schweizerische Friedsensstiftung/Institut für Koflictlösung.

Behar, R., & Gordon, D. A. (Eds.). (1995). *Women writing culture*. Berkeley: University of California Press.

Bloom, L. R. (1998). *Under the sign of hope: Feminist methodology and narrative interpretation*. Albany: State University of New York Press.

Bondi, L., Avis, H., Bankey, R., Davidson, J., Duffy, R., Einagel, V. I., Green, A.-M., Johnston, L., Lilley, S., Listerborn, C., McEwan, S., Marshy, M., O'Connor, N., Rose, G., Vivat, B.,

& Wood, N. (2002). *Subjectivities, knowledges and feminist geographies: The subjects and ethics of social research*. Boulder, CO: Rowman & Littlefield.

Braidotti, R. (1994). *Nomadic subjects: Embodiment and sexual difference in contemporary feminist theory*. New York: Columbia University Press.

Braidotti, R. (2003). Becoming woman: Or sexual difference revisited. *Theory, Culture & Society, 20*(3), 43–64.

Bray, A., & Colebrook, C. (1999). The haunted flesh: Corporeal feminism and the politics of (dis)embodiment. *Signs, 24*(1), 35–67.

Broad, K. L., & Joos, K. E. (2004). Online inquiry of public selves: Methodological considerations. *Qualitative Inquiry, 10*(6), 923–946.

Brossard, N. (2000). A state of mind in the garden. *Journal of Lesbian Studies, 4*(4), 35–40.

Browne, K. (2003). Negotiations and fieldworkings: Friendship and feminist research. *ACME: An International E-Journal for Critical Geographies, 2*(2), 132–146.

Buchanan, I., & Colebrook, C. (2000). *Deleuze and feminist theory*. Edinburgh, UK: University of Edinburgh Press.

Byrne, B. (2003). Reciting the self: Narrative representation of the self in qualitative interviews. *Feminist Theory, 4*(1), 29–49.

*Canadian Geographer*. (1993). Feminism as method. *Canadian Geographer, 37*, 48–61.

Chapman, T. K. (2005). Expressions of "voice" in portraiture. *Qualitative Inquiry, 11*(1), 27–51.

Clarke, L. H. (2003). Overcoming ambivalence: The challenges of exploring socially charged issues. *Qualitative Health Research, 13*(5), 718–735.

Colebrook, C. (2002). *Understanding Deleuze*. Crows Nest, New South Wales, Australia: Allen & Unwin.

Colebrook, C. (2004). The sense of space: On the specificity of affect in Deleuze and Guattari. *Postmodern Culture, 15*(1). (Available through Project Muse.)

Collins, V. T. (1999). The speaker respoken: Material rhetoric as feminist methodology. *College English, 61*(5), 545–573.

Cook, J. (2000). Dangerously radioactive: The plural vocalities of radio talk. In A. Lee & C. Poynton (Eds.), *Culture and text: Discourse and methodology in social research and cultural studies* (pp. 59–80). Lanham, MD: Rowman & Littlefield.

Deem, R. (2002). Talking to manager-academics: Methodological dilemmas and feminist research strategies. *Sociology, 36*(4), 835–855.

Deleuze, G., & Guattari, F. (1987). *A thousand plateaus: Capitalism and schizophrenia*. Minneapolis: University of Minnesota Press.

DeVault, M. L. (1999). *Liberating method: Feminism and social research*. Philadelphia: Temple University Press.

Diprose, R. (2000). What is (feminist) philosophy? *Hypatia, 15*(2), 115–132.

Dixson, A. D. (2005). Extending the metaphor: Notions of jazz as portraiture. *Qualitative Inquiry, 11*(1), 106–137.

Dobscha, S., & Ozanne, J. L. (2001). An eco-feminist analysis of environmentally sensitive women using qualitative methodology: The emancipatory potential of an ecological life. *Journal of Public Policy & Marketing, 20*(2), 201–214.

Dominelli, L. (1991). *Women across continents: Feminist comparative social policy*. New York: Harvester Wheatsheaf.

Dyck, I. (1993). Ethnography: A feminist method. *Canadian Geographer, 37*(1), 52–57.

Dyck, I., Kontos, P., Angus, J., & McKeever, P. (2005). The home as a site for long-term care: Meanings and management of bodies and spaces. *Health & Place, 11*, 173–185.

Eadie, J. (2001). Boy talk: Social theory and its discontents. *Sociology, 35*(2), 575–582.

*Feminist Theory*. (2001). Special section. Response to But the empress has no clothes! *Feminist Theory, 2*(1), 79–111.

Ferber, M. A., & Nelson, J. A. (Eds.). (2003). *Feminist economics today: Beyond economic man*. Chicago: University of Chicago Press.

Gailey, C. W. (1998). Feminist methods. In H. R. Bernard (Ed.), *Handbook of methods in cultural anthropology* (pp. 203–233). Lanham, MD: Altamira Press.

Gatenby, B., & Humphries, M. (2000). Feminist participatory action research: Methodological and ethical issues. *Women's Studies International Forum, 23*(1), 89–105.

Gibbs, A. (2003). Writing and the flesh of others. *Australian Feminist Studies, 18*(42), 309–319.

Greenhouse, C. J., & Mertz, E. (Eds.). (2002). *Ethnography in unstable places: Everyday lives in contexts of dramatic political change*. Durham, NC: Duke University Press.

Grosfoguel, R., & Cervantes-Rodríguez, A. M. (Eds.). (2002). *The modern/colonial/capitalist world-system in the twentieth century: Global processes, antisystemic movements, and the geopolitics of knowledge*. Westport, CT: Greenwood Press.

Haraway, D. (1988). Situated knowledges: The science question in feminism and the privilege of partial perspective. *Feminist Studies, 14*(3), 575–599.

Harding, H. A. (2005). "City girl": A portrait of a successful white teacher. *Qualitative Inquiry, 11*(1), 52–80.

Harding, J. (1997). Bodies at risk: Sex, surveillance and hormone replacement therapy. In A. Petersen & R. Bunton (Eds.), *Foucault, health and medicine* (pp. 134–150). London: Routledge.

Harding, S. (1987). Introduction: Is there a feminist method? In S. Harding (Ed.), *Feminism and methodology* (pp. 1–14). Bloomington: Indiana University Press.

Hawkesworth, M. E. (1990). *Beyond oppression*. New York: Continuum.

Henderson, J. (2002). The tidiest revolution: Regulative feminist autobiography and the defacement of the Australian women's movement. *Australian Literary Studies, 20*(3), 178–191.

Horne, S., Mathews, S., Detrie, P., Burke, M., & Cook, B. (2001). Look it up under "f": Dialogues of emerging and experiences feminists. *Women & Therapy: A Feminist Quarterly, 23*(2), 5–18.

Humble, A. J., & Morgaine, C. A. (2002). Placing feminist education within the three paradigms of knowledge and action. *Family Relations, 51*(3), 199–205.

Hyams, M. (2004). Hearing girls' silences: Thoughts on the politics and practices of a feminist method of group discussion. *Gender, Place & Culture, 11*(1), 105–119.

Johnston, H. B., Ved, R., Lyall, N., & Agarwal, K. (2003). Where do rural women obtain postabortion care? The case of Uttar Pradesh, India. *International Family Planning Perspectives, 29*(4), 182–187.

Kindon, S. (2003). Participatory video in geographic research: A feminist practice of looking? *Area, 35*(2), 142–153.

Knapp, K. K. (2000). Still office flowers: Japanese women betrayed by the Equal Employment Opportunity Law. In A. K. Wing (Ed.), *Global *critical race feminism: An international reader* (pp. 409–423). New York: New York University Press.

Koikari, M., & Hippensteele, S. K. (2000). Negotiating feminist survival: Gender, race and power in academe. *Violence Against Women, 6*(11), 1269–1296.

Kwan, M.-P. (2002). Feminist visualization: Re-envisioning GIS as a method in feminist geographic research. *Annals of the Association of American Geographers, 92*(4), 645–661.

Kwan, M.-P., & Moss, P. (2003, March). *Women, new information technologies and the geographies of everyday life.* Paper presented at the annual meeting of the Association of American Geographers (AAG), New Orleans, LA.

Lanser, S. (1999). Feminist criticism, "The Yellow Wallpaper," and the politics of color in America. In S. Hesse-Biber, C. Gilmartin, & R. Lydenberg (Eds.), *Feminist approaches to theory and methodology: An interdisciplinary reader* (pp. 195–215). New York: Oxford University Press.

Larson, J. L. (1999). Josephine Butler's *Catharine of Siena*: Writing (auto)biography as a feminist spiritual practice. *Christianity and Literature, 4894,* 445–471.

Lather, P. A. (1991). *Getting smart: Feminist research and pedagogy with/in the postmodern.* New York: Routledge.

Lawrence-Lightfoot, S. (2005). Reflections on portraiture: A dialogue between art and science. *Qualitative Inquiry, 11*(1), 3–15.

Lawrence-Lightfoot, S., & Davis, J. H. (1997). *The art and science of portraiture.* San Francisco: Jossey-Bass.

Lentin, R. (2000). Constructing the self in narrative: Feminist research as auto/biography. In A. Byrne & R. Lentin (Eds.), *(Re)searching women: Feminist research methodologies in the social sciences in Ireland* (pp. 247–264). Dublin, Ireland: Institute of Public Administration.

Letherby, G. (2004a). Quoting and counting: An auto-biographical response to Oakley. *Sociology, 38*(1), 175–189.

Letherby, G. (2004b). Reply to Ann Oakley. *Sociology, 38*(1), 193–194.

Lock, M. (2004). Living cadavers and the calculation of death. *Body & Society, 10*(2–3), 135–152.

Lopez, A. S. (2000). Comparative analysis of women's issues: Toward a contextualized methodology.

In A. K. Wing (Ed.), *Global critical race feminism: An international reader* (pp. 67–80). New York: New York University Press.

Lynch, K. (2000). The role of emancipatory research in the academy. In A. Byrne & R. Lentin (Eds.), *(Re)searching women: Feminist research methodologies in the social sciences in Ireland* (pp. 73–104). Dublin, Ireland: Institute of Public Administration.

Magarey, S., & Round, K. (2004). From autobiography to biography: Roma the First. *Australian Feminist Studies, 19*(43), 87–101.

McDowell, L. (1992). Doing gender: Feminism, feminists and research methods in human geography. *Transactions, Institute of British Geographers, 17,* 399–416.

Mies, M. (1983). Towards a methodology for feminist research. In G. Bowles & R. Duelli Klein (Eds.), *Theories of women's studies* (pp. 117–139). London: Routledge & Kegan Paul.

Moss, P. (2002). Taking on, thinking about, and doing feminist research in geography. In P. Moss (Ed.), *Feminist geography in practice: Research and methods* (pp. 1–17). London: Blackwell.

Moss, P. (2003). *In search of housing for women in transition . . . Notes from focus sessions with four groups.* Unpublished manuscript, Studies in Policy & Practice, University of Victoria, Canada.

Moss, P. (2005). A bodily notion of research: Power, difference, and specificity in feminist methodology. In L. Nelson & J. Seager (Eds.), *A companion to feminist geography* (pp. 41–59). London: Blackwell.

Moss, P., & McMahon, M. (2000). Between a flake and a strident bitch: Making "it" count in the academy. *Resources for Feminist Research/ Documentation sur la Recherche Féministe, 28*(1–2), 15–32.

Mouffe, C. (1992). Feminism, citizenship and radical democratic politics. In J. Butler & J. W. Scott (Eds.), *Feminists theorize the political* (pp. 369–384). New York: Routledge.

Mountz, A., Miyares, I. M., Wright, R., & Bailey, A. J. (2003). Methodologically becoming: Power, knowledge and team research. *Gender, Place & Culture, 10*(1), 29–46.

Murphy, K. (2001). What does John Gray have to say to feminism? *Continuum: Journal of Media & Cultural Studies, 15*(2), 159–167.

Naples, N. A. (2003). *Feminism and method: Ethnography, discourse analysis, and activist research.* New York: Routledge.

Oakley, A. (2004). Response to quoting and counting: An autobiographical response to Oakley. *Sociology, 38*(1), 191–192.

Pillow, W. (2003). "Bodies are dangerous": Using feminist genealogy as policy studies methodology. *Journal of Education Policy, 18*(2), 145–159.

Potts, A. (2004). Deleuze on Viagra (or, What can a "Viagra-body" do?). *Body & Society, 10*(1), 17–36.

Pratt, G., & Kirby, E. (2003). Performing nurses: BC union's nurses theatre project. *ACME: An International E-Journal for Critical Geographies, 2*(1), 14–32.

Probyn, E. (2004). Teaching bodies: Affects in the classroom. *Body & Society, 10*(4), 21–43.

*Professional Geographer.* (1995). Should women count? The role of quantitative methodology in feminist geographic research. *Professional Geographer, 47,* 426–466.

Ramazanoğlu, C. (with Holland, J.). (2002). *Feminist methodology: Challenges and choices.* Thousand Oaks, CA: Sage.

Reinharz, S. (1992). *Feminist methods in social research.* New York: Oxford University Press.

Ribbens, J., & Edwards, R. (Eds.). (1998). *Feminist dilemmas in qualitative research: Public knowledge and private lives.* London: Sage.

Riley, R., & Manias, E. (2003). Snap-shots of live theatre: The use of photography to research governance in operating room nursing. *Nursing Inquiry, 10*(2), 81–90.

Rivera-Fuentes, C. (2000). Doing sym/bio/graphy with Yasna. In T. Cosslett, C. Lury, & P. Summerfield (Eds.), *Feminism and autobiography: Texts, theories, methods* (pp. 247–251). London: Routledge.

Rose, G. (1997). Situating knowledges: Positionality, reflexivities and other tactics. *Progress in Human Geography, 21,* 305–320.

Roulston, K. (2001). Data analysis and "theorizing as ideology." *Qualitative Research, 1*(3), 279–302.

Ryan, L. (2004). Mother and daughter feminist, 1969–1973. Or why didn't Edna Ryan join women's liberation? *Australian Feminist Studies, 19*(43), 75–85.

Sandoval, C. (2000). *Methodology of the oppressed.* Minneapolis: University of Minnesota Press.

Schuurman, N., & Pratt, G. (2002). Care of the subject: Feminism and critiques of GIS. *Gender, Place and Culture, 9*(3), 291–299.

Scott, J. W. (2002). Feminist reverberations. *Differences: A Journal of Feminist Cultural Studies, 13*(3), 1–23.

Shildrick, M. (1997). *Leaky bodies and boundaries: Feminism, postmodernism and (bio)ethics.* London: Routledge.

Shildrick, M. (2002). *Embodying the monster: Encounters with the vulnerable self.* London: Sage.

Smith, D. (1974). Theorizing as ideology. In R. Turner (Ed.), *Ethnomethodology* (pp. 41–44). Harmondsworth: Penguin.

Solórzano, D. G., & Yosso, T. J. (2002). Critical race methodology: Counter-storytelling as an analytical framework for education research. *Qualitative Inquiry, 8*(1), 23–44.

Speer, S. A. (2002). What can conversation analysis contribute to feminist methodology? Putting reflexivity into practice. *Discourse & Society, 13*(6), 783–803.

Squire, S. (2002). The personal and the political: Writing the theorist's body. *Australian Feminist Studies, 17*(37), 55–64.

Stanley, L., & Wise, S. (2000). But the empress has no clothes! Some awkward questions about the "missing revolution" in feminist theory. *Feminist Theory, 1*(3), 261–288.

Stokoe, E. H., & Weatherall, A. (2002). Gender, language, conversation analysis and feminism. *Discourse & Society, 13*(6), 707–713.

Sullivan, N. (2002). Queer material(ities): Lyotard, language and the libidinal body. *Australian Feminist Studies, 17*(37), 43–54.

Teghtsoonian, K. (2003). W(h)ither women's equality? Neoliberalism, institutional change and public policy in British Columbia. *Policy, Organisation and Society, 22*(1), 26–47.

Valentine, G. (2002). People like us: Negotiating sameness and difference in the research process. In P. Moss (Ed.), *Feminist geography in practice: Research and methods* (pp. 116–126). London: Blackwell.

Van Steveren, I. (1997). Focus groups: Contributing to a gender-aware methodology. *Feminist Economics, 3*(2), 131–135.

Visweswaran, K. (1994). *Fictions of feminist ethnography.* Minneapolis: University of Minnesota Press.

Walls, E. M. (2002). "A little afraid of the women today": The Victorian New Woman and the rhetoric of British modernism. *Rhetoric Review, 21*(3), 229–246.

Wang, C. C., & Redwood-Jones, Y. A. (2001). Photovoice ethics: Perspectives from Flint Photovoice. *Health Education & Behavior, 28*(5), 560–572.

Wilkinson, S. (1999). How useful are focus groups in feminist research? In R. S. Barbour & J. Kitzinger (Eds.), *Developing focus groups research: Politics, theory and practice* (pp. 64–78). Thousand Oaks, CA: Sage.

Wolf, D. L. (1996). Situating feminist dilemmas in fieldwork. In D. L. Wolf (Ed.), *Feminist dilemmas in fieldwork* (pp. 1–55). Boulder, CO: Westview Press.

Ylönen, M. E. (2003). Bodily flashes of dancing women: Dance as a method of inquiry. *Qualitative Inquiry, 9*(4), 554–568.

Young, I. M. (1990). *Justice and the politics of difference*. Princeton, NJ: Princeton University Press.

# 18

## FEMINIST PERSPECTIVES ON SOCIAL MOVEMENT RESEARCH

SARAH MADDISON

## THE FIELD OF SOCIAL MOVEMENT RESEARCH

The field of social movement studies has, at least in part, been characterised by intense debates about the validity and usefulness of various theoretical approaches. For some scholars, this conflict has amounted to nothing more than "theory bashing" (see, e.g., Lofland, 1993). However, in their recent collection devoted to methods of social movement research, Bert Klandermans and Suzanne Staggenborg (2002) argue that this conflict has in fact served to advance the study of social movements, particularly where an openness to new approaches has been accompanied by a willingness to test new ideas in the field (p. ix). Importantly in this context, feminist social movement scholars such as Verta Taylor (2000; Rupp & Taylor, 1987; Taylor & Rupp, 2002), Myra Marx Ferree (1987; Ferree & Martin, 1995; Ferree & Merrill, 2000; Ferree & Gamson, 2003), Nancy Whittier (1995), Mary Margaret Fonow (2003), and Belinda Robnett (1997), among others, have brought a lively empirical rigour to the field, in ways that have provided an important critique of the gendered assumptions underpinning much previous social movement research.

To some extent, empirical studies of social movements have mirrored the much-discussed conflicts between the European and North American schools of theory. Methods developed in Europe include Alberto Melucci's (1989, 1996) emphasis on videotaped focus group discussion and Alain Touraine's (1981, 2000) highly innovative "intervention sociologiques." A sociological intervention as outlined by Touraine involves the researcher providing analytical feedback and even direction to social movement groups based on their observations of the group's activities. This method of direct intervention is designed to "bring actors to 'discover' the highest possible meaning of their own action" (Touraine, 2000, p. 905). Although this method has been used to produce compelling results by scholars such as Kevin McDonald (1999) in his study of young peoples' "struggles for subjectivity," these methods have not gained wide acceptance among North American social movement researchers (Johnston, 2002, p. 83).

Similarly, methods that were developed by resource mobilization and political process scholars, such as Shorter and Tilly's (1974) method of "protest event analysis," have not been taken up by researchers working in the European "new" social movement approach. Protest event analysis uses newspapers, police files, and reports of press agencies as data sources in which the protest event itself is the unit of analysis (Klandermans & Staggenborg, 2002, p. xii). The focus of protest event analysis is on the "quantification of many properties of protest, such as frequency, timing and duration, location, claims, size, forms, carriers, and targets, as well as immediate consequences and reactions" (Koopmans & Rucht, 2002, p. 231). The macrodimensional focus of the North American scholars and the microdimensional focus of much European scholarship saw research on the two continents take divergent paths.

Other differences have emerged as, over time, scholars' attitudes towards social movements have changed, and theoretical developments have created a range of different "lenses" through which these phenomena may be observed and interpreted (Goodwin & Jasper, 2003, p. 5). James Jasper (1997) describes some of these lenses:

> Quantitative approaches may give special attention to resources, the most measurable dimension. Historical approaches might recommend closer attention to political structures and the strategic interactions by which they are created and transformed. Ethnographic and participant research allow more than a crude reckoning of explicit beliefs. (p. 334)

One outcome of these differences is that the field of social movement scholarship remains refreshingly free of "methodological dogmatism" (Klandermans & Staggenborg, 2002, p. xii). Although David Meyer (2002, p. 3) advocates greater connection between scholars researching social movements in order to create a "larger whole" that is as "inherently collective" as the object of our study, it would seem to me that given the multifaceted complexity of social movements as an empirical phenomenon, a plurality of methodological approaches must remain an imperative.

My own research, as outlined in this chapter, takes a feminist cultural approach. I consider it crucial that the field of social movement studies should involve activists—as the subjects of our research—both in the research process and as a critical audience. Such involvement will

inevitably focus our attention on our "local knowledge" rather than our "general knowledge" (Jasper, 1997, p. 377) as it develops in dialogue with the activists themselves, from their perspective and giving them a voice in the process. The cultural lens brings into focus a far wider range of social movement activity, including those activities that take place quietly, "behind the scenes," and yet without which no publicly visible movement could be possible. Such focus, on what Melucci (1985) calls "submerged networks" (p. 800), constitutes social movement actors as "diffuse and decentralized" (Taylor, 2000, p. 222) and takes account of periods away from the public spotlight.

Moreover, such a perspective does much to explain the continuity and survival of social movements around the world. For example, in their study of the survival of the women's movement in the United States and the United Kingdom, Joyce Gelb and Vivien Hart (1999) argue that the maintenance of "networks of women [that] have been sustained locally and nationally and also across differences of ethnicity, nationality, sexuality, and class" (p. 181) has been vital for movement continuity. This perspective recognises that social movements need to adopt different "structural forms and strategies" at different periods depending on whether they are "in a stage of formation, success, continuation and survival or decline" (Rupp & Taylor, 1987, p. 9).

This chapter discusses my approach to the study of social movements as one that is feminist, cultural, constructivist, and grounded in standpoint theory. My perspective is one that begins by acknowledging and privileging an *activist standpoint*. In explaining this approach I will consider the intersections between feminist standpoint theory and the idea of social movement collective identity *as a process*. In the following sections, I will consider the importance of feminist theory to social movement research and argue for the importance of an activist standpoint in the study of movements. I will then outline my own methods for researching activism from this perspective, specifically through the case studies of two submerged networks of contemporary young feminist activists in Australia, considering the ways in which feminism has influenced my approach to these methods.

# FEMINIST SOCIAL MOVEMENT RESEARCH

A feminist approach to the study of social movements remains a challenging and important enterprise. Verta Taylor and Nancy Whittier (1998) argue,

> Analyzing social movements as simultaneously political and gendered raises sweeping and exciting challenges for both fields. Scholars grounded in social movements and gender have begun to bring together the concerns and analytical approaches of the two fields. . . . Feminist reconceptualizations of the state, cultural hegemony, discourse, identity, and organization challenge social movement approaches that treat these institutions as gender neutral. (p. 622)

I concur with Taylor and Whittier's suggestion that a feminist approach that takes account of gender, along with its intersections with race, class, ethnicity, and sexuality, and places these concerns at the centre of social movement analysis "poses unresolved questions" (p. 622). Such an approach suggests considerable challenges to previous understandings of social movement processes. A desire to challenge gender-neutral assumptions about social movements has been one of the important factors in shaping my own research practice.

There has been a considerable amount of feminist scholarship that has considered social research methods in the light of feminist epistemological understandings (see, e.g., Stanley, 1990; Fonow & Cook, 1991, inter alia). Indeed, questions of method and methodology continue to engage feminist scholars such as Jane Ribbens and Rosalind Edwards (1998), Anne Byrne and Ronit Lentin (2000), and Caroline Ramazanoğlu and Janet Holland (2002), among others. Shulamit Reinharz (1992) suggests certain themes that are present in much discussion of feminist social research, specifically, feminism is a perspective, not a research method; feminist research uses a multiplicity of research methods and involves an ongoing criticism of nonfeminist scholarship guided by feminist theory; feminist research may be transdisciplinary; feminist research aims to create social change and strives to represent human diversity;

feminist research includes the researcher as a person and frequently attempts to develop special relations with the people studied (in interactive research); and, finally, feminist research frequently defines a special relation with the reader (p. 240).

That Reinharz specifically claims that feminist research aims to create social change underscores the importance and usefulness of considering feminist approaches to the study of activism. Feminist research methodologies are often "impelled by a concern with social justice" and therefore "are designed to reveal the gender problematic through prioritising women's lived experience of the social, telling this experience 'in their own voice'" (Byrne & Lentin, 2000, p. 7). Iris Marion Young (1997) also argues that feminism is "a mode of questioning, an orientation and set of commitments" that entails "a commitment to ameliorating . . . harms and disadvantages" that women experience (p. 3). Young also points out, however, that applying this commitment to feminist scholarship should not be understood as implying "a claim to common attributes, circumstances or harms that all women share" (p. 6). In other words describing a commitment to social justice through feminist research and scholarship should not be read as a universalising claim regarding women's needs or lived experiences. Nevertheless, this commitment to social justice suggests that feminist approaches to research have much to contribute to the field of social movement research more generally.

As Jennifer Somerville (1997) points out, "Feminism as a social movement is rich in descriptive, historical accounts," but these accounts are generally "atheoretical," and very few use the concept of social movement "analytically" (pp. 673–674). Without exception, recent examinations of Australian feminist activism (such as Bulbeck, 1997; Kaplan, 1996; Lake, 1999) start from the assumption that the women's movement is a defined object for study that can be explored in terms of history, goals, and achievements. According to Alberto Melucci (1995), however, this approach is inadequate because it can never

> answer the questions of how social actors come to form a collectivity and recognise themselves as

being part of it; how they maintain themselves over time; how acting together makes sense for the participants in a social movement; or how the meaning of collective action derives from structural preconditions or from the sum of individual motives. (p. 42)

Constructivist "new" social movement theory offers an approach to answering these questions, both for activists and for researchers. Melucci (1996) argues that by shifting from a "monolithic and metaphysical idea of collective actors" (p. 43) to a more "processual" approach that uses the concept of collective identity as an analytical tool, we are able to better understand how it is that collective mobilisation can occur and be sustained in complex societies (Melucci, 1995, 1996).

## COMMON GROUND: FEMINIST EPISTEMOLOGIES AND COLLECTIVE IDENTITY AS A PROCESS

My approach to the study of social movements is—first and foremost—informed by feminist epistemological assumptions. In other words, I begin with the assumption that knowledge and the production of knowledge are inherently gendered. Further, I remain convinced that feminist epistemologies have enormous potential to subvert and transgress traditional, disciplinary knowledge, creating new spaces for theory and research practice (Chapman, 1995; Reinharz, 1992). The common ground I suggest in this section is that, to me, there seems a very obvious and important link to be made between the subversive potential of feminist *thinking* and the subversive potential of social movement *activism*. Feminist social movement research has an outstanding capacity to draw these links in ways that can only enrich the field of social movement studies.

Despite feminist (and other) challenges, there is still considerable faith in the universal, sex-neutral subject and in neutral, transparent methodologies and techniques whereby the product (i.e., knowledge) is also considered value neutral (Longino, 1993). These assumptions operate to maintain belief in a "reality" or a "truth" that can be discovered through rational

knowledge (Silverman, 1992) and thus create a hegemony of all aspects of knowledge: what it is, how it is made, and who can make it. These assumptions do not recognise that knowledge *does things*; it is an activity, not just thought and reflection (Grosz, 1993). Given this implicit, but often unrecognised, control over knowledge production, it is hardly surprising that the types of knowledges that have been produced, particularly about gender (and in this case gender and activism), have reinforced and reified the same paradigms within which they were made.

The feminist manoeuvre of valorising experience is a radical departure from these terms and these ways of validating knowledge. This "reversal strategy" assumes that women's experience is drastically different from academic knowledges and that it potentially offers a critique of these knowledges (Waldby, 1995, p. 16). However, these methodological departures have been criticised for making certain assumptions about the nature of experience, which, it is argued by critics, should not be understood as either transparent or unequivocal. This is not the same criticism as the rationalist dismissal of experience as being entirely perspectival and without objective merit. Rather, it points to the fact that choosing to validate a particular standpoint as epistemologically privileged requires social theory in order to understand social positioning and powerlessness and thus grant this privilege (Longino, 1993). Here the site of epistemic privilege shifts from the group as defined objectively (i.e., women) to the group defining itself subjectively as a collective political agent or as holders of a particular form of political consciousness (in this case, feminists). The claim is not to a universal "women's standpoint" but to a politicised and partial "feminist standpoint."

If a feminist standpoint can be described as being "derived from a committed feminist exploration of women's experiences of oppression" (Stanley & Wise, 1990, p. 27), I am proposing that an *activist standpoint* can be conceived as a transformative exploration of activists' experiences of *resistance* to oppression. In this theoretical context, Alberto Melucci's processual approach to understanding movement collective identity can allow for the standpoints of feminist and other activists to be revealed through an analysis of the ways in which they construct their own experiences and understandings. Melucci's approach offers a theory and method that can, in turn, illuminate standpoint theory, revealing the processes behind the articulation of a politicised collectivity.

The process of collective identity is one of the most significant and yet most misunderstood elements of the "new" social movement approach to analysing collective action. In large part, the misunderstandings surrounding the term arise from the use of the word *identity* with its psychological overtones, and a problem arises when scholars overly psychologise the concept of collective identity[1] rather than acknowledge its fundamentally political character. As Stacey Young (1997) points out, this "misses the efforts of movements (particularly the feminist and the lesbian, bisexual, and gay movements) to analyse in social and political terms oppression and resistance grounded in identity" (p. 20). In similar terms, Aldon Morris (1992) argues that differing forms of what he terms "political consciousness" arise from different standpoints or real experiences of particular forms of domination: racial consciousness as a response to racial domination, gender consciousness as a response to male domination, and so on (pp. 360–372).

Collective identity should not be understood as a "thing to be studied" (Melucci, 1995, p. 46) but rather as a tool for understanding processes that produce a set of reflexively constructed and negotiated definitions regarding the "field of opportunities and constraints offered to collective action" (Melucci, 1985, p. 793). These processes, which occur in specific contexts, organisations, and locations (Whittier, 2002, p. 298) that may or may not constrain diversity, are "experienced [by movement participants] as an action rather than a situation" (Melucci, 1995, p. 51), in that they constitute an important function in and of themselves. Collective identity in this sense is "fluid and relational," involving acts of "perception and construction" (Polletta & Jasper, 2001, p. 298). Understanding processes of collective identity in this way allows us to "get at" the ways in which social movements determine such issues as membership and activities (Laraña, Johnston, & Gusfield, 1994) or agree on the fundamental question of "who they are" (Taylor & Whittier, 1992, p. 105) while also allowing for the constantly debated and

contested nature of these agreements. As Whittier (1995) points out,

> In the process of constructing a collective identity, challenging groups adopt labels for themselves (such as "feminist"), draw lines between insiders and outsiders, and develop interpretive frameworks, a political consciousness through which members understand the world. Of course "collective identities" exist only as far as real people agree upon, enact, argue over, and internalise them; group definitions have no life of their own, and they are constantly changing rather than static. (p. 15)

Ultimately, the fact that we are able to observe the action of social movements in the form of organisational structures *presupposes* processes of collective identity and is therefore a goal in its own right (Gamson, 1992; Melucci, 1995).

Conflict and disagreement play an important role in processes of collective identity. Jodi Dean (1997) argues that in feminist politics, for example, differences between women have often been "experienced as conflicts that threatened both the integrative role of the groups and the individual woman's sense of self" (p. 245). To many participants these experiences of conflict appeared to clash with notions of unity, solidarity, and sisterhood that were deemed essential to successful feminist praxis and, therefore, the conflicts themselves were repressed or smothered wherever possible. Attempts to repress conflict, however, do not recognise its significance as a creative force in social movement processes of collective identity. In the case of the women's movement, Dean argues that

> there is no "feminism" to be defined and solidified once and for all. Instead, it is always in process, the continuing accomplishment of our discussions and reflections. So, rather than viewing criticism as potentially disruptive, a solidarity of differences employs it to further our recognition of each other. (p. 254)

In other words, through conflicts over differences to do with identity ("race," class, sexuality, and age), meaning, goals, and strategy, movement actors are able to conceive of new forms of social existence and produce new understandings of social, cultural, and political life that have implications beyond the movement itself. It is in the reflexive processes of collective identity that these conflicts are able to occur. Further, these conflicts indicate a movement's continued relevance and vitality and, as such, should be seen as both productive and integral to movement survival, rather than as something to be resolved and put aside. It is my contention that this attention to conflict as a constituent component of feminist and other processes of collective identity goes some way towards overcoming the perceived problem with the feminist standpoint, that being the failure of such a perspective to acknowledge the existence of multiple standpoints. Any collective identity developed in any movement must make space for a range of standpoints, which may in turn be debated and contested as a part of these processes. This process makes women's experiences explicit and offers a lens for revealing not only the differences between women but also the ways in which these differences and conflicts can work to produce a collective—yet continually contested—identity.

David Snow (2001) is critical of this focus on social movement processes over what he perceives as the end result or "product" of these processes. Snow argues that it is "both questionable and unnecessary to contend that the process is more fundamental than the product to understanding the character and functionality of collective identity" (p. 3). However, this perspective implies that, over time, processes of collective identity may produce an identity that is a stable and homogeneous "social object" allowing Snow to argue,

> Although collective identities can congeal in various aggregations and contexts, they appear not to do so on a continuous basis historically. Instead, their emergence and vitality appear to be associated with conditions of sociocultural change or challenge, socio-economic and political exclusion, and political breakdown and renewal, thus suggesting that they cluster historically in social space. (p. 4)

Such a claim can only be made, however, if one views collective identity as an *object*. As a

*process* collective identity can be seen to be "vital" (if not "emerging" in the sense of being publicly visible) even in times of movement decline or abeyance and in between-the-waves moments such as the one in which the contemporary Australian women's movement is currently located. While this claim may not be true of all social movements all of the time, an understanding of collective identity as a process does not restrict the study of it to periods of high profile social movement activism.

Whittier (1995) argues that the concept of collective identity is vital to understanding "new" social movements, such as the women's movement, that are engaged in politics beyond institutional transformation. It is this lens that allows researchers to recognise movement continuity and to identify struggles that occur in culture and everyday life (p. 24). Melucci (1995) outlines the processes of collective identity as requiring the following factors:

1. "Cognitive definitions concerning the ends, means, and field of action" that are constructed through interaction and compromise

2. "A network of active relationships" of which styles of organisation, leadership, and communication are constitutive parts

3. "A degree of emotional investment, which enables individuals to feel like part of a common unity" (pp. 44–45)[2]

It is through a reflexive engagement with these factors that social movements are able to present an empirical unity. But Melucci (1995) emphasises that this apparent unity should be considered a "result rather than a starting point, a fact to be explained rather than evidence" (p. 43). Continued debate about these factors is an indication of a movement's ongoing vitality and relevance or that the collective identity in question, such as "feminist," still "means something" (Whittier, 1995, p. 18). Collective identity suggests that structural position is not enough to mobilise a group's members; rather, it is the continual reformulation and discussion in groups about "sameness and difference, homogeneity and diversity" that determine the "central questions" of personal, social, and political action (Whittier, 1995, pp. 56–58).

The nexus of this processual, constructivist methodological approach to collective identity with the feminist standpoint epistemology discussed above allows for a privileging of the activist standpoint that can guide research practice in this field. Recognising this common methodological ground can in turn lead to a consideration of *how* such research might be conducted and how research data may be analysed.

## RESEARCHING CONTEMPORARY YOUNG FEMINIST ACTIVISM

The research project that I will focus on for the remainder of this chapter emerged from my desire to begin documenting the types of activism being practised by young women in the contemporary Australian women's movement. In the mid- to late 1990s, the Australian women's movement, like the women's movements in the United States and the United Kingdom, had been consumed by suggestions of intergenerational warfare. Questions had been raised about the presence and visibility of young women in the movement, and assertions that some forms of feminist praxis were "good," and some were not, began to undermine the value of the important work being done in this "between the waves" moment. My hope was that by developing an understanding of what young women are doing *now* we might begin to conceptualise what a resurgence of highly visible feminist activism might look like in the future. Further, I hoped this knowledge would assist both older and younger feminists to recognise their points of connection and similarity as well as their points of difference.

On the basis of these hopes, I posed a number of specific research questions:

1. What role are young women playing in constructing and maintaining the contemporary Australian women's movement?

2. How do social movements sustain themselves during periods without highly visible activism?

3. How can we distinguish processes of social movement continuity from the failure or demise of a movement?

4. What role does conflict between women have in feminist processes of collective identity?

5. How do these processes facilitate social movement continuity?

From the outset I was clear that this would be a qualitative study. I was not interested in "how many?" young women were in the Australian women's movement (nor "where?" nor "when?"), but rather, I wanted to know *how* certain groups of young women were constructing themselves as a collectivity within the Australian women's movement and how they dealt with conflict as a part of their processes of collective identity. Bringing a feminist standpoint to the study of collective identity would facilitate a unique qualitative methodological approach to answering these questions, specifically by seeking to understand "political actors as conscious social beings who shape the world of politics as well as being shaped by it" (Devine, 1995). Fiona Devine suggests that qualitative methods "capture meaning, process, and context" and are most appropriately used in research where the aim is to "explore people's subjective experiences and the meanings they attach to those experiences." Devine also suggests that qualitative methods are appropriate in the study of processes, thereby making them appropriate to my concern with activists' processes of collective identity. Minichiello, Aroni, Timewell, and Alexander (1995) add that qualitative research allows for an understanding of how experience, feelings, meaning, and process in turn influence the *actions* of research participants (p. 10).

With this in mind I chose two case studies for this research, in very different locations, with two very different groups of young women. The first was a campus-based group, the Cross Campus Women's Network (CCWN), operating primarily in metropolitan Sydney, and second was the Young Women Who Are Parents Network (YWWAPN), operating from a women's health centre in an economically disadvantaged suburb on Sydney's southwestern outskirts. The two groups represented different strands and trajectories of the Australian women's movement. The CCWN represented the strand of the women's movement that both grew out of and remains a constituent part of the student movement. Both the CCWN and the student movement consider themselves to be a part of the broad left in Australia and work in coalition with other groups and movements across a range of issues. By contrast, the YWWAPN represented the strand of the movement that developed into the women's health movement and remains concerned with service provision and local community development with women. Both groups were highly politicised but in relation to very different issues. The ages of the women in both groups ranged from 17 up to 23. The two cases provided interesting comparative material because of the differing socioeconomic status of the participants and the diverse range of issues that concern them. As "critical cases" (Snow & Trom, 2002, p. 158), they suggest particular features that are of empirical significance rather than being seen as in any way typical or representative of young women in the contemporary Australian women's movement.

The following sections detail the research methods in this project.

## Feminist Case Study Methodology

In considering the role of qualitative methods in the study of social movements, Kathleen Blee and Verta Taylor (2002) suggest that these methods are often used to "uncover the essential features of a case or number of cases" (p. 111) and that these cases may then be used to exemplify "more general theoretical processes pertaining to social movements" (p. 111). David Snow and Danny Trom (2002) suggest that case studies should not be understood as a research method but rather as "a research strategy that is associated with a number of data-gathering methods or procedures" (p. 151). Snow and Trom provide a workable and clear definition of a case study as including the following:

(a) investigation and analysis of an instance or variant of some bounded social phenomenon that (b) seeks to generate a richly detailed and "thick" elaboration of the phenomenon studied through (c) the use and triangulation of multiple methods or procedures that include but are not limited to qualitative techniques. (p. 147)

The aim of case study research should be to produce "a holistic—that is, a richly or thickly contextualized and embedded—understanding of the phenomenon or system under investigation" (Snow & Trom, 2002, p. 150). This goal and the definition above nicely summarise my approach to the case studies in this project. In addition, I would argue that, as Reinharz (1992) points out, "case studies are important for putting women on the map of social life" (p. 174). More specifically, one of the goals of this research was to put contemporary young feminist activists on the "map" of the Australian women's movement.

Feminist interest in case study research stems in part from a desire to document women's experiences and achievements "for future secondary analysis and future action on behalf of women" (Reinharz, 1992, p. 171). Where the subject of the research is the women's movement itself, a case study approach is particularly appropriate, given the often dispersed nature of movement organisations and groups. As Nancy Whittier (1995) points out in her study of the radical women's movement in the United States, the fact that the movement has traditionally been based in "grassroots, loosely organized groups" means that "any study of radical feminism is thus, by necessity, a local case study" (p. 5). Similarly, in Australia, there is no centralised organisation that can claim to constitute the women's movement, nor has such an organisation ever really existed.[3] Further, the questions with which this research was concerned arose largely from the apparent invisibility of groups of young feminist activists to the broader women's movement. These case studies, therefore, were an effort to increase the visibility of young women in the movement by documenting the work that they were doing.

## Participant Observation

To build up a suitably holistic and "thick" elaboration of these cases, I chose to engage in participant observation with both groups of young women. While there is, as Paul Lichterman (2002) notes, "more than one way to do participant observation" (p. 119), the general intention is for researchers to "immerse" themselves into the social setting of their field site, thereby "observing people in their own milieux and participating in their activities" (Devine, 1995, p. 137). Participant observation "opens a window on lived experience"

(Lichterman, 2002, p. 121), providing a unique source of research data. Lichterman describes it as follows:

> Listening to people talking in their own settings, on their own time, participant-observers have the opportunity to glean the everyday meanings, tacit assumptions, ordinary customs, practical rules of thumb that organize people's everyday lives. (p. 138)

As Nancy Whittier (1995) notes, it is through the observable "concrete lived experience of organizing a challenge together, not an abstract 'spirit of the times,'" that processes of collective identity are revealed to a researcher and movement participants negotiate their "shared world-view" (p. 17). Of particular importance to this study was the fact that participant observation allowed for a unique perspective on the influence of social movements over time. As Lichterman (2002) argues, through participant observation social movement researchers can observe the "enduring influence of a movement on everyday life, years after the movement's height of visibility and political influence" (p. 141).

I engaged in participant observation with both groups in this study over a 12-month period during 2001 and into early 2002. In the case of the CCWN, I attended their fortnightly meetings and participated in other activities such as mail outs and planning meetings. I also attended the annual Network of Women Students Australia (NOWSA) conference, appropriately titled "Which Way Forward for Women's Liberation?" in which I participated by giving a paper and through discussion on the conference floor and in workshops. In addition, I participated on the e-mail lists both for the CCWN and for NOWSA, which were active sites of contestation to do with the group's processes of collective identity. In the case of the YWWAPN, I spent 1 day a week in Campbelltown, where I attended network meetings and engaged more informally with the young women in the program. Over the course of the year, I participated with both staff and young women in the program through activities such as working with the young women to produce an orientation booklet for new members, conducting program evaluation, and running a workshop on "gender issues" as a part of their Opportunities and Choices training course. Through participant observation, I also identified key informants who were invited to participate in in-depth interviews towards the end of the research process.

## In-Depth Interviewing

Lichterman (2002) argues that participant observation evidence and interview evidence can be combined "judiciously to create a richer account of lived experience" (p. 141). According to Blee and Taylor (2002), an interview is simply "a guided conversation"; however, the difference between an interview and other forms of conversation is the need on the part of the interviewer to "elicit specific kinds of information" (p. 92). It is important to note the distinct difference in method between structured or survey interviews that are used in quantitative research and the type of qualitative, unstructured interviews conducted in the fieldwork for this project. Feminists such as Ann Oakley (1981) suggest that structured interviews rest on positivist assumptions about research and can be disempowering for participants. In contrast, feminists have written extensively on the benefits of unstructured interviews for providing "access to people's ideas, thoughts and memories in their own words rather than in the words of the researcher," which can be seen as an important historical corrective to the marginalisation of women's voices in traditional research (Reinharz, 1992, p. 19). Minichiello et al. (1995) argue that this type of interviewing "empowers participants in the same way as other forms of participatory research" (p. 7).

In contrast to the use of structured interviews in the study of social movements, Blee and Taylor (2002) suggest that unstructured or semi-structured interviews "provide greater breadth and depth of information [and] the opportunity to discover the respondent's experiences and interpretations of reality" (p. 92). They argue that the unstructured form of such interviews allows respondents to "generate, challenge, clarify, elaborate, or recontextualize understandings of social movements based on earlier interviews, documentary sources, or observational methods" (p. 94). In this study, the amount of time that I had already spent as a participant observer prior to conducting the interviews served to locate these conversations in a relational context. In this way the two research methods worked to complement one another extremely well, enhancing the breadth and depth of my findings. Blee and Taylor also suggest that this type of interviewing can allow researchers to

> gain insight into the individual and collective visions, imaginings, hopes, expectations, critiques of the present, and projections of the future on which the possibility of collective action rests and through which social movements form, endure, or disband. . . . [Interviews] can illuminate how activists are mobilized or politically sustained during periods of relative quiescence or abeyance. (p. 95)

Certainly, the women I interviewed for this project were astonishingly thoughtful and reflexive in their consideration of these issues, and these qualities added greater richness and depth to the case studies.

I conducted three in-depth interviews with women who were associated with the CCWN, which were supplemented by e-mail discussion and interviews with six other women who had attended the NOWSA conference. At the Young Women Who Are Parents Program I selected three key staff members and three long-term network members to participate in interviews. As "key informants," these participants were chosen from both groups because of their particular experiences in the movement organisations, rather than because they were necessarily representative of the wider membership of their groups (Blee & Taylor, 2002, p. 100). As Blee and Taylor point out, the criteria for selecting key informants is different from the criteria needed to select a representative sample of interviewees. For key informant selection, the crucial consideration is "the amount of knowledge [the informant] has about a topic and his or her willingness to communicate with the researcher" (p. 105).

The interviews ranged in length from 1 to 2 hours and were unstructured in their form. Due to my (by then lengthy) involvement with each organisation, the interviews felt like a continuation of ongoing conversations with the participants.

Each interview ranged across a wide variety of themes. While there was some variation in these themes for each organisation, the following themes were almost always present:

- The history of each interviewee's involvement with that particular organisation and with activism more broadly
- The interviewee's reflection on what it meant to "be a feminist"
- The challenges and problems that each interviewee had experienced in her activism
- The interviewee's thoughts about the role of organisational location, structure, and processes in determining the scope and focus of her activism
- The challenges that the interviewees had experienced as arising from differences and conflict between women in the movement to do with ideology, goals, and strategy
- The challenges to feminist activism that each interviewee had experienced in trying to organise around intersections of "race," class, sexuality, and so on
- The interviewee's views about the future possibilities for feminist activism in Australia

### Triangulation and Textual Analysis

Despite this emphasis on participant observation and in-depth interviewing, I would suggest that my research strategy in this project should more accurately be described as one of triangulation or multiple-methods research, so that the textual analysis that formed an important part of my analysis is not overlooked. As Reinharz (1992) argues, "Multimethod research creates the opportunity to put texts or people in contexts, thus providing a richer and far more accurate interpretation" (p. 213). I see the inclusion of textual material as entirely compatible with the activist standpoint approach. The primary textual material that informed this research included historical interview and autobiographical texts that allowed me to trace feminist processes of collective identity from the 1970s to the present, along with the organisational documents that I studied during my time in the field. These organisational documents included minutes from meetings, newsletters, annual reports, planning and evaluation reports, conference proceedings, research reports, and publicity or information materials for the general public. The detail in these documents allowed me to supplement and verify the information gathered from participant observation and interviewing. This approach is not unusual in the study of social movements, as Blee and Taylor (2002, p. 111) point out, because triangulation significantly increases the amount of detail researchers can bring to their analysis. Blee and Taylor argue,

> The combination of participant observation or document analysis with semi-structured interviewing can be a useful means of analysing the specific contexts within which participants in social movements construct their understandings of these movements. (p. 112)

In relation to young women in the contemporary Australian women's movement, a significant part of this context is the contentious history of the women's movement itself. Second-wave Australian feminism has generated a significant quantity of autobiographical or biographical material that has not been subject to any significant analysis. Susan Mitchell (1984), Jocelynne Scutt (1987), and Jan Bowen (1998) provide fairly raw interview material, and autobiographies from Zelda D'Aprano (1995), Anne Summers (1999), Susan Ryan (1999), and Wendy McCarthy (2000), inter alia, contribute to a growing body of literature that allows feminists to speak in their own words and is fertile ground for social movement analysis. I considered these texts "documents of interaction" (Angrosino, 1989, p. 4), a category that covers biography, autobiography, life history, and personal narratives and refers to "the interaction between the individual reliving and reinterpreting life experiences and the individual whose *active* responses to that telling become an integral part of its process of creation" (p. 4). Inherent to this perspective is the understanding that interview and autobiographical material, as acts of sharing, presuppose an interested audience and therefore primarily include deliberately chosen facets of an individual's experience. I cannot, therefore, analyse this material uncritically as a historical "truth" (Angrosino, 1989, pp. 5–8).

Margaret Henderson (2002) is critical of these particular texts exactly because she feels that they represent a version of feminist activism that has been "made comprehensible and palatable to the mainstream." Henderson argues that if we were to rely on these accounts alone, then the second wave of the Australian women's movement "should be renamed the 'tidiest revolution'" (p. 181). For the purposes of this study, however, I was able to use these documents as individualistic accounts that, taken together, provided richly personal data entirely suitable for an activist standpoint analysis that certainly did not reveal the "tidiness" of these women's experiences of feminist activism in the 1970s. When analysed in relation to feminist processes of collective identity and the scholarly histories of the period, what are most apparent are the confusion and difficulty that many of these women experienced in dealing with conflict between their "sisters."

## PRIVILEGING AN ACTIVIST STANDPOINT

Together these research methods generated a wealth of data. I had extensive field notes from the participant observation phase, interview transcripts, organisational documents, historical material, and records from e-mail discussion lists. Using the analytic method described in the first half of this chapter, I was then able to consider the processes of collective identity that the young activists in the two networks were engaged in and to situate these processes in the historical context of the Australian women's movement. My analysis derived from the "activist standpoint" described earlier in the chapter in which I privileged the perspectives of the young women themselves as knowing, politicised subjects who articulated their processes of collective identity through their feminist discourse and action. For a researcher, such an approach depends on a certain humility, what Cynthia Kaufman (2003) describes as "a sense that no matter how much we know, other people have experiences and perspectives that we have much to learn from" (p. 4). A humble approach to research and analysis, from an activist perspective, provides the space and opportunity to "give the voice back to the protestors we study" (Jasper, 1997, p. 379). An analysis of processes of collective identity from this perspective can allow researchers the opportunity to observe and document what Chela Sandoval (2000) describes as the "differential mode of consciousness" that "depends on a form of agency that is self-consciously mobilized" (p. 58). This consciousness, which Sandoval describes as "processual and differential," bears striking parallels with Melucci's processes of collective identity. Both suggest the fluid and strategic nature of collective identity and reveal that any such identity is itself created from social and political struggle (Taylor & Whittier, 1992, p. 110).

For the young women who participated in this research project, these struggles are a part of their everyday experiences as activists. The women in the CCWN, for example, often experience their activism to be frustrating, isolating, and paralysing. They battle continuously with ideological and strategic dilemmas, as well as issues of inclusion and coalition that would sound very familiar to many feminists of the second wave. With little support they struggle to find ways of making their actions seem meaningful to a broad category of women, whilst their heightened awareness of debates around difference, and inclusion and exclusion, sometimes threaten to silence them altogether. The pressure that some of these young women place on themselves is, at times, quite extraordinary. For example, Fiona feels that she is active on a personal level but feels guilty that she does not "do more" and "would like to be more active on a political level." She then went on to describe her activism:

Nike blockades each week and I am involved in mass protests, like S11 and M1. I expect to go on Reclaim the Night. I go to Critical Mass (a bike rally), do volunteer work at a food co-op and tutor a young woman in literacy once a week. I think that volunteer work in my local community is very important and has more of a connection than just big rallies. I'm vegetarian and choose to shop at the co-op and local IGA. I don't use plastic bags and try to buy organic food. . . . Other consumer choices include not consuming much, and when I do I choose not to spend money with companies that have bad human-rights records [such as] Nestle, Nike, Sussan, Shell. . . . I think that self-education is important. I choose to live with queer women and spend time in the women's department at uni. This gives me strength and inspiration. I hope to become more active as Bloody

Feminists starts up again on campus. I'm also running as women's officer next year. My honours thesis (in linguistics) is on a gender issue and I try to live my political commitments every day.

This commitment to incorporating feminist politics into all aspects of their daily lives is typical of the young women who participated in this research, and, as in the case of Fiona, it is hard to imagine many of them having any time left to become *more* politically active.

And yet this sense of inadequacy is a theme for the young women in the CCWN. In her end of year report as convenor for 2001, Pru expressed her feeling that she has "probably disappointed many comrades" by not achieving more during the year and expresses the hope that her colleagues understand that "even the revolution goes on holiday." There is a constant tension for Pru in wanting to always "be active where I'm at in my everyday life" and the recognition that there are also other things she wants to do with her life, including activism on other issues. These activists have a strong sense of responsibility to the broader women's movement, especially in terms of maintaining a feminist political space. As Mari expresses it,

Yeah, sometimes I think it would be easier if you just didn't care but the fact is I do care, so I can't quit. . . . Recently I was thinking, "Why am I still doing women's stuff? There's a huge refugee movement starting at the moment, I could be out there calling actions that thousands of people turn up to. Why am I doing what I'm doing?" And I thought . . . someone's got to do it otherwise no one will be doing it. And it's not like I can't still be involved in the other things as well. . . . And it also means at the very least that if something big . . . happens and women are the focus of it then at least there will be a base of people who do have that consciousness and are prepared to act on it.

For Pru, however, one of the difficulties is that campus activism is so "insular" and yet the demands on young feminists seem so great:

It's hard because you want to sort of look beyond the square you're in but at the same time taking on the world is really difficult when there's no base for doing that. . . . So we need to learn from what we've been doing and sort of look at other movements a bit as well, seeing where they're going. It's just hard. It's really difficult . . . I know so many feminists who are . . . depressed in a clinical sense and I think one of the issues there is that women's lives are just so hectic.

In the more supported environment of the YWWAPN, the challenges of feminism are different, primarily due to the different social location of the young women involved. The older women who work to support the young women's program have an enormous sensitivity about the disturbing, and often distressing, effects that developing a feminist consciousness can have on the young, working-class women in the program. This experience is one that is common to many women, as program director Maggie explains:

It's profoundly disturbing I think when any of us start to realise how oppressed women are. Profoundly disturbing. It shakes the way you look at the world and the way you see the world. And once you do that there is absolutely no going back. And I think it's the same for these women; it questions their relationships, how they've been treated, and the future they've pictured for themselves or had painted for them. It's huge.

Maggie also explains that the program prepares for the potential effects of this new awareness and "take[s] into account the fact that the participants are going to be profoundly shaken up."

Kerry is one young woman in the YWWAPN who experienced these personal challenges of "coming to feminism":

It was a really traumatic time in my life. I was searching for who am I outside of being my partner's girlfriend and my child's mother. I didn't even realise I was supposed to be someone outside of these other roles. That's when I started learning and reading about what was happening in the world with women and the roles that women play in men's lives. This radar came up and I felt really naked and exposed and really aware of what was going on around me—it was really scary.

For these young women, their "new feminism" is also tempered by the common, negative stereotypes about feminism that they are so familiar with; as Suszy says,

I've realised that I am a feminist and that I hadn't realised it before. I actually think it's really sad that I didn't know that. It's sad to me that the community in general doesn't understand what it is and that we're all so focussed on [the myth that] feminism means you've got a shaved head and you burn your bra. It seems ridiculous to me that feminism is such a valid argument [but] when we think about society that's what people see and I think it's really sad.

Kerry's new knowledge about herself and the world is also tainted by a sense of confusion about why so many people in the community reject feminism:

When people say you're a feminist they can mean it in such horrible ways. Like we're some really weird thing. I'm not saying *they're* weird, I'm just saying I can't understand why they're not saying what we're saying. It's out there every day and they're just so blind to it.

These small vignettes reveal a great deal about the deep commitment that these young women bring to their activism. In their struggles over processes of collective identity, they consistently demonstrate an ethic of care for the work that they do that illuminates the importance of their work both for broader feminist struggles and in social movement communities more generally. Of course the relationship that we had mutually constructed meant that, in some senses, neither I nor the young women in the project could be truly "ourselves" or be "objective" about the research experience. The nature of research means that the sort of action and interaction that I was participating in, observing, and documenting was itself somewhat artificial in character. However, this acknowledgement that research does not "mirror 'true' reality" (Melucci, 1996, p. 390) is not intended to invalidate the research findings or undermine the importance of the activist standpoint. Rather, this acknowledgement brings us closer to a recognition of what research actually is: "namely, that it is a social activity, a self-reflexive process constructed within the possibilities and constraints of a social field" (p. 390). Further, acknowledging the constructed nature of the research process is ultimately beneficial because it can provide both the researcher and the research participants with a "welcome space for reflection" (Lichterman, 2002, p. 127)—on the research process itself and on the broader context of social movement activism.

It was my hope that, through this research process, the young women in the two case studies would have an opportunity to reflect on and develop their local practices and strategies that will assist them to achieve their goals for feminist social and political change. Conversations with some of the research participants since the completion of the project suggest that this may indeed be the case, at least for some of them who have really enjoyed reading their case studies and reflecting on my analysis. Certainly it has been my goal to give these young feminists a greater voice of their own in conceptualising, theorising, and organising the social conditions in which their activism may flourish and be recognised. More broadly, however, I again agree with Melucci (1996) when he suggests that "analysis of movements provides insights that point behind the back of the collective actors as empirical facts" (p. 380). Behind the young women who participated in this study is a diversity of young feminist praxis that deserves a wealth of scholarly attention.

Alain Touraine (1985) has argued that the concept of social movement should be centrally important to sociological enquiry because it can act as a "bridge between the observation of new technologies and the idea of new forms of political life" (p. 782). Melucci (1996) goes further by suggesting that the sort of focus on the "plurality and tensions constituting collective life" that I have advocated in this chapter can "contribute to a practice of freedom" (p. 397). To layer a feminist perspective on this project once more, as researchers we must remember that "the aim of feminist research is liberation" (Fonow & Cook, 1991, p. 6). As David Meyer (2002) reminds us, in the study of social movements:

> It is too easy to forget the critical importance of what we study. The people who make social movements are trying to change the world, trying

to promote their visions of peace, justice, and social progress—sometimes at great personal risk. This means that we start with subjects invested with emotion, import, conflict, and tension from the outset. I hope that the work of scholars can be more clearly animated by the importance of such commitments, treating the puzzles of collective action with the passion employed by activists about their own efforts. (p. 20)

Considering the study of social movements from an activist standpoint can give activists themselves a voice in articulating their commitment, highlighting their strategic and fluid engagement with a differential consciousness and revealing the processes by which they construct their collective identities. In this humble researcher's opinion, the rest of us have much to learn.

## NOTES

1. For a discussion of the ways in which collective identity is considered analytically distinct from both individual and public identity, see Laraña, Johnston, and Gusfield (1994).

2. The study of emotion as a vital component of social movement processes is seeing something of a return to favour after the dominance of studies of structure and rationality in the field in recent decades. In a recent collection devoted to this task, Jeff Goodwin, James Jasper, and Francesca Polletta (2001) express their hope that "emotions, properly understood, may prove once again to be a central concern of political analysis" (p. 2).

3. The closest thing to a national or centralised organisation in the women's movement that Australia has seen was the Coalition of Australian Participating Organisations of Women (CAPOW!), which was formed in 1991. CAPOW! was an attempt by a range of organisations in the Australian women's movement to form a national networking coalition. While CAPOW! played an important coordinating role in the lead up to the United Nations Conference for Women in Beijing in 1995, it was the first women's organisation to be defunded by the Howard government in 1996. The death of Helen Leonard (CAPOW! convenor and one of Australia's most active feminists) in 2001 has meant that the organisation continues to exist in name only.

# REFERENCES

Angrosino, M. V. (1989). *Documents of interaction: Biography, autobiography, and life history in social science perspective.* Gainesville: University of Florida Press.

Blee, K. M., & Taylor, V. (2002). Semi-structured interviewing in social movement research. In B. Klandermans & S. Staggenborg (Eds.), *Methods of social movement research* (pp. 92–117). Minneapolis: University of Minnesota Press.

Bowen, J. (1998). *Feminists fatale: The changing face of Australian feminism.* Sydney, New South Wales, Australia: HarperCollins.

Bulbeck, C. (1997). Living feminism: The impact of the women's movement on three *generations of Australian women.* Cambridge, UK: Cambridge University Press.

Byrne, A., & Lentin, R. (Eds.). (2000). *(Re)searching women: Feminist research methodologies in the social sciences in Ireland.* Dublin, Ireland: Institute of Public Administration.

Chapman, J. (1995). The feminist perspective. In D. Marsh & G. Stoker (Eds.), *Theory and methods in political science* (pp. 94–114). Basingstoke, UK: Macmillan.

D'Aprano, Z. (1995). *Zelda.* Melbourne, Victoria, Australia: Spinifex Press.

Dean, J. (1997). The reflective solidarity of democratic feminism. In J. Dean (Ed.), *Feminism and the new democracy: Resisting the political* (pp. 244–264). Thousand Oaks, CA: Sage.

Devine, F. (1995). Qualitative analysis. In D. Marsh & G. Stoker (Eds.), *Theory and methods in political science.* Basingstoke, UK: Macmillan.

Ferree, M. M. (1987). Equality and autonomy: Feminist politics of the United States and West Germany. In C. Mueller & M. Katzenstein (Eds.), *The women's movements of the United States and Western Europe* (pp. 172–195). Philadelphia: Temple University Press.

Ferree, M. M., & Gamson, W. (2003). The gendering of governance and the governance of gender: Abortion politics in Germany and the USA. In B. Hobson (Ed.), *Recognition struggles and social movements.* New York: Cambridge University Press.

Ferree, M. M., & Martin, P. M. (Eds.). (1995). *Feminist organizations: Harvest of the new women's movement.* Philadelphia: Temple University Press.

Ferree, M. M., & Merrill, D. (2000). Hot movements, cold cognition: Thinking about social movements in gendered frames. *Contemporary Sociology: A Journal of Reviews, 29,* 454–462.

Fonow, M. M. (2003). *Union women: Forging feminism in the United Steelworkers of America.* Minneapolis: University of Minnesota Press.

Fonow, M. M., & Cook, J. A. (1991). Back to the future: A look at the second wave of feminist epistemology and methodology. In M. M. Fonow & J. A. Cook (Eds.), *Beyond methodology: Feminist scholarship as lived research.* Bloomington: Indiana University Press.

Gamson, W. (1992). The social psychology of collective action. In A. D. Morris & C. M. Mueller (Eds.), *Frontiers in social movement theory* (pp. 53–76). New Haven, CT: Yale University Press.

Gelb, J., & Hart, V. (1999). Feminist politics in a hostile environment: Obstacles and opportunities. In M. Guigni, D. McAdam, & C. Tilly (Eds.), *How social movements matter.* Minneapolis: University of Minnesota Press.

Goodwin, J., & Jasper, J. M. (2003). (Eds.). *The social movements reader: Cases and concepts.* New York: Blackwell.

Goodwin, J., Jasper, J. M., & Polletta, F. (2001). *Passionate politics: Emotions and social movements.* Chicago: University of Chicago Press.

Grosz, E. (1993). Bodies and knowledges: Feminism and the crisis of reason. In L. Alcoff & E. Potter (Eds.), *Feminist epistemologies* (pp. 187–215). New York: Routledge.

Henderson, M. (2002). The tidiest revolution: Regulative feminist autobiography and the defacement of the Australian women's movement. *Australian Literary Studies, 20*(3), 178–191.

Jasper, J. (1997). *The art of moral protest: Culture, biography and creativity in social movements.* Chicago: University of Chicago Press.

Johnston, H. (2002). Verification and proof in frame and discourse analysis. In B. Klandermans & S. Staggenborg (Eds.), *Methods of social movement research* (pp. 62–91). Minneapolis: University of Minnesota Press.

Kaplan, G. (1996). *The meagre harvest: The Australian women's movement 1950s–1990s.* Sydney, New South Wales, Australia: Allen & Unwin.

Kaufman, C. (2003). *Ideas for action: Relevant theory for radical change.* Cambridge, MA: South End Press.

Klandermans, B., & Staggenborg, S. (Eds.). (2002). *Methods of social movement research.* Minneapolis: University of Minnesota Press.

Koopmans, R., & Rucht, D. (2002). Protest event analysis. In B. Klandermans & S. Staggenborg (Eds.), *Methods of social movement research* (pp. 231–259). Minneapolis: University of Minnesota Press.

Lake, M. (1999). *Getting equal: The history of Australian feminism.* Sydney, New South Wales, Australia: Allen & Unwin.

Laraña, E., Johnston, H., & Gusfield, J. R. (Eds.). (1994). *New social movements: From ideology to identity.* Philadelphia: Temple University Press.

Lichterman, P. (2002). Seeing structure happen: Theory-driven participant observation. In B. Klandermans & S. Staggenborg (Eds.), *Methods of social movement research* (pp. 118–145). Minneapolis: University of Minnesota Press.

Lofland, J. (1993). Theory-bashing and answer-improving in the study of social movements. *American Sociologist, 24*(2), 37–58.

Longino, E. H. (1993). Subjects, power and knowledge: Description and prescription in feminist philosophies of science. In L. Alcoff & E. Potter (Eds.), *Feminist epistemologies* (pp. 101–120). New York: Routledge.

McCarthy, W. (2000). *Don't fence me in.* Sydney, New South Wales, Australia: Random House.

McDonald, K. (1999). *Struggles for subjectivity, identity, action and youth experience.* Cambridge, UK: Cambridge University Press.

Melucci, A. (1985). The symbolic challenge of contemporary movements. *Social Research, 52*(4), 789–815.

Melucci, A. (1989). *Nomads of the present: Social movements and individual needs in contemporary society.* Philadelphia: Temple University Press.

Melucci, A. (1995). The process of collective identity. In H. Johnston & B. Klandermans (Eds.), *Social movements and culture.* Minneapolis: University of Minnesota Press.

Melucci, A. (1996). *Challenging codes: Collective action in the information age.* Cambridge, UK: Cambridge University Press.

Meyer, D. S. (2002). Opportunities and identities: Bridge-building in the study of social movements. In D. S. Meyer, N. Whittier, & B. Robnett (Eds.), *Social movements: Identity, culture and the state* (pp. 3–24). New York: Oxford University Press.

Minichiello, V., Aroni, R., Timewell, E., & Alexander, L. (1995). *In-depth interviewing: Principles, techniques, analysis* (2nd ed.). Melbourne, Victoria, Australia: Addison-Wesley Longman.

Mitchell, S. (1984). *Tall poppies.* Ringwood, Victoria, Australia: Penguin.

Morris, A. (1992). Political consciousness and collective action. In A. Morris & C. Mueller (Eds.), *Frontiers in social movement theory.* New Haven, CT: Yale University Press.

Oakley, A. (1981). Interviewing women: A contradiction in terms. In H. Roberts (Ed.), *Doing feminist research.* London: Routledge & Kegan Paul.

Polletta, F., & Jasper, J. M. (2001). Collective identity and social movements. *Annual Review of Sociology, 27,* 283–305.

Ramazanoğlu, C., & Holland, J. (2002). *Feminist methodology: Challenges and choices.* London: Sage.

Reinharz, S. (1992). *Feminist methods in social research.* New York: Oxford University Press.

Ribbens, J., & Edwards, R. (Eds.). (1998). *Feminist dilemmas in qualitative research: Public knowledge and private lives.* London: Sage.

Robnett, B. (1997). *How long? How long? African American women in the struggle for civil rights.* New York: Oxford University Press.

Rupp, L. J., & Taylor, V. (1987). *Survival in the doldrums: The American women's rights movement, 1945 to the 1960s.* New York: Oxford University Press.

Ryan, S. (1999). *Catching the waves: Life in and out of politics.* Sydney, New South Wales, Australia: HarperCollins.

Sandoval, C. (2000). *Methodology of the oppressed.* Minneapolis: University of Minnesota Press.

Scutt, J. (Ed.). (1987). *Different lives: Reflections on the women's movement and visions for its future.* Ringwood, Victoria, Australia: Penguin.

Shorter, E., & Tilly, C. (1974). *Strikes in France, 1830–1968.* Cambridge, UK: Cambridge University Press.

Silverman, K. (1992). *Male subjectivity at the margins.* New York: Routledge.

Snow, D. (2001). Collective identity and expressive forms. *Centre for the Study of Democracy Papers.* Retrieved October 22, 2004, from http://repositories.cdlib.org/csd/01-07

Snow, D. A., & Trom, D. (2002). The case study and the study of social movements. In B. Klandermans & S. Staggenborg (Eds.), *Methods of social movement research*. Minneapolis: University of Minnesota Press.

Somerville, J. (1997). Social movement theory, women and the question of interests. *Sociology, 31*(4), 673–695.

Stanley, L. (Ed.). (1990). *Feminist praxis: Research, theory, and epistemology in feminist sociology*. London: Routledge.

Stanley, L., & Wise, S. (1990). Method, methodology and epistemology in feminist research processes. In L. Stanley (Ed.), *Feminist praxis: Research, theory, and epistemology in feminist sociology* (pp. 20–60). London: Routledge.

Summers, A. (1999). *Ducks on the pond: An autobiography 1945–1976*. Ringwood, Victoria, Australia: Viking.

Taylor, V. (2000). Mobilizing for change in a social movement society. *Contemporary Sociology, 29*(1), 219–230.

Taylor, V., & Rupp, L. (2002). Loving internationalism: The emotion culture of transnational women's organizations. *Mobilization, 7*(2), 141–158.

Taylor, V., & Whittier, N. (1992). Collective identity in social movement communities: Lesbian feminist mobilization. In A. D. Morris & C. M. Mueller (Eds.), *Frontiers in social movement theory* (pp. 104–129). New Haven, CT: Yale University Press.

Taylor V., & Whittier, N. (1998). Guest editors' introduction [Special issue on gender and social movements]. *Gender and Society, 12*(6), 622.

Touraine, A. (1981). *The voice and the eye*. Cambridge, UK: Cambridge University Press.

Touraine, A. (1985). An introduction to the study of social movements. *Social Research, 52*(4), 749–787.

Touraine, A. (2000). A method for studying social actors. *Journal of World Systems Research, 1*(3), 900–918.

Waldby, C. (1995). Feminism and method. In B. Caine & R. Pringle (Eds.), *Transitions: New Australian feminisms* (pp. 15–28). Sydney, New South Wales, Australia: Allen & Unwin.

Whittier, N. (1995). *Feminist generations: The persistence of the radical women's movement*. Philadelphia: Temple University Press.

Whittier, N. (2002). Meaning and structure in social movements. In D. S. Meyer, N. Whittier, & B. Robnett (Eds.), *Social movements: Identity, culture and the state*. New York: Oxford University Press.

Young, I. M. (1997). *Intersecting voices: Dilemmas of gender, political philosophy, and policy*. Princeton, NJ: Princeton University Press.

Young, S. (1997). *Changing the wor(l)d: Discourse, politics and the feminist movement*. New York: Routledge.

# 19

# INSTITUTIONAL ETHNOGRAPHY

## From a Sociology for Women to a Sociology for People

### DOROTHY E. SMITH

I want to emphasize from the outset that I do not view institutional ethnography as a sociological method so much as a sociology that proceeds by inquiry rather than by establishing from the outset a theoretical framework for the interpretation of people's behaviour. It is often described as a methodology and appears sometimes in discussions of qualitative methods in sociology, but it aims to go beyond that to a reconstruction or reorganization of the social relations built into a systematically developed knowledge of the social. Sociology for the most part does start with concepts established historically in various sociological communities—positivist orientations relying primarily on quantitative methods, structural approaches, symbolic interaction, ethnomethodology, and so on. It seeks to explain or otherwise understand people's social life, whether at the level of direct interchange among people or of larger historical structures. Whatever the approach, sociology for the most part makes people its objects; they are what sociology studies. Institutional ethnography, by contrast, is consciously designed to start in people's everyday lives and with their experience of them; it

problematizes the social relations and organization that extend beyond experience and coordinates our lives with those of others elsewhere and elsewhen. In other words, it proposes to explore into the social *from where we are* in our everyday lives and to discover how what we experience locally is shaped by what we cannot know directly.

My title implies that institutional ethnography is not strictly speaking a feminist sociology or a feminist method. It is, however, feminist in three respects:

1. It originated in and was developed from the logic of the politics of consciousness-raising that was so central to the women's movement in its early days.

2. Its design problematizes the conceptual strategies and methods of sociologies that alienate people from their experience and proposes as an alternative an inquiry that works from and learns from people's experience of the actualities of our everyday lives.

3. People are the knowers, the subjects of knowledge rather than the objects of study.

I'm going to proceed in a quasi-autobio-graphical fashion to make the linkages between my own experiences as a sociologist who is a woman or a woman who is a sociologist and the kind of sociology that has emerged from these experiences and from the immensely rich dialogue I have enjoyed with others using this approach.

For some reason, when I was in graduate school at the University of California at Berkeley (in a sociology department at that time far from supportive of women), I worried about the gap between the world that sociology could know and the world that I lived in and experienced in my body.[1] The experience of learning survey and mathematical sociologies had its intellectual charms but seemed disconnected from my every-day life. To use a phrase from the Yorkshire of my childhood, sociology lacked bottom. I couldn't find how it was grounded in the actualities of experience. Erving Goffman (1959, 1963) had discovered for us a whole region of everyday experience that had simply not been present for sociology until his radically innovative work. But the trick for those that followed still seemed to be that of somehow finding a concept to isolate and dramatize sociologically an aspect of human social life that the genius of the researcher had made visible (an approach systematized in the methods of grounded theory).

The women's movement transformed my modest intradisciplinary concern into something quite different. The disconnection between the theories and concepts organizing sociological discourse metamorphosed: It was not just some-thing to think about; it was something I was living. It was not only that the discipline was thought and dominated by men and women who did our work on their ground. It was something else. When I looked for where I was in my disci-pline I discovered that I was not there. My world with my children and my work in the house was where I was as a woman. The embodied woman disappeared from view when I went to work in the text-based world of sociology.

## TALKING EXPERIENCE

It is easy to forget now what the women's move-ment of the late 1960s and early 1970s was up against—the historical sedimentation of an intellectual, cultural, and political universe that excluded us as subjects. We did not at that time even have a language for our condition. We had at first no language to express ourselves as women other than the one that already confined us. So we spoke our experience to each other to find a place to stand that had not been corrupted and to discover ways of speaking of what we were sharing. It was an essentially dialogic process in which we spoke our experience to each other and took sides with our bodies against the abstract. Talking, writing, reading, and in some way or other sharing our experience as women were foundational to discovering what it might mean, how to speak of it, and how to frame and organize action. Exploring our experience as women was foundational to the politics of the women's movement in the early days.

Feminist sociologists of this period were dis-covering multiple problems with sociology.[2] Where were the women in its stories? We were hardly mentioned. Some sociologists were dis-covering peculiarities of its conceptual structures and regions of the social that were totally absent or diminished. Since that time, sociology has been transformed by feminist or feminist-influenced work. My own direction was deter-mined by my rediscovery as a feminist of the gap between sociology and the actualities of our lives. I began to examine sociology from a standpoint in my experience as a woman, in my body, with my children, at work in my home, in the local particularities of my life. I began to be able to see sociology as my and other people's local prac-tices, in our bodies, our subjectivities coordinated by its texts, and I began to want a sociology that could see what I was learning in the dialogic of women's experience (Bakhtin, 1981).

## SOCIOLOGY WITHOUT WOMEN

The problem with sociology was not just the masculine warping of its topics. It had come to embody conceptual/theoretical and method-ological practices that had precluded speaking from people's experience, let alone women's experience. It could make use of people's expe-rience as data interpreted to fit its frameworks; it could not take on people's experience as its own starting point. I had in that period of change many occasions of encounter with sociological discourse that raised questions for me (I was learning from these). I saw how political intentions were irrelevant once the sociological activist engaged her sociological gears. In the university, I supervised young women who wanted to do politically relevant research. Some wanted to study the movements they were active in from the perspective of sociology's theory of *social movements*. This came to seem strange to me. How was it that if you were involved in the women's movement as an activist, you'd want to make that your *object* of sociological investigation? And while I was not particularly paranoid at that time (now I'd be more so), I couldn't but wonder to whom such research might be relevant. Who would want to know about social movements in our societies?

From thinking about these kinds of issues, I came to want to know what it was about sociology that turned the movement these women were part of into the *object* of investigation. How did it do that? And could a different kind of sociology be written?

## Remaking Sociology From Women's Standpoint

When as activists we turned, as sociologists, our own political involvements into objects of investigation, we were captured by sociology's conceptual practices—I no less than the students I supervised. Sociology's conceptual practice automatically constituted people and our doings as the objects of study. We didn't have to think about it; we didn't even recognize that that was what was happening. The sociologist, as subject, was perched outside the world she or he was a part of, and that's where we were situated once we engaged the discourse. Hence, inventing a sociology that would start in people's lives and with our experience meant designing alternative conceptual and methodological practices.

I discovered in the women's movement how to experience myself as a woman, and along with that I discovered that I experienced myself as a woman only in those aspects of my life in which the immediacies of my bodily being came into play. This, then, was the standpoint

from which a different sociology must be written. This is where a sociology in which women could be subjects had to begin, in the local actualities of people's embodied being.

My first step was to revisit what Marx and Engels wrote of making a social science grounded not in theory, concepts, speculation, or imagination but in actual people's activities and the conditions of those activities.

The second step was learned from the women's movement. It was a move that Marx did not make—to place people's embodied experience at the foundation. Making a sociology *for* women entails taking a standpoint in the actualities of people's embodied being, in our everyday lives.

These together are the basis of the approach called institutional ethnography. It explores the social world as it is known experientially, and it explores it as people's activities or doings in the actual local situations and conditions of our lives. The idea is to discover and map that world so that how it is being put together can be made observable from the point of view of those caught up in it.

## The Everyday World as Problematic

Since the earlier days of the women's movement, we have learned much from women's experience in different settings of our lives, in different parts of society, and in different parts of the world. Sociology has learned how to take up people's experience that was not recognized earlier and honours it in ways that we had not known how to do. Institutional ethnography takes that move one step further. People know a great deal; indeed, in a sense, we are all experts in our everyday lives. Of course, we're not always conscious of all we know because most of the time it doesn't become spoken, but it is always available to us in what we do. What is obscure to us are the relations and organization that are present in and organize our everyday worlds and activities and that coordinate what we are doing with what others are doing elsewhere and elsewhen. We don't know them for the most part, and often we are not even aware of their existence. The relations that organize our connections are translocal, that is, they coordinate across the local settings of our everyday lives and experience.

We don't need sociologists to tell us how to find our ways around our everyday lives. There, we are the experts and they must learn from us. It's another matter when it comes to how translocal relations organize and shape what we do and experience and what we participate in without knowing more than those strands that come within our scope. Institutional ethnography takes this general property of our contemporary world as its problematic (Smith, 1987), that is, as a general focus for inquiry and discovery. In particular and from the point of view of those involved, it focuses on the objectified forms of consciousness and organization based on textual technologies of various kinds (print, computers, film, television, audio, etc.). These include many of the regions explored by cultural studies but, perhaps more important, those ordinarily identified in sociology with formal or large-scale organization, bureaucracy, discourses of all kinds, professional organization, and so on. These translocal forms of organization are called the *ruling relations* (Smith, 1995), and the institutions to be explored ethnographically are functionally specialized complexes within the ruling relations: education, health care, government, law, business corporations, and so on. Institutions are not treated as independent units; it is important to avoid isolating them and to keep in focus the ways in which they are tied, on the one hand, in a wider organization of interconnecting translocal relations and, on the other, into the social relations of capital (these are not, of course, independent of one another). We become subjects and agents within the ruling relations and their institutions; we may also become objects; in any of these ways, they bring our everyday activities into a coordinated relation with those of others.

These are generally regions that the social sciences appropriate theoretically. Institutional ethnography adopts a different strategy. It is one of ethnographic discovery. Sociological ethnographies focus for the most part on what lies within the observational reach of the researcher. Institutional ethnography adopts the commitment to learning from people and how people go about their lives, but it has developed conceptual practices that reach beyond the local. There are two principal notions:

1. One is that of social relations much as Marx conceived them. These are not to be confused with relationships such as those between mothers and daughters. They are, strictly speaking, not entities to be examined as such, but they are sequences of action in which people are involved at different stages but not necessarily directly engaged in a shared work process (Smith, 1995). The importance of the concept is in the direction of research that it proposes. Starting in the everyday experience of people caught up or otherwise participating in an institutional process, it directs the researcher to explore how their activities are articulated to and coordinated with the relations that are institutionalized. Thus, when Alison Griffith and I (Griffith & Smith, 2005) decided to learn more about how mothers' work contributed to their children's schooling, we started with women's experience of that work and proceeded from there to ask how schools worked with what they had contributed (more about this study later). So simple a matter as the ability of a school to start the school day on time and to run a strict schedule of time allocated to different topics depended on the work (usually of mothers, sometimes of both parents) of getting their children to school on time. Note that the concept of social relations oriented us away from treating the school day as an institutional "thing" and to seeing it as coordinating the activities that accomplished its daily reality.

2. The second is the recognition and developing of means of analysing texts as part of the action. Texts are present as material objects in our local worlds, and at the same time they create as they are read, watched, or listened to connections with others who are not present to us. Texts' capacity to replicate the same words, images, or sounds in multiple settings is essential to the very existence of institutions; they are integral to institutional processes and forms of action. For example, one essential configuration of institutional practices is that of entering actualities into the textual forms in which they can be made institutionally actionable. The forms we are so used to filling in are one notable everyday example of this. The ethnographic trick is to see how the text that the ethnographer

can sometimes observe in "action" or find out about by talking with those involved enters into the organization of institutional sequences of action. More on this topic later.

Thus, institutional ethnography goes to work at the point where people's everyday experience is joined to and shaped by relations and organization that coordinate what we do with others' work elsewhere and elsewhen. It is a method of inquiry that starts and works with and through people's experience. The ethnography it creates explores and explicates social relations and powers from the standpoint of people in their everyday worlds. The ethnographer learns from the actualities of what people are doing and from what they have to tell her or him about their everyday lives.

## A Brief Guide

- An institutional ethnography starts with people's experience of some issue or problem in an institutional setting. That becomes the problematic of the research.
- It takes a standpoint in people's experience and learns from their knowledge of their everyday world, their work, and the institutional relations in which they participate (people often don't know how much they know until they start talking about it).
- Then, the ethnography builds on what has been learned to "explore" the relations that are coordinating their work with institutional relations. What has been learned at one stage becomes the basis for formulating questions to be asked and issues to be raised at the next (always working with people's experiential knowledge of their everyday world).
- Institutions depend on texts, and institutional ethnography draws the texts that are key in coordinating people's work into the scope of the ethnography study. Texts are seen as an integral aspect of people's activities.
- Then, the resulting account of how the institutional processes work can provide for people a way of expanding their own knowledge of their everyday world; it creates something like a map of regions we cannot see directly.

## Two Examples

### Example 1

Ellen Pence was part of a group in Duluth, Minnesota, that had been providing advocacy support for women whose partners had been charged with domestic abuse. Those working in this way had ample experience of how little even the improved efficacy of the judicial process contributed to women's safety. Pence's (1996, 2002) study drew on that experience, supplemented by rare opportunities for observation and participation. She makes the texts, so ubiquitous in the judicial process, an integral part of her observational and analytic focus. Her study of the judicial process traces it from the moment the dispatcher receives a 911 call to sentencing. She never sees the problems as those of individuals. Rather, she examines the interlocking textually coordinated sequences of action that relate the law to the work of the police, lawyers, probation officers, women's advocates, judges, social workers, and so on. The work organization is not an effect of a single unit regulating the various functions within a corporate entity. The work in each site is coordinated with others through the texts that each is accountable for reading, responding to, and sometimes producing at various stages of the overall process. Each textual step is the basis on which the next step is taken.

The standpoint Pence adopted was that of women caught up in the judicial process whose partners had been charged with domestic abuse. The police responding to the 911 call that initiates the process in most cases translate what they discover in the setting and the events that occur there in their presence into a report. George Smith (1988) has made a detailed analysis of this step in his study of charges brought against gay men engaged in sexual activity in a bathhouse in Toronto in the 1980s. He shows the police report as constructed to select those aspects of what the police saw and how they attended to what could be fitted to the law under which the men were charged.

In the instance of domestic abuse, the process is initiated by someone present at the scene, sometimes one of the adult participants, sometimes a child, occasionally a neighbour. The work of the police in rendering the local particularities of events into textual form is critical in the initiation of the judicial sequence of action, and their report, as Pence shows, plays a critical role in coordinating the work of others. The report standardizes for all involved what is known of the incident for the prosecuting attorney, for the lawyer for the defence, for social services (particularly if children are present), and so on. If someone is arraigned for trial, this report will have played a central part.

Pence was able to demonstrate how women's experience of the violence they had been subjected to was excluded from the process. Hence, the degree of violence and the degree of danger they might be exposed to never became in practice an issue in the law enforcement process. Women's safety was not an issue, and women were only marginally visible in the crucial process of sentencing. Her critiques of police procedures and of the preparation of sentencing reports by probation officers have resulted in changes in Duluth, and the Duluth police practices have become a model for law enforcement in this area in the United States.

## Example 2

The second example draws on Michel Foucault's (1970, 1972a, 1972b) concept of discourse. Institutional ethnography understands *discourse* not just as ideas, conventions, statements, forms of knowledge, and so on, or indeed as an order (Foucault, 1981), but as an integral dimension of the ruling relations and hence as definite forms of social relations based in texts that coordinate how people speak, write, and calculate in the local settings of their work. Furthermore, it explores the relations of discourse from a standpoint in people's experience, starting with an actual situation in someone's or some people's experience that is embedded in an institutional regime in some way.

This example draws on my own and Alison Griffith's experience of an institutional ethnography (referred to above) of the work that mothers do in relation to their children's schooling and its implications for schools. We were both single parents. We found that schools thought that single parents damaged their children; when our children were in trouble at

school, they blamed us. So we decided to try to find out what was so special about the "normal" family with both parents present. Why was that kind of family so important to schools (Griffith & Smith, 2005)?

We started by talking to women members of normal families with children in elementary schools about the work they did in relation to their children's schools. One group was drawn from parents with children at a school in a low-income area and the other from a school in a middle to affluent area. In the course of our research, the ruling relations popped up in a way we had not foreseen.

Alison came back from an interview very upset. She had been talking to a mother who had everything she did not have: This mother was married to a professional man and did not work outside the home; she spent a great deal of time doing educational work with her children, including consulting with them about which of Shakespeare's plays to go to at a nearby Shakespeare festival (remember these are kids in elementary school). Alison was on welfare; she had neither the time nor the financial resources to do this kind of educational work, yet she felt acutely guilty because she was not able to meet the standards set by someone with time and finances at her disposal.

We had learned from the women's movement not to take guilt for granted, so we talked about what was going on here. The difference between the two situations was plain. So why did Alison feel this way? In exploring further, we discovered in the new work of feminist historians what we came to call the *mothering discourse* (Griffith & Smith, 1987). It was invented early in the 20th century in North America in association with the public school system, and it was aimed at mobilizing and training mothers to orient their work with children towards schooling. Although it originated in a movement largely of middle-class white women, it was developed in academic settings mostly by men working in psychology, educational theory, child development, and so on.

An important aspect of this discourse was that mothers were to blame if things did not go right with their children in school. The conditions such as a family's earnings *did not count*; every mother must measure her performance against the best done under maximally favourable conditions. Both Alison and I were trained by the texts of the discourse just as were other women in North America, including those we talked to in our study; we'd read the books on child rearing, we read the stories in women's magazines, and we knew (and others knew) we were to blame if anything was not as it should be.

Notice how the text-based discourse standardized subjectivities! We were not the only women reading the texts of the mothering discourse; probably, the vast majority of at least middle-class women in North America participated in that discourse through its texts. The discourse mobilized and coordinated the unpaid work of women in the home in relation to the public school system. It is an integral component of the school system's institutional character.

Discovering the mothering discourse helped us to moderate its effects in our feelings; it did not, however, undo the problem that its presuppositions had been built into our research. Fortunately, since we were working ethnographically, that did less damage than it might have done if we'd been using a more structured approach. Indeed, our discovery expanded our understanding of the institutional complex we were examining. We would not have been aware of this dimension if Alison's experience had not opened it up for investigation.

This experience taught us one major merit of doing institutional ethnography: When you are committed to discovering just how things are being put together, you can make discoveries that overturn what you took for granted and thought you knew. From such discoveries, more is learned about that institutional complex of the ruling relations than the researcher had known how to ask at the outset.

## CONCLUSION

These are examples of explorations that open up from the everyday worlds of people's experience into organization and relations that are indeed in them and part of them, and in which those involved participate. Our everyday lives and work are shaped to coordinate with the work of others we do not know. This is a reality of our contemporary world.

We might think of these effects in terms of power, but that concept is entirely inadequate to

discovering how things are actually put together so that they work as they do in our lives. Ellen Pence (1996, 2002) explores the work that people do in law enforcement in relation to domestic abuse cases. It is their coordinated work that produces the outcomes for women, whose safety from abusers it does not protect. In seeking change, we have to look at the textual forms of coordination and the intertextuality of law and procedures. What Alison and I learned—both the larger study and our discoveries of the operation of the mothering discourse—has been passed on in various ways: Alison has used our research in teaching teachers; we've both spoken about our findings to a variety of women's groups. On one occasion, three women with children in the same school spoke up after our talk to say that their children had had problems in school for which they blamed themselves. They had not been able to talk to each other or to other mothers about them because to do so would show them as guilty. Revealing the mothering discourse enabled them to come together to talk about problems *in* the school rather than in their relationships with their children.

Rather than making people its objects of study, institutional ethnography aims to expand people's knowledge of how translocal relations organize their everyday worlds. The researchers' choice of research is essentially political. They may be working with activists, have concerns in a particular institutional area, or have had experiences of their own that become a focus. The work of research may be technical. Its academic exposition may also be technical, but because it is based on people's own knowledge of their local practices and explicates and expands that knowledge, it translates readily back into what is familiar. The academic product, if indeed there is one, is only one step in the process of opening up for people the ruling relations that organize their lives and showing how they exist as products of people's local work and how it is organized textually.

## NOTES

1. There were others with analogous concerns, notably Aaron Cicourel (1964) and Harvey Sacks

(1963), who wrote a paper for the *Berkeley Journal of Sociology* (a student publication) in an issue that I lost in a flood in my apartment and have not been able to locate.

2. Marcia Millman and Rosabeth Moss Kanter's (1975) collection of feminist papers was a major event in this process.

# References

Bakhtin, M. M. (1981). *The dialogic imagination: Four essays* (Caryl Emerson, Trans.). Austin: University of Texas Press.

Cicourel, A. V. (1964). *Method and measurement in sociology.* New York: Free Press of Glencoe.

Foucault, M. (1970). *The order of things: An archaeology of the human sciences.* London: Tavistock.

Foucault, M. (1972a). *The archaeology of knowledge.* New York: Pantheon Books.

Foucault, M. (1972b). *The discourse on language.* New York: Pantheon Books.

Foucault, M. (1981). The order of discourse. In R. Young (Ed.), *Untying the text: A poststructuralist reader* (pp. 51–78). London: Routledge.

Goffman, E. (1959). *The presentation of self in everyday life.* Garden City, NY: Doubleday.

Goffman, E. (1963). *Behavior in public places; notes on the social organization of gatherings.* New York: Free Press of Glencoe.

Griffith, A., & Smith, D. E. (1987). Constructing cultural knowledge: Mothering as discourse. In J. Gaskell & A. McLaren (Eds.), *Women and education* (pp. 87–103). Calgary, Alberta, Canada: Detselig.

Griffith, A., & Smith, D. E. (2005). *Mothering and schooling.* New York: Routledge.

Millman, M., & Kanter, R. M. (Eds.). (1975). *Another voice: Feminist perspectives on social life and social science.* Garden City, NY: Doubleday.

Pence, E. (1996). *Safety for battered women in a textually-mediated legal system.* Unpublished doctoral dissertation, Sociology in Education, University of Toronto, Toronto, Ontario, Canada.

Pence, E. (2002). Safety for battered women in a textually mediated legal system. *Studies in Cultures, Organizations, and Societies, 7*(2), 199–229.

Sacks, H. (1963). Sociological description. *Berkeley Journal of Sociology, 8,* 1–16.

Smith, D. E. (1987). *The everyday world as problematic: A feminist sociology.* Toronto, Ontario, Canada: University of Toronto Press.

Smith, G. W. (1988). Policing the gay community: An inquiry into textually mediated social relations. *International Journal of the Sociology of Law, 16,* 163–183.

Smith, G. W. (1995). Accessing treatments: Managing the AIDS epidemic in Ontario. In M. Campbell & A. Manicom (Eds.), *Knowledge, experience, and ruling relations: Studies in the social organization of knowledge* (pp. 18–34). Toronto, Ontario, Canada: University of Toronto Press.

# PART III

## FEMINIST PERSPECTIVES ON THE RESEARCH PROCESS

*Issues and Insights*

# 20

# Core Feminist Insights and Strategies on Authority, Representations, Truths, Reflexivity, and Ethics Across the Research Process

Sharlene Nagy Hesse-Biber
Abigail Brooks

In Part II of the *Handbook*, we observed how research methods in the hands of feminists become flexible and fluid. Feminist researchers bend their methods to answer a range of new research questions, sometimes finding that they need to combine methods, or create emergent methods, to get at subjugated knowledge. Feminists use a diverse range of methods, but they also share some epistemological concerns across the spectrum of their methods practices. In Part III, the authors confront issues of truth and morality, power and representation, and knowledge and authority at all stages of the research process, and they explore the implications of these epistemological dimensions for *research praxis.*

In her chapter, "Authority and Representation in Feminist Research," Judith Roof reminds us of the significance of personal, lived experience, or what she terms the "personal model,"

for building knowledge and traces the different ways in which women have used the personal model as an effective "strategy of persuasion" throughout the 20th and 21st centuries. Pioneering women, Virginia Woolf, Simone de Beauvoir, and Betty Friedan among them, have drawn from their own personal experiences to successfully challenge dominant gender norms and ideologies and to critique the exclusion and misrepresentation of women in a range of disciplines and professions. Women's application of the personal model has also produced new approaches to ethics, morality, and knowledge building. By centering her research on women's personal experiences, thoughts, and feelings, for example, Carol Gilligan (1982, cited by Preissle) discovered an alternative to Lawrence Kohlberg's (1981, cited by Preissle) model of morality, a model based on the value of relationships in contrast to abstract principles.

419

Further, as Roof points out, personal experience can serve as a powerful source of evidence of oppression—a mode of "authorizing its authenticity"—and a means to galvanize resistance against it. In cases where it may not be possible, or safe, for many to speak out, one woman's personal experience, for example, may come to represent the experiences of many women—and this is the "value of testimony based on individual experience."

On the other hand, Roof also illuminates the importance of attending to difference among and across women's experiences: Women do not share one lived experience or position but experience multiple social, economic, cultural, and racial realties. Women's diverse experiences have been articulated in new branches of feminist standpoint theory, and feminist theorists of the body are exploring women's subjectivities and different ways of knowing through their bodies. Feminist artists and aesthetic theorists are devising new and different ways of understanding women's art as "multiple, dispersed, tactile, often crafts based, and nonobjectifying." But irrespective of whether a woman's lived experience is individual or reflected in the lives of many other women, personal experience is no longer "an overlooked and ignored resource"—it has become instead "a rhetorical guarantee of authenticity not easily countermanded. Who, after all, can argue with a person's experience?"

According to Kathy Charmaz, all researchers are "intertwined with what we study and how we study it," but it is the active incorporation of personal experience into the research process that makes it *feminist*. A feminist researcher's personal, lived experience and situated perspective may guide her to particular research topics over others. Her gendered lens—or "way of seeing and understanding the world"—influences what questions she asks and how she gathers, analyzes, and interprets her data. And increasingly, as Charmaz points out, feminist researchers openly acknowledge and reflect on their personal experiences and perspectives *in writing*.

In her chapter "What's Good Writing in Feminist Research? What Can Feminists Learn About Good Writing?" Charmaz explores how feminist researchers actually go about integrating their personal experiences and perspectives into the writing process and asks, In what ways do personal experience and perspective shape feminist texts? By sharing their own personal experiences and perspectives with readers, Charmaz argues, authors may actually improve the credibility of their research. Like Roof, Charmaz equates personal experience with authenticity: "Knowing that the author held a personal stake in the topic once marked research as biased. Increasingly, however, readers see a personal stake as a mark of authorial credibility rather than bias." On the one hand, as Charmaz points out, an author who openly shares her "standpoints and starting points" and "concerns and commitments" enables readers to "place the narrative into perspective and delineate the boundaries"—to understand what the author hopes to accomplish and to evaluate it accordingly. On the other hand, authors who reveal their personal experiences and perspectives can create connections and build a rapport with readers. For example, by sharing her own personal struggles and anxieties about her hair, the feminist researcher Rose Weitz (2004, cited by Charmaz) gains the trust of her readers and lends credibility to her study about women and their relationship to their hair. Finally, Charmaz also illustrates how feminists make creative use of several other literary techniques and narrative devices—from metaphors and similes to word and title choices—to reach out to readers and to make their writing more engaging and effective. As an example, Michelle J. Budig and Paula England (2001, cited by Charmaz) use provocative questions and words such as "free riders" and "we" to gain readers' attention and draw them into their argument. As Charmaz puts it, "*We* have taken a place in the argument; it no longer merely refers to a category of people out there somewhere. Budig and England enter the narrative and bring their argument home—to us."

Laurel Richardson's piece, "Reading for Another: A Method for Addressing Some Feminist Research Dilemmas," also heightens our attention to the active role that personal experience and situated perspective play in the practice of feminist research. As Richardson embarks on a quest to know her mother—a quest that engages a variety of media, including her own dreams and therapy sessions, reading a novel that she knew her mother had read, and *writing this piece*—she finds that her own personal experience and situated perspective serve as both an aid and a hindrance to her quest. She attempts to read Alan Paton's (1953, cited by Richardson) *Too Late the Phalarope* "through her mother's eyes" and to seek out characters her mother may have identified with. But as Richardson tries to get inside her mother's head, she finds it difficult to separate her mother's thoughts and feelings from her own: "In reading for my mother, I've been reading for and from myself. I superimpose my world, my feelings, my point of view onto her." On the other hand, it is Richardson's own self—her subconscious, her dreams, and her identity as a feminist—that summons her mother to her and enables her to feel empathy for her mother's position as a woman and to respect her mother's strength and courage in standing up to her father. As Richardson explains, "We're always writing about ourselves. Subjectivity is always present. But this is not bad. This is what makes our work feminist. We can see ourselves in others, see others in ourselves."

But Richardson's exercise in "qualitative methodological writing practice" also teaches us about multiple selves—what she calls the "slipperiness" of the self—and the capacity for self-transformation. As she revisits her mother's life, Richardson draws from her own feminist identity and from her understanding of the personal as political, in an effort to better understand her mother's choices and experiences. At the same time, however, it is in the process of seeking connection to her mother that Richardson sees her mother in a new light. As Richardson explains, "Reading for Mother through 'the phalarope,' I have constructed her as a compassionate, complex, smart, and honorable woman— not the repressed mother I have carried in my mind's eye." And as Richardson comes to understand her mother's life from a fresh perspective—as her feelings about her mother change and as her relationship to her mother takes on a different form—her own identity morphs and changes. In fact, Richardson's quest to (re)discover her mother also reveals new and different versions of "the truth." Poststructuralist theory becomes practice—truth is fluid, mutable, and subject to interpretation— because what Richardson felt to be true about her mother before differs from what she perceives to be true about her mother now.

In her piece, "Truth and Truths in Feminist Knowledge Production," Mary Hawkesworth addresses the relationship between positionality, truth, and knowledge production in feminist research. Hawkesworth distinguishes feminist research from positivist, postpositivist, and critical rationalist approaches to knowledge building. While postpositivists and critical rationalists critique positivism for failing to produce value-free research, they suggest corrective measures and stricter methodological techniques that will improve the potentiality of achieving value-free, objective results. Feminists, on the other hand, not only critique positivism's failure to achieve objective, value-free findings but also question the viability and utility of conducting neutral, value-free research altogether. In fact, as Hawkesworth points out, specific political convictions, such as the desire to "eliminate male domination in all its various manifestations," inspire the existence of "*feminist research* [italics added]." Thus, far from being a "source of bias and distortion," feminist convictions and principles "are deemed an asset to the research."

But even if most feminist researchers share some basic goals and convictions, they may have different perspectives and approaches to achieving these goals and convictions. Mary Hawkesworth turns to Helen Longino's concept of "cognition as human practice" to help us understand feminist research and analysis as a rich and varied tradition. Understanding cognition as human practice means rejecting the possibility of fact, or an "unmediated knowledge of the world," in favor of multiple and competing theoretical formulations, explanations, and interpretations of social reality (Hawkesworth). If, however, we accept a plurality of feminist approaches to knowledge building, does that mean we also give up the potential for achieving common ground? What about coming together across difference to fight for social change? And what of notions of truth and objectivity—are they simply unattainable?

Hawkesworth confronts these questions head-on and urges feminists to incorporate what Helen Longino has called a process of "critical and intersubjective reflection" into the research process. Only by engaging in ongoing and reflexive dialogue with ourselves and other researchers about our positions, viewpoints, and values can we hope to build connections and construct common ground. We must continue to question our own "tacit assumptions and foundational beliefs of various disciplines" if we hope to achieve objectivity, albeit in a new form. This new objectivity demands inclusivity, embraces "diversity as means," and incorporates transformative critique: "A method of inquiry is objective to the extent that it permits transformative criticism" (Longino, 1990, p. 75, cited by Hawkesworth).

Integrating reflexivity into the research process certainly improves the capacity for "transformative criticism." In their chapter, "Holistic Reflexivity: The Feminist Practice of Reflexivity," Sharlene Nagy Hesse-Biber and Deborah Piatelli describe the practice of reflexivity as a potentially "transformative process for researchers, participants, and the larger community of knowledge builders." Through tracing feminist reflexivity in practice, Hesse-Biber and Piatelli demonstrate its effectiveness as a "methodological tool for deconstructing power throughout the entire research process." Whether practicing reflexivity takes the form of critical self-reflection and internal conversations within the self (on the part of the researcher self or the participant self) or active dialogue and discussions between researcher and participant, identities are unhinged. Reflexive interrogation shakes up the boundaries between researcher and participant and the taken-for-granted role of the researcher as a questioner of others. Roles are exchanged—researcher as participant and participant as researcher. And it is this fluidity, this crossing of boundaries and borders, that creates a potential common space for knowledge building (Hesse-Biber & Piatelli).

Practicing reflexivity can lead to a heightened awareness of the differences between participant and researcher, to change and transformation on the part of the researcher or the participant or both, and to the construction of common ground between them. As Hesse-Biber and Piatelli illuminate, commonalities discovered in the process of reflexive dialogue between researcher and participant can serve as important sources of rapport and as tools for diffusing power differentials. On the other hand, assuming commonality based on a "single dimension of identity" can be "detrimental to the project of deconstructing power relations

and co-constructing knowledge." Researchers must also be respectful and mindful of difference. This means acknowledging that there is an aspect of lived experience that is invisible to those "who possess neither the language nor the cultural equipment either to elicit or understand that experience" (Rhodes, 1994, p. 549, cited by Hesse-Biber & Piatelli).

Understanding the reality of difference, however, does not necessarily translate into a "failure to study across difference" (Hesse-Biber & Piatelli). By openly acknowledging difference, and through engaging in discussion and dialogue with participants about their differences, researchers may be more able to develop trust and build rapport with their participants (see, e.g., the following cited by Hesse-Biber & Piatelli: Anderson, 1998; Edwards, 1990). Further, an honest admission of difference may also make it easier for both participants and researchers to recognize any potential commonalities between them (see the following cited by Hesse-Biber & Piatelli: Dunbar, Rodriguez, & Parker, 2000; Ralston, 2001). Finally, successful study across difference also may require paying attention to a diverse range of verbal and nonverbal communication modes (see the following cited by Hesse-Biber & Piatelli: DeVault, 1990; Dunbar et al., 2000).

But how do feminist researchers actually go about integrating reflexivity into their research practice? Hesse-Biber and Piatelli review a range of reflexive, methodological techniques used by feminist researchers throughout all stages of the research process—from "reflexivity sampling" (Hesse-Biber & Piatelli) and "collaborative interviewing" (see the following cited by Hesse-Biber & Piatelli: Charmaz, 2000; DeVault, 1990) to "interpretative focus groups" (see Dodson & Schmalzbauer, 2005, cited by Hesse-Biber & Piatelli). Hesse-Biber and Piatelli also highlight feminist ethnographers' inclusion of both the researcher and the participant's interpretations in the written text (see Kirsch, 1999, cited by Hesse-Biber & Piatelli) and the construction of messy, open texts.

Attending to the relationship between researcher and participant continues to be a fundamental aspect of feminist research. According to Judith Preissle, this responsiveness to the researcher-researched relationship reflects a unique set of feminist ethics—an ethics of care versus an ethics of principle, a "situated ethics" versus a "detached ethics" (Vivat, 2002, cited by Preissle). In her chapter, "Feminist Research Ethics," Preissle draws from the work of feminist psychologist Carol Gilligan (1982) and feminist philosopher Nell Noddings (1984) to construct a cogent feminist ethics framework. Gilligan's (1982) research reveals that for women, morality is characterized by actively caring for others and by connected networks and webs or reciprocities rather than by adhering to "rule-governed hierarchies of authority and obedience among separate individuals" (Gilligan, 1982, as paraphrased by Preissle). Similarly, Noddings (1984) argues that women engage in a practical ethics that is focused on relationships with others as opposed to the adherence to universal principles of morality or reason. This practical ethics, or "ethics of care," is motivated not by the pursuit of some universal principle but by an active and ongoing commitment to "the development of another" (Noddings, 1984, as paraphrased by Preissle).

Preissle does not wish to imply that feminists ignore the relevance of universal principles, such as justice, or to deny that feminists also draw on the ethics of principle as a rationale for their research. However, it is the ethics of care—attending to the researcher-participant relationship and responding to the goals of participants—Preissle argues, that motivates many feminist researchers and makes feminist research unique. Integrating an ethics of care into the research process is a complex and challenging task, and in some respects, an ethics of care is more demanding than an ethics of principle. Greater value placed on the relationship between the researcher and the participant requires greater responsibility—in short, an ethics of care does not "eliminate our ethical dilemmas" (Preissle).

Taking an ethics of care seriously means being receptive to the "*situation-specific* [italics added] quality of human relationships" (Preissle). There is no one answer, universal principle, or set of questions that teaches us how to cultivate the researcher-researched relationship or how to attend to the well-being, goals, and needs of participants. Different approaches, methods, questions, and decisions may be required in different contexts and with different communities of participants. Researchers must evaluate each case

based on its particularity and situated location—an approach to cultivating a respectful relationship between the researcher and her participant may succeed in one community but alienate another. For example, some feminist researchers engage in self-reflexive critique (see the following cited by Preissle: Ellis, 2004; Fine, 1994; Visweswaran, 1994), share their own experiences with respondents (see Seibold, 2000, cited by Preissle), and actively collaborate with, and include, respondents' voices and interpretations in research texts (see Blakeslee, Cole, & Conefrey, 1996, cited by Preissle). On the other hand, feminist researchers may decide not to share data with participants in order to protect their physical safety, psychological well-being, and privacy (see the following cited by Preissle: Hopkins, 1993; Robertson, 2000).

In this section, the authors interrogate epistemologies of truth, knowledge, power, and morality from a feminist perspective. The traditional meanings of these terms are challenged, reworked, and re-invented as the authors explore their implications for *feminist research praxis*. In and through the practice of feminist research, truth is transformed from universal applicability to situated location, knowledge from objectivity and value neutrality to lived experience and personal perspective. Personal experience becomes a source of authenticity rather than a contaminant, and by honestly acknowledging her situated perspective, a researcher increases the validity and legitimacy of her research project. Morality shifts from the realm of abstract principles to living, human relationships, and issues of power and representation are problematized throughout all stages of the research process.

Feminists' perspectives on these epistemological issues are multiple and complex, however, and feminists continue to engage in dialogue and debate on how best to address, confront, and translate issues of truth, knowledge, and power into their research practices. And as feminists reconceptualize these epistemological meanings and work them into their research practices, new questions, demands, and challenges arise. Practicing feminist ethics, for example, requires acute attention to the "situation-specific" quality of each researcher-researched relationship, and the practice of reflexivity alternatively involves sharing, collaboration, and a heightened sensitivity to difference. Further, if knowledge and truth are based in personal experience and situated perspective, is there any room for seeking commonalities and shared knowledge between and across these experiences and situations? And if authenticity is rooted in situated perspective and personal experience, what happens if perspectives and experiences change? The authors in this section begin to tackle these kinds of questions by illuminating not only the "situated" self but also the "slippery" self and by embracing "diversity as a means"— dialogue and constructive critique across and among diverse perspectives bring potential change and transformation. But feminists continue to wrestle with these important epistemological themes, to contribute to our understanding of their relevance and implications for feminist research and to confront how best to re-invent and incorporate these themes into the practice of feminist research.

# 21

# AUTHORITY AND REPRESENTATION IN FEMINIST RESEARCH

JUDITH ROOF

Feminist research is an invention of the 20th century. As such it participates in the assumptions and methods of (primarily Western) thought that dominate the era. These include empirical scientific methods of showing various sex/gender functions and inequities (sociology, biology, anthropology) and more abstract philosophical- and linguistic-based interrogations of sex/gender focused on various aspects of representation (images of woman and gender, the gender bias of underlying assumptions in the arts, literature, film, theater, and culture broadly speaking). The first set is considered "objective" and scientific and assumes the transparency of all representations (words and people mean what they say). The second, the humanist, investigates the ways structures, organizations, ideologies, and representations are anything but transparent, exploring the various ways both cultural material and our ways of thinking about such material already depend on assumptions about and evaluations of gender. In these two different approaches, authority derives from the slightly different assumptions about what truth is and how it is discerned. Science asserts fact and method as the basis for its authority. The humanist derives authority from the logical power of its more analogical or paradigmatic

arguments and insights. In both cases, an investigator's authority is augmented by many factors: the soundness of method, the clarity and indisputability of facts, the persuasive elegance of argument, the professional reputation of the speaker, the effectiveness of rhetoric, and the identitarian affiliations (gender, race, ethnicity, class, national origin, age, religion) of the speakers themselves. Finally, authority and power depend on historical circumstances—on how timely an argument is and how ready audiences are to hear it.

Feminist research is also in itself a set of representations, both in the ways in which research is communicated and in the tendency to represent the experiences and situations of individual women, identifiable interest groups, and general populations. The presentation of research both follows the prescribed modes of various disciplines—empirical reportage of the sciences, analysis and critique in the humanities—and begins to devise more feminist formulations of communication, including more work produced cooperatively, more personalized modes of presenting arguments, and mixing of genres (empirical research and autobiography, testimony and statistics, life writing and criticism) as ways of making representation itself more closely aligned with feminist thought and drawing attention to the inherent phallocentrism of traditional academic forms. Feminist experiments in representing work are sometimes rhetorical, that is, sometimes serve as ways of enacting the "personal is political" assumptions of a feminist program. They also sometimes represent new modes of cooperative inquiry or the need to treat a different subject matter (women) differently. In all cases, modes of communicating research are most often inextricable from the research they present.

That feminist research often calls for mixed media in its representation points to the ways feminism itself requires a mixing of disciplines. Although empiricism and the humanities seem to represent opposing methodologies with conflicting assumptions, feminist research has often combined the two, seeing that neither in itself can account for the complex difficulties presented by the pervasive gender asymmetries underwriting human cultures. In addition, feminist researchers have questioned the possible "objectivity" of either approach, suggesting that what we regard as objective or universal veils the privileges of patriarchal organizations and male speakers. Challenging notions of objectivity, neutrality, or universality, feminist research often combines objective approaches with experiential strategies, balancing the empirical with the subjective, receptivity with authority, and the power of discourse with the irresistible evidence of women's lives. This has resulted not only in expanding disciplinary inquiry and questioning traditional assumptions but also in the combination of personal, group, and contextualized representations of research both in the rhetoric and style of communication and in challenges to the universality of any kind of "truth." Because feminism is itself a critique of the ways power and authority are distributed in relation to the gendered structures of patriarchy, feminist research and the representations of feminist research have had to walk a fine and self-critical line between the attractions of the authorized universal subject wielding Enlightenment logics and traditional authoritarian rhetoric and the insights feminist research itself has gained by attending to the subjective, the instinctive, and the disempowered.

Power and authority in feminist research have seemed to exist, thus, in a paradox, trading between the authority of science and the power of experience as well as the impersonal practices of generalization and the more problematic questions of rhetoric and representation. Although we tend to assume that power and authority follow one from the other, the projects of feminist research have critiqued the intrinsic gender biases of that relation, have shown various ways in which authority may be gained without power, have empowered alternative modes of authority, have devised alternative distributions of power, and have offered alternative visions of what might constitute research itself. These projects represent multiple approaches to the problems of (1) wielding authority while questioning it, (2) deploying traditional scientific approaches or critical theories as a means of critiquing gendered practices of power and authority, (3) developing convincing alternative theories and methods of inquiry, and (4) devising new techniques of persuasion and representation. What is clear is that feminist research in general believes in the power of critique and inquiry to change materially the structures of culture and the lives of individuals.

## Questioning the Bases of Authority

Although feminist pioneers such as Mary Wollstonecraft, Charlotte Perkins Gilman, and Susan B. Anthony observed the unhappy effects of patriarchy on women of all classes, it is not until Virginia Woolf (1929) writes her famous *A Room of One's Own* that the observation of inequality is joined by a systematic interrogation of the conditions and assumptions by which gender inequities are produced and sustained. Woolf's queries, followed and deepened in her 1938 exposition, *Three Guineas* (Woolf, 1938), begin the unraveling of privilege, authority, and material conditions premised on and alibied by gender myths. *A Room of One's Own* is famous for its concluding proposition that with a yearly income of £500 and a room of her own, a woman might be as inquiring, creative, and authoritative as a man. The essay is, however, also an insightful exploration of the assumptions and presumptions grounding patriarchal authority itself.

Looking to the wisdom of male writers, sociologists, historians, and critics, Woolf finds a universal misogyny seemingly established only through the angry repetition of cultural assumptions. The gender bias of male thinkers, she realizes, becomes the means of such experts' assumption of authority. She counters these forays into the masculinist universe of scholarly inquiry with insights gained from her own observations about the effect material conditions have on an individual's ability to indulge in scholarly or creative activities. Noting that women in general rarely have the education, income, or opportunity to write or create, Woolf describes the institutional and material disadvantages of women—like Shakespeare's apocryphal sister—that prevent them from easily exploring their own talents. Her recommendation of privacy and sustenance depends finally on the experiential observation that the hungry, overworked, and dispossessed can hardly be expected to be the equals of their much better fed and equipped male counterparts.

Combining the experience and observation of a woman with a rhetoric of open-minded exploration—combining the personal and the fictive with the more generally political—*A Room of One's Own* commences nearly a century of feminist critique of the unchallenged alignment of authority, power, masculinity, privilege, and wealth. Woolf's project, furthered by her own insights in *Three Guineas,* instigates Simone de Beauvoir's (1949) extended inquiry into the theoretical and methodological bases of women's oppression in *The Second Sex.* Trained as a philosopher, de Beauvoir systematically addresses every mode of post-Enlightenment analysis, from the empiricisms of biology and sociology to the theoretical interventions of psychoanalysis and Marxism. De Beauvoir's investigation is divided into two parts: Book 1 is an interrogation of the "facts and myths" through which the category "woman" has been understood in biological, historical, sociological, anthropological, literary, psychoanalytic, and Marxist terms. De Beauvoir's mode of analysis is a critical interrogation of the ways these discourses and methods assume, depend on, naturalize, and reproduce specific myths of the inferiority, inabilities, and patriarchal dispositions of women. Her authority is based on her knowledge of these fields as well as on her ability to demonstrate consistently the self-contradictory

way all these disciplines understand woman. In other words, her authority is premised on the persuasiveness of her analysis combined with the pervasiveness of her findings. The representation of de Beauvoir's authority comes through her masterful deployment of forms of traditional argument. Unlike Woolf, de Beauvoir does not resort to fiction or the personal but instead performs inquiry through the presentation of logic.

Showing the systematic bias of multiple disciplines provides de Beauvoir with the platform from which she can launch the argument of Book 2 of her project, *Woman's Life Today,* which, more exhaustively than Woolf's essays, presents the category "woman" as a cultural production. "One is not born," she says, "but rather becomes, a woman" (p. 249). This second section, like the first, is an exhaustive counter-reading of cultural myths and attitudes, engaging alike expert opinion and popular fantasy. De Beauvoir devises the position from which she speaks as a combination of her own perspective and the rapier incisiveness of an acute, penetrating observer. Her rhetoric is the construction of a commanding, authoritative voice whose mustering of facts, phenomena, and argument displays an estimable intelligence. In other words, de Beauvoir represents authority herself in the very way she writes the book.

Woolf and de Beauvoir, thus, employ the persona of the brilliant and capable woman to counteract myths about women's ability to do what each accomplishes in her books. The representational strategy combines analysis, rhetoric, and the performance of an authoritative persona, humble in the case of Woolf, masterful in the case of de Beauvoir, but both in a position to observe from a more reasoned, less biased perspective. Because a large portion of their work shows that the perspective of patriarchal culture is indeed biased, they position their own observations as less biased correctives.

Woolf and de Beauvoir's works begin the wave of feminist examinations of the biases inherent to patriarchal authority and the illogical inequality of women in Western culture. Many of the influential works that follow in this vein—Betty Friedan's (1963) *The Feminine Mystique,* Germaine Greer's (1971) *The Female Eunuch,* Jill Johnston's (1973) *Lesbian Nation,* and Kate Millet's (1970) *Sexual Politics*, for example—continue the process of demythologizing myths about woman through reasoned counteranalysis. Friedan grounds her authority in being a representative—the spokeswoman for a large underrepresented group of women. Beginning her exploration with an evocation of women's daily lives, Friedan uses her own experience, glossed as a quasi-objective interviewing method, as a way of organizing and dismantling literary, historical, and cultural myths about the proper roles and abilities of women. Although Friedan occasionally cites studies from sociology, her arguments are based on an appeal to the comments of real people she gathered through interviews with women who may, it is implied, be more willing to talk to Friedan than to male researchers. For example, Friedan begins her chapter on sexuality with the following nod to the sources of her authority:

> I did not do a Kinsey study, but when I was on the trail of the problem that has no name, the suburban housewives I interviewed would often give me an explicitly sexual answer to a question that was not sexual at all. (p. 247)

Although very few of her conclusions are based on the opinions she gathered, her appeal to the disenfranchised masses augments her authority as analyst.

Millett, Greer, and Johnston all perform extended analyses of social practices, institutions, and representations, designed to demonstrate the pervasive existence of misogyny as a condition of social existence. Their various analyses depend on the performance and representation of insightful counter-reading made persuasive through the persona of the writer and the trenchancy of her observations. They all share in the combination of empirical methodologies (i.e., survey facts, interviews, other sociological texts) and the kinds of critical analyses practiced by de Beauvoir, as deftly managed by an insightful critic whose first imprimatur of authority consists in her mastery of argument and style. Because each of these figures is among the first to argue publicly for radical feminist analyses, they also gain power through our perception of them as brave and pioneering. At the same time, the power of their analyses

also comes from their readers' recognition that someone is finally describing their own experience of the world. In this latter sense, such analyses gain their authority from the burgeoning feminist interest in "consciousness-raising" as a countermode of authority based on experience. These works and others pave the way for contemporaneous kinds of critical work that deploy critical and disciplinary strategies to make visible the endemic sexism of both methodologies and fields of knowledge.

## The Power of Feminist Critique

The power of feminist critique derives from the masterful deployment of critical and disciplinary methodologies, first, to discern and correct the systematic omission of women and, second, to correct the sexist and misogynist practices and assumptions associated with specific modes of research. Almost all of this work represents a moment in which political necessity makes analysis relevant and desirable across a range of disciplines from the recovery projects of feminist history, sociology, anthropology, philosophy, and literary studies to discipline-based analyses of gender in culture as performed by sociologists, historians, political scientists, anthropologists, philosophers, and literary, media, and cultural theorists to extended feminist critiques of such discourses as philosophy, social policy, law, psychology and psychoanalysis, and medicine. All these projects base their authority on the responsible, reasoned, and expert practice of disciplinary methodologies. All gain power from the timing of their appearance in the late 1970s to mid-1980s, the quality of their inquiry, the persuasiveness of their argument, and the effectiveness of their rhetoric. In other words, as correctives and critiques, they premise authority on the very same qualities by which such authority has been traditionally granted, with the difference being that these analyses are focused on women and presented primarily (though not exclusively) by women in explicit relation to issues of gender and sexuality.

Although critiques of disciplinary assumptions rely less on experience than on reason, recovery projects in which the omitted or underrepresented experiences of women are made visible do presume the authoritative presence of alternative perspectives. In fact, the reason for collecting them, apart from providing a more balanced view of humanity, is to demonstrate the previous bias of scholarly inquiry, which had omitted both the accomplishments of influential women and the women's meaningful participation in larger cultural processes. Endeavors to collect and present lost women's traditions in history, sociology, anthropology, culture, literature, and film began in the early 1970s and continue even now. Feminist scholars began a process of making women and their role in history, society, and culture visible.

The impetus of feminist recovery projects is corrective. Its authority derives from both a belief in the bias of traditional disciplines and the sheer quantity of material these projects exhume. That there were numerous important and influential women in history justifies and empowers the project of finding them. Building an archive of previously ignored historical figures, writers, and artists produces a counter-history in which the rediscovered figures also speak for themselves. Like most historical scholarship, feminist recovery projects depend on the authority of historical texts, basing any claims about the value and importance of women figures on what the figures themselves have said and done. Incorporating this rediscovered material revises understandings of the historical, political, social, and literary contexts in which they were produced. Newer understandings of context invite further investigation, so that what might appear to be simply the authority garnered through corrective rediscovery of lost women figures is in fact a complicated renegotiation of entire fields where power and authority rest equally on the presentation of new material and the reinterpretation of the old in light of the new.

Often, though not always, these recovery projects have been undertaken by women scholars, presumed by an incipient identity politics (which assumes a naturalized and identificatory link between subjective identity and objects of interest) to be especially interested in the process. Such endeavors undertaken by male scholars increasingly came under suspicion as appropriative, preemptive, or dismissive. The tendency to associate the gender of authors with

their "right" to wield an authority marks the incipient stages of the kinds of identity politics that become pronounced in the 1980s as guaranteeing authority in themselves.

Although all these recovery projects were implicitly political insofar as the idea of finding lost women's traditions assumes and acts on their previous exclusion, some are more overtly feminist than others, combining an analysis of women's oppression with the process of bringing women's roles and achievements to light. Juliet Mitchell's (1971) *Women's Estate* and Vivian Gornick and Barbara Moran's (1971) *Woman in Sexist Society* both reread history as an analysis of distributions of power and disadvantage. Elizabeth Janeway's (1971) *Man's World, Woman's Place* provides a rereading and analysis of gender relations in social history, following the much earlier work of Anna Spencer's (1925) *Women's Share in Social Culture*. Sociologists and political scientists begin to focus on accounts of women's roles in social and political processes. Feminist collectives begin to ameliorate the dearth of information available about women's health in forms accessible to women in the landmark *Our Bodies, Ourselves* (1971), first published in 1971 and continually expanded and updated. Early 1970s feminist literary criticism splits its energies between rediscovering lost or underappreciated women authors such as Aphra Behn, Virginia Woolf, Charlotte Perkins Gilman, and Gertrude Stein and forging a critical practice that takes gender as its central concern (Brown & Olson, 1978; Cornillon, 1972; Spacks, 1975).

The authority of these texts comes from their construction of a specific female viewpoint understood as perceiving women differently and more accurately than traditional scholarship. The sense, too, that many women scholars put their careers on the line to engage in studies about women lends these projects the credibility of bravery and sacrifice. In addition, producing explicitly women's texts, especially as *Our Bodies, Ourselves* does in a collective, low-budget, straightforward way, elicits the sway of the credible friend who has no motive other than the philanthropy of feminist activism grounding the project. In other words, the power and authority of these earlier projects derives from the politicized circumstances of their very production as a feminist act. Their modes of representing knowledge as accessible, friendly, and familiar produce a style of feminist representation that enacts a democratization of knowledge and a sense of communal sharing. Their persuasiveness is produced by their appeal to the practical.

Just as the process of recovery has been itself both a political action and a political critique, so too does it accompany a reevaluation of the various disciplinary methods and assumptions by which women and their accomplishments were initially excluded. This process occurs in every discipline, though various factors such as the traditional presence of women in the field, the relative influence of the area, and the extent to which traditional forms of inquiry and method were entrenched influenced how quickly disciplines accepted feminist correction and critique. History, sociology, and literature participate in the earliest recovery projects, whereas the method-centered fields of science and philosophy attracted analyses correcting the assumptions by which their disregard of women and gender as a category had produced skewed studies and theories. In these fields, knowing disciplinary assumptions and methodology became the primary basis for critiquing omissions and conclusions. Continuing the work of Simone de Beauvoir, Mary Daly examines the concatenation of religions and patriarchy in *Beyond God the Father: Toward a Philosophy of Women's Liberation.* Other feminist philosophers such as Marilyn Frye, Sarah Hoagland, and Alison Jaggar continued the examination of the presumptions of Western metaphysics as well as forging a specifically feminist philosophy (Frye, 1983; Hoagland, 1988; Jaggar, 1984). This philosophy focused on issues of ethics and epistemology as the specific sets of questions by which patriarchal and sexist assumptions might be challenged and altered.

Philosophy exudes the authority of metaphysics, of a reasoning process presumably untainted by specific content or bias. The same is true of science, which like philosophy was challenged as a set of methods and an epistemology by feminist philosophers and scholars of science. The interrogation of the gender bias of the scientific method and its exclusion of women came later, however, than a set of inquiries into the status of women in science,

which occurred through the 1970s and early 1980s. The initial work on women and science was concerned with the relative absence of women working as scientists, assuming that fuller participation by women would correct some of the field's sexist biases. Thus bypassing issues of method in favor of the gender identity of researchers, early surveys of women in science identified the problem as literally a problem of women's absence from scientific fields (Cole, 1979; Fausto-Sterling & English, 1985; Haas & Perrucci, 1984; Rossiter, 1982; Schilling & Hunt, 1974).

By the early 1980s, however, feminist scholars began to question the gender bias of science's assumptions and methods. Deploying a mode of feminist critique that reads "across" a discipline's own assertions and claims, feminist critics merged an authority premised on a thorough knowledge of a field with the power of feminist critique, especially in the way such a critique made visible and apparent sexist assumptions and exclusions of scientific thought and practice. Biology was a natural first target insofar as it deals most directly with issues of sex. Ruth Bleier's (1984) *Science and Gender: A Critique of Biology and Its Theories* commenced a series of feminist interrogations of science in general, including Evelyn Fox Keller's (1985) *Reflections on Women in Science*, Sandra Harding's (1986) *The Science Question in Feminism*, Donna Haraway's (1989) *Primate Visions: Gender, Race, and Nature in the World of Modern Science*, Nancy Tuana's (1989) collection of essays, *Feminism and Science*, and Mary Jacobus and Sally Shuttleworth's (1990) anthology *Body/ Politics: Women and the Discourses of Science.*

A similar questioning of exclusion and method occurred contemporaneously in the social sciences. Less concerned with the absence of female researchers, political scientists and sociologists also began questioning the gender bias of disciplinary assumptions. Susan Okin's (1979) *Women in Western Political Thought* was followed by Judith Evans's (1986) *Feminism and Political Theory* and Diana Coole's (1988) *Women in Political Theory: From Ancient Misogyny to Contemporary Feminism* as interrogations of the gendered biases of political thinking. Sociological methodologies and assumptions were queried by Nancy Fraser (1989) in *Unruly Practices: Power,*

*Discourse, and Gender in Contemporary Social Theory*, while Henrietta Moore's (1988) *Feminism and Anthropology* approaches similar problems in anthropology. Kathleen Weiler's (2001) collection, *Feminist Engagements: Reading, Resisting, and Revisioning Male Theorists in Education and Cultural Studies*, questions the sexist assumptions of education and cultural studies.

Generally, the projects of recovery and disciplinary critique draw their authority from the disciplines themselves, entering and altering the field's own conversations. At the same time, however, they constitute the field of women's studies from which they gain an additional institutional authority. Although all the scientific, social, and humanities disciplines interrogated by feminist scholars have constituted themselves in one way or another through the exclusion of women and a reliance on gender-biased assumptions, most critique itself derived from one of two sets of assumptions about authority itself. Although we may map the disciplines according to whether we understand their endeavors as empirical or representational, science or humanism, the basic sets of questions applied derive either from a belief in the defining capacities of human psychology or from the credibilities attributed to historical circumstances and material conditions. For this reason, the discourses of psychoanalysis and historical materialism have occupied a central place as both modes and objects of feminist critique.

Psychoanalysis is the study of the human subject with an eye toward treating mental illness. As Sigmund Freud formulated his understandings of how the human psyche formed and functioned, gender and sexuality constituted a large part of the subject's conscious and unconscious mental structure. Although credited with the line "biology is destiny," Freud saw very clearly that individual bodies and desires did not necessarily align into neat binaries. His formulations about gender and sexuality, however, assumed a male subject as his unquestioned model. Although a significant portion of Freud's work on sexuality focused on femininity and female sexuality, he was never able to theorize either adequately. Because psychoanalysis— and particularly Freudian psychoanalysis— seemed to have a profound influence on the normativizing impetuses of analysts, medical practitioners, and social policymakers and because it was so overtly focused on gender and sexuality, it was one of the first targets of feminist critique. From the earliest moments, however, that critique was ambivalent, accepting the idea of a subjective structure and the unconscious while trying to expose and revise the sexist assumptions of such founding fathers as Freud and Havelock Ellis.

After Simone de Beauvoir devotes a chapter to "The Psychoanalytic Point of View" in *The Second Sex*, feminist thinkers such a Kate Millett, Betty Friedan, and Phyllis Chesler take on its authority by showing the intrinsic patriarchalism of some of Freud's conclusions (Chesler, 1972; Friedan, 1963; Millett, 1970). Both Millett and Friedan blame Freud for providing a new and scientized authority for traditional beliefs about the second-class status of women. Pointing to such formulations as "anatomy is destiny" and "penis envy," Millett and Friedan demystify Freudian psychoanalysis as thinly veiled patriarchal ideology, especially in the apparent sexism of its more publicly bruited conclusions. Understanding psychoanalysis itself as an authority to be defeated if women were to achieve any measure of equality, Freud became one focus of early feminist attack.

Freud and psychoanalysis were not, however, without their feminist defenders, scholars such as Juliet Mitchell, Jacqueline Rose, Ellie Ragland-Sullivan, Teresa Brennan, Jane Gallop, and others, who saw in Freudian psychoanalysis a mode of analysis and an understanding of the subject that left room for a much more sophisticated and open understanding of the relations among subjects, genders, and sexualities (Brennan, 1989; Gallop, 1982; Mitchell, 1975; Mitchell & Rose, 1985; Ragland-Sullivan, 1986; Rose, 1986). This kind of work, which began with Mitchell's (1975) *Psychoanalysis and Feminism*, continued through the 1980s as feminist scholars argued that the various psychoanalytic methods might become a mode of authority for feminist work. Certainly, most understandings of textual analysis are derived from a psychoanalytic model in the first place— a model in which one reads a text's symptoms to discern its operation and less obvious meanings. Feminist modes of reading across and against texts depended on understanding this kind of analysis as something that showed a text's underlying assumptions and enabled both critique and revision.

The authority of psychoanalysis as wielded by feminist thinkers was increased by the dissemination of the thought of Jacques Lacan, whose understandings of sexuation, sexuality, and subjectivity engaged more contemporary theories of language and image. Although feminist thinkers charged Lacan with the same kind of patriarchalism as Freud, many literary, film, and feminist psychoanalytic scholars such as Rose, Ragland-Sullivan, Kaja Silverman, Laura Mulvey, Brennan, Gallop, Elizabeth Grosz, and Judith Butler saw Lacan's insights as opportunities for a more feminist and less patriarchal understanding of the dynamics of gender, sexuality, and the development of various forms of the female subject (Brennan, 1993; Butler, 1990; Gallop, 1985; Grosz, 1990; Mulvey, 1989; Rose, 1986; Ragland-Sullivan, 1986; Silverman, 1983). This understanding depended on seeing the dynamics of process as more important than the sometimes sexist conclusions derived therefrom. This meant that psychoanalytic ideas, assumptions, and methods could be turned to a feminist use, along with the authority psychoanalysis connoted.

While textual and film critics developed a feminist psychoanalytic method of criticism, others, such as Carol Gilligan, Nancy Chodorow, and Jessica Benjamin, devised new psychological theories of female development. Still premised on the methods and assumptions of psychoanalysis, these female-centered theories considered a different set of influences and values that might account for and to some extent liberate possibilities for female subjects. Both Chodorow's (1978) *The Reproduction of Mothering* and Gilligan's (1982) *In a Different Voice: Psychological Theory and Women's Development* provided new bases for feminist authority over the female subject. At the same time, feminist psychologists such as Sue Cox and Jessica Benjamin developed specifically feminist understandings of female psychology, and others such as Anica Mander and Anne Rush devised modes of feminist clinical practice (Benjamin, 1988; Cox, 1976; Mander & Rush, 1974).

Because psychoanalysis' understandings of gender were so closely allied to issues of sexuality, feminist researchers also took on their own

examination of the otherwise underconsidered realm of female sexuality. Nancy Friday (1973) gathered specifically women's sexual fantasies in the 1973 *My Secret Garden,* and Shere Hite, a sex researcher, published her landmark study of female sexuality, *The Hite Report: A Nationwide Study on Female Sexuality,* in 1976 (Hite, 1976). The development of a feminist psychology and studies of sexuality, though derived from the insights of psychoanalysis, also depended largely on collecting the experiences of women. Their authority, then, begins a shift toward women's experience as a primary basis for the authority of feminist research, especially in areas of social and psychological study. Representations of this research mixed accounts of women's experience with more empirical arguments and analyses.

A psychoanalytic focus on the subject, however, did not address other possible theories for the conditions within which women lived. Whereas psychoanalytic theorists saw the ways we think about gender, sexuality, and the subject itself as correctible vectors of oppression, historical materialists sought the reasons for sexism in the class divisions and material conditions of women's lives. As she did with psychoanalysis, Simone de Beauvoir recommences this kind of analysis in *The Second Sex,* though she picks up a debate begun earlier by Emma Goldman (1906–1917) in her monthly periodical, *Mother Earth,* published from 1906 to 1917 and in her writings collected later in *The Traffic in Women and Other Essays* (1970). Although, as de Beauvoir points out, Marxism itself does not address gender directly, its analysis of the oppressive effect of class relations provides a model for understanding the interrelations among gender, class, and capitalist practices that provide women with a very different material experience of the world. Women become cheap labor in a system in which patriarchy is wed to capitalism.

The study of the material conditions of women's lives stems from this understanding and provides another kind of authority for feminist analyses based on the material conditions of women as a class as well as another motive for recovering and documenting the lives and experiences of women. Making visible and accessible the lives of otherwise unrepresented women changes the way we might conceive of gender relations as well as the stakes involved in social change. Seeing, for example, the ways women are the objects of exchange between men, as Luce Irigaray and Gayle Rubin do, situates gender relations as market relations, women as objects instead of subjects, and reveals the masculinist and homosocial bases of Western culture (Irigaray, 1977; Rubin, 1996). Such critics as Lillian S. Robinson, Judith Newton, and Rosemary Hennessey present a materialist feminist view of both Western representations of women and feminist practice itself, premising their analyses on Marxist insights about class (Hennessey, 2000; Newton, 1978; Robinson, 1978).

The processes of feminist recovery and the critique of existing discourses locate authority in feminist critics' ability to wield traditional disciplinary assumptions and methods both to make visible the women's lives, experience, and accomplishments that have been ignored and as a way of pointing out and correcting the sexist assumptions of traditional fields. Adding women to fields themselves has the effect of changing the ways such disciplines as biology, history, sociology, anthropology, and literature conceive of their subject matter as well as the ways they understand their own methods. The power of considering women's points of view as both subject and method of inquiry alters the ways such inquiries are conducted but also raises additional questions about the value and effect of different kinds of experience, the ethics of using traditional methodologies, and the modes of communicating thought to feminist audiences.

## ALTERNATIVE THEORIES AND METHODS OF INQUIRY

In an influential essay titled "The Master's Tools," poet and critic Audre Lorde (1984) raises the question of what the relation might be between traditional modes of thinking and the conclusions researchers might draw between conventional modes of universalizing rhetoric and the empirical impersonalities of science and presumptions of mastery. How, in other words, might feminists "use the master's tools" to build anything other than the master's house? Or what

other tools, ways of thinking, and modes of representation might feminist researchers employ that would have persuasive power and authority? The process of rediscovering women's lives and experiences provided one an authority based on experience itself. Experience became an important basis for challenging the impersonal conclusions of traditional scholars, providing an authority for a feminist account of the world, breaking down oppressive stereotypes and patriarchal conclusions of uniformity and forging a theory based on the imagined practicalities of women's existence instead of on the more metaphysical and less relevant pronouncements of conventional institutions such as religion, philosophy, law, and aesthetics. Making theory personal meant making it real, practical, and immediate. It also meant making it less universalized, which both enabled a different mode of more personal argument and allowed more broadly accessible forms of representation that often involved group projects (e.g., the Combahee River Collective) or personal essays such as Lorde's own collection or Gloria Anzaldúa's (1987) *Borderlands/La Frontera: The New Mestiza*.

In the 1960s the American women's movement declared that the "personal is political," an idea that not only made relevant previously trivialized aspects of women's lives but also empowered their speech as if from a new kind of subject. This new liberationist subject became immediately expert about her own experience, encouraged to recognize her difficulties, trials, and frustrations as a more profound version of truth than the cultural ideologies of feminine domesticity by which those perceptions had been dismissed as neurotic, spoiled, weak, or imaginary. The authority of the personal was encouraged by the emergence of consciousness-raising groups where women got together, talked, and found that their experiences often contradicted the lauded happiness of suburbia, the securities of happy marriage, or the myths of survival in the business world. It was also encouraged by an incipient flood of popular press material such as Friedan's *The Feminine Mystique* that put those frustrations and contradictions in print.

Spurred by a new sense of communal vigor and source of support, women began working with other women to address issues such as rape, incest, battery, poverty, exploitation, racism, job discrimination, and sexual frustration—all problems previously ignored or suppressed by mainstream culture. The consciousness-raising group gave women a place to voice their problems, uncertainties, and fears, often finding others whose experience ratified their own—producing, then, groups of women whose perceptions of the world were reinforced by one another's experiences, which enabled the more public dissemination of what Friedan calls "the problem that has no name," and culminating in forms of feminist activism focused on rendering women's lives and problems visible. While publication and popular media attention cultivated an audience of women liberated through self-recognition (or women devoutly hunkered in defense and denial), personal testimony became a primary source of power and authority for women's liberation. Women talking to other women became an effective vector for female enlightenment.

One collection of personal experiences and analysis, Robin Morgan's (1970) *Sisterhood Is Powerful,* had a profound effect on the burgeoning women's movement by showing that women's voices and experiences are indeed valuable, catalyzing forces for change. Morgan's collection was joined by an increasing number of small press publications and periodicals by and for women—*The Ladder* (1956–1972), *Voice of the Women's Liberation Movement* (1968–1969), *Off Our Backs* (1970–), *It Ain't Me Babe* (1970–1971), *Battle Acts* (1970–1974), *The Way We See It* (1970), *Womankind* (1971–1973), *Mother Lode* (1971–1973), *The Furies* (1972–1973), *Lavender Woman* (1971–1976), *Amazon Quarterly* (1972–1975)—that continued the promulgation of women's experiences and analyses of various forces of oppression. By providing publication opportunities, small presses and journals provided a site of empowerment for feminist researchers who needed a better way to reach audiences and whose work and ideas were likely to be censored by mainstream modes of publication.

The mainstream itself, however, picked up this new market of women interested in women's issues. With Random House's publication of *Sisterhood Is Powerful,* women authors found new and effective outlets for their work. *Ms.* magazine began its mainstream publication in 1972. Nancy Friday, Marilyn French, Erica Jong, and Rita Mae Bown began publishing fiction focused on women's experiences, and the poets Nikki Giovanni, Judy Grahn, Audre Lorde, and Adrienne Rich gained a new visibility and wider audience. Women artists such as Judy Chicago made quite visible the differences in perception and aesthetics that emerge from women's experience. All this production authorized continued exploration of women's expression. The more evident presence of women-centered art in turn authorized an expanding field of women artists and writers who themselves made women's experience and vision the subject and aesthetic of their works.

This burgeoning artistic activity fed into developing women's studies programs at universities, which, defined already by their recovery projects, found new terrain for feminist scholarship. The links between feminist community activities such as rape crisis centers, women's newspapers and bookstores, women's concerts, women's centers, women's studies programs, and other women-centered endeavors not only produced a system of mutual support but also authorized and empowered women's political initiatives such as the fight for the Equal Rights Amendment (ERA) and reproductive rights, lobbying for more protective domestic relations laws, fairer social security and other benefits, child care programs, and better health care for women. Women's studies programs began national conferences in 1977, and music festivals such as the Michigan Women's Music Festival started in the same year to bring women together from all over the United States.

Politically, such public conversations among women produced action groups such as the National Organization for Women (NOW), begun in 1966 by Betty Friedan and others. NOW lobbied first for the ERA, then for reproductive rights and against discrimination. Other "official" women-centered activities such as International Women's Year in 1975 brought attention to the plight of women in nonindustrialized countries. The national organization, visibility, and public endorsement of women's perspectives additionally authorized feminist research as respectable and almost mainstream.

As a mode of authority, visibility was central in the 1970s, especially as women's difficulties had been convincingly presented by Friedan and others as partly a problem of anonymity and invisibility. In addition, the increasing importance of media visibility in general in the 1970s as television became more central and pervasive made media attention necessary to certify the significance of events and causes.

As the consolidation of feminist communities brought together women of different backgrounds, classes, and races, so too did differences among women and their experiences become more evident. If experience could authorize speech, community, and political action, it also showed disparate needs, interests, and perspectives. Thus, as a mode of representative authority, experience was a two-edged sword. On the one hand it countered more overtly ideological versions of women's truth and enabled the development of communities of individuals with common problems, anxieties, and experiences that seemed to support the truth of lived experience. On the other hand, the different experiences of women also demonstrated that the category itself was full of variations and even clashes in class, opportunity, race, sexualities, regional and ethnic interests, religious affiliations, and understandings of the relative importance of gender itself. In other words, representations of the issues as personal demonstrated how representative experiences might be as well as how idiosyncratic and unrepresentative they often were. Experiences of gender oppression themselves differed for women of different races, ages, sexualities, and classes as did ideas about the urgency and proper mode of addressing sexism. Trying to subsume all under the rubric of "women" became, thus, increasingly difficult as feminists began to perceive the pervasiveness of oppressions.

African American women, sometimes already engaged in the ongoing civil rights movement, readily pointed out the disparities among women, questioning assumptions about the universality of women's experience of oppression. Most often, African American women's objections were themselves based on experience, inflected with an acute understanding of the effects of racism. Already in the early 1970s, African American women made their perspectives clear. Angela Davis (1971) called for antiracist activism in her letter from prison, while such writers as Gloria Hull, Sonia Sanchez, and Alice Walker published poetry and stories and Toni Cade Bambara edited a collection of essays and stories about black women (Bambara, 1970; Davis, 1971). As experience itself became more obviously complex and contradictory, its authorizing aegis was defined more and more in relation to imagined degrees of oppression. Privileged white women began to feel less authorized to speak from their own experience in light of the more difficult lives of other women. If oppression was ultimately the subject of feminist research and if experience of oppression was a primary mode of authorization, then less oppressed women experienced a species of de-authorization. In addition, the practice of academic authority, especially as perceived as universalizing and exclusive, was discredited by some as itself oppressive to women.

The recognition of women's vastly different experiences, then, led to the development of new modes of feminist authority, representation, and rhetoric. Experience became a matter of subject position in a politics of identity in which one's experience and insights were linked to categories of race, ethnicity, class, and sexuality. Traditional academic theories not only were examined for their sexist bias but also became suspect for some as intrinsically oppressive, catalyzing the development of specifically feminist theories or the adoption of approaches that seemed less authoritative, universalist, and expert and more experiential, democratic, and accessible. The valorization of identity as determining experience resulted in identity politics and standpoint epistemologies on the one hand, while suspicion and critique of the intrinsic sexist bias in theorizing led to alternative ways of theorizing on the other.

Some feminists, such as those deploying psychoanalytic or Marxist analyses, understand experience as simultaneously individual and an effect of social organizations such as patriarchy or capitalism. For these scholars, the individual becomes the nexus of conflicting forces, and though neither mode of analysis believes that individual experience represents broader truth, they, as well as many feminists, regard personal experience as a mode of authority. The value of this experience as a mode of authorizing lies more in its imagined authenticity than in any representative capability. Those who testify about their experiences as women speak bravely from a site of oppression about events and feelings only women in their position can understand and communicate. Because it is their experience and because the speakers have most often been disenfranchised in one way or another, these experiences and feelings are presumed to be genuine and unmediated—that is, oppressed people are more capable than others of communicating their experiences without inflecting these experiences with dominant ideologies or self-interest. They are imagined to speak from the heart, although, of course, their testimony has no more claim to truth than that of anyone else. Situating such testimony as unassailable displaces issues of authority into the identities of those often deemed to be "other." Despite the fact that making explicit the fantasy subtending this idea of authenticity produces an inevitable hint of cynicism, the fantasy nonetheless underwrites many populist conceptions of the unassailable value of testimony based on experience (as with victims of the Holocaust) and powerlessness, defined as differences in relation to a middle-class, white, Christian majority.

These experiences are not only authoritative in themselves; they testify as well on behalf of the sociocultural position of the speaker. What began as individual testimony is transformed into a speech representing grids of sociocultural presence defined in terms of those categories believed to be oppressed in and of themselves. Nonwhite speakers, for example, inevitably speak as oppressed racial others, lower-class people as oppressed poor people. The experience of individuals is subsumed by the position from which they are imagined to speak, and this position becomes what authorizes and authenticates their testimony. The equation of individuals and subject positions has the effect of erasing idiosyncrasy while appealing to difference and diversity. At the same time, it encourages individual responsibility for a consciousness of the effects of sociocultural positioning on beliefs, experience, and authority. It suggests that only those approaching a social phenomenon from a specific position may speak from and for that position. It

suggests, in other words, that the distribution of authority through culture is not only inequitable, it is also appropriative, dismissive, and dependent on the invisibility of those whom it oppresses to secure its power.

That the relations between a speaker's "identity" and the status and authority of what she says themselves represent a set of problems, however, might also be an inevitable conclusion of feminist theorizing. If patriarchy depends on an oppressed class of gendered others whose speaking for themselves might begin their liberation, then this same model works for other situations of oppression. Although displacing the locus of authority from experience to the schematized categories of economic, racial, and ethnic intersection from which individuals are imagined to speak dissolves individual experiences into the truths of political theories of oppression, it is precisely this conflation of witness and oppression that is understood to combat the universalizing erasure of other perspectives. One's speech is then understood to be not only testimony but also the inevitable product of subject position. This set of connections suggests that individuals can only speak authoritatively from their own subject positions. In addition, however, it also suggests that some subject positions are more "positioned" to see the truth of oppression than are other positions. In other words, those who are understood as more oppressed are more likely to see this oppression than those located on the side of the oppressors. If subject positions are imagined in relation to their imagined access to power (i.e., in relation to economic, social, racial, and ethnic regimes of privilege), then those more enfranchised to speak perceptively about oppression are those in positions of less advantage.

The problem with this is that it both represents and depends on the same modes of oppression that it tries to critique. On the one hand, seeing authority in relation to oppression enables many to speak powerfully. On the other, this mode of enfranchisement assumes rather than questions the bases by which certain subject positions are constructed as well as the terms through which both oppression and concepts of the subject itself are understood. Only certain kinds of difference and oppression are acknowledged; the theoretical bases by which these positions are constructed remain fairly invisible or are themselves authorized by the ratifying self-identifications of subjects who understand themselves to occupy those positions. Finally, position, understood in terms of a few categories of social oppression such as race, class, gender, and ethnicity, becomes coterminous with identity. Group politics becomes a matter of sorting individuals by identity category.

Obviously, there is an absurdity to this collapse, in the shorthand of any notion of identity premised primarily on stereotyped categorization and the assumption that all members of categories share similar experiences. The reduction of authorization to a semaphore of identity categories became a way of short-circuiting individual experience in favor of the imaginary authorizations of particular theories of relative oppression. The idea that individuals perceive the world itself according to these identity categories produces a notion of a "standpoint epistemology," a way of knowing the world from a specific, identifiable point defined as the intersection of certain kinds of socially relevant categories such as race, class, and gender. Discussions about the validity of standpoint epistemologies took center stage in the early 1990s, as the idea of standpoint epistemology represents both the apotheosis of the logic of identity politics and a delimiting factor for any universalizing practices. Collections such as Roof and Wiegman's (1995) *Who Can Speak? Authority and Critical Identity* and Alcoff and Potter's (1993) *Feminist Epistemologies* identify and explore the complex issues of identity, ethics, authority, and representative speech.

Standpoint epistemologies become eventually a matter of an ethical recognition of both the differences of others and one's own production as subject in relation to cultural forces. At the same time, standpoints are increasingly collapsed into bodies themselves as sites that indicate subjective standpoint. Shane Phelan's (1994) *Getting Specific* argues for a thorough and responsible accounting for differences, while feminist theories of the body provide a different kind of challenge to the systems of thought by which identity categories are produced in the first place.

Just as feminist challenges to the theoretical bases of authority push feminist researchers toward personal experience as one mode of

validation, so too do they push feminist researchers to devise explicitly feminist theories. As bodies define sociocultural and political positions, and as familial and economic organizations such as patriarchy and capitalism depend on the same subjugation of bodies, the sites of the body, the family, and economies seem the most propitious sites for feminist interventions. If, for example, we believe that ways of knowing come from the subject's experience of her body, then feminist thinkers employ the female body as the place from which a different way of knowing might be authorized. French feminist theorists such as Julia Kristeva, Luce Irigaray, and Hélène Cixous all devised countertheories of subjectivity, epistemology, and aesthetics from the female body as a distinctly different experience of the world. Kristeva (1984) devised an understanding of poetics in relation to the different relation between female bodies and language (*Revolution in Poetic Language*), while Irigaray (1977, 1985) assails psychoanalysis and Western philosophy from an assumption that women's bodies experience existence as essentially more multiple and decentered than male bodies (*This Sex Which Is Not One, Speculum of the Other Woman*). Cixous devises alternative theories of literature and aesthetics based on an understanding of the different relations between women's bodies, language, and aesthetics (Cixous, 1994; Cixous & Clément, 1986).

Feminist artists and aesthetic theorists likewise devise new understandings of a feminist aesthetic based on the differences in perception and bodily experience of women, which itself represents a form of authority. Judy Chicago's *Dinner Party* (1979) and *The Birth Project* (1985) as well as writing by women authors, artists, playwrights, and filmmakers, devise theories of feminist praxis whose power is specifically womanist—addressing and appealing to women. On the basis of this rich new tradition of feminist artistic work, feminist theorists devise different ways of understanding a feminist aesthetics, premised on the works' foregrounding of styles, colors, themes, and stories associated with and focusing on women, women's bodies, and women's experiences. Understood as multiple, dispersed, tactile, often crafts based, and nonobjectifying, women's art is formulated in feminist theories of women's art as a medium of communication, a mode of authority, a site of both individual and group self-representation, a means of community building, and occasionally a marker of separatist difference, speaking to women only or primarily and eschewing both the supposed universalism and rebellious Oedipality of mainstream artistic production. Like the body or the identitarian speaker, feminist art is often imagined to speak from beyond the structure of oppression as sincere, perceptive, heartfelt, and true. Of course, like all other modes of sincere or presumably "unmediated" communication, artistic expression constitutes a mode of critique and self-expression that often represents the perspective of many while simultaneously effecting an individual vision. Its authority lies in its appeal to the sense and the visceral, while its power lies in its ability to capture and express what appear to be the insights of individual and group experience.

Understanding art as a mode of communal authority requires some reconsideration of the function of art itself as well as adjusting and valorizing a specifically womanist or feminist aesthetic practice, which simultaneously envisions and critiques, expresses, and enables a different kind of vision understood specifically as female. This retheorizing of the aesthetic occurs in all media, from music (see, e.g., Sally MacArthur's [2002] *Feminist Aesthetics in Music*; MacArthur & Cate Poynton's [1999] *Music and Feminisms*), theater (*Theatre and Feminist Aesthetics* edited by Karen Laughlin & Catherine Schuler, 1995), film (see Mary Gentile, 1985, *Film Feminisms: Theory and Practice*), and more general feminist aesthetic theories in Gisela Ecker's (1985) *Feminist Aesthetics*, Peg Brand and Carolyn Korsmeyer's (1995) *Feminism and Tradition in Aesthetics*, Tuzyline Allen's (1995) *Womanist and Feminist Aesthetics*, and *Aesthetics in a Feminist Perspective,* edited by Hilde Hein and Carolyn Korsmeyer (1993), *The Power of Feminist Art: The American Movement of the 1970s, History and Impact,* edited by Norma Broude and Mary Garrard (1994), and *Women Making Art: Women in the Visual, Literary, and Performing Arts since 1960,* edited by Deborah Johnson and Wendy Oliver (2001).

Just as the body provides a site on which different theories of feminist epistemology and

practice might be premised, privileging the maternal offers a challenge to patriarchal dominance in thought and social organization. Modeled on mother–daughter relations, woman-to-woman relations enable feminists to reconceive relations among women and envision a more generous, selfless culture based on sharing and nurturing instead of selfishness and single-minded ego. Mother–daughter relations ground Nancy Chodorow's theory of female psychological development in *The Reproduction of Mothering,* as well as understandings of literary and artistic production. Marianne Hirsch (1989), for example, deploys the maternal model as a way of reading women's literature in *The Mother/Daughter Plot*, and Madelon Sprengnether (1990) begins from the mother as a way of rereading Freud in *The Spectral Mother: Freud, Feminism, and Psychoanalysis.* Understanding the maternal as an ethic of selfless interrelation, feminist theories often read women's interrelations, particularly relations among generations, as maternal. This produces a critical practice in which earlier generations become sites of empathy and admiration, and ideally ideas are shared and nurtured among many. This Utopian and often separatist ideal gains its authority from the alternative to patriarchy it seems to offer, especially as most such theories ignore maternal difficulties and mother–daughter strife, dismissing both as effects of patriarchy.

Matriarchy also encompasses social organizations in which the singularity of patriarchal nuclear families gives way to expansive, cooperative communities, imagined at least in literature such as Monique Wittig's (1975) *The Lesbian Body* or Rita Mae Brown's (1978) *Six of One.* Feminist social theorists undertake rethinking the family (*Rethinking the Family: Some Feminist Questions;* Thorne & Yalom, 1982), while ecofeminists deploy a feminist ethic of sharing and coexisting in revisioning the relations among humans, spirits, and the world (Carol Adams, 1993, *Ecofeminism and the Sacred*; Carolyn Merchant, 1992, *Radical Ecology*; Diamond & Orenstein, 1990, *Reweaving the World: The Emergence of Ecofeminism*; Greta Gaard, 1993, *Ecofeminism: Women, Animals, Nature*).

Finally, some feminist thinkers ground an alternative ethic in an appeal to a different cosmology, governed by female principles and the goddess. This specifically feminist spirituality authorizes practices of generosity and sharing as well as witchcraft, womanist rituals, and empowering transformations. Like all religions, the power of feminist spirituality lies in its appeal to a truth beyond proof, to feeling, sensing, and communing with something beyond. Feminist spirituality avoids the patriarchal imperatives of monotheisms by countering with a more pervasive, nourishing spirit world (see, e.g., Wendy Griffin, 2000, *Daughters of the Goddess: Studies of Healing, Identity, and Empowerment*; Wendy Roberts, 1998, *Celebrating Her: Feminist Ritualizing Comes of Age*; Carol Christ, 1997, *Rebirth of the Goddess: Finding Meaning in Feminist Spirituality*).

## TECHNIQUES OF PERSUASION

The range of authorizing structures empower a rethinking of patriarchal culture, assumptions about women's lives, ways of reading culture, and presumptions about ethics and justice. The "master's tools," however, still dominate actual practices of empowerment, especially modes of public persuasion. Logics, theories, and rhetorical practices conform to familiar patterns as a part of their persuasive operation. Even if feminist thinkers bring alternative theories to light, communicating those theories—outside feminist artistic practices—becomes difficult within traditional conventions of argumentation.

Virginia Woolf's presentation of the difficulties faced by creative women took the form of personal essays in which the protagonist sought out most of the forms of traditional authority in her quest to understand why there have not been more women artists and thinkers. In *A Room of One's Own,* Woolf contrasts conventional "authorities" with her own experience and that of other women to forward her theory that poor material conditions and lack of personal freedom make it difficult for women to be artists. Using a first person narrator to contrast an experience of pinching poverty with the misogynistic pronouncements of pampered experts, Woolf's essays deploy the personal as a most influential mode of persuasion.

Woolf's use of the personal model has become a persuasive trope for feminist writers

and researchers. If women's experience and insight have been omitted in favor of a universalizing masculinist view, what better way to begin to correct the situation than through the very voices and experiences that have been squelched? Not simply an overlooked and ignored resource, personal experience becomes a rhetorical guarantee of authenticity not easily countermanded. Who, after all, can argue with a person's experience?

We can, however, take exception to conclusions drawn from that experience; so feminist persuasion also bolsters experience with the expert practice of disciplinary conventions for argument, evidence, and objectivity. Feminist researchers rarely conform to disciplinary conventions without also signaling their consciousness of the potentially nonobjective character of those conventions. In other words, feminist researchers often practice a self-conscious disciplinarity in which they can use the persuasive techniques of fields of study while indicating their own positions as researchers and their knowledge that techniques and methods may incorporate power disparities.

The simultaneous feminist use and critique of disciplinary methods and assumptions occurs in most disciplines—in history (e.g., Joan Scott, 1999), literary history and criticism (e.g., Gilbert & Gubar, 1979), anthropology and folklore (e.g., Behar & Gordon, 1995), philosophy (e.g., Frye, 1983), psychoanalysis (e.g., Rose, 1986), and science (e.g., Harding, 1986). Like de Beauvoir, contemporary feminist theorists and critics straddle the line between disciplinary "soundness" and responsibility and disciplinary critique as itself a mode of feminist authority. In this way, feminist criticism accomplishes a double labor. Not only does it attend to a more comprehensive disciplinary study that includes previously elided viewpoints and subjects, it also demonstrates the assumptions and practices that have enabled the exclusion and mischaracterization of women for so long.

One crucial disciplinary authorizing technique is the citation of the work and ideas of predecessors. While in traditional disciplines that precedent often reflects the sexist ideologies of the field, feminist researchers deploy alternative and often previously ignored work by pioneering women and others. Establishing a feminist history has been important not only as a way of recovering lost experiences and lives but also as a way of supporting the insights of more contemporary thought. The work of other feminist thinkers serves as well to produce a burgeoning field of expertise that begins to authorize itself.

The personalizing impetus in much feminist research is also related to the exigencies of identity politics as positionality itself becomes a primary mode of authorizing. When the personal is the political, then the positional aspects of the personal become authorizing categories of an insight and expertise about the lives of variously oppressed groups or groups engaged in alternative or nontraditional modes of life. Researchers must speak with care of experiences and cultural sites not their own. Positioning oneself as a part of a ritual of writing becomes a preliminary mode of self-authorization.

Rhetorical techniques such as the insertion of autobiographical detail and experience, the ritual self-positioning of authors, and references to sets of preeminent feminist thinkers become shorthands for authority. Power, however, comes from clarity, timeliness, generosity, and care.

## References

Adams, C. (Ed.). (1993). *Ecofeminism and the sacred.* New York: Continuum.

Alcoff, L., & Potter, E. (1993). *Feminist epistemologies.* New York: Routledge.

Allen, T. (1995). *Womanist and feminist aesthetics.* Athens: Ohio University Press.

*Amazon Quarterly* [Periodical]. (1972–1975). Oakland, CA: Amazon Press.

Anzaldúa, Gloria. (1987). *Borderlands/la frontera: The new mestiza.* San Francisco: Spinsters/Aunt Lute.

Bambara, T. C. (1970). *The black woman.* New York: Penguin Books.

*Battle Acts* [Periodical]. (1970–1974). New York: Women of Youth Against War and Fascism.

Behar, R., & Gordon, D. (Eds.). (1995). *Women writing culture.* Berkeley: University of California Press.

Benjamin, J. (1988). *The bonds of love: Psychoanalysis, feminism, and the problem of domination.* New York: Pantheon.

Bleier, R. (1984). *Science and gender: A critique of biology and its theories.* New York: Pergamon Press.

Brand, P., & Korsmeyer, C. (Eds.). (1995). *Feminism and tradition in aesthetics.* University Park: Penn State University Press.

Brennan, T. (Ed.). (1989). *Between feminism and psychoanalysis.* New York: Routledge.

Brennan, T. (1993). *History after Lacan.* New York: Routledge.

Broude, N., & Garrard, M. (Eds.). (1994). *The power of feminist art: The American movement of the 1970s, history and impact.* New York: H. N. Abrams.

Brown, C., & Olson, K. (Eds.). (1978). *Feminist criticism: Essays on theory, poetry, and prose.* Metuchen, NJ: Scarecrow.

Brown, R. M. (1978). *Six of one.* New York: Harper & Row.

Butler, J. (1990). *Gender trouble: Feminism and the subversion of identity.* New York: Routledge.

Chesler, P. (1972). *Women and madness.* Garden City, NY: Doubleday.

Chodorow, N. (1978). *The reproduction of mothering: Psychoanalysis and the sociology of gender.* Berkeley: University of California Press.

Christ, C. (1997). *Rebirth of the goddess: Finding meaning in feminist spirituality.* Reading, MA: Addison-Wesley.

Cixous, H. (1994). *The Hélène Cixous reader* (S. Seller, Trans. & Ed.). New York: Routledge.

Cixous, H., & Clément, C. (1986). *The newly born woman* (B. Wing, Trans.). Minneapolis: University of Minnesota Press.

Cole, J. (1979). *Fair science: Women in the scientific community.* New York: Free Press.

Combahee River Collective. (1986). *The Combahee River Collective statement: Black feminist organizing in the seventies and eighties.* New York: Kitchen Table Women of Color Press.

Coole, D. (1988). *Women in political theory: From ancient misogyny to contemporary feminism.* Brighton, UK: Wheatsheaf Books.

Cornillon, S. (Ed.). (1972). *Images of women in fiction: Feminist perspectives.* Bowling Green, OH: Bowling Green University Press.

Cox, S. (1976). *Female psychology: The emerging self.* Chicago: Science Research Associates.

Daly, M. (1973). *Beyond god the father: Toward a philosophy of women's liberation.* Boston: Beacon Press.

Davis, A. (1971). *A letter from Angela to Ericka.* New York: New York Committee to Free Angela Davis.

de Beauvoir, S. (1949). *The second sex* (H. M. Parshley, Trans.). New York: Knopf.

Diamond, I., & Orenstein, G. (Eds.). (1990). *Reweaving the world: The emergence of ecofeminism.* San Francisco: Sierra Books.

Ecker, G. (Ed.). (1985). *Feminist aesthetics* (H. Anderson, Trans.). London: Women's Press.

Evans, J. (1986). *Feminism and political theory.* London: Sage.

Fausto-Sterling, A., & English, L. (1985). *Women and minorities in science: An interdisciplinary course.* Wellesley, MA: Wellesley College Center for Research on Women.

Fraser, N. (1989). *Unruly practices: Power, discourse, and gender in contemporary social theory.* Minneapolis: University of Minnesota Press.

Friday, N. (1973). *My secret garden: Women's sexual fantasies.* New York: Pocket Books.

Friedan, B. (1963). *The feminine mystique.* New York: Dell.

Frye, M. (1983). *The politics of reality: Essays in feminist theory.* Trumansburg, NY: Crossing Press.

*The Furies* [Periodical]. (1972–1973). Washington, DC: Furies Collective.

Gaard, G. (1993). *Ecofeminism: Women, animals, nature.* Philadelphia: Temple University Press.

Gallop, J. (1982). *The daughter's seduction: Feminism and psychoanalysis.* Ithaca, NY: Cornell University Press.

Gallop, J. (1985). *Reading Lacan.* Ithaca, NY: Cornell University Press.

Gentile, M. (1985). *Film feminisms: Theory and practice.* Westport, CT: Greenwood Press.

Gilbert, S., & Gubar, S. (1979). *The madwoman in the attic.* New Haven, CT: Yale University Press.

Gilligan, C. (1982). *In a different voice: Psychological theory and women's development.* Cambridge, MA: Harvard University Press.

Goldman, E. (1906–1917). *Mother earth.* New York: Author.

Goldman, E. (1970). *The traffic in women and other essays on feminism.* New York: Times Change Press.

Gornick, V., & Moran, B. (Eds.). (1971). *Woman in sexist society.* New York: Basic Books.

Greer, G. (1971). *The female eunuch.* New York: McGraw-Hill.

Griffin, W. (2000). *Daughters of the goddess: Studies of healing, identity, and empowerment.* Walnut Creek, CA: AltaMira Press.

Grosz, E. A. (1990). *Jacques Lacan: A feminist introduction.* New York: Routledge.

Haas, V., & Perrucci, C. (1984). *Women in scientific and engineering professions.* Ann Arbor: University of Michigan Press.

Haraway, D. (1989). *Primate visions: Gender, race, and nature in the world of modern science.* New York: Routledge.

Harding, S. (1986). *The science question in feminism.* Ithaca, NY: Cornell University Press.

Hein, H., & Korsmeyer, C. (Eds.). (1993). *Aesthetics in a feminist perspective.* Bloomington: Indiana University Press.

Hennessey, R. (2000). *Profit and pleasure: Sexual identities in late capitalism.* New York: Routledge.

Hirsch, M. (1989). *The mother/daughter plot.* Bloomington: Indiana University Press.

Hite, S. (1976). *The Hite report: A nationwide study on female sexuality.* New York: Macmillan.

Hoagland, S. (1988). *Lesbian ethics: Toward a new value.* Palo Alto, CA: Institute of Lesbian Studies.

Irigaray, L. (1977). *Ce sexe qui n'en est pas un.* Paris: Editions de Minuit.

Irigaray, L. (1985). *Speculum of the other woman* (G. Gill, Trans.). Ithaca, NY: Cornell University Press.

*It Ain't Me Babe* [Periodical]. (1970–1971). Berkeley, CA: W. L. P. B. Collective.

Jacobus, M., & Shuttleworth, S. (Eds.). (1990). *Body/politics: Women and the discourses of science.* New York: Routledge.

Jaggar, A. (1984). *Feminist frameworks: Alternative theoretical accounts of the relations between men and women.* New York: McGraw-Hill.

Janeway, E. (1971). *Man's world, woman's place.* New York: Morrow.

Johnson, D., & Oliver, W. (Eds.). (2001). *Women making art: Women in the visual, literary, and performing arts since 1960.* New York: Peter Lang.

Johnston, J. (1973). *Lesbian nation.* New York: Simon & Schuster.

Keller, E. F. (1985). *Reflections on women in science.* New Haven, CT: Yale University Press.

Kristeva, J. (1984). *Revolution in poetic language* (M. Waller, Trans.). New York: Columbia University Press.

*The Ladder* [Periodical]. (1956–1972). New York: Arno Press.

Laughlin, Karen, & Schuler, C. (1995). *Theatre and feminist aesthetics.* Madison, NJ: Fairleigh Dickinson University Press.

*Lavender Woman* [Periodical]. (1971–1976). Chicago: Lavender Woman Collective.

Lorde, A. (1984). *Sister outsider: Essays and speeches.* Trumansburg, NY: Crossing Press.

MacArthur, S. (2002). *Feminist aesthetics in music.* Westport, CT: Greenwood Press.

MacArthur, S., & Poynton, C. (1999). *Music and feminisms.* Sydney, New South Wales, Australia: Australian Music Centre.

Mander, A., & Rush, A. (1974). *Feminism as therapy.* New York: Random.

Merchant, C. (1992). *Radical ecology.* New York: Routledge.

Millett, K. (1970). *Sexual politics.* Garden City, NY: Doubleday.

Mitchell, J. (1971). *Women's estate.* New York: Pantheon.

Mitchell, J. (1975). *Psychoanalysis and feminism.* New York: Penguin Books.

Mitchell, J., & Rose, J. (1985). *Feminine sexuality: Jacques Lacan and l'école freudienne.* New York: Norton.

Moore, H. (1988). *Feminism and anthropology.* Cambridge, UK: Polity Press.

Morgan, R. (Ed.). (1970). *Sisterhood is powerful.* New York: Vintage.

*Mother Lode* [Periodical]. (1971–1973). San Francisco: Mother Lode.

Mulvey, L. (1989). *Visual and other pleasures.* Bloomington: Indiana University Press.

Newton, J. (1978). *Women, power, and subversion: Social strategies in British fiction 1778–1860.* Athens: University of Georgia Press.

*Off Our Backs* [Periodical]. (1970–). Washington, DC: Off Our Backs.

Okin, S. (1979). *Women in Western political thought.* Princeton, NJ: Princeton University Press.

*Our bodies, ourselves.* (1971). Boston: Boston Women's Health Book Collective.

Phelan, Shane. (1994). *Getting specific.* Minneapolis: University of Minnesota Press.

Ragland-Sullivan, E. (1986). *Jacques Lacan and the philosophy of psychoanalysis.* Champaign: University of Illinois Press.

Roberts, W. (1998). *Celebrating her: Feminist ritualizing comes of age.* Cleveland, OH: Pilgrim Press.

Robinson, L. (1978). *Sex, class, and culture.* Bloomington: Indiana University Press.

Roof, J., & Wiegman, R. (1995). *Who can speak? Authority and critical identity.* Champaign: University of Illinois Press.

Rose, J. (1986). *Sexuality in the field of vision.* London: Verso.

Rossiter, M. (1982). *Women scientists in America: Struggles and strategies to 1940.* Baltimore: Johns Hopkins University Press.

Rubin, G. (1996). The traffic in women: Notes on the "political economy" of sex. In J. Scott (Ed.), *Feminism and history* (pp. 157–210). New York: Oxford University Press.

Schilling, G. F., & Hunt, M. K. (1974). *Women in science and technology.* Santa Monica, CA: Rand.

Scott, J. (1999). *Gender and the politics of history.* New York: Columbia University Press.

Silverman, K. (1983). *The subject of semiotics.* New York: Oxford University Press.

Spacks, P. (1975). *The female imagination.* New York: Knopf.

Spencer, A. (1925). *Women's share in social culture.* Philadelphia: Lippincott.

Sprengnether, M. (1990). *The spectral mother: Freud, feminism, and psychoanalysis.* Ithaca, NY: Cornell University Press.

Thorne, B., & Yalom, M. (Eds.). (1982). *Rethinking the family: Some feminist questions.* New York: Longman.

Tuana, N. (Ed.). (1989). *Feminism and science.* Bloomington: Indiana University Press.

*Voice of the Women's Liberation Movement* [Periodical]. (1968–1969). Chicago: Voice of the Women's Liberation Movement.

*The Way We See It* [Periodical]. (1970). Springfield, MA: Springfield Women's Liberation.

Weiler, K. (Ed.). (2001). *Feminist engagements: Reading, resisting, and revisioning male theorists in education and cultural studies.* New York: Routledge.

Wittig, M. (1975). *The lesbian body* (David LeVay, Trans.). Boston: Beacon Press.

*Womankind* [Periodical]. (1971–1973). Chicago: Chicago Women's Liberation Union.

Woolf, V. (1929). *A room of one's own.* London: Hogarth.

Woolf, V. (1938). *Three guineas.* London: Hogarth.

# 22

# WHAT'S GOOD WRITING IN FEMINIST RESEARCH? WHAT CAN FEMINIST RESEARCHERS LEARN ABOUT GOOD WRITING?

KATHY CHARMAZ

Good writing in feminist research unites perspective with writing practices. Feminist perspectives inform a rich research literature and inspire innovative ideas about writing research. Does a feminist perspective ensure good writing? No. Does research from other perspectives exemplify good writing? Yes, of course (see, e.g., Bosk, 1979; Duneier, 1999; Stearns, 1994).[1] Nonetheless, feminist researchers have advanced current trends to produce good writing. Numerous feminist researchers aim to make their writing clear, crisp, engaging, and effective—all criteria for good writing. Yet how they meet these criteria remains invisible.

Epistemological challenges about scientific roles and representation of subjects have had fundamental consequences for writing feminist research. Increasingly, we appear in our texts as thinking, acting—and feeling—participants rather than as disembodied reporters of collected facts. Lines between the subjective and objective blur. Feminist research and writing ranges on a continuum from seemingly external examinations of specific topics that affect women such as job discrimination or caregiving to authors' autobiographical reflections in which they themselves become the object of inquiry and the center of the examined text. Many studies at both objective and subjective ends of the continuum provide valuable contributions—but other studies produce mundane statements.

- What makes feminist research compelling to read?
- How do feminist researchers construct their writings?
- How can feminist researchers use writing strategies to advance their work?

Author's Note: I thank Sharlene Hesse-Biber, Bonnie Massey, Virginia Olesen, and members of the Sonoma State University Faculty Writing Program, Teresa Ciabatarri, James Dean, Dolly Friedel, and Andrew Roth, for their views of an earlier version of this chapter. Andrew Roth suggested using similar questions in the title.

To address these questions, we can study feminist research reports and explicate the writing practices embedded in them. These reports reflect if, when, how, and where their authors enter the research scene as well as the views and values they bring with them. Thus, I take a short step back and discuss entering the scene before analyzing how feminist researchers adopt literary conventions and writing strategies to express their thoughts. Throughout the chapter, I explore how taken-for-granted use of language imparts meanings and messages and start by looking at what titles of research studies say. Next I explicate how several reports exemplify writing strategies, whether or not their authors consciously invoked these strategies. I emphasize metaphor and style in my assessments of why these authors' writings work and show how their writing strategies produce memorable arguments. In short, I concentrate on *how* these authors write rather than on what they write.[2] Last, I conclude the chapter with some advice for writing and for managing to write.

By developing a strong authorial voice, offering fresh metaphors, interrogating taken-for-granted metaphors, and adopting writers' strategies and rhetorical devices—what Carroll (2000) calls "writer's tricks"—authors construct memorable arguments. We can blend a repertoire of writers' tricks with social scientific evidence and reasoning to strengthen our writing and to expand our audiences. This approach broadens the discourse about writing feminist research, challenges taken-for-granted assumptions about writing and research, and suggests ideas for handling writing projects.

Effective writing necessitates balancing the author's style with the audience's desire for clarity, insight, and usefulness. True, not all writing is effective. Captive, rather than captivated, audiences allow some academic authors to forego clarity. Academic fiefdoms allow imposing an arcane language on novices confined within the castle towers. Both ruling authorities and their underlings living in the castle lose touch with ordinary language and discourse beyond the moat. Not everyone, however, can afford to let her or his writing remain obscure and opaque.[3] Researchers who wish to reach new or broader audiences, including the people they studied, must attend to their writing.

They invite their readers into the narrative and keep them engaged. Their narratives spark readers' interest, kindle their curiosity, and ignite their imaginations. The writing evokes new images or casts familiar images in new light and does so with brilliant clarity.

Aiming for clarity does not mean reducing theoretical ideas to simplistic description. It does mean stating these ideas in the most simple, direct terms possible and providing readers with an analytic path to understand them. Researchers can construct an analytic path with clear definitions, sound evidence, and effective reasoning. When they use writers' strategies to traverse their analytic path, they can create new views for their readers. Novices can learn these strategies to increase the power and significance of their writing.

Might feminist researchers attend more closely to the writing process than their nonfeminist counterparts? Many feminist researchers do. Does feminist writing differ from other forms of writing? Not always. Must we claim subjectivist proclivities in our writing? Not necessarily. We can take a middle ground between the objectivist reporter and the subjectivist narrator (see Charmaz & Mitchell, 1996), and from this middle ground, we can assess our data, analyses, and audiences. Feminist researchers have challenged conventional positivistic assumptions about speaking with and speaking for research participants. Yes, we place ourselves in the research process and try to maintain allegiances as we create images of those we study and represent their situations in words, tables, or diagrams. In keeping with Lather (2001), feminist researchers understand complexity, acknowledge partial truths, and recognize multiple subjectivities—and we can write them into our research narratives.

Before we embark on our scrutiny of feminist writing, we need to consider gender. Contested, contingent, and reconstructed notions of gender shape or underlie feminist inquiry (Glenn, 2002; Olesen, 2000, 2005). Gender is more than a variable. It is a way of seeing and experiencing the world. As evident in *The Gender Lens* series (Pine Forge Press/Sage Publications) and the subtitle of Judith A. Howard's book coauthored with Jocelyn A. Hollander (Howard & Hollander, 1997), gender provides a lens through which seeing and knowing occur. Interactional patterns and institutional practices become visible. Yes, we see gender differences, but a gender lens also enlarges the scope of our vision and sharpens our view of power, privilege, and priorities. Although we may shift the lens and change its focus, gender provides a powerful tool in research and analysis. A gender lens brings women into the center of analysis focusing on women's—and men's—lives, concerns, and the institutional arrangements that affect them. Adopting a gender lens can lead to taking a wider view that brings differences such as race, class, or age into focus.

A gender lens makes diverse standpoints visible—the researcher's as well as the research participants' (Harding, 1991; Hartsock, 1998; Smith, 1987, 1999). Feminist researchers have made concerted efforts to show how their standpoints spawn beliefs and practices and to push beyond the taken-for-granted middle-class, white, heterosexist, and more recently, age and able-bodied biases embedded in earlier writings. When researchers do not recognize their standpoints and do not take a reflexive stance toward them, they risk reproducing the assumptions given in these standpoints (Charmaz, 2005, 2006). A gender lens has long prompted such reflexivity. Charles Bosk (2003) looked back on his 1979 study of surgical residents through a gender lens. He now regrets that he had not seen the lone female resident's situation from her perspective. By not taking gender into account, he had reproduced the attending physicians' negative judgments of her.

## ENTERING THE SCENE

Feminist ethnographers increasingly write about how they enter their research scene and what their personal experience has been within it. This trend has spread throughout feminist research but takes a different tack than traditional social research. Social scientists have long acknowledged and sometimes advocated that researchers pursue topics of personal interest in their empirical studies. Lofland and Lofland (1995) and Lofland, Snow, Anderson, and Lofland (2006) urge novice qualitative researchers to draw on their experiences when selecting a topic, and thus these authors title their first chapter, "Starting Where You Are."

Many feminist researchers start where they are but do much more: They subject this starting point to rigorous scrutiny. Increasingly, as feminists, we position ourselves, our lives, and our goals in relation to the topic, particularly in books.[4] Thus, we show how we entered the scene and what happened after we arrived there. From the start, our authorial voices take hold of the narrative.

This positioning means acknowledging values and ideological positions. Such positioning is becoming prerequisite in feminist scholarly studies and may also appear in methodological treatises. In both types of works, feminist allegiances may be understood but not necessarily fully articulated because they permeate the entire structure of the work. For example, in her methodological treatise that extends grounded theory, Adele E. Clarke (2005) expresses her appreciation of participating in a special research group on "Feminist Epistemologies and Methodologies." She says, "We focused on research methods and feminist scholarship, informing my earliest work on this book" (p. xix) without specific iteration of how this scholarship contributed to her reconstruction of grounded theory.

Authors who reveal their starting points and standpoints—and concerns and commitments—permit readers to assess both their approach and the quality of their content.[5] An articulated position then becomes an anchor point for the observations and interpretations that follow. Readers then can place the narrative into perspective and delineate the boundaries of generalizations within it.

Certain topics—particularly those that address hierarchical relations in organizations—result in taking sides. As feminist researchers, we often position ourselves and our work with the underdog. Such positioning is not new; some ethnographers have long taken it as prerequisite for obtaining certain types of data, much less to endorse ethical preferences or claim political allegiances. Goffman (1989), for example, argues that to understand what life looks like at the bottom of a hierarchy, ethnographers must align themselves with the people there and live as they do. We researchers may have present or potential advantages and privileges that our research participants will never enjoy, such as health, education, and opportunities. Although feminist researchers seldom live as participants do, we often align ourselves with research participants who are at the bottom of a hierarchy—and position our work accordingly. Such positioning must be more than ideological when the researcher's empirical observations and knowledge arise from this location. In her book, *Women Without Class: Girls, Race, and Identity,* Julie Bettie (2003) states,

> I want to acknowledge the principal and the unit administrators, who gave me their trust, allowed me to conduct my research at their school, tolerated my presence, and made me feel welcome. Because I am narrating a story largely through the eyes of students and simply because I am performing a critical analysis, I "other" teachers at times, and I apologize for this necessary betrayal. These were warm people with the best intentions who, I recognize, were working very hard at their jobs. My analysis is not meant to be critical of individual people, but of the social systems, processes, and ideologies present in our culture to recruit individual actors and inform their actions. (p. x)

Positioning oneself in relation to research participants assumes particular significance for any study, like Bettie's, that entails insider-outsider relationships and is crucial for gaining an insider's view. Hence, this positioning includes when, how, and to what extent a researcher can claim having achieved an insider's view. Such positioning allows readers to understand what an author attempts to accomplish and to evaluate it accordingly.

For other kinds of topics, feminist researchers have firsthand knowledge of the studied experience and state how the experience has affected them. Such statements convey the author's sincerity and, often, imply a sense of fairness. The author tells her or his story because the research participants have told their stories. In an author-meets-critics session (April 18, 2005) on her book, *Rapunzel's Daughters: What Women's Hair Tells Us About Women's Lives* (2004), Rose Weitz talked about her study of 74 interviews and many informal conversations with women and girls about their hair. Weitz described herself as a private person but said she knew that her own experiences with hair had to

be a part of this book. In the preface Weitz wrote,

> At one level, the story of my hair is purely personal, reflecting the particular constellation of people and events in my life. But this story also reflects internal struggles and external pressures that all American women share. In the same way that Rapunzel's hair both defined her—how much of the story do you remember, other than her hair?—and helped her find her prince and escape from the witch's tower, it sometimes seems as if our hair both defines us and offers us a key for improving our lives. As a result, all of us sooner or later obsess about our hair. We agonize over how to style it and whether to color it, measuring ourselves against other girls and women, and believing that our hair says something important about us. (p. xi)

Pressures to position oneself in relation to the studied experience can arise from other sources than self or colleagues. Editors may request it. Readers identify with an author who has shared the studied experience. For trade and crossover books, such positioning may serve to establish the author's voice in the narrative and add to the book's market appeal.

Feminist researchers often study a topic from a position they had experienced earlier in their lives. Exploring topics of profound subjective meaning can illuminate how difficult experiences have shaped researchers as well as research participants' lives. Knowing that the author held a personal stake in the topic once marked research as biased. Increasingly, however, readers see a personal stake as a mark of authorial credibility rather than bias. Lynn Davidman (2000) sheds light on how enforced silences about her mother's death complicated her grief and rendered it inaccessible. She writes,

> This book, on growing up motherless, forces me to probe into my memories and confront my feelings about my mother's death and its impact on my life, a subject which has been deeply repressed by me and my family. The silences around my mother's sickness and death began when she became ill. I was not told what was wrong with her, and when I guessed it was cancer (what else was un-nameable in the late 1960s?),

my father and aunt denied it. . . . Needless to say, I was shocked when she died. The silences surrounding her illness and death have continued until very recently; my brothers and I have almost never discussed our mother, nor was it a topic I brought up even with my closest friends. (p. 8)

Through entering the scene, we tell *how* it has affected us rather than hiding underneath our scientific mantle. *Which* topic a researcher chooses, how we study it, and what sense we make of our subsequent data are not neutral decisions. Rather a feminist perspective in research commits scholars to reveal circumstances in women's—and, increasingly, men's—lives and to create knowledge that can improve them. Like Weitz's study, feminist research often arises from shared experiences of the body (Hesse-Biber, 1996; Rothman, 1982; Smith, 1987, 1999), honors stories (Riessman, 1990), opens silences (Charmaz, 2002; DeVault, 1991, 1999), and brings hidden institutional practices into view (Smith, 1987).

Feminist writers have been at the forefront of epistemological developments during the past 35 years. The objective, disinterested, neutral observer resides in the past. We are part of the research process; we are intertwined with what we study and how we study it (Charmaz, 2005, 2006). Any study occurs under specific historical, cultural, and situational conditions. Whether we study small groups, historical documents, questionnaire results, or people in natural settings, we bring our perspectives not only into the research process but also into how we write our research products. Feminist researchers often write how they experienced being part of the process into their research narratives (Krieger, 1991). The words we choose and the concepts we adopt suggest who we are as well as the subject matter we choose to write about.

## WRITING THOUGHTS

### Titles Talk

Titles talk. A title can tell more than what a paper or book is about. A title may reveal the author's point of view, political stance, and tribal connections, as well as current disciplinary trends. The wording of a title may state a feminist approach, such as Marjorie DeVault's (1999) *Liberating Method: Feminism and Social Research.* DeVault's title announces her allegiances and promises to free the reader from conventional methodological constraints. Sharlene Hesse-Biber's title, *Am I Thin Enough Yet? The Cult of Thinness and the Commercialization of Identity,* suggests feminist inquiry of experiences with weight and a critique of cultural prescriptions about it. Who else but girls and women asked this question in the 1990s? Who but a feminist would devote a major research project to it? Framing the main title as a question reveals that the issue is gendered. The question echoes what the teenage girls in her study say and simultaneously foretells the direction of the book.

What makes a title work? Effective titles reflect contemporary concerns and reproduce common parlance, if these titles are clear and concrete.[6] Arlie Hochschild's titles *The Time Bind: When Work Becomes Home and Home Becomes Work* (1997) and *The Second Shift: Working Parents and the Revolution at Home* (1989) both work because they are specific and speak to problematic situations that readers share. For many North Americans, the years of a 40-hour work week have passed long ago as work hours and workweeks have stretched. Many women work a second shift at home, and as jobs increasingly require a second unpaid shift, family work goes to a third shift. Note that these titles each imply a point of view—that something is amiss. The *Time Bind* also asserts that social change is happening, and the *Second Shift* announces that an upheaval has occurred.

At times, a title suggests an ironic twist. Sue Fisher (1986) takes a wry stance in her title, *In the Patient's Best Interest: Women and the Politics of Medical Decisions.* In the narrative, she decimates beliefs that male doctors act in the best interests of their women patients. Hochschild's (1973) title *The Unexpected Community: Portrait of an Old Age Subculture* casts a note of surprise on the discovered community of elderly working-class women who lived in a small apartment complex. But who was surprised? The sociologist or the residents?

Many authors play on words in their titles. Sue Fisher (1995) plays on what nurses do, the tensions between nurses and doctors, and their relationships with women patients in her title *Nursing Wounds: Nurse Practitioners, Doctors, Women Patients, and the Negotiation of Meaning*. Mary R. Jackman (1994) attests to her concerns and alludes to the "iron hand" in her title *The Velvet Glove: Paternalism and Conflict in Gender, Class, and Race Relations*. Some titles play with topics and play on readers' taken-for-granted assumptions. Creating surprise invites a browser to read further. Verta Taylor and Leila J. Rupp's (2005) article title catches readers' attention: "When the Girls Are Men: Negotiating Gender and Sexual Dynamics in a Study of Drag Queens."

Titles reflect trends. Used carefully, a trend can help authors to position their work—in the title and throughout the narrative. Attempts to be trendy, however, rapidly date a book or article as fads rise and fall. Some authors ride fads to heights of fame; other authors crash with a falling fad. What started out as an innovative direction can become a convenient peg on which an author hangs his or her work. In the 1970s, studies with the term *identity* in the title gained popularity. More recently, the terms, *race, class,* and *gender* took hold of considerable theorizing and book titles throughout the social sciences and humanities. Jennifer Crewe (2004), the editorial director at Columbia University Press, recounts:

> A few years ago the words race, class, and gender graced the title or sub-title of almost four hundred submissions I received in a single year in literary studies. Some of these scholars even seemed to have forced consideration of race or class into a book that actually had a largely different focus. A couple of years later postcoloniality was the term in the vast majority of titles of books submitted to me in this field. Ten years before that, almost every submission had a portion of a word in the title in parentheses or featured a slash or two. . . . As you can imagine, these books all sound alike to an editor after the first dozen or so. Our eyes glaze over and we're inclined to reject the book right away. (pp. 136–137)

Titles that bored Crew touted trends and tribal connections. Titles designed to capture the point of the research may also be ineffective when they are ambiguous, incomplete, or misleading. Many of us have a string of misguided titles trailing behind us. As a graduate student, I conducted a small study of working-class adults who provided care to dying elderly relatives (Calkins, 1972). At that time, qualitative researchers who used grounded theory methods sought to identify one basic social process that accounted for all their data.[7] My professor insisted that the basic social process I had discovered was "shouldering a burden." I realized that the stories of caregiving contained some burdening of family members—and much more. A number of interview participants viewed being the chosen caregiver as an honor. The daily acts of caregiving represented a symbolic completion of a cherished relationship, which I mentioned in the article. Because I could not find a single basic process, I accepted my professor's title—a mistake. The data belied its negative images of caregiving. The title of the article also erred in not providing sufficient information to illuminate the topic. Subsequently, gerontologists ignored it.[8] Except for being reproduced in one collection, the article failed to command much attention.

My title captured neither the full range of significant responses nor the specific experiences; however, the idea of adopting a pointed cliché, common term, or familiar metaphor can make a snappy title.[9] Dana Rosenfeld (2003) adopts "the changing of the guard" as the main title of her book. She aims to theorize generational change by examining discontinuous identity cohorts among gay and lesbian elders and, hence, offers a subtitle: *Lesbian and Gay Elders, Identity, and Social Change*.

Titles are growing longer. In his recent editorial about titles in the *American Sociological Review*, Howard S. Becker (2003) points out that titles have grown longer, advertise more key words, and frequently consist of two "colonized" (p. iv) clauses, one catchy, one scientific. Becker believes this trend emerged because academic departments make hiring and career decisions based on their candidates' citation counts. Thus, he hastens to absolve authors of blame for putting everything that could possibly be of interest in their titles. Becker's 29-word title of his three-page editorial underscores his point.

Authors use subtitles to provide telling words that clarify what the piece is about and to pick up analytic slack in their titles. Marketing directors may add an explanatory subtitle or change a title to fit their conceptions of market demand. Marketing concerns may not coincide with prescriptions for good writing. Researchers may choose a title that alludes to the purpose of the book or their position on the topic. Publishers aim to maximize the market and, thus, may advocate a general, recognizable—and mundane—title. Such titles identify the topic but flatten the content. A crisp, catchy title may have worked better.

## Creating Original Metaphors and Similes

Original metaphors and similes can make a piece distinctive. A metaphor makes an implicit comparison by taking a term that ordinarily has one meaning and using it to designate another. A simile compares and likens two fundamentally dissimilar things. Writers construct original metaphors and similes to serve specific purposes, including evoking a particular response from readers.

What makes a metaphor work? How does it help you make a point? How have feminist researchers used original metaphors and similes to advance their ideas? Rosanna Hertz (2002) evokes a powerful simile in her study of single mothers who chose to have known or unknown donors father their child. How can the sociologist portray this relationship? What images does the donor dad evoke? To what can his presence be likened? Hertz creates a compelling simile in the following way:

> The known donor's image is as a negative of a photograph. On a negative, light and shadow are the reverse of the positive generated from it. The negative offers a glimpse of a person who was there but missing. The child knows his or her genetic identity, but the man remains in shadow socially. Ironically, the mother knows him as a whole person (the positive print) because of a shared past relationship. The child still must imagine what it would be like to have a dad, even if the mother's history and memory form the basis of talk with the child about her imagined father. . . .
> The known donor appears visible on the unprinted negative, forming an image for the child but not as the developed self of the dad. (p. 17)

By likening the donor's image to a negative of a photograph, Hertz's simile reproduces the ambiguity of the child's relationship to his or her donor father. She draws a picture for the reader using outline and shadow. Depth and detail blur in the image of the photographic negative, as does the child's relationship to the donor dad. The blurred image reveals the father's phantom presence but conceals the quirks and qualities that would enliven his image and make him real. This simile works because it captures the problematic and ambiguous relationship in condensed form. It evokes an image the reader can grasp and envision and melds this image in Hertz's narrative. The simile extends the analysis and deepens the narrative.

Hertz's simile does more than provide an intriguing image. Rather, the shadow image of the donor then becomes a metaphor for the child-father relationship. Hertz uses the metaphor of the ambiguous negative to intrigue the reader and to build her argument. She thus informs and locates the reader's knowledge of the ambiguous role of the blurred dad as well as of the child's understanding about what a family is. The child learns that traditional forms of family roles and boundaries do not hold in his or her family.

All kinds of metaphors and similes reside in research narratives. It matters whether authors construct metaphors and similes with forethought or invoke them unwittingly. Hertz constructs the simile to clarify her analysis. Writers create metaphors to reveal a deeper meaning, a hidden truth. They invoke metaphors unwittingly when they assume that the metaphor *is* the truth. Metaphor and reality merge. Emily Martin (1999a) conveys an exquisite awareness of the power of taken-for-granted metaphors and creates an original metaphor to depict them. Martin points out that literary conventions refer to "dead" metaphors, but she finds "sleeping metaphors in science" and challenges feminists to "awaken" them (p. 25). These metaphors appear in the writing of scientific text but lie hidden within the content. Martin uses sleep and wakefulness as metaphors for our language use and narrative understanding. Words that are asleep still lie there seemingly inert, but they have not died.

Sleeping metaphors wield power precisely because they remain tacit: They shape the text and, moreover, our conceptions of the realities it addresses. Such metaphors shape *what* we see and *how* we see it and contain hidden reasons that explain, justify, and perpetuate *why* we see it that way.

## Uncovering Taken-for-Granted Metaphors

Writers invoke taken-for-granted metaphors when they say one thing *means* or *symbolizes* another. These metaphors merge separate entities such as masculinity and aggressiveness or take one characteristic of a process or an object as the whole, such as saying "aging is deterioration." We can extend Martin's (1999a) concept of sleeping metaphors to include all those metaphors we take for granted. Implicit meanings embedded in these metaphors slip by as they become an unexamined part of everyday discourse. How are taken-for-granted metaphors used? When do research participants and writers invoke them? To what extent are they shared throughout a group or setting? How do they influence what we do? We all use metaphors—often unconsciously. Uncovering hidden and not so hidden metaphors reveals perspectives and shows how they inform practices.

Metaphors not only shape images of specific phenomena but also persuade audiences. Martin (1999b) found that metaphors of women's bodies in medical and popular texts shape the very way we see women's bodies. After examining the language authors adopt, Martin takes diffuse images and information through the texts and re-presents them in condensed conceptualized form. See how Martin articulates implied metaphors and makes them visible in the following examples:

[Female brain-hormone-ovary system] So this is a communication system organized hierarchically, not a committee reaching decisions by mutual influence. The hierarchical nature of the organization is reflected in some popular literature meant to explain the nature of menstruation simply: "From first menstrual cycle to menopause, the hypothalamus acts as a conductor of a highly trained orchestra. Once its baton signals the downbeat to the pituitary, the hypothalamus-pituitary-ovary axis is united in purpose and begins to play its symphonic message, preparing a woman's body for conception and child-bearing." (p. 292)

[Menopause] In both medical texts and popular books, what is being described is the breakdown of a system of authority. The cause of ovarian decline is the "decreasing ability of the aging ovaries to respond to pituitary gonadotropins." At every point in this system, functions "fail" and falter: Follicles "fail to muster the strength" to reach ovulation. As functions fall, so do the members of the system decline: "breasts and genitals organs gradually atrophy," "wither," and become "senile." (p. 293)

By garnering evidence and presenting it systematically, Martin transforms conventional images and descriptions, assembles them, and creates an impressive argument.

The basic images chosen here—an information-transmitting system with a hierarchical structure—have an obvious relation to the dominant form of organization in our society. What I want to show is how this set of metaphors, once chosen as the basis for the description of physiological events, has profound implications for the way in which a change in the basic organization of the system will be perceived. In terms of female reproduction, this basic change is of course menopause. Many criticisms have been made of the medical propensity to see menopause as a pathological state. I would like to suggest that the tenacity of this view comes not only from negative stereotypes associated with aging women in our society, but as a logical outgrowth of seeing the body as a hierarchical information processing system in the first place. (p. 292)

Martin traces the language flowing from these metaphors, which in turn give rise to more metaphors, including "unresponsive" ovaries that "regress," and then become "senile," a hypothalamus "addicted" to estrogen that gives "inappropriate orders," and a system that "fails" (p. 293). By bringing these sleeping metaphors to life, she shows how the texts impart a fundamentally sexist analysis.

## MAKING MEMORABLE ARGUMENTS

### Invoking Metaphors as Markers and Measures

The best writers construct arguments we remember. How might they craft an argument through telling an analytic story? What role might metaphor play in telling an analytic story and in advancing an argument?

Writers can tell a story with a fresh metaphor or simile that simultaneously marks their work and makes it distinctive. The story serves as a means of setting the stage for the argument to come and, when successful, does so with a fresh twist. Hochschild (1997) tells a story about an incident in the day care center of a company where she was observing. She moves from dialogue to explanatory description as she takes the reader into Cassie's relationship with her mother, Gwen Bell, and into the day care center.

At 7:40 A.M. four-year-old Cassie sidles in, her hair half-combed, a blanket in one hand, a fudge bar in the other. "I'm late," her mother explains to Diane [the childcare worker]. "Cassie wanted the fudge bar so bad, I gave it to her," she adds apologetically—though Diane has said nothing.

"Pleeese, can't you take me with you?" Cassie pleads.

"You know I can't take you to work," Gwen replies in a tone that suggests she's heard this request before. Cassie's shoulders droop in defeat. She's given it a try, but now she's resigned to her mother's imminent departure, and she's agreed, it seems, not to make too much of a fuss about it. Aware of her mother's unease about her long day at childcare, however, she's struck a hard bargain. Every so often she gets a morning fudge bar. This is their deal, and Cassie keeps her mother to it. As Gwen Bell later explained to me, she continually feels that she owes Cassie more time than she actually gives her. She has a time-debt to her daughter. If many busy parents settle such debts on evenings or weekends when their children eagerly "collect" promised time, Cassie insists on a morning down payment, a fudge bar that makes her mother uneasy but saves her the trouble and embarrassment of a tantrum. (pp. 4–5)

Hochschild (1997) weaves fresh metaphors and creates similes in her description and punctuates them with familiar metaphors. Debts take the form of time. The fudge bar symbolizes a hard bargain. Hochschild treats adversarial bargaining as a dominant metaphor and slips it into her narrative through the description itself. She adopts related metaphors that measure this bargaining when she tells of a "hard bargain," "time-debt," "defeat," and "down payment." Hochschild gives adversarial bargaining a new twist: It proceeds from taken-for-granted assumptions about children's rights to have their parents' sustained attention and parental obligations to give it. From this perspective, Gwen fails Cassie, and Cassie knows it. The tensions and contests involved in time bargaining emerge at the day care center. Hochschild's words convey the struggles between Cassie and her mother. Cassie "pleads," is "resigned," makes a "deal," "keeps her mother to it," and "insists on a morning down payment." Gwen "owes" more time but trades an "uneasy" bargain and "saves" herself "trouble." The metaphor of bargaining shapes and unifies the narrative.

Note that Hochschild "represents" each actor—and their silent witnesses—in the scene but she does so through describing the incident. Her even style and tone make her voice creditable and the story believable. She stands in the scene but does not enter the story. As Hochschild presents the scenario at the daycare center, she represents Cassie and Gwen. Diane's silent presence, but imagined or perhaps visible judgment, frames Gwen's apologies. Does Hochschild retell everything that occurred during this incident? Probably not. More likely, she distills the incident to bare essentials. She lets Gwen and Cassie speak in their own voices—*while they deliver their most revealing lines*. No irrelevant small talk disrupts the tale. The dialogue in Gwen and Cassie's story consists of only four sentences; Hochschild's voice forms the rest of the anecdote. Yet we gain a sense of who Cassie and Gwen are and what their respective actions mean through Hochschild's rendering of the scene.

A few deft sentences paint images of the actors in the scene; however, their actions take precedence and shape this story. In turn, the story tells a larger tale than the idiosyncratic actions of individuals. Readers understand that Cassie's payoff results from the bargaining about

Gwen's time bind. Hochschild *shows* us the incident concretely, rather than relating it in general terms. We gain sufficient sense of the actors and the scene that we believe her portrayal of it.

The balance between dialogue and description permits Hochschild to use her research participants' direct statements without usurping their meaning. Meaning lies in the action and scene, as well as in research participants' statements. The story of the incident allows us to locate their statements because of how Hochschild tells the tale. As she creates and connects images in this story, Hochschild constructs and strengthens her analytic narrative. Later Hochschild directs the reader back to Gwen Bell's time bind: "Cassie still stands at the front door holding her fudge bar like a flag, the emblem of a truce in a battle over time" (p. 11). A fudge bar flags the truce but marks the battle.

## Using Rhetorical Devices

Good writers of all kinds use a variety of rhetorical devices to interest their readers and to make memorable arguments. Hochschild (1997) used the narrative above to establish her idea of the time bind and to launch her argument about it. Although Hochschild does not enter the narrative, she brings a persuasive authorial voice to it. Authors of quantitative reports can also build a strong authorial voice into their narratives and use rhetorical devices to further their objectives. They too build images but with numbers and explanations. They can ask rhetorical questions and provide unexpected answers.[10]

Rather than starting with a strong thesis sentence, as writing handbooks prescribe, Michelle J. Budig and Paula England (2001) begin their article with a provocative question: "Does motherhood affect an employed woman's wages?" (p. 204). This question sparks readers' interest and engages them in the article. The authors then state a clear purpose for the article and list five possible explanations for it:

We provide evidence of a penalty for the cohort of American women currently in their child-bearing years, and we investigate its causes. Five explanations for the association between motherhood and lower wages have been offered. First, many women spend time at home caring for children, interrupting their job experience, or at least interrupting full-time employment. Second, mothers may trade off higher wages for "mother-friendly" jobs that are easier to combine with parenting. Third, mothers may earn less because the needs of their children leave them exhausted or distracted at work, making them less productive. Fourth, employers may discriminate against mothers. Finally, perhaps the association is not really a penalty *resulting* from motherhood and its consequences at all. What appears in cross-sectional research to be a causal effect of having children may be a spurious correlation; some of the same unmeasured factors (such as career ambition) that discourage child-bearing may also increase earnings. (p. 204)

Observe Budig and England's brisk wording of their finding and how they use it to frame the purpose for this article. They do not waste words or time. After listing four one-sentence possible explanations, they state the fifth and most contentious explanation. By placing this explanation last and giving it the most space, Budig and England create rhythm and balance in the paragraph, provide a logical ordering of the explanations, and set the stage for juxtaposing their argument against it.

Before delving into their analysis, Budig and England argue that readers should care about this wage penalty because of gender inequality. Rather than stating this argument in general terms, they introduce novel ideas:

Good parenting, for example increases the likelihood that a child will grow up to be a caring, well behaved, and productive adult. This lowers crime rates, increases the level of care for the next generation, and contributes to economic productivity. Most of those who benefit—the future employers, neighbors, spouses, friends, and children of the person who has been well reared—pay nothing to the parent. Thus, mothers pay a price in lowered wages for doing child rearing, while most of the rest of us are "free riders" on their labor. (p. 205)

Readers share Budig and England's starting premise. Their outline of benefits of good parenting extends our agreement. Then they spring the real economic point on us—most beneficiaries pay nothing. By interjecting a surprising fact into their reasoning, they rivet our attention. While we absorb this surprising news, Budig and England tweak us further by calling us "free riders." *We* have taken a place in the argument; it no longer merely refers to a category of people out there somewhere. Budig and England enter the narrative and bring their argument home—to us.

In a short paragraph, Budig and England catch their potential adversaries and force them to rethink if not reverse their views. Because the authors do not exempt themselves from the free rider label, they simultaneously establish a link to their readers and give us a glimpse of who they are. Then they recede from view. More often, writers align themselves with their readers through the topic, personal experience, and voice. Carol Brooks Gardner (1995) uses each as she opens her narrative and charts its course. She starts with an epigraph[11] quoting an innocuous flirtation and next recounts an incident that occurred while she was traveling. A young male attendant had teased her when she was paying for gas. After she had completed the transaction with her credit card, he proffered the card and then waved it out of her reach. She states,

> Feminist perspectives inform research topics, but also imbue the logic of inquiry and the development of the argument. I want to think of myself more as a citizen than as a source for gender games. That fact alone probably accounts for my fascination with public places, where rituals—sometimes argued by women and men alike to be innocuous, even flattering, or explained away as the province only of the lower classes or the youthful—can be transformed into full-fledged verbal abuse or can escalate into unambiguous physical assault, even rape. And although this book focuses on the routine troubles of women, I could also write about some of the routine pleasures of public places. For women and those in other social categories who are disadvantaged in public places, even these routine pleasures will be experienced with knowledge of what *can* occur. A counterpoint to the opening epigraph is this informant's narrative:

> About a year ago, I was aerobic-walking near a mall, for exercise. It wasn't very late, just past dusk. It was the summertime. It was nice out. As I went by one of the stores, a man standing outside said hello to me, and just to be polite, I smiled and said hello back. Then he started to follow me, keeping talking to me. I was only a few blocks away from home, so I started to run. The man started to run too, and he caught me and raped me. At gunpoint. They never caught him. (p. 2)

Gardner invites readers to identify with her experience in a public place while she establishes the public realm as a particular site. Within public places, trivial incidents are linked with terrifying events. See how Gardner foreshadows the last incident. She builds progressive intensity into the narrative by moving from innocuous flirtation to an irritating gender game to sexual assault. Gardner gives us warnings. Like a novelist, she foreshadows the impending violence by intensifying force in her terms. Her verbs shift from a neutral to foreboding tone. Telling verbs build momentum and add suspense. Certain incidents can be "explained away," but ritual public harassment can "escalate." Then, by defining the outcomes of escalation ("unambiguous physical assault, even rape"), Gardner establishes the seriousness of her topic and underscores it with how "the knowledge of what *can* occur" casts an ominous cloud over women in public.

Gardner introduces another voice, another view with her informant's story. It simultaneously magnifies all that precedes and shrinks the shift from innocuous interaction to horrific assault. Does Gardner's skillful foreshadowing prepare us for the rape? Not entirely. The narrative still imparts an element of shock and horror. The innocence of the woman's voice magnifies her innocent action, and for a moment, we feel disarmed. Then we sense the full meaning of her story as she says, "He caught me and raped me. At gunpoint."

## Attending to Language

Writers who attend to their research participants' language—and their own—have the makings of a memorable argument. Key terms that participants use to describe their actions and each other reveal divisions between groups, ideologies, and practices. Writers can use their analyses of these terms to frame their studies and present the terms as compelling evidence.

Anne Arnett Ferguson (2000) looks at meanings and consequences of African American school-boys being "at risk," "inappropriate," "educable," and exhibiting "needy behavior" and links them to the social structure of the school. These links allow Ferguson to see beyond and through school officials' views of the boys' behavior as identifying them as troubled and troublesome. Ferguson says of one boy, "So Donel is marked as 'inappropriate' through the very configuration of self that school rules regulate: bodies, language, presentation of self" (p. 92).

Like Ferguson, we can attend to our research participants' language and portray them through their words. Building the analysis on participants' words encourages both writer and reader to sense or see implicit meanings. This approach also can resolve two other writing problems that feminist researchers face. First, a researcher's commitments to social justice can spawn nagging questions about representing research participants: "How can I do justice to their experience? How can I find words to express it?" An artful weaving of participants' words in the research narrative shows the rhythm, grace, and expressiveness of their voices and the passion in their words. They speak for themselves; the writer creates the stage and focuses the spotlight. Second, studying research participants' language illuminates how they make sense of their situations and, in some cases, explains how they may perpetuate disadvantages that affect them (Lively, 2001; Murray, 2000). Murray (2000) provides the following story:

> When members of the Child Care Worker Organizing Committee were invited to talk to child care staff interested in unionization, the discussions often evolved into debates about teacher salaries and parents' fees. During these debates it was not uncommon to hear teachers defending their current low wages with statements about emotional rewards and self-sacrificing values. When an increase in teacher salaries meant an increase in parents' fees, teachers often appeared unwilling to make that demand of parents.

| | |
|---|---|
| Alice [union organizer]: | Do you realize that you're supplementing their child care costs by accepting low wages? |
| Mary [neighborhood teacher]: | It's not like they [the parents] have any money either. We're not here to complain about wages. We love this work, that's enough. What we really want is more respect. |
| Jeffery [union organizer]: | Getting paid livable wages is about respect. |
| Sarah [neighborhood teacher]: | I get paid each time a child smiles at me. (p. 154) |

## WRITING ADVICE

Feminist researchers are not all alike. Our relative access to time, privileges, and resources varies enormously. How can feminist researchers with heavy workloads maintain a writing agenda despite isolation and lack of resources? What helps feminist researchers become accomplished and published writers? What distinguishes good writing from mundane reporting? How can feminist researchers improve their work?

Advice books for scholarly writers seldom address their readers' situations and hence offer acontextual prescriptions, impose general standards of success, and individualize blame for problems in making progress (see, e.g., Zerubavel, 1999). Similarly, advice from senior scholars may reflect their circumstances of long ago and current privileges, not your situation. A heavy workload may vitiate usual prescriptions such as "Write every day." Is it possible?

Writing every day is sound advice if you can do it but leads to guilt and frustration when you cannot. The structure of your day—and night—alone may squash hopes of writing when long hours of meetings, organizational housekeeping, classes, and office hours fill your days and endless grading, preparation, e-mails, and clerical tasks consume your nights and weekends. Organizational deskilling has serious consequences for aspiring writers and differentially affects those who already have little time. Perhaps you can simplify or eliminate some tasks, but perhaps not. The common prescription to squeeze in 15 minutes of writing here and there works for didactic pieces and departmental business—anything you can treat as straightforward and routine. This prescription rarely works when you struggle with ambiguous meanings and theoretical interpretations. So how do you manage to write?

Two recommendations may help. First, make writing a collaborative venture, whether or not you collaborate on writing projects. Writing is an inherently social act. We build on past works and write for specific readers. Make some of those readers local and immediate through finding a writing partner or forming a supportive writing group. Then be accountable to each other for giving and receiving constructive critiques. Accountability will get you started; accountability with caring will keep you going—and keep *you* caring about your research. Second, learn to take full advantage of the times you can write: develop a writing rhythm, a way of immersing yourself in the task so the words flow from you.[12] It takes practice, but your doctoral studies have given you a head start. Having a writing rhythm increases your comfort with writing and helps you to resume your work after periods when daily demands precluded writing. Studying your schedule—and your writing practices—helps, too. You can discern when and how you compose new ideas and what encourages you to return to old drafts. Rather than struggling to compose complex ideas in those scarce minutes you carve out, revising and editing may make more productive use of your time.

Writing teachers have long known that writing consists of two phases: a learning phase and a revising phase (Ede, 2004; Elbow, 1981; Provost, 1980). In the learning phase, you make discoveries as you compose. During the revising phase, you clarify, organize, and tighten your writing for an audience, although new ideas may surface. Granted, ready-made disciplinary templates outline traditional research reports, but learning and innovation emerge within the content. In any form of writing, the location, concentration, and amount of time that you require for composing and revising may differ. Awareness of such differences can help you construct realistic time projections and schedules. Learning *how* you write will help you manage *to* write.

Last, I offer some writing strategies to help you improve your writing:

- Study effective writing
- Critique other writers' work in progress
- Write for yourself first
- Write in active voice
- Use strong, descriptive nouns and verbs
- Show, don't just tell your reader
- Provide concrete evidence
- Impose organization after composing a draft
- Revise for clarity and power
- Eliminate needless words, sentences, and passages
- Revise for your specific audience.

*Enjoy the process!*

## Notes

1. To save space, my citations throughout this chapter are illustrative rather than comprehensive.

2. For specific guidelines on creating arguments, writing a literature review, and constructing a theoretical framework, see Charmaz (2006).

3. Mentors who published their doctoral dissertations decades ago may be unaware of what their students need to do today. These mentors may offer their students poor advice about submitting manuscripts for publication review, such as sending a dissertation off to a publishing house without revising it (Charmaz, 2006). Standards for writing have risen, as has competition to publish in good venues.

4. Researchers now make candid statements about how their race, social class, age, and, when they deem it relevant, sexual orientation influence the direction and content of their studies. Positioning oneself in relation to one's research could affect present or potential employment and has affected certain feminist researchers in both explicit and elusive ways. Susan Krieger (1997), who has had a long and productive career, states that being a lesbian, but not being either an entrepreneurial or a male model lesbian, hurt her chances of receiving a permanent position in a desirable locale and institution. When employers welcome diversity, stating one's positions and standpoints may help an author. Still, how potential colleagues and administrators interpret these positions and standpoints can vary and remain elusive. For example, the implications of acknowledging invisible disability and chronic illness remain murky.

5. Many readers and researchers assess standpoints and starting points to ascertain the validity of the research. Such an assessment presupposes that researchers can obtain valid results albeit within the general and specific conditions that shaped the study.

6. The emphasis on contemporary concerns is not limited to social scientists and professionals interested in pressing problems. Historians' titles often reflect a contemporary interest or current topic but may document and explain their historical emergence or significance in a particular time and place. See, for example, Beauchamp (1998) and Dubinsky (1993).

7. The search for a single basic social process or social psychological process was a standard prescription for developing grounded theories (Glaser, 1978; Glaser & Strauss, 1967). Now many of us, including Glaser (2001) himself, disavow the notion of a unitary process (see, e.g., Charmaz, 2003, 2006; Clarke, 2005).

8. Another reason why gerontologists ignored the article stemmed from the deep division between the study of aging and the study of death and dying. Separate literatures and traditions had developed. By publishing the piece in a journal on death and dying, I unwittingly foreclosed getting it to the most relevant audience. Nonetheless, the paper went to an editor, Richard Kalish, who evinced interest in my work and created a painless path through the publication process. Then as now, positive experiences with editors and journals were career shaping for doctoral students new to the vicissitudes of publishing, and particularly so for a new qualitative researcher then. At that time, doctoral students rarely published and journal editors seldom sought qualitative research by unknown authors.

9. Think about whether your title fits the situation where it appears. "Shouldering a Burden" would have worked much better as a title for a conference session on family care for elderly relatives than for an article.

10. Rhetorical devices can serve both qualitative and quantitative researchers; however, quantitative researchers may not attend to them as closely.

11. An epigraph is a quotation at the beginning of a narrative that sets forth its theme.

12. This flow is unlikely to be fluent. That's all right. Aim to get words on screen and paper. You do not need to share your scribbles and meanderings with anyone. At first, each word may first seem to be wrung out of you drop by drop, but with practice you will increase the flow.

## REFERENCES

Beauchamp, Cari. (1998). *Without lying down: Frances Marion and the powerful women of early Hollywood.* Berkeley: University of California Press.

Becker, Howard S. (2003). Long-term changes in the character of the sociological discipline: A short note on the length of titles submitted to the *American Sociological Review* during the year 2002. *American Sociological Review, 68*(3), iii–v.

Bettie, Julie. (2003). *Women without class: Girls, race, and identity.* Berkeley: University of California Press.

Bosk, Charles L. (1979). *Forgive and remember: Managing medical failure.* Chicago: University of Chicago Press.

Bosk, Charles L. (2003). *Forgive and remember: Managing medical failure* (2nd ed.). Chicago: University of Chicago Press.

Budig, Michelle J., & England, Paula. (2001). The wage penalty for motherhood. *American Sociological Review, 66,* 204–225.

Calkins, Kathy. (1972). Shouldering a burden. *Omega, 3,* 16–32.

Carroll, David L. (2000). *A manual of writer's tricks.* New York: Paragon House.

Charmaz, Kathy. (2002). Stories and silences: Disclosures and self in chronic illness. *Qualitative Inquiry, 8,* 302–328.

Charmaz, Kathy. (2003). Grounded theory. In J. A. Smith (Ed.), *Qualitative psychology: A practical guide to research methods* (pp. 81–110). London: Sage.

Charmaz, Kathy. (2005). Grounded theory in the 21st century: Applications for advancing social justice studies. In Norman K. Denzin & Yvonna S. Lincoln (Eds.), *Handbook of qualitative research* (3rd ed., pp. 507–535). Thousand Oaks, CA: Sage.

Charmaz, Kathy. (2006). *Constructing grounded theory: A practical guide through qualitative analysis.* London: Sage.

Charmaz, Kathy, & Mitchell, Richard G. (1996). The myth of silent authorship: Self, substance, and style in ethnographic writing. *Symbolic Interaction, 19,* 285–302.

Cheney, Theodore A. Rees. (1983). *Getting the words right: How to rewrite, edit & revise.* Cincinnati, OH: Writer's Digest Books.

Clarke, Adele E. (2005). *Situational analysis: Grounded theory after the postmodern turn.* Thousand Oaks, CA: Sage.

Crewe, Jennifer. (2004). Caught in the middle: The humanities. In B. Luey (Ed.), *Revising your dissertation: Advice from leading editors* (pp. 131–147). Berkeley: University of California Press.

Davidman, Lynn. (2000). *Motherloss.* Berkeley: University of California Press.

DeVault, Marjorie L. (1991). *Feeding the family: The social organization of caring as gendered work.* Chicago: University of Chicago Press.

DeVault, Marjorie L. (1999). *Liberating method: Feminism and social research.* Philadelphia: Temple University Press.

Dubinsky, Karen. (1993). *Improper advances: Rape and heterosexual conflict in Ontario, 1880–1929.* Chicago: University of Chicago Press.

Duneier, Mitchell. (1999). *Sidewalk.* New York: Farrar, Straus, & Giroux.

Ede, Lisa. (2004). *Work in progress: A guide to academic writing and revising* (6th ed.). Boston: Bedford/St. Martin's.

Elbow, Peter. (1981). *Writing with power.* New York: Oxford University Press.

Ferguson, Anne Arnett. (2000). *Bad boys.* Ann Arbor: University of Michigan Press.

Fisher, Sue. (1986). *In the patient's best interest: Women and the politics of medical decisions.* New Brunswick, NJ: Rutgers University Press.

Fisher, Sue. (1995). *Nursing wounds: Nurse practitioners, doctors, women patients, and the negotiation of meaning.* New Brunswick, NJ: Rutgers University Press.

Gardner, Carol Brooks. (1995). *Passing by.* Berkeley. University of California Press.

Glaser, Barney G. (1978). *Theoretical sensitivity.* Mill Valley, CA: Sociology Press.

Glaser, Barney. (2001). *The grounded theory perspective: Conceptualization contrasted with description.* Mill Valley, CA: Sociology Press.

Glaser, Barney G., & Strauss, Anselm L. (1967). *The discovery of grounded theory.* Chicago: Aldine.

Glenn, Evelyn Nakano. (2002). *Unequal freedom: How race and gender shaped American citizenship and labor.* Cambridge, MA: Harvard University Press.

Goffman, Erving. (1989). On fieldwork. *Journal of Contemporary Ethnography, 18,* 123–132.

Harding, Sandra. (1991). *Whose science, whose knowledge?* Ithaca, NY: Cornell University Press.

Hartsock, Nancy C. M. (1998). *The feminist standpoint revisited and other essays.* Boulder, CO: Westview Press.

Hertz, Rosanna. (2002). The father as an idea: A challenge to kinship boundaries by single mothers. *Symbolic Interaction, 25,* 1–31.

Hesse-Biber, Sharlene. (1996). *Am I thin enough yet? The cult of thinness and the commercialization of identity.* New York: Oxford University Press.

Hochschild, Arlie. (1973). *The unexpected community.* Englewood Cliffs, NJ: Prentice Hall.

Hochschild, Arlie. (1983). *The managed heart: Commercialization of human feeling.* Berkeley: University of California Press.

Hochschild, Arlie. (1989). *The second shift: Working parents and the revolution at home.* New York: Viking.

Hochschild, Arlie. (1997). *The time bind: When work becomes home and home becomes work.* New York: Metropolitan Books.

Howard, Judith A., & Jocelyn A. Hollander. (1997). *Gendered situations, gendered selves: A gender lens on social psychology.* Thousand Oaks, CA: Sage.

Jackman, Mary R. (1994). *The velvet glove: Paternalism and conflict in gender, class, and race relations.* Berkeley: University of California Press.

Krieger, Susan. (1991). *Social science & the self: Personal essays on an art form.* New Brunswick, NJ: Rutgers University Press.

Krieger, Susan. (1997). Lesbian in academe. In B. Laslett & B. Thorne (Eds.), *Feminist sociology: Life histories of a movement* (pp. 194–208). New Brunswick, NJ: Rutgers University Press.

Lather, Patti. (2001). Postmodernism, post-structuralism and post(critical) ethnography: Of ruins, aporias and angels. In P. Atkinson, A. Coffey, S. Delamont, J. Lofland, & L. Lofland (Eds.), *Handbook of ethnography* (pp. 477–492). London: Sage.

Lively, Kathryn J. (2001). Occupational claims of professionalism: The case of paralegals. *Symbolic Interaction, 24,* 343–366.

Lofland, John, & Lofland, Lyn H. (1995). *Analyzing social settings: A guide to qualitative observation and analysis* (3rd ed.). Belmont, CA: Wadsworth.

Lofland, John, Snow, David, Anderson, Leon, & Lofland, Lyn H. (2006). *Analyzing social settings: A guide to qualitative observation and analysis* (4th ed.). Belmont, CA: Wadsworth/Thomson Learning.

Martin, Emily. (1999a). The egg and the sperm: How science has constructed a romance based on stereotypical male-female roles. In S. Hesse-Biber, C. Gilmartin, & R. Lyndenberg (Eds.), *Feminist approaches to theory and methodology: An interdisciplinary reader* (pp. 15–25). New York: Oxford University Press.

Martin, Emily. (1999b). Medical metaphors of women's bodies: Menstruation and menopause. In Kathy Charmaz & Debora Paterniti (Eds.), *Health, illness, and healing: Society, social context, and self* (pp. 292–293). Los Angeles: Roxbury.

Mitchell, Richard G., Jr., & Charmaz, Kathy. (1996). Telling tales, writing stories: Postmodernist visions and realist images in ethnographic writing. *Journal of Contemporary Ethnography, 25,* 144–166.

Murray, Susan B. (2000). Getting paid in smiles: The gendering of child care work. *Symbolic Interaction, 23,* 135–160.

Olesen, Virginia L. (2000). Feminisms and qualitative research at and into the millennium. In Norman K. Denzin & Yvonna S. Lincoln (Eds.), *Handbook of qualitative research* (2nd ed., pp. 215–255). Thousand Oaks, CA: Sage.

Olesen, Virginia. (2005). Early millennial feminist qualitative research: Challenges and contours. In Norman K. Denzin & Yvonna S. Lincoln (Eds.), *Handbook of qualitative research* (3rd ed., pp. 235–278). Thousand Oaks, CA: Sage.

Provost, Gary. (1980). *Make every word count.* Cincinnati, OH: Writer's Digest Books.

Riessman, Catherine Kohler. (1990). *Divorce talk: Men and women make sense of personal relationships.* New Brunswick, NJ: Rutgers University Press.

Rosenfeld, Dana. (2003). *The changing of the guard: Lesbian and gay elders, identity, and social change.* Philadelphia: Temple University Press.

Rothman, Barbara Katz. (1982). *In labor: Women and power in the birthplace.* New York: Norton.

Smith, Dorothy E. (1987). *The everyday world as problematic: A feminist sociology.* Boston: Northeastern University Press.

Smith, Dorothy E. (1999). *Writing the social: Critique, theory and investigations.* Toronto, Ontario, Canada: University of Toronto Press.

Stearns, Peter. (1994). *American cool: Constructing a twentieth century emotional style.* New York: New York University Press.

Taylor, Verta, & Rupp, Leila J. (2005). When the girls are men: Negotiating gender and sexual dynamics in a study of drag queens. *Signs: The Journal of Women in Culture & Society, 30,* 2115–2139.

Weitz, Rose. (2004). *Rapunzel's daughters: What women's hair tells us about women's lives.* New York: Farrar, Straus and Giroux.

Zerubavel, Eviatar. (1999). *The clockwork muse: A practical guide to writing theses, dissertations, and books.* Cambridge, MA: Harvard University Press.

# 23

# Reading for Another

## A Method for Addressing Some Feminist Research Dilemmas

Laurel Richardson

This chapter demonstrates how the application and integration of two feminist strands can help resolve some recurrent feminist research dilemmas. The first strand—"the personal is the political"—shaped second-wave feminism. This strand holds that one's personal experiences and memories are routes into consciousness-raising about the structures and cultures of oppressions. The personal, therefore, is not marginalized, but is recognized as a theoretical and political strategy (Fonow & Cook, 1991; Taylor, Whittier, & Pelak, 2004). The second strand is feminist-poststructuralism. Feminist-poststructuralist theory holds that no theory or method has a corner on the truth. No writing is innocent. Power, language, and subjectivity are intertwined; the self is fluid; and knowledge is local, partial, and contextual (see Foucault, 1978).

These two strands met in the 1980s and have since reshaped the theory and practice of feminist qualitative research (Denzin & Lincoln, 2002). For example, poststructuralist theory of feminist research warrants autoethnography (Bochner & Ellis, 2002; Ellis & Bochner, 2000), as well as alternative ways of writing that research. Indeed, writing is itself positioned as a

*method of inquiry,* a method of discovery (Richardson, 2000; St. Pierre, 2000). Narrative analysis becomes another method for constructing theory (Chase, 1995; Davies, 1992; Ellis & Bochner, 2000), and positivist assumptions about how to conduct social research are sidelined. Feminist qualitative research has become a site of multiple interpretive practices (Denzin & Lincoln, 2002), a site that illustrates Sandra Harding's (1987) idea of "transitional epistemology." The conversation with hard scientists that controlled much of feminist qualitative research in the past has been superseded by conversations within qualitative research regarding interpretive moves, subjectivity, and power interests in the construction of knowledge.

Although there has been this radical revision of what constitutes social research, there are few texts that demonstrate a *method* through which the feminist qualitative researcher can make visible her own slippery subjectivity, power interests, and limitations—the recognition that her knowledge production is partial, contextual, and inevitably flawed. It is quite a different enterprise to present theory and critique research texts, a fairly standard practice, than it is to produce research texts that exemplify that theory.

But without such examples, I would contend that the theory is in effect "untested," and so then is its value for feminist projects.

An example of poststructural theory *as qualitative methodological writing practice* can accomplish the pedagogical, political, and intellectual work normally assigned to theorizing, however. Such examples can provide pathways through feminist research dilemmas by demonstrating (rather than talking about) the intersectionalities of subjectivity, gender, race, culture, class, ethnicity, and sexuality. Moreover, such examples warrant others—nonacademics, even—to theorize how the stories of their lives map onto stories of other people's lives.

This article offers an example of feminist-poststructural theory ensconced in a methodological writing practice. I withhold further description or analysis until the conclusion of the chapter, for an essential element of this poststructural methodology is the invitation to readers to "read for" themselves.

## READING FOR MOTHER

Mother's in my dreams, again. She is sitting next to me in my therapy session, wearing a dark suit skirt, her hair permed and dyed flat black in that 1950s beauty shop way. Supposedly her problem is that she can't control her swearing, but she doesn't say a word. "I am done with my dream work," I tell Belinda, the therapist in the dream. "No, you're not," she says. She's right.

Soon after I dream that a tall brunette woman with astigmatism (which is how I might be described) is outraged when I suggest she can afford to fix her eyesight. How do I know what it will cost her? Don't I know she has her mother to take care of? She is furious. "I've given you my vita," she yells, "and you've done nothing for me." I'm in the backseat of the car she drives over a cliff into a river. I awake thinking, well at least I am "still alive."

And just in case I haven't gotten the dream message, I dream that Mother looks like Whistler's mother, stoic and patient, and I look like Audrey Hepburn, which I did during my teen years—and especially so the year I turned 15 and went off to college. Mother and I sit posed, she looking toward the camera, me in profile, looking at her. We're a still life. Still alive.

"What have you learned about ways of being in the world from your mother?" Belinda, the real life therapist, asks. One might think Belinda's question would elicit fear and loathing, on my part—or to be less dramatic, boredom. But it doesn't. Her question lightens my mood and lifts my spirits. Her question contests the Story of My Life. It contests my lifetime belief that I have rejected my mother wholesale. How helpful—how nice—how exhilarating to think that there is something positive of my mother in me.

I go to sleep thinking about my mother, hoping a dream will come. I remember so little about her. Dailiness is difficult to recall, sort out, differentiate, remember in concrete detail; specifics blur into a generalized memory of sorts. The traumas and major life passages, in which she played a part, I remember. But how little I can say about her internal life. Did she have one? Does my silly little child, still alive within me, refuse to give my mother a life? Feelings? Beliefs? Ideas? A life worth living? Or do I not remember because I never knew?

"Oh silly Mimi," I say to my cat, as I start down the stairs, awake, disappointed to be dreamless. Mimi darts up the stairs, "me-meing," asking me in her cat way to come up and make my bed, with her in it. "Too late," I say, and then from seemingly nowhere, I add, "the phalarope."

"Do you remember the novel *Too Late the Phalarope?*" I ask Ernest at breakfast.

"One of those 1950s best sellers," he says, "by the author of *Cry the Beloved Country*. Why do you ask?"

"I associate it with my mother."

Mother checked best sellers out on 2-day loans from the Broadway Lending Library. Hundreds of books in and out of her hands; yet *Too Late the Phalarope* is the only title I remember. Why?[1]

After breakfast, I walk to my public library and take out a 1953 first edition (!) of Alan Paton's (1953) *Too Late the Phalarope*. I immerse myself in it for the rest of the day, trying to read it through my mother's eyes. With what character(s) would she have identified? What situations would she recognize as variants of her own life? This is an audacious act of co-optive reading, on my part, I know, but it might give me clues to her life—and yes, clues to how I have lived my own life.

I am reading *for* my mother.

The novel is set in South Africa, post World War II. The main character Pieter, a police lieutenant, rules over the Blacks with ease and restraint. Pieter cares about his wife and children; he cares about the old Black woman, Esther, the "only soul still alive" who witnessed the whites' trek across the grasslands; and he cares about Esther's "niece," the alternately "smiling and frowning" Stephanie, a single mother of a "sole child." Pieter, raised by a Bible-fearing father, a gentle mother, and a smothering maiden aunt, never talks about that which matters to him. His aunt, the narrator of the story, says of him:

> He was always two men. The one the soldier of the way, with all the English ribbons his father hated; the lieutenant in the police, second only to the captain; the great rugby player, hero of thousands of boys and men. The other was the dark and silent man, hiding from all men his secret knowledge of himself, with that hardness and coldness that made men afraid of him, afraid even to speak to him. (p. 2)

Indeed, "not speaking" is the book's central theme and emotional core. The aunt's voice begins the book: "Perhaps, I could have saved him, with only a word, two words, out of my mouth. Perhaps I could have saved us all. But I never spoke them" (p. 1).

Nor does Pieter ever *say* the "word or two" that might have "changed it all." His wife, Nella, only rarely gives her body/soul over to him. He can't speak to her about his longing, nor can he speak to the new minister, the police captain, his aunt, or his friends—Kaplan the Jewish shopkeeper and Jappie the social worker—about this or his obsessive desire for the Black woman, Stephanie.

Pieter succumbs to his desire and therewith violates the "Immorality Act," copulation between the races, a crime punishable by imprisonment for only a year or two, but in his community, a life sentence, "never forgiven, never forgotten." Pieter's father silently crosses

out Pieter's name from the family bible. Pieter never lived, will never again be spoken of, and all remnants of his existence will be destroyed. No one in the household will ever again speak to anyone outside the household; the front door is permanently locked. Pieter's shamed wife and children must leave the city. Pieter's sister terminates her engagement to the young minister, refusing to speak to him about it. And his aunt—who still obsessively loves Pieter—is declared dead, exiled, and never to be spoken of again, either.

I don't know if my father's passion for "other women" equaled his passion for helping the poor, needy, and those accused of crimes, for although I knew of his successes in the courtroom, he only talked about his successes with "other women" to my brother, who recoiled in anger and disgust. I do know that I could never understand why my father married my mother. She had an eighth-grade education, he was an attorney; she was dark and Jewish, he was fair and English-Irish; she was a Russian immigrant, he was from pre-Revolutionary War stock. When I asked him, he answered, "Because I always favor the underdog."

Here I am trying to read through my mother's eyes and I move so readily into my father's. But perhaps I am still in mother's eyes. A few hours before my first wedding, Mother took me aside and spoke to me about marriage. "You don't know what things you'll have to put with up," she said. "But you put up with them. You don't marry the man, you marry the life."

Did she know that my father thought of her as an "underdog"? Let me put some words into my mother's mouth: "Actually, Tyrrell, my marriage to you has allowed me to escape my origins—and you (you stupid fool), you have lost your underdog. Does that mean you will try to find another?"

My mother never swore—at least I never heard her swear. Nor did I, until graduate school. For me, eschewing clichéd swearwords was an intellectual badge of honor, proof of a nuanced sensibility. For Mother, I think, not swearing was a symbol of a genteel womanhood, proof of her passage into the American middle class. But I wax romantic here. No one swore in the house. Father sent me to my room if I used teen slang such as "screw you!" which

I certainly didn't know had a sexual meaning; once, I was excused from the table for saying "laid"—apparently in a context that had a sexual innuendo. I still struggle with the conjugations of "lie" and "lay." Not swearing, then, I think became a habit of mind.

How good it feels now to give Mother the swear words she never would have uttered: "Damn you, Tyrrell! You and your underdogs!"

My feather pillow cradles my neck, my head filled with Mother and Father. I dream that in a backyard, enclosed by a stone fence and gate, there is a mangy black and white dog with soulful eyes and matted fur, hungry, dirty. I bring the dog into my house, but I can't find a comb for its fur—and I don't know if the dog is mine or not. I don't even know if I have a dog. In the dream, I am deeply puzzled: How can I not know whether I have a dog or not?

My mind returns to a Monday in April, when I was 14. Mother had lost a pin in her glasses and Father instructed me to get a replacement pin from the optometry where I worked after school. On Monday night, I came into the house. "Hi," I yelled up the staircase. And then, remembering, yelled, "I'm sorry I forgot to get the pin."

My father stormed out of my parents' bedroom, yelling, "You're a spoiled, inconsiderate brat. You never think of anyone but yourself." He had never talked to me this way before.

"I'm sorry. And I'm not inconsiderate." My stomach cramped.

"You're a slothful, indolent child," he yelled coming down the stairs with his silk robe half tied. Mother came, too.

"No, I'm not," I said, heading to the living room, baffled by Father's outburst. How could he expect me to remember everything all the time?

I tried to defend myself, but I don't remember a word I said. But father's words still resound: "insolent," "disrespectful," "selfish."

I imagine I went into freeze response, like the rabbit in the headlights, quieting my heart, lowering my blood pressure, glowering, all of which must have been as maddening to my father as his eruption was infuriating, and confusing, to me. My father, I knew, championed "fair trials," the "rights of the accused," "innocent until proven guilty," "compassion in judgment," "second chances," "the

underdog," and above all, reasoned, thoughtful action. He believed in restraint and moderation in all things. Now, he was out of control and yelling. No one in my family ever yelled.

"You're irredeemable. You belong in a juvenile detention home." He went to the phone, called someone, and I heard him say, "Pick her up. Now. She's incorrigible."

Mother was crying and arguing with father. I had never before seen my parents argue. Then, Mother took a determined breath, and said, "If you send her away, I will leave you, Tyrrell." That she cared about me more than her marriage astounded me.

I didn't go to a juvenile home, Mother didn't leave Father, and I didn't talk to him for months after his explosive rage. Father said I was breaking Mother's heart.

When my father died 21 years later (3 years after my Mother's death), a woman claiming to be his long-term mistress appeared. She said that a son, Richard, was born to them in April, the year I turned 14—the year father called me incorrigible and accused me of breaking Mother's heart.

Were mother and father talking about Richard when I happened up the stairs, pinless? Was she threatening to leave him? Did father project his own insolence onto me? Father was bringing a "bastard" into my mother's life and exiling her own daughter. I wonder if through Mother's oblique promise not to leave him, I became the linchpin in their marriage. Or had I become a kind of scrappy "underdog"?

Is letting the scrappy dog from my recent dream into my house—not sure if it belongs to me and not having the tools to clean it up—my unconscious's attempt to bring that part of my mother/me out of the shadow, into my consciousness?

So while the door is open and before it is too late, let me go on reading for Mother in *Too Late the Phalarope*.

Likely, Mother identified Father with the book's main character, Pieter. My father, like Pieter, was a decorated soldier, an athlete, handsome and charming, a respected member of the "law and order" brigade, and a lawbreaker, himself. Like Pieter, my Father was estranged from his father; his mother—I don't know—maybe dead and gone, a woman without power. And, of course, both Pieter and my father had proper middle-class homes and families, yet lusted for other women.

The comparisons between Pieter and my Father are patently true and an obvious first literary analytic move. My mother's first "reading," too, I think, would have focused on the husband. "You don't marry the man, you marry the life."

But, then, could the sermon delivered by the young dominee (minister) have spoken to her? "Was there a husband . . . who would wish . . . his wife to know what the world, or some stranger, knew about him?" (Paton, 1953, p. 81).

What did the "other woman" know about my Father and his life that was closed to my mother? The "other woman" worked in a law office downtown near my father's office. She was privy, then, to the law talk—my father's "other" life, a life from which Mother would be at best one step removed and at worse, shut out. How could she not be angry with a husband who gave the "other woman" so much?

Let me give her a name—Dorothy. I'll call her Dorothy O'Connor. After my father died, I met her. Spoke with her.

"I'd see you downtown with your dad on Saturdays," she said.

"How did she know about those Saturdays?" I say to myself.

"I'd get a first peek of you coming out of his car. I'd be waiting in the garage."

Stalking him? I wonder.

"He bought my theater tickets, too."

No, not stalking. Invited.

"You looked so pretty in your red coat with its leopard fur lining. You wore it to *The Red Shoes* premier."

What? I am thinking. *The Red Shoes* was not just any movie—it shaped my destiny. From it I got an idea about how I might live my life differently than my mother's. Not understanding, then, the true thrust of the movie—thinking it was only the shoes that were dancing away into oblivion—I imagined that a woman could have both a marriage and a career—which is what I have done.

"I sat behind you, and stroked your coat's fur lining," Dorothy continues.

My mind goes to how I begged my mother to buy me that expensive coat. A perfect fit!

I was 10, and this was the first time we had gone shopping downtown. I had never had a new coat. Being the youngest of a large extended "fictive kin" family, I was the sole recipient of everyone's hand-me-downs. Oh how I wanted something brand new. Mother bought me the coat from her "allowance," and I loved her that day. I promised I would not grow for 2 years—the only promise I have made to anyone that I have not kept.

"You loved the movie. You wanted to stay and see it again," Dorothy says. A Cheshire smile on her face.

Yes, that's true. I did. I did.

As I write this, I allow my submerged feelings to surface. Father had invited Dorothy into my life, to invade my privacy. Were my "special times" with my father opportunities for him to share experiences with Dorothy? And if so—and apparently so—then my father shared with Dorothy more than the courtroom and the bedroom. She knew more about my "special times" with my Father than my mother did. I am saddened and outraged and humiliated—and I begin to understand violation of trust. This part of the "story of my life" will need to be renarrativized, too.

But not now. Now, I must return to Mother's eyes. How difficult it is to stay in her world; to see through her eyes. How easily I am drawn into my father's life and my own.

Yet writing of Dorothy's presence in my child life, unknown to me at the time, brings me to my mother's experience. Her trust was violated. Her life—her "things"—the leopard lined coat, her husband—were touched. Invaded.

Yet still, men of my father's generation and social class routinely had "mistresses." Second lives with second wives.

"Your father supported me in Chicago," Dorothy said. "And he always spent Christmas with me."

My mind turns to one particular Christmas when father was gone most of the day—"gone to see a man about a dog"—but presumably imbibing Christmas cheer with the uncles. He returned late in the evening bearing a large ceramic cat as a gift for my mother, like a peace offering. It seemed a strange gift and I wondered where he could have bought it because stores were closed on Christmas Day. Perhaps, I think now, it was a gift to him from Dorothy. Or even a gift to me. She probably knew how much I loved cats.

That Cheshire cat sits atop my bookcase, now. My granddaughter Katya wants to play with it, but I wont let her. I tell her it's too fragile—yet I let her play with other fragile bric-a-brac; accept the broken pieces; ask Ernest to glue them back together. But no, she can't play with the Cheshire cat. Too fragile. Perhaps, I have always known but didn't know until I wrote this, how fragile my life was at that time.

The social world of my childhood did not have a "color line" because Chicago's version of apartheid, segregated neighborhoods, was not a "line" but a brick wall through which a white child living on the north side, such as myself, would never even see a Black child. But there was a "religion line." Gentile on one side of the line, Jew on the other. Each school year, I would count the number of Gentiles and Jews in my class. The same number of each. And then, I'd keep the balance—"half Jew/half Gentile." A child of a Jewish mother and a Gentile Father, unwilling to deny either heritage, I was a religious half-caste. A not-to-be-dated outcast.

But I digress. Or do I? *Too Late the Phalarope* is sympathetic to the suffering of the Jews and to reconciliation between Jews and Christians. Surely Mother would have noted it. Pieter's family and minister were "not against the Jews, as they were in some other places." Nor did they countenance any "secret plans" against or hatred of the Jews because the Bible "came from the Jews" who had "suffered and died to win the Holy Land." Christians, too, were "a people of Israel." The brothers Abraham and Matthew Kaplan were town stalwarts. Abraham's gifted daughter played the violin "like the cries and lamentations of men and nations forsaken, rising and rising until you felt you could bear them no longer and would die if they did not fall." Mathew Kaplan was empathetic, generous, smart, kind—and Pieter's best friend (Paton, 1953, pp. 24–26).

To escape the pogroms Gramma came to America from a stetl near Kiev. She brought her 8-year-old daughter, Rose, with her. If she had not, my mother Rose would have been buried at Babi Yar and I would not be here. That is a sentence I have felt compelled to write often. It is not a new thought but, still, writing it always humbles me—rekindles my gratitude.

Father's best friend was Mike, a Jewish intellectual. They met at "bug-house square," a site of free speech in Chicago during the 1920s. Mike was also my mother's brother. Father became a boarder at Gramma's house where he met my mother. And then they married. Father got his "underdog," but why did Mother do this?

By marrying my Gentile father, Mother ensured her entry and her children's entry into mainstream America. That is the story I always tell, anyway. It is a sociological one. Not knowing what my mother thought, I have liked folding her life into the generic second-generation immigrant's story.

"Tell me about your life in Russia," I asked my mother the year she died.

"I don't remember," she said.

I didn't understand then about survivors. I didn't understand then that if Mother allowed even a bit of a memory to surface the rest would come flooding back and overwhelm her in grief. So I persisted, deploying my interviewing skills.

"I'd like to know," I said.

"Who would want to know about those terrible things!?!" she yelled.

I had never heard her yell before.

Now, I take out a photo album to look at three full-length pictures of my mother in her young twenties. She's at the beach, in a black wool bathing suit. In the profile picture, her black hair, loose, falls below her breasts. Head cocked, she looks downward toward her hand, palm out, barely resting on her tilted hip. Her legs are long, her toes pointed. She looks like a vamp or a Russian ballet dancer, intense and sensuous. In another picture, she is sitting on the sand, legs spread-eagle, head down, securing her hair in a bun. She looks self-absorbed—contemplative, perhaps. In the third, she and two female friends are rolling in the sand, their bodies touching. Mother's head is back and she is smiling. I imagine a deep throat laugh the likes of which I never heard from her.

These are photos of the Mother I never knew. The emotionally complex woman, fully present in her intensity, pensiveness, and exuberance. A woman fully present to herself and others—the self-contained yet engaged woman playing in the sand.

Would this woman—this Mother I never knew—the one I am happy to believe once lived inside the Mother I did know—have found in Stephanie, the alternately "frowning and smiling" black girl in *Too Late the Phalarope,* a kindred spirit? Would she not have identified with Stephanie?

Stephanie is often imprisoned for illegally making and selling whiskey, which she does to support her child and the old Black woman Esther. When the magistrate mentioned her child, Stephanie "was immediately another woman, and she looked around the court with wary eyes, as an animal might look round when it is hunted" (Paton, 1953, p. 65). The magistrate warns Stephanie that if she doesn't find legal employment, the government "may take away your child." Stephanie looks at the magistrate, smile gone, unbelieving. "*Dis my engiste kind,*" she says—"This is my only child" (p. 66).

Before long, The Women's Welfare League prepares to remove Stephanie's child from her care. Sergeant Steyn, a man whose hatred for Pieter knows no bounds and who suspects Pieter of consorting with Stephanie, approaches her with a secret plan. She can keep her child if she tricks Pieter into meeting her, again, and reports him as a violator of the Immorality Act. Although Pieter has been her benefactor, she reports him. Once the accusation is in writing, it cannot be revoked. Pieter's family is destroyed. Stephanie keeps her child.

For Mother to identify with this "other woman," she would have to remap her horrible experiences as a Jew in Russia onto the horrible experiences of a Black woman in South Africa. She might have identified superficially with Pieter's emotionally repressed wife, but her inner self must have resonated with Stephanie's exuberance and sorrow—the alternately "smiling and frowning" underdog. And how could she not see the parallels between Stephanie's devotion to her child and her own willingness to chose a child's life—mine—over any attachments to a man, benefactors, or vows? Gramma had done this, too, and so had I, many years later, when—for the sake of my son—I divorced my first husband.

When Mother's breast cancer metastasized to her brain, *her three* children, gathered by her hospital bed, listened to her screaming,

"Remember, Tyrrell. There are *four children.* Love all four." I like to think the fourth was Richard, father's child. In *Too Late the Phalarope,* Pieter's crime would "not be forgotten, not be forgiven." Mother did not forget, either, but she did forgive.

I, too, have not forgotten the child. Not Richard. No. I mean the child that my mother should have been.

In Kiev, there is now a Jewish kindergarten—Hatikvah, "the hope." I help it survive. On my wall is a photo of the children coloring. They are dark-haired, intense, alive, beautiful. They look at their work and at each other. They could be my mother's great-grandchildren.

And so I end my outrageous project of trying to read for mother. In some ways, a failed project. Doomed from the start. For as you have heard, in reading for my mother, I've been reading for and from myself. I superimpose my world, my feelings, my point of view onto her. I don't even know if she finished the book, much less what she thought about it.

Yet I would insist that in a larger sense the project has not failed. It demonstrates the slipperiness of representing anyone's life. We're always writing about ourselves. Subjectivity is always present. But this is not bad. This is what makes our work feminist. We can see ourselves in others, see others in ourselves.

More particularly, this work has been for me a surprise, a pleasure, a success. Reading for Mother through "the phalarope," I have constructed her as a compassionate, complex, smart, and honorable woman—not the repressed mother I have carried in my mind's eye. Through the reading/writing I have acquired a second innocence, a place from which I can want her to live on in me.

When I was 13 and swimming competitively, I would silently recite a mantra with each stroke, "Mother-water hold me, mother-water hold me." Although I am a good swimmer, in my dreams I am always drowning. The night I finished this piece, I dreamt that I am at the bottom of the ocean. It is beautiful, blue, and warm. But I am not drowned. I am immersed in my mother.

There is a "strange power" between people, which makes "quite ordinary things impossible to speak of . . . and because of that power I was silent" (Paton, 1953, p. 2). So says the narrator of *Too Late the Phalarope*. And so my mother, too, had been silent. Why I am dreaming and thinking about her, I do not know. But I do know I cannot be silent now.

## Discussion

This project addresses dilemmas in feminist social research by providing an example of a feminist-poststructural method of reading/ writing. In it, I situate myself in my interior life—dreams, therapy, and writing projects. I fully acknowledge that I am writing from "somewhere"—my particular subjective state (see Bordo, 1990). Because I do not know where my writing will take me, my position is one of vulnerability. This is an appropriate stance for a feminist researcher to take; any other stance necessarily insulates, separates, and elevates her above her "subject(s)." This stance, furthermore, creates conditions through which the research can change the researcher, a desirable, nay necessary, outcome of feminist research (Fonow & Cook, 1991). Without vulnerability, how can there be change?

Furthermore, the text demonstrates how a researcher can move from "unknowing" to "knowing" to "unknowing." That is, the structure of the text helps the author escape from the conundrum of claiming "ignorance" from a position of "knowing." What the author knows is discovered, constructed, during the writing, and is, therefore, subject to renarrativization. The text, thus, models the local, specific, and temporariness of knowing as an appropriate and useful feminist epistemological stance.

The writing exemplifies, moreover, the new ways and new territories to which social researchers lay claim. One is always present in one's writing/research; to deny that is either unethical, or unscientific, or both. Through the pages of the narrative, the writer's self shifts, alters, relocates, and shifts again. The story I tell moves through decades, peoples, and continents. It illustrates "the personal as the political." Surely, I am not the only feminist woman who has identified with her father and rejected her mother. Surely, I am not the only feminist woman who has come to understand, not

through Freudian psychology, but through reflexive writing, specificities through which she can reproduce her "good" mother. Does not learning to see "the mother" as a woman with agency making moral choices contribute to a rethinking of feminist consciousness?

Finally, I offer a methodology that has effectively demonstrated the intersectionality of gender, race, class, and colonial/patriarchal cultures. *Reading for* builds on and extends autoethnographic strategies by focusing on a reader and book outside the autoethnographer. Yet it doesn't fall prey to colonializing the mind-of-the-other because the outrageousness of the strategy is forefront. The reader knows that the writer is constructing how another might read. The leap to knowing that writers always construct how others might read anything is a small one. An appropriate one, for it limits the truth-claims of the writer while at the same time displaying how those truth-claims have been made.

In the case of this autoethnographic social research, "Reading for Another," I am able to specify the interlinkings between class, ethnicity, and gender, and map one woman's experiences of culturally produced and socially sustained violence onto another's. I am not able to see clearly through my mother's eyes, for that is an impossibility, but I can see through my own eyes the parallels of oppressive violence through time and space, from the Russian pogroms to South African Apartheid—and, yes, to the violence against women locally and globally. Most important to me in terms of feminist social research and dealing with its dilemmas, though, is that this method of writing/research sparks identification. It offers an expanded feminist consciousness and a method for other feminists to make sense of their worlds in ways that connect us to one another in common cause.

## Note

1. In the novel, Pieter and his father go together to see, too late, the phalarope, a bird misidentified in an English bird book. Of interest, although not part of Paton's subtext, is that the male phalarope tends the nest.

## REFERENCES

Bochner, Arthur P., & Ellis, Carolyn. (Eds.). (2002). *Ethnographically speaking: Autoethnography, literature and aesthetics.* Walnut Creek, CA: AltaMira Press.

Bordo, Susan. (1990). Feminism, postmodernism, and gender-sceptism. In Linda J. Nicholson (Ed.), *Feminism/postmodernism* (pp. 133–156). New York: Routledge.

Chase, Susan. (1995). *Ambiguous empowerment: The work of narratives of women school superintendents.* Amherst: University of Massachusetts.

Davies, Bronwyn. (1992). Women's subjectivity and feminist stories. In Carolyn Ellis & Michael G. Flaherty (Eds.), *Investigating lived subjectivity: Research on lived experience* (pp. 53–78). Newbury Park, CA: Sage.

Denzin, Norman K., & Lincoln, Yvonna S. (2002). Introduction: The discipline and practice of qualitative research. In Norman K. Denzin & Yvonna S. Lincoln (Eds.), *Handbook of qualitative research* (2nd ed., pp. 1–29). Thousand Oaks, CA: Sage.

Ellis, Carolyn, & Bochner, Arthur. (2000). Autoethnography, personal narrative, reflexivity: Researcher as subject. In Norman K. Denzin & Yvonna S. Lincoln (Eds.), *Handbook of qualitative research* (2nd ed., pp. 733–768). Thousand Oaks, CA: Sage.

Fonow, Mary Margaret, & Cook, Judith A. (Eds.). (1991). *Beyond methodology: Feminist scholarship as lived research.* Bloomington: Indiana University Press.

Foucault, Michel. (1978). *The history of sexuality: An introduction.* New York: Pantheon.

Harding, Sandra. (1987). Conclusion: Epistemological questions. In Sandra Harding (Ed.), *Feminism and methodology* (pp. 181–190). Bloomington: Indiana University Press.

Paton, Alan. (1953). *Too late the phalarope.* New York: Scribner.

Richardson, Laurel. (2000). Writing: A method of inquiry. In Norman K. Denzin & Yvonna S. Lincoln (Eds.), *Handbook of qualitative research* (2nd ed., pp. 923–949). Thousand Oaks, CA: Sage.

St. Pierre, Elizabeth A. (2000). Nomadic inquiry in the smooth spaces of the field: A preface. In Elizabeth A. St. Pierre & Wanda S. Pillow (Eds.), *Working the ruins: Feminist poststructural theory and methods in education* (pp. 258–283). New York: Routledge.

Taylor, Verta, Whittier, Nancy, & Pelak, Cynthia Fabrizio. (2004). The woman's movement: Persistence through transformation. In Laurel Richardson, Verta Taylor, & Nancy Whittier (Eds.), *Feminist frontiers* (6th ed., pp. 515–531). Boston: McGraw-Hill.

# 24

## TRUTH AND TRUTHS IN FEMINIST KNOWLEDGE PRODUCTION

MARY HAWKESWORTH

*The project of feminist theory is to write a new encyclopedia. Its title:* The World, According to Women.

— Frye (1993, p. 104)

By situating feminist scholarship in the tradition of the radical 18th-century French *encyclopédistes*, whose objective was to systematize all human knowledge, Marilyn Frye illuminates the enormity of the task of feminist inquiry: to develop an account of the world that places women's lives, experiences, and perspectives at the center of analysis and, in so doing, corrects the distorted, biased, and erroneous accounts advanced by men. By suggesting that scholarship by men has gotten things wrong and that scholarship that starts from women's lives will get them right, Frye acknowledges that the quest for truth lies at the heart of the feminist project. She also invokes a conception of truth tied to the philosophical enterprise first developed in ancient Greece. Truth is understood as *alethia*, that which remains when all error is purged. Thus, Frye construes feminist scholarship as a maieutic art, a form of inquiry that begins with claims that are widely accepted, subjects them to critical scrutiny, and demonstrates defects in their assertions.

Feminist scholarship has grown exponentially over the past three decades, transforming knowledge in the humanities, social sciences, and natural sciences. Cutting across the divisions of knowledge that structure contemporary universities, feminist inquiry has been characterized as oppositional research because it challenges the right of the powerful across these diverse disciplines to define realities (DeVault, 1999, p. 1). To interrogate the dominant paradigms in their disciplines, feminist scholars have to develop expertise in the modes of analysis, investigation, and interpretation accredited within their fields. Thus, any account of "truth" in feminist research practices must be attuned to commonalities and diversities, explicating that which feminist scholars share in common as well as the points of divergence and disagreement across complex modes of intellectual life. This chapter will begin with an exploration of assumptions about knowledge production shared by feminist scholars and then probe a range of debates about the nature of truth and the possibilities for discerning truth in feminist research.

## FEMINIST METHODOLOGY

The French philosopher Michele LeDoeuff (1991) has defined a feminist as "a woman who does not leave others to think for her" (p. 29). Interrogating accepted beliefs, challenging shared assumptions, and reframing research questions is a characteristic of feminist inquiry regardless of specialization. Feminist scholars have taken issue with dominant disciplinary approaches to knowledge production. They have contested androcentric "ways to truth," which universalize the experiences of a fraction of the human population. They have challenged the power dynamics structuring exclusionary academic practices, which have enabled unwarranted generalizations to remain unchallenged for centuries or indeed millennia. They have sought to identify and develop alternative research practices that further feminist goals of social transformation.

To probe the common dynamics of diverse feminist research practices, scholars interested in the philosophy and sociology of inquiry have initiated debates on "feminist methodology," probing ideas about the theories of knowledge, strategies of inquiry, and standards of evidence appropriate to the production of feminist knowledge. Noting the enormous range of feminist research, many scholars who have written on the question of feminist methodology have taken an inclusive approach, describing the variety of methods feminists have deployed and tracing connections between the specific methods and kinds of research questions they are particularly suited to answer (DeVault, 1999; Fonow & Cook, 1991; Hesse-Biber, Gilmartin, & Lydenberg, 1999; Hesse-Biber & Leavy, 2004; Oakley, 2000; Reinharz, 1992; Windance Twine & Warren, 2000; Wolf, 1996). The range of questions and the scope of feminist research are extensive. Archaeological, autobiographical, biographical, biological, case study, causal, comparative, cultural, dialectical, deconstructive, demographic, discursive, econometric, ethnographic, experimental, genealogical, geographical, gynocritical, hermeneutic, historical, institutional, intertextual, legal, materialist, narrative, phenomenological, philosophical, primatological, psychoanalytic, psychological, semiotic, statistical, structural, survey, teleological, theoretical, and textual analyses have all been deployed successfully by feminist scholars across a range of disciplines. While such an enumeration highlights the breadth of feminist inquiry, it does not resolve the question of how feminist appropriations of these diverse methods are distinctive.

Thinking about methodology in a slightly different way, then, might help to illuminate common dimensions of feminist inquiry amid this diversity. Etymologically, the term *methodology* arises from the conjunction of three Greek concepts: *meta*, *hodos*, and *logos*. When used as a prefix in archaic Greek, *meta* typically implied "sharing," "action in common," or "pursuit or quest." *Hodos* was usually translated as "way," but when combined with *logos*, which was variously translated as "account," "explanation," or "truth," *hodos* suggested a very particular way to truth about the essence of reality (Wolin, 1981). Bringing the three Greek terms together opens up possibilities for a variety of interpretations of methodology: "a shared quest for the way to truth," "a shared account of truth," or "the way a group legitimates knowledge claims."

The Greek roots of the term are particularly helpful in laying the groundwork for an exploration of the distinctive aspects of feminist methodology because the etymology makes clear that methodologies are group specific and as such political. The appropriate methodology for any particular inquiry is a matter of contestation because scholars often disagree about the "way to truth." Strategies that are accredited as legitimate means to acquire truth gain their force from the decisions of particular humans; thus, there is a power element in the accreditation of knowledge. Power is never the only factor involved, but neither is it a negligible factor.

Like all methodologies, then, feminist research is informed by a politics. But unlike methodologies developed in accordance with positivist assumptions about knowledge production, which explicitly deny any political dimension to "scientific" inquiry, feminist research acknowledges that particular political convictions inspire its existence. As a political movement, feminism seeks to eliminate male domination in all its various manifestations. Knowledge production is a rich terrain for feminist engagement because the authoritative accounts of the world accredited by academic disciplines, whether in the humanities, social sciences, or natural sciences, have profound effects on women's lives. "What constitutes feminist work is a framework that challenges existing androcentric or partial constructions of women's lives" (Geiger, 1990, p. 169).

In an effort to explicate how feminist principles could contribute to academic research, Adrienne Rich (2003) noted suggestively that "a politicized life ought to sharpen both the senses and the memory" (p. 454). Feminist convictions attune scholars to power dynamics that structure women's lives, which can generate challenges to dominant accounts and new questions for research.

> It is the political commitment that feminists bring to diverse fields that motivates them to focus attention on lines of evidence others have not sought out or thought important; to discern patterns others have ignored; to question androcentric or sexist framework assumptions that have gone unnoticed or unchallenged; and sometimes to significantly reframe the research agenda of their discipline in light of different questions or an expanded repertoire of explanatory hypotheses. (Wylie, 2000, p. 16)

In recognizing the role of the researcher's values in the logic of discovery, feminist research has a great deal in common with the postpositivist philosophy of science. There is another dimension of feminist scholarship, however, that goes well beyond claims concerning the value-laden origins of research. Feminist scholarship suggests that a particular politics embedded in the research process improves the quality of analysis, heightens objectivity, and enhances the sophistication of research findings. Far from being a source of bias and distortion, feminist convictions and principles are deemed an asset to research. In the words of Linda Nochlin (1971/1988),

> Natural assumptions must be questioned and the mythic basis of so much so-called fact brought to light. And it is here that the very position of women as an acknowledged outsider, the maverick "she" instead of the presumably neutral "one"—in reality the white-male position accepted as natural, or the hidden "he" as the subject of all scholarly predicates—is a decided advantage, rather than merely a hindrance or a subjective distortion. (p. 152)

In marked contrast to positivist conceptions of science, Kantian conceptions of moral reasoning,

and the tenets of new criticism within literary theory, feminist scholarship suggests that a commitment to struggle against coercive hierarchies linked to gender, race, and sexuality, a commitment to promote women's freedom and empowerment, and a commitment to revolt against institutions, practices, values, and knowledge systems that subordinate and denigrate women enhance the truth content and deepen the insights of feminist accounts of the world. Despite widely divergent disciplinary and interdisciplinary backgrounds, feminist scholarship involves "disidentification" from some of the guiding precepts of positivism such as value neutrality and from the norms of distanced, dispassionate research and the quest for universal explanations characteristic of many disciplines. To understand how feminist scholars came to recognize the necessity of this disidentification, it is helpful to consider their sustained engagement with dominant conceptions of objectivity.

## POSITIVIST AND FEMINIST CONCEPTIONS OF OBJECTIVITY

Objectivity has been a regulative ideal in philosophical and scientific investigations, ethical and judicial deliberations, and bureaucratic practices. Objectivity gains its purchase within these diverse domains on the basis of specific promises. In the context of philosophical and scientific investigations, for example, an objective account implies a grasp of the actual qualities and relations of objects as they exist independent of the inquirer's thoughts and desires regarding them (Cunningham, 1973). Objectivity, then, promises to free us from distortion, bias, and error in intellectual inquiry, to provide a path to truth that transcends the fallibility of individual knowers.

Feminist critiques of objectivity have been triggered by breach of promise. Feminist scholars have demonstrated that observations, beliefs, theories, methods of inquiry, and institutional practices routinely labeled "objective" fall far short of the norm. A significant proportion of feminist scholarship involves detailed refutations of erroneous claims about women produced in conformity with the prevailing disciplinary standards of objectivity. The pervasiveness of the mistakes about the nature of women and their roles in history, politics, and society, as well as the imperviousness of mistaken views to refutation, has led some feminist scholars to examine the conception of objectivity accredited within positivist conceptions of knowledge production.

## Positivism

The term *positivism* was first coined by the French sociologist Auguste Comte, who suggested that scientific understanding operates in the realm of the "positive," which denotes "real" or "actual" existence. By eschewing the metaphysical and theological and relying solely on observable facts and the relations that hold among observed phenomena, scientific inquiry could discover the "laws" governing empirical events. Within the field of philosophy of science "logical positivism" was further elaborated in the 1920s by the members of the Vienna Circle, who further restricted the possibilities for valid knowledge by elaborating the *verification criterion of meaning*, which stipulated that a contingent proposition is meaningful if and only if it can be empirically verified, that is, if there is an empirical method for deciding if the proposition is true or false. While the logical positivists sought to explicate methodological concepts in formal, logical terms, empirical researchers within the natural sciences and the social sciences drew on positivist precepts to legitimate particular methodological techniques to generate objective knowledge. Chief among these were the fact/value dichotomy and the hypothetico-deductive model of scientific inquiry. According to positivist precepts, differentiating between factual claims and evaluative judgments is the first step in the scientific process, which culminates in the vindication of empirical propositions as objective representations of the world. Categorizing claims as empirical, that is, as statements that can be verified by sensory inspection, and separating them from those that are normative constitutes a crucial precondition for the acquisition of valid knowledge, because it demarcates the range of propositions amenable to scientific investigation. Induction, a method of knowledge acquisition grounded on systematic observation of particulars as the foundation for empirical generalizations, was taken to provide the key to scientific investigations.

Within the positivist framework, the task of science was understood to be the inductive discovery of regularities existing in the external world. Scientific research sought to organize in economical fashion those regularities that experience presents in order to facilitate explanation and prediction. To promote this objective, positivists endorsed and employed a technical vocabulary, clearly differentiating facts (empirically verifiable propositions) and hypotheses (empirically verifiable propositions asserting the existence of relationships among observed phenomena) from laws (empirically confirmed propositions asserting an invariable sequence or association among observed phenomena) and theories (interrelated systems of laws possessing explanatory power). Moreover, the positivist logic of scientific inquiry dictated a specific sequence of activities as definitive to "the scientific method."

According to the positivist model, the scientific method began with the carefully controlled, neutral observation of empirical events. Sustained observation over time would enable the regularities or patterns of relationships in observed events to be revealed and thereby provide for the formulation of hypotheses. Once formulated, hypotheses were to be subjected to systematic empirical tests. Those hypotheses that received external confirmation through this process of rigorous testing could be elevated to the status of scientific laws. Once identified, scientific laws provided the foundation for scientific explanation, which, according to the precepts of the "covering law model," consisted in demonstrating that the event(s) to be explained could have been expected, given certain initial conditions ($C_1$, $C_2$, $C_3$, . . .) and the general laws of the field ($L_1$, $L_2$, $L_3$, . . .). Within the framework of the positivist conception of science, the discovery of scientific laws also provided the foundation for prediction, which consisted in demonstrating that an event would occur given the future occurrence of certain initial conditions and the operation of the general laws of the field. Under the covering law model, then, explanation and prediction have the same logical form; only the time factor differs: Explanation pertains to past events, whereas prediction pertains to future events. Positivists were also committed to the principle of the "unity of science," that is, to the belief that the logic of scientific inquiry was the same for all fields. Whether natural phenomena or social phenomena were the objects of study, the method for acquiring valid knowledge and the requirements for explanation and prediction remained the same. Once a science had progressed sufficiently to accumulate a body of scientific laws organized in a coherent system of theories, it could be said to have achieved a stage of "maturity" that made explanation and prediction possible. Although the logic of mature science remained inductive with respect to the generation of new knowledge, the logic of scientific explanation was deductive. Under the covering law model, causal explanation, the demonstration of the necessary and sufficient conditions of an event, involved the deductive subsumption of particular observations under a general law. In addition, deduction also played a central role in efforts to explain laws and theories: The explanation of a law involved its deductive subsumption under a theory, and the explanation of one theory involved its deductive subsumption under wider theories.

## Critiques of Positivism

The primary postulates of positivism have been subjected to rigorous and devastating critiques (Popper, 1959, 1972a, 1972b). Neither the logic of induction nor the verification criterion of meaning can accomplish positivist objectives; neither can guarantee the acquisition of truth. The inductive method is incapable of guaranteeing the validity of scientific knowledge owing to the "problem of induction" (Hume, 1748/1927). Because empirical events are contingent, that is, because the future can always be different from the past, generalizations based on limited observations are necessarily incomplete and, as such, highly fallible. For this reason, inductive generalizations cannot be presumed to be true. Nor can "confirmation" or "verification" of such generalizations by reference to additional cases provide proof of their universal validity. For the notion of universal validity invokes all future, as well as all past

and present, occurrences of a phenomenon; yet no matter how many confirming instances of a phenomenon can be found in the past or in the present, these can never alter the logical possibility that the future could be different, that the future could disprove an inductively derived empirical generalization. Thus, a demonstration of the truth of an empirical generalization must turn on the identification of a "necessary connection" establishing a causal relation among observed phenomena.

Unfortunately, the notion of necessary connection also encounters serious problems. If the notion of necessity invoked is logical necessity, then the empirical nature of science is jeopardized. If, on the other hand, positivism appeals to an empirical demonstration of necessity, it falls foul of the standard established by the verification criterion of meaning, because the "necessity" required as proof of any causal claim cannot be empirically observed. As Hume (1748/1927) pointed out, empirical observation reveals "constant conjunction" (a correlation in the language of contemporary social science); it does not and cannot reveal necessary connection. As a positivist logic of scientific inquiry, then, induction encounters two serious problems: It is incapable of providing validation for the truth of its generalizations, and it is internally inconsistent, because any attempt to demonstrate the validity of a causal claim invokes a conception of necessary connection that violates the verification criterion of meaning.

The positivist conception of the scientific method also rests on a flawed psychology of perception. In suggesting that the scientific method commences with "neutral" observation, positivists invoke a conception of "manifest truth," which attempts to reduce the problem of the validity of knowledge to an appeal to the authority of the source of that knowledge (e.g., "the facts 'speak' for themselves"). The belief that the unmediated apprehension of the "given" by a passive or receptive observer is possible, however, misconstrues both the nature of perception and the nature of the world. The human mind is not passive but active; it does not merely receive an image of the given but rather imposes order on the external world through a process of selection, interpretation, and imagination. Observation is always linguistically and culturally mediated. It involves the creative imposition of expectations, anticipations, and conjectures on external events.

Scientific observation, too, is necessarily theory laden. It begins not from "nothing" or from the "neutral" perception of given relations but rather from immersion in a scientific tradition that provides frames of reference or conceptual schemes that organize reality and shape the problems for further investigation. To grasp the role of theory in structuring scientific observation, however, requires a revised conception of "theory." Contrary to the positivist notion that theory is the result of observation, the result of systematization of a series of inductive generalizations, the result of the accumulation of an interrelated set of scientific laws, theory is logically prior to the observation of any similarities or regularities in the world; indeed, theory is precisely that which makes the identification of regularities possible. Moreover, scientific theories involve risk to an extent that is altogether incompatible with the positivist view of theories as summaries of empirical generalizations. Scientific theories involve risky predictions of things that have never been seen and hence cannot be deduced logically from observation statements. Theories structure scientific observation in a manner altogether incompatible with the positivist requirement of neutral perception, and they involve unobservable propositions that violate the verification criterion of meaning: Abstract theoretical entities cannot be verified by reference to empirical observation.

That theoretical propositions violate the verification criterion is not in itself damning, because the verification criterion can be impugned on a number of grounds. As a mechanism for the validation of empirical generalizations, the verification criterion fails because of the problem of induction. As a scientific principle for the demarcation of the "meaningful" from the "meaningless," the verification criterion is self-referentially destructive. In repudiating all that is not empirically verifiable as nonsense, the verification criterion repudiates itself, because it is not a statement derived from empirical observation nor is it a tautology. Rigid adherence to the verification criterion, then, would mandate that it be rejected as metaphysical nonsense. Thus, the positivist conflation of that which is not amenable to empirical observation with nonsense simply will not withstand scrutiny. Much (including the verification criterion itself) that cannot be empirically verified can be understood, and all that can be understood is meaningful.

## Critical Rationalism

As an alternative to the defective positivist conception of science, Karl Popper (1972a, 1972b) advanced "critical rationalism." In this view, scientific theories are bold conjectures that scientists impose on the world. Drawing insights from manifold sources to solve particular problems, scientific theories involve abstract and unobservable propositions that predict what may happen as well as what may not happen. Thus, scientific theories generate predictions that are incompatible with certain possible results of observation, that is, they "prohibit" certain occurrences by proclaiming that some things could not happen. As such, scientific theories put the world to the test and demand a reply. Precisely because scientific theories identify a range of conditions that must hold, a series of events that must occur, and a set of occurrences that are in principle impossible, they can clash with observation; they are empirically testable. While no number of confirming instances could ever prove a theory to be true because of the problem of induction, one disconfirming instance is sufficient to disprove a theory. If scientific laws are construed as statements of prohibitions, forbidding the occurrence of certain empirical events, then they can be definitively refuted by the occurrence of one such event. Thus, according to Popper, "falsification" provides a mechanism by which scientists can test their conjectures against reality and learn from their mistakes. Falsification also provides the core of Popper's revised conception of the scientific method.

According to the "hypothetico-deductive model," the scientist always begins with a problem. To resolve the problem, the scientist generates a theory, a conjecture, or a hypothesis, which can be tested by deducing its empirical consequences and measuring them against the world. Once the logical implications of a theory have been deduced and converted into predictions concerning empirical events, the task of science is falsification. In putting theories to the test of experience, scientists seek to falsify predictions, because that alone enables them to learn from their mistakes. The rationality of science is embodied in the method of trial and error, a method that allows error to be purged through the elimination of false theories.

In mandating that all scientific theories be tested, and in stipulating that the goal of science is the falsification of erroneous views, the criterion of falsifiability provides a means by which to reconcile the fallibility of human knowers with a conception of objective knowledge. The validity of scientific claims does not turn on a demand for an impossible neutrality on the part of individual scientists, on the equally impossible requirement that all prejudice, bias, prejudgment, expectation, or value be purged from the process of observation, or on the implausible assumption that the truth is manifest. The adequacy of scientific theories is judged in concrete problem contexts in terms of their ability to solve problems and their ability to withstand increasingly difficult empirical tests. Those theories that withstand multiple intersubjective efforts to falsify them are "corroborated," identified as "laws" that with varying degrees of verisimilitude capture the structure of reality and for that reason are tentatively accepted as "true." But in keeping with the critical attitude of science, even the strongest corroboration for a theory is not accepted as conclusive proof. Popperian critical rationalism posits that truth lies beyond human reach. As a regulative ideal that guides scientific activity, truth may be approximated, but it can never be established by human authority. Nevertheless, error can be objectively identified. Thus, informed by a conception of truth as a regulative ideal and operating in accordance with the requirements of the criterion of falsifiability, science can progress by the incremental correction of errors and the gradual accretion of objective problem-solving knowledge.

Although Popper subjected many of the central tenets of logical positivism to systematic critique, his conception of critical rationalism shares sufficient ground with positivist approaches to the philosophy of science that it is typically considered to be a qualified modification of, rather than a comprehensive alternative to, positivism (Stockman, 1983). Indeed, Popper's conception of the hypothetico-deductive model has been depicted as the "orthodox" positivist conception of scientific theory (Moon,

1975, pp. 143–187). Both positivist and Popperian approaches to science share a belief in the centrality of logical deduction to scientific analysis, both conceive scientific theories to be deductively related systems of propositions, both accept a deductive account of scientific explanation, both treat explanation and prediction as equivalent concepts, and both are committed to a conception of scientific progress dependent on the use of the hypothetico-deductive method of testing scientific claims (Brown, 1977, pp. 65–75; Stockman, 1983, p. 76). In addition, both positivist and Popperian conceptions of science are committed to the correspondence theory of truth, which holds that a statement (proposition, idea, thought, belief, opinion) is true if that to which it refers (corresponds) exists: That is, truth lies in correspondence with facts. Thus, both positivist and Popperian approaches also accept the corollary assumption that the objectivity of science ultimately rests on an appeal to the facts. Both are committed to the institutionalization of the fact/value dichotomy to establish the determinate ground of science. Both accept that once safely ensconced within the bounds of the empirical realm, science is grounded on a sufficiently firm foundation to provide for the accumulation of knowledge, the progressive elimination of error, and the gradual accretion of useful solutions to technical problems. And although Popper suggested that reason could be brought to bear on evaluative questions, he accepted the fundamental positivist principle that, ultimately, value choices rested on nonrational factors.

## Feminist Critiques of Positivist Approaches

Ruth Berman (1989) identified three core assumptions of objectivity within positivist approaches to scientific inquiry:

> that a rational method of investigation, the scientific method, exists, which can be utilized regardless of social context or the phenomenon being investigated; that any "good," well-trained, honest scientist can apply this well-defined, neutral method to the object being investigated and obtain objective, unbiased data; and that the "facts"

(data) are the facts: the results reported are hard, immutable and unaffected by personal concerns. (p. 236)

Numerous feminist scholars have taken issue with each of these assumptions.

In contrast to broad construals of the scientific method in terms of formulating, testing, and falsifying hypotheses, feminist scholars have pointed out that "science has many methods," all of which are discipline specific and most of which are closely linked to the nature of the phenomenon under study (Fee, 1983; Harding, 1986; Longino, 1990, 2002). Moreover, irrespective of whether the specific method of investigation involves induction, deduction, or controlled experimentation, no method can guarantee the validity of its results. The attainment of truth cannot be ensured by adherence to a simple procedural formula. Thus, conceptions of objectivity that turn on adherence to an appropriate disciplinary method are seriously defective. Nor can positivists save the belief that the scientific method guarantees objectivity of results by appealing to replicability. Intersubjective testing and confirmation cannot be taken as reliable tokens of truthfulness. As the history of scientific and philosophical claims about women so clearly demonstrates, conventional misogyny has sustained verifications of erroneous views (Ruth, 1981). Multiple investigators deploying identical techniques may produce the same conclusions, but such intersubjective consensus cannot attest to the veracity of the claims.

It could, of course, be argued that adherence to an invariant scientific method is not a criterion of objectivity in science but that belief in such a method is an artifact of certain reconstructions of science characteristic of the philosophy of science. What is central to scientific objectivity is the neutrality of precise methods within the various scientific disciplines. Adherence to a neutral, public methodology devised to control for the idiosyncrasies of the individual inquirer produces credible scientific results. In response to this kind of claim, many feminist scholars have devoted a good deal of attention to the examination of methodological "neutrality" in the natural and social sciences. Their investigations have revealed extensive androcentrism in diverse scientific methods, manifested in the selection of scientific problems deemed worthy of investigation, research design, definition of key terms and concepts, decisions concerning relevant evidence and counterexamples, data collection and analysis, interpretations of results, and assessments of practical falsifications (Bleier, 1979, 1984; Eichler, 1980; Fausto-Sterling, 1986; Hubbard, Hennifin, & Fried, 1982; Stanley & Wise, 1983; Westkott, 1979). Contrary to claims of neutrality, their researches have demonstrated a pervasive level of sexism in scientific research, which renders women invisible, ignores women's concerns, precludes elicitation of certain kinds of information about women, reproduces gender stereotypes in the operationalization of terms, denies that gender might serve as an explanatory variable in any instance, and reverts to functionalist explanations that accredit the status quo (Benston, 1982; Farganis, 1989; Kelly, Ronan, & Cawley, 1987; Vickers, 1982). Sandra Harding (1986) has suggested that not only are the concepts, methods, and conclusions of inquiry permeated by androcentrism; sexism also influences the recruitment of personnel in science and the evaluation of the significance of scientists' research.

> If women are systematically excluded from the design and management of science and their work devalued, then it appears that neither the assignment of status to persons within science nor the assessment of the value of the results of inquiry is, or is intended to be, value-neutral, objective, socially impartial. (p. 67)

And Margaret Benston (1982) has concluded that "present science practices a kind of 'pseudo-objectivity' where because they are not taken explicitly into account, subjective factors are uncontrolled and unaccounted for."

If the disciplinary techniques devised to investigate the natural and social worlds are value permeated rather than value neutral, then perhaps the best hope for objectivity lies in the attitude of the investigator. Berman's reference to any "honest scientist" reflects the belief that the critical, nondogmatic, skeptical stance of scientists themselves can serve as a guarantor of objectivity. In disciplinary discussions of objectivity, it is not uncommon to find a peculiar displacement. In the absence of a neutral method, descriptions of the qualities of "objective knowledge" are offered as clues to the appropriate means to its attainment. Disinterestedness, dispassionateness, detachment, impersonality, and universality have been put forward as model deportment for researchers on the assumption that if the inquirer emulates the qualities attributed to objective knowledge, then the results of inquiry will be imbued with those characteristics. Feminist investigations have raised logical and empirical objections to this construal of objectivity as well. Logically, displacing the characteristics of objective knowledge onto the attitudes of "objective" inquirers can no more guarantee the attainment of truth than can a clearly elucidated research method. Empirically, there are good reasons to doubt that scientists conform to these model traits. In contrast to systematic skepticism, many scientists not only never question popular gender stereotypes but also incorporate culturally specific gender roles in their hypotheses about various animal species, cellular organisms, and social systems (Haraway, 1989; Martin, 1990; Strum & Fedigan, 2000). Claims of detachment, disinterest, distance, and universality merely serve as mechanisms for male hegemony, substituting certain men's perspectives for the "view from nowhere" (Nagel, 1986).

Like many postpositivist critics, feminist scholars have pointed out that norms of value neutrality pertaining to either methods of inquiry or attitudes of inquirers seriously misconstrue the nature of cognition, creating a false dichotomy between emotion and rationality, overlooking the theoretical presuppositions that shape perception and interpretation, masking individual creativity, and concealing the politics of disciplinary practices (Grant, 1993; Hawkesworth, 1989, 2006; Jaggar, 1989; Longino, 1990, 2002). They have also pointed out that the continuing invocation of conceptions of objectivity rooted in erroneous notions of value neutrality can have pernicious consequences.

> Commonly, women's perspectives of social reality have been denied, suppressed, or invalidated and women have been labeled "deviant" or "sick" if they have refused to accept some dominant definition of their situation. Commonly, too, theories have been put forward in the name of "science" or "objectivity" which have not only denied or distorted female experience but have also served to rationalize and legitimize male control over women. (Grimshaw, 1986, p. 254)

Several feminist scholars have suggested that rather than producing accurate depictions of the natural and social worlds, allegedly objective scientific inquiry has produced propaganda that serves the purpose of social control (Harding, 1986, p. 67). Scientifically accredited "facts" are not the hard, incontrovertible, immutable givens they are purported to be but rather ideological fragments that promote male dominance (Fox Keller, 1985; Mies, 1984). Rather than capturing things as they are, appeals to objectivity "bolster the epistemic authority of the currently dominant groups, composed largely of white men, and discredit the observations and claims of the currently subordinate groups including, of course, the observations and claims of many people of color and women" (Jaggar, 1989, p. 158). In this view, the dominant conceptions of objectivity serve "as a potent agent for maintaining current power relationships and women's subordination" (Berman, 1989, p. 224), precisely because they accord authority to androcentric claims not merely by masking their bias but also by certifying their "neutrality."

Feminist scholarship across the disciplines has revealed that misogyny routinely blinds "objective" investigators. In addressing the "Woman Question," philosophers and scientists often ignore or violate the methodological constraints of their fields, generate contradictory claims about women that undermine the internal consistency of their arguments about human beings, and fail to notice that the hypotheses they advance about women are inadequately warranted. The frequency with which such problems arise in the context of objective modes of inquiry implies both that existing strictures of objectivity are insufficient to attain truth and that there are serious deficiencies in the dominant conceptions of objectivity.

Feminist scholarship offers a critique of dominant, disciplinary conceptions of objectivity that illuminates the role of social values in cognition and that has important implications beyond investigations in which women are the objects of inquiry. It has already been noted that feminists have identified a number of faulty inferences that can explain how investigators committed to objective inquiry and acting in good faith can generate erroneous claims. The assumption that emulation of the qualities of objective knowledge can ensure its attainment and the belief that adherence to specific research techniques can guarantee the validity of the results both reflect mistakes about the requirements of objectivity. Although they arise in different problem contexts, both also manifest an erroneous understanding of the social constitution of knowledge and its implications for objective inquiry.

Conceptions of objectivity premised on self-purging of bias, value, or emotion and conceptions of objectivity dependent on intersubjective correction of the same sources of error imply that the fundamental threat to objectivity is idiosyncrasy. Both share the Baconian view of subjectivity as an obscuring, "enchanted glass, full of superstition and imposture, if it be not delivered and reduced" (Bacon, 1861, p. 276). Both locate the chief obstacle to the acquisition of truth within the individual researcher. Thus, the techniques of objective inquiry, whether conceived in terms of acts of pure intellect or intersubjective emendation, are designed to protect against "the capacity of the knower to bestow false inner projections on the outer world of things" (Bordo, 1987, p. 51).

The feminist discovery of persistent patterns of sexist error in objective inquiry suggests that the target of the various corrective strategies has been mislocated. The conviction that the central problem of objectivity lies with the emotional and perceptual quirks of the subjective self that distort, confuse, and interfere with objective apprehension of phenomena neglects the social dimensions of inner consciousness. Situating the issue of objectivity in a contest between the inner self and external reality masks the social constitution of subjectivity. The recurrence of a profound degree of sexism that filters perceptions, mediates philosophical arguments, structures research hypotheses, and "stabilizes inquiry by providing assumptions that highlight certain kinds of observations and experiments in light of which data are taken as evidence for hypotheses" (Longino, 1990, p. 99) indicates a remarkable uniformity in the kinds of distortion that impede the acquisition of truth. Such uniformity challenges the myth of radical idiosyncrasy. One need not be committed to the full implications of Foucault's view of subjectivity as normalizing practice to accept the feminist argument that even one's innermost consciousness is culturally freighted.

If social values incorporated within individual consciousness present an important obstacle to objective knowledge, then norms of objectivity that blind the individual to their role or suggest that intersubjective consensus is a sufficient remedy will fail to produce objective accounts of the world. If social values structure conceptions of self and perceptions of the social and natural worlds, then neither isolated acts of pure intellect nor intersubjective testing will suffice to identify them. On the contrary, the belief that subjectivity is the fundamental obstacle to objectivity will preclude detailed investigations of shared assumptions and observations as well as intersubjectively verified theories. Rather than being perceived as a potential source of error, values such as sexism and racism that are widely held will escape critical reflection. Their very popularity will be taken to certify their validity, thereby truncating further inquiry into their merits.

Feminist scholars have illuminated the numerous points at which social values infiltrate discourses on women. Helen Longino (1990, 2002) has drawn on these insights to develop an account of objectivity that can coexist with a clear understanding of the social and cultural construction of science. Longino identifies the crucial role played by social values in framing research questions, characterizing the objects of inquiry, accrediting forms of explanation, demarcating credible evidence, structuring modes of argumentation, and reducing a discipline's vulnerability to maverick claims. The point of Longino's investigation is not to demonstrate the impossibility of objectivity but rather to illuminate the complexity of its attainment. Only heightened awareness of the multiple sources of error and the complexity of problems of knowledge can sustain adequate strategies to achieve objectivity. And only repudiation of the naive faith that adherence to a simple method can guarantee the acquisition of truth can help cultivate the sophistication essential to objective inquiry.

At the heart of this feminist conception of objectivity is a conception of cognition as a human practice, a conception that recognizes the complex interaction among traditional assumptions, social norms, theoretical conceptions, disciplinary strictures, linguistic possibilities, emotional dispositions, and creative impositions in every act of cognition. Operating in the context of cognition as complex social practice, the quest for objectivity entails the cultivation of the intellect. To track the multiple sources of error in a specific field of inquiry requires far more than intellectual engagement within a narrow sphere of specialization. Sensitivity to distortion and bias presupposes an intellect informed by systematic study of a chosen field, familiar with the strengths and weaknesses of a wide range of methodological tools and sufficiently knowledgeable across disciplines to analyze the role of social values in constituting the research object (Alcoff, 2000; Hawkesworth, 1989; Longino, 2002).

A capacity for critical reflection is central to this feminist conception of objectivity, but it is not the sole requirement. Intersubjectivity also plays a key role. "A method of inquiry is objective to the extent that it permits transformative criticism" (Longino, 1990, p. 75). The point of intersubjectivity within this framework is not the confirmation of shared assumptions about what is normal, natural, or real, but rather to subject precisely what seems least problematic to critical scrutiny. Awareness of the role of social values in naturalizing oppressive practices leads feminists to emphasize the importance of critical intersubjectivity in probing tacit assumptions and foundational beliefs of various disciplines.

If objective inquiry depends on systematic probing of precisely that which appears unproblematic, then who does the probing may be a matter of central concern to those committed to objective inquiry. For what is taken as given, what appears to be natural, what seems to fall outside the legitimate field of investigation may be related to the gender, race, class, and historical situatedness of the investigator. Feminist scholars have argued that the attainment of objectivity by means of probing and sophisticated intersubjective critique has implications that transcend the quest for an appropriate intellectual procedure. Convinced that "methodological constraints are inadequate to the task of ruling values out of scientific inquiry" (Longino, 1990, p. 15), feminists have argued that objectivity demands inclusivity. Objective inquiry cannot be attained within the preserve of privilege—whether it be the privilege of whites, the middle class, or men. The feminist argument for the inclusion of women and people of color within academic disciplines can thus be understood in terms of the demands of objectivity. To the extent that social values mediate perception and explanation, exclusionary practices can only help insulate questionable assumptions from scrutiny. A commitment to objectivity conceived as sophisticated intersubjective critique embraces diversity as a means. More and different "guides to the labyrinths of reality" (Stimpson, 1991) may help us to confront the contentious assumptions most deeply entrenched in our conceptual apparatus. The inclusion of people from different social backgrounds, different cultures, different linguistic communities, and different genders within science and philosophy cannot guarantee, but it might foster, sustained critique of problematic assumptions long entrenched in the academic disciplines (Alcoff, 2000).

A feminist conception of objectivity does not offer an authoritative technique that can guarantee the production of truth. In lieu of a simple method, it calls for the cultivation of sound intellectual judgment. It demands a level of sophistication that can be cultivated only by sustained study across an array of disciplines. It presupposes a reconceptualization of the relation between inner self and external world. Moreover, it demands the expansion of the scientific and philosophical communities to encompass formerly excluded groups. Thus, this feminist conception of objectivity cannot be easily attained. It remains at odds with the excessive specialization of contemporary academic training, with the naive conviction that truth lies in the application of an accredited method, and with the renewed commitment to preserve white, middle-class, male hegemony in philosophy, science, and society at large. Despite such marked differences from dominant trends, the strength of this feminist conception of objectivity lies in its promise of fostering the benign aspirations and objectives of objectivity where traditional conceptions have failed.

## CONTEXTUALIZING TRUTH CLAIMS: FEMINIST ANTIFOUNDATIONALISM

Feminist scholarship across a wide range of disciplines involves a break with traditional assumptions about the possibility and the necessity of value neutrality in research. It is also characterized by a rejection of "foundationalism," the notion that there is an absolute ground for truth claims, whether that ground is understood in terms of a permanent, transhistorical "Archimedean point," the capaciousness of rationality, or the systemic powers of observation. Critiques of foundationalism have emphasized that the belief in a permanent, ahistorical, Archimedean point that can provide a certain ground for knowledge claims is incompatible with an understanding of cognition as a human practice. They have suggested that the belief that particular techniques of rational analysis can escape finitude and fallibility and grasp the totality of being misconstrues both the nature of subjective intellection and the nature of the objective world (Code, 1991; Hawkesworth, 1989; Tanesini, 1999).

Standard critiques of foundationalism question the adequacy of deductive and inductive logic as the ground of objective knowledge. To challenge rationalists' confidence in the power of logical deduction as a method for securing the truth about the empirical world, critics typically point out that the truth of syllogistic reasoning is altogether dependent on the established truth of the syllogism's major and minor premises. Yet, when one moves from the relations of ideas governed by logical necessity to a world of contingency, the "established truth" of major and minor premises is precisely what is at issue. Thus, rather than providing an impeccable foundation for truth claims, deduction confronts the intractable problems of infinite regress, the vicious circle, or the arbitrary suspension of the principle of sufficient reason through appeals to intuition or self-evidence (Albert, 1985; Hume, 1748/1927).

Attacks on induction have been equally shattering. It has been repeatedly pointed out that inductive generalizations, however scrupulous and systematic, founder on a host of problems: Observation generates correlations that cannot prove causation; conclusions derived from incomplete evidence sustain probability claims but do not produce incontestable truth (Albert, 1985; Popper, 1972a). Moreover, where rationalism tends to overestimate the power of theoretical speculation, empiricism errs in the opposite extreme by underestimating the role of theory in shaping perception and structuring comprehension. Thus, as noted above, the "objectivity" of the positivist project turns on the deployment of an untenable dichotomy between "facts" and "values"—a dichotomy that misconstrues the nature of perception, fails to comprehend the theoretical constitution of facticity, and uncritically disseminates the "myth of the given" (Sellars, 1963).

As an alternative to conceptions of knowledge that depend on the existence of an unmediated reality that can be grasped directly by observation or intellection, antifoundationalists suggest a conception of cognition as a human practice. In this view, "knowing" presupposes involvement in a social process replete with rules of compliance, norms of assessment, and standards of excellence that are humanly created. Although humans aspire to unmediated knowledge of the world, the nature of perception precludes such direct access. The only possible access is through theory-laden conventions that organize and structure observation by according meanings to observed events, bestowing relevance and significance on phenomena, indicating strategies for problem solving, and identifying methods by which to test the validity of proposed solutions. Knowledge, then, is a convention rooted in the practical judgments of a community of fallible inquirers who struggle to resolve theory-dependent problems under specific historical conditions. In contrast to the correspondence theory of truth, which assumes that it is possible to measure claims about reality against what actually exists, the conception of cognition as a human practice relies on a coherence theory of truth premised on the recognition that all human knowledge depends on theoretical presuppositions whose congruence with external reality cannot be established conclusively by reason or experience.

Acquisition of knowledge occurs in the context of socialization and enculturation to determinate traditions that provide the conceptual frameworks through which the world is viewed. As sedimentations of conventional attempts to comprehend the world correctly, cognitive practices afford the individual not only a set of accredited techniques for grasping the truth of existence but also a "natural attitude," an attitude of "suspended doubt" with respect to a wide range of issues based on the conviction that one understands how the world works. In establishing what will be taken as normal, natural, real, reasonable, expected, and sane, theoretical presuppositions camouflage their contributions to cognition and mask their operation on the understanding. Because the theoretical presuppositions that structure cognition operate at the tacit level, it is difficult to isolate and illuminate the full range of presuppositions informing cognitive practices. Moreover, any attempt to elucidate presuppositions must operate within a "hermeneutic circle." Any attempt to examine or to challenge certain assumptions or expectations must occur within the frame of reference established by mutually reinforcing presuppositions. That certain presuppositions must remain fixed if others are to be subjected to systematic critique does not imply that individuals are "prisoners" trapped within the cognitive framework acquired through socialization (Bernstein, 1983). Critical reflection on and abandonment of certain theoretical presuppositions is possible within the hermeneutic circle, but the goal of transparency, of the unmediated grasp of things as they are, is not; for no investigation, no matter how critical, can escape the fundamental conditions of human cognition.

Thus, the conception of cognition as a human practice challenges the possibility of unmediated knowledge of the world, as well as notions such as "brute facts," the "immediately given," "theory-free research," "neutral observation language," and "self-evident truths," which suggest that possibility. Because cognition is always theoretically mediated, the world captured in human knowledge and designated "empirical" is itself theoretically constituted. Divergent cognitive practices rooted in conventions such as common sense, religion, science, philosophy, and the arts construe the empirical realm differently, identifying and emphasizing various dimensions, accrediting different forms of evidence, different criteria of meaning, different standards of explanation, different tokens of truthfulness. Such an understanding of the theoretical constitution of the empirical realm in the context of specific cognitive practices requires a reformulation of the notion of facts. A *fact* is a theoretically constituted proposition, supported by theoretically mediated evidence, and put forward as part of a theoretical formulation of reality. A fact is a contestable component of a theoretically constituted order of things.

A coherence theory of truth accepts that the world is richer than the theories devised to grasp it; it accepts that theories are underdetermined by facts and, consequently, that there can always be alternative and competing theoretical explanations of particular events. It does not, however, imply the relativist conclusion that all theoretical interpretations are equal. That there can be no appeal to neutral, theory-independent facts to adjudicate between competing theoretical interpretations does not mean that there is no rational way of making and warranting critical evaluative judgments concerning alternative views. Indeed, presupposition theorists have pointed out that the belief that the absence of independent evidence necessarily entails relativism is itself dependent on a positivist commitment to the verification criterion of meaning. Only if one starts from the assumption that the sole test for the validity of a proposition lies in its measurement against the empirically "given" does it follow that in the absence of the given, no rational judgments can be made concerning the validity of particular claims (Bernstein, 1983, p. 92; Brown, 1977, pp. 93–94; Gunnell, 1986, pp. 66–68; Stockman, 1983, pp. 79–101).

Once the myth of the given (Sellars, 1963, p. 164) has been abandoned and once the belief that the absence of one invariant empirical test for the truth of a theory implies the absence of all criteria for evaluative judgment has been repudiated, it is possible to recognize that there are rational grounds for assessing the merits of alternative theoretical interpretations. To comprehend the nature of such assessments it is necessary to acknowledge that although theoretical presuppositions structure the perception of events, they do not create perceptions out of nothing. Theoretical interpretations are "world-guided" (Williams, 1985, p. 140). They involve both the pre-understanding brought to an event by an individual perceiver and the stimuli in the external (or internal) world that instigate the process of cognition. Because of this dual source of theoretical interpretations, objects can be characterized in many different ways, "but it does not follow that a given object can be seen in any way at all or that all descriptions are equal" (Brown, 1977, p. 93). The stimuli that trigger interpretation limit the class of plausible characterizations without dictating one absolute description.

Assessment of alternative theoretical interpretations involves deliberation, a rational activity that requires that imagination and judgment be deployed in the consideration of the range of evidence and arguments that can be advanced in support of various positions. The reasons offered in support of alternative views marshal evidence, organize data, apply various criteria of explanation, address multiple levels of analysis with varying degrees of abstraction, and employ divergent strategies of argumentation. This range of reasons offers a rich field for deliberation and assessment. It provides an opportunity for the exercise of judgment and ensures that when scientists reject a theory, they do so because they believe they can demonstrate that the reasons offered in support of that theory are deficient. That the reasons advanced to sustain the rejection of one theory do not constitute absolute proof of the validity of an alternative theory is simply a testament to human fallibility. Admission that the cumulative weight of current evidence and compelling argument cannot protect scientific judgments against future developments that may warrant the repudiation of those theories currently accepted is altogether consonant with the recognition of the finitude of human rationality and the contingency of empirical relations.

The recognition that all cognition is theory laden has also generated a critique of many traditional assumptions about the subject/self that undergird rationalist, empiricist, and materialist conceptions of knowing. Conceptions of the "innocent eye," the "passive observer," and the mind as a "tabula rasa" have been severely challenged (Brown, 1977; Stockman, 1983). The notion of transparency—the belief that the individual knower can identify all his or her prejudices and purge them in order to greet an unobstructed reality—has been rendered suspect. Conceptions of an atomistic self who experiences the world independent of all social influences, of the unalienated self who exists as a potentiality awaiting expression, and of a unified self who can grasp the totality of being have been thoroughly contested (Benhabib, 1986). The very idea of the "subject" has been castigated for incorporating assumptions about the "logic of identity" that posit knowers as undifferentiated, anonymous, and general, possessing a vision independent of all identifiable perspectives (Megill, 1985; Young, 1986). Indeed, the conception of the knowing subject has been faulted for failing to grasp that rather than being the source of truth, the subject is the product of particular regimes of truth (Foucault, 1980).

In addition to challenging notions of an unmediated reality and a transparent subject/self, the conception of cognition as a human practice also takes issue with accounts of reason that privilege one particular mode of rationality while denigrating all others. Attempts to reduce the practice of knowing to monadic conceptions of reason fail to grasp the complexity of the interaction between traditional assumptions, social norms, theoretical conceptions, disciplinary strictures, linguistic possibilities, emotional dispositions, and creative impositions in every act of cognition. Approaches to cognition as a human practice emphasize the expansiveness of rationality and the irreducible plurality of its manifestations within diverse traditions. Perception, intuition, conceptualization, inference, representation, reflection, imagination, remembrance, conjecture, rationalization, argumentation, justification, contemplation, ratiocination, speculation, meditation, validation, deliberation—even a partial listing of the many dimensions of knowing suggests that it is a grave error to attempt to reduce this multiplicity to a unitary model. The resources of intellection are more profitably considered in their complexity, because what is involved in knowing is heavily dependent on what questions are asked, what kind of knowledge is sought, and the context in which cognition is undertaken (Cavell, 1979).

The conception of cognition as a human practice suggests that feminist critique is situated within established traditions of cognition even as it calls those traditions into question.

Defects in traditional accounts of knowledge engender critical feminist reflection that relies on a range of traditional analytical techniques to criticize the limitations of received views. Thus, feminists must deal deftly with the traditions that serve both as targets of criticism and as sources of norms and analytic techniques essential to the critical project. The conception of cognition as a human practice also suggests that feminist analysis can itself be understood as a rich and varied tradition. To understand the specific conceptions of truth operative in feminist research practices, then, would require careful consideration of the diverse cognitive practices that already structure feminist inquiry. Questions concerning the subject of inquiry, the level of analysis, the degree of abstraction, the type of explanation, the standards of evidence, the criteria of evaluation, the tropes of discourse, and the strategies of argumentation deployed within feminist investigations of concrete problems would be necessary to develop a full account of competing conceptions of truth operative within specific modes of feminist inquiry.

## AREAS OF CONTESTATION IN FEMINIST DEBATES ABOUT TRUTH

Although commitments to value-critical research, antifoundationalism, and plurality characterize feminist inquiry, there remains a good deal of contestation among feminist scholars concerning the nature of truth and the possibility of attaining it. In a pathbreaking work that launched the field of feminist epistemology, Sandra Harding (1986) mapped conflicting conceptions of truth that distinguished three approaches to feminist scholarship: feminist empiricism, feminist standpoint theory, and feminist postmodernism. While the parameters of these approaches have been the subject of rich and productive debate over the past two decades, the distinctions Harding identified help to illuminate the central points of contention in contemporary feminist accounts of truth.

### Feminist Empiricism

Empiricism is an old and rich epistemological tradition that dates back at least to Aristotle.

Many versions of empiricism suggest that the senses can generate reliable knowledge concerning facts as well as values and material as well as immaterial reality. While versions of empiricism dating from the 19th century severely constricted what the senses can know, as the discussion of positivism above makes clear, postpositivist versions of empiricism are attuned to the value ladenness of perception and the theoretical constitution of facticity and the underdetermination of theory by evidence.

Contemporary feminist empiricism accepts the insights of postpositivism while also incorporating the tenets of philosophical realism (which posits the existence of the world independent of the human knower) and empiricist assumptions about the primacy of the senses as the source of all knowledge about the world (Longino, 1990; Nelson, 1990; Oakley, 2000; Walby, 2001; Wylie, 2000). Feminist empiricists emphasize the complexity and diversity of empirical strategies of knowledge production and note that conflict, contestation, argument, and disagreement are both central to and productive for the practices of scientific inquiry. Through such intersubjective contestations, truth claims are adjudicated.

Feminist empiricists suggest that systematic inquiry to "unbury" the data of women's lives is crucial, precisely because women have so often been omitted from scientific studies. Through empirical investigation, feminist scholars seek to discover and articulate patterns in women's experiences, judge the strength and scope of these patterns, locate particularity and deviations from these patterns, and attempt to understand the patterns and variations from them in all their complexity (Frye, 1993, p. 108). Keenly attuned to problems of bias and distortion that result from inadequate evidence and overgeneralization, feminist scholars have been remarkably innovative in devising concepts and research strategies to describe and explain dimensions of women's realities that encompass questions of embodied existence, health, divisions of labor and power, structures of inequality, violence, reproduction, and mothering.

Within the frame of feminist empiricism, scholars working with specific methods have identified different tokens of truthfulness. Ethnographers, for example, generate "thick descriptions" (Geertz, 1994), detailed descriptions of a particular mode of life that attempt to situate social practices within the cultural norms and values of a particular group. To test the validity of their accounts, ethnographers often appeal to the judgment of the group being studied, presenting their analysis to their research subjects to see if they find the account adequate to their understanding of their cultural practices (Wolf, 1996). Feminist sociologists interested in analyzing the interaction of multiple forms of structured inequality, such as race, class, and gender in particular regions of the United States, have developed sophisticated quantitative techniques to investigate multiple groups, examine the relations among them, control for a range of interaction effects, and develop systematic comparisons that help to identify the dimensions and causes of inequality (McCall, 2001). To heighten the validity of their causal claims, some feminist scholars in the social sciences and the natural sciences use experimental methods that allow sustained observation under controlled conditions. Randomized controlled trials, which investigate the causal effects of particular interventions, such as the effects of tamoxifen on breast cancer or the effects of increased welfare payments on the work incentives of the poor, involve the comparison of particular groups of randomly selected research subjects to isolate particular cause-effect relations while controlling for the effects of chance (Oakley, 2000). Recognizing that the specific method of empirical inquiry chosen in a particular research context depends on the specific research question they seek to answer, feminist empiricists concur in their judgment that these diverse methods can generate reliable knowledge about the world. Working within an antifoundationalist frame, feminist empiricists investigate a rich and complex array of issues, generating truths of critical importance to the health, livelihoods, and well-being of women in the contemporary world.

## Feminist Standpoint Theories

Drawing on historical materialism's insight that social being determines consciousness, feminist standpoint theories reject the notion of an "unmediated truth," arguing that knowledge is always mediated by a host of factors related to an individual's particular position in a determinate sociopolitical formation at a specific point in history. For example, class, race, and gender necessarily structure the individual's understanding of reality and hence inform knowledge claims. Although feminist standpoint epistemologies repudiate the possibility of an unmediated truth, they do not reject the notion of truth altogether. On the contrary, they argue that while certain social positions (e.g., the oppressor's) produce distorted ideological views of reality, other social positions (e.g., the oppressed's) can pierce ideological obfuscations and generate a more comprehensive understanding of the world (Collins, 1990; Harding, 1993; Hartsock, 1983; Sandoval, 2000; Smith, 1979).

While some early proponents of standpoint theory seemed to suggest that the "standpoint of women" could be explained in terms of particular facets of women's lives, such as the unification of manual, mental, and emotional capacities in women's traditional activities; the sensuous, concrete, and relational character of women's labor in the production of use values and in reproduction; or the multiple oppressions experienced by women that generate collective struggles against the prevailing social order, these accounts were criticized for falling prey to essentialist assumptions about women that failed to recognize hierarchical structures of difference among women. They also presupposed too simple a relation between oppression and truth, suggesting that certain forms of adversity afford epistemic privilege, which could free the oppressed from confusion, error, distortion, contradiction, and fallibility (Grant, 1993; Hawkesworth, 1989; Hekman, 1997; Longino, 1993).

Over the past two decades more sophisticated and nuanced accounts of standpoint theory have been developed, which scrupulously avoid

essentialist definitions of the social categories or collectivities in terms of which epistemically relevant standpoints are characterized . . . [and] any thesis of automatic epistemic privilege, any claim that those who occupy particular standpoints (usually subdominant, oppressed, marginal standpoints) automatically know more, or know better, by virtue of their social, political location. (Wylie, 2000, p. 2)

Within this frame, feminist scholars deploy a conception of standpoint to investigate

> how power relations inflect knowledge; what systematic limitations are imposed by the social location of different classes or collectivities, or groups of knowers; and what features of location or strategies of criticism and inquiry are conducive to understanding this structured epistemic partiality. (Wylie, 2000, p. 7)

Thus proponents of standpoint inquiry acknowledge that "it is an empirical question exactly what historical processes create hierarchically structured relations of inequality and what material conditions, socio-political structures, and symbolic or psychological mechanisms maintain them in the present" (Wylie, 2000, p. 4).

Standpoint theory on this construal serves as an analytical tool, a heuristic device that illuminates areas of inquiry, frames questions for investigation, and identifies puzzles in need of solution and problems in need of exploration and clarification. Standpoint theory also provides concepts and hypotheses to guide research (Hawkesworth, 1999, 2006). Accepting plurality as an inherent characteristic of the human condition, inquiry guided by standpoint theory recognizes that scholars must attend to the views of people in markedly different social locations. Investigation of multiple interpretations of the same phenomenon helps to illuminate the theoretical assumptions that frame and accredit the constitution of facticity within each account. Analyzing and comparing competing claims requires the researcher to engage questions concerning the adequacy, internal consistency, and explanatory power of alternative accounts as a way to adjudicate the truth of competing interpretations.

Concerns with ideological distortion and ideology critique have been central to projects that involve standpoint analysis. While conceptions of ideology are themselves a subject of contestation, proponents of standpoint theory agree that ideologies involve systems of representation and material practices that structure beliefs and that legitimate systemic inequalities. By advocating modes of research that challenge dominant ideologies, proponents of standpoint theory suggest that feminist knowledge production can do more than describe and explain the empirical world; it can contribute to human emancipation, generating insights that can enable people to free themselves from ideological distortion and various modes of domination. Thus, the conception of truth embedded in feminist standpoint theory links claims about existing structures of inequality to modes of critical reflection that can empower people to transform existing social relations.

## Feminist Postmodernism

Informed by a Nietzschean conception of perspectivism, feminist postmodernism rejects the very possibility of a truth about reality. Feminist postmodernists use the "situatedness" of each finite observer in a particular sociopolitical historical context to challenge the plausibility of claims that any perspective on the world could escape partiality. Extrapolating from the disparate conditions that shape individual identities, they raise grave suspicions about totalizing notions of human consciousness or the human condition. In addition, feminist postmodernists emphasize that knowledge is the result of invention, the imposition of form on the world rather than the discovery of something pregiven, some "natural order of being." As an alternative to the futile quest for an authoritative truth to ground feminist theory, feminist postmodernists advocate a profound skepticism regarding universal (or universalizing) claims about the existence, nature, and powers of reason (Flax, 1986, 1987; Hekman, 1992; Yeatman, 1994). Rather than succumb to the authoritarian impulses of the "will to truth," they urge instead the development of a commitment to plurality, multivocity, and the play of difference (Nicholson, 1990).

Discussions of the situatedness of knowers suggest that the claims of every knower reflect a particular perspective shaped by social, cultural, political, and personal factors and that the perspective of each knower contains blind spots, tacit presuppositions, and prejudgments of which the individual is unaware (Buker, 1990; Moi, 1985). The partiality of individual perspectives in turn suggests that every claim about the world, "every account can be shown to have left something out of the description of its object and to have put something in which others regard as nonessential" (White, 1978, p. 3). Recognition of the selectivity of cognitive accounts, in terms of conscious and unconscious omission and supplementation, has led some postmodern thinkers to characterize the world in literary terms, to emphasize the fictive elements of fact; the narrative elements of all discourse—literary, scientific, historical, social, political; and the nebulousness of the distinction between text and reality. The move to "intertextuality" suggests the world be treated as text, as a play of signifiers with no determinate meaning, as a system of signs whose meaning is hidden and diffuse, as a discourse that resists decoding because of the infinite power of language to conceal and obfuscate. Postmodernist discourses emphasize the human capacity to misunderstand, to universalize the particular and the idiosyncratic, to privilege the ethnocentric, and to conflate truth with those prejudices that advantage the knower. Indeed, postmodernist insights counsel the abandonment of the very notion of truth as a hegemonic and, hence, destructive illusion.

Feminist postmodernists call attention to the hubris of scientific reason and the manifold ways in which scientism sustains authoritarian tendencies. By merging of the horizons of philosophical and literary discourses, feminist postmodernists loosen the disciplinary strictures of both traditions and produce creative deconstructions of the tacit assumptions that sustain a variety of unreflective beliefs. By taking discourse—structures of statements, concepts, categories, and beliefs that are specific to particular sociohistorical formations—as the primary object of analysis, postmodernists seek to heighten our understanding of the integral relations between power and knowledge and the means by which particular power/knowledge constellations constitute us as subjects in a determinate order of things (Scott, 1988, 1992).

Two analytic techniques have been central to postmodern feminist inquiry: deconstruction and genealogy. Both seek to disrupt widely accepted understandings of the world by denaturalizing categories, destabilizing meaning, unmasking the will to truth that informs particular discursive formations, and exposing the operation of power in knowledge production itself. Deconstruction is a method of discursive analysis developed by French philosopher Jacques Derrida (1979, 1980, 1981a, 1981b), which challenges the idea that language merely describes or represents what exists, suggesting instead that language is constitutive of reality. Within this framework, meaning is created through implicit and explicit contrasts structured by language. Binaries, such as man/woman, define terms by creating oppositions that are hierarchically ordered and that privilege the first term, insinuating that priority implies primacy and that the residual term is derivative or inferior. As an analytical technique, deconstruction involves the interrogation of binaries, examining how meaning is constrained, how mistaken assumptions of homogeneity inform each term of the binary, and how the binary form exudes faulty notions that it exhausts the full range of categorical possibilities.

Informed by the works of Nietzsche (1969) and Foucault (1977), genealogy is a unique form of critique premised on the assumption that what is taken for granted—objects, ideas, values, events, and institutions—has been constituted contingently, discursively, and practically. Described as diagnostic histories of the present, genealogies seek to undermine the self-evidences of the present and to open up possibilities for the enhancement of life. Unlike traditional techniques of historical analysis, genealogy rejects any search for origins, notions of progress or unilinear development, and assumptions concerning definitive causes and unbroken continuity. Genealogy's unit of analysis is not "the past" as it was lived (which is taken to be unknowable) but the historical record, the arbitrary assemblage of documents and narratives with which people make sense of their pasts. Following Nietzsche, genealogists problematize such established discourses, insisting that historical narratives are framed by questions that reflect the preoccupations and concerns of the writers. Thus, the genealogist attempts to identify the conditions under which particular discourses arise, illuminate multiplicity and randomness at the point of emergence, interrogate the interests that inform the narrative, and question the values that sustain the discursive formation. In an effort to trace complexity and disparity, genealogists begin their analysis with particularity, chance, disjuncture, and accidents, dredging up forgotten documents and apparently insignificant details in order to re-create forgotten historical and practical conditions for contemporary existence. In seeking to reveal the arbitrariness of what appears "natural" and "necessary," the genealogist aspires to open up possibilities, by disrupting dominant discourses and stimulating reflection on and resistance against what is taken for granted about the world and about ourselves. In this sense, genealogical narratives are oriented toward the enhancement of life by releasing us from the strictures of the past and orienting us toward the possibilities for innovation and invention. Postmodernists caution, however, that all new discursive formations produce new power/knowledge constellations.

While proponents of postmodern feminist modes of analysis explicitly challenge the legitimacy of all truth claims, some scholars have pointed out that the modes of critique they embrace presuppose the possibility of evaluating the comparative merits of various forms of knowledge (Walby, 2001). Thus, their analytic practices suggest implicit criteria for assessing "better, not merely different" knowledge claims. Indeed, the assertion that postmodern research strategies are appropriate for the analysis of the will to power in knowledge production can itself be interpreted as a claim to truth about the nature of intellectual inquiry and the analytic techniques best suited to engage that reality.

## Conclusion

Despite continuing contestation about the best strategies for feminist knowledge production, feminist scholarship has made huge strides over the past 30 years. Theoretical developments within women's and gender studies have been rich and profound. Feminist scholars have developed systematic critiques of androcentric bias in theoretical assumptions, interpretive strategies, genres, styles of representation, rhetoric of inquiry, problem selection, standards of evidence, models of explanation, research design, data collection, analysis of results, narrative strategies, and discursive formations. Attuned to the damage done by false universals;

biological determinism; essentialism; a colonizing gaze; heteronormativity; and insensitivity to race, class, ethnicity, disability, nationality, and other critical markers of difference, feminist scholars have developed multiple epistemic communities to interrogate disciplinary and interdisciplinary knowledge production.

Feminist scholars have struggled over the past 30 years to learn lessons from their own mistakes, their omissions, distortions, and myopias, calling into question the most basic categories of analysis, including "woman," "women," "gender," "race," and "nation." They have developed analytical tools to help frame new research questions by problematizing the given and denaturalizing what is taken for granted. Intellectual vistas have expanded with intensive debates over concepts such as intersectionality, gender analysis, standpoint theory, feminist epistemology, gynocriticism, sister/outsider, the lesbian continuum, mestiza consciousness, triangulated consciousness, the reproduction of mothering, domestic labor, technologies of gender, feminization of poverty, domestic violence, heterosexism, heteronormativity, women's double duty and triple shift, the glass ceiling and the sticky floor, situated knowledges, the ethics and politics of care, gender regimes, reproductive freedom, the subaltern, sexual harassment, gendered institutions, negotiated identities, homosocial environments, scopophilia, sexual objectification, phallogocentrism, the logic of identity, faces of oppression, gender mainstreaming, the politics of parity, the dream of a common language, world traveling theories, a feminist imaginary, and resisting subjects.

Deploying gender *and* intersectionality as analytical tools, feminist scholars have raised new questions about the social constitution of subjectivity; the materialization and stylization of the body; the identities of desiring subjects; the designation of desirable objects; patterns of desire; sexual practices; gendered performances; the terms and conditions of sexual exchange; the asymmetries of power in public and private spheres; the politics of reproduction; the distributions of types of work; the organization of domestic activity; the divisions of paid and unpaid labor; the structures of the formal, informal, and subsistence economies; the segregation of labor markets; patterns of production and consumption; the terms and conditions of labor exchange; opportunities for education, employment, and promotion; the politics of representation; the structures and outcomes of public decision making; the operating procedures of regulatory and redistributive agencies; the dynamics of diasporas and decolonization; the potent contradictions of globalization, war making, and militarization; and women's manifold resistances against the oppressive forces structuring and constraining their life prospects. Feminist knowledge production in all these spheres has raised and continues to raise powerful challenges to established disciplines in the humanities, social sciences, and natural sciences.

It has also demonstrated that the numerous obstacles to women's full participation in social, political, and economic life are humanly created and hence susceptible to alteration. In providing sophisticated and detailed analyses of concrete situations, feminists have dispelled distortions and mystifications that abound in malestream thought.

Based on a consistent fallibilism consonant with life in a world of contingencies, feminists need not claim universal, ahistorical validity for their analyses. They need not assert that theirs is the only or the final word on complex questions. In the absence of claims of universal validity, feminist accounts derive their justificatory force from their capacity to illuminate existing social relations, to demonstrate the deficiencies of alternative interpretations, and to debunk opposing views. Precisely because feminists move beyond texts to confront the world, they can provide concrete reasons in specific contexts for the superiority of their accounts. Such claims to superiority are derived from the ability to demonstrate point by point the deficiencies of alternative explanations. At their best, feminist analyses engage both the critical intellect and the world; they surpass androcentric accounts because in their systematicity more is examined and less is assumed.

# References

Albert, Hans. (1985). *Treatise on critical reason* (Mary Varney Rorty, Trans.). Princeton, NJ: Princeton University Press.

Alcoff, Linda. (2000). On judging epistemic credibility: Is social identity relevant? In Naomi Zack (Ed.), *Women of color and philosophy* (pp. 235–262). Oxford, UK: Blackwell.

Bacon, Francis. (1861). Advancement of learning, Book II. In James Spedding & Robert Ellis (Eds.), *Works*. Boston: Brown & Taggard.

Benhabib, Seyla. (1986). *Critique, norm and utopia*. New York: Columbia University Press.

Benston, Margaret. (1982). Feminism and the critique of scientific method. In Geraldine Finn & Angela Miles (Eds.), *Feminism in Canada*. Montreal, Quebec, Canada: Black Rose Books.

Berman, Ruth. (1989). From Aristotle's dualism to materialist dialectics: Feminist transformation of science and society. In Alison Jaggar & Susan Bordo (Eds.), *Gender/body/knowledge: Feminist reconstructions of being and knowing* (pp. 224–255). New Brunswick, NJ: Rutgers University Press.

Bernstein, Richard. (1983). *Beyond objectivism and relativism: Science hermeneutics and praxis*. Philadelphia: University of Pennsylvania Press.

Bleier, Ruth. (1979). Social and political bias in science. In Ethel Tobach & Betty Rosoff (Eds.), *Genes and gender* (pp. 58–59). New York: Gordian Press.

Bleier, Ruth. (1984). *Science and gender: A critique of biology and its theories on women*. New York: Pergamon Press.

Bordo, Susan. (1987). *The flight to objectivity*. Albany: SUNY Press.

Brown, H. (1977). *Perception, theory and commitment: The new philosophy of science*. Chicago: Precedent.

Buker, Eloise. (1990). Feminist social theory and hermeneutics: An empowering dialectic? *Social Epistemology, 4*(1), 23–39.

Cavell, Stanley. (1979). *The claim of reason: Wittgenstein, skepticism, morality and tragedy*. New York: Oxford University Press.

Code, Lorraine. (1991). *What can she know?* Ithaca, NY: Cornell University Press.

Collins, Patricia Hill. (1990). *Black feminist thought*. New York: Routledge.

Cunningham, Frank. (1973). *Objectivity in social science*. Toronto, Ontario, Canada: University of Toronto Press.

Derrida, Jacques. (1979). *Spurs/eperons*. Chicago: University of Chicago Press.

Derrida, Jacques. (1980). *The archaeology of the frivolous*. Pittsburgh, PA: Duquesne University Press.

Derrida, Jacques. (1981a). *Dissemination*. Chicago: University of Chicago Press.

Derrida, Jacques. (1981b). *Positions*. Chicago: University of Chicago Press.

DeVault, Marjorie. (1999). *Liberating method: Feminism and social research*. Philadelphia: Temple University Press.

Eichler, Margaret. (1980). *The double standard: A feminist critique of social science*. New York: St. Martins Press.

Farganis, Sondra. (1989). Feminism and the reconstruction of social science. In Alison Jaggar & Susan Bordo (Eds.), *Gender/body/knowledge* (pp. 207–223). New Brunswick, NJ: Rutgers University Press.

Fausto-Sterling, Ann. (1986). *Myths of gender*. New York: Basic Books.

Fee, Elizabeth. (1983). Women's nature and scientific objectivity. In Marian Lowe & Ruth Hubbard (Eds.), *Women's nature: Rationalizations of inequality* (pp. 9–28). New York: Pergamon Press.

Flax, Jane. (1986). Gender as a social problem: In and for feminist theory. *American Studies/Amerika Studien, 31*(2), 193–213.

Flax, Jane. (1987). Postmodernism and gender relations in feminist theory. *Signs, 12*(4), 621–643.

Fonow, Mary Margaret, & Cook, Judith. (1991). *Beyond methodology: Feminist scholarship as lived research*. Bloomington: Indiana University Press.

Foucault, Michel. (1977). *Discipline and punish*. New York: Vintage Books.

Foucault, Michel. (1980). *The history of sexuality*. New York: Vintage Books.

Fox Keller, Evelyn. (1985). *Reflections on gender and science*. New Haven, CT: Yale University Press.

Frye, Marilyn. (1993). The possibility of feminist theory. In Alison Jaggar & Paula Rothenberg (Eds.), *Feminist frameworks* (3rd ed., pp. 103–112). Boston: McGraw-Hill.

Geertz, Clifford. (1994). Thick description: Toward an interpretive theory of culture. In Michael Martin & Lee C. McIntyre (Eds.), *Readings in the philosophy of social science* (pp. 213–232). Cambridge: MIT Press.

Geiger, Susan. (1990). What's so feminist about women's oral history. *Journal of Women's History, 2*(1), 169–182.

Grant, Judith. (1993). *Fundamental feminism: Contesting the core concepts of feminist theory*. New York: Routledge.

Grimshaw, Jean. (1986). *Philosophy and feminist thinking*. Minneapolis: University of Minnesota Press.

Gunnell, John. (1986). *Between philosophy and politics*. Amherst: University of Massachusetts Press.

Haraway, Donna. (1989). *Primate visions*. New York: Routledge.

Harding, Sandra. (1986). *The science question in feminism*. Ithaca, NY: Cornell University Press.

Harding, Sandra. (1993). Rethinking standpoint epistemology: What is strong objectivity? In Linda Alcoff (Ed.), *Feminist epistemologies* (pp. 49–82). New York: Routledge.

Hartsock, Nancy. (1983). The feminist standpoint: Developing the ground for a specifically feminist historical materialism. In Sandra Harding & Merrill B. Hintikka (Eds.), *Discovering reality: Feminist perspectives on epistemology, metaphysics, methodology and philosophy of science* (pp. 283–310). Boston: Reidel.

Hawkesworth, Mary. (1989). Knowers, knowing, known: Feminist theory and claims of truth. *Signs, 14*(3), 533–557.

Hawkesworth, Mary. (1999). Analyzing backlash: Feminist standpoint theory as analytical tool. *Women's Studies International Forum, 22*(2), 135–155.

Hawkesworth, Mary. (2006). *Feminist inquiry: From political conviction to methodological innovation*. New Brunswick, NJ: Rutgers University Press.

Hekman, Susan. (1992). *Gender and knowledge*. Boston: Northeastern University Press.

Hekman, Susan. (1997). Truth and method: Feminist standpoint theory revisited. *Signs, 22*(2), 341–365.

Hesse-Biber, Sharlene, Gilmartin, Christina, & Lydenberg, Robin. (1999). *Feminist approaches to theory and methodology: An interdisciplinary reader*. New York: Oxford University Press.

Hesse-Biber, Sharlene, & Leavy, Patricia. (2004). *Approaches to qualitative research*. New York: Oxford University Press.

Hubbard, Ruth, Hennifin, Mary Sue, & Fried, Barbara. (1982). *Biological woman: The convenient myth*. Cambridge, MA: Schenkman.

Hume, David. (1927). *An enquiry concerning human understanding* (L. A. Selby-Bigge, Ed.). Oxford, UK: Clarendon Press. (Original work published 1748)

Jaggar, Alison. (1989). Love and knowledge: Emotion in feminist epistemology. In Alison Jaggar & Susan Bordo (Eds.), *Gender/body/knowledge* (pp. 145–171). New Brunswick, NJ: Rutgers University Press.

Kelly, Rita, Ronan, Bernard, & Cawley, Margaret. (1987). Liberal positivistic epistemology and research on women and politics. *Women and Politics, 7*(3), 11–27.

LeDoeuff, Michele. (1991). *Hipparchia's choice: An essay concerning women, philosophy, etc.* (Trista Selous, Trans.). Oxford, UK: Blackwell.

Longino, Helen. (1990). *Science as social knowledge.* Princeton, NJ: Princeton University Press.

Longino, Helen. (1993). Feminist standpoint theory and the problems of knowledge. *Signs, 19*(1), 201–212.

Longino, Helen. (2002). *The fate of knowledge.* Princeton, NJ: Princeton University Press.

Martin, Emily. (1990). The egg and sperm: How science has constructed a romance based on stereotypical male and female roles. *Signs, 16*(3), 485–501.

McCall, Leslie. (2001). *Complex inequality: Gender, race, and class in the new economy.* New York: Routledge.

Megill, Allan. (1985). *Prophets of extremity: Nietzsche, Heidegger, Foucault, Derrida.* Berkeley: University of California Press.

Mies, Maria. (1984). Toward a methodology for feminist research. In Edith Hoshino Altbach, Jeanette Clausen, Dagmar Schultz, & Naomi Stephan (Eds.), *German feminism.* Albany: State University of New York Press.

Moi, Toril. (1985). *Sexual/textual politics.* New York: Methuen.

Moon, J. Donald. (1975). The logic of political inquiry: A synthesis of opposed perspectives. In Fred I. Greenstein & Nelson W. Polsby (Eds.), *Handbook of political science* (Vol. 1, pp. 131–228). Reading, MA: Addison-Wesley.

Nagel, Thomas. (1986). *The view from nowhere.* Oxford, UK: Oxford University Press.

Nelson, Lyn. (1990). *Who knows: From Quine to a feminist empiricism.* Philadelphia: Temple University Press.

Nicholson, Linda. (1990). *Feminism/postmodernism.* New York: Routledge.

Nietzsche, Friedrich. (1969). *On the genealogy of morals* (Walter Kaufman, Trans.). New York: Vintage Books.

Nochlin, Linda. (1988). Why have there been no great women artists? In *Women, art and power and other essays* (pp. 145–178). New York: Harper & Row. (Reprinted from *Art News, 69*(9), January 1971)

Oakley, Ann. (2000). *Experiments in knowing: Gender and method in the social sciences.* New York: New Press.

Popper, Karl. (1959). *The logic of scientific discovery.* New York: Basic Books.

Popper, Karl. (1972a). *Conjectures and refutations* (4th Rev. ed.). London: Routledge & Kegan Paul.

Popper, Karl. (1972b). *Objective knowledge: An evolutionary approach.* Oxford, UK: Clarendon Press.

Reinharz, Shulamit. (1992). *Feminist methods in social research.* New York: Oxford University Press.

Rich, Adrienne. (2003). Notes toward a politics of location. In Carole R. McCann & Seung-Kyung Kim (Eds.), *Feminist theory reader: Local and global perspectives* (pp. 447–459). New York: Routledge.

Ruth, Sheila. (1981). Methodocracy, mysogyny and bad faith: The response of philosophy. In Dale Spender (Ed.), *Men's studies modified.* Oxford, UK: Pergamon.

Sandoval, Chela. (2000). *Methodology of the oppressed.* Minneapolis: University of Minnesota Press.

Scott, Joan. (1988). Deconstructing the equality vs. difference debate: Or the uses of poststructuralist theory for feminism. *Feminist Studies, 14*(1), 575–599.

Scott, Joan. (1992). Experience. In Judith Butler & Joan Scott (Eds.), *Feminists theorize the political* (pp. 22–40). New York: Routledge.

Sellars, Wilfred. (1963). *Science, perception and reality.* New York: Humanities Press.

Smith, Dorothy. (1979). A sociology for women. In Julia A. Sherman & Evelyn Torton Beck (Eds.), *The prism of sex: Essays in the sociology of knowledge* (pp. 137–187). Madison: University of Wisconsin Press.

Stanley, Liz, & Wise, Susan. (1983). *Breaking out: Feminist consciousness and feminist research.* London: Routledge & Kegan Paul.

Stimpson, Catharine. (1991, January). *On cultural democracy and the republic of letters.* Phi Beta Kappa Lecture, University of Louisville, Louisville, KY.

Stockman, Norman. (1983). *Anti-positivist theories of science: Critical rationalism, critical theory and scientific realism.* Dordrecht, the Netherlands: Reidel.

Strum, Shirley, & Fedigan, Linda. (2000). *Primate encounters: Models of science, gender, and society.* Chicago: University of Chicago Press.

Tanesini, Allesandra. (1999). *An introduction to feminist epistemologies.* Oxford, UK: Blackwell.

Vickers, Jill M. (1982). Memoirs of an ontological exile: The methodological rebellions of feminist research. In Geraldine Finn & Angela Miles (Eds.), *Feminism in Canada* (pp. 27–46). Montreal, Quebec, Canada: Black Rose Books.

Walby, Sylvia. (2001). Against epistemological caverns: The science question in feminism revisited. *Signs, 26*(2), 486–509.

Westkott, Marcia. (1979). Feminist criticism of the social sciences. *Harvard Educational Review, 49,* 422–430.

White, Hayden. (1978). *Tropics of discourse.* Baltimore: Johns Hopkins University Press.

Williams, Bernard. (1985). *Ethics and the limits of philosophy.* Cambridge, MA: Harvard University Press.

Windance Twine, Frances, & Warren, Jonathan. (2000). *Racing research, researching race.* New York: NYU Press.

Wolf, Diane. (1996). *Feminist dilemmas in fieldwork.* Boulder, CO: Westview Press.

Wolin, Sheldon. (1981). Max Weber: Legitimation, method, and the politics of theory. *Political Theory, 9*(3), 401–424.

Wylie, Alison. (2000, December). *Why standpoint matters.* Paper presented at the annual meeting of the American Philosophical Association, Eastern Division, New York.

Yeatman, Anna. (1994). *Postmodern revisionings of the political.* New York: Routledge.

Young, Iris. (1986). Impartiality and the civic public: Some implications of feminist critiques of moral and political theory. *Praxis International, 5*(4), 381–401.

# 25

## HOLISTIC REFLEXIVITY

### *The Feminist Practice of Reflexivity*

SHARLENE NAGY HESSE-BIBER

DEBORAH PIATELLI

| Sharlene | Deb |
|---|---|
| I am conducting participant observations of and interviews with African American girls between the ages of 11 and 18 at an inner city community center that houses an after-school program for youths. What is it like for young teens to "come of age" in their community? I have been hanging out at the center for over a month now, meeting with the girls once or twice a week. Sometimes they ask me to join them in playing basketball, or I watch them practice their "stepping" routines. I tutor the younger children once a week. | On entering my research with a peace and justice network, I considered myself both an insider and outsider to this community of activists. I shared their perspectives and values, yet I was not a part of this community. Although I anticipated sharing many cultural and structural experiences of the majority of the activists who were white, middle-class women, there would be a number of activists with whom I would not find an apparent commonality. Equipped with the insights from feminist researchers, I entered the field acknowledging that there would be differences in our lived experiences. I was prepared to openly share my research interests, my background, and my commitment and work through any power imbalances that arose during the research process. I understood that when working across differences, there would be many moments when I would need to listen more and talk less. |
| The neighborhood surrounding the center had several drive-by shootings, and last week one of the girls mentioned that a male youth was recently shot outside the center's back door. One girl told me she rarely goes out after school except when she comes to the community center. What is it like for young girls to have their day-to-day mobility so restricted? How does violence in their community affect peer group interactions? How do girls cope with the high levels of violence on their doorstep? | Despite this reflexive work, my access and initial conversations were problematic. Members |

*(Continued)*

(Continued)

| Sharlene | Deb |
|---|---|
| Today, Norah, my research assistant, and I are the only two white people in the entire community center, and I have been dealing with feelings of being on the margins, concerned that my whiteness and my difference in age and social class is affecting my ability to listen to the girls. How can I bridge the differences divide? Do I expect too much of myself? Of them?<br><br>I usually stay in my car before pulling out of the community center driveway. I have a tape recorder to capture my reflections. The following are reflections on a meeting Norah and I had with the girls one Friday afternoon:<br><br>Norah: I think the girls were more open this time. I don't know if it was just because we bought them pizza, but I think that it was the fact that they have seen a lot of us and we are showing interest in the boys there as well and I felt that they were open to talking about things like discrimination and white people and I didn't feel like there was as much tension around us being white.<br><br>Sharlene: I really felt the girls opened up to me today. I think that one of the keys, it kind of fell into our laps, was that by not excluding the boys who happened to walk into our room today, we gave legitimacy to the girls being there with us, because the boys wanted to be there as well. I think it made it an important thing that day. In a crazy way, the boys legitimized the whole thing.<br><br>As I reflected on my conversation with Norah, I realized that I had not thought about what our presence at the center meant for the boys who were also there. Our talking exclusively to the girls served to "de-center" the boys, and they became quite curious about what we were doing there. In fact, our openness to having the boys hang out with all of us for a brief time allowed them to know us a little and provided an opportunity to ask them if we could talk with them as well at a later point in our visit. There were things that the girls would say | responded negatively to my attendance at meetings and requests for interviews. My activist identity and the desire to collaborate and produce a useful product for this community did not seem to be enough to gain the trust of these members. I began to take their refusals to meet and the distancing at meetings personally until I attended a workshop as part of a forum that this community sponsored. The purpose of the workshop was to bring academics and activists in conversation with each other. What transpired within the first 20 minutes of that session revealed to me the invisible barrier I was facing in my own work. I began to see myself through the eyes of these activists, and I did not like what I witnessed. I began to understand their resistance in trusting academics.<br><br>As is customary in many community and academic settings, we went around the room and introduced ourselves. Thirty-five of the forty-four people in the room identified themselves as academics first, activists second. Eight identified themselves solely as activists. I followed suit—officially, I was not yet an academic; rather, I was an activist and graduate student. Two academics facilitated the session. We went around the room once again, and each of us was asked to identify an issue plaguing the Left. However, what began as a participatory conversation quickly came to a halt as several academics began constructing "research questions" appropriate for academics to undertake "to help activists." One woman (an activist) raised her hand and said, "Those questions are great, but if you really want to help us, come do the work." One of the academic facilitators responded by saying "Well, that's what we're trying to do. We [academics] have the intellectual skills and the resources, and so our time is best spent researching these issues and telling you how to solve them." The eight self-identified activists stood up and walked out. The academics looked puzzled; however, they |

| Sharlene | Deb |
|---|---|
| about the boys, especially around issues of body image and appearance, and this gave us an opportunity to see how their perceptions matched up to how the boys felt about what they found attractive in a female.<br><br>One of the issues I was hoping the girls would bring up was that of what it meant to be a black female within their community. Today, one of the girls actually talked about this issue. It came up when one of the girls touched on what it meant be an African American female. This moment provided me with an opportunity to directly ask the girls what being black and being female meant to them and whether they felt that one identity was first and the other second. I reflected on this interview moment.<br><br>Sharlene: I found it interesting that all the girls said they considered themselves black first and female second. In most cases they responded that above all they were black. They attributed this feeling to the fact that being black fundamentally shaped their sense of self and the way in which others perceived them, much more so than their gender. Related to this is the way in which the girls equated being black with a sense of strength. Many of the girls indicated that a defining factor of African American womanhood was strength, not only for themselves but also for their families and the community.<br><br>I also reflected on what it meant for a white researcher to ask this question. What assumptions was I making concerning race and gender? Would I ask such a question if my respondents were white? How does my own positionality reflect my agenda? | continued on with their conversation. I was horrified.<br><br>I wondered—was this the way I was being perceived and identified in the community, as a disconnected intellectual not willing to do the dirty work of organizing and suggesting that I had the answers to their issues? A few days later, I was invited to speak briefly at one of the network's weekly planning meetings. I discussed my experience in the workshop, but instead of professing my sincerity and commitment, I listened to their interpretations of my experience. By dialoguing about the workshop and not specifically about my access, individuals more freely expressed their concern with the role of academics in activist communities. Through this conversation, I was able to reflexively view myself through their eyes and better understand what I needed to do to gain their trust.<br><br>After 18 months in the field I am neither insider nor outsider. My researcher identity remains and interacts with my other identities, acting sometimes as an asset and other times as a hindrance. Although I spend much time reflecting about my social location, the power I hold as a researcher, and how I present myself in the field, I also consider the power others have in defining who I am, why I am there, and how much access I am allowed. By extending reflexivity outward, I am able to shift the angle of vision from analyzing my own self-presentation to also considering how I am being defined and why. My positionality continues to be both the subject and the object of study. |

Reflexivity exposes the exercise of power throughout the *entire* research process. It questions the authority of knowledge and opens up the possibility for negotiating knowledge claims as well as holds researchers accountable to those with whom they research. Reflexivity addresses two central questions that concern feminist researchers—what can we know and how do we know it? These epistemological and ontological questions about power and knowledge have long been the subject matter for social theorists. Although reflexivity is not a new concept, feminist researchers bring a unique perspective to the understanding and practice of reflexivity. In the following, we explore the historical discourse from which contemporary feminist conceptualizations of reflexivity have emerged. Using the insights and practices of feminist researchers that have greatly affected our approach to research, we illustrate how reflexivity can serve as a methodological tool for deconstructing power throughout the entire research process. Last, drawing from the practice of "experience sampling,"[1] we suggest a practical method of *reflexivity sampling* that allows researchers to "experience sample" their own reflexive moments. Experiencing and practicing *reflexivity in the moment*,[2] as demonstrated in the excerpts of our field notes above, can uncover new angles of vision, reveal invisible barriers of power or ethical concerns, and lead to greater understandings, less hierarchical relationships, and more authentic research.

## FEMINIST CONTRIBUTIONS: BUILDING ON HISTORICAL DISCOURSE

### A Reflexive Methodology

> It [reflexivity] permeates every aspect of the research process challenging us to be more fully conscious of the ideology, culture, and politics of those we study [with] and those whom we select as our audience.
>
> —*Hertz (1996, p. 5)*

Reflexivity is a holistic process that takes place along all stages of the research process— from the formulation of the research problem, to the shifting positionalities of the researcher and participants, through interpretation and writing. A reflexive methodology offers the opportunity for raising new questions, engaging in new kinds of dialogue, and organizing different kinds of social relations (Collins, 1998, 2000; Harding, 1991, 1993; Smith, 1987). For the feminist, reflexive researcher, the process of reflection begins prior to entering the field. Reflexivity, at one level, is a self-critical action whereby the researcher finds that the world is mediated by the self—what can be known can only be known through oneself, one's lived experiences, and one's biography. Through self-critical action, reflexivity can help researchers explore how their theoretical positions and biographies shape what they choose to be studied and the approach to studying it. Reflexivity is also a communal process that requires attentiveness to how the structural, political, and cultural environments of the researcher, the participants, and the nature of the study affect the research process and product. Reflexivity at this level fosters sharing, engaged relationships and participatory knowledge building practices, hence, producing less hierarchical and more ethical, socially relevant research. The practice of reflexivity can bring alternative forms of knowledge into public discourse. The reflexive researcher acknowledges that "all knowledge is affected by the social conditions under which it is produced and that it is grounded in both the social location and the social biography of the observer and the observed" (Mann & Kelley, 1997, p. 392). A methodology that is reflexive can be a transformative process for researchers, participants, and the larger community of knowledge builders.

> Reflexivity can lead to the "development of critical consciousness of both researcher and participants, improvement of the lives of those involved in the research process, and transformation of fundamental societal structures and relationships."
>
> —*Maguire (1987, p. 29)*

A reflexive methodology challenges the status quo of scientific inquiry—inquiry that rests on the foundation of positivism. A positivist methodology has been critiqued by those supporting alternative paradigms such as an interpretative approach, critical theory, and constructivism (Denzin & Lincoln, 2000; Guba & Lincoln, 2000). In addition to criticisms of an ontological nature, these alternative paradigms have challenged the model's commitment to replication and neutrality. Feminists have also challenged positivism and argue that its principles of objectivity, detachment, value neutrality, and universality are rooted in a historical, gendered, scientific paradigm that results in unequal power relations between the researcher and the participants involved in the inquiry (Harding, 1991, 1993; Hartsock, 1998; Reinharz, 1992; Smith, 1987). A feminist epistemology questions the proposition that the social world is one fixed reality that is external to individual consciousness and suggests that it is socially constructed, consisting of multiple perspectives and realities. To propose that an objective social reality exists is to deny that reality is humanly and socially constructed within a historical context. It also denies the importance of human subjectivity and consciousness as part of knowledge creation. Without considering values and interests, a positivist methodology can produce distorted research and exclude the problematic, the knowledge, and the voices of those on the receiving end of relations of the ruling.[3]

---

The idea of a social world to be known implies a knower; the knower is the expert, and the known are the objects of someone else's knowledge, not, most importantly, of their own.

—*Oakley (1998, p. 710)*

---

## Moving Toward a "Stronger Science"[4]

Objectivity implies a separation of ideology and science, an observation of the world without the infectivity of political and individual beliefs. To study the social, feminists argue for a reflexive science, or, as Sandra Harding (1986) suggests, a "stronger science." This reflexive science is one that better reflects the world around us and one that acknowledges that researchers bring their biographies, their experiences, and their knowledge into the field of research. As theorists of reflexivity and reflexive researchers grapple with one's social biography and its role in the research process, they find that ideological and personal beliefs muddy the waters of knowledge production. Separation of science and ideology becomes impossible and theoretically untenable, a fact that many theorists have accepted and articulated. Pierre Bourdieu (1993) stepped away from the more rigid definitions of objective knowledge. He

argued that there are objects of knowledge to be understood by the sociologist, but also that the sociologist is an active participant within these objects and fields of knowledge, which are the patterns of habitus. Reflexive researchers and writers are responsible for and indebted to the very texts that they shape, because it is the text and in it the reflexive self that is externalized, taking on a material life of its own. Within Bourdieu's analysis there is a deep sense that power is "relational or process oriented . . . [where power] is a function of relations between subjects and so power must be seen to function through a multiplicity of relations" (Everett, 2002, p. 57). The destructive force of objectivity can be contrasted with the potential for a transcendent force of reflexivity, where the world could be transformed by transforming its representation. If we accept with Bourdieu that the social world of interactions and meanings are directly linked to the cognitive knowing of this world, then through the symbolic world of language and representation the known world is dominated, subordinated, and controlled. However, to work and aim to be a critical theorist, one must, according to Bourdieu, examine "one's relation to the research object." In other words, the researchers must reflect the scientific gaze back on themselves, on the objectifying gaze of sociology.

Feminists, most notably Harding (1993), argue that the scientific model of objectivity needs to be replaced by a *strong objectivity*, an objectivity that can be found in feminist epistemologies. From her grounding aim of strong objectivity, Harding moves reflexivity in a slightly different direction, describing *strong reflexivity* where the researcher/theorist's own conceptual framework is the subject of critique. Additionally, strong objectivity can be achieved not by removing oneself from the world, but by acknowledging our situated location and being reflexive of our position within it. Harding conceptualizes this beyond what has been critiqued as confessional discourse toward a more potent form of objectivity. Strong objectivity is built on the sustainable desire for critical self-reflection and an attempt at liberatory social change, starting from women's lives. Harding (1992) speaks of reflexivity as "self criticism in the sense of criticism of the widely shared values and interests that constitute one's own institutionally shaped research assumptions" (p. 569). Harding's own gaze is turned toward the critique of the social sciences just as Bourdieu (1993) employs the turning of the sociological gaze back on itself. Harding (1993) sees "the grounds for knowledge are fully saturated with history and social life rather than abstracted from it" (p. 57). The singularity and universality of Truth is in question here, for when the door is open to interpretation of knowledge and facts, a single Truth cannot be obtained. The purpose of research is not to validate a Truth, but to enable different forms of knowledge to challenge power. Multiple truths and diverse knowledges become the actual product of research when the subjectivity, location, and humanness of the knower are included. Dorothy Smith (1987) asks that we not wrestle with notions of Truth, but more with how to "write a sociology that will lay out for people how our everyday worlds are organized and how they are shaped and determined by relations that extend beyond them" (p. 121). A stronger, reflexive science becomes one that reconstructs or reorganizes the social relations of building knowledge (Harding, 1986; Smith, 1987).

## Interrogating the Self or Selves

Alfred Schutz (1964) argued that both experience and biography play a direct role in the knowing of the social world. Bringing one's "own being in the world" to the research endeavor can redirect positivist conceptualizations of objectivity. Like Schutz, feminists ask that researchers be critically self-reflexive of personal and cultural biases in the formation of their theoretical perspectives of the social world. However, feminists push researchers further and ask them not only to bring themselves into the research, but also to acknowledge that

> we cannot rid ourselves of the cultural self we bring with us into the field any more than we can disown the eyes, ears, and skin through which we take in our intuitive perceptions about the new and strange world we have entered. (Olesen, 1998, pp. 314–315)

One phase of reflexivity is the methodological interrogation of the researcher's positionality, namely that of insider or outsider.[5]

> I, the human being, born into the social world, and living my daily life in it, experience it as built around my place to it, as open to my interpretation and action, but always referring to my actual biographically determined situation.
>
> —*Schutz (1964, p. 314)*

In the early 20th century, traditional ethnographic researchers positioned themselves as the detached observer, Schutz's (1964) "stranger," some standing outside the culture gazing on it, while others submersed themselves in the culture. Whether or not one was a professional stranger or had simply gone native, the ethnographer was expected to "maintain a polite distance from those studied and to cultivate rapport, not friendship; compassion, not sympathy; respect, not belief; understanding, not identification; admiration, not love" (Tedlock, 2000, p. 457). At the end of the day, the lone ethnographer transformed his or her observations of the other into text, and this text became the authoritative representation of the other. Shaped by the legacy of colonialism, classic ethnographic writing became the inscription of an observed other.

Many critics have raised concerns about the positionality of the objective observer or the immersed native. Robert Merton (1972) questioned the epistemic privilege claims of the "insider doctrine" and argued that researchers "unite" their insider or outsider identities and "consider their distinctive and interactive roles in the process of truth seeking" (p. 36). Although Merton saw the multiplicity of "contrasting statuses" that each individual holds, feminists have argued that he did not acknowledge the fluid and shifting nature of these identities based on a multitude of reasons such as one's social location and knowledge of participants, issues, and organizational culture. Moreover, not only do we as researchers attempt to define our role; how others see us is also in flux (Acker, 2000; Kondo, 1990; Marx, 2000). Feminists also have pointed to the danger of self-identifying as an insider or outsider prior to entering the research setting. Feminists argue that researchers can only come to understand themselves as subject/object, insider/outsider by reflexively examining the continuously shifting nature of one's role in the field. Power relations occur between the researcher and research participants and exploitative processes bound forth. Hence, not only must the reflexive researcher examine his or her own biography, but also the unequal power relationship between the knower and the known. In considering positionality, one must not take for granted that we are insiders as we may make false assumptions, blind ourselves to important insights and viewpoints, or simply ask the wrong questions. However, if we stand back and distance ourselves as outsiders, we are in danger of producing the very barriers we wish to deconstruct (Anderson, 1998; Edwards, 1990; Riessman, 1987). Interrogating the self or selves is more than just examining one's social location and its effect on the field; rather, this reflexive process also involves negotiating one's positionality and recognizing the shifting nature of power relations from site to site.

---

Immersion may be a useful strategy to attempt to view a culture from within, and it may position the researcher in a way that differs from a more distant participant-observer, but it does not basically alter the researcher's positionality, which remains part of her in the field to which she returns in full when she is finished. Changing locations does not fundamentally alter one's positionality or the situatedness of one's knowledge.

—*Wolf (1996, p. 10)*

---

In writing on her research experience in Iowa, Nancy Naples (1996, 2003) draws our attention to the importance of continuous self-reflection and the duality of the insider/outsider phenomenon. Naples describes her feelings of outsider status on entering the research setting. She was an urban type, not familiar with the rural way of life. However, as she progressed through her fieldwork she found that she was also considered an insider by community members who felt alienated from their community. Furthermore, Naples found varying degrees of insiderness/outsiderness among community members based on shifting power relations and patterns of inequality in these small towns. It is the multiple aspects of our

identity, she says, not necessarily the insider/outsider perspective, that shape our research experience, and this identity continuously shifts throughout the research process. Researchers are never fully insiders or outsiders. By allowing herself to reflect on and experience the fluidity of her positionality throughout the research process, she was able to gain greater insight about her own biases and assumptions as well as explore the similarities and differences between herself and the community members she encountered.

In her ethnography of young Indian women's experiences and meanings given to their reading of Western romance novels, postcolonial feminist scholar Radhika Parameswaran (2001) stresses the importance of examining our positionality within the research setting, whether we are studying within our own culture or whether we have stepped outside the familiar boundaries of our identities. Although comfortable within the boundaries of sharing her Indian heritage with her participants, Parameswaran found this insider identity worked against her when talking with male "gatekeepers" who questioned her research and position as well as with the parents of some of the women who accused her of generating problems for them and their daughters. She also found that she was vulnerable to the parents and relatives of her informants who wanted to manipulate her for their own purposes. To deal with issues of power and authority, she continuously had to negotiate both her identity and positionality. Parameswaran reminds us that concepts such as "insider and outsider," "native and Western," "self and other" are not binary concepts, but are fluid and are subject to negotiation within the research setting. Like Naples (1996, 2003), the researcher can be an insider in one time and place and an outsider in another.

## Negotiating Power and Co-constructing Knowledge

An array of interlocking identities, such as race, gender, and class, influence the research process, and insider/outsider positionalities become more complicated as the researcher ventures into relationships across difference. Therefore, assuming commonality based on a single dimension of identity is detrimental to the project of deconstructing power relations and co-constructing knowledge

(Anderson, 1998; Beoku-Betts, 1994; Collins, 2000; Dunbar, Rodriguez, & Parker, 2000; Edwards, 1990; Riessman, 1987). To minimize power differentials in knowledge construction one must acknowledge difference. Acknowledging difference involves reflecting about one's situatedness in a complicated, shifting *matrix* of social locations and conversing openly with the research participants about that difference (Collins, 2000; Edwards, 1990). In her experience interviewing Afro-Caribbean women, Rosalind Edwards (1990) found that assuming commonality based on gender and shared experience as a mother or student was not conducive to building rapport across difference. Her privilege as a white, middle-class woman clearly offered her a different mothering and academic experience than that of her participants. She states,

> I realized that rapport was easier after I had signaled not a nonhierarchical, nonexploitative, shared-sex relationship, but rather an acknowledgement that I was in a different structural position to them with regard to race and did not hold shared assumptions on that basis. My placing was not just as a woman but as a white woman. (p. 486)

By acknowledging difference rather than similarity in their experiences, Edwards found that the women in her study were open to meeting with her and spoke more freely during their conversations. Similarly, Margaret Anderson (1998) found that by reflexively interrogating her own privilege as a white researcher and the barriers this placed on her relationships, she was able to more easily enter the research site and build relationships with the women of color in her study. Placing a conventional methodological approach aside, Anderson engaged in open, dialogical conversations with participants; exchanging and co-constructing knowledge by revealing her own biography, experiences, and opinions.

---

A researcher can overcome the structural constraints of power by negotiating a role consistent with the respondent's level of power, both improving the quality of interactions and enriching the research process.

—*Marx (2000, p. 132)*

---

Acknowledging difference also involves understanding that there is an aspect of lived experience that is invisible to those "who possess neither the language nor the cultural equipment either to elicit or understand that experience" (Rhodes, 1994, p. 549). However, this inability to readily unveil the invisible does not translate into a failure to study across difference. What this implies is that researchers must undertake reflexive projects and navigate the research process through both their own shifting positionalities as well as those of the participants to produce relationships that are less hierarchical and research that is more inclusive and less distorted. Working across difference depends not only on possessing common language and cultural knowledge, but also on establishing trust and engaging in dialogical relationships (Collins, 2000; Rhodes, 1994). Difference mediates the meaning of questions that are asked and how those questions are answered and interpreted. In her study on overt and perceived racism on a college campus, Dalia Rodriguez describes "the reflexive interplay between background knowledge derived ethnographically and experientially and the personal narratives generated by way of interview questions" (Dunbar et al., 2000, p. 285). By reflexively drawing from and sharing her experiences, Rodriguez was able to find common experiential ground with the people of color she engaged with, but at the same time vocalized the differences in their experiences. Using her knowledge of the "racialized subject," which she acquired "experientially and ethnographically," she was able to place the participants' experiences into social context, thereby better informing her listening skills, choice of language, and questions as well as her interpretation of the experiences of these students of color (Dunbar et al., 2000). Moreover, by reflexively engaging her experiential knowledge she gained outside the interview setting, Rodriguez was better able to notice and interpret the silences and find alternative approaches for engaging participants. Similarly, Helen Ralston (2001) drew on her experiential knowledge as a white, middle-class, British-colonized Australian migrant to Canada when interviewing urban, middle-class South Asian women from the Indian subcontinent about their experiences of migration to Canada, Australia, and

New Zealand. Although sharing class and migration experience, Ralston was attentive to how color and language shaped their differing skin experiences. Ralston used her experiential knowledge, but reflexively placed it within a political, structural, and cultural context to bring into view the institutional and structural barriers that these women faced in their lives. By doing so, Ralston was better able to appropriately "record the stories of their lived experience from their standpoint" (p. 219).

---

Taking the standpoint of the immigrant woman involves an initial and ever developing awareness of the personal and structural barriers and boundaries of the interviewer and interviewee.

—*Ralston (2001, p. 221)*

---

Marjorie DeVault (1990) argues that oftentimes words are not available to describe lived experience and that researchers must "develop methods for listening around and beyond words" (p. 101). DeVault stresses the importance of collecting embodied texts—texts that are grounded in lived experiences and produced physically as well as verbally. Christopher Dunbar (Dunbar et al., 2000) relates his own experiences in interviewing persons of color across class and calls attention to the importance of "observing facial expressions, vernacular voice intonations, nonverbal cues, and other forms of body language" when interviewing across difference (p. 293). Attentiveness to physical cues can alert the researcher to hidden feelings or culturally sensitive questions that are not apparent in the ordinary course of the conversation.

| Sharlene | Deb |
|---|---|
| How does one really listen? How do I listen in a way that the girls feel they are being heard? How do I listen to them across our many differences?<br><br>I remember walking into the community center feeling "the outsider" as a white, middle-class researcher. My concerns centered on trying very hard not to have a strict agenda—a set of prepackaged questions I would ask all of them, reminiscent of a survey where there is little room for the voices of those I interview to be heard outside my own agenda of questions. I also wanted to position myself in the setting so that I would be able to break down somewhat the power and authority that is often inherent in the researcher-researched relationship.<br><br>As that Friday afternoon progressed, the girls talked about their feelings of being "black girls" and the racial discrimination they experience. At one point, Tasha expressed how difficult it was to be a black female and to keep the fiber of the black community together. Racial discrimination is a constant issue the girls bring up—for example, being watched when they go | As a peace activist and a scholar of social movements, I approached my research project holding the belief that sustained collective action around an antiwar agenda would eventually force a change in U.S. intervention around the world. Although committed to supporting an antiwar agenda, I also understood the links between militarism and domestic policy and that U.S. foreign policy was racist, in that its prey was overwhelmingly people of color. Furthermore, I agreed with many critics of the peace movement that to fulfill its agenda, the movement needed to shed its white, middle-class identity and work to become more diverse. In my fieldwork, I was interested in learning exactly how activists within a particular peace and justice network were attempting to do just that. However, through reflexive listening, my views have shifted and in turn so have my research and consciousness.<br><br>During my conversations in the field, I began to note that people spoke about peace work and approached organizing in very different |

*(Continued)*

(Continued)

| Sharlene | Deb |
|---|---|
| into a predominately white downtown mall. Tasha comments, "Society is in my face, in front, in back, on the side, telling me how I should be. It won't let me be, ya know? They said, 'You are gonna steal from this store and we're here to prevent you from doing it'; it's not, 'We're here to welcome you.'"<br><br>Listening to Tasha, Norah and I reflected on our own white privilege living our lives in predominately white middle-class communities.<br><br>Norah: I cannot imagine that these girls are only 13, 14, 15, and 16, and I almost felt like they have lived more of a life than mine. They have so much more experience and knowledge. I didn't have to worry about things like going to the mall because I grew up in white suburbia; my parents had money. I was with white people everywhere I went, so I never experienced those things, it wasn't a problem.<br><br>Sharlene: White women don't have to deal with our whiteness. We don't have to feel the eyes of white surveillance on a daily basis.<br><br>As I began to pull my car out of the driveway of the center, I realized that the world in which these girls lived was less than 5 miles from my house. The children in my neighborhood don't have to leave their homes, as one of the girls I interviewed put it, "looking to the left and then to the right" to make sure a bullet was not coming her way. I wanted to delve deeper into the impact of violence on the girls' lived experience. We began to touch on some of these issues in my conversations with them, but the girls were guiding me to ask deeper questions on issues of community violence as well as the overall impact of discrimination on their day-to-day lives. | ways. Initially, I thought it was simply because people had different political experiences and that these experiences led them to different forms of organizing. However, by listening more closely, openly sharing biographies, and encouraging participants to question my beliefs, I began to understand that people's understanding of peace work shaped their approaches to organizing and that these beliefs and practices were products of different structural, lived experiences in a racialized, classed, and gendered society.<br><br>Through these reflexive relationships, I was challenged to examine my own social biography—not just how it shaped what I asked and how I heard others but also how my social location, my white privilege in particular, shaped my views. Through this different angle of vision, I began to construct an alternative definition of peace work—one that began to see the limited gains an antiwar agenda can make in constructing a more democratic, just society. I began to realize that working across difference not only has to do with deconstructing individual barriers but also has to do with interrogating one's social biography and becoming conscious of how one's knowledge is shaped. Examining my own privilege as a white, middle-class woman facilitated the transformation of my worldview, my activism, and the research project. No longer was the research focused simply on organizational practices that could hinder or foster work across difference; rather, I began to consider the broader structural and cultural forces shaping differing worldviews and hence our efforts to build relationships and alliances across differences. Practicing reflexive listening across the entire research process asks that the researcher not only interrogate her or his positionality and social location but also engage in a dialogical practice of sharing with others. A dialogical relationship can identify points of connection that can cultivate changes in thinking, leading to actions and experiences that can alter consciousness. |

In reflexive relationships, the researcher experiences a moment or moments during the conversation where an exchanging of roles occurs—the researcher as participant, the participant as researcher. This fluidity of roles in the process of constructing knowledge occurs when the researcher is reflexive about the interview relationship and the social conditions that affect the conversation. Because we carry our biographies and presumptions into the interview setting, we must problematize all positions whether shared or not to create a nonhierarchical environment conducive to sharing. In the excerpts above, we suggest that by reflexively listening and engaging in dialogical relationships with our participants, we can bring our presuppositions into view and radically change the way we know and what we know. Working across difference requires entering another's personal space. By entering either experientially, like Rodriguez (Dunbar et al., 2000) or Ralston (2001), or finding innovative ways of listening and interpreting, like DeVault (1990) and Dunbar et al. (2000), the researcher must not only reflexively interrogate her or his positionality, but also engage in the communal processes of crossing borders and boundaries and creating a common space for building knowledge.

---

The researcher is transformed in the process of research—influenced and taught by her respondent-participants as she influences them.

—*Gorelick (1991, p. 469)*

---

## Authenticating Voice

Negotiating power is not simply changing the relationship between researcher and researched. Feminist research values and brings alternative forms of knowledge to the forefront of public discourse. Dorothy Smith (1987) and Patricia Hill Collins (2000) use the concept of bifurcated consciousness when discussing the life experience of subjugated individuals. Smith's (1987) *insider sociology* and Collins's (2000) *outsider within perspective* both suggest that subjugated knowledge is produced from a different angle of vision that reveals certain

aspects of power relations. Rooted in Marxian theory, feminist standpoint epistemology privileges the knowledge of persons whose standpoints arise from positions of intense subordination in the intersection of the vectors of oppression. Dorothy Smith (1987) states that a woman's location and experience is distinctive, and Collins (2000) suggests that the lived experience of the *other* can shape a consciousness that is counterhegemonic because it is from a special vantage point—the lived experience of the dominated rather than the dominant. However, although subjugated knowledge provides critical insight into understanding how oppressive social relations operate, we must acknowledge that each unique, situated standpoint is only a partial perspective as there is not one way, but many ways of knowing (Collins, 2000; Haraway, 1988; Hartsock, 1993; Smith, 1987). Although it is tempting to claim that the most subjugated voices have a more accurate view of oppression, we must not rank human oppression (Collins, 2000). Instead, we must consider the subjugated voices from every group, their unique standpoint, and their own partial and situated knowledges. Validating and legitimizing the knowledge that emerges from the everyday life experiences of *outsiders within* and moving subjugated knowledge *from the margin to the center* of social inquiry is one of the ways in which feminism has broadened the theorizing of reflexivity (Collins, 2000; hooks, 1984). Nancy Hartsock (1993) states,

> We [researchers] need to develop our understanding of difference by creating a situation in which hitherto marginalized groups can name themselves, speak for themselves and participate in defining terms of interaction, a situation in which we can construct an understanding of the world that is sensitive to difference. (p. 545)

The purpose of research, then, is not to construct grand generalizations, but to work closely with people, maintaining an inclusive reality, open and flexible, consisting of a diversity of perspectives, and enhancing their understanding and ability to control their own reality.

Participatory action research is one example of social inquiry in which researchers reflexively seek to authenticate the voices of those with whom they study (Lykes & Coquillon, this volume; Maguire, 1987; Reason, 1998; Stringer, 1996). Participatory action research is an iterative process that combines dialogue, reflection, and action. Participants assess their situation, analyze data they have collected themselves, and act on the findings. Participatory research results in action at the local level, seeking to involve people as active participants in the research process. It seeks to "promote collective processes of inquiry that expose the ideological, political, and social processes underlying and permeating systems of inequality" (Lykes & Coquillon, this volume). The role of the participatory action researcher is not that of an observer or external consultant, but that of an engaged participant who works as an interactive partner with community members. Researchers encourage participation, promote dialogue, and foster relationships. Process is as important as product, and knowledge is a collaborative process. Through these participatory processes, people explore the ways in which their lives are shaped and constrained by extra-local processes and find ways to either change or work within them (Lykes, 1997; Lykes & Coquillion, this volume; Maguire, 1987; Reason, 1998; Stringer, 1996).

## Representing the Social: Interpretation and Writing

From the moment the researcher engages in the research project, to the probing and asking of questions, through the transcription of field notes, the voices of the participants have already been interpreted. Even when employing participatory methods, the researcher ultimately holds authority over the interpretation and writing of the final research product. Can the researcher, during the process of interpretation and writing, find ways to share power as well as find ways to better represent people's lives? Gaining an understanding of the reality of people's lives within its structural and cultural contexts was at the center of Max Weber's (1921) inquiry. His concept of *verstehen* was a significant contribution to the methodology of contemporary sociology. However, whether or not the researcher has the ability to know another's experience or has the authority to give voice continues to remain the subject of debate within methodological discourse across disciplines. Can we really know another's experience or are we simply able to just "hear voices that we record and interpret"? (Riessman, 1993, p. 8).

---

Verstehen: we cannot understand what people do without some sense of how they subjectively interpret their own behavior.

—*Weber (1921)*

---

In her much-cited essay, Judith Stacey (1991) draws our attention to the multiple ways in which the researcher holds power over the participants in the research process and argues that critical self-reflection is not enough to ease the power difference between researcher and participant. Stacey argues that the highly personalized relationship between ethnographer and participant masks actual differences in power, knowledge, and structural mobility and places research subjects at grave risk of manipulation and betrayal by the ethnographer. Even though a researcher may wish to establish an egalitarian relationship with participants, the researcher has the power to determine what is recorded and what is not as well as how things are interpreted. Furthermore, participants become extremely vulnerable and trust becomes an issue when participants feel encouraged by researchers to share the most intimate and confidential details of their lives (Kirsch, 1999; Pini, 2004). The published ethnography becomes an "intervention into the lives and relationships of its subjects" (Stacey, 1991, p. 114). Although innovative approaches to interpretation and writing attempt to deconstruct the author's authority, the research product is ultimately that of the researcher, whether it is coauthored by the participant or not. Researcher power over what is written (or not written) is unavoidable. Similarly, Carol Warren (2000) states that the danger for exposure of both *the other* and *the self* begins with the writing of our field notes. She points to the tension between the need for thick description and the desire to protect the identity of both the research setting and the participants. She asks us to consider how much the altering of the site and participants' identifying information distorts the meaning of people's lived experiences. Moreover, Warren argues that in writing the other, we also write the self. She asks, how can researchers resolve the tension between "revelation and concealment" of the one's identity—how can one inscribe the self, without erasing the voice of the participant? Jayati Lal (1996) speaks of the problems of self-reflexivity in that it can give more voice to the author and less to the subject. She argues that the researcher should attempt to employ both narrative and reflexivity, but at the same time not selectively choose participants' voices to buttress the researcher's arguments. Lal states,

> Researchers contributing to debates in feminist methodology and experimental ethnography point to the strategies of polyvocality and suggest giving research subjects a voice in a move to decolonize the subject, yet we often fail to take account of the challenges to modes of representations and contestations for meaning by research subjects who provide their own self presentations. We need to acknowledge this agency, to treat the researched as subjects with whom we are engaged in a mutual, though unequal power-charged social relation of conversation. (p. 205)

## REFLEXIVE INTERPRETIVE PROCESSES

Interpretation involves translation as researchers do not have direct access to another's experience. The reflexive researcher not only must listen for "the everyday processes of translation" that are a part of one's speech, but also convert that speech into readable text (DeVault, 1990, p. 102). Catherine Riessman (1993) argues that there are at least five levels of representation in the research process: attending to experience or the choice in what you notice and select to tell, telling, transcribing, analyzing, and reading. Researchers, then, are interpreting and creating texts at every juncture of the process. DeVault (1990) further describes the process of translation as listening, editing, and writing. In her research on the work of feeding a family, DeVault reflexively drew on her own personal experiences as a resource for listening to how women searched for and used "close enough" language to describe their everyday experiences, thereby enhancing her ability to hear participants in new ways. She was attentive to preserving the "messiness of everyday talk," enabling her to extend beyond

presumptions and focus on what was being said as well as what was not. In her research on chronic illness, Kathy Charmaz (2000) found that a research relationship that honors respect for emotionality and fosters an environment that is conducive to sharing can provide greater insight on the part of both the researcher and the participant. Through reflexive listening and approaching interviews as "contextualized conversations" (Stage & Mattson, 2003), DeVault (1990) and Charmaz (2000) were able to better understand the experiences of their participants.

Language is embedded in cultural contexts. The work of translation becomes further complicated when working across language and cultures. Bogusia Temple (1997) discusses the problematics that might arise when researchers rely on interpreters or even do the work of language translation themselves. She cautions researchers to question the familiar as they label and name experience, because words and concepts "have a history specific to the society they originate from" (p. 611). When doing the process of translation, she suggests that researchers engage in examining and sharing their "intellectual autobiographies" to explore the different perspective individuals bring to the process of translation. Dealing with interpretive conflict is an issue many researchers confront in the processes of translation and interpretation. Gesa Kirsch (1999) relates her experience negotiating with a participant over the interpretation of her experience. Although she attempted to negotiate her interpretation with that of the participant, they both remained polarized in their interpretations. Kirsch was faced "with the dilemma of interpreting another woman's experience and presuming interpretive powers that transcended hers" (p. 49). In her text, Kirsch decided to place the interpretations side by side, allowing readers to evaluate the two different readings.

---

Intellectual autobiography: "An analytic (not just descriptive) concern with the specifics of how we come to understand what we do, by locating acts of understanding in an explication of the grounded contexts these are located in and arise from."

—*Kirsch (1990, p. 608), quoting Liz Stanley*

Researchers working with vulnerable populations have been required to find innovative ways to do the work of translation. Building on more conventional methods of focus groups and member checking, Lisa Dodson and Leah Schmalzbauer (2005) use an innovative method of "interpretive focus groups" to give greater understanding to the voices and experiences of people in their studies.[6] In their work with women in low-income communities, oftentimes across language and cultures, Dodson and Schmalzbauer use a collaborative, communitarian, participatory methodology in their research. Seeking "co-analysis, not confirmation of data previously gathered," interpretive focus groups engage community members who have not participated in the data gathering phase to fulfill the role of expert interpreter. Vulnerable populations tend to hide the real experiences of their everyday lives and rightly so. These "habits of hiding" show up as silences, contradictions, or selective telling in conversations (Dodson & Schmalzbauer, 2005; Scott, 1990). Dodson and Schmalzbauer (2005) embarked on their research to provide accurate descriptions of the experiences of low-income families in America, decentering the distorted visions that affect social policy on a daily basis. Respecting the right of these women to disclose or not disclose their private experiences, Dodson and Schmalzbauer found that interpretive focus groups were able to safely bring their experiences into discourse without causing harm or risking exposure. Interpretive focus groups seek a "communitarian approach to analysis and multivocal representation of the meaning of data."

## Writing the Reflexive

In their controversial text *Writing Culture: The Poetics and Politics of Ethnography*, James Clifford and George Marcus (1986) raised the question of the researcher's power and authority over ethnographic representation. Influenced by the writings of the French poststructuralists, Clifford and Marcus questioned the reproduction of culture and knowledge by the objective social researcher. Ethnographic writing is not simply cultural reportage; it is "always caught up in the invention, not the representation of cultures" (p. 2). They called for ethnographers to "avoid a detached posture of neutral observation, and acknowledge their subjects as collaborators in a project that the researcher can never fully control" (Stacey, 1991, p. 115). They argued that the other can never be fully experienced; hence, any interpretive work will always be a partial truth (Marcus, 1994). These writings raised important questions about the validity and existence of a True, complete ethnographic account. Reflexivity, then, became a tool for critical self-reflection in the writing process.

Feminists had addressed issues of power and representation long before this new critique of ethnography surfaced. Dating back to the 19th century, feminists were rejecting the disinterested and omniscient observer and calling for researchers to reveal the social location from which they were speaking, share their emotional responses to the field experience, and engage in analytical dialogue with their participants (Cooper, 1892; Martineau, 1836; Perkins-Gilman, 1898; Tristan, 1844). Speaking from the position of the other, these first-wave feminists questioned the construction of the woman as the other not only in the experience of otherness, but also with the inscription of women as other in language and discourse. In her autobiographical work *A Voice from the South by a Black Woman from the South*, Anna Julia Cooper (1892), an African American woman and associate of W. E. B. DuBois, called for the necessity of hearing the black woman's voice to understand the raced, classed, and gendered nature of American society (Lemert & Bahn, 1988). Cooper argued that "only the Black woman can say when and where I enter, in the quiet, undisputed dignity of my womanhood, without violence and without suing on special patronage, then and there the whole Negro race enters with me" (Lemert & Bahn, 1988, p. 63, quoting Cooper, 1892). For these women, the role of the researcher was not an objective, value-neutral one; it was engaged, rooted in everyday life experiences, and gave voice to those who had been silenced. Contemporary feminist writings on the woman as other can be traced back to as early as the 1950s with Simone de Beauvoir's (1953) *The Second Sex,* which called for women to speak for and claim themselves as subjects (Mascia-Lees, Sharpe, & Cohen, 1989). Attention to voice and representation was a primary focal point for second-wave feminists.

This self-critical reflexive turn in ethnographic writing, or an "experimental moment in the human sciences," resulted in a reexamination of the writing of ethnography and produced a genre of scholars calling for researchers to experiment with alternative forms of representation by employing a polyvocality to their writing and performing a critical self-analysis of their experiences in the field (Marcus & Fischer, 1999). Early ethnographic texts or realist tales took the form of a dispassionate, third person narration (Van Maanen, 1988, p. 45). These realist tales performed what Donna Haraway (1988) called the "god trick," writing the other from nowhere and reflecting the textual authority of the researcher. In these texts, the other's words, experiences, and behaviors were called on to verify or validate the researcher's interpretations. This literary format produced and reproduced, when read by others, the power imbalance inherent in ethnographic research. At the other extreme, confessional tales were considered "highly personalized styles" and "self-absorbed" texts (Van Maanen, 1988, p. 73). These self-reflective writings positioned the self front and center and described the decisions and dilemmas of the fieldwork experience and the impact that the field had on the researcher. Confessionals were often written in addition to the realist account and were attempts to reveal the biases and biography of the researcher to allow the reader to evaluate the validity of the text. Although produced to deconstruct the power of the researcher, these texts actually rendered the other more invisible.

More experiential forms of writing have attempted to bring researcher and participant together in representational form. These texts pay attention to critical self-reflection as well as multiplicity and partiality instead of singularity and universality. They range in form from the literary to the coauthorship of research texts.[7] These messy texts are

> messy because they insist on an open-endedness, an incompleteness, and an uncertainty about how to draw a text/analysis to a close. Such open-endedness often marks a concern with an ethics of

> dialogue and partial knowledge that a work is incomplete without critical, and differently positioned, responses to it by its (one hopes) varied readers. (Marcus, 1994, p. 567)

These new forms are concerned with exposing the power relations embedded in ethnographic writing. A reflexive text attempts to deconstruct power relations between the researcher and participants by decentering the authority of the researcher's voice.

Writing is biographical work. At the moment of inscription, the other becomes vulnerable, and when we write the other, we also write the self (Coffey, 1999; Fine, 1998; Warren, 2000). Amanda Coffey (1999) draws our attention to the relationship between the self and the field and asks researchers to write reflexively by interrogating our own biography. We must ask, How has our presence affected the field, but also how has the field affected us? The central concern for the reflexive writer is deconstructing power—who has it, how it is used, and for what purposes. Although new ethnographic writing or what is sometimes referred to as the *literary turn* in ethnographic writing allows for writing the self into the text, we always are writing the self because our biography shapes what we see and hear, how we interpret, and how we choose what to write. Typically, ethnographers have kept personal field notes separate from their ethnographic observations and interactions and have carried this forward in their writings. Coffey offers field notes, partial autobiographical accounts, and tales of the self as alternatives to writing the self into an ethnography. Writing in the self can be a good practice in reflexivity. Reflexivity, she says, is "having an ongoing conversation experience while simultaneously living in the moment—and voice—presenting the author's self while simultaneously writing the respondents' accounts and representing their selves" (p. 132). The boundaries between self-indulgence and reflexivity are blurred. There will always be a struggle with how much to reveal or silence.

---

The presence of the voice, which the reader is meant to experience as the voice of a real rather than fictional person, is the mark of a desire not to be silenced or defeated, to impose oneself on an institution of power and privilege from the position of the excluded, the marginal, the subaltern.

*—Beverly (2000, p. 556)*

How does one bear witness and accurately represent people's lives? One form of writing is the testimonio,[8] where the researcher brings the voices of those who are silenced and marginalized into public discourse. The uniqueness of the form of the testimonio is the presence of *an I* that *"demands to be* recognized, that wants or needs to stake a claim on our attention" (Beverly, 2000, p. 556). In situations of oppression, where it may not be safe or possible for an oppressed group to speak, the testimony of one becomes representative of the testimony of many others. The narrator is the "real protagonist or witness of the events she or he recounts" and this involves the tape-recording, transcription, and editing of an oral account by the researcher (p. 555). The testimonio subdues the presence and authority of the author and instead affirms the authenticity of lived experience within political, social, and cultural contexts. The testimonio allows subalterns to speak in their own voices and on their own terms (Spivak, 1988).

## Transforming Lives: Transforming the Social

As ethnographers we want to learn about our informants but as reflexive ethnographers we also learn about our own lives in the process of grasping how the lives of others could teach us something about all lives. Here lies that potential for change inherent in the reflexive stance—the learning itself is viewed as empowering the scholar while the recording is a political act, and thus may help change the informants' lives.

*—Wasserfall (1993, p. 27)*

Feminist researchers argue that the ultimate goal of sociology is the creation of a more just society (Collins, 2000; Harding, 1992; Mertens, 2003; Reinharz, 1992; Smith, 1987). Socially just research can foster changed consciousness, encourage collective empowerment, and transform both researcher and participants in the research process. A reflexive methodology seeks to describe reality within its multiple contexts, encourages interaction between the research and participants, and strives to minimize power differentials during the research process (Eichler, 1997; Harding, 1991). Reflexive researchers acknowledge that "knowledge is not neutral but is influenced by human interests, that all knowledge reflects the power and social relationships within society, and that an important purpose of knowledge construction is to help people improve society" (Mertens, 2003). Whether transforming sociology, methods, or people's lives, a reflexive methodology works to create a more democratic, just society. While diverse in approaches and aims, reflexive researchers are socially engaged, committed activists in their own disciplines and in society at large. For instance, institutional ethnography has radically transformed the practice of social research by providing "the empirical investigation of linkages among local settings of everyday life, organizations, and translocal processes of administration and governance" (DeVault & McCoy, 2000, p. 751). Beginning with people's everyday lives, institutional ethnography "problematizes the social relations and organization that extend beyond experience," looking to "discover how what we experience locally is shaped by what we cannot know directly" (Smith, this volume). By uncovering how extra-local relations organize people's lives, institutional ethnography can expand local knowledge, empower local change strategies, and reveal the interconnectedness of translocal communities (Campbell & Manicom, 1995; DeVault & McCoy, 2000; Smith, 1987, 2002, this volume).

## REFLEXIVITY SAMPLING: A PRACTICAL METHOD

What the methodological examples presented in this chapter demonstrate is that reflexivity is necessary and vital to research practice. Reflexive researchers continue to seek innovative techniques to negotiate power, minimize harm, and illuminate and transform the social structures that oppress people on a daily basis. A reflexive methodology can allow the researcher to "become aware of, and diminish the ways in which domination and repression are reproduced in the course of research and in the products of their work" (Naples, 2003, pp. 37–38). However, power cannot be entirely eliminated from the research process. Differences of culture, ethnicity, race, and class place strains on the research process. Although the practice of reflexivity can enable researchers to become more sensitive to power relations and see how their own social location shapes the research process, it cannot completely eradicate power differences between the researcher and participants or between participants in the study (Stacey, 1991; Wasserfall, 1993; Wolf, 1996). Adopting a reflexive perspective in practice is often one where the researcher becomes both insider and outsider, taking on a myriad of different standpoints and negotiating these identities simultaneously. In many instances, the researcher must take a more flexible and fluid approach to her or his reflexive practice. This is aptly expressed by Trinh T. Minh-ha's concept of multiple subjectivities:

> Working right at the limits of several categories and approaches means that one is neither entirely inside or outside. One has to push one's work as far as one can go: to the borderlines, where one never stops, walking on the edges, incurring constantly the risk of falling off one side or the other side of the limit while undoing, redoing, modifying this limit." (Trinh, 1991, p. 218)

Attention to doing necessary "border work" has been at the forefront of feminist practice, most notably in postcolonial feminist research (Anzaldúa, 1987; Trinh, 1991; Parameswaran, 2001; Patai & Gluck, 1991; Spivak, 1988). This "border work" also requires attention to and reassessment of our own disciplinary practices and how tightly bound one has become to the specific methodological practices and conceptual definitions of our own disciplines. As feminist researchers are most often interested in issues that cross disciplines, they often draw on interdisciplinary theory to interpret their data,

and this process exposes them to alternative methods. As we mentioned at the outset of this chapter, reflexivity is not a one-shot process; it should ideally take place along the research process continuum. Psychologists Tamlin Conner and Eliza Bliss-Moreau (2006) provide us with an excellent method of practicing reflexivity across a research project. *Experience sampling*, a method used by psychologists to capture subjective experience in the moment, uses a variety of technological devices to sample and record experience in naturalistic settings over time, such as the use of palm pilots, tape recorders, or journaling in an ongoing diary. Conner and Bliss-Moreau argue that experience sampling can resolve lapses in memory or the loss of emotive feelings that can occur in one-time measurements of experience during an interview or in a laboratory setting when one is asked to recall experiential moments. Participants in an experience sampling study are "signaled" at various moments throughout the day and prompted to answer questions, designed by the researcher, about their experiences as they go about their daily routine.

We suggest an adaptation of the experience sampling method and ask that researchers practice *reflexivity sampling*. While we certainly are not suggesting researchers attach a beeper to themselves or have someone monitor them over the course of the day or research period, we are suggesting that throughout the research process, researchers "check in" with themselves and reflect on how the research process is going. These reflections should be ongoing throughout the project and occur not only in the writing of field notes and memos, but also "in the moment." Practically speaking, how does *reflexivity sampling* work? Based on our experiences practicing reflexivity in this way, we suggest the following practices researchers might consider.

A helpful practice is to maintain a reflexive diary, separate from your research journal and field notes. One may even consider working with a technological device such as a palm pilot that is quite portable, or even a cell phone for that matter. If you feel you need prompting, these devices can send out a signal to you throughout the given course of your research project that reminds you to check in periodically with yourself, by answering a series of key questions that you write in your diary or key into the device itself. Deb prefers a sampling method based on events, as the signaling process can be disruptive when she is in the field.[9] Sharlene uses a tape recorder whenever she can and often sets a timer on her cell phone to prompt her with several reflexive questions she wants to cover over the course of her research rounds. Sometimes the prompting can be disruptive. To prevent this she changes the time intervals so she doesn't unduly disrupt her ongoing interactions and observations in the field.

Your questions should be structured in a way to allow you to capture your feelings in the moment as well as allow time for later reflection. You might also want to record the context within which these issues and feelings emerge. This will enable you to reflect later on how your experiences about the research may shift over time in specific contexts. Practicing reflexivity in the moment is not only helpful for later interpretation and writing; it can also alert you to unconscious feelings or practices and allow you to make immediate changes in the conduct of the research or the wording of questions or help to anticipate or address ethical dilemmas that inevitably arise without warning.

What might these questions look like? Drawing on the feminist research depicted in the preceding sections, we offer a sampling of questions that we used in our research experiences to provoke reflexive thinking:

- Know your standpoint prior to entering the research project.[10] To what extent do you recognize, examine, and comprehend how your own socioeconomic background and assumptions about the researched affect the type of question(s) you seek to ask and the question(s) you choose not to ask? What particular biases do you bring to/impose on your research? How does your epistemology affect the types of questions you ask, and how you intend to approach the research process? Whom is this research for?

- Examine your positionality and role in the field. To what extent do you make visible your own social locations and identities during the research process? How does your positionality shift from site to site, participant to participant, and why?

- Monitor your relationship with participants. To what extent do you interact with participants? How often did you answer a question from the participants or share a piece of your social biography? What is the quality of rapport you have developed between yourself and the participants?

- Listen to your participants. Are you providing an environment for participants to freely express their attitudes and feelings? Are there silences, hesitations? Is the participant expressing discomfort with the conversation? Are you attentive to participants' probes for information?

- Listen to yourself. Are you confused, unclear about something the participant said or didn't say? Why? Are you feeling personal discomfort? Why?

- Be attentive to difference. What are the differences that matter, given your research question? Are you making assumptions based on your similarities/differences? Are you conversing openly with the research participants about that difference? Are you considering political, social, and cultural contexts as you converse and observe? Am I awarding epistemic privilege to any particular group?

- Reflexively interrogate your data. What are your specific analytic and social biases? How do you respond emotionally and intellectually to these data? Are there ways to bring participants into the interpretation of the data? The writing of the report?

## Notes

1. For more information on the history and method of experience sampling, see Conner and Bliss-Moreau (2006).

2. See Guillemin and Gillam (2004) for their important reflections and insights on reflexivity and ethically important moments.

3. The feminist contributions and critiques of positivism are too numerous to mention here, but most notable are Harding (1986, 1991, 1993), Hartsock (1998), Oakley (1998), Reinharz (1992), and Smith (1987).

4. See Harding (1986).

5. There have been writings on the insider/outsider concept. We highlight in this chapter some of

the most influential in our work: Acker (2000), Collins (1998), Cook and Fonow (1986), Griffith (1998), Naples (1996), Reinharz (1992), and Stanley and Wise (1993).

6. Lisa Dodson (1998) developed this method of interpretive focus groups during the many years she has worked with low-income women. Leah Schmalzbauer (in press) uses this method in her study of survival strategies of poor Honduran transnational families.

7. There are many examples of innovative writing techniques. Of particular note: Anzaldúa (1987), Behr (1993, 1996), Ellis and Bochner (2000), Lather and Smithies (1997), Richardson (2000), and Wolf (1992).

8. See Beverly (2000) for citations of exemplary forms of testimonios.

9. For instance, Deb will reflexivity sample each time she encounters a different venue, participant, conflict, and emotion. See Conner and Bliss-Moreau (2006) for more on various experience sampling methods.

10. Kirk and Miller (1986) suggest that in addition to Type I and Type II errors found in quantitative research, there is another type of error, Type III, where the researcher asks the wrong question—that is, just asking the *wrong* research question. One important guard against this type of error is for each researcher to be reflexive about her or his own standpoint.

# REFERENCES

Acker, Sandra. (2000). In/out/side: Positioning the researcher in feminist qualitative research. *Resources from Feminist Research Journal, 28*(1/2), 189–208.

Anderson, Margaret. (1998). Studying across difference: Race, class and gender in qualitative research. In Maxine Baca Zinn, Pierette Hondagneu-Sotelo, & Michael A. Messner (Eds.), *Through the prism of difference: Readings on sex and gender* (pp. 70–78). Boston: Allyn & Bacon.

Anzaldúa, Gloria. (1987). *Borderlands/la frontera: The new mestiza.* San Francisco: Aunt Lute.

Behr, Ruth. (1993). *Translated woman: Crossing the border with Esperanza's story.* Boston: Beacon Press.

Behr, Ruth. (1996). *The vulnerable observer: Anthropology that breaks your heart.* Boston: Beacon Press.

Beoku-Betts, J. (1994). When black is not enough: Doing field research among Gullah women. *NWSA Journal, 6*(3), 413–433.

Beverly, John. (2000). Testimonio, subalternity, and narrative authority. In Norman K. Denzin & Yvonna S. Lincoln (Eds.), *Handbook of qualitative research* (pp. 555–565). Thousand Oaks, CA: Sage.

Bourdieu, Pierre. (1993). Structures, habitus, practices. In Charles Lemert (Ed.), *Social theory: The multicultural and classical readings* (pp. 479–484). Boulder, CO: Westview Press.

Campbell, Marie, & Manicom, Ann. (Eds.). (1995). *Knowledge, experience, and ruling relations: Studies in the social organization of knowledge.* Toronto, Ontario, Canada: University of Toronto Press.

Charmaz, Kathy. (2000). Grounded theory: Objectivist and constructivist methods. In Norman K. Denzin & Yvonna S. Lincoln (Eds.), *Handbook of qualitative research* (pp. 509–535). Thousand Oaks, CA: Sage.

Clifford, James, & Marcus, George E. (Eds.). (1986). *Writing culture: The poetics and politics of ethnography.* Berkeley: University of California Press.

Coffey, Amanda. (1999). *The ethnographic self: Fieldwork and the representation of identity.* Thousand Oaks, CA: Sage.

Collins, Patricia Hill. (1998). *Fighting words: Black women and the search for justice.* Minneapolis: University of Minnesota Press.

Collins, Patricia Hill. (2000). *Black feminist thought* (2nd ed.). New York: Routledge.

Conner, Tamlin, & Bliss-Moreau, Eliza. (2006). Sampling human experience in naturalistic settings. In Sharlene Nagy Hesse-Biber and Patricia Leavy (Eds.), *Emergent methods in social science research* (pp. 109–129). Thousand Oaks, CA: Sage.

Cook, Judith, & Fonow, Mary Margaret. (1986). Knowledge and women's interests: Issues of epistemology and methodology in feminist sociological research. *Sociological Inquiry, 56*(1), 2–29.

Cooper, Anna Julia. (1892). *A voice from the south by a black woman from the south.* Xenia, OH: Aldine.

de Beauvoir, Simone. (1953). *The second sex.* New York: Knopf.

Denzin, Norman K., & Lincoln, Yvonna S. (2000). Introduction: Entering the field of qualitative research. In Norman K. Denzin & Yvonna S. Lincoln (Eds.), *Handbook of qualitative research* (pp. 1–28). Thousand Oaks, CA: Sage.

DeVault, Marjorie. (1990). Talking and listening from women's standpoint. *Social Problems, 37,* 96–116.

DeVault, Marjorie, & McCoy, Lisa. (2000). Institutional ethnography: Using interviews to investigate ruling relations. In *Handbook of interview research: Context and method* (pp. 751–776). Thousand Oaks, CA: Sage.

Dodson, Lisa. (1998). *Don't call us out of name: The untold lives of women and girls in poor America.* Boston: Beacon Press.

Dodson, Lisa, & Schmalzbauer, Leah. (2005). Poor mothers and habits of hiding: Participatory methods in poverty research. *Journal of Marriage and Family, 67.*

Dunbar, Christopher J., Rodriguez, Dalia, & Parker, Laurence. (2000). Race, subjectivity, and the interview process. In J. F. Gubrium & J. A. Holstein (Eds.), *Handbook of interview research: Context and method* (pp. 279–298). Thousand Oaks, CA: Sage.

Edwards, Rosalind. (1990). Connecting methods and epistemology: A white woman interviewing black women. *Women's Studies International Forum, 13*(5), 477–490.

Eichler, Margrit. (1997). Feminist methodology. *Current Sociology, 45*(2), 9–36.

Ellis, Carolyn, & Bochner, Arthur. (2000). Autoethnography, personal narrative, reflexivity: Researcher as subject. In Norman K. Denzin & Yvonna S. Lincoln (Eds.), *Handbook of qualitative research* (2nd ed.) (pp. 733–768). Thousand Oaks, CA: Sage.

Everett, Jeffery. (2002). Organizational research and the praxeology of Pierre Bourdieu. *Organizational Research Methods, 5*(1), 56–80.

Fine, Michelle. (1998). Working the hyphens: Reinventing self and other in qualitative research. In Norman K. Denzin & Yvonna S. Lincoln (Eds.), *The landscape of qualitative research* (pp. 130–155). Thousand Oaks, CA: Sage.

Gorelick, Sherry. (1991). Contradictions of feminist methodology. *Gender & Society, 5*(4), 459–477.

Griffith, Alison I. (1998). Insider/outsider: Epistemological privilege and mothering work. *Human Studies, 21,* 361–376.

Guba, Egon, & Lincoln, Yvonna S. (2000). Competing paradigms in qualitative research. In Norman K. Denzin & Yvonna S. Lincoln (Eds.), *Handbook of qualitative research* (pp. 105–117). Thousand Oaks, CA: Sage.

Guillemin, Marilys, & Gillam, Lynn. (2004). Ethics, reflexivity, and "ethically important moments" in research. *Qualitative Inquiry, 10*(2), 261–280.

Haraway, Donna. (1988). Situated knowledges: The science question in feminism and the privilege of partial perspective. *Feminist Studies, 14*(3), 575–599.

Harding, Sandra. (1986). *The science question.* Ithaca, NY: Cornell University Press.

Harding, Sandra. (1991). *Whose science, whose knowledge? Thinking from women's lives.* Ithaca, NY: Cornell University Press.

Harding, Sandra. (1992). After the neutrality ideal: Science, politics, and "strong objectivity." *Social Research, 59*(3), 567–587.

Harding, Sandra. (1993). Rethinking standpoint epistemology: What is strong objectivity? In Linda Alcoff & Elizabeth Porter (Eds.), *Feminist epistemologies* (pp. 49–82). New York: Routledge.

Hartsock, Nancy. (1993). Foucault on power: A theory for women. In Charles Lemert (Ed.), *Social theory: The multicultural & classic readings* (pp. 545–554). Boulder, CO: Westview Press.

Hartsock, Nancy. (1998). *The feminist standpoint revisited.* Boulder, CO: Westview Press.

Hertz, Rosanna. (1996). Introduction: Ethics, reflexivity, and voice. *Qualitative Sociology, 19*(1), 3–9.

hooks, bell. (1984). *Feminist theory: From margin to center.* Boston: South End Press.

Kirk, Jerome, & Miller, Marc L. (1986). *Reliability and validity in qualitative research.* Newbury Park, CA: Sage.

Kirsch, Gesa. (1999). *Ethical dilemmas in feminist research: The politics of location, interpretation, and publication.* Albany: State University of New York Press.

Kondo, Dorinne K. (1990). *Crafting selves: Power, gender, and discourses of identity in a Japanese workplace.* Chicago: University of Chicago Press.

Lal, Jayati. (1996). Situating locations: The politics of self, identity, and other in living and writing the text. In Diane Wolf (Ed.), *Feminist dilemmas in fieldwork* (pp. 185–214). Boulder, CO: Westview Press.

Lather, Peggy, & Smithies, C. (1997). *Troubling the angels: Women living with HIV/AIDS.* Boulder, CO: Westview Press.

Lemert, Charles, & Bahn, Esme. (Eds.). (1988). *The voice of Anna Julia Cooper.* Baltimore: Rowman & Littlefield.

Lykes, Brinton. (1997). Activist participatory research among the Maya of Guatemala: Constructing meanings from situated knowledge. *Journal of Social Issues, 53*(4), 725–746.

Maguire, Patricia. (1987). *Doing participatory research.* Amherst: University of Massachusetts.

Mann, Susan A., & Kelley, Lori. (1997). Standing at the crossroads of modernist thought: Collins, Smith, and the new feminist epistemologies. *Gender & Society, 11*(4), 391–408.

Marcus, George E. (1994). What comes (just) after "post"? The case of ethnography. In Norman K. Denzin & Yvonna S. Lincoln (Eds.), *Handbook of qualitative research* (pp. 563–574). Thousand Oaks, CA: Sage.

Marcus, George E., & Fischer, Michael M. J. (Eds.). (1999). *Anthropology as cultural critique* (2nd ed.). Chicago: University of Chicago Press.

Martineau, Harriet. (1836). *Society in America.* New York: Saunders & Otley.

Marx, Marcia. (2000). Invisibility, interviewing, and power: A researcher's dilemma. *Resources for Feminist Research, 28*(3/4), 131–152.

Mascia-Lees, Frances, Sharpe, Patricia, & Cohen, Colleen Ballerino. (1989). The postmodernist turn in anthropology: Cautions from a feminist perspective. *Signs, 15*(1), 7–33.

Mertens, Donna M. (2003). Mixed methods and the politics of human research: The transformative-emancipatory perspective. In Abbas Tashakkori & Charles Teddlie (Eds.), *Handbook of mixed methods.* Thousand Oaks, CA: Sage.

Merton, Robert. (1972). Insiders and outsiders: A chapter in the sociology of knowledge. *American Journal of Sociology, 78*(1), 9–47.

Naples, Nancy A. (1996). The outsider phenomenon. In Carolyn D. Smith & William Kornblu (Eds.), *In the field* (pp. 139–149). Westport, CT: Praeger.

Naples, Nancy A. (2003). *Feminism and method: Ethnography, discourse analysis, and activist research.* New York: Routledge.

Oakley, A. (1998). Gender, methodology and people's way of knowing: Some problems with feminism and the paradigm debate in social science. *Sociology, 32*(4), 707–732.

Olesen, Virginia. (1998). Feminisms and models of qualitative research. In Norman K. Denzin & Yvonna S. Lincoln (Eds.), *The landscape of qualitative research* (pp. 300–332). Thousand Oaks, CA: Sage.

Parameswaran, Radhika. (2001). Feminist media ethnography in India: Exploring power, gender and culture in the field. *Qualitative Inquiry, 7*(1), 69–103.

Patai, Daphne, & Gluck, Sherna B. (Eds.). (1991). *Women's words: The feminist practice of oral history.* New York: Routledge.

Perkins-Gilman, Charlotte. (1898). *Women and economics.* Boston: Small & Maynard.

Pini, Barbara. (2004). On being a nice country girl and an academic feminist: Using reflexivity in rural social research. *Journal of Rural Studies, 20*(2), 169–179.

Ralston, Helen. (2001). Being a white Australian-Canadian feminist doing research with South Asian women of color in the Diaspora: Crossing borders and boundaries, creating spaces. In Vasilikie Demos & Marcia Texler Segal (Eds.), *Advances in gender research: Vol. 5. International challenge to theory* (pp. 213–231). Oxford, UK: Pergamon Press.

Reason, Peter. (1998). Three approaches to participative inquiry. In Norman K. Denzin & Yvonne S. Lincoln (Eds.), *Strategies of qualitative inquiry* (pp. 923–948). Thousand Oaks, CA: Sage.

Reinharz, Shulamit. (1992). *Feminist methods in social research.* New York: Oxford University Press.

Rhodes, P. (1994). Race of interviewer effects in qualitative research. *Sociology, 28*(2), 547–558.

Richardson, Laurel. (2000). Writing a method of inquiry. In Norman K. Denzin & Yvonna S. Lincoln (Eds.), *Handbook of qualitative research* (pp. 923–948). Thousand Oaks, CA: Sage.

Riessman, Catherine. (1987). When gender is not enough: Women interviewing women. *Gender & Society, 1*(2), 172–207.

Riessman, Catherine. (1993). *Narrative analysis.* Newbury Park, CA: Sage.

Schmalzbauer, Leah. (in press). *Striving and surviving: A daily life analysis of Honduran transnational families.* New York: Routledge.

Schutz, Alfred. (1964). *Collected papers* (Arvid Brodersen, Ed.). The Hague, the Netherlands: Martinus Nijhoff.

Scott, J. (1990). *Domination and the arts of resistance: Hidden transcripts.* New Haven, CT: Yale University Press.

Smith, Dorothy. (1987). *The everyday world as problematic: A feminist sociology.* Boston: Northeastern University Press.

Smith, Dorothy. (2002). Institutional ethnography. In Tim May (Ed.), *Qualitative research in action* (pp. 17–52). Thousand Oaks, CA: Sage.

Spivak, Gayatri Chakravorty. (1988). Can the subaltern speak? In Cary Nelson & Lawrence Grossberg (Eds.), *Marxism and the interpretation of culture* (pp. 271–313). Urbana: University of Illinois Press.

Stacey, Judith. (1991). Can there be a feminist ethnography? In Daphne Patai & Sherna B. Gluck (Eds.), *Women's words: The feminist practice of oral history* (pp. 111–119). New York: Routledge.

Stage, Christina W., & Mattson, Marifran. (2003). Ethnographic interviewing as contextualized conversation. In Robin Patric Clair (Ed.), *Expressions of ethnography: Novel approaches to qualitative methods* (pp. 97–105). Albany: State University of New York Press.

Stanley, Liz, & Wise, Sue. (1993). *Breaking out again: Feminist ontology and epistemology.* New York: Routledge.

Stringer, Ernest. (1996). *Action research: A handbook for practitioners.* Thousand Oaks, CA: Sage.

Tedlock, Barbara. (2000). Ethnography and ethnographic representation. In Norman K. Denzin & Yvonna S. Lincoln (Eds.), *Handbook of qualitative research* (2nd ed., pp. 455–486). Thousand Oaks, CA: Sage.

Temple, Bogusia. (1997). Watch your tongue: Issues in translation and cross-cultural research. *Sociology, 31*(3), 607–618.

Trinh, Minh-ha, T. (1991). *Framer framed.* New York: Routledge.

Tristan, Flora. (1844). *The workers union.* Urbana: University of Illinois Press.

Van Maanen, John. (1988). *Tales of the field: On writing ethnography.* Chicago: University of Chicago Press.

Warren, Carol A. B. (2000). Writing the other, inscribing the self. *Qualitative Sociology, 23*(2), 183–199.

Wasserfall, Rahel R. (1993). Reflexivity, feminism, and difference. *Qualitative Sociology, 16*(1), 23–41.

Weber, Max. (1921). *Economy and society.* Totowa, NJ: Bedminster Press.

Wolf, Diane. (1996). Situating feminist dilemmas in fieldwork. In Diane Wolf (Ed.), *Feminist dilemmas in fieldwork* (pp. 1–55). Boulder, CO: Westview Press.

Wolf, Margery. (1992). *A thrice told tale: Feminism, postmodernism, and ethnographic responsibility.* Stanford, CA: Stanford University Press.

# 26

# FEMINIST RESEARCH ETHICS

JUDITH PREISSLE

Helen is dying of breast cancer. Facing her own mortality uncertainly, she struggles with how to help her young children through this experience. A few miles away a research ethics board hesitates about approving a study of the relationship between dying parents and young children. Approaching people at their most vulnerable to request consent to study them and their family seems crass at best. How could the risk of intrusion possibly balance any benefit from what might be learned?

Ethics and moral theory are about making judgments, especially judgments informed by some explicit framework. Feminism and the varieties of feminisms themselves constitute such moral and ethical frameworks because they each represent value positions on the experiences and places of women around the world. I agree with the pragmatist feminist Charlene Haddock Seigfried (1996) that all feminisms seek to improve the lot of women. Making gender a basic category of analysis, of course, also revalues women in relationship to men and leads to interrogating the categories of sex and gender themselves (Butler, 1990). As Tong (1998)

emphasizes, feminisms vary in how women's revaluation, empowerment, and emancipation ought to be formulated, accomplished, and assessed. Liberal feminists are said to advocate social reform of existing social arrangements, socialist and Marxist feminists advocate restructuring society, and so forth.

In this chapter, I explore the development of feminist research ethics over the past several decades in the context of two influences: the increasing worldwide attention to responsible conduct of research and feminist ethics more generally. Feminist ethics developed in part as an explicit challenge to conventional patterns of Western epistemology and ethics and thus has its roots in two feminist projects. The first is work by psychologists such as Carol Gilligan and philosophers such as Nel Noddings who have formulated an ethic of care believed to better characterize the moral decision making of females than the modernist variety of Western moral theories centered in abstract principles. This project posits differences between how men and women conceptualize and practice ethics and morality. The second feminist project, discussed more fully in other chapters in

Author's Note: I want to acknowledge the assistance of Youngsek Kim in collecting material for this manuscript and the critical questions and generous care provided by Sharlene Hesse-Biber throughout its preparation. The work has benefited enormously from my mentors in philosophy, Victoria M. Davion and Beth F. Preston, who have no responsibility for any of my philosophical errors and misconceptions.

this handbook and treated only tangentially here, is work by feminist social theorists and philosophers who have contributed to the efforts of poststructuralists, postcolonialists, and postmodernists to challenge the epistemological assumptions of modern scientific practice. Calling into question presuppositions about the nature of human beings, about the efficacy of positivist and postpositivist research models, and about the relationship of knower to known, these feminist thinkers propose alternative ways to define, create, and assess human knowledge.

## How Can She Judge?

With apologies to Lorraine Code (1991) for adapting the title of her cogent consideration of feminist epistemology, I offer here my own position in the array of feminisms and the approach I took in developing a chapter on ethics in feminist research.

Where do I position myself as a feminist? At times I must admit to an eclectic feminism because my positioning has varied by time, place, circumstances, and people. Having grown up in a conventional 1950s, upwardly mobile, European American family, I have lived an adulthood that some of those family members still consider unconventional: 40 years a teacher, 30 years an academic, childless, divorced twice and married thrice. In my role as a social-foundations-of-education scholar, I aspire to be a multicultural and global feminist. In my role as a qualitative research methodologist, this feminism blends with critical and postmodern perspectives and philosophical pragmatism. Educated as a progressive teacher in the 1960s and radicalized by women's liberation in the 1970s, I view change and continuity as the result of the dynamic dialectic among individuals in their ongoing and ever-changing groups, communities, and collectivities.

How does any of this qualify me to comment on feminist research ethics and to make feminist ethical judgments? My preparation as a scholar was in educational research from an anthropological and ethnographic perspective. I have been conducting and teaching qualitative research from a feminist perspective—sometimes explicit and other times tacit—for 30 years. For the past 15 of those 30 years, I have

served on my university's institutional review board, the human subjects research review committee for U.S. universities, the same board that decided to approve the study of dying mothers and their young children. At the start of the new century I won a year's support to study philosophy, working principally with a feminist ethicist and an epistemologist with feminist leanings. Writing this chapter has provided me an opportunity to synthesize several literatures: feminist theory, feminist social research, feminist research methods, qualitative research methods and design at its many intersections with feminism, general research ethics, feminist ethics within the general area of ethics, and moral theory from philosophy. The material that I cite throughout the chapter reflects both general reading in these areas and the results of specific searches on feminist research ethics.

Finally, I offer some comments about what I think I have learned about ethics over the years. First, ethics at best are frameworks that guide decision making. They are not rules, regulations, or laws. Even ethicists who claim absolute values struggle with how those values apply in any given situation. What makes ethical decisions difficult is that several competing "goods" may be at stake or several simultaneous "bads" are to be avoided. I may arrive at an adequate answer, but it is rarely ideal. Second, a review of a research plan for protection of human participants provides only input from other researchers on obvious problematic issues; it does not guarantee that the researcher will have no further ethical challenges. Third, feminist values of whatever kind provide us with ethical frameworks for our decision making, but we must still prioritize those values and decide how they are at play in any given situation.

## Feminism and Ethics

Two scholars, Carol Gilligan and Nel Noddings, epitomize the challenge of 20th-century feminism to modernism's principle-based models of moral theory. Although many others have contributed to a relationship-based ethics, Gilligan and Noddings are responsible for producing what are now recognized as alternative feminist approaches to the European frameworks organizing ethics around such principles as rights, duties, virtues, and consequences (Tong, 1993). In this section I describe their orientations as presented in two seminal texts and compare and contrast their ideas to previous moral theory, moral development theory, and some of the philosophical premises underlying these ideas.

## A Gendered Moral Development

Working with Lawrence Kohlberg and collecting interviews on moral decision making herself, Gilligan (1982) reported consistent empirical patterns of differences between the reasoning of the men she studied and that of the women. She rejected Kohlberg's idea of universally invariant stages of development for a developmental model that accommodates the differing patterns of men and women, pointing out that Kohlberg had selected white, middle-class males for his work.

### Kohlberg's Moral Development

Lawrence Kohlberg (1981), in the mid-20th century, following up with Jean Piaget's notions of moral decision making as a developmental process from simpler to more complex, formulated a theory to explain how people reason through their ethical choices (Colby & Kohlberg, 1987). He believed that all people mature through six invariant stages of moral decision making as they grow up. The six stages of moral development are interdependent with parallel development of cognitive abilities, and some people never reach the highest stages of functioning. Kohlberg grouped the six stages of moral reasoning in three levels: preconventional, conventional, and postconventional. These levels represent a maturation in concern from the self, to the community, and to an abstracted all or universal. According to Kohlberg, only a few people reach the final postconventional stage, the universal ethical principle orientation where individuals make moral decisions on the basis of principles they have adopted for their own, such as the Golden Rule.

### Relationship Versus Principle

At both the conventional and postconventional levels, Kohlberg saw people making decisions on the basis of rules, laws, and principles.

Women consistently scored lower on his measures of moral decision making because maintaining and fostering relationships were central to their responses. His premise that the most ethical person acts from universally applicable rights or virtues or obligations is consistent with the modernist assumption that human behavior, including ethical imperatives, is governed by universal laws. However, Gilligan insisted that women's most sophisticated moral decision making was based on the value for relationship, not the value for principle. Contingencies such as gender challenge the possibility of universality in human behavior and thus undermine expectations for certainty and predictability in human activity.

Gilligan explains the differences between how men and women make moral decisions and accounts for overlaps in their maturation by relying on psychodynamic (Chodorow, 1978) and psychodevelopmental theories (Erikson, 1968; Levinson, 1978) of gender. Males and females often have different patterns of early experiences in the family, centering on attachment and separation, and hence may view the world differently. She supplements this framework with a sociohistorical approach in considering how differential experiences and views may have developed in 19th- and 20th-century U.S. society.

Women, according to Gilligan, begin their moral development interviews by asking more questions about the details of a decision, especially probing for the human relationships involved. As they reason through their choices and the justifications for these choices, they focus on relationships among people and not just the rules, norms, or laws that might operate in a given situation. Although aware of fairness as one priority in an ethical dilemma, women more commonly than men privilege the value of caring. They ask, "Does the decision indicate people's caring for one another?" rather than merely "Is the decision fair to everyone?" Among women, relationships are more likely to be conceptualized as connected networks or webs of reciprocities than as rule-governed hierarchies of authority and obedience among separate individuals.

Gilligan formulates women's decision making as maturing through three stages according to how women think through their views of selfishness and responsibility. An initial focus on the self and on self-interested decisions where the good is what is good for the individual is succeeded by a focus on others and on self*less* decisions where the good is what is good for the individual's network or web of others. In the third stage, women recognize a responsibility to self as well as others and seek to make decisions where the good is a caring choice for everyone that allows networks of relationships to be maintained. As the individual struggles to balance self with other, the conformity and desire to be "good" of the middle stage develops into a desire for honesty and truth in the third stage. In the third stage, women critically examine their personal needs for care and compassion, assess intentions and consequences independent of how they might be viewed by others, transform their notion of reciprocity into an understanding of interdependence, and come to a sense of responsibility and integrity for their choices. Gilligan concludes that balancing rights and duties is the challenge for all adults, male and female, but that men and women formulate these values and how to prioritize them differently. Individuals learn that the ideals of care and fairness can never be achieved fully for everyone in any particular decision, but that care, responsibility, fairness, and rights all enter the mix when autonomous choices are to be made.

Both Kohlberg and Gilligan show that the competing normative moral theories of rights, duties, consequences, and such come alive in alternatives when people are making real ethical choices. What Gilligan does, however, is challenge some of the philosophical premises underlying Kohlberg's more rigid and narrow view of moral decision making. In her 1982 text, Gilligan argued against privileging the abstract over the concrete, the principle over the relationship, the absolute over the relative, the universal over the particular, the objective over the subjective, and the cognitive over the affective. She discussed real people in their material worlds, making decisions by trying to achieve multiple values and make wise choices for satisfying lives. These decisions undermine such assumed binaries as objective and subjective or even absolute and relative and reveal them more as ideal, if contradictory, states to which we aspire but which we never reach. Such

challenges to philosophical premises embedded in Gilligan's work were approached more directly by Nel Noddings in her 1984 formulation of caring.

## An Ethic of Care

Noddings begins by observing that contemporary ethics has been dominated by choices over the right normative principle, whether rights, justice, consequences, or something else, and by a focus on logical reasoning believed to contribute to making decisions based on the right principle. She calls these "the language of the father." She proposes introducing into ethics the "mother's voice." The feminine approach to ethics Noddings endorses is rooted in the relationship of caring and being cared for. In a recent edition of her text (2003), she emphasizes that "relations, not individuals, are ontologically basic" to ethical decisions (p. xiii). When caring must be prescribed as an obligation or duty, then the relation is with social expectations and not the other, not the *thou*, and what Nodding calls natural caring is diverted into something like the virtue principle: People behave in a caring manner because that is the *right* thing to do.

Noddings labels her endeavor a "practical ethics" conceptualized from what she believes women commonly do when faced with ethical dilemmas. Although they may consider principles and may reason through decisions, women consider the feelings involved and the relationships among the people in the situation. The caring relationship involves the *one-caring* and the *cared-for* in an interaction to which both contribute, but often asymmetrically. The one-caring, a generic *she* in Noddings's account, acts from the satisfaction of experiencing the feeling of care and from an interest, absorption, or engrossment in the cared-for, Noddings's generic *he*. The motive to care comes from previous experiences of being cared for and caring. It is an affective aspiration lodged in relationship rather than a pursuit of some principle, such as fairness or virtue.

Although caring is a feeling accessible to all, judgments based on caring are particular to a given situation and may not be applicable to other situations where the particulars are different. Here, Noddings rejects the binary of objectivism and relativism by noting how both may operate in any given circumstances. Likewise, she notes that she depends on intuitionism and emotivism as well as rationality to build her case for the ethic of caring—an eclectic mix that refuses only absolutism. Caring, according to Noddings, is a commitment to the development of another.

An ethic of care begins with what Noddings (1984) believes is common to all humans, "a longing for goodness" (p. 27). It relies on the capacity for empathy, a receptiveness to the experience of another that is both affective and cognitive. Like Gilligan, she prefers a psychodynamic explanation for caring, finding its source in the early development of the child in the family, but she precludes neither biological nor social conditions as contributing to it. Men as well as women develop the capacity to care, but Noddings views caring as the predominant response of women to ethical decisions.

She then takes the human commitment to care as a framework for an *ethical ideal* that guides decision making. The ethical ideal is an image people have of themselves as the one-caring, whose priority is to maintain relationship, "guided in what we do by three considerations: how we feel, what the other expects of us, and what the situational relationship requires of us" (p. 46). The ethical ideal is less a virtue than an internalization of people's selves in their best caring experiences. Conventions and other social norms can be helpful in setting boundaries for care, but moral decision making is guided by caring and by the affective and cognitive requirements for caring. Caring is what Noddings calls a "constrained ideal," riddled with the guilt aroused from the necessity of selecting among competing priorities and from facing the conflicts inherent to everyday living, but sustained by the joy of positive feelings from and intense engagement with another.

Thus, both Noddings and Gilligan shift the focus of ethics from principles and argumentation to relationships and exploration of particulars. Neither gives up principles and arguments because consideration of both is necessary for deciding what is in the best interest of those in relationship and for weighing the conditions and particulars that contribute to competing priorities. The traditions of principle-based, Western

ethical thought are present in the feminist approach to ethics exemplified by these two scholars, but they are framed differently. These traditions contribute to alternative ways of formulating what is positive in a relationship, rather than as standards to emulate in decision making. Noddings's philosophical assumptions, similar to the epistemological contributions of such philosophers as Bordo (1987) and Code (1991), are inclusive and multidimensional, resisting such binaries as objective and subjective, absolute and relativistic, for a more faceted consideration of what is at play in the assumptions about how we experience the world and develop knowledge that underlie how we make ethical choices (see the chapters in Part I).

Noddings and Gilligan together offer a feminist ethic based in relationship that challenges the principled ethics of rights, justice, consequences, and such. Interpreted by some as suggesting essentialist assumptions that reduce human behavior to the unchangeable determinism of genetic sex typing (cf. Fuss, 1989, for an antiessentialist argument on the positive contributions of essentialism to feminist thought), both scholars argue that patterns of difference need not mean mutually exclusive thinking and action; both also emphasize the complicated and socially embedded nature of moral decision making (cf., however, Lloyd's [1996] challenge to the dichotomy underlying the separation of thought from emotion, of reason from intuition, in both conventional ethics and relational ethics). Their formulations of an ethic of care have since been refined and elaborated by others (e.g., Brabeck, 1989).

But how does their thinking contribute to a feminist *research* ethic? To address this question, I first summarize the development of a tradition of ethics for research practice. My focus on the United States is intended as one case among the cases worldwide of concerns for ethical research practice, not as the only way societies and scholars have developed research ethics. I argue later that the principled orientation to research ethics as it has developed in the United States in the past quarter century has been challenged and, in some cases, has been reformulated by feminist ethics—by the concern with relationship, particularity, constraint, and inclusion.

## Research Ethics in the United States

Throughout the 20th century, a collection of established status hierarchies were challenged, and in many cases the authority of these structures was overturned. Political colonialism was dismantled; ethnic and racial civil rights movements around the world won civil liberties and political participation for many; various worldwide women's movements challenged and even overturned patriarchal structures. In Western societies, one of the hierarchies so challenged was the subject-researcher relationship. An ethic of authority, where researchers decided what was best for those they studied, has been replaced by a participatory ethic, where researchers' plans are scrutinized by colleagues before being reviewed by potential participants, who are expected to make their own free and informed decisions about consenting to the research.

Consequently most discussions of ethics in social science and professional research focus on who is being studied—the human subjects, participants, or coresearchers. How people are sought, studied, and recompensed for research studies became such a crucial ethical issue in the 20th century that nations such as the United States developed federal guidelines regulating research on human beings. The relationship between the studied and the studier, between the inquirer and those inquired about, is a defining attribute of research in the human, social, and professional sciences, but it has been abstract principle rather than caring that frames most conventional thought about this relationship (e.g., National Research Council, 2003). In this section, I address the ethical problems and controversies that ongoing human relationships pose, but I add to this the ethical implications of formulating research goals and of representing those studied in research reports. Of course goals, relationships, and representations are not mutually exclusive categories of research conduct; they are all interacting facets of the research experience. I separate them for heuristic purposes to ensure that the ethical implications of each are addressed directly.

### Ethics of Research Purpose

What is the value of conducting research with human beings? Why should we do this at all? What is right and wrong about studying people? What is intrinsically moral and ethical about inquiry into human endeavors, and how do we make that decision? Why should feminists distract themselves from more important tasks to conduct research? My argument is that, although different feminists may find different values in their research purposes, all feminists understand that research itself is value laden rather than value neutral and hence are attempting to realize some value through their research.

Some have addressed the question of research value by claiming that knowledge is superior to ignorance—that understanding by itself has intrinsic value. The normative codes adopted by such professional research organizations in the United States as the American Anthropological Association (1998), the American Educational Research Association (2000), the American Psychological Association (2002),[1] and the American Sociological Association (1997) prescribe knowledge generation as good.[2]

Many feminists likewise value knowledge over ignorance. Much of the initial feminist research in the 1970s, for example, focused on differential patterns of experience and behavior among men and women (e.g., Goetz, 1978; Goetz & Grant, 1988) to demonstrate that scholarship on men could not be assumed to represent knowledge about women. Gilligan's (1982) work in women's moral development exemplifies this pattern.

Another justification for research appeals to nature. Our animal physiology and development revolves around sensing the environment, storing and using the information acquired, and learning from this process. We could argue that, as particular kinds of beings, we are predisposed genetically to seek information, to know, to understand. Although this natural law justification frames much of 19th-century feminist demand for equality of treatment (Traina, 1999), most feminist thought is ambivalent about appeals to biology. This may be changing with such feminist challenges to conventional evolutionary theory as that of Gowaty (1997) and Waage and Gowaty (1997), whose genetic research disputes sexist assumptions about biology in the notion of biology as destiny (cf. Haraway, 1989; Harding, 1998).

Most cultures around the world incorporate in their ideology, their belief systems, some presumption of an intrinsic value of knowledge—knowledge is good. Here it is a virtue, and that becomes its justification. Or because knowledge is taken as inherently good, we can understand it as a duty to pursue. The Western scientific movement (Harmon, 1996) arising during the European Enlightenment was based on the idea that knowledge is freeing—that it provides an alternative to superstition, to religious orthodoxy, and to feudal authority. This assumption of the intrinsic value of knowledge is deeply embedded in feminist thought. Around the world, women's access to knowledge and to education provides the means to improving their lives (Bloom, 1998; Martin, 1985; Sexton, 1976). DeVault (1999), in her survey of feminism and social research, stresses the value of revealing hitherto invisible knowledge. Throughout her text, she emphasizes not only neglected experiences but also corrective research—studies that provide views of women's experiences that are alternatives to gender-insensitive portrayals.

Nevertheless, cultures often offer the antithesis of knowledge being good as a second attribute. Knowledge can be bad—it can be painful, disillusioning, frightening, and destructive. Fonow and Cook (1991) briefly acknowledge how the intimate and personal nature of what many participants reveal in feminist research may generate knowledge that they and other women might prefer to avoid. This suggests that the intrinsic nature of knowledge may be neither good nor bad—but good or bad according to its content and the purposes to which it is put, in context and in relation to the knower and the known. Knowledge per se then becomes integral to other values, and knowledge as inherently political is a fundamental claim of 20th-century Western feminisms (e.g., Harding, 1987; Stanley & Wise, 1993).

The idea of an intrinsic value of knowledge is related to the view of knowing and the search for truth as constituting a form of worship. In revealing the mystery of life and of others, the knower is affirming a value beyond self—god, nature, community, or cosmos. However, the value is conceptualized; the search is a way of respecting and honoring god, nature, community, cosmos, or other value beyond self. Among feminists, Mary Daly's (1978) mystical formulation of an essential, natural female beingness provides such an ethical purpose for the inquirer. Daly's work, generally grouped with radical feminism, embraces gender separatism as best promoting the interests of women, a position some other feminists find objectionable. Such profound disagreements prompt the question of what values are served by the quest for knowledge.

During the Enlightenment, the religious premise—service to god—became a service to the human community, and the idea was transformed into the consequentialist philosophy of right action being what benefits the community. Here, what made knowing and inquiry good were more or less direct consequences—study is good because it promotes more effective behavior or better solutions to human problems (Reason, 1996). Seeking knowledge that fosters social change and the transformation of societies into better places for women to live, where they may "liberate themselves from oppression" (Tong, 1998, p. 280), is arguably one of the common threads among many feminisms. In her characterization of feminist research, Reinharz (1992, p. 240) likewise includes "creation of social change" as one of 10 common themes. However, the question of who benefits from research requires that we also ask who may be harmed by the inquiry and the knowledge produced, and what benefits are privileged at the cost of alternative goods. Feminist researchers vary in how they conceptualize harms and benefits and thus how they frame their studies (see Hesse-Biber & Leckenby, 2004, for commonalities among the diversity of feminist social research).

Addressing the cost-benefit issue requires consideration of relationships of power. How power and the distribution of resources are considered among feminists varies, of course. Among Marxist, socialist, and postmodern feminists concern for power differentials is commonly integrated into research goals (Naples, 2003), often with the intention of disturbing or dismantling conventional arrangements of power, as Fine (1992) has attempted in a number of her research endeavors and as many standpoint theorists advocate (e.g., Harding, 2004).

The call for research to serve women's interests has come from many feminist scholars, and justifications for feminist research are as diverse as feminism itself, or feminisms themselves. Eichler (1988) proposes nonsexist inquiry, including women's perspectives to achieve a more representative knowledge of humanity, a goal reflecting issues of fairness or justice. However, Du Bois (1983) has sought research that would "address women's lives and experience *in their own terms*, to create theory grounded in the actual experience and language of women" (p. 108), moving the emphasis from creating balance to valuing research on women for its own sake. Here, a concern for justice or fairness, in Eichler's rationale, becomes care for or interest in the particular. In Smith's (1987) formulation, women's positions, experiences, and views of the world are standpoints that lack cultural representation:

> The issue is more than bias. It is more than simply an omission of certain kinds of topics. It involves taking up the standpoint of women as an experience of being, of society, of social and personal process that must be given form and expression in the culture, whether as knowledge, as art, or as literature or political action. (p. 36)

Smith and other standpoint theorists (e.g., Harding, 2004) insist that research is always carried out by someone in a particular position and that understanding the purpose of a study requires understanding the position of the researcher.

Like Du Bois and Smith, Lather (1991) denies neutrality in research. She calls for "research as praxis," or research to serve the purposes of social justice, for a feminist research to put gender at the center of inquiry. The intent is both to make the gendered facet of human identity clear in any study of humans and to redress implicit and explicit gender inequities. Lather proposes that, to assure awareness of choice in the values directing any study, feminist researchers must consider and reconsider their own purposes and approaches in self-reflexive critique (cf. Doucet & Mauthner, 2002). Collins (1990) elaborates the feminist agenda by cautioning that studying gender without concern for race and class merely privileges some experiences of marginality without addressing the complexities of human oppression. Longino (1994) likewise

compares racial and gender biases in her discussion of how researchers' assumptions, questions, procedures, and conceptualization of data reflect social values that prejudice the knowledge generated. Roman and Apple (1990) offer a set of questions for feminist researchers to consider in assessing how well their endeavors serve the integrity and purposes of their participants (cf. Grossman et al., 1997; Massat & Lundy, 1997). Finally, Allen and Baber (1992) summarize the limitations of goals, such as those voiced by feminists, that seek to transform the lives of others— risks of homogenizing diversity among women, of co-opting or subverting others' visions of themselves and goals for themselves, of losing public relevance in overemphasizing the personal, of trading the universal for the particular. Acker, Barry, and Esseveld (1991), for example, in their study of women's entry and reentry into the labor force, found that women participants do not always share researchers' desires for their emancipation.

Feminist researchers from a variety of disciplines have tried to assure that their studies serve women's purposes by including participants in the formulation, planning, conduct, and analysis of the work. Some scholars may formulate this as a kind of feminist participatory action research (PAR), but others consider it integral to the feminism they practice (Tolman & Brydon-Miller, 2001). Fine (1992), for example, builds a strong case that conventional and interpretive research, however much influenced by feminist perspectives, cannot relieve women's oppression as effectively as does activist participatory feminist research.

Participatory feminist research has had mixed success, depending on research participants' interest in and commitment to the endeavor. As might be expected, this varies greatly. For example, Seibold's (2000) study of the experience of menopause of single midlife women was assured some value for women because she herself had experienced menopause as a single middle-aged woman and because participant concerns guided her selection, collection, and analysis of information. Paradis (2000), on the other hand, had not experienced the homelessness she wanted to study in an urban setting, and she details the variety of issues that feminist professionals face when trying to plan a study both *on* and *for* homeless women. McGraw, Zvonkovic, and Walker (2000) increased interest in their study of work and family life among Northwest fishing families by adding to their objectives a goal specified by their female participants that could be construed as antifeminist by some. However, both this study and another by Skelton (2001) of female youth in Wales indicate how researchers must prioritize even feminist goals. Both studies show researchers focusing on how women want to view goals they themselves formulate, regardless of how well these goals fit a particular feminist agenda.

Ironically, feminist principles or policies may or may not foster feminist care. Patai (1991) believes that the undeniable and inevitable inequities between researchers and those they study make unavoidable a certain level of exploitation in research. She counsels humility in our claims to benefit others and courage to continue research that is ethical enough without being ethically perfect (cf. Gillies & Alldred, 2002).

In this section, I have explored what I have called the ethics of research purpose. Feminist scholars from the spectrum of feminisms have formulated their research purposes for the values they seek to realize, and these are ethical choices. The ethics of principle, especially social justice, and the ethics of care have been the predominant rationales used by feminist researchers to justify their endeavors. Feminist research in the 1970s and 1980s, with its focus on sex differences, was more explicitly concerned with equity per se. We sought to expose inequalities in resources and power and to discredit claims that women were somehow lesser men. More recent feminist research, informed by Gilligan, Noddings, and others, has been more preoccupied with a responsive research that attends to the goals of participants.

However, the goals and objectives of research are only one facet of the ethical issues in research. Feminists and other emancipatory theorists share additional concerns. What interests are served and what are ignored or imperiled in a particular study? Who will have access to the knowledge produced, who decides this, and how is it decided? Who gets to be the inquirer and who is the inquired about? What

balances of resources and decision making do these roles represent? These questions are addressed in part by consideration of the researchers' roles and interactions with those researched. Feminists have been at the forefront of challenging conventional researcher roles and interactions with those researched, just as they have been at the forefront of challenging the neutrality of research purpose.

## Ethics of Research Roles and Conduct

In the past 30 years ethical codes provided by the U.S. government and various U.S. professional groups have regulated the participation of people in research studies. Such codes have set parameters for the conduct of research that constrain all scholars, and the codes themselves may be challenged by emerging feminist practices. The current professional standards of research conduct toward study participants have been influenced by 20th-century transgressions of human rights, neglect of respect for others, and violations of conventional standards of decency in the United States and elsewhere (Jones, 1981; War Crimes Tribunal, 1947; World Medical Association, 1975). The Kantian ethical imperative (Tong, 1993) that people be treated as ends, rather than as means, was ignored in the name of research time and again over the course of the 20th century.

The National Research Act, a U.S. law passed in 1974, resulted in the development of a set of principles, summarized in the Belmont Report, governing human participation in research studies: respect for persons, beneficence, and justice (National Commission for the Protection of Human Subjects of Medical and Behavioral Research, 1979). These principles frame a code of conduct requiring informed consent of those studied, assessment of the balance of risk to benefit in any research, and fairness in selection of human participants. This is the guide used around the United States by the institutional review boards (IRBs) charged with the protection of human subjects of research by reviewing and approving research proposals. Its focus is on what happens during the period when data are collected. Although beneficence requires researchers to consider the morality of the research itself—Will the presumed benefits outweigh any harm to participants?—the emphasis is on the people directly involved. Likewise, the justice principle is often interpreted to mean justice for those involved, rather than justice more broadly; this may be changing as concerns have increased about funding for offshore research in circumstances less regulated than in the United States.

Much of the initial feminist commentary on research relationships occurred within the same time frame—the 1980s and into the early 1990s—that IRBs were being set up around the United States. I believe that feminist researchers were responding, in part, to the same climate of criticism of conventional research practice and policy (Barnbaum & Byron, 2001) that prompted governmental intervention: concern over a proliferation of research studies that manipulated and endangered people.

The feminist response to protection based on principle is a challenge to the assumed division between who is the researcher and the knower and who is the researched or the known. The principles themselves may be inoffensive, even desirable, given our history of research abuses, but they assume a relationship and an ethics governing relationship that many feminist scholars have found problematic (e.g., Edwards & Mauthner, 2002; England, 1994; Robertson, 2000). An initial challenge to the researcher as detached, protective expert is Oakley's (1981) classic comment on interviewing. In a study of expectant mothers, Oakley found herself restricted by expectations of distance and detachment from her participants and especially hampered by the asymmetry of the interviewer as the questioner and the respondent as the answerer. She found these expectations contradictory to her commitment to caring about the women as individuals, to establishing authentic relationships with them, and to offering whatever she knew that might improve their lives (cf., however, Oakley's [2000] reconsideration of the deeper gender assumptions underlying such dichotomies as qualitative and quantitative research). Stacey (1991) took this argument further, finding that fieldwork requires researchers to misrepresent themselves and to manipulate participants. Her second issue with a feminist ethnography is that the product, the ethnography, is a representation of participants and their lives that is ultimately controlled by the researcher. I elaborate on the latter concern in the next section.

In 1981, Oakley found the conventional research *relationship* unfeminist, but a decade later, Stacey questioned whether conventional research itself might be unfeminist (however, cf. Kirsch, 1999, pp. 42–43, for how the vagaries of ordinary relationships are inevitable in research relationships too, and Wolf, 1996, for how research conventions may be used to further feminist efforts in fieldwork). Between these positions are efforts of many feminist researchers to reform the exploitative hierarchy of the researcher and the researched, and these efforts have affected a generation of feminist practice (Romyn, 1996). Fisher (2000), for example, endorses a process that brings research participants into the moral decision making such that the ethics of any study may be considered not only by researchers and peer review boards, but also by those to be studied.

What happens when feminist researchers strive to put these policies of reciprocity into practice? As might be expected, this varies. Gatenby and Humphries (2000), in their PAR with Maori participants in higher education, report a level of success that may have been fostered by a study of women educating themselves in ways they themselves selected. Knight (2000) similarly engaged members of an education community to improve and to document their work with diverse communities and thus drew on participants' own aspirations in framing her research. On the other hand, Morris-Roberts (2001) was challenged to maintain equity in her relationships with the teenage girls she was studying when she began to observe some of them bullying others and felt impelled to intervene. In another study of young women, Morris, Woodward, and Peters (1998) also report being challenged for their affiliation among the participants in the study. These studies suggest that reducing the ethical tensions of unequal status may only open the way to the ethical dilemmas of living among peers. Choices in affiliation are complicated further when the researcher is operating across levels of institutional status, as Weinberg (2002) reports in a study of a facility for single mothers in Ontario. She was pressed to balance her allegiance between the female clients and the female staff. How ethical decisions may vary according to the differing interests of diverse research participants and the variety of contexts researchers may encounter is illustrated well by Vivat's (2002) ethnographic study of a hospice in Scotland; Vivat uses the notion of "situated ethics" as a contrast with a principle-based "detached ethics."

Robertson's (2000) study of bulimia among adult women indicates other issues when studying individuals from an assumed position of equity. First, as a recovered bulimic, she notes the researcher's care of self as part of a responsibility to protect everyone in a research endeavor, echoing both Gilligan's and Noddings's emphasis on self-care as an indication of maturity. Second, she found that sharing data and results with some participants put them at risk of psychological distress that contributing information had not. Third, a request from a participant to interview the researcher about her own experience with bulimia permitted Robertson a view of her ethical practice she had not previously had. Finally, like Patai (1991), Robertson emphasizes the ethical considerations in ending the research relationship. This is yet another power difference between researchers and their participants.

Intimate, equitable relationships pose ethical dilemmas that distant, hierarchical relationships may avoid (see Avis, 2002). Birch and Miller (2002) and Duncombe and Jessop (2002) report experiences with attempting to put their feminist principles into practice that indicate the pitfalls and hazards of all human relationships. Bingley (2002) suggests incorporating approaches from psychotherapy into research practice so as to better address these pitfalls and hazards. De Laine (2000) provides extensive examples of the assault on a researcher's psyche such difficulties create. Wolf (1996) discusses the disadvantages that fieldworkers who are members of a field community encounter because of the conflicts between their insider role and their researcher role and stresses what she considers as power differentials between researchers and participants that complicate friendships in the field. What all these examples suggest is that moving from a codified and principle-based set of ethical standards to an ethic of care does not resolve ethical dilemmas.

The principle-based ethics of respect for persons, beneficence, and justice helps researchers to consider those they are studying as fellow human beings with their own goals, priorities, and agendas. They aid feminist researchers, for example, in balancing feminist agendas with those claimed by the women we may be studying. What principle-based ethics do not do is address the situation-specific quality of human relationships and interactions. The ethic of care provides a systematic model for an engaged and reciprocal relationship with research participants. It gives us a set of priorities for decision making that takes into account the specifics of who we are while we study ourselves and our similar-to-different others (Gluck & Patai, 1991a). Nevertheless, feminist ethnographer Bell (1993), who summarizes her development over a period of years from a "naïve feminist empiricist stance" to an appreciation of how the politics of feminism and power differentials operate in field situations, cautions that "feminist ethnography opens a discursive space for the 'subjects' of the ethnography and as such is simultaneously empowering and destabilizing" (p. 31).

Although the ethic of care permits us to judge the quality of our researcher roles and human interactions in a research study, it does not eliminate our ethical dilemmas. The challenges of research remain, the asymmetries created by the different interests of researchers, participants, and even researcher-participants are inevitable, and unanticipated issues may plague researchers who have added new sets of expectations to their notions of ideal research practice. The principle of respect for persons that I discussed previously as guiding U.S. informed consent may be a less demanding ethical precept for research conduct than is the ethic of care, which demands that we acknowledge a relationship of whatever kind we seek. To the extent that an ethic of care becomes the major influence on our research conduct, our responsibilities are much greater (Gluck & Patai, 1991b). Publishing and otherwise presenting or disseminating the research adds to the levels of complexity in ethical decision making. I turn to this next.

## Ethics of Representation

The ethics of representation is the good or ill that results from how participants are represented in publications, presentations, and other reports of research. Feminists have a particular stake in the ethics of representation because of what many of us believe to have been misrepresentations of women and our experiences. The androcentric scholarship that feminist thinkers such as Code (1991, 1995) find so objectionable both ignores and distorts women's lives and views (cf. Richardson, 1997). Feminists have led the way in challenging how people are represented in the human and professional sciences. Will research participants be distressed when they learn how they are described, characterized, and interpreted? Will they agree with how they are represented? Will individuals be placed at risk from others in their situation or from the general public by how they are presented? Will other people—other teenagers, others suffering from bulimia, other single mothers, for example—face difficulties in their lives because of how those who share their attributes are represented?

The feminist ethic of care provides moral justification for the concern expressed by scholars such as Hopkins (1993) for relationships with research participants and for the desire to support their pride and avoid embarrassing them. Another ethical challenge to feminist representations is the assumption of homogeneity among women whose points of view and experiences vary considerably by race, ethnicity, class, religion, sexual orientation, and their ability-disability conditions. Having objected to being portrayed as no different than men in social science research, white women scholars have been challenged by scholars of color, by queer theorists, and by others with divergent points of view to honor, respect, and celebrate the diversity of women's experiences and views of the world (e.g., hooks, 1984; Lewin, 1995).

In a now-classic formulation about representing others in what we write and present about them, Fine (1994) struggles with the conventions, positioning, and hierarchies that produce a mostly offstage author writing a tidy image of players. The writing itself, who writes whom, creates imbalances in power and an inevitable "othering" of participants. Fine advocates addressing this issue by "working the hyphens." She does this by presenting material that defies stereotypes and conventional images of people,

material that critiques those who create these conventional images, and material that calls for direct action to rectify inequities. She struggles to address our multiple, interacting identities as women, individuals whose abilities, ethnic and racial backgrounds, religious affiliations, and sexual orientations vary. She advocates studying the powerful as well as the powerless.

Fine stresses that although our identities are fluid and changeable, they nevertheless associate us more with some in our communities than with others. These groups and affiliations can be caricatured and stereotyped in ways that hamper and hurt both individuals and communities. Even more important is positioning of self and other at what Fine calls "the hyphen." This metaphor invites the reader to reflect on the self as other and the other as self. How might I write differently about my experiences with my research participants if I write about "we" or if I write about an "I and thou" relationship? The ethics of relationships provide models of connections with those we study. These sources and the other strategies Fine suggests permit us to work the hyphen, to problematize rather than to assume the relationships between researcher and researched (cf. Alldred & Gillies, 2002). Thus, Robertson (2000) is working the hyphen when she agrees to be interviewed by a research participant about her own struggle with bulimia. Stacey (1991) works the hyphen by insisting that feminist ethnographers take responsibility for an ethically imperfect research practice.

Wolf's (1992) representation of a young mother's unconventional behavior in a village in Taiwan through three different genres—field notes, a conventional ethnographic report, and a short story—was intended to illustrate many of the complications of the ethics of representation. She discusses the "double responsibility" of "feminists doing research on women," responsible both to their women participants and to the broader world of women whose lives we hope to improve. She cautions that power is not merely held by researchers over participants but by participants who make their own decisions about what to share with, withhold from, or distort for investigators. Having shown the multiple and competing views of one woman's interactions with her neighbors, Wolf nevertheless worries about the academic consequences to feminist scholars of being forthright about acknowledging the power that participants may exert.

Some feminist researchers attempt to address the ethics of representation by limiting their studies to collaborative research or PAR or to such personal endeavors as autoethnography (Ellis, 2004) and experimental ethnography (Visweswaran, 1994). Others ask research participants to "vet" or otherwise edit or approve data and even interpretations that involve them. Disputed material may be omitted or disagreements about material may be included in reports. Reports and presentations may be composed so as to include multiple voices and commentators—researcher, researched, and other stakeholders (Blakeslee, Cole, & Conefrey, 1996). Researchers Kirsch (1999) and Mortensen and Kirsch (1996) examine the multiple ways researchers have struggled with the moral and ethical issues of representation and conclude that every alternative has its strengths and limitations.

In a study of women activists on both sides of the abortion debate, Ginsburg (1993) considers the issue of representation as broader than the particular individuals directly involved in her study; she uses the notion of polyphony, developed by the Russian literary scholar Mikhail Mikhailovich Bakhtin, to generate a multifaceted and heterogeneous presentation of her research. Zeni, Prophete, Cason, and Phillips (2001) similarly apply Collins's (1990) analysis of African American feminists to represent multiple perspectives held by individuals in diverse communities. In contrast, Mills (2002) finds the authentic representation of even a single individual to pose a challenge to the skills and knowledge of researchers—how to move from autobiography to biography in a way faithful and respectful of the subject. Jacobs (2004) recounts a different issue in representation in her study of the experiences of females during the Holocaust where the death of those she studies does not relieve her sense of ethical obligation to them. The tension expressed by all these researchers is underscored by their relationships to those they study. In representing their participants, they are also representing themselves and facets of themselves that they share with the participants. Similarity and difference merge, and the ethics of research become the ethics of everyday life.

## CONCLUSION

What I have tried to do in this chapter, first, is show the connections and disconnections between the Western approach to ethics developed in academic philosophy, especially as it applies to women, and the challenge to that ethics posed in the 20th century by feminist ethicists. Carol Gilligan and Nel Noddings challenged the privileging of principle-based decision making, and they reconceptualized moral theory to include the ethics of relation. Second, I have linked this to general research ethics as applied by many social scientists and to ethical practices developed among researchers using an explicitly feminist approach. Although many feminist researchers continue to be guided by such ethical principles as justice, most have integrated an ethic of care and relationship into their conduct of research. In this chapter, I have examined how these two frameworks play out in how we feminists formulate our research purposes, how we work with others in the research, and how we represent those we study in our research reports.

However, feminist ethics do not resolve moral dilemmas in research. Women studying women, about women or with women, for the purpose of relieving women's oppression and reconfiguring androcentric knowledge into a more inclusive understanding of "huwomanity," complicates the research process. This is the pattern attested to by many of the feminist researchers I have cited here. Feminist ethics likely generate as many issues as they may help either avoid or address. This is particularly evident in trading a detached, distant, and hierarchical stance for an intimate, close, and equitable position. Distance and intimacy create their own problems.

Even within sets of coherent guidelines lie troubling tensions. The feminist project is deeply grounded in the principle of justice. Women's rights have traditionally been justified by the values of equity and equality. The ethic of care and relationship does not preclude consideration of principle but may provide a parallel formulation of human rights and responsibilities to one another. Nevertheless, philosophers such as Jean Grimshaw (1991) caution feminists about the implications of claiming an ethics that may place women back into a gendered ghetto.

Similarly the conventional binaries of universal and particular, relativism and absolutism, objectivism and subjectivism, realism and idealism—like that of man and woman—may no longer adequately represent conceptual positions that admit subjectivity to objective study or locate categories of particulars as universals. Feminist ethicists (e.g., Held, 1987) and feminist epistemologists (e.g., Moody-Adams, 1997) are rejecting the view of ethical frameworks as either inevitably universal, absolute, objective, and real or alternatively particular, relative, subjective, and ideal. The ethics of relationship that Gilligan and Noddings have pioneered are grounded in the subjective, the particular, and the relative, but neither scholar denies the relevance of a universal principle like justice.

Likewise the formal and static roles once assumed in research designs have given way to circumstances where the researcher may research herself, where she may be researching others while others research her, or where research itself becomes part and parcel of everyday public and private life—no longer limited to the purview of an expert with esoteric training unavailable to ordinary people (see Benhabib, 1992). However, even with such an expansion and democratization of inquiry, ethical dilemmas and issues will still arise. Balancing the interests of individuals and communities is an ongoing human enterprise. Ameliorating old oppressions and preventing new forms of exploitation is a global endeavor. Satisfying what can be competing needs for knowledge of and action for the oppressed and exploited in situations where people disagree among themselves about what is happening to them makes ethical choices complex. Attending to both secular and sacred human interests when people dispute which of these should prevail is an ongoing challenge. What the ethics of relationship have added to the ethics of principle is a complementary framework that permits a different layer of consideration in these thorny difficulties.

## Notes

1. The American Psychological Association has also published an anthology on feminist ethics in psychology (Brabeck, 2000).

2. Noticeably missing from this list is the National Women's Studies Association (NWSA). NWSA does have an ethics policy (see www.nwsa .org/govern/policy.php#ethics, retrieved December 14, 2005), but it focuses on relationships among members and says nothing directly about research ethics.

## References

Acker, J., Barry, K., & Esseveld, J. (1991). Objectivity and truth: Problems in doing feminist research. In M. M. Fonow & J. A. Cook (Eds.), *Beyond methodology: Feminist scholarship as lived research* (pp. 133–153). Bloomington: Indiana University Press.

Alldred, P., & Gillies, V. (2002). Eliciting research accounts: Re/producing modern subjects? In M. Mauthner, M. Birch, J. Jessop, & T. Miller (Eds.), *Ethics in qualitative research* (pp. 146–165). London: Sage.

Allen, K. R., & Baber, K. M. (1992). Ethical and epistemological tensions in applying a postmodern perspective to feminist research. *Psychology of Women Quarterly, 16*(1), 1–15.

American Anthropological Association. (1998). *Code of ethics of the American Anthropological Association.* Retrieved December 14, 2005, from www.aaanet.org/committees/ethics/ethcode.htm

American Educational Research Association. (2000). *Ethical standards of AERA.* Retrieved December 14, 2005, from www.aera.net/about aera/?id=222

American Psychological Association. (2002). *Ethical principles of psychologists and code of conduct.* Retrieved December 14, 2005, from www.apa .org/ethics/code2002.html

American Sociological Association. (1997). *Code of ethics.* Retrieved December 14, 2005, from asanet .org/page.ww?section=Ethics&name=Ethics

Avis, H. (2002). Whose voice is that? Making space for subjectivities in interviews. In L. Bondi, H. Avis, R. Bankey, A. Bingley, J. Davidson, R. Duffy, et al. (Eds.), *Subjectivities, knowledges, and feminist geographies: The subjects and ethics of social research* (pp. 191–207). Lanham, MD: Rowman & Littlefield.

Barnbaum, D. R., & Byron, M. (2001). *Research ethics: Text and readings.* Upper Saddle River, NJ: Prentice Hall.

Bell, D. (1993). Yes, Virginia, there is a feminist ethnography: Reflections from three Australian fields. In D. Bell, P. Caplan, & W. J. Karim (Eds.), *Gendered fields: Women, men and ethnography* (pp. 28–43). London: Routledge.

Benhabib, S. (1992). *Situating the self: Gender, community and postmodernism in contemporary ethics.* New York: Routledge.

Bingley, A. (2002). Research ethics in practice. In L. Bondi, H. Avis, R. Bankey, A. Bingley, J. Davidson, R. Duffy, et al. (Eds.), *Subjectivities, knowledges, and feminist geographies: The subjects and ethics of social research* (pp. 208–222). Lanham, MD: Rowman & Littlefield.

Birch, M., & Miller, T. (2002). Encouraging participation: Ethics and responsibilities. In M. Mauthner, M. Birch, J. Jessop, & T. Miller (Eds.), *Ethics in qualitative research* (pp. 91–106). London: Sage.

Blakeslee, A. M., Cole, C. M., & Conefrey, T. (1996). Constructing voices in writing research: Developing participatory approaches to situated inquiry. In P. Mortensen & G. E. Kirsch (Eds.), *Ethics and representation in qualitative studies of literacy* (pp. 134–154). Washington, DC: National Council of Teachers of English.

Bloom, L. R. (1998). *Under the sign of hope: Feminist methodology and narrative interpretation.* Albany: State University of New York Press.

Bordo, S. R. (1987). *The flight to objectivity: Essays on Cartesianism and culture.* Albany: State University of New York Press.

Brabeck, M. M. (Ed.). (1989). *Who cares? Theory, research, and educational implications of the ethic of care.* New York: Praeger.

Brabeck, M. M. (Ed.). (2000). *Practicing feminist ethics in psychology.* Washington, DC: American Psychological Association.

Butler, J. (1990). *Gender trouble: Feminism and the subversion of identity.* New York: Routledge.

Chodorow, N. (1978). *The reproduction of mothering: Psychoanalysis and the sociology of gender.* Berkeley: University of California Press.

Code, L. (1991). *What can she know? Feminist theory and the construction of knowledge.* Ithaca, NY: Cornell University Press.

Code, L. (1995). How do we know? Questions of method in feminist practice. In S. Burt & L. Code (Eds.), *Changing methods: Feminists transforming*

*practice* (pp. 13–44). Peterborough, Ontario, Canada: Broadview Press.

Colby, A., & Kohlberg, L. (1987). *The measurement of moral judgment: Vol. 1. Theoretical foundations and research validation.* Cambridge, UK: Cambridge University Press.

Collins, P. H. (1990). *Black feminist thought: Knowledge, consciousness, and the politics of empowerment.* London: HarperCollinsAcademic.

Daly, M. C. (1978). *Gyn/ecology, the metaethics of radical feminism.* Boston: Beacon Press.

de Laine, M. (2000). *Fieldwork, participation and practice: Ethics and dilemmas in qualitative research.* London: Sage.

DeVault, M. L. (1999). *Liberating method: Feminism and social research.* Philadelphia: Temple University Press.

Doucet, A., & Mauthner, N. (2002). Knowing responsibly: Linking ethics, research practice and epistemology. In M. Mauthner, M. Birch, J. Jessop, & T. Miller (Eds.), *Ethics in qualitative research* (pp. 123–145). London: Sage.

Du Bois, B. (1983). Passionate scholarship: Notes on values, knowing and method in feminist social science. In G. Bowles & R. D. Klien (Eds.), *Theories of women's studies* (pp. 105–116). London: Routledge & Kegan Paul.

Duncombe, J., & Jessop, J. (2002). "Doing rapport" and the ethics of "faking friendship." In M. Mauthner, M. Birch, J. Jessop, & T. Miller (Eds.), *Ethics in qualitative research* (pp. 107–122). London: Sage.

Edwards, R., & Mauthner, M. (2002). Ethics and feminist research: Theory and practice. In M. Mauthner, M. Birch, J. Jessop, & T. Miller (Eds.), *Ethics in qualitative research* (pp. 14–31). London: Sage.

Eichler, M. (1988). *Nonsexist research methods: A practical guide.* New York: Routledge.

Ellis, C. (2004). *The ethnographic I: A methodological novel about autoethnography.* Thousand Oaks, CA: Sage.

England, K. V. L. (1994). Getting personal: Reflexivity, positionality, and feminist research. *Professional Geographer, 46*(1), 80–89.

Erikson, E. H. (1968). *Identity: Youth and crisis.* New York: Norton.

Fine, M. (1992). *Disruptive voices: The possibilities of feminist research.* Ann Arbor: University of Michigan Press.

Fine, M. (1994). Working the hyphens: Reinventing self and other in qualitative research. In N. K. Denzin & Y. S. Lincoln (Eds.), *The handbook of qualitative research* (pp. 70–82). Thousand Oaks, CA: Sage.

Fisher, C. B. (2000). Relational ethics in psychological research: One feminist's journey. In M. M. Brabeck (Ed.), *Practicing feminist ethics in psychology* (pp. 125–142). Washington, DC: American Psychological Association.

Fonow, M. M., & Cook, J. A. (1991). Back to the future: A look at the second wave of feminist epistemology and methodology. In M. M. Fonow & J. A. Cook (Eds.), *Beyond methodology: Feminist scholarship as lived research* (pp. 1–15). Bloomington: Indiana University Press.

Fuss, D. (1989). *Essentially speaking: Feminism, nature & difference.* New York: Routledge.

Gatenby, B., & Humphries, M. (2000). Feminist participatory action research: Methodological and ethical issues. *Women's Studies International Forum, 23*(1), 89–105.

Gillies, V., & Alldred, P. (2002). The ethics of intention: Research as a political tool. In M. Mauthner, M. Birch, J. Jessop, & T. Miller (Eds.), *Ethics in qualitative research* (pp. 32–52). London: Sage.

Gilligan, C. (1982). *In a different voice: Psychological theory and women's development.* Cambridge, MA: Harvard University Press.

Ginsburg, F. (1993). The case of mistaken identity: Problems in representing women on the right. In C. B. Brettell (Ed.), *When they read what we write: The politics of ethnography* (pp. 163–176). Westport, CT: Bergin & Garvey.

Gluck, S. B., & Patai, D. (1991a). Introduction. In S. B. Gluck & D. Patai (Eds.), *Women's words: The feminist practice of oral history* (pp. 1–5). New York: Routledge.

Gluck, S. B., & Patai, D. (1991b). Part I: Language and communication. In S. B. Gluck & D. Patai (Eds.), *Women's words: The feminist practice of oral history* (p. 9). New York: Routledge.

Goetz, J. P. (1978). Theoretical approaches to the study of sex-role culture in schools. *Anthropology and Education Quarterly, 9*(1), 3–21.

Goetz, J. P., & Grant, L. (1988). Conceptual approaches to studying gender in education. *Anthropology and Education Quarterly, 19*(2), 182–196.

Gowaty, P. A. (1997). Sexual dialectics, sexual selection, and variation in mating behavior. In P. A. Gowaty (Ed.), *Feminism and evolutionary biology* (pp. 351–384). New York: Chapman & Hall.

Grimshaw, J. (1991). The idea of a female ethic. In P. Singer (Ed.), *A companion to ethics* (pp. 491–499). Oxford, UK: Blackwell.

Grossman, F. K., Gilbert, L. A., Genero, N. P., Hawes, S. E., Hyde, J. S., & Maracek, J. (1997). Feminist research: Practice and problems. In J. Worell & N. G. Johnson (Eds.), *Shaping the future of feminist psychology: Education, research, and practice* (pp. 73–91). Washington, DC: American Psychological Association.

Haraway, D. (1989). *Primate visions: Gender, race, and nature in the world of modern science.* New York: Routledge.

Harding, S. (1987). Conclusion: Epistemological questions. In S. Harding (Ed.), *Feminism and methodology: Social science issues* (pp. 181–190). Bloomington: Indiana University Press.

Harding, S. (1998). *Is science multicultural? Postcolonialisms, feminisms, and epistemologies.* Bloomington: Indiana University Press.

Harding, S. (2004). Introduction: Standpoint theory as a site of political, philosophical, and scientific debate. In S. Harding (Ed.), *The feminist standpoint theory reader: Intellectual and political controversies* (pp. 1–15). New York: Routledge.

Harmon, W. W. (1996). The shortcomings of Western science. *Qualitative Inquiry, 2*(1), 30–38.

Held, V. (1987). Feminism and moral theory. In E. F. Kittay & D. T. Meyers (Eds.), *Women and moral theory* (pp. 111–128). Totowa, NJ: Rowman & Littlefield.

Hesse-Biber, S. N., & Leckenby, D. (2004). How feminists practice social research. In S. N. Hesse-Biber & M. L. Yaiser (Eds.), *Feminist perspectives on social research* (pp. 209–226). New York: Oxford University Press.

hooks, b. (1984). *Feminist theory: From margin to center.* Boston: South End Press.

Hopkins, M. C. (1993). Is anonymity possible? Writing about refugees in the United States. In C. B. Brettell (Ed.), *When they read what we write: The politics of ethnography* (pp. 121–129). Westport, CT: Bergin & Garvey.

Jacobs, J. L. (2004). Women, genocide, and memory: The ethics of feminist ethnography in Holocaust research. *Gender & Society, 18*(2), 223–238.

Jones, J. (1981). *Bad blood: The Tuskegee syphilis experiment: A tragedy of race and medicine.* New York: Free Press.

Kirsch, G. E. (1999). *Ethical dilemmas in feminist research: The politics of location, interpretation, and publication.* Albany: State University of New York Press.

Knight, M. G. (2000). Ethics in qualitative research: Multicultural feminist activist research. *Theory Into Practice, 39*(3), 170–176.

Kohlberg, L. (1981). *Essays on moral development: Vol. 1. The philosophy of moral development: Moral stages and the idea of justice.* New York: Harper & Row.

Lather, P. (1991). *Getting smart: Feminist research and pedagogy with/in the postmodern.* New York: Routledge.

Levinson, D. J. (1978). *The seasons of a man's life.* New York: Knopf.

Lewin, E. (1995). Writing lesbian ethnography. In R. Behar & D. A. Gordon (Eds.), *Women writing culture* (pp. 322–335). Berkeley: University of California Press.

Lloyd, G. (1996). The man of reason. In A. Garry & M. Pearsall (Eds.), *Women, knowledge, and reality: Explorations in feminist philosophy* (pp. 149–165). New York: Routledge.

Longino, H. (1994). Gender and racial biases in scientific research. In K. Shrader-Frechette (Ed.), *Ethics of scientific research* (pp. 139–151). Lanham, MD: Rowman & Littlefield.

Martin, J. R. (1985). *Reclaiming a conversation: The ideal of the educated woman.* New Haven, CT: Yale University Press.

Massat, C. R., & Lundy, M. (1997). Empowering research participants. *Affilia: Journal of Women and Social Work, 12*(1), 33–56.

McGraw, L. A., Zvonkovic, A. M., & Walker, A. J. (2000). Studying postmodern families: A feminist analysis of ethical tensions in work and family research. *Journal of Marriage and Family, 62*(1), 68–77.

Mills, E. (2002). Hazel the dental assistant and the research dilemma of (re)presenting a life story: The clash of narratives. In W. C. van den Hoonaard (Ed.), *Walking the tightrope: Ethical issues for qualitative researchers* (pp. 107–123). Toronto, Ontario, Canada: University of Toronto Press.

Moody-Adams, M. M. (1997). *Fieldwork in familiar places: Morality, culture, and philosophy.* Cambridge, MA: Harvard University Press.

Morris, K., Woodward, D., & Peters, E. (1998). "Whose side are you on?" Dilemmas in conducting feminist ethnographic research with young women. *Social Research Methodology, 1*(3), 217–230.

Morris-Roberts, K. (2001). Intervening in friendship exclusion? The politics of doing feminist research with teenage girls. *Ethics, Place & Environment, 4*(2), 147–153.

Mortensen, P., & Kirsch, G. E. (Eds.). (1996). *Ethics and representation in qualitative studies of literacy.* Washington, DC: National Council of Teachers of English.

Naples, N. A. (2003). *Feminism and method: Ethnography, discourse analysis, and activist research.* New York: Routledge.

National Commission for the Protection of Human Subjects of Medical and Behavioral Research. (1979). *The Belmont report: Ethical principles and guidelines for the protection of human subjects of research.* Retrieved December 14, 2005, from ohsr.od.nih.gov/guidelines/belmont.html. Washington, DC: Department of Health, Education, and Welfare.

National Research Council. (2003). *Protecting participants and facilitating social and behavioral sciences research.* Washington, DC: Author.

Noddings, N. (1984). *Caring: A feminine approach to ethics & moral education.* Berkeley: University of California Press.

Noddings, N. (2003). *Caring: A feminine approach to ethics & moral education* (2nd ed.). Berkeley: University of California Press.

Oakley, A. (1981). Interviewing women: A contradiction in terms. In H. Roberts (Ed.), *Doing feminist research* (pp. 30–61). London: Routledge & Kegan Paul.

Oakley, A. (2000). *Experiments in knowing: Gender and method in the social sciences.* New York: New Press.

Paradis, E. K. (2000). Feminist and community psychology ethics in research with homeless women. *American Journal of Community Psychology, 28*(6), 839–858.

Patai, D. (1991). U.S. academics and Third World women: Is ethical research possible? In S. B. Gluck & D. Patai (Eds.), *Women's words: The feminist practice of oral history* (pp. 137–153). New York: Routledge.

Reason, P. (1996). Reflections on the purposes of human inquiry. *Qualitative Inquiry, 2*(1), 15–28.

Reinharz, S. (1992). *Feminist methods in social research.* New York: Oxford University Press.

Richardson, L. (1997). *Field of play: Constructing an academic life.* New Brunswick, NJ: Rutgers University Press.

Robertson, J. (2000). Ethical issues and researching sensitive topics: Mature women and "bulimia." *Feminism and Psychology, 10*(4), 531–537.

Roman, L. G., & Apple, M. W. (1990). Is naturalism a move away from positivism? Materialist and feminist approaches to subjectivity in ethnographic research. In E. W. Eisner & A. Peshkin (Eds.), *Qualitative inquiry in education: The continuing debate* (pp. 38–73). New York: Teachers College Press.

Romyn, D. M. (1996). Problems inherent in the epistemology and methodologies of feminist research. In J. F. Kikuchi, H. Simmons, & D. Romyn (Eds.), *Truth in nursing inquiry* (pp. 140–149). Thousand Oaks, CA: Sage.

Seibold, C. (2000). Qualitative research from a feminist perspective in the postmodern era: Methodological, ethical and reflexive concerns. *Nursing Inquiry, 7*(3), 147–155.

Seigfried, C. H. (1996). *Pragmatism and feminism: Reweaving the social fabric.* Chicago: University of Chicago Press.

Sexton, P. C. (1976). *Women in education.* Bloomington, IN: Phi Delta Kappa Educational Foundation.

Skelton, T. (2001). Girls in the club: Researching working class girls' lives. *Ethics, Place, and Environment, 4*(2), 167–173.

Smith, D. E. (1987). *The everyday world as problematic: A feminist sociology.* Boston: Northeastern University Press.

Stacey, J. (1991). Can there be a feminist ethnography? In S. B. Gluck & D. Patai (Eds.), *Women's words: The feminist practice of oral history* (pp. 111–119). New York: Routledge.

Stanley, L., & Wise, S. (1993). *Breaking out again: Feminist ontology and epistemology.* London: Routledge.

Tolman, D. L., & Brydon-Miller, M. (Eds.). (2001). *From subjects to subjectivities: A handbook of interpretive and participatory methods.* New York: New York University Press.

Tong, R. (1993). *Feminine and feminist ethics.* Belmont, CA: Wadsworth.

Tong, R. (1998). *Feminist thought: A more comprehensive introduction* (2nd ed.). Boulder, CO: Westview Press.

Traina, C. L. H. (1999). *Feminist ethics and natural law: The end of the anathemas.* Washington, DC: Georgetown University Press.

Visweswaran, K. (1994). *Fictions of feminist ethnography.* Minneapolis: University of Minnesota Press.

Vivat, B. (2002). Situated ethics and feminist ethnography in a west of Scotland hospice. In L. Bondi, H. Avis, R. Bankey, A. Bingley, J. Davidson, R. Duffy, et al. (Eds.), *Subjectivities, knowledges, and feminist geographies: The subjects and ethics of social research* (pp. 236–252). Lanham, MD: Rowman & Littlefield.

Waage, J., & Gowaty, P. A. (1997). Myths of genetic determinism. In P. A. Gowaty, (Ed.), *Feminism and evolutionary biology* (pp. 585–613). New York: Chapman & Hall.

War Crimes Tribunal. (1947). *The Nuremberg code.* Retrieved December 14, 2005, from www.hhs .gov/ohrp/references/nurcode.htm

Weinberg, M. (2002). Biting the hand that feeds you, and other feminist dilemmas in fieldwork. In W. C. van den Hoonaard (Ed.), *Walking the tightrope: Ethical issues for qualitative researchers* (pp. 79–94). Toronto, Ontario, Canada: University of Toronto Press.

Wolf, D. L. (1996). Situating feminist dilemmas in fieldwork. In D. L. Wolf (Ed.), *Feminist dilemmas in fieldwork* (pp. 1–55). Boulder, CO: Westview Press.

Wolf, M. (1992). *A thrice told tale: Feminism, postmodernism, and ethnographic responsibility.* Stanford, CA: Stanford University Press.

World Medical Association. (1975). *World Medical Association declaration of Helsinki: Ethical principles for medical research involving human subjects.* Retrieved December 14, 2005, from www .wma.net/e/policy/b3.htm

Zeni, J., Prophete, M., Cason, N., & Phillips, M. (2001). The ethics of cultural invisibility. In J. Zeni (Ed.), *Ethical issues in practitioner research* (pp. 113–112). New York: Teachers College Press.

# PART IV

Commentaries on Future
Directions in Feminist Theory,
Research, and Pedagogy

# 27

# DIALOGUING ABOUT FUTURE DIRECTIONS IN FEMINIST THEORY, RESEARCH, AND PEDAGOGY

SHARLENE NAGY HESSE-BIBER

From its inception, feminist theory and research practices sought to disrupt, modify, and trouble dominant categories of theorizing and the practices of research inquiry. Part IV of this *Handbook* provides a space for dialogue around some unresolved feminist dilemmas in knowledge building. We address some of the tough questions and issues within the feminist community of knowledge builders and examine future directions of feminist theorizing and research for and about women and other oppressed groups. In addition, we explore pedagogical lessons and insights from the women's studies classroom.

Part IV of this *Handbook* is not necessarily a place where feminists are in agreement. There are many points of disagreement, sometimes contentious, at other times conciliatory, and at some points expressions of outright disdain for those who disagree with the other's point of view. Part IV contains only a *few* of the many feminist voices at the center and at the margins of discourse on knowledge building.

## DIALOGUE VERSUS DISCUSSION: WHAT'S THE DIFFERENCE?

To dialogue means to "invite in" ideas and interactions regarding points of view, to lay bare one's thinking about an issue and be willing to change course, be ready to make discoveries—be willing to entertain multiple points of view, not just similarities, but also differences. To discuss, on the other hand, means to defend a position, not listen to others but argue for a specific point of view, defend one's turf, state definitive conclusions, debate to hold to a position with the object of "winning."

Bell hooks (1994) stresses the importance of dialogue and describes it as "one of the simplest ways we can begin as teachers, scholars, and critical thinkers to cross boundaries, the barriers that may or may not be erected by race, gender, class, professional standing, and a host of other differences" (p. 130). Through dialoguing, we express our beliefs and uncertainties, as well as gain better insight into other viewpoints.

Dialogue's purpose is not necessarily to shift our beliefs, but to shift our mode of communication by creating conversational practices that prevent unnecessary and destructive debate, and instead foster a constructive exchange of ideas and collaboration.

To gain legitimacy for knowledge within the feminist community of theory and practice means an openness to critique. To what extent are feminists responsive to each other's versions of reality? To what extent do feminists envision themselves as a community of knowledge builders? And to what extent are these communities inclusive of differing points of view?

The goal in Part IV of this *Handbook* is to harness the wisdom within the feminist community of theory building and praxis through dialogue. Bell hooks (1994) articulates the sentiments of women's studies students who come to their classes only to find that the articles they read do not connect to their own lived experiences:

> Students most of whom are female, come to Women's studies classes and read what they are told is feminist theory only to feel that what they are reading has no meaning, cannot be understood, only when understood in no way connects to "lived" realities beyond the classroom. (pp. 64–65)

Dialoguing then becomes a means to empower the field of feminist research, by drawing on the strengths of its diversity—not to divide but to unite feminists in their quest to uncover the reality of oppression, and to produce more authentic and trustworthy research that can lead to the betterment of society.

## Entry Points for Dialoguing

**Conundrum #1.** Can feminists advocate for a feminist methodology without compromising on some of the basic tenets of scientific knowledge: truth, reason, and logic? Does practicing a feminist methodology mean one gives up on the practice of science? Is a feminist epistemic community possible?

We begin Part IV of this *Handbook* with several feminist views as to whether or not a feminist

epistemology helps or hinders our understanding of women's concerns and issues; and subsequently, we look at the prospects of the viability of a feminist epistemic community. Helen Longino's chapter, "Reason, Truth, and Experience: Tyrannies or Liberation?" states that while there is no one feminist epistemology, feminists engage with concepts of truth, rationality, and experience in the service of women.

In an earlier work, Longino (1989) asserts that science does not operate within a value-free environment; it is impossible for science, what she terms "constitutive values," to block the influence of "contextual values," those that are part of the sociocultural environment. She further notes: "Scientific inquiry takes place in a social, political and economic context which imposes a variety of institutional obstacles to innovation, let alone to the intellectual working out of oppositional and political commitments" (p. 55). Constitutive values reflect what research questions we ask and what questions become priorities for us. Longino suggests that we can choose our communities of knowledge building. In her words, "We can continue to do establishment science, comfortably wrapped in the myths of scientific rhetoric or we can alter our intellectual allegiances" (p. 54). For Longino, knowledge is based within a community of scholars, not individual scientists, and reflects a community's set of assumptions and norms. To get an understanding from this perspective on science demands that each science be open to self-reflection from its community. In a later work, Longino (2002) lays out specific norms of operation of communities of knowledge building as they go about their discussions: "There must be publicly recognized forums for the criticism of evidence, of methods, and of assumptions and reasoning" (p. 129). "There must be uptake for criticism" (p. 129). "There must be publicly recognized standards by reference to which theories, hypotheses, and observational practices are evaluated and by appeal to which criticism is made relevant to the goals of the inquiring community" (p. 130). "Communities must be characterized by equality of intellectual authority" (p. 131).

Feminist philosopher Noretta Koertge, on the other hand, argues that there is a definite detriment to taking on an epistemology that claims to be feminist (this volume). In her view, feminist epistemologists have given in too easily to the idea that science is "underdetermined," and by doing so, they invite bias into the scientific enterprise from the start. She notes that practicing a feminist epistemology fosters among feminists a "suspicion of logic and science." She is against an epistemology that borders on advocating a "feminist science."

For Longino (this volume), science becomes a "critical engagement with philosophical questions about knowledge in light of commitment to one or more of a family of positions claimed as feminist." According to Longino, feminists do not throw out reason and logic, truth or experience. These still remain at the center of feminist inquiry. For Longino, the heart of a feminist epistemology lies in the questions feminists engage in that make their epistemology feminist.

Yet there remain some thorny issues for feminist theorists to ponder. It is here that I believe there is common ground for Longino and Koertge to dialogue about. They both hold out the perspective that science must search for truth, rationality, and logic in the research process. However, Longino (this volume) is also aware of how pursuit of truth within science has, at times, also served to "delegitimize women's cognitive abilities and performances." Koertge is critical of how feminists' use of epistemologies has been detrimental in the other direction, with the practices of some feminists undermining women's concerns and issues.

Helen Longino's concept of an *epistemic community* becomes relevant to this discussion. What is the scholarly community of science that feminist epistemology is embedded in? That traditional science is embedded in? In terms of theorists like Émile Durkheim, a major proponent of the scientific method and advocate of the practice of "rules" for sociological methods, we might ask: Where is the community of knowledge builders that agrees on these rules and why? Under what conditions do these rules apply in practice? Not apply? If there are abstract laws that science seeks to understand, who determines what laws are given priority in our search?

Noretta Koertge finds that one hopeful sign within the community of feminist epistemologists is the distinction that they make between "feminist science" and "doing science as a feminist." She prefers the latter term, however, as she states that her ultimate "goal would be to simply have 'feminists doing science.'"

Alison Wylie's chapter "The Feminism Question in Science: What Does It Mean to 'Do Social Science as a Feminist?'" takes us through the tensions within the community of feminist science building. Wylie is interested in exploring what it means "to do science as a feminist." She acknowledges the reservations Noretta Koertge grapples with and notes, "The anxiety that haunts these discussions is that if research is guided by explicitly feminist values, its epistemic credibility is irrevocably compromised." What Wylie provides in her commentary is a set of specific practices that counters this concern. She also discusses some exemplary examples of how feminists have addressed these epistemic concerns. Additionally, she believes a reformulation of standpoint theory can also serve to counteract these critiques of feminist inquiry, by suggesting that new formulations of feminist standpoint can be a "pivotal" tool by providing a "transformative critique." Feminist standpoint's emphasis on "situated knowledge" provides a location from which to access differences in our "strengths and liabilities . . . as epistemic agents."

Nancy Naples's commentary provides important insights in understanding why standpoint epistemologies, in particular those "embodied standpoints of subordinates[, are] powerful . . . [and] can help transform traditional categories of analyses that originate from dominant groups." She notes that what is most characteristic about standpoint theory's approach is its dialogic process. She states, "Given standpoint theory's emphasis on a process of dialogue, analysis, and reflexivity, the approach has proven extremely vibrant and open to reassessment and revision."

Liz Stanley and Sue Wise's "Commentary: Using Feminist Fractured Foundationalism in Researching Children in the Concentration Camps of the South African War (1899– 1902)" (this volume) urges feminists to examine the feminist epistemology in research practice. They are concerned that debates and arguments have been "bogged down in reformulations of abstract ideas and debates about epistemology rather than exploring new developments in practice." It is the praxis that reveals how feminism interacts with the scientific method. They develop a framework for "grounded feminist research practice" termed *"feminist fractured foundationalism* (FFF)." This term recognizes that all research is situated in a social/economic political context. FFF is a set of research procedures, in their words, "a set of procedural strategies that enable research conceptualisation, grounded research practices, writing about research data, and theorising from these, to be brought together and thought about as a coherent whole."

Stanley and Wise provide an in-depth example of FFF in practice by unearthing the lived experience of children residing in concentration camps during the South African War (1899–1902), basing their research on archival data. Their goal was to focus primarily on children "because previous research has looked at the war and the camps from the perspective of adults, even though the overwhelming majority of those who died were children." They conclude that using an FFF framework made researchers more accountable "for the what and how and why of our research practices." In addition, applying an FFF framework provided "a very powerful incentive to make what we were doing as accountable as possible." An FFF framework also allowed them a means for "bringing into focus the most vulnerable and least powerful . . . this is children." Using an FFF framework also had it drawbacks: "There were also times when we experienced the FFF framework as overly constraining . . . we were left wondering whether we had written about the most important things about the research."

Feminist research must continue to challenge conventional ideas about what constitutes knowledge building while dealing with the tensions and dilemmas they will confront within their pursuit of partial truths. Knowledge building is a "messy" operation, but it is within and between these partial truths that we come to a greater understanding of the diversity of women's lived experiences.

**Conundrum #2.** What does acknowledging difference mean to feminist researchers? Does embracing difference mean there is no identity politics for women? What are the consequences of embracing difference for research praxis? How do feminist researchers engage with issues of difference in their research and activist pursuits without losing the power of a gendered analysis?

The 1980s and 1990s were characterized by a turn toward difference among feminist researchers:

> Feminists working in and across many disciplines began developing new ways of thinking about, writing about, and researching women and their lives. For example, in the late 1980s and early 1990s, sociologist Patricia Hill Collins . . . began uncovering black women's subjugated knowledge when she created a black women's epistemological standpoint she termed the "outsider within." With this epistemology she criticized the white middle-class feminists who overgeneralized without reference to the diversity of women's lives. (Hesse-Biber & Yaiser, 2004, p. 101)

Early efforts on the part of feminists to conceptualize difference served more to stereotype and generalize "the other." In the introduction to their volume *Feminist Approaches to Theory and Methodology*, Hesse-Biber, Gilmartin, and Lydenberg (1999) comment on this aspect of the difference conundrum as follows:

> Efforts to represent difference . . . often fell into stereotypes and generalizations that . . . obscured the specificity of difference. Mohanty describes, for example, the "discursive colonization" by which "material and historical heterogeneities" of third-world women's experiences were lost in Western feminists' construction of a "composite, singular Third World Woman." (pp. 4–5)

The postmodern turn (e.g., Butler, 1993) transformed our understanding of the category of gender as socially constructed, not a fixed category of analysis, and brought feminists face-to-face with the political aspects of embracing difference: If feminists cannot accept that the category of gender is based on women's lived experience, then what is the "'essence' of feminist praxis" (see Hesse-Biber et al., 1999, p. 4)?

The authors who address Conundrum #2 find common ground with each other in acknowledging the importance of difference in understanding women's lives and underscore their concerns about how to bridge the divide between theory and praxis of difference; but there is some contention around how best to do this.

We start off with Diane Reay's chapter, "Future Directions in Difference Research: Recognising and Responding to Difference." Reay suggests that the current challenge of feminism in the 21st century is in finding ways to embrace diversity without abandoning the category of "gender." She advocates feminists continue to move toward new conceptualizations of difference. In her words, "The challenge is to build towards an understanding of the complex of differences as both a set of dynamic relationships and operating within specific contexts." Reay also stresses that for the past several decades feminist research did not deal with issues of class as an important difference within social research. As Reay notes, class is a primary division of understanding women's lives, comparable to difference issues along gender and race as well as sexual preference.

While Reay draws attention to the issue of class, she also cautions against the old "additive model of addressing difference" and argues that feminist research must consider the context of difference because "different differences are stressed or muted depending on the social context." She provides some important examples of research praxis that take account of social class in addition to other differences that matter— such as ethnicity, sexuality, and age—and provides us with some specific practices that support dealing with differences in theory and practice. Reay offers what she calls the "3Rs" approach to feminist research: "recognition, respect, and response." Recognition of difference requires "feminist vigilance" of those differences within ourselves. Reflexivity is the process that the researcher uses to reevaluate her or his own standpoint. A larger response, however, is required of academic researchers to bridge the theory and praxis divide, and that is for them to become activists within the academy by pushing for continued diversity within the academic community of feminist scholars.

Michelle Fine's chapter, "Feminist Designs for Difference," provides yet another avenue for bridging the divide between theory and praxis of difference. Unlike Diane Reay's emphasis on the "3Rs," she asserts that the roots to conceptualizing

and practicing difference are through participatory action research (PAR) projects (see also the chapter by Lykes & Coquillon, in Part II of this volume). Fine notes:

> PAR projects document the grounds for collective dissent and collective desires by creating a process for pooling "private" troubles among very different women and revealing their common, public roots. . . . PAR shatters the false consensus of complicity by interrogating and denaturalizing the conditions of everyday oppression.

Michelle Fine presents snapshots of her 4-year longitudinal research work on the impact of college on women in prisons and their children as well as prison personnel (officers), in addition to postrelease outcomes for these women. She stresses the importance of dialoguing across differences, and in practicing PAR, she is aware of the "chasm between feminist theorizing and practice" of difference research and notes:

> As powerful as PAR has been . . . fantasies of our collective freedom to study, write, and speak were naive. We were reminded frequently that the prisoners were always more vulnerable than we were as outsiders . . . in the praxis "gap" lie the bodies and vulnerabilities of those most oppressed.

Katherine Borland's chapter, "Decolonizing Approaches to Feminist Research: The Case of Feminist Ethnography," offers yet another point of dialogue to address how to acknowledge difference in the research process. Like Diane Reay, she stresses the need to use a dynamic and fluid conceptual framework of difference and also the need for self-reflectivity on the part of the researcher. She is particularly interested in the issue of representation of the other in the research process and takes up how the researcher's authority affects interpretation, especially as this pertains to the practice of feminist ethnography. She provides a series of research examples and a number of very useful guideposts that ethnographers can use in decolonizing their research practices. In particular, Borland reverses the problem of difference from the researcher's gaze on the field back onto herself. She employs difference to practice critical self-reflection and interrogation on one's privilege and authority and its effect on how we research and represent those whom we claim we are "speaking for."

Bonnie Thornton Dill, Amy McLaughlin, and Angel David Nieves's commentary, "Future Directions of Feminist Research: Intersectionality" (this volume), advocates an "intersectional" approach to knowledge building, which takes into account how differences such as race, class, and gender "combine to create new and distinct social, cultural, and artistic forms." To get at the fluid nature of difference, in terms of its multidimensionality—the fact that the individual occupies both a privileged and an oppressed positionality—the authors provide a specific history of the growth of intersectional research and note that there is a paradigm shift taking place in higher education that is especially prevalent in "the field of identity studies, work that engages with globalization/transnationalism(s), sexualities/ queer studies, and new ways of linking theory and practice." They discuss issues in conducting research within an intersectional paradigm, and among these is the problem of authenticity and representation, as well as the lack of commitment on the part of some academic institutions to embrace intersectional research. Like Helen Longino, Bonnie Thornton Dill and her colleagues call for participation in a "community" of knowledge building in order to transform traditional ways of knowing to incorporate issues of difference and social justice. An "intersectional" perspective sees interdisciplinary scholarship as a key way to restructure academic knowledge building. These authors note that more work must focus on

> the historical and geographical context of events, attitudes, and cultures, and work that breaks out of the academic mold to join forces with the communities whose internal knowledge is indispensable to the project. Thus, this scholarship has the capability to transform rigid boundaries between departments, between universities and their neighboring communities, and, in general, what is viewed as valid and worthy of support in the academy and what is not.

The movement toward intersectionality requires a deep change in current course curricula as well as academic transformation on the part of key faculty toward making a commitment to interdisciplinary scholarship "by founding and leading intersectionally oriented research centers."

Kum-Kum Bhavnani's chapter, "Interconnections and Configurations: Toward A Global Feminist Ethnography," is in agreement that difference must be a central concept in our understanding of women's experiences and takes up Diane Reay's challenge to feminists to "work toward new conceptual frameworks" for understanding difference. Bhavnani's chapter starts out with the question of "whether feminism can ever be more than critique." She believes, like Katherine Borland, that feminist praxis must make women's experiences visible and audible by specifically focusing on issues of representation. She notes that we must ask:

> Which women's lives are being analyzed, interrogated, and even evaluated? In which parts of the world? Which aspects of their lives? Which voices? Who edits the documentation? And, indeed, are there any continuities in the lived experiences of women across class, region, nation, sexuality, and race/ethnicity?

Bhavnani is particularly concerned that we expand our vision of difference to include global differences. Bhavnani seeks to reconceptualize difference within a global context by offering a global feminist ethnographic approach she terms "Women, Culture, Development (WCD)." She conceptualizes difference as "interconnections" across "axes of difference/inequality" that provide women with agency and a dialogic perspective by promoting active listening across these differences, such that the full range of women's lived experiences is taken into account, particularly as this pertains to the study of women and global issues. She provides some in-depth exemplary studies that begin to capture a "transnational" perspective on women and development, by stressing that oppression cannot be understood locally; feminists need to step out of their microlocation to observe the macrolinkages that traverse cultures, nationalities, and geographical space. Kum-Kum Bhavnani's commentary on difference provides an important perspective on and segue into the issue of difference in a global context, which is the subject of Conundrum #3.

**Conundrum #3.** How can feminists develop an empowered feminist community of researchers across transnational space? How can feminists reach out across their own differences to begin to globalize their understanding of women's standpoint and oppression?

Feminists' discussion of this conundrum is in agreement on the importance of expanding our vision globally. Where there is much disagreement is around the questions feminists should be asking regarding globalization, as well as how to carry out research on a global scale, and for what ends. Some feminists advocate a research agenda that is political and activist; others are more cautious in approach, seeking to gather knowledge locally, without necessarily drawing on its more global and political ramifications.

Postcolonial feminists study relations of power and knowledge within a global context paying specific attention to differences among women that result from what Patricia Hill Collins (2000) terms a "matrix of domination." Feminist theorists Jacqui Alexander and Chandra Talpade Mohanty (1997) state that the "conception of the international [in international feminism] has been the notion of a universal patriarchy operating in a transhistorical way to subordinate all women" (p. xix). The authors stress the need for rethinking international feminism, not as a global essential sisterhood, but as one that encompasses a "transnational" feminism. A transnational feminist perspective traverses boundaries of nationality and geographical region; it rejects binary thinking and stresses the need to understand women's experiences through acknowledging their different degrees of disadvantage and privilege in an unequal, historically created system of oppression.

Patricia Hill Collins (2000) envisions a transnational perspective on empowerment by noting that "we must find common differences that characterize an intercontinental movement, one that responds to intersecting oppressions that are differently organized via a global matrix of domination" (p. 238), and, quoting Angela Miles, says that we must find "shared political issues that constitute a potential basis for common political struggle. Global feminisms are the result of this common struggle grounded in diverse local realities" (p. 240). Collins suggests developing a "transversal politics" that "emphasizes coalition building that takes into account the specific positions of political actors" (p. 245) and empowers women's issues and concerns.

How do we begin to move toward a transnational feminism and develop a new mode of consciousness, one that erases boundaries and empowers and unites people in common struggles against oppression? In their chapter, "Feminizing Global Research/Globalizing Feminist Research: Methods and Practice Under Globalization," Jennifer Bickham Mendez and Diane Wolf ask whether feminists can realign the ways in which they theorize and practice research with a more expanded awareness of globalization. How can a global understanding of women's issues and concerns catalyze a rethinking of analytical categories, such as the concept of "place" and "community," as well as affect how feminists practice their research? Expanding one's vision globally enables one to see the interconnections among and between women suffering under globalized systems of oppression. Power and resistance become "multisited, ever-shifting, and 'situated and contextualized within particular intersubjective relationships,'" thereby opening up new research alliances among and between transnational feminists. Acknowledging how globalization changes the meaning of "place" and "community" complicates the notion of insider or outsider and yet at the same time offers feminists multiple spaces for dialogue and collaboration.

Maria Mies's chapter, "A Global Feminist Perspective on Research," reminds us that feminist research grew out of political activism of the women's movement in the 1960s, which also made an international impact. These early international roots of the 1960s' activism are part of the legacy of feminism, and it is from this place in history that Mies suggests feminists can also draw on thinking about the intersection between feminism and globalization.

She relates her own narrative as a feminist activist and methodologist in Germany during the 1970s and 1980s, from which grew her "seven postulates on feminist research." From this historical vantage point onto globalization, Mies is concerned that as a group many feminist scholars have "uncritically joined the 'mainstream.'" Someplace along the way, feminists have lost their political grounding and have become complacent in challenging status quo policies of a "global, neoliberal capitalism." She believes that there needs to be a re-emergence of feminists who spend time on the "university of the street." She notes:

People learn more about modern economics and about globalization policies than what they would learn in an economics course at the university. . . . I don't see a global perspective for feminist research unless more women move out of the sterility of the academic ivory towers . . . [and recognize the globalizing structures] under which more and more people, including women, are now suffering.

Lynn Weber, in her commentary "Future Directions of Feminist Research: New Directions in Social Policy—The Case of Women's Health" (this volume), stresses, as does Maria Mies, the importance of feminists strengthening the scholarship/activism connection that specifically focuses on public policy issues that promote social justice. She examines the case of inequities in women's health, especially as this pertains to race, ethnicity, gender, and social class. She suggests three specific ways in which feminist scholars and researchers can strengthen this connection: (1) making a stronger critique of status quo research and policy, bringing into focus the globalizing structures that influence social policy research and debates; (2) making some specific improvements on how we theorize and practice research by focusing on what she terms the "intersections" between differences within and among groups and using a range of methods across the quantitative/qualitative divide; and (3) building links and coalitions across different activist groups to promote social change. Weber also speaks of the importance of dialogue as an integral part of coalition/alliance building across difference.

Mies's cautionary about women's positionality has implications for the way that we teach in our women's studies programs. How do academic feminists impart their knowledge building and their practices on how to get at these issues in the "real world"? This is the subject of Conundrum #4.

**Conundrum #4.** How can feminists convey the range of women's scholarship that differentiates it from the charge that women's studies scholarship conveys only ideology, not knowledge? Has women's studies drifted away from activism, and should there be a place for activism in the women's studies classroom? To what extent is

there dialogue across differences within the women's studies classroom?

In this last section, we take up feminist pedagogy as praxis. This section covers practical issues of teaching women's studies and also aims to address the "messy" issues of teaching women's studies that are left out of more mainstream pedagogical discussions, including the lived experiences of teachers within the women's studies classroom, where feminist research and theory meet the road of the lived classroom experience.

Debra Kaufman's commentary, "From Course to Discourse: Mainstreaming Feminist Methodology," relates her pedagogical experiences in teaching feminist methodology. At the outset, she declares her teaching to be "as political as it was academic." She raises the question of politics and research this way: "In what ways, we asked our students, are we historical and political subjects when *we* do our research? How do our life histories and stage of career affect our choice of topic and how we formulate research problems?" Kaufman relates her own research journey in which she confronts issues of political difference in conducting ethnographic research on Orthodox Jewish women who embrace Jewish fundamentalism and its opposition to equality between women and men for her book *Rachael's Daughters*.

Kaufman's research leads her to ask a number of crucial questions about how to study and teach about difference, by noting:

> How do we "do" research on those whose identity politics are different from ours? Or put another way, how do I do socially committed work as a feminist activist and still respect the integrity of my respondents who differ from me politically? Feminist practice demands we make the lived experiences of women visible and give them voice. When we study women who advocate and support fundamentalist traditions, we help to make vocal and visible the narratives of those whose politics we do not share. This dilemma was not lost on students.

She further notes that the identity tensions around these differences provide her with some important pedagogical research moments, which she then takes back with her into the women's studies classroom on feminist methodology. The first lesson was that very few researchers are "value neutral." The second point is that "the way we theorize our research often shapes the way in which we do our research." Kaufman notes that at the time she was conducting research on fundamentalist women, little was known about their lived experiences apart from the fact that they participated in antifeminist activities. She notes that it would be easy to assume from this that such women "were assuredly antifeminists." Kaufman learned that assuming a priori ideas about these women without delving into their lived experiences may "limit the world to male images of women . . . [and we may] assume that the parameters of women's experiences are set by male exploitation alone" (Kaufman, 1990, p. 126, cited in Kaufman, this volume).

The third pedagogical lesson Kaufman takes into the women's studies classroom is the idea that "we often must go beyond our disciplinary boundaries to put into context the lives we wish to explore." In her research on *Rachael's Daughters*, taking a multidisciplinary perspective allows her to raise new research questions. She notes:

> Jewish feminists' *theological* conclusions about the oppression of orthodox women posed the beginning of important *sociological* feminist questions. Do women experience orthodoxy in the ways in which they are theologically described by those in religious studies? Are they simply passive recipients of theological interpretations? Are they victims of a false consciousness created by male ideology?

The fourth methodological insight coming out of her research work is the idea that "those we research are agents in the making of their worlds as much as they are subjects." Those Jewish Orthodox women she studies are not "passive" agents of their religion. On the contrary, she found that

> despite their seemingly "antifeminist" attitudes, many of the women I interviewed used the rhetoric of feminism and often offered a direct critique of male, secular normative models to explain

their choice of Jewish orthodoxy. They compared a male normative secular world of individualistic and competitive striving with the spiritual, modest, "feminine," and communally oriented world of Jewish Orthodoxy.

Kaufman's fifth pedagogical lesson reminds her students that all knowledge is historically situated. Taking such an approach allows the researcher to look at the wider macrohistorical and social factors that also play a role in women's lived experiences and allows for the asking of yet other questions about their experiences, such as "What were the specifics of the relationships, at both the personal and institutional level, that maintained/sustained these women?"

Coming back to Kaufman's comments on her teaching, "[It] was as political as it was academic," reminds us that to make our own scholarship more subject to rigor requires facing our own set of values and attitudes and dealing with them up front, both in our own research and in the teaching of women's studies scholarship. Kaufman states:

> As teachers and scholars we must see ourselves as historical and political subjects. We must make explicit how we have come to our topics of inquiry and the disciplinary tools we choose or even more important disregard in our scholarly journeys. We must be self-reflexive in our research process and aware of the political repercussions, not only within our disciplines, but also within the very communities we are investigating. For whom is our research important? Have we built a wide enough audience, both within the academy and outside of it, to ensure that we can survive beyond this particular political and historical moment?

Daphne Patai, in her chapter, "Feminist Pedagogy Reconsidered," starts out her commentary with a set of questions regarding how adding the term *feminism* in front of the words research and teaching changes the meaning of these two terms. She asks: "Does feminist-inspired pedagogy create problems that differ fundamentally from those attending conventional teaching and research?" She views a definite clash between feminist politics, research, and teaching. She notes: "The political engagement underlying feminism in the academy is bound to set up a highly tendentious model for research and teaching, a paradigm most feminists would hardly accept were its objectives contrary to their own." She does not agree with what she sees as the argument by feminists that knowledge building of the past has been exclusively male biased and exclusive of women's concerns and interests. She notes:

> They [feminists] insist that in the routine practices of the old dispensation, teaching and research have always been, and still are, biased, exclusionary, and inimical to the interests of women. In short, they are "masculinist." To many feminists, this is a decisive claim. For only when academic procedures can be portrayed in such starkly negative terms is the feminist agenda seen as a corrective: legitimate, appropriate, fair, salutary, and urgently necessary.

From Patai's perspective, "What the term *feminist* introduces into the classroom is a patently political project driving its sense of the aims of education and the pursuit of knowledge." She argues that another perspective on teaching and research is needed, one that requires a different starting point, namely, that

> teaching and research are not, and ought not to be, either feminist or masculinist and that despite the historical exclusion of women, the substance of a liberal education and the ideas on which it rests have not been entirely and always flawed—the adjective *feminist* begins to look less like a salutary corrective and more like the calamitous imposition of a political point of view. Why calamitous? Because the great thing about the university is that it provides that rare space in which emphasis can be on *how* to think, not *what* to think, on acquiring intellectual tools, not accepting hand-me-down political doctrines.

Patai's chapter is an important critique against feminists whose research and teaching practices often assume a tight link between knowledge and politics. For Patai, even if all knowledge building of the past were male biased, it does not behoove feminism to do the same and err in the opposite direction. She notes:

To assert that indoctrination is what men have in fact traditionally perpetrated in all fields and that it is now the turn of women to do the same, even if this assertion were accurate, is a weak defense, since it would turn the feminist program into a replica of a practice considered flawed and even malevolent. Surely the appropriate response to whatever are deemed to be the shortcomings of traditional teaching is not simply to reverse the biases of the past but rather to surpass them.

She does not buy into the feminist viewpoint that "all teaching is political."

Patai sees little dialogue occurring among and between women's studies scholarship and teaching, and amid those who argue against a feminist point of view on a range of scholarship presented in the women's studies classroom. She notes: "While progress occurs in many other fields, consequent on the extraordinary scientific and sociopolitical advances of our time, many teachers of women's studies, like other ideologues, prefer simply to dismiss whatever ideas seem to threaten their closed worldview."

Daphne Patai's perspective, at its core, asks whether or not feminism is compatible with scientific inquiry when it is unable to adequately critique its own "pet ideas." She further notes: "Aren't standards of evidence and objective investigation crucial to all women (to all people) as they attempt to combat prejudice and ignorance?" Patai queries whether or not students in women's studies classes are able to be critical of feminist ideas by noting, more specifically, if they can "develop the capacity of independent judgment and appraisal that might challenge the feminist presuppositions on which their courses rest."

Patai also talks about her own lived experiences as a scholar whose critiques of feminism have found her and other critics of feminist practice labeled as backlashers, who are "an enemy of feminism, a 'conservative,' or a reactionary trying to force women back to the kitchen."

Patai's chapter questions the extent to which feminists are willing to engage in dialogue rather than discussion with one another. What are the points of convergence and divergence in Patai's argument for mainstream teachers of feminism? Is there any common ground on which to dialogue across the range of feminist perspectives on knowledge building? What is the best course of action feminists of different persuasions can take when they don't agree?

Judith Cook and Mary Margaret Fonow end this section with their commentary, "A Passion for Knowledge: The Teaching of Feminist Methodology." Earlier, they had published a now classic anthology, *Beyond Methodology: Feminist Scholarship as Lived Research* (Fonow & Cook, 1991). What they point to is the fluid and ever-changing aspects of feminist knowledge building. They note: "We are often asked to define and defend feminist methodology as a unique methodology, and we have always resisted giving a precise response because we do not want to foreclose new avenues of inquiry and discovery" (Cook & Fonow, this volume).

Their teaching of feminist methodology is guided by a set of principles that can apply to a range of qualitative and quantitative methods, and they note:

> We are more concerned that students understand how to select and defend their choices in the design, collection, representation, and interpretation of data. We ask them to consider the following questions: What methods will help you to answer your research question, and what is your rationale for selecting this approach? How are you, as the researcher, situated in this project? What ethical safeguards are you planning for your study, and how do they reflect feminist ethics? What are your responsibilities as a feminist researcher? How does your approach address difference (marked and unmarked)? Will research subjects play a role in the research, and what are some of the dilemmas of involving research subjects? How do you plan to represent your findings, and what are the politics involved in such a representation?

This set of commentaries and range of conundrums reminds us that there is no one feminist point of view and that feminists engage with each other, sometimes dialoguing, at other times in contentious discussion; and it is through these interactions that the landscape of feminist theory and praxis is ever evolving. It is this changing nature of feminisms that often gets lost in critiques and understandings of what feminisms are in theory and practice.

## REFERENCES

Alexander, M. Jacqui, & Mohanty, Chandra Talpade. (1997). *Feminist genealogies, colonial legacies, democratic futures.* New York: Routledge.

Butler, Judith. (1993). *Bodies that matter: On the discursive limits of "sex."* New York: Routledge.

Collins, Patricia Hill. (2000). *Black feminist thought* (2nd ed.). New York: Routledge.

Fonow, Mary Margaret, & Cook, Judith A. (1991). *Beyond methodology: Feminist scholarship as lived research.* Bloomington: Indiana University Press.

Hesse-Biber, Sharlene Nagy, Gilmartin, Christina, & Lydenberg, Robin. (Eds.). (1999). *Feminist approaches to theory and methodology: An interdisciplinary reader.* New York: Oxford University Press.

Hesse-Biber, Sharlene Nagy, & Yaiser, Michelle L. (2004). Difference matters: Studying across race, class, gender, and sexuality. In Sharlene Nagy Hesse-Biber & Michelle L. Yaiser (Eds.), *Feminist perspectives on social research* (pp. 101–120). New York: Oxford University Press.

hooks, bell. (1994). *Teaching to transgress: Education as the practice of freedom.* New York: Routledge.

Longino, Helen E. (1989). Can there be a feminist science? In Nancy Tuana (Ed.), *Feminism & science* (pp. 45–57). Bloomington: Indiana University Press.

Longino, Helen E. (2002). *The fate of knowledge.* Princeton, NJ: Princeton University Press.

# 28

# REASON, TRUTH, AND EXPERIENCE

## *Tyrannies or Liberation?*

HELEN E. LONGINO

The concepts of reason, truth, and experience, contested as they are, have been at the heart of Western epistemological reflection. Their analysis provides answers to the question of how and what humans know, and epistemological positions are distinguished by the varying claims made about them. Feminists, too, have entered the debates, linking positions both to their distinctive research aims and to the social and political values associated with feminism. Of course, there is only partial agreement as to what those aims and values are or should be and, hence, no single epistemological approach that could be labeled feminist epistemology. Instead, feminist epistemology is better thought of as critical engagement with philosophical questions about knowledge in light of commitment to one or more of a family of positions claimed as feminist. In this brief comment, I wish to review why reason, truth, and experience remain at the center of epistemological reflection, suggest some of the traditional difficulties in arriving at adequate understandings of them and the specific challenges to them raised by feminist theorists, and indicate some of the questions that remain for feminist epistemologists.

## PHILOSOPHICAL PRELIMINARIES

### Reason and Rationality I

Efforts to formalize logic have seemed to straightjacket reason and rationality, forcing good reasoning into patterns sanctioned by one or another formalization—whether Aristotelian syllogisms or Frege and Russell's truth functions. In addition, the use of *rational* as a term of commendation for both action and belief has engendered much confusion—is "rational" a substantive or a procedural concept? A descriptive or a normative one? It is used in all these ways, and any one sense can be criticized on grounds more appropriate to one of the others. *Reason* suffers from equivocations as well. Of this, more presently. Why should we care about reason? Minimally, the notion refers to a basic and fairly general human capacity to connect ideas in some nonarbitrary way, subject to rules. This minimal characterization must be filled in with a specification of what such rules are and what their actual role might be. Setting these questions aside, the bare capacity is what enables us to see one thing as grounds for believing or disbelieving another—the presence of a stain on a table clean 2 hours previously as grounds for believing that someone or something has been in the room since then or for rejecting the claim that no one or nothing has been. Minimal reason, as a bare capacity, enables us to go beyond immediate experience, to bring the past to bear on our beliefs about the present, the near to bear on our beliefs about the distant, the present to bear on our expectations about the future. Part of the function of rules would be to specify what ways of bringing beliefs to bear on one another give reliable results and what ways don't. Whether these are explicit components of reasoning or criteria of evaluation and whether reasoning requires certain levels of linguistic capacity or not remain open questions. Given that the content of human knowledge extends or is hoped to extend beyond the immediate moment, the capacity to reason is nevertheless a central topic for epistemological reflection.

## Truth I

One cannot know what is false: If my keys are locked in my office, I cannot know, although I may believe, that they are in the briefcase I am carrying as I exit the building. There is what the philosopher Alvin Goldman would call a veritistic component of knowledge. Part of what we mean when we claim to know something or claim that another knows something is that what we claim to know or to be known by another is as we say it is—in other words, that it is true. This is so whether our claim concerns the location of keys or the extent of poverty or health or oppression in a population. As with *reason*, what is or could be meant by *true* is up for philosophical grabs, but it is central to the concept of knowledge.

## Experience I

Here again is an expression with many meanings. In a job advertisement it means past acquaintance with, performance of activities, and use of equipment associated with the occupation in question. In personal terms, it may mean what happened, in whole or in part, as in "not in all my experience have I seen such a storm" or "my experience at the University of X was tumultuous." While these are epistemologically relevant senses, the more traditional epistemological meaning is

narrower, referring to sense experience, something like sense perception—how we are in the moment affected by the world through our receptive capacities of taste, smell, hearing, touch, and vision. Sense experience is our mode of access to, or interaction with, the world around us. Through experience we come to know the grass is green, the vegetables salty, a hawk's cry piercing.

So we might be tempted to say something like the following: Our (sense) experience gives us the raw materials, or basic ingredients, that we connect by use of reason to articulate/construct/rely on (what we hope to be) truths about the world. The use of the terms *raw* and *basic* already evoke problematic philosophical positions—it's hard to elaborate their meaning without falling into some kind of foundationalism, but there is surely something commonsensical in this proposal. The challenge has been to preserve the common sense while giving content to its key ideas in a way that escapes contradiction, excessive limitation, or excessive inclusiveness.

## FEMINIST ENGAGEMENTS

Feminist scholars have been especially concerned with excessive limitation and the ways in which analyses of reason, truth, and experience have been used to delegitimize women's cognitive abilities and performances. The historian of philosophy Genevieve Lloyd (1984) showed how reason and masculinity have remained metaphorically associated with each other through multiple changes in the understanding of each. This association is part of a conceptual orientation that includes associating womanhood with unreason and unreason with emotions, or with unruly or base emotions, or with the body, or with materiality. Investigation of philosophical systems operative in most historical periods reveals pairs of contrasts that taken together systematically elevate men and masculinity and debase women and femininity. While these conceptual categories only imperfectly fit actual human beings, their effects are to support the subordination and disempowerment of women. No wonder (some) feminists have reacted by celebrating emotion and subjectivity and rejecting rationality and objectivity. To do so, however, is in the end to collude with our cognitive subordination. The task should be instead to develop analyses of the components of our concept of knowledge that do not support either symbolic or material gender inequalities.

This is, of course, just what feminist epistemologists have been doing. Practitioners of the natural and social sciences, feminist theorists, and feminist philosophers have struggled with the concepts of reason, rationality, truth, objectivity, and experience in an effort to legitimate feminist knowledge projects without running afoul of familiar philosophical obstacles or newer ones posed by postmodernist challenges to philosophical orthodoxy.

## Reason and Rationality II

Feminists have objected to efforts to treat reason, rationality, and reasoning as cold-blooded calculation, divorced from values and emotion. They have also objected to characterizations of rationality that essentially privilege the status quo, by treating as rational what is consistent with generally accepted ideas. Because generally accepted ideas have historically served to perpetuate male privilege and the subordination of women, rationality under this description is hardly a feminist desideratum. And general acceptance, while considered universal among the acceptors, is usually general only in a particular cultural context. What's worth noting is that the first-mentioned concept— reason as calculation—is the concept of a procedure, while the second kind of rationality is attributed to outcomes—beliefs or actions—and is done so as a mode of appraisal. To say that something is rational in this sense is to say that it is not self-defeating, that it either is consistent with or advances the agent's self-interest, or is consistent with or follows from the agent's other beliefs or values. To make such a judgment requires either knowing the agent's beliefs and values or attributing some to the agent. And it is in that attribution that generally accepted ideas enter, because they seem the most probable to assume (e.g., as per Donald Davidson's principle of charity). It is easy to see how the use of *rational* and *rationality* can be co-opted in preservation of the status quo, but then it is also easy to defend against it. The problematic aspects of the procedural sense of *rational*, *rationality*, and *reason* are a little subtler, and

this is because the procedural sense can be meant descriptively or prescriptively—as the name of a process or as the name of successful versions or performances of that process.

All three of these senses of *reason*—attribute of belief or action, name of a process, favorable judgment on a version or performance of a process—can be conflated when defending or critiquing either rationality and reason or conceptions of these. In general, feminist repudiations of reason tend to be directed at the first and third of these, especially at conceptions of success that valorize and entrench the status quo. Reformist efforts are directed at conceptions of the second, that is, at conceptions of the reasoning process that either blatantly or subtly privilege men and/or masculinity or disparage women and/or femininity. Two related aspects of concepts of reason have particularly attracted feminist attention: the concept of reason as disembodied and the concept of reason as value-free, that is, proceeding from or determined by high-level principles but remaining clear of values or value-laden principles or assumptions in the course of particular performances of reasoning. Feminists have rejected *tout court* the treatment of reason and other cognitive phenomena as disembodied, seeing here the old association of men with the mental and cognitive and women with the material and emotional. Reformist efforts, thus, have been directed at showing the consequences of understanding reason as embodied. Feminists in philosophy of science have argued that reasoning engages values or value-laden assumptions or that good reasoning can and does include values or value-laden assumptions. Reasoning allegedly value-free usually incorporates the generally accepted, hence invisible, values of the reasoner's culture. The work of Phyllis Rooney (1992), Lynn Hankinson Nelson (2001), Alison Wylie (2002), Janet Kourany (2003), and Elizabeth Anderson (2004) seeks to understand and articulate through case studies how reasoning to conclusions in scientific contexts involves values and how such value-laden reasoning produces better conclusions than allegedly value-free reasoning. Alison Jaggar (1989) has argued for the constructive role of emotions in knowledge, as have feminist scholars seeking to bring the work of Carol Gilligan to bear on knowledge (Belenky,

Clinchy, Goldberger, & Tarule, 1986). Others, for example, Longino (1990, 2002), have argued that reasoning is not a solitary, individualistic practice but a social, interactive one. While there is no unanimity of opinion, this is an area of investigation that feminists have found very fruitful.

## Truth II

Truth is imperiled in part by its association with objectivity. Ever since Evelyn Fox Keller's (1985) exposure of masculinist dimensions of this concept, objectivity has been problematic, if not anathema, to feminists. One sense of *objective* is true, as in "objectively true," which just means "really true." In this sense, to say that a claim is objective is to say that it is verified by some state of the world. (See Lloyd, 1995, for a critical analysis of the multiple senses of objectivity.) Feminist examination of the history of the concept of objectivity has found it to be associated with an ideal of domination of the natural world (and, through the identification of women with the natural body, of women). Truth, by association, has also been associated with domination, an association reinforced by poststructuralist thinkers such as Michel Foucault and philosophers attracted to postmodernist themes, such as Richard Rorty.

Feminists have given more direct attention to objectivity and have been relatively successful in articulating alternative conceptions of objectivity, introducing them into feminist methodological discussion and somewhat less so into mainstream philosophical conversation. These redefinitions of objectivity tend to focus on objectivity of method, rather than objectivity of content (see Longino, 1993, for a discussion of this distinction; also Lloyd, 1995).[1] Because truth is associated with objectivity of content, these alternatives do not as such advance a feminist understanding of truth. Truth and falsity are attributed to the outcomes of our cognitive efforts. Successful outcomes are true, unsuccessful ones false. Thus, our concept of truth must be linked to our concept of the aims of our cognitive pursuits, aims in light of which success or failure is judged. Within traditional analytic philosophy we find correspondence, coherence, and deflationary concepts of truth, absolutist and relativist concepts. There are pragmatist definitions of truth and postmodernist deconstructions of the concept. Currently, feminist philosophy offers defenses of relativism[2] regarding truth (Code, 1995), of coherence[3] as the meaning of truth (Alcoff, 1996), and of conformation[4] as the meaning of epistemic success (Longino, 2002). These must be regarded as initial investigations. One of the outcomes of feminist discussion so far is the importance of articulating the cognitive goals that motivate inquiry. Future discussion of the concept of truth, including critical and comparative evaluation of the just mentioned and other analyses of truth or epistemic success, will have to take into account what feminist knowledge goals are and ought to be.

## Experience II

As noted above, the term *experience* has multiple meanings differently relevant to the theory of knowledge. Feminist standpoint theorists placed women's experience at the center of theorizing—whether about social relations or about knowledge. In this context experience is understood thickly, to borrow a term from the anthropologists, as a person's lived history understood from her or his perspective. It includes judgments, values, and emotional responses, as well as actions and events. Feminist standpoint theorists argued that mainstream theorizing, reflecting a masculinist or androcentric perspective, begins at a fairly high level of abstraction that already incorporates implicit judgments endorsing sexual distributions of labor, value, burden, and benefit. The experience of those whose oppression is both ratified and masked by those judgments constitutes, according to standpoint theorists, a better starting point, less likely to perpetuate the distortions required to sustain systems of domination. Standpoint theory took many forms and underwent many modifications in the course of its history: from a method of evaluating conclusions to a point about the relative (but not absolute) advantage of certain social positions or situations vis-à-vis certain kinds of objects of knowledge, from a single standpoint afforded by women's experience presumed as a universal to multiple standpoints reflecting the variety of women's race, class, and national identities.

Even with these modifications, standpoint theory ran into trouble from another direction. In a frequently cited and reprinted article, as well as in exchanges with other historians, Joan Scott (1991) took the invocation of experience to task for its naïveté. Uncritical use of subjects' reports of their experience as evidence by historians and social scientists reifies the social categories through which experience is understood, such as gender, instead of exhibiting them for critique. Rather than repeating and collating narratives, historians and social scientists should be examining the production of experience by discourse. This approach, however, delegitimizes the oppressed as authoritative sources about their lives and, thus, seems, to some, to reinforce their oppression rather than helping to expose and end it. One of the more effective rebuttals to Scott comes from Chandra Mohanty (1991), who notes that one of the strategies of members of oppressed groups is to share experiences with each other. Out of this kind of interchange emerges a critical understanding of the strategies, including discursive ones, of domination. Narrative understandings of experience collaboratively produced are not slavish reinscriptions of oppressive social categories but the result of a collective critical interrogation of experience and the categories through which it is lived. The concern with experience in this sense reflects feminist theorists' continuing interest in the tensions between postmodernist and liberationist approaches to theory and has implications for how the results of many feminist social research methods are to be evaluated and for how to understand documents such as the *testimonios* of representatives of oppressed populations.

One intriguing exploration of experience notes the focus on propositional knowledge at the expense of practical knowledge (Dalmiya & Alcoff, 1993). Practical or skill knowledge is almost entirely manifest in the actions of its possessor. Women, historically excluded from formal education, have, in cultural contexts elevating theoretical, propositional knowledge over skills and know-how, been doubly disadvantaged: prevented from acquiring propositional knowledge and disparaged for the knowledge they do have.

Neither the debate about experience as evidence nor the observations about practical knowledge, however, do anything to clarify the nature of perceptual or sensory experience or its role in knowledge. It does draw attention to the need to think through the implications of using one or another concept. Sensory experience has been pronounced by (some) philosophers to be as illusory as Scott (1991) finds personal narratives. It is nevertheless central to the various forms of feminist empiricism, one or another of which has found favor among feminist social researchers. Analyses of sensory experience include sense data theories, which try to reduce experience to indubitable raw feels—for example, sensing redly or greenly. These raw feels are then used to construct ideas of independently existing, three-dimensional objects not directly perceived. These theories place the guarantors of belief in sensations internal to cognitive agents and place at risk our beliefs about the so-called external world. At the other end of the spectrum are nonreductive causal realist theories, which hold that objects existing independently of us cause our sensations of them. These theories place the guarantors of belief in the external world. Somewhere in between are theories about the necessity of some conceptual organization to provide order to experience. An example would be the Kantian account of the conceptual categories necessary for any possible experience. In addition, advances in the biology and psychology of perception establish limits and suggest alternatives to the philosophical views on offer. The task for feminist philosophers is to think about which conceptions of experience privilege mainstream or masculinist values and which are compatible with or even advance feminist cognitive goals. Of course, this is a moving target, because changing conditions change the relations among epistemological concepts, masculinist values, and feminist cognitive goals. The work of feminist scholars will not cease until gender ceases to be a significant axis of power and privilege.

Reason, truth, and experience are, as mentioned earlier, central to conceptions of knowledge. I've tried to show the ways in which they are variously understood, identify feminist interests in and challenges to them, and suggest questions that remain to be addressed. Researchers in the various empirical disciplines must devise methods that enable them to answer the questions they address to their subject matter. These methods and their implementation assume the meaningfulness of the epistemological concepts. The challenge for feminist philosophers is to provide analyses of these concepts capable of underwriting feminist methodologies, broad enough to accommodate the variety of these methodologies, and open to debate about what feminist cognitive goals are and should be.

## NOTES

1. Objectivity of method concerns the reliability and freedom from subjective bias or preference of the methods used to investigate a phenomenon or validate claims about it. Objectivity of content concerns the relation between the content of a claim and what it is about, regardless of methods of investigation or validation.

2. Code explicates her relativism as anti-universalism.

3. Coherence is attributed to a belief set and is generally understood as mutual consistency of the members of the set. Alcoff prefers an analysis of coherence as mutual explanatoriness.

4. Conformation is a hybrid of correspondence and pragmatist conceptions and is pluralistic rather than absolutist or relativist.

## REFERENCES

Alcoff, Linda. (1996). *Real knowing*. Ithaca, NY: Cornell University Press.

Anderson, Elizabeth. (2004). Uses of value judgments in science. *Hypatia, 19,* 1.

Belenky, Mary Field, Clinchy, Blythe, Goldberger, Nancy, & Tarule, Jill. (1986). *Women's ways of knowing*. New York: Basic Books.

Code, Lorraine. (1995). Must a feminist be a relativist after all? In Lorraine Code (Ed.), *Rhetorical spaces: Essays on gendered locations* (pp. 185–207). New York: Routledge.

Dalmiya, Vrinda, & Alcoff, Linda. (1993). Are old wives tales justified? In Linda Alcoff & Elizabeth Potter (Eds.), *Feminist epistemologies* (pp. 217–244). New York: Routledge.

Jaggar, Alison. (1989). Love and knowledge in feminist epistemology. In Alison Jaggar & Susan Bordo (Eds.), *Gender/body/knowledge* (pp. 145–171). New Brunswick, NJ: Rutgers University Press.

Keller, Evelyn Fox. (1985). *Reflections on gender and science*. New Haven, CT: Yale University Press.

Kourany, Janet. (2003). A philosophy of science for the 21st century. *Philosophy of Science, 70,* 1.

Lloyd, Elisabeth. (1995). Objectivity and the double standard for feminist epistemologies. *Synthese, 104,* 351–381.

Lloyd, Genevieve. (1984). *The man of reason*. Minneapolis: University of Minnesota Press.

Longino, Helen E. (1990). *Science as social knowledge*. Princeton, NJ: Princeton University Press.

Longino, Helen E. (1993). Essential tensions. In Louise Antony & Charlotte Witt (Eds.), *A mind of one's own*. Boulder, CO: Westview Press.

Longino, Helen E. (2002). *The fate of knowledge*. Princeton, NJ: Princeton University Press.

Longino, Helen E. (2005). How values can be good for science. In Peter Machamer & Gideon Wouters (Eds.), *Values, objectivity and science* (pp. 127–142). Pittsburgh, PA: University of Pittsburgh Press.

Mohanty, Chandra. (1991). Cartographies of struggle. In Chandra Mohanty, Ann Russo, & Lourdes Torres (Eds.), *Third world women and the politics of feminism* (pp. 1–47). Indianapolis: Indiana University Press

Nelson, Lynn Hankinson. (2001). Relativism and science studies scholarship. In Nancy Tuana & Sandra Morgen (Eds.), *Engendering rationalities* (pp. 175–194). Albany: State University of New York Press.

Rooney, Phyllis. (1992). Values in science. In David Hull, Micky Forbes, & Kathryn Okruhlik (Eds.), *PSA 1992* (Vol. 1, pp. 13–22). East Lansing, MI: Philosophy of Science Association.

Scott, Joan. (1991). The evidence of "experience." *Critical Inquiry, 17,* 773–797.

Wylie, Alison. (2002). *Thinking from things*. Los Angeles: University of California Press.

# 29

# Critical Perspectives on Feminist Epistemology

Noretta Koertge

In a useful encyclopedia article on feminist epistemology, Elizabeth Anderson (2004) writes, "Feminist epistemology and philosophy of science studies [*sic*] the ways in which gender does and *ought to* [italics added] influence our conceptions of knowledge, the knowing subject, and practices of inquiry and justification" (p. 1). Thanks in large part to the contributions of people working in women's studies, the claim that gender *does* influence inquiry is no longer surprising. However, the normative claim that gender *ought to* play a role in our best epistemic practices is extremely controversial. In a short essay, one cannot hope to survey the variety of epistemic approaches that label themselves as feminist. What I will do instead is critically discuss three important examples of feminist theorizing taken from the works of Andrea Nye, Sandra Harding, and Helen Longino. Each believes that dominant knowledge practices disadvantage women and so a feminist epistemology is needed. My conclusion, however, will be that trying to gender epistemology can in fact be very detrimental to women.

## WHEREIN IDENTITY POLITICS BEGAT WOMEN'S STUDIES, WHICH BEGAT GENDER STUDIES, WHICH BEGAT FEMINIST EPISTEMOLOGY

Mainstream philosophical approaches to the nature of knowledge propose universally applicable criteria for good evidence and good arguments. Thus, to understand the roots of and motivation for feminist epistemology, we need to survey the context in which it arose.

It is well-known that the late 1960s saw the rise of what came to be called "identity politics"—the attempt to analyze political issues and organize groups to act politically along the lines of race (black power), gender (women's liberation), and sexual orientation (gay liberation). What happened in the 1970s was the establishment of various new "studies" programs in the university.

Women's studies (WOST) initiatives were enormously successful. Like Afro-American studies programs and the less numerous gay (later queer) studies courses, these programs had an explicit double agenda: They were to foster new directions in research and teaching, but they were also to promote political activism. In WOST, there was a popular slogan that appeared in official mission statements: "Women's Studies is the academic arm of the Women's Movement."

Thus issues of political expediency could legitimately be invoked at every stage: Who should be hired (was a PhD necessary or could experience as an activist be equally relevant?); how should curriculum requirements be set (would interning at a battered women's shelter count for academic credit?); and how should essay prizes be awarded (what if the writing was good but the woman seemed not to be an active feminist?).[1]

The weight awarded to such political considerations varied greatly from university to university and over time in a single university, but they could never be ruled irrelevant once and for all. The issue of how much a given academic decision should be shaped according to what was perceived as good for the movement was always a live one.

WOST programs and departments self-consciously set out to effect a revolution in scholarship as well. At the very first, people simply set out to study *women*—their lives, past and present; their biological, psychological, and sociological development in various cultures; and how they talk, think, worship, and what have you. Here, the emphasis was on filling in the gaps and noting how dominant narratives or theories or models would have to be changed if women were to be included.

But very quickly, the focus shifted to gender—and the new mantra became "RCG," the study of race, class, and gender. Some programs renamed themselves "Gender Studies," and their research came to include the study of the social construction of "maleness" (how males define themselves in part out of fear of being thought female) and "whiteness" (how part of white identity can be a sense of relief at not being like colored folk)—and how each of these constructions varies by class.

Because the majority of feminist scholars were trained in the humanities, they relied heavily on evidence from "texts" and—here is the connection to postmodernism—learned to read "silences" when there was no overt mention of

RCG in their sources. Like Sherlock Holmes, who found great significance in "the dog who failed to bark in the night," they deconstructed references to race-gender-class where they were to be found and recorded absences when they were not.

This distinction between bias against women (leaving unquestioned the criteria of excellence) and bias against gendered attributes (thus advocating a change in the criteria themselves) is important to remember when we turn to feminist epistemology. Early on, WOST had developed models of "women's ways of knowing" and theories of feminist pedagogy.[2] Put in a nutshell, what these approaches tended to do was to positively affirm various stereotypes about female mentality and "valorize" them. Women supposedly responded well to noncompetitive, cooperative learning situations with a "guide by the side" instead of a "sage on the stage." They liked to learn experientially, not through abstract analysis. They wanted their knowledge to be concretely applicable and used for humane purposes.

But if such an account of female cognition is in any way close to being correct, we immediately see a strong clash between so-called women's ways of knowing and traditional accounts of reasoning in logic, mathematics, and science. Feminists were quick to conclude that not only were the standard pedagogical approaches to these subjects gender biased in a way that posed barriers for students; there was also something inherently flawed about the disciplines themselves. A striking example of this kind of feminist critique is Andrea Nye's (1990) commentary on deductive logic, which is often assumed to lie at the very core of rationality. It will illustrate nicely both the rhetorical appeal of such feminist attacks on traditional epistemology and what I will argue are the retrogressive political effects.

## IS LOGIC AN INSTRUMENT OF PATRIARCHAL OPPRESSION?

Logic is the systematic study of patterns of correct inference. The first treatise on logic is Aristotle's (1964) *Prior and Posterior Analytics*, written around 350 BCE, and there are remarkable similarities between the way he presented his theory of valid arguments and the way it is still taught today. He analyzes the *form* of various inferences and then illustrates them with concrete examples. He begins with very simple cases:

> If no B is A, neither can any A be B . . . e.g. if no pleasure is good, no good will be pleasure.
>
> If some B is not A, it does not follow that some A is not B. By way of illustration let B stand for animal and A for man: not every animal is a man, but every man is an animal. (p. 5)

Aristotle's exposition of syllogistic reasoning was at the center of what came to be called the organon, the instrument of demonstrative reasoning, and logic was an honored member of the trivium, which functioned as the "core curriculum" throughout the Middle Ages. Today, students are still strongly encouraged to take logic—at my university, beginning logic is required for undergraduates majoring in nursing, physical therapy, and social work. As was the case with claims made about studying Latin, it is very difficult to provide compelling evidence for the salutary influence of the study of logic on human reasoning in ordinary life situations, but it clearly does help students do well on the Graduate Record Exam and the Law School Admission Test. For this reason alone, one might well expect feminists to urge women students to take logic courses and to point out that it is not just women students who find logic difficult.

Unfortunately, the predominant feminist response has been to attack logic and other traditional canons of rationality as sexist. We will look at two separate lines of critique, the first dealing with the way logic is taught—I call this the problem of sexist syllogisms. The other, more radical objection is directed at the discipline itself. Here the claim is that by regimenting reasoning logic becomes a tool of oppression.

Sexist Syllogisms: Logic textbooks are full of exercises that give the student practice in translating strings of ordinary English sentences into logical notation and then appraising the formal correctness of the resulting inferences. Many of the examples are now classics—who has not heard the syllogism about Socrates and

his mortality? But there is also a tradition among textbook writers of generating witty examples that are intended to keep students awake as they work their way through Venn diagrams, truth tables, or natural deduction schemata. So, for example, the exercises in Lewis Carroll's (1958) 19th-century logic book include whimsical sentences such as these:

> No lizard needs a hairbrush. (p. 130)
>
> Guinea-pigs are hopelessly ignorant of music. (p. 115)
>
> My dreams are all about Bath-buns. (p. 120)

As the last example about Bath buns (British breakfast rolls) illustrates, these little student exercises provide us with glimpses of both the author's psychology and contemporary popular culture.

Post-World War II American texts also reflect the concerns of the time, but now gender roles are a major topic of interest. Copi's exercises include the following:

> A communist is either a fool or a knave. (Copi, 1979, p. 77)
>
> The United Nations will become more responsible or there will be a third world war. (Copi, 1979, p. 11)
>
> If any husband is unsuccessful then if some wives are ambitious he will be unhappy. (Copi, 1979, p. 89)
>
> All members are both officers and gentlemen. (Copi, 1979, p. 77)
>
> Whoso findeth a wife findeth a good thing. (Copi, 1979, p. 71)
>
> All popular girls are good conversationalists. (Copi, 1968, p. 159)
>
> All successful executives are intelligent men. (Copi, 1968, p. 134)
>
> All tenors are either overweight or effeminate. (Copi, 1979, p. 83)

A similar pattern is found in other well-respected books of the period. Women or girls do not figure at all in most of the exercises, and when they do appear they are almost always in passive, trivial, or demeaning roles:

> Single women are decorous only if they are chaperoned. (Kalish & Montague, 1964, p. 98)

> Women without husbands are unhappy unless they have paramours. (Kalish & Montague, 1964, p. 98)

> Simone de Beauvoir is not a great writer. (Suppes, 1957, p. 107)

> If either red-heads are lovely or blondes do not have freckles, then logic is confusing. (Suppes, 1957, p. 18)

There is no question that the exercises employed in these logic books reinforced traditional sexual stereotypes. Whether this fact played a significant role in deterring women from liking logic is less clear. As the last example above reminds us, many students, male and female, find logic confusing, boring, or difficult. What we can conclude, however, is that in America today, thanks to the success of the women's movement, students are now sensitized to gender stereotypes and find sentences such as "every girl loves a sailor" to be inappropriate. And more recent books, such as the fifth edition of Kahane's (1986) *Logic and Philosophy,* portray women and men in a wider variety of roles:

> Art watched "General Hospital," but Betsy didn't. (p. 33)

And in Kahane's dialogue about the Liar's Paradox, it is Bonny who says "I know," and provides the proof, whereas Charlie says things like "Maybe yes, maybe no" and "I don't know why" (p. 193).

Although women students are not well served by being encouraged to melt down at the first sight of a sexist syllogism, there is no reason why they or any other group of students should be distracted by a barrage of examples that they find to be insulting. And as my little survey of the change in textbooks over time suggests, authors are responding to these concerns.

I wish I could end the story of the feminist critique of logic on this happy note. Unfortunately, however, some feminists have claimed that not just the homework exercises but the very

enterprise of characterizing the formal structure of logical inference cannot be separated from sexism, racism, and totalitarianism.

Logic as a Tool of Oppression: Conflict between rationalists and romantics, those who would rely on reason versus those who would privilege feelings, predate feminism, but feminists have added some new arguments and lots of new anger to the debate. Nye's (1990) *Words of Power*, published in Routledge's *Thinking Gender* series, provides a good example of a radical feminist critique. Because it is more clearly written and argued than most (Nye has not entirely abandoned her traditional training!), it is worth examining in some detail.

Nye begins with a story about the feelings she had in her logic class, how there was only one other woman in her class, how she was too unsure of herself to raise her hand in class, and how difficult it was to think in the way required. When confronted with the example "Jones ate fish with ice cream and died," Nye, who had come to philosophy from literature, finds her mind wandering off into speculation about why Jones ate such a bizarre dish and why death was the consequence. The difficulty she experienced in representing the structure of the sentence with $p$'s and $q$'s raised a troubling question in Nye's mind: "Is it because I, as a woman, had a different kind of mind, incapable of abstraction and therefore of theorizing, [or] is it because I was too 'emotional'?" (p. 2).

Many women have had such doubts. The liberal feminist reply is an analysis of how logical pedagogical styles as well as societal gender stereotypes make women feel alienated from logic. Nye's response is to put the shoe of blame on the other foot. She argues that given its historical development from the time of the Greeks, logic as we know it today is not only alienated from women but also has been and continues to be a weapon of oppression.

Nye's first complaint is a familiar one to logic teachers—by requiring that sentences be formalized, logicians strip away nuances and metaphorical meanings. As Nye puts it: "The philosopher who combs the tangles from language must also be a butcher who trims away the fleshy fat of ordinary talk to leave the bare bones of truth" (p. 33).

Nye believes that training in logic makes us focus too much on *what* is said instead of on *who* said it or *why*. As an example she cites the success of the Willie Horton ad in the 1988 Bush-Dukakis campaign. Nye believes that listeners behaved too much like logicians in their processing of the commercials; i.e., they concentrated too much on the arguments about parole policies and too little on the emotional impact of the pictures. (Needless to say, a logician would immediately point out the existence of what are technically called "hidden lemmas" [unstated assumptions] in the Willie Horton argument and conclude that the listeners were not being logical enough!)

Nye's second objection is directed at Aristotle's law of the excluded middle, a favorite target of feminists who see it as the basis of patriarchal dualistic thinking. The law of the excluded middle simply says that everything is either A or not-A. It would be a contradiction to say of something that it is at once A and not-A. But Nye argues that this logic does not apply to "ambiguous bodily individuals who so often both are and are not what we desire of them" (p. 51). Many lay criticisms of the law of the excluded middle are based on a crude confusion between contraries and contradictories. The classic law does *not* claim that everything is either black or white and that there are no shades of gray. What it *does* say is that everything is either black or not-black, white or not-white, gray or not-gray. Aristotle's logic does not rule out the possibility of hermaphrodites, lukewarm baths, or wars that end with no victor.

However, logicians themselves have had many interesting discussions of all of Aristotle's laws of negation. Some are worried about the proper analysis of intrinsically vague terms, such as *city* (How big must a town be before it counts as a city?), and have developed a formal analysis in terms of what are called *fuzzy sets*. Others have resisted the idea that every sentence is either true or false and have experimented with so-called three-valued logics. Philosophers of science have tried to develop a measure of "verisimilitude" that would permit us to say of two false sentences that one has a higher truth content than the other. Logic has more resources and more flexibility than are dreamt of in most feminist philosophy.

We now come to Nye's original criticism of logic, one based on an unusual reading of its history, starting with the Greeks, progressing through the Middle Ages, and then jumping to the early 20th century. Nye proudly owns up to committing the genetic fallacy and arguing ad hominem (p. 174) because she believes that the historical context in which a theory develops and the character of the person who originates it *are* relevant to the evaluation of the truth of that view. (The logician's response, I suppose, would be that such historical and psychological factors might well be relevant to our understanding of *what* the person was trying to say but are totally irrelevant to whether the view is well argued.)

So when Nye describes Aristotle's syllogism, she also describes his theory of reproduction, according to which the active male semen impresses its form on passive female matter, and his doctrine of the "natural slave." We learn not only of Abelard's struggle to reconcile Stoic logic with Aristotelianism but also of his dialectical assault on Heloise. And it is claimed (I confess I couldn't follow the argument) that the racist sentiments in Frege's private diary are somehow relevant to his approach to mathematical logic.

Nye (1990) finds even more damning the uses to which logic was put. Thus, she claims, as logical discourse came to be admired in Hellenic law courts or public fora, those who did not follow the prescribed modes were disenfranchised: "Logic rendered them all speechless, unable to voice their reservations and scruples, unable to validate or refute what had been said from their own experiences. And it was this dazzlement and this silencing that logic was *meant* [italics added] to create" (p. 79).

The book culminates by positing a link between Frege, a giant of early 20th-century logic, and Hitler:

> Hitler . . . guided by sentiments not unlike the ones expressed in Frege's diary, worked out the master-logic of National Socialism . . . National Socialism thought like Frege's, did not concern itself with empirical content. . . . No personal experience could negate [its] body of truth. The applications of logic to action that Frege had promised came readily to hand. If Jews are a mongrel race, they must be exterminated. "A thought like a hammer" [Frege's phrase] demanded instant obedience to the dictates of logic. (p. 169)

Nye's feminist reading of the history of logic ends with these words: "Logic in its final perfection is insane" (p. 171).

But are her interpretations of sources at all plausible? If we go back to Frege's (1977) own essay, we find little solace for the authoritarian. Frege begins his final paragraph this way:

> How does a thought act? By being grasped and taken to be true. . . . If, for example, I grasp the thought we express by the theorem of Pythagoras, the consequence may be that I recognize it to be true, and further that I apply it in making a decision. (pp. 28–29)

So far Frege has focused on the inner world of the individual thinker and how our judgments of truth may influence our actions. He then goes on to describe how thoughts are passed on to others.

> The influence of man on man is brought about for the most part by thoughts. People communicate thoughts. . . . Could the great events of world history have come about without the communication of thoughts? And yet we are inclined to regard thoughts as unactual, because they appear to do nothing in relation to events, whereas thinking, judging, stating, understanding, in general doing things, are affairs that concern men. How very different the actuality of a hammer appears, compared with that of a thought! (p. 29)

Nye would have us believe that this essay about the reality of ideas and their influences on the lives of individuals who judge them to be true should be read as a recipe for brainwashing and extermination camps! It is, of course, impossible to refute a "reading." But perhaps the quotations I have displayed might prompt some readers to read Frege for themselves. The question of the historical use and misuse of the tools of logical analysis and inference is an interesting and legitimate one, and I found much of what Nye said about Greek and medieval law thought provoking. But let us not omit the liberating moments in history. Let us also trace the connections between John Stuart Mill's *System of Logic* and the way he argues in *On Liberty* and note the influences of rationalist philosophers of the Enlightenment on the writers of our

Bill of Rights. Let us tell our women students who admire Adrienne Rich's "Dream of a Common Language" that Leibniz and d'Alembert had a related dream and discuss the similarities and differences.

And most important of all, let us stress the use of logic as an instrument of criticism. Nye is correct in saying that too often logic is viewed as a hammer—if you accept these premises, then by God (and by modus ponens) you've got to accept these logical consequences. But modus tollens is a rule of logic, too. And modus tollens says that if a logically correct argument leads to a false conclusion, then by God (or by Goddess!) something is wrong with the premises. Here, logic is acting like a tiny sharp needle—the discovery of one little falsehood can discredit an enormous deductive system. That is why understanding logic is an invaluable tool for groups of people who have little physical or economic strength but do have sharp wits and a rigorous mind.

Let us now turn to some representative feminist critiques of traditional canons of scientific reasoning.

## FEMINIST INCURSIONS INTO PHILOSOPHY OF SCIENCE: RESONANCES WITH POST-KUHNIAN CONCERNS

Just as Nye argued that traditional logic was damaging to women, some feminists claimed that if more women were ever to take part in science, then science itself had to change. To quote a National Science Foundation report by Sue V. Rosser, science had to become more "female-friendly." She called for less emphasis on dissecting frogs and controlled experiments and more fieldwork and science-for-the-people projects.[3] (Note the tendency to speak of "women" instead of "female gender," but if pressed, most authors would switch to gender talk to avoid the charge of "essentialism.")

There developed a vast array of feminist critiques of science, many of them originating from people who had little knowledge of either science or its history, sociology, or philosophy. And their goal sometimes appeared to be to dismantle the authority of and support for science. But influential work was also done by people who had classical training in various branches of what we now call science studies, and in these cases the authors wanted to understand science better and perhaps improve its efficiency, as well as promote political goals. In the sections below, I will concentrate on the works of two noted feminist philosophers of science: Sandra Harding and Helen Longino.[4] But back to my historical narrative.

As long as one focuses on issues of *women* in science, there is no tradition within philosophy of science that would make it plausible that one would turn up anything of particular philosophical relevance. The whole point of the scientific method is to render the personal characteristics of the scientist irrelevant. But when we switch to talk of *gender* and science, the feminist program looks more promising.[5] In what is sometimes called the "historical" approach to philosophy of science (an approach that pays a great deal of attention to past—and present—scientific practice), there had been a lot of interest in documenting the role of what is loosely called "metaphysics" on the development of science. If prescientific conceptions of the nature of matter influence the development of chemistry and ideas about the cosmos influence astronomy, then even nonfeminists should expect gender ideology to have an influence on the development of scientific accounts of reproduction in biology, theories about the relationship between males and females in anthropology, theories about the family in sociology, and models of child development and in a myriad of other places in the social sciences.

And such cases were in fact easy to find— one favorite is Aristotle's account of the passive female egg, which supplied the inert matter, and the active male, which supplied the form. But it was not at all clear what moral should be drawn from such case studies. Philosophers of science from the historical school were interested in questions about discovery, pursuit, how long metaphysically based preconceptions continued to play a role as evidence was collected, questions about incommensurability between conceptual schemes, and so on. Here the cases of apparent influence of ideas about gender seemed completely unremarkable, especially because mistaken ideas that arose from gender stereotypes were removed and corrected

through the normal internal criticism characteristic of the scientific approach.

Those who were specifically interested in gender for other reasons were hoping to draw other morals, namely that the influence of gender ideology was especially ubiquitous and especially powerful. But even in the history of reproduction that case was surprisingly difficult to make! Just as conceptions of matter oscillated between atomistic and continuum theories and optics wrestled with wave versus particle conceptions, so biologists sometimes flirted with accounts that gave the *egg* pride of place over the sperm! Were we to say that 17th- and 18th-century preformationist and ovular accounts of embryology flourished at a period when patriarchy had somehow lost its grip?

Nevertheless, there developed a kind of urban legend about gender and the history of reproduction that even found its way into *Newsweek*.[6] It goes roughly like this: Positivism said that science was not influenced by ideology, but feminists have revolutionized our understanding of how science works. For centuries, scientists thought the egg was passive and it was the sperm which actively went courting and eventually penetrated the egg. But now (the implication being that this happened after the rise of feminism in the mid-20th century) scientists are realizing that the egg also has a say and actively envelopes the sperm of its choice.

But the most that such a feminist research program, no matter how successful, could show was that societal ideas about sex and gender have some sort of impact (we could argue about how much) on the scientific study of subject matter having to do with sex and gender (which admittedly covered a pretty wide domain). But what about physics? And chemistry, and geology? What could gender feminism possibly say about them?

Here some feminist scholars took a quasi-Freudian approach to gender and found influences everywhere, as in Luce Irigaray's attempt to argue that the history of hydrodynamics was influenced, and impeded, by male scientists' fear of soft, yielding fluids and their fixation on models employing rigid bodies.[7] Using a similar approach one could plunk for a steady state cosmology, arguing that some of the appeal of the big bang theory was its masculinist associations.

However, the most interesting and sophisticated move was to see whether there might be something distinctively gendered about research methodology itself.

Because women are more apt to be female gendered (and because there was already all of this early research on women worthies in science), one started looking for distinctive features of their overall approach. Some of the results were interesting additions to the history of science, but their philosophical significance was less clear. Barbara McClintock may indeed have had a "feeling for the organism" and been good at imagining jumping genes, but Albert Einstein (who now turns out to be a right old chauvinist pig) had a "nose for problems" and relied on *Fingerspitzgefuehl* while visualizing rides on light rays. As more histories of antireductionist and antimechanistic approaches to science, including so-called romantic science and Naturphilosophie, were written, it became obvious that the leaders of such movements showed few signs of being protofeminists. There may indeed be some interesting variations in approaches to science—one often speaks of "lumpers" versus splitters, Aristotelians versus Platonists, algebraic versus geometric methods, top-down versus bottom-up approaches to problem solving—but none of these mapped onto masculine versus feminine.

## DO RCG GROUPS HAVE A PRIVILEGED STANDPOINT?

Sandra Harding[8] (1991) proposed a more sophisticated and interesting approach to studying gender and science, which she called "standpoint epistemology"—what you see, what you find important, and how you understand the world depends on your "standpoint." Just as Marx claimed that the standpoint of the proletariat is privileged on economic matters and Hegel argued that sometimes slaves have a clearer picture of what's really going on than masters do (we could also draw examples from the BBC series *Upstairs, Downstairs,* featuring the servants in an Edwardian household), so Harding argues, women and other oppressed groups have distinctive viewpoints to contribute to science. Thus, she calls for what she terms

*strong objectivity:* If present science is distorted by the predominance of male perspectives, would not science become more objective by the deliberate inclusion of views from the standpoint of women, minorities, workers, and any other group that is underrepresented in today's scientific community?

A familiar example that appears to support Harding's thesis is the work of primatologist Jane Goodall, who is noted for her studies of the social organization of chimpanzees. On the face of it, it might appear that much of her success can be attributed to her female standpoint: She exhibited exquisite patience (a stereotypical female virtue) in observing her chimpanzees. (Or was it doggedness, an attribute with less pleasant connotations?) And true, she did focus in on the roles of females and the nature of family relationships, thus perhaps reflecting her "standpoint" as a woman.

But Goodall also documented aggression, murder, and even cannibalism among her beloved chimps. Does being prepared to notice cannibalism also reflect a gendered "standpoint"? Or was she just a careful scientist! Yet what about her empathy with her subjects and her intense commitment to saving their habitat? How can one look at her face on CNN and not see her female-gendered perspective shining through!

Don't get me wrong—to me, Jane Goodall is a saint—a much better role model than Mother Teresa—but how different is her standpoint from that of Jacques Cousteau, who also did naturalistic field work, observed all sorts of new behaviors of the great white shark, and formed the Cousteau Society to save the oceans, all the while exhibiting a typical Gallic chauvinist flair?

But even if one could document that females bring a distinctive perspective to scientific inquiry, postpositivist philosophers of science have a blasé reply: Well, we all know (following Kuhn) that disciplinary commitments influence science and that other perspectives may well play a role in the formative stages, but then as evidence piles up these extraneous influences disappear. Either the distinctive approach stands up to severe tests or it doesn't. To revise a common aphorism, man—or woman—proposes, but Nature disposes.

It is all too easy to assume that certain standpoints have privileged access to the truth. I am reminded of what people used to say about simplicity—surely God would not allow the true picture of the universe to be so complex that we could not understand it. Similarly, one might believe that a goddess would not design a universe that could be accurately described by sociobiology, or a world in which there were socially relevant kinds of genetic influences on intelligence, ability in mathematics, or tendencies to commit violent crimes. If one were to adopt such an article of faith, then just as people used to take simplicity as one indicator of truth, one would now take political progressiveness as an indicator of empirical adequacy!

Let me sum up by noting that Harding's call for the inclusion of a plurality of viewpoints is surely a good idea. Science thrives on the competition among a variety of approaches to solving the problems at hand. And in applied science it becomes especially important to seek input from the users who will actually be working with the innovation. Too often those who would export technology to developing countries have made terrible blunders that could have been avoided if they had worked more closely with people on the ground.

But it would be dubious epistemological advice to recommend that people construct their beliefs on the basis of a particular standpoint, whether it be the one they were born into or one that they deliberately construct. Early feminism urged women to trust their own experience and feelings. This may have been good therapeutic advice for certain individuals who had been brainwashed by authoritarian religions and families. But the whole purpose of education is to supersede provincialism. Too often, feminist pedagogy encourages treating the standpoint of one's own race, class, or gender group as privileged or as a badge of identity. Participants in the Midwest division of the Society for Women in Philosophy (SWIP) often begin papers by declaring their standpoint—"speaking as a Chicana Lesbian Mother."[9] But if we are interested in scientific knowledge, a standpoint is at best a starting point!

## SHOULD POLITICAL COMMITMENTS PLAY A ROLE IN EPISTEMOLOGY?

Helen Longino[10] offers an epistemological approach that diverts attention from the mental processes of the individual knower and instead looks at the shared epistemic values of the scientific community, for example, desiderata such as empirical adequacy, simplicity, and explanatory power. She then argues that the space of scientific hypotheses would be enriched if one looked seriously at theories that conformed to standards exemplified in the work of feminist scientists and commentators. These include *novelty* (a deliberate break with the approaches prevalent in the male-dominated history of science), *ontological heterogeneity* (resistance to models that gloss over individual differences), *complexity of relationship* (recognition of the importance of interactions), and *applicability to current human needs* (Longino, 1995). Longino also suggests a variety of ways of improving the ways in which scientific hypotheses are discussed and evaluated, which I will not summarize here.

Note that, as I have described it thus far, Longino's epistemology is *feminist* in only a rather sophisticated (or should I say attenuated?) sense. No longer are we trying to attribute to women special ways of knowing, such as intuitive or qualitative or holistic. Nor are we trying to describe gendered differences in knowing—one is not claiming that there is something masculinist about liking the big bang theory or the mechanics of billiard balls. Rather, it seems to me, Longino is making a historical point about the inspiration for her epistemology. At this point in time feminists have been at the forefront of criticizing certain approaches to anthropology, biology, and psychology. Longino has extracted from those critiques a list of values that she believes are different from those embedded in mainstream science. She then proposes that science would be enriched by actively pursuing hypotheses that score well on the values that she extracted from the writings of feminists.

The issue of the uniquely feminist status of such values is perhaps less important than their intrinsic merits. Let's look at them briefly in turn. *Novelty* is a value touted by all would-be scientific revolutionaries. In some cases, it leads to progress—if epicycles seem to be multiplying without end, then maybe it's time to look beyond Ptolemaic astronomy. But every crank theory ever proposed also measures up well on the novelty scale.

The usefulness of encouraging *ontological heterogeneity* also depends on circumstances: Many scientific breakthroughs involve a reduction of heterogeneity—we now know that organic compounds do not require a vital force for their synthesis; they obey the same laws as inorganic compounds. But in other cases, more ontological heterogeneity *is* needed. One thinks of the introduction of new fundamental particles—a neutron is not just a combo of the familiar proton and electron; it is a different kind of particle. Similar considerations accrue to the value of *complexity of relationship*. There are generally methodological advantages to starting out with simple models, but they don't always capture the phenomena.

As for *applicability to current human needs*, since the time of Bacon both scientists and funding agencies have shared this value. Where it gets tricky is in prioritizing needs and guessing which lines of research are most likely to pan out. Applying this criterion is also complicated by the fact that so-called basic or pure research often turns out to be exceedingly useful in improving the human condition. I once heard a talk that tried to analyze the research leading to the birth control pill into steps that were mission directed and steps that had been taken with no such purpose in mind. What was striking to me was that the story of the birth control pill was not, as I expected, a tale that began with scattered pure research that was followed by an intense period of applied or development activity. Rather, there was a continuous interjection of, and reliance on, research results that had no intentional connection to the quest for a pill. In this case too much emphasis on Longino's norm of applicability to human needs would probably have slowed the development of a method of birth control that had an enormous liberating effect on women.

Leaving aside the issue of what we should make of Longino's list of proposed new epistemic values, we can surely agree with her point that they might inspire new approaches to current scientific problems, and she is certainly right to argue that a free-ranging debate that paid respectful attention to a plurality of viewpoints would certainly be of *epistemic* benefit to science (no matter how conservative our conception of scientific inquiry might be). Because

women's perspectives have historically been neglected, including them would be one obvious way of diversifying the pool of hypotheses that would then be scrutinized by scientists in their search for good scientific theories. But Longino goes on to make remarks that are consistent with the radical proposal that we should include the likely political repercussions of a scientific research program as a relevant factor in our internal evaluations of it.

Longino's stance vis-à-vis this proposal is very unclear because her discussions of theories she dislikes (e.g., man-the-hunter and linear-hormonal models) show their empirical flaws as well as their purported political infelicities. Perhaps Longino is simply reminding us of type II statistical error and urging us to adopt a precautionary strategy: If a theory is likely to have bad social consequences we should be especially cautious in basing policy on it—while adding the warning that sometimes even to raise a question that cannot be quickly answered can cause harm. Traditional philosophy of science readily admits the important role of social values in the context of application of scientific results; it is more controversial to suggest that we rule out certain kinds of research problems simply because we are afraid of what we may find—certainly Alfred Kinsey would have objected!

But Longino also seems to be suggesting that we add political progressiveness to the traditional list of cognitive virtues that are used to evaluate scientific hypotheses. If that is her intent, then she is indeed proposing a radical feminist account of scientific rationality, one that puts a specific political agenda right at the justificatory heart of the search for knowledge. Let us briefly document what Longino says on this issue. (Her precise view is not easy to interpret.) We will then go on to criticize the position that feminists might easily take away from reading Longino.

Longino's (1990) book *Science as Social Knowledge: Values and Objectivity in Scientific Inquiry* contrasts what she calls constitutive and contextual values. Constitutive values include empirical adequacy, accuracy, breadth, and predictive power; contextual values are those current in the social and cultural environment in which science operates at a given time and place

(p. 4). Traditional normative accounts of the development of science would caution us to keep contextual values out of our appraisals of the epistemic merits of scientific hypotheses. Longino's social epistemology finds this prophylactic approach both unrealistic and undesirable: "The idea of a value-free science is not just empty but pernicious" (p. 191).

Her own positive account of the proper role of contextual values is not clearly spelled out. But the following quotes provide some hints: "When faced with a conflict between these commitments and a particular model of brain-behavior relationships we allow the political commitments to guide the choice" (pp. 190–191). How exactly are political commitments supposed to guide the choice between competing theories? Since Longino considers herself to be an empiricist, Anderson finds the concerns of critics such as me to be baseless. After all, Longino lists empirical adequacy as a core constitutive value for science. So wouldn't whatever emphasis she places on other values in the end be trumped by how well the theory is supported by evidence? Yet one of the distinctive features of Longino's epistemology is her emphasis on a variety of other values, and as Anderson (2004) herself reports,

> Feminist epistemologists have also sometimes used the term "context of justification" to refer to more than the process of determining the truth or warrant of theories. Theories are evaluated with respect to *all* of the goals for which they were constructed.[11]

So let us read further in Longino.

Longino ends her chapter on science and ideology this way (my comments are interspersed between sentences that were contiguous in the original): "The theory which is the product of the most inclusive scientific community is better, other things being equal, than that which is the product of the most exclusive" (p. 214). (The things that must be equal presumably include how well the theory measures up to constitutive values, such as empirical adequacy.)

But then Longino continues: "It [the theory] is better not as measured against some independently accessible reality but better as measured against the cognitive needs of a genuinely democratic community." (Here we see contextual values being brought into play—the more theories conform to the needs of a community, the better they are, other things being equal. We may be taken aback when we recall that Nazi Germany had a cognitive need for theories of Aryan superiority and that the Kansas School Board has a need for research showing the inadequacy of neo-Darwinism. Longino, however, insists that science only needs to appraise theories in response to the cognitive needs of *genuinely democratic* communities.)

She concludes: "This suggests that the problem of developing a new science is the problem of creating a new social and political reality." Here we have a stirring call for feminist action—by improving society we will make possible an improved science. Yet Longino's proposal raises all the concerns that go along with utopian dreams. Even if one cedes for the sake of argument that incorporating political values into science would be OK in a "genuine" democracy, nothing follows about whether it is wise to let a society's cognitive needs play a role in theory appraisal within an imperfect democracy. Is the promise of research on adult stem cells as contrasted with embryonic stem cells to be influenced by what today's society *wants* to be the case? Or to pick examples that would appear to satisfy more progressive cognitive needs: Should we judge the economic and technological feasibility of hydrogen fuel cells partly in terms of our nation's energy needs?

I think not. From the early days of the Royal Society, scientists have realized that it is much more difficult to reach consensus about religious and political matters than it is to agree on the empirical adequacy and explanatory power of competing scientific accounts. Not only are our wishes about how we want the world to be completely irrelevant to the way the world actually is, it is impractical to make scientific appraisals dependent on political agendas. The one thing you can be sure of in a genuine democracy is that science policy about futuristic science agendas will be highly contested and subject to change! Science can help society improve itself by providing feedback on the viability of various scenarios. As we have seen with NASA in recent years, when a science program tries too hard to accommodate contextual values, its rockets may not work![12]

## CONCLUSION

So where do matters stand today with feminist perspectives on scientific reasoning, logic, and theories of rationality? And what should we expect in the future? The prevalent picture of science in the humanities today is strongly influenced by feminist research, reinforced, of course, by the writings of postmodernists and social constructionists.[13] Students and faculty alike often expect a philosophy of science course to deal with feminist perspectives on science as well as critiques of technoscience. Textbooks today reflect that market and typically have a section at the end dealing with social constructivism and feminism. The second edition of Kourany's (1998) anthology, by contrast, not only begins with a section on the social context in which scientific knowledge is produced, but also integrates essays written from feminist and social constructivist perspectives into units on the traditional topics of the empirical basis and validation of scientific knowledge.

At this point in time, it seems to me that the future of feminist perspectives on science is closely bound up with the fate of postmodernism and the variants of social constructionism that have played such an important role in the so-called science wars. As a partisan in those wars who is very critical of feminist, postmodernist, and constructivist understandings of science, I am perhaps overly optimistic about their quick demise! But I do think there are sociological as well as intellectual reasons for feminists not to place all their bets on those lines of research! Anderson's (2004) encyclopedia article points out that some feminist philosophers are making a distinction between "feminist science" and "doing science as a feminist" and recommending the latter (p. 19). This is a hopeful sign, although I think the appropriate goal would be to simply have "feminists doing science." We can find a parallel threefold distinction in the current debates about evolution in the schools: Some advocate "creationist science"; recently, people such as Michael Behe could be described as "doing science as a Christian"; others, such as Kenneth Miller, are simply "Christians doing science."

In epistemology proper (as opposed to the broader field of science studies), some authors who self-identify as feminist, such as Longino, are read with respect. However, as our brief look at Longino bears out, although she is obviously influenced by academic feminism, her views on social epistemology can be understood and evaluated without referencing any specifically feminist concerns. It is an epistemology that extols theoretical pluralism and wants science to be more responsive to democratic values. If I were to teach a seminar on Longino, I might pair her new book (Longino, 2001), *The Fate of Knowledge,* with Philip Kitcher's (2003) *Science, Truth, and Democracy*, a book without feminist roots.[14] So while feminist concerns may continue to play a heuristic role in the current epistemological line of research, I anticipate that the intellectual connection between feminism and epistemology proper will weaken, although the label will continue to be used for pragmatic epistemic approaches that place an emphasis on the social dimension of inquiry.

So what are those who remain concerned about the underrepresentation of women in the physical and cognitive sciences to do? Do women's studies or gender studies have anything to contribute? My recommendations will sound terribly old-fashioned, and they may not be esoteric enough to get anyone tenure in today's terribly, terribly sophisticated university. As Hippocrates said long ago, first let us do no harm. Even if one sincerely and thoughtfully believes that there are special and superior women's ways of knowing, let us not put barriers in the way of women's learning to play the violin or do physics in a supposedly patriarchal fashion! Women are alienated enough without making them feel like a gender traitor if they like logic or appreciate abstract mathematical theories. And women are smart enough to be "bilingual" learners, to appreciate the beauty of a Euclidean proof as well as the beauty of a patchwork quilt!

If one sincerely and thoughtfully believes that there are special and superior women's ways of knowing, then let us do research to show their benefits and then make them available to all students. But let us not automatically conclude that every mental habit of women or of the female gender *is* superior. Oppression can lead to stunted development as well as clever survival skills.

And in an age that expects convenience in every aspect of human existence, let us remember that not every bump in one's educational journey is the result of patriarchy or prejudice. Some concepts are intrinsically difficult to grasp (the Greeks were smart, but an understanding of probabilities only began in the 17th century), and intellectual work, whether it is writing poetry or understanding thermodynamics, is difficult and time-consuming. Women's studies, with its natural emphasis on the barriers women have faced, and its understandable urge to provide students with a sympathetic classroom environment, may all too easily lead students to believe that if life is hard that means something is unfair, that they're being victimized, and that they should assertively demand change. As the women's movement becomes more and more successful—and there's all sorts of evidence showing that it is—it becomes less and less likely that the major cause of the difficulties encountered by a given young woman is either overt bias or so-called structural discrimination. Our foremothers knew very well that when the going gets tough, the tough get going. They were not afraid to be better than their peers if that's what it took. That's still good advice for anyone, male or female, black or white, today. To teach young women that they are in fact epistemically privileged but have trouble in certain classes because those disciplines are intrinsically patriarchal or cater to male knowers is not only to act on a speculative feminist conjecture that has been seriously criticized but also to impart advice that can do great harm.

Thoughtful feminist philosophers of science do not intend their writings to harm would-be women scientists or educated laywomen. They are writing to oppose what they consider to be a male-dominated philosophical tradition. But they must become more aware of how their views are bowdlerized and simplified in women's studies classes and nonprofessional feminist writings. The climate in WOST still reflects its historical suspicion of logic and science. Feminist epistemologists are well situated to change that legacy, but to do so, they must confront feminist falsehoods.

## NOTES

1. For a fuller discussion of the climate in early women's studies programs see Patai and Koertge (2003).

2. See the further discussion in Patai and Koertge (2003, chap. 7).

3. See Patai and Koertge (2003, chap. 12).

4. For a broader critical survey of feminist epistemological views, see Pinnick, Koertge, and Almeder (2003). Anderson's (2004) encyclopedia article provides a useful taxonomy of competing feminist epistemologies and extensive references to sympathetic feminist commentaries.

5. A former colleague of mine reports that one day he realized he needed a new file folder, one labeled "Gender and Science," to accompany his "Women and Science" offprints. It was only then that he realized the philosophical relevance of feminist commentaries on science.

6. For an amusing account of the history of the sperm-egg saga, see Paul Gross's article "Bashful Eggs, Macho Sperm, and Tonypandy" (Koertge, 1998, chap. 4).

7. This approach was further developed by Katherine Hayles. For a critical analysis, see "An Engineer Dissects Two Case Studies: Hayles on Fluid Mechanics, and MacKenzie on Statistics," in Koertge (1998, chap. 5).

8. Sandra Harding, now Director of the UCLA Center for the Study of Women, made notable contributions to traditional philosophy of science early in her career (see Harding, 1976). But she is best known for her work on feminist and postcolonialist critiques of science. Her standpoint epistemology has received a good deal of critical attention. For a good introduction to the issues, see Parsons (2003), who provides excerpts from Harding's own writings and then comments on them.

9. For more on feminist philosophy organizations, see Patai and Koertge (2003, p. 209).

10. Longino is a distinguished philosopher of science who draws inspiration from current feminist perspectives. For a good introduction to her epistemology, see the interview posted at www.stanford.edu/group/dualist/vol10/longino.html. Longino recently moved from Minnesota to Stanford.

11. See the review of Pinnick et al. (2003) posted on her Web site: www-personal.umich.edu/~eandersn

12. For a further discussion, see Koertge's "Feminist Values and the Value of Science" in Pinnick et al. (2003) and Koertge (2002).

13. I have not dwelt on them here. For a thoroughgoing critique see Koertge (1998) and Parsons (2003).

14. As editor of *Philosophy of Science*, I was privileged to be able to arrange a lengthy interchange

between Longino and Kitcher. See *Philosophy of Science, 69*(4), 2002, 549–573.

# REFERENCES

Anderson, Elizabeth. (2004). Feminist epistemology and philosophy of science. http://plato.stanford.edu/archives/spr2004/entries/feminism-epistemology.

Aristotle. (1964). *Prior and posterior analytics* (John Warrington, Trans.). London: J. M. Dent & Sons.

Carroll, Lewis. (1958). *Symbolic logic and the game of logic.* New York: Dover.

Copi, Irving M. (1968). *Introduction to logic* (3rd ed.). New York: Macmillan.

Copi, Irving M. (1979). *Symbolic logic* (5th ed.). New York: Macmillan.

Frege, Gottlob. (1977). *Logical investigations* (P. T. Geach & R. H. Stoothoff, Trans.). Bristol, UK: Western Printing Services.

Gross, Paul R. (1998). Bashful eggs, macho sperm, and tonypandy. In Noretta Koertge (Ed.), *A house built on sand: Exposing postmodernist myths about science* (pp. 59–70). New York: Oxford University Press.

Harding, Sandra. (Ed.). (1976). *Can theories be refuted? Essays on the Duhem-Quine thesis.* Dordrecht, the Netherlands: Reidel.

Harding, Sandra. (1991). *Whose science? Whose knowledge? Thinking from women's lives.* Ithaca, NY: Cornell University Press.

Kahane, Howard. (1986). *Logic and philosophy: A modern introduction* (5th ed.). Belmont, CA: Wadsworth.

Kalish, Donald, & Montague, Richard. (1964). *Logic: Techniques of formal reasoning.* New York: Harcourt, Brace & World.

Kitcher, Philip. (2003). *Science, truth, and democracy.* New York: Oxford University Press.

Koertge, Noretta. (Ed.). (1998). *A house built on sand: Exposing postmodernist myths about science.* New York: Oxford University Press.

Koertge, Noretta. (2002). How might we put gender politics into science? *Philosophy of Science Proceedings 2002, 71,* 868–879.

Kourany, Janet A. (1998). *Scientific knowledge: Basic issues in the philosophy of science* (2nd ed.). Belmont, CA: Wadsworth.

Longino, Helen E. (1990). *Science as social knowledge: Values and objectivity in scientific inquiry.* Princeton, NJ: Princeton University Press.

Longino, Helen, E. (1995). Gender, politics, and the theoretical virtues. *Synthese, 104,* 383–397.

Longino, Helen E. (2001). *The fate of knowledge.* Princeton, NJ: Princeton University Press.

Nye, Andrea. (1990). *Words of power: A feminist reading of the history of logic. Thinking gender.* New York: Routledge.

Parsons, Keith. (Ed.). (2003). *The science wars: Debating scientific knowledge and technology.* Amherst, NY: Prometheus Books.

Patai, Daphne, & Koertge, Noretta. (2003). *Professing feminism: Education and indoctrination in women's studies.* Lanham, MD: Lexington Books.

Pinnick, Cassandra L., Koertge, Noretta, & Almeder, Robert F. (Eds.). (2003). *Scrutinizing feminist epistemology: An examination of gender in science.* New Brunswick, NJ: Rutgers University Press.

Suppes, Patrick. (1957). *Introduction to logic* (J. L. Kelly & P. R. Halmos, Eds.). Princeton, NJ: D. Van Nostrand.

# 30

## THE FEMINISM QUESTION IN SCIENCE

### *What Does It Mean to "Do Social Science as a Feminist"?*

ALISON WYLIE

From the time feminists turned a critical eye on conventional practice in the social sciences, they have asked what it would mean to do better, more inclusive research. For many, initially the challenge was to counteract sexist, androcentric erasure and bias in conventional research. Practical guidelines and handbooks proliferated, like Eichler's (1988) *Nonsexist Research Methods*, codifying principles many of which are now widely accepted. But for others the challenge was to think beyond conventional practice: What forms of social science do we need to develop to be effective in addressing questions that have largely been left out of account, questions that particularly matter for understanding, with precision and explanatory force, the systems of social differentiation and conditions of life, the forms of experience and identity, that are, to varying degrees and in diverse ways, oppressive for those categorized as women or as sex/gender variant? It was this question that became the focus of sustained discussion through the 1980s and early 1990s in the context of the feminist method debate: the "feminism question in science," as I will refer to

it, inverting the question Harding (1986) poses in *The Science Question in Feminism*.

I focus here on two broad strategies of response: Longino's discussion of what it means to "do science as a feminist," and a distillation of the guidelines for practice proposed by feminist social scientists. I then consider examples of feminist research that both exemplify and put epistemically consequential pressure on these principles. The anxiety that haunts these discussions is that if research is guided by explicitly feminist values, its epistemic credibility is irrevocably compromised. The methodological principles I will consider illustrate how this worry is countered in practice; I conclude with an argument for a reformulation of feminist standpoint theory that captures the wisdom implicit in this practice.

## METHODOLOGICAL ESSENTIALISM AND THE VALUE(S) OF SCIENCE

One family of answers to my central question has long been highly contentious: that feminists must seek a distinctive form of practice, a

567

uniquely "feminist science," because conventional strategies of research practice in the social sciences are inherently patriarchal and cannot be recuperated. Those who might be interpreted as holding such a position, a view more often attributed to feminists than exemplified by their practice, include feminist critics of the social sciences who saw these disciplines as one node in a network of "ruling practices" that operate by "eclipsing" women's roles and contributions, marginalizing their experience, and trivializing their self-understanding (Smith, 1978)—as an enterprise animated by interests that are systematically obscured by a positivist rhetoric of objectivity and value neutrality (Mies, 1983; Stanley & Wise, 1983b).[1] As one example of a more general antipathy for the sciences, such a stance, and its presumed implication for practice—that feminists must seek a distinctively feminist form of practice—has been sharply criticized by epistemic conservatives, who reject the very idea of feminist science on the ground that it is a contradiction in terms. To take one prominent example, Haack (1993) objects that any intrusion of gender-specific interests into the sciences can only compromise their integrity; to advocate a feminist methodology or a feminist science is to abandon "honest inquiry"—inquiry inspired by a "genuine desire to find out how things are"—in favor of a dogmatic commitment to "make a case for a foregone conclusion" ("sham" research). Moreover, Haack argues, the quest for feminist forms of practice presupposes an untenable gender essentialism: that women *qua* women must share a distinctively female or feminine "way of knowing" and that women scientists must rely on feminine forms of intuition and (non)reason that have been (in Haack's view, rightly) ignored by traditional theories of knowledge and marginalized within mainstream science.

In fact, feminists were among the earliest and most uncompromising critics of gender essentialism, and some of the sharpest challenges to the quest for a distinctively feminist method came from advocates of feminist practice in the social sciences. One catalyst for the feminist method debate was the question, why limit feminist initiatives to one particular set of methods or research strategy (Jayaratne, 1983)? By the early 1990s, Reinharz (1992a) could identify feminist uses of virtually every research method

and methodology available in the social sciences; and by the end of the 1990s, Gottfried (1996) concluded that feminist practitioners had made a decisive "move from singularity to plurality" (p. 12). Parallel arguments had been made a decade earlier by Harding (1987) and by Longino (1987), who argued that there is no brief for positing "a distinctive female way of knowing"; why should feminists allow methodological commitments to define in advance the scope of their research agenda? Was this not simply to re-entrench at the core of feminist research programs the mystification of method that feminists found so debilitating in the sciences they hoped to reform (Harding, 1987, p. 19)? Longino (1987) urged that questions about the nature and direction of feminist research be reframed: We should ask not what it means to build or to do "feminist science" but what is involved in "doing science as a feminist" (p. 53). By extension, we should be prepared to recognize that what "doing research as a feminist" means in practice will be as diverse as what it means to be a feminist and as situationally specific as the fields in which feminists have undertaken to "do science."

While Haack and like-minded critics might be reassured by this repudiation of essentialism, they would no doubt find just as worrisome the endorsement of pluralism, predicated as it is on the conviction that scientific inquiry is always *relative to* context, if not *relativist* (Hesse, 1980, p. 181). But *contra* Haack, far from being a marginal extreme, the arguments for a pragmatic, contextualist turn in thinking about the sciences—for recognizing that the sciences are historically contingent and deeply structured by context-specific interests and values—are by now generic to the philosophy of science (Lloyd, 1995).[2] Arguments from such canonical philosophical theses as Quine-Duhem holism, the theory ladenness of evidence, and the underdetermination of theory by evidence establish that cognitive, evidential, and logical factors rarely, if ever, determine theory choice: "whatever grounds for knowledge we have, they are not sufficient to warrant the assertion of claims beyond doubt" (Longino, 1994, p. 472). Crucially, this is not just a matter of the underdetermination of content, such that contextual factors must take up the slack in determining the significance of empirical data as evidence. It is, in addition, a matter of meta-underdetermination: The cognitive and epistemic values presumed to be constitutive of well-functioning (unbiased, objective) science are themselves underdetermined as guidelines for practice. Such widely cited principles as a commitment to maximize the empirical adequacy, predictive and explanatory power, intertheoretic consistency, and internal coherence of scientific theories, as well as quasi-aesthetic values such as simplicity or formal elegance, are by no means transparent; they require interpretation and typically cannot be simultaneously maximized (Doppelt, 1988; Kuhn, 1977, p. 322; Longino, 1995; Wylie, 1995). What counts as meeting a requirement of empirical adequacy, for example, is by no means given by the facts themselves or by abstract ideals of rationality. Standards of empirical adequacy are context specific and evolve within distinct research traditions, in response to goals and interests that are external to inquiry as well as to internal theoretical and technical considerations. And when epistemic values come into conflict, as when a commitment to formal idealization (e.g., to expand explanatory and predictive scope) requires a trade-off of localized empirical adequacy, the question of which constitutive value should take precedence must generally be settled by appeal to the noncognitive goals and values that inform the research program.

Doing (social) science as a feminist is a matter, then, of insisting that we be accountable for the values and interests that shape not just our choice of research questions but also the whole range of decisions and conventions that constitute our research practice. Far from seeing this pragmatism as grounds for despair, or for outrage (in the case of Haack), I join a growing contingent of science studies theorists who argue that we should regard contextual values as a crucial condition for the success of the sciences, not only (or always) as a source of compromising contamination (Wylie & Nelson, in press).

## THE FEMINIST QUESTION IN (SOCIAL) SCIENCE

Consider, then, two ways in which feminists have articulated a mandate for "doing research as a feminist": Longino's philosophical account of the community values that inform the research undertaken by feminists in the sciences generally and the methodological guidelines developed by feminist social scientists.

Longino has identified six community values—or "theoretical virtues"—as characteristic of the work of feminist scientists (1987, 1990, 1994; Wylie, 1995). There is some ambiguity about the status of these virtues: whether they describe what feminist practitioners actually do (in an unspecified range of sciences) or are intended to capture what feminists could or should do. And they are strikingly free of any explicit feminist content. They cluster around three focal concerns:

1. *Epistemic values*: Longino finds feminists committed, first and foremost, to a fundamental requirement of empirical adequacy and to a preference for novel hypotheses (Longino, 1994, p. 476, 1995, p. 386).

2. *Ontological*: She identifies, as well, a preference for hypotheses that take full account of diversity in the objects of study—that allow "equal standing for different types"—and that treat "complex interaction as a fundamental principle of explanation" (Longino, 1994, pp. 477–478; see also Longino, 1995, pp. 387–388).

3. *Normative and pragmatic values*: She finds feminist research animated by a commitment to use the tools of scientific inquiry to generate knowledge that is "applicab[le] to current human needs" (Longino, 1994, p. 476, 1995, p. 389) and to democratize the production of knowledge in ways that foster an "equality of intellectual authority" (Longino, 1990, pp. 78–81, 1993a, 1993b, 1995, p. 389).

Even this last, most explicitly normative, commitment is warranted not because it makes scientific practice a site for institutional change along lines advocated by feminists in other contexts, but because it provides for a redistribution of power and resources within the sciences that Longino (1990, pp. 76–80) believes will enhance the epistemic integrity of inquiry. It counteracts the reification of epistemic authority, expanding the range of perspectives brought to bear on conventional assumptions; it reinforces a recognition that knowledge production is a pluralistic enterprise that serves divergent goals ("cognitive needs"), engaging dissent seriously and fostering if not an idealized "view from everywhere," at least "views from many wheres" (Longino, 1993b, p. 113; see the elaboration of these epistemic norms in Longino, 2002, pp. 128–135).

The sense in which these community values are *feminist* is that they embody what Longino (1994) describes as a "bottom line" feminist commitment. They have the effect of "prevent[ing] gender from being disappeared," and in this they are evaluative standards that "mak[e] gender a relevant axis of investigation" (p. 481). So, for example, the preference for novelty counteracts the conservative, gender-disappearing effects that can be expected to follow from the more typical directive to maximize consistency with other well-established theories (given that these are likely to be predicated on just the kinds of gender-conventional wisdom feminists are intent on challenging). The preference for ontological and causal complexity likewise counters conventions of practice that privilege the sorts of simplifying idealization Smith (1978) found responsible for the sociological "eclipsing" of women's experience. And a commitment to democratize scientific practice, while justified on gender-neutral epistemic grounds, puts the onus on the scientific community to ensure that marginal voices are not systematically silenced, including the voices of women. Longino (1994) adds to these principles and the "bottom line" maxim one further metaprinciple: *epistemic provisionalism*. Each of the other community values must be held open to revision in light of what feminists learn from practice (p. 483).

In the context of feminist social science, Longino's community values find their clearest articulation in the guidelines for nonsexist research mentioned at the outset, where the goal is to improve research by conventional standards. Feminist interests and values figure as a resource; they draw attention to gaps and distortions in conventional research and to aspects of the subject domain and explanatory possibilities that have been overlooked. In practice, however, feminist research has been animated by much more explicitly feminist goals than these; the principles articulated in the context of the method debate are broadly consistent with Longino's community values but go well beyond them. I identify four widely shared commitments

around which the overlapping systems of general principles, ideals, maxims, and guidelines for feminist research have coalesced since the early 1980s.

The principle to which feminist social scientists typically give first priority is a specification of explicitly *feminist goals*: The "human needs" that feminist researchers should be concerned to address when they practice as feminists are those of women and, more generally, those oppressed by gender-structured systems of inequality. Sometimes these feminist goals have been articulated as a requirement that feminist research should be "movement-generated"; not only should it expose the sexism inherent in extant institutions—"muckraking research" (Ehrlich, 1975, p. 10)—it should also generate strategies for changing these institutions (p. 13). The other orienting principles are articulations of how best to realize feminist goals however these are defined.

The second is a directive to *ground feminist research in women's experience*: to take "as our starting point" women's experience and everyday lives (Smith, 1974, 1987, p. 85). In effect, Longino's (1994, p. 481, 1995, p. 391) "bottom line maxim" is reframed as a commitment, not just to ensure that gender is "not disappeared," but also to treat gendered experience and self-understanding as a crucial resource in developing a systematic understanding of the gendered dimensions of community life and institutions, systems of belief, social differentiation, and inequality. Sometimes this principle counters the second, ontological cluster of values Longino (1994, pp. 477–478, 1995, pp. 387–388) identifies. Rather than advocate ontological heterogeneity and multidirectional causality as desirable in themselves, it suggests that feminists should build into their theories whatever degree of complexity (or simplification) is necessary to do justice to women's experience and the sex/gender systems that structure their lives.

A third cluster of principles specify ethical commitments that give further content to Longino's (1994, p. 478, 1995, p. 389) normative and pragmatic values. They require that feminists hold themselves *accountable to research subjects*, broadly construed. At the very least the research process should not oppress or exploit research subjects; ideally, it should empower them, particularly when they are themselves oppressed by sex/gender systems. Feminist practitioners often insist, more ambitiously, that they should make research practice a site for instituting feminist social and political values: They should deliberately counteract the hierarchical structures that make social science a "ruling practice" and implement egalitarian, participatory forms of knowledge production. Here, a general argument for democratizing research practice is specified as a commitment to break down the (gendered) hierarchies of power and authority that operate in much conventional research; in the ideal, research subjects and those affected by research should play an active, collaborative role at all stages of research design, data collection, analysis, and authorship.

Fourth, virtually every set of published guidelines for feminist research in the social sciences emphasizes the importance of cultivating a stance of sustained and critical *reflexivity*. As Narayan (1988) puts it, "One of the most attractive features of feminist thinking is its commitment to contextualizing its claims" (p. 32). At the very least, this requires feminist social scientists to "state their premises rather than hide them" (Reinharz, 1992b, p. 426). On stronger formulations, it requires that feminists, *qua* feminists, take into account the various ways in which their own social locations, their interests and values, are constitutive of the research process and of the understanding it produces (e.g., Cook & Fonow, 1986; Fonow & Cook, 1991; Mies, 1983). Standpoint theorists specify what this involves in terms of a requirement for "strong objectivity": The tools of jointly empirical and conceptual inquiry should be applied (reflexively) to the research process itself (Harding, 1993). With this, Longino's (1994, p. 483) principle of "methodological provisionalism" is reframed as a requirement, not just that feminists should be willing to revise orienting principles but that they should subject them, actively and continuously, to conceptual, empirical scrutiny.

## DOING SOCIAL SCIENCE AS A FEMINIST, IN PRACTICE

The research projects that most straightforwardly realize these principles and that stood as an ideal for much early feminist social science were various forms of community self-study: *research undertaken by women, on women, for women* (Gorelick, 1991, p. 459; e.g., Jacobson, 1977). Here, women's experience gives rise directly to the questions asked; inquiry is motivated by explicitly activist objectives and designed with the aim of leveling the hierarchy of authority inherent in traditional "expert" forms of social scientific research. The use of qualitative, participatory methods of inquiry (e.g., oral history, ethnography, discourse analysis) serves not only to engage research subjects directly in the research process but also to resituate the particularities of women's experience and self-understanding at the center of inquiry, counteracting the "eclipsing" of this experience and its assimilation to gender-conventional categories of description and analysis (Smith, 1974, 1978). In some cases, these projects were directly inspired by consciousness-raising practice conceived as a matter of "grasp[ing] the collective reality of women's condition from within the perspective of that experience" (MacKinnon, 1982, p. 536), bearing witness to the particularities of women's lives and critically situating these in the frame of broader patterns of gender politics and gendered institutions (Wylie, 1992, p. 237). A classic example is the grassroots research on workplace environment issues—the "chilly climate" that women encounter in academia and other traditionally male-dominated professions—that proliferated in the late 1970s and 1980s (Chilly Collective, 1995). In these projects the four methodological principles I have identified are given a literal interpretation and are mutually reinforcing.

At the same time, however, feminists were exploring a range of questions and research strategies that pointed up ambiguities inherent in the interpretation of these principles and showed how they might come into conflict with one another. Consider, specifically, some examples that put pressure on a literal reading of the directive to ground feminist research in women's experience—the most contentious of the four principles where worries about epistemic integrity and objectivity are concerned.

### The Subject of Research

First, and perhaps most obviously, if the goal of feminist research is to address questions that are relevant for understanding and ultimately changing gendered systems of oppression, it does not follow that women must always be the primary subject of feminist inquiry. Stanley and Wise (1979, 1983a, 1983b) argued, in this connection, that if feminists are to understand the hostility to women that underpins patriarchal culture, it will be necessary to study the attitudes and behaviors of sexist and misogynist men; this was the rationale for their early work on obscene telephone calls. The course of development of "chilly climate" research makes it clear how important comparison with male peers is in discerning conditions that reproduce inequality, some of which are effective precisely because they are opaque to women (Wylie, 2004).

But beyond changing the subject, feminist practitioners often draw on women's experience as a source of research questions and interpretive insight rather than taking it as a direct subject of inquiry. This opens up space for feminist research in fields where women themselves, and the experiential dimensions of social life, are often inaccessible, as in archaeology (Wylie, 2001), or where the subject of inquiry is projectively gendered, as in primatology (Strum & Fedigan, 2000). It also throws into relief the potentially radical implications of a thoroughgoing commitment to epistemic provisionalism. Those who undertake research as feminists routinely discover that what they most need to understand, to address a problem initially identified in gender terms, are the dynamics of class formation and the emergence and maintenance of systemic racism, along with myriad other forms of social differentiation that are mutually constitutive of contemporary sex/gender systems. The lessons from queer theory and transnational feminisms make it especially clear that a sophisticated understanding of gender inequality cannot be expected to arise from research that focuses narrowly on gendered institutions, symbolic economies, roles, and identities. Far from dogmatically recapitulating foregone conclusions, the substantive results of feminist research frequently destabilize—even "disappear"—the categories that originally gave it direction.

## Critiques of Experientialism

Even when women and gender are the primary subject of analysis, there are two further reasons to resist a literal reading of the directive to ground research in women's experience. One targets an early construal of the "grounding" requirement that took it to be a proscription against questioning women's experience, as when Stanley and Wise (1983a, 1983b) insisted that in countering sexist assumptions about the credibility and significance of women's self-reports—in treating women as authorities about their own experience—feminist researchers must never "go beyond" women's experience. The pitfalls of such "experientialism" became an immediate focus of attention in the feminist method debate (e.g., Brunsdon, 1978; Grant, 1987). In her classic article, "The Evidence of Experience," Scott (1991) objects that "when experience is taken as the origin of knowledge, the vision of the individual subject becomes the bedrock on which explanation is built," foreclosing questions about the "constructed nature of experience, about how subjects are constituted different in the first place, about how one's vision is structured" (p. 776). "Giving voice is not enough" (Gorelick, 1991, pp. 463, 477), even when the goal of research is to bear witness to forms of community life and experience that have been systematically marginalized in a sexist, heteronormative society.

The practical implications of this critique are evident, for example, in the care with which Kennedy and Davis (1993) scrutinize their subjects' recollections of a working-class lesbian community that grew up in Buffalo in the 1940s and 1950s. They worry about the vagaries of memory, where interviewees were asked to recall events and conditions of life from 30 or 40 years earlier, and about the impact on these memories of fundamental changes in social and cultural conceptions of what it means to be a lesbian that had emerged in the intervening years. They employ a strategy of triangulation, systematically cross-checking interviewees' accounts to ensure the factual accuracy of the historical ethnography they constructed. It is precisely because they respect their subjects and the larger community they represent that Kennedy and Davis insist on the need to treat these experiential accounts judiciously, not disrespectfully but with critical caution.

Similar principles are operative in the context of feminist research that is explicitly designed as a form of therapeutic and activist intervention.

The staff of the Battered Women's Advocacy Center (BWAC) in London (Ontario, Canada) developed a standardized intake form, which made it possible to collect information about the demography, family histories, experiences of violence, and strategies of response of the women making use of BWAC's services. While this form provided crucial support for the research mandate of the agency, the front-line advocates and counselors reported that it also served an important counseling function (Greaves, Wylie, & the staff of the BWAC, 1995). Sometimes questions about particular aspects of a recent violent episode or about long-term patterns of physical and collateral forms of abuse (economic control, social isolation, psychological abuse) would elicit an overall picture that was starkly at odds with an interviewee's initial self-report. The shock of recognition, when a standardized question draws attention to some hitherto unacknowledged or unspoken aspect of a woman's experience, does more than any general assurance could to make it clear that however unique a woman might think her own experience of violence, it is often by no means idiosyncratic. In short, "going beyond" our experience—questioning it, rethinking it, putting it in perspective, asking how and why it arises— is a crucial part of coming to terms with the sex/gender oppression of a heteronormative society.

A second, related concern often raised about strong experientialist readings of the second principle is that any directive to "ground feminist research in women's experience" must be articulated with some care if it is not to prove perniciously parochial, reproducing and reifying precisely the conditions of oppression that feminists ought to challenge. In *White Women, Race Matters*, Frankenberg (1993) reads her subjects' testimony against the grain with an eye to discerning the contours of race privilege, including the privileges of ignorance, that define the lives of white women. She focuses on contradictions inherent in first-person accounts that reveal the unacknowledged "racial geography" of her interviewees' lives. Critiques of the early 1990s generalize the methodological point implicit here, drawing attention to the inherent elitism of inquiry grounded in the experience of those relatively privileged women who are most likely to be in a position to undertake systematic empirical research (Mohanty, 1991) or to

be recruited as research subjects (Cannon, Higginbotham, & Leung, 1991). Women's experience may offer a crucial corrective to the systems of common sense and scientific knowledge that render it invisible and inauthoritative, but it is always intersectionally partial, and in this, it offers, at most, a point of departure, not an end point for feminist inquiry (Bannerji, 1991, p. 67; Smith, 1974, pp. 12–13).

The upshot is that the liberatory goals of feminist research—articulated as the first principle—put considerable pressure on any literal or essentialist reading of the second principle (the requirement for experiential grounding). Effective activism depends on understanding accurately and in detail how "specific form[s] of oppression originated, how [they have] been maintained and all the systemic purposes [they] serve" (Narayan, 1988, p. 36), and this routinely requires that feminists go substantially beyond women's experience and self-understanding in a number of senses. They must expand the range of experience on which they ground social research, on the principle that all experience reflects the partiality of location. They must be prepared to critically interrogate this experience, on the principle that it is often the opacity of social institutions and practices that makes them effective in conditioning our self-understanding. And they must contextualize it, on the principle that we need to grasp "how [the world of everyday experience] is put together," to posit the socioeconomic order that lies "in back" of and that makes possible and organizes immediate experience (Gorelick, 1991, pp. 463–466; Smith, 1974, pp. 12–13).

Crucially, it is not only the subjects' gendered experience that must be situated, read against the grain, treated as a point of departure and not a destination; it is also the researcher's own experience and self-understanding that require scrutiny in all these ways. What practitioners rely on when they do social science are, therefore, the resources of a feminist standpoint, not just a gendered social location.

## CONCLUSION

Two epistemic implications follow from these observations about feminist practice in the social sciences. First, far from illustrating a sad decline into cynical dogmatism—a state in which, Haack (1993) feared, "foregone conclusions" would dictate not only the goals but also the outcomes of research—the dominant effect of feminist community values has been to mobilize transformative critique (Longino, 1990, pp. 73–76). Feminist commitments have catalyzed much more searching critical scrutiny of the presuppositions of research—including those that inform feminists' practice as well as the conventions they challenge—than conventional epistemic virtues had done or faith in the self-correcting capacity of scientific method seems likely to do.

Second, the feminist standpoint that, as I have suggested, is pivotal to this enterprise need not be construed in essentialist terms or be accorded any automatic epistemic privilege—the key features that worry critics like Haack (1993).[3] Central to this conception of a feminist standpoint is a situated knowledge thesis: what we experience and understand, the differential strengths and liabilities we develop as epistemic agents, are systematically shaped by our location in hierarchically structured systems of power relations, the material conditions of our lives, the relations of production and reproduction that shape our social interactions, and the conceptual resources we rely on to interpret and represent these relations. Gender is one dimension along which our lives are structured in epistemically consequential ways. What feminist standpoint theory adds to this account of situated knowledge is an inversion thesis. Those who are subject to structures of domination that systematically marginalize and oppress them may in fact have substantial (contingent) epistemic advantage relative to those who are comparatively privileged (and who enjoy a presumption of epistemic authority on this basis); they may have access to an expanded range of evidence and interpretive heuristics, as well as a critical perspective on otherwise unacknowledged framework assumptions, by virtue of what they typically experience and how they understand their experience (Wylie, 2004, pp. 32–39).

Two points follow where the specifics of "doing social science as a feminist" are concerned. First, the directive to ground feminist research in women's experience should be construed, in standpoint terms, as a recommendation to treat the situated knowledge of gendered subjects as a resource (not a foundation) for understanding the form and dynamics of the sex/gender systems that shape their lives. Second, Longino's (1994, 1995) commitment to epistemic provisionality should be framed as a substantive requirement that feminists develop an explicitly feminist standpoint on knowledge production; they should build into their research enterprise a critical consciousness of our social location(s) and the difference it makes epistemically. Far from signaling an abdication of epistemic responsibility, these guidelines for doing research as a feminist effectively raise the epistemic bar (see Harding, 1993, on "strong objectivity"); they direct feminists to make discerning use of contingent epistemic advantages that may accrue to them by virtue of their gendered social locations and hard-won feminist standpoint.

## NOTES

1. In fact, Smith, Mies, and other feminist social scientists writing in the 1970s and 1980s argued that their critiques called not for wholesale abandonment of the tools of social scientific inquiry but for the judicious use of those forms of inquiry—typically qualitative, participatory methods—best suited to the task of countering the entrenched sex/gender biases of conventional research (Hesse-Biber, Leavy, & Yaiser, 2004, p. 14; Naples, 2003; Smith, 1974, p. 8, 1987, pp. 61–69).

2. Indeed, there are good reasons to regard Haack's (1993) diatribe against cynical critics of the authority of science as a sustained argument against a straw opponent, predicated on an implausibly narrow view of the range of epistemic positions that may reasonably be taken by those who reject the Enlightenment ideals she defends (Anderson, 1995, pp. 34–42, 2004; Wylie, 1995, p. 347).

3. I summarize here an argument developed in more detail in "Why Standpoint Matters" (Wylie, 2003).

## REFERENCES

Anderson, Elizabeth. (1995). Knowledge, human interests, and objectivity in feminist epistemology. *Philosophical Topics, 23,* 29–58.

Anderson, Elizabeth. (2004). Review of Cassandra Pinnick, Noretta Koertge, and Robert Almeder, eds., *Scrutinizing Feminist Epistemology*. *Metascience, 13*. (An extended critical notice is available at www-personal.umich.edu/%7Eeandersn/hownotreview.html)

Bannerji, Himani. (1991). But who speaks for us? Experience and agency in conventional feminist paradigms. In Himani Bannerji, Linda Carty, Kari Dehli, Susan Heald, & Kate McKenna (Eds.), *Unsettling relations: The university as a site of feminist struggle* (pp. 67–108). Toronto, Ontario, Canada: Women's Press.

Brunsdon, Charlotte. (1978). It is well known that by nature women are inclined to be rather personal. In Women's Studies Group, Centre for Cultural Studies, University of Birmingham (Eds.), *Women take issue: Aspects of women's subordination* (pp. 18–34). London: Hutchinson.

Cannon, Lynn Weber, Higginbotham, Elizabeth, & Leung, Marianne L. A. (1991). Race and class bias in qualitative research on women. In Mary Margaret Fonow & Judith A. Cook (Eds.), *Beyond methodology: Feminist scholarship as lived research* (pp. 107–118). Bloomington: Indiana University Press.

Chilly Collective. (Eds.). (1995). *Breaking anonymity: Anonymity: The Chilly Climate for Women Faculty*. Waterloo, Ontario, Canada: Wilfrid Laurier Press.

Cook, Judith A., & Fonow, Mary Margaret. (1986). Knowledge and women's interests: Issues of epistemology and methodology in feminist sociological research. *Sociological Inquiry, 56,* 2–29.

Doppelt, Gerald D. (1988). The philosophical requirements for an adequate conception of scientific rationality. *Philosophy of Science, 55*(1), 104–133.

Ehrlich, Carol. (1975). *The conditions of feminist research* (Research Group One Report No. 21). Baltimore: Vacant Lots Press.

Eichler, Margrit. (1988). *Nonsexist research methods: A practical guide*. Boston: Allen & Unwin.

Fonow, Mary Margaret, & Cook, Judith A. (Eds.). (1991). Back to the future: A look at the second wave of feminist epistemology and methodology. In *Beyond methodology: Feminist scholarship as lived research* (pp. 1–15). Bloomington: Indiana University Press.

Frankenberg, Ruth. (1993). *White women, race matters: The social construction of whiteness*. Minneapolis: University of Minnesota Press.

Gorelick, Sherry. (1991). Contradictions of feminist methodology. *Gender & Society, 5,* 459–477.

Gottfried, Heidi. (Ed.). (1996). *Feminism and social change: Bridging theory and practice*. Urbana: University of Illinois Press.

Grant, Judith. (1987). I feel therefore I am: A critique of female experience as the basis for a feminist epistemology. *Women and Politics, 7*(3), 99–114.

Greaves, Lorraine, Wylie, Alison, & the staff of the Battered Women's Advocacy Clinic. (1995). Women and violence: Feminist practice and quantitative method. In Sandra D. Burt & Lorraine Code (Eds.), *Changing methods: Feminists transforming practice* (pp. 301–326). Peterborough, ON: Broadview Press.

Haack, Susan. (1993). Knowledge and propaganda: Reflections of an old feminist. *Partisan Review, 60,* 556–565. (Reprinted in *Scrutinizing feminist epistemology: An examination of gender in science*, by Cassandra Pinnick, Noretta Koertge, & Robert Almeder, Eds., 2003, New Brunswick, NJ: Rutgers University Press)

Harding, Sandra. (1986). *The science question in feminism*. Ithaca, NY: Cornell University Press.

Harding, Sandra. (1987). The method question. *Hypatia, 2,* 19–36.

Harding, Sandra. (1993). *Whose science? Whose knowledge? Thinking from women's lives*. Ithaca, NY: Cornell University Press.

Hesse, Mary. (1980). In defense of objectivity. In *Revolutions and reconstructions in the philosophy of science* (pp. 167–186). New York: Harvester Press.

Hesse-Biber, Sharlene Nagy, Leavy, Patricia, & Yaiser, Michelle L. (2004). Feminist approaches to research as a *process*: Reconceptualizing epistemology, methodology, and method. In Sharlene Nagy Hesse-Biber & Michelle L. Yaiser (Eds.), *Feminist perspectives on social research* (pp. 3–26). New York: Oxford University Press.

Jacobson, Helga E. (1977). *How to study your own community: Research from the perspective of women*. Vancouver, British Columbia, Canada: Vancouver Women's Research Centre.

Jayaratne, Toby Epstein. (1983). The value of quantitative methodology in feminist research. In Gloria Bowles & Renate Duelli Klein (Eds.), *Theories of women's studies* (pp. 140–162). London: Routledge & Kegan Paul.

Kennedy, Elizabeth Lapovsky, & Davis, Madeline D. (1993). *Boots of leather, slippers of gold: The history of a lesbian community*. New York: Penguin Books.

Kuhn, Thomas. (1977). Objectivity, value judgment, and theory choice. In *The essential tension: Selected studies in scientific tradition and change* (pp. 320–339). Chicago: University of Chicago Press.

Lloyd, Elisabeth. (1995). Objectivity and the double standard for feminist epistemologies. *Synthese, 104*(3), 351–381.

Longino, Helen. (1987). Can there be a feminist science? *Hypatia, 2*(3), 51–64.

Longino, Helen. (1990). *Science as social knowledge: Values and objectivity in scientific inquiry*. Princeton, NJ: Princeton University Press.

Longino, Helen. (1993a). Feminist standpoint theory and the problems of knowledge. *Signs, 19*, 201–212.

Longino, Helen. (1993b). Subjects, power and knowledge: Description and prescription in feminist philosophies of science. In Linda Alcoff & Elizabeth Potter (Eds.), *Feminist epistemologies* (pp. 101–120). New York: Routledge.

Longino, Helen. (1994). In search of feminist epistemology. *The Monist, 77*(4), 472–485.

Longino, Helen. (1995). Gender, politics, and the theoretical virtues. *Synthese, 104*, 383–397.

Longino, Helen. (2002). *The fate of knowledge*. Princeton, NJ: Princeton University Press.

MacKinnon, Catherine. (1982). Feminism, Marxism, method and the State: An agenda for theory. *Signs, 7*, 515–544.

Mies, Maria. (1983). Towards a methodology for feminist research. In Gloria Bowles & Renate Duelli Klein (Eds.), *Theories of women's studies* (pp. 117–139). London: Routledge & Kegan Paul.

Mies, Maria. (1991). Women's research or feminist research? The debate surrounding feminist science and methodology. In Mary Margaret Fonow & Judith A. Cook (Eds.), *Beyond methodology: Feminist scholarship and lived research* (pp. 60–84). Bloomington: Indiana University Press.

Mohanty, Chandra Talpade. (Ed.). (1991). Under Western eyes: Feminist scholarship and colonial discourses. In Chandra Talpade Mohanty, Ann Russo, & Lourdes Torres (Eds.), *Third world women and the politics of feminism* (pp. 51–80). Bloomington: Indiana University Press.

Naples, Nancy A. (2003). *Feminism and method: Ethnography, discourse analysis, and activist research*. New York: Routledge.

Narayan, Uma. (1988). Working together across difference: Some considerations on emotions and political practice. *Hypatia, 3*(2), 31–48.

Reinharz, Shulamit. (1992a). *Feminist methods in social research*. New York: Oxford University Press.

Reinharz, Shulamit. (1992b). The principles of feminist research: A matter of debate. In Cheris Kramarae & Dale Spender (Eds.), *The knowledge explosion: Generations of feminist scholarship* (pp. 423–437). New York: Teachers College Press.

Scott, Joan W. (1991). The evidence of experience. *Critical Inquiry, 17*, 773–797.

Smith, Dorothy E. (1974). Women's perspective as a radical critique of sociology. *Sociological Inquiry, 44*, 7–13.

Smith, Dorothy E. (1978). A peculiar eclipsing: Women's exclusion from man's culture. *Women's Studies International Quarterly, 1*, 281–295. (Reprinted in Smith, 1987)

Smith, Dorothy E. (1987). *The everyday world as problematic: A feminist sociology*. Toronto, Ontario, Canada: University of Toronto Press.

Stanley, Liz, & Wise, Sue. (1979). Feminist research, feminist consciousness and experiences of sexism. *Women's Studies International Quarterly, 2*, 359–374.

Stanley, Liz, & Wise, Sue. (1983a). "Back into the personal" or: Our attempt to construct "feminist research." In Gloria Bowles & Renate D. Klein (Eds.), *Theories of women's studies* (pp. 192–209). London: Routledge & Kegan Paul.

Stanley, Liz, & Wise, Sue. (1983b). *Breaking out: Feminist consciousness and feminist research*. London: Routledge & Kegan Paul.

Strum, Shirley C., & Fedigan, Linda M. (Eds.). (2000). *Primate encounters: Models of science, gender, and society*. Chicago: Chicago University Press.

Wylie, Alison. (1992). Reasoning about ourselves; feminist methodology in the social sciences. In Elizabeth Harvey & Kathleen Okruhlik (Eds.), *Women and reason* (pp. 225–244). Ann Arbor: University of Michigan Press.

Wylie, Alison. (1995). Doing philosophy as a feminist: Longino on the search for a feminist epistemology. *Philosophical Topics, 23*(2), 345–358.

Wylie, Alison. (2001). Doing social science as a feminist: The engendering of archaeology. In Angela Creager, Elizabeth Lunbeck, & Londa Schiebinger (Eds.), *Feminism in twentieth century science, technology, and medicine* (pp. 23–45). Chicago: Chicago University Press.

Wylie, Alison. (2003). Why standpoint matters. In Robert Figueroa & Sandra Harding (Eds.), *Philosophical explorations of science, technology, and diversity* (pp. 26–48). New York: Routledge.

Wylie, Alison. (2004, February). *The gender of science: Chilly climate issues for women in science.* Lecture presented to the Barnard Center for Research on Women (BCRW) and summarized in the description of the BCRW conference, Women, Work and the Academy, December 2004. (Available at www.barnard.edu/bcrw/womenandwork)

Wylie, Alison, & Nelson, Lynn Hankinson. (in press). Coming to terms with the values of science: Insights from feminist science scholarship. In Harold Kincaid, John Dupre, & Alison Wylie (Eds.), *Value free science: Ideal or illusion?* Oxford, UK: Oxford University Press.

# 31

# STANDPOINT EPISTEMOLOGY AND BEYOND

NANCY A. NAPLES

F eminist standpoint theory is a broad categorization that includes somewhat diverse theories ranging from Nancy Hartsock's (1983) *feminist historical materialist* perspective, Donna Haraway's (1988) analysis of *situated knowledges*, Patricia Hill Collins's (1990) *black feminist thought*, Chela Sandoval's (2000) explication of Third World feminists' *differential oppositional consciousness*, and Smith's (1987, 1990a, 1990b) *everyday world sociology*. Sandra Harding (1986) first named feminist standpoint theory as a general approach within feminism to refer to the many different theorists who argued for the importance of situating knowledge in women's experiences. Standpoint theorists are found in a wide variety of disciplines and continue to raise important questions about the way power influences knowledge in a variety of fields. In fact, feminist standpoint theories are among the most influential approaches in feminist social science scholarship today.[1] However, feminist postmodernist scholars have generated a series of charges against standpoint epistemology that has led to reformulations and rearticulation of various standpoint approaches. Ironically, many theorists whose work has been identified with standpoint epistemologies contest this designation.

Smith (1992) has been particularly vocal about the limits of this classification. She writes,

> If I could think of a term other than "standpoint," I'd gladly shift, especially now that I've been caged in Harding's (1986) creation of the category of "standpoint theorists" and subjected to the violence of misinterpretation, replicated many times in journals and reviews, by those who speak of Hartsock and Smith but have read only Harding's version of us (or have read us through her version). (p. 91)

In this chapter, I will provide an overview of the different approaches to standpoint epistemology, elaborate some of the critiques of standpoint theorizing, and highlight the tension between modernist and postmodernist constructions. I will conclude with a discussion of contemporary feminist theoretical formulations that build on as well as go beyond feminist standpoint articulations.

## MARXIST HISTORICAL MATERIALISM AND STANDPOINT THEORIZING

Feminist standpoint theory was initially developed in response to debates surrounding Marxist

---

Author's Note: Portions of this chapter are adapted from Naples (2003).

feminism and socialist feminism in the 1970s and early 1980s. In reworking Marx's historical materialism from a feminist perspective, standpoint theorists' stated goal is to explicate how relations of domination are gendered in particular ways. Standpoint theory also developed in the context of Third World and postcolonial feminist challenges to the so-called dual systems of patriarchy and capitalism. The dual systems approach was an attempt to merge feminist analyses of patriarchy and Marxist analyses of class to create a more complex socialist feminist theory of women's oppression. Critics of the dual systems approach pointed out the lack of attention paid by socialist feminist analyses to racism, white supremacy, and colonialism. In contrast, feminist standpoint theory offers an intersectional analysis of gender, race, ethnicity, class, and other social structural aspects of social life without privileging one dimension or adopting an additive formulation (e.g., gender plus race). Contemporary approaches to standpoint theory retain elements of Marxist historical materialism for their central premise, namely, that knowledge develops in a complicated and contradictory way from lived experiences and social historical context (Harding, 2004).

Despite the diverse perspectives that are identified with standpoint epistemology, all standpoint theorists emphasize the importance of experience for feminist theorizing. In this regard, many point out the significance of the connection between standpoint analysis and consciousness-raising (CR), the women's movement's knowledge production method. CR was a strategy of knowledge development designed to help support and generate women's political activism. By sharing what appeared as individual level experiences of oppression, women recognized that their experiences were shaped by social structural factors. The CR process assumed that problems associated with women's oppression needed political solutions and that women acting collectively are able to identify and analyze these processes (Fisher, 2001). The CR group process enabled women to share their experiences, identify and analyze the social and political mechanisms by which women are oppressed, and develop strategies for social change.

Standpoint theorists assert a link between the development of standpoint theory and feminist political goals of transformative social, political, and economic change. Harding (1986) describes this connection as follows:

> Feminism and the women's movement provide the theory and motivation for inquiry and political struggle that can transform the perspective of women into a "standpoint"—a morally and scientifically preferable grounding for our interpretations and explanations of nature and social life. (p. 26)

From the perspective of feminist praxis, standpoint epistemology provides a methodological resource for explicating how relations of domination contour women's everyday lives. With this knowledge, women and others whose lives are shaped by systems of inequality can act to challenge these processes and systems (Weeks, 1998, p. 92). One example of this point is found in Ellen Pence's (1996) work. Pence created an assessment of how safe battered women remain after they report abuse to the police. She drew specifically on Smith's (1987) approach to shift the standpoint on the process of law enforcement to the women who the law attempts to protect and to those who are charged with protecting them. Pence developed what she termed "a safety audit" to identify how criminal justice and law enforcement policies and practices can be enhanced to ensure the safety of women and to ensure the accountability of the offender. Pence's safety audit has been used by police departments, criminal justice and probation departments, and family law clinics in diverse settings across the country. Pence asserts that her approach is not an evaluation of individual workers' performances but an examination of how the institution or system is set up to manage domestic violence cases.

Standpoint theorists are critical of positivist scientific methods that reduce lived experiences to a series of disconnected variables such as gender, race, or class. For example, Harding (1986) has written extensively about the limits of positivism and argues for an approach to knowledge production that incorporates the point of view of feminist and postcolonial theoretical and political concerns. She argues that traditional approaches to science fail to acknowledge how the social context and perspectives of those who generate the questions, conduct the research, and interpret the findings shape what counts as knowledge and how data are interpreted. She argues for a holistic approach instead that includes greater attention to the knowledge production process and to the role of the researcher. Harding (1986) and Smith (1987) both critique the androcentric nature of academic knowledge production. They argue for the importance of starting analysis from the lived experiences and activities of women and others who have been left out of the knowledge production process rather than start inquiry with the abstract categories and a priori assumptions of traditional academic disciplines or dominant social institutions.

## DIFFERENT CONCEPTUALIZATIONS OF STANDPOINT

Despite the shared themes outlined above, the notion of standpoint is conceptualized differently by different standpoint theorists. Nancy Naples (2003) has identified three different approaches to the construction of standpoint: as embodied in women's social location and social experience, as constructed in community, and as a site through which to begin inquiry. Many feminist theorists understand standpoint as embodied in specific actors who are located in less privileged positions within the social order and who, because of their social locations, are engaged in activities that differ from others who are not so located. The appeal to women's embodied social experience as a privileged site of knowledge about power and domination forms one central thread within standpoint epistemologies. Critics of standpoint theory point out that the reliance on a notion of women or any other marginalized group as having an identifiable and consistent standpoint leads to the trap of essentialism. For example, feminist scholars who center the role of mothering practices in generating different gendered ways of knowing (Belenky, Clinchy, Goldberger, & Tarule, 1986; see also Ruddick, 1989) or who argue that there are gendered differences in moral perspective (Gilligan, 1982) have been criticized for equating such gendered differences with an essentialized female identity (Spelman, 1988). In contrast to this assessment, many

feminist theorists who contribute to the embodied strand of standpoint theorizing argue that due to relations of domination and subordination, women, especially low-income women of color or others located in marginalized social positions, develop a perspective on social life that differs markedly from that of men, middle-income people, and upper-income people.[2] Black feminist and Chicana standpoint theorists assert that the political consciousness of women of color develops from the material reality of their lives.

Both Collins and Hartsock emphasize that there is a difference between a so-called women's standpoint and a feminist standpoint. Alison Jaggar (1989) points out that a women's standpoint is different from women's viewpoint or women's specific experiences. In contrast, these authors argue that a standpoint is achieved and is a consequence of analysis from the point of view of a specific social actor, social group, or social location, rather than available simply because one happens to be a member of an oppressed group or share a social location. Political theorist Kathi Weeks (1998) also considers the conceptualization of feminist standpoint "as an achieved, constructed collectivity" useful for "the feminist political project" (p. 8). She explains that this conceptualization of a feminist standpoint "can serve as an inspiring example of a collective subject, a subject that is neither modeled after the individual, and thus somehow unitary and homogeneous, nor conceived as spontaneous and natural community" (p. 8). These standpoint theorists emphasize that perspectives from the vantage point of the oppressed remain partial and incomplete (see also Haraway, 1988). A central problematic feature of feminist standpoint analyses is determining how partial particular perspectives are. For example, Patricia Clough (1994) aims her criticism of Collins's approach right to the heart of embodied standpoint analyses when she emphasizes that privileging experience in any form, even with attention to the partiality of that experience, is a problematic theoretical move. However, rather than view standpoints as individual possessions of disconnected actors, most standpoint theorists attempt to locate standpoint in specific community contexts with particular attention to the dynamics of race, class, and gender.

This second strand of feminist standpoint epistemology understands standpoint as a relational accomplishment or as one generated by and on behalf of a particular community. Using this approach, the identity of "woman" or other embodied identities is viewed as constructed in community and therefore cannot be interpreted outside the community context. Collins's (1990) approach to community development of black feminist thought involves a collective process through which individuals come to represent themselves in relation to others with whom they share similar experiences. Collins (1997) argues that a standpoint is constructed through "historically shared, *group*-based experiences" (p. 375). Like the embodied approach to standpoint theorizing, group-based approaches have also been criticized for unproblematically using women's class and racial identities to define who is or is not part of a particular group. However, those who draw on a relational or community-based notion of standpoint emphasize the collective analytic process that must precede the articulation of a standpoint. Both Sandoval (2000) and Collins (1990) use this approach to standpoint. Although Sandoval does not describe her approach as a "standpoint epistemology," it does share many of the features outlined above. Sandoval's (2000) analysis of oppositional consciousness has much in common with Hartsock's and Collins's approach in that her analysis of oppositional consciousness focuses on the development of Third World feminism as a methodology by which oppressed groups can develop strategies for political resistance. Sandoval's model offers a methodological strategy that contests previously taken-for-granted categorizations of women's political practice such as liberal, radical, or socialist. The oppositional methodology she presents draws on multiple political approaches such as equal rights or liberal, revolutionary, and separatist political strategies. Rather than privilege one approach, Sandoval argues that oppressed peoples typically draw on multiple strategies to form an oppositional methodology. Sandoval treats experience as simultaneously embodied and strategically created in community and concludes that this dynamic interaction affects the political practice of Third World women. Although Sandoval locates her analysis in a

postmodern frame and Hartsock resists such a move, the legacy of historical materialism links their work within a broadly defined feminist standpoint epistemology. In fact, Hartsock (1996) acknowledges the power of Sandoval's analysis for challenging essentialized views of identity and identity politics.

The third strand of feminist standpoint epistemology, most associated with Smith's (1987) everyday world sociology, provides a framework for capturing the interactive and fluid conceptualization of community and resists attaching standpoint to particular bodies, individual knowers, or specific communities or groups. Here standpoint is understood as a site from which to begin a mode of inquiry as in Smith's everyday world institutional ethnographic approach to epistemology. Smith (1992) explains that her approach does not privilege a subject of research whose expressions are disconnected from her social location and daily activities. Rather, Smith starts inquiry with an active knower who is connected with other people in particular and identifiable ways. This mode of inquiry calls for explicit attention to the social relations embedded in women's everyday activities. Smith's (1992) analysis of standpoint as a mode of inquiry offers a valuable methodological strategy for exploring how power dynamics are organized and experienced in a community context.

## POSTMODERN CRITIQUES OF STANDPOINT THEORY

Postmodern feminist critics argue against the construction of standpoint epistemologies as "science" in search of "truth." For example, sociologist of law Carol Smart (1995) criticizes "standpointism" for requiring "precise rules" for the production of knowledge and requiring that a feminist academic "act as interpreter and disseminator of this knowledge" (p. 11). Here Smart is referring primarily to criminologist Maureen Cain's (1990) analysis of standpoint epistemologies as a successor science. Smart explains that this approach "participates in creating hierarchies of knowledge" that are supported by "the promise of a good political outcome." However, she contrasts this promise with postmodern or poststructuralist feminism that offers "no programmes of action and Utopian visions" (p. 11).

Postmodern theorists are especially critical of standpoint theory for presuming that it is possible to identify and locate what are socially constructed and mobile social positions (Clough, 1994; King, 1994). For example, in her critique of standpoint theory, Katie King (1994) notes the "difficulties with conceptualizing the feminist standpoint as a constructed and mobile position" (p. 71). In response to the poststructuralist arguments that standpoint theories remain hopelessly modernist, standpoint theorists like Smith, Hartsock, and Collins find postmodern interventions suspect, given, as Collins (1998) asks, "Who might be most likely to care about decentering [the subject]—those in the centers of power or those on the margins?" (p. 127). Collins is concerned that "postmodern views of power that overemphasize hegemony and local politics provide a seductive mix of appearing to challenge oppression while secretly believing that such efforts are doomed." She concludes that "depoliticized decentering disempowers Black women as a group while providing the illusion of empowerment" (p. 137).

The few feminist postmodernists who offer alternative research strategies often limit their approaches to textual or discursive modes of analysis. For example, following an assessment of the limits and possibilities of feminist standpoint epistemologies for generating what she calls a "global social analytic," literary analyst Rosemary Hennessy (1993) posits "critique" as materialist feminist "reading practice" as a way of recognizing how consciousness is an ideological production. She argues that, in this way, it is possible to effectively resist the charge of essentialism that has been leveled against standpoint epistemology. In revaluing feminist standpoint theory for her method, she reconceptualizes feminist standpoint as a "critical discursive practice." Hennessy's methodological alternative effectively renders other methodological strategies outside the frame of materialist feminist scholarship.

However, even poststructural critics of feminist standpoint epistemology within the social sciences also conclude their analyses with calls for discursive strategies. For example, Clough (1994) calls for shifting the starting point of sociological investigation from experience or social activity to a "social criticism of textuality and discursivity, mass media, communication technologies and science itself" (p. 179). In contrast, standpoint theory, especially Smith's approach, offers a place to begin inquiry that envisions subjects of investigation who can experience aspects of life outside discourse. Standpoint theorists like Smith tie their understanding of experience to the collective conversations of the women's movement that gave rise to understandings about women's lives that had no prior discursive existence. In this way, despite some important theoretical challenges, standpoint theory continues to offer feminist analysts a theoretical and methodological strategy that links the goals of the women's movement to the knowledge production enterprise.[3]

Political scientist Sonia Kruks (2001) defends the project of standpoint theory against its critics, arguing as follows:

> Because it begins from the social division of labor and from accounts of social reality that emerge from different social practices, there is nothing intrinsic to the theory that would preclude developing an account of a multiplicity of women's standpoints, which would perhaps overlap in some aspects and diverge radically in others. (p. 112)

Kruks points to Haraway's work on "situated knowledges" to demonstrate the usefulness of "certain postmodern sensibilities" for "acknowledging a multiplicity of different epistemological locations for a non-dominative feminism" (p. 113). Given the effective challenges posed to standpoint theorizing by feminist postmodern theorists, many standpoint theorists, like Kruks, have begun to revision standpoint epistemology to take account of these critiques, especially as they relate to analyses of discourse and power and the fluidity of subjectivities. At the same time, feminist postmodern theorists are addressing one of the major critiques of their approach, namely, the failure to attend to or account for material social inequalities and to contribute effectively to feminist praxis. These efforts are coming together in a new approach to materialist feminism.

## Standpoint Epistemology and Beyond: The Case for Materialist Feminist Standpoint Epistemology

Postmodern feminist scholars emphasize the ways disciplinary discourses shape how researchers see the worlds they investigate and how "without critique of the metanarratives that theoretically and practically sustain the structures and discourses of" academia, research operates to reinsert power relations, rather than challenge them (Luke, 1992, p. 37; see also Kondo, 1990; Visweswaran, 1994). Sociologist Diane Wolf (1996) explains that some feminist scholars "have found useful the sensitivity postmodernism demonstrates toward a greater multiplicity of power relations" and that "postmodernist theorizing has created opportunities for further innovation in research methods and the post-fieldwork process, particularly representation and writing" (p. 6). However, many other feminist scholars "are concerned that the overly textual focus of postmodernism renders the lived realities of women irrelevant" (p. 6). In addition, sociologist Carolyn Sachs (1996) argues that a postmodern emphasis on "fractured identities" and "the multitude of subjectivities" could lead to "total relativism" that precludes political activism (p. 19). Furthermore, women's studies scholars Jacqui Alexander and Chandra Mohanty (1997) express concern that

> postmodern theory, in its haste to dissociate itself from all forms of essentialism, has generated a series of epistemological confusions regarding the interconnections between location, identity, and the construction of knowledge. Thus, for instance, localized questions of experience, identity, culture, and history, which enable us to understand specific processes of domination and subordination, are often dismissed by postmodern theories as reiterations of cultural "essence" or unified, stable identity. (p. xvii)

Concerns about the depoliticizing consequences of postmodern theories are a consistent thread in feminist debates on the value of postmodernist theories for feminist praxis. Alexander and Mohanty (1997) address this tension between feminist political goals and "postmodernist discourse [that] attempts to move beyond essentialism by pluralizing and dissolving the stability and analytic utility of the categories of race, gender, and sexuality." They argue that "this strategy often forecloses any valid recuperation of these categories or the social relations through which they are constituted" (p. xvii). Alexander and Mohanty caution that "the relations of domination and subordination that are named and articulated through the processes of racism and racialization still exist, and they still require analytic and political specification and engagement" (p. xvii; see also Fraser & Nicholson, 1990).

Naples's (2003) strategy for negotiating these challenges has been one of praxis, namely, generating a materialist feminist standpoint that speaks to the empirical world in which her research takes place. She argues that by foregrounding the everyday world of poor women of different racial and ethnic backgrounds in both the rural and urban United States and by exploring the governing practices that shape their lives, it is possible to develop a class-conscious and antiracist methodological approach (see also Alexander & Mohanty, 1997). This materialist feminist approach to standpoint epistemology draws on the power of the so-called modernist insights of standpoint theory and postmodernist approaches to power, knowledge, and subjectivity.[4]

In their introduction to *Materialist Feminism: A Reader in Class, Difference, and Women's Lives*, Rosemary Hennessy and Chrys Ingraham (1997a) describe materialist feminism as "the conjuncture of several discourses— historical materialism, Marxist and radical feminism, as well as postmodern and psychoanalytic theories of meaning and subjectivity" (p. 7). Materialist feminists view agency "as complex and often contradictory sites of representation and struggle over power and resources" (Hesford, 1999, p. 74). Materialist feminism, as in Naples's (2003) reconstruction of its intellectual history, has its roots in socialist feminist theories and has been particularly influenced by the theoretical critiques of African American, Chicana, and Third World feminists[5] who, in turn, contributed to the development of diverse feminist standpoint epistemologies as discussed above.[6] For example, in the preface to *This Bridge Called My Back*, Moraga (1981) passionately ties the political consciousness of women of color to their lived experiences. This "politics of the flesh" (p. xviii) does not privilege one dimension and artificially set it apart from the context in which it is lived, experienced, felt, and resisted. In fact, literary scholar Paula Moya (1997) argues that Moraga's "theory in the flesh" provides a powerful "non-essentialist way to ground . . . identities" (p. 150) for the purposes of resistance to domination.[7] Contemporary formulations of materialist feminism[8] are also informed by Michel Foucault's analysis of discourse. For example, Sandoval (2000) argues that "the theory and method of oppositional and differential consciousness is aligned with Foucault's concept of power, which emphasizes the figure of the very *possibility* of positioning power itself" (p. 77).[9] Foucault is an unlikely resource for feminist praxis, given two features of his work: his neglect of the dynamics of gender in his analysis of power and his displacement of the subject as a central agent for social change. However, Hennessy (1990) finds that "Foucault's project *has* opened up productive avenues for developing materialist feminist theory" (p. 254). However, she argues for "an alternative post-Althusserian analytic" that is "more in keeping with a feminism that aims to come to terms with the materiality and politics of difference" (p. 254). In contrast, Naples (2003) found in Foucault's approach to discourse a powerful methodological tool for materialist feminist analysis when grounded in a multidimensional standpoint epistemology that can explicate how "discursive and nondiscursive practices" relate to "the materiality of discourses and the materiality of institutions" (Hennessy, 1990, p. 266). Furthermore, as Vikki Bell (1993) points out, "Foucault's politics . . . has its emphasis on local resistance and the questioning of discursive categories that surround us"—two political projects that have much in common with feminist praxis (p. 55).[10] Foucault argues that

> the key to power is not overt domination of one group by another, but the acceptance by all that there exists "an ideal, continuous, smooth text that runs beneath the multiplicity of contradictions, and resolves them in the calm unity of coherent

thought." (Foucault, 1971, quoted in Worrall, 1990, pp. 8–9)

Discourses are defined as "historically variable ways of specifying knowledge and truth—what is possible to speak of at a given moment" (Ramazanoğlu, 1993). They are not merely "groups of signs (signifying elements referring to contents or representations) but [are] practices that systematically form the objects of which they speak" (Foucault, 1972, p. 49). Using a Foucauldian articulation of power, education theorist Jennifer Gore (1992) analyzes power "as exercised, rather than as possessed" (p. 59). This approach, she argues, requires more attention to the microdynamics of the operation of power as it is expressed in specific sites.

A *materialist feminist standpoint theory* that incorporates important insights of postmodern analyses of power, subjectivity, and language is a powerful framework for exploring the intersection of race, class, gender, sexuality, region, and culture in different geographic and historical contexts. Naples's (2003) development and elaboration of different dimensions of standpoint epistemology revealed a tension between theorists who considered standpoint theory to be firmly grounded in the modernist concerns of feminist political goals and those who viewed standpoint epistemology as anticipating many of the postmodern calls to avoid grand narrative constructions of identity and construct power as multiple and productive. Consequently, feminist standpoint theory offers a powerful tool for exploring the "microdynamics of the operation of power."[11] Yet the power of standpoint theorizing can be enhanced by incorporating insights from postmodern perspectives on power, subjectivity, and language, especially to explore the way power infuses investigation and the textual products of such efforts.

## CONCLUSION

In sum, standpoint theorists typically resist focusing their analyses on individual women removed from their social context. Knowledge generated from embodied standpoints of subordinates is powerful in that it can help transform traditional categories of analyses that originate from dominant groups. However, as many feminist standpoint theorists argue, it remains only a partial perspective (Haraway, 1988). By placing the analysis within a community context, it is possible to uncover the multiplicity of perspectives along with the dynamic structural dimensions of the social, political, and economic environments that shape the *relations of ruling* in a particular social space (Naples, 2003). Haraway (1988), along with other standpoint theorists, explains that situated knowledges are developed collectively, rather than by individuals in isolation. Hartsock (1983) and Collins (1990) both emphasize that standpoints are achieved in community, through collective conversations and dialogue among women in marginal social positions. According to Collins, standpoints are achieved by groups who struggle collectively and self-reflectively against *the matrix of domination* that circumscribes their lives. Hartsock also emphasizes that a feminist standpoint is achieved through analysis and political struggle.

Given standpoint theory's emphasis on a process of dialogue, analysis, and reflexivity, the approach has proven extremely vibrant and open to reassessment and revision. As a consequence, standpoint theory remains an extremely important approach within feminist theory that has been further enriched by reflective incorporation of postmodern analyses of power, subjectivity, and discourse. This new approach refuses the so-called modernist or postmodernist divide to produce a materialist feminism that retains a link to the political goals of the women's movement while recognizing the multiple ways that power operates through discourse and nondiscursive processes to reveal the shifting patterns of gender, race, class, and region, among other social structural forces that shape everyday life.

## NOTES

1. Other influential approaches include feminist symbolic interactionism (see Fenstermaker & West, 2002), the gender and power approach developed by R. W. Connell (1987, 1995), and feminist social constructionism (see, e.g., Lorber, 1995).

2. See Collins (1990), Moya (1996), and Sandoval (2000).

3. See also Barrett and Phillips (1992), Butler and Scott (1992), Clough (1994), di Leonardo (1991),

Hartsock (1987b), McNay (1992), Nicholson (1990), Smith (1999), and Visweswaran (1994).

4. See, for example, Ferguson (1991), Hennessy and Ingraham (1997b), and Weedon (1987).

5. See G. Joseph (1981), Mohanty (1991a, 1991b), and Spivak (1988).

6. See also A. Ferguson (1991) and Hennessy (1993).

7. Sandoval (2000) asserts that Moraga's (1981) "theory in the flesh" is "a theory that allows survival and more, that allows practitioners to live with faith, hope, and moral vision in spite of all else" (p. 7). Moraga's "theory of the flesh" and Anzaldúa's (1987) construction of *la conciencia de la mestiza* are built from "gut-wrenching struggle," as communication scholar Jacqueline Martinez (2000, p. 83) explains. Martinez cautions us that "The attention to the embodied flesh that is the substance and methodology of much of Chicano feminist theorizing must not be theorized away in abstract language that allows for a distanced and removed engagement" (p. 84).

8. See Hennessy (1993) and Landry and MacLean (1993). Philosopher Ann Ferguson (1991) defines "feminist-materialism" as follows:

> [It] assumes that male power (a) is based on social practices rather than simply in biological sex differences; (b) connects to systematic inequalities in the exchange of work between men and women in meeting material needs; and (c) involves historically specific rather than universal systems of male dominance. (p. 1)

While indebted to postmodern theories that reject "an essential and unitary theory of self," Ferguson argues that her approach retains "a totalist project in ways that many postmodernist approaches would reject" (pp. 25–26).

9. Sandoval (2000) defines her complex project in *Methodology of the Oppressed* as exploring "the mobile interchange between the sovereign, Marxist, and postmodern conceptions of power" in order to explicate the development and political potential of "differential consciousness" (p. 77).

10. See also McNay (1992).

11. See, especially, Smith (1990a, 1990b, 1999).

## REFERENCES

Alexander, M. Jacqui, & Mohanty, Chandra Talpade. (1997). Introduction: Genealogies, legacies, movements. In M. Jacqui Alexander & Chandra

Talpade Mohanty (Eds.), *Feminist genealogies, colonial legacies, democratic futures* (pp. xiii–xlii). New York: Routledge.

Anzaldúa, Gloria. (1987). *Borderlands/la frontera: The new mestiza.* San Francisco: Spinsters/Aunt Lute.

Barrett, Michelle, & Phillips, Anne. (Eds.). (1992). *Destabilizing theory: Contemporary feminist debates.* Stanford, CA: Stanford University Press.

Belenky, Mary Field, Clinchy, Blythe McVicker, Goldberger, Nancy Rule, & Tarule, Jill Matuck. (1986). *Women's ways of knowing.* New York: Basic Books.

Bell, Vikki. (1993). *Interrogating incest: Feminism, Foucault and the law.* New York: Routledge.

Butler, Judith, & Scott, Joan. (Eds.). (1992). *Feminists theorize the political.* New York: Routledge.

Cain, Maureen. (1990). Realist philosophy and standpoint epistemologies or feminist criminology as a successor science. In Louraine Gelsthorpe & Alison Morris (Eds.), *Feminist perspectives in criminology* (pp. 120–140). Maidenhead, UK: Open University Press.

Clough, Patricia Ticiento. (1994). *Feminist thought.* Cambridge, MA: Blackwell.

Collins, Patricia Hill. (1990). *Black feminist thought: Knowledge, consciousness, and the politics of empowerment.* Boston: Unwin Hyman.

Collins, Patricia Hill. (1997). Comment on Hekman's "Truth and method: Feminist standpoint theory revisited": Where's the power? *Signs: Journal of Women in Culture and Society, 22*(2), 375–381.

Collins, Patricia Hill. (1998). *Fighting words: Black women and the search for justice.* New York: Routledge.

Connell, R. W. (1987). *Gender & power.* Stanford, CA: Stanford University Press.

Connell, R. W. (1995). *Masculinities.* Berkeley: University of California Press.

di Leonardo, Micaela. (Ed.). (1991). *Gender at the crossroads of knowledge: Feminist anthropology in the postmodern era.* Berkeley: University of California Press.

Fenstermaker, Sarah, & West, Candace. (Eds.). (2002). *Doing gender/doing difference.* New York: Routledge.

Ferguson, Ann. (1991). *Sexual democracy: Women, oppression, and revolution.* Boulder, CO: Westview Press.

Fisher, Berenice Malka. (2001). *No angel in the classroom.* Lanham, MD: Rowman & Littlefield.

Foucault, Michel. (1972). *The archaeology of knowledge and the discourse on language.* New York: Harper & Row.

Fraser, Nancy, & Nicholson, Linda J. (1990). Social criticism without philosophy: An encounter between feminism and postmodernism. In Linda J. Nicholson (Ed.), *Feminism/postmodernism* (pp. 19–38). New York: Routledge.

Gilligan, Carol. (1982). *In a different voice: Psychological theory and women's development.* Cambridge, MA: Harvard University Press.

Gore, Jennifer M. (1992). What we can do for you! What can "we" do for "you"? Struggling over empowerment in critical and feminist pedagogy. In Carmen Luke & Jennifer Gore (Eds.), *Feminisms and critical pedagogy* (pp. 54–73). New York: Routledge.

Haraway, Donna. (1988). Situated knowledges: The science question in feminism and the privilege of partial perspective. *Feminist Studies, 14*(3), 575–599.

Harding, Sandra. (1986). *The science question in feminism.* Ithaca, NY: Cornell University.

Harding, Sandra. (2004). *The feminist standpoint theory reader: Intellectual and political controversies.* New York: Routledge.

Hartsock, Nancy. (1983). *Money, sex and power: Toward a feminist historical materialism.* New York: Longman.

Hartsock, Nancy. (1987a). The feminist standpoint: Developing the ground for a specifically feminist historical materialism. In Sandra Harding (Ed.), *Feminism & methodology* (pp. 157–180). Bloomington: Indiana University Press.

Hartsock, Nancy. (1987b). Rethinking modernism: Majority theories. *Cultural Critique, 7,* 187–206.

Hartsock, Nancy. (1996). Theoretical bases for coalition building: An assessment of postmodernism. In Heidi Gottfried (Ed.), *Feminism and social change: Bridging theory and practice* (pp. 256–274). Urbana: University of Illinois Press.

Hennessy, Rosemary. (1990). Materialist feminism and Foucault: The politics of appropriation. *Rethinking Marxism, 3*(3–4), 252–274.

Hennessy, Rosemary. (1993). *Materialist feminism and the politics of discourse.* New York: Routledge.

Hennessy, Rosemary, & Ingraham, Chrys. (1997a). Introduction: Reclaiming anticapitalist feminism. In Rosemary Hennessy & Chrys Ingraham (Eds.), *Materialist feminism: A reader in class, difference, and women's lives* (pp. 1–14). New York: Routledge.

Hennessy, Rosemary, & Ingraham, Chrys. (Eds.). (1997b). *Materialist feminism: A reader in class, difference, and women's lives*. New York: Routledge.

Hesford, Wendy S. (1999). *Framing identities: Autobiography and the politics of pedagogy*. Minneapolis: University of Minnesota Press.

Jaggar, Alison. (1989). Love and knowledge: Emotion in feminist epistemology. In Alison M. Jaggar & Susan R. Bordo (Eds.), *Gender/body/knowledge: Feminist reconstructions of being and knowing* (pp. 145–171). New Brunswick, NJ: Rutgers University Press.

Joseph, Gloria. (1981). The incompatible ménage à trois: Marxism, feminism, and racism. In Lydia Sargent (Ed.), *Women and revolution* (pp. 91–108). Boston: South End Press.

King, Katie. (1994). *Theory in its feminist travels: Conversations in U.S. women's movements*. Bloomington: Indiana University Press.

Kondo, Dorinne K. (1990). *Crafting selves: Power, gender, and discourses of identity in a Japanese workplace*. Chicago: University of Chicago Press.

Kruks, Sonia. (2001). *Retrieving experience: Subjectivity and recognition in feminist politics*. Ithaca, NY: Cornell University Press.

Landry, Donna, & MacLean, Gerald. (1993). *Materialist feminism*. Oxford, UK: Blackwell.

Lorber, Judith. (1995). *Paradoxes of gender*. New Haven, CT: Yale University Press.

Luke, Carmen. (1992). Feminist politics in radical pedagogy. In Carmen Luke & Jennifer Gore (Eds.), *Feminisms and critical pedagogy* (pp. 25–53). New York: Routledge.

Martinez, Jacqueline. (2000). *Phenomenology of Chicana experience and identity: Communication and transformation in praxis*. Lanham, MD: Rowman & Littlefield.

McNay, Lois. (1992). *Foucault and feminism: Power, gender and the self*. Boston: Northeastern University Press.

Mohanty, Chandra Talpade. (1991a). Cartographies of struggle: Third World women and the politics of feminism. In Chandra Talpade Mohanty, Ann Russo, & Lourdes Torres (Eds.), *Third World women and the politics of feminism* (pp. 1–50). Bloomington: Indiana University Press.

Mohanty, Chandra Talpade. (1991b). Under western eyes: Feminist scholarship and colonial discourses. In Chandra Talpade Mohanty, Ann Russo, & Lourdes Torres (Eds.), *Third World women and the politics of feminism* (pp. 51–80). Bloomington: Indiana University Press.

Moraga, Cherríe. (1981). Introduction. In Cherríe Moraga & Gloria Anzaldúa (Eds.), *This bridge called my back: Writings by radical women of color* (pp. xiii–xix). Watertown, MA: Persephone Press.

Moya, Paula M. L. (1997). Postmodernism, "realism," and the politics of identity: Cherrie Morago and Chicana feminism. In M. Jacqui Alexander & Chandra Talpade Mohanty (Eds.), *Feminist genealogies, colonial legacies, democratic futures* (pp. 125–150). New York: Routledge.

Naples, Nancy A. (2003). *Feminism and method: Ethnography, discourse analysis, and activist research*. New York: Routledge.

Nicholson, Linda J. (Ed.). (1990). *Feminism/postmodernism*. New York: Routledge.

Pence, Ellen. (1996). *Safety for battered women in a textually mediated legal system*. Unpublished doctoral dissertation, Graduate Department, Sociology in Education, University of Toronto, Ontario, Canada.

Ramazanoğlu, Caroline. (1993). Introduction. In Caroline Ramazanoğlu (Ed.), *Up against Foucault: Explorations of some tensions between Foucault and feminism*. New York: Routledge.

Ruddick, Sara. (1989). *Maternal thinking: Toward a politics of peace*. New York: Ballantine Books.

Sachs, Carolyn. (1996). *Gendered fields: Rural women, agriculture and environment*. Boulder, CO: Westview Press.

Sandoval, Chela. (2000). *Methodology of the oppressed*. Minneapolis: University of Minnesota Press.

Smart, Carol. (1995). *Law, crime and sexuality: Essays in feminism*. Thousand Oaks, CA: Sage.

Smith, Dorothy E. (1987). *The everyday world as problematic: A feminist sociology*. Toronto, Ontario, Canada: University of Toronto Press.

Smith, Dorothy E. (1990a). *Conceptual practices of power*. Boston: Northeastern University Press.

Smith, Dorothy E. (1990b). *Texts, facts, and femininity: Exploring the relations of ruling*. New York: Routledge.

Smith, Dorothy E. (1992). Sociology from women's experience: A reaffirmation. *Sociological Theory, 10*(1), 88–98.

Smith, Dorothy E. (1999). *Writing the social: Critique, theory, and investigations*. Toronto, Ontario, Canada: University of Toronto Press.

Spelman, Elizabeth V. (1988). *Inessential woman: Problems of exclusion in feminist thought*. Boston: Beacon Press.

Spivak, Gayatri Chakravorty. (1988). *In other worlds: Essays in cultural politics*. New York: Routledge.

Visweswaran, Kamala. (1994). *Fictions of feminist ethnography*. Minneapolis: University of Minnesota Press.

Weedon, Chris. (1987). *Feminist practice and post-structuralist theory*. New York: Blackwell.

Weeks, Kathi. (1998). *Constituting feminist subjects*. Ithaca, NY: Cornell University Press.

Wolf, Diane L. (1996). Situating feminist dilemmas in fieldwork. In Diane L. Wolf (Ed.), *Feminist dilemmas in fieldwork* (pp. 1–55). Boulder, CO: Westview Press.

Worrall, Anne. (1990). *Offending women: Female lawbreakers and the criminal justice system*. London: Routledge.

# 32

## COMMENTARY

## *Using Feminist Fractured Foundationalism in Researching Children in the Concentration Camps of the South African War (1899–1902)*

LIZ STANLEY

SUE WISE

Some people, particularly in a North American context, may be surprised at the appearance of the words *concentration camp* in our title, concerning events in southern Africa, many years before the Shoah and the Nazi version of concentration camps in Europe.[1] However, the term came into existence to characterise internment camps that "concentrated" people by removing them from their farms; and like other military uses of a concentration policy at this time, such as in Cuba, the policy pursued during the South African War was disastrous because epidemics of measles, typhoid, and diphtheria spread quickly and many inhabitants, particularly children, died after catching a succession of these diseases. Later, because of political alliances between nationalists in South Africa and prominent Nazis in the early 1930s, the Nazis came to call their labour and death camps by the same name as part of a propaganda exercise. There is an extremely large literature by historians, sociologists, and others concerning the South African

War and its concentration camps, which will not be discussed here but which forms the backcloth to our commentary,[2] which relates to a joint research project concerned with children during the South African War and textual and photographic representations of their lives, and sometimes their deaths.

Through our long-standing collaborative project of formulating a feminist methodology and epistemology,[3] we have developed a framework for a grounded feminist research practice termed *feminist fractured foundationalism* (FFF).[4] Most recently, we argued there is an impasse in present thinking about feminist research (Wise & Stanley, 2006a, 2006b) because it is bogged down in reformulations of abstract ideas and debates about epistemology rather than exploring new developments in practice (the purpose of this volume and our contribution). We discuss here some aspects of our operationalisation of FFF in the project we conducted in South Africa in 2004, describing how the framework shaped up when used in our archive-based research and discussing its possibilities and limitations.

"Fractured foundationalism" is our characterisation of social life, the fundamental "it" feminist researchers grapple with understanding: Social life is both founded in a material factual reality and also involves disagreements and disjunctures between people's views of "the facts." The term thus recognises both that there is a materially grounded social world that is real in its consequences *and* insists that differently situated groups develop often different views of the precise realities involved. For us, the resultant complexities of interpretation have to be responded to in ways that do not position feminist researchers as a priori overriding the understandings of "the researched," and therefore FFF involves eschewing assumptions of epistemic privilege. However, feminist researchers who reject a normative or realist epistemology (a conventional form of foundationalism) for feminism, as we do, still need to have a reasoned grounding for this alternative epistemological position—fractured foundationalism provides such grounding and also recognises social constructionism.[5]

FFF proceeds from making transparent the practices and understandings of feminist research. However, FFF is not "a method"; it can be utilised in feminist survey research as much as feminist interviewing and ethnography, as much as feminist historiography. Neither is it straightforwardly "an epistemology" because, although having epistemological underpinnings, it contains broad precepts for operationalising feminist research in practice. It is instead "a methodology," a set of procedural strategies that enable research conceptualisation, grounded research practices, writing about research data, and theorising from these, to be brought together and thought about as a coherent whole. Succinctly, FFF is a *feminist* epistemology and methodology because it involves research carried out by feminist practitioners explicitly putting "feminism into practice" in their research practices, specifically because FFF is organised around a number of principles or strategies that make feminist researchers accountable, including analytical reflexivity around the use of retrievable data.[6] In this short commentary on putting the FFF framework into practice, we are unable to discuss in any more

detail the strategies that compose it, although we have discussed them in other publications,[7] and instead focus on "putting it into practice."

The immediate backcloth to the research involves the events of the South African War (1899–1902), particularly its "scorched earth" phase, when the British military burned many Boer[8] farms, and women, children, and elderly people were removed to camps of tents, situated along railway lines so that they could be provisioned. More than 4,000 women and 22,000 children died[9] when a succession of major epidemics—measles, diarrhoea, enteritis, typhoid, and pneumonia—occurred, spread when people were moved from one concentration camp to another to be closer to their original homes. These events, together with how they were remembered and used within the development of nationalism and racial segregation in South Africa, have been the subject of Liz's recent research.[10] The other element of the backcloth is formed by Sue's long-standing research and writing on feminist social work, and her interest in social justice regarding the treatment and welfare of children.[11]

When we decided to "test" FFF in grounded research practice, we pooled our respective interests: We designed a small project focusing on the experiences of children during the South African War, in the concentration camps in particular, because in that war (as in others before and since) it was children who "bore the brunt," while adults were not willing to end it without capitulation from the other side.[12] We also made an in-principle decision to focus the project on children because previous research has looked at the war and the camps from the perspective of adults, even though the overwhelming majority of those who died were children.[13]

## THE RESEARCH PROCESS

Britain provoked the South African War (1899–1902) against the two Boer republics of the Orange Free State and South African Republic and annexed these as the Orange River (ORC) and Transvaal colonies as part of its imperialist expansionist project in Southern Africa. The war, however, did not end. Boer commandos continued fighting; the British "scorched earth" policy and the creation of concentration camps as internment camps for Boer civilians was a response. Our camp children project was designed with two interrelated components, concerned with the main ways that experiences of children were represented following the removal of people to the concentration camps: the official records, and photograph collections.

The official records were kept by British administrators at the local level in the approximately 40 Boer concentration camps and also in the headquarters of each newly annexed colony.[14] These were records of an organisational apparatus concerned with maintaining and regulating the "removed" population, with accountability ultimately held by the British government in Whitehall, but beneath this by the colony governments[15] and their chief administrators of the camps, and then beneath this by the superintendents or administrators of each camp. There are many extant records—"returns" of information and also summarising registers.[16] We picked one element of these records, in one of the annexed colonies, for detailed investigation: the "minutes" or files of enquiries between the Chief Superintendent of Refugee Camps (SRC), and the superintendents in charge of the ORC's 11 camps. In the SRC archive collection, there are nearly 11,000 such enquiries, some of which are specifically concerned with children's lives, illnesses, or deaths.

The second component of the research involves archive collections of photographs.[17] These were taken primarily by professional photographers, who travelled to war locations and routinely visited the camps, selling their photographs to newspapers worldwide and to British soldiers and Boer commandos and people living in the camps. There are three main collections of South African War photographs in South Africa holding around 80,000 photographs of "the war."[18] The collection held by the Free State Archives Depot in Bloemfontein (VAB) covers the same camps as the SRC records of enquiries, and consequently it became the focus of our investigation. The photographs throw a different light on the concentration camps from the official records, the enquiries concerning children in particular, because they feature a much wider range of children's presence and activities. This is absolutely *not* to suggest that the photographs are more "real" than the official records (or vice

versa) but to emphasise that the two sources have different origins and purposes, and the photographs witness camp inhabitants more involved in choosing how they were represented; it is also witnessed in keeping these as mementoes post-war.

Many of the total set of SRC enquiries cover matters including or of relevance to children because children composed the large majority of the populations of all the camps. However, our interest was in those enquiries where children were the *specific* focus, so while in the Bloemfontein Archives Depot,[19] we worked through detailed notes on them all to identify this smaller group, using Liz's previous research on the collection. Then we read the enquiry papers for each of the children's enquiries identified in detail, using other SRC records to generate additional information where available;[20] Table 32.1 summarises the concerns of these.

These 49 enquiries were discussed in detail, including in relation to wider aspects of the war and the camps. From this, 7 enquiries were selected because discussion of these would enable covering the broad distribution of enquiries in Table 32.1.[21] A piece of retrievable data for each of them was identified from the enquiry papers, a document that would help signal to readers a range of issues to be discussed. From the outset, we had decided to write up the project using "retrievable data," to tie the discussion as closely as possible to original documents that "stand for" or exemplify wider aspects of the research and our interpretations of it, so readers could evaluate our arguments against their own. We do not claim referentiality for retrievable data—such texts are not directly reflective of "the real happenings" that gave rise to them. Nor are they the total evidence we wanted to draw on in discussing the children's enquiries. However, providing original documentation helps show something of the evidential base being worked from, provides a flavour of what working with this encompasses, and enables a more informed readerly evaluation of interpretations and conclusions.

A similar procedure was adopted regarding the VAB photograph collection, which neither of us had worked on before. The result was the identification of 116 concentration camp photographs, in 61 of which children appeared, with the classification of these shown in Table 32.2.

**Table 32.1** SRC Enquiries Concerned With Children

| Area of Concern | Number |
| --- | --- |
| Policy and practice regarding orphans[a] | 15 |
| Child mortality issues | 8 |
| Formal enquiries and postmortems | 7 |
| Specific children in/out camps | 5 |
| Administrative issues and misrecords | 4 |
| Illegitimacy | 3 |
| Children's rations | 2 |
| Miscellaneous | 5 |
| Total | 49 |

a. The majority of these enquiries were raised after peace was declared, on June 1, 1902.

Our principled decision to use retrievable data meant considerable discussion of the photographs with children in them, including in relationship to the SRC enquiries coterminously being worked on, to narrow the choices down. As with the enquiries, photographs were selected to broadly reflect the distribution of subjects across the whole set, resulting in our selection of eight photographs.[22]

Finally, back in the United Kingdom and during the initial writing-up stage, with some reluctance we decided to focus down on three enquiries and three photographs around which to discuss putting FFF into practice, as a small enough number to provide readers with specific examples and the interpretations based on these. However, we rapidly realised that even this was too many when working within constrained word limits. The result was the decision to base the discussion around one enquiry and one photograph, but still to provide retrievable data for the more representative group of seven enquiries and eight photographs. This we thought would enable readers to place the two cases discussed in a broader context because we supplemented it by footnoting comments on the other six enquiries and seven photographs at appropriate points in the discussion, a simple form of "hypertexting" linkages across the enquiries we had worked on in depth.[23]

The enquiry was selected first, on the basis that it raised the widest range of issues; this was the Swart[24] case, with the retrievable data here provided in Appendix A. It is a letter from the superintendent of Harrismith camp, Arthur Bradley, written on December 25, 1901, to the ORC's Chief Superintendent, Captain Trollope, concerning the events occurring around the death from typhoid of 13-year-old Christina Swart. Then the photograph was selected, to raise different issues about a different camp, Kroonstad; this photograph is of the mundane activity of distributing firewood and is provided as Appendix B.

Christina Swart's parents failed to report her illness for 3 weeks, with what they thought were her best interests at heart. As other filed documentation shows, they had deliberately hidden Christina from the daily "sick call" carried out by Boer probationer nurses[25] and secretly buried her typhoid-infected faeces. Also, while the postmortem shows that Christina had been fed on solids, her mother's sworn statement mentions feeding liquids but not solid food: It seems Mrs. Swart was aware of the strict advice to starve typhoid patients, but her wish to do her best for her daughter had overridden this and she thought the doctors, rather than her feeding her daughter, had killed Christina.[26]

**Table 32.2**    VAB Concentration Camp Photographs

| Subjects | Numbers | Totals |
|---|---|---|
| Views | 14 | 14 |
| Adults | | 41 |
| • Employees and others | 20 | |
| • Camp inhabitants | 12 | |
| • Relief Committee[a] members | 9 | |
| Children | | 61 |
| • Posed (formal, informal) | 14 | |
| • Playing | 2 | |
| • Working | 9 | |
| • School/Sunday school | 3 | |
| • Soup distribution[b] | 2 | |
| • "Relief" activities | 12 | |
| • Peace Day[c] | 3 | |
| • Sick and hospital | 2 | |
| • Views with people, including children | 14 | |
| Total | 116 | 116 |

a. Because this camp was close to the town, a local relief committee played a high-profile role in organising funding for and the distribution of "extras" to rations.
b. This was done by camp authorities, concerned that the individualised approach to cooking and eating in most camps led to children being inadequately fed.
c. Celebrations were held in all camps after peace was declared on June 1, 1902.

The superintendent's letter implies his response to the doctors was purely a humanitarian one about Christina, but he had other motives too. Thus, it is clear he actually *intervened* only because of the importance of Christina's uncles in the camp. Also, his letters indicate his pressing practical concern with "managing" men in the camp like the Swart brothers and preventing their "discontent." In addition, other filed documents show him "covering his back" by masking the fact that Mrs. Swart had reported Christina's sickness to him before the doctors found out about it.

And further complexity can be added by taking the best possible view of why the doctors acted as they did.[27] There had been an immense rise in the camp's death rate from November on. The doctors' various evidence comments that

the Swarts had buried Christina's typhoid-infected faeces in the area of their tent; for them it was self-evident that the Swarts were likely to have been responsible for part of Harrismith's hugely increased death rate in December and January, shown in Table 32.3.

Reading the full documentation of the Swart enquiry, what comes across is that all the adults involved had good (but different) moral reasons for acting as they did; however, their same actions can also all be seen as morally wrong when looked at from a different angle. The superintendent had good humanitarian reasons for resisting the doctors' decision—but he only acted on his sympathetic response because Christina's uncles were powerful in the camp. The doctors were battling with rampant typhoid and bringing

**Table 32.3**   Harrismith Deaths and Death Rates, May 1901 to March 1902

| | Camp Population | Deaths | Death Rates[a] |
|---|---|---|---|
| May 1901 | — | — | — |
| June | 656 | 1 | 18 |
| July | 927 | 3 | 38 |
| August | 1,134 | 5 | 52 |
| September | 1,304 | 2 | 18 |
| October | 1,596 | 5 | 37 |
| November | 1,650 | 13 | 94 |
| December | 1,623 | 63 | 761 |
| January 1902 | 1,470 | 32 | 261 |
| February | 608 | 4 | 79 |
| March | 348 | 1 | 34 |

SOURCE: From Hobhouse (1902, pp. 341–344); the information is taken from the UK Government "Blue Books" or Command Reports.

a. These death rates are per 1,000 population and are annual rates: If deaths continued at this level, in the course of a year 761 people out of each 1,000 would die. In some camps, death rates at the peak of the epidemics were extremely high, and in Kroonstad (referred to later) reached more than 1,100 per 1,000 per annum.

the death rates down—but they wanted to be top dogs in the official hierarchy, despised the peasant medical beliefs of Boer farming people, and forced the removal of Christina even though she was dying. Mrs. Swart comes across as a woman of considerable determination, and it is impossible not to feel sympathy for both the Swart parents in wanting to protect their daughter—but they probably killed dozens of other people in the process, while Christina might have survived had she gone into hospital.[28]

FFF is a political and analytical position, not a representation of the world according to women, and we are concerned with the most vulnerable and least powerful person involved: the dying Christina Swart. Christina appears in the enquiry documents only as a cipher, an "absent presence" at the heart of events; and adults, particularly her parents, attribute feelings and motives to her, rather than her speaking "in her own right."[29] So, might it be possible to read the enquiry documents to bring Christina into view? We concluded it was not and that

doing this requires consideration of other situations where children became the focus to understand more of the dynamics at work.

A less fully documented but more notorious case of a child whose death was disputed between adults involves Lizzie van Zyl, a young girl from Bloemfontein camp. There is a much republished photograph of a skeletal Lizzie, with her appearance almost automatically assumed to "show starvation" by adults on all sides.[30] Through publication of this photograph in the international press in early 1902, Lizzie's illness and death became caught up in a two-sided propaganda battle. Like Christina Swart, Lizzie van Zyl "vanished" in these disputes between adults, except that her pitiful photograph remains (and is still used, in both senses of the word[31]). Even when children were the focus, we conclude this was still overwhelmingly as they were seen and positioned (and "voiced") by adults.[32]

In thinking through the dynamics of the Swart enquiry as represented in the extant documentation, it is clear that unless the focus of a research project is based entirely on retrievable documentary sources, it is really not possible to provide readers with the entirety of relevant evidence.[33] It is therefore useful to explore the process of "knowing" around an archive source we know no more about than readers. This is a photograph that archive information states was taken in Kroonstad camp, shown in Appendix B.[34] Kroonstad was a bigger camp than Harrismith and had many extremely poor Boer people living in it;[35] consequently, using a retrievable document concerning Kroonstad provides a means of recognising the experiences of Boer people very different from the Swarts. Also the photograph's mundane content—distributing wood and people queuing— provides a direct contrast to the dramatic and upsetting events of the Swart enquiry and enables some of the more everyday and routine aspects of camp life to be—literally—seen.

This photograph illustrates the orderliness and routinisation that characterised much, indeed most, of camp life. Many of the "views with people" across the three archive collections are of this kind and suggest, first, that "ordinary life" continued, because cooking, eating, and keeping warm remained priority activities; and second, that concentration introduced new levels of regulation (e.g., rations of wood) and routinisation (e.g., times and places for their distribution). Also like other "views with people" in the collections, the photograph witnesses the significant presence of able-bodied men, whereas received wisdom is that the camps were composed of women and children and very elderly people and all Boer men were loyalists on commando duty. It also shows the highly gendered division of labour at an everyday level—men and boys in the foreground are sorting and apportioning the firewood, while women and female children in the background are queuing and waiting to be given the appropriate ration.

There are two further matters worth commenting on, neither "there" in the photograph itself but important to interpreting it. The first concerns the women and children standing in line and queuing. This of course *can* be seen: But what is not visible is what this *meant* for the camp inhabitants. Queuing was a raced activity in the Boer republics, with such "lowly" tasks done by black people, not whites. It was a highly resented aspect of life in all the camps, because it indicated not being treated as "superior" in race terms and was seen as part of the inexplicable and

unforgivable "topsy-turvy" consequence of the war in overturning the assumed natural order. The second is what this and other photographs by professional photographers indicate about the openness of the camps to people from "outside." There is little sense that photographing in the camps was subject to any stringent controls. Thus, looking at photographs in a sequence (some of which are numbered), it is clear the photographer in question was walking about the camp, taking photographs as different activities and "scenes" met his eye.[36] And the photographers were by no means the only visitors: Most camps were routinely visited by members of local Relief Committees, journalists, "do-gooders" from abroad, shopkeepers, and peddlers.

## COMMENTARY

Operationalising the FFF framework has made us very careful about the "how" of presenting our camp children project for an audience, by requiring us to do so within the terms set by this framework so that readers are able to assess what we have written against the strategic components of FFF. Having readers in mind in this way was a very powerful incentive to make what we were doing as accountable as possible. As part of this, we were equally careful about the selections of enquiries and photographs made and how these would "fit" the specifications of the FFF framework, and we shifted and changed these selections many times as a consequence. In relation to these matters, we concluded that FFF was useful to think with, encouraged accountability, and constrained carefulness in fulfilling the requirements attached to this framework.

As we interpret it, the FFF framework shapes up most powerfully as a way of rethinking who and what the feminist research process is concerned with representing. We are interested in FFF providing a means of bringing into focus the most vulnerable and least powerful, and in the project reported on here this is children rather than women. One of the consequences of knowing "what came after" in the South African case is that it becomes difficult to see Boer women one-dimensionally as heroines or victims; and it was children who definitely bore the brunt of politically and morally objectionable conduct by adults, of both genders, on both sides. This was a very powerful aspect of the process and one we welcome—it made us very aware of "adultism" both in the contemporary documents (including the photographic sources, although to a perhaps lesser extent than written documentation) *and* in the assumptions and focuses of researchers, ourselves included.

Using the FFF framework with its emphasis on the multifaceted character of social life made us closely attend to at the time reality-claims and to the complexities, fractures, and disjunctures surrounding these. It is one thing to say that social life is both materially grounded *and* socially constructed, but it is another to grasp the nettle of this, and working within the FFF framework really did enable us to see how complicated reality issues and truth claims were, even within the context of their representation in the organisational documents we were working with.

The doctoral research process requires the basis of knowledge and the methodological and other competence underpinning this to be fully demonstrated, having to be accountable about such matters because they will be interrogated as part of the oral examination of the eventuating thesis. However, beyond this, it is salutary to note that the more experienced researchers are, the more other people are expected to take their research practices on trust and to bracket many of the things that thesis examiners would expect to be fully accounted for. Another strength of the FFF framework, then, is that it requires experienced researchers to be more fully accountable for the what and how and why of our research practices.

One aspect of this that needs separate mention concerns readers. We see FFF as a process as well as a framework, a process that is accountable in part to even up the usual vast academic power imbalance between writers and readers, in which readers are given products, the production of which they are required to take on trust. FFF provides something, but certainly not all, of this process. Knowing that readers can read at least some of the same documents means that readers are kept in mind throughout the process, and operationalising FFF definitely made us attentive to what readers would need to know to be able to read actively. At the same time, it also led us to find ways of weaning readers away from the usual "take it on trust, or reject it out of hand" way of reading academic work, requiring

readers to be active and enquiring and to think precisely about what they are reading. If FFF requires active and accountable writing, it also requires active accountable readership—moral epistemology cuts both ways.

However, there were also times when we experienced the FFF framework as overly constraining. Increasingly, as we used it we concluded that in spite of our efforts, it was actually more an epistemology than a methodology, and in order to "work" as a methodology we had to rework it by focusing on the methodological dimensions of its nine composing strategies and strip away from these their, at times, too dominating epistemological concerns. As a consequence, operationalising FFF shaped a very great deal of what and how we wrote about what we have, so much so that at the end of the process we were left wondering whether we had written about the most important things about the research carried out. Although a conclusion about this is "still pending," we are certain that the substantive and conceptual issues would have been written about in a very different way, and rather different things highlighted, if we had started from the research and our ideas (before, during, and after the archival fieldwork) about it.

At the end of the process, we conclude that using the FFF approach certainly evens up things for the reader, in particular by providing retrievable data and working this in analytically reflexive ways (and we are very interested in how readers of Wise & Stanley, 2006a, 2006b, experience this and see the pros and cons). It evens things up by putting the spotlight on the researchers and their research practices and making researchers be much more accountable; however, does it do this at the expense of sidelining the details of the research itself? Certainly operationalising FFF made us contemplate and write about things we would not have ordinarily done and, particularly with regard to children and the "narratively dispossessed" more generally, we think this is worth the constraints involved; but we are also aware there are important aspects of both the enquiries and the photographs that have not even been mentioned in passing, and we regret this. So is it simply a matter of gaining on the swings but losing on the roundabouts? For us, "the jury is still out" here.

There are also issues concerning the use of retrievable data within the FFF framework.

Initially, we thought there was a problem in using retrievable data, that this was suitable only for discussing technical matters that are entirely recoverable from within a single document or other data source—all the time, we felt the need to adduce wider knowledge to understand what was readable or observable in these. However, further thought suggests that the problem is actually much simpler and concerns word constraints—that is, it would be relatively easy to write a book around a collection of retrievable data and in relation to which the reader really would be an active agent with regard to the researchers' argument and interpretation. However, in the short length of an article or chapter, it is necessary to explain the background rather than provide a succession of retrievable documents around which their explication would supply this. At the same time, it is worth making a caveat here: Having considered that there are special requirements concerning research on the "long ago and far away" and that research on the "here and now" could trade on common knowledge, we now think it is mistaken to assume that "everyone knows," not least because potential readers are of all ages and come from many different cultures and different parts of the world.[37]

## Appendix A: SRC 17/6922 [also Col Sec 14/02] Refugees Refusing to Report Cases of Sickness

Supt's office
Harrismith
23 12 01

Dear Capt Trollope,

A Mrs Swartz reported to me this morning that her daughter aged 13 had been ordered into Hospital, and asked me to go to her Tent. I informed her that as the Medical Officer had ordered the child into Hospital, that [sic] her only course was to let the child go. It was apparent to everyone that the child was dying, and I wrote to the S.M.O. the letter that I now enclose for your perusal. I received no written reply, but my clerk informed me that the Doctor still insisted on the removal of the child.

The child was absolutely terrified at the idea of being removed, and I never remember seeing such a pitiful sight, as I saw on the attempted removal and which resulted in the death of the child, before the bed sent for it was clear of the Tent.

Mrs Swartz then came to me again in great distress and asked me for an independent Post Mortem. This I referred to the Resident Magistrate, as being my next immediate superior, and he ordered the Post Mortem to be held.

The Medical Officers were extremely incensed with me, and were very insulting, and used language which culminated in my telling Dr Rossiter, that if he could not control himself he had better leave my office. I take it, that my duty to these poor people requires me to take steps to look into any grievance they report to me, and in my opinion, this was a case in which more humanity might have been shown.

The Resident Magistrate is holding an inquiry into the whole facts of the case, and the proceedings will be laid before you in due course.

I take it, that I acted correctly in reporting the matter to the R.M. as the burial was about to take place.

All the people here are now well in hand, and are in a large majority well disposed towards the British occupation, all my orders are obeyed, and the men work willingly, and a lot more can be effected with them by kindness, than by the use of harshness, and I dont [sic] want to see them lapse back into the old discontented state.

I quite recognize that the people are very loath to report sickness, and I always impress on them the necessity of at once reporting, and I entirely support the M.O.s in this, & in getting them into Hospital, but I would ask you to impress on them, that the people are to be as considerately treated as possible, and any insubordination can be referred to me.

I would ask you to administer a rebuke to Dr Rossiter for his insolent language to me, and inform him that the people are justified in coming to me with their grievances, if they desire so to do, as he disputes this point.

This occurrence is also unfortunate, from the fact that there are 5 Brothers Swartz in Camp, & they are all wealthy men & large landowners in this District, with considerable influence & following, and I have been doing all I can to propitiate them, with a view to the future settlement of the Colony.

Yours faithfully
Arthur William Bradley, Lieut I.Y.

## Appendix B: VAB 2920

SOURCE: Reproduced by kind permission of the Free State Archives Depot, Bloemfontein, South Africa.

## Notes

1. Although now it is almost impossible not to read the term through knowledge of the Nazi work and death camps, it is important to keep in mind, first, that the term had no such associations at the time and, second, that Goebbels deliberately labelled the Nazi camps as he did as part of anti-British propaganda, of a "they had them too, how dare they criticize us" kind.

2. Useful reading includes Cuthbertson, Grundlingh, and Suttie (2002), Hanekom and Wessels (2000), Jackson (1999), Nasson (1999), Pretorius (2001), and Spies (1977).

3. Including Stanley and Wise (1979, 1983a, 1983b, 1990, 1992, 1993, 2000).

4. Including in Stanley and Wise (1993, 2000) and Wise and Stanley (2003).

5. As explored in detail in Wise and Stanley (2005a).

6. These strategies are discussed in detail in Wise and Stanley (2006b), and the details of their practical application in the camp children project are provided in Wise and Stanley (2006a). They are concerned with the feminist research labour process, grounding feminist knowledge, unalienated

knowledge, the knowing subject, the fractured ontological base, knowers and competing knowledge-claims, moral epistemology, analytical reflexivity, and a modest "internalist" approach to feminist knowledge production.

7. See Note 4 for the key references.

8. Literally, farmer; by the 1890s, this people, later known as Afrikaners, also included an urban educated class.

9. Postwar, there was the suppression of male death rates in the camps because of the political mythology that all Boer men were loyalists on commando duty.

10. See Stanley (2002a, 2002b, 2002c, 2004, 2005, 2006a, 2006b), Stanley and Dampier (2005), and Dampier and Stanley (2006). See also Dampier (2005a, 2005b).

11. See Wise (1990, 1991, 1995, 1999).

12. This applied to women too: Indeed, contemporaries saw Boer women as more militant than their menfolk; *The Brunt of the War and Where It Fell* is the title of a 1902-published book by Emily Hobhouse (1902).

13. Interesting reading, which departs from the usual "adultist" concerns with childhood, includes

all the contributions to Christensen and James (2000); also Ferguson (2004), James and Prout (1990), James, Jenks, and Prout (1998), Qvortrup, Bardy, Sgritta, and Wintersberger (1994), and Strange (2002).

14. Some were informal while others were started but then moved, so tracking the exact number is complicated, not least because some parts of the records were lost en route to being archived postwar. The key collections are the Director of Burgher Camps Collection, Transvaal Archives Depot; and Superintendent of Burgher Camps Collection, Free State Archives Depot, Bloemfontein; both are in South Africa. Helpful reading on imperial and other archives includes Bartel (1996), Cohn (1990, 1996), Crais (2002), McEwan (2003), Richards (1993), Rose (2000), and Starn (2002).

15. Following annexation, these were mixed military and civil governments.

16. These concern sicknesses and deaths, rations distribution, supplies arriving, people (often black) employed to provide services needed to run the camps, passes to work in local towns or visit husbands at the front, the array of goods for sale in camp shops, camp schools, and more.

17. Relevant reading on using photographs includes Brink (2000), Bugin (1982), Paris (2003), Pols (2002), Riches and Dawson (1998), Rose (2000), Sontag (1977, 2003), and Walker and Moulton (1989).

18. These are Fotosversameling, Transvaal Archives Depot, Pretoria; Fotosversameling, Free State Archives Depot, Bloemfontein; and Fotosversameling, War Museum of the Boer Republics, Bloemfontein, all in South Africa.

19. Fieldwork took place from June to the end of September 2004.

20. Some records were lost en route to being archived when political control was gained in elections by the Afrikaner majority populations.

21. These are one enquiry concerning adoption of an orphan, one enquiry concerning mortality rates, two formal enquiries regarding suspected unlawful killings, one administrative enquiry about misrecording, one administrative enquiry regarding nonroutine events and expenditure, and one enquiry around a major dispute that enables many of these concerns and also important issues for FFF to be raised.

22. These are a posed group, doing domestic chores, helping distribute firewood, a young African servant washing clothes, inside a camp school, soup distribution, a wealthy family group, and a "view with people."

23. And concerning which active readership by readers is required in two respects: the whole set of retrievable documents provide a broader informational context for readers to locate the Swart case and the Kroonstad photograph in; and the footnotes provide our summarising interpretations of these and, to grasp these, readers need to have read the retrievable documents themselves.

24. The name appears variously, mainly as Swartz, but was actually Swart.

25. Actually, more akin to health visitors.

26. On the "clash of medical cultures" involved, see Van Heyningen (1999, 2001).

27. It is easy to think the worst because of the effects on Christina Swart, but they were working in an extreme situation.

28. Political rumour had it that children were deliberately killed in the hospitals, whereas the actuality is that survival rates in hospitals were many times better than when people stayed in their tents (see Stanley, 2006b, chap. 6).

29. For an interesting discussion of how children are denied a "voice" in the making of history, see Hendrick (2000); for an insightful discussion of the "narratively dispossessed" more generally, see Baldwin (2006).

30. Such children were a considerable moral as well as epidemiological problem: Why did they "fade away" and who was responsible? The basic problem was probably the ubiquitous prevalence of enteritis, dysentery, and other diseases involving diarrhoea, noted by some medical officers including in the black camps immediately after civil control was instituted in late February 1901.

31. Discussed in Stanley (2006b, chap. 6).

32. On ways of rethinking "narrative voice," see Baldwin (2006).

33. Use of retrievable data was pioneered by conversational analysis, focused on technical matters concerning the structural aspects of transcribed talk and written documents, with content mainly a background matter; we are interested in using it in contexts where content is of the essence, thus the problem.

34. The photograph was taken by a professional photographer who would have sold the image—a printed caption appears at the bottom with its number in a sequence.

35. It also had a phenomenally high death rate (from measles in particular) from June 1901 to January 1902, reaching 1,173 per thousand per annum in August 1901.

36. All the known professional photographers in the ORC camps were male. The travelling photographers would have needed permission from the camp superintendent to carry out their activities. However, many of them would have been English speakers, perhaps the source of their "freedom to roam."

37. A separate project that Sue carried out concurrently with our joint camp children research was concerned with South African street children contemporaneously. We discussed in detail how we would operationalise FFF in relation to this and rapidly concluded that the same need to explain events, processes, and structures for nonfamiliar audiences existed.

## REFERENCES

Baldwin, Clive. (2006). The narrative dispossession of people living with dementia: Thinking about the theory and method of narrative. In Kate Milnes, Christine Horrocks, Nancy Kelly, Brian Roberts, & David Robinson (Eds.), *Narrative, Memory and Knowledge* (pp. 101–110). Huddersfield, UK: University of Huddersfield Press.

Bartel, Diane. (1996). *Historic preservation: Collective memory and historical identity*. New Brunswick, NJ: Rutgers University Press.

Brink, Cornelia. (2000). Secular icons: Looking at photographs from Nazi concentration camps. *History and Memory, 12*, 135–150.

Bugin, Victor. (Ed.). (1982). *Thinking photography*. London: Macmillan.

Christensen, Pia, & James, Allison. (Eds.). (2000). *Research with children: Perspectives and practices*. London: Falmer Press.

Cohn, Bernard. (1990). *An anthropologist among the historians and other essays*. Delhi, India: Oxford University Press.

Cohn, Bernard. (1996). *Colonialism and its forms of knowledge: The British in India*. Princeton, NJ: Princeton University Press.

Crais, Clifton. (2002). *The politics of evil: Magic, state power, and the political imagination in South Africa*. Cambridge, UK: Cambridge University Press.

Cuthbertson, Greg, Grundlingh, Albert, & Suttie, Mary-Lynn. (Eds.). (2002). *Writing a wider war: Rethinking gender, race, and identity in the South African War, 1899–1902*. Cape Town, South Africa: David Philip.

Dampier, Helen. (2005a). *Women's personal testimonies of the South African War concentration camps, 1899–1902 and after*. Doctoral dissertation, University of Newcastle, UK.

Dampier, Helen. (2005b). Everyday life in Boer women's testimonies of the concentration camps of the South African War, 1899–1902. In Graeme Dunstall & Barry Godfrey (Eds.), *Crime and empire 1840–1940: Criminal justice in local and global context* (pp. 202–223). Cullompton, UK: Willan.

Dampier, Helen, & Stanley, Liz. (2006). Simulacrumdiaries; knowledge, the "moment of writing" and the diaries of Johanna Brandt-Van Warmelo. In Kate Milnes, Christine Horrocks, Nancy Kelly, Brian Roberts, & David Robinson (Eds.), *Narrative, Memory and Knowledge* (pp. 27–40). Huddersfield, UK: University of Huddersfield Press.

Ferguson, Harry. (2004). *Protecting children in time: Child abuse, child protection and the consequences of modernity*. Basingstoke, UK: Palgrave Macmillan.

Hanekom, Leandré, & Wessels, Elria. (2000). *Valour, thy name is woman: An overview of the role of Afrikaner women and children inside and outside Anglo-Boer War concentration camps 1899–1902*. Bloemfontein, South Africa: War Museum of the Boer Republics.

Hendrick, Harry. (2000). The child as social actor in historical sources: Problems of identification and interpretation. In Pia Christensen & Allison James (Eds.), *Research with children: Perspectives and practices* (pp. 36–61). London: Falmer Press.

Hobhouse, Emily. (1902). *The brunt of the war and where it fell*. London: Methuen.

Jackson, Tabitha. (1999). *The Boer War*. London: Channel 4 Books.

James, Allison, Jenks, Chris, & Prout, Alan. (1998). *Theorizing childhood*. Cambridge, UK: Polity Press.

James, Allison, & Prout, Alan. (Eds.). (1990). *Constructing and reconstructing childhood*. London: Falmer Press.

McEwan, Cheryl. (2003). Building a postcolonial archive? Gender, collective memory and citizenship in post-apartheid South Africa. *Journal of Southern African Studies, 29*, 739–757.

Nasson, Bill. (1999). *The South African War 1899–1902*. London: Arnold.

Paris, Heather. (2003). "Lifting up the little form": Victorian images of childhood and death 1870–1900. *Sociological Research Online, 8*(3). Retrieved from www.socresonline.org.uk/8/3/paris.html

Pols, Robert. (2002). *Family photographs 1860–1945*. Richmond, UK: Public Record Office Publications.

Pretorius, Fransjohan. (Ed.). (2001). *Scorched earth*. Cape Town, South Africa: Human & Rousseau.

Qvortrup, Jens, Bardy, M., Sgritta, G., & Wintersberger, H. (Eds.). (1994). *Childhood matters: Social theory, practice and politics*. Aldershot, UK: Avebury.

Richards, Thomas. (1993). *The imperial archive: Knowledge and the fantasy of empire*. London: Verso.

Riches, Gordon, & Dawson, Pamela. (1998). Lost children, living memories: The role of photographs in processes of grief and adjustment among bereaved parents. *Death Studies, 22*, 121–140.

Rose, Gillian. (2000). Practising photography: An archive, a study, some photographs and a researcher. *Journal of Historical Geography, 24*, 555–571.

Sontag, Susan. (1977). *On photography*. Harmondsworth, UK: Penguin.

Sontag, Susan. (2003). *Regarding the pain of others*. New York: Picador.

Spies, S. B. (1977). *Methods of barbarism: Roberts, Kitchener and civilians in the Boer republics January 1900–May 1902*. Kaapstad, South Africa: Human & Rousseau.

Stanley, Liz. (2002a). Women's South African War testimonies: Remembering, forgetting and forgiving, In *Should We Forget? Tydskrif vir Nederlands en Afrikaans (TN&A), 9*, 93–118.

Stanley, Liz. (2002b). A "secret history" of local mourning: The South African War, the Vroue Monument and state commemoration. *Society in Transition: Journal of the South African Sociological Association, 19*, 1–22.

Stanley, Liz. (2002c). Mourning becomes . . . : The work of feminism in the spaces between lives lived and lives written. *Women's Studies International Forum, 25*, 1–17.

Stanley, Liz. (2004). Black labour and the concentration system of the South African War. *Joernaal vir Eietdse Geskiedenis/Journal of Contemporary History, 28*, 190–213.

Stanley, Liz. (2005). Emily Hobhouse, moral life and the concentration camps of the South African War, 1899–1902. *South African Historical Journal, 52*, 60–81.

Stanley, Liz. (2006a). Looking at the taciturn exterior: On legendary topography, the meta-narrative of commemoration and palimpsest monuments of the concentration camps of the South African War. *Journal of Visual Culture, 5*.

Stanley, Liz. (2006b). *Mourning becomes . . . Post/memory and the concentration camps of the South African War*. Manchester, UK: Manchester University Press.

Stanley, Liz, & Dampier, Helen. (2005). Aftermaths: Post/memory, commemoration and the concentration camps of the South African War 1899–1902. *European Review of History, 12*, 89–113.

Stanley, Liz, & Wise, Sue. (1979). Feminist research, feminist consciousness and experiences of sexism. *Women's Studies International Quarterly, 2*, 259–274.

Stanley, Liz, & Wise, Sue. (1983a). *Breaking out: Feminist consciousness and feminist research*. London: Routledge.

Stanley, Liz, & Wise, Sue. (1983b). Back into the personal, our attempt to construct feminist research. In Gloria Bowles & Renate Duelli Klein (Eds.), *Theories of women's studies* (pp. 192–209). London: Routledge.

Stanley, Liz, & Wise, Sue. (1990). Method, methodology and epistemology in feminist research processes. In Liz Stanley (Ed.), *Feminist praxis: Research, theory and epistemology in feminist sociology* (pp. 20–60). London: Routledge.

Stanley, Liz, & Wise, Sue. (1992). Feminist epistemology and ontology. *Indian Journal of Social Work, 53*, 343–365.

Stanley, Liz, & Wise, Sue. (1993). *Breaking out again: Feminist ontology and epistemology*. London: Routledge.

Stanley, Liz, & Wise, Sue. (2000). But the Empress has no clothes! Some awkward questions about the "missing revolution" in feminist theory. *Feminist Theory, 1*, 261–288.

Starn, Randolph. (2002). Truths in archives. *Common Knowledge, 8*, 387–401.

Strange, Julie-Marie. (2002). "She cried very little": Death, grief and mourning in working-class culture, c. 1880–1914. *Social History, 27*, 143–161.

Van Heyningen, Elizabeth. (1999). The voices of women in the South African War. *South African Historical Journal, 41,* 22–43.

Van Heyningen, Elizabeth. (2001). British doctors versus Boer women: Clash of medical cultures. In Fransjohan Pretorius (Ed.), *Scorched earth* (pp. 178–197). Cape Town, South Africa: Human & Rousseau.

Walker, Andre, & Moulton, Rosalind. (1989). Photo albums: Images of time and reflections of self. *Qualitative Sociology, 12,* 155–182.

Wise, Sue. (1990). Becoming a feminist social worker. In Liz Stanley (Ed.), *Feminist praxis: Research, theory and epistemology in feminist sociology* (pp. 236–249). London: Routledge.

Wise, Sue. (1991). *Child abuse: The NSPCC version* (Feminist Praxis 32). Manchester, UK: University of Manchester.

Wise, Sue. (1995). Feminist ethics in practice. In Richard Hugman & David Smith (Eds.), *Ethical issues in social work* (pp. 104–119). London: Routledge.

Wise, Sue. (1999). Reading Sara Scott's "Here be dragons." *Sociological Research Online,* 4(1). Retrieved from www.socresonline.org.uk/4/1/wise.html

Wise, Sue, & Stanley, Liz. (2003). Looking back and looking forward: Some recent feminist sociology reviewed. *Sociological Research Online,* 8(3). Retrieved from www.socresonline.org.uk/8/3/wise.html

Wise, Sue, & Stanley, Liz. (2006a). Using feminist fractured foundationalism in researching children in the concentration camps of the South African War 1899–1902. *Sociological Research Online, 11.* Retrieved from www.socresonline.org.uk/11/1.stanley.html

Wise, Sue, & Stanley, Liz. (2006b). Having it all: Feminist fractured foundationalism. In Kathy Davis, Mary Evans, & Judith Lorber (Eds.), *Sage handbook of gender and women's studies* (pp. 435–456). London: Sage.

# 33

# FUTURE DIRECTIONS IN DIFFERENCE RESEARCH

## Recognising and Responding to Difference

DIANE REAY

This chapter focuses on differences among women and the tensions that are generated within feminist research that attempts to address these differences. It draws on existing feminist research that engages with a range of difficult differences. While the chapter has a particular emphasis on social class as a marginalised but enduring difference, it also examines differences of ethnicity, sexuality, and age, and their consequences, not only for feminist methodology but also for actual research processes and practices. All too often, the high moral ground of feminist theory is lost in the messy realities of fieldwork because the differences so neatly captured in our texts spiral either out of control or out of vision. The chapter looks at feminist accounts that have, with varying degrees of success, attempted to deal with problematic differences within the field. It concludes by suggesting some research practices that support feminist research in bridging theory and praxis and by mapping out feminist ways of working in the field for the 21st century.

As Loraine Gelsthorpe (1992) notes, "women are never just women"—we have a class, a sexuality, an ethnicity, often national, religious, and cultural affiliations, and all these, and many other aspects of difference, affect our situation and views. Historically, feminism has been overshadowed by a neglect of difference. While notions of difference have long constituted important issues for feminist theory, politics, and practice, the overriding preoccupation with sexism has far too often resulted in feminists ignoring differences of race, class, ethnicity, age, (dis)ability, sexuality, and nationality. For example, second-wave Western feminists prioritised sex/gender relations and inequalities, arguing against the conceptualisation of women as other in relation to a male norm. One consequence in both the United States and the United Kingdom has been that the histories of the feminist movement have been fraught with racism, homophobia, and exclusionary practices (Bryan, Dadzie, & Scafe, 1985; Collins, 1990; Davies, 1982; Ware, 1992). Feminism has long had a tendency to remake all women in its own image. Bhavnani (1993) writes that feminist accounts have frequently erased, denied, ignored, or tokenised the contradictory and conflicting interests that women have.

However, during the 1980s, feminist debate moved on to an engagement with the power differentials and inequalities that exist between women. Particularly influential has been Haraway (1988), who argues for an engagement with difference that enshrines responsibility and accountability; feminists need to become "answerable for what we learn to see" (p. 583). So recognising differences is a vital first step but a wholly inadequate one on its own. Too often faced with the impossibility of addressing the limitless permutations of difference, feminists have resorted to "the mantra approach" to difference—reeling them off, then relegating most of them to the sidelines of the research endeavour. Cealey Harrison and Hood-Williams (1998) criticise the notion that we as researchers could possibly work with all the differences out in the research field. After arguing that sexuality, (dis)ability, age, gender, social class, and ethnicity are the relevant forms of social classification in the current sociological lexicon, they continue:

> Given that these groups themselves contain a greater number of different subject positions within them (perhaps only two for sexual orientations, perhaps as many as nine for ethnicity) and that it is possible to belong to any combination of groups, the total combinatory of positions created by intersections that are fundamental to a full understanding is actually likely, at a conservative estimate, to be around 288. Depending on the "intersections" one defines and the variant forms of positionality within them there is no mathematical limit to the social divisions thus produced. (pp. 2–3)

Cealey Harrison and Hood-Williams (1998) clearly underestimate the different subject positions within sexuality and ethnicity, but factoring more subject positions into the feminist research landscape only serves to reinforce their original point. How can we do more than pay lip service to difference if we play a numbers game? The additive model of addressing difference ignores the myriad ways in which experience is transformed by identity factors (Francis, 2001).

So at the beginning of the 21st century, feminism is struggling to understand patterns of inequalities in a context of a heightened awareness of individual and multiple differences. In particular, the rise of postmodernism and the deconstruction of grand narratives within feminist theorising (Butler, 1997) have granted theoretical prominence to notions of difference and the multiplicity of identities and inequalities (Archer, Hutchings, & Leathwood, 2001), but they have left us bereft of any guidance on the vital theoretical and methodological issues facing feminist thought. For instance, how do we understand and theorise feminist solidarity if the supposedly inclusive *we* of feminism is revealed to be partial and excluding (Soper, 1990)? The vexing problem Susan Bordo (1990) identified is still with us. Then as now, the issue was one of how feminists could theorise difference without losing the analytic force of gender analysis. I would argue that the challenge is to respect cultural difference and diversity without abandoning cross-cultural categories such as gender. But that has become a difficult enterprise within contemporary feminisms in particular because of the power of postmodern theorising and its influence on feminist thought.

## IMPLICATIONS OF DIFFERENCE FOR FEMINIST THEORISING

It may seem that we are stuck in a feminist quagmire, but there are ways forward. One positive direction is to work towards new conceptual frameworks. We require analytic concepts that allow us to examine how any one difference is affected by and affects all of the other aspects of difference in multiple ways. The challenge is to build towards an understanding of the complex of differences as both a set of dynamic relationships and operating within specific contexts. Hesse-Biber and Yaiser (2004) stress the importance of recognising that differences are contextual, emphasising that they are constantly undergoing change "as the economy changes, politics shifts, and new ideological processes, trends and events occur" (p. 108). They argue that researchers and feminist academics need to work with dynamic fluid definitions and theories that are a reflection of society and have political, historical, and social significance. Similarly, Candice West and Sarah Fenstermaker (2002) argue against the additive approach to differences, positing a view of differences as ongoing accomplishments that cannot be understood apart from the context in which they are accomplished. As I will illustrate later in relation to both others' and my own research, different differences are stressed or muted depending on the social context.

Susan Heckman (1999) declares that it is time for feminists to stop arguing about differences and get on with the task of devising a theory and method for differentiation. She goes on to argue,

> An epistemology of differences must develop a conception of subjectivity that defines differences as constitutive rather than marginal. The defining feature of the Cartesian subject is the stability of its identity, it assumes a universal human essence. By contrast the subject of difference is unstable—its identity varies according to an array of differences, only one of which is gender. (p. 42)

This is similar to Kathy Ferguson's (1993) argument that feminists need to conceive of subjectivity as mobile—temporal, relational, and shifting yet enduring, ambiguous, messy, and multiple (p. 153). Such interpretations complement those of Hesse-Biber and Yaiser (2004). Different aspects of self become more prominent in some contexts than in others. Our social class positioning, age, ethnicity, and sexuality are foregrounded in some interactions and muted in others, while gender can become particularly salient in certain contexts but relatively unimportant in others.

This is no fragmentary postmodern approach to difference. I, and many other feminists, have no desire to lose sight of "woman" and desperately wish to revitalise feminist politics. But we need to recognise the complexities of feminist subjectivities and the myriad competing interests and loyalties we endlessly struggle with. To state it baldly, differences operate differently in different contexts, and we have to develop analytic tools to make sense of this.

Instead of separating out a multiplicity of differences, one approach is to draw difference in as an expression of a relationship, moving beyond description to "an analysis of the forces producing those differences and relationships and the dynamic structure of which they are a changing part" (Gorelick, 1996, p. 41). Gorelick draws on the example of the concept of compulsory heterosexuality, arguing that

when Adrienne Rich moved beyond complaining about the exclusion of lesbians from feminist writing to analysing "compulsory heterosexuality," lesbians—and indeed feminism itself—moved beyond discussing "difference" to analysing the determinants of lesbian existence. More than that: The concept of compulsory heterosexuality examines not only lesbianism but also heterosexuality as a set of institutions and ideological practices. (p. 41)

So theory building is vital to the feminist enterprise of addressing differences. Adrienne Rich's concept of compulsory heterosexuality has spoken to the experience of both lesbians and heterosexual women. There have been further key conceptual developments that address other aspects of difference. For example, Beverley Skeggs's (2004) feminist reworking of Marxist use and exchange value has progressed feminist understandings of the mediation of social class on gender. Both Rich and Skeggs's concepts meet Patricia Hill Collins et al.'s (2002) criteria that any feminist analysis must remain rooted in the question of how differences are put to use in defending unequal power relations. This means for Collins and her colleagues that power relations and material inequalities must be kept firmly in the feminist research frame. The theoretical challenge for feminisms remains one of how to hold together conceptions of difference and structural inequalities. Feminisms need to continue to develop and expand insights in relation to both epistemology and methodology but always keeping power relations in view.

## WORKING IN THE FIELD WITH DIFFICULT DIFFERENCES

I have discussed the difference differences make to feminist methodology and theorising. I now want to focus on how differences are played out in more mundane everyday research processes and practices. As we know so well from mainstream academic theorising and practice, there is far too often a chasm between what we write and theorise about and our actual practice. Key questions for feminist research are how and to what extent our research deals with differences within the research encounter, particularly the power differentials that these differences generate.

This is not just an issue of recognising differences within fieldwork, analysis, and writing but a much more holistic concern that spans the affective as well as the intellectual, encompassing concerns with philosophical issues of ethics and morality. Such a concern stretches from theory to the mundane everyday microdetails of fieldwork—what data we include and exclude in our analyses and why, who we like and dislike in our interactions in the field and how we deal with our affective responses. To engage with the consequences of differences for everyday research processes and practices, in the next three sections I look at three feminist accounts of research that attempt to deal with difficult differences in the field. I conclude by drawing on the insights from these studies to suggest some research practices that support feminist research in bridging theory and praxis.

## Taking Up Different Positionings Within the Research Relationship

The first project, carried out by Louise Archer (2004), is one in which where there are clear differences of ethnicity and culture between researcher and researched. In the other two projects, the differences are more blurred. In my own research with working-class women (Reay, 1998), my positioning as a once working-class woman comes powerfully into play but not always as a source of strength and empathy as I had anticipated. Molly Andrews's (2002) research foregrounds differences of values and attitudes and illuminates how these more "individual" differences, despite being frequently overlooked in research accounts, are just as salient as categorical differences for feminist research.

Louise Archer (2004) draws on her own research experience of interviewing young Asian women to illustrate the utility of Brah's (1999) application of the Urdu terms of *ajnabi*, *apna*, and *ghair*. Brah uses the three terms to capture emotional relations of difference across structural locations of difference. While *ajnabi* is "a stranger; a newcomer but one who holds the promise of friendship, love and intimacy, *apna* [italics added] is 'one of our own' " (p. 19). In contrast, *ghair* walks the tightrope between insider and outsider. It is a form of irreducible,

opaque difference. Archer (2004) fruitfully draws on Brah's conceptual terminology to make sense of complex and shifting differences within the research relationship. She identified herself as initially occupying an *ajnabi* or *ghair* position in relation to her young Asian respondents but describes how shifting power relations and, in particular, the opening up of herself for interrogation by the respondents meant she moved between *ajnabi*, *ghair*, and *apna* positions. Relatedly, her Asian coresearcher's positioning as *apna* "was sometimes disrupted as psychosocial/emotional differences were opened up in terms of her own differing religious identification, lifestyle choices and/or gendered sexual values" (p. 464). As a consequence, she moved between *apna* and *ghair* positions over the course of the fieldwork. There are issues here of context and temporality in which different aspects of difference such as religious affiliation become more salient in different research contexts and at different times.

## Dealing With the Seductions of "Knowing Better"

Molly Andrews (2002) addresses a difference that is rarely articulated in feminist research—the difference between feminists and non- and antifeminists (but see also Millen, 1997). We are talking about not only key differences of age and generation (these women were all more than 60 years old, while Andrews was a young doctoral student) (Andrews, 1991) but also differences of consciousness, beliefs, and values, where feminist researchers confront very different problems from those usually posed through difference research. Her research raises the issue of how feminist researchers can maintain a commitment simultaneously to the expressed viewpoint of participants and the causes of feminisms in general. Andrews (2002) faced what Liz Kelly and her colleagues (Kelly, Burton, & Regan, 1994) have called

> the troubling issue of what we do when our understandings and interpretations of women's accounts would either not be shared by some of them, and/or represent a form of challenge or threat to their perceptions, choices and coping strategies. (p. 37)

The majority of Andrews's (2002) respondents rejected feminist identification, and those who did accept it were liberal feminists pushing for progress within existing systems. For Andrews there was a continual tension between her interpretation of her respondents' experiences and the meaning the participants themselves tended to attribute to their experience, since the majority of them did not analyse these experiences in terms of patriarchy or sex-gender systems but considered them to be individualised or as "just something that had to be coped with." Andrews's work reminds us that the seductions of "knowing better" rather than knowing differently are ever present, but it also provides us with a way of rethinking differences that does not lapse into hierarchy. Andrews draws on Nancy Chodorow's (1996) work to generate a productive tension in her research in relation to difference. Following Chodorow, Andrews (2002) develops an analysis in which both knowledge and gender are situated: "Gender is a situated phenomenon, both in itself, as it can be more or less salient in different arenas or at different times of life, and in respect to other aspects of social and cultural categorisation and identity" (Chodorow, 1996, p. 43).

As a result, cultural and historical processes as well as social situation make certain conceptualisations and not others probable (Chodorow, 1996). Andrews's (2002) research highlights the importance of context for consciousness, because she recognises that not only are the views of her respondents historically and culturally situated, but so are her own. However, we can extend and develop Chodorow's (1996) insights about the importance of context and situatedness to all other aspects of difference. All aspects of our identity become more salient in some contexts than in others. I draw on an example of the perils of foregrounding some aspects of our female identity at the expense of others by examining my own fieldwork with working-class women.

## THE PERILS OF ASSUMED COMMONALITIES

Even when feminists are sensitised to difference, there still remain the perils of assumed commonalities—the hidden differences we often don't want to see. Joanne Braxton (1989),

describing her responses to other black women's texts, writes, "I read every text through my own experience, as well as the experiences of my mother and my grandmothers" (p. 1). The affirmation of finding yourself at the core of other women's accounts contains enormous power. We can read our centrality where previously there had only been partiality. However, as well as strengths, there are also the hazards of neglecting mundane everyday differences. As we can see from Andrews's (2002) research, these small, more individual differences of perspective, postionality, disposition, and beliefs are just as important as the macrocategorical and group differences of race, sexuality, nationality, and class. However, while for Andrews the differences in opinion and perspective between herself and the women she interviewed were always evident, in my own research I often lost sight of such differences in a desire for commonality.

As a once working-class woman I have often had a strong sense of identification with the working-class women I have interviewed, preferring not to focus on how differently they would perceive me (Reay, 1996). A particularly telling case of assuming sameness when my respondent was asserting difference was my analysis of Lisa's interview. Lisa, a working-class single mother, told me:

> Do the ignorant ever look around London when they talk about inner cities? Everywhere is so different, they talk as if it's just the same, when really it's such a mixture. They never seem to see that there's lots of good people out there.

My aim was to give voice to working-class women, but as Sherry Gorelick (1996) points out, "Giving voice is fraught with interpretation" (p. 38). In my initial analysis, I (mis)analyse Lisa's comment as a criticism of other, less reflexive working-class people. In doing so, I fail to hear Spivak's (1993) caution to avoid reshaping the subaltern as object, but even more to the point I have actually failed to hear what Lisa is saying. However, when I went back to the transcripts later, I realised that I had imposed an interpretation on Lisa's words that was rooted in my own current positioning as a privileged academic. I had not adequately listened to what Lisa had said because she refers to the ignorant later on in her interview in a context where it is obvious that she is discussing the middle classes. She is talking about middle-class stereotyping of the working classes, and in imposing my privileged feminist standpoint on what she said I had either omitted her challenges to dominant discourses and prevailing class inequalities or reduced them to irrelevancies and false consciousness. My interpretation denies Lisa her subversive reading of the status quo. And these are the women whose side I see myself as being on! I offer this example to reinforce my point that there can never be too much scrutiny of our feminist practices, and it is often those areas where we feel most confident of our practice, where we feel assured of the "comforts of proximity," that we should open up to the greatest scrutiny. Barbara Du Bois (1983) succinctly captures this danger of proximity:

> The closer our subject matter to our own life and experience, the more we can probably expect our own beliefs about the world to enter into and shape our work—to influence the very questions we pose, our conceptions of how to approach those questions, and the interpretations we generate from our findings. (p. 105)

What I have learnt from my own experiences is that empathy and identification with respondents can also be problematic if they become subsumed under our political agendas and pioneering zeal. We can overlook the difference we don't want to see. There is a thin dividing line between the understandings that similar experiences of respondents bring to the research process and the element of exploitation implicit in mixing up one's own personal history with apparently similar yet still markedly different female experiences. This also brings me back to the point I made earlier, in relation to Molly Andrews's (2002) research, about context and the salience of different aspects of our identities in different social situations. In interviews with working-class women, my working-class background becomes salient in a way that it ceases to be in many middle-class contexts. While this can be a strength, it can also, as I have tried to show, be a liability, especially if it results in a blindness about current privilege. Feminist reflexivity is knowing the difference between the two.

In this section, I have examined three very different feminist attempts to address difficult differences in the field. In Archer's (2004) work, beyond the focus on context for feminist research, we gain a sense of the importance of temporality, of differences that shift and transform over time as well as space. Andrews's (2002) research suggests a means of thinking of difference in nonhierarchical ways, through a focus on the situatedness of both gender and knowledge. Both studies work with strong boundaries and easily recognised differences in the research field. In contrast, my own research problematises commonalities and attempts to make explicit the perils of denying difference for feminist research.

## FUTURE DIRECTIONS FOR DIFFERENCE RESEARCH

Perversely, after criticising the "counting" approach to difference at the beginning of this chapter, I want to argue for what I call the 3Rs approach to feminist research. But whereas the 3Rs usually conjures up images of the basics, the 3Rs I have in mind—recognition, respect, and response—ensure that complexities, context, and change are all addressed. First, we need to recognise differences within the research field, not only the multiple differences among women but also the difference our own differences make. This entails a particular kind of feminist vigilance: the hard work of constant scrutiny and socioawareness. There also needs to be a response that comes from respecting the differences between the researcher and the women she is researching. Commitment to feminisms means a commitment to respecting the ways in which women who are different both experience and describe their lives (Chodorow, 1996). So I am arguing for a very particular reflexivity and feminist ethic. This should also embrace a focus on the differences within as well as without. We need to pay attention to the internally complex nature of subjectivity and how this is worked through at the level of self-understanding and practice. As I have tried to show in the examples from my own research and that of Louise Archer (2004), certain aspects of self become far more salient at particular times and in specific contexts.

We need to be attuned to these psychic shifts and changes if we are to be reflexive feminist researchers.

Reflexivity has become a commonplace requirement for social justice research. On a fundamental level, reflexivity is about giving as full and honest an account of the research process as possible, in particular explicating the position of the researcher in relation to the research. However, there is a paradox implicit in reflexivity. We explicate the processes and positions we are aware of being caught up in. But inevitably some of the influences arising from aspects of social identity remain beyond the reflexive grasp.

There is always a need for continuous interrogation. The 3Rs I elaborated on earlier are not discrete stages of research or targets to be achieved. Rather, they are complex and constantly shifting processes that require constant monitoring and reevaluation.

However, there needs to be a further approach in addition to individual reflexive feminist practice—a collective working towards changing the institutions we work in to make them more representative of the differences we find all around us in the wider social world. Until academia has far more black minority faculty, women from working-class backgrounds, and disabled and lesbian women, the sad paradox remains that differences may have proliferated in the wider social world but within academia there is still a stifling homogeneity, even among women faculty and researchers. There may be a growing willingness to research differences out there, but within academic feminisms the individuals doing the researching are predominantly white, middle-class, able-bodied, and heterosexual. So our feminist project for the 21st century needs to be two-pronged—working on both the feminist self and the wider feminist academic community.

# References

Andrews, M. (1991). *Lifetimes of commitment: Aging, politics, psychology.* Cambridge, UK: Cambridge University Press.

Andrews, M. (2002). Feminist research with non-feminist and anti-feminist women: Meeting the challenge. *Feminism & Psychology, 12*(1), 55–77.

Archer, L. (2004). Re/theorising "difference" in feminist research. *Women's Studies International Forum, 27,* 459–473.

Archer, L., Hutchings, M., & Leathwood, C. (2001). Engaging with commonality and difference: Theoretical tensions in the analysis of working-class women's educational discourses. *International Studies in Sociology of Education, 11*(1), 41–62.

Bhavnani, K. (1993). Tracing the contours of feminist research and feminist objectivity. *Women's Studies International Forum, 6*(2), 95–104.

Bordo, S. (1990). Feminism, postmodernism and gender-scepticism. In L. Nicholson (Ed.), *Feminism/postmodernism* (pp. 133–176). New York: Routledge.

Brah, A. (1999). The scent of memory: Strangers, our own and others. *Feminist Review, 61,* 4–26.

Braxton, J. (1989). *Black women writing autobiography: A tradition within a tradition.* Philadelphia: Temple University Press.

Bryan, B., Dadzie, S., & Scafe, S. (1985). *The heart of the race: Black women's lives in Britain.* London: Virago.

Butler, J. (1997). *Excitable speech: A politics of the performative.* New York: Routledge.

Cealey Harrison, W., & Hood-Williams, J. (1998). More varieties than Heinz: Social categories and sociality in Humphries Hammersley and beyond. *Sociological Research Online, 3*(1). Retrieved May 22, 2005, from www.socresonline.org.uk/3/1/contents

Chodorow, N. (1996). Seventies questions for thirties women: Some nineties reflections. In S. Wilkinson (Ed.), *Feminist social psychologies: International perspectives* (pp. 21–50). Milton Keynes, UK: Open University Press.

Collins, P. (1990). *Black feminist thought: Knowledge, consciousness and the politics of empowerment.* New York: Routledge.

Collins, P. H., Maldonado, L., Takagi, D., Thorne, B., Weber, L., & Winant, H. (2002). Symposium on West and Fenstermaker's "Doing Difference." In S. Fenstermaker & C. West (Eds.), *Doing gender, doing difference* (pp. 81–94). New York: Routledge.

Davies, A. (1982). *Women, race and class.* London: Women's Press.

Du Bois, B. (1983). Passionate scholarship: Notes on values, knowing and method in feminist social science. In G. Bowles & R. Klein (Eds.),

*Theories of women's studies* (pp. 105–116). London: Routledge & Kegan Paul.

Ferguson, K. (1993). *The man question: Visions of subjectivity in feminist research.* Berkeley: University of California Press.

Francis, B. (2001). Commonality and difference? Attempts to escape from theoretical dualisms in emancipatory research in education. *International Studies in Sociology of Education, 1*(2), 157–172.

Gelsthorpe, L. (1992). Response to Martyn Hammersley paper on feminist methodology. *Sociology, 26*(2), 213–218.

Gorelick, S. (1996). Contradictions of feminist methodology. In H. Gottfried (Ed.), *Feminism and social change: Bridging theory and practice* (pp. 23–45). Champaign: University of Illinois Press.

Haraway, D. (1988). Situated knowledges: The science question in feminism and the privilege of partial perspective. *Feminist Studies, 14,* 575–599.

Heckman, S. (1999). *The futures of differences: Truth and method in feminist theory.* Cambridge, UK: Polity Press.

Hesse-Biber, S., & Yaiser, M. (2004). Difference matters: Studying across race, class, gender and sexuality. In S. Hesse-Biber & M. Yaiser (Eds.), *Feminist perspectives on social research* (101–120). New York: Oxford University Press.

Kelly, L., Burton, S., & Regan, L. (1994). Researching women's lives or studying women's oppression? Reflections on what constitutes feminist research. In M. Maynard & J. Purvis (Eds.), *Researching women's lives from a feminist perspective* (pp. 27–48). London: Taylor & Francis.

Millen, C. D. (1997, November). *Using the "F" word: Women scientists and ideas of feminism.* Paper presented at the Women in Higher Education Network Conference, University of Salford, Greater Manchester, UK.

Reay, D. (1996). Insider perspectives or stealing the words out of women's mouths: Interpretation in the research process. *Feminist Review, 53,* 57–73.

Reay, D. (1998). *Class work: Mothers' involvement in their children's schooling.* London: University College Press.

Skeggs, B. (2004). *Class, self, culture.* London: Routledge.

Soper, K. (1990). Feminism, humanism and post-modernism. *Radical Philosophy, 55,* 11–17.

Spivak, G. (1993). Can the subaltern speak? In P. Williams & L. Chrisman (Eds.), *Colonial discourse and post-colonial theory* (pp. 66–111). London: Harvester Wheatsheaf.

Ware, V. (1992). *Beyond the pale: White women, racism and history.* London: Verso.

West, C., & Fenstermaker, S. (2002). Doing difference. In S. Fenstermaker & C. West (Eds.), *Doing gender, doing difference* (pp. 55–80). New York: Routledge.

# 34

# FEMINIST DESIGNS FOR DIFFERENCE

MICHELLE FINE

*Before they seize power and establish a world according to their doctrines, totalitarian movements conjure up a lying world of consistency.*

—Hannah Arendt, *The Origins of Totalitarianism*

Born from the soil of discontent, *participatory action research* (PAR) projects are designed through difference and to amplify voices of desire from the margins and the bottom; voices of dissent and radical entitlement. Based largely on the theory and practice of Latin American activist scholars, PAR draws from neo-Marxist, feminist, indigenous, queer, and critical race theorists (Anzaldúa, 1997; Cahill, 2004; Collins, 1998; Crenshaw, Gotanda, Peller, & Thomas, 1995; Davis, 2003; Fine, Bloom, Burns, Chajet, Guishard, Payne, et al., 2005; Fine & Carney, 2001; Lykes, 2001; Matsuda, 1995; Tolman & Brydon-Miller, 2001; Torre, 2005; Torre & Fine, 2006). PAR projects document the grounds for collective dissent and collective desires by creating a process for pooling "private" troubles among very different women and revealing their common, public roots (Mills, 1959). PAR shatters the false consensus of complicity by interrogating and denaturalizing the conditions of everyday oppression, challenging Arendt's "lying world of consistency."

A methodological stance rooted in the belief that valid knowledge is produced only in collaboration and in action, PAR recognizes that those "studied" harbor critical social knowledge and as such should be repositioned as architects rather than "subjects" of research (Fals-Borda, 1979; Fine, 1998; Freire, 1982; Martín-Baró, 1994; Torre, 2005). Legitimating democratic inquiry within institutions and from the outside, PAR excavates knowledge "at the bottom" (Matsuda, 1995) and "at the margins," signifying a fundamental right to ask, investigate, dissent, and demand what could be (Torre, 2005). PAR moves a series of feminist commitments—difference, critique, action, and solidarity—into a radical practice of method.

Over the past decade, members of the Participatory Action Research Collective at the Graduate Center have designed a number of PAR projects in a women's prison in New York State, documenting the impact of college on women in prison, the prison environment, and the women's postrelease outcomes; in wealthy desegregated schools, documenting the persistent segregation within these schools; and in impoverished communities, excavating evidence of systematic educational injustice (see www.changingminds.ws

for the women's prison project; see *Echoes of Brown: Youth Documenting and Performing the Legacy of Brown v. Board of Education* by Fine, Roberts, Torre, Bloom, Burns, Chajet, Guishard, & Payne, 2004; Fine et al., 2005; see Fine, Freudenberg, Payne, Perkins, Smith, & Wanzer, 2002, for youth research on the politics of racial/class injustice in public education; see Guishard et al., 2003, for participatory projects by youth activists in the South Bronx). Grounded in feminist and critical race theory, in each setting, we work intensively with an explicitly "diverse" collection of insiders—women in prison, students in and dropouts from high schools, activists in communities—designing a series of 2-day "methods camps" so that we can learn, together, the local history of struggle and develop a shared critical language of social theory, feminist theory, critical race theory, and methodology. Working through issues of power and difference, these participatory research collectives are designed toward radical inclusion and intentional interrogation of power and "difference" (Fraser, 1990; Smith, 1999, 2001; Torre, 2005). When PAR collectives are organized as "contact zones," purposely diverse communities are gathered to explicitly examine the fault lines of power, knowledge, and privilege within the group (see Pratt, 1991) and use these differences as resources to further the social justice agenda of the research (Torre, 2005). But creating the "we" under the heavy weight of "difference" and power inequities constitutes serious feminist labor.

We offer below a series of snapshots from our work in the Bedford Hills Correctional Facility, a maximum security prison for women in New York State, where we documented, over the span of 4 years, the profound impact of a college-in-prison program on women, their children, the officers, and the women's postrelease outcomes (see Fine & Carney, 2001; Fine, Torre, Boudin, Bowen, Clark, Hylton, Martinez, "Missy," Rivera, Roberts, Smart, & Upegui, 2003; Torre, 2005).

## A History of Desire: College in Prison

The 1980s and 1990s in the United States were decades of substantial public and political outcry about crime and about criminals. During these years, stiffer penalties were enforced for crimes, prisons were built at unprecedented rates, parole was tougher to achieve, "three strikes and you're out" bills were passed, and college was no longer publicly funded for women and men in prison. Indeed, with the signing of the Violent Crime Control and Law Enforcement Act, President Bill Clinton stopped the flow of all federal dollars (in the form of Pell Grants) that had enabled women and men in prison to attend college. It was then up to the states, simply, to finalize the closing of most prison-based college programs around the nation.

At Bedford Hills Correctional Facility, a vibrant college program had been coordinated by Mercy College for more than 15 years. In 1995, this program, like more than 340 others nationwide, was closed. This decision provoked a sea of disappointment, despair, and outrage from the women at Bedford Hills who had been actively engaged in higher education and in GED/ABE preparation. Within months, a group of prisoners met with the superintendent and, later, an active community volunteer, and soon they, with Marymount Manhattan College, resurrected college, as a private, voluntary consortium of colleges and universities dedicated to prisoner education.

The design of the college was conceptualized through pillars of strong, ongoing participation by the prison administration, staff, prisoners, university administrators and faculty, and community volunteers, called "civilians." Students, in particular, are expected to "give back" in any number of ways. They teach, mentor, pay the equivalent of a month's wages for tuition, give back while in prison, and demonstrate high levels of community engagement once they are released. With a commitment to participatory governance, the college administrators at Bedford Hills Correctional Facility (BHCF) met regularly with the prison administration, the Inmate Committee, and a representative of the board to create and sustain a "safe" context for serious conversation—reflection, revision, and re-imagining of the college program. It was essential to build the program on a base of broad and deep participation from every constituency. Many, including the long-termers who witnessed the loss of college, did not want the younger women to ever take the program for granted, assume its permanence, forget its fragility, or view it as an entitlement. And all of us wanted to inspire a sense of broad-based responsibility and accountability for sustaining college in prison. The greater the number of constituencies that "own" the program, the more porous will be the walls of prison, and the less likely are Abu-Ghraib-like atrocities to occur without comment.

The women at Bedford have, for the most part, spent the better (or worst) part of their lives under the thumbs of poverty, racism, and men. In college in prison, in contrast, they could "hear my own voice" or "see my own signature" or "make my own decisions"—re-viewing themselves as agents who make choices, take responsibility, create change for self and others (e.g., family, children, and younger women at Bedford), and design a future not overdetermined by the past (see Gordon, 1997).

At its heart, this college program has not simply been about the taking of courses but about deep immersion in an intellectual and ethical community of scholars. The physical space of the Learning Center—equipped with nonnetworked computers (no Internet), secondhand books, magazines, newspapers, flags from colleges and universities in the consortium—holds a sense of community, a place where, the women will attest, "if I need help I can find it—even if that means someone to kick me in the ass to get back to work and finish my papers." This intellectual community also spills out onto the "yard," where you can overhear study groups on Michel Foucault, qualitative research, or Alice Walker, or in the cell block, where the ticking of typewriter keys can be heard late into the night; or a "young inmate may knock softly on [my] wall, at midnight, asking how to spell or punctuate."

When I was asked to conduct the empirical documentation of the impact of college on the women, it seemed clear that a participatory design behind bars would be nearly impossible—and essential. We consulted with the superintendent, who agreed with the design, after the New York State Department of Correctional Services had provided official approval.

## DESIGNING FOR DIFFERENCE

The original research collective, Kathy Boudin, Iris Bowen, Judith Clark, Aisha Elliot, Donna

Hylton, Migdalia Martinez, "Missy," and Pamela Smart, and the original group from the Graduate Center, Michelle Fine, Melissa Rivera, Rosemarie A. Roberts, Maria Elena Torre, and Debora Upegui, gathered as a group of very different women, brought together by anger at the prison industrial complex and a desire for college to be resurrected within the walls of hell. We were half prisoner and half not. Among us, as a team, we met often, sometimes once a month, sometimes more often, and sometimes less. Encumbered by limitations on privacy, freedom, contact, and time, we were profoundly moved by the desire to climb over the walls that separate and carve a small delicate space of trust, inquiry, and radical action for women's lives.

In this space for critical inquiry, we walked across barbed wires outside the windows and inside the room, through our racialized and classed histories, between biographies filled with too much violence and too little hope and biographies lined with too much privilege and too little critique. We engaged in what Paulo Freire (1982) would call "dialogue," a "relation of 'empathy' between two 'poles' who are engaged in a joint search." The task, then, was not merely to educate us all to "what is," but to provoke analysis of "what has been" and release, as Maxine Greene would invite, our imagination for "what could be."

## AND YET: BETWEEN US

> This space of radical openness is a margin—a profound edge. Locating oneself there is difficult yet necessary. It is not a "safe" place. One is always at risk. One needs a community. (bell hooks, 1984, p. 149)

We were, at once, a team of semifictional coherence, and, on the ground, a group of women living very different lives, defined in part by biographies of class, race, and ethnic differences. Half of us went home at night; half of us remained in the prison. Many of us brought personal histories of violence against women to our work, while all of us worried about violence against, and sometimes by, women. Some of us had long-standing experience in social movements for social justice; others barely survived on the outside. Some of us were white, Jewish,

Latina, Caribbean, or African American, and some were mixed. Most of us were from the mainland of this country, a few were born outside the borders of the United States. The most obvious divide among us was free or imprisoned, but the other tattoos and scars on our souls wove through our work, worries, writings, and our many communities. Usually, these differences would enrich us. Sometimes they distinguished us. At moments, they separated us. We understood ourselves to carry knowledge and consciousness that are, at once, determined by where we come from and shaped by who we choose to be (Harding, 1991; Hartsock, 1983; Smith, 1987).

Using focus groups; interviews with women, corrections officers, the children of prisoners, and women postrelease; and a quantitative longitudinal analysis of recidivism rates for women with and without college, we worked to produce (a) a policy document on the impact of college on women in prison, which was sent to all the New York State legislators and every governor in the country; (b) a set of scholarly chapters; (c) a Web site (www.changingminds.ws); and (d) a set of activist brochures in English and Spanish. Our intimate relationships brought both a passion and a fever to the work, as the future of the program moved between solid and unstable ground. We brought fear, despair, desire, and outrage to the table, which we had to balance among us, for we were always being watched. Too many tears or too much "obvious" food could provoke an officer to shut us down. Emotions that flowed unchecked could destroy our research effort. In a research meeting, it was common for us to jog between hope and despair, possibility and fear as we faced the realities of our relationships to the college program, the research, each other, and the superintendent. These emotions and our commitments to the work at times left us numb—the result of too many feelings, jockeying despair, desire, and rage. Sometimes in a research meeting or the prison-based graduate course on methods, we would pause as a research member detailed the difficulty of registering new students eager to start the program with one or two courses, because she silently feared the program might close before these students graduate; as another wept because her parents had traveled from

Nevada to visit and the officer "lost" the paperwork; as we listened to details of a botched kidney transplant; as we held each other because a mother serving 20 to life had just learned her son was selling drugs and she couldn't stop him; as we discovered that one of our students was sent to the Solitary Housing Unit because she had tried to cut herself. Other times we deliberately stayed clear of conversations that were too painful, keeping on task as a way to feel control when there is little available. The context and physical environment of our research was harsh, noisy, and without privacy, by design.

At our rectangular, cramped, uneven wooden table in the Learning Center, we huddled around smuggled fruits and "butter-tastes-like-this-now?" cookies, and our writing. There was a chemistry—a witches' brew, the guards might have thought—steaming among us. As we pressed on our common concerns, the shards of difference would rise, and we would proceed forward and back with caution.

I remember the long, extended conversations held at that Learning Center table, as other women completed research papers, studied for the GED, tutored new women, or cared for their seeing-eye dogs in training. Among our research collective, we would each bring in the writing we had done, focused on our distinct sections and concerns. Two snippets of conversation come to mind, revealing the thick, delicate nature of participatory work behind bars, exposing the messy tensions that lie inside feminist praxis.

*November 1999.* We had just completed the interviews and focus groups, all collaboratively facilitated by a prisoner researcher and a (outside) graduate student researcher. The transcriptions were complete and our analyses emerging. Those of us on the outside, from the Graduate Center, brought the codes into the prison to see if the women would agree with the coding scheme. It seemed all was going well when, suddenly, Judy asked, "So we get to collect the data, but you do the analysis? What kind of division of labor is that?" In the name of ethics and confidentiality, we had (unwittingly?) separated the "brawn" from the "brains," the data collection from the political and theoretical work of analysis. And so a long talk about power, process, and democracy ensued.

We struggled to figure out a way to bring the transcribed interviews into the prison and leave them there (prisoners have no access to locked cabinets, and confidentiality would be violated if these interviews were allowed to lie around for public viewing). With prisoner and outside collaborative wit, we figured it out.

*March 2000.* Later in our research process, we had completed the research and we were trying to figure out how to write our text—single voiced or multivoiced? Filled with a voice of feminist self-reflection or of empirical authority?

We had multiple goals, including the basic desire to convince the New York State legislature to restore funds for college in prison programs. So we decided to craft multiple products. Our primary document would be a single-voiced, gorgeous, and authoritative report, available widely as a Web site (www.changingminds.ws), with quotes and endorsements from people on the political Left and Right. The prisoners wanted Michelle Fine to be the first name, and "Missy" insisted that that was the name she would use. This report was distributed to every governor in the United States and all the New York State senators and members of the Assembly. We would, as well, construct additional essays on feminist methodology (see, e.g., Fine et al., 2003), in which our contradictions would be interrogated, and we produced 1,000 organizing brochures in English and Spanish that carried a strong voice of advocacy, demands for justice and action.

As we struggled with the section on who is the "we" of the research collective, I naively offered, "What if we write, something like, 'We are all women concerned with violence against women; some of us have experienced, most of us have witnessed and all are outraged.'" I had proudly snuck this text beyond the barbed wire, past the slamming steel doors, and under the eyes of the guards. I awaited the women's response, when Donna said, "Michelle, please don't romanticize us. Your writing is eloquent, but you seemed to have left out the part that some of us are here for murder. When we're not here, in the college, and we're alone in our cells we have to think about the people affected by our crimes. We take responsibility and we need you to represent that as well as our common concerns as women, as feminists, as political. . . ."

This moment is critical because it revealed another "space" in the chasm between feminist theorizing and practice. The women were explicit—*Don't romanticize us! Please explain that structural conditions radically limited our freedom and yet we made terrible mistakes. Don't theorize us out of personal responsibility!* The final report and our collaborative chapters marinate in a language of personal responsibility, remorse, and accountability far more thoroughly than the Graduate Center researchers would have written on their own, but the women inside the prison insisted. At the heart of our collaboration—between the ether of the feminist academy and life on the streets and in prisons—important debates flourished about the origins of social problems, structural determinism, and existential freedom. In participatory research, there is an obligation to enter those debates and not write over them. In struggling through the "we" and issues of power and privilege, there were tough, important, troubling conversations to be had about guilt, blood, pain, oppression, freedom, and possibility.

As powerful as PAR has been behind bars, fantasies of our collective freedom to study, write, and speak were naive. We were reminded frequently that the prisoners were always more vulnerable than we were as outsiders. Their poetry books, journals, favorite seasonings, letters from home, and private documents were searched, ransacked, and tossed out when the administration decided to exert power or tried to warn us abusively, in the sadomasochistic rhythm of prison about our writings. And with the critical consciousness that accompanies participatory research came anger, outrage, and a raw recognition of injustice that boiled in prison. We mark, then, another dilemma in the relation of feminist theory and practice—in the praxis "gap" lie the bodies and vulnerabilities of those most oppressed.

## REFLECTIONS

PAR offers feminists a radical methodology to reveal the underbelly of social injustice. Participatory projects gather up the stories of lives, legitimate underground knowledges, and spark the flames of social movements. Refusing hegemonic discourses about women, crime, and punishment, challenging what Arendt calls the "lying world of consistency," this PAR project dared to examine critically "what is" and launch, with a passionate sisterhood across barbed wire, "what could be" (see Harris, Carney, & Fine, 2001).

In the midst of a struggle against the mass incarceration of people of color, and women in particular, this project offered an electric current through which critique and possibility traveled, providing an interior legacy and power—within the prison and outside—of respect for insider knowledge and recognition of prisoner authority. But the struggles between what "should be" and "what is"—between feminist theory and praxis—continually scratch at our memory. We have highlighted here a series of such struggles that others need to reflect on as they design participatory projects in spaces of surveillance, injustice, and abuse. Within a research collective, it's important to (a) continually interrogate privilege and power within the research collective; (b) make sure that collaboration defines every phase of research; (c) take up routinely and deliberately the hard conversations about difference, power, and politics; (d) remember that vulnerability is distributed in inverse proportion to power; and (e) remember that action—policy change, organizing, programmatic revisions, protest, small moves—is the "validity check" for participatory action research. And remember always the words of Maxine Greene (1995): "A world may come into being in the course of a continuing dialogue" (p. 196).

## References

Anzaldúa, G. E. (1997). *Words of women quotations for success*. San Francisco: Power Dynamics.

Cahill, C. (2004). Defying gravity? Raising consciousness through collective research. *Children's Geographies, 2*(2), 273–286.

Collins, P. H. (1998). *Fighting words: Black women and the search for justice*. Minneapolis: University of Minnesota Press.

Crenshaw, K., Gotanda, N., Peller, G., & Thomas, K. (1995). *Critical race theory: The key writings that formed the movement* (pp. 63–79). New York: New Press.

Davis, A. (2003). *Are prisons obsolete?* New York: Seven Stories Press.

Fals-Borda, O. (1979). Investigating the reality in order to transform it: The Colombian experience. *Dialectical Anthropology, 4,* 33–55.

Fine, M. (1998). *Framing dropouts*. Albany: State University of New York Press.

Fine, M., Bloom, J., Burns, A., Chajet, L., Guishard, M., Payne, Y., et al. (2005). Dear Zora: A letter to Zora Neal Hurston fifty years after Brown. *Teachers College Record, 107*(3), 496–528.

Fine, M., & Carney, S. (2001). Women, gender, and the law: Toward a feminist rethinking of responsibility. In R. Unger (Ed.), *Handbook of the psychology of women and gender* (pp. 388–409). New York: Wiley.

Fine, M., Freudenberg, N., Payne, Y., Perkins, T., Smith, K., & Wanzer, K. (2002). "Anything can happen with police around": Urban youth evaluate strategies of surveillance in public places. *Journal of Social Issues, 59,* 141–158.

Fine, M., Roberts, R. A., Torre, M. E., Bloom, J., Burns, A., Chajet, L., Guishard, M., & Payne, Y. (2004). *Echoes of Brown: Youth documenting and performing the legacy of Brown v. Board of Education.* New York: Teachers College Press.

Fine, M., Torre, M. E., Boudin, K., Bowen, I., Clark, J., Hylton, D., Martinez, M., "Missy," Rivera, M., Roberts, R. A., Smart, P., & Upegui, D. (2003). Participatory action research: Within and beyond bars. In P. Camic, J. E. Rhodes, & L. Yardley (Eds.), *Qualitative research in psychology: Expanding perspectives in methodology and design* (pp. 173–198). Washington, DC: American Psychological Association.

Fraser, N. (1990). Rethinking the public sphere: A contribution to the critique of actually existing democracy. *Social Text, 25/26,* 56–80.

Freire, P. (1982). Creating alternative research methods: Learning to do it by doing it. In B. Hall, A. Gillette, & R. Tandon (Eds.), *Creating knowledge: A monopoly*. New Delhi, India: Society for Participatory Research in Asia.

Gordon, A. F. (1997). *Ghostly matters: Haunting and the sociological imagination*. Minneapolis: University of Minnesota Press.

Greene, M. (1995). *Releasing the imagination: Essays on education, the arts, and social change*. San Francisco: Jossey-Bass.

Guishard, M., Fine, M., Doyle, C., Jackson, J., Roberts, R., Staten, S., et al. (2003, May). "As long as I got breath, I'll fight": Participatory action research for educational justice. The Family Involvement Network of Educators. Harvard Family Research Project. Retrieved March 2005 from www.gse.harvard.edu/hfrp/projects/fine/resources/digest/par.html

Harding, S. (1991). *Whose science? Whose knowledge?* Ithaca, NY: Cornell University Press.

Harris, A., Carney, S., & Fine, M. (2001). Counter work: Introduction to "Under the covers: Theorizing the politics of counter stories." *International Journal of Critical Psychology, 4,* 6–18.

Hartsock, N. (1983). *Money, sex and power.* New York: Longman.

hooks, b. (1984). *Feminist theory: From margin to center.* Boston: South End Press.

Lykes, M. B. (2001). Activist participatory research and the arts with rural Maya women: Interculturality and situated meaning making. In D. L. Tolman & M. Brydon-Miller (Eds.), *From subjects to subjectivities: A handbook of interpretive and participatory methods* (pp. 183–199). New York: New York University Press.

Martín-Baró, I. (1994). *Writings for a liberation psychology.* Cambridge, MA: Harvard University Press.

Matsuda, M. (1995). Looking to the bottom: Critical legal studies and reparations. In K. Crenshaw, N. Gotanda, G. Peller, & K. Thomas (Eds.), *Critical race theory: The key writings that formed the movement* (pp. 63–79). New York: New Press.

Mills, C. W. (1959). *The sociological imagination.* London: Oxford University Press.

Pratt, M. L. (1991). Arts of the contact zone. *Profession, 91,* 33–40.

Smith, D. (1987). *The everyday world as problematic: A feminist sociology.* Boston: Northeastern University Press.

Smith, L. T. (1999). *Decolonizing methodologies: Research and indigenous peoples.* London: Zed Books.

Smith, L. T. (2001). Troubling spaces. *International Journal of Critical Psychology, 4,* 167–182.

Tolman, D., & Brydon-Miller, M. (2001). *From subjects to subjectivities: A handbook of interpretive and participatory methods* (pp. 183–199). New York: New York University Press.

Torre, M. (2005). The alchemy of integrated spaces: Youth participation in research collectives of difference. In L. Weis & M. Fine (Eds.), *Beyond silenced voices* (pp. 251–256). Albany: State University of New York Press.

Torre, M., & Fine, M. (2006). Researching and resisting: Democratic policy research by and for youth. In S. Ginwright, P. Noguera, & J. Cammarota (Eds.), *Beyond resistance! Youth activism and community change* (pp. 269–285). New York: Routledge.

# 35

# DECOLONIZING APPROACHES TO FEMINIST RESEARCH

## The Case of Feminist Ethnography

KATHERINE BORLAND

Authority to speak and to write as and for women has been a crucial subject of feminist theorizing since Virginia Woolf (1929/1991) first identified the woman novelist's problem as an excess of critical self-consciousness. Woolf enumerated the material and psychic conditions necessary for cultivating her own voice. The feminist ethnographer recognizes an even more difficult task: How to speak or write authoritatively as a feminist while at the same time preserving the authority of the subjects one studies. Over the last 35 years, feminist ethnographers have moved from a confident identification *with* their research subjects to a recognition of their own involvement in hierarchical relations of power during the research encounter. They have tempered the goal of achieving empathy with a concern for maintaining a respectful distance. In the process, feminist ethnographers have debated the virtues of using accessible versus theoretically sophisticated language, and they have weighed the relative merits of championing the marginal or critiquing hegemonic institutions. They have recognized that issues of authority and of representation are intimately intertwined. In this review, I will quickly trace our increasingly

sophisticated understanding of ethnographic authority and representation and suggest a productive overlap with decolonizing approaches to research, approaches that have sometimes been described as antagonistic to feminism.

During the 1970s, the issue of ethnographic and representational authority remained largely unproblematized. As feminists recognized that the male bias in existing scholarship systematically ignored, trivialized, or distorted women's perspectives, they sought to correct or complete the record—to make it more truly *objective*—by recording and positively evaluating women's knowledge, experience, and contributions. In other words, feminist ethnographers regarded the women they researched as cultural authorities within a larger social and scholarly environment in which women were not so regarded. Although such an approach has sometimes been disparagingly labeled "add women and stir," it significantly challenged existing institutions of knowledge by revealing the partial nature (in both senses of the word) of what had been masquerading as universal truth. For instance, in 1975, a special issue of the *Journal of American Folklore* was titled *Women and Folklore: Images and Genres.* Editor Claire Farrer argued that traditional folklore scholarship focused largely on performances in the male-dominated public arena. Yet women's artistry might occur in locations at the periphery of the scholarly gaze. By taking women's words and performances seriously, contributors both expanded the ethnographer's field of inquiry and challenged the view that men's performances could be taken as representative of the whole.

At the same time that they were identifying women's forms of cultural expression, feminists sought to avoid what many regarded as masculine research styles that privileged the researcher's interpretive skills over those of the researched subject. While feminists had already identified the patriarchal nature of language as a barrier to theorizing a new order, a strong populist strain in the movement favored the representational styles of transparent realism. Because this early work assumed a shared identity between the speaking woman and her feminist scribe, it did not adequately account for potential differences or conflicts between them.

By the 1980s, privileged white feminists were shaken from their delusions of alliance with women of the world on a number of fronts simultaneously. First world women of color, lesbians, and women from formerly colonized areas vehemently resisted the constructions of womanhood produced by a mostly white, middle-class, westernized feminist movement. Audre Lorde admonished attendees at the Second Sex Conference that the movement had failed to adequately include alternate voices. Moraga and Anzaldúa's (1983) edited collection *This Bridge Called My Back: Writings by Radical Women of Color* forcefully introduced the perspectives of women who had been marginalized and silenced within the rhetoric of universal sisterhood.

Simultaneously, feminist ethnographers began to reflexively critique their own assumptions about the ethical superiority of engaged, collaborative methodologies. Claiming that "elements of inequality, exploitation and even betrayal are endemic to ethnography," Stacey (1988) argued that research based on a model of intimacy and engagement is potentially more abusive to its subjects than one predicated on maintaining a respectful distance. Moreover,

she pointed out that rather than reinforcing one another, the ethnographic and feminist obligations of the researcher often conflict. These problems are only magnified in cross-cultural work, asserted Patai (1991). The systematic inequalities that enable U.S. academics to study impoverished Third World women reiterate the exploitative pattern of First World/Third World exchange. That is, the raw materials are extracted for subsequent refashioning, packaging, and sale to a distant consumer. Patai concluded that under such circumstances ethical research is impossible. Nevertheless, neither Stacey nor Patai advocate abandoning feminist ethnography. Instead, they admonish feminists to cultivate humility in the following ways: by acknowledging our privilege within the research encounter, by ceasing to claim our research improves the lives of those we study, and by recognizing the gap between a researcher's intentions and the actual consequences of her work.

Another challenge to feminist ethnography arose with the publication of Clifford and Marcus's (1986) *Writing Culture.* The authors in this collection, after rediscovering the close association between the study of anthropology and colonial structures of domination, attempted to decolonize ethnographic texts through experiments in representation. They rejected what they viewed as an outmoded objective stance for a more literary approach to ethnographic writing. Acknowledging the partial nature of all claims to knowledge, they emphasized the ways in which knowledge is intersubjectively produced. And yet they traced their intellectual foundations almost entirely through the white male line, ignoring the significant early formulations of the problems of subjectivity within feminist and black studies (de Beauvoir, 1949/1971; Du Bois, 1903/2003; Fanon, 1963, 1952/1968). Early literary experiments with ethnography by women, such as Hurston's (1935/1978) *Mules and Men* and Fernea's (1965/1989) *Guests of the Sheik* go unmentioned. The special insights of insider-outsiders remain unexplored (Nájera-Ramírez, 1999; Narayan, 1993). As bell hooks (1990) pointed out, *Writing Culture* "in no way challenges the assumption that the image/identity of the ethnographer is white and male" (p. 126). In fact, feminist scholars interpreted Clifford's famous apology for their exclusion from serious consideration as a highly unreflexive replication of hierarchical relations within the academy that attribute cutting-edge scholarship to the men in charge (Bell, 1993; Gordon, 1995; Lutz, 1995).

Two feminist critiques of *Writing Culture*, Bell, Caplan, and Karim's (1993) *Gendered Fields: Women, Men and Ethnography* and Behar and Gordon's (1995) *Women Writing Culture*, explore how relations of privilege—the authority to speak and be heard—are reproduced both within and through research. Like the experimental ethnographers, the contributors to these essay collections challenge the inherited canon. Yet they also recover the work of earlier women scholars that had been overlooked, ignored, or devalued in the canon-building process. This distinction between the feminist and postmodernist projects is an important one. Feminists remain acutely aware that an alternate intellectual heritage has been repeatedly obscured by relations of inequality. We know that reclaiming that heritage leads to greater empowerment. New theories that deconstruct the canon without providing opportunities for reconstructions that include alternate voices do not ultimately challenge existing hierarchies of cultural authority.

For this reason, many feminist social scientists remained cautious about the compatibility of feminism with postmodernism. In their influential article "The Postmodernist Turn in Anthropology: Cautions from a Feminist Perspective," Mascia-Lees, Sharpe, and Ballerino Cohen (1989) point out that while the postmodern decentering of the Cartesian subject promises the decentering of the master figure, actual postmodern *writing* may effect the opposite by privileging the Western male experience of fragmentation as the only legitimate truth. In this way, the literary turn in anthropology may mask existing power relations rather than empower new actors. One advantage of feminist ethnography, they point out, is that it knows its own politics. Abu Lughod (1990) further suggested that feminist ethnography might productively inform anthropological postmodernism by conceptualizing a self that participates in multiple identifications simultaneously, a self (woman) that recognizes difference (race and class) in sameness. She concludes, "What

feminist ethnography can contribute to anthropology is an unsettling of the boundaries that have been central to its identity as a discipline of the self studying other" (p. 26).

With reciprocal ethnography, Elaine Lawless (1992, 1993) offered a feminist revision of the postmodern call for reflexive and polyvocal texts by extending the dialogue established between researched women and the ethnographer during fieldwork to the writing and revision of ethnography. A text so produced provides the opportunity for the researched subject to review and modify a researcher's preliminary understandings. Moreover, it can reveal the points at which the perspectives of researcher and researched diverge. Yet Lawless points out that new methodologies cannot resolve all women's differences in happy collaboration or equal time for opposing viewpoints. She concludes, "the feminist scholar looking at an oppressive situation for women has both the right and obligation to point out that the situation *is* oppressive, and that the women involved may justifiably fear repercussions for their actions" (1992, p. 312).

The paradox of ethnographic authority, then, remains: The feminist's ethical commitment to reveal the relations of women's oppression will at times conflict with her commitment to honor voices and experiences of other women with whom she collaborates. A case in point is the controversy about Diane Bell and Topsy Nelson's (1989) article, "Speaking About Rape Is Everybody's Business," which sought to bring attention to an alarming rate of violence against women in an aboriginal community. Women active in the aboriginal rights movement criticized Bell, the white anthropologist, for appropriating Nelson, the aboriginal woman's voice, to authorize her own position. They further argued that speaking out about rape created harmful divisions within the aboriginal community (Huggins et al., 1991). For her part, Bell charged her critics with attempting to silence Nelson and deflect attention away from the critical issue of culturally sanctioned violence against women. Ahmed (2000) explains that by naming Nelson as a coauthor rather than an informant,

> Bell is implicated in the postmodern fantasy that it is the "I" of the ethnographer who can undo the power relations that allowed the "I" to appear.

Such a fantasy allows the ethnographer to be praised for her or his ability to listen well. So it remains the ethnographer who is praised: praised for giving up her or his authority. (p. 64)

In this way, Ahmed reiterates earlier feminists' calls for greater humility in cross-cultural, cross-class exchanges. The move in reflexive ethnography to name one's informants as authorial equals fails to overcome colonial relations of exchange in the ethnographic encounter. Clearly, feminist ethnographers are engaged in the politics of cultural representation in contexts that display cross-cutting fields of oppression.

It goes without saying that how we represent our research will be governed by what we want to communicate. By the early 1990s, a new concern with epistemology, or how we know what we know, identified the failures in feminist ethnography not to develop new, more egalitarian methods of research but to interrogate our own epistemological and representational assumptions. Visweswaran (1994a), for instance, challenges the early feminist model of giving voice to an *other* by positing that a woman might find power not in self-revelation but in self-concealment. "Perhaps," Visweswaran suggests, "a feminist ethnography can take the silences among women as the central site for the analysis of power between them. We can begin to shape a notion of agency that, while it privileges speaking, is not reducible to it" (1994a, p. 51).

Moreover, Visweswaran (1994b) insists that recognizing the ethical conflicts inherent in the unequal research exchange does not resolve them. She therefore contends that a feminist ethnography based on "fieldwork" will not produce a substantially different (or "decolonized") ethnography, but a feminist ethnography characterized by what she calls "homework" might. On the other hand, Nash (1997) faults anthropologists who too readily abandon fieldwork for the "homework" of theoretical inquiry. Characterizing anthropology as a field in which old theories are constantly overturned by new ones, Nash insists that what remains important is the development of an ethnographic record. Since we know that the written record has powerfully bolstered Western patriarchal authority, the production of alternative histories and perspectives remains an urgent task, even if the resulting record contains its own blind spots and flaws. Nevertheless, it remains possible to conduct "homework" that is also "fieldwork." Crewe and Harrison (1998) have provided a good example in their ethnography of Western aid institutions operating to address the "plight of Third World women." Their work reveals the patriarchal structures of such institutions, highlighting the disparity between what Western institutions preach and what they practice.

The tension between those who privilege politically grounded work and those who struggle to develop new theoretical formulations also expresses itself in different representational styles. Noting some feminists' resistance to textual experimentation, Lather cautions that the "plain speaking" of ethnographic realism masks its own mastery, allowing the author to hide behind the voices of others. By "troubling" the text, Lather (1996) aims to draw attention to the ways in which truth claims are always partial and constructed. Lather's ethnography of women living with AIDS, cowritten with Chris Smithies, provides an example of such an antihumanist text, and has provoked strong reactions on the part of readers. Combining the stories of women with AIDS, her own accounts of research, scientific factoids about AIDS, and passages on angelology, Lather (2001) asserts,

> The text works toward constructing a respectful distance between the reader and the subject of the research, producing a kind of gap between text and reader that is about inaccessible alterity, a lesson in modesty and respect, somewhere outside of the "murderous mutuality" presumed by empathy (Sommer, 1994, p. 547). Incited by the demand for voice and situatedness, but perverting, inverting, redirecting that demand, the book attempts to complicate the question of ethnographic representation. (p. 214)

As a consequence, however, Lather (2001) admits that she produces not the Wal-Mart text that the AIDS women had requested of her—a text that might reach a broad, popular audience—but a difficult, challenging interrogative text instead. Whether such a text more successfully induces social change than one that employs techniques of transparent realism remains a subject for continuing debate.

In another stylistic experiment, Stewart (1996) explores how residents of a West Virginia coal camp generate their subjectivity through "back talk" against externally generated discourses that demean and distort them. This *new ethnography* aims to represent both the process of subject formation and the equality of subject's and author's discourse through a stylistic heteroglossia that interweaves the words of subject and researcher even in the same sentence. Yet the experiment ultimately succumbs to the structures of power it seeks to reveal. Some local participants read the resulting style as yet another parody of their cultural expression.

Recognizing the inherent dialogism both of a person's self-construction and of the ethnographic interaction, Patricia Sawin (2004) explores the subject formation of a single woman singer through a technique she labels dialogic ethnography. This approach, Sawin argues, "liberates the ethnographer from the impossible quest for perfect representation or natural context" (p. 17). Sawin imagines her project as an act of listening and responding to her subject, Bessie Eldreth, even as she acknowledges the constraints of conversational interaction, particularly those arising from the different intentions and goals of conversants.

While each of these experiments has merit, ultimately the feminist ethnographer's search for a uniform or uniquely feminist approach has been replaced by the recognition that feminist ethnography is not so much a matter of adopting a particular style as it is maintaining a political commitment, a commitment that results in a standpoint that both recognizes the distortions and erasures of existing structures of knowledge and works to build an alternative legacy (Harding, 2003).

Decolonizing researchers also adopt a particular standpoint predicated on the right of indigenous people to self-representation. However, these researchers appear to conceptualize their relations with existing feminist theory differently. In her recent article "A Few Cautions at the Millennium on the Merging of Feminist Studies with American Indian Women's Studies," Mihesuah (2000) bemoans the continuing production of scholarship about natives by nonnatives that perpetuates damaging stereotypes of reservation life or that appropriates

native knowledge and religious practices in ways that disempower native people. She insists that outsider scholars become more responsible in three ways: They must recognize the validity of oral history, they must engage with real people, and they must allow their research to be reviewed by native authorities. Once again, we are reminded that working across differences of class, race, and culture demand sensitivity, reflexivity, and humility. In addition, working with real people in real communities creates the possibility of irreconcilable conflicts. And yet I would contend that Mihesuah's first two demands constitute a well-established practice for feminist ethnographers. Both reciprocal and dialogic ethnographers stipulate consultation with the ethnographic subject or community through the entire process of research and writing. Such consultation does not grant absolute authority to the ethnographic subject, because it recognizes that neither party in the research exchange is the sole arbiter of truth. Instead, these ethnographic models assume that communicating across cultural divides constitutes an ongoing negotiation of difference that is unevenly successful but worth doing nonetheless.

Tuhiwai Smith (1999), another indigenous scholar, acknowledges that decolonizing methodologies draw on a legacy of feminist and critical theory to build the foundations for a different, non-Western scholarship. *Decolonizing* signals both the continuing relations of domination and subordination between the North and the South, between the Western academy and indigenous communities, and the need for research to actively transform those relations. Decolonizing researchers call for research that addresses the material, cultural, and spiritual impoverishment of contemporary indigenous communities—research that results in the recovery of lands, languages, histories, and identities—research that allows indigenous peoples to create their own futures. Arguing that Western research has often been detrimental to the health and self-concept of those being studied, decolonizing methodologies insist that research must first and foremost benefit the researched community. Such a project mirrors feminist ethnographers' concerns with honoring and strengthening "local knowledge" not simply as a fixed artifact from the past—a tradition—but as a dynamic, evolving counterpoint to dominant discourses that seek to define and contain the marginal other (Hufford, 1996).

Feminists have extended their dialogue with the researched subject from fieldwork to the writing of ethnography. Decolonizing researchers would extend that dialogue backward to the planning and goals of research itself. Both acknowledge that no method or representational model can avoid the ethical dilemmas involved in politically committed research with others. A reflexive awareness of our multiple roles and identities—as both insiders and outsiders—can help us more successfully produce scholarship that matters to communities.

# REFERENCES

Abu Lughod, L. (1990). Can there be a feminist ethnography? *Women and Performance, 9*, 7–27.

Ahmed, S. (2000). *Strange encounters: Embodied others in post-coloniality.* London: Routledge.

Behar, R., & Gordon, D. (Eds.). (1995). *Women writing culture.* Berkeley: University of California Press.

Bell, D. (1993). Introduction 1: The context. In D. Bell, P. Caplan, & W. J. Karim (Eds.), *Gendered fields: Women, men and ethnography* (pp. 1–18). London: Routledge.

Bell, D., Caplan, P., & Karim, W. J. (Eds.). (1993). *Gendered fields: Women, men and ethnography.* London: Routledge.

Bell, D., & Nelson, T. (1989). Speaking about rape is everybody's business. *Women's Studies International Forum, 12*(4), 403–447.

Clifford, J., & Marcus, G. E. (Eds.). (1986). *Writing culture: The poetics and politics of ethnography.* Berkeley: University of California Press.

Crewe, E., & Harrison, E. (1998). *Whose development? An ethnography of AID.* London: Zed Books.

de Beauvoir, S. (1971). *The second sex* (H. M. Parshley, Trans.). New York: Alfred A. Knopf. (Original work published 1949)

Du Bois, W. E. B. (2003). *The souls of black folk.* New York: Barnes and Noble Classics. (Original work published 1903)

Fanon, F. (1963). *The wretched of the earth.* New York: Grove Press.

Fanon, F. (1968). *Black skin, white masks* (C. Farrington, Trans.). New York: Grove Wiedenfield. (Original work published 1952)

Fernea, E. (1989). *Guests of the sheik: An ethnography of an Iraqi village.* New York: Anchor Books. (Original work published 1965)

Gordon, D. (1995). Conclusion: Culture writing women: Inscribing feminist anthropology. In R. Behar & E. Gordon (Eds.), *Women writing culture* (pp. 429–442). Berkeley: University of California Press.

Harding, S. (2003). How standpoint methodology informs philosophy of social science. In S. N. Hesse-Biber & P. Leavy (Eds.), *Approaches to qualitative research: A reader in theory and practice* (pp. 62–80). New York: Oxford University Press.

hooks, b. (1990). Culture to culture: Ethnography and cultural studies as critical intervention. In *Yearning: Race, gender and cultural politics* (pp. 123–133). Boston: South End Press.

Hufford, M. (1996). Context. *Journal of American Folklore, 108*(430), 528–549.

Huggins, J., et al. (1991). [Letter to the editor.] *Women's Studies International Forum, 14*(5), 505–513.

Hurston, Z. N. (1978). *Mules and men.* Bloomington: Indiana University Press. (Original work published 1935)

Lather, P. (1996). Troubling clarity: The politics of accessible language. *Harvard Educational Review, 66*(3), 525–545.

Lather, P. (2001). Postbook: Working in the ruins of feminist ethnography. *Signs: Journal of Women in Culture and Society, 27*(1), 199–227.

Lawless, E. J. (1992). "I was afraid someone like you . . . an outsider . . . would misunderstand": Negotiating interpretive differences between ethnographers and subjects. *Journal of American Folklore, 105*(417), 302–314.

Lawless, E. J. (1993). *Holy women: Wholly women: Sharing ministries of wholeness through life stories and reciprocal ethnography.* Philadelphia: University of Pennsylvania Press.

Lorde, A. (1983). The master's tools will never dismantle the master's house. In C. Moraga & G. Anzaldúa (Eds.), *This bridge called my back: Writings of radical women of color* (pp. 98–101). New York: Kitchen Table Women of Color Press.

Lutz, C. (1995). The gender of theory. In R. Behar & D. Gordon (Eds.), *Women writing culture* (pp. 249–266). Berkeley: University of California Press.

Mascia-Lees, F., Sharpe, P., & Ballerino Cohen, C. (1989). The postmodernist turn in anthropology: Cautions from a feminist perspective. *Signs: Journal of Women in Culture and Society, 15*(11), 7–33.

Mihesuah, D. A. (2000). A few cautions at the millennium on the merging of feminist studies with American Indian women's studies. In J. A. Howard & C. Allen (Eds.), *Feminisms at the millennium* (pp. 239–243). Chicago: University of Chicago Press.

Moraga, C., & Anzaldúa, G. (Eds.). (1983). *This bridge called my back: Writings by radical women of color* (3rd ed.). New York: Kitchen Table Women of Color Press.

Nájera-Ramírez, O. (1999). Of fieldwork, folklore, and festival: Personal encounters. *Journal of American Folklore, 112*(444), 183–199.

Narayan, K. (1993). How native is a "native" anthropologist? *American Anthropologist, 95*(3), 671–686.

Nash, J. (1997). When isms become wasms: Structural functionalism, Marxism, feminism and postmodernism. *Critique of Anthropology, 17*(1), 11–32.

Patai, D. (1991). U.S. academics and third world women: Is ethical research possible? In S. Gluck & D. Patai (Eds.), *Women's words: The feminist practice of oral history* (pp. 137–153). New York: Routledge.

Sawin, P. (2004). *Listening for a life: A dialogic ethnography of Bessie Eldreth through her stories and songs.* Logan: Utah State University Press.

Stacey, J. (1988). Can there be a feminist ethnography? *Women's Studies International Forum, 11*(1), 21–27.

Stewart, K. (1996). *A space by the side of the road: Cultural politics in an "other" America.* Princeton, NJ: Princeton University Press.

Tuhiwai Smith, L. (1999). *Decolonizing methodologies: Research and indigenous peoples.* New York: Zed Books.

Visweswaran, K. (1994a). Betrayal: An analysis in three acts. In *Fictions of feminist ethnography* (pp. 40–59). Minneapolis: University of Minnesota Press.

Visweswaran, K. (1994b). Feminist ethnography as failure. In *Fictions of feminist ethnography* (pp. 95–113). Minneapolis: University of Minnesota Press.

Woolf, V. (1991). *A room of one's own.* New York: Harcourt Brace Jovanovich. (Original work published 1929)

# 36

# FUTURE DIRECTIONS OF FEMINIST RESEARCH

## *Intersectionality*

BONNIE THORNTON DILL
AMY E. MCLAUGHLIN
ANGEL DAVID NIEVES

Intersectionality is grounded in feminist theory, asserting that people live multiple, layered identities and can simultaneously experience oppression and privilege. It is an approach to creating knowledge that has its roots in analyses of the lived experiences of women of color—women whose scholarly and social justice work reveal how aspects of identity and social relations are shaped by the simultaneous operation of multiple systems of power. Intersectional scholarship is interdisciplinary in nature and focuses on how structures of difference combine to create new and distinct social, cultural, and artistic forms. It is intellectually transformative not only because it centers the experiences of people of color and locates its analysis within systems of ideological, political, and economic power as they are shaped by historical patterns of race, class, gender, sexuality, nation, ethnicity, and age, but also because it provides a platform for uniting different kinds of praxis in the pursuit of social justice: analysis, theorizing, education, advocacy, and policy development.

Over the past two decades, intersectional approaches have expanded considerably, evolving in many different fields and across the humanities and social sciences, including women's studies, American studies, law, history, sociology, education, African American studies, anthropology, literature, ethnic studies, English, architecture, and more. As its utility in revealing the complexities and multidimensionality of experience has become apparent, other identity groups and bodies of scholarship have utilized intersectional analysis to shed light on their particular experiences (i.e., queer studies, disability studies, and cultural studies). In addition, as scholars producing intersectional work began to apply their insights to the institutions where they worked—institutions of higher education—they began to speak and write about the challenges and opportunities that exist within and through the academy. Thus, intersectional scholarship is engaged in transforming both theory and practice in higher education across the disciplinary divide, offering a wide range of methodological approaches to the study of multiple, complex social relations.

In this chapter, we are charged with suggesting future directions of intersectional scholarship; Part 1 will offer speculation on future intersectional analyses, along with a few words of caution, and Part 2 will focus on the institutionally transformative character of intersectional work.

## PART 1: INTELLECTUALLY TRANSFORMATIVE ROOTS AND HISTORY

Intersectionality has grown out of the work of feminists of color who have theorized about the interrelationship of race, class, gender, and other dimensions of difference.[1] These scholars began their work by theorizing the experience of women of color who had been ignored in the scholarship on race and on gender. What distinguished these women was that their lives could not be understood through a unidimensional analysis focusing exclusively on either race or gender. Intersectionality instead builds on a U.S. scholarly tradition that began in the 19th century with women like Sojourner Truth, Maria Stewart, Anna Julia Cooper, and men like W. E. B. Du Bois—intellectuals who first articulated the unique challenges of Black women facing the multiple and simultaneous effects of race, gender, and class. Contemporary women of color have continued this legacy through landmark scholarship of lived experience at the intersections of race, gender, ethnicity, class, and sexuality.

The people engaged in this work do so out of strong commitments to diversity, multiculturalism, and human rights and a desire to create a more equitable society that recognizes, validates, and celebrates difference. The social justice agenda of this scholarship is crucial to its utility in analyzing inequalities of power and privilege, and it is of interest to persons outside the academy who share concerns that underlie this scholarship.

## Growth, Dissemination, and the Future

Because the contemporary growth of this approach is relatively recent and has developed in a number of different fields, future growth is largely defined by the trajectories of current debates and inquiries. Some of these directions were revealed in a study conducted by Bonnie Thornton Dill (2002) that investigated the current state of intersectional scholarship through interviews with 70 faculty members and a few graduate students at 17 universities and colleges. This report, and the developments that have occurred since that time, form the basis of our assessments of current and future directions in scholarship and pedagogy in those academic departments and institutions wherever intersectionality has gained an intellectual foothold.

Areas of scholarship where important debates are occurring and/or new combinations of intellectual and political insights are being combined are in the field of identity studies, work that engages with globalization/transnationalism(s), sexualities/queer studies, and new ways of linking theory and practice. Within each of these topics are disagreements about approach and perspective, but the debates and discussions contribute to the vibrancy of the topic.

### Identity Studies

To a large extent, intersectional work is about identity, and identity politics has been the subject of considerable scholarly and popular debate over the past two decades. While identities and identity politics remain contested and much debated, the constructions and discourses about intersectionality as a tool for illuminating the nature of both individual and group identity is central to work in this area. Intersectionality in identity studies helps us understand the multidimensional ways people experience life—how people see themselves and how they are treated by others—and provides a particularly useful lens for examining the category of race. This interrogation not only must take place on the individual level but also must question how economic, political, and ideological structures construct and perpetuate group identities. Patricia Hill Collins (1998) writes,

> The fluidity that accompanies intersectionality does not mean that groups themselves disappear, . . . [but] deepens the understanding of how the actual mechanisms of institutional power can change dramatically even while they reproduce long-standing group inequalities of race, class, and gender. (pp. 205–206)

In the discourse surrounding identity, it is the tension between intersectionality as a tool for illuminating group identities that are not essentialist, and individual identities that are not so fragmentary as to be meaningless, that provides the energy to move the concept forward to the future. At the individual level, identity studies continue to call attention to dimensions of difference that have been largely unexplored and ignored. As Dill has pointed out, long neglected social groups at undiscovered points of intersection reveal the complexity of their lived experience, in particular "people whose identity crosses the boundaries of traditionally constructed groups" (Dill, quoted in Leslie McCall, 2005). Among the newer areas that are rapidly developing are disability and queer studies, where an intersectional analysis reveals the importance of individual difference and experience. At the same time, the methods by which these and other dimensions of difference are organized into systems of structured social inequality are essential to understanding the meaning of these categories and their particular histories. Uncovering and analyzing the linkages between these two kinds of analysis continues to drive the push toward social justice and human rights in this scholarship.

As a cautionary note, much intersectional work does currently focus on the individual/experiential level. More pathways need to be forged methodologically and theoretically to apply intersectional analyses of identities at the structural and political levels of analysis. This may mean using multiple methods in the same analysis, including ethnographic (and even autoethnographic) quantitative research.

### Globalization/Transnationalism(s)

Work that examines international and global perspectives is another area that advances this scholarship. For example, work examining the social construction of blackness within a global context, along with work on African, Latino, Asian, and other diasporic groups, is seen as developing important new insights, not only for understanding the world outside the United States but for understanding the U.S. context as well. Chandra Mohanty (2003) uses the phrase "comparative women's studies" to describe

intersectional scholarship. She argues that in addition to conceptualizing identity in multiple categories, it helps foreground ideas of nationhood and citizenship that may in turn be used to elucidate the position of women of color throughout the United States. The work on Third World women has emphasized the existence and importance of indigenous-based feminisms, within broader comparative hemispheric considerations, further stressing the importance of a global perspective on intersectional scholarship.

An intersectional approach also contributes to an understanding as to how dimensions of difference operate in different societies. One provocative example is the construction of race in the United States as compared with its construction in Bosnia-Herzegovina. Intersectionality reminds us that each cultural framework must be understood within its own context, regardless of whether the focus is on individuals, groups, or, in the case of Bosnia-Herzegovina, across nation-states.

One final caveat regarding globalization and transnationalism is this: We cannot allow the growing interest in this work to have us overlook the structural inequalities within the United States, and the identities and social dilemmas that continue to exist here. The recent widespread interest in transnational research—across our own borders and through the constant flow of human capital and resources—tends to submerge the embedded matrices of inequality and oppression originating here in the United States. It is perhaps easier to look outside our own borders without doing the necessary work to change, and even challenge, ourselves and the continuing power constructions of U.S. imperialism, consumerism, and economic elitism (Butler, 2001).

### Sexualities/Queer Studies

The developing study of sexuality broadens our understandings of gender, breaking down some of the traditional borders between the sexes and our notions of sexual desire. Intersectional approaches are beginning to illuminate the relationships between sexuality, race, power, identity, and social organization. An example is the work of historian John D'Emilio, whose current work on the life of labor and civil rights activist Bayard Rustin examines the complex ways race, gender, and sexuality intersected in Rustin's life and affected key strategies and actions of the civil rights movement. Rustin's identity as a gay man cannot be easily separated from his race or class or be distinguished from his work as an active member of the civil rights movement. Rustin's sexuality, examined through an intersectional analysis, reveals how integral his identity was in his framing of civil rights as a human rights movement. Roderick Ferguson (2003), in his book *Aberrations in Black: Toward a Queer of Color Critique*, develops an approach he calls "queer of color analysis" that reveals the interconnections among sexuality, economic inequality, and race not only in the history of American labor but also within various forms of knowledge production. His book lays out the historical role sociology has played in labeling African American culture as deviant, and, by carefully highlighting this process, Ferguson reveals how identity is inextricably linked to power, political representation, and the ever-shifting power dynamics of identity politics.

Salvador Vidal-Ortiz's (2004) article, "On Being a White Person of Color: Using Autoethnography to Understand Puerto Ricans' Racialization," is an example of current intersectional scholarship that challenges classical definitions of race, ethnicity, and nationality, while also repositioning debates about identity politics in the United States. Vidal-Ortiz argues that an alternative racialization process occurs when Puerto Ricans represent themselves while living in the United States, contrasted with living on the island. By studying the impact of more than one racialization system, it then becomes possible to see how categories of analysis like gender, class, and sexuality may depend entirely on one's own geopolitical positionalities (i.e., imagined realities, physically or rooted, through political participation).

Work in the area of queer studies may require some precautions. For example, changes in language appropriation/usage and terminology, from "gay" to "queer," or as Ferguson suggests, a "queer of color analysis," may lead to the erasure of the experiences of transgender or intersexed individuals who have been actively involved in the struggle over equal marriage rights for couples regardless of their gendered identities. As Rhonda M. Williams has suggested,

although *queer* is seen as a "necessarily expansive impulse," we must understand how it still also reflects and, in some cases, might blur the complexities of sexual orientations and racial politics among Black gays and lesbians (Harper, cited in Williams, 1998).

### Linking Theory and Practice

Because this knowledge is grounded in the everyday lives of people of diverse backgrounds, it is seen as an important tool linking theory with practice. Intersectional work can validate the lives and histories of persons and subgroups previously ignored or marginalized, and it is used to help empower communities and the people in them.

An example can be found in the work of Professors Barbara Ransby, Elsa Barkley-Brown, and Deborah King, who organized a national response to the Anita Hill/Clarence Thomas controversy. Ransby, Barkley-Brown, and King prepared a public statement that applied an intersectional analysis to the vilification of Anita Hill as well as Clarence Thomas's distorted use of the concept of lynching. Signed by more than 1,600 African American women scholars, the statement offered an interpretation of those events that went beyond the singular focus on sexual harassment that had become the overriding concern of many White feminists, and the concurrent racial victimization evoked by Clarence Thomas's "high-tech lynching" claim. Their statement argued that constructs of race and gender intersected in the treatment of Anita Hill to demean and discredit her in a way that was consistent with the historical pattern of treatment of Black women who speak out on sexual matters or publicly criticize Black men. The statement, published in the *New York Times* and six African American newspapers, offered a perspective on the case that had been totally omitted from public discourse and debate.

Scholars whose work is intersectional acknowledge their intellectual, social, and personal debt to civil rights, women's, peace, gay/queer rights, labor, and other social justice movements. It is worth noting, however, that scholars on an academic career track do theory-practice connections on their own; in most academic locations, they will not get credit for the practical/applied side of their work. Social justice work is not as well regarded or as well rewarded as publishing, and junior scholars are often warned against "widening their focus" beyond the traditional requirements for tenure. In addition, this work takes a sustained investment of time and personal energy to ensure that it maintains its focus on social justice and outcomes that affect the everyday lives of people. This kind of work grows out of lived experience of people from disadvantaged social, political, and economic locations; therefore, research must be conducted in such a way that it is neither intrusive nor exploitive of the community on which it is focused. Developing the linkages between scholarship and praxis takes an inordinate amount of time and requires the nurturing necessary to ensure some benefit to local communities. In short, these projects should benefit the community as much or perhaps even more than the individual researcher or team.

In sum, the future looks promising for intersectional scholarship. The field continues to diversify, and new knowledge is being produced across a wide range of fields. In each expanding area, scholars are staying true to the intersectional commitment to interrogating power, privilege, and oppression and working toward equitable forms of social justice.

## Precautions, Problems, and Misappropriations

### Authenticity and Representation

As much as issues of authenticity and representation are debated as they concern national, international, and global affairs, they are also debated in scholarship and in the hiring, tenure, and promotion of faculty. Among these debates is the issue of who studies whom, and who speaks for whom—that is, who represents the "authentic" voice or voices of a particular community or communities. Within this scholarship, questions of speaking for and writing about "the other" have been central to its development. As scholars have sought to reclaim and present the stories and lives of previously silenced groups, and to define new areas of scholarship such as Black feminist studies, Chicana studies, American Indian studies, Latino studies, and so on, questions of identity, assimilation, essentialism, and who can claim membership in these groups have been highly contested.

Faculties and departments with a growing emphasis on scholarly questions related to race and ethnicity face a limited supply of faculty of color and find themselves grappling with these issues in hiring decisions, reappointment, promotion, and tenure. Once hired, faculty of color most often come to realize that they are expected to "represent" people of color as a kind of "spokesperson," in a variety of service capacities, none of which are incorporated fully into their compensation or tenure evaluations. Even departments and institutions with good intentions of making race, ethnicity, and difference central to their work rely heavily on a very small number of scholars of color who are personally committed to institutional change (Benjamin, 2000).

### Relationship to the Organization and Structure of the Academy

A second area of controversy centers on the nature and structure of the academy itself and the place of intersectional studies within it. In general, the interviews with faculty of color across the United States convey the belief that intersectional work remains at the outermost margins of the academic enterprise. Although scholars acknowledge that strides have been made, that the amount of scholarship is growing, and that various institutions have begun to support some aspects of this work, those engaged in it feel that it continues to be far more peripheral to the central mission and activities of colleges and universities today than is appropriate or acceptable. The reasons for this are both intellectual and organizational (as well as financial) and cannot be discussed in depth here, but the next section details some of the progress that intersectional work is making in the academy and the challenges that remain.

## PART 2: TRANSFORMING THE ACADEMY/INSTITUTIONALLY TRANSFORMATIVE

Intersectional work primarily takes place in the academy, communities, foundations, and social justice organizations dedicated to bringing about change. This analysis focuses on institutions of higher education because universities and colleges are an important site for the production of knowledge, have links to these other institutions, and have traditionally been the location where much intersectional scholarship is produced. They are also a site where the influence of the scholars doing this work can be felt in subsequent changes that have an effect on the mission, engagement, and daily operations of these institutions. The analysis of the institutionally transformative aspects of intersectional knowledge presented here can be used as a basis for analyses of other institutions, most likely those formally connected to universities and colleges, as they engage with this scholarship and work at the intersections.

But arguing that this scholarship is institutionally transformative is not to say that it has already transformed the academy; to the contrary, the process remains at an early stage of development. To create and discover previously unlooked for analyses and histories using an intersectional framework means more interdisciplinary work, more work that focuses on the historical and geographical context of events, attitudes, and cultures, and work that breaks out of the academic mold to join forces with the communities whose internal knowledge is indispensable to the project. Thus, this scholarship has the capability to transform rigid boundaries between departments, between universities and their neighboring communities, and, in general, between what is viewed as valid and worthy of support in the academy and what is not.

## Interdisciplinarity

Fundamentally, this body of scholarship connects ideas across disciplines and interlaces constructs that have customarily been treated as separate and distinct. It is, in essence, an interdisciplinary exercise. Within the conventionally structured academy, interdisciplinary studies have been gaining in popularity and, attesting to this, the Academy of Sciences released a report in 2004 that urges universities to promote successful interdisciplinary research (National Academy of Sciences, 2005) because it

[has] an impact on multiple fields or disciplines and produce[s] results that feed back into and enhance disciplinary research. It will also create researchers and students with an expanded research vocabulary and abilities in more than one discipline and with an enhanced understanding of the interconnectedness inherent in complex problems. (Klein & Newell, 1998, p. 3)

And yet this growth is taking place with little recognition of the departments and programs that have been interdisciplinary from their inception. These continuing programs may benefit as barriers fall, but much of the new interest reinscribes existing institutional power relations in the academy. Interdisciplinary programs that have an intersectional/social justice agenda are precariously placed and continue to be viewed with skepticism; yet they are the location of much cutting-edge scholarship that confronts entrenched disciplinary dogma.

Intersectional interdisciplinarity is transformative because of its commitment to a social justice agenda—one that draws on new connections and exchanges of ideas that take place when scholars from different institutional locations work together. In addition, nontraditional strategies are introduced, such as shared hires and recruitment targeting relatively newer disciplines (e.g., ethnic studies, women's studies, American studies, etc.), which contain within them opportunities for destabilizing the traditional ways of producing knowledge. This may require a department to support a scholar whose work crosses conventional boundaries and, perhaps, necessitates engaging in a mutually beneficial relationship with another campus program, department, or institution.

## Curriculum Transformation

For a variety of educational, social, economic, and political reasons, colleges and universities are increasingly working to develop programming and public images that highlight diversity. Most often this notion of diversity focuses on improving human relations throughout the campus by increasing awareness, acceptance, understanding, and appreciation of human differences. Rarely does it focus on the inequalities of power and resources embedded in these differences; even more rarely is the expertise of intersection scholars seen as central to this enterprise. The push for diversity and multiculturalism coincides with a push toward a more business-centered and entrepreneurial academy; rising tuition and fees; reduced state and federal support; and increasing student debt. It is not coincidental that these problems have reached crisis proportions at a time when corporate (e.g., privatized) solutions to the funding and organization of universities are seen as a corrective. In today's university there is (according to many) greater emphasis on "treating students as consumers and education as a commodity that produces credentials" (Hollander & Saltmarsh, 2000, para. 13). Intersectional work can belie the push toward corporatism as it is a contextualized approach that engages extensively with its subject. By its own definition, it is scholarship produced in pursuit of social justice that must question how power infiltrates the research and funding processes. Intersectional work often engages with off-campus communities and integrates nonacademic voices and experiences into its findings. The results aim to fuel changes in unjust practices across a wide variety of dimensions of social and political life.

Yet its ability to perform this function is hampered by the disproportionate underrepresentation of faculty color—the very faculty members most likely to bring this theoretical and applied perspective to their work. Nevertheless, revising campus curricular requirements is an important avenue toward an academy representative of all society (e.g., the University of Maryland's record of awarding Ph.D.s in 2004 was 5% African American, 5% Asian American, 1% Hispanic, and 0.2% American Indian—obviously not reflective of an increasingly diverse society), and for giving students the tools to become critical thinkers on their own merits. In addition, a diversified curriculum will increase and support the development of future intersectional scholars and activists.

## Faculty Interventions

Some faculty create direct interventions into the production of knowledge on their campuses by founding and leading intersectionally oriented research centers, having joint appointments with traditional departments and newer departments, and promoting new approaches that integrate professional organizations. These centers will influence different academic arenas and change the campus intellectual climate by incorporating new forms of knowledge production, taking intersectional work outside of the academy, and shaping public policy and additional approaches to social justice.

The work of The Latino Critical Race Studies Group (LatCrit) at the University of Miami Law School provides an example. LatCrit, a national organization of law professors and students, seeks to use critical race theory to develop new conceptions of justice. To do this, the organization is actively engaged in what it terms "anti-essential community building." LatCrit (http://personal.law.miami.edu/~fvaldes/latcrit) has two main goals:

> (1) To develop a critical, activist and interdisciplinary discourse on law and policy towards Latinas/os, and (2) to foster both the development of coalitional theory and practice as well as the accessibility of this knowledge to agents of social and legal transformation. LatCrit theorists aim to center Latinas/os' multiple internal diversities and to situate Latinas/os in larger intergroup frameworks, both domestically and globally, to promote social justice awareness and activism.

No single community can produce a theory about intergroup justice without connections to and across other groups, and yet every single social justice movement has had a problem of essentialism, giving primacy to some aspects of their identity while ignoring others that intersect with and re-form that primary identity. As a result, LatCrit seeks quite consciously to consider Latino identity as a multifaceted, multilayered intersectional reality. Latinos, they argue, are Black, Asian, Gay, and straight and speak many different languages. Thus, in all their conferences, debates, and activities they seek to keep all of these differences actively engaged in the conversation.

At the University of Maryland, College Park, the Consortium on Race, Gender and Ethnicity (CRGE) is an interdisciplinary institution that works to promote intersectional theory, pedagogy, and methodology (www.crge.umd.edu). Founded in 1998, CRGE has been working to develop a national reputation as a leader in intersectional scholarship, while promoting and disseminating work that uncovers how systems of race, gender, ethnicity, and other dimensions of inequality mutually shape experience, identity, and social organization. In so doing, CRGE has become vital to the fulfillment of the University of Maryland's mission of achieving excellence and diversity in areas of research, scholarship, teaching, and community service by providing a foundation for the University's ability to attract and retain graduate students and faculty of color. CRGE's mission, therefore, is unique among research centers nationwide because it produces pathbreaking research and scholarship while mentoring and training faculty and graduate students of color, promoting scholarly collaborations across the campus, and applying its research and scholarship to issues of public policy.

Grant monies from the Ford Foundation provided for further development of CRGE as a research center as well as for funding of the *Curriculum Transformation Project* and the Department of African American Studies. With CRGE's share of the grant money, the Center established itself with three faculty, two full-time staff members, and two graduate students, and funded 21 Research Interest Groups on campus among faculty from more than 25 departments to study issues related to race, gender, and ethnicity. Centers like CRGE are the kinds of institutional interventions that have made credible inroads in transforming the dialogue of social justice and diversity at universities across the country.

## CONCLUSION

In sum, intersectionality is a body of scholarship that continues to be explored and expanded across a number of fields. This chapter has examined the directions that this scholarship might take; yet we believe only a glimmer of its bright future can now be envisioned across the numerous fields and disciplines where intersectionality is establishing itself. As an "emerging paradigm," intersectionality is unique in its versatility and ability to produce new knowledge (Collins, 1998). We remain optimistic about the future of intersectionality, particularly if this scholarship respects its crucial commitments to laying bare the roots of power and inequality while continuing to pursue an activist agenda of social justice.

## NOTE

1. The following list is not meant as exclusive or exhaustive but as a reflection of the breadth of early intersectional scholarship. See, for example, Patricia Hill Collins (1990), Kimberlé Crenshaw (1989), Gloria Anzaldúa (1987), Maxine Baca Zinn and Bonnie Dill (1996), Angela Y. Davis (1981), Cherríe Moraga (1983), Chela Sandoval (1991), Chandra Talpade Mohanty (1988), and bell hooks (1984).

## REFERENCES

Anzaldúa, G. (1987). *Borderlands/la frontera: The new mestiza.* San Francisco: Aunt Lute.

Benjamin, B. (2000). Race-related service and faculty of color: Conceptualizing critical agency in academe. *Higher Education, 39,* 363–391.

Butler, J. (2001). *Color-line to borderlands: The matrix of American ethnic studies.* Seattle: University of Washington Press.

Collins, P. H. (1990). *Black feminist thought: Knowledge, consciousness, and the politics of empowerment.* Boston: Unwin Hyman.

Collins, P. H. (1998). *Fighting words: Black women and the search for justice.* Minneapolis: University of Minnesota.

Crenshaw, K. (1989). Demarginalizing the intersection of race and sex: A black feminist critique of antidiscrimination doctrine, feminist theory, and antiracist politics. *University of Chicago Legal Forum,* 139–167.

Davis, A. Y. (1981). *Women, race, and class.* New York: Random House.

Dill, B. T. (2002). *Work at the intersections of race, gender, ethnicity and other dimensions of identity in higher education.* Consultant report to the Ford Foundation.

Ferguson, R. (2003). *Aberrations in black: Toward a queer of color critique.* Minneapolis: University of Minnesota Press.

Hollander, E. L., & Saltmarsh, J. (2000, July/August). The engaged university. *Academe, 86*(4). Retrieved December 3, 2005, from www.aaup .org/publications/Academe/2000/00ja/JA00Holl .htm hooks, b. (1984). *Feminist theory: From margin to center*. Cambridge, MA: South End Press.

Klein, J. T., & Newell, W. H. (1998). Advancing interdisciplinary studies. In W. H. Newell (Ed.), *Interdisciplinarity: Essays from the literature* (pp. 3–22). New York: College Entrance Examination Board.

McCall, L. (2005). The complexity of intersectionality. *Signs: Journal of Women in Culture and Society, 30*(3), 1774.

Mohanty, C. T. (1988). Under Western eyes: Feminist scholarship and colonial discourses. *Feminist Review, 30*, 61–88.

Mohanty, C. T. (2003). *Feminism without borders*. Durham, NC: Duke University Press.

Moraga, C. (1983). *Loving in the war years*. Boston: South End Press.

National Academy of Sciences. (2005). *Facilitating interdisciplinary research*. Washington, DC: Author.

Sandoval, C. (1991). U.S. Third World feminism: The theory and method of oppositional consciousness in the postmodern world. *Genders, 10*, 1–24.

Vidal-Ortiz, S. (2004). On being a white person of color: Using autoethnography to understand Puerto Ricans' racialization. *Qualitative Sociology, 27*(2), 179–203.

Williams, R. M. (1998). Living at the crossroads: Explorations in race, nationality, sexuality, and gender. In W. Lubiano (Ed.), *The house that race built*. New York: Vintage.

Zinn, M. B., & Dill, B. T. (1996). Theorizing differences from multi-racial feminism. *Feminist Studies, 22*(2), 321–331.

# 37

## INTERCONNECTIONS AND CONFIGURATIONS

### *Toward a Global Feminist Ethnography*

KUM-KUM BHAVNANI

A frequently encountered puzzle for feminist scholarship is whether feminism can ever be more than critique. Although it is clear that the work of critique is important in and of itself, it is also the case that feminist scholarship offers, through a reflection on empirical work, the real-life implications of feminist critique. This is a key reason why feminist scholars in the late 1980s and into the 1990s wrote so extensively on feminist epistemology methods and methodology, namely, to discover what might (and might not) constitute feminist research (e.g., Behar, 1993; Bhavnani, 1993; Code, 1991; Harding, 1991; Lather, 1991; Longino, 1993; Nicholson, 1994; Reinharz, 1992; Smith, 1990; Stacey, 1988; Stanley & Wise, 1990; Trujillo, 1991). In these attempts at definition and specification, much thought has gone into delineating the criteria and enumerating what the range of approaches to feminist research could include. Such discussions are not without their detractors, among them feminist scholars. For example, Evelyn Fox Keller (1996) asks if there is a conflict between a commitment to feminism and a commitment to science. She suggests that when critiques of

*positivist* (my adjective) objectivity emerge from feminist work, the result of such critiques is that science is seen as a pure social product and that the rigors of "science then dissolve into ideology and objectivity loses all intrinsic meaning" (p. 31). Many disagree with Fox Keller's approach to objectivity. Below, I discuss the classic essay by Donna Haraway (1988), which offers the possibilities of moving beyond the apparent binary between feminist and other forms of science put forward by Fox Keller (1996).

As a quick summary, feminist scholars tend to agree that scholarship rooted in feminist epistemologies is characterized by an antipositivist philosophy of science, discussions as to whether the subjects of feminist research are exclusively women (e.g., many suggest that feminist research does include research on men and masculinity, even when conducted by men); whether the researchers have to be exclusively women; and, perhaps the greatest conundrum of all, how to talk about the category "woman" given its embeddedness in, and impetus for, all discussions of difference as they are expressed through power inequalities. Such puzzles have been tackled by Mary Maynard (1994), who poses the question of how feminist scholars might ground notions of difference in empirical work, as well as others working in different disciplinary areas, who engage issues of race/ethnicity, racism, nation, sexuality, class, and difference in their writings (e.g., Bhavnani, 1993, 2001b; Collins, 1990; duCille, 1999; Freeman, 2001; James, 1998; Lewis, 1996; Moore, 1994; Narayan, 1997; Pajaczkowska & Young, 2000; Spelman, 1997). More recently, some have also turned their attention to the dilemmas in conducting feminist research (e.g., Twine & Warren, 2000; Wolf, 1996). What is agreed on, however, is that feminist approaches contribute to documenting the visibility of women's lives and making women's voices audible.

Visibility and audibility have many layers. For example, Hammonds (1995), in her discussion of black female queer sexualities, points out that while visibility is often a goal of much feminist research, what is often not attended to are the consequences of such visibility. She writes, "Visibility in and of itself does not . . . challenge the structure of power and domination, symbolic and material, that determines what can and cannot be seen" (p. 143). Gillian Rose (1997) has also noted the dangers of not seeing difference. She does this by discussing the "myth of community"—a myth because she argues that the overused concept of community leads to a denial of difference. Her suggestion for remedying this myth is that feminist scholars build a "politics of voice and translation" in empirical research. It now becomes clear that feminist research is not simply or merely about visibility but is simultaneously about *how* those voices and lives are represented (Lewis, 1996) and what critical/feminist objectivity can be in practice.

There seems to be little to disagree with so far. Yet this agreement is also in need of much refinement—which women's lives are being analyzed, interrogated, and even evaluated? In which parts of the world? Which aspects of their lives? Which voices? Who edits the documentation? And, indeed, are there any continuities in the lived experiences of women across class, region, nation, sexuality, and race/ethnicity? My argument will be that feminist ethnographies (they can also be thought of as narrative

approaches to research) that pay attention to the axes of inequality listed above as well as to regional and national locations as contours of difference offer the possibility of glimpsing where continuities and discontinuities in women's lives might speak to each other. They do not speak past each other and are thus able to help in working through why we still draw on the category "woman" when we are so aware of its limitations and possibilities for masking power inequalities among women (examples of such scholarship include Aggarwal, 2000; Castillo, Gomez, & Delgado, 1999; Kempadoo, 1999; Nnaemeka, 2001; Puar, 1998; Puri, 2002; Robertson, 2000; Smith, 2002).

In some of the more interesting discussions on difference (e.g., Crenshaw, 1989), attention is paid to the intersection of points of difference along axes of inequality. Difference is imagined as being synonymous with such axes of inequality, and examples are offered to show how axes of difference/inequality are not discrete from each other but intersect each other. Audre Lorde is one such person who in herself, and in her work, embodies(d) difference in a number of ways. I myself have argued that these interconnections must form the focus of feminist analysis. In 1997, I wrote that the task of feminist work, inside and outside the academy, "should be to concentrate on how 'race,' class, ethnicity, and sexuality shape and influence each other, alongside gender" (Bhavnani, 1997, p. 46).

To further develop this attempt to refine contemporary feminist thinking, I addressed the notion of interconnections along axes of difference/inequality at the United Nations World Conference Against Racism (Bhavnani, 2001a). There, I suggested that to conceptualize the linkages of difference as intersections, rather as one views road intersections, tends toward constituting the subject as a victim rather than also as an agent. I argue this because a discourse of intersectionality that draws on a crossroads metaphor—for example, race and gender intersecting at a crossroads with the race-d/gender-ed person standing at the meeting point of those crossroads—directs the gaze to the intersections of the roads and the directions in which they travel and meet. This emphasis can lead to losing sight of the person, a human being with desires, motivations, fears, and so on, that is, as someone with agency, who stands at those crossroads. This matters because if we are not only to analyze the world but also to change it, then the easiest way to imagine the shifts in the relationships between race/ethnicity and gender is to imagine the roads being moved to form new intersections. In this way, the person at the crossroads is seen from a different angle, and in addition, his or her own perspective/view/gaze of the crossroads also shifts.

However, in such a metaphor, the person who is standing at the intersection does nothing—it is just that the roads are shifted. That is why I have suggested that a more agentic way for thinking about inequalities might be as "interconnections" that configure each other—because *interconnections that configure* connotes more movement and fluidity than lies in the metaphor of intersection, as well as offering a way of thinking about how not only race and gender but also nation, sexuality, and wealth all interconnect, configure, and reshape each other. *Interconnections that configure each other* also implies a notion of active engagement, with a consequent attribution of agency to the subjects of the configurations. From this standpoint, the term *intersectionality* is too static and too close to losing sight of agency of human beings.

It is also the case that feminist scholars have been analyzing how to understand projects of development and global processes more accurately in the past two decades by suggesting that a feminist approach allows a clearer vision of the impact of these projects and processes on people's actual lives (e.g., Antrobus, 2004; Beneria, 2003; Bhavnani, Foran, & Talcott, 2005; Enloe, 2004; Mayo, 2005; Moghadam, 2005; Peterson, 2003). Often, work on development, global processes, neoliberalism, and the gendered consequences of such processes (especially when focused on the Third World) is necessarily replete with statistical information that some might consider to be "objective" in a positivistic sense; yet it is crucial that, at the same time, if one is to engage with issues in the Third World *qua* feminists, that is, as issues that are best understood from the point of view of the *lived experiences* of the poor, we must seek to integrate our notions of objectivity so that we are able to consider all levels of analysis.

The issue is how do feminist scholars conduct research that is global in its approach while remaining feminist in its epistemology? Ethnographic research is one obvious way of conducting this type of research. While there are many discussions as to whether feminist research is *by definition* ethnographic in its orientation, I will not take up that debate here. Rather, I want to sketch out what a global feminist ethnography might look like.

## ETHNOGRAPHY

A chapter in a handbook of this sort is not the place in which to lay out the variety of discussions on ethnography—its origins (see, e.g., Asad, 1973; Clifford, 1988), whether ethnography is necessarily a liberatory approach, or, indeed, from the perspective of the positivist social scientist, whether ethnography offers anything more than anecdotal and nonreliable data. What I want to do is to see what it is that ethnographic research can offer and, in so doing, suggest how feminist global ethnography might lead us to see the world through a different set of lenses.

George Marcus (1998) argues that the ethnographer is a midwife who is able, through words, to help give birth to what is happening in the lives of the oppressed. Beverley Skeggs (1994) has proposed that ethnography is, in itself, "a theory of the research process," and I have suggested that it is the power inequalities in the conduct of ethnographies that open up possibilities for seeing the world in a new and different way (Bhavnani, 1993): ethnography as midwife, ethnography as theory, ethnography as offering new lenses. But what is it that we look at with ethnography, and what is it that we wish to analyze?

In the past 5 years, I, along with coauthors, have been working on a new paradigm we call Women, Culture, Development (WCD) (e.g., Chua, Bhavnani, & Foran, 2000; Bhavnani, Foran, & Kurian, 2003; Bhavnani, Foran, Kurian, & Munshi, in press). This paradigm focused on women in the Third World and was initiated from our research, teaching, and writing about development, which may be thought of here as planned social transformation. We suggest that a WCD approach is suggestive of substantive, theoretical, and methodological concerns across many arenas, not only development (e.g., Bhavnani & Chua, 2000). Here, I offer a brief summary of WCD with an emphasis on its methodological implications.

WCD argues that it is crucial in the 21st century to attend to how Third World development since the 1950s has failed in its goals of ameliorating poverty (at the time of writing, 2.8 billion people were living on less than $2 per day) and offering chances for human beings to extend themselves beyond the day-to-day practices of their lives—to develop their creativity. We argue that this failure is due to overly economistic assumptions on the part of development theories and policies. Further, we demonstrate that this failure of development also lies in the exclusion of women from projects of development or in viewing women either as wives and mothers or as laborers and not integrating women's reproductive and productive contributions. We argue, therefore, that it is not that development policies, projects, and theories make women invisible but, rather, that the visibility of women within development does not shed light on their lives in all the wonderful complexity of the following interconnected configurations: production and reproduction, the lived experience of women, and their agency. We suggest that a focus on women need not exclude men but is simply one starting point that is then able to illuminate the circumstances of all people's lives, including men's lives. We argue that to focus on women within development in this way offers prospects for seeing the lives of people as more tangled and therefore as richer than has hitherto been suggested. Thus, the WCD paradigm applies to both women and men.

The methodological consequences of such an approach are what concern me here. To tease out the relationship between production and reproduction, to ensure that the agency of people is captured, and to see the tangle of the interconnected configurations of axes of inequality require that we conduct our empirical research by interrogating the actual lived experience of people. It is these requirements that form, nowadays for me, the basis of feminist research.

## RETRACING THE CONTOURS

Over 10 years ago, I wrote "Tracing the Contours" (Bhavnani, 1993), in which I spelt out some implications of the argument that all knowledge is historically contingent and, therefore, that the processes of knowledge production are situated. In that article, I wondered if it is possible to identify the criteria that could delineate feminist objectivity and how those criteria could be put into practice by feminist scholars who conduct empirical research.

My argument emerged after I read Donna Haraway's (1988) "Situated Knowledges" piece, in which she points to scientists' partiality—"being answerable for what we see"—and scientists' positioning—"limited location"—as key markers for maintaining feminist objectivity (p. 583). In being explicit as to how she is using *situated* in the title of her essay, the brilliance of Haraway's argument is that partiality is not only offered in contrast to prevailing visions of objectivity that promise "a transcendence . . . of all limits and responsibility" (p. 582) but also that the particularities of knowledge production do not lie in the characteristics of individuals. Rather, knowledge production is "about communities, not about isolated individuals" (p. 590).

My understanding is that the idea of situated knowledges does not refer to what sometimes passes for "reflexivity." At times, to be reflexive, researchers note their racial/ethnic identity, sex/gender, age, class, ability (i.e., they list biographical aspects of themselves and present these aspects as essential and unchanging factors) and then move on to discuss their research as if objectivity is possible as a transcendent vision. Or they discuss the research as if it can be only the analysis of *one* individual, whose social context and intellectual biographies mean that other approaches to the issue under discussion are equally valid. I have referred to this as "absolute relativism" (Bhavnani, 1993), which Alcoff and Potter (1993) refer to as "extreme relativism." It was my discomfort with reflexivity as personal biography and with absolute relativism that led me to wonder how to work with Haraway's (1988) elements of accountability, positionality, and partiality. I asked this question: "What are the principles that flow from these elements and that, in turn, indicate the criteria according to which research can be defined as 'feminist'?"

Based on my own empirical work with working class youth in England in the mid-1980s, I suggested that Haraway's (1988) notion of being answerable for what we see—accountability—can be engaged with in empirical research through the idea of reinscription. Accountability is often discussed as accountability to an individual or to one constituency. I took the view that there are many constituencies to which all academic researchers are accountable, and a key element in feminist research is that researchers be aware of the many constituencies to which they are accountable—for example, their own institution and colleagues, colleagues within their "discipline," the idea of rigorous research, integrity, and academic freedom in research, as well as the people with whom the research is being conducted. The last constituency is a site where the feminist researcher, in order to be accountable, is publicly aware of the prevailing images of the research group and examines whether her own research reinscribes the group into dominant stereotypes. For example, if a study focuses on South Asian women and reinscribes the women simply as victims of patriarchal cultures and as people who are also sexually exotic and erotic, then that research reinscribes South Asian women into dominant representations and so may not be thought of as feminist. This is because this reinscription undermines a fundamental tenet of feminist approaches—that of *comprehending* why things are the way they are (Are the women passive in their social contexts? Are they critical of the power inequalities? How do they express agency, autonomy, and resistance?), not merely describing them in terms of essential categories. I am not, here, suggesting that feminist research adopt a romantic approach. What I am saying is that whatever the findings of an empirical study that claims feminist scholarship as its basis, the study has to be accountable to a notion of feminism that *interrogates* prevailing representations rather than simply reproducing them.

Haraway (1988) also discussed the significance of positionality for feminist objectivity. Here, she suggested that it is the researcher's knowledge of her own "limited location" that creates objectivity. In other words, knowing the limitations of one's structural position as a researcher contributes to objective research because, again, there is no "god trick" (which, she explains, is like "seeing everything from nowhere," p. 582). I took this idea and suggested that for research to be feminist, this limited location implied that the researcher analyze the micropolitics of the research situation—that is, that researchers explore, in public, what power dynamics come into play and when, how they shift, and what their consequences might be in the many different parts of their research.

Finally, Haraway (1988) argued that partiality of vision is the third element in being objective in the sense of a "particular and specific embodiment . . . [not as a] false vision promising transcendence of all limits and responsibilities" (p. 580). She urges an explicit partiality of vision not for its own sake "but for the sake of the connections and unexpected openings [that] situated knowledges make possible" (p. 590). I argued that to ensure a partiality of vision did not mean a partiality of theorizing (a caution also presented by Haraway, 1988) but that partiality of vision demands an active engagement with difference. I therefore proposed that all research examine difference within its empirical work and try to tease out some of the interconnected configurations of difference.

In rereading Haraway's work and "Tracing the Contours," I now understand that it is not only accountability, partiality, and positionality that can be translated into ideas for empirical research. If I am honest, in 1990 (when I started to write "Tracing the Contours") it was also the idea of unexpected openings and connections that resonated with me. This was a period when I was at the point of completing my book manuscript (Bhavnani, 1991) and was therefore a time when I was intellectually confident that scholarly research must (I use the imperative here with deliberation) offer innovative and dynamic ways of seeing the world. I did not, however, 10 years ago, know how to take such unexpected openings and connections further. Having taught feminist epistemologies to some wonderful classes of graduate students at the University of California at Santa Barbara since then, which inevitably have given rise to thought-provoking discussions, I am now able to grapple with the idea of contradictions, linkages, and unexpected connections and to see how interconnections and configurations are central to such work. Below, I discuss the work of a newer generation of scholars whose work *starts* with these notions in mind.

FEMINIST GLOBAL ETHNOGRAPHY:
THREE EXAMPLES

## Partial Vision: Condom Matters and Social Inequalities: Inquiries Into Commodity Production, Distribution, and Advocacy Processes

Peter Chua's (2001) multisited ethnography focuses on condoms as commodities in a global context. His work examines the production, distribution, consumption, and advocacy of condoms. His far-reaching field work, including interviews and archival analysis, was undertaken at four sites—Bangkok, Manila, Delhi, and San Francisco—and his goal was to understand how social processes in these regions both inform and influence each other and are simultaneously shaped by global and local imperatives.

Chua (2001) offered three types of conclusions from his research. First, he suggested that one could see how the production of condoms affects the lives of those who make them as well as those who do and those who do not use them. For example, one part of his dissertation follows the racial, economic, and cultural transformations in Dothan, Alabama—a southern black-white Christian town, which has two multinational condom factories and is "the condom production capital of the world." He not only examines the labor process in his analysis but also broadens it by investigating simultaneously the industrial waste created by condom manufacture, as well as the social and medical consequences of these waste products for the workers and the communities in which they live.

Chua's (2001) second main type of conclusion is in regard to the social marketing of contraceptives, condoms in particular, where he focuses on the marketing strategies developed to ensure that condoms are used. To arrive at this conclusion, he analyzed the behaviorist strategies that underlie condom education and argued that the reason such education is often unsuccessful in achieving behavioral change—a lack of success that is often puzzling for many health educators and policymakers—is that it pays little or no attention to the agency of target groups or to the fluidity of the identities of the target groups. He arrives at this conclusion through his extensive interviewing of many groups of condom users and advocates.

Chua's (2001) final conclusion interrogated how and why condoms are distributed as part of development aid through, for example, the United States Agency for International Development (USAID). In so doing, he notes that a major assumption underlying all such aid is that Third World women and *all* gay men are seen as the cause of almost all social problems that are health related. In addition, by analyzing the linkages between condom distribution and condom advocacy, Chua demonstrates how international agreements that contain clauses on condoms as aid strongly influence, and at times determine, how Third World nation-states organize their social welfare and health systems.

In sum, Chua (2001) teases out how global neoliberalism, sexualities, labor processes, privatization, ethnicity, and immigration are not merely discrete processes that shape contemporary understandings of a commodity such as the condom, but are also processes that are intimately imbricated within each other. What is so excitingly innovative about Chua's work is that he does not simply reiterate the existence of the interconnections but, rather, because of the specific focus of his study on condoms—partiality of vision—he is able to *specify* the ways in which these interconnections configure each other and, therefore, how they operate. He achieves this by drawing on comparative perspectives: not only geographically comparative but also comparative in terms of labor process analysis, critique of behavioral social marketing techniques, interviews, and institutional analysis. Because he juxtaposes and links often incommensurate sites such as condom production in Alabama and condom advocacy in Thailand, Chua offers us a window into the ways in which condoms are actually used and commodified by constituencies as seemingly disparate as USAID, advocacy groups in India, truck drivers in Zimbabwe, and the workers who make condoms in Alabama. In other words, Chua documents how a vision of one commodity, the condom, leads to views about many aspects of health around the world.

## Limited Location: Laboring Districts, Pleasuring Sites: Hospitality, "Gay" Life, and the Production of Urban Sexual Space in Manila

Dana Collins (2002) interrogates current work on sex tourism by exploring male-to-male sex tourism in her ethnography of gay men's lives in the Malate and Ermita districts in Manila, the Philippines—a research project informed by sociology, cultural studies, feminist analysis, and political economy.

In this research, Collins (2002) examined gay districts that are also tourist districts in Manila. She conducted an ethnography of gay life in Malate and Ermita, with a view to specifying the interconnections among gay life, tourism, urban space, and globalization. For this ethnography she combined sociological and anthropological methods—that is, she kept detailed and numerous field notes, "hung out" in appropriate places, and conducted formal and informal interviews, while simultaneously collecting documents from a number of sources, including the Philippine government, the Internet, and libraries, as well as a number of groups who work and reside in the two neighborhoods. Her informal and formal interviews were with gay hosts in the Malate and Ermita districts; male tourists from outside the Philippines; local activists; and the business owners who run cafes, bars, restaurants, and clubs for gay men.

From this extensive ethnographic research, Collins (2002) concluded that gay sexuality is performed differently in the Philippines compared with its performance in countries of the North and the West, and she documents these differences. However, because of her exploring many sources of data, her research was not confined to performance alone. As she noted differences in performativity, she also noted that despite the 1990s' state clampdown on "immorality" in these districts, gay bars, cafes, and clubs were thriving due to the simultaneous attempts by the Philippine state to revitalize business in Malate and Ermita. She then probed this contradiction—between a clampdown on "immorality" and the desirability of having gay businesses help develop a run-down area. She suggested that because Malate and Ermita are viewed as "open" and "Bohemian" areas of Manila—characteristics that are desirable precisely because they embrace and sidestep discussions of immorality—they form the underpinnings for commercialization and gentrification, particularly with an eye to tourist development. Thus, the categorization of a district as open and Bohemian, combined with the state's desire to revitalize entrepreneurship, has led to an increase in gay social venues. Furthermore, because Malate is a complex mixture of Spanish, North American, and Asian influences, gay life is explicitly configured by a range of racialized ethnicities that Collins makes key to her work.

In addition to looking at gay life in the context of ethnicity, commercialization, space, and globalization, Dana Collins's (2002) work also explores class relationships. She does this by comparing the clientele of two key gay bars—Piggy's (the bar that is viewed as the "hustler" bar by many) and Joy (a more subdued bar)—to see how class shapes and is shaped by the friendships that develop in these two sites. The way in which she has read the discursive patterns of behaviors in the two bars is instructive. For example, her work shows that tourist men often talk about their fear of being "ripped off" (e.g., cheated out of their money) by call boys in Piggy's and try to avoid being "taken for a ride" in this way. However, it is clear that these same men tourists do not go to other bars to distance themselves from the call boys in Piggy's, despite their stated fears. She saw this because it is the call boys in Piggy's who told her about their long-term and long-distance relationships with gay men living outside the Philippines whom the hosts had met when the men were tourists. That is, the call boys are sought out as gay hosts by tourists, despite the latter's fears of being ripped off or hustled.

This study is significant because it does not start from a heterosexual approach to sex tourism and sex work. It is doubly significant because Dana Collins (2002) examines how the structures of urban space affect the very sex work they house. In other words, the limited location of her work (Malate and Ermita in Manila) has actually permitted her to make unexpected connections and thus see how larger theoretical approaches to "gay," "place," and "space" can be reconfigured.

## Unexpected Connections: Forest Politics, Gendered Subjects: Local Knowledge and the Negotiated Meanings of Development in Rural Dominican Republic

With a theoretical emphasis on local knowledges, Light Carruyo (2002) argues that economic development strategies developed by the Dominican state and discourses of environmental conservation have focused on rescue—in this case, the rescue of the forest in the Dominican Republic from peasant subsistence practices. This is being done by the state with an eye to permitting the peasants to enter the Dominican economy as "productive citizens." From her field work—conducted in La Cienaga (a rural community located on the edge of the Armando Bermúdez National Park in the Cordillera Central), Light Carruyo shows how the state and discourses of environmental conservation have *jointly* created a category of rural citizenship—mediated through legislation, military force, and more recently, development projects—that undermines both local subsistence practices and understandings of masculinity and womanhood. Her argument is persuasively documented thorough interviews, field notes, historical and institutional analysis, and archival material, as well as through her participation in a training for ecotourism guides. Her work also innovates by laying out what might be thought of as "webs of interest" (Carruyo, personal communication, November 2005) among forest politics, tourism and nation building, and micro-enterprise to suggest how definitions of citizenship, development, and women are both created and contested in the Dominican Republic.

Carruyo (2002) began the research by studying local-level, grassroots development strategies in a small town—La Cienaga—and examining the accomplishments of the community organization

Asociación Nueva Esperanza, whose leadership is made up of poor women. She argues that notions of "progress" in La Cienaga are defined by residents through their own relationship to conservation strategies, the presence of tourists in the region, and the possibilities for setting up micro-enterprise ventures.

By analyzing her interviews in a profoundly organic manner—that is, she looked at, and specified, the words, discourses, and contexts in which the words were spoken; by whom they were spoken; and the interviewee's relationship to the issue as well as to other people in the community—Carruyo (2002) interweaves discussions of development strategies with the politics of forest conservation to demonstrate that these webs of interest are interconnected, dynamic, and configured by each other. This means that they can allow, for example, definitions of development to move away from being solely about access to cash and toward notions of development as well-being. An analysis of locally based social movements that challenge some of the tenets of globalizing processes is an important part of her work—and she grounds these discussions by critically examining what "local knowledges" might mean, in all their romantic and contradictory connotations.

Because local voices are often unexpected and complex, Carruyo (2002) demonstrates that it is necessary to specify the links between historically crafted identities and current development as they exist in the lived practices of local peoples. It then becomes possible to imagine well-being as a process that emerges from local knowledge rather than as a condition that results from rescue. Finally, she complicates her timely narrative so that what one sees is not merely a recitation of facts but an engaging analysis of how and why trees are so important in the history, present, and sociology of this country— a series of unexpected connections from which she draws some wonderful insights into the actions of the state as well as into people's lived experience of their community.

## CONCLUSION

A feminist global ethnography is now in the making. The works of the scholars above suggest the promise it holds: We can discern some of its contours through their engagement with partiality of vision, limited location, and unexpected connections—Haraway's concepts for creating objectivity without the "god trick"—as they are refracted through the lens of transnational feminisms. The rigorous and creative empirical studies of Light Carruyo (2002), Peter Chua (2001), and Dana Collins (2002) ground these ideas in lived experiences and structures of feeling, showing the affinity of global feminist ethnography with the insights of WCD. Through the interconnected configurations that help us see how inequalities are shaped and resistances are actively forged, this new ethnography offers us a glimpse into the possibilities of a world in which scholarship and people's lives speak more directly with each other.

# REFERENCES

Aggarwal, Ravina. (2000). "Point of departure": Feminist locations and the politics of travel in India. *Feminist Studies, 26*(3), 535–562.

Alcoff, Linda, & Potter, Elizabeth. (Eds.). (1993). Introduction: When feminisms intersect epistemology. In *Feminist epistemologies* (pp. 1–14). New York: Routledge.

Antrobus, Peggy. (2004). *The global women's movement: Origins, issues and strategies.* London: Zed Press.

Asad, Talal. (Ed.). (1973). *Anthropology and the colonial encounter.* New York: Humanities Press.

Behar, Ruth. (1993). *Translated woman: Crossing the border with Esperanza's story.* Boston: Beacon Press.

Beneria, Lourdes. (2003). *Gender, development and globalization: Economics as if people mattered.* New York: Routledge.

Bhavnani, Kum-Kum. (1991). *Talking politics: A psychological framing for views from youth in Britain.* Cambridge, UK: Cambridge University Press.

Bhavnani, Kum-Kum. (1993). Tracing the contours: Feminist research and feminist objectivity. *Women's Studies International Forum, 16*(2), 95–104.

Bhavnani, Kum-Kum. (1997). Women's studies and its interconnections with "race," ethnicity and sexuality. In Diane Richardson & Victoria Robinson (Eds.), *Thinking feminist* (pp. 27–48). New York: New York University Press.

Bhavnani, Kum-Kum. (2001a). *"Difference" and racism.* Paper presented at the UNRISD Conference at UNWCAR, Durban, South Africa.

Bhavnani, Kum-Kum. (Ed.). (2001b). *Feminism and "race."* Oxford, UK: Oxford University Press.

Bhavnani, Kum-Kum, & Chua, Peter. (2000). From critical psychology to critical development studies. *International Journal of Critical Psychology, 1*(1), 62–78.

Bhavnani, Kum-Kum, Foran, John, & Kurian, Priya. (2003). *Feminist futures: Re-imagining women, culture, development.* London: Zed Press.

Bhavnani, Kum-Kum, Foran, John, Kurian, Priya, & Munshi, Debashish. (Eds.). (in press). *On the edges of development: Critical interventions.* New York: Routledge.

Bhavnani, Kum-Kum, Foran, John, & Talcott, Molly. (2005). The red, the green, the black and the purple: Reclaiming development, resisting globalization. In Richard Appelbaum & William I. Robinson (Eds.), *Critical globalization studies* (pp. 323–332). New York: Routledge.

Carruyo, Light. (2002). *Forest politics, gendered subjects: Local knowledge and the negotiated meanings of development in rural Dominican Republic.* Doctoral dissertation, Department of Sociology, University of California at Santa Barbara.

Castillo, Debra A., Gomez, Maria Gudelia Rangel, & Delgado, Bonnie. (1999). Border lives: Prostitute women in Tijuana. *Signs: Journal of Women in Culture and Society, 24*(21), 387–422.

Chua, Peter. (2001). *Condom advocacy, its arguments, its organizations, and its representations: A comparative study of health promotion campaigns in Bangkok, Manila, New Delhi, and San Francisco.* Doctoral dissertation, Department of Sociology, University of California at Santa Barbara.

Chua, Peter, Bhavnani, Kum-Kum, & Foran, John. (2000). Women, culture, development: A new paradigm for development studies? *Ethnic and Racial Studies, 23*(5), 820–841.

Clifford, Jim. (1988). *The predicament of culture: Twentieth century ethnography, literature and art.* Cambridge, MA: Harvard University Press.

Code, Lorraine. (1991). *What can she know?* Ithaca, NY: Cornell University Press.

Collins, Dana. (2002). *Laboring districts, pleasuring sites: Hospitality, "gay" life, and the production of urban sexual space in Manila.* Doctoral dissertation, Department of Sociology, University of California at Santa Barbara.

Collins, Patricia Hill. (1990). *Black feminist thought: Knowledge, consciousness and the politics of empowerment.* Boston: Unwin Hyman.

Crenshaw, Kimberle. (1989). Demarginalizing the intersection of race and sex: A black feminist critique of antidiscrimination doctrine, feminist theory and antiracist politics. In University of Chicago Legal Forum (Ed.), *Feminism in the law: Theory, practice, and criticism* (pp. 139–167). Chicago: University of Chicago Law School.

duCille, Ann. (1999). Black Barbie and the deep play of difference. In Morag Schiach (Ed.), *Feminism and cultural studies* (pp. 106–132). Oxford, UK: Oxford University Press.

Enloe, Cynthia. (2004). *The curious feminist: Searching for women in a new age of empire.* Berkeley: University of California Press.

Fox Keller, Evelyn. (1996). Feminism and science. In Evelyn Fox Keller & Helen E. Longino (Eds.), *Feminism and science* (pp. 28–40). Oxford, UK: Oxford University Press.

Freeman, Carla. (2001). Is local:global as feminine:masculine? Rethinking the gender of globalization. *Signs, 26*(4), 1007–1038.

Hammonds, Evelynn. (1995). Black (w)holes and the geometry of black female sexuality. *Differences, 6*(2,3), 126–145.

Haraway, Donna. (1988). Situated knowledges: The science question in feminism and the privilege of partial perspective. *Feminist Studies, 14*(3), 575–600.

Harding, Sandra. (1991). *Whose science? Whose knowledge?* Ithaca, NY: Cornell University Press.

James, Stanlie. (1998). Shades of othering: Reflections on female circumcision/genital mutilation. *Signs: Journal of Women in Culture and Society, 23*(4), 1031–1048.

Kempadoo, Kamala. (Ed.). (1999). *Sun, sex and gold: Tourism and sex work in the Caribbean.* Lanham, MD: Rowman & Littlefield.

Lather, Patricia. (1991). *Getting smart: Feminist research and pedagogy with/in the postmodern.* New York: Routledge.

Lewis, Reina. (1996). *Gendering orientalism.* London: Routledge.

Longino, Helen. (1993). Feminist standpoint theory and the problems of knowledge. *Signs, 19*(1), 201–212.

Marcus, George E. (1998). *Ethnography through thick and thin.* Princeton, NJ: Princeton University Press.

Maynard, Mary. (1994). "Race," gender and the concept of difference in feminist thought. In Haleh Afshar & Mary Maynard (Eds.), *"Race," gender and difference in feminist thought.* London: Taylor & Francis.

Mayo, Marjorie. (2005). *Global citizens: Social movements and the challenge of globalization.* New York: Zed Books.

Moghadam, Valentine. (2005). *Globalizing woman: Transnational feminist networks.* Baltimore: Johns Hopkins University Press.

Moore, Henrietta. (1994). *A passion for difference.* Bloomington: Indiana University Press.

Narayan, Uma. (1997). *Dislocating cultures: Identities, traditions and Third World feminism.* New York: Routledge.

Nicholson, Linda. (1994). Interpreting gender. *Signs, 20*(1), 79–105.

Nnaemeka, Obioma. (2001). If female circumcision did not exist, Western feminism would invent it. In Susan Perry & Celeste Schenk (Eds.), *Eye to eye: Women practicing development across cultures* (pp. 171–189). New York: Zed Books.

Pajaczkowska, Clare, & Young, Lola. (2000). Racism, representation and psychoanalysis. In E. Ann Kaplan (Ed.), *Feminism and film* (pp. 356–374). Oxford, UK: Oxford University Press.

Peterson, V. Spike. (2003). *A critical rewriting of global political economy.* London: Routledge.

Puar, Jasbir. (1998). Transnational sexualities: South Asian (trans)nation(alism)s and queer diasporas. In David L. Eng & Alice Y. Hom (Eds.), *Queer in Asian America* (pp. 405–422). Philadelphia: Temple University Press.

Puri, Jyoti. (2002). Concerning *Kamasutras*: Challenging narratives of history and sexuality. *Signs: Journal of Women in Culture and Society, 27*(3), 603–639.

Reinharz, Shulamit. (1992). *Feminist methods in social research.* New York: Oxford University Press.

Robertson, Jennifer. (2000). Dying to tell: Sexuality and suicide in imperial Japan. In Cindy Patton & Benigno Sanchez-Eppler (Eds.), *Queer diasporas* (pp. 38–70). Durham, NC: Duke University Press.

Rose, Gillian. (1997). Performing inoperative community: The space and the resistance of some community arts projects. In Steve Pile & Michael Keith (Eds.), *Geographies of resistance* (pp. 184–202). London: Routledge.

Skeggs, Beverley. (1994). Situating the production of feminist ethnography. In Mary Maynard & June Purvis (Eds.), *Researching women's lives from a feminist perspective*. London: Taylor & Francis.

Smith, Andrea. (2002). Better dead than pregnant: The colonization of native women's reproductive health. In Jael Silliman & Annanya Bhattacharjee (Eds.), *Policing the national body: Race, gender and criminalization* (pp. 123–146). Cambridge, MA: South End Press.

Smith, Dorothy, E. (1990). *Texts, facts and femininity: Exploring the relations of ruling*. London: Routledge.

Spelman, Elizabeth V. (1997). *Fruits of sorrow*. Boston: Beacon Press.

Stacey, Judith. (1988). Can there be a feminist ethnography? *Women's Studies International Forum, 11*(1), 21–27.

Stanley, Liz, & Wise, Sue. (1990). Method, methodology, and epistemology in feminist research processes. In Liz Stanley (Ed.), *Feminist praxis: Research, theory and epistemology in feminist sociology* (pp. 20–60). London: Routledge.

Trujillo, Carla. (1991). *Chicana lesbians: The girls our mothers warned us about*. Berkeley, CA: Third Woman Press.

Twine, France Winddance, & Warren, Jonathan. (Eds.). (2000). *Race-ing research: Methodological and ethical dilemmas in critical race studies*. London: Routledge.

Wolf, Diane L. (Ed.). (1996). Situating feminist dilemmas in fieldwork. In *Feminist dilemmas in fieldwork* (pp. 1–55). Boulder, CO: Westview Press.

# 38

## FEMINIZING GLOBAL RESEARCH/GLOBALIZING FEMINIST RESEARCH

### Methods and Practice Under Globalization

JENNIFER BICKHAM MENDEZ
DIANE L. WOLF

I ncreased awareness of globalization has prompted a critical reevaluation of notions of place, community, and "the local." The study of global processes has altered feminist thinking, creating a new wave of scholarship that enriches our theoretical, analytical, and empirical understandings of the interactions between global structures and gendered practices. Feminists have explored and raised questions about global economic, social, and cultural impacts on women in different localities, by race and ethnicity, and what globalization has meant for gendered ideologies, practices, and political organizing. Despite these important efforts, we have not seen a parallel rethinking of feminist methods in a globalized political economy.

The gendered dimensions of globalization compel us to reconsider some of the main issues in feminist methods and research. Recent scholarship and our own research demonstrate how globalization may offer possibilities for expanding and reconceptualizing feminist research projects. For example, transnational collaborations,

coalitions, and alliances among organizations and researchers offer new sites of intervention and possibilities for collaboration for feminist researchers.

In this chapter, we envisage how a more global approach can inform and affect feminist methods and praxis by taking up the following questions: How does globalization affect the contradictions, dilemmas, and possibilities of feminist research practices? What does this imply for future research? How might we conceptualize new modes of praxis for future scholars?

Our own backgrounds situate our approach, and our particular sensibilities and feminist politics have compelled us to consider critically feminist research methods as well as issues related to epistemology and positionality in our work on globalized transformations. A generation of feminist theory has shown that there is no singular feminism, but a multitude of ways to be and act feminist. This insight as well as our own experiences as feminists "in the field" lead us to see the development of globalized feminist research methods as a continually evolving "strategy" that involves balancing a series of issues related to accountability, feminist principles, and disciplinary research practices (DeVault, 2004, p. 227).

In our discussion of the implications of globalization for feminist research, we maintain that a conceptualization of power as a zero-sum game in which research by First World feminists *always* victimizes Third World respondents is not useful. Rather, we envisage power as multisited, ever-shifting, and "situated and contextualized within particular intersubjective relationships" (Bloom, 1998, p. 35). Such a conceptualization moves us away from a unidirectional view of power and assumptions that seriously underestimate Third World peoples' resistance capabilities and also present First World feminist researchers as an undifferentiated category (Blacklock & Crosby, 2004, p. 57). Thus, global feminist research practices must include a recognition not only of how research relations are constituted within particular structures that constrain and dominate, but also that participants are not merely the "objects" of research but also subjects who exert some level of control over the research encounter (Kondo, 1986, p. 80).

In our view, cooperative attempts at seeking and obtaining more input from those being researched and endeavoring to establish non-hierarchical relationships between researcher and researched, while important to pursue, on their own cannot change broader power relations. Neither can consciousness-raising be the sole strategy for feminist research to become feminist praxis. Just as there are multiple feminisms, globalized feminist research methods must take multiple forms if they are to be effective tools for generating knowledge and contributing to social transformation (Lather, 1991).

We argue that designing and implementing globalized feminist research must involve a strategic awareness of the contradictions and problems embedded in research relationships and how power under globalization may affect them. Researchers must devise feminist research practices with constant attention paid to the ways in which global processes interact with local ones in a given political and historical conjuncture—how local settings shape the dynamics of global processes "on the ground."

In our final section, we highlight sophisticated research that has contributed to the field both as models of what we consider exemplary global feminist scholarship and as springboards for future endeavors.

## GLOBALIZATION'S CHALLENGE TO RESEARCH METHODS

For the sake of conceptual clarity, in this chapter globalization refers to the historical, economic, social, and cultural processes through which individuals, groups, and institutions are increasingly interconnected on a worldwide scale. Thus, the scope of global processes reaches (or nearly reaches) the entire globe largely without reference to specific national territories or localities, and global flows are to a great extent without boundaries (Glick Schiller, 1999).

Globalization disrupts underlying assumptions of what constitutes a society, traditionally defined as the confines of a nation-state, and destabilizes embedded notions of "place" and "community." Thus, globalization calls into question the primary subject of analysis of social science, and in so doing challenges researchers to reconfigure their units of analysis for scholarly inquiry and rethink methodologies (Albrow, 1997; Gille & Riain, 2002; Marcus, 1995).

Some theorists of globalization have focused attention on the interconnections and interplay between the global and the local or national (Guidry, Kennedy, & Zald, 2000; Sassen, 2001). Increasingly, global connections, the products or flows of people, ideas, and things, have become the subject of ethnographic investigation (see Burawoy et al., 2000; Freeman, 2000). Calling attention to the ways in which global processes are localized, transnational studies ground the abstract and general notion of globalization and center analysis on the ways in which everyday people react to, engage with, and even re-create and influence global processes (Basch, Glick Schiller, & Blanc, 1994; Glick Schiller, 1999; Smith & Guarnizo, 1998).

Gender has clearly been and continues to be an integral part of globalization; globalization is gendered and gender ideologies are globalized. Such ideologies and gendered power structures that devalue women and their work make up a kind of foundation on which the global economy rests. Women constitute the bulk of cheap labor that continues to serve transnational capital, which seeks a young and "docile" labor force. Under the global hegemony of neoliberalism, women have increasingly taken on breadwinner roles in ways that both draw on and undermine traditional gender roles (Peterson & Runyan, 1999, pp. 130–147). Furthermore, in the current global context, women make up a large proportion of migrants, setting up transnational families, and leaving their children behind to work abroad and send remittances home (Parreñas, 2001). Care work has also gone transnational, and women from poorer countries leave home and families to care for children or the elderly in wealthier countries (Hondagneu-Sotelo, 2001); indeed, in Israel the term *Filipina* is synonymous with a caregiver, usually for the elderly.

## FEMINIST RESEARCH METHODS

Power issues within the research process are closely linked to epistemological understandings of how knowledge is generated, which in turn are tied to methodological perspectives and the politics of representation (Hesse-Biber & Leckenby, 2004, pp. 209–210; Naples, 2003, pp. 4–5). Feminist researchers engage with these issues by directly confronting the ways in which power shapes the research process. In endeavoring to construct projects "by, for and about women," they have struggled to develop research methods that challenge and break down "the dualities between 'theory' and 'praxis,' researcher and researched, subject and object" (Richardson, 1997, p. 55). Some feminist researchers approach their methods and resultant research relations as feminist practice in and of itself with the potential to promote respondents' gaining a deeper understanding of their situations through self-reflection that might lead to their seeking change in their lives—that is, consciousness-raising.

By challenging assumptions about knowledge production and raising questions about the purpose of research and whose voices are privileged in the production of scholarship, feminist writings have undoubtedly opened important dialogues. Feminist researchers have used reflective strategies to promote awareness of and minimize the ways in which hierarchies of power and domination are reproduced through the course of research, but it is less clear whether they have succeeded in designing research methodologies that overcome the contradictions that stem from race, class, nationality, and other differences within their projects. Scholars continue to address this Achilles' heel in feminist research by striving to develop research practices that reflect feminist principles.

## GLOBALIZING FEMINIST RESEARCH, FEMINIZING ACTION RESEARCH

*Action research* represents a rather misleading, general rubric that refers to a broad and messy array of disciplinary approaches, schools of thought, and methodological practices—sometimes known as "activist," "participatory," or "community-based" research. The unifying goal of this type of work, however, is a reconfiguration of knowledge production, so as to shift power and control into the hands of the poor, oppressed, or marginalized, thereby creating a space for the expression of "subjugated knowledges" (Collins, 1990) and in so doing transform oppressive social structures (Fals-Borda, 1991; Maguire, 1987; Park, 1993; Park, Brydon-Miller, Hall, & Jackson, 1993; Stoecker, 1999).

Although feminist and action research both seek to expose the myth of value-free knowledge production through the pursuit of positive social change, the literatures on and practices of action research have not always included women, gender issues, or feminist orientations (Maguire, 1996, 2001). As Maguire so astutely points out, feminist perspectives are in fact integral to action research in that they highlight not just the power in the social construction of knowledge, but the ways in which power is multifaceted and intersectional, shaped by race, class, gender, and other dimensions. Feminism(s) have called attention not only to whose voices are missing or marginalized from knowledge production but how categories like "community," "the oppressed," or "the poor" might obfuscate differences of power and perspective.

Feminist advocates for action research argue for incorporating (multiple) feminist perspectives—including the second-wave feminist principle that the personal is political—into research models, raising questions about who exactly in the community is empowered by action research (Maguire, 1996, p. 111; Naples, 2003). Researchers place emphasis on the *process* of collective endeavors as empowering and more than simply a means to an end. As Hesse-Biber and Leckenby (2004) point out, "this positions feminist research at the crossroads of intellectual endeavors within a community of academics and social change endeavors within a community of activists" (p. 223).

Both feminist critics and globalization theorists have challenged notions of bounded, homogeneous "local" communities (see Burawoy, 2000; Maguire, 2001). Globalization's disruption of simplistic notions of community "belonging" adds new dimensions to power issues confronted by activist researchers, such as the multiple power differentials that crosscut organizations and communities and the consequences of research in communities to which one belongs as opposed to those in which the researcher is a "foreigner" or outsider. For example, economic globalization has resulted in a process of "Third-Worlding" of urban and even suburban areas in the United States and Europe. Thus, the "Third World" becomes a process, not a fixed, geographical location. Corporations can outsource jobs to "Third World" locations to reduce labor costs, or in the case of industries such as meatpacking and the hotel industry in the United States they can "import" Third World workers and work conditions.

Thus, under globalization geography becomes disassociated from community "belonging." This disassociation also has implications for qualitative feminist methodologies because it highlights what feminist researchers have already called attention to—the limits of a bipolar construction of insider/outsider. As Naples (2004) points out, "insiderness and outsiderness are not fixed or static positions, rather, they are ever-shifting and permeable social locations that are differentially experienced and expressed by community members" (p. 373). Thus, the ethnographer continually negotiates and renegotiates her insiderness and outsiderness within a context of interacting and shifting power relations.

In an era of globalization these interactions become complex and entail transnational dimensions and contextual definitions of "belonging." In Jennifer's current research with Latino/a migrants in Williamsburg, Virginia, home of Colonial Williamsburg, in which she works in collaboration with a community organization that provides support services to low-income families, she has had to negotiate her insiderness and outsiderness in surprising ways. Class and racial differences clearly divide her from the immigrant women who have participated in her study. But commonalities and connections have arisen in ways that reflect the particularities of transnational processes in Williamsburg, a historically monolingual community in which Latinos are newcomers and "race" has historically meant "black or white." Jennifer's position as a mother with young children whose father is Central American, her language abilities in Spanish, and her familiarity with Mexican and Central American culture has shaped her relations with the participants in this community-based research project in ways that at times differentiate her as a cultural "insider" as contrasted with the professional staff from the nonprofit organization who work with these Latina mothers on a regular basis but who do not speak Spanish.

## SPACES FOR GLOBALIZED FEMINIST RESEARCH

The uneven expansion of global capitalism has brought with it new contradictions and interactions among capitalist, nationalist/racist, and patriarchal systems of domination, reconfiguring preexisting power structures and giving rise to new dimensions and scales of power. And yet globalization also has brought about some new and exciting possibilities for unsettling systems of domination, including "cross-race and cross-national projects, feminist movements, anticolonial struggles and politicized cultural practices" (Lowe & Lloyd, 1997, p. 25). Global forces have sparked the growth of increasingly transnational public spheres (Guidry et al., 2000).

The explosion of nongovernmental organizations (NGOs) onto the political stage represents an important element of this process. Reflecting what has become a globalized civil society, these increasingly active groups have undertaken a wide array of social, political, and even economic functions. Indeed, NGOs are significant actors in transnational politics and have successfully deployed transnational strategies to gain influence in national as well as international political circles.

Globalization has given rise to shifts in relations between civil societies and nation-states. States have experienced a decrease in some aspects of their sovereignty and have increasingly eschewed welfare functions. Despite these changes, nation-states remain extremely powerful regulators and continue to exert a great deal of control over their national populations. The way in which they do so, however, has been affected by the emergence of a more universalized set of international norms and rules. Based on liberalism and a notion of individual bearers of unalienable rights, these norms have transformed the sphere of international political activity. In addition, the globalized discourse of human rights has become a crucial idiom for disenfranchised groups as they frame their claims and demands. While this language of rights—be they civil or human—converges with the discursive frameworks of neoliberal state regimes and multilateral donor organizations, the language holds radically different meanings for social movements that posit alternative conceptions of citizenship, even as they use the same language as state actors (Schild, 1998).

Globalized norms and discourses surrounding conceptions of rights and citizenship have been important tools for women's transnational political networks (Keck & Sikkink, 1998). The strategies and collaborations of groups within such alliances have been facilitated by the emergence of telecommunications technologies and the dramatic decrease of transportation costs, both of which have stimulated the circulation of ideas, discourses, resources, and people across national, regional, and international sites (Appadurai, 1996). Wielding information as an instrument of power, social movement organizations use diffuse, transnational links with organizations in other national contexts (often using e-mail and the Internet) to transmit information and reach other national or transnational public spheres and "foreign reference publics" (Keck & Sikkink, 1998). The practices involved in such politics include negotiation, lobbying, and media campaigns with the goal of exerting impact through persuasion and changing perceptions and values by challenging the meaning of democracy under global capitalism (Schild, 1998).

Information plays a major role in the coalitions of the transnational feminist/women's movement. Feminist discourses and ideas about feminist politics have circulated within an increasingly globalized sphere, and transnational linkages among feminists have become increasingly important and more easily facilitated under globalization. Transnational linkages and regional and "world" conferences have resulted in what Alvarez (1998) calls "the multiplication . . . of the spaces and places in which women who call themselves feminists act" (p. 294). The transnational feminist movement, then, also becomes a logical space for globalized feminist research to contribute to social justice projects.

As Keck and Sikkink (1998, p. 16) point out, through transnational advocacy campaigns NGOs gain influence by serving as alternative sources of information, but to achieve leverage the information produced must be reliable and well documented. Thus, there is an increasing need for NGOs and social justice organizations to know how to gather and effectively "package" information to access national and transnational public spheres. In a context of the rolled-back welfare state and the hegemony of neoliberal political and economic policies that privilege the private sector, then, the "NGOization" of women's movements has been accompanied by increased import placed on research "from below." And more and more NGOs have research wings or have taken on research as a major facet of their work, creating potentially important spaces for feminist, global research (Gaventa, 1993, pp. 31–32; Harper, 2001).

Charting the complex interactions of institutional power at the transnational, national, and local levels could be an important contribution of feminist research, which could serve resistance efforts through the identification of multiple sites of intervention and the development of strategies (Marchand & Runyan, 2000a). Raising the awareness of policymakers about the gendered aspects of the global economy is another area of activism to which feminist research can contribute. As Marchand and

Runyan (2000b) point out, there has been a recent shift in the balance of power within states and multilateral organizations to ministries of finance and economic affairs. Such institutional spaces are dominated by the view that "gender issues, finance and the global economy are totally unrelated" (p. 20).

Economic globalization produces problems that manifest themselves in intensely local forms but have implications that are anything but local and which are not always readily observable to people on the ground. Feminist researchers could support locally engaged political actors in placing their local experiences into a global framework. During Jennifer's field research in Nicaragua she found organizers of maquila workers wanting to understand better global connections between the work conditions and experiences of women in maquilas located in Nicaragua and those in other contexts (see Mendez, 2005). In the words of one organizer, "we all have to be political economists now." The antisweatshop movement has highlighted the radical democratic potential of workers' and community members' linking "local" issues, such as work conditions within a factory, to a picture of worker vulnerability and and flexible capitalist production. By integrating local workplace grievances within a global framework of resistance, networks such as Coalition for Justice in the Maquilas can function "like a transnational counter-public with cosmopolitan citizens and trans-cultural values" (Bandy, 2004).

Such efforts to create a "culture of solidarity" (Fantasia, 1988) also serve a counterhegemonic purpose of creating alternatives for resistance and opposition to the dominant neoliberal paradigm. Further, coalitions like the Network of Central American Women in Solidarity with Maquila Workers illustrate that the culture of solidarity that results from placing local stories within a global framework creates a space for dialogue and exchange and makes possible difficult coalitions across barriers of national origin, race, gender, and class (Bandy & Mendez, 2003).

Spaces that permit and foster solidarity and exchange in which groups and individuals link local issues, grievances, and even identities to an understanding of global processes become fertile ground for the creation of counter-hegemonies. This practice mirrors feminist consciousness-raising—linking personal transformation to broader issues of gender inequalities. Making explicit global/local connections in women's lives "allows for the subversive possibility of women seeing beyond the local to the global" (Eisenstein, 1997, p. 147). Likewise, as Eschle (2001, p. 96) points out, such strategies are predicated on the feminist notion that the means and ends of struggle are interrelated.

Globalization also holds important implications for constructing a "politics of accountability with those with whom we work" (Blacklock & Crosby, 2004, p. 69). The increase and intensification of global communications and travel mean that research respondents increasingly have access to and entrées into the worlds of feminist researchers. In the words of Thayer (2004, p. 1), "We can no longer write with impunity." Indeed, in a context of intensified transnational links among women's organizations and the reliance of groups in the South on funding and support from NGOs in the North, women in the South rightly perceive the stakes of control over representations of themselves and their work in the research of First World academics as increasingly high, given the potential to jeopardize relationships with potential donors (Thayer, 2004; see also Mendez, 2005). And consequently, organizers in the South may actively seek to limit the most well-meaning researcher's access to information or activities, as they recognize that they have little control over how the information may be used or presented once it reaches a transnational public sphere.

For the "global ethnographer" (Burawoy, 2000), "the field" becomes an ever more politicized arena, and departure from her geographical "field site" does little to extract her from the political implications of her research or engagements with the political issues that she analyzes. In the case of transnational, feminist activist projects, academics are not the only ones who travel within transnational circuits. And researchers may unexpectedly come into contact with "respondents" at conferences or in other forums. Respondents are more likely than before to read our writings or at least hear about something that we communicated in a public forum due to transnational social and activist networks.

In some ways globalization and transnational communications and networks enforce accountability, making researchers more aware than ever of the political implications of their research. This is especially the case for feminist activist/researchers who collaborate with and study women's movements. In these cases transnational communications and activism have given a voice to feminist activists in the South who can engage in dialogue with the researcher about the findings of the research as well as its political implications, which clearly represents a positive step toward more accountability and equality within research relationships. At the same time, such enforced accountability also opens up new dilemmas and questions. Feminist activist researchers who work with transnational feminist struggles must decide what to do when their analytical interpretations do not match those of their respondents or when participants disagree with researchers' findings. In some cases negotiations about access or publications might be crystal clear, but in others the waters are muddier. At best researchers run the risk of committing political faux pas. At worst researchers could unintentionally damage an organization's chances at securing funding or even undermine the political strategy of a movement.

## GLOBAL FEMINIST RESEARCH

Much of the feminist research related to globalization focuses on emergent configurations of work and gender and the ideologies that develop alongside these changes. The best examples of scholarship in this area reflect a deep understanding of these shifting and often contradictory ideologies and how they play out in the daily lives and practices of those involved (Lee, 2000; Freeman, 2000). Still, the global assembly line remains a vivid site for feminist research (Collins, 2003; Mendez, 2005; Salzinger, 2002), and the so-called sweatshop issue is a compelling one for transnational political activism. The issues seem straightforward and easily bifurcated into what's right—better wages and work conditions for workers producing brand-name apparel—and what's wrong—purchasing goods that workers produce under poor work conditions while receiving "sweatshop" wages.

However, feminist research has also uncovered how important these jobs are for women despite low and exploitative wages. In some cases women's incorporation into the labor force, a process facilitated by the globalization of the economy, has empowered them economically and has even provided them with "the means to generate solidarity across class and gender lines" (Giles & Hyndman, 2004, p. 303). Given other available alternatives in the labor market, for women workers who are the only breadwinners in their large families the maquila industry often presents them with the best survival strategy. Boycotts by well-meaning students and labor organizers in the North could end up hurting the very workers they are trying to help by contributing to factory closures and moves to ever cheaper locales. As Kabeer (2004) notes, boycotting campaigns are "blunt instruments" that leave little room for "nuanced, balanced and differentiated accounts of ground-level realities in low-income countries" (p. 179).

Thus, this kind of earnest activism is not risky for U.S. university student-activists, but the possible and unexpected deleterious effects on women workers need to be acknowledged. The antisweatshop movement cannot ignore the fact that the majority of workers in free trade zones are, in fact, brown, black, or Asian women whose gendered responsibilities as caretakers of the home contribute to their facing the harsh reality of having to choose between the opportunity to work and the struggle to improve work conditions (Kabeer, 2004, p. 187).

Although women in Southeast and East Asia have been prominent in research on factory labor as well as the sex trade, another area has brought the effects of globalization into focus—that of the export of women for marriage and for domestic work. The globalized marriage market (Constable, 2003) draws from women in China, the Philippines, and elsewhere such as the former Soviet Union to fulfill Western ideologies of romance as well as a traditional sexual division of labor. Tens of thousands of Filipina women (Constable, 1997; Parreñas, 2001) constitute an extremely lucrative state export for yet another niche and are in demand as servants in many advanced industrial economies around the globe. Up until now, Hong Kong, Italy, and the United States have been studied, but important sites such as Taiwan, Japan, Israel, and other countries in the Middle East have not yet been mined.[1] It would be extremely useful to understand the interactions between Filipina domestics and different state-society configurations.

Women laboring in sex work, factories, and domestic service or doing emotional labor is perhaps the main focus thus far of the majority of research in the field of gender and globalization; however, the realm of consumption begs attention. Bonnie Adrian's (2003) *Framing the Bride* focuses on the particularly excessive consumption of highly artificial bridal photographs in Taiwan's bridal industry based on globalized images of beauty. A focus on global consumption practices in traditionally female arenas such as weddings, birthing, and motherhood represent opportunities for further feminist theorizing on globalized gender ideologies as well as the body.

Gender and nationalism, war, and the military have been a focus of feminist scholarship in years past, but since 9/11 and the global upheaval created by the so-called war on terrorism, these topics merit yet another look through feminist lenses, particularly in regard to the Middle East, to further our understanding of international politics, neocolonialism, and the militaristic turn (Lentin, 2000). A focus on gender and war has zeroed in on (1) women as warriors and soldiers, (2) women's bodies as the site of war-making, and (3) the effects of war and genocide on women and their families (Sancho, 1997). The current war in Iraq, especially the sexual abuse of male prisoners at Abu Ghraib, invites a feminist analysis of this particular mélange of power, sexualities, gender and the body, and imperialism.[2] The topic of gender and war and/or genocide in sites such as Bosnia-Herzegovina (Boric, 1997), Rwanda, Sudan, Palestine, and elsewhere deserve more attention and should rank high on the feminist agenda. A focus on war and genocide leads to other topics such as immigration, flight, displacement, asylum, and the plight of refugees in camps and in exile. Again, feminists have turned their lens to this topic with regard to refugees (Julian, 1997) and refugee camps (Hans, 2004; Hyndman, 2004), but this topic has not been fully explored yet. Indeed, the gendered aspects of exile, memory, and diasporas have not been mined in the literatures on these topics. One exception is a recent emergence of writings by Iranian women in exile such as Marjane Satrapi's (2003, 2004) series *Persepolis I and II*, or Azar Nafisi's (2003) *Reading Lolita in Tehran*, welcomed contributions that can and should be connected to scholarly works on gender, nationalism, and exile.

## Conclusion

> What is a feminist ethnography? . . . Perhaps the best way to describe a feminist ethnography is to define what it is not. A feminist ethnography is not certain, institutional, unchallenged, contained, uncomplicated or value-free. It does not "give voice" but hopefully opens up spaces for the contestation of oppositionally defined identities and how voices are not only represented but accessed and interpreted. (Tracy Smith, UC Davis, June 15, 2004, in her final paper for a seminar on Gender and Globalization)

What do we tell our feminist students, neophyte researchers who want to venture into a world that is much more complicated and contradictory than ever before and clearly more challenging to those with a critical and feminist approach? The demands on feminist researchers to be ever-conscious about their self-presentation, their interrelations, the possibility of exploitation, power, and accountability may be overwhelming. We would stress the following: First, process is as important as results, and the search for a "pure" feminist methodology with "absolute" transformative potential is a fruitless one. Researchers should approach the design of feminist methods as neither theory nor practice, but a strategy constructed out of political engagement within global and grounded, local contexts. If we choose to design and implement methods that involve collaborations with community organizations, then we must do so strategically with an awareness of the contradictions and problems embedded in these relationships, and we must do so guided by a set of principles established through dialogue and exchange with our collaborators. We should avoid the trap of an idealized notion of "grassroots" communities as homogeneous entities free from power differentials and detached from a global context. Researchers should endeavor to engage in dialogue about research as part of a grounded, political strategy that includes mechanisms for researcher accountability to those studied.

Second, although some may feel intimidated by all the "demands" of global feminist research outlined in this chapter, it is also important to remember that this is a new frontier for feminists engaged in global research with more possibilities than ever before. There is perhaps more room for yet unimagined global linkages and connections as well as for creative interweavings of resources, organizations, strategies, and perspectives. Feminist theory and scholarship give us tools to confront different, ever-shifting situations while engaged in global feminist research. We must use our critical faculties to recognize power in its multiple forms, not just as an "external" force present in global capitalism, but also as constituted within intersubjective relations and microlevel dynamics, that involve the specific ways in which global and local power structures interact.

In the tradition of feminism we must endeavor to connect theory and practice by applying our theoretical findings about the way that power works to situational analyses to engage in dialogue with our respondents about their perspectives and to build strategies for social change. By connecting feminist insights about multiple ways to be and act feminist with what we know about how global processes and the gendered experiences of men and women are lived on the ground, we can confront the challenges that will emerge in the field. We cannot expect to know how to "do feminism," or for that matter "feminist research," as disconnected from grounded situations. But we can build on the work of those who came before us and be open to dialogue and future imaginings of what feminist research could look like were it to embody feminist principles within a context of globalization.

## NOTES

1. Most Filipinas who emigrated to the United States after 1965 were educated professionals and did not become domestic servants; thus the United States is most likely not the most profitable research site for this focus.

2. Though not a specifically feminist analysis, Lisa Hajjar's (2005) penetrating ethnography of

Israeli military courts deals almost entirely with males—both as Israeli soldiers and as Palestinian prisoners. Applying Lentin's more critical feminist and postcolonialist analysis to Hajjar's data and topic would be but a small step.

## REFERENCES

Adrian, Bonnie. (2003). *Framing the bride*. Berkeley: University of California Press.

Albrow, Martin. (1997). *The global age: State and society beyond modernity*. Stanford, CA: Stanford University Press.

Alvarez, Sonia. (1998). Latin American feminisms "go global": Trends of the 1990s and challenges for the new millenium. In Sonia E. Alvarez, Evelina Dagnino, & Arturo Escobar (Eds.), *Culture of politics/politics of cultures: Revisioning Latin American social movements* (pp. 293–324). Boulder, CO: Westview Press.

Appadurai, Arjun. (1996). *Modernity at large: Cultural dimensions of globalization*. Minneapolis: University of Minnesota Press.

Bandy, Joe. (2004). Paradoxes of transnational civil society: The coalition for justice in the maquiladoras and the challenges of coalition. *Social Problems, 51*(3).

Bandy, Joe, & Mendez, Jennifer Bickham. (2003). A place of their own? Women organizers negotiating the local and transnational in Nicaragua and Northern Mexico. *Mobilization, 8*(2), 173–188.

Basch, Linda, Glick Schiller, Nina, & Blanc, Cristina Szanton. (Eds.). (1994). *Nations unbound: Transnational projects, postcolonial predicaments and deterritorialized nation-states*. Langhorne, PA: Gordon & Breach.

Blacklock, Cathy, & Crosby, Alison. (2004). The sounds of silence: Feminist research across time in Guatemala. In Wenona Giles & Jennifer Hyndman (Eds.), *Sites of violence: Gender and conflict zones* (pp. 45–72). Los Angeles: University of California Press.

Bloom, L. R. (1998). *Under the sign of hope: Feminist methodology and narrative interpretation*. Albany: State University of New York Press.

Boric, Rada. (1997). Against the war: Women organizing across the divide in the countries of the former Yugoslavia. In Ronit Lentin (Ed.), *Gender and catastrophe* (pp. 165–182). London: Palgrave & Macmillan.

Burawoy, Michael. (2000). Introduction: Reaching for the global. In Michael Burawoy, Joseph A. Blum, Sheba George, Zsuzsa Gille, Teresa Gowan, Lynne Haney, et al., *Global ethnography: Forces, connections, and imaginations in a postmodern world* (pp. 1–40). Berkeley: University of California Press.

Burawoy, Michael, Blum, Joseph A., George, Sheba, Gille, Zsuzsa, Gowan, Teresa, Haney, Lynne, et al. (2000). *Global ethnography: Forces, connections, and imaginations in a postmodern world.* Berkeley: University of California Press.

Collins, Jane L. (2003). *Threads: Gender, labor, and power in the global apparel industry.* Chicago: University of Chicago Press.

Collins, Patricia Hill. (1990). *Black feminist thought.* London: HarperCollins Academic.

Constable, Nicole. (1997). *Maid to order in Hong Kong: Stories of Filipina workers.* Ithaca, NY: Cornell University Press.

Constable, Nicole. (2003). *Romance on a global stage.* Berkeley: University of California Press.

DeVault, Marjorie L. (2004). Talking and listening from women's standpoint: Feminist strategies for interviewing and analysis. In Sharlene Nagy Hesse-Biber & Michelle L. Yaiser (Eds.), *Feminist perspectives on social research* (pp. 227–250). New York: Oxford University Press.

Eisenstein, Zillah. (1997). Women's publics and the search for new democracies. *Feminist Review, 57,* 140–167.

Eschle, Catherine. (2001). *Global democracy, social movements, and feminism.* Boulder, CO: Westview Press.

Fals-Borda, Orlando. (1991). Some basic ingredients. In Orlando Fals-Borda & Mohammad Anisur Rahman (Eds.), *Action and knowledge: Breaking the monopoly with participatory action-research* (pp. 3–12). New York: Apex Press.

Fantasia, Richard. (1988). *Cultures of solidarity: Consciousness, action, and contemporary American workers.* Berkeley: University of California Press.

Freeman, Carla. (2000). *High tech and high heels in the global economy: Women, work and pink-collar identities in the Caribbean.* Durham, NC: Duke University Press.

Gaventa, John. (1993). The powerful, the powerless and the experts: Knowledge struggle in an information age. In Peter Park, Mary Brydon-Miller, Budd Hall, & Ted Jackson (Eds.), *Voices of change: Participatory research in the United States and Canada* (pp. 21–40). Westport, CT: Bergin & Garvey.

Giles, Wenona, & Hyndman, Jennifer. (2004). New directions for feminist research and politics. In Wenona Giles & Jennifer Hyndman (Eds.), *Sites of violence: Gender and conflict zones* (pp. 301–316). Berkeley: University of California Press.

Gille, Zsuzsa, & Riain, Sean Ó. (2002). Global ethnography. *Annual Review of Sociology, 28,* 271–295.

Glick Schiller, Nina. (1999). Transmigrants and nation-states: Something old and something new in the U.S. immigrant experience. In Charles Hirschman, Philip Kasinitz, & Josh Dewind (Eds.), *The handbook of international migration: The American experience* (pp. 94–119). New York: Russell Sage.

Guidry, John A., Kennedy, Michael D., & Zald, Mayer N. (2000). Globalizations and social movements. In John A. Guidry, Michael D. Kennedy, & Mayer N. Zald (Eds.), *Globalizations and social movements: Culture, power, and the transnational public sphere* (pp. 1–32). Ann Arbor: University of Michigan Press.

Hajjar, Lisa. (2005). *Courting conflict: The Israeli military court system in the West Bank and Gaza.* Berkeley: University of California Press.

Hans, Asha. (2004). Escaping conflict: Afghan women in transit. In Wenona Giles & Jennifer Hyndman (Eds.), *Sites of violence: Gender and conflict zones* (pp. 232–248). Berkeley: University of California Press.

Harper, Caroline. (2001). Do the facts matter? NGOs, research and international advocacy. In Michael Edward & John Gaventa (Eds.), *Global citizen action* (pp. 247–258). Boulder, CO: Lynne Rienner Press.

Hesse-Biber, Sharlene Nagy, & Leckenby, Denise. (2004). How feminists practice social research. In Sharlene Nagy Hesse-Biber & Michelle L. Yaiser (Eds.), *Feminist perspectives on social research* (pp. 209–226). New York: Oxford University Press.

Hondagneu-Sotelo, Pierrette. (2001). *Doméstica: Immigrant workers cleaning and caring in the shadows of affluence.* Berkeley: University of California Press.

Hyndman, Jennifer. (2004). Refugee camps as conflict zones: The politics of gender. In Wenona Giles & Jennifer Hyndman (Eds.), *Sites of violence: Gender and conflict zones* (pp. 193–212). Berkeley: University of California Press.

Julian, Roberta. (1997). Invisible subjects and the victimized self: Settlement experiences of refugee women in Australia. In Ronit Lentin (Ed.), *Gender and catastrophe* (pp. 193–216). London: Palgrave & Macmillan.

Kabeer, Nalia. (2004). Labor standards, women's rights, basic needs: Challenges to collective action in a globalizing world. In Lourdes Benería & Savitri Bisnath (Eds.), *Global tensions: Challenges and opportunities in the world economy* (pp. 173–192). New York: Routledge.

Keck, Margaret, & Sikkink, Kathryn. (1998). *Activists beyond borders: Transnational advocacy networks in international politics.* Ithaca, NY: Cornell University Press.

Kondo, Dorinne K. (1986). Dissolution and reconstitution of self: Implications for anthropological epistemology. *Cultural Anthropology, 1*(1), 74–88.

Lather, Patti. (1991). *Getting smart: Feminist research and pedagogy with/in the postmodern.* New York: Routledge.

Lee, Chin-Kwan. (2000). *Gender and the South China miracle.* Berkeley: University of California Press.

Lentin, Ronit. (2000). *Israel and the daughters of the Shoah: Reoccupying the territories of silence.* New York: Berghahn Books.

Lowe, Lisa, & Lloyd, David. (1997). Introduction. In Lisa Lowe & David Lloyd (Eds.), *The politics of culture in the shadow of capital* (pp. 1–32). Durham, NC: Duke University Press.

Maguire, Patricia. (1987). *Doing participatory research: A feminist approach.* Amherst: University of Massachusetts, School of Education, Center for International Education.

Maguire, Patricia. (1996). Considering more feminist participatory research: What's congruency got to do with it? *Qualitative Inquiry, 2*(1), 106–118.

Maguire, Patricia. (2001). Uneven ground: Feminisms and action research. In Peter Reason & H. Bradbury (Eds.), *Handbook of action research* (pp. 59–69). London: Sage.

Marchand, Marianne H., & Runyan, Anne Sisson. (Eds.). (2000a). *Gender and global restructuring: Sightings, sites and resistances.* New York: Routledge.

Marchand, Marianne H., & Runyan, Anne Sisson. (2000b). Introduction. In Marianne H. Marchand & Anne Sisson Runyan (Eds.), *Gender and global restructuring: Sightings, sites and resistances.* New York: Routledge.

Marcus, George E. (1995). Ethnography in/of the world system: The emergence of multi-sited ethnography. *Annual Review of Anthropology, 24,* 95–117.

Mendez, Jennifer Bickham. (2005). *From the revolution to the maquiladoras: Gender, labor and globalization in Nicaragua.* Durham, NC: Duke University Press.

Nafisi, Azar. (2003). *Reading Lolita in Tehran: A memoir in books.* New York: Random House.

Naples, Nancy A. (2003). *Feminism and method: Ethnography, discourse analysis, and activist research.* New York: Routledge.

Naples, Nancy A. (2004). The outsider phenomenon. In Sharlene Nagy Hesse-Biber & Michelle L. Yaiser (Eds.), *Feminist perspectives on social research* (pp. 373–381). New York: Oxford University Press.

Park, Peter. (1993). What is participatory research? A theoretical and methodological perspective. In Peter Park, Mary Brydon-Miller, Budd Hall, & Ted Jackson (Eds.), *Voices of change: Participatory research in the United States and Canada.* Westport, CT: Bergin & Garvey.

Park, Peter, Brydon-Miller, Mary, Hall, Budd, & Jackson, Ted. (Eds.). (1993). *Voices of change: Participatory research in the United States and Canada.* Westport, CT: Bergin & Garvey.

Parreñas, Rhacel Salazar. (2001). *Servants of globalization: Women, migration, and domestic work.* Stanford, CA: Stanford University Press.

Peterson, V. Spike, & Runyan, Anne Sisson. (1999). *Global gender issues.* Boulder, CO: Westview Press.

Richardson, John T. E. (Ed.). (1997). *Handbook of qualitative research methods for psychology and the social sciences* (2nd ed.). Leicester, UK: British Psychological Society, Blackwell Publishers.

Salzinger, Leslie. (2002). *Gender in production: Making workers in Mexico's global factories.* Berkeley: University of California Press.

Sancho, Nelia. (1997). The comfort women system in World War II: Asian women as targets of mass rape and sexual slavery by Japan. In Ronit

Lentin (Ed.), *Gender and catastrophe* (pp. 217–235). London: Palgrave & Macmillan.

Sassen, Saskia. (2001). Spatialities and temporalities of the global: Elements for a theorization. In Arjun Appadurai (Ed.), *Globalization* (pp. 260–278). Durham, NC: Duke University Press.

Satrapi, Marjane. (2003). *Persepolis.* New York: Pantheon.

Satrapi, Marjane. (2004). *Persepolis II.* New York: Pantheon.

Schild, Veronica. (1998). New subject of rights? Women's movements and the construction of citizenship in the "new democracies." In Sonia E. Alvarez, Evelina Dagnino, & Arturo Escobar (Eds.), *Culture of politics/politics of cultures: Re-visioning Latin American social movements* (pp. 93–117). Boulder, CO: Westview Press.

Smith, Michael Peter, & Guarnizo, Luis Eduardo. (Eds.). (1998). *Transnationalism from below.* New Brunswick, NJ: Transaction.

Stoecker, Randy. (1999). Are academics irrelevant? Roles for scholars in participatory research. *American Behavioral Scientist, 42*(5), 840–854.

Thayer, Millie. (2004). *Negotiating the global: Northeast Brazilian women's movements and the transnational feminist public.* Unpublished doctoral dissertation, University of California, Berkeley.

# 39

# A GLOBAL FEMINIST PERSPECTIVE ON RESEARCH

MARIA MIES

I t is important to remind ourselves that feminist research did not grow out of academia but was a child of the women's movement. It was a result of women's struggles against patriarchal oppression and exploitation, struggles whose arena was the street rather than the classroom or research institutes. This patriarchal oppression was experienced by women first at the personal level: violence against women in the family and in public, discrimination of women at all levels of social life, in production, at the place of work, in the family where housework was not counted as work, in the area of reproduction with prohibition of abortion, and generally with control of women's bodies by state, religion, and the medical establishment. The slogan "the personal is political" expresses adequately this concern with the personal, everyday problems of women. Research at that level therefore had a clear practical goal, namely the solution of these issues.

Yet although the feminist movement and research centred on the most personal, intimate social relations, the man-woman relation had at the same time immediately an international reach. Not only in the countries of the North but also in the South women's movements emerged that began to fight the most burning problems stemming from patriarchal relationships at the

cultural-political level. These movements were not just a copy of the Northern movements but were aimed at the exploitative and oppressive structures typical for their own cultures. Examples are the campaigns of the Indian feminist movement against dowry, against mass rape of women, against discrimination of girls, against wife burning, against abortion of female foetuses, and so forth. As in the countries of the North, these practical struggles in the streets were accompanied by analysis and by research and were followed by publications (feminist journals and books), by women's shelters, and by a host of feminist projects and initiatives to change patriarchal society. All these projects and initiatives sprang up and maintained themselves for a long time without being financially supported either by the state or by sponsors from the business community.

Looking back at this early time of the feminist movement and research all over the world, we can see that women started with the personal but were at the same time truly internationalist—today one would say global. As in the West, this research was inspired by what I called *Betroffenheit*, concern and the desire to change things. Feminist researchers were not mainly interested in careerism and academic fame. Apart from their local commitment, they understood themselves as part of an international movement. Hence, the slogan *the personal is political* could have been accompanied by the slogan *the personal is international.*

It is in this historical context that I developed my ideas about a new methodology for feminist research. The *Methodological Postulates on Feminist Research* (Mies, 1978, 1983, 1996), first published in Holland and Germany and later in English, were inspired by my own Betroffenheit, the concern and anger I experienced during the time when my students and myself struggled to establish the first shelter for battered women in Germany (1976). During this struggle, I gained a number of theoretical and methodological insights, which I presented at the first meeting on women's studies in Germany in 1977. An English translation of these Methodological Postulates can be found in Bowles and Klein's (1983) *Theories of Women's Studies.* In the following, I'll give a brief exposition of the seven *postulates*:

1. The postulate of value-free research, of "objectivity," neutrality, and indifference of the researcher vis-à-vis the "research objects" has to be replaced by consciously taking sides for the oppressed.

2. The vertical relationship between the researcher and the researched, the *view from above,* must be replaced by the *view from below.*

3. The contemplative, uninvolved "spectator knowledge" must be replaced by active participation in actions, movements, and struggles for women's liberation. Research must become an integral part of such struggles.

4. Participation in actions and movements and the integration of research into these processes further implies that the change of the status quo becomes the starting point for a new research process. The motto for this approach could be "If you want to know a thing, you must change it."

5. The research process must become a process of *conscientization* (Freire, 1972) for both the researcher and those on whom she or he does researches (e.g., other women).

6. The collective conscientization of women, initiated by the women's movement and furthered by a problem formulating and solving research methodology, must be accompanied by the study of women's individual and social history.

7. Women cannot appropriate their own history unless they collectivize their own experiences. Women's studies therefore must strive to overcome the individualism, competitiveness, and careerism prevalent among male scholars.

The knowledge on which these postulates are based is first and foremost *experiential knowledge* due to the contradictions felt by all women, students, and teachers alike in all existing academic and research institutions worldwide today. June Nash had called these contradictions *double consciousness* (Nash & Safa, 1976). Double consciousness means that women in the universities have to follow the rules of "objective," "rational," indifferent scientific methods of "spectator knowledge" from outside and from above if they want to be accepted as serious scholars. This means they have to "forget" their own subjectivity, their feelings, and the experiences of their everyday life as women. However, instead of considering this split in ourselves as an obstacle only, with June Nash and others I began to see it as an opportunity to develop a new paradigm of research altogether.

This new approach to integrate action into research, or rather research into action, was inspired by, among others, concerned activist scholars like Gerrit Huizer from the University of Nijmegen, the Netherlands. He told me about his experiences as a researcher among poor peasants in South America. I learned from him concepts like "view from below and within," "experiential knowledge," and "change of the status quo in order to understand a situation" (Huizer, 1973; Huizer & Mannheim, 1979). They helped me greatly to analyse the experiences of our struggles against violence against women. He was one of the rare male scholars at that time who not only supported the feminist movement but was also keen to learn from feminist scholars.

As soon as my seven postulates on feminist research became known, a heated and long-lasting debate started among feminist scholars and activists, first in Holland and Germany, then also in other countries. The thrust of these postulates was to overcome the sterile division between action and reflection, practice and theory, research and politics. In the United States, this methodology was later referred to as *standpoint research*, or *standpoint theory*, because it was based on a clear standpoint. Those who wanted simply to give women more space in academia and those who did not want to revolutionize the existing research paradigm were totally against this approach. Again and again I was asked to respond to my critics. A summary of my arguments can be found in Mies (1991). Though this new feminist approach to doing research was widely criticized, it also inspired many women to follow this new paradigm. They saw it as a true liberation from the fetters of meaningless and sterile accumulation of irrelevant knowledge. I myself used this methodology not only in my research in India (Mies, 1982, 1986), but also in my teachings in Germany and the Netherlands (1979–1982). I found that the potential of this new methodology was not just to help women and other oppressed groups to become aware of the causes of their helplessness and despair but also to be able to overcome this situation. Moreover, it gave all who were involved in this action research process a wider and deeper and, hence, a more comprehensive understanding of reality, an understanding traditional research can never achieve.

## NEOLIBERAL GLOBALIZATION AND FEMINIST RESEARCH

In those years the term *globalization* was not yet known by most people. But already in 1990, I was invited by Norwegian feminists to talk about theoretical and methodological problems of doing global feminist research (Mies, 1990). For me this was an opportunity to reflect on the various feminist and ecological movements in the world which I knew and which had inspired me. But I could not yet refer to a comprehensive global theory that could explain what was going on in the world from a feminist perspective. Even a conference on feminist economics that took place in Amsterdam in the early 1980s had only partially opened my eyes. It had the title "Out of the Margin—Into the Mainstream." This conference marked a total U-turn, a rollback of

feminist theory and research to the positivistic paradigm that had been rejected by many feminists in the earlier years of the women's movement. More radical positions like the one I have described above were considered "marginal." Now feminists were mobilized to strive for the "mainstream." But what was this "mainstream"?

In economics this concept signified the neoliberal, globalized model of universal free trade, of deregulation and liberalization of all laws that stand in the way of the free flow of capital and goods, including labour laws and environmental rules and regulations, the reduction of state interference in the realm of economics, furthering competition of small and big enterprises across national borders and privatization of state-owned enterprises. Neoliberal economic theory is based above all on the ideas of Adam Smith (1723–1790), David Ricardo (1772–1823), and others. These ideas have been modernized by economists like Hayek (1899–1992), Friedman, and the so-called Chicago School of Economics. The main principles of this new/old economic theory had been laid down in the *Washington Consensus*. This theory had already been developed earlier by think tanks in the United States and the United Kingdom. It was first put into practice by Pinochet in Chile (1973), by Ms. Thatcher in the United Kingdom (1979), and by Mr. Reagan (1980). The ultimate goal of these new "reforms," as this policy has been called, was the dismantling of all traces of the Keynesian welfare state. (The new principles included a tax reform in favour of big enterprises.)

Although women in the West should have known that the dismantling of the welfare state would be to their disadvantage, many of them welcomed this new economic paradigm. They seemed to believe the promises of the propagators of global neoliberalism, that globalization and free trade would lead to more jobs and hence to more wealth. Inequality between poor and rich countries and poor and rich sections of the society would disappear, democracy would be furthered, and finally this would lead to peace in the world. People—not only women—were mislead by such promising slogans as "when the tide rises, not only the luxury yachts rise but also the small fishing boats." This new version of the old trickle-down theory was accepted. Moreover, after the fall of the Berlin Wall in 1989 and the breakdown of socialism in Eastern Europe people tended to believe Thatcher's slogan, that there was no alternative to global, neoliberal capitalism.

Combined with a lack of critical information and discussion it is not surprising that many feminists accepted these economic "reforms," as they were called, as inevitable. Not only the academic establishment but also the mainstream media everywhere uncritically preached that the neoliberal philosophy and policies were beneficial and without an alternative. This acceptance was furthered in the United States by certain "policies" by which women seemed to benefit. Women's unemployment was reduced by what has been called *McJobs*. A woman needs at least three of them to make a living.

The neoliberal global policies also had an immediate impact on women's studies and women's research in the universities. First, there was an ideological and theoretical shift by which more radical, Marxist, and activist orientations of women's studies were gradually eliminated. Feminists who still followed this line were marginalized or lost their jobs. Radical left theory and practice disappeared from the campus. It was substituted by the new postmodern and gender discourse. Maybe it was this ideological shift that made feminists in the academy unaware of and insensitive to the actual historical context within which economic and social relations and structures were totally transformed. An Australian friend reported in 1986: "If you want a job in any women's studies program in the Anglo-Saxon world today, you must accept postmodernism as your basic theoretical framework."

What strikes me most about these ideological changes is on the one hand the tempo with which they occurred—not only in the United States and the United Kingdom but also practically all over the world—and on the other hand the depth of their impact on people's, especially women's, consciousness. This can be seen clearly if one looks at certain concepts that were common up to 1990. Concepts and terms like *capitalism, patriarchy, oppression, exploitation, class, race, colonialism,* and many others disappeared from the public and theoretical discourse, including from

feminist research. This process could be observed more in the industrialized countries than in countries of the South where the process of neoliberal globalization was hitting poor women much more drastically.

The ideological shift could be most clearly observed in the context of the new *gender discourse*. This discourse had been introduced by feminists before these economic changes took place. With the new economic "reforms," however, this discourse became a kind of *lingua franca* in academic studies as well as in economics and politics. Expressions like *discrimination against women* were replaced by *gender discrimination*, programs for *women's studies* mutated to *gender studies programs*, politicians trying to win over female votes talked of *gender mainstreaming*. Part of the funds earmarked for developing countries were given to *gender training programs*. Even the term *woman* disappeared more and more from the public discourse. The abstractness of the term *gender* not only made room for all kinds of manipulations; it also suggests that men have the same problems as women. Hence, *gender equity* or *gender democracy* is seen as the right policy to solve the women's question, as it was called in the 19th and 20th centuries. What is worst perhaps is that the gender discourse again obscures *women* from public and political perceptions. Women's anger, their creativity and resistance, their *Betroffenheit* and subjectivity disappear behind the smoke screen of gender. This means they become politically invisible, and as feminists, apathetic. One of my friends from Bangladesh, Farida Akhter, wrote to me recently: "I am a woman, not a gender!"

I do not want to further elaborate my critique of postmodernism and the gender theory here. I only want to ask whether this kind of feminist discourse and research is able to stimulate an impulse towards criticism and resistance to globalized, neoliberal capitalism under which more and more people, including women, are now suffering. After about 15 years of economic "reforms" based on the rules of radical free market principles, it has become clear that none of the neoliberal promises has been realized: There is more inequality between countries and within countries than before. Poverty has risen dramatically even in rich countries. The gap between those who have profited from globalization and the victims of globalization has widened everywhere. These facts are admitted today by the United Nations, the World Bank, and even the governments. In many countries unemployment has risen to unprecedented heights. In Germany, it is more than 5 million, a number never experienced before. States and communities are indebted and we have entered a new phase of wars (Mies, 2004).

Women are suffering more than other groups from these developments. And yet in the protest movements against this neoliberal globalization one does not find many feminists. In the growing new social movements that started in the 1990s with the successful campaign against the Multilateral Agreement in Investment and that continued with the protests against the World Trade Organization and its various agreements; against genetically manipulated organisms; against the World Bank and the International Monetary Fund, the annual World Economic Forums, and other gatherings of the global players, one does find many young people, among them also many young women. Yet most of them would not want to be identified as feminists, let alone feminist researchers. They have mostly joined these movements because they want to fight against injustice in the world, the erosion of democracy, and the destruction of the environment. They do not see a connection between these issues and patriarchal and capitalist social relations. They do not understand that the deterioration of women's position in their own countries as well as in the countries of the South is a direct consequence of the neoliberal, globalized patriarchal and capitalist economy.

This lack of understanding may be due to the fact that feminist scholars, as was mentioned before, have mostly uncritically joined the "mainstream." It may also be due to the postmodern discourse in academia. By elimination of concepts like "patriarchy," "capitalism," "system," "exploitation," "oppression," and "solidarity" from public awareness, not only women but also people at large lack analytical tools to express what they are fighting against and fighting for.

These movements and struggles of civil society are an excellent opportunity, however, to begin a new learning process from below and from within. The rallies, marches, and gatherings are indeed what I call the *university of the street*. In this university of the street, people learn more about modern economics and about globalization policies than what they would learn in an economics course at the university. It is in this university of the streets that I learned all I know about neoliberal economics and politics, where I rediscovered again the fruitfulness of my earlier feminist activist research methodology. It is here that *activist scholars* like Vandana Shiva, Arundhati Roy, Medha Patkar, Farida Akhter, and many others get their training and become teachers, researchers, and mobilizers at the same time. It is such women who are able to remake the connections that modern science and capitalist economics have severed: The connection between nature and humans, between women's oppression and the rise of multinational corporations, between people from the North and the South, between city and countryside, the obscene wealth of some and the lack of the basic necessities for large numbers of others. Such women are really signs of hope for many, many people, particularly young women.

I don't see a global perspective for feminist research unless more women move out of the sterility of the academic ivory towers and join the young people in the university of the street.

## REFERENCES

Bowles, G., & Klein, R. D. (1983). *Theories of women's studies*. Boston: Routledge & Kegan Paul.

Fonow, M. M., & Cook, J. A. (Eds.). (1991). *Beyond methodology: Feminist scholarship as lived research*. Bloomington: Indiana University Press.

Freire, P. (1972). *Cultural action for freedom*. Middlesex, UK: Penguin Books.

Huizer, G. (1973). *Peasant rebellion in Latin America*. Middlesex, UK: Penguin Books.

Huizer, G., & Mannheim, B. (Eds.). (1979). *The politics of anthropology*. The Hague, the Netherlands: Mouton.

Mies, M. (1978). Methodische Postulate zur Frauenforschung; dargestellt am Beispiel der Gewalt gegen Frauen. *Beiträge zur feministischen Theorie und Praxis*, *1*, 41–63.

Mies, M. (1982). *The lace makers of Narsapur: Indian housewives produce for the world market*. London: Zed Books.

Mies, M. (1983). Towards a methodology of feminist research. In Gloria Bowles & Renate Duelli-Klein (Eds.), *Theories of women's studies* (pp. 117–139). London: Routledge & Kegan Paul.

Mies, M. (1986). *Indian women in subsistence and agricultural labour*. Geneva, Switzerland: International Labour Office.

Mies, M. (1990). Theoretical and methodological problems of doing global feminist research. *Nytt om Kvinee-Forskning, 14*(2), 13–20.

Mies, M. (1991). Women's research or feminist research? The debate surrounding feminist science and methodology. In M. M. Fonow & J. A. Cook (Eds.), *Beyond methodology: Feminist scholarship as lived research* (pp. 60–84). Bloomington: Indiana University Press.

Mies, M. (1996). Liberating women, liberating knowledge. *Atlantis: A Women's Studies Journal, 2*(1), 10–24.

Mies, M. (2004). *Krieg ohne Grenzen: Die neue Kolonisierung der Welt*. Köln: Papy Rossa.

Nash, J., & Safa, H. (1976). A critique of social science roles in Latin America. In J. Nash & H. Safa (Eds.), *Sex and class in Latin America*. New York: Praeger.

# 40

# FUTURE DIRECTIONS OF FEMINIST RESEARCH

*New Directions in Social Policy— The Case of Women's Health*

LYNN WEBER

To provide effective solutions to the deeply embedded structured inequalities that characterize the 21st century, social policy must derive from what feminist scholarship has come to understand about race, class, gender, sexuality, nation, and other intersecting systems of inequality. These systems are complex, pervasive, persistent, mutually constituted, socially constructed power relationships (see Collins, 2000a; Weber, 1998, 2001). Without taking into account the complex nexus of systemic inequalities within which these relationships are embedded, trying to understand women's lives and to develop social policy to redress women's oppression is like trying to clean the air on one side of a screen door.[1]

Since the 1960s, feminists have sought to promote just social policies through their scholarship and activism. These scholar-activists have emphasized the need to combine macrolevel policies with a localized and complex understanding of people's lives—eschewing both an expert-centered approach that fails to engage the people and a grassroots approach that fails to engage the broader structural

environment for macrolevel policies (see Naples, 2003). But even though feminist scholarship has influenced public policies and advanced understanding of social inequalities of gender and its intersections, it has done so largely outside the mainstream of public funding for research and outside legitimized avenues for shaping social policy. In health research, for example, the biomedical paradigm and its social science offshoots solidly dominate major research funding, prestigious publications, and public policy (see Institute of Medicine, 2002; Weber, 2006).

In this chapter, I suggest some ideas for situating feminist scholarship more solidly in the foreground of social science and more centrally in the dialogue and debate that constitutes the public policy process. New directions will obviously derive from the interplay of the social, economic, and political forces shaping the policy context; from awareness of and dialogue about the strengths and limitations of the various paradigms addressing social inequalities; and from the efficacy of efforts to strengthen the scholarship and activism connection in ways that shape policies to promote social justice.

To contextualize the broader arguments about ways to increase the impact of feminist scholarship on social policy, a useful case to examine is the arena of women's health and health disparities of race, ethnicity, gender, and social class.[2] First, health research is the best-funded research in all of academia. Second, the positivist biomedical paradigm solidly dominates the intellectual terrain of women's health and health disparities scholarship and policy, so much so that the social science of health has largely evolved as an emulation of that paradigm—despite its nominal effectiveness at reducing health disparities (see Weber & Parra-Medina, 2003). Third, despite the hegemony of the positivist biomedical paradigm, the women's health movement—integrally tied to the development of second-wave feminism—has had a significant impact on women's health policy, health care institutions, and a wide variety of medical practices and feminist theory, particularly intersectional theory (Morgen, 2002, 2006; Ruzek, 1978; Ruzek & Becker, 1999).

To further the impact of feminist scholarship on social policy, we must

- Sharpen our critique of status quo research and policy
- Improve our research theory and practice
- Develop alliances and principled coalitions for change

## SHARPENING OUR CRITIQUE OF STATUS QUO RESEARCH AND POLICY

Building effective social policy requires that feminist scholars continually monitor and seek to understand the macrolevel shifts in social conditions that shape fundamental social inequalities and thus the contexts within which social policy is constructed. In recent years, such processes include globalization and attendant wealth concentration, the growth of fundamentalist movements, increased class and race divides between professionals and the working class and poor populations whose lives the professionals shape—in part through the social policy process and the aging of the U.S. population amidst the relative youth of non-Western nations (see Mullings, 2005; Ruzek, 2004; Ruzek & Becker, 1999).

Each of these trends has evolved over a long time; contributes to increased gender, race, class, and national inequality; and will likely persist as a fundamental challenge to a just social order for years to come. In this context, the need for perspectives on health that recognize the complexities and differences in women's life circumstances becomes even more apparent (Ruzek, Clarke, & Olesen, 1997). Yet despite increased public awareness and outcry, concern among researchers and government funding agencies, and years of funding of social science research on health inequalities, health disparities across race and ethnicity, class, and gender have not abated (Hofrichter, 2003; House, 2002; House & Williams, 2000; Smedley, Stith, & Nelson, 2003). One clear culprit in this failure has been the positivist biomedical paradigm and its hegemony over the research and policy landscape. Even the prestigious Institute of Medicine (IOM) of the National Academies of Science,[3] for example, has begun to recognize the need for new approaches to public health and health disparities. In a recent report, *The Future of the Public's Health in the 21st Century* (IOM, 2002), the Institute points to the dominance of the biomedical paradigm as a *cause* of the gap between U.S. health-related expenditures—roughly 13% of our gross domestic product, more than any other industrialized nation—and our health status, which lags behind that of many nations:

> The vast majority of health care spending, as much as 95 percent by some estimates, is directed toward medical care and biomedical research. However, there is strong evidence that behavior and environment are responsible for over 70 percent of avoidable mortality, and health care is just one of several determinants of health. (p. 2)

The biomedical paradigm obscures the social bases of health and facilitates the shift of national resources away from the fundamentals of health and toward an overmedicalized, highly technical, and socially unequal health care system that works well for the privileged few. But women, especially poor, working-class, immigrant, and racial or ethnic women, remain at equal risk with many Third-World countries in basic health indicators, including infant mortality, HIV infection, cardiovascular disease and stroke, obesity, diabetes, and other chronic diseases (House & Williams, 2000; National Institutes of Health, 2001; Ruzek, Olesen, & Clarke, 1997; Smedley et al., 2003).

How the biomedical paradigm could be a part of the problem of unequal health in the United States becomes somewhat clearer when we compare the epistemologies, methodologies, and theoretical premises of a feminist intersectional paradigm—which emerged from a social-justice impulse—to those of the positivist biomedical paradigm, which views advocacy as antithetical to science. In so doing, we not only sharpen our critique of status quo research paradigms and policy and highlight weaknesses in our own approaches but also uncover arenas of potential convergence with other alternative paradigms that may catalyze future alliances for change.

## Feminist Intersectional and Positivist Biomedical Paradigms

Although important variations exist among them, mainstream social science studies of health disparities typically employ standards reflecting the ideals of a positivist biomedical paradigm and share common assumptions, conceptualizations, and methodologies. Below I summarize key differences in positivist biomedical (PB) and feminist intersectional (FI) approaches to the study of health disparities across race, class, gender (RCG), and other dimensions of inequality.

| Motivation | PB | Knowledge accumulation |
| --- | --- | --- |
|  | FI | Social justice |
| Researcher stance | PB | Affective neutrality; researcher "expert" controls research |
|  | FI | Engaged subjectivity, reflexivity; researcher collaborates with researched |
| Methodology | PB | Emphasizes measurement, quantification; individuals as units; surveys and randomized controlled trials |
|  | FI | Emphasizes holistic representation of meaning in individual lives and institutional arrangements; multimethod |
| Inequality measures | PB | Resource differences among individuals (e.g., levels of education, income) |
|  | FI | Power relations of dominance and subordination between groups at macro- and microlevels |
| Goal of analysis | PB | Separate independent effects of RCG on health outcomes; identify more proximate causes (e.g., stress, health behaviors) between social inequality and health |
|  | FI | Explicate interconnected nature of RCG at macrosystemic and microindividual levels |
| Change strategies | PB | Interventions designed to change proximate causes |
|  | FI | Interventions designed to change broad systems of RCG, including those outside health (e.g., economy, jobs, education, law) that shape health (for a more complete comparison of these paradigms, see Weber, 2006; Weber & Parra-Medina, 2003) |

The strengths of a feminist intersectional approach to understanding and developing effective policies to challenge health disparities rest precisely in the ways this approach contrasts with the dominant biomedical paradigm. Sandra Morgen (2006) recently demonstrated the strengths of an intersectional paradigm for addressing health disparities by contrasting two recent reports on the issue: an IOM report, *Unequal Treatment: Confronting Racial and Ethnic Disparities in Health Care* (Smedley et al., 2003), published by the National Academy of Sciences, and a publication prepared for the National Colloquium on Black Women's Health (NCBWH), an event and publication cosponsored by the National Black Women's Health Project (NBWHP), the Congressional Black Caucus Health Brain Trust, and the U.S. Senate Black Legislative Staff Caucus (NBWHP, 2003). The IOM report clearly approaches the question of health disparities from the positivist biomedical framework while the Colloquium on Black Women's Health takes a feminist intersectional approach.

By directly comparing the two approaches, the limitations of the IOM report as a guide for research to address health disparities stand out in bold relief. Morgen (2006) notes three critical problems with the positivist biomedical paradigm in the IOM report, each of which distinguishes it from an intersectional approach:

(1) The extraction of race/ethnicity from the complex matrix of power relations that characterize and shape inequality in the United States; (2) the reduction of structural/systemic inequalities to individual-level problems of bias, stereotyping, and discriminatory behavior; and (3) framing issues in a putatively objective, scientific manner that also tends to mute the urgency and mask the human costs of injustice. (p. 408)

In contrast, the NCBWH focused on the intersectional character of black women's health and the macrostructural conditions of racism, sexism, and classism and promoted an activist goal of eliminating inequalities in health care and the health status of multiply oppressed groups. In so doing, it identified such key factors in black women's health as the historical convergence of a variety of social policies— eugenics, family planning, welfare "reform," differential opportunities for access to health care coverage—that represent the institutional mechanisms of race, class, gender, and religious inequalities in black women's lives. As Morgen (2006) notes, the impact of these policies on health disparities are rarely mentioned in the IOM report because they are deemed to be outside its purview.

As Morgen has done, we can sharpen our critique of status quo research and policy by engaging critically with dominant paradigms— in this case the positivist biomedical paradigm—in direct comparison with a feminist intersectional approach. Unfortunately, feminist scholars have often eschewed this process. As Patricia Hill Collins notes (2000b), "Mainstream science operates as such a powerful discourse and set of social practices that, to many, it appears to be invincible" (p. 275). It is so powerful and ubiquitous, in fact, that even many feminist scholars whose work is deeply critical of mainstream science unwittingly contribute to its dominance by simply rejecting science out of hand and refusing to engage in dialogue at all. Postmodernist theories, for example, have become popular in feminist circles in part because by minimizing the importance of science's power over the intellectual landscape, these theories simultaneously avoid addressing the role of power relationships in shaping feminists' own critical knowledge (Collins, 2000b). While comfortably isolating postmodernist scholars from critical self-reflection on the role of class, race, sexuality, gender, and national power in shaping their own theories and research, these approaches do little to challenge science for its biases. But engaging with the dominant science paradigm suggests avenues for strengthening feminist scholarship and practice itself.

## IMPROVING FEMINIST INTERSECTIONAL SCHOLARSHIP

Two avenues seem particularly important for moving feminist intersectional scholarship into the foreground of health disparities research and policy:

1. Explicating power relationships and the mechanisms of oppression

2. Improving research methods and practices

## Explicating Power Relationships and the Mechanisms of Oppression

As the complex experiences of scholar activists demonstrate, recognizing *that* power relations are a central dynamic in race, class, and gender structures is not the same as demonstrating *how* power relations are co-constructed, maintained, and challenged. And explicating how these systems operate—the *mechanisms* that constitute and connect them—is a critical challenge before feminist and other scholars (Mullings, 2005; Naples, 2003; Reskin, 2003). For example, recognizing the ongoing problem of race- and gender-based workplace discrimination in the presence of formal legal structures prohibiting it, Reskin (2003) argued that we need to shift our attention away from the *motives* for discrimination and to its *mechanisms*. We should not ask *why* allocators (people in positions of power) in the workplace produce inequality by making decisions that effect unequal outcomes for women and people of color (i.e., their motives) but should ask instead *how* their actions produce inequality—stated otherwise, *what* actions or processes produce the inequalities (i.e., the mechanisms). Conversely, we should also ask what actions produce equitable outcomes (e.g., blind assessments, formalization of reward systems).

Much like the traditional research on workplace discrimination that focused on changing the motives of individual allocators (e.g., through diversity training), health interventions emerging from a biomedical paradigm tend to focus on changing the values, behaviors, cognitions, or even biochemical processes of individuals. Understanding the mechanisms of power relationships enables us to entertain different kinds of interventions by shifting the balance of power away from the biomedical paradigm with its focus on medical care and biomedical research to the social contexts of and prerequisites for

health[4]—away from individual bodies and to healthy communities.

When social inequalities are viewed as power relationships, the ways in which dominant groups benefit from denying others adequate child care, medical access, and so on, become a focus of attention. So changes that might alter the balance of power—a living wage; shifts in workplace control; universal, affordable, quality child care; accessible public transportation; safe and affordable housing; equal access to quality education; and universal prevention-focused health care—become the preferred interventions. While individual approaches may change the lives of those involved in targeted programs, power-based approaches are more likely to effect change that would significantly reduce health disparities.

## Improving Research Methods and Practice

Recent reviews of feminist methodology affirm the now common assumption in feminist scholarship that no single methodology is uniquely feminist even though qualitative methodologies have heavily dominated feminist research generally and intersectional research specifically (DeVault, 1999; Fonow & Cook, 2005; Naples, 2003; Weber & Parra-Medina, 2003). Furthermore, both the intersectional and interdisciplinary thrusts of feminist research have spawned new methods and encouraged the use of multiple methods for the critical analysis of systems of inequality.

Today's methodological challenges lie not in making a simple choice between qualitative and quantitative approaches but in selecting a variety of methods from among the many at our disposal—many of which blur the distinction between quantitative and qualitative research. Yet our selections of methods are complicated by the very power dynamics and value conflicts that shape the broader terrain of knowledge production.

In *Feminism and Method: Ethnography, Discourse Analysis, and Activist Research*, for example, Nancy Naples (2003) complicates the rather straightforward and seemingly uncomplicated argument in most social science methods texts that research methods should be chosen that are appropriate for the research questions asked. While not disagreeing with that statement, Naples points out,

> The methods we choose are not free of epistemological assumptions and taken-for-granted understandings of what counts as data, how the researcher should relate to the subjects of research, and what are the appropriate products of a research study. Furthermore, seldom do the authors of traditional methods books acknowledge that the questions researchers ask are inevitably tied to particular epistemological understandings of how knowledge is generated. (p. 5)

When social activism and social policy are the goals, researchers value strategies such as dialogue and consciousness-raising that are designed to minimize the inequities in the knowledge production process and to enable a critical assessment of the ways that dominant discourses infuse our own understandings of what counts as data and whose voices are privileged in our ethnographic accounts (Naples, 2003). Egalitarian research practices are also increasingly common and called for in public health research, for example, in community-based participatory action research (CBPAR). Furthermore, as a complement to the microfocus of CBPAR, many public health and feminist scholars now call for multilevel and multisite research, even engaging communities and scholars transnationally (e.g., to trace the impact of globalization on women workers) (Barndt, 2002; Fonow & Cook, 2005; Townsend, Zapata, Rowlands, Alberti, & Mercado, 1999).

Feminist activist research that employs multiple methods inevitably invites tough questions about the limits and uses of particular methods, and these limits must be examined in light of the power inequities in the structure of dominant knowledge-producing institutions (Fonow & Cook, 2005). Blee (2004) argues, for example, that we must rethink the traditional view of qualitative research: That it is an appropriate prelude to quantitative research wherein hypotheses are developed and relationships are examined on a small scale that can actually be tested with quantitative research. This view places qualitative research in the role of a "maidservant" to the more powerful quantitative master. But qualitative research can also be used

to interrogate more fully systematic empirical relationships revealed in quantitative studies. And this use of qualitative research was what Reskin (2003) concluded is necessary to uncover the mechanisms of discrimination. Specifically, she argued that focus on these mechanisms will require more research at the firm and organizational level in order to see patterns of discrimination, as well as qualitative and ethnographic research to reveal the mechanisms at work—a call that was recently affirmed by a National Science Foundation report on the scientific foundations of qualitative research (Ragin, Nagel, & White, 2004) and by IOM and National Institutes of Health (NIH) reports (NIH, 2001; Smedley & Syme, 2000; Smedley et al., 2003).

Awareness of the relative power attached to the use of qualitative and quantitative methods is especially critical for feminist policy studies because traditional, narrowly construed "scientific" research designs remain highly valued in U.S. policy arenas even though other countries rely more on qualitative and consensus studies in setting their public policy agendas and enacting corresponding legislation (Fonow & Cook, 2005, p. 2230).

This power imbalance in methodology is one that feminist scholars should continue to challenge directly by critically assessing the strengths and weaknesses of both dominant and feminist research approaches and by asking how we can use multiple methods together effectively without privileging one method and thus one set of research questions. Biomedical health research, for example, can become so fixed on measurement and quantification that it impedes acting to eliminate hierarchies of health—actions that themselves can lead to a better understanding of these hierarchies. In contrast, intersectional scholarship's heavy reliance on qualitative methodologies has too often focused primarily on revealing the meaning, mechanisms, and experience of social inequalities without documenting or assessing the efficacy of different approaches to social change (Collins, 2000a; DeVault, 1999; Mies, 1983).

To strengthen our research practice we need to focus on explicating our theories of change, our epistemological assumptions, their connections with methods, and our assessments of change. Transnational, multilevel, multisite, participatory action research can be a solid foundation for developing and implementing policies and practices that promote social justice. Effective research that challenges the hegemony of traditional approaches especially in the policy arena will also require that we develop and sustain coalitions with others working for justice from multiple perspectives.

## DEVELOPING ALLIANCES AND PRINCIPLED COALITIONS FOR CHANGE

The social movements of the Civil Rights Era have demonstrated both the possibility of change for justice and the long-range difficulty of sustaining and building on that change (see Morgen, 2002, 2006; Mullings, 2005; Naples, 2003; Omi & Winant, 1994; Ruzek & Becker, 1999). One clear message that has emerged from intersectional scholars' understandings of this history and their involvements in activist scholarship is that effective scholarship and policy for the future will depend on our ability to develop strong, principled alliances and coalitions (Collins, 2000a; Morgen, 2002, 2006; Naples, 2003; Ruzek, 2004; Schulz & Mullings, 2006; Weber, 2006; Weber & Parra-Medina, 2003).

If we hope to develop a more equitable and engaged scholarship and practice to eliminate health disparities, we must promote a more inclusive intellectual landscape to support dialogue and collaboration across intersectional, critical public health and biomedically derived paradigms.

These coalitions will involve scholars with a justice agenda who may be working from different disciplinary approaches as well as community groups whose engagement we need to sharpen our critique of the status quo, to improve our own scholarship, and to identify paths to effective activism and change.

In fact, the call for alliances is so widespread that the critical question today is not *should* we develop alliances for change, but *how* do we go about bridging our differences to effectively promote change that furthers social justice? What are the processes we should engage? With whom is it most fruitful to engage? And how do we know when those differences are unbridgeable

or if bridging them might impede or divert rather than promote social justice?

Three areas show promise for building and sustaining effective, principled coalitions for social justice:

1. Promising points of convergence in health research

2. Methodological advances in bridging disciplinary and social boundaries

3. Development of bridging organizations and outlets

### Promising Points of Convergence in Health Research

Several recent reports of the IOM and the NIH, while still quite different in approach from feminist intersectional approaches, call for changes to the traditional biomedical paradigm in health research, policy, and education—changes that converge with key elements of both intersectional and other critical public health paradigms. These reports have called for

- An ecological approach to health research, policy, and education that incorporates "upstream" factors such as social contexts and public policies even in sectors beyond health that nonetheless shape it, such as law, economy, education, and media
- Community-based collaborative research
- Multilevel, multimethod (including qualitative and quantitative methods), interdisciplinary research (IOM, 2002, 2003; NIH, 2001; Smedley & Syme, 2000; Smedley et al., 2003)

These reports reflect growing recognition among scholars both critical of and immersed within the biomedical paradigm that understanding and reducing or eliminating health disparities requires new directions (see the reports above and Weber, 2006).

To some extent, these calls also reflect the impact on dominant health research institutions of feminist and other alternative, justice-oriented public health approaches to health disparities that differ in significant ways from the biomedical paradigm: ecological (Glanz et al., 1995; McLeroy, Bibeau, Steckler, & Glanz, 1988;

Parra-Medina & Fore, 2004), technoscience (Clarke & Olesen, 1999; Shim, 2002), social capital (Wallack, 2000), community-based participatory research (McLeroy, Norton, Kegler, Burdine, & Sumaya, 2003; Minkler & Wallerstein, 2003), and social justice (Hofrichter, 2003).

One common theme in these alternative approaches is that they shift the focus of attention away from individual bodies as primary loci of health and from biomedical research as the best way to understand and to improve a nation's health. Instead, as Ruzek (2004) notes, they attend to the social production of health and illness, social equity in access to health care, education, and other determinants of health, and the power dynamics shaping knowledge production and health promotion institutions.

## Methodological Advances in Bridging Disciplinary and Social Boundaries

To build successful partnerships and alliances for change across the unequal power relations that structure research and social life, intersectional and other critical, justice-oriented scholars contend that we must engage in what is variously labeled "border work," "boundary-crossing," "bridging," and "trans-ing" social and disciplinary divides and of doing so by inhabiting "in-between spaces" or "outsider-within locations" (Anzaldúa, 1987; Collins, in press; Dill, 2002; Pryse, 2000; Yuval-Davis, 1997). Many feminist communities, both here and across the globe, have sought to identify ways to "bridge" race, class, gender, sexuality, and disciplinary boundaries to achieve truly interdisciplinary thought and effective social action. As Ruzek, Clarke, and Olesen (1997) describe, "the challenge is to find new ways to grow beyond our differences while not evading or ignoring them" (p. 83). Identifying and refining strategies for initiating and nurturing these principled coalitions or "multivocal" alliances is one of the most difficult challenges for feminist research (Naples, 2003).

Israeli feminist Nira Yuval-Davis, for example, calls for "transversal politics" as a method for bridging these barriers. In transversal politics each participant brings with her the *rooting* in her own social location and identity but at the same time

tries to *shift* to put herself in a situation of exchange with others who have a different social location and identity. By combining *shifting* to understand and incorporate the views of others with a *rooted* critical self-awareness of our race, gender, class, nation, discipline, and other sources of identity and by employing the "shifting" skills that intersectional scholars develop as they seek to work across disciplinary boundaries, we have the potential to develop what Collins (2000a) calls principled coalitions. Such coalitions are based not on the exploitation of power differentials but on self-awareness, self-respect, and a genuine appreciation of others.

Another new interdisciplinary method is "intertextuality"—deconstructing symbolic representations to reveal the ideological processes of the production of hierarchy. Intertextuality is the study of how symbolic codes in one text are related to those in another, allowing the researcher to compare and contrast similar themes within or among different genres or media (Fonow & Cook, 2005). Continued work to improve on existing methods and to develop new methods for bridging the researcher-researched, race, class, gender, nation, and disciplinary divides is key to increasing the effectiveness of our activism and the impact of feminist scholarship on public policy.

## Development of Bridging Organizations and Outlets

A growing number of feminist policy and other activist organizations and communication and publication outlets are working to support and to promote alliances and coalitions that seek social justice. The National Council for Research on Women, a member organization of 3,000 individuals and organizations and 92 research centers and institutes, focuses on advocacy for women and girls. The Institute for Women's Policy Research conducts research, publishes policy reports, and organizes scholar-activist-policymaker meetings to promote understanding and collaborations to advance progressive social change. *Women, Politics and Policy*, co-edited by Heidi Hartman and Carol Hardy-Fanta, is a new scholarly journal whose first issue highlights recent policy developments in Europe, Latin America, and the United States around a variety of issues, including citizenship, elections, social capital, human rights, and women's roles in policy implementation.

In the women's health arena both long-standing grassroots organizations and more recently developed professional health equity organizations populate the policy landscape. The Boston Women's Health Book Collective, Federation of Feminist Women's Health Centers, DES Action, National Women's Health Network, National Black Women's Health Project, National Latina Health Organization, National Asian Women's Health Organization, and Native American Women's Health Education Resource Center are just some of the many grassroots women's health advocacy groups whose work has shaped women's health and public policy (see Morgen, 2002).

Since the 1990s, the health policy terrain has become immensely more complicated by the growth of women's health organizations that are typically professionalized, disease specific (e.g., breast cancer, cervical cancer, AIDS), and more attached to biomedicine and to corporate sponsors (Ruzek & Becker, 1999). Developing principled coalitions across these groups is both a challenge and a necessity, especially in the age of the Internet, where all comers can claim organizational status and gain instant worldwide recognition. One challenge for women's health policy advocates will be to remain key information brokers on women's health given the increasingly complex array of women's health information.

To bridge the divides of race, class, gender, nation, discipline, and organization, feminist intersectional scholars must continue to develop our intellectual base and critique of the status quo, methodological expertise, and organizational strategies. Our success in these ventures will determine how effective we can be at placing our work more solidly in the center of health disparities research and policy and in promoting health equity and social justice in the years ahead.

## Notes

1. This analogy was inspired by Jean Anyon's (1997, p. 168) statement on fixing inner-city schools.

2. *Health disparities* is the terminology currently used by the government and medical establishment to refer to differences in the incidence, prevalence, mortality, and burden of diseases and other adverse health conditions that exist among specific population groups in the United States.

3. The IOM, solidly entrenched in the positivist biomedical paradigm, is designed to provide scientific advice for policy development. In its own words, "The Institute provides unbiased, evidence-based, and authoritative information and advice concerning health and science policy to policy-makers, professionals, leaders in every sector of the society, and the public at large" (www.iom.edu/CMS/3239.aspx).

4. The World Health Organization, which proposes a much broader definition of health than the biomedical paradigm, defines the prerequisites of health as freedom from the fear of war; equal opportunity for all; satisfaction of basic needs for food, water, and sanitation; education; decent housing; secure work and a useful role in society; and political will and public support (for a detailed discussion, see Downie, Fyfe, & Tannahill, 1990).

## References

Anyon, J. (1997). *Ghetto schooling: A political economy of urban educational reform.* New York: Teachers College Press, Columbia University.

Anzaldúa, G. (1987). *Borderlands/la frontera: The new mestiza.* San Francisco: Spinsters/Aunt Lute.

Barndt, D. (2002). *Tangled routes: Women, work, and globalization on the tomato trail.* Lanham, MD: Rowman & Littlefield.

Blee, K. M. (2004). Evaluating qualitative research. In C. Ragin, J. Nagel, & P. White (Eds.), *Workshop on scientific foundations of qualitative research* (pp. 55–57). Washington, DC: National Science Foundation.

Clarke, A., & Olesen, V. (Eds.). (1999). *Revisioning women, health, and healing: Feminist, cultural, and technoscience perspectives.* New York: Routledge.

Collins, P. H. (2000a). *Black feminist thought* (2nd ed.). New York: Routledge.

Collins, P. H. (2000b). Moving beyond gender: Intersectionality and scientific knowledge. In M. M. Ferree, J. Lorber, & B. Hess (Eds.), *Revisioning gender* (pp. 261–284). Lanham, MD: Rowman & Littlefield.

Collins, P. H. (in press). Pushing the boundaries or business as usual? Race, class, gender studies and sociological inquiry. In C. Calhoun (Ed.), *Sociology in America: A history*. Chicago: University of Chicago Press.

DeVault, M. L. (1999). *Liberating method: Feminism and social research*. Philadelphia: Temple University Press.

Dill, B. T. (2002). *Work at the intersections of race, gender, ethnicity and other dimensions of identity in higher education*. College Park: University of Maryland, Consortium for Research on Race, Gender, and Ethnicity.

Downie, R. S., Fyfe, C., & Tannahill, A. (1990). *Health promotion models and values*. New York: Oxford University Press.

Fonow, M. M., & Cook, J. A. (2005). Feminist methodology: New applications in the academy and public policy. *Signs: A Journal of Women in Culture and Society, 30*(4), 2211–2236.

Glanz, K., Lankenau, B., Foerster, S., Temple, S., Mullis, R., & Schmid, T. (1995). Environmental and policy approaches to cardiovascular disease prevention through nutrition: Opportunities for state and local action. *Health Education Quarterly, 22*(4), 512–527.

Hofrichter, R. (2003). The politics of health inequities: Contested terrain. In R. Hofrichter (Ed.), *Health and social justice: Politics, ideology, and inequity in the distribution of disease* (pp. 1–56). San Francisco: Jossey-Bass.

House, J. S. (2002). Understanding social factors and inequalities in health: 20th century progress and 21st century prospects. *Journal of Health and Social Behavior, 43*(2), 125–142.

House, J. S., & Williams, D. R. (2000). Understanding and reducing socioeconomic and racial/ethnic disparities in health. In B. D. Smedley & S. L. Syme (Eds.), *Promoting health: Intervention strategies from social and behavioral research* (pp. 81–124). Washington, DC: National Academy Press.

Institute of Medicine. (2002). *The future of the public's health in the 21st century*. Committee on Assuring the Health of the Public in the 21st Century. Washington, DC: National Academy of Sciences.

Institute of Medicine. (2003). *From neurons to neighborhoods: The science of early childhood development*. Washington, DC: National Academy of Sciences.

McLeroy, K. R., Bibeau, D., Steckler, A., & Glanz, K. (1988). An ecological perspective on health promotion programs. *Health Education Quarterly, 15*(4), 351–377.

McLeroy, K. R., Norton, B. L., Kegler, M. C., Burdine, J. N., & Sumaya, C. V. (2003). Community-based interventions. *American Journal of Public Health, 93*(4), 529–533.

Mies, M. (1983). Towards a methodology for feminist research. In G. Bowles & R. D. Klein (Eds.), *Theories of women's studies* (pp. 117–139). London: Routledge & Kegan Paul.

Minkler, M., & Wallerstein, N. (Eds.). (2003). *Community-based participatory research for health*. San Francisco: Jossey-Bass.

Morgen, S. (2002). *Into our own hands: The women's health movement in the United States 1969–1990*. New Brunswick, NJ: Rutgers University Press.

Morgen, S. (2006). Movement-grounded theory: Intersectional analysis of health inequities in the United States. In A. Schulz & L. Mullings (Eds.), *Race, class, gender and health* (pp. 394–423). San Francisco: Jossey-Bass.

Mullings, L. (2005). Interrogating racism: Toward an antiracist anthropology. *Annual Review of Anthropology, 34*, 667–693.

Naples, N. (2003). *Feminism and method: Ethnography, discourse analysis, and activist research*. New York: Taylor & Francis.

National Black Women's Health Project. (2003). *National colloquium on black women's health*. Washington, DC: Congressional Black Caucus Health Brain Trust and U.S. Senate Black Staff Legislative Caucus.

National Institutes of Health/Office of Behavioral and Social Science Report. (2001). *Towards higher levels of analysis: Progress and promise in research on social and cultural dimensions of health: Executive summary* (NIH Publication No. 21-5020). Washington, DC: Author.

Omi, M., & Winant, H. (1994). *Racial formation in the United States: From the 1960s to the 1990s*. New York: Routledge.

Parra-Medina, D., & Fore, E. (2004). Behavioral studies. In B. M. Beech & M. Goodmand (Eds.), *Race and research* (pp. 101–112). Washington, DC: American Public Health Association.

Pryse, M. (2000). Trans/feminist methodology: Bridges to interdisciplinary thinking. *NWSA Journal, 12*(2), 105–118.

Ragin, C., Nagel, J., & White, P. (Eds.). (2004). *Workshop on scientific foundations of qualitative research*. Washington, DC: National Science Foundation.

Reskin, B. (2003). Presidential address: Including mechanisms in our models of ascriptive inequality. *American Sociological Review, 68*(1), 1–21.

Ruzek, S. (1978). *The women's health movement.* New York: Praeger.

Ruzek, S. (2004). How might the women's health movement shape national agendas on women and aging? *Women's Health Issues, 14,* 112–114.

Ruzek, S., & Becker, J. (1999). The women's health movement in the U.S.: From grassroots activism to professional agendas. *Journal of American Medical Women's Association, 54*(1), 4–8, 40.

Ruzek, S., Clarke, A., & Olesen, V. (1997). What are the dynamics of difference? In S. Ruzek, V. Olesen, & A. Clarke (Eds.), *Women's health: Complexities and differences* (pp. 51–95). Columbus: Ohio State University Press.

Ruzek, S., Olesen, V., & Clarke, A. (Eds.). (1997). *Women's health: Complexities and differences.* Columbus: Ohio State University Press.

Schulz, A., & Mullings, L. (Eds.). (2006). *Race, class, gender and health.* San Francisco: Jossey-Bass.

Shim, J. (2002). Understanding the routinised inclusion of race, socioeconomic status and sex in epidemiology: The utility of concepts from technoscience studies. *Sociology of Health and Illness, 24*(2), 129–150.

Smedley, B. D., Stith, A. Y., & Nelson, A. R. (Eds.). (2003). *Unequal treatment: Confronting racial and ethnic disparities in health care.* Washington, DC: National Academy Press.

Smedley, B. D., & Syme, S. L. (Eds.). (2000). *Promoting health: Intervention strategies from social and behavioral research.* Washington, DC: National Academy Press.

Townsend, J. G., Zapata, E., Rowlands, J., Alberti, P., & Mercado, M. (1999). *Women and power: Fighting patriarchies.* New York: Zed Books.

Wallack, L. (2000). The role of mass media in creating social capital: A new direction for public health. In B. D. Smedley & S. L. Syme (Eds.), *Promoting health: Intervention strategies from social and behavioral research* (pp. 337–365). Washington, DC: National Academy Press.

Weber, L. (1998). A conceptual framework for understanding race, class, gender, and sexuality. *Psychology of Women Quarterly, 22,* 13–32.

Weber, L. (2001). *Understanding race, class, gender, and sexuality: A conceptual framework.* New York: McGraw-Hill.

Weber, L. (2006). Reconstructing the landscape of health disparities research: Promoting dialogue and collaboration between the feminist intersectional and positivist biomedical traditions. In A. Schulz & L. Mullings (Eds.), *Race, class, gender and health* (pp. 21–59). San Francisco: Jossey-Bass.

Weber, L., & Parra-Medina, D. (2003). Intersectionality and women's health: Charting a path to eliminating health disparities. In V. Demos & M. T. Segal (Eds.), *Advances in gender research: Gender perspectives on health and medicine* (pp. 181–230). Amsterdam: Elsevier.

Yuval-Davis, N. (1997). Women, ethnicity and empowerment: Towards trans-versal politics. In N. Yuval-Davis (Ed.), *Gender and nation* (pp. 116–133). Thousand Oaks, CA: Sage.

# 41

## FROM COURSE TO DISCOURSE

### *Mainstreaming Feminist Methodology*

DEBRA RENEE KAUFMAN

If the past is prologue to the future, then my 15 years of experience as a teacher of feminist methodology may prove useful in contemplating whether feminist methodology will be accepted into mainstream, disciplinary analyses, or, as with other critical views, be relegated to the margins of the disciplines. Currently, sociological analysis is statistically driven and technologically sophisticated. Although statistics and technology are not inherently inimical to feminist modes of analyses, logical positivism's insistence on the separation of moral concerns, value commitments, and the researcher from the scientific inquiry, emphatically is.[1] The questions we ask (or do not ask) and the moral imperatives that provoke that inquiry are as important to feminist scholars and teachers as are the answers we find. As feminists we are committed to the dictum that *how* we study determines *what* we know. Therefore, it is critical that feminist methodology survive as a critical part of any curriculum if the feminist perspective is to have any academic base.

Some years ago I was asked to write a piece for the *Journal of Radical Education and Cultural Studies* (1996) about feminist pedagogy. In that piece I argued that we must "trouble" our disciplinary categories by decentering

the theories and methods that reproduce scholarship according to a white male normative model, a model that neglects and devalues the female experience. My politics were clear. We were to make room for women not only as scholars within the academy, but also as subjects known on their own terms, in their own voices, and through their own experiences. Although the initial formulation was naive, since I had failed to specify whose experiences, whose voices, and whose agency represented women and men, I had little doubt that the ideas formulated in the academy needed to be placed in touch with the outside world. Our theories and methods were tied to real-life policies, experiences, and applications. It is the tie between the "real" world and the world of the academic that the now hundreds of students I have encountered in feminist classes find so compelling and simultaneously vexing. The first task for those of us teaching feminist methodology is to rethink and reflect on and, eventually, rewrite the texts that lie at the very foundations of our specific disciplines.

Although sociology, my own discipline, had a history of self-conscious critique, especially between the functionalists and conflict theorists, it was the work of feminist thinkers, particularly outside the social sciences, which gave me the language to formulate a critique of positivist social science. Until then, "I had been operating (albeit freely) within the boundaries of established paradigmatic parameters. With feminism, I learned not only to 'cross the borders' but to dissolve the boundaries between them" (Kaufman, 1996, pp. 166–167). The first feminist methodology course I taught was called Feminist Methodologies: New Ways of Knowing and Doing. Reading and reflecting on the writings of leading feminist thinkers from disciplines both within and outside of the social sciences helped me and my coteacher, Christine Gailey, an anthropologist, to design our syllabus to challenge and rework the disciplinary assumptions within each of our disciplines. The classroom itself was designed to examine assumptions about the relationship between private and public, between the classroom and the community, and between the teacher and the student. The pedagogy was informed by feminist methodological assumptions about the social world and the way in which we were to study it as feminists. Traditional binaries were questioned, and established hierarchies were flattened. For instance, since feminist inquiry asserts that all research/ scholarship is value laden, some of our first questions were as follows: For whom was the curriculum designed and for what purpose? Whose voice, whose text, and whose interests predominated? And implicitly, what (who) was missing?

Since feminist inquiry insists that all scholarship/research is a social process filled with power dimensions, we structured the classroom in ways that helped eliminate the distance between teacher and student. We sat in a circle and we called each other by our first names. Because feminist inquiry demands that the researcher and the "researched" are mutually constitutive, we redesigned some of the syllabus and added texts, as we discovered students' interests and concerns. Just as feminist researchers recognize the importance of social position, of power, and of control in research practice, we were aware of the very same issues in the classroom. As teachers, we tried to position ourselves as experienced readers of the material and as experienced scholars, but not as authoritarian experts. We understood that the very class we were teaching had a historical

place in feminist scholarship within our university and within the larger context of feminist inquiry. We raised consciousness about the very politics that made and/or unmade the teaching of feminist methodology. We were all actors in this project of discovery.

The multidisciplinary representation of faculty and students (our classes served male and female students from outside our disciplines as well) led to a classroom rife with assumptions about and explanations for almost every topic under investigation. Every process of inquiry needed to be deconstructed according to level of analysis, disciplinary assumptions, and subjective experiences. No term could be understood at face value. No topic was off-limits for investigation. The only rule that applied across topics and disciplines was the need to historically locate and critically scrutinize the assumptions about gender within each investigation and the ideas that supported it. Since our disciplines often led us to focus on different issues in the presentation of material, Christine and I often differed in our points of emphasis and in our interpretations. "Our best discussions (according to the students)," I wrote, "came when we [Christine and I] disagreed with each other's interpretations of the readings, thereby setting the stage for one of the key principles of feminist pedagogy, the notion of de-centering authority by presenting multiple voices and therefore multiple interpretations" (1996, p. 169). In this way, "We were able to lay bare the assumptions deeply embedded in our own feminist understanding(s) of our disciplinary texts and the methods . . . used" (Kaufman, 1996, p. 169). Because our classroom was filled with students from a variety of ethnic and racial groups, "voice" became an important dimension of our classroom discussions. We self-consciously raised the issues of race, class, and gender as positional markers in the social process called feminist inquiry.

Our pedagogy was as political as it was academic. We wished to develop a future audience for, as well as active scholars of, feminist scholarship and research. In what ways, we asked our students, are we historical and political subjects when *we* do our research? How do our life histories and stage of career affect our choice of topic and how we formulate research problems?

Since "good" feminist methodology, and hence "good" methodology in general, requires that we be self-reflexive from the beginning to the end of our research journeys, students often asked us how we had come to our research. They wanted us to give them the "insider" information about the trials and tribulations of "doing" feminist research. How had our feminist concerns become one with our intellectual interests? Often such retrospection elicited issues we had either forgotten or long repressed.

One pedagogical tool I have used in all my classes is to respond to student-generated questions through empirical examples. In the early 1990s, I wrote *Rachel's Daughters*, a book about the "return" to Jewish Orthodoxy during the closing decades of the 20th century by once secular, highly assimilated, highly educated, middle-class, white, Jewish women. Perhaps no research is better positioned to touch on the knottiest of feminist methodological issues than the exploration of women, religion, and politics. The early work on fundamentalist and presumably "antifeminist" women is perhaps even more intriguing today than it was some 15 years ago. Consider for a moment what we "knew" or thought we knew about the attitudes, behaviors, and everyday experiences of religious right women at that time. Questions, primarily taken from quantitative surveys, were aimed at "objectively" measuring the attitudes, values, and behaviors associated with patriarchal living. What we knew about women who had turned to the right we knew primarily from their activities in antifeminist contexts. We knew very little about them in their own voices, and even less about their everyday lives as religious women. Indeed, there was little in the feminist lexicon to help us, beyond vague references to "false consciousness" and monolithic models about patriarchy and oppression to explain this phenomenon.

The study of women who embrace and advocate for patriarchal religious traditions presents several interrelated problems for us as feminist empirical researchers and a plethora of questions for our students. It provokes the most basic pedagogical question. How do we "do" research on those whose identity politics are different from ours? Or put another way, how do I do socially committed work as a feminist activist and still respect the integrity of my respondents who differ from me politically? Feminist practice demands we make the lived experiences of women visible and give them voice. When we study women who advocate and support fundamentalist traditions, we help to make vocal and visible the narratives of those whose politics we do not share. This dilemma was not lost on students.

The women I wrote about in *Rachel's Daughters* had embraced the denomination of Judaism most opposed to equality between men and women at the very same time that such inequalities were breaking down both within other denominations in Judaism and in the secular world. As a committed Jewish feminist, I wished to know more about the ways in which feminism, and especially, Jewish feminism, had failed them. The return of many once feminist women, or indeed any women, to the most traditional arm of Judaism in their young adult years surprised, perplexed, and worried me. Children of the New Left and inheritors of a nascent Jewish feminist movement, these women had turned away from the very social forces that had pulled me into the women's movement and later into feminist academic work. I was anything but a neutral observer or agent in this research process. Several key issues facing us when we teach our students how to "do" feminist research emerge when we look at empirical data from the "inside," as my students refer to it.

The first teaching issue is that few investigations are "value neutral." What is in need of an explanation is always a problem or of interest to someone, to some class of people, or to some nation. As noted above, early work on religious right women is laden with issues about the value and possibility of "neutral" science. What often surprised many of us doing feminist research on fundamentalist women in the early 1990s was the way in which our most basic assumptions were often offset by how our subjects formulated issues about family and gender relations. Many of my interviewees, for instance, used feminist rhetoric and a woman-centered focus in their narratives about life as religious right women that resonated with domestic feminists of the late 19th century as well as some contemporary feminists (Kaufman, 1993). Judith Stacey (1990) coined the term *protofeminist* to describe the Pentecostal women she studied.

The second pedagogical point an exploration of fundamentalist women makes is that the way we theorize our research often shapes the way in which we do our research. Because there was little data available at the time of my research on fundamentalist women apart from their involvement in antifeminist activities, many others and I assumed a priori that such women were assuredly antifeminists. In a chapter I wrote some years ago about feminist methodology and family theory, I argued that

> feminist-interpretive methodology, developed from theoretical assumptions about grounding theory in the actual lives women lead, insists that we not limit the world to male images of women nor that we assume that the parameters of women's experiences are set by male exploitation alone. (Kaufman, 1990, p. 126)

If we do so, we "transform women's history into a subcategory of the history of male values and behavior" (Smith-Rosenberg, 1980, p. 56). In a sophisticated rendering of her distinction between a priori categories substituting for interpersonal relations, Chandra Mohanty (1988) suggests that if we assume that women are a unified, powerless group prior "to the historical and political analysis in question," then we have specified "the context after the fact" (p. 68). She writes that such women "are now placed in the context of the family, or in the workplace, or within religious networks, almost as if these systems existed outside the relations of women with other women, and women with men" (p. 68). Abstract or political designations are no match for "voice" and lived experience.

The third feminist methodological lesson to offer was that we often must go beyond our disciplinary boundaries to put into context the lives we wish to explore. For instance, for me, Jewish feminists' *theological* conclusions about the oppression of Orthodox women posed the beginning of important *sociological* feminist questions. Do women experience Orthodoxy in the ways in which they are theologically described by those in religious studies? Are they simply passive recipients of theological interpretations? Are they victims of a false consciousness created by male ideology? Using a feminist methodological framework, I wanted to

move beyond abstract claims in describing these women's lives (what Leacock, 1977, refers to as unwarranted teleology) to the actual and complex lives women lead. Where might preaching and practice differ? All empirical work must be placed within a specific political, historical, and sociological context. This demands the insights and tools of a multidisciplinary perspective.

The fourth pedagogical lesson of my research journey was that those we research are agents in the making of their worlds as much as they are subjects. While feminist methodology cautions that we are never just observers when we do our research, it is clear that those under scrutiny are never just subjects. They are not passive, unthinking recipients of theological discourse and patriarchal structure. I found, for instance, that despite their seemingly "antifeminist" attitudes, many of the women I interviewed used the rhetoric of feminism and often offered a direct critique of male, secular normative models to explain their choice of Jewish Orthodoxy. They compared a male normative secular world of individualistic and competitive striving with the spiritual, modest, "feminine," and communally oriented world of Jewish Orthodoxy. Because they came to their Orthodoxy as young adults, they were able to offer critiques of both the secular and the religious worlds that resonated with feminist rhetoric and criticism. Many women claimed that they preferred the "patriarchal devils" within Orthodoxy to those outside of it (Kaufman, 2002).

The fifth lesson to be learned from my pedagogical narrative was that all research is historically specific. The "return to Orthodoxy" for these women came within a specific sociohistoric moment. It was a time of turning inward, a time of great gender role upheaval, and a time when we were experiencing a "turn to the right" both politically and religiously. What were the specifics of the relationships, at both the personal and institutional level, that maintained/sustained these women? How did these women compare to and differ from 19th-century domestic feminists who argued strenuously for a woman-centered world in contrast to a world gone awry with male values? How did these women compare to and differ from women living in other contemporary, sex-segregated religious communities in different geographic, class, and racial contexts? How did they disrupt the categories of patriarchy, motherhood, and sex segregation in ways that are both familiar and unfamiliar? How did their narratives compare to contemporary radical lesbian feminists who extol the virtues of women's bodies and sexuality, as did these women? In short, how did the specific historical and political contexts of their embracing Orthodoxy affect their "patriarchal" experiences?

If we do not differentiate by time, place, and politics, we end up disguising rather than explaining the effects of the structure of patriarchy on religious discourses about gender relations or how religious rituals are used in everyday life. Elizabeth Brusco (1986), for instance, discovered that the growth of Evangelicalism among Colombian women was, in part, a way these "born-again" women held "impious men" to "pious" rules through adherence to the religious dictates of the church not to smoke, drink, or gamble. It serves as an important lesson in the meaning and measure of patriarchy. In part, the growth of Protestant fundamentalism was a way, argues Brusco, to combat the "machismo" of the Catholic Church. However, what we also learn here is the way in which patriarchal rule varies between two equally patriarchal churches.

Uma Narayan (1989) warns that patriarchal resolutions and strategies vary. She suggests that what might be good within Western countries may backfire in non-Western ones. She cautions that "it may be politically counterproductive for nonwestern feminists to echo uncritically the terms of western feminist epistemology that seeks to restore the value . . . of 'women's experience' because it only 'values women's' place as long as she keeps to the place prescribed" (p. 259). She continues her warning by noting that she is "inclined to think that in nonwestern countries feminists must still stress negative ideas of the female experience" within their cultures. The time for a more sympathetic evaluation is not, in her words, "quite ripe" (p. 259).

In the 15 years I have taught feminist methodology at Northeastern University, I have cotaught only once with a woman of color, a black social psychologist. Increasingly the lack of a multicultural base either in the curriculum or within the mix of teachers and students has been a much-vaunted problem across major universities. When I joined the faculty of the Graduate Consortium on Women's Studies at Radcliffe, I found a more diverse faculty with whom to teach the feminist methodology course. I was forced to address the ways in which the feminist curriculum had (or had not) responded to a growing critique from within. That critique highlighted many more lessons in how to "do" feminist research. Multiculturalism was the new buzzword in feminist teaching and research. Uma Narayan (2000) warned us, however, not to replace gender essentialism with "culture-specific essentialist generalizations" (p. 81), such as Western women and non-Western women. Such categories, she argues, "conflate the abstract, socially dominant norms in operation within any one culture" for the reality of practices within each. As such, the "social construction of culture, its history and politics" are lost in our theoretical and methodological models (p. 84). She further argues, as I did earlier with reference to much of the scholarly work done (or more precisely not done) on "born-again" women, that cultural essentialism promotes the discovery of differences a priori, before the "kind and quality of real differences" can emerge (p. 85). We are caught in the dilemma of trying to capture experience before theory constructs it (Kaufman, 1990). A series of essays in response to Susan Okin's (1999) lead essay in *Is Multiculturalism Bad for Women?* raised controversial issues, at both the theoretical and empirical levels, for the feminist study of multiculturalism, and they have raised many questions among our students. Whose voice and whose everyday experiences do we investigate, theorize about, and value in our inquiries? Okin's challenge to reconcile egalitarian principles with cultural and/or religious diversity is parallel to feminist debates about reconciling feminism and the politics of universalistic and particularistic claims. For instance, it raises the issue of how to avoid relativism when doing comparative research on gender and sexuality. The questions Okin poses bring into focus the theoretical issues critical to the development of a feminist practice that is able to form alliances across class, race, national, and international boundaries (and as noted earlier, disciplinary boundaries). Her choice of what she sees as the most blatant of gender inequalities—child marriages, forced marriages, divorce systems biased against women, polygamy, and clitoridectomy—present some of the most heated debates I have experienced within the classroom.

For many, especially, Western-trained students, there are clear directives. We must put all our efforts into eliminating such inequalities and oppressive practices. For others, we must locate the *specific* historic and political context within which such practices take place and salvage that which can be maintained as central components of cultural identity without being inimical to women. A feminist approach, as Narayan (2000) suggests, can discover the historical and political processes that make culturally dominant norms of femininity central components of cultural identity, and, thereby, uncover how dominant groups misuse, romanticize, reinvent, and/or present cultural practices as unchanging to their own advantage.

Feminist historical and political inquiries can make clear how radically changed cultural practices (often quite inimical to women) can remain hidden under the label of cultural preservation (Narayan, 2000). Theoretical questions about the meaning of epistemic advantage and the place of women's everyday experience and language are critical to this balancing act. Perhaps the most troubling of the issues raised in these multicultural debates is the possibility of ever being able to generalize beyond the particular set of voices under consideration. If we are unable to speak of women as a category, how do we act on our political behalf? Similarly, if we are unable to speak of a culture, how can we make claims for equity among its members? Narayan (2000) offers a not-altogether-satisfying response. She writes,

I believe that antiessentialism about gender and about culture does not entail a simple-minded opposition to *all generalizations,* but entails instead a commitment to examine both their empirical accuracy and their political utility or risk. It is seldom possible to articulate effective political agendas, such as those pertaining to human rights, without resorting to a certain degree of abstraction, which enables the articulation of salient similarities between problems suffered by various individuals and groups. On the other hand, it seems arguably true that there is no need to portray female genital mutilation as an "African cultural practice" or dowry murders and dowry related harassment as a "problem of Indian women" in ways that eclipse the fact that not *all* "African women'" or "Indian women" confront them in identical ways, or in ways that efface local contestations of these problems. (2000, p. 97)

Multicultural debates evoke many questions from students. How might we find a common ground for a "practice" politics, which honors the particular without "otherizing" or "romanticizing" it? Need we throw out the liberal baby with the Western bathwater? Robert Post (1999, p. 67) suggests that liberal multiculturalism both sustains and constrains individual freedom. The struggle, both within the classroom and outside of it, to distinguish between enabling and oppressive cultural norms, demands that all cultural and institutional structures be placed within *their own historical evolution.* The classroom then becomes the place where we struggle to move beyond the "Western/non-Western" dichotomy and to find the balance between particular integrity and universal solidarity—the place where the universal and the particular meet (Kaufman, 2002).

Teaching with colleagues from different disciplinary perspectives parallels many of the issues raised when addressing multiculturalism and feminist scholarship and practice. How do we understand the "other" when teaching with colleagues and to students from disciplines "other" than our own? Often a multidisciplinary teaching team creates tensions similar to those created by a multicultural set of voices within our texts and empirical research. Each discipline poses its own hierarchy of values and concerns that dictate the choice of materials to be taught and the "voice" from which it will be taught. Students face similar issues in placing their teachers' comments in a perspective that is compatible with the values and issues they have come to recognize as disciplinarily important to them. The multicultural issues raised by Okin are particularly exacerbated when we combine humanists, scientists, and social scientists in the same classroom. Students are frequently caught between competing claims and different levels of analysis in coming to terms with feminist policy on gender patterns not only in cultures different from theirs, but also from different disciplinary perspectives.

All methodological choices have consequences. That recognition is critical to a feminist consciousness. The issues raised in this essay move beyond feminist methodology. They raise questions about the power politics inherent in academic life and in the making of knowledge. They raise questions about the price we pay for leaving the safety of our disciplines and for making "cutting-edge" choices. For whom and to whom do we write and teach as feminists? At times I am at a loss to answer this question. I often feel that I have lost my academic compass, not quite sure for whom I am writing or, more important, for whom my writing is important.

As teachers and scholars we must see ourselves as historical and political subjects. We must make explicit how we have come to our topics of inquiry and the disciplinary tools we choose or, even more important, disregard in our scholarly journeys. We must be self-reflexive in our research process and aware of the political repercussions, not only within our disciplines, but also within the very communities we are investigating. For whom is our research important? Have we built a wide enough audience, both within the academy and outside of it, to ensure that we can survive beyond this particular political and historical moment? Does multidisciplinary teaching and interdisciplinary inquiry open new audiences for our work or does it muddy the process whereby we can mainstream our scholarship and teaching?

We have come full circle to my question at the beginning of this essay. Will feminist methodology ever be accepted into mainstream, disciplinary analyses, or, as with other critical views, will it be relegated to the margins of the disciplines? Need it remain marginal to traditional disciplinary canons to evoke an epistemological revolution? Perhaps the more critical question is, What will happen should feminism find its way to the center of disciplinary traditions?

There is little to indicate that feminist methodology will be brought into the mainstream of most disciplinary discourses any time soon. Mohanty (1988) claims that "feminist scholarly practices exist within relations of power—relations which they counter, redefine, or even implicitly support" (p. 62). The future promises no easy resolution of these inherent tensions, but rather a continuing dialogue and a lively set of debates among and between feminists, our students, and the academy.

## NOTE

1. It is important to note here, however, that positivism is not the only source of critical concern for feminists and that it may present a different set of issues for Third World women (see Narayan, 1989).

## REFERENCES

Brusco, Elizabeth. (1986). Colombian Evangelicalism as a strategic form of women's collective action. *Feminist Issues, 6*(2), 3–13.

Kaufman, Debra Renee. (1990). Engendering family theory. In Jetse Sprey (Ed.), *Fashioning family theory* (pp. 107–135). Newbury Park, CA: Sage.

Kaufman, Debra Renee. (1993). *Rachel's daughters: Newly orthodox Jewish women.* New Brunswick, NJ: Rutgers University Press.

Kaufman, Debra Renee. (1996). Rethinking, reflecting, rewriting: Teaching feminist methodology. *Journal of Radical Education and Cultural Studies, 181,* 165–174.

Kaufman, Debra Renee. (2002). Better the devil you know and other contemporary identity narratives: Orthodoxy and reform Judaism. In Dana Evan Kaplan (Ed.), *Platforms and prayer books: Theological and liturgical perspectives on reform Judaism* (pp. 251–260). Lanham, MD: Rowman & Littlefield.

Leacock, E. (1977). The changing family and Levi-Strauss, or whatever happened to fathers. *Sociological Research, 44,* 235–289.

Mohanty, Chandra. (1988). Under Western eyes: Feminist scholarship and colonial discourses. *Feminist Review, 30,* 61–88.

Narayan, Uma. (1989). The project of feminist epistemology: Perspectives from a nonwestern feminist. In Alison Jaggar & Susan Bordo (Eds.), *Gender/body/knowledge* (pp. 256–269). Princeton, NJ: Rutgers University Press.

Narayan, Uma. (2000). Essence of culture and a sense of history: A feminist critique of cultural essentialism.

In Uma Narayan & Sandra Harding (Eds.), *Decentering the center: Philosophy for a multicultural, postcolonial, and feminist world* (pp. 80–100). Bloomington: Indiana University Press.

Okin, Susan Moller. (Ed.). (1999). *Is multiculturalism bad for women?* Princeton, NJ: Princeton University Press.

Post, Robert. (1999). Between norms and choices. In Susan Moller Okin (Ed.), *Is multiculturalism bad for women?* (pp. 65–68). Princeton, NJ: Princeton University Press.

Smith-Rosenberg, C. (1980). Politics and culture in women's history: A symposium. *Feminist Studies, 6*(1), 55–64.

Stacey, J. (1990). *Brave new families*. New York: Basic Books.

# 42

# FEMINIST PEDAGOGY RECONSIDERED

## DAPHNE PATAI

What happens when feminism pervades academic research and teaching? Does feminist-inspired pedagogy create problems that differ fundamentally from those attending conventional teaching and research? I want to approach these questions by reflecting on the consequences of placing the qualifier *feminist* before the nouns *teaching* and *research*.

As innumerable women's studies course descriptions, mission statements, and Web sites attest,[1] the adjective *feminist* adds—and is intended to add—something highly programmatic to whatever nouns it modifies—namely, a deliberate purpose, a project of political advocacy. The activist design underlying women's studies has been present since its earliest days, when the new field was defined as "the academic arm of the women's movement," but its expression has grown ever more blatant over the years, as current women's studies self-descriptions make plain. In the classroom, feminist politics expresses itself, and at the least, as a commitment to fundamental feminist positions and teaching practices, at the most, as an unyielding ideological drive. Does such an orientation prove problematic to conscientious teaching and research? Not inevitably, perhaps, but very likely. And that is so because the political engagement underlying feminism in the

academy is bound to set up a highly tendentious model for research and teaching, a paradigm most feminists would hardly accept were its objectives contrary to their own. But rather than attack this dilemma directly, women's studies prefers to measure itself against the past. And this backward-looking gauge, in turn, rests on a sweeping (and self-promoting) claim about all non- and prefeminist teaching and research.

To justify and defend the introduction of *feminist* as a legitimate modifier of their *teaching* and *research*, feminists have had to greatly exaggerate the flaws affecting the pre- or non-feminist model they are contesting. They insist that in the routine practices of the old dispensation, teaching and research have always been, and still are, biased, exclusionary, and inimical to the interests of women. In short, they are "masculinist." To many feminists, this is a decisive claim. For only when academic procedures can be portrayed in such starkly negative terms is the feminist agenda seen as a corrective: legitimate, appropriate, fair, salutary, and urgently necessary.

Thus, what the term *feminist* introduces into the classroom is a patently political project driving its sense of the aims of education and the pursuit of knowledge. This project has a broad range of objectives—from the basic pedagogical goals of "liberal feminism" or "equality for women," which are often derided and dismissed in more radical feminist circles, to the extreme views associated with such writers as Catharine MacKinnon, who disdainfully treats the concept *liberal* as a disguise for the exercise of patriarchal privilege. MacKinnon (1987) entitled one of her books *Feminism Unmodified* precisely because her position is that her own brand of feminism alone is the genuine article and therefore tolerates no qualifier.

If we start, however, with a different set of assumptions—namely, the suppositions that teaching and research are not, and ought not to be, either feminist or masculinist and that despite the historical exclusion of women, the substance of a liberal education and the ideas on which it rests have not been entirely and always flawed— the adjective *feminist* begins to look less like a salutary corrective and more like the calamitous imposition of a political point of view. Why calamitous? Because the great thing about the university is that it provides that rare space in which emphasis can be on *how* to think, not *what* to think, on acquiring intellectual tools, not accepting hand-me-down political doctrines. To assert that indoctrination is what men have in fact traditionally perpetrated in all fields and that it is now the turn of women to do the same, even if this assertion were accurate, is a weak defense, since it would turn the feminist program into a replica of a practice considered flawed and even malevolent. Surely the appropriate response to whatever are deemed to be the shortcomings of traditional teaching is not simply to reverse the biases of the past but rather to surpass them.

But this imperative presents a major conundrum for the feminist project, and it is precisely to avert the consequences of this conundrum that feminists have resorted to the proposition that "all teaching is political,"[2] which allows them to represent their own academic activism as no less legitimate than earlier academic procedures. For if all these activities are inherently political, and they have been so in a way that has oppressed women, then the feminist-inspired activist classroom is a corrective required by both justice and fairness. This is the argument that anchors and justifies the feminist position on education.[3]

Is it, then, true that all education and research are "political" and at best (or worst) manage to conceal their biases? Though in particular cases a political slant may be demonstrated, it seems to me absurd to insist that this distortion is omnipresent and feminists alone face up to it (and embrace it). Only by turning itself into mere triviality can the "all education is political" claim survive scrutiny. To be sure, in some general sense almost everything can be shown to have a political aspect. But only by means of gross extrapolation from the subject at hand can one paint all past knowledge with such a broad brush. To offer one instance of such strained extrapolation, when I made this very point on an online "chat" sponsored by the *Chronicle of Higher Education*, the example I used in my counterargument to "everything is political" was of the periodic table.[4] Where, exactly, I wondered, is the "unacknowledged political agenda" (mentioned by one of the discussants) inherent in the periodic table? I quickly got my answer from one women's studies professor:

> Doesn't the teaching of the Periodic Table imply that "man's" appropriate relationship with "nature" is one of dominance? And that we should search for the meaning of existence through science? Since when are such humanist assertions free from political implications?

Here, in a few sentences, is laid out the confusion routinely warned against by philosophers of science—namely, the confounding of the *content* of science with the *context* in which scientific work is done and disseminated. It is hardly reassuring to think that college students are being encouraged to repeat such a wrongheaded argument without recognizing its inherent logical fallacy. But this attitude toward science—indeed toward knowledge generally— seems actually to be a requisite of women's studies. The philosopher of science Noretta Koertge (2003) has explained why taking on science has been a particular goal of feminists:

> Scientific inquiry embodied all of the so-called masculine virtues that feminism most wanted to challenge—objectivity (vs. subjectivity), the power of reason (instead of intuition), problem solving through logical analysis and the weighing of evidence (vs. conflict resolution through empathy and plumbing the depths of oppression). (p. 321)[5]

If feminists could demonstrate that even science—supposedly the most rational human pursuit—is at its core political and that claims to objectivity are always fraudulent, they could then justify similar critiques of other domains of knowledge *a fortiori*, thus undergirding their own legitimacy and warding off suspicions that they are engaged in special pleading.[6] And for that very reason, hostility to science, as it emerges from a host of feminist writings and teaching materials, is in my view an important criterion for judging the intellectual integrity that feminists bring to the classroom.

But isn't the charge that feminism is hostile to science a mere caricature? Or a part of the "backlash"? Let us see. Leaving aside such well-known critiques as that by Alan Sokal and Jean Bricmont of renowned French feminists' garbled and ignorant claims about physics,[7] I turn to the evidence of discussions taking place in women's studies classes everywhere, discussions about sex. Women's studies programs and the books on their reading lists treat as a matter of orthodoxy the view that gender differences are always socially constructed. However, unlike earlier second-wave feminist work that attempted to distinguish between gender (social) and sex (biological), many women's studies teachers these days have extended social constructionism to the point where it engulfs biology altogether.[8]

A few years ago, on the Women's Studies e-mail list (WMST-L), I questioned the utility of spending much class time on Anne Fausto-Sterling's work (2000; extremely popular in women's studies courses then and now), which argues that there are more than two sexes (p. 20).[9] The existence of a very small percentage of infants born with sexual anomalies, I stated, in no way challenges the reality of sexual dimorphism as a biological fact. Angry denunciations of my comment poured into the list, one of which even accused me of attacking the civil rights of minorities. But more than the tone, what startled me about these responses was the categorical insistence that Fausto-Sterling demonstrates that our very bodies are "socially constructed" as binary, the apparent underlying assumption being that "biology" itself was somehow inimical to feminist interests and had to be reconceived. This conviction led to some astonishing messages,

accusing me of reiterating *with no evidence* that sexual dimorphism is indeed a biological fact.[10]

At last, a biologist (Ruthann Masaracchia, 2001), who was also directing a women's studies program, wrote in to say that she was appalled at the lack of basic knowledge of biology demonstrated in the discussion. Offering to explain the reality of sexual dimorphism, she asked:

> So where would you like to start—dimorphism in utero, chromosomes and chromosomal diversity, differentiation and development? I will try to be succinct but I will also provide some facts that many of you (based on your comments) aren't going to like.

Few people took her up on the offer. Instead, she was denounced in short order for claiming to have expertise and soon decided, sensibly, to stop wasting her time on the list.[11]

I recount this episode to convey the mood and characteristic reactions among faculty members most involved in teaching women's studies—those who regularly participate on the WMST-L (which at that time had about 4,500 subscribers and in 2005 was up to about 5,000)—and thereby provide a fascinating portrait of the attitudes and postures prevalent in that field. But it's important to add here that even while being denounced on the list, I often get a few "behind the scenes" messages of support from women's studies faculty members and graduate students, who tell me privately that they share my concerns, are made uneasy by the dogma of social constructionism or other favored tenets of women's studies, but feel unable to say so openly for fear of jeopardizing their careers. As I argued long ago, little tolerance inhabits women's studies, and the fears expressed by young or future faculty members demonstrate that this has not changed.

The result is that while progress occurs in many other fields, consequent on the extraordinary scientific and sociopolitical advances of our time, many teachers of women's studies, like other ideologues, prefer simply to dismiss whatever ideas seem to threaten their closed worldview. The science writer Deborah Rudacille is one who demonstrates the oddness of the feminist rejection of biology. In her recent book *The

*Riddle of Gender: Science, Activism, and Transgender Rights*, Rudacille (2005) argues against the social constructionist orthodoxy so prevalent in the past few decades. "Today," she writes, "the pendulum in gender research is slowly swinging back to biology. Hormones acting under the influence of genes are now thought to be the primary architects of gender identity" (pp. 138–139), although the exact developmental mechanisms are not yet clear.[12]

Many feminist academics, however, evidently have great difficulty leaving their core ideas behind, no matter how anachronistic they have become. This is readily apparent when one turns to publications on science in the field of women's studies. In Mary F. Rogers and C. D. Garrett's (2002) book *Who's Afraid of Women's Studies: Feminisms in Everyday Life*, for example, it is stated flatly that "sexual identities have been culturally constructed" (p. 49). Another book, *Feminist Science Studies: A New Generation* (Mayberry, Subramaniam, & Weasel, 2001), similarly reveals the feminist desire to dismiss science and put in its place politically agreeable notions. In the latter book, which purports to present the latest thinking in the burgeoning field of science studies, the three editors describe feminist science studies as committed to exploring "situated knowledges," in which the relationship between feminism and science and "the intersections between race, class, gender, and science and technology" are examined and which aims at a "disruption of the dichotomy between scientific inquiry and policy" (pp. 5, 6). As the introduction explains, *Feminist Science Studies* aims at nothing less than to provide "progressive, positive readings of science, and of reconstructions of science consistent with feminist theories, ideals, and visions" (p. 10).[13] The extraordinary nature of this objective seems not to trouble the field of feminist science studies, nor has it hindered the uncritical adoption of articles in this field in the "multidisciplinary" women's studies courses typically taught by nonscientists.

Martha Whitaker (2001), in her essay in *Feminist Science Studies*, affirms that Anne Fausto-Sterling's work (2000) has been of special importance "in helping me to understand that scientists' analyses and quantification of earth and natural processes *are* social and political

processes" (p. 49)—a perfect expression, this, of the reigning approach to science among feminists. Still another contributor (Subramaniam, 2001) aims to go beyond feminist science studies' penchant for "taking apart the visible workings of science to highlight the invisible factors that shaped the interconnections between nature and culture, science and society." Her project is "one of reconstruction—to use [the] insights of deconstruction to rebuild a practice that was scientifically rigorous but also informed by the rigors of feminist politics and scholarship" (p. 57)—as if the problem were not precisely that the "rigors" of these different endeavors are hardly to be compared.[14]

Particularly revealing is an article by Rebecca M. Herzig (2001) describing her Introduction to Women's Studies course at Bates College. Aiming to dispel students' notion that biology exists "outside the effects of culture and history," Herzig provides her class with "modules" complete with guided readings designed to help students "query received knowledge about 'the female body.'" While this appears to be an unobjectionable aim, Herzig's true goals are apparent in her tendentious module on "Sexual Dimorphism," which relies heavily on readings by Fausto-Sterling and a few others who emphasize the existence of intersexed humans. Here is how the module presents the problem:

> Lurking in most contemporary discussions about gender and sexuality in the United States [but not elsewhere?] is a presumption of the universal, timeless dimorphism between human males and females. How empirically sound are these dualistic categories? What evidence has been presented for and against universal human sexual dimorphism? How might cross-cultural ethnographic evidence challenge biomedical assumptions of a strict two-sex model? How does the presumption of sexual dimorphism inform our understandings of human sexuality? (pp. 183–192)[15]

The last question of course gives the agenda away: It is important to attack the notion of biological dimorphism because the fact of dimorphism is essential to our history of sexual reproduction. And sexual reproduction, from a biological point of view, confirms the normalcy, indeed the ordinariness, of heterosexuality, which is the very thing that academic feminists routinely identify as the "institution" at the root of women's "oppression." Biology thus presents a particularly intractable problem for feminist analysis, and it is not surprising that many feminists spend considerable energy arguing that biology is merely one more ingredient in the formidable ideology sustaining patriarchy. Readers who note the contradictions in the feminist attack on biology should be reassured: These dodges seem not to be a problem for feminists who denounce the existence of biological "facts" while, at the same time, having constant recourse to essentialist—and always negative—characterizations of "males" and their intrinsic nature.[16]

There is, then, a deep and—for many feminists—vital link between attacking the biology of sex differences and undermining the "institution" of heterosexuality, seen as the linchpin to male dominance. I have documented elsewhere this salient tendency within much contemporary feminism.[17] But lest readers think that arguments against biology come only from a few doctrinaire radical feminists now perhaps out of fashion, I turn to a standard reference work, the Houghton Mifflin *Reader's Companion to U.S. Women's History*,[18] whose entry on "Heterosexuality" (Trimberger, 1998) reveals that statements perhaps once thought to be controversial within feminism can these days be affirmed without qualification:

> Sexuality is not private, but is political and related to power. "Compulsory heterosexuality" is part of a power structure benefiting heterosexual males at the expense of women and homosexuals. This inequity is justified by an ideology that sees heterosexuality as natural, universal, and biologically necessary, and homosexuality as the opposite. The system also is reinforced by legal sanctions and violence against women (rape, battering, incest, and murder) and against lesbians, gays, and transgendered persons (verbal harassment, physical assault, and murder). (p. 255)

The author spells out why it is important for feminists to press such an argument: "If our sexuality is socially constructed it can also be de- and reconstructed"—a clear indication, this, of feminism's urgent need to reconstitute everything about men and women's lives that it sees as hindering its own project of social transformation.

If even in relation to biology feminist educators do not shrink from their tendentious and often ill-supported arguments, we can expect comparable procedures to drive other feminist endeavors to reshape education. It should be, but isn't, needless to say that the integrity of education is always in danger when politics or ideology supersede rational inquiry and the careful consideration of evidence. Twentieth-century history has demonstrated this peril in abundance, and it is distressing that academic feminists have not taken these cautionary instances to heart.

Still, one may ask: Does it really matter that virtually all feminist teachers believe teaching to be invariably political? That they hold fairness and claims of objectivity in research to be mere illusions, if not outright frauds? I answer: Yes, definitely it matters, because teachers who hold these beliefs are left incapable of even attempting to recognize their own biases, let alone transcend them. Worse, they are programmatically committed to propagating their biases, which is exactly what they do in the "feminist classroom." Thus, women's studies teachers openly declare their objective to make students confront their "privilege" or recognize the "institutional" causes of their unprivileged status.[19] And in the name of multi- or interdisciplinarity, they pass on to their students all manner of research the merits of which they are not able to evaluate but that is accepted or rejected on political grounds. In such classes, students rarely encounter criticisms of feminist-inspired work, nor are they encouraged to develop the capacity of independent judgment and appraisal that might challenge the feminist presuppositions on which their courses rest.[20] Women's studies prides itself on constantly challenging Western society—but the one thing it shrinks from challenging is its own pet ideas.

Having written about these issues for the past 15 years, I am well aware that the usual response to criticisms of this type—and often merely to raising these issues—is that the writer is an enemy of feminism, a "conservative," or a reactionary trying to force women back to the kitchen, and so on—all of which are feeble rejoinders designed to avoid engaging with the very real problems caused by the intentional politicizing of research and teaching. Not surprisingly, whole books have been devoted to attempting to prove that criticisms such as the ones I and others have made are merely examples of "backlash."[21] Indeed, the very word *backlash* has acquired a sacramental aura in feminist circles, obviating even the expectation of a reasoned response to the specific criticisms that have been voiced. And as scholars who had formerly devoted years to the advancement of feminism in the academy express their dissatisfaction with where politicized teaching has taken us, they too can expect to be vilified by the feminist academics still defending their turf. Though what such scholars really want is to see research and teaching liberated from feminism's (and other identity groups') political advocacy, deviation from the feminist educational agenda is enough to have one's writing dismissed out of hand and one's character impugned.

Despite this predictable response, some well-known senior scholars closely associated with feminism in the academy have in recent years felt moved to object to the politicizing of education. In the Summer 2000 issue of *Signs*, devoted to dozens of essays on feminism and the academy, Elaine Marks, a widely recognized lesbian critic, who until her death in late 2001 was Germaine Brée professor of French and women's studies at the University of Wisconsin, Madison, complained that she was beginning to feel "isolated in Women's Studies," where she had come to be perceived as "a closet conservative." Why? Because she deplored the prevalence of identity politics in literature courses and now agreed with Harold Bloom (1994) that "to read in the service of any ideology is not, in my judgment, to read at all" (p. 29). Marks confessed that she herself used to have politically correct responses, the kind that seek, in any work of literature, traces of the dreaded *isms* (sexism, racism, etc.). But she was no longer satisfied with such approaches. Hence, her decision to air in public some of what she considered to be "feminism's perverse effects" in the academy.

"It is no simple matter," Marks (2000) concluded, "in this millennial fin de siècle, to criticize certain tendencies in cultural studies or Women's Studies or ethnic studies without being accused of

participating in a conservative political agenda" (p. 1163). And she is right. In the topsy-turvy world of academe, to call for an education not bound to a political agenda is tantamount to being "conservative." Moreover, the fact that *conservative* has become a label of instant dismissal in academe exemplifies the ideological rigidity that now disfigures the one arena that was supposed to fearlessly and openly explore ideas and knowledge claims on their own merits.[22]

The philosopher Susan Haack is one critic whose work should be indispensable reading for every feminist who aspires to scholarly integrity. Her 1998 book, *Manifesto of a Passionate Moderate: Unfashionable Essays*, is filled with challenges to the notion that a "feminist" perspective strengthens intellectual work, the sorts of challenges routinely ignored in women's studies classrooms. To Haack (1998b), "the politicization of inquiry, . . . whether in the interests of good political values or bad, is always epistemologically unsound" (p. 119).[23] Haack (1998a) considers that "the rubric 'feminist epistemology' is incongruous on its face, in somewhat the way of, say, 'Republican epistemology'" (p. 124; see also Noretta Koertge, this volume). Haack (1998a) explains:

> The profusion of incompatible themes proposed as "feminist epistemology" itself speaks against the ideas of a distinctively female cognitive style. But even if there were such a thing, the case for feminist epistemology would require further argument to show that women's "ways of knowing" . . . represent better procedures of inquiry or subtler standards of justification than the male. And, sure enough, we are told that insights into the theory of knowledge are available to women which are not available, or not easily available, to men. (p. 126)

Dismissing "the egregious assumption that one thinks with one's skin or one's sex organs," Haack (1998b) in another essay stresses that

> this form of argument, when applied to the concepts of evidence, truth, etc., is not only fallacious; it is also pragmatically self-undermining. . . . For if there were no genuine inquiry, no objective evidence, we couldn't know what theories are such that their being accepted would conduce to women's interests, nor what women's interests are. (p. 118)

Haack (1998a) denounces the "ambition of the new, imperialist feminism to colonize epistemology," and then makes the telling comment: "There would be a genuinely feminist epistemology if the idea could be legitimated *that feminist values should determine what theories are accepted*" (p. 128). And, indeed, precisely such a destructive idea is regularly embraced in women's studies circles, where few seem to note that it will undermine the ground of their own pedagogy.

In recent years, I have not seen any evidence that women's studies teachers have modified their antagonism toward claims to positive knowledge in particular and scientific reasoning in general.[24] And, not surprisingly, they are now finding themselves in some company they may not choose to keep. As "creation science," recast these days as "intelligent design," extends its reach and threatens the teaching of basic science (reduced to a competing ideology) in the United States, its defenders make comments about the status of evolution—that it is "just a theory," for example, though one that claims for itself a privileged status—that are remarkably similar to the feminist depreciation of science.[25] Like creationists, many feminists have shown contempt for evidence—when it did not support their preconceptions. They may misunderstand science (perhaps intentionally), denounce its procedures, and ignore its commitment to self-correction—all in order to be able to characterize it as ideology and not even as honest a one as their own feminist ideology, which acknowledges its political interests.

But the rejection of the ideals of objective knowledge (however imperfectly attainable) and the deployment of the admitted limitations of knowledge into a weapon against past knowledge, to be dismissed as the product of patriarchal dead white men, along with the disdain for standards of evidence and logic, gain feminists only an illusory victory. It may leave them free to defend and promote their agenda, but it also renders them vulnerable to ignorant or politically motivated calumnies directed against them. For how will feminists respond when, with the next cultural turn, we are once again told that the blood of menstruating women causes milk to curdle? Aren't standards of evidence and objective investigation crucial to all

women (to all people) as they attempt to combat prejudice and ignorance?

Because I have often observed feminists readily veering from one line of argument to another (e.g., resorting to biological determinism when denouncing men while insisting on social constructionism—the official feminist orthodoxy—most of the time), I have concluded that caring more about achieving "feminist" goals than about meeting the obligations of scrupulous teaching and research leads to an opportunistic intellectual stance in the academy and—most harmfully—in the classroom. One example of this is the reality that these days feminist advocacy must increasingly depend on a gross misrepresentation of the status of women in North American society generally and in the university in particular. An egregious example of this distortion is the claim made—presumably with a straight face—by some feminist scholars in the United States that "the academy remains an essentially single sex institution. It is male-dominated, and that domination exerts itself in both numbers and power" (Scollay & Bratt, 1997, p. 274). Such misrepresentations of the real-life situation of women, which are common to this day, as feminist writings on higher education reveal, should not be seen as a pathological inability to recognize the profound changes and improvements that have occurred over the past few decades but merely as a tactical necessity for women's studies.

But as feminist pedagogues continue to rely on scare statistics regarding rape while ignoring, say, research on woman-initiated domestic violence,[26] and as women's studies courses claim multidisciplinary expertise while often resting on multidisciplinary ignorance, the result of feminist teaching is a pedagogy ever more at odds with observable reality, steeped in ever less-authentic-sounding pronouncements. Never mind the massive evidence—statistical, judicial, and legislative, as well as anecdotal—of enormous and ongoing improvement in women's status in the United States (and many other parts of the world). Society has changed, but feminist activists seem determined either not to notice or not to admit it.[27] Instead, self-serving stereotypes about male violence and female victimization and oppression are repeated as though they were startling insights.[28]

Oddly enough, women's studies seems to have learned little from its own criticisms of what happens when education is governed by political agendas. Nor do many feminist teachers appear to have grasped the implications of such illuminating 20th-century cases as Lysenkoism in the USSR, a stellar example of science "reconstructed" so as to be "consistent with" a reigning political ideology—the overt goal, as we saw earlier, of the volume *Feminist Science Studies* (Mayberry et al., 2001). Embracing, as feminism in the academy does, the principle that all education is political (and declining to explore just how this might be true, to what extent, in what circumstances, and at what costs) makes it impossible for women's studies and other politically inspired programs to respond convincingly to political pressures from the other side. It also forces disingenuous misrepresentations of challenges to current orthodoxies. Thus, David Horowitz's (2003) *Academic Bill of Rights*, for example, with its demand for political diversity in the name of academic freedom, is routinely charged by multicultural/feminist/left-liberal professors with being a thinly disguised effort to enforce his own (conservative) politics. Despite his careful delineation of his proposal, Horowitz is constantly depicted as attacking academic freedom in that hitherto pristine bastion of intellectual exploration, the university.

Of course, some state legislators who support the Academic Bill of Rights (ABOR) may well be motivated by the desire to ensure space in the classroom for conservative political ideas. And why not? After all, those who claim that all education is political hardly have grounds for objecting to the inclusion of some mainstream—or even conservative—political views not currently fashionable in the academic world. If feminists really believe in their characterization of nonfeminist education, why are they (like many academic organizations) in a panic over the ABOR? The fact is that Horowitz has stolen the high ground from those who might now, opportunistically, wish to reclaim it. For while the campus left has, as we have seen, affirmed that all education is political, Howoritz is in fact relying on definitions of academic freedom that have a long and distinguished lineage. And even worse, when feminists themselves are now forced to resort to

the same sort of claims in an effort to combat him, they are easily exposed by charges of utter hypocrisy and bad faith.[29]

And if feminists and other politically committed teachers are worried about being sued by students disgruntled with their one-sided representations of knowledge (as a bill introduced in Florida would have allowed), why haven't they objected to the widespread adoption of harassment policies and speech codes in academe, under which scores of professors have already been subjected to censure, loss of job, and legal action because a woman was offended by, say, a professor's nonfeminist discussion of abortion or rape? I have not seen women's studies teachers rush to protect academic freedom and uninhibited class discussion for those whose views contradict their own. Quite the contrary, as I have documented at length (see Patai, 1998).

Where, one might well ask, will feminists be able to go in this struggle over which ideas should be protected in the academy? Presumably, feminists would respond that *their* ideas are true or better. But to sustain this claim, they would be forced to resort to high standards of evidence, rigorous logic, and fair evaluation not in thrall to political predispositions. Yet these are the very procedures feminist academics have so often attacked. In combating other ideologues and their claims, the feminist promotion of subjectivity, value-laden theory, or "standpoint epistemology"—all still very much in vogue—will not serve them well. For their own practice has helped create a conflict with no rules, only with competing political passions and varieties of belief.

As many commentators have observed, feminism itself could not even have gotten started without embracing claims resting on objective conditions and drawing on supposedly unbiased research said to accurately assess the situation of women vis-à-vis men. In light of feminism's path, therefore, the present assertions of feminist pedagogy seem not only tendentious but also disingenuous. The feminist promotion of subjectivity, of standpoint epistemology, and of the paradigm that "everything is political" is, thus, at best situational. It hardly justifies the pedagogy that has grown up around it. Of course, women's studies is not alone in promoting these habits. Postmodernist fashions have made a variety of vulnerable intellectual and pedagogical approaches acceptable and widely used. And this is the case even among feminist critics of postmodernism, who while decrying its alienating and pretentious vocabulary, and its distance from everyday political struggles, nonetheless adopt its practices whenever they prove convenient. Postmodernism's indiscriminate rejection of significant distinctions, its obsession with power, and its habit of dogmatic assertion (the very thing, ironically, that postmodernism claims to "interrogate") have influenced feminist academics' own critiques, though, of course, this at times contravenes an agenda that would be meaningless without some firm convictions about the real world and our ability to obtain communicable knowledge of it.

To sum up, feminist pedagogues by their own accounts indulge in a series of wide-ranging self-destructive habits. They dismiss logic as so much phallocentric baggage. They celebrate emotion and intuition, as if there were no pertinent historical examples of what actually happens when a society obeys its passions and its "gut" feelings. They (though not only they) assume that identity politics tells us most of what we need to know for adjudicating among competing views and knowledge claims. (How this can happen within the context of a postmodernism that has challenged the very notion of a stable identity is not clear but isn't much of a problem once logic and coherence are rejected as "masculinist.") They appeal to cultural relativism when it serves some immediate purpose and deny it when it doesn't. They welcome "local knowledges" in relation to Third World "others" but rigidly resist them when they come from disapproved groups within Western societies.[30] Distinctions fall by the wayside: Ear piercing and breast implants are equivalent to clitoridectomy; high-heeled shoes hardly differ from Chinese footbinding. Double standards prevail. The "authority of experience," so praised by feminists in their struggle to have women's voices heard (logocentrism notwithstanding), is subjected to cynical deconstruction when the proclaimed experience is not one that suits the feminist causes of the moment.

What all this means in practice is that there prevails an opportunism at the heart of feminist pedagogy today. To me, the evidence for this conclusion is utterly convincing. I also believe, however, that the many failures of this state of affairs are becoming more and more evident. Thus, feminist pedagogy, if it wants to have any credibility outside its own clique-like circles, will have to begin to hold itself to a higher standard. Only professors dedicated more to their teaching than to their politics—and able to tell the difference—provide us with reason for hope.

Teaching and the research on which it rests are noble pursuits. To commit oneself to fostering the intellectual development of one's students is no small or unworthy task. And, contrary to what many feminists believe, this task requires something other than political advocacy. Though women's studies programs typically refuse to recognize the fact, there are vital distinctions to be drawn between teaching that is informed and conscientious and teaching that attempts to persuade students to sign on to a particular political vision. The important role of educators is precisely not to deny but to embrace these distinctions, to observe them, and indeed to cherish them.

## NOTES

1. Women's studies mission statements these days typically embrace the word *feminism* and proudly declare their programs' political commitments. See, for numerous examples, Daphne Patai and Noretta Koertge (2003b, chaps. 10, 11), a much expanded edition of our 1994 book. The present essay draws on this work, which may be consulted for a more detailed discussion of the issues raised here. Feminist scholars usually retort that there are many feminisms, not one, and that it is an unstable and constantly developing field. All this may be true, and new debates may evolve (e.g., conflicts among different or newly emerging identity groups), but it does not alter the fact that there are underlying and characteristic views, positions, and beliefs—especially in relation to the nonfeminist and prefeminist world—that represent the prevailing orthodoxy.

2. This notion (resting on a vast feminist literature) underlies numerous books and is regularly repeated by feminists in academe. For recent examples of this position, from various English-speaking countries, see the Women's Studies e-mail list at www .wmst-l@listserv.umd.edu, August 22–25, 2005. The

posting by J. L. Tallentire (2005; a graduate student in history) is a particularly clear exposition of the feminist claim as it is absorbed by students. After announcing that all education is political, she summarizes:

> Anyone who complains about the "proselytizing" in some classrooms but not others is simply mistaken about the nature of teaching. Feminists have seen fit to face it and embrace it, because we recognize that politics has *always* been in the classrooms we attended—a politics that left women and marginalized peoples out, usually—and we needed to get our own in there too.

Does she believe this is true of all subjects, always? Evidently.

> So can we please stop pretending there's a neutral and nonpolitical (and thus more ethical) set of ideas, theories, teaching styles, and classroom activities? Because there isn't. Not in social sciences, humanities, fine arts, sciences, whatever.

3. See, for example, Gayle Letherby's (2003) assertion: "Feminist work highlights the fact that the researchers' choice of methods, of research topic and of study group population are always political acts" (p. 4). The adversarial stance celebrated by feminist teachers can be seen in the Women's Studies e-mail list discussion of "poverty activities" in the classroom. One professor supported such exercises because they "force privileged students to step outside their privilege for a few minutes" (J. Musial, 2005). Another wrote: "I have a responsibility to encourage my students (and the wider public where I can) to think outside the dominant views (lies) about 'reality'" (B. Winter, 2005). This professor also wrote: "I think challenging the bullshit that our culture—'high' and 'low'—produces to prop up the abuse of women, including through education, is the most important and useful thing a feminist academic can do" (B. Winter, 2005).

4. See Patai (2000) and http://research.umbc.edu/~korenman/wmst/patai1.html. For a clear analysis of the issue, see Paul A. Boghossian (2001, pp. 6–8).

5. Koertge (2003) goes on to analyze three books (including Anne Fausto-Sterling's [2000] discussed below) that represent some of the most widely known feminist works on science, demonstrating the faulty research strategies each engages in. In an earlier chapter, Koertge and I analyze the very popular book *Women's Ways of Knowing* and its profound impact on feminist teaching (Patai & Koertge, 2003a). Cassandra L. Pinnick (2000), in her review essay "Feminist Philosophy of Science: High Hopes," takes on the claim made by feminists that feminist science is better than ordinary science.

6. Though some feminists attempt to deny this problematic feminist "contribution," many textbooks demonstrate how mainstream the feminist critique has by now become. See, for example, Amy Koerber and Mary M. Lay (2002), in which the view that "science and technology seek to control and dominate nature and by extension the so-called feminine aspects of societies" (p. 82) is repeated without criticism and with the usual references to Sandra Harding and Evelyn Fox Keller. Or consider the simple assertion made by Philip Rice and Patricia Waugh (2001) that "scientific knowledge can be no more 'objective' than aesthetic knowledge" (p. 449). They go on to assert that "science constructs the shape of nature."

7. See Alan Sokal and Jean Bricmont (1998, p. 109 ff), who include devastating analyses of claims such as Luce Irigaray's (1987) that $E = mc^2$ is a "sexed equation." Irigaray writes,

> Is $E = mc^2$ a sexed equation? Perhaps it is. Let us make the hypothesis that it is insofar as it privileges the speed of light over other speeds that are vitally necessary to us. What seems to me to indicate the possibly sexed nature of the equation is not directly its uses by nuclear weapons, rather it is having privileged what goes the fastest. (p. 110)

8. For an intriguing and amusing critique of the zealous embrace of social constructionism, see Ian Craib (1997). Craib asks what anxieties might give rise to comforting collective beliefs not open to rational debate and suggests that extreme social constructionism (which he calls a "manic psychosis") allows us to fantasize control over change that we do not, in fact, possess (pp. 10, 11).

9. In various of her publications, Fausto-Sterling has provided different figures for the prevalence of sexual anomalies among neonates, ranging from 1 or 2 in 2,000 to 4 in 100. To make the case against sexual dimorphism as the natural condition of humans, women's studies courses are likely to select the higher figures, though even these hardly challenge the reality of sexual dimorphism. And such teachers are unlikely to mention the many serious critics of Fausto-Sterling's claims, statistics, and shifting terminology and criteria.

10. See, for example, Susan Kane (2001) to the Women's Studies e-mail list. I have discussed this episode in detail in "Policing the Academy" (Patai, 2003). See also Koertge's (2003) "Feminists Take on Science." Meanwhile, denunciations of others' defective feminism continue unabated on the WMST-L, with the same sorts of arguments, name calling, and feminist grandstanding made again and again. See, for example, the exchanges in early August 2005 under the subject "Transgender Discussion."

11. Ruthann Masaracchia (2001) to the Women's Studies e-mail list (WMST-L). To make crystal clear my own position, I append one of my messages, labeled "Biology and Silence," posted on the WMST-L (Patai, 2001):

I would like once again to state that in no sense have I suggested it's not interesting or valuable to study anomalies. Nor have I attacked "free inquiry" or intellectual curiosity. And, of course, I have never suggested that transgendered or homosexual or any other minority should be persecuted or treated badly.

What I have written, consistently for quite some time, has constituted a criticism of the *pretense*—for it seems clearly to be that—that the anomalies are more important and more central in women's studies than the norms and that the anomalies are to be stressed and insisted on in feminist classrooms.

I got this sense from the discussions on this very list, from people's enthusiasm for Anne Fausto-Sterling's (2000) work, from their own comments about how terrific it was to teach this work in their courses because it upset their students' ideas of sex and gender. But my point was a simple one: Students who believe that the vast majority of humans are biologically male and female are correct in their beliefs and do not need re-educating. When those beliefs are assailed, as this list shows they often are in women's studies, the agenda is political, not educational. That is what I am criticizing.

It has been fascinating for me to see how Ruthann Masaracchia's knowledgeable postings (the last one on August 2, 2001) usually end the discussion. No one asks how these biological facts can be incorporated into introductory women's studies classes and how they might be integrated into more complicated visions that do not misrepresent the facts to students. Instead, after days of debate, there is silence—as if this information

were irrelevant to women's studies—until the next round of a similar discussion in which the same dynamics arise again, the same challenges to the biological facts, again erroneously presented as social constructions, and on and on.

Let me note that last winter, when I wrote something similar, a List member wrote back that I kept asserting the fact of sexual dimorphism without providing evidence. I refer readers to (1) our reality, notwithstanding postmodernist debates, and (2) the thousands of books, articles, and studies in the field of biology.

As to Fausto-Sterling's (2000) writing—on which many women's studies people seem to be resting their beliefs—I note her habit of verbal slippage: From a discussion of truly constructed, that is, imposed through surgery, sexual identity on infants born with anomalies, she generalizes (often in the same paragraph) to the constructed nature of male/female, period. I see the interest in learning about these intersexed or otherwise "different" people, and I also understand and sympathize with the desire to call the treatment they've received into question—but I continue to *not* understand how this can be used to challenge the "normalcy" of male/female.

Fausto-Sterling (2000), in her book, at various times criticizes scholars (e.g., Diamond) for falling into the language of "normal" in their writing—as if "normal" were always a moral judgment and not also a statistical one. I've at times wondered if the whole point of the feminist attack on science is to clear the field for any and every claim without any standard of evidence, since all can be dismissed as masculinist or patriarchal.

I read Fausto-Sterling's (2000) work looking for some evidence that her argument was being misused by people on this List for their own purposes, but I concluded that it was not being misused and that she does indeed in the end make the same sort of case. A close analysis of her book's rhetoric shows a constant slippage from the anomalies to the norm—thus inviting women's studies professors to make the very moves they are repeatedly making on this List, which is to take the anomalies as somehow casting doubt on the biological reality of the norms.

This is not a useful debate. The only reason I bother about it is because I am concerned about what is being taught to students and what is passing as feminist education—which I believe dishonors both feminism and any notion of intellectual integrity.

A pithy rejoinder to Fausto-Sterling's (2000) views is David Barash's (2001) letter to the editor. Responding to an interview with Fausto-Sterling (January 2, 2001), Barash, the author of several dozen books on biology, psychology, and peace studies, acknowledged the interest of examining intermediate cases of all natural phenomena and then commented:

Nonetheless, scientists and laypeople alike would be seriously misled if they were to respond to the existence of rare in-between cases by questioning the legitimacy, or even the existence, of the baseline situations from which these cases depart. Imagine a meteorologist who was so intrigued with dawn and dusk that she insisted that we abandon the categories day and night, or that we consider them to be "socially constructed." (p. F3)

12. Rudacille's work aims at gaining tolerance for transgendered individuals. As she puts it, "Nature may provide the architecture of gender, but culture does the decorating." Still, she has no trouble asserting that "as seems increasingly certain, [gender identity] is hardwired into the brain at birth" (p. 292).

13. Throughout the book, the same few feminist science scholars (Barad, Bleier, Fausto-Sterling, Fox Keller, Haraway, Harding) are cited again and again.

14. See Raymond Tallis (2000) for a brief but telling description of the crucial distinction between these two modes of inquiry.

15. While often claiming to have superseded a simple distinction between the biological and the social, the real agenda clearly emerges in such feminist teachers' own discussions of the subject. For simplistic core feminist beliefs about the natural sciences, intended for consumption by undergraduates, see Elizabeth L. MacNabb et al. (2001, p. 159 ff).

16. For feminist stereotypes of men, see Alice Echols (1989), who notes the confusion between essentialism and social constructionism in the work of radical feminists such as Andrea Dworkin and Catharine MacKinnon. Although they indignantly proclaim that they are not essentialists, these writers see male dominance as "eternal and unchanging." Echols comments that if the social structure is "as impervious to change as [they] suggest, it might as well be biologically fixed" (pp. 362–363). Today, positions that used to be identified with radical

feminism often appear institutionalized within women's studies programs.

17. See Daphne Patai (1998), from which some passages in the present essay are adapted.

18. Amazon.com's current listing for this book includes a review in the *School Library Journal* by Mary H. Cole, of the Polytechnic Preparatory Country Day School, recommending the volume for Grades 7 and up.

19. These examples can be found on the Women's Studies e-mail list discussion of "poverty activities" in the classroom. As one professor put it (J. Hatten, 2005),

The beauty of the "Life Happens" exercise is that privileged students can see how they've benefited from their privilege and those who have struggled with these issues can get beyond the self-blame/self-doubt instilled in them by the individualistic notion of the "American Dream." When students are shown how institutional forces control more of their life circumstances than often their own efforts, it is very freeing for them—I've also seen this exercise promote a lot of social activism from students.

20. For an interesting example of a women's studies reader that does register a bit of criticism of the field, see Sheila Ruth (1998). Ruth includes my essay "What's Wrong With Women's Studies?" and positions it between one by Susan Faludi about "pod feminists" and "pseudofeminists" and one by Suzanne L. Cataldi dismissing charges of "male bashing" in women's studies. Even so, she does not trust students to draw their own conclusions: Her introductory comments to my essay alert students that my critiques "fit within the genre delineated in the previous selection by Susan Faludi." By contrast, her agreement with Faludi and Cataldi is evident in the phrasing of her introductions to their essays.

21. See, for example, Rogers and Garrett (2002) and Note 13 above.

22. See, for example, the reactions to David Horowitz's (2003) *Academic Bill of Rights*, discussed below.

23. For an example of work that incorporates critiques of science without falling prey to what she calls the "New Cynicism," see Haack (2003).

24. In July 2005, in response to negative comments made on the Women's Studies e-mail list to a query of mine regarding "Darwinian feminism,"

I received an interesting private message from a student of bioinformatics on the West Coast who had encountered hostility in women's studies students to any discussion of evolution.

> As a biologist/computer scientist-in-training I am deeply concerned by the near total absence of women in my classes. In fact, the more rigor required the fewer women are interested in the courses. To wit, in some of the more "woodsy" biology courses I've taken there was, what seemed to me, a reasonable representation of women. In my calculus, programming and the more mathematical of my biology courses (like population genetics) there are far fewer women. The issue concerns me because I believe that, without realizing it, some feminists are actively discouraging women from studying scientific subjects and then encouraging young women (I am nearly forty, returning to school) to hold forth on subjects that they know nothing about—or in many cases would be better off if they didn't know anything about the subject than the wild inaccuracies they hold now.

25. See, for example, PBS's *NewsHour With Jim Lehrer* (2005), "Evolution Debate." For a thorough analysis of the flaws of the controversy surrounding the teaching of intelligent design, which has implications for the feminist attack on "positive" knowledge generally, see Jerry Coyne (2005).

26. The literature on violence initiated by women is extensive. See, for example, Martin S. Fiebert (1997), Martin S. Fiebert and D. M. Gonzalez (1997), and Philip W. Cook (1997). On lesbian violence, see, for example, Janice L. Ristock (2002). Women's studies scholars, however, typically reject this work—judging by the hostility to it evinced on the WMST-L and in feminist publications.

27. See, for example, U.S. Department of Education (2003):

> Between 1987–88 and 2000–01, the number and proportion of degrees awarded to women rose at all levels. In 2000–01, women earned the majority of associate's, bachelor's, and master's degrees, 45% of doctor's degrees, and 46% of first professional degrees. Between 2000–01 and 2012–13, continued increases are expected in the number of degrees awarded to women at all levels. (para. 4)

For employment trends in academe, see the *NEA Advocate Online* (Clery & Topper, 2005, Table 4, p. 13), which shows that the number of women faculty continues to increase. At public institutions, full-time women faculty have increased 49% in the past 15 years, while the number of men has decreased by 3%. Women are at parity with men at community colleges but are underrepresented elsewhere, with the greatest gender disparity appearing in doctoral universities. (By contrast, minority faculty continue to be very much underrepresented.) At private and public 4-year colleges, women now constitute about 40% of the faculty (higher than 50% at junior colleges) and only about 35% at doctoral-granting schools. As for salaries, women as a whole continue to earn less than men in almost all sectors—particularly at doctoral universities, where their salaries are 78% to 79% of men's (2003–2004), while lower-level schools show smaller discrepancies. These data are not sorted by field, however.

Parity is not being reached in specific academic fields, and there is considerable feminist resistance to plain talk about the possible reasons for this. Because the prevailing contention of feminists is that disparity necessarily equals discrimination, even as notable a figure as Lawrence H. Summers, president of Harvard University, can be cowed by feminist critics into abject apologies merely for wondering, at a conference on diversifying the science and engineering workforce, if innate differences might explain why fewer women than men pursue careers in science and math. See Claudia Goldin and Lawrence F. Katz (2005). Summers's comments were apparently intolerable to a feminist scientist so sensitive that, according to her own account, she had to flee the room before vomiting or blacking out. What is most telling about the episode, however, is the power of feminists—who continue to cry that universities are unwelcoming places for them—to force not only an apology from Summers but also a pledge of $50 million to make the Harvard faculty more "diverse." More shocking still, this entire episode led to Summers's resignation as president of Harvard. So much for the ability of the most famous school in America to tolerate free speech and controversy.

28. See, for example, Jane Pilcher and Imelda Whelehan (2004), who assert the "close links between masculinities and violence" (p. 175).

29. For the text of and debates on Horowitz's (2003) Academic Bill of Rights, see www.studentsfor academicfreedom.org and www.FrontPagemag.com. For an example of how a college professor defends her

teaching against Horowitz's efforts, see www.common dreams.org/views05/0328-30.htm. Consider also the statement made by Ann Ferguson, then director of the Women's Studies Program at the University of Massachusetts, Amherst, in defending a document that would have given campus feminists wide-ranging oversight of academic programs. When concerns about "academic freedom" were raised at a Faculty Senate meeting, Ferguson responded, "We can't lose track of the wider goal in order to defend some narrow definition of academic freedom, which might amount to a right not to have to respond to new knowledges that are relevant to someone's own field of expertise." See discussion of the "Vision 2000" documented in "Policing the Academy" (Patai, 2003).

30. For an analysis of the retrograde effects on less developed countries of anti-Western, antiscience, and postmodernist fashions (including feminist critiques of science), see the important work of Meera Nanda (1998, 2003).

## REFERENCES

Barash, D. (2001, January 9). [Letter to the editor.] *New York Times*, p. F3.

Bloom, H. (1994). *The Western canon: The books and school of the ages*. New York: Harcourt Brace.

Boghossian, P. A. (2001, February 23). What is social construction? Flaws and contradictions in the claim that scientific beliefs are "merely locally accepted." *Times Literary Supplement,* pp. 6–8.

Clery, S. B., & Topper, A. M. (2005, Summer). Faculty salaries: 2004–2005. *National Education Association Advocate Online,* pp. 7–26. Retrieved May 20, 2006, from www2.nea.org/he/healma2k6/images/a06p7.pdf

Cook, P. W. (1997). *Abused men: The hidden side of domestic violence*. Westport, CT: Praeger.

Coyne, J. (2005, August 22). The faith that dare not speak its name. *The New Republic*. Retrieved May 19, 2006, from www.tnr.com/doc.mhtml?i=20050822&s=coyne082205

Craib, I. (1997). Social constructionism as a social psychosis. *Sociology, 31*(1), 1–15.

Echols, A. (1989). *Daring to be bad: Radical feminism in America, 1967–1975*. Minneapolis: University of Minnesota Press.

Fausto-Sterling, A. (2000). *Sexing the body: Gender politics and the construction of sexuality*. New York: Basic Books.

Fiebert, M. S. (1997). References examining assaults by women on their spouses or male partners: An annotated bibliography. *Sexuality and Culture, 1,* 273–286.

Fiebert, M. S., & Gonzalez, D. M. (1997). Women who initiate assaults: The reasons offered for such behavior. *Psychological Reports, 80,* 583–590.

Goldin, C., & Katz, L. F. (2005, January 23). Summers is right. *Boston Globe*.

Haack, S. (1998a). Knowledge and propaganda: Reflections of an old feminist. In *Manifesto of a passionate moderate: Unfashionable essays* (pp. 123–136). Chicago: University of Chicago Press.

Haack, S. (1998b). Science as social?—Yes and no. In *Manifesto of a passionate moderate: Unfashionable essays* (pp. 104–122). Chicago: University of Chicago Press.

Haack, S. (2003). *Defending science—within reason: Between scientism and cynicism*. Amherst, NY: Prometheus Books.

Hatten, J. (2005, August 24). Message posted to Women's Studies electronic mailing list, archived at www.wmst-l@listserv.umd.edu

Herzig, R. M. (2001). What about biology? Building sciences into introductory women's studies curricula. In M. Mayberry, B. Subramaniam, & L. H. Weasel (Eds.), *Feminist science studies: A new generation* (pp. 183–192). New York: Routledge.

Horowitz, D. (2003). *Academic bill of rights*. Retrieved May 19, 2006, from www.students foracademicfreedom.org

Irigaray, L. (1987). Sujet de la science, sujet sexué? [Is the subject of science sexed?]. In *Sens et place des connaissances dans la société* (pp. 95–121). Paris: Centre National de Recherche Scientifique.

Kane, S. (2001, February 24). Message posted to Women's Studies electronic mailing list, archived at www.wmst-l@listserv.umd.edu

Koerber, A., & Lay, M. M. (2002). Understanding women's concerns in the international setting through the lens of science and technology. In M. M. Lay, J. Monk, & D. S. Rosenfelt (Eds.), *Encompassing gender: Integrating international studies and women's studies* (p. 82). New York: Feminist Press.

Koertge, N. (2003). Feminists take on science: Tilting at the evil empire. In D. Patai & N. Koertge,

*Professing feminism: Education and indoctrination in women's studies* (Rev. ed., pp. 321–362). Lanham, MD: Lexington Books.

Letherby, G. (2003). *Feminist research in theory and practice.* Buckingham, UK: Open University Press.

MacKinnon, C. A. (1987). *Feminism unmodified: Discourses on life and law.* Cambridge, MA: Harvard University Press.

MacNabb, E. L., et al. (2001). *Transforming the disciplines: A women's studies primer.* New York: Haworth Press.

Marks, E. (2000). Feminism's perverse effects. *Signs: Journal of Women in Culture and Society, 25*(4), 1161–1166.

Masaracchia, R. (2001, March 1). Message posted to Women's Studies electronic mailing list, archived at www.wmst-l@listserv.umd.edu

Mayberry, M., Subramaniam, B., & Weasel, L. H. (Eds.). (2001). Adventures across natures and cultures: An introduction. In *Feminist science studies: A new generation* (pp. 1–11). New York: Routledge.

Musial, J. (2005, August 23). Message posted to Women's Studies electronic mailing list, archived at www.wmst-l@listserv.umd.edu

Nanda, M. (1998). The epistemic charity of the social constructivist critics of science and why the Third World should refuse the offer. In N. Koertge (Ed.), *A house built on sand: Exposing postmodernist myths about science* (pp. 286–311). New York: Oxford University Press.

Nanda, M. (2003). *Prophets facing backward: Postmodern critiques of science and Hindu nationalism in India.* New Brunswick, NJ: Rutgers University Press.

Patai, D. (1998). *Heterophobia: Sexual harassment and the future of feminism.* Lanham, MD: Rowman & Littlefield.

Patai, D. (2000). *The state of women's studies.* Retrieved May 19, 2006, from http://chronicle.com/colloquylive/transcripts/2000/10/20001004patai.htm

Patai, D. (2001, August 5). Biology and silence. Message posted to Women's Studies electronic mailing list, archived at www.wmst-l@listserv.umd.edu

Patai, D. (2003). Policing the academy. In D. Patai & N. Koertge, *Professing feminism: Education and indoctrination in women's studies* (Rev. ed., pp. 275–320). Lanham, MD: Lexington Books.

Patai, D., & Koertge, N. (2003a). "Mirror, mirror on the wall": Feminist self-scrutiny. In D. Patai & N. Koertge, *Professing feminism: Education and indoctrination in women's studies* (Rev. ed., 158–182). Lanham, MD: Lexington Books.

Patai, D., & Koertge, N. (2003b). *Professing feminism: Education and indoctrination in women's studies* (Rev. ed.). Lanham, MD: Lexington Books.

PBS *NewsHour With Jim Lehrer.* (2005, March 28). Evolution debate. Retrieved May 19, 2006, from http://www.pbs.org/newshour/bb/education/jan-june05/creation_3-28.html

Pilcher, J., & Whelehan, I. (2004). *Fifty key concepts in gender studies.* London: Sage.

Pinnick, C. L. (2000). Feminist philosophy of science: High hopes. *Metascience, 9*(2), 257–266.

Rice, P., & Waugh, P. (Eds.). (2001). *Modern literary theory: A reader* (4th ed.). London: Arnold.

Ristock, J. L. (2002). *No more secrets: Violence in lesbian relationships.* New York: Routledge.

Rogers, M. F., & Garrett, C. D. (2002). *Who's afraid of women's studies? Feminisms in everyday life.* Walnut Creek, CA: AltaMira Press.

Rudacille, D. (2005). *The riddle of gender: Science, activism, and transgender rights.* New York: Pantheon Books.

Ruth, S. (Ed.). (1998). *Issues in feminism: An introduction to women's studies* (4th ed.). London: Mayfield.

Sax, Leonard. (2002). How common is intersex? A response to Anne Fausto-Sterling. *Journal of Sex Research, 39*(3), 174–179. Retrieved May 20, 2006, from www.findarticles.com/p/articles/mi_m2372/is_3_39/ai_94130

Scollay, S. J., & Bratt, C. S. (1997). Untying the Gordian knot of academic sexual harassment. In B. R. Sandler & R. J. Shoops (Eds.), *Sexual harassment on campus: A guide for administrators, faculty, and students* (pp. 261–277). Boston: Allyn & Bacon.

Sokal, A., & Bricmont, J. (1998). *Fashionable nonsense: Postmodern intellectuals' abuse of science.* New York: Picador.

Subramaniam, B. (2001). And the mirror cracked! Reflections of natures and cultures. In M. Mayberry, B. Subramaniam, & L. H. Weasel (Eds.), *Feminist science studies: A new generation* (pp. 55–62). New York: Routledge.

Tallentire, J. L. (2005, August 24). Message posted to Women's Studies electronic mailing list, archived at www.wmst-l@listserv.umd.edu

Tallis, R. (2000). Evidence-based and evidence-free generalisations. In M. Grant (Ed.), *The Raymond Tallis reader* (pp. 309–329). Hampshire, UK: Palgrave.

Trimberger, E. K. (1998). Heterosexuality. In W. Mankiller et al. (Eds.), *Reader's companion to U.S. women's history* (p. 255). Boston: Houghton Mifflin.

U.S. Department of Education. (2003). *Projections of education statistics to 2013*. National Center for Education Statistics, Washington, DC.

Retrieved May 19, 2006, from http://nces.ed .gov/programs/projections/ch_4.asp#2

Whitaker, M. P. L. (2001). Oases in a desert: Why a hydrologist meanders between science and women's studies. In M. Mayberry, B. Subramaniam, & L. H. Weasel (Eds.), *Feminist science studies: A new generation* (pp. 48–51). New York: Routledge.

Winter, B. (2005, August 23, 25). Message posted to Women's Studies electronic mailing list, archived at www.wmst-l@listserv.umd.edu

# 43

# A Passion for Knowledge

## The Teaching of Feminist Methodology

Judith A. Cook

Mary Margaret Fonow

I n 1991, we published *Beyond Methodology: Feminist Scholarship as Lived Research*, an anthology that addressed the challenges of conducting feminist research in the social sciences.[1] Our ideas about feminist methodology have evolved over the years, and we reflect on those changes and identify newer developments in feminist methodology in a special issue of *Signs: Journal of Women in Culture and Society* devoted to the dilemmas of feminist research practices (Fonow & Cook, 2005). Our commentary here will focus more directly on teaching feminist methodology to graduate students and training feminist policy researchers in a range of settings and contexts, including seminars, workshops, conferences, and research and training institutes.

We are often asked to define and defend feminist methodology as a unique methodology, and we have always resisted giving a precise response because we do not want to foreclose new avenues of inquiry and discovery. Feminist methodology, we believe, involves the description, explanation, and justification of techniques used in feminist research and scholarship and is an abstract classification that refers to a

variety of methodological stances, conceptual approaches, and research strategies. Feminist methodologies include epistemological arguments on how to apprehend the social; the evaluation of specific research techniques and practices; the formulation of research questions and designs that capture the historical, intersectional, and transnational dimensions of women's lives and gender relations; attention to the ethical and policy implications of research; acknowledgment of the representational quality of research and scholarship; and attention to the outcomes of research, including the development of multiple strategies for the dissemination of research findings.

## A Graduate Seminar on Feminist Methodology

In 2001, Fonow and Lather, her colleague at Ohio State, designed a feminist methodology course for graduate curriculum in women's studies at Ohio State University. Lather (Lather, 2001; Lather & Smithies, 1997) is a professor of cultural studies in education and an international expert on critical and feminist methodology. We did not intend the course to be a practical, "how-to" course but rather a course that used feminist insights to theorize about the conduct of inquiry and in the process open new paths of discovery. We sought to establish an interdisciplinary feminist plane from which we could analyze research practices in women's studies and in education and make informed decisions about our individual projects. Readings for the course focused on the methodological implications of feminist epistemologies; the ethical dilemmas and politics of feminist inquiry; the strategies involved in collecting, interpreting, and analyzing primary material; reflexivity; and issues in representation. We used texts that include methodological reflections and analysis of race, class, gender, nation, and sexuality in the production of social and cultural knowledge.

The seminar explored the pleasures and anxieties of doing research through exercises and activities that afforded students the opportunity for a backstage view of knowledge production. We demystified the research process by inviting researchers to share earlier versions of our own research, by having students deconstruct a published text by feminist scholars, and by staging a miniconference at the end of the course, which re-created a typical professional meeting, complete with organizers and discussants and with each student presenting his or her final paper.

For example, Valerie Lee (1996), a feminist folklorist and literary critic, discussed with us the field work for her book *Granny Midwives and Black Women Writers: Double-Dutched Readings*. Lee used archival records, literary criticism, and oral history interviews to examine the lived experiences of African American midwives and the fictional representations of midwives in the novels of black women writers. She talked to the seminar about her trip to Mississippi to interview a 90-year-old country midwife who turned the table on the scholar by asking her to demonstrate her "smarts." Lee generously shared what she had learned in her odyssey to the imagined community of her roots in the black rural south, a landscape made familiar in the fiction of black women writers such as Toni Morrison and Gloria Naylor. Inviting faculty and visiting scholars to class to reflect on their struggles to create knowledge allowed

students greater access to the process of research and writing. Students had the opportunity to ask questions, and guests had the freedom to talk about the pleasures and pain of their work.

The seminar situated feminist methodology within the context of early feminist critiques of science, particularly the critiques of positivism. To make the debates about positivism intelligible to students, we showed the 1965 film *Obedience*, a documentary about the famous Milgram laboratory experiments that were conducted at Yale. The grainy, black-and-white film features a researcher in a white lab coat who tells subjects to administer electrical shocks to research confederates when they make a mistake in matching pairs of nonsense words. We used the film as a springboard to discuss the logic of experimental design (sampling, conceptualization, operationalization, cognitive authority, norms of science, etc.) and to discuss the ethical implications of human subject research and the university's human subject review process. Two recent articles on research ethics (Halse & Honey, 2005; Kirsch, 2005) from the special issue of *Signs* on feminist methodology could be assigned at this point in the course.

Next, the course introduces some of the epistemological issues associated with feminist methodology. We view epistemology at the most general level as the framework for specifying the generation of knowledge: How does the knower come to understand and interpret the nature of reality? We see the domain of epistemology as concerned with larger philosophical questions: What is knowledge? Who can know and by what means? How do we recognize, validate, and evaluate knowledge claims? Women of color have raised important questions concerning the epistemologies of the oppressed: Do oppressed people, by virtue of their knowledge of both the oppressor's views of reality and those of their own subjugated groups, have access to truer or better knowledge of reality? Who is privileged in an epistemological sense—feminists, women of color, lesbians, working-class women, postcolonials? Who can speak for whom (Fonow & Cook, 2005)?

The actual methods we cover vary and are chosen more to reflect the general principles of feminist methodology than a comprehensive review of all the possibilities. Graduate students are encouraged to seek broad training in research methods through research seminars and other methodology courses in historiography, visual and textual analysis, survey, ethnography, and so on. We are more concerned that students understand how to select and defend their choices in the design, collection, representation, and interpretation of data. We ask them to consider the following questions: What methods will help you to answer your research question, and what is your rationale for selecting this approach? How are you, as the researcher, situated in this project? What ethical safeguards are you planning for your study, and how do they reflect feminist ethics? What are your responsibilities as a feminist researcher? How does your approach address difference (marked and unmarked)? Will research subjects play a role in the research, and what are some of the dilemmas of involving research subjects? How do you plan to represent your findings, and what are the politics involved in such a representation?

## TRAINING FEMINIST POLICY RESEARCHERS

As a feminist sociologist whose professional life has been spent in the realm of policy research in the field of mental health disability, Cook has been successful in obtaining and maintaining significant national funding regardless of the political climate. She believes that feminists engaged in policy research, especially in organizations that rely on external funding, must be both methodologically rigorous and politically astute to assure that their results can be heard by policymakers and that their findings are given the appropriate weight.

For Cook, it is important for policy researchers to begin with a thorough understanding of the policy to be investigated. Feminist policy researchers must be able to read and understand policy material written in bureaucratic language that is often tedious and uninteresting. Useful questions to ask oneself include the following: How does the language of the law read? How have federal or state agencies interpreted the law? What do regulations or directives based on the law require? How are local administrators using them? What has been the impact on the individuals with whom the feminist researcher is concerned—for example, a mentally ill woman who is not permitted to stay at a homeless shelter?

The next step involves a review of the previous research used to construct the policy you are concerned about—its quality, who conducted it and why, how it was conducted, and what the findings were. This is equally important whether the researcher respects or agrees with the research, the researcher, and the findings or believes that the prior research came from a nonfeminist or other ideological view. In the case of a policy the researcher wants to see changed, it is often very important to see why and how the supporters of the current policy used the earlier research. The feminist researcher should keep in mind that research used to support a policy may not have been designed to be policy research; nevertheless, as soon as it is used to set policy, it has become policy research.

Externally funded research comes with built-in challenges—funding agents may not want to support long-term studies, and policymakers cannot wait for a longitudinal study. The researcher will have to balance what the policymakers need with the knowledge that the methods required in that timeframe may not be ideal. When reviewing prior research, the researcher may want to remember that quick-and-dirty techniques may have been used and may not be a sound basis for the policy.

Sometimes reviewing the primary documents and past research is not sufficient, and researchers may have to contact individuals—individuals who do not necessarily support their point of view—to assist their understanding of the policy and its purpose. Careful preparation will be required because some individuals are not accustomed to and will not welcome such interviews. Another approach is to find a mentor who knows the policy and can guide their interpretation—someone who can say, for example, what Congress meant when the law was written or who can describe what is happening on the ground now that regulations are out. Researchers must be aware of not only their own bias but also the bias these informants may bring to their interpretation of the policy and of its aims and realities.

Once the policy is thoroughly understood, the researcher can begin to frame questions that elucidate the policy and its outcomes and to design methodological approaches. Researchers must be careful in thinking about policy questions because their findings may have implications for other policies; the research must answer the primary question but the researcher should think in advance about other implications of the findings. Sometimes research findings around the primary question do not support the policy's goal, but the research may show unintended positive consequences. For example, a government-funded preschool intervention program did not lead to higher test scores, but it had other positive outcomes—the children's parents were more active at the school and the home lives of these children were more stable. The positive family results may be enough to support ongoing funding, and the agency providing the program can now seek ways to use the family benefits to lead to increased test scores.

In the Center we often find it helpful to employ multiple methods. The researcher must know how policymakers are using research to determine what kind of data they find useful and how they used it. Sometimes policymakers are less persuaded by numbers than by personal stories, but that is an individual question; if they have not used quotes from interviews, they may not be open to qualitative approaches. Qualitative approaches alone may be persuasive when the findings are egregious or unanimous. For example, if in-depth interviews with 25 welfare recipients revealed that every one cited some form of coercion by her caseworker, while the researcher cannot hypothesize about the prevalence of coercion overall, the finding may warrant further investigation by the policymakers. Sometimes policymakers are able to use the stories gleaned from qualitative research to convince their constituencies that a change is needed.

A frequently untapped resource is large data sets; interesting or radical stories may be hiding in the data. Sometimes these data sets are the sole source of information on a problem, and, if researchers understood the data better, they could demonstrate findings that no prospective data collection can. Feminists may be able to effect policy change by studying large data sets to see whether counterarguments can be made,

by using the data set to answer new questions, and by thinking about new ways to use the data.

Feminists engaged in policy research have an opportunity to change the minds of policymakers in a positive direction; however, this usually cannot be accomplished using theory that is too abstract or by a direct request to adopt a contradictory policy that may threaten the stakeholders of the status quo. The policy researcher must understand the position of those supporting the current policy and the research that helps them maintain their position. Then the researcher can do similar research with similar methods and determine whether the initial findings hold.

Sometimes it is possible to influence policymakers by noting that the research covers only a few years of follow-up. The researcher may propose extending the timeline to show that better outcomes could be achieved. Creative researchers look for opportunities, for example, to fund longer-term research or to include a different population in the research. Even policymakers who have drawn their "line in the sand" may support policy changes if the researcher provides the evidence to support a different approach. For example, if your research shows that homeless women with mental health disabilities do not require additional costly social services if they receive less-expensive self-help support from women peers, a policymaker may be motivated to make a fiscal argument to justify a policy change that funds more peer support programs.

Several pitfalls await the unprepared policy researcher. Most policymakers prefer a simple, useful answer, while research findings seldom provide one central finding and may often be complex or ambiguous. We train our graduate students to develop complex research designs; and while this is a good thing, we must also train them to think about how policymakers can make use of the data. A related pitfall is presenting too much research to policymakers or presenting research with the kind of hedging that is appropriate for a scholarly journal but not for policymakers. They need to know what, overall, is the effect of the policy on the stakeholders or constituency represented by the policymaker. The findings must be presented with qualifications that are appropriate. The ethical standards of policy research are demanding.

Researchers must be able to recognize their investment in the research and manage both their biases and sometimes their disappointment in their results. Feminist researchers often care deeply about the issue and the participants in their research; nevertheless, it is critical to be careful and reflective about how the caring might influence the inquiry or the way findings are presented. The researcher may have difficulty in knowing whether their bias is present.

Management of disappointment is also important; research findings may provide evidence for the policy status quo when the researcher expected the opposite. It may be tempting not to report the findings, but this would be dishonest. Instead, the report can include a discussion of design weaknesses or other biases that call study findings into question. Also included can be other research that showed the expected findings.

We often find it helpful to check in with both allies and rivals to help decide where the ethical center is. Reviewing the evidence and discussing interpretations can help create a report that is accurate and meets ethical requirements. For example, the researcher's data find a program approach is doing x when everyone wants y. Talking to others, explaining what might be going on in the data that ameliorates the findings, and hearing their response can provide input in how to report the findings. If they grant some bias, researchers are on sounder ground releasing the findings with caveats.

In presenting findings, it is well to remember that policymakers are, by and large, well educated and bright individuals. It is not necessary in some cases to interpret the data; instead, the researcher can present factual information in such a way that the facts lead to obvious policy conclusions. One research project, for example, showed the unemployed affected by a certain policy. Had the report concluded that the policy was motivating people to remain unemployed the policymakers might not have agreed. The report was therefore structured to lead deductively to that conclusion without having to state it. In this case, the policymakers concluded that they were actually paying people not to work. We were able to say that was one way to interpret the data. The well-prepared researcher can help policymakers reach their own understanding.

When a research topic is controversial or has political implications, for example, HIV, reproductive choice, or welfare reform, researchers should anticipate how their findings can be used or abused and prepare for news media attention. When interview requests are made, the well-prepared researcher will learn who the journalist is (newspaper, TV, freelance?), the vehicles and audiences for which they write (*Good Housekeeping* or the *Washington Post*?), and what their perspective or possible biases are. Preparing sound bites is helpful to avoid being misunderstood or misquoted. For example, suppose the findings show that people with mental health disabilities have a high quit rate in their first job but that over time they stay longer and get paid more. Stating the finding chronologically may lead the press to emphasize the quit rate. Instead the researcher can prepare a sound bite such as "people with mental health disabilities go on to longer term, better paid employment even though they start with higher quit rates." Such a sound bite accurately reflects the research findings while it helps the media select the more positive results. Last, researchers should think about what do to if findings are abused, often by partial use of findings. Some strategies include seeking a correction, talking to other media to obtain accurate coverage, and contacting related organizations that can refute the abusive statements, for example, by quoting the rest of your data. The results of policy research can often be used to support a number of arguments; researchers must recognize this and be prepared to handle such issues.

Policy research is quite complex, and it will be difficult to help students actually conduct research in one semester. Curriculum redesign may be required to teach feminist methodology effectively. We recommend that courses teach multiple methods to increase the versatility of students; requiring use of both quantitative and qualitative methods shows students experientially the limitations of using one or the other. If a student is new to a policy area, using multiple methods can be an effective way to get a good introduction. We discussed large data sets earlier and we recommend teaching the skills needed to do data mining. Students should be able to read policy and related material, conduct interviews, and collect, digest, and analyze both quantitative and qualitative data. Students could benefit from increasing their research-related creativity by exploring additional data sets with the same questions and methods to see if new results emerge. They should learn how different statistical approaches may lead to contradictory findings, how significant effects seen in smaller data sets may disappear when doing policy research on a large scale, and how statistical techniques can be used to control for the "messiness" often found in real-world data. Ideally, courses will guide them through different stages of policy research and expose them to typical issues in design/execution/interpretation of research using case examples of different policy studies. For example, students may be assigned to look for bias in how a question was phrased. Next, they may be required to produce a policy report, an executive summary, and presentation of findings. We can also benefit our students greatly by introducing them to the special realities of externally funded policy research, such as how to stand out when the researcher is unknown or when the findings or approach are not notable; and the importance of understanding the sponsor's culture and worldview to understand their likely responses, objections, and concerns. These are aspects that do not influence the methodologies and yet are important to obtaining and maintaining resources.

Most policy researchers learn best by doing. Internships and pro bono support to organizations are two ways to begin to do policy research. Students might intern at a state agency or in Washington, D.C., to learn about different sources of data and types of research and to see how findings are used by political decision makers. Identify and volunteer at organizations that do policy research. Examples include the research department of departments of health that are affecting policy, for example, around HIV prevention. Municipal, federal, and state courts often have staff who collect data to assist the judges. Local nonprofit organizations and nongovernmental organizations can provide fruitful internships and can be good places to learn about the need for evaluation and the data they use. Remember too that some policy research goes by other names: Program evaluation research is often to support policy. Needs assessment can be used as support to policy.

After three decades of conducting research as feminist sociologists in a variety of contexts, we have come to the realization that training students and young policy researchers is an ongoing project. Feminist methodology can be taught in courses and in workshops, but much of it only makes sense when the researcher is in the thick of conducting research. We know the future will involve preparing researchers to think about gender in an increasingly complex world, and while this will be challenging work, we don't have to do it alone and we don't have to start from scratch.

## NOTE

1. Debates, critiques, and reflections on the meaning and scope of feminist methodology have greatly expanded since the publication of our collection (Bloom, 1998; DeVault, 1999; Generett & Jeffries, 2003; Gottfried, 1996; Hesse-Biber & Yaiser, 2004; Hunter, 1999; Jacobs, 2002; Lather, 2001; Letherby, 2003; McCall, 2005; Naples, 2003; Parker, Deyhle, & Villenas, 1999; Ramazanoğlu & Holland, 2002; Sandoval, 2000; D. Smith, 1999, 2005; L. Smith, 1999; Sprague, 2005; St. Pierre & Pillow, 2000; Tuana & Morgen, 2001; Twine & Warren, 2000). Discussions about feminist methodology are being presented at professional meetings and published in new anthologies, in special issues of scholarly journals, and in monographs.

## REFERENCES

Bloom, Leslie Rebecca. (1998). *Under the sign of hope: Feminist methodology and narrative interpretation.* Albany: State University of New York Press.

DeVault, Marjorie L. (1999). *Liberating method: Feminism and social research.* Philadelphia: Temple University Press.

Fonow, Mary Margaret, & Cook, Judith A. (2005). Feminist methodology: New applications in the academy and public policy. *Signs: Journal of Women in Culture and Society, 30*(4), 2211–2236.

Generett, G., & Jeffries, R. (Eds.). (2003). *Black women in the field: Experiences understanding ourselves and others through qualitative research.* Cresskill, NJ: Hampton Press.

Gottfried, Heidi. (Ed.). (1996). *Feminism and social change: Bridging theory and practice.* Urbana: University of Illinois Press.

Halse, C., & Honey, A. (2005). Unravelling ethics: Illuminating the moral dilemmas of research ethics. *Signs: Journal of Women in Culture and Society, 30*(4), 2141–2162.

Hesse-Biber, Sharlene Nagy, & Yaiser, Michelle L. (2004). *Feminist perspectives on social research.* New York: Oxford University Press.

Hunter, Lynette. (1999). *Critiques of knowing: Situated textualities in science, computing, and the arts.* New York: Routledge.

Jacobs, Merle. (Ed.). (2002). *Is anyone listening? Women, work and society.* Toronto, Canada: Women's Press.

Kirsch, Gesa E. (2005). Friendship, friendliness, and feminist fieldwork. *Signs: Journal of Women in Culture and Society, 30*(4), 2163–2172.

Lather, Patti. (2001). Postbook: Working the ruins of feminist ethnography. *Signs: Journal of Women in Culture and Society, 27*(1), 199–228.

Lather, Patti, & Smithies, Chris. (1997). *Troubling the angels: Women living with HIV/AIDS.* Boulder, CO: Westview Press.

Lee, Valerie. (1996). *Granny midwives and black women writers: Double-dutched readings.* New York: Routledge.

Letherby, Gayle. (2003). *Feminist research in theory and practice.* Buckingham, UK: Open University Press.

McCall, Leslie. (2005). The complexity of intersectionality. *Signs: Journal of Women in Culture and Society, 30*(3), 1771–1800.

Naples, Lynn H. (1990). *Who knows? From Quine to a feminist empiricism.* Philadelphia: Temple University Press.

Naples, Nancy A. (2003). *Feminism and method: Ethnography, discourse analysis, and activist research.* New York: Routledge.

Parker, Laurence, Deyhle, Donna, & Villenas, Sofia. (Eds.). (1999). *Race is . . . race isn't: Critical race theory and qualitative studies in education.* Boulder, CO: Westview Press.

Ramazanoğlu, Caroline, & Holland, Janet. (2002). *Feminist methodology: Challenges and choices.* London: Sage.

Sandoval, Chela. (2000). *Methodology of the oppressed.* Minneapolis: University of Minnesota Press.

Smith, Dorothy. (1999). *Writing the social: Critique, theory, and investigations.* Toronto, Ontario, Canada: University of Toronto Press.

Smith, Dorothy. (2005). *Institutional ethnography: Sociology for people.* Lanham, MD: AltaMira Press.

Smith, Linda Tuhiwai. (1999). *Decolonizing methodologies: Research and indigenous peoples.* London: Zed Press.

Sprague, Joey. (2005). *Feminist methodologies for critical researchers: Bridging differences.* Lanham, MD: AltaMira Press.

St. Pierre, Elizabeth A., & Pillow, Wanda S. (Eds.). (2000). *Working the ruins: Feminist poststructural theory and methods in education.* New York: Routledge.

Tuana, Nancy, & Morgen, Sandra. (Eds.). (2001). *Engendering rationalities.* Albany: State University of New York Press.

Twine, France Winddance, & Warren, Jonathan W. (Eds.). (2000). *Racing research/researching race: Methodological dilemmas in critical race studies.* New York: New York University Press.

# AUTHOR INDEX

Abbate, J., 226
Abu-Lughod, L., 163, 165, 167, 623
Acker, J., 159, 178, 200, 316, 522
Acker, S., 207, 498
Adam, B., 379
Adams, C., 438
Adams, V., 361–362
Addams, J., 176, 267
Adelman, C., 297
ADMI, 311
Adorno, T., 76
Adrian, B., 658
Agarwal, K., 373
Aggarwal, R., 640
Agronick, G., 331
Ahmed, S., 623–624
Akhter, F., 666–667
Alarcón, N., 115
Albert, H., 480
Alberti, P., 674
Albrecht, L. ., 184
Albrow, M., 652
Alcoff, L., 178, 437, 479, 550–551, 642
Alexander, J., 541, 584
Alexander, L., 397
Alexander, M. J., 96–97, 184
Alexander, P., 230
Alldred, P., 523, 526
Allen, J. A., 124, 126–128, 130
Allen, K. R., 522
Allen, P., 177
Allen, T., 438
Alreck, P. L., 200, 211
Altman, R., 231, 242
Alvarez, S., 655
Amos, V., 110–111
Anderson, E., 549, 553, 563–564
Anderson, G., 166, 423
Anderson, L., 445
Anderson, M., 50, 499–500

Andrews, L. B., 236
Andrews, M., 608–610
Angel, J., 337
Angroino, M. V., 401
Angus, J., 372
Annells, M., 350
Anthony, S. B., 426
Antony, L. M., 31–32, 34, 41–42
Antrobus, P., 641
Anzaldúa, G., 2–4, 12, 128, 159, 162,
        184, 299, 433, 509, 613, 622, 676
Appadurai, A., 655
Apple, M. W., 522
Archer, L., 606, 608, 610
Arendell, T., 180
Arendt, H., 184, 613
Aristotle, 547, 554–555, 557, 559
Armstrong, B., 242
Aroni, R., 397
Arriata, M., 308
Asad, T., 641
Ashe, A., 333
Aspin, L., 234
Association of American University Women, 233
Atkinson, P., 144, 346–347
Auerbach, C. F., 353
Austen, S., 352, 361
Avila, M., 313
Avis, H., 525
Avorn, J., 226

Babbie, E., 215
Baber, K. M., 522
Bacon, F., 478
Bahn, E., 506
Baier, A, 34
Bailar, J. C., 231
Bailey, A., 383
Baker, D. G., 381
Baker, Q., 313

Baker Collins, S., 316, 319
Bakhtin, M. M., 527
Balin, J., 335
Ballerino Cohen, C., 623
Bambara, T. C., 435
Bamberger, M., 291–292
Bandy, J., 656
Banks, R., 190
Bannerji, H., 187, 189, 573
Barad, K., 348
Barandun, P., 379
Barker, D., 50
Barkley-Brown, E., 632
Barnaby, F., 226
Barnbaum, D. R., 524
Barndt, D. ., 674
Barrett, M., 11
Barron, M., 264
Barry, K., 178, 200, 316, 522
Bart, P., 177
Barthes, R., 81, 89–90
Bartow, A., 335
Bartunek, J. M., 312
Basch, L., 115, 245, 652
Batt, S., 231
Bauman, Z., 79–80
Beardsley, R., 291
Beasley, C., 90
Becker, H. S., 356, 448
Becker, J., 670, 675, 677
Behar, R., 159, 165, 180, 184,
        374, 439, 623, 639
Behe, M., 564
Behn, A., 429
Belenky, M. F., 159, 549, 581
Bell, D., 525, 623
Bell, G., 451–452
Bell, S. G., 185, 265
Bell, V., 585
Beneria, L., 283, 641
Benet, J., 258
Benhabib, S., 77, 482, 528
Benjamin, B., 633
Benjamin, J., 432
Bennington, G., 94, 96
Benoliel, J. Q., 345, 350
Benston, M., 476
Benz, C., 327, 330
Beoku-Betts, J., 179, 500
Berelman, R. L., 229
Berg, A. J., 226
Berger, P., 348
Berkeley, .G., 30
Berman, J., 241
Berman, R., 475, 477

Bernard, C., 334
Bernstein, R., 481
Best, A., 183
Bettie, J., 446
Beverly, J., 508
Bhabha, H., 113
Bhavnani, K. K., 8–9, 13–14,
        281, 362, 540, 605, 639–643
Biagioli, M., 59
Bibeau, D., 675
Biemer, P. P., 210
Bierema, C., 283
Bigby, C., 180, 184
Biklen, S. K., 176, 183
Bingley, A., 525
Biology and Gender Study Group, 30
Birch, M., 525
Birke, L., 224
Blacklock, C., 652, 656
Blair, J., 200, 210
Blakeslee, A. M., 527
Blanc, C. S., 115, 652
Blank, R. M., 283
Blauner, R., 52–53
Blee, K. M., 180, 183, 398–401, 674
Bleier, R., 224, 232, 237, 430, 476
Bliss-Moreau, E., 509
Bloom, H., 694
Bloom, J., 613–614
Bloom, L. R., 371, 521, 652
Blum, L., 263
Blumer, H., 348, 356
Bluming, A. Z., 239
Bochner, A. P., 459
Bodker, S. ., 235
Bogdan, R. C., 174, 176
Boler, M., 77
Bondi, L., 371
Bone, D., 351
Booth, K., 263–264
Bordo, S. R., 13, 98, 466, 478, 519, 606
Boric, R., 658
Borland, K., 16, 539–540
Bosk, C. L., 443, 445
Boston Women's Health Book Collective, 306
Boudin, K., 614–615
Bourdieu, P., 497–498
Bové, P. A., 82
Bowen, I., 614–615
Bowen, J., 401
Bowen, K., 280, 286–287
Bowers, B., 349
Bowker, G., 347, 352, 356
Bowles, G., 9, 664
Boxer, M., 248

Boyatzis, R. E., 330
Brabeck, M. M., 519
Bradbury, H., 298
Brah, A., 608
Braidotti, R., 87, 95, 100, 383
Brand, P., 438
Bratt, C. S., 695
Bratteteig, T., 238
Braxton, J., 609
Bray, A., 95, 383
Brée, G., 694
Brennan, T., 431–432
Bricmont, J., 691
Brisolara, S., 145–146, 148,
    151, 278–280, 291
Britzman, D., 81, 97
Broad, K. L., 379
Brodribb, S., 95
Brooks, A., 22
Brossard, N., 372
Broude, N., 438
Brown, C., 429
Brown, H., 475, 481–482
Brown, J. C., 267
Brown, R. M., 434, 438
Brown, W., 100, 129, 131
Brown-Collins, A., 203
Browne, K., 374
Bruce, J., 283
Bruckman, A., 241
Brun, E., 240
Brunsdon, C., 572
Brusco, E., 685
Bryan, B., 605
Bryant, A., 345, 350
Brydon-Miller, M., 297, 301, 522, 613, 653
Bryron, M., 524
Buchanan, I., 383
Budig, M. J., 420, 452–453
Buehler, J. W., 229
Buker, E., 485
Bulbeck, C., 108, 113–114, 393
Bulkin, E., 184
Bunster, X., 311
Buraway, M., 652, 654, 656
Burdine, J. N., 676
Burke, M., 381
Burns, A., 303, 613–614
Burns, N., 329
Burris, M., 310
Burt, S., 15
Burton, S., 608
Bushman, C., 267
Busia, A. P., 109
Buss, D. M., 216

Butler, J., 12, 71–72, 74, 77, 80–81, 83, 86, 92–93,
    96, 98–99, 127, 167, 240–241, 243, 348, 432,
    515, 538, 606
Bwyer, D., 283
Byrne, A., 393
Byrne, B., 379
Byrne, S., 265–266

Cahill, C., 613
Cain, M., 582
Calkins, K., 448
Calle-Gruber, M., 89
Campbell, D. T., 258, 277
Campbell, G. ., 225
Campbell, K., 240
Campbell, M., 63, 146, 186, 189, 362, 508
Campbell, R., 36–37, 42, 202, 209
Cancian, F., 314, 317
Candela, M. A., 163
Canguihem, G., 356
Cannon, L. W., 573
Caplan, P., 623
Capra, F., 237
Carby, H. V., 109
Carney, S., 613–614, 618
Caro, R., 228
Caro-Bruce, C., 303
Caron, S., 261
Carpenter, L., 261
Carr, D., 334, 340
Carrette, J. R., 85
Carroll, D., 444
Carroll, L., 555
Carruyo, L., 646–647
Carter, G. L., 231
Cason, N., 527
Casper, M. J., 347, 360
Cassaro, D., 282, 292
Castillo, D. A., 640
Castor, L., 72
Catens, M., 98
Cavell, S., 482
Cawley, M., 476
Cealey Harrison, W., 606
Cervantes-Rodríguez, A. M., 375
Chafetz, J. S., 205
Chajet, L., 613–614
Chanda, I., 115
Chaney, E. M., 311
Chapman, J., 394
Chapman, T. K., 382
Charmaz, K., 22, 144, 347–348, 352,
    361, 420, 444–445, 447, 505
Chase, S. E., 176, 181, 459
Chaudhry, L. N., 162, 163, 165

Chavez, V., 313–314
Chavis, D., 316
Cherny, L., 266
Chesler, P., 431
Chicago, J., 434, 437
Chilly Collective, 571
Chin, F., 133
Chodorow, N., 127, 224, 235,
    260, 432, 438, 517, 609–610
Choi, Y., 268–269
Chomsky, N., 41–42
Chrisman, L., 299
Christ, C., 439
Christian, B., 179
Chu, S. Y., 229
Chua, P., 641, 644
Chuaprapaisilp, A., 307
Cixous, H., 11, 75, 89, 95–96, 437
Clark, J., 614–615
Clarke, A. E., 144–145, 150, 231, 345,
    347–349, 351–353, 357–358,
    360–361, 445, 670–671, 676
Clarke, L. H., 372
Cleaver, F., 316–317
Clément, C., 75, 81, 437
Clifford, J., 158, 184, 506, 622, 641
Clinchy, B. M., 159, 549, 581
Clinton, W. J., 614
Clough, P. T., 83, 88, 100, 178, 189, 581, 583
Clough, S., 31
Cockburn, C., 226, 228, 235, 240, 310, 317, 320
Code, L., 9, 15, 36, 47, 184, 480, 516, 519, 526,
    550, 639
Coffey, A., 144, 346, 507
Cohen, C. B., 179, 507
Cohen, C. J., 333
Cohen, J., 230
Colby, A., 517
Cole, C. M., 527
Cole, E. R., 8, 149, 205, 337, 361
Cole, J., 430
Colebrook, C., 87, 95, 383
Collins, D., 645, 647
Collins, J., 186
Collins, P. H., 12–13, 15, 46, 61, 108–110, 127,
    144–145, 148, 156, 162, 174, 187, 229, 265,
    299–300, 304, 361–362, 379, 484, 496, 500,
    503, 508, 522, 527, 538, 541, 579, 581–583,
    586, 605, 607, 613, 630, 636, 640, 653, 657,
    669, 672, 674–676
Commission for Historical Clarification, 311
Comte, A., 7, 472
Condit, C., 337
Condor, S., 203
Conefrey, T., 527

Conley, V. A., 89
Conner, T., 509
Conrad, E., 202–203, 328, 340
Constable, N., 269–270, 657
Contratto, S., 260
Converse, J., 201
Cook, B., 381
Cook, J. A., 15, 159, 161–162, 165–166, 380–381,
    393, 404, 459, 466, 470, 521, 545, 571,
    673–674, 676, 705–707
Cooke, B., 319
Cooke, J. A., 345
Coole, D., 430
Cooper, A. J., 506, 630
Copeland, B., 189
Copi, I. M., 555
Coquillon, E., 145–146, 148, 150–151, 504, 539
Corbin, J., 144, 345, 347, 350
Corea, G., 233
Cornell, D., 77
Cornillon, S., 429
Cornwall, A., 309, 317, 319
Cortina, L. M., 329, 335–336
Cott, N., 127
Cousins, B., 285
Cousteau, J., 560
Cowan, R. S., 226, 234
Cox, S., 432
Crawford, M., 202
Crawley, H., 309
Creager, N. H., 224
Crenshaw, K. W., 110, 127, 613, 640
Cresswell, J. W., 345
Crewe, E., 624
Crewe, J., 448
Crissman, L., 244
Crooks, D. L., 348, 350
Crosby, A., 652, 656
Cseh, M., 283
Cunningham, F., 471
Currie, D., 261–262, 309, 312
Czaja, R., 200, 210

Dadzie, S., 605
Dalmiya, V., 178, 551
Daly, K., 352
Daly, M., 238–239, 521
Dan, A., 248
Daniels, A. K., 258
D'Aprano, Z., 401
Davidman, L., 446
Davidson, D., 549
Davies, A., 605
Davies, B., 11, 14, 16, 19–20, 73–74, 81–84, 90–92,
    99, 160, 350, 459

Davis, A., 162, 299, 435, 613
Davis, J. H., 382
Davis, M. D., 572
Dawkins, R., 231
Day, S., 184
Dean, J., 395
Deanes, R., 225
Debbink, G., 308
de Beauvoir, S., 1, 3, 156, 233–234, 419, 427–428,
    430–432, 439, 506, 622
de Coutrivon, I., 95
Deem, R., 381
De Laine, M., 525
de la Maza, I., 308
Delamont, S., 346
de Lauretis, T., 23, 113, 240–241
Deleuze, G., 85, 87, 95–96, 383
Delgado, B., 640
Delgado-Bernal, D., 162
Delgado-Gaitan, C., 162–163
D'Emilio, J., 631
Denzin, N. K., 76, 158, 166, 300, 361, 459, 496
Derrida, J., 85–86, 95–96, 241, 279, 486
Desai, M., 188
Descartes, René, 41
Detrie, P., 381
DeVault, M. L., 15–16, 110, 144, 146, 148–149,
    151, 173, 176, 183–186, 192, 371, 447,
    469–470, 501, 503, 505, 508, 521, 652,
    673–674
Devine, F., 397–398
Dey, E. L., 218
Diamond, A., 177
Diamond, I., 438
Diamond, L., 332
Diamond, T., 186
DiBenedetto, T., 266
Dick, B., 301
Diley, R., 372
Dill, B. T., 6, 13, 540, 630–631, 676
Dillman, D. A., 200, 209
Dilorio, J., 260
Dinnerstein, D., 235
Diprose, R., 376–377
DiStefano, C., 59
Dixson, A. D., 382
Dobscha, S., 372
Dodson, L., 148, 506
Doell, R., 33
Doll, R., 242
Dominelli, L., 375
Donolo, A. L., 209
Dooley, D. A., 215
Doppelt, G. D., 569
Doucet, A., 522

Drasgow, F., 336
Dreifus, C., 234
Dua, E., 175
Du Bois, B., 214, 299, 522
DuBois, W. E. B., 176, 506, 622, 630
duCille, A., 114, 640
Duelli-Klein, R. D., 9
Dunbar, C. J., 500–501, 503
Duncan, L., 331, 338
Duncombe, J., 525
Duneier, M., 443
Duran, B., 313
Duran, J., 34, 40
Durham, R., 350
Durkheim, É., 537
Dworkin, A., 233, 237
Dyck, I., 372

Eadie, J., 374
Easlea, B., 232
Ecker, G., 438
Ecumenical Women's Team Visit, 310
Ede, L., 455
Edin, K., 328, 339
Edwards, E., 374
Edwards, L. R., 177
Edwards, R., 181, 393, 422, 499–500, 524
Ehrenreich, B., 228, 231, 234, 245
Ehrlich, C., 570
Eichler, M., 4, 149, 190, 202, 211–212, 216, 476,
    508, 522, 567
Eikeland, O., 297
Einstein, A., 560
Eisenstein, H., 227
Eisenstein, Z., 32, 155–156, 656
Elam, D., 20, 86, 94–96, 125
Elbow, P., 455
Eldreth, B., 625
Elkins, R., 351
Elliott, A., 615
Ellis, C., 459, 527
Ellis, H., 431
Elson, D., 245
Emberley, J. V., 113
Eng, D., 133–134
Engels, F., 46, 411
England, K. V. L., 524
England, P., 285, 339, 420, 452–453
English, D., 234, 245
English, L., 430
Enloe, C., 228, 641
Erhardt, A., 226
Eribon, D., 84
Erikson, E. N., 517
Eschle, C., 656

Esseveld, J., 178, 200, 316, 522
Esterberg, K. G., 176
Evans, J., 430
Evans, S. M., 299
Evans-Winters, V., 160, 166
Everett, J., 497
Ewald, F., 86

Faden, R., 229
Fals-Borda, O. R., 298, 308, 613, 653
Fanon, F., 134, 622
Fantasia, R., 656
Farganis, S., 476
Farrer, C., 622
Fassinger, R. E., 352
Fausto-Sterling, A., 37, 40, 55, 223–224, 232, 282,
    430, 476, 691–692
Featherman, D., 327
Fedigan, L. M., 477, 572
Fee, E., 214, 224, 237, 476
Feiner, S. F., 50
Fenstermaker, S., 348, 606
Ferber, M. A., 374
Ferguson, A. A., 237, 454
Ferguson, K., 82, 164, 607
Ferguson, R., 632
Fernea, E., 622
Ferree, M. M., 391
Ferrell, R., 235
Fetterman, D. M., 279, 285
Fiene, J. I., 352
Figert, A., 360
Figueroa, R., 46
Finch, J., 362
Fine, M., 148, 165–166, 203, 263, 300–301, 304,
    312–313, 315, 328–329, 335, 354, 507,
    521–522, 526, 539, 613–618
Finkenthal, M., 124–125
Fiore, Q., 271
Firestone, R., 237
Firestone, S., 247, 299, 309
Fish, S., 129
Fisher, B. M., 580
Fisher, C. B., 524
Fisher, M. M. J., 507
Fisher, S., 447
Fishman, J. R., 351–352
Fitzgerald, L. F., 336
Flax, J., 59–60, 79, 81, 168, 485
Folbre, N., 283
Fonow, M. M., 15, 161–162, 165–166, 345, 391,
    393, 404, 459, 466, 470, 521, 545, 571,
    673–674, 676, 705–706
Foran, J., 641
Ford-Gilboe, M., 350

Fore, E., 676
Forsythe, D. E., 360
Fosket, J. R., 352, 357–358
Foucault, M., 77–78, 80, 83–85, 87,
    92–98, 100, 178, 241, 279, 355–357,
    414, 482, 486, 550, 615
Fowler, F. J., 211–213
Fox, B. J. ., 263
Fox, M., 227, 304
Fox-Genovese, E., 278, 282
Francis, B., 91, 606
Frank, A. G., 61
Frankenberg, R., 147, 181, 573
Fraser, N., 77, 430, 584
Frazer, N., 614
Freeman, C., 640, 652
Freeman, H. E., 277
Freeman, J., 299
Frege, G., 547, 557–558
Freire, P., 46, 159, 297–298, 303, 305, 308–309,
    613, 615, 664
French, M., 434
Freud, S., 48, 54, 134, 235, 279, 431
Freudenberg, N., 614
Friday, N., 432, 434
Fried, B., 476
Friedan, B., 2–3, 177, 225, 260, 299,
    419, 427–428, 431, 433–434
Friedman, M., 665
Frieze, I. H., 210
Frissen, V., 243
Frye, M., 240, 430, 439, 469, 483
Fuentes, A., 228, 231
Fullarton, J. E., 236
Fuss, D., 519

Gaard, G., 438
Gailey, C. W., 371, 374, 376
Gallop, J., 431–432
Gamson, J., 345
Gamson, W., 391, 395
Gane, N., 79
Gannon, S., 11, 14, 16, 19–20, 73,
    81, 83–84, 90, 99
Gardner, C. B., 453
Garrard, M., 438
Garrett, C. D., 692
Gatenby, B., 379, 524
Gatens, M., 87
Gatley, C., 682
Gaventa, J., 304, 655
Gay, J., 245
Geertz, C., 483
Gelb, J., 392
Gelder, K., 345

Gelsthorpe, L., 605
Gentile, M., 438
Gergen, M., 330
Gibbs, A., 383
Gibson, C. M., 338
Gibson-Davis, C. M., 339
Gibson-Graham, J. K., 109
Giddings, P., 259
Gilbert, S., 439
Giles, W., 657
Gille, Z., 652
Giller, J. E., 310
Gillespie, M. A., 244
Gillies, V., 523, 526
Gilligan, C., 48, 93, 127, 159, 340, 419, 423, 432,
    515–520, 523, 525, 527–528, 549, 581
Gilman, C. P., 267, 380, 426, 429
Gilmartin, C., 11, 18, 470, 538
Ginsburg, F., 183, 527
Ginzberg, E. A., 331
Giovanni, N., 434
Glanz, K., 675
Glaser, B. G., 144, 345–350
Glenn, E. N., 444
Glick Schiller, N., 652
Gluck, S. B., 15, 185, 189, 299, 509, 525
Goetz, J. P., 520
Goffman, E., 348, 410, 445
Goldberger, N. R., 159, 549, 581
Goldman, A., 548
Goldman, E., 432
Goldsen, R., 258
Gomez, M. G. R., 640
Gonick, M., 99
Goodall, J., 284, 560
Goodwin, D. H., 352
Goodwin, J., 392
Gordon, A. F., 182, 615
Gordon, D. A., 159, 165, 184, 374, 439, 623
Gordon, S. M., 328
Gore, J., 585
Gorelick, S., 178, 199, 204, 207,
    312, 503, 571–573, 607, 609
Gornick, V., 177, 429
Gossett, J., 265–266
Gotanda, N., 613
Gottfried, H., 205, 207, 300, 568
Gowaty, P. A., 520
Grady, K. E., 204, 215
Grahame, K. M., 186
Grahn, J., 434
Gramsci, A., 355
Grant, J., 477, 484, 572
Grant, L., 520
Greaves, L., 573

Green, E., 235
Greenbaum, J., 235, 243
Greene, J., 279, 289–290
Greene, M., 615
Greenhouse, C. J., 374
Greenwood, D., 297
Greer, G., 427–428
Gregor, F., 146, 186
Gregor, G., 362
Grewal, I., 107–109, 113–114, 117, 119,
    126–128, 130, 136–137, 191, 244
Grieco, L., 353
Griffin, W., 439
Griffith, A. I., 176, 183, 237, 412, 414
Grimshaw, J., 527
Grobbee, D. E., 225, 233
Grosfoguel, R., 375
Gross, G., 16, 148–149, 151, 174
Gross, P. R., 63
Grossman, F. K., 522
Grosz, E., 81, 87–88, 94, 97–99, 242, 394, 432
Groves, R., 200–201, 205, 209, 212–215
Gruber, S. H., 239, 267
Guarnizo, L. E., 652
Guattari, F., 87, 383
Guba, E. G., 328, 496
Gubar, S., 439
Gubrium J. F., 176
Guidry, J. A., 652, 654
Guijt, I., 309, 319
Guinier, L., 335
Guishard, M., 613–614
Gunell, J., 481
Gunew, S., 241
Gurin, P., 218
Gurwitz, J. H., 226
Gusfield, J. R., 395
Gustafsson-Larsson, S., 352
Gustavsen, B., 297
Gutman, S. A., 353

Haack, S., 568, 569, 574, 694–695
Haas, V., 430
Habermas, J., 76
Hacker, S., 238
Hacking, I., 348
Hagg, K., 353
Hall, B., 653
Hall, S., 111, 112
Halse, C., 706
Hamber, B., 315
Hamilton, J., 226
Hammarstrom, A., 352
Hammonds, E., 357, 640
Hanson, S., 116

Haraway, D. J., 8–9, 45–47, 58, 60, 81, 87,
        112–113, 127, 130, 144, 202, 207–208,
        224, 237, 246–247, 269, 345, 348, 354,
        375, 430, 477, 503, 507, 520, 579, 581,
        583, 586, 606, 639, 642–643, 647
Harcourt, W., 270–271
Harding, S., 5, 8–10, 16, 19, 30–32, 40, 42, 45–46,
        51–52, 55, 59, 61, 63, 112, 130, 143–145, 149,
        157, 174, 177, 200–203, 205, 207, 214,
        224–225, 229, 237, 244, 281, 284–285, 291,
        299, 328, 354, 371, 374, 376, 382, 430, 439,
        445, 459, 476–477, 483–484, 496–498, 508,
        520–522, 553, 560–561, 567–568, 574,
        579–581, 616, 625, 639
Hardy-Fanta, C., 676
Harmon, W. W., 521
Harper, C., 655
Harré, R., 73
Harris, A., 618
Harris, J. R., 242
Harrision, R., 352
Harrison, E., 624
Hart, B., 339
Hart, V., 392
Hartmann, H., 8, 201, 204, 208, 218, 227, 676
Hartsock, N. C., 19, 45–46, 59, 61, 143,
        202, 283–284, 445, 484, 497, 503,
        579, 581–583, 586, 616
Haskell, M., 258
Hassard, J., 357
Hateman, W., 261
Haug, F., 76, 91, 99
Hausman, B. L., 345
Hawkesworth, M. E., 22, 279, 281, 284–285,
        375, 421–422, 477, 479–480, 484–485
Hawthorne, S., 246–247
Hayek, F., 665
Healy, B., 233
Healy, J. M., 331
Heasley, C., 100
Heckman, S., 607
Hegel, G. W. F., 560
Heilbrun, C., 185
Hein, H., 438
Hekman, S. J., 63, 79, 85, 484–485
Held, V., 528
Helson, R., 330, 331, 339–340
Hempel. C., 334
Henderson, D. J., 320
Henderson, J., 381
Henderson, M., 401
Hennessy, R., 433, 583–585
Hennifin, M. S., 476
Henriques, J., 76
Hepburn, A., 460

Hernández, D, 137
Herring, S., 266
Herrnstein, R. J., 216
Hertz, R., 449, 496
Herzig, R. M., 692
Hesford, W. S., 584
Hess, D. J., 46
Hesse-Biber, S. N., 11, 14, 17–18, 22, 152,
        199–200, 203, 207, 231, 422, 447, 470,
        521, 538, 606–607, 653, 654
Hey, V., 161
Higginbotham, E., 573
Hill, A., 632
Hintikka, M., 47
Hinton, W., 177
Hippensteele, S. K., 379
Hirsch, M., 12, 438
Hirschmann, N., 59
Hite, S., 432
Hitler, A., 557
Hoagland, S. L., 240, 430
Hochschild, A., 447, 451–452
Hodson, R., 334
Hofrichter, R., 670, 676
Holland, C., 393
Hollander, E. L., 635
Hollander, J. A., 444
Hollway, W., 76
Holmes, H. B., 234
Holstein, J. A., 176
Holtzman, N. A., 236
Hondagneu-Sotelo, P., 188, 191, 300, 653
Honey, A., 706
Hood, D., 282, 292
Hood-Williams, J., 606
hooks, b., 2–3, 12, 15, 109, 162,
        229, 299, 503, 535–536, 615, 622
Hope, A., 308–309
Hopkins, M. C., 526
Hopper, G., 246
Horkheimer, M., 76
Horne, S., 381
Horner, M. S., 329
Horowitz, D, 696
House, E. R., 285
House, J. S., 670–671
Howard, J. A., 444
Howe, K. R., 285
Hrushesky, W. J. M., 238–239
Hubbard, R., 47, 232, 237, 476
Huddy, L., 329
Hufford, M., 625
Huggins, J., 623
Hughes, E. C., 357
Hulbert, K. D., 330

Hull, G., 435
Hulzer, G., 664
Humble, A. J., 379
Hume, D., 30, 34, 473, 480
Humphries, M., 379, 524
Hundelby, C., 19
Hunt, M. K., 430
Hurd, T., 316
Hurston, Z. N., 176, 622
Hurtado, A., 113, 282
Hurtado, S., 218
Huston, A. C., 338
Hutchings, L., 606
Hutchings, M., 606
Hutchinson, S. A., 349, 351
Hyams, M., 379
Hylton, D., 614–615
Hyndeman, J., 657–658

Ingraham, C., 584
Ingram, D., 351
Institute for Policy Research, 339
Institute of Medicine, 669
Irigaray, L., 11, 87, 95, 241–242,
    433, 437, 559
Irwin, K., 351

Jackman, M. R., 448
Jackson, T., 653
Jacobs, H., 1, 3
Jacobs, J. L., 527
Jacobson, H. E., 571
Jacobson, J. L., 245, 308
Jacobus, M., 430
Jaggar, A., 9, 45, 47, 55, 223, 225,
    230, 237–239, 284, 430, 477, 549, 581
James, S. M., 109, 640
Jameson, F., 46, 52, 61, 241
Janeway, E., 429
JanMohammed, A., 113–114
Jasper, J. M., 392, 395, 401
Jayaratne, T. E., 8, 149, 203–205,
    208, 216–218, 328–329, 340, 568
Jefferson, T., 352
Jenkins, S. R., 331
Jenks, C., 348
Jessop, J., 525
Jick, T. D., 337
Johnson, D., 227, 266, 438
Johnson, M., 333
Johnson-Bailey, J., 162
Johnston, H. B., 373, 391, 395
Johnston, J., 427–428
Jones, J. H., 214, 231, 523
Jong, E., 434

Joos, K. E., 379
Jordan, B., 239
Jordan, J., 184
Julian, R., 658

Kabeer, N., 657
Kaczala, C. M., 217–218
Kahane, H., 556
Kahn, R., 209
Kalish, D., 556
Kamuf, P., 86
Kandiyoti, D., 13
Kaneko, L., 133
Kant, E., 48, 551
Kanter, R. M., 5
Kaplan, C., 107–109, 113, 115, 117, 119,
    126–128, 130, 136–137, 175, 191
Kaplan, G., 393
Karim, W. J., 623
Karlberg, K., 360
Karner, T. X., 176
Karon, S., 259
Kasama, H., 91
Kass, N., 229
Katz, C., 115, 116–117
Kaufman, C., 401
Kaufman, D. R., 542–543, 682–686
Kearney, M. H., 350–351
Keating, A., 184
Keck, M., 655
Keddy, B., 350
Kegler, M. C., 676
Keller, E. F., 12, 47, 202, 224, 235,
    237, 284–285, 430, 550, 639
Kelley, L., 496
Kelly, A., 206
Kelly, L., 608
Kelly, R., 476
Kelly-Gadol, J., 6
Kelsey, S. F., 226
Kempadoo, K., 640
Kendall, L., 266
Kennedy, C., 350
Kennedy, E. L., 572
Kennedy, M. D., 652
Kenney, S., 63
Khanna, R., 298, 306–307
Kidder, L., 203, 315
Killion, C. M., 338
Kim, H. S., 14, 16, 20
Kim, S. K., 137, 268
Kimmel, M., 260, 264
Kim-Puri, H. J., 108, 115, 118–119
Kincheloe, J., 11, 76
Kindon, S., 319, 372

King, D., 109–110, 632
King, K., 583
King, M. C., 232
King, Y., 232
Kingston, M. H., 133
Kinsella, H., 63
Kinsey, A., 562
Kirby, E., 372
Kirkup, G., 243
Kirsch, G. E., 504–505, 524, 527, 706
Kitch, S. L., 20–21, 124, 126–128, 130
Kitcher, P., 564
Klandermans, B., 391–392
Klatch, R. E., 180, 183
Klein, J. T., 124–126, 634
Klein, R. D., 131, 234, 246–247, 664
Klonoff, E. A., 203
Knapp, K. K., 376
Knight, M. G., 524
Knights, J. J., 230
Koblinsky, M., 245
Koertge, N., 536–537, 690, 694
Kohlberg, L., 48, 419, 517–518
Koikari, M., 379
Kondo, D. K., 162–163, 165–166, 498, 584, 652
Konik, J., 8, 149, 210
Kontos, P., 372
Kools, S., 349, 350
Koopmans, R., 392
Korsmeyer, C., 438
Kothari, U., 319
Kourany, J. A., 549, 564
Kramarae, L., 266
Kriby, V., 97–98
Krieger, S., 447
Kristeva, J., 11, 95, 241, 437
Kruks, S., 583
Kuhn, T. S., 32–35, 46, 57, 216, 569
Kulick, R., 147, 151
Kuni, V., 248
Kurian, P., 641
Kushner, K. E., 350, 351, 352
Kwan, M. P., 373

Lacan, J., 95, 134, 279, 432
Ladner, J., 177
Lai, J., 505
Lakatos, I., 57
Lake, M., 393
Lal, J., 151
Lamphere, L., 15
Lancan, J., 241
Lancaster, J., 224
Lander, J., 315
Landrine, H., 203–204, 212, 215

Lanser, S., 380
Lapointe, J., 4
Laraña, E., 395
LaRosa, J., 233
Larrabee, M. J., 233
Larson, P. A., 381
Lather, P., 15, 72, 76–78, 81, 97, 99,
    147, 165, 167, 285, 348, 354, 361–362,
    374, 444, 522, 624, 639, 652, 705
Laughlin, K., 438
Laughlin, P., 305
Law, J., 348, 357
Law, L., 188
Lawless, E., 623
Lawrence, D. H., 174
Lawrence-Lightfoot, S., 382
Lawson, V., 116
Lay, M. M., 128
Lazreg, M., 187–188
Leach, M., 161
Leacock, E., 684
Leathwood, C., 606
Leavitt, R., 224
Leavy, P., 11, 199, 470
Leck, G. M., 159
Leckenby, D., 17–18, 152, 521, 653, 654
LeDoeuff, M., 469
Lee, A., 133
Lee, C. K., 657
Lee, V., 706
Leibowitz, L., 224
Leiter, V., 360
Lemert, C., 506
Lemish, D., 264
Lempert, L., 351
Lentin, R., 381, 393, 658
Lenz-Taguchi, H., 86
Lerman, N., 227
Lesser, M., 239
Lessor, R., 362
Leung, M. L. A., 573
Levin, M., 297
Levinson, D. J., 339, 517
Levitt, N., 63
Lewin, E., 526
Lewis, H. M., 304
Lewis, R., 113, 362, 640
Lichterman, P., 398–399, 404
Lifton, R. J., 269
Lin, A. C., 328, 332, 334–335, 337
Lincoln, Y. S., 76, 158, 300, 328, 361, 459, 496
Linden, R. R., 165, 184, 187
Lin-Fu, J. S., 226
Linker, M., 39–40
Linnenberg, K., 339

Lippman, M. E., 242
Lively, K. J., 454
Lloyd, D., 654
Lloyd, E., 568
Lloyd, G., 55, 266–267, 519, 548, 550
Lock, M., 383
Locke, J., 30
Locke, K., 345
Loevinger, J., 339
Lofland, J., 391, 445
Lofland, L. H., 445
London, A., 188
Long, J., 185
Longino, H. E., 30, 33, 35–37, 39, 43, 47, 143,
        223–224, 394, 421–422, 476, 477–479,
        483–484, 522, 536–537, 540, 549–550,
        553, 561–564, 568–571, 574, 639
Lopata, H., 177
Lopez, A. S., 375
Lorde, A., 2–3, 109, 128, 162, 182,
        184, 299, 433, 434, 622, 640
Louis, M. R., 312
Love, S. M., 231, 232
Lovelace, A., 246
Lowe, L., 654
Lowenberg, J., 349
Luckman, T., 348
Lugones, M., 109, 174
Lukacs, G., 46
Luke, C., 584
Lunbeck, E., 224
Lundy, M., 522
Luttrell, W., 183
Lutz, C., 186, 623
Lyall, N., 373
Lyberg, L. E., 210
Lydenberg, R., 11, 18, 470, 538
Lykes, M. B., 145–146, 148, 150–151, 202,
        300, 311, 313–315, 329, 504, 539, 613
Lynch, K., 379
Lyotard, J. F., 79, 241

MacArthur, S., 438
MacDonald, A. L., 232, 234
MacDonald, M, 350
MacKenzie, D., 227–228
MacKinnon, C., 48, 50, 233, 237–239, 571, 690
MacLure, M., 161
Maddison, S., 146–147, 148, 151
Madonna, 261
Magee, W. J., 340
Magley, V. J., 329
Maguire, P., 46, 150, 299, 301, 303,
        305, 316–318, 496, 504, 653–654
Mahler, S., 116

Malcom, S., 226
Malson, H., 99
Mama, A., 110
Mamo, L., 351–352
Mander, A., 432
Mani, L., 108
Manias, E., 372
Manicom, A., 63, 146, 508
Manji, A., 307
Mann, S. A., 496
Mannheim, K., 46
Mannheim, M., 664
Mansbridge, J., 177
Mararey, S., 381
Marcellus, L., 350
Marchand, M. H., 109, 655
Marcus, G. E., 158, 184, 506, 507, 622, 641, 652
Marcuse, H., 76
Marecek, J., 202, 203–204, 215, 315
Marks, E., 95, 694
Martin, E., 6–7, 30–31, 186, 224, 449–450, 477
Martin, J. R., 521
Martin, K. A., 329
Martin, M., 298, 318
Martin, P. M., 391
Martín-Baró, I., 613
Martineau, H., 258–259, 267, 506
Martinez, M., 614–615
Marx, K., 10, 46, 48, 54, 284,
        411–412, 498, 500, 560, 580
Masaracchia, R., 691
Mascia-Lees, F. E., 179, 507, 623
Mason, J., 362
Massat, C. R., 522
Massey, D., 108, 115
Massumi, B., 354
Mathews, S., 381
Matsuda, M., 613
Mattson, M., 505
Matusov, E., 163
Mauthner, N., 522, 524
May, T., 176
Mayberry, M., 692, 696
Maynard, M., 15, 203, 204, 640
Mayo, C., 146, 150, 163–164
Mayo, M., 641
Mazowiecki, T., 310
McCall, L., 484, 631
McCall, R. B., 218
McCann, C., 137
McCarthy, D., 348, 353
McCarthy, M., 350
McCarthy, T., 76
McCarthy, W., 401
McClintock, A., 134–135, 237

McClintock, B., 284, 560
McCloskey, D. N., 189
McCoy, L., 146, 185–186, 508
McCreadie, J., 303
McDonald, K., 391
McDonald, S., 316, 318
McDowell, L., 116, 374
McGraw, D., 229
McGraw, L. A., 523
McIntosh, P., 13
McIntyre, A., 300–301, 305, 315–316
McKeever, P., 372
McLanahan, S., 339
McLaren, A. E., 177
McLaren, P., 11, 76
McLaughlin, A., 13, 540
McLeroy, K. R., 675, 676
McLoyd, V. C., 338
McLuhan, M., 271
McMahon, M., 384
McMillan, D. W., 316
McMillan, S., 353
McNay, L. ., 93
McRobbie, A., 160, 166, 261
McTaggart, R., 46, 279, 306
McVicker, J., 128
Mead, G. H., 347–348
Megill, A., 482
Mehta, B. J., 244
Meijer, I. C., 99
Melia, K. M., 350
Mellon, J., 258
Melucci, A., 391–396, 402–404
Mendez, J. B., 13, 541, 656–657
Mercado, M., 674
Merchant, C., 232, 237, 438
Merrifield, J., 304
Merrill, D., 391
Merritt-Gray, M., 350, 351
Mertens, D. M., 149, 285, 508
Merton, R. K., 46, 312, 498
Mertz, E., 374
Metzl, J. M., 337
Meyer, D., 392, 404
Microsysters, 237
Midgley, C., 134
Mies, M., 61, 144, 148, 283, 284, 372,
    541–542, 568, 571, 664–665, 667, 674
Mihesuah, D. A., 625
Miles, A., 541
Milgram, S., 214
Mill, J. S., 225, 558
Millar, M., 246–247
Millen, C. D., 608
Miller, K., 299, 564

Miller, M., 291
Miller, S., 351
Miller, T., 525
Miller, V., 303
Milles, S., 113
Millet, K., 258, 428, 431
Millman, M. ., 5
Mills, C. W., 354
Mills, E., 527
Mills, S., 85, 92, 362
Miner-Rubino, K., 8, 149, 331
Minichiello, V., 397, 399
Minkler, M., 305–306, 306, 676
Miranda, M. K., 160, 166
Mirza, H. S., 107, 110–112
Mishler, E., 184
Mishler, E. G., 176, 331
Mitchell, C., 299
Mitchell, J., 429, 431
Mitchell, K., 115, 118
Mitchell, R. F., 381
Mitchell, R. G., 444
Mitchell, S., 401
Mitchell, V., 339
Miyares, I. M., 383
Moghadam, V., 641
Mohanty, C. T., 12–13, 96–97, 107–108, 111,
    113–115, 126, 128, 175–176, 186–187,
    188, 228, 244, 541, 551, 573, 584, 631,
    684–685, 687
Mohun, A., 227
Moallem, M., 115
Moi, A., 348
Moi, T., 83, 95, 485
Money, J., 226
Monhanty, C. T., 14, 191–192, 299
Monk, J., 128
Montague, R., 556
Montini, T., 357–358
Moody-Adams, M. M., 528
Moore, H., 431, 640
Moore, L. J., 352, 360
Moraga, C., 159–160, 162, 165,
    184, 299, 584, 622
Moran, B. K., 177, 429
Moran, J., 124–125, 127, 129
Morawski, J. G., 329
Morgaine, C. A., 379
Morgan, D. L., 176, 330
Morgan, R., 434
Morgen, S., 670, 672, 675, 677
Morris, A., 395
Morrison, C., 225
Morrison, T., 706
Morris-Roberts, K., 524

Morrow, R., 350, 351
Mortensen, P., 527
Moser, C., 283
Moses, C. G., 96
Moses, R., 228
Moshner, K., 350
Moss, P., 149, 371, 373, 375, 379, 384
Mother Teresa, 560
Moucault, M., 585
Mouffe, C., 375
Mountz, A., 383
Moya, P. M. L., 178, 585
Mullings, L., 352, 362, 670, 673, 675
Mulvey, L., 128, 432
Munshi, D., 641
Murphy, K., 382
Murphy, S., 351
Murray, C., 216
Murray, P., 243
Murray, S. B., 454
Musgrave, A., 57
Mutulsky, A. G., 236
Myers, N., 188

Nagar, R. A., 107, 115–116
Nagel, J., 674
Nagel, M., 114
Nagel, T., 477
Nájera-Ramirez, O., 622
Nananda, F. C., 226
Nanda, M., 63
Napier-Klemic, J., 353
Naples, N. A., 10, 14–16, 110, 188–189, 299,
    313, 317, 320, 362, 371, 499, 509, 521,
    537, 581, 584–586, 654, 669, 673–676
Narayan, K., 622
Narayan, U., 61, 108–109, 111, 113–114,
    187–188, 571, 573, 640, 685–686
Narrigan, D., 233
Nash, J., 624, 664
Nash, K., 113
National Academy of Sciences, 634
National Breast Cancer Coalition, 236
National Institutes of Health (NIH), 671
National Library of Medicine, 247
National Science Board, 248
National Science Foundation, 225
Naylor, G., 706
Needham, J., 58
Negrey, C., 260
Nelson, A. R., 670
Nelson, J. A., 374
Nelson, L. H., 32, 36–42, 47, 483, 549
Nelson, T., 623
Neuman, W. L., 7

Neurath, O., 31
Newbrough, J. R., 316
Newcomb, H., 258
Newell, W. H., 634
Newman, I., 327, 330
Newton, J., 433
Nicholson, L. J., 158, 485, 584, 639
Nielson, J. M., 15
Nietzsche, F., 486
Nieves, A. D., 13, 540
Nightingale, F., 267
Nip, J., 268
Nnaemeka, O., 640
Nochlin, L., 471
Noddings, N., 423, 515–516,
    518–519, 523, 525, 527–528
Noffke, S., 279
Norberg, K., 354
Norman, C., 226
Norton, B. L., 676
Norwood, C., 233
Novick, P., 55
Nye, A., 553–554, 556–558
Nzegwu, N., 111

Oakley, A., 15, 143, 148–149, 158,
    165, 177–178, 399, 470, 483–484, 497, 524
O'Brien, M., 233
Office of Human Rights of the Archdiocese of
    Guatemala [Oficina de Derechos Humanos
    del Arzobispado de Guatemala], 311
Ogunyemi, C., 244
Ohman, A., 353
Okin, S., 430, 685
Okome, M. O., 108, 112–113
Okruhlik, K., 31–33, 35
Old Boys Network, 247
Oldenziel, R., 227
Olesen, V. L., 231, 349, 351, 361,
    444, 498, 670–671, 676
Oliver, W., 438
Olshansky, E. F., 350
Olson, K., 429
Olson, L. C., 182
Omi, M., 675
Ong, A., 108, 113
Ontai, L. L., 333
Orestein, G., 438
Ormer, S., 260
Ornelas, A., 308
O'Shaughnessy, E., 349
Ospina, S., 318
Ostrander, S. A., 176
Oswald, R., 352
Owen, J., 235

Oyewumi, O., 111–112
Ozanne, J. L., 372

Pace, S., 353
Paget, M., 181
Pain, D., 235
Pajaczkowska, C., 640
Papart, J. L., 283
Paradis, E. K., 522
Parameswaran, R., 499, 509
Park, P., 653
Park, Y., 112–113
Parker, L., 352, 500
Parmar, P., 110–111
Parpart, J. L., 319, 321
Parr, J., 351
Parra-Medina, D., 670, 673, 675–676
Parreñas, R. S., 653, 657
Patai, D., 160, 185, 189, 299, 301,
    509, 523, 525, 543–544, 622, 696
Pateman, C., 127
Paterson, N., 246
Patillo-McCoy, M. E., 333
Patkar, M., 667
Paton, A., 420, 460, 464–465
Patton, M. Q., 283, 285, 290, 292
Pattrow, L. M., 230
Payne, Y., 613–614
Peake, L., 115
Pearce, K. C., 266
Pedhazur, E. J., 216
Pelak, C., 459
Peller, G., 613
Pence, E., 186, 190, 413–414, 580
Peplau, L. A., 202–203, 328, 340
Perkins, T., 614
Perkins-Gilman, C., 506
Perrucci C., 430
Personal Narratives Group, 299
Pessar, P., 116
Peters, E., 524
Peterson, B. E., 340
Peterson, V. S., 641, 653
Petraka, V., 258
Petras, E. M., 46
Pew Research Center, 209
Phelan, S., 437
Phillips, A., 11
Phillips, M., 527
Piaget, J., 48, 517
Piatelli, D., 17, 21–22, 422
Pierce, K., 261
Pigg, S. L., 361, 362
Pillow, W. S., 15, 78, 99, 146,
    150, 157, 162, 166, 375

Pini, B., 504
Pinn, V., 233
Pinochet, A., 665
Pitts, V., 352
Podems, D., 291–292
Polletta, F., 395
Popper, K., 33, 473–475, 480
Porpora, D. V., 46
Post, R., 686
Potter, E., 437, 642
Potts, A., 383
Poynton, C., 438
Pratt, G., 115, 116, 372
Pratt, M. B., 184
Pratt, M. L., 614
Pratt, P., 374
Preissle, J., 22, 419, 422
Press, A. L., 337, 361
Prins, B., 99
Probyn, E., 87, 98, 372
Proctor, R., 55
Prophete, M., 527
Provost, G., 455
Pryse, M., 676
Puar, J., 640
Puri, J., 640
Purvis, J., 15

Quina, K., 211–212
Quine, W. V. O., 30, 32, 34, 36, 42

Rabinowitz, V. C., 327, 329
Radcliffe, S., 108, 113, 115
Raffaelli, M., 333
Ragin, C., 674
Ragins, B. R., 329
Ragland-Sullivan, E., 431–432
Ragone, H., 15
Rahman, M. A., 298, 308, 313, 653
Rajan, S. ., 112
Raju, S., 115
Ralston, H., 500–501, 503
Ramazanoğlu, C., 15, 96–97,
    371, 393, 585
Ransby, B., 632
Rapp, R., 224
Rappaport, J., 318
Rasinski, K., 200
Rawls, J., 48
Reagan, R., 665
Reagon, B. J., 182
Reason, P., 284–285, 298, 504, 521
Reay, D., 539, 540, 608–609
Redwood-Jones, Y. A., 372
Regan, L., 608

Rehman, B., 137
Reiche, C., 247
Reid, I. S., 177
Reid-Walsh, J., 299
Reimer, M. ., 186
Reinharz, S., 15–16, 143–144, 147, 151, 157, 160,
      162, 204–205, 214–216, 257, 259, 281, 284,
      292, 299, 329, 371, 393–394, 398–400,
      470, 497, 508, 521, 568, 571, 639
Reskin, B., 673–674
Reynolds, T., 111
Rhodes, P., 500
Rhondes, P., 239
Riain, S. O., 652
Ribbens, J., 374, 393
Ricardo, D., 665
Rich, A., 128, 434, 471, 558, 607
Richardson, L., 22, 73, 88, 159, 165–166,
      189, 283, 420–421, 459, 526, 653
Richie, B., 350
Riessman, C. K., 176, 179, 185,
      189, 213, 345, 499–500, 505
Riger, S., 205
Rips, L., 200
Rivera, M., 614
Rivera-Fuentes, C., 381
Roberts, H., 15, 299
Roberts, R. A., 614–615
Roberts, W., 439
Robertson, J., 524–525, 526, 640
Robinson, L. S., 433
Robnett, B., 391
Robrecht, L., 350
Rodriguez, D., 500, 503
Rogers, M. F., 692
Rogers, T. F., 209
Roldan, M. ., 283
Rollins, J., 188
Roman, L. G., 522
Romero, M., 188
Romich, J., 338–339
Romyn, D. M., 524
Ronan, B., 476
Roodt, M J., 308
Roof, J., 16, 22, 419–420, 437
Rooney, P., 34–36, 40, 41–43, 549
Rorty, R., 550
Rose, G., 115, 374, 640
Rose, H., 45, 47, 223, 227
Rose, J., 431–432, 439
Rose, N., 94
Rose, S., 223
Rosen, P., 239
Rosen, R., 299
Rosenbaum, M., 351

Rosenfeld, D., 448
Rosenfelt, D. S., 128
Rosser, S. V., 8, 143–144, 223–225,
      227, 230, 232, 237, 248, 558
Rossi, P. H., 277
Rossiter, M., 225, 430
Roth, P., 41
Rothfield, P., 241
Rothman, B. K., 234, 447
Roulston, K., 380
Round, K., 381
Rowan, J., 284–285
Rowell, S., 232
Rowell, T., 224
Rowlands, J., 674
Roy, A., 667
Roy, D., 290
Royle, N., 85–86
Rubin, A., 215
Rubin, G., 237, 433
Rubin, L., 181
Rucht, D., 392
Rudacille, D., 691–692
Ruddick, S., 46, 581
Runyan, A. S., 109, 653, 655–656
Rupp, L. J., 391–392, 448
Rush, A., 432
Russell, B., 547
Rustin, B., 632
Ruth, S., 476
Ruzek, S., 670–671, 675, 677
Ryan, L., 381
Ryan, S., 401
Ryff, C. D., 340

Sachs, C., 584
Sacks, W., 61
Safa, H. I., 283, 664
Said, E., 113, 356
Saltmarsh, J., 635
Saltzman, J. C., 8
Salzinger, L., 657
Samik-Ilbrahim, R. M., 361
Sanchez, S., 435
Sancho, N., 658
Sanders, J., 165
Sandoval, C., 42, 61, 108–109, 113,
      299, 375, 402, 484, 579, 582, 585
Sangari, K., 115
Sapiro, V., 329
Sarachild, K., 177
Sasson, S., 652
Satrapi, M., 658
Saussure, F. de, 86
Sawin, P., 625

Scafe, S., 605

Schatzman, L., 347, 350

Schiebinger, L., 224

Schild, V., 655

Schiller, N. G., 115

Schilling G. F., 430

Schlenker, J., 261

Schlozman, K., 329

Schmalzbauer, L., 506

Schmelkin, L. P., 216

Schmidt, M., 352

Schreiber, R. S., 345, 350

Schrock, S., 352

Schuler, C., 438

Schulz, A. J., 352, 362, 675

Schuman, H., 212

Schuster, D. T., 330

Schutte, O., 113

Schutz, A., 498

Schuurman, N., 374

Schwalbe, M., 352

Schwartz, R. D., 258

Schwarz, N., 212–213

Scollay, S. J., 695

Scott, E., 188

Scott, J. W., 9, 178, 347, 373, 384, 439, 486, 506, 551, 572

Scriven, M., 289

Scutt, J., 401

Seager, J., 308

Sechrest, L., 258

Segrest, M., 184

Seibold, C., 522

Seigart, D., 145–146, 148, 151, 278, 280, 291

Seigfried, C. H., 348, 515

Selin, H., 46

Sellars, W., 480

Seller, S., 89

Sen, A. K., 283

Senie, R., 239

Settle, R. B., 200, 211

Sexton, P. C., 521

Shah, M. K., 309, 319

Sharpe, B., 179

Sharpe, J. P., 113

Sharpe, P., 507, 623

Sherif, C. W., 6, 202–203, 329

Shibutani, T., 357

Shildrick, M., 383

Shim, J. K., 352, 361

Shiva, V., 61, 667

Shorter, E., 391

Shuttleworth, S., 430

Sigel, R., 336

Sikkink, K., 655

Silverman, K., 394, 432

Silverstein, L. B., 353

Simmel, G., 46

Sims, S., 350

Sinclair, C., 266

Singer, B., 340

Skeggs, B., 607, 641

Skelton, T., 523

Sleckler, A., 675

Sleeter, C., 305

Smart, B., 85

Smart, C., 582

Smart, P., 614–615

Smedley, B. D., 670–672, 674–675

Smith, A., 640, 665

Smith, B., 184

Smith, C. A., 210

Smith, C. K., 447

Smith, D. E., 2–3, 9–10, 19, 45–48, 51, 111, 143–148, 150, 162, 176–179, 183, 185–187, 189, 191–192, 203, 213, 262, 271, 281, 285, 299–300, 311, 329–330, 353, 362, 380, 412, 445, 447, 484, 496–498, 503, 508, 522, 568, 570–571, 573, 579, 581–583, 639

Smith, E., 231

Smith, G., 413

Smith, K., 614

Smith, L. T., 2, 15, 53, 614

Smith, M. P., 163, 652

Smith, S., 306

Smith, T., 625, 658

Smithies, C., 99, 147, 165, 167, 348, 361–362, 624, 705

Smith-Rosenberg, C., 684

Snow, C. P., 125

Snow, D. A., 396, 398, 445

Sobstyl, E., 40–41

Socrates, 555

Sohn-Rethel, A., 48

Sokal, A., 691

Solomon, M., 35, 37–39

Solórzano, D. G., 372

Somerville, J., 393

Somerville, M., 98

Somerville, S., 132–133

Søndergaard, D. M., 99

Soper, K., 606

Sorenson, K., 236

Sothern, R. B., 239

Spacks, P., 429

Spanier, B., 224

Spatler-Roth, R., 8, 201, 204, 208, 218

Speer, S. A., 380

Spelman, E. V., 109, 299, 316, 581, 640

Spencer, A., 429

Spender, D., 5, 127, 266–267
Spivak, G. C., 13, 86, 96, 108–109, 113–114, 126, 244, 508, 509, 609
Sprague, J., 8–9, 149, 200
Sprengnether, M., 438
Springer, H., 267
Springer, K., 188
Springer, M., 267
Squire, S., 379
St. Pierre, E. A., 15, 78–79, 82, 84, 87–88, 94–95, 97, 100, 165, 459
Stacey, J., 151, 165, 167, 315, 345, 504, 506, 509, 524, 526, 622, 639, 683
Stachel, D. L., 335
Stack, C., 328
Staeheli, L., 107
Stage, C. W., 505
Staggenborg, S., 391–392
Stake, R., 289
Stangor, C., 210
Stanley, A., 246
Stanley, L., 9, 15, 149, 205, 282, 284, 393, 394, 476, 505, 521, 537–538, 568, 572, 591, 598, 639
Star, S. L., 345, 347–348, 351–353, 356–357
Statham, A., 159
Steady, F., 229, 244
Stearns, P., 443
Stein, G., 429
Steinberg, R. J., 204
Steiner, L., 268
Stern, P. N., 345, 349, 350
Stern, S., 313
Stewart, A. J., 8, 149, 202–205, 209–210, 216, 299, 328–331, 340
Stewart, K., 625
Stewart, M., 630
Stitcher, S., 283
Stith, A. Y., 670
Stocking, S. H., 218
Stockman, N., 475, 481–482
Stoecker, R., 653
Stokoe, E. H., 379
Stone-Mediatore, S., 179
Stooke, R., 186
Stracuzzi, N., 263
Strander, S. A., 176
Strauss, A. L., 144, 345–351, 353, 362
Stringer, E., 504
Strum, S. C., 477, 572
Stryker, S., 241
Subramaniam, R., 692
Suchman, L., 237, 239
Suleri, S., 113, 114
Sullivan, N., 372

Sumaya, C. V., 676
Summers, A., 401
Sunder Rajan, R., 112–113
Suppes, P., 556
Swart, C., 594, 596
Swiss, S., 310
Sylvester, C., 111, 113
Syme, A. Y., 674–675
Szalacha, L. A., 330–332

Talburt, S., 162
Talcott, P., 641
Tambe, A., 115, 117
Tanesini, A., 480
Tangri, S. S., 331
Tarule, J. M., 159, 549, 581
Tashakkori, A., 327, 330–331, 337, 340
Tate, B., 189
Taylor, S. J., 174, 176
Taylor, V., 268, 391–393, 395, 398–402, 448, 459
Teddlie, C., 327, 330–331, 337, 340
Tedlock, B., 498
Teghtsoonian, K., 379
Teiter, R., 50
Temple, B., 505
Terre Blanche, M., 315
Thatcher, M., 665–666
Thayer, M., 656
Thein, V., 352
Themba, M. N., 306
Thomas, C., 632
Thomas, D. S., 354
Thomas, H. G., 208
Thomas, K., 613
Thomas, W. I., 354
Thompson, C., 362
Thompson, M., 259
Thompson, S., 352
Thoresen, K., 238
Thorne, B., 159, 438
Thornton, S., 345
Tickner, J. A., 55
Tilly, C., 391
Tilly, L., 258
Timewell, E., 397
Timmel, S., 308–309
Timmermans, S., 347, 360
Timyan, J., 245
Tischler, C., 280
Titchen, A., 306
Tolman, D. L., 330–332, 522, 613
Tong, R. P., 72, 83, 96–97, 233, 515, 517, 521, 523
Torges, C., 331
Torre, M. E., 304, 613–615
Torres, M. N., 305

Touraine, A., 391, 404
Tourangeau, R., 200
Townsend, J. G., 674
Traina, C. L. H., 520
Traustadóttir, R., 184
Trautmann, M. T., 208
Travers, A., 267, 270
Trimberger, E. K., 693
Trinh, M. T., 2–3, 73, 88, 90, 96, 113, 163, 299, 509
Tristan, F., 506
Trivers, R. L., 231
Trom, D., 398
Trotz, A., 175
Trotz, D. A., 115
Trousdale, A. M., 353
Trujillo, C., 639
Truman, C., 281–282, 289, 291–292
Truth, S., 630
Tuana, N., 6, 42, 224, 348, 430
Tuchman, G., 258
Turing, A., 241
Turkle, S., 269
Twine, F. W., 362, 640

Unger, R. K., 318, 329
Upegui, D., 614–615
Urwin, C., 76
U.S. Bureau of the Census, 201
Ussher, J. M., 81
Uttal, L., 188

Valentine, G., 379
Vandewater, E. A., 330–331
Van Maaneen, J., 507
Van Steveren, I., 378
van Zyl, L., 596
Ved, R., 373
Venn, C., 76
Verba, S., 329
Veronesi, U., 242
Vetter, B., 225
Vickers, J. M., 476
Vidal-Ortiz, S., 632
Villenas, S., 162–163, 165–166
Visweswaran, K., 162–163, 165–167, 354, 384, 527, 584, 624
Vivat, B., 525
Vogt, W. P., 211

Waage, J., 520
Wajcman, J., 227–228
Walby, S., 63, 483, 487
Walker, A. J., 112, 128, 162, 435, 523, 615
Walker, G., 191
Walkerdine, V., 76, 81, 160

Wallack, L., 676
Wallerstein, I., 61
Wallerstein, N., 305–306, 313, 676
Walls, E. M., 379
Wallston, B. S., 204, 215, 329
Walters, D., 261–262
Wang, C. C., 310, 338, 372
Wanzer, K., 614
War Crimes Tribunal, 523
Ward, K., 282–286, 291
Ware, V., 605
Warren, C. A. B., 176, 504, 507
Warren, J. N., 362, 470, 640
Wasco, S. M., 202
Washburn, J., 245
Wasserfall, R. R., 151, 508–509
Waugh, P., 91
Wax, R., 163, 167
Weasel, L. H., 692
Weatherall, A., 379
Webb, B., 176
Webb, E., 258
Webb, S., 176
Weber, L., 542, 669–670, 673, 675
Weber, M., 504
Weber, R., 234
Webster, J., 227, 239–240, 242–243
Weedon, C., 83, 91
Weeks, K., 60, 580–581
Weiler, K., 267, 431
Weinberg, M., 524
Weingart, P., 124
Weis, L., 329
Weise, E. R., 266
Weisner, T., 338
Weiss, G., 124–126
Weiss, H. B., 279
Weiss, R. S., 176
Weisstein, E., 6
Weisstein, N., 329
Weitz, R., 258, 420, 446
Welbourne, A., 306–307
Wellman, D., 52–53
Wells, I. B., 259
Weseen, S., 327, 329
West, C., 348, 606
Westkott, M., 476
Wheatley, E., 345
Whitaker, M., 692
White, H., 486
White, P., 674
Whitier, N., 395–396
Whitmore, E., 279, 280, 285
Whittier, N., 268, 391, 393, 398–399, 402, 459
Whyte, W. F., 297

Wickham, J., 243
Wiegman, R., 437
Wildby, C., 394
Wiley, A., 483–485
Wilkinson, S., 378
Willett, W., 242
Williams, B., 127, 482
Williams, J., 146
Williams, J. H., 329
Williams, J. W., 313–314
Williams, P., 229, 244, 299
Williams, R. M., 632
Williams D. R., 670–671
Willis, P., 159
Wilshire, D., 72
Wilson, E. O., 231
Wilson, H., 349
Winant, H., 675
Windance Twine, F., 470
Wing, A. K., 128
Winig, M., 438
Wise, S., 9, 15, 149, 205, 282, 284, 394, 476,
    521, 537–538, 568, 572, 591, 598, 639
Wittig, M., 202
Wodak, R., 124–126
Wolf, D. L., 13, 15, 53, 144, 372, 470,
    484, 509, 524, 525, 541, 584, 640
Wolf, M., 147, 499, 526
Wolin, S., 470
Wolkomir, M., 352
Wollstonecraft, M., 225, 426
Women of Photovoice, 311
Woodward, D., 524
Woofsey, C., 230
Woolf, V., 1, 3, 186, 419, 426, 429, 439, 621
World Medical Association, 523

Wright, R., 383
Wuest, J., 350, 351
Wylie, A., 14, 16, 537, 549, 569, 571–574

Xiang, Y., 310

Yaiser, M. L., 11, 18, 199, 538, 606–607
Yalom, M. ., 438
Yeatman, A., 485
Yeoh, B., 115
Yerkes, R. M., 223
Yllo, K., 329
Ylönen, M. E., 372
Yohalem, A. M., 331
Yosso, T. J., 372
Young, I. M., 375, 393, 482
Young, K., 309, 311
Young, L., 640
Young, S., 395
Youngs, G., 266
Yunus, M., 308–309
Yuval-Davis, N., 676

Zald, M. N., 652
Zapata, E., 674
Zavella, P., 15, 179
Zeichner, K., 297, 302–303
Zeni, J., 527
Zerai, A., 190
Zerubavel, E., 454
Zima, P. V., 76
Zimmerman, B., 225
Zimmerman, M. A., 318
Zimmerman, M. K., 8–9, 149, 200
Zita, J., 99
Zvonkovic, A. M., 523

# SUBJECT INDEX

*Aberrations in Black: Toward a Queer of Color Critique* (Ferguson), 632
"Absolute relativism," 642
Absolutist concept of truth, 550
*Academic Bill of Rights* (Horowitz), 696
Accountability, in interviewing, 190–192
Accuracy, predictive, 35
"Achievement motivation," 329
Action research, 149
    evaluation research and, 285, 288–290
    global, 653–654
    *See also* Participatory and action research
Active listening, 149
Activist standpoint, 392, 394, 401–404
Additive model, 606
Advice writing, 454–455
*Aeneid* (Homer), 30
*Aesthetics in a Feminist Perspective* (Hein and Korsmeyer), 438
Affirmative action, 218
African American feminists, 52, 229–231.
    *See also* Black feminists
Afrocentric theories, 20, 109–112, 162
AIDS/HIV:
    community-based participatory research and, 302, 306
    content analysis on, 263
    ethnography on, 165
    healthcare research on, 229, 233
    mixed-methods research on, 333
"Alterity," 244
"Alternative sociology," 185
*Amazon Quarterly,* 434
*Ambiguous Empowerment* (Chase), 181
*Ambition and Accommodation: How Women View Gender Relations* (Sigel), 336
American Anthropological Association, 520
American Civil Liberties Union (ACLU), 230
American Educational Research Association, 520
American Evaluation Association, 278

American Psychological Association (APA), 128, 218, 520
American Sociological Association, 520
*American Sociological Review,* 448
*Am I Thin Enough? The Cult of Thinness and the Commercialization of Identity* (Hesse-Biber), 447
Androcentric bias of research, 4–7
*Another Voice: Feminist Perspectives on Social Life and Social Science* (Millman and Kanter), 5
Anthropometric data, 234
Anthropomorphism, 30
Antifoundationalism, 480–483
Antipositivist philosophy of science, 639
ARPANET (Advanced Research Projects Agency Network), 226
Authority issues, 16–17, 520, 621. *See also* Representation
Autobiographic writing, 381–382
Autoethnography, 459, 466, 527

Bates College, 692
Bat Shalom feminist Web site, 267
Battered women, 186
Battered Women's Advocacy Center (BWAC), London, Ontario, 573
*Battle Acts,* 434
Bedford Hills Correctional Facility, New York, 614–615
Beijing Conference of 1993, 245
Belmont Report (National Commission for the Protection of Human Subjects of Biomedical and Behavioral Research), 214–215, 523
*Beyond God and Father: Toward a Philosophy of Women's Liberation* (Daly), 430
*Beyond Methodology: Feminist Scholarship as Lived Research* (Fonow and Cook), 15, 545, 705
"Bias paradox," 31
Binary metaphors, 73–74, 91, 109
Biological determinist model, 36, 235

Biomedical model, 232, 383, 670–672
Biomedicine, 246
Birth Project, The (Chicago), 437
Black feminists:
    Afrocentric standpoint theory of, 109–112
    experimental research and, 229–231
    globalization and, 107–109
Black Feminist Thought: Knowledge,
    Consciousness, and the Politics of
    Empowerment (Collins), 15
Blacksburg Electronic Village, 230
Body/Politics: Women and the Discourses of Science
    (Jacobus and Shuttleworth), 430
Boer War, 135
Borderlands/La Frontera: The New Mestiza
    (Anzaldúa), 433
Boston Women's Health Book Collective, 677
Boundaries of Blackness, The (Cohen), 333
Breaking Out: Feminist Consciousness and Feminist
    Research (Stanley and Wise), 15
Breaking Out Again: Feminist Ontology and
    Epistemology (Stanley and Wise), 15
Breast cancer research, 231. See also
    Healthcare research
Brown v. Board of Education, 304, 613–614

C. Wright Mills Award, 360
CAMERA (Committee for Accuracy in Middle East
    Reporting in America), 271
Can the Subaltern Speak? (Spivak), 114
Capitalism, 3, 81, 107, 432. See also Globalization
Cartographies of Struggle (Mohanty), 191
Causality, 7, 570
Celebrating Her: Feminist Ritualizing Comes of Age
    (Roberts), 439
Cellular biology, 30
Centers for Disease Control and
    Prevention (CDC), 229
Central European University (Hungary), 21,
    135–137
Central tendency measures, 355
Centre of African Studies, University of
    Copenhagen, 321
Changing Methods: Feminist Transforming Practice
    (Burt and Code), 15
Chicago School of Economics, 665
Chicano movement, 52
"Chilly climate," in academia, 571–572
Chronicle of Higher Education, 690
Cinderella Was a Wuss: A Young Girl's Responses to
    Feminist and Patriarchal Folktales (Trousdale
    and McMillan), 353
Circumfession (Bennington and Derrida), 93
City University of New York (CUNY), 304
Class hierarchy, 46–47, 50

Closed-ended questions, in surveys, 212, 215
Coalition Politics: Turning the
    Century (Reagon), 182
Cognition, 482
Coherence theory of truth, 480–481, 550
"Collaborators," survey respondents as, 215
Collective analysis, 378, 383–384
Collective identity, 395–396, 402
Colonialism, 13, 79, 108, 113, 319–320
"Colonial" research processes, 52–56
Columbia University, 331, 448
Combahee River Collective, 177
Committee for Accuracy in Middle East Reporting
    in America (CAMERA), 271
Community-based participatory action research
    (CBPAR), 674
Community-based participatory
    research (CBPR), 306
Community development, 308–312, 316–317
Computers, 209, 233, 235–236
Confessionals, 507
Conflict theory, 681
Congressional Black Caucus Health Brain Trust, 672
"Conscientization," 664
Consciousness, differential oppositional, 579
Consciousness-raising, 177
Consortium on Race, Gender, and Ethnicity
    (CRGE), University of Maryland, 635–636
"Constant conjunction," 473
Constructivist research methods, 147, 334, 394, 496
Contemporary theory, 89
Content analysis, 147, 257–275
    feminist, 258–260
    knowledge production and, 266–271
    non-neutrality in, 271–272
    representation in, 260–266
Context:
    of discovery, 54–55, 328
    of justification, 203
    research, 375, 377–378
Contingency, in research, 375, 377–378
Contingent Foundations (Butler), 83
Contraceptive research, 234
Convenience sampling, 210
Conversation analysis, 379–381
Coresearchers, 314–315
Cornell University, 301
Corporate culture, colonialism as, 79
Corporeal feminism, 98
Correspondence theory of truth, 480, 550
Cosmopolitanism, 108
Cousteau Society to Save the Oceans, 560
Covering law model, 472
Critical action evaluation research, 279
Critical inquiry, 615

Critical race feminism (CRF), 128
Critical rationalism, 474–475
Critical theory, 11, 496
    explanation of, 76–78
    interdisciplinarity and, 99–100
    materiality erasure and, 97–99
    morality and ethics in, 93–95
    patriarchal theory *versus*, 95–96
    principles of, 71–75
    relativism and politics in, 92–93
    relevance of, 96–97
    *See also* Postmodern theory;
        Poststructural theory
Cross Campus Women's Network (CCWN),
    Sydney, Australia, 397, 399–400, 402
Cross-disciplinary approaches, 125.
    *See also* Interdisciplinary approaches;
        Transdisciplinary approaches
*Cry the Beloved Country* (Paton), 460
Cultural imperialism, 111
Cultures, visual and narrative (VNC), 132.
    *See also* Ethnography
Curriculum Transformation Project, 634–636
Cyber communication, 151
Cyberfeminism, 246–248, 267–269
*Cyberfeminism: Next Protocols* (Old Boys
    Network), 247–248

Dalara Talsepo feminist Web site, 268
*Daughters of the Goddess: Studies
    of Healing, Identity, and
    Empowerment* (Griffin), 439
Debriefing, as research method, 372
Decolonization, 112–115
Decolonizing approaches, 621–627
    authority and, 621
    ethnography and, 622–625
    reflexive critique toward, 622
    standpoints in, 625–626
*Decolonizing Methodologies: Research and
    Indigenous Peoples* (L. T. Smith), 15
Deconstruction:
    analysis of, 347
    ethics and, 95
    postmodern theory and, 486
    poststructural strategy of, 85–90
    women's bodies as tool of, 96
    *See also* Poststructural theory
"Deficit hypothesis," 217
Deflationary concept of truth, 550
Deleuzean-inspired inquiries, 383
Democratic evaluation research, 285
DES Action, 677
*Destabilizing Theory: Contemporary Feminist
    Debates* (Barrett and Phillips), 11

*Diagnostic and Statistical Manual of Mental
    Disorders* (DSM-III-R), 360
Dialoguing, 535–545
    discussion *versus,* 535–536
    on difference, 538–540
    on feminist methodology, 536–538
    on transnational research, 540–542
    on women's scholarship *versus*
        women's studies, 542–545
Difference research, 605–619
    assumed commonalties in, 609–610
    designing, 615–617
    dialoguing on, 538–540
    example of, 614–615
    feminist research and, 12–13
    feminist theorizing and, 606–607
    field work in, 607–608
    future directions of, 610–611
    "knowing better" in, 608–609
    positionings in, 608
    reflections on, 617–618
    standpoint theory and, 62–63
Differential oppositional consciousness, 579
"Digital default," 230
Dimorphism, 37
*Dinner Party* (Chicago), 437
Disability issues, 180, 184
*Discipline and Punish* (Foucault), 92
Disciplines, feminist research and, 17
Discourses, 82, 184–186
Discovery, context of, 54–55, 328
Discrimination, 110
Diversity, team, 230, 338–339
Diversity inclusive evaluation research, 285
*Doing Feminist Research* (Roberts), 15
Domestic violence, 190
Domination, matrix of, 586
*Do Promise Keepers Dream of Feminist Sheep?*
    (Silverstein, Auerbach and Grieco), 353
Double consciousness, 664
*Dream of a Common Language* (Rich), 558
"Duhem-Quine thesis," 31

*Echoes of Brown: Youth Documenting and
    Performing the Legacy of Brown v. Board of
    Education* (Fine, Torre, Bloom, Burns, Chajet,
    Guishard, and Payne), 613–614
Ecofeminism, 232
*Ecofeminism: Women, Animals, Nature* (Gaard), 438
*Ecofeminism and the Sacred* (Adams), 438
Economic liberalism, 107
Education:
    intersectionality in, 634–635
    methodology in, 682–685
    participatory and action research in, 302–305

Emancipation, 11
  critical, postmodern, and poststructural
      theories and, 73, 79, 92
  emergent research methods and, 382
  evaluation research for, 279
  movements for, 52–53
  social science and, 149
Emergent research methods, 371–389
  autobiographic writing as, 381–382
  collective analysis as, 383–384
  conversation analysis as, 379–381
  Deleuzean-inspired inquiries as, 383
  feminist questions about, 371–373
  for focus groups, 377–379
  overview of, 373–375
  portraiture as, 382–383
  spaces for, 376–377
  understanding, 375–376
Emotion, rationality *versus,* 8–9
Empiricism, 7–8, 29–44
  conceptions of truth and, 483
  controversies about, 39–42
  humanities combined with, 426
  knowledge building and, 483–484
  naturalism *versus,* 34–35
  radical future of, 42–43
  scientific sexism and, 30–31
  social agency and, 37–39
  standpoint theory challenges to, 59
  survey research and, 203
  theoretical values of, 35–37
  traditional resource of, 31–32
  underdeterminism *versus,* 32–34
Empowerment:
  black feminist, 110
  concepts of, 319
  conflict in, 311
  feminist perspective of, 3, 19
  global action research for, 654
  liberatory pedagogy and, 308
  metaphor for, 14
  participation and, 319–320
Empowerment evaluation research, 279, 285, 289
Epidemiological approaches, 242–243
Epigraphs, 453
Epistemic community, 537
Epistemic provisionalism, 570, 572, 574
Epistemology, 553–566
  conceptions of truth and, 483
  conclusions about, 564–565
  definition of, 3
  feminist, 7–10
  foundations of, 553–554
  logic and, 554–558
  methodology as, 130–131

philosophy of science and, 558–560
political commitments in, 561–563
positioning of, 382
social movement research and, 394–397
survey research and, 202–203
transitional, 459
  *See also* Standpoint epistemology
Equal Rights Amendment, 248, 434
Error in research, 205–206, 218, 478
Essentialism, 19
  black women and, 111
  experimental research and, 231–233
  multiculturalism *versus,* 685
  science and, 567–569
  standpoint theory and, 60
Ethics, 16–17, 515–532
  critical, postmodern, and poststructural
      theories and, 78, 93–95
  "detached," 423
  ethic of care as, 22, 127
  feminism and, 516–519
  Human Subject Review process and, 706
  in interviewing, 186–189
  men's decisions as, 48
  principle of justice and, 527–528
  representation and, 525–527
  research conduct and, 523–525
  research purpose and, 520–523
  research relationships and, 163
  science principles of, 570
  situated, 525
  survey research participants and, 214–215
  technological developments and, 240–241
Ethnic conflict, 310–311
Ethnography, 115, 155–171
  analyzing, 165–166
  autoethnography in, 459, 527
  clarifying quantitative data
      with, 328, 334–335
  decolonizing approaches in, 622–625
  ending, 166–167
  evaluation research and, 284
  feminist, 157–161
  grounded theory and, 347
  in-depth, 333
  insider/outsider researchers in, 654
  observations in, 301, 334
  participant interpretations in, 422
  purposes and practices of, 161–165
  researcher position in, 498
  "ruins" of, 167–168
  situated ethics in, 525
  social movement research and, 392
  "thick descriptions" of, 483–484
  *See also* Institutional ethnography

Ethnography, global, 639–649
    conclusions from, 646–647
    contours of, 642–644
    description of, 639–642
    examples of, 644–646
Evaluation research, 146, 149, 277–295
    challenges to, 288–290
    feminism in, 278–279
    future of, 293
    implementing, 290–292
    incorporating feminist concepts
        in, 286–288
    mixed methods for, 338
    survey research and, 217–218
    theoretical grounding of, 279–286
*Evidence of Experience, The* (Scott), 178
Existentialist feminism, 233–235
Experientialism, 572–573
Experiential knowledge, 664
Experimental ethnography, 527
Experimental research, 223–256
    African-American/womanist feminism and,
        229–231
    cyberfeminism and, 246–248
    essentialist feminism and, 231–233
    existentialist feminism and, 233–235
    lesbian separatism and, 240–241
    liberal feminism and, 225–227
    omitting females from, 143–144
    postcolonial feminism and, 243–246
    postmodern or poststructural feminism
        and, 241–243
    psychoanalytic feminism and, 235–237
    queer and transgender theories and, 241
    radical feminism and, 237–240
    socialist feminism and, 227–229
Exploratory research, 208.
    *See also* Survey research

*Family Violence and the Women's Movement*
    (Walker), 191
*Fate of Knowledge* (Longino), 564
Federation of Feminist Women's
    Health Centers, 677
*Feeling for the Organism, A* (McClintock), 237
*Female Eunuch, The* (Greer), 427
*Feminine Mystique, The* (Friedan),
    260, 427, 433
*Feminism and Anthropology* (Moore), 431
*Feminism and Method: Ethnography,*
    *Discourse Analysis and Activist*
    *Research* (Naples), 15, 673
*Feminism and Methodology* (Harding), 5
*Feminism and Political Theory* (Evans), 430
*Feminism and Science* (Tuana), 6, 430

*Feminism and Tradition in Aesthetics*
    (Brand and Korsmeyer), 438
*Feminism and Youth Culture* (McRobbie), 160
*Feminism in Twentieth-Century Science, Technology,*
    *and Medicine* (Creager, Lunbeck, and
    Schiebinger), 224
*Feminism & Psychology,* 299
*Feminist Aesthetic in Music* (MacArthur), 438
*Feminist Aesthetics* (Ecker), 438
*Feminist Approaches to Theory and*
    *Methodology* (Hesse-Biber, Gilmartin,
    and Lydenberg), 11, 18, 538
*Feminist Contentions* (Benhabib, Butler, Cornell,
    and Fraser), 77
*Feminist Dilemmas in Fieldwork* (Wolf), 15
*Feminist Engagements: Reading, Resisting, and*
    *Revisioning Male Theorists in Education and*
    *Cultural Studies* (Weiler), 431
*Feminist Epistemologies*
    (Alcoff and Potter), 437
Feminist fractured foundationalism (FFF),
    538, 591, 597–598
*Feminist Grounded Theory Revisited* (Wuest and
    Merritt-Gray), 351
*Feminist Interviewing: Experience, Talk, and*
    *Knowledge* (DeVault and Gross), 16
*Feminist Methodology: Challenges and Choices*
    (Ramazanoğlu), 15
*Feminist Methods in Social Research* (Reinharz),
    15–16, 299
*Feminist Perspectives on Social Research*
    (Hesse-Biber, Leavy, and Yaiser), 11, 18
*Feminist Praxis: Research, Theory, and*
    *Epistemology in Feminist Sociology*
    (Stanley), 15
Feminist research, 1–26
    androcentric bias *versus,* 4–7
    epistemologies and methodologies of, 7–10
    globalization in, 13–14
    handbook of, 17–23
    postmodern, 10–12
    practice of, 14–17
    theory and practice differences of, 12–13
    visions of, 1–4
*Feminist Research Methods: Exemplary Readings in*
    *the Social Sciences* (Nielson), 15
*Feminist Science Studies: A New*
    *Generation* (Mayberry, Subramaniam,
    and Weasel), 692, 696
*Feminist Theory: From Margin to*
    *Center* (hooks), 15
*Feminist Theory Reader: Local*
    *and Global Perspectives*
    (McCann and Kim), 137
Fertilization, 30–31

*Few Cautions at the Millennium on the Merging of Feminist Studies with American Indian Women's Studies, A* (Mihesuah), 625

*Film Feminisms: Theory and Practice* (Gentile), 438

*Florida Enchantment, A,* 133

Focus groups, 211, 377–379, 616

Food and Drug Administration (FDA), 358

Ford Foundation, 636

"Foreign reference publics," 655

Fragile Families and Child Wellbeing Study, 339

*Framing Dropouts* (Richardson), 165

*Framing the Bride* (Adrian), 658

Frankfurt School of Social Research (Germany), 76

Freirian pedagogical practice, 303

*Furies, The,* 434

*Future Directions for Feminist Research* (Dill, McLaughlin, and Nieves), 540

*Future of the Public's Health in the Twenty-First Century* (Institute of Medicine, National Academy of Sciences), 670

"Gail model," 352

*Gendered Fields: Women, Men, and Ethnography* (Bell, Caplan, and Karim), 623

*Gender in the Prozac Nation* (Blum and Stracuzzi), 263

*Gender Lens series, The* (Pine Forge Press/Sage Publications), 444

*Gender & Society,* 119

Genealogy, 85

"Generative grammars," 130

Georgia Institute of Technology, 241

*Getting Smart: Feminist Research and Pedagogy With/in the Postmodern* (Lather), 15, 77

*Getting Specific* (Phelan), 437

Global ethnography. *See* Ethnography, global

Globalization, 116–117
    feminist research on, 13–14, 540–541
    gay life and, 645
    gendering of, 109
    inequalities caused by, 107–108
    intersectionality and, 631

Global research, 651–668
    action research in, 653–654
    challenges of, 652–653
    conclusions on, 658–659
    feminist, 653, 657–658
    methodology for, 663–665
    neoliberal, 665–667
    spaces for, 654–657

Google search engine, 257

Grameen Bank, 308–309

*Granny Midwives and Black Women Writers: Double Dutched Readings* (Lee), 706

*Gratz v. Bollinger,* 218

Great Depression, 304

Grounded theory, 345–353
    conclusions about, 361–362
    description of, 346–347
    emergent research methods on, 382
    feminist characteristics of, 347–349
    feminist development of, 349–353
    inductive approach to, 144–145
    postmodern extension of, 150
    *See also* Situational analysis

*Grounded Theory and Gender Relevance* (Glaser), 350

*Grounded Theory of Flow Experiences of Web Users, A* (Pace), 353

*Grutter v. Bollinger,* 218

*Guests of the Sheik* (Fernea), 622

"Habits of hiding," 506

*Handbook of Qualitative Research* (Denzin and Lincoln), 361

"Hard systems" design approach, to computers, 235–236

*Has Feminism Changed Science?* (Schiebinger), 224

Health Care for Women International, 350

Healthcare research, 144, 669–679
    coalitions for change in, 675–677
    critique of, 670–672
    intersectional scholarship and, 672–675
    participatory and action research in, 305–308

Hierarchical research models, 315

Highlander Research and Education Center, New York, 304

*Hite Report: A Nationwide Study on Female Sexuality, The* (Hite), 432

HIV/AIDS:
    community-based participatory research and, 302, 306
    content analysis on, 263
    ethnography on, 165
    healthcare research on, 229, 233
    mixed-methods research on, 333

Holistic reflexivity, 493–514
    example dialogue in, 493–495
    interpretive processes in, 505–506
    interrogation in, 498–499
    methodology of, 496–497
    power and knowledge from, 499–503
    sampling by, 508–510
    "stronger science" and, 497–498
    voice in, 503–504
    writing from, 504–508
    *See also* Reflexivity

Hull House, 176

Human Genome Era, 232, 247–248

Human Subject Review process, 706

Hybridity, 108
Hypotheses in survey research, 207–209, 211, 217
"Hypothetico-deductive model," 474

Identity studies, 630–631
Immersion, in ethnography, 499
Imperialism, 13, 108, 111
*Imperial Leather: Race, Gender, and Sexuality in Colonial Conquest* (McClintock), 134
"Implicated actors," in situational analysis, 357
*In a Different Voice: Psychological Theory and Women's Development* (Gilligan), 432
Indian Health Service, 245
Inductive method, 472–473
"Inessential women," 112–115
Insiders/outsiders, researchers as, 162, 166, 312–313, 498–499, 654
Institute for Women's Policy Research, 676
Institute of Medicine,
    National Academy of Science, 670
Institutional ethnography, 409–416
    everyday world, 411–413
    examples of, 413–415
    guide to, 413
    interviewing in, 178, 185
    levels of inquiry in, 146, 149–150
    sociology from women's standpoint
        and, 410–411
    talking experience in, 410
Institutional Review Boards, 214, 523–524
Intellectual property rights, 228
Interdisciplinary approaches, 99–100, 634
    Central European University example of, 135–137
    description of, 124–127
    feminist perspectives on, 127–130
    methodologies in, 130–131
    Ohio State University example of, 131–135
    transdisciplinarity and, 137–138
International Monetary Fund, 667
International Women's Day, 320
International Women's Year, 434
Internet:
    cyberfeminism and, 246–247, 267–269
    Google search engine on, 257
    history of, 226
    pornography on, 264–266
*Interpreting Women's Lives*
    (Personal Narratives Group), 185
Interpretivist methods, 328, 335, 496
Intersectionality, 629–637
    ethnography and, 640
    feminism and feminist theory and, 156
    healthcare research and, 671–675
    history of, 630–633

identity markers and, 127
institutional transformation and, 634–636
multiple social identity study and, 330
Interviewing, 173–197
    accountability in, 190–192
    active listening in, 149
    conduct of, 179–182
    discourse structure in, 184–186
    feminist methodology of, 174–176
    grounded theory and, 347
    in-depth, 328
    influences on, 213–214
    listening in, 182–184
    moral development, 517
    prison college and, 616
    research ethics of, 186–189
    social movement research and, 399–400
    survey research, 189–190, 209
    telling "experiences" through, 176–179
    training for, 201
*Interviewing Women: A Contradiction in Terms?*
    (Oakley), 15, 178
*In the Patient's Best Interest: Women and the Politics of Medical Decisions* (Fisher), 447
*Is Female to Male as Nature is to Culture?* (Ortner), 260
*Is Multiculturalism Bad for Women?* (Okin), 685
*It Ain't Me, Babe*, 434

John Radcliffe Hospital, Oxford, England, 306
Joint Primary Aircraft Training System, 234
*Journal of American Folklore*, 621
*Journal of Radical Education and Cultural Studies*, 681
Justification, context of, 203

Kansas School Board, 563
Knowledge building, 19–21, 469–491
    antifoundationalism and, 480–483
    content analysis and, 266–271
    contingency in, 375
    critical rationalism and, 474–475
    critiques of positivism and, 475–480
    evaluation research and, 283–285, 287–288
    feminist empiricism and, 483–484
    feminist methodology in, 469–471
    holistic reflexivity and, 495, 499–503
    interviewing for, 175
    positivism and, 472–474
    postmodern theories and, 485–487
    propositional *versus* practical, 551
    reflexivity and, 148
    relational, 191
    research ethics and, 520
    situated, 127, 208, 537

spectator, 664
standpoint theories of,
    50, 62–63, 484–485
"subjugated," 110
*See also* Interdisciplinary approaches;
    Methodologies; "Women's ways of
    knowing"
Kohlberg's moral development, 517
Ku Klux Klan, 183

*Ladder, The,* 434
Language:
    barriers in, 314
    critical, postmodern, and poststructural
        theories and, 75, 80, 88
    cultural context of, 505
    nonoppressive, 212
    postcolonial, 246
    writing and, 453–454
Latino Critical Race Studies Group (LatCrit),
    University of Miami, 635
*Lavender Woman,* 434
*Lesbian and Gay Elders, Identity, and Social
    Change* (Rosenfeld), 448
Lesbian and Gay Pride movement, 52
*Lesbian Body, The* (Wittig), 438
*Lesbian Nation* (Johnston), 427
Lesbian separatism, 240–241
Liberal feminism, 225–227
*Liberating Methods: Feminism and
    Social Research* (DeVault), 15, 447
Libertarian feminists, 237
Linear-hormonal model, 36
Listening, in interviewing, 149, 182–184
Lived experiences, 147
Logic, epistemology and, 554–558
*Logic and Philosophy* (Kahane), 556
Logic of inquiry, 47–52, 61

Male theory, 95–96
*Manifesto of a Passionate Moderate: Unfashionable
    Essays* (Haack), 694
*Man of Reason, The* (Lloyd), 266
*Man's World, Women's Place* (Janeway), 429
"Man-the-hunter" perspective, 31
Mapping, 191, 353, 372
Marginalized social groups, 46, 109, 111, 200, 301
Market economies, globalization of, 107
Marxist theory, 227, 579–581
Marymount Manhattan College, 614
Master-slave relationship, 19
*Materialist Feminism: A Reader in Class,
    Difference, and Women's Lives* (Hennessy and
    Ingraham), 584
Materialist standpoint epistemology, 584–585

Materiality erasure, 97–99
Matrix of domination, 586
Meaning, verification criterion of, 472–473
Medica Women's Centre, Bosnia, 320
*Medium Is the Message, The*
    (McLuhan and Fiore), 271
Mehila Samakkhya organization, India, 116
*Men's Studies Modified: The Impact of Feminism on
    the Academic Disciplines* (Spender), 5, 127
Mercy College, 614
Metaphors and similes, in writing, 449–451
*Methodological Postulates on Feminist Research*
    (Mies), 664
Methodological provisionalism, 571
Methodologies, 7–10, 681–688, 705–711
    bridging disciplines by, 676
    case study, 398
    dialoguing on, 536–538
    essentialism in, 567–569
    holistic reflexivity, 496–497
    in interdisciplinary approaches, 130–131
    interviewing, 174–176
    knowledge building, 469–471
    multiculturalism and, 685–687
    pedagogy and, 682–685
    seminar in, 705–707
    sociological, 681–682
    survey research, 200, 206–207
    training in policy, 707–710
Michigan Women's Music Festival, 434
Milgram laboratory experiments,
    Yale University, 706
Mitigated relativism, 9–10
Mixed-methods research designs, 279. *See also*
    Narratives and numbers
Modern Language Association (MLA), 128
*Modest_Witness@Second_Millenium. FemaleMan©_
    Meets_OncoMouse™: Feminism and
    Technoscience* (Haraway), 247
Morality. *See* Ethics
Morally engaged evaluation research, 279
*Mother/Daughter Plot, The* (Hirsch), 438
*Mother Earth* (Goldman), 432
"Mothering" discourse, 93, 260, 414–415
*Mother Lode,* 434
Motivation, achievement, 329
*Mules and Men* (Hurston), 622
Multicenter AIDS Cohort Study (MACS), 229
Multiculturalism, 685–687
Multidirectional causality, 570
Multidisciplinary approaches, 125. *See also*
    Interdisciplinary approaches;
    Transdisciplinary approaches
Multilateral Agreement in Investment, 667
Multimethod research, 675

*Music and Feminisms*
(MacArthur and Poynton), 438
Mutuality of interaction, to reveal gender, 37
*My Secret Garden* (Friday), 432
*Myth of Community, The: Gender*
*Issues in Participatory Development*
(Guijt and Shah), 309

Narratives and numbers, 327–344
clarifying quantitative data with ethnography,
334–335
conclusions from, 340–341
diversity of, 337–338
framing qualitative data by quantitative data,
332–334
introduction to, 327–330
parallel studies of, 335–337
quantitative data as, 339–340
survey research for, 203–204
team approach to, 338–339
transforming qualitative data into quantitative
data, 330–332
visual and narrative cultures (VNC) and, 132
National Academy of Engineers (NAE), 230
National Academy of Sciences, 634, 670, 672
National Asian Women's Health
Organization, 677
National Black Women's Health
Project (NBWHP), 672
National Colloquium on Black Women's Health
(NCBWH), 672
National Commission for the Protection of Human
Subjects of Biomedical and Behavioral
Research (Belmont Report), 214–215, 523
National Council for International Health
Conference on Women's Health of 1991, 245
National Council for Research on Women, 676
*National Geographic,* 186
National identity, 13
National Institutes of Health (NIH), 233, 239, 674
National Latina Health Organization, 677
National Organization for Women (NOW), 434
National Research Act of 1974, 523
National Science Foundation, 558, 674
National Women's Health Network, 677
Native American Women's Health Education
Resource Center, 677
Naturalism, feminist, 34–35
categorization and, 178
empiricism and, 39
grounded theory and, 347
rationalism supported by, 41–42
Nebraska Feminist Collective, 187
Neocolonialism, 244
Neo-Darwinism, 563

Network of Central American Women in Solidarity
with Maquila Workers, 656
Network of East-West Women (NEWW) feminist
Web site, 267
Network of Women Students Australia, 399–400
*New Directions for Evaluation* (Seigart and
Brisolara), 278, 290–291
New Hope Project poverty
intervention program, 338–339
*New Scientist,* 263
*Newsweek,* 559
New York State Department of Correctional
Services, 615
New York State Legislature, 617
*New York Times,* 263, 333
No Child Left Behind Act, 303
Nomadism, 87–88
Nonexploitive research, 165
Nongovernmental organizations (NGOs), 654
Nonoppressive language, 212
Nonprobability sampling, 210
*Nonsexist Research Methods* (Eichler), 567
Normal curves, in situational analysis, 355–356
Northeastern University, 685
Norwegian Institute of Technology, 236
Novelty, to reveal gender, 37, 561
Numbers. *See* Narratives and numbers;
Quantitative analysis
*Nursing Wounds: Nurse Practitioners,*
*Doctors, Women Patients, and the*
*Negotiation of Meaning* (Fisher), 448

Obedience, 706
Objectivity, 55–56
challenging, 426
critical, postmodern, and poststructural
theories of, 72
detached relationship and, 147
male-oriented theories and, 224
positivist assumptions of, 475–476, 479–480
redefinition of, 550
survey research, 202
*See also* Empiricism; Knowledge building
*Odyssey* (Homer), 30
*Off Our Backs,* 434
*Of Grammatology* (Spivak), 85
Ohio State University, 21, 131–135, 705
*On Being a White Person of Color: Using*
*Autoethnography to Understand Puerto*
*Rican's Racialization* (Ortiz), 632
*On Liberty* (Mill), 558
*On the Treatment of Sexes in Research* (Eichler and
Lapointe), 4
Ontological heterogeneity, to reveal gender,
37, 561–562, 570

Open-ended questions, in surveys,
212, 215, 331
Operationalization, in survey research, 211
"Opportunity gap," 304
Oppositional consciousness, differential, 579
Oppressed people, in feminist research, 3, 10,
109–112, 673
Organizational deskilling, 454
"Othering" practice, 93, 244, 526
*Our Bodies, Ourselves* (Boston Women's Health
Book Collective), 306, 429
Outsiders/within, researchers as,
162, 312–313, 498

Participatory and action research, 149, 297–326
community-based, 674
designing, 312–317
difference research in, 613
education and, 302–305
health and, 305–308
holistic reflexivity in, 504
local communities and, 308–312
praxis in, 299–302
research ethics in, 522
social injustice revealed by, 617
social movement research and, 392
transformational praxis in, 317–321
values and goals of, 298–299
Participatory evaluation research, 279
Participatory rural appraisal (PRA), 298
Patriarchal theory, 95–96, 156
Peace Accords of 1996, 311
Pedagogy, 689–704
feminism in, 689–691
methodology and, 682–685
multidisciplinary, 695–697
postmodern theory and, 697
sexuality and, 693–695
women's studies and, 691–693
Personal Narratives Group, 185, 299
Perspectivism, 485
Persuasion techniques, 439–440
Philosophy of science, 558–560, 639, 690
Photovoice narratives, 301, 372
Physicians' Health Study Group, 227, 233
Place making, 116–117
Policy research, 707–710
Polyphony, 527
Polyvocality, 148, 507
Populations, vulnerable, 506
Pornography, 264–266
Portraiture research methods, 382–383
Positivism, 7–8, 334
biomedical model and, 670–672
critique of, 475–480, 496

experimental research and, 223
feminism commitment to, 96
knowledge building and, 472–474
objectivity in, 568
qualitative and quantitative studies and, 340
research designs and, 300
research participants and, 444
sociology and, 409
standpoint theory *versus,* 14–15, 59, 580
survey research and, 201
value-neutral researcher and, 12
Postcolonial approaches, 299, 580
experimental research and, 243–246
globalization as, 107–109
inessential women in, 112–115
poststructural theory and, 96–97
projects in, 61
relativism of, 57
theory of, 14
Postmodern theory, 10–12
conceptions of truth in, 483
deconstruction in, 486–487
difference research and, 607
ethnography and, 158
experimental research and, 241–243
explanation of, 78–80
interdisciplinarity in, 99–100
knowledge building in, 485–487
materiality erasure in, 97–99
morality and ethics in, 93–95
patriarchal theory *versus,* 95–96
pedagogy and, 696–697, 697
positivism *versus,* 14
power differentials in, 521, 672
principles of, 71–75
queer theory grounded in, 268
relativism in, 90–93
relevance of, 96–97
standpoint epistemology and, 582–583
standpoint theory in, 57, 59–60, 583
transdisciplinary approaches and, 129
women's studies and, 666
*See also* Critical theory; Grounded theory;
Poststructural theory; Situational analysis
*Postmodern Turn in Anthropology: Cautions from a
Feminist Perspective* (Mascia-Lees, Sharpe,
and Cohen), 623
Postpositivism, 281, 286, 300, 340, 483
Poststructural theory, 11
analytic strategies of, 85–90
autoethnography in, 459–460
concepts of, 82–85
ethnographic writing and, 506
experimental research and, 241–243
explanation of, 80–82

interdisciplinarity and, 99–100
materiality erasure and, 97–99
morality and ethics in, 93–95
patriarchal theory *versus,* 95–96
principles of, 71–75
queer theory grounded in, 268
relativism in, 90–93
relevance of, 96–97
standpoint theory and, 583
truth and domination in, 550
*See also* Critical theory; Postmodern theory
Poverty intervention programs, 338–339
Power, 16–17
critical, postmodern, and poststructural
theories of, 11, 84
differentials in, 521, 525, 607
evaluation research and, 282–283, 287
exclusionary practices of, 470
feminist research and, 426
gender, 134
geographies of, 115–116
holistic reflexivity and, 495, 499–503
interrogating, 318–319
interviewing and, 175
knowledge link to, 50
participatory and action research
and, 312–317
postmodern theory on, 672–673
relational, 191
research relationships and, 161
retrodictive, 35
*Power of Feminist Art: The American Movement
of the 1970s, History and Impact*
(Broude and Garrard), 438
Pragmatism, 347
Praxis in feminist research, 21–22, 143–153
future of, 151–152
process of, 145–150
social justice from, 150–151
synergistic perspective on, 14–17
*See also* Participatory and action research
*Precarious Life* (Butler), 93
Predictive accuracy, of science, 35
Pretesting surveys, 213
*Primate Visions: Gender, Race, and Nature in the
World of Modern Science* (Haraway), 430
Primatology, 224
*Prior and Posterior Analytics* (Aristotle), 554
Prison reform, 92
Privatization, 228
Probability sampling, 210
Probe Ministries, 271
"Processes of recolonization," 97
*Protean Self, The* (Turkle), 269
"Protofeminist," 683

Provisionalism, 570–572, 574
*Prozac on the Couch* (Metzl), 337
*Psychoanalysis and Feminism* (Mitchell), 431
Psychoanalytic feminism, 235–237
Purdue University, 300

Qualitative analysis, 149, 173, 189, 445.
*See also* Narratives and numbers
Quantitative analysis, 149, 392. *See also*
Experimental research; Narratives and
numbers; Survey research
Queer and transgender theories, 241
*Queering the Color Line: Race and the Invention of
Homosexuality in American Cultures*
(Somerville), 132
Queer Sisters (Hong Kong), 268
Questions, research, 207–209, 212–213, 331, 452

Race, class, gender studies (RCG), 554
*Rachel's Daughters* (Kaufman), 542–543, 683
*Racial Castration: Management Masculinity in
Asian America* (Eng), 133–134
Radcliffe College, 18, 685
*Radical Ecology* (Merchant), 438
Radical feminism, 237–240
"Radicalized patriarchy," 156
Random error in research, 206
Random House Publishers, 434
Randomized controlled trials, 484
Random sampling, 210
*Rapunzel's Daughters: What Women's Hair Tell Us
About Women's Lives* (Weitz), 446
Rationalism:
critical, 474–475
emotion *versus,* 8–9
naturalism *versus,* 41–42
reason and, 547–550
standpoint theory challenges to, 59
Weberian concept of, 5
*Reader's Companion to U.S. Women's History*
(Houghton Mifflin), 693
Reading for another, 459–467
Reason, 547–552
*Rebirth of the Goddess: Finding Meaning in
Feminist Spirituality* (Christ), 439
Reciprocal ethnography, 623, 625
Reciprocity, 163, 524
"Recolonization," 97
*Red Shoes, The,* 463
*Reflections on Women in Science* (Keller), 430
Reflexivity, 16–17
decolonizing approaches and, 622
difference research and, 611
ethnography and, 159
evaluation research and, 292

interviewing for, 181
knowledge building and, 148
limits to analysis and, 379
mixed methods research and, 330
participatory and action research
    and, 313–314
power and, 147
reciprocal ethnography and, 623, 626
research dialogue of, 421–422
researcher biography for, 642
research relationships and, 165–166
standpoints and, 539
sustained and critical, 571
*See also* Holistic reflexivity
Refugees, 116, 658
Relational knowledge, 191, 315–316, 356
Relationship, complexity of, 561–562
Relations of ruling, 412, 586
Relativism:
    absolute, 642
    concept of truth in, 550
    mitigated, 9–10
    politics and, 92–93
    social action and, 90–92
    standpoint theory and, 56–59
Reliability of research results, 211
Replication, 496
Representation, 425–442
    alternative method of inquiry and, 433–439
    content analysis to show, 260–266
    ethics in, 525–527
    feminist critique and, 428–433
    intersectionality and, 633
    persuasion techniques and, 439–440
    questioning authority for, 426–428
    research relationships and, 161, 163
*Reproduction of Mothering, The*
    (Chodorow), 432, 438
*Researching Women's Lives from a Feminist
    Perspective* (Maynard and Purvis), 15
Research process, 22–23. *See also* Feminist
    research; specific types of research
Research questions, 207–209, 212–213, 331, 452
Responsive evaluation research, 277
*Rethinking the Family: Some Feminist Questions*
    (Thorne and Yalom), 438
Retrodictive power, 35
*Revolution in Poetic Language* (Kristeva), 437
*Reweaving the World: Emergence of Ecofeminism*
    (Diamond and Orestein), 438
Rhetorical devices, in writing, 452–453
Rhizoanalysis, 87–88
*Riddle of Gender: Science, Activism, and
    Transgender Rights* (Rudacille), 692

*Room of One's Own, A* (Woolf),
    426–427, 439
*Rules of Sociological Method, The* (Durkheim), 7
Ruling relations, 412, 586
Rural community development, 308–309

Sampling:
    achievement motivation study and, 329
    grounded theory and, 346
    reflexivity, 421–422, 496, 508–510
    survey research, 201, 210
SARTHI organization, India, 307
Satipatthana process in participatory and
    action research, 307
Science, 7, 567–577
    antipositivist philosophy of, 639
    antireductionist and antimechanistic
        approaches to, 560–561
    feminist question in social, 569–571
    methodological essentialism in, 567–569
    philosophy of, 558–560, 690
    practice of, 571–573
    predictive accuracy of, 35
    "science of subjectivity" and, 181
    sexism in, 30–31
    standpoint theory for, 61–62, 580
    "stronger," 497–498
    value-neutral, 8, 12, 563
    verb-sense of, 34–35
    *See also* Empiricism; Ethnography;
        Experimental research
*Science, Truth, and Democracy* (Kitcher), 564
*Science and Gender: A Critique of Biology and Its
    Theories* (Bleier), 430
*Science as Social Knowledge: Values and
    Objectivity in Scientific Inquiry*
    (Longino), 562
*Science Question in Feminism, The* (Harding),
    47, 430, 567
*Scientific Foundations of Qualitative Research*
    (Ragin, Nagel, and White), 674
*Second Sex, The* (Beauvoir), 427, 431–432, 506
*Second Shift: Working Parents and the Revolution at
    Home, The* (Hochschild), 447
*Seventeen* magazine, 261
Sexist error, 190
"Sexual contract," 127
Sexual harassment, 130, 335
Sexualities and Latina/Black Women's Studies, 133
Sexuality/queer studies, 631–632
*Sexual Politics* (Millet), 428
*Signs: Journal of Women in Culture and Society,*
    299, 694, 705–706
Similes and metaphors, in writing, 449–451

*Sisterhood is Powerful* (Morgan), 434
*Situated Actions and Vocabularies of
    Motive* (Mills), 354
Situated knowledge, 127, 208
*Situated Knowledge* (Haraway), 354, 641
*Situated Lives: Gender and Culture in Everyday Life*
    (Lamphere, Ragone, and Zavella), 15
Situational analysis, 150, 353–362
    conclusions about, 361–362
    description of, 353
    difference research on, 609
    feminist characteristics of, 354–357
    feminist development of, 357–361
    postmodern theory and, 485
    *See also* Grounded theory
*Six of One* (Brown), 438
Sleeping metaphors, 450
Smith College, 240
Snowball sampling, 210
Social action, 90–92. *See also* Survey research
Social agency, 37–39
Social-cognitive model, 36
*Social Construction of Reality, The* (Berger and
    Luckmann), 348
Social constructivism, 35
*Social Empiricism* (Solomon), 37–38
Social groups, marginalized, 46, 200, 301, 673
Socialist feminism, 227–229, 521
Social justice, 49, 286
Social movement research, 391–407
    activist standpoint in, 401–404
    description of, 391–392
    epistemologies of, 394–397
    feminist, 393–394
    young feminist activism and,
        397–401
Social policy. *See* Healthcare research
Social worlds theory, 358–360
Society for Women in Philosophy, 561
Sociology:
    alternative, 185
    everyday world, 579, 582
    methodologies in, 681–682
    science, 35
    symbolic interactionist, 347–348
    without women, 410–411
    women's standpoint of, 411, 413
*Sociology of Feeling and Emotion: Selected
    Possibilities* (Hochschild), 5
"Somatophobia," 88, 97
*Speaking About Rape is Everybody's
    Business* (Bell and Nelson), 623
"Speaking bitterness," 177
Specificity, in research, 375, 377–379

"Spectator knowledge," 664
*Spectral Mother: Freud, Feminism, and
    Psychoanalysis* (Sprengnether), 438
*Speculum of the Other Woman* (Irigaray), 437
*Sperm Tales: Social, Cultural and
    Scientific Representations of
    Human Semen* (Moore), 352
"Spin doctors," 135
Stakeholder evaluation research, 277
Standpoint epistemology, 560–561, 579–589
    conceptualizations of, 581–582
    conclusions about, 585–586
    Marxist materialism in, 579–581
    materialist, 584–585
    pedagogy and, 696
    postmodern critiques of, 582–583
Standpoint theory, 10, 45–69
    activist, 392, 394, 401–404
    Afrocentric, 109–112, 162
    "colonial" research processes *versus,* 52–56
    conceptions of truth in, 483
    decolonizing approaches in, 625–626
    difference issues in, 16, 62–63
    epistemology in, 560–561
    essentialism of, 19, 60
    Eurocentric, 60
    global research and, 665
    knowledge building in, 62–63, 484–485
    logic of inquiry in, 47–52
    mainstream theorizing and, 550
    modern *versus* postmodern, 59–60
    natural sciences and, 61–62
    new branches of, 420
    origins of, 45–47
    positivism *versus,* 14–15
    postcolonial projects and, 61
    reflexivity in, 539
    relational, 12
    relativism of, 56–59
    situated knowledge in, 537
    sociology and, 411, 413
    survey research and, 202
    "women's ways of knowing" in, 60–61
Statistics, 201, 216–217. *See also*
    Narratives and numbers
*Still Lifting, Still Climbing: African American
    Women's Contemporary Activism,*
    (Springer), 188
Storytelling, as research method, 372
"Stronger science," 497–498
Strong Program of sociology of science, 35
*Structure of Scientific Revolutions, The* (Kuhn),
    17, 33, 57
Subjectification, 82

Subjectivity, science of, 181
"Subjugated knowledge," 110, 503
Suffragettes, 82
Survey research, 189–190, 199–222
    construction of, 210–213
    data analysis and interpretation in, 215–217
    data collection in, 213–215
    dissemination of results of, 217–219
    feminist and mainstream similarities in, 202–209
    feminist criticism of, 202–205, 205–206
    feminist methodologies in, 206–207
    history of, 201–202
    key concepts of, 200–201
    research questions and hypotheses in, 207–209
    sampling for, 210
    types of, 209–210
Symbolic interactionist sociology, 347–348
Systematic error in research, 205–206
*System of Logic* (Mill), 558

*Talking and Listening from Women's Standpoint*
    (DeVault), 183
Team diversity, 230, 338–339
*Teen* magazine, 261
Telephone surveys, 209
Teleworking, 243
*Telling the Truth After Postmodernism*
    (D. E. Smith), 179
*Telling Women's Lives* (Long), 185
Terrorism, 658
Testing, 35–36
Textual analysis research designs, 400–401
*Theories of Women's Studies*
    (Bowles and Klein), 664
"Thick descriptions" in ethnography,
    483–484, 504
*Thinking Gender series* (Routledge), 556
*This Bridge Called My Back* (Moraga and
    Anzaldúa), 159, 584, 622
*This Discussion is Going Too Far! Male Resistance
    to Female Participation on the Internet*
    (Herring et al.), 266
*This Sex Which Is Not One* (Irigaray), 437
*Three Guineas* (Woolf), 426–427
Time, Love, Cash, Care, and Children (TLC3)
    Study, 339
*Time Bind: When Work Becomes Home and Home
    Becomes Work, The* (Hochschild), 447
Titles, writing, 447–449
*Together Place Women* (Reid), 177
*Tomorrow's Tomorrow* (Ladner), 177
*Too Late the Phalarope* (Paton), 421,
    460, 462, 464
Topography, critical, 116–117

*To Prove Them Wrong Syndrome: Voices from
    Unheard African American Males in
    Engineering Disciplines* (D. E. Smith), 353
*Tracing the Contours* (Haraway), 643
*Traffic in Women and Other Essays,
    The* (Goldman), 432
*Training for Transformation*
    (Hope and Timmel), 309
Transdisciplinary approaches, 126
    Central European University example of,
        135–137
    future of, 137–138
    Ohio State University example of, 131–135
Transformational praxis, 317–321
Transformative criticism, 422
Transformative evaluation research, 285
Transgender theories, 241
Transitional epistemology, 459
*Translated Woman* (Behar), 180
Transnational feminist perspectives, 20,
    107–109, 115–119
Transparency, 482
Triangulation research designs, 205, 331,
    400–401, 572
Truth, theories of, 480, 547–552
*Turning Game, The* (Turing), 241
Tuskegee syphilis study, 214, 231

Underdeterminism, 32–34
*Understanding Women's Recovery from Illness and
    Trauma* (Kearney), 351
*Under Western Eyes* (Mohanty), 113
*Undoing Gender* (Butler), 93
*Unequal Treatment: Confronting
    Racial and Ethnic Disparities in
    Health Care* (Smedley et al.), 672
*Unexpected Community, The* (Hochschild), 447
United Nations, 667
United Nation's Children's Fund (UNICEF), 310
United Nations Development Fund for Women
    (UNIFEM), 267
United Nations World Conference Against Racism
    of 2001 (UNWCAR), 640
United States Agency for International Development
    (USAID), 644–645
Universalization, 111
University of California at Berkeley, 410
University of California at San Francisco, 349
University of California at Santa Barbara, 643
University of Chicago, 201
University of Copenhagen, 321
University of Maine, 261
University of Maryland, 635–636
University of Miami, 635

University of Michigan, 218

University of Nijmegen, the Netherlands, 664

University of Wisconsin, 694

Unninet Sisters' Village feminist Web site, 268

*Unruly Practices: Power, Discourse, and Gender in Contemporary Social Theory* (Fraser), 430–431

U.S. Congress, 225, 358, 707

U.S. Department of Defense, 226

U.S. Senate Black Legislative Staff Caucus, 672

U.S. Supreme Court, 218

Utilization evaluation research, 277


Validity of research results, 211

Value-neutral research:
    disidentification from, 471
    feminist social science *versus,* 664
    impossibility of, 207, 683
    positivism concept of, 8, 12, 568
    scientific inquiry based on, 496
    *See also* Empiricism; Objectivity

Vanangana organization, India, 116

*Velvet Glove: Paternalism and Conflict in Gender, Class, and Race Relations, The* (Jackman), 448

Verification criterion of meaning, 472–473

Vienna Circle, 31, 472

Violent Crime Control and Law Enforcement Act, 614

*Visible Human Project* (Reiche), 247

Visual and narrative cultures (VNC), 132

VNX Matrix, Australia, 246

Voice:
    community survival and, 311
    in holistic reflexivity, 503–504
    multiplicity of, 314–315
    research relationships and, 161, 163
    rhetorical devices as, 453

*Voice from the South by a Black Woman from the South, A* (Cooper), 506

*Voice of the Women's Liberation Movement,* 434

*Voices and Images: Mayan Ixil Women of Chajal* (Women of Photovoice/ ADMI and Lykes), 311

*Volatile Bodies* (Grosz), 87

Voting patterns, 127

Vulnerable populations, 506


War on terrorism, 658

*Washington Consensus,* 665

*Way We See It, The,* 434

Weberian concept of rationality, 5

Web surveys, 209. *See also* Internet

Welfare state, 665

Western New Mexico University, 305

*What Can She Know? Feminist Theory and the Construction of Knowledge* (Code), 9

*When Black is Not Enough* (Beoku-Betts), 179

*When Gender is Not Enough* (Riessman), 179

*When the Girls Are Men: Negotiating Gender and Sexual Dynamics in a Study of Drag Queens* (Taylor and Rupp), 448

*White Women, Race Matters* (Frankenberg), 573

*Who Can Speak? Authority and Critical Identity* (Roof and Wiegman), 437

*Who's Afraid of Women's Studies? Feminisms in Everyday Life* (Rogers and Garrett), 692

*Woman in the Body, The* (Martin), 6

*Womanist and Feminist Aesthetics* (Allen), 438

Womanist feminism, 229–231

*Womankind,* 434

"Woman-the-gatherer" perspective, 31

Women, inessential, 112–115

*Women, Politics, and Policy* (Hartman and Hardy-Fanta), 676

*Women and Folklore: Images and Genres* (Farrer), 621–622

*Women in Black* (Scott), 384

*Women in Political Theory: From Ancient Misogyny to Contemporary Feminism* (Coole), 430

*Women in Sexist Society* (Gornick and Moran), 429

*Women in Western Political Thought* (Okin), 430

*Women Making Art: Women in the Visual, Literary, and Performing Arts Since 1960* (Johnson and Oliver), 438

*Women's Activism and Globalization* (Naples and Desai), 188

*Women's Estate* (Mitchell), 429

Women's Health Initiative, NIH, 233, 238

Women's magazines, 260–263

*Women's Share in Social Culture* (Spencer), 429

Women's studies (WOST):
    double agenda in, 553–554
    pedagogy of, 691–693
    postmodern theory in, 666
    women's scholarship *versus,* 542–545

"Women's ways of knowing," 60–61, 159. *See also* Knowledge building

*Women's Words: The Feminist Practice of Oral History* (Gluck and Patai), 15

*Women Without Class: Girls, Race, and Identity* (Bettle), 446

*Women Writing Culture* (Behar and Gordon), 159, 165, 623

*Words of Power* (Nye), 556
*Working the Ruins: Feminist Poststructural Theory and Methods in Education* (St. Pierre and Pillow), 15
World Bank, 667
World Economic Forums, 667
"World systems theory" (Marx), 61
World Trade Organization, 667
Writing, 443–458
    advice, 454–455
    autobiographic, 381–382
    deconstructive, 88–90
    entering the scene, 445–447
    holistic reflexivity, 504–510
    language in, 453–454
    metaphors and similes, 449–451

    rhetorical devices, 452–453
    titles, 447–449
*Writing Culture: The Poetics and Politics of Ethnography* (Clifford and Marcus), 158–159, 506, 622–623

Xerox PARC, 239

Yale University, 706
*Yearning: Race, Gender, and Cultural Politics* (hooks), 15
*Yellow Wallpaper, The* (Gilman), 380
Young Women Who Are Parents Network (YWWAPN), Sydney, Australia, 397, 400, 403
Youth Research Community, City University of New York (CUNY), 304

# ABOUT THE EDITOR

**Sharlene Nagy Hesse-Biber** is Professor of Sociology at Boston College and Director of the Women's Studies Program. She is founder and director of the National Association for Women in Catholic Higher Education. She is coeditor of several books, including *Feminist Perspectives on Social Research* (2004); *Approaches to Qualitative Research* (2004); *Women in Catholic Higher Education: Border Work, Living Experiences and Social Justice* (2003); and *Feminist Approaches to Theory and Methodology* (1999). She is coauthor of *The Practice of Qualitative Research* (Sage, 2006), *Emergent Methods in Social Research* (Sage, 2006), *Working Women in America: Split Dreams* (2005), and the forthcoming *Feminist Research Practice: A Primer* (Sage). She is the author of *Am I Thin Enough Yet?* (1996) and an upcoming revised edition of that book titled *The Cult of Thinness* (2006). She has written numerous articles in the fields of body image, qualitative methods, and computer approaches to qualitative data analysis. She is codeveloper of HyperRESEARCH (for MAC/WINDOWS) (www.researchware.com), a computer software program for qualitative data analysis, and HyperTranscribe (MAC/WINDOWS), a stand-alone transcription software tool for transcribing digitized audio and video files.

# ABOUT THE CONTRIBUTORS

**Kum-Kum Bhavnani** is Professor of Sociology at the University of California at Santa Barbara and chairs the program in Women's Culture and Development in Global and International Studies. She has written books, articles, and essays on several topics, including feminist methodologies, women in prison, and feminist theory. She has also been studying the relationships between interconnected configurations of "race"/ethnicity, gender, sexuality, and class. She now conducts research on women in the Third World where she, along with coauthors Peter Chua, John Foran, Priya Kurian, and Debashish Munshi, has been developing a new approach to development studies—the women, culture development paradigm. From that theoretical frame, she has recently completed a 2006 documentary, *The Shape of Water* (http://www.theshapeofwatermovie.com), which centers women making change in Brazil, India, Jerusalem, and Senegal.

**Katherine Borland** is Associate Professor of Comparative Studies in the Humanities at Ohio State University at Newark, where she teaches Folklore, World Literature, and Post-development Theory. She has published articles in the *Radical History Review*, the *Journal of American Folklore*, and several edited collections. She has also published two ethnographically grounded, book-length studies: *Unmasking Class, Gender and Sexuality in Nicaraguan Festival* (2006) and *Creating Community: Hispanic Migration to Southern Delaware* (2001). She is currently embarking on an ethnography of the salsa scene in North Jersey. Outside the academy, she has worked as a public folklorist and as director of a nonprofit educational organization serving inner-city youth.

**Sharon Brisolara** is a program evaluator, and she founded and owns Evaluation Solutions, an evaluation organization operating in Northern California. Her areas of expertise include feminist evaluation, participatory evaluation, qualitative methodology, and mixed-method studies. She is an active member of the American Evaluation Association and of the Feminist Evaluation Topical Interest Group (TIG), and she is currently serving as the group's program chair. She coedited *Feminist Evaluation: Explorations and Experiences: New Directions for Evaluation* (2002) with Dr. Denise Seigart and has written and presented in various forums on feminist evaluation and feminist theory. She received her doctorate from Cornell University in program evaluation and planning with concentrations in women's studies and rural sociology.

**Abigail Brooks** is a PhD candidate in sociology at Boston College. Her areas of interest include feminist theory, sociology of gender, critical gerontology and feminist age studies, sociology of the body, science and technology studies, and social theory. Her dissertation investigates women's lived experiences and interpretations of growing older against the contextual backdrop of growing prevalence, acceptance, and approval of cosmetic surgery. She recently published an article titled "'Under the Knife and Proud of It': An Analysis of the Normalization of Cosmetic Surgery" in the *Journal of Critical Sociology*.

**Kathy Charmaz** is Professor of Sociology and Coordinator of the Faculty Writing Program at Sonoma State University, a program to assist faculty in writing for publication. She has written or coedited six books, including her 2006 volume, *Constructing Grounded Theory: A Practical Guide Through Qualitative Analysis* (Sage, London) and *Good Days, Bad Days:*

*The Self in Chronic Illness and Time*, which won awards from the Pacific Sociological Association and the Society for the Study of Symbolic Interaction. She has also written numerous papers on grounded theory methods as well as on medical sociology and social psychology. She serves as vice president of Alpha Kappa Delta, the international honorary society for sociology, and she has served as president of the Pacific Sociological Association, vice president of the Society for the Study of Symbolic Interaction, editor of *Symbolic Interaction*, and chair of the Medical Sociology Section of the American Sociological Association.

**Adele E. Clarke** is Professor of Sociology and Adjunct Professor of History of Health Sciences at the University of California, San Francisco. Her work centers on studies of science, technology, and medicine (with special emphasis on medical technologies and women's health) and qualitative research methods. Her latest book is *Situational Analysis: Grounded Theory After the Postmodern Turn* (Sage, 2005). She is best known for her study of the reproductive sciences in biology, medicine, and agriculture, *Disciplining Reproduction: American Life Scientists and the "Problem of Sex"* (1998). She coedited *Revisioning Women, Health and Healing: Cultural, Feminist and Technoscience Perspectives* (1999) with Virginia Oleson and a forthcoming book, *Biomedicalization: Technoscience and the Transformation of Health and Illness in the U.S.*, with Janet Shim, Laura Mamo, Jennifer Fosket, and Jennifer Fishman (2006).

**Elizabeth R. Cole** is Associate Professor of Women's Studies and Afro-American and African Studies at the University of Michigan. She coauthored *Speaking of Abortion: Television and Authority in the Lives of Women* with Andrea Press (1999). She and Joan Ostrove coedited an issue of the *Journal of Social Issues* (Vol. 59, No. 4, 2003) that focused on the psychological meanings of social class in educational contexts. She earned her BA from Boston University and received her doctorate in psychology from the University of Michigan. Her research focuses on how individuals' sense of themselves as connected to social groups (such as race, gender, or social class) is related to how they understand their social environments, issues of public concern (such as abortion or affirmative action), and their choices about political participation.

**Judith A. Cook** is a professor of psychiatry at the University of Illinois at Chicago. She directs the Center on Mental Health Services Research and Policy, and her recent research explores the lives of women with psychiatric disabilities and those living with HIV/AIDS. She is also focusing much of her research on the intersection of gender, class, and race in health and human services public policy.

**Erzulie Coquillon** holds a master's degree in counseling psychology from Boston College and a BA in history from Harvard College.

**Bronwyn Davies** is Professor and chair of the Narrative, Discourse and Pedagogy Research Unit at the University of Western Sydney, Australia. Her publications include *Poststructural Theory and Classroom Practice* (1994), *(In)scribing Body Landscape Relations* (2000), *A Body of Writing* (2000), and *Gender in Japanese Preschools: Frogs and Snails and Feminist Tales in Japan* (2004), and she has also published second editions of *Frogs and Snails and Feminist Tales* (2003) and *Shards of Glass* (2003). She coauthored the chapter on "Feminism/Poststructuralism" in *Research Methods in the Social Sciences* (2005) with Susanne Gannon, and they also coedited the book *Doing Collective Biography* (2006).

**Marjorie L. DeVault** is Professor of Sociology and a member of the Women's Studies Program at Syracuse University. Her research has explored women's "invisible work" in families and in the historically female field of dietetics and nutrition education. Trained in the Chicago-School fieldwork tradition and deeply influenced by the feminism of the 1970s, she has written extensively on qualitative and feminist methodologies. She has been learning about institutional ethnography (IE) from Dorothy Smith and others in the "IE network" since the 1980s, and she currently works with graduate students on IE projects. She also maintains an IE Web site at http://faculty.maxwell.syr.edu/mdevault. She is the author of *Feeding the Family: The Social Organization of Caring as Gendered Work* (1991) and *Liberating Method: Feminism and Social Research* (1999).

**Bonnie Thornton Dill** is Professor and Chair of the Women's Studies Department and Program and Director of the Consortium on Race, Gender, and Ethnicity at the University of Maryland. Her research focuses on intersections of race, class, and gender with an emphasis on African American women and families and has been reprinted in numerous collections and edited volumes. Before coming to Maryland in 1991, she was professor of sociology at the University of Memphis, where she founded and directed the Center for Research on Women. Under her leadership, this organization gained national prominence for outstanding work on the intersections of race, class, and gender. Her more recent publications include "Disparities in Latina Health: An Intersectional Analysis" (with R. E. Zambrana) in A. Schulz and L. Mullings, *Gender, Race, Class & Health* (2006), "Between a Rock and a Hard Place: Motherhood, Choice and Welfare in the Rural South" (with T. Johnson), in Sharon Harley et al. (Eds.), *Sister Circle: Black Women and Work* (2002), and "Poverty in the Rural U.S.: Implications for Children, Families and Communities," in Judith Blau (Ed.), *Blackwell Companion to Sociology* (2001). Her work has also been published in journals, including *Signs, Feminist Studies, The Journal of Family History*, and *The Journal of Comparative Family Studies*, and these articles are widely reprinted. She has received several prestigious awards, including the Distinguished Contributions to Teaching Award and the Jessie Bernard Award for research in gender studies. These were both given by the American Sociological Association.

**Michelle Fine**, Distinguished Professor of Social Psychology, Women's Studies and Urban Education at the Graduate Center, City University of New York (CUNY), has taught at CUNY since 1990. Her recent publications include *Working Method: Social Research and Social Injustice* (2004, with L. Weis), *Off White: Essays on Race, Privilege and Contestation* (2004, with L. Weis, L. Powell Pruitt, & A. Burns), *Brown v. Board of Education* (2004), and *Changing Minds: The Impact of College in Prison* (2001, with Kathy Boudin, Iris Bowen, Judith Clark, Donna Hylton, Migdalia Martinez, "Missy," Rosemarie Roberts, Pamela Smart, Maria Torre, & Debora Upegui).

**Mary Margaret Fonow** is Professor and Director of the Women and Gender Studies Program at Arizona State University. Her research areas include global unions, feminist methodology, and social movements. She is the author of *Union Women: Forging Feminism in the United Steelworkers of America* (2003), and she is currently writing a book about feminists' roles within global union networks as advocates for women's transnational labor rights.

**Susanne Gannon** lectures in the School of Education at the University of Western Sydney, Australia. She is a founding member of the Narrative, Discourse and Pedagogy Research Unit. Her doctoral research examined writing practices through feminist poststructural theory. She has published studies on research methodology and feminist approaches to embodiment and writing in a range of journals, including *Sex Education, Qualitative Inquiry, Qualitative Studies in Education*, and *Auto/Biography*. She coauthored the chapter on "Feminism/Poststructuralism" in *Research Methods in the Social Sciences* (2005) with Bronwyn Davies, and they also coedited the book *Doing Collective Biography* (2006).

**Glenda Gross** is a doctoral student in sociology at Syracuse University. Her research interests include feminist theory; qualitative methods and feminist methodologies; race, class, gender, and work; studies in the social organization of knowledge; institutional ethnography; and antiracist feminist pedagogies. Her work explores the social organization of antiracist feminist educators' work in U.S. colleges and universities. She earned her MA in sociology, with a certificate of advanced studies (CAS) in women's studies.

**Sandra Harding** teaches philosophy of social science and postcolonial and feminist studies at the University of California at Los Angeles. She has written or edited 14 books and special issues of journals that focus on feminist and postcolonial epistemology, methodology, and philosophy of science. *The Feminist Standpoint Theory Reader: Intellectual and Political Controversies* was published in 2004, and *Science and Social Inequality: Feminist and Postcolonial Issues* appeared in April 2006. She coedited *Signs: Journal of Women in Culture and Society* from 2000 to 2005, and she is currently working on *Women, Science, and Modernity*.

**Mary Hawkesworth** is Professor of Women's and Gender Studies at Rutgers University. Her teaching and research interests include feminist theory, women and politics, contemporary political philosophy, philosophy of science, and social policy. Her major works include *Globalization and Feminist Activism* (2006); *Feminist Inquiry: From Political Conviction to Methodological Innovation* (2006); *Beyond Oppression: Feminist Theory and Political Strategy* (1990); *Theoretical Issues in Policy Analysis* (1988); and *The Encyclopedia of Government and Politics* (1992; 2nd revised edition, 2003). She is currently the editor of *Signs: Journal of Women in Culture and Society*.

**Catherine Hundleby** is Assistant Professor in Philosophy and cross-appointed with Women's Studies at the University of Windsor, Canada. She focuses on feminist naturalism and feminist standpoint theory, with special attention to the relationships between cognitive and sociopolitical values. Her papers on these topics have appeared in *Hypatia, Social Epistemology,* and *Women & Politics*. She received her doctorate in philosophy from the University of Western Ontario, and her research focuses on feminist epistemology from an analytical perspective.

**Toby Epstein Jayaratne** is currently a research psychologist at the University of Michigan and directs the Beliefs and Understanding of Genetics Project, a study exploring Americans' perceptions about possible genetic influences on perceived gender, class, and race differences and on sexual orientation. Her academic interests focus on the use of genetic explanations to justify and support various social and political ideologies. She has written and presented several papers on the topic of feminist methodology. She received her PhD in developmental psychology from the University of Michigan.

**Debra Renee Kaufman** is the former founder and Director of Women's Studies, a Matthews Distinguished University Professor, and Professor of Sociology at Northeastern University. Among her award nominated and selected books are *Achievement and Women* (coauthored with Barbara Richardson, honorable mention,

C. W. Mills Award), *Rachel's Daughters: Newly Orthodox Jewish Women* (nominated for three awards), and an invited guest-edited edition of *Contemporary Jewry* titled *Women and the Holocaust*. Her commitment to feminist scholarship is evident in her published articles and chapters on post-Holocaust Jewish identity politics and her forthcoming books *From the Protocols of Zion to Holocaust Denial: Challenging the Media, the Law and the Academy* (coedited with G. Herman, J. Ross, and D. Phillips) and *Post Holocaust Identity and an Ever-Dying People: Contemporary Narratives*. She is currently researching intergenerational ties among adult Jewish daughters and their mothers.

**Hyun Sook Kim** is Chair and Professor of Sociology at Wheaton College in Massachusetts. She teaches a range of courses in sociology, women's studies, and Asian/American studies. Her research and publications have focused on postcolonial and transnational feminist studies of nation/state violence, gender, ethnic conflicts, nationalism, and history writing. She recently coedited a special issue (April 2005) of *Gender & Society* that calls for retheorization of the linkages between "Gender-Sexuality-State-Nation" and the development of transnational feminist sociology.

**Sally L. Kitch** is a Professor in and former Chair of the Department of Women's Studies at Ohio State University. Her other articles and book chapters on interdisciplinary feminist scholarship include "PhD Programs and the Research Mission of Women's Studies: The Case for Interdisciplinarity" (2003) and "Disciplined by Disciplines? The Need for an Interdisciplinary Research Mission in Women's Studies" (1998, coauthor Judith Allen). Both of these articles appeared in *Feminist Studies*. Her research focuses on the mechanisms by which women in various historical and cultural contexts have exerted pressure on gendered expectations and developed their own strategies of resistance. She has published numerous articles and three books of transdiciplinary scholarship analyzing gender, feminism, and utopianism: *Chaste Liberation: Celibacy and Female Cultural Status*; *This Strange Society of Women: Reading the Lives and Letters of the Woman's Commonwealth*; and *Higher Ground: From Utopianism to Realism in American Feminist Thought and Theory*. Her current book project analyzes the gendered foundations of racial ideology in the United States as well as women's strategies for resisting them. In 2006–2007, Kitch will become founding Director of the Institute for Humanities and Research and College Professor of Women's and Gender Studies at Arizona State University.

**Noretta Koertge** is Professor Emeritus in History & Philosophy of Science at Indiana University and has written extensively on the relationship between scientific research and social values. Her coauthored and edited books include *Professing Feminism* (1994, 2003), *A House Built on Sand* (1998), *Scrutinizing Feminist Epistemology* (2003), and *Scientific Values and Civic Virtues* (2005). After working in chemistry, she studied philosophy of science in London during the time when Popper, Lakatos, and Feyerabend were very influential. Her earlier publications address problems in scientific methodology and social science with an emphasis on the conceptual issues that arise in the study of homosexuality. Although she has taught in Turkey, England, and Canada, she has spent most of her academic life at Indiana University. After receiving tenure, she published two novels that deal with the lesbian experience in pre- and post-Stonewall America: *Who Was That Masked Woman?* (1981) and *Valley of the Amazons* (1984). She is the current editor of *The New Dictionary of Scientific Biography*.

**Julie Konik** is now a Scholar in Residence at Antioch College, where she is continuing her research on social identity and well-being, with a special focus on sexual minorities. Her recent research examines the role of individual differences in the development of sexual identity and the lived experiences of sexual minorities in a variety of contexts. She completed a PhD in psychology and women's studies from the University of Michigan, where her dissertation focused on the negative effects of sexual harassment and heterosexist harassment in the workplace.

**Rachel Kulick** is currently a doctoral candidate in sociology at Brandeis University. Her areas of interest include feminist theory and methodology, visual sociology, media democracy, and globalization. Her current research examines the ways in which feminist artists aesthetically confront injustices and asymmetries of power across national, gendered, and racial borders. She holds a master's degree in education from Harvard Graduate School of Education.

**Helen E. Longino** is Professor of Philosophy at Stanford University. Her teaching and research interests are in philosophy of science, social epistemology, and feminist philosophy. She is the author of *Science as Social Knowledge* (1990), *The Fate of Knowledge* (2001), and many articles in the philosophy of science, feminist philosophy, and epistemology. Her many coedited volumes include *Feminism and Science* (with Evelyn Fox Keller, 1996) and *Osiris 12: Women, Gender and Science* (with Sally Gregory Kohlstedt, 1997), and the forthcoming *Scientific Pluralism* (Vol. 19) of the Minnesota Studies in Philosophy of Science (with Stephen Kellert & C. Kenneth Waters, 2006). She is currently completing a book-length comparative analysis of four approaches in the sciences of human behavior, focusing on research on aggression and research on sexual orientation. This analysis includes both an examination of the logical structures and interrelations of these approaches and study of their social and cultural reception and uptake.

**M. Brinton Lykes** is Professor of Community-Cultural Psychology at the Lynch School of Education and Associate Director of the Center for Human Rights and International Justice at Boston College. She is an activist scholar whose research explores the interstices of indigenous cultural beliefs and practices and those of Western psychology, toward collaborating in the design and development of community-based programs that respond to the effects of war in contexts of transition and transformation and in the development of training programs and postgraduate diplomas for psychosocial trauma workers. She has published extensively about this work in journals and edited volumes and is also a community activist, cofounder, and participant in many local, national, and international NGOs. These organizations include the Boston Women's Fund, Women's Rights International, and the Ignacio Martín-Baró Fund for Mental Health and Human Rights.

**Sarah Maddison** is Lecturer in the School of Politics and International Relations at the University of New South Wales. She is currently working on the focused audits for women and sexual minorities for the Democratic Audit of Australia (http://democratic.audit.anu.edu.au) and is engaged in ongoing research on Australian Indigenous activism. She has been active in the Australian Women's Movement since 1995, and she has served as a national media spokesperson for the Women's Electoral Lobby since 1999. She has published many works in the areas of young women and feminist activism, social movements, nongovernment organizations, and democracy. Her first book, *Activist Wisdom: Practical Knowledge and Creative Tension in Social Movements* (2006, with Sean Scalmer), addresses important questions concerning the ways that activists manage tension and conflict in social movements. Her forthcoming book, *Silencing Dissent: How the Howard Government Is Eroding Democracy in Australia* (coedited with Clive Hamilton) is due in early 2007.

**Cris Mayo** is Associate Professor in the Department of Educational Policy Studies and the Gender and Women's Studies Program at the University of Illinois at Urbana-Champaign. Her work includes *Disputing the Subject of Sex: Sexuality and Public School Controversies* (2004) as well as articles in the areas of philosophy of education, sexuality studies, gender studies, and multicultural theory.

**Amy E. McLaughlin** is Associate Director of the Consortium on Race, Gender and Ethnicity (CRGE) and works to further the organization's agenda of theoretical, methodological, and pedagogical insights into intersectionality. Her research agenda uses an intersectional lens to examine the symbolic and physical role that violence plays in the lives of women. She also pursues an interest in processes of institutional change and is currently working on a life history analysis of faculty members who engage in advocacy for social justice on university campuses.

**Jennifer Bickham Mendez** is Associate Professor of Sociology at the College of William and Mary. She wrote *From the Revolution to the Maquiladoras: Gender, Labor and Globalization in Nicaragua* (2005), which presents an ethnographic case study of a Nicaraguan working women's organization to demonstrate how globalization affects grassroots advocacy for social justice, particularly as it relates to the situation of women maquila workers. She has published articles in *Social Problems, Organization, Mobilization, Identities*, and other journals. Her current work focuses on Latino/a migration to Williamsburg, Virginia, and explores migrants' experiences of exclusion and incorporation in this new immigration receiving site.

**Maria Mies** is former Professor of Sociology of the Faculty of Applied Social Sciences at the University of Applied Social Sciences, Cologne. She worked for 5 years as a lecturer of German at the Goethe Institute in Pune, India. On her return, she wrote her PhD dissertation on "Indian Women and Patriarchy" (1972). Her study of Indian patriarchy helped her discover German patriarchy, and this encouraged her to become active in the international women's movement and other various social movements. She always combined theoretical work with social activism. In 1979, she initiated the program "Women and Development" at the Institute of Social Studies in The Hague, the Netherlands. It is the first of its kind in the world. She is the author of several works, including *Women: The Last Colony, Patriarchy and Accumulation on a World Scale, Ecofeminism* (with V. Shiva), and *The Subsistence Perspective*.

**Kathi Miner-Rubino** is currently Assistant Professor of Psychology at Western Kentucky University. She teaches courses in social psychology, psychology of women, and research methods. She has published several papers in the areas of gender, social class, and psychological well-being. Her most recent publications focus on vicarious exposure to the mistreatment (i.e., incivility and harassment) of women in work settings. She received her PhD in psychology and women's studies from the University of Michigan.

**Pamela Moss** is Professor in the Studies in Policy and Practice Program, Faculty of Human and Social Development, University of Victoria, Canada. Her research coalesces around themes of power and body in different contexts— feminist methodology, constructs of contested illness, and activist practices. She draws on

feminism and poststructural thinking to make sense of women's experiences of changing environments and uses autobiographical writing analytically in her empirical and theoretical work. She is also active in feminist politics on issues of chronic illness and invisible or unapparent disabilities. She edited *Placing Autobiography in Geography* (2001) and *Feminist Geography in Practice* (2002). She also coauthored *Women, Body, Illness: Space and Identity in the Everyday Lives of Women With Chronic Illness* (2003) with Isabel Dyck.

**Nancy A. Naples** is Professor of Sociology and Women's Studies at the University of Connecticut where she teaches courses on feminist theory; feminist methodology; sexual citizenship; gender, politics, and the state; and women's activism and globalization. She is the author of *Feminism and Method: Ethnography, Discourse Analysis, and Activist Research* (2003) and *Grassroots Warriors: Activist Mothering, Community Work, and the War on Poverty* (1998). She is also the editor of *Community Activism and Feminist Politics: Organizing Across Race, Class, and Gender* (1998). She is coeditor of *Women's Activism and Globalization: Linking Local Struggles and Transnational Politics* and *Teaching Feminist Activism*. Her next book, *Restructuring the Heartland: Racialization and the Social Regulation of Citizenship*, focuses on a long-term ethnographic study of economic and social restructuring in two small towns in Iowa. She is currently working on a comparative intersectional analysis of sexual citizenship and immigration policies.

**Angel David Nieves** is Assistant Professor in the School of Architecture, Planning, and Preservation at the University of Maryland, College Park. He is an affiliate faculty member in the Departments of American Studies, Women's Studies, African American Studies, and Anthropology. He is also an affiliate member of the Center for Heritage Resource Studies. He completed his doctoral work in architectural history and Africana studies at Cornell University in 2001. His book manuscript, *"We Gave Our Hearts and Lives To It": African American Women Reformers and Nation-Building in the Post-Reconstruction South, 1877-1968*, is currently being revised for publication. His scholarly work and activism critically engages with issues of heritage preservation, gender, and nationalism at the intersections of race and the built environment in the Global South.

**Daphne Patai** is Professor of Brazilian Literature and Adjunct Professor of Comparative Literature at the University of Massachusetts, Amherst. She spent 10 years in the Women's Studies Program before deciding to leave it for reasons that are explained in her chapter in this volume. She is the author and editor of 11 books, including *Heterophobia: Sexual Harassment and the Future of Feminism* (1998). Her 1994 critique of academic feminism, written with Noretta Koertge, was recently reissued in a new and expanded edition as *Professing Feminism: Education and Indoctrination in Women's Studies* (2003). Her latest book, coedited with Will H. Corral, is *Theory's Empire: An Anthology of Dissent* (2005). Many of her essays on academic foibles have appeared in *The Chronicle of Higher Education*. A recipient of fellowships from the Guggenheim Foundation, the National Endowment for the Humanities, and the National Humanities Center (all for feminist projects), she has come to appreciate that education and politics are not the same thing.

**Deborah Piatelli** is an activist and doctoral candidate in sociology at Boston College. She is currently writing her dissertation on the challenges contemporary mobilizations for peace and social justice face as they work across race, class, and gender. She works with the Global Justice Project at Boston College (an undergraduate student-led program) and a local community group of the United for Justice With Peace coalition based in Boston. Taking a feminist, participatory approach, she collaborated with activists over a 2-year period and uncovered how hidden cultures of privilege were preventing collective work across difference. Through participatory discussions with activists, this work has opened up a space for activists to reflect and exchange dialogue to potentially transform their beliefs, practices, and identities.

**Wanda S. Pillow** is Associate Professor in the Department of Educational Policy Studies at the University of Illinois at Urbana-Champaign. She is author of *Unfit Subjects: Educational Policy and the Teen Mother* (2004) and coeditor of *Working the Ruins: Feminist Poststructural Theory and Methods in Education* (2000).

**Judith Preissle** (formerly Preissle Goetz) is the 2001 Distinguished Aderhold Professor in the Qualitative Research Program at the College of Education, University of Georgia (UGA), and she is an affiliated faculty member of UGA's Institute for Women's Studies. Although she began her career teaching middle grades in 1965, Preissle has worked at UGA since 1975 and teaches, researches, and writes in educational anthropology, qualitative research, gender studies, and ethics. She founded the qualitative research program at UGA that now offers a graduate certificate program. She is the coauthor of *Ethnography and Qualitative Design in Educational Research* (1984, 1993), which was translated into Spanish in 1988, and coeditor of *The Handbook of Qualitative Research in Education* (1992). Her most recent book, coauthored with Xue Lan Rong, is *Educating Immigrant Students* (1998). She and her spouse, a computer network manager at UGA, have two miniature schnauzers and two Chinese pugs. All five share her interest in philosophical quandaries.

**Diane Reay** is Professor of Education at Cambridge University. She is a feminist sociologist working in the area of education but is also interested in broader issues of the relationship between the self and society, the affective and the material. Her priority has been to engage in research with a strong social justice agenda that addresses social inequalities of all kinds. She is particularly interested in developing theorizations of social class and the ways in which it is mediated by gender and ethnicity, and she has worked extensively with Pierre Bourdieu's conceptual framework. Recent research includes understanding white-middle-class identities in multiethnic urban spaces and the experiences of working-class students in higher education. Her most recent book (with S. Ball & M. David) is *Degrees of Choice: Social Class, Race and Gender in Higher Education* (2005).

**Shulamit Reinharz** is the Jacob Potofsky Professor of Sociology at Brandeis University.

She directed the Brandeis University Women's Studies Program in the 1990s and founded the Hadassah-Brandeis Institute (HBI) in 1997 to develop fresh ways of thinking about Jews and gender worldwide. In 2001, she founded the Women's Studies Research Center (WSRC) where research, art, and activism converge. The WSRC is housed in a 10,000-square-foot facility, which she designed and for which she raised all the funds. Both the HBI and the WSRC are members of the National Council for Research on Women. Reinharz is the author/editor of 10 books, including *On Becoming a Social Scientist* (1979/1984), *Qualitative Gerontology* (1987), *Feminist Methods in Social Research* (1992), and *American Jewish Women and the Zionist Enterprise* (2005). She is also the chief editor of the *Brandeis Series on Jewish Women.*

**Laurel Richardson** is Professor Emeritus of Sociology at the Ohio State University. She specializes in the sociology of knowledge, gender, and qualitative methods. She has been honored with visiting lectureships in many countries and has published over 100 articles—many of them demonstrating alternative writing formats, including poetic representations. She is the coeditor of *Feminist Frontiers* and author of seven other books, including *The New Other Woman* (translated into seven languages) and the Cooley award winning book *Fields of Play*: *Constructing an Academic Life.* Her most recent book, *Travels With Ernest: Crossing the Literary/Sociological Divide* (2004), was coauthored with novelist Ernest Lockridge and models a new writing format that preserves the individual voice, breaks down hierarchies, and demonstrates feminist communication strategies across gender and disciplines. Her current research expands her interest in alternative reading/writing practices through an ethnographic and textual study of Altered Books.

**Judith Roof** is Professor of English and Film Studies at Michigan State University. She is the author of *A Lure of Knowledge: Lesbian Sexuality and Theory*, *Come as You Are: Narrative and Sexuality*, *All About Thelma and Eve: Sidekicks and Third Wheels*, and the forthcoming *The Poetics of DNA.* She is coeditor (with Robyn Wiegman) of *Who Can Speak? Authority and Critical Identity.*

**Sue V. Rosser** has served as Dean of the Ivan Allen College of Liberal Arts at Georgia Tech since 1999, where she is also Professor of Public Policy and of History, Technology, and Society. The author of nine books, Rosser has also written more than 120 refereed journal articles on issues of women and feminism in science, technology, and health. Her most recent book is *The Science Glass Ceiling: Academic Women Scientists and Their Struggle to Succeed* (2004).

**Denise Seigart** is Professor in the Health Sciences Department at Mansfield University, Pennsylvania, and is currently serving there as Interim Associate Provost. She has been an active member of the American Evaluation Association and has served as Chair and Program Chair of the Feminist Issues in Evaluation Topical Interest Group. In collaboration with Dr. Sharon Brisolara, she edited *Feminist Evaluation: Explorations and Experiences: New Directions for Evaluation*, a critical work regarding Feminist Evaluation, which was published in December, 2002. She received her PhD in human service studies/program evaluation from Cornell University in 1999.

**Dorothy E. Smith** is Professor Emeritus at the University of Toronto and Adjunct Professor at the University of Victoria. Her published books include *Women Look at Psychiatry: I'm Not Mad, I'm Angry* (coedited with Sara David, 1975); *Feminism and Marxism*: *A Place to Begin, A Way to Go* (1977); *El Mundo Silenciado de las Mujeres* (1985); *The Everyday World as Problematic: A Feminist Sociology* (1987); *The Conceptual Practices of Power: A Feminist Sociology of Knowledge* (1990); *Texts, Facts, and Femininity: Exploring the Relations of Ruling* (1990); *Eine Soziologie Für Frauen* (translated and edited by Frigga Haug, 1998); *Writing the Social: Critique, Theory and Investigations* (1999); *Mothering for Schooling* (coauthored with Alison Griffith, 2005); *Institutional Ethnography: A Sociology for People* (2005); and an edited collection of essays by institutional ethnographers, *Institutional Ethnography as Practice* (2006).

**Liz Stanley** is Professor of Sociology at the University of Edinburgh. Her main research and writing interests focus on the questions of methodology and epistemology, and many projects were produced with Sue Wise. Substantively, her research has been on historical topics for the last two decades, in particular, regarding South Africa. Relevant books include *Imperialism, Labour and the New Woman: Olive Schreiner's Social Theory* (2002) and *Mourning Becomes . . . Post/Memory, Commemoration & the Concentration Camps of the South African War 1899-1902* (2006).

**Abigail J. Stewart** is Sandra Schwarz Tangri Professor of Psychology and Women's Studies at the University of Michigan and director of the UM ADVANCE project, supported by the NSF ADVANCE program on Institutional Transformation. She was director of the Women's Studies Program (1989–1995) and the Institute for Research on Women and Gender (1995–2002), and she is a former Associate Dean in the College of Literature Science and the Arts at the University of Michigan (2002–2004). She has published many scholarly articles and several books that focus on the psychology of women's lives, personalities, and adaptations to personal and social changes. Her current research combines qualitative and quantitative methods and includes comparative analyses of longitudinal studies of educated women's lives and personalities; a collaborative study of race, gender, and generation in the graduates of a Midwest high school; and research and interventions on gender, science, and technology with adolescent girls, undergraduate students, and faculty.

**Lynn Weber** is Director of the Women's Studies Program and Professor of Sociology at the University of South Carolina. She is cofounder of the Center for Research on Women at the University of Memphis, and her research and teaching has explored the intersections of race, class, gender, and sexuality for over 20 years. Since the publication of *Understanding Race, Class, Gender, and Sexuality: A Conceptual Framework* (2001), her work has focused on bringing the insights of intersectional scholarship to the problem of persistent social inequalities in health. Her recent publications include "Intersectionality and Women's Health: Charting a Path to Eliminating Health Disparities" in *Advances in Gender Research* and "Reconstructing the Landscape of Health Disparities Research: Promoting Dialogue and Collaboration Between the Feminist Intersectional and Positivist Biomedical Traditions" in *Race, Class, Gender and Health,* edited by Amy Schulz and Leith Mullings. She is also coauthor of *The American Perception of Class.*

**Sue Wise** is Professor of Social Justice at Lancaster University, the United Kingdom. She is interested in all aspects of social justice and teaches and writes on social divisions and social diversity. The oppression and exploitation of children is a particular interest. She has written many books and articles on feminist epistemology and ontology with Liz Stanley. One of their most noted collaborations is *Breaking Out Again: Feminist Ontology and Epistemology* (1993).

**Diane L. Wolf** is Professor of Sociology at the University of California, Davis. She edited *Feminist Dilemmas in Fieldwork* (1996) and authored *Factory Daughters* (1992) and *Beyond Anne Frank: Hidden Children, Family Reconstruction and the State in Post-war Holland* (2006, in press). With Judith Gerson, she coedited *Sociology Confronts the Holocaust: Identities, Memories and Diasporas* (2007, in press). She also studies the children of Filipino and Vietnamese immigrants in California.

**Alison Wylie** is Professor of Philosophy at the University of Washington. She is interested in philosophical questions raised by archaeological practice and by feminist research in the social sciences. Her work on evidential reasoning in archaeology is collected in *Thinking From Things: Essays in the Philosophy of Archaeology* (2002), and her essays on the philosophical implications of feminist research practice and feminist critiques of science appear in *Science and Other Cultures* (2003), *The Difference Feminism Has Made* (2001), *Primate Encounters* (2000), and *Changing Methods* (1995). She has also been active on equity issues as organizer of "Women, Work and the Academy" (2005; www.barnard.edu/bcrw/women andwork) and as contributing coeditor of *Breaking Anonymity: The Chilly Climate for Women Faculty* (1995). She is currently working on a monograph on feminist standpoint theory, *Standpoint Matters, in Feminist Philosophy of Science.*